PUBLISHER
Andrew McDowall

EDITOR
Philip van Zyl

ASSOCIATE EDITORS
Jos Baker, Tim James, Cathy van Zyl

TASTERS
Michael Fridjhon, Angela Lloyd; Master of Wine Cathy van Zyl; Cape Wine Masters Winnie Bowman, Greg de Bruyn, Tim James, Christine Rudman, Irina von Holdt (2008 edition) and Meryl Weaver; David Biggs, David Clarke, Christian Eedes, Higgo Jacobs, Cathy Marston, Fiona McDonald, Ingrid Motteux, Khuselo Mputa (2010 edition), Gregory Mutambe, Roland Peens (2010 edition), Jörg Pfützner, James Pietersen & Dave Swingler.

CONTRIBUTORS
Christian Eedes, Lynne Kloot, Greg Landman, Cathy Marston, Lindsaye McGregor, Joanne Gibson & Wendy Toerien

COORDINATORS
Ina de Villiers (information), Christina Harvett (wine & tasting) & Ina Smith (regional tasting)

DATABASE, WEB & QR CODES
Sean de Kock, Alex Maughan (Digital Energy Media), Tracy Frayne (Tracy Frayne Digital Design), Ben van Rensburg (Modern Web Presence)

TYPESETTING & MAPS
Gawie du Toit, Ryk Taljaard, Heinrich Schloms (VinPro)

PHOTOGRAPHY
Teddy Sambu & Athol Moult

ADVERTISING
Linda Ransome · T +27 (0)82-412-3048 · lindar@wineonaplatter.com

SALES
Linda Butler · T +27 (0)83-462-8172 · lindab@wineonaplatter.com

© John Platter SA Wine Guide (Pty) Ltd 2014
PO Box 1466 Hermanus 7200
Tel: +27 (0)28-316-3210/+27 (0)82-490-1820 · Fax: +27 (0)86-513-3908
andrew@wineonaplatter.com

🌐 www.wineonaplatter.com
f Facebook: http://www.facebook.com/platterswineguide
t Twitter: @wineonaplatter

ISBN 978-0-9870046-2-8

Platter's

SOUTH AFRICAN

WINES

2 0 1 4

THE GUIDE TO CELLARS, VINEYARDS,

WINEMAKERS, RESTAURANTS

AND ACCOMMODATION

Focus on Rainbow Wine Nation

John Platter SA Wine Guide (Pty) Ltd
www.wineonaplatter.com

CONTENTS

PHOTO GALLERY

    Away from the media headlines trumpeting conflict and discord, South Africans from a diversity of backgrounds are drawn together every day by their love of wine — be they members of the industry involved in making, marketing or selling wine, or consumers enjoying a glass of their favourite drink. Twenty years on from democracy and South Africa's return to the international community, we celebrate the cultural kaleidoscope that constitutes this flourishing 'rainbow nation of wine' and highlight how some wine businesses embody, support or promote its unique spirit.

For my family – and in an African sense this is very much an extended family – food and eating have always been a very important part of our culture. We like eating together, and this is as much for the social interaction as for the meal itself.

So when I first opened the now famous Mzoli's Place in Gugulethu on 15 December 1999, my first priority was to have some really good food on the table. The concept was simple: have the best meat available for people to choose with their eyes, then prepare and cook it really well, always remembering that there are no short cuts to excellence.

My late son Mandisi was the driving force behind looking at wine as something that would go well with my 'mix' in the future. Mandisi, as a new-generation South African, understood about retaining the traditional but adding the excitement of change. So, together with Charles Withington, he started the ball rolling and the two of them became great friends in the process. On 27 November 2006, we held our first wine presentation at Mzoli's and it was a huge success.

On 27 June 2009, Mandisi died in a car accident – a terrible, terrible loss. As a family we decided to keep this wine project going in memory of him. We now have some of our own wines and have also instigated the Mzoli's Gugulethu Wine Show . . . and more is still to come.

You might ask why I see a growth in wine in a culture which seemingly does not have a great wine following. Let me tell you that the African way of eating is ideally suited to wine for the simple reason that our meals are very much a social and sharing process. At Mzoli's the norm is that the meat comes in a single bowl and is passed continually round the table, adding more meat when necessary. This way of eating is very social. Wine is also a very social drink – it always has been and always will be. Unlike beer, cider and the like, where you all clutch your single bottle to yourself, wine is poured and shared, which almost becomes a ritual in itself.

Over and above our own house wines, the Mandisi Merlot and Unathi red blend, I plan to carry a small selection of hand-selected wines at Mzoli's, which will increasingly become a part of the meal. I also feel that we must go further than a single wine show to showcase wine's appeal, and I am looking at hosting some winetastings or wine-and-food pairing events. Nothing has been finalised yet but all I can promise is that it will be good and it will be different!

Finally, I would also like to mention that when we started out, and not really coming from a wine background, I needed some sort of reference and so I was introduced to the Platter's South African Wine Guide. This was what was needed. It has simply everything on the South African wine industry, and is easy for anyone to read, understand and refer to. As Archbishop Desmond Tutu said after our historically successful hosting of the FIFA Soccer World Cup in 2010: 'We South Africans continue to amaze ourselves.' So when I see the Platter Guide I am amazed but then, being South African, would we expect anything less?

Mzoli Ngcawuzele
Owner of Mzoli's Wines and Mzoli's Place in Gugulethu, Cape Town

We last featured brandy and sherry-styles, wine's grape-derived sibling beverages, in the 1997/8 editions as a series of general notes written by Dave Hughes, an acknowledged expert on South African spirits and fortified wines, and sometime member of our wine-tasting team. This guide, the 34th, sees brandy and sherry-styles making a return in an expanded and higher-profile format, with comprehensive tasting notes and ratings incorporated into the A–Z listing of producers and their bottlings.

We're delighted to welcome Dave back to the team as an adviser and constant reference to tasters and Cape Wine Masters Winnie Bowman, Tim James and Christine Rudman. The trio reviewed 62 brandies and grappa-styles, and 9 sherry-styles, and the fruits of their labours are listed under the producer entries on pages 15 to 523.

By publishing the brandy and sherry notes alongside those for the wines, we're hoping to create a sense of discovery and excitement among our readers (Nederburg does brandy?! Who knew?), and hopefully prompt further exploration of South Africa's internationally acclaimed brandy and sherry-style offerings.

See the notes about our tasting procedure and the main stylistic categories of brandy and sherry-styles on page 570.

Speaking of welcome returns, we're very pleased to have up-and-comer Teddy Sambu back as photographer for the full-colour Photo Gallery. The young lensman debuted in these pages last edition under the mentorship of Cape Town artist and photographer Athol Moult with a series of images inspired by the general theme of the 2013 edition, namely 'Backstories'. See our Facebook page for an album of these portraits.

The theme for this book is 'Rainbow Wine Nation' and in our opinion Teddy, final-year student at the Cape Town School of Photography and protégé of the Imara Lightwarriors initiative, has created a collection of truly memorable images.

Regarding the tastings for this edition, our aim and approach have remained unchanged, namely to taste, rate and describe as many as possible South African-made wines available during the currency of the book, both locally and overseas.

Much as we'd like to, the number of individual wines precludes us from re-tasting/rating vintages which have been submitted previously yet will still be available for sale during the book's currency. Only wines which last year were reviewed as tank or barrel samples, and thus rated provisionally (or considered too young and unformed to rate), or wines we believe we may have miscalled last time, are revisited for the current book. New and previously untasted vintages are, of course, reviewed as normal.

It bears repeating that the rankings reflected in the book are the result of a process beginning towards the end of June, when we mobilise our team of tasters. The results of their work are reflected in the A–Z section, along with news about the wineries and winemakers, general information about products, vinification facilities, vineyards, amenities available to visitors and more. (Scores for all wines in the A–Z are also listed separately for convenience in the section named 'This Year's Ratings Summarised' on page 527.)

For visitors in search of wine-route information, we've incorporated GPS coordinates for as many as possible of the wineries open to the public at set hours or by appointment. The maps have again been fully updated, along with the quick-lookup tables which furnish key visitor information about the wineries of a particular area, such as whether or not they are open on weekends and public holidays, offer meals or refreshments, specifically cater for children, or are friendly to individuals with reduced mobility. The maps and tables have been moved to the very back of the book, where hopefully they will be easier and quicker to find.

Our initiative to provide professionally conducted audits of winetasting areas, cellar tours and other visitor facilities in the winelands in conjunction with accessibility specialist Disability Solutions is highlighted on page 609.

Also of interest to tourists and wine-ramblers are the Restaurants and Accommodation sections, featuring hotels, B&Bs, restaurants, delis and a plethora of other dining and unwinding venues among the vines. Well-qualified Jos Baker edits the (sponsored) entries.

Our wine ranking system remains the same as last year. We cover the full spectrum, from wines we consider 'somewhat less than ordinary' (and award 0 stars) to 'superlative Cape classics', worthy of a full 5 stars. Wines rated ★★★★ or higher are usually listed first in each entry, and set in red type. However, wines debuting as barrel/tank previews and therefore provisionally rated 4 or more stars remain in black type. Vintages deviating from the general rating are individually starred in the text. Very good/promising wines and more modest examples (★★★☆ or fewer) are included in the 'run-on' listings at the end of entries. For easy identification, the quaffing best-buys are boxed together and individually labelled with the wallet-cordial ☺ sign. See also the section 'How to Use the Guide' on page 7.

Because of deadlines, many wines in the guide are tasted freshly bottled or as works-in-progress; any considered unrateable as a result are noted as such in the text. It's worth mentioning that we taste from the end of June to mid-August. Except for the bottlings assessed for five stars (see the preamble to the Wines of the Year on page 10), all wines are tasted 'sighted' (with labels exposed) and the name of the producer known. As a control, we also double-blind taste hundreds of wines in the course of our assessments. In these corroborative reviews, tasters have no information about the wine save what's in the glass. Because of the subjective element associated with wine assessment, we strongly recommend you view our rankings as adjuncts to the tasting notes rather than as oracular pronouncements. And we continue to urge you, in the words of a local winery's marketing slogan, to 'trust your taste'.

Wines featured in this edition were assessed by a team whose professionalism and unflagging enthusiasm we gratefully acknowledge. Their initials appear below the wines they tasted, as follows: Michael Fridjhon (MF), Angela Lloyd (AL); Master of Wine Cathy van Zyl (CvZ); Cape Wine Masters Winnie Bowman (WB), Greg de Bruyn (GdB), Tim James (TJ), Christine Rudman (CR) and Meryl Weaver (MW); also David Biggs (DB), Christian Eedes (CE), Higgo Jacobs (HJ), Cathy Marston (CM), Fiona McDonald (FM), Ingrid Motteux (IM), Jörg Pfützner (JPf), James Pietersen (JP), Dave Swingler (DS) and newcomers David Clarke (DC) and Gregory Mutambe (GM). For potted biographies of the tasters, see page 524.

In a further endeavour to ensure the fairest possible ratings for wines debuting this edition, or returning after a gap, we've again assembled small panels of tasters to carry out the reviews. Regional tastings (in Worcester, Robertson, Olifants River, Klein Karoo, Tulbagh and the southern Cape/Elim) are also done by small teams.

Warm thanks to the rest of the splendid team, specially to associate editors Tim James (also proofreader) and Jos Baker; Christian Eedes, Joanne Gibson, Lynne Kloot, Greg Landman, Cathy Marston, Lindsaye McGregor and Wendy Toerien; information coordinator Ina de Villiers, regional tasting coordinator Ina Smith, wine coordinator Christina Harvett and assistants Yolandi Barnard, Jessica Garlick, Wilbe Myburgh, JC Rademeyer, MF Schoeman, Wilhelm Schultz, Stephan Steyn, Annette van Zyl and Michelle Waldeck; map and typesetting guru Gawie du Toit; light warriors Teddy Sambu and Athol Moult; the two Lindas (Ransome and Butler) for advertising and sales respectively; Lara Philp and Johan Rademan of Vineyard Connection for the use of their excellent facilities; Lauren de Kock for indexing and fact-checking; Mark Whyte and XtraSmile Couriers; Danie Pretorius and the Brandy Foundation; Ryk Taljaard (Geo-Logic Mapping) and Heinrich Schloms (VinPro) for the Wine of Origin maps; Ben van Rensburg (Modern Web Presence) for QR code; Alex Maughan (Digital Energy Media) and Tracy Frayne (Tracy Frayne Digital Design) for web/mobi site design; the ever-helpful SAWIS; and Michael Bucholz and Jacques de Klerk for the calibration wines. Special thanks to Sean 'Anything Is Possible' de Kock for 24 x 7 help with the database, intranet and website.

Most of all, loving thanks to Cathy, wife of 25 wonderful years, associate editor and regional tasting team leader who completely outdid herself this edition by juggling a day job, Platter's and at least half-dozen other roles and responsibilities with style, grace, humour and truly baffling efficiency; and to son Luke, 17 this year and now holder of a Student Pilot Licence – living the dream he's had since age 5!

Certainly not least, sincere thanks to South Africa's wine producers and negociants, without whose support the book could not be produced.

Finally, an invitation to join us on the web, Facebook and Twitter (see page 2 for details), and to look for our apps on the AppStore and Google Play.

Philip van Zyl

Our Track-Record-Based Rating System

All wines rated 4 stars or more are set in red type

General rating ★★★★ **Caldera**

For 4-star or better wines, we give the 'track-record rating' over two or more vintages in the margin.

Vintage-specific rating **06 (★★★☆)**

Any differences from the general rating noted in brackets beside the particular vintage

★★★★★	Superlative. A South African classic
★★★★☆	Outstanding
★★★★	Excellent
★★★☆	Very good/promising
★★★	Characterful, appealing
★★☆	Good everyday drinking
★★	Pleasant drinking
★☆	Casual quaffing
★	Plain and simple
☆	Very ordinary
No star	Somewhat less than ordinary

Symbols

Winery symbols

♠	Bottles own wine on property
�	Open for tasting (no fee unless noted)
☕	Restaurant/refreshments
⌂	Accommodation
◉	Other tourist attractions/amenities on the property
⛷	Bring your own (BYO) picnic
☆	Child friendly
♿	Wheelchair friendly (see page 609)

Wine symbols

⊟	Screwcapped
✓	Good value
☺	Exceptionally drinkable and well priced
NEW	New wine
⊛	Wine still selling, not retasted
✾	Organic
◎	Biodynamic
⧄	Certified as sustainable (see www.swsa.co.za)

Abbreviations

% alc	Percentage alcohol by volume
1stB	First bottled vintage
BEE	Black Economic Empowerment
BWI	Biodiversity & Wine Initiative
BYO	Bring your own (wine, picnic)
Cs	Cases
CWG	Cape Winemakers Guild
CWM	Cape Wine Master
Est	Date established
g/l	Grams per litre
IPW	Integrated Production of Wine
IWC	International Wine Challenge
IWSC	International Wine & Spirit Competition
LBV	Late Bottled Vintage
Malo	Malolactic fermentation
MCC	Méthode cap classique
MW	Master of Wine
NLH	Noble Late Harvest
NV	Non-vintage. Year of harvest not stated on label
RS	Residual sugar
SAA	South African Airways (selected for First or Premium Class)
SLH	Special Late Harvest
Veritas	SA National Bottled Wine Show
WIETA	Wine & Agricultural Ethical Trade Association
WO	Wine of Origin

cabernet/cab	cabernet sauvignon
pinot	pinot noir
chenin	chenin blanc
sauvignon/sauv	sauvignon blanc
touriga	touriga nacional
tinta	tinta barocca

Location: nearest major centre to winery, vyd, head office. Map: See Maps section for winery's position.
WO: Wine of Origin geographical unit, region, district or ward; wines described/rated bear the first-mentioned WO certification unless noted.

Producer's name

Total hectares/hectares under vine (not necessarily in production); main varieties planted

GPS coordinates, based on Datum WGS 84

Our track-record-based rating system
See previous page for an explanation

Unless noted, red wines wooded; whites unoaked

Wine name, vintage, colour & style

Listings of wines available during the currency of the book

Symbols
See previous page for a complete list

Abbreviations
See previous page for a list of abbreviations

Date established

T = Telephone number
F = Fax number

The text used here is illustrative and not complete. See A–Z for full details.

Fairview

Location/WO: Paarl • Map: Paarl & Wellington • E
30min before closing • Fee R25 or R60 • Closed Eas
Groups by appt only • Tasting & sales of Fairview cl
Anthony de Jager (Dec 1996), with Adele Dunbar (
Mouton • 500ha/300ha (cab, barbera, merlot, m
sauv, viog) • 1 850t 80% red 15% white 5% rosé •
accredited • Export brand: Six Hats • PO Box 583 Su
S 33° 46' 19.5" E 018° 55' 28.0" • **T 021-863-24:**

Fresh life is being fed into the enti
Paarl's distinctive granite dome and
form of uprooting blue gum trees ar
dry as long as Charles Back can reca
plantings of Grenache blanc and rous
first tempranillo went to barrel.

Fairview range

★★★★ **Cabernet Sauvignon** ✓ Renamed S
some & approachable. Silky tannin frame from 5
★★★★ **Cyril Back** Flagship homage to Back
but gentle texture. Complex, dense & concentra
fruit. 18 mths in 30% new Fr oak. Needs time.
★★★★ **Sauvignon Blanc** ✓ 🍴 🧊 Fig & gr
tact adds body to mid-palate. All Darling fruit.

Darling Chenin Blanc ☺ 🍴 🧊 ★★★ A
minerality with honeysuckle hint. Broad palate

Barbera ★★★★ **08** has ripe mulberry succulence
mths old Fr oak. **Stellenbosch Merlot** 🍴 ★★★
tar intensity. Fr oak, 20% new, yr. **Mourv** NEW "d
08. Concentrated & slightly chunky but elegant. Y
08's bold structure & density tempered by plum
Straw Wine ✓ ★★★★ Exotic lavender floral nos
Vanilla wafer too. Sweet (136g RS) but long, dry fi

False Bay Vineyards

Location: Somerset West • WO: Coastal/Western
Boutinot • Winemaker(s) Werner Engelbrecht (20
70% white • PO Box 2093 Somerset West 7129 •
T 021-858-1292 • F 021-858-1293

A consistent range for the UK-owned
lar of sibling Waterkloof - with the s
and often with the natural ferm
Engelbrecht. The grapes are, howeve

Tastings, sales & cellar tour times (closed Saturdays & Sundays but open public holidays unless noted)

Symbols
See previous page for a complete list

Other attractions or activities available on the property

🍴 🍷 📷 ♿

▪ 1stB 1974 ▪ Tasting & sales daily 9–5, last tastings …c 25, Jan 1 ▪ The Goatshed (see Restaurants section) ▪ …wner(s) Charles Back ▪ Winemaker(s) Charles Back & …tephanie Betts (2010) ▪ Vineyard manager(s) Donald …t sirah, ptage, shiraz, chard, chenin, grenache b&n, …2001 & HACCP certified; IPW & BWI member; WIETA …17624 ▪ info@fairview.co.za ▪ www.fairview.co.za ▪ …1-863-2591

Names of owner, winemaker, viticulturist & consultant/s; year/month of appointment in brackets

Postal & email address, website
(see www.wineonaplatter.com for social media details)

…view ecosystem on the rear slopes of …tain. On the natural front it took the … vegetation that has seen riverbeds — …n with water again. In the cellar, new …were vinified for the first time, and the

All wines dry unless noted

b. **08** is bold, leafy cassis & fruitcake galore. Sleek, lis-
…, brl-ferm fruit. 16 mths in 25% new Fr oak.

07's waxy plum segues to blueberry & pepper. Firm
… yet full-bodied. Basket-pressed Paarl & Swartland

…crispness on **10**. Lemon & flint minerality. Lees con-

Exceptionally drinkable & well priced

…anadilla & grapefruit zip on unoaked **10**. Fresh
…contact.

…mon spice over cocoa oak notes. Fine tannin from 12
…lling 08. Cocoa earthiness set against ripe mulberry,
★☆ Savoury soy & earth over black pepper & plum on
Petite Sirah ★★★☆ Floral lavender & blueberry.
… Long mocha tail. Yr Fr oak, 40% new. **Hanepoot**
…ysugar, jasmine, ginger & peach abundance on **08**.
…epoot grapes ex-swartland. — FM

Taster/s initials

🎤

…/1stB 2000 ▪ Tasting at Waterkloof ▪ Owner(s) Paul
…culturist(s) Werner Engelbrecht ▪ 60,000cs 30% red
…erkloofwines.co.za ▪ www.waterkloofwines.co.za ▪

Production, in tons and/or 6-bottle cases (cs) and red:white ratio

…outinot portfolio and made in the cel-
…ttention to detail as the estate's wines
…n favoured by winemaker Werner
…e widely sourced.

Brief introduction/news update

In the course of tasting and rating potentially 7,000 wines for this edition, the members of our team individually identified a limited number of bottlings showing exceptional quality. These were entered into a second round of tasting, open only to finished/bottled wines, available during the currency of the book. The short-listed wines were tasted 'blind' (without sight of the label) by an assembled panel, and those regarded as superlative in a South African context awarded the guide's highest grading — five stars. These standouts are listed below under the heading 'Five Stars'. The highest-scoring five star wines were subjected to a further evaluation to determine the overall top scorer. The two wines which emerged this year from the stringent selection represent the pinnacle of SA winemaking and are the joint recipients of the guide's highest accolade: Wines of the Year.

The wines which did not make the five star selection, but which are extremely fine and collectible in their own right, are listed immediately below the Five Stars under the heading 'Highly Recommended'.

Implicit in wines of this calibre is the potential to improve with further bottle-maturation — say 8–10 years, perhaps more, in the case of the reds and fortifieds, and around 4-6 years for the whites. (Proper storage is, of course, vital for sound maturation.) During the cycle of tasting, our team identified a number of bottlings, over and above the candidate five stars, which show particular potential for cellaring. These ageworthy wines are listed separately under the heading 'Buy Now, Drink Later'.

Also listed is a selection of entry-level wines offering exceptional drinkability at budget prices. The 'Superquaffer of the Year' provides the best overall value and quaffability in this category.

There is, too, the prestigious 'super award', Winery of the Year, in recognition of a winegrowing team who, in the opinion of the editor, are ambassadors par excellence for South African wine.

Further details about all releases listed in this section will be found under the names of the relevant producers in the A–Z directory. The five-star tasting is audited by PKF (Cpt) Inc.

Winery of the Year

Mullineux Family Wines

To think it nearly didn't happen. He on a path to accounting, she reaching for the stars as an aspirant astronaut. But good fortune (theirs and ours) set them on converging courses in wine, and today Chris and Andrea Mullineux are partners in life and in a Swartland boutique venture whose modest quantities completely belie their stellar quality. This edition's haul of four maximum ratings gives them an astonishing 11 five stars to date, and places them firmly in the league of the greatest modern-era wineries. This in just seven years of operation. Reassuring (and thrilling!) to know not only that Chris and Andrea are still full of youth and vigour, but with typical forethought and meticulousness they've lined up a new generation to keep the family business up in the firmament.

Wines of the Year

FIVE STARS & RED WINE OF THE YEAR

Pinot Noir
- Newton Johnson Windansea 2012

FIVE STARS & WHITE WINE OF THE YEAR

White Blend
- DeMorgenzon Maestro 2012

Five Stars

Cabernet Franc
- Raats Family 2011
- Warwick 2010

Cabernet Sauvignon
- Boekenhoutskloof 2011

- Cederberg Five Generations 2011
- Ernie Els Proprietor's 2011

Five Stars (continued)

- Neil Ellis Vineyard Selection 2010
- Stark-Condé Three Pines 2011

Pinotage

- Chateau Naudé Le Vin de François 2011
- Rijk's Reserve 2009
- Spioenkop '1900' 2012

Pinot Noir

- Newton Johnson Family Vineyards 2012

Shiraz

- Cederberg CWG Auction Reserve Teen die Hoog 2011
- Eagles' Nest 2010
- Fable Syrah 2011
- Hilton The Dalmatian 2010
- Mont Destin Destiny 2009
- Mullineux Family Schist Syrah 2011
- Mullineux Family Granite Syrah 2011
- Rust en Vrede Single Vineyard Syrah 2011
- Stark-Condé Three Pines Syrah 2011
- Saronsberg 2011
- Sijnn 2011

Red Blends

- Bouchard Finlayson Hannibal 2011
- Chamonix Troika 2011
- Delaire Graff Botmaskop 2011
- Eikendal Classique 2011
- Ken Forrester Three Halves 2009
- Thelema Rabelais 2009
- Windmeul Reserve Cape Blend 2012

Chardonnay

- Chamonix Reserve 2012
- Hamilton Russell 2012
- Newton Johnson Family Vineyards 2012
- Richard Kershaw Elgin Clonal Selection 2012

Chenin Blanc

- Alheit Radio Lazarus 2012
- Beaumont Hope Marguerite 2012
- Botanica Old Vine 2012
- DeMorgenzon Reserve 2012
- Jean Daneel Signature 2012
- Kleine Zalze Family Reserve 2012
- Mullineux Family Schist 2012
- Opstal Carl Everson 2012
- Reyneke 2012
- Sadie Family Skurfberg 2012
- Stellenrust 48 Barrel Fermented 2012

Grenache Blanc

- The Foundry 2012
- AA Badenhorst Family CWG Auction Reserve White Grenache Vuilgoed 3 2012

Roussanne

- Simonsig CWG Auction Reserve The Russety One 2012

Sauvignon Blanc

- Cederberg David Nieuwoudt Ghost Corner Wild Ferment 2012
- Klein Constantia Perdeblokke 2012
- Kleine Zalze Family Reserve 2012
- Mulderbosch 1000 Miles 2012
- Tokara Walker Bay 2013

Semillon

- Constantia Uitsig 2012

White Blends

- Cape Point Isliedh 2012
- Cederberg David Niewoudt Ghost Corner Bowline 2012
- David Aristargos 2012
- Fable Jackal Bird 2012
- Fairview Nurok 2012
- Flagstone Treaty Tree Reserve 2011
- Nederburg Ingenuity 2012
- Nitida Coronata Integration 2012
- Rall 2012
- Reyneke Reserve White 2011
- Sadie Family Palladius 2011
- Tokara Director's Reserve 2012

Méthode Cap Classique

- Klein Constantia Brut 2010
- Silverthorn The Green Man Blanc de Blancs 2010

Dessert Wine, Fortified

- Alvi's Drift Muscat de Frontignan White 2010

Dessert Wine, Unfortified

- Delheim Edelspatz Noble Late Harvest 2012
- Fleur du Cap Noble Late Harvest 2012
- KWV The Mentors Noble Late Harvest 2012
- Mullineux Family Straw Wine 2012
- Nederburg Eminence 2012
- Nederburg Edelkeur 2012
- Nederburg Winemaster's Reserve Noble Late Harvest 2012

Port-Style

- Axe Hill Cape Vintage 2011
- De Krans Cape Vintage Reserve 2011
- KWV Cape Tawny NV

Brandy

- Boplaas Potstill 20 Years Brandy
- KWV 15 Year Old Alambic
- KWV 20 Year Old
- Oude Meester Souverein
- Van Ryn 12 Year Distillers Reserve
- Van Ryn 20 Year Collectors Reserve
- Van Ryn Au.Ra

Highly Recommended

Cabernet Franc
- Rainbow's End Limited Release 2011
- Raka 2011

Cabernet Sauvignon
- Flagstone Music Room 2010
- Kleine Zalze Family Reserve 2009
- Restless River 2009
- Rudera 2011

Grenache
- David 2012
- Neil Ellis Vineyard Selection 2011

Merlot
- Shannon Mount Bullet 2011

Pinotage
- Diemersfontein Carpe Diem 2011
- Flagstone Time Manner Place 2010
- Kanonkop 2011
- L'Avenir Single Block 2010
- Nederburg Private Bin R172 2010

Pinot Noir
- Bouchard Finlayson Galpin Peak 2011
- Chamonix Reserve 2012
- Crystallum Cuvée Cinéma 2012
- Crystallum Bona Fide 2012
- Iona Limited Release 2011
- Meerlust 2012
- Shannon Rockview Ridge 2012

Shiraz
- Boekenhoutskloof 2011
- De Trafford 393 2011
- Fairview The Beacon 2010
- Fairview Cyril Back 2009
- GlenWood Grand Duc Syrah 2011
- Hartenberg Gravel Hill 2009
- Luddite 2009
- Mullineux Family Syrah 2011
- Rijk's Private Cellar 2008
- Simonsig Merindol 2011
- Strandveld Syrah 2010
- Vergelegen Reserve 2010
- Vins d'Orrance Cuvée Ameena 2011

Red Blends
- AA Badenhorst Family Red 2010
- Anthonij Rupert Blend 2007
- Buitenverwachting Christine 2009
- De Toren Fusion V 2011
- Dornier Wines CMD 2011
- Druk My Niet T3 2010
- Ernie Els CWG Auction Reserve 2011
- Hillcrest Hornfels 2011
- Jean Daneel Signature 2009
- Jordan Cobblers Hill 2010
- Jordan Sophia 2010

- Kaapzicht Steytler Vision 2010
- Kanonkop Paul Sauer 2010
- Ken Forrester The Gypsy 2010
- Luddite Saboteur 2009
- Meerlust Rubicon 2009
- Mvemve Raats MR De Compostella 2011
- Nico van der Merwe Mas Nicolas Cape 2008
- Reyneke Reserve 2010
- Sadie Family Columella 2011
- Spier Frans K. Smit 2008
- Strandveld The Navigator 2011
- Van Biljon Cinq 2011
- Vergelegen Vergelegen V 2009
- Vergelegen Vergelegen V 2008

Chardonnay
- De Wetshof The Site 2012
- GlenWood Grand Duc 2011
- Groot Constantia 2012
- Jordan CWG Auction Reserve 2012
- Paul Cluver CWG Auction Reserve Wagon Trail 2012
- Rustenberg Five Soldiers 2011
- Vins d'Orrance Cuvée Anaïs 2012

Chenin Blanc
- Alheit Cartology 2012
- Cederberg Five Generations 2011
- Ken Forrester The FMC 2011
- KWV Cathedral Cellar 2012
- Raats Family Old Vine 2012
- Remhoogte Honeybunch 2012
- Sadie Family Mev. Kirsten 2012

Sauvignon Blanc
- Bartinney 2013
- Cape Point Reserve 2012
- De Grendel Koetshuis 2013
- Diemersdal 8 Rows 2013
- Diemersdal Reserve 2013
- Diemersdal MM Louw 2012
- Graham Beck Pheasant's Run 2013
- Quoin Rock The Nicobar Reserve 2012
- Quoin Rock Cape South Coast 2012
- Reyneke Reserve White 2012
- Shannon Sanctuary Peak 2013
- Strandveld Pofadderbos 2012
- Warwick Professor Black 2012

White Blends
- AA Badenhorst Family White 2011
- Avondale Cyclus 2011
- Chamonix Reserve White 2012
- Cape Point CWG Auction Reserve 2012

Platter's SOUTH AFRICAN WINE GUIDE HIGHLY RECOMMENDED

Highly Recommended *(continued)*

- Cape Rock GRV 2013
- Delaire Graff Reserve 2011
- Lammershoek Roulette Blanc 2011
- Mullineux Family White Blend 2012
- Savage 2012
- Steenberg Magna Carta 2011
- Vergelegen GVB 2012
- Vergelegen GVB 2011

Méthode Cap Classique

- Colmant Brut Chardonnay NV
- Graham Beck Cuvée Clive 2007
- Silverthorn Jewel Box 2010

Dessert Wine, Unfortified

- Badsberg Badslese 2012
- Boekenhoutskloof Noble Late Harvest 2010

- Donkiesbaai Hooiwijn 2012
- Fairview La Beryl Blanc 2012
- Jordan Mellifera 2012
- Klein Constantia Vin de Constance 2008
- Meinert Semillon Straw Wine 2012
- Miles Mossop Kika 2012
- Paul Cluver Noble Late Harvest 2012
- Quoin Rock Vine Dried Sauvignon Blanc 2012
- Vergelegen Semillon Straw Wine 2011

Dessert Wine, Fortified

- Nuweland Muscat de Frontignan 2009
- Nuy Red Muscadel Limited Release NV

Port-Style

- Boplaas Family Cape Vintage Reserve Show Selection 2010

Buy Now, Drink Later

Barbera

- Idiom 900 Series 2009

Cabernet Franc

- Camberley 2010
- Nelson Family Lisha Nelson Signature 2010
- Rainbow's End 2011
- Val de Vie Polo Club 2011

Cabernet Sauvignon

- Akkerdraai 2009
- De Trafford 2011
- De Wetshof Naissance 2011
- Edgebaston David Finlayson 'GS' 2011
- Fleur du Cap Unfiltered 2011
- Graceland 2011
- Graham Beck Coffeestone 2011
- Kanonkop 2010
- Le Riche Reserve 2010
- Napier 2011
- Overgaauw 2011
- Rickety Bridge Paulina's Reserve 2010

Grenache

- Vriesenhof 2011

Merlot

- Bein Reserve 2011
- Catherine Marshall Peter's Vision Reserve 2011
- GlenWood 2012
- Groot Constantia 2011
- Lourensford Winemaker's Selection 2011

Mourvèdre

- Raka 2011

Petit Verdot

- Springfontein Terroir 2010

Pinotage

- Beyerskloof Diesel 2011

- DeWaal Top of the Hill 2011
- Dornier 2011
- Windmeul Reserve 2012
- Kaapzicht Steytler 2010
- Lanzerac Pionier 2010
- Pulpit Rock Reserve 2012

Pinot Noir

- AntHill Long John Silver 2010
- Creation Reserve 2012
- Paul Cluver CWG Auction Reserve 2011
- The Winery of Good Hope Freedom 2012

Shiraz

- Cirrus 2010
- Fairview Eenzaamheid 2011
- La Motte 2011
- Land's End 2011
- Lazanou Organic 2011
- Spice Route 2010
- Stony Brook Reserve 2010
- Tamboerskloof Kleinood 2009
- The Three Foxes Castillo Syrah 2010
- Lomond Cat's Tail 2011

Red Blends

- Anwilka 2011
- Ataraxia Serenity 2010
- Cape Rock SMV 2012
- Darling Cellars Sir Charles Henry Darling 2011
- De Toren Z 2011
- Durbanville Hills Caapmans Vineyard Selection Cabernet Sauvignon-Merlot 2011
- Gabriëlskloof Five Arches 2010
- Hidden Valley Hidden Gems 2011

Platter's
SOUTH AFRICAN WINE GUIDE
BUY NOW, DRINK LATER

Buy Now, Drink Later – Red Blends *(continued)*

- Keermont 2011
- Laborie Jean Taillefert 2011
- Luddite CWG Auction Reserve Just Alice Shiraz-Mourvèdre 2010
- Marianne Floreal 2010
- Meinert Synchronicity 2009
- Neethlingshof Short Story Collection Caracal 2011
- Painted Wolf The Black Pack Pictus III 2011
- Schalkenbosch Cumulus 2010
- Solms-Delta Hiervandaan 2011
- Somerbosch Kylix 2010
- Stellenbosch Ridge 2011
- The High Road Director's Reserve 2009

Chardonnay

- Buitenverwachting 2012
- Glen Carlou Quartz Stone 2012
- Julien Schaal 2012
- Mulderbosch Barrel Fermented 2012
- Sumaridge 2011

Chenin Blanc

- Bosman Family Special Vineyard Optenhorst 2011
- Old Vines 2012
- Rudera Robusto 2011
- Saltare 2011
- Teddy Hall Dr Jan Cats Reserve 2011

Riesling

- Nitida 2013

Sauvignon Blanc

- Iona 2012
- Jordan The Outlier 2012
- Hillcrest Relief 2012

Semillon

- Vergelegen Reserve 2011
- Zonnebloem Limited Edition 2012

Viognier

- Spice Route 2012
- Idiom 2011

White Blends

- Black Oystercatcher White Pearl 2010

Méthode Cap Classique

- Saxenburg Private Collection NV

Dessert Wine, Unfortified

- Post House Treskilling Yellow 2012

Dessert Wine, Fortified

- Boplaas Muscadel Reserve 2010

Port

- Landskroon Cape Vintage 2010

Superquaffer of the Year

Chenin Blanc

- Boland Kelder Five Climates 2013

Platter's
SOUTH AFRICAN
WINE GUIDE
SUPERQUAFFERS
☺

Exceptionally Drinkable & Well Priced

Cabernet Sauvignon

- Kaapzicht Kaleidoscope 2011

Pinotage

- Groot Parys Die Tweede Droom 2013

Red Blends

- Jordan Chameleon Cabernet Sauvignon-Merlot 2011
- Schalkenbosch Edenhof Nighthawk 409 2011
- Villiera Down to Earth 2012

Chardonnay

- The Winery of Good Hope Unoaked 2012

Chenin Blanc

- Spier Signature 2013
- Van Zylshof 2013

Pinot Gris

- Flat Roof Manor 2013

Sauvignon Blanc

- Backsberg 2013
- Helderberg Wijnmakerij 2013
- Lutzville Cape Diamond 2013
- Ken Forrester Petit 2013

White Blends

- AntHill Pieces of 8 2011

AA Badenhorst Family Wines

Location: Malmesbury ▪ Map: Swartland ▪ WO: Swartland/Voor Paardeberg/Coastal ▪ Est 2007 ▪ 1stB 2006 ▪ Tasting, sales & tours by appt ▪ Closed all pub hols ▪ Conferences ▪ Function venue for 130 people ▪ Conservation area ▪ Guest cottages ▪ Owner(s) Adi & Hein Badenhorst ▪ Winemaker(s) Adi Badenhorst (2006), with Jasper Wickens (2008) ▪ Viticulturist(s) Pierre Rossouw (Jan 1975) ▪ 60ha/23ha (cinsaut, grenache, shiraz, chard, chenin, rouss) ▪ 40,000cs own label 60% red 40% white ▪ PO Box 1177 Malmesbury 7299 ▪ adi@iafrica.com ▪ www.aabadenhorst.com ▪ S 33° 32' 38.01" E 018° 49' 7.42" ▪ **T +27 (0)82-373-5038** ▪ F +27 (0)21-794-5196

Seats are limited at the monthly Saturday morning tastings followed by brunch, Swartland style - waterblommetjie quiche and boerewors, and wine - at the Badenhorst family's Kalmoesfontein farm on Perdeberg. But there's plenty of space in the cellar, where half of the second attempt at a bottle-fermented sparkling was lost... in a series of messy explosions. 'The combination of slightly too much sugar and "dodgy" bottles was, well, fun,' recalls co-owner and winemaker Adi Badenhorst. A master of refined and textured wines from Rhône varieties and chenin, Adi has a healthy appreciation for the classics. But he never strays too far from the fun side, so there's always something funky to hand, like the detonating 'Perdeberg Pop' and, 'if my flor doesn't die again!', a sherry-style wine.

AA Badenhorst range

★★★★☆ **CWG Auction Reserve LDR Shiraz** NEW 'Light Dry Red' unseriously serious Adi Badenhorst's description for **11**'s amazing delicacy & poise. Light-textured but taut shiraz from mature bushvines on elevated granitic site, bunch ferment; bone-dry, appealing 'oystershell' persistence & Rhône-like stemmy grip.

★★★★☆ **Red** Wonderfully fresh & light-footed (13.5% alcohol) **10**, shiraz-led blend with usual grenache, cinsaut, plus tinta instead of previous'mourvèdre. Only larger & older oak for wine of effortless, savoury contemplation. Less sugar, as much restraint as seamless **09**.

★★★★★ **CWG Auction Reserve White Grenache Vuilgoed 3** NEW Classy, misnamed **12** actually as-yet-unrecognised grenache gris. Voor Paardeberg fruit, bunch pressed without settling (hence 'Dirty'). Perfectly judged acidity & pithy texture, nutty complexity. Delicious now but will reward ageing 3+ years.

★★★★☆ **White** Typically one third chenin & drop each 8 other varieties, fermented/aged in 60 year old casks. Gloriously scented **11** has great presence & length; far more savoury & mineral than its fruity bouquet suggests, like unshowy yet rich **10** (★★★★★), which stepped up as a new SA classic. Voor Paardeberg grapes.

Funky White Wine Next awaited. **Méthode Ancestrale** NEW ★★★☆ 'Méthode Platteland', 'Perdeberg Pop' - who knows what eventual name will be for quirky bubbles from muscat, chenin, verdelho. Underwent primary ferment in bottle (unlike MCC), **13** fresh & foamy, fun, & very dry. 'No two bottles taste the same.'

Secateurs range

★★★★ **Red Blend** 🏷 Only large older oak for shiraz-led 5-way blend (with drop pinotage). Soulful & finely textured **12** as good as spicy & fresh **11** but more fruit-filled & very drinkable.

★★★★ **Chenin Blanc** 🏷 27 different Swartland/Perdeberg parcels; mostly natural ferment in concrete tanks & old casks. Multi-layered **13** wonderful concentration, similar masterly balance to **12**.

Rosé 🏷 ★★★☆ Bollywood pink **13** seriously styled cinsaut, shiraz & grenache combo, with pleasing nudge tannin, extra weight (not sweetness) from 5.8 g/l sugar. — CvZ

Aaldering Vineyards & Wines

Location/map/WO: Stellenbosch ▪ Est 2004 ▪ 1stB 2007 ▪ Tasting & sales Mon-Thu 9-5 Fri 9-3 Sat (Nov-Apr) 9-3 ▪ Closed all pub hols ▪ Cellar tours by appt ▪ Owner(s) Marianne & Fons Aaldering ▪ Cellarmaster(s)/winemaker(s)/viticulturist(s) Dustin Osborne (Jul 2011) ▪ 20ha/19.7ha (cab, merlot, ptage, syrah, chard, sauv) ▪ ±120t/±18,300cs own label 70% red 30% white ▪ IPW ▪ PO Box 1068 Stellenbosch 7599 ▪ estate@aaldering.co.za, dustin@aaldering.co.za ▪ www.aaldering.co.za ▪ S 33° 55' 9.81" E 018° 49' 8.14" ▪ **T +27 (0)21-865-2495**

Dutch businessman Fons Aaldering doesn't mince his words when it comes to his ambitions for the Devon Valley property he acquired in 2004: 'I want to be considered among the top 10 in South Africa'. Winemaker Dustin Osborne came across from Franschhoek in mid-2011 and wine quality seems to be on the rise.

★★★★ **Lady M** NEW Unwooded pinotage, 3 months lees-aged. **12** dark cherry & tilled earth aromas. Good concentration, fresh acidity, firm but fine tannins. No undue embellishment.

★★★★ **Shiraz** Red & black fruit, hint of vanilla plus attractive floral note on **10**. Clean & fresh, with fine spicy tannins. Return to form after less convincing **09** (★★★★).

★★★★ **Sauvignon Blanc 12** is weighty yet balanced, with notes of green melon, granadilla & pineapple, nicely tangy acidity.

Pinotage ★★★★ Intense black fruit & attractive oak spice on **10**. Carries 15% alcohol relatively well. More deftly managed than rustic **09** (★★★). **Cabernet Sauvignon-Merlot** ★★★★ Classically styled **10** shows red & black fruit, touch of iodine. Good intensity, nice freshness, oak well judged. Step up on more modest **09** (★★★). **Pinotage Blanc** NEW ★★★★ Highly unusual style, juice quickly drawn off the skins, **12** is quirky but likeable. Peach & spice flavours, thick texture. **Chardonnay** 🖉 ★★★★ **12** shows citrus, peach, hint of vanilla plus a subtle leesy note - much more expressive than previous. — CE

Aan de Doorns Cellar 🍷♿

Location/map/WO: Worcester ▪ Est 1954 ▪ Tasting & sales Mon–Fri 8–5 Sat 10-1 ▪ Closed all pub hols ▪ Tours during harvest by appt ▪ Owner(s) 58 members ▪ Cellarmaster(s) Johan Morkel (Nov 1993) ▪ Winemaker(s) Gert van Deventer (Sept 1997) & Ryno Booysen (Jan 2007) ▪ Viticulturist(s) Pierre Snyman ▪ 1,494ha (cab, ptage, chard, chenin, cbard) ▪ 30,868t/22,400cs own label ▪ PO Box 235 Worcester 6849 ▪ info@aandedoorns.co.za ▪ www.aandedoorns.co.za ▪ S 33° 41' 47.0" E 019° 29' 26.2" ▪ **T +27 (0)23-347-2301** ▪ F +27 (0)23-347-4629

A third of the land farmed by Aan de Doorns' Worcester grower-owners is under chenin, making cellarmaster Johan Morkel's eyes sparkle, given the variety's recent good press. Equal cause for optimism are increased yields in 2013, and the partnership with FirstCape, hugely successful supplier to UK supermarkets.

★★★★ **Muscat d'Alexandrie** ✓ 🖉 Honey, sultanas & jasmine - the whole scented nine yards in **12** fortified. Unctuous, rich, yet wonderfully fresh. Light (for style) alcohol extends the sunset sipping. No **11**.

> **Doornroodt** ☺ 🖉 ★★★ **12**'s equal mix ruby cab & merlot maintains quaffability quotient, a cranberry tang keeping things lively. **Colombar Semi-Sweet** ☺ 🍴 🖉 ★★★ Delightful **13** preview, tropical fruit salad in a bottle, subtler & better balanced than last. **Sparkling Demi Sec** ☺ 🖉 ★★★ Pretty, pink & bubbly, **NV** perfect for sweet-toothed party animals.

Pinotage 🖉 ★★★ Upbeat everyday sipper offering choc-sprinkled mulberries & plums, **12** to enjoy soon. **Blanc de Noir** 🍴 🖉 ★★★ Charming, well-made **13** preview packed with juicy strawberries & raspberries. **Chenin Blanc** 🍴 🖉 ★★ Lively, lightish **13** perfect for seafood braais, unusual peach also good with summer salads or solo. **Sauvignon Blanc** 🍴 🖉 ★★ Probably won't be going viral among sauvignon fans, but **13** perfectly pleasant dry white. **Red Muscadel** ✓ ★★★★ Pre-bottling, **12** fortified very sweet, but deft fortification ensures each mouthful is fresh & moreish. **Cape Ruby** ★★★ Softly dry **12** port-style from tinta & touriga. Latest preview is deeper, more complex, a fireside comforter par excellence. — DB, CvZ

■ **Abbotsville** see Org de Rac

Abbottshill 🍾🍷⛩

Location/WO: Malmesbury ▪ Map: Swartland ▪ Est/1stB 2004 ▪ Tasting, sales & tours by appt ▪ BYO picnic ▪ Owner(s) Dynadeals One (Pty) Ltd ▪ Winemaker(s)/viticulturist(s) CA Bain ▪ 112ha/10ha (cab, mourv, shiraz) ▪ 1,250cs own label 100% red ▪ PO Box 433 Malmesbury 7299 ▪ cameron@empa.co.za ▪ S 33° 29' 26.4" E 018° 39' 25.3" ▪ **T +27 (0)82-492-0692**

'We're still tiny but time is short,' says winemaker/viticulturist Cameron Bain, who therefore asked 'one of the new kids on the Swartland block' to help him last year. Already making wine under his own label, Bryan MacRobert persuaded him to try harvesting earlier. 'It's a different style for me but the wine's tasting okay!'

> **Shiraz** ☺ ★★★ Now **NV** (blend of **10** & **11**). In the glass, salty meat, cloves, black pepper & dark cherries unfold to show intriguingly different & tasty wine.

Cabernet Sauvignon ⨁ ★★★ Mid-2010 unwooded preview **09** looked promising, yet needed time to show its best. **Shiraz-Cabernet Sauvignon** Next awaited, as for **Bosstok Boogie** & **Rosé**. — DB

Abingdon Wine Estate

Location: Lions River ▪ Map: KwaZulu-Natal ▪ Est 2004 ▪ 1stB 2007 ▪ Tasting room & restaurant open Sat/Sun & pub hols 10-5 for personalised tastings & fresh country meals ▪ Weekday visits by appt ▪ Weddings & corporate functions ▪ Self-catering accommodation ▪ Owner(s) Ian & Jane Smorthwaite ▪ Winemaker(s)/viticulturist(s) Ian Smorthwaite ▪ 7ha/3ha (cab, shiraz, chard, sauv, viog) ▪ Lions River KZN Midlands ▪ jane@abingdonestate.co.za, ian@abingdonestate.co.za ▪ www.abingdonestate.co.za ▪ S 29° 26' 36.71" E 030° 09' 14.18" ▪ T +27 (0)33-234-4335/+27 (0)83-463-8503 (Jane) ▪ F +27 (0)86-572-6877

It took belief in the wine potential of this KwaZulu-Natal Midlands property for pioneer owners Ian and Jane Smorthwaite to set up operation here, and a loyal following, including restaurant listings, has confirmed their vision. High altitude (1,140m) and cooler temperatures give their wines Old World restraint, and to date these are the only registered estate single-vineyards in the province.

▪ Above the Mist *see* Retief Wines

Accolade Wines South Africa

Stellenbosch ▪ Owner(s) Champ Private Equity based in Australia ▪ Winemaker(s) Bruce Jack, Gerhard Swart, Ben Jordaan & Karen Bruwer ▪ Viticulturist(s) Chris Keet ▪ 6.4m cs own label ▪ PO Box 769 Stellenbosch 7599 ▪ flagstone@accolade-wines.com ▪ www.accolade-wines.com ▪ T +27 (0)21-852-5052 ▪ F +27 (0)21-852-5085

Owned by Champ Private Equity of Australia, Accolade Wines South Africa is part of the global drinks company Accolade Wines, whose portfolio contains some of the world's best-known wine brands. The South African business, based in Stellenbosch, is responsible for big-selling entry-level brand Kumala, mid-tier Fish Hoek, and highly regarded Flagstone pinnacle wines. See separate listings.

Adoro Wines

Location: Stellenbosch ▪ WO: Western Cape/Coastal ▪ Est 2005 ▪ 1stB 2004 ▪ Closed to public ▪ Owner(s) Intra International ▪ Winemaker(s) Ian Naudé (May 2005) ▪ Viticulturist(s) Lucas de Kock (Aug 2005) ▪ 40% red 60% white ▪ PO Box 982 Stellenbosch 7599 ▪ adorowines@iafrica.com ▪ www.adorowines.co.za ▪ T +27 (0)83-630-3794 ▪ F +27 (0)21-880-1585

Adoro Wines was born of the view that blended wine – mindful of the influence of soil, grape and man – is greater than the sum of its parts. It owns no vines but has long-term relationships with grape growers in a wide variety of regions. Each parcel is vinified separately, giving vintner Ian Naudé a multitude of elements with which to build his compositions.

★★★★ **Sauvignon Blanc** ⓐ ▥ **10** (★★★★) steely but not as penetrating as **09**, thanks to fleshy fruit & the softening effect of bottle-maturation at the cellar.

★★★★☆ **Naudé White** ⓐ ▥ Lightly oaked chenin, semillon, sauvignon, roughly equal portions. **10**'s chalk, mineral, floral & fruity elements held together by fresh acidity, & background wood.

Red Blend ★★★★ Ready for drinking **07** equal cab & merlot, plus shiraz. Soft, plump red berry fruit in harmony with yielding tannins, all-new oak (18 months) absorbed into medium frame. **Natural Sweet Mourvèdre** ★★★★ A made-for-cheese wine, 'neither fortified nor overly dry or sweet'. **10** individual; mocha-tinged ripe fruit toned with oak, 62 g/l residual sugar refreshed by natural acidity. WO Coastal. — DS

Aeternitas Wines

Location: Strand ▪ Map: Helderberg ▪ WO: Swartland ▪ Est 2005 ▪ 1stB 2007 ▪ Tasting by appt ▪ Closed all pub hols ▪ Owner(s) Johan & Michelle Grimbeek ▪ Cellarmaster(s)/winemaker(s) Johan Grimbeek ▪ Viticulturist(s) Various ▪ 4t/640cs own label 50% red 45% white 5% rosé + 8,000cs for clients ▪ 21 Livingstone Street, Strand 7140 ▪ aeternitaswines@telkomsa.net ▪ S 34° 6' 3.3" E 018° 49' 35.6" ▪ T +27 (0)82-714-2095

Wine dominates the lives of husband-and-wife team Johan and Michelle Grimbeek: he winemaker at Kanu, she local head of the Cape Wine Academy. The Aeternitas wines, made in their suburban garage, are maturing nicely, just needing someone who has what they don't have... time to market them!

Syrah ⊕ ★★★★ Delectable **08** is plush & utterly moreish. Heaped with sweet mulberry fruit, it has poise & finesse, despite 15% alcohol. Wild ferment, like **07** (★★★☆). **Blanc** ⊕ 🍽 🧊 ★★★★ **10** from chenin billows summer fruit, shows amazing balance considering ripeness, oak & 14% alcohol. — DS

▪ **A Few Good Men** *see* Riebeek Cellars
▪ **Africa** *see* Waterstone Wines
▪ **Africa Five** *see* Waterstone Wines
▪ **African Dawn** *see* Rooiberg Winery
▪ **African Gold** *see* Old Bridge Wines
▪ **African Lizard** *see* Waterstone Wines

African Pride Wines

Location: Constantia ▪ WO: Western Cape/Coastal ▪ Est/1stB 2002 ▪ Closed to public ▪ Owner(s) Afrifresh Group ▪ Winemaker(s) Mike Graham (May 2002) ▪ 480,000cs ▪ PO Box 518 Constantia 7848 ▪ info@ africanpridewines.co.za ▪ www.africanpridewines.co.za ▪ **T +27 (0)21-887-2204** ▪ F +27 (0)21-887-2204

A large-scale export brand with a presence in 37 countries around the globe, African Pride is one of the industry's recent success stories. Look out for one of their labels if you find yourself in Estonia, Iceland, India or even Latvia. As part of a local drive, Antony Eva has been appointed South African sales chief.

Lady Anne Barnard range

★★★★ **Sauvignon Blanc** ✓ 🧊 **12** (★★★☆) a tad off serious **10**. Capsicum & tropical fruit flavours, bracing acidity needs time to integrate. Elgin vines (Coastal WO). **11** sold out untasted.
Cabernet Sauvignon Next awaited, like **Shiraz**.

Footprint range

> **Chenin Blanc-Semillon** ☺ 🍽 🧊 ★★★ Fruity & fragrant **12** quaffer trumps previous.

Merlot-Pinotage New bottling not ready.

Cape Grace Sugarbird range

> **Shiraz** ☺ 🍽 🧊 ★★★ **12** offers sweet, soft dark fruit & fynbos, smoky end. **Chenin Blanc** ☺ 🍽 🧊 ★★★ Improved light & fruity **13**, easy summer sipper.

Pinotage 🍽 🧊 ★★ Unoaked, as all in range. Perky **12** with understated dry plum flavours.

Footprint Long Walk range

> **Cabernet Sauvignon** ☺ 🧊 ★★★ Berry fruit & fresh herb appeal on **12**, unoaked as all in this range.
> **Shiraz** ☺ 🧊 ★★★ Juicy-fruity **12** is smoother than last, with brambly flavours. Perfect for the braai.
> **Sauvignon Blanc** ☺ 🧊 ★★★ Fragrant tropical fruit aromas on **13**, lean & dry finish.

Merlot 🧊 ★★ **12** upfront perky fruit yet a dry, very firm finish. **Pinotage Rosé** 🍽 🧊 ★★ **13** is bright pink, fruit-shy & dry. **Chardonnay** Await new vintage. — WB

▪ **African Roots** *see* Seven Sisters
▪ **African Star** *see* Stellar Winery

African Terroir

Location: Paarl ▪ Map: Paarl & Wellington ▪ WO: Western Cape/Paarl/Voor Paardeberg/Elgin ▪ Est/1stB 1991 ▪ Tasting, sales & cellar tours Mon-Fri 8.30-4 strictly by appt ▪ Closed all pub hols ▪ Conferences ▪ Functions ▪ Conservation area ▪ Owner(s) Jacques Germanier ▪ Winemaker(s) Jaco Marais (Nov 2012), with Marco Swartz (Feb 2009) ▪ Viticulturist(s) Johan Barnard (Nov 2009) ▪ 75ha (cab, merlot, ptage, shiraz, chard, cbard, sauv, viog) ▪ 540t ▪ Brands for clients: Hunting Owl (Woolworths), Mwitu (USA), Tribal (Spar) ▪ ISO 22000, BWI, Fairtrade certified, FOA, HACCP, IPW, Organic ▪ PO Box 2029 Windmeul Paarl 7630 ▪ office@african-terroir.co.za ▪ www.african-terroir.co.za ▪ S 33° 37' 1.8" E 018° 50' 38.4" ▪ **T +27 (0)21-869-8103** ▪ F +27 (0)21-869-8104

On the farm Sonop near Paarl, African Terroir is Swiss owned but incorporates the 'spirit of Africa' – compassion for the environment and those who inhabit it – into everything it does. Hence its commitment to organic farming and its upliftment project, the Winds of Change/Communal Property Association. Previously focused on the offshore market, it's striving to share more of its spirit locally.

Out of Africa range

Cabernet Sauvignon ⑨ ★★★ Unoaked **11**, ex-tank mid-2011, strawberry toned with affable grip. WO Elgin. **Shiraz** ⑨ 🍴 ★★ **11** comfortingly familiar: savoury, ripe & very firm on release. **Chardonnay** ★★★ Previewed **13** displays more serious intent in creamy body, ripe peachy fruit & long nutty tail showing well-judged oaking. **Sauvignon Blanc** ★★★ Ex-tank **13** seems programmed for sushi given its seaweed-like & green olive savouriness on the palate.

Sonop Organic range

Cabernet Sauvignon ⑩ ★★★ Displaying improved form, **13** preview already shows complexity in its violet-perfumed ripe fruit, promise of further improvement if allowed time. From Voor Paardeberg, like Merlot & Shiraz. **Merlot** ⑩ ★★★ Another label on the up & up. Preview **13** very ripe aromatic fruit flavours (cherry, plum & raspberry), firm but very approachable tannins & good balance. **Pinotage** ⑨ 🔥 📖 ★★ Lemony acidity on strawberry-infused **10**. **Shiraz** ⑩ ★★★★ More serious than last **10** (★★★), & styled for the longer haul, **13**'s fruit is full & mocha-rich, poised to unfold. Tasted pre-bottling, rating provisional. **Viognier-Merlot Rosé** ⑨ 🍴 🔥 📖 ★ Perfumed dry **10** lacks verve. **Chardonnay** ⑨ 🍴 🔥 📖 ★★ **10** wallet-friendly unwooded easy-drinker. **Sauvignon Blanc** ⑨ 🔥 📖 ★★ **10** is zesty, with khaki bush notes. WO Paarl, as all this range's wines still selling/not retasted. **Viognier** ⑨ 🔥 📖 ★★★ **11** engaging orange & apricot, good weight & length.

Tribal range

Cabernet Sauvignon 🍴 📖 ★★★ Immediate pleasure delivered by juicy, cassis & vanilla-toned **12**; tug of tannin adds to the appeal. **Merlot** ⑨ 🍴 ★★ Further bottling of **11**, preview is fruity with rustic tannins. **Pinotage** 🍴 📖 ★★ Made for early & easy drinking, **12** delivers with simple but juicy & ample fruit. **Shiraz** 🍴 📖 ★★★ Showy **12**, plummy & perfumed, effortless medium-bodied red with nutmeg/white pepper sensation. **Dry Red** ★★ Now vintage-dated, **12** mixes capsicum & cherries in lightish bodied quaffing wine. **Semi Dry Red** In abeyance, like **Rosé** & **Semi Dry White**. **Chardonnay** ⑨ 🍴 📖 ★★ Lightly wooded **11** tank sample's light fruit still meshing with oak mid-2012. **Chenin Blanc** ⑨ 🍴 📖 ★★ Khaki bush aroma on sweet-fruited **11** preview. **Sauvignon Blanc** Await next, as for **Sauvignon Blanc-Colombard Fairtrade**, **Chenin Blanc-Colombar**, **African White**, **Sparkling Rosé Dry**, **Sparkling White Dry** & **Sparkling Semi-Sweet**. **Dry White** ★★ Unwooded **13**, ripe & tropical, aromatic with grapefruit finish.

Winds of Change Fairtrade Organic range

Cabernet Sauvignon ⑨ 🔥 ★★★ **10** has spice highlights to red fruit. **Merlot** ⑨ 🔥 ★★ **10**'s soft plums offset by firm tannin. **Pinotage** ⑨ 🔥 ★★ Lemon acidity adds zest to strawberry flavours in **10**. **Shiraz** ⑨ 🔥 ★★★ Scrub & sour cherry notes, firm tannins on **10**. **Pinotage-Shiraz** ⑨ 🔥 📖 ★★★ Friendly **11** supple & juicy, slips down easily. **Chardonnay** ⑨ 🔥 📖 ★★ Further bottling of **11** is nutty, some woody notes, brief. **Sauvignon Blanc** ⑨ 🔥 ★★ Grassy **10** tangy & dry. **Chardonnay-Viognier** ⑨ 🔥 📖 ★ Fragrant **11** preview previously had bold, plump palate. WO Paarl. **Sparkling Cabernet Sauvignon Rosé** ⑨ 🔥 📖 ★★ NV sparkler an appealing celebration package. — GM

African Wines & Spirits

Cape Town ▪ Est 1999 ▪ Closed to public ▪ Owner(s) Edward Snell & Co ▪ Directors D Asherson, DV Hooper, IV Hooper, JM Pousson & CC Weeden ▪ 40% red 60% white ▪ PO Box 318 Paarden Eiland ▪ chrisw@esnell.co.za ▪ **T** +27 (0)21-506-2600 ▪ F +27 (0)21-510-4560 / +27 (0)86-682-4922

This wholesaling and marketing company is owned by Edward Snell & Co, and responsible for the separately listed good-value range, Craighall, among others.

▨ **Agaat** *see* Truter Family Wines
▨ **Agterkliphoogte** *see* Wandsbeck Wyne Koöp Bpk

Agterplaas Wines

Location: Stellenbosch ▪ WO: Western Cape/Stellenbosch ▪ 1stB 2003 ▪ Tasting by appt ▪ Owner(s)/winemaker(s) James Basson ▪ 2t/300cs own label 60% red 40% white ▪ PO Box 863 Stellenbosch 7599 ▪ agterplaas@adept.co.za ▪ **T** +27 (0)21-886-5446 ▪ F +27 (0)21-886-5446

No new wines this edition - demand for his services as an architectural designer left James Basson with scant time for winemaking in his 'agterplaas' (backyard) in Stellenbosch, but 'Watch this space for exciting changes'.

Cabernet Sauvignon ① ★★★★ Fruit-forward & rounded **10**, mocha & blackberry juiciness, friendly ripe tannins on finish. **Agterplaas** ① ▤ ★★★ Mainly cab & merlot, dashes cab franc, malbec & petit verdot. When last tasted, **06** savoury plum spice, silky tannin & integrated oak. **Chenin Blanc** ① ★★★ Oatmeal & apricot on toasty backing of wooded **10**. Good length & structure, tangy acidity adds freshness. — DB

Akkerdal Wine Estate

Location/map/WO: Franschhoek ▪ Est 2000 ▪ 1stB 2001 ▪ Tasting & sales Mon-Fri 10-4 ▪ Fee R20pp ▪ Closed all pub hols ▪ Self-catering chalet ▪ Owner(s)/cellarmaster(s)/winemaker(s) Pieter Hanekom ▪ Viticulturist(s) Pieter Hanekom, advised by Eben Archer, Bennie Liebenberg & Dawid Saayman ▪ 18ha (barbera, cab f, carignan, durif, grenache, malbec, merlot, mourv, p verdot, roobernet, shiraz, tannat, tempranillo, chard, nouvelle, sauv, sem, viog) ▪ 6,000cs own label 95% red 4% white 1% rosé ▪ IPW ▪ PO Box 36 La Motte 7691 ▪ wine@akkerdal.co.za ▪ www.akkerdal.co.za ▪ S 33° 52' 50.9" E 019° 3' 3.8" ▪ **T +27 (0)21-876-3481/+27 (0)82-442-1746** ▪ F +27 (0)21-876-3189

Pieter Hanekom is the proud owner, and master of all trades, at Franschhoek boutique winery Akkerdal. He cultivates some unusual varieties, selling what he doesn't need for his own characterful, critically acclaimed bottlings. A range of wines is planned to honour the role of his staff in the success of the enterprise.

Limited Releases

★★★★ **Kallie's Dream** ① ▨ Shiraz-led blend, rest mourvèdre, grenache, carignan, viognier. Pure & very expressive **10** with red fruit, fynbos & some toasty oak. Permeated with fresh acidity & fine spicy tannins. **TDT** ▨ ★★★★ **12** unusual blend of tempranillo, durif & tannat has intriguing dark perfumed fruit & supple tannins. Succulent, balanced but still youthful, with potential. Step up on **10** (★★★★). No **11**.

Akkerdal range

★★★★ **Syrah** Returns after a break with **12**, still tight but shows intriguing white pepper, fennel & savoury tones, from dash of mourvèdre. Dry tannins & oak (18 months) show underlying seriousness. Needs cellar time.

★★★★ **Wild Boar** ① **09** conforms to no conventional template, with 5 different varieties including roobernet & tempranillo. Fruit driven but not facile, with fresh acidity, dry finish. No **07**, **08**.

Merlot ▨ ★★★★ **12**, first since **05**, is balanced with a smooth creamy texture & minted red fruit. Polished & approachable, ready to enjoy. **Petit Noir** ① ▨ Malbec-led **10** Bordeaux red shows dark fruit, herbal note on nose & palate. Rustic but not without charm. **Passion Reserve** ▨ ★★★ Was 'Passion Red', **11** malbecled Bordeaux red quartet. Recently bottled, with tight tannin structure & savoury, smoky tone. Needs time to reveal its charms. **Kallie's Dream Red** Await next, like **Sauvignon Blanc**. **Sophie's Blush** ▨ ★★★★ Back after a break, **13** rosé from shiraz & grenache has savoury cranberry flavours woven into succulent structure. A hint of tannin adds earnest intent & longevity. — MW

Akkerdraai

Location/map: Stellenbosch ▪ WO: Western Cape ▪ Est 1956 ▪ 1stB 2007 ▪ Tasting Mon-Fri 9-5 Sat 9-12.30 ▪ Closed Easter Fri-Mon, Dec 25 & Jan 1 ▪ Fee R20, waived on purchase ▪ Walks/hikes ▪ Owner(s)/cellarmaster(s) Salie de Swardt ▪ Winemaker(s) Ronell Wiid (consultant), with Salie de Swardt (Jan 2004) ▪ Viticulturist(s) Ronell Wiid (consultant) ▪ 1.5ha (cab) ▪ 12t 100% red ▪ PO Box 22 Lynedoch 7603 ▪ saliedes@mweb.co.za ▪ S 33° 59' 53.52" E 018° 49' 50.94" ▪ **T +27 (0)21-881-3861/+27 (0)83-264-1463** ▪ F +27 (0)21-881-3861

Now abetting Stellenbosch boutique vintner Salie de Swardt's goal of 'turning every vintage into a masterpiece' is former Diners Club laureate Ronell Wiid. Where others who plough money into wine talk of ROI (return on investment) or ROE (return on ego), this retired media man's capital and labour are directed towards ROJ: 'the joy we give a small group of winelovers at an affordable price'.

★★★★ **Cabernet Sauvignon** Blackcurrant, cassis richness on complex, refined palate with spice, fynbos twist on long tail. Sleek, harmonious **09** follows similar class act & elegance of **08**. — FM

■ **Alexanderfontein** *see* Ormonde Private Cellar

AlexKia Estate

Location/WO: Robertson ▪ Est 2004 ▪ 1stB 2006 ▪ Tasting by appt at La Verne Wine Boutique, Robertson ▪ Owner(s) Carla Maestroni ▪ Winemaker(s) André van Dyk (Rooiberg) ▪ ±90ha/7ha (cab, chard) ▪ ±70t/ 10,000cs own label 50% red 50% white + 8,000cs for clients ▪ PO Box 101 Robertson 6705 ▪ franco@alexkia. co.za ▪ www.alexkia.co.za ▪ **T +27 (0)82-575-9578/+27 (0)82-783-9825**

'A marriage of Mediterranean heritage and modern taste' is how Franco and Carla Maestroni describe their wine and rosemary farm – named after grand-daughters Alexandra and Chiara – in Robertson's Eilandia Valley.

Alexandra Cabernet Sauvignon Await new vintage, as for **Merlot Reserve**. **Chiara Chardonnay** 🍷 ▨ ★★★ Unoaked **13** raises the bar with harmonious citrus & cream glassful for solo sipping. —DB,CvZ

Alheit Vineyards

Location: Hermanus ▪ Map: Elgin, Walker Bay & Bot River ▪ WO: Western Cape/Bottelary ▪ Est 2010 ▪ 1stB 2011 ▪ Tasting by appt only ▪ Owner(s)/winemaker(s) Chris & Suzaan Alheit ▪ Cellarmaster(s) Chris Alheit ▪ 11t/ 1,120cs own label 100% white ▪ PO Box 711 Hermanus 7200 ▪ chris@alheitvineyards.co.za ▪ www. alheitvineyards.co.za ▪ S 34° 20' 35.56" E 019° 18' 11.30" ▪ **T +27 (0)83-274-6860**

Chris and Suzaan Alheit, young themselves, have a genuine passion for old vine-yards – like the neglected, doomed chenin bushvines high on Stellenbosch's Bottelary Hills that they stumbled on during their searches. Named jointly for the vineyard's resurrection and the radio beacon nearby, the resulting wine, Radio Lazarus, now appears as the first in a projected portfolio of single-origin bottlings added to the Cartology regional blend - which received unprecedented local and international praise in its maiden release. Back at the cellar (rented space in the Hemel-en-Aarde area) minimal intervention marks the vinification of the precious grapes: no yeast inoculation, no additives, only old oak barrels. The finished wines are generally bottled unfined and unfiltered. It's those old vines that matter.

★★★★★ **Cartology 12** (★★★★★) from 4 old blocks of chenin, one (14%) of semillon. A touch drier than maiden **11**, which adds to the steely, stony tautness in brilliant equipoise with supple fruit. Lovely but not facile, with subtle, complex intensity, great length. Like a sunny, scrubby hillside. Try to resist for a year or 10.

★★★★★ **Radio Lazarus** NEW **12** is intriguing & expressive - of what? Surely of the resurrected Bottelary Hills chenin vines which yield juice so sparingly. A little earthier than Cartology, perhaps more depth & richness, similar purity & supple ease. Intense, but no exaggeration or ingratiation. Both need time; decant now. — TJ

Alkmaar Boutique Vineyard

Location/WO: Wellington ▪ Map: Paarl & Wellington ▪ Est 2001 ▪ 1stB 2005 ▪ Tasting & sales Mon-Fri 10-4 Sat 10-2 ▪ Closed all religious pub hols ▪ Cellar tours by appt ▪ Walks (part of Wellington Wine Walk) ▪ Owner(s) Bouwer & Janet Nell ▪ Winemaker(s) Pieter-Niel Rossouw (Jan 2010, consultant), with Dawid Futhwa (Jan 2010) ▪ Viticultur-ist(s) Dawid Futhwa (Jan 2003) ▪ 9.9ha (cab, merlot, mourv, p verdot, ptage, shiraz, chard, viog) ▪ 50t/900cs own label 83% red 17% white + 12,000L bulk ▪ PO Box 1273 Blouvlei Road Wellington 7654 ▪ janet@alkmaarwines. co.za ▪ www.alkmaarwines.co.za ▪ S 33° 39' 37.98" E 019° 1' 55.14" ▪ **T +27 (0)21-873-0191**

Bouwer and Janet Nell have embraced not just the story behind their boutique wine brand, namely a 19th century school building on their Wellington prop-erty, but also 'the moral fibre and principles' of that institution's Dutch founder, Marinus Stucki, 'by creating opportunities for individuals and empowering our people'. The Nells pay homage to another local hero, Prof Izak Perold, Wellington-schooled viticulturist and father of pinotage, in their new release.

The Old School Professor NEW ★★★★ Typical plum & cherry notes on no-nonsense, appealing **11** pinotage. Medium body, fresh acidity, nicely dry on finish. **The Old School Master** 🍷 ★★★ Bordeaux-style red **10** ultra-ripe to the point of jammy, also slightly minty, finishes a little short. **The Old School Mistress** 🍷 ★★★★ Well-assembled Rhône-style red, **10** medium bodied with red fruit & touch of spice, fresh acidity & fine tannins. **The Old School Reunion** 🍷 ★★★ Uncomplicated **12** chardonnay, true-to-variety citrus, light vanilla, moderate acidity. —CE

Allée Bleue Wines

Location/map: Franschhoek ▪ WO: Franschhoek/Walker Bay/Stellenbosch/Piekenierskloof/Western Cape ▪ Est 1690 ▪ 1stB 2001 ▪ Tasting & sales Mon-Fri 9-5 Sat 10-5 Sun 10-4 ▪ Fee R20/4 wines ▪ Closed Good Fri ▪ Cellar tours by appt ▪ Bistro Allée Bleue (see Restaurants section) ▪ Wine tasting courtyard with kiddies corner, light lunches in summer ▪ Picnics - booking required ▪ Jungle gym ▪ Tour groups by appt ▪ Gifts ▪ Farm produce ▪ Conferences ▪ Weddings ▪ Allée Bleue Kendall Cottage & Manor House (see Accommodation section) ▪ Owner(s) DAUPHIN Entwicklungs-und Beteiligungs GMH (Germany) ▪ Winemaker(s) Van Zyl du Toit (Jul 2009) ▪ Viticulturist(s) Douw Willemse (Sep 2008) ▪ 135ha/25ha (cab, merlot, ptage, pinot, shiraz, chard, chenin, sauv, sem, viog) ▪ 380t/46,000cs own label 34.5% red 55% white 5% rosé 5% MCC 0.5% fortified ▪ IPW ▪ PO Box 100 Groot Drakenstein 7680 ▪ info@alleebleue.com ▪ www.alleebleue.com ▪ S 33° 51' 29.0" E 018° 59' 12.9" ▪ **T +27 (0)21-874-1021** ▪ F +27 (0)21-874-1850

Named after the bluegums lining the avenue to the Franschhoek estate, German-owned Allée Bleue has a diverse portfolio including wine, accommodation, weddings and functions, fresh herbs, and an extensive cellardoor offering that showcases a 300-year heritage. The improving wines, friendly and accessible, are made in rapidly increasing quantities by Van Zyl du Toit, who dreams of taking his team to Côte Rôtie someday - after he's paid off his speeding fines!

Allée Bleue range

★★★★ **Pinotage** ⓘ Juicy plums, berries & lively spice, punchy **09** bursts with luscious flavour through to a firm but amenable conclusion. WO Piekenierskloof.

★★★★ **L'Amour Toujours** Flagship blend of cab, cab franc & merlot with a tweak of petit verdot, **10** (★★★★★) improves on **09** with darkly fruited notes of blackcurrants & cherries swathed in smooth & spicy oak, all beautifully integrated & structured. WO Stellenbosch.

★★★★ **Chenin Blanc** ✓ 🍴 Accomplished **12** shows plenty of soft yellow apple & lime cordial. Partial oaking & 7% viognier add ginger biscuit spice. Follows bold **10**, also ex Walker Bay & Franschhoek.

★★★★ **Sauvignon Blanc 13** layers of lovely fresh fruit (gooseberry, grapefruit & guava) with racy acidity & tingling length. Dash of semillon adds depth, rounded by touch of sugar. WO Walker Bay.

★★★★ **Isabeau** 🍴 Classy blend chardonnay & semillon with 6% viognier, **12** rich, almost savoury spiced yellow fruit & lime marmalade notes. Elegant partner for fish & seafood. Walker Bay & Coastal vines.

Shiraz ★★★★ Crowd-pleasing, soft & juicy **11** has plenty of clove spice, black berries & a raisined finish. **Cabernet Sauvignon–Merlot** ✓ ★★★★ **11** is delicious cherry/berry mouthful with choc-mint notes waiting in the wings. Elegant tannins & lengthy finish suggest further pleasure in store. Stellenbosch grapes. Notch up on **10** (★★★★). **Brut Rosé Méthode Cap Classique** ⓘ ★★★★ Dry bottle-fermented sparkling from pinotage, chenin & pinot noir. **11** onionskin hue with strawberry & green apple, fine creamy mousse & zesty finish. Franschhoek & Walker Bay vines. **Brut Méthode Cap Classique** ⓘ ★★★★ Creamy-dry bubbly **10** from pinot & chardonnay with Golden Delicious apple & vanilla biscuit flavours. WO Walker Bay. **Cape Ruby** ⓘ 🍴 ★★★ Port-style **11** from pinotage is light & full fruited, with a spirited finish.

Starlette range

> **Pinotage** ☺ 🍴 ★★★ Juicy quaffer **12** with lots of jammy red fruit & soft ripe tannins making for delicious braai wine. Some Paarl grapes. **Rosé** ☺ 🍴 ★★★ Bright watermelon pink **13** from 100% shiraz has bags of red plum fruit & touch of sweetness. Lively & refreshing.

Rouge ★★★ **11** friendly blend of cab, merlot & shiraz for everyday drinking. **Blanc** ✓ 🍴 ★★★★ Step-up **13** blend of sauvignon & chenin a delicious fruit cocktail of apple, pineapple & guava. Superior summer sipper. — CM

Allegria Vineyards

Location/map: Stellenbosch ▪ WO: Polkadraai Hills ▪ Est 2005 ▪ 1stB 2010 ▪ Tasting by appt ▪ Conferences ▪ Allegria Guest House ▪ Owner(s) Jan & Annemarie Zevenbergen ▪ Winemaker(s) Louis Nel (Nov 2009, consultant) ▪ Viticulturist(s) Francois Hanekom (Sep 2009, consultant) ▪ 2ha/0.5ha (shiraz) ▪ ±3,500kg/±160cs own label 100% red ▪ PO Box 24 Vlottenburg 7604 ▪ wine@allegria.co.za ▪ www.allegriavineyards.co.za ▪ S 33° 57' 29.79" E 018° 45' 31.63" ▪ **T +27 (0)21-881-3389** ▪ F +27 (0)21-881-3210

On Stellenbosch's scenic and viticulturally auspicious Polkadraai Hills, Jan and Annemarie Zevenbergen's shiraz grapes are husbanded and vinified by advisers

Francois Hanekom and Louis Nel respectively. To taste the resulting wine, check into their luxury guest house or find it on a select wine list.

★★★★ **Shiraz** Last time a preview, now bottled **11** (★★★★) somewhat curious in showing pronounced herbaceous character along with dark fruit. Not quite as elegant as **10**. — CE

Allesverloren

Location: Riebeek West ▪ Map/WO: Swartland ▪ Est 1704 ▪ Tasting & sales Mon-Fri 8.30–5 Sat 8.30–2 ▪ Fee R15pp charged only for groups of 10/more ▪ Closed Easter Fri/Mon, Dec 25 & Jan 1 ▪ Cellar tours by appt ▪ Pleasant Pheasant Restaurant Tue 10.30–3 Wed-Sat 9-3 & 6-10 Sun 9-4 ▪ Facilities for children ▪ Conferences ▪ Weddings/functions ▪ Owner(s) Malan Boerdery Trust ▪ Cellarmaster(s) Danie Malan (Nov 1987) ▪ Winemaker(s) Danie Malan (Nov 1987), with Armand Lacomme (Aug 2012) ▪ 227ha/187ha (cab, shiraz & various port varieties) ▪ 100,000cs own label 100% red ▪ PO Box 23 Riebeek West 7306 ▪ info@allesverloren.co.za ▪ www.allesverloren.co.za ▪ S 33° 21' 32.5" E 018° 52' 24.1" ▪ **T +27 (0)22-461-2320** ▪ F +27 (0)22-461-2444

It doesn't get much more old-school than Allesverloren on the slopes of Swartland's Kasteelberg. The property was acquired by Daniel François Malan in 1872 and has remained in the family ever since. Current cellarmaster Danie is the sixth generation to farm here and he's been turning out honest, unshowy wines since he took over as viticulturist and winemaker in 1987. Time alone will tell if the much-vaunted 'Swartland Revolution' of recent times will take effect here.

★★★★ **Shiraz** 🔲 **11** (★★★★) has red & black fruit, mild spice. Clean & fresh, well assembled but a bit short on wow-factor. Lacks nuance of **10**.

★★★★ **Fine Old Vintage** Enduring port-style from tinta (50%), touriga & souzão. **09** is a return to form after lighter **08** (★★★★). Plums, prunes, nuts & spice. Good palate weight while fresh acidity lends balance.

Cabernet Sauvignon ⓣ ★★★ **10** is rich & full but lacks focus & purity as result of slightly raisined fruit, drying on finish. **Tinta Barocca** ⓣ ★★★ **10** lightly fruity, hint of spice but rather plain, bare boned. **Touriga Nacional** 🔲 ★★★ Dark cherry, fresh acidity, appealing tannic grip on robust **11**. **Danie's Backyard Blend** 🔲 ★★ Shiraz-based combo, **11** has some dark fruit but it's overshadowed by charry oak. **Tinta Barocca Rosé** NEW Export label, missed our deadline. — CE

Alluvia Winery & Private Residence Club

Location/map: Stellenbosch ▪ WO: Banghoek/Western Cape ▪ Est 2002 ▪ 1stB 2005 ▪ Sales daily 9-5 ▪ Tasting & cellar tours by appt ▪ Fee R30 ▪ Closed Good Fri & Dec 25 ▪ Two 5-star self-catering houses & five 4-star suites ▪ Breakfast baskets for stay-over guests ▪ Day & estate spa ▪ Facilities for children ▪ Tour groups ▪ Picnics by appt ▪ Conferences ▪ Hiking & mountain biking trails ▪ Helipad ▪ Fly fishing ▪ PGA golf tee & green ▪ Owner(s) Brugman family ▪ Cellarmaster(s) Delarey Brugman ▪ Winemaker(s) Delarey Brugman & Neil Moorhouse ▪ Viticulturist(s) Bennie Booysen (Jan 2009, consultant) ▪ 11ha/7ha (cabs s/f, sauv) ▪ 30t/3,600cs own label 85% red 10% white 5% straw wine ▪ PO Box 6365 Uniedal 7612 ▪ wine@alluvia.co.za ▪ www.alluvia.co.za ▪ S 33° 55' 4.7" E 018° 55' 37.1" ▪ **T +27 (0)21-885-1661** ▪ F +27 (0)21-885-2064

Learning in 2002 that his wife Sandie was expecting twin girls, co-owner/cellarmaster Delarey Brugman decided to create a legacy and safe, nurturing environment for them, and Alluvia in Stellenbosch's Banhoek Valley is the result. The wines are named after family members, and the residence club has attracted likeminded people. The Give Me A Chance range funds a social upliftment programme.

Princess range

★★★★ **Ilka Cabernet Sauvignon** 🔲 In contrast with its sibling red, **11** ex barrel is a serious fellow. Layered blackcurrants & cedar, whiffs of scrub but firm tannins not integrated. Good potential, all it's missing is time.

★★★★ **Lisa Vineyard Cabernet Franc** 🔲 One of a growing number of varietal bottlings. Barrel sample **11** has fruitcake richness, attractive succulence & oak backing the fruit, providing definition. Varietal true, ripe & generous.

★★★★ **Ilka Sauvignon Blanc** Ex-tank **13** (★★★★) shows apple & melon styling, ripe figs & an ample fresh-toned roundness. Less intense than **10**.

Queen range

★★★★☆ **Sandie Viognier Straw Wine** ✓ Boldly styled in colour, alcohol & sweetness, yet **11** ex-barrel is sublime. Liquidised apricots, honey, quince preserve & barley sugar, but the palate surprises, sweetness with focus thanks to 18 months in barrel. 375 ml. WO Western Cape.

Give Me A Chance range

Red Blend Await next release. **Sauvignon Blanc** New vintage not available. — CR

■ **Almara** *see Southern Sky Wines*

Almenkerk Wine Estate   🍷 🥂 🎋 📷

Location/WO: Elgin ▪ Map: Elgin, Walker Bay & Bot River ▪ Est 2004 ▪ 1stB 2009 ▪ Tasting, sales & cellar tours Wed-Sun 10-4 (Sep-May) & Tue-Sat 10-4 (Jun-Aug) ▪ Open pub tasting except on Mon/Tue ▪ Meals/picnics by prior booking (min 20 pax) or BYO picnic ▪ Walking/hiking trails ▪ Conservation area ▪ Heliport ▪ Boules court ▪ Owner(s) Van Almenkerk family ▪ Cellarmaster(s) Joris van Almenkerk ▪ Winemaker(s) Joris van Almenkerk, with Danver van Wyk (Feb 2009) ▪ Viticulturist(s) Neil de Beer (May 2010) & Kevin Watt (consultant) ▪ 104.2ha/15ha (cabs s/f, malbec, merlot, mourv, p verdot, shiraz, chard, sauv, viog) ▪ 100t/1,600cs own label 65% red 30% white 5% rosé ▪ Brands for clients: De Mikke Patron, Pot Luck Club ▪ BWI ▪ PO Box 1129 Grabouw 7160 ▪ info@almenkerk.co.za ▪ www.almenkerk.co.za ▪ S 34° 12' 55" E 019° 01' 57" ▪ **T +27 (0)21-848-9844** ▪ F +27 (0)86-523-0877

The Belgian/Dutch van Almenkerk family arrived in South Africa in 2002. Two years of intense searching led them to this old apple farm, some of which - 'just enough for profit' - they turned to vineyards. Joris van Almenkerk, a lawyer, then worked at other cellars to ensure this change in career was what he wanted, before studying viti/viniculture at Stellenbosch University. Learning continues with their growing winemaking services and cellar rental business.

Almenkerk Estate range

★★★★ **Syrah** NEW Delicate yet compelling **10** with unusual 15% cab franc. Pure yet subtle spice, red fruits perfume, finely etched structure & elegant freshness eloquently express its cool origin. No new oak.

★★★★ **Chardonnay** Obvious buttery, leesy barrel-ferment character currently prominent on **12**; more limy elegance, bracing acid refresh, trim usual few grams sugar. Natural ferment, 25% new oak.

★★★★ **Sauvignon Blanc** Incisive flinty, mineral tones plus naturally cool feel return **12** to form after **11** (★★★). Has benefited from time in bottle at the cellar. From farm's most exposed block.

Lace range

Red Blend 🍴 ★★☆ Uncomplicated **11**, mainly merlot & shiraz; fresh & fruity; just off-dry. **Rosé** 🍴 ★★★ Shy, smooth & savoury mix merlot, cab & sauvignon blanc. **12** pleasantly just-dry. **Sauvignon Blanc** 🍴 ★★★ Previously 'White'. Early reticence yields to tropical tones & toasty lees hints on gently fresh **12**. Fruit lengthened by few grams sugar. — AL

■ **Alta Casa** *see Darling Cellars*

Alto Wine Estate   🍷 🥂 📷

Location/map/WO: Stellenbosch ▪ Est 1693 ▪ 1stB 1921 ▪ Tasting & sales Mon-Fri 9–5 Sat/Sun 10–4 ▪ Fee R10 wine/port tasting ▪ Closed Good Fri & Dec 25 ▪ Pâté & wine pairing R50pp, advance booking required ▪ Hiking trail ▪ MTB track ▪ Owner(s) Lusan Premium Wines ▪ Cellarmaster(s)/winemaker(s) Schalk van der Westhuizen (Jun 2000) ▪ Viticulturist(s) Schalk van der Westhuizen & Danie van Zyl ▪ 191ha/83ha (cabs s/f, merlot, shiraz) ▪ 800t/100,000cs own label 100% red ▪ PO Box 104 Stellenbosch 7599 ▪ info@alto.co.za ▪ www.alto.co.za ▪ S 34° 0' 10.4" E 018° 50' 49.4" ▪ **T +27 (0)21-881-3884** ▪ F +27 (0)21-881-3894

The original farm was granted in 1693, but the title 'oldest red wine estate in South Africa' refers to a subdivided portion on which the Malans first made wine in the 1920s. They named it Alto, alluding to the farm's altitude on the slopes of the Helderberg Mountain and their aspirations. Under Lusan Premium Wines ownership, the property maintains its reputation for classically styled red wines, including Alto Rouge, a popular label for more than 50 years.

★★★★ **Cabernet Sauvignon** ⊕ Dark & dense in warmer **10** (★★★★) vintage, with molten liquorice & cassis in firm tannic embrace. Sacrifices some of the classical elegance of **09** & previous. Needs time.

★★★★ **Alto Rouge** ✓ 🖾 **11** is a 5-way blend of mostly cab franc & shiraz. This renowned & dependable steakhouse standard is structured, smooth & flavoursome. **10** sold out untasted.

Shiraz ★★★★ Riper & bolder in **11**. Dark, dense & brooding liquorice tones, with robust structure & alcohol. Needs time to harmonise. **MPHS** Occasional release, like **Port**. — MW

Altydgedacht Estate

Location/WO: Durbanville ▪ Map: Durbanville, Philadelphia & Darling ▪ Est 1698 ▪ 1stB 1981 ▪ Tasting & sales Mon-Fri 9-5 Sat 9-3 ▪ Closed Easter Fri/Sun, Dec 25 & Jan 1 ▪ Cellar tours by appt ▪ B'fast & light lunches Mon-Sat 9.30-4 (T +27 (0)21-975-7815/eat@altydgedacht.co.za) ▪ Facilities for children ▪ Conferences ▪ Weddings/functions ▪ Conservation area ▪ Owner(s) Parker family ▪ Cellarmaster(s) Oliver Parker (1981) ▪ Winemaker(s) Etienne Louw (Jan 2006) ▪ Viticulturist(s) John Parker (1981) ▪ 412ha/180ha (16 varieties, r/w) ▪ 1,500t total 160t/22,000cs own label 30% red 65% white 5% rosé ▪ Other export brand: Ralph Parker ▪ PO Box 213 Durbanville 7551 ▪ info@altydgedacht.co.za ▪ www.altydgedacht.co.za ▪ S 33° 50' 46.6" E 018° 37' 26.4" ▪ **T +27 (0)21-976-1295** ▪ F +27 (0)86-218-5637

The Parker family have been farming their enviable 400 ha-plus spread, tucked into the suburban edge of Durbanville, since 1852. Fifth-generation Oliver (cellarmaster) and John (viticulturist) have always taken roads less travelled: dry gewürztraminer, varietal barbera, aromatic blends for spicy food; these were their hallmarks of the early 1990s and - fans will be pleased to know - the current releases are equally fragrant, cuisine-friendly and delicious.

Parker Family Reserve range

★★★★ **Tintoretto** Top-notch Cape Blend of pinotage, barbera, cab & shiraz, **12** is satisfyingly full bodied & ripe. Deep & dark, with solid black fruit, yet elegantly aromatic.

★★★★ **The Ollo Estate White** 🍴 Barrel-fermented chardonnay, viognier, semillon, chenin, **12** top-tier white blend brings out the best of each: ripe tropical fruit, creamy richness & steely, focused acidity.

Weisser Riesling 🍴 ★★★★ Good varietal definition on spare frame, dry **13** has delightfully piercing acidity with spicy marmalade notes. **Méthode Cap Classique Blanc de Blanc** Not tasted. **Semillon Noble Late Harvest** ★★★★ Barrel-fermented botrytis dessert. Mulled honey with nougat nuttiness brings charm to ultra-sweet **12**, rounding out to pineapple syrup & marzipan on finish.

Altydgedacht Estate range

★★★★ **Pinotage** Decidedly fruit-focused **12** has charming sweet spice & savoury mix, plumply rounded body & silky tannin structure. Forceful but elegant expression of variety.

★★★★ **Sauvignon Blanc** 🍴 Stridently pungent aromatic assault from **13** (★★★★) follows to full, complex palate with wild tertiary flavours. **12** less extreme.

Barbera ★★★★ Pioneer producers of north Italian variety celebrate 20th vintage with quirky, spicy **12**. Stewed rhubarb laced with mocha, after richer **11** (★★★★). **Gewürztraminer** 🍴 ★★★ Seductively floral, persistently dry, **13** is light bodied & fragrantly aromatic. Fresh, crisp & unpretentious.

Ralph Parker range

Cabernet Sauvignon Limited Release ★★★★ Leafy, herbaceous **11** offers succulent juicy fruit but lacks ripeness & intensity, finishing with tough, chewy tannins. **Merlot Limited Release** ★★★ **11** shows oak spice & tobacco aromas, following to angular, sinewy body. Meaty & raw, with chewy tannins. **Shiraz** ★★★★ Smoked bacon notes on dense, full-bodied **11**, with sour cherries, wild herbs & sweet oak vanilla spiciness.

Tygerberg range

Cabernet Franc Blanc de Noir 🍴 ★★★ Tinsel-pink, dry **13** has dusty, earthy tones & forthright blackcurrant fruit. Real character & summertime appeal. **Chatelaine** 🍴 ★★★ Brightly fragrant, aromatic off-dry **13** riesling, muscat, gewürztraminer blend, styled for spicy Eastern food. Discontinued: **Gamay Noir**, **Blanc de Blanc**, **Blanc de Blanc Sparkling**. — GdB

Alvi's Drift Private Cellar

Location/map/WO: Worcester ▪ Est 1928 ▪ 1stB 2004 ▪ Tasting, sales & tours by appt ▪ Closed all pub hols ▪ Farm produce ▪ Owner(s) Bertie, Alvi & Johan van der Merwe ▪ Cellarmaster(s) Henk Swart ▪ Winemaker(s) Henk Swart, Alvi van der Merwe & Linley Schultz, with Anton Trollip ▪ Viticulturist(s) Pierre Snyman (consultant) & Jan du Toit ▪ 6,000ha/420ha (ptage, shiraz, chard, chenin, muscat de F) ▪ ±7,500t/400,000cs own label ▪ IPW ▪ PO Box 126 Worcester 6850 ▪ info@alvisdrift.co.za ▪ www.alvisdrift.co.za ▪ S 33° 46' 25.8" E 019° 31' 53.7" ▪ **T +27 (0)23-340-4117** ▪ F +27 (0)86-654-9425

Alvi van der Merwe was a medical doctor who always loved working in the vineyards established by his grandfather on the family farm. His brother Johan was a lawyer with a particular interest in business. Linley Schultz was chief winemaker at Distell with a yearning for a brand of his own. Their recent collaboration has resulted in what they say is 'an authentic family-owned wine business providing great wines at reasonable prices' and 'the biggest and best producer' in Worcester's Scherpenheuvel wine ward, specialising in pinotage, chenin and viognier.

AD range

★★★★ **Drift Fusion** ⊕ Suave combo cab, pinotage &, in **09**, shiraz. Berry & clove appeal, supportive tannins, savoury & dry finish despite grain sugar & dash new American oak.

★★★★ **Chardonnay** 🍴 🏠 Vanilla-seamed **12**'s (★★★) intense flavours & syrupy texture almost parody the variety, soupçon sugar more overt than in **11**. Lees-aged with oak-chips versus previous' barrels.

★★★★ **CVC** 🍴 🏠 Attractive white blend, aged in 30% new barrels giving vanilla-tinged creamy plushness to **12**'s lemon & white peach. Chardonnay upped to 50%, equal viognier & chenin.

Premium Selection

★★★★☆ **Muscat de Frontignan White** ✓ 🏠 Alluring fortified dessert, small-oak matured. Glorious copper hue of **10** (★★★★★) only one of its charms: 'dry' notes of tealeaf, figs & cherry tobacco, 'moist' honey, fig jam & sultana, & gingery caramel tail. What an endless, unctuous mouthful! Easily trumps last **07**.

Signature range

★★★★ **Viognier** 🍴 🏠 Hedonistic **13**'s nectarine & apricot richness enlivened by fresh acidity & careful oaking. Unsubtle but typical & delicious.

Cabernet Sauvignon ⊕ 🍴 🏠 ★★★ Fruit bomb **10** dusted with oak spice, very drinkable. Lightly oak-chipped, like other reds, Chardonnay & Viogner. **Pinotage** 🍴 🏠 ★★★ Step-up **12** savoury & earthy with spiced plum finish; 'perfect with duck' say its creators. **Shiraz** ⊕ 🍴 🏠 ★★★ Faint 'wild' hint on cherry-fruited **10**. **Chenin Blanc** ✓ 🍴 🏠 ★★★★ Floral **13** is fruity & generous, with nutty highlights & crisp acidity. **Sauvignon Blanc** ✓ 🍴 🏠 ★★★★ Like many of these, **13** punches above its price. Pungent capsicum & nettle, bold flavours, balanced vinosity & weight at just 12% alcohol. **Chardonnay-Viognier** ✓ 🍴 🏠 ★★★★ Improved **12** (90% chardonnay) barrel-aged for rounded & creamy mouthfeel. Appetising bakery/confectionery store aromas, noticeably sweetish but balanced farewell.

Naughty Girl range

Sparkling Sahara NEW 🏠 ★★ NV celebratory tipple drier than siblings, slightly more alcohol with tannic nudge. **Sparkling Rosé** 🏠 ★★★ The original 'Naughty Girl', now renamed but still a low-alcohol, gently sweet NV sparkler with flirty cherry flavours. **Sparkling Nude** NEW 🏠 ★★★ Appley aromas waft from cheerful NV sweet bubbly, just 7.5% alcohol & ready to party. — DB, CvZ

◼ **Amandalia** *see* Rooiberg Winery

Amani Vineyards 🍴🍷🎴🏠📷🍵🍴🛒

Location/map: Stellenbosch ▪ WO: Stellenbosch/Western Cape/Upper Hemel-en-Aarde Valley ▪ Est/1stB 1997 ▪ Tasting, sales & cellar tours Mon-Sat 9-5 ▪ Closed Easter Fri-Mon, Dec 25/26 & Jan 1 ▪ Mini cheese platters @ R35, pre-booking essential ▪ Facilities for children ▪ BYO picnic ▪ Walks/hikes ▪ Owner(s) Lynde & Rusty Myers ▪ Cellarmaster(s) Carmen Stevens (Jul 2005) ▪ Winemaker(s) Carmen Stevens (Jul 2005), with Chris van Reenen (Jan 2011) ▪ Viticulturist(s) JD Stassen (Apr 2006) & Chris Keet (2012, consultant) ▪ 38ha/32ha (cabs s/f, merlot, mourv, shiraz, chard, sauv, viog) ▪ 217t/20,000cs own label 70% red 29% white 1% rosé ▪ EnviroWines ▪ PO Box 12422 Die Boord 7613 ▪ wine@amani.co.za ▪ www.amani.co.za ▪ S 33° 57' 54.3" E 018° 43' 59.5" ▪ **T +27 (0)21-881-3930** ▪ F +27 (0)21-881-3931

There's a clear aesthetic at this boutique winery on Stellenbosch's Polkadraai Hills, where the grapes off the sustainably farmed vineyards are skilfully vinified by Carmen Stevens and Chris van Reenen. The wines are generally very ripe, richly fruited and powerful yet soft, with a touch of gratifying sweetness; oaking is mostly restrained. Sentiment is not forgotten, with wines named for the children of owners Lynde and Rusty Myers: Kenzie (only in US), Jordan, and the late Forest.

★★★★ **Merlot** Powerful, alcoholic **11**, the ultra-ripe sweet fruit also giving plenty of flavour but less freshness, all supported by sensibly restrained oaking. With a lean muscularity allowing for ageing.

★★★★ **Cabernet Franc-Merlot** ⏱ Enticing **10** (★★★☆) last year, with dollops cab & malbec, but less classic than **09**. Fresh, spicy-leafy aromas; succulent flavours with modest savoury grip. WO W Cape.

★★★★ **Forest Myers** Amani's ripe charm on **11** from shiraz & mourvèdre, the blend giving some complexity. Typical fruit intensity too, quite soft though powerful; strong acid a bit awkward. Sweet finish.

★★★★ **I Am 1** Good-natured **11** cab-based Bordeaux blend with a drop of shiraz, offering spicy, sweet-fruited, bright charm in the most restrained & balanced of the reds. Ready now, but could keep.

★★★★ **Chardonnay** ▦ As was lively **11**, **12** (★★★☆) naturally fermented & with only older barrels used for maturation. Easygoing balance of structure & fruit, gently rich, soft textured.

★★★★ **Kamili Chardonnay-Viognier** ⏱ ▦ Last ed, **11** (★★★☆) almost semi-sweet, unlike **10**, with easy charm. Structure from chardonnay & light oaking, with viognier's peachy richness, but no intensity. **Cabernet Sauvignon** NEW ★★★☆ Pleasing blend of savoury & berry notes on firmly built, muscular **11**. Needs a few years for acid & tannin to harmonise, but there's enough fruit to allow it. **Pinotage** NEW ★★★ Ripe, easy, fruity, mildly sweetish **11** (though packing an alcoholic punch). A cheerful offering from Hemel-en-Aarde grapes. **Pendana Shiraz** ▦ ★★★ Ripe, fruity, smoky aromas on **11** lead to flavourful, chunky, sweetish, soft but rather acidic palate. Dollop of cab & other grapes. **Jordan Myers** Occasional release. **Poppy Blush** ▦ ★★ Mildly fruity, off-dry **12** rosé. **Sauvignon Blanc** ▦ ★★★ A tiny oak influence adds broadness to the green-tinged tropical character on pleasantly fresh, soft & lightish **12**. — TJ

Amares Wines

Location/map: Stellenbosch ▪ WO: Simonsberg-Stellenbosch/Stellenbosch ▪ Est 2005 ▪ 1stB 2006 ▪ Tasting, sales & cellar tours Mon-Sat by appt ▪ Closed all pub hols ▪ Cheese & olive platters by appt ▪ Owner(s) Amares Wines (Pty) Ltd ▪ Winemaker(s) Neville Koudstaal (Mar 2006), Sally Noel & Renier Pienaar ▪ Viticulturist(s) Amares Wines ▪ 5ha/2ha (cab) ▪ 4t/750cs own label 100% red ▪ PO Box 7253 Stellenbosch 7599 ▪ info@amares.co.za ▪ www. amares.co.za ▪ S 33° 54′ 30.30″ E 018° 53′ 27.21″ ▪ **T +27 (0)21-887-9414** ▪ F +27 (0)21-413-0854

A partnership of 'family and friends who cherish all things decadent' was established on this tiny farm surrounded by Stellenbosch's famous Rustenberg estate. There's a few hectares of cabernet here, and vegetables and free-range chickens too. The operation is small-scale and hands-on, guided by organic principles.

Cabernet Sauvignon ⏱ ★★★☆ Like previous vintage, **09** solid, sweet-fruited, powerful & oak-influenced; a few years should help soften the slightly drying finish. **Syrah** ⏱ ★★★☆ Big, exuberant, deep-coloured **09**; lots of savoury-edged ripe fruit, lots of power. High alcohol adds sweetness. WO Stellenbosch. — TJ

■ **Ama Ulibo** see Goedverwacht Wine Estate

Ambeloui Wine Cellar

Location: Hout Bay ▪ Map: Cape Peninsula ▪ WO: Western Cape ▪ Est 1994 ▪ 1stB 1998 ▪ Tasting by appt ▪ Owner(s) Nick & Ann Christodoulou ▪ Cellarmaster(s)/viticulturist(s) Nick Christodoulou (1994) ▪ Winemaker(s) Nick Christodoulou (2005), with Alexis & Christo Christodoulou ▪ 1ha/0.5ha (pinot, chard) ▪ 15t/3,000cs own label 5% white 95% MCC ▪ PO Box 26800 Hout Bay 7872 ▪ wine@ambeloui.co.za ▪ www. ambeloui.co.za ▪ S 34° 0′ 49.5″ E 018° 22′ 55.4″ ▪ **T +27 (0)21-790-7386/+27 (0)82-880-1715/+27 (0)82-460-8399** ▪ F +27 (0)88-021-790-7386

Nick Christodoulou came to Cape Town's Hout Bay to find a home by the sea. Soon its 'little vineyard' ('ambeloui' in Cypriot) fired a bubbly passion and a cellar was excavated under the house... Twenty years on, Nick and charming family have run out of new offspring after whom to name the vintages, but not regular customers who fill their car boots on the traditional sale day, the first Saturday in November.

★★★★☆ **Méthode Cap Classique Rosanne Rosé** ✓ **NV** sparkling from chardonnay (55%) & pinot noir, base wine lightly oaked. Thrilling latest release offers delicate red fruit flavours, silky texture & refreshing dry mousse. Complex & most satisfying.

★★★★☆ **Méthode Cap Classique** ✓ Stylish chardonnay-pinot noir (55/45) bubble, 10% of base wine wooded; includes grapes from other growers. Rich & aromatic **10** 'Miranda' has a plush brioche/baked apple character from 3 years on lees. **11** 'Max' is younger, tighter; both are exquisitely focused, mouthwatering. — DS

■ **Amistad Wine Company** see The Amistad Wine Company

Anatu Wines 🍷 🍴

Location: Stellenbosch ▪ Map: Helderberg ▪ WO: Coastal ▪ Est/1stB 2002 ▪ Tasting, sales & cellar tours by appt ▪ Closed all pub hols ▪ Owner(s) André & Freda Hamersma ▪ Winemaker(s) Micu Narunsky (Jan 2009) ▪ 40t/5,600cs own label 40% red 40% white 20% rosé ▪ Other export brand: Sereia ▪ Postnet Suite 246 Private Bag X5061 Stellenbosch 7599 ▪ sales@anatu.co.za ▪ www.anatu.co.za ▪ S 34° 1' 52.20" E 018° 50' 46.73" ▪ **T +27 (0)83-307-9333** ▪ F +27 (0)86-577-5019

Anatu is a story of two people from different backgrounds and careers drawn together by a passion for wine: former banker André Hamersma and jazz pianist Micu Narunsky, who fell in love with wine while touring the French vineyards. They make a formidable pair, believing that blending - not only complementary varieties but also grapes from different areas - gives best results.

Family Blend range

★★★★☆ **Red** ⑫ Full-bodied **10** (★★★★) mix grenache & shiraz from Wellington & Stellenbosch, concentrated black fruit & good oaking, with warmish finish. Attractive, but misses the complexity of last-tasted **08**.

★★★★ **White 12** (★★★★) chiefly chenin, with grenache blanc & colombard, briefly oaked, is understated, savoury. Intended to be accessible young, but pre-bottling is actually quite esoteric, lacks primary fruit of **11**.

Rosé ★★★☆ Carefully conceived **12** preview from grenache, shiraz, mourvèdre, lightly wooded, shows strawberry & spice. Clean, fresh & dry, with good length.

Fugue range

★★★★☆ **Red** ⑫ Super debut **10**, shiraz & grenache from Stellenbosch & Wellington, is restrained, combining clean black fruit, meat & wild game aromas. Full-bodied, concentrated fruit flavours with a delicious core of well-judged oak. Alcohol (15.5%) well hidden.

★★★★☆ **White** ⑫ **11** blend of roussanne, chenin & grenache blanc; rich, vibrant & full bodied, waxy ripe-fruit flavours supported by precise oaking & firm minerality. Elegant, with an unflagging end.

Rosé ★★★ **12** from partly wooded shiraz, mourvèdre & grenache is pleasantly rustic, with red & black cherry, some earthiness, moderate acidity. Discontinued: **Shiraz**. — CE

◼ **Ancient Earth** see Bellingham

Andersons Wines 🍷

Location/WO: Plettenberg Bay ▪ Map: Klein Karoo & Garden Route ▪ Est 2008 ▪ 1stB 2011 ▪ Tasting by appt ▪ Fee R5/wine ▪ Closed all pub hols ▪ Owner(s) Ian Anderson ▪ Winemaker(s) Anton Smal (Bramon Wines) ▪ Viticulturist(s) Ian Anderson, assisted by Anton Smal ▪ 22ha/2.5ha (sauv) ▪ 5.5t/600cs own label 100% white ▪ PO Box 2564 Plettenberg Bay 6600 ▪ ian@app.co.za ▪ S 33° 59' 17.7" E 023° 27' 15.1" ▪ **T +27 (0)44-534-8873/+27 (0)83-453-3624** ▪ F +27 (0)44-534-8873

Owner Ian Anderson planned to retire on his Plettenberg Bay property but now finds himself nurturing young and promising sauvignon vines, assisted by Anton Smal of Bramon Wines. 'We are very proud to be in the wine business in our area,' says Ian, whose wine is named after the endemic Ghost Moth.

Leto Venus Sauvignon Blanc 🏛 ★★★ Challenging, bird-marauded **13** preview is deftly handled, shows riper white peach flavours, & more typical Plettenberg racy freshness & seafood compatibility. — HJ,CvZ

Andreas Wines 🍷🍴

Location/WO: Wellington ▪ Map: Paarl & Wellington ▪ Est 2003 ▪ 1stB 2004 ▪ Tasting & sales by appt Mon-Fri 9–5 ▪ Fee R10 ▪ Closed all pub hols ▪ Cellar tours by appt ▪ Accommodation ▪ Weddings/functions ▪ Owner(s) Jan & Anita Bokdal ▪ Cellarmaster(s) Howard Heughs & Eugenie Ellis ▪ Winemaker(s) Howard Heughs & Ettienne Malan (consultant) ▪ Viticulturist(s) Howard Heughs ▪ 6ha/4.5ha (mourv, shiraz) ▪ 48t/3,168cs own label 100% red ▪ PO Box 892 Wellington 7654 ▪ andreas@ezinet.co.za ▪ www.andreas.co.za ▪ S 33° 37' 52.0" E 019° 2' 50.1" ▪ **T +27 (0)21-873-2286** ▪ F +27 (0)86-664-5087

Swedish couple Jan and Anita Bokdal realised a lifelong ambition of owning an operational wine farm when they acquired Groenendal in Wellington's Bovlei Valley in 2005. A single shiraz is made from the property's small vineyard.

★★★★ **Andreas Shiraz** ⑫ Distinctive super-silky styling continues in **10**, intense choc-dipped wild berry & liquorice, well-judged oak & wine's signature spicy blackberry liqueur aftertaste. — WB

Andy Mitchell Wines

Location: Greyton ▪ Map: Southern Cape ▪ WO: Swartland/Walker Bay/Western Cape ▪ Est/1stB 2003 ▪ Tasting, sales & cellar tours by appt ▪ Closed Easter Fri/Sun & Dec 25 ▪ Owner(s) Andy & Vikki Mitchell ▪ Cellarmaster(s) Andy Mitchell (Jan 2003) ▪ Winemaker(s) Andy Mitchell (Jan 2003), with Olivia Mitchell (Jan 2008) ▪ 1st own label 42% red 21% white 13% rosé 24% MCC + 200cs for clients ▪ PO Box 543 Paarden Eiland 7420 ▪ andy@andymitchellwines.com ▪ www.andymitchellwines.com ▪ S 34° 2' 26.3" E 019° 37' 2.6" ▪ **T +27 (0)28-254-9045** ▪ F +27 (0)86-611-3106

The Mitchell boutique family vintners in pastoral Greyton upped production from usually widely sourced grapes with their first locally grown (WO Greyton) shiraz, from nearby Heuningkloof, proposed new home for the cellar/tasting room. Daughter Olivia survived a dunking in fermenting pinot noir. Her new mobile didn't. 'Supposedly punching down, probably tweeting!' teases dad Andy.

★★★★ **Swartland Chenin Blanc** ⓐ 🏠 40 year old Malmesbury bushvines; cask-fermented **11** generous fruit yet appealing minerality, lees complexity, dry tail. Greater dimension than **09** (★★★★). No **10**.

Elgin Pinot Noir Await next, as for **Crooked Path Pinot Noir**, **Breakfast Rock Syrah** & **Nerina Shiraz Rosé**. **Crooked Path Shiraz** Current **07** untasted. **Syrah-Grenache-Mourvèdre** NEW ★★★ **12** cherry fruit, meat & tobacco tones; juicy farewell curtailed by strong tannins. WO W Cape. **Walker Bay Chenin Blanc** NEW 🏠 ★★★★ Oak spice coats **12**'s ripe peachy fruit, imparts weight & depth as well as oily/waxy texture. Mouthfilling, with food-friendly vinosity. — WB, GdB

Angels Tears Wines

Location: Franschhoek ▪ WO: Western Cape ▪ Closed to public ▪ Owner(s) Dutch & Belgium consortium ▪ Cellarmaster(s)/winemaker(s)/viticulturist(s) Karl Lambour (May 2012) ▪ 32ha/22ha (cab, merlot, chard, sauv) ▪ 600t/60,000cs own label 30% red 60% white 10% rosé ▪ PO Box 102 Franschhoek 7690 ▪ reservations@grandeprovence.co.za ▪ www.angelstears.co.za ▪ **T +27 (0)21-876-8600** ▪ F +27 (0)21-876-8601

Debuting in our 1989 guide as Larmes des Anges, this big-selling second-tier range from Grande Provence recalls the legend that on tasting the fruits of a fine vintage, the angels weep for joy.

Merlot-Cabernet Sauvignon-Shiraz-Petit Verdot ★★ Good everyday red, **12** fruity, easy, with smooth curves & food-inviting savouriness. **Rosé** ★★ Light berry tones on **12** off-dry quaffer. **Sauvignon Blanc** ★★★ Sugarcane & cut grass, soft acidity & gentle pithy grip, **12** is easy to sip. **Muscat d'Alexandrie-Chenin Blanc** ★★ Aromatic semi-sweet since 1989. Muscat & white pepper spice, lemon flavours in **12** incarnation. As ever, drink soon. — CvZ

■ **Ankerman** see uniWines Vineyards

Annandale Wines

Location/map: Stellenbosch ▪ WO: Stellenbosch/Coastal ▪ Est/1stB 1996 ▪ Tasting, sales & cellar tours Mon-Sat 9-5 ▪ Fee R20 ▪ Closed Easter Fri-Mon, Ascension Day & Dec 25 ▪ Farm produce ▪ BYO picnic ▪ Owner(s) Hempies du Toit ▪ Winemaker(s)/viticulturist(s) Hempies du Toit (1996) ▪ 72ha/45ha (cabs s/f, merlot, shiraz) ▪ 250t/10,000cs own label 100% red ▪ PO Box 12681 Stellenbosch 7613 ▪ info@annandale.co.za ▪ www.annandale.co.za ▪ S 33° 59' 49.2" E 018° 49' 50.9" ▪ **T +27 (0)21-881-3560** ▪ F +27 (0)21-881-3562

Hempies du Toit, owner, winemaker and viticulturist of boutique winery Annandale, traces his heritage in wine back to the earliest days of the Cape settlement. The ever-exuberant rugby legend's rustic estate on the Helderberg is notable for resolutely traditional winemaking and extended barrel maturation.

★★★★ **Cabernet Sauvignon** ⓐ Serious-minded & classically styled. A melange of dark cherry & cassis on bold, spicy **04**, bottled after 7 years in barrel & showing similar fine form to previous.

★★★★ **Shiraz** ⓐ Spicy, oaky complexity adds to black pastille fruit on solid, unshowy & firmly structured **04**. Made to last.

★★★★ **Nostalgia** ⓐ Tribute to old-style Cape reds & the founders of Alto Estate. From cab, shiraz & cinsaut - latter adding charming wild, raspberry notes in **NV**. From various years, is mature but still vibrant.

Merlot ⓐ ★★★★ Big, burly **05**'s herbal-edged fruit has survived 6 years in oak, still some freshness. Ready now, but like all these should keep well. **Cavalier** ⓐ ★★★★ **04** Bordeaux-style blend with shiraz oozes spice & black fruit. Big & sturdy, yet balanced & smooth with lots of life after 7 years in barrel. More complex than **01** (★★★☆). Great with a roast. **Sauvignon Blanc** ⓟ ★★★☆ Unusual, successful take on variety in **11**. Oxidative styling lessens fruitiness, not flavour. Lightly rich, dry, savoury. Coastal WO. **CVP** ⓟ ★★★☆ 'Cape Vintage Port' from shiraz; **04** offers spicy fruitcake flavours, vibrant raisins & spirity grip. — WB

Annex Kloof Wines

Location: Malmesbury ▪ Map: Swartland ▪ WO: Swartland/Western Cape ▪ Est/1stB 2006 ▪ AnnexKloof stall on N7: sales daily; tasting Fri 8-5.30 Sat 8-3 Sun 9-5 ▪ Farm: tasting, sales & cellar tours by appt only ▪ Closed Easter Fri-Mon, Ascension Day, Pentecost, Dec 16/25/26 & Jan 1 ▪ BYO picnic ▪ Walks/hikes ▪ 4x4 trail ▪ Conservation area ▪ Owner(s) Toeloe Basson with sons Thys, Hugo & Tobie ▪ Winemaker(s) Hugo Basson (Jan 2006) ▪ 450ha (cab, malbec, merlot, ptage, shiraz, chard, chenin, sauv) ▪ 4,300t/1,250cs own label 95% red 5% white ▪ PO Box 772 Malmesbury 7299 ▪ hugo@annexkloofwines.co.za ▪ www.annexkloofwines.co.za ▪ S 33° 30' 39.1" E 018° 48' 22.5" (estate), S 33° 21' 5.69" E 018° 42' 36.87" (farmstall) ▪ **T +27 (0)22-487-3870** ▪ F +27 (0)86-569-3957

This is a story of three brothers, Thys, Tobie and Hugo Basson, on three Swartland farms, each having vineyards with individual characters and which provide fruit for both big-brand buyers and the range below, made by Hugo. Bottling under the Annex Kloof label is up - 'thanks to demand, especially from abroad,' says Hugo.

Annex Kloof range
★★★★ **Malbec** The cellar's calling card. Aromas of sage & liquorice on **11** (★★★☆) lead to rather less than usual flavour intensity, more prominent austerity. A few years may help - but less complex than last-tasted **09**.
Tulu ★★★☆ Was 'Red Blend'. Shiraz with mourvèdre, grenache. **11** brighter, more fruit-forward than **10**; plenty of flavour satisfaction with balanced freshness, grip, for current enjoyment. **Port** Await next.

Xenna range
★★★★ **Chenin Blanc** ✓ 🍴 **13** fine example of unoaked old-vine chenin. Incredible concentration; flavour richness of pristine spicy pear, green apples all delivered with freshness, persistence & just 13% alcohol.

> **Cabernet Sauvignon** ☺ 🍴 ★★★ Pleasantly rugged & unpretentious **11**. Warm dark earth smells; flavoursome with supple, chunky tannins. WO W Cape, as for Chenin.

Pinotage ✓ 🍴 ★★★☆ Generous luscious dark cherries, mulberries just cover **11**'s big 15% alcohol. Rounding in old oak lends polished, smooth feel, making for good drinking now & another year or two. **Shiraz** ⓟ 🍴 ★★★☆ **11** in honest, rustic style. Rich, savoury flavours backed by rumbling tannins. Rounded by older oak. — AL

AntHill Wines 🍷

Location: Somerset West ▪ WO: Stellenbosch/Elgin ▪ Est 1999 ▪ 1stB 2000 ▪ Tasting by appt ▪ Owner(s) Mark Howell & Hylton Schwenk ▪ Winemaker(s) Mark Howell (Feb 2000) ▪ 600cs own label 100% red ▪ 19 Immelman Rd Somerset West 7130 ▪ www@telkomsa.net ▪ S 34° 4' 30.8" E 018° 52' 37.6" ▪ **T +27 (0)82-895-9008** ▪ F +27 (0)86-668-4566

Truly boutique in style, Anthill was part of the dawn of the garagiste movement in South Africa. Mark Howell, partner and winemaker, is now fully self-employed and this 'will allow the time to possibly increase the volumes slightly'.

★★★★ **Cabernet Sauvignon Entre Nous 10** (★★★★) shade off **09**. Refreshing on the palate, packed with pure blackcurrant fruit & oak flavours. Soft-textured & harmonious, but a swift farewell.
★★★★ **Long John Silver Pinot Noir** NEW ✓ **10** from Elgin, soft, savoury strawberry compote with vanilla oak perfume. Elegant & delicate yet serious, with depth & long savoury finish.

> **Pieces of 8** NEW ☺ 🍴 ★★★ Bright & cheerful chardonnay-led **11** blend will bring a smile to your face with juicy ripe fruit & vanilla oak flavours. Delicious &, winemaker says, great with sushi.

The Persian Shiraz In abeyance, like **Davey Jones Locker**. — WB

Anthonij Rupert Wyne

Location/map: Franschhoek ▪ WO: Western Cape/Coastal/Citrusdal Mountain/Franschhoek/Stellenbosch/Swartland/Elandskloof/Overberg ▪ Est 1714 ▪ 1stB 1982 ▪ Two tasting rooms: Anthonij Rupert Mon-Sat 10-4.

30; Terra del Capo Tue–Sun 10-4.30 ▪ Fee R10-R60 per flight ▪ Closed Good Fri & Dec 25 ▪ Antipasti Bar for light meals & refreshments ▪ Cheese, olive oil & honey ▪ Franschhoek Motor Museum T +27 (0)21-874-9002 Mon-Fri 10-4 Sat/Sun 10-3; admittance R60pp, seniors R50 & children (3-12 yrs) R30 ▪ Owner(s) Johann Rupert ▪ Winemaker(s) Dawie Botha (Jan 2005), Zanie Viljoen (Jan 2007) & Vernon van der Hoven (2012) ▪ 4 farms: total ±1,100ha/±210ha (cabs s/f, carignan, cinsaut, grenache, merlot, mourv, pinot, sangio, shiraz, chard, chenin, pinot grigio, rouss) ▪ ISO 14001:2009 ▪ PO Box 435 Franschhoek 7690 ▪ tasting@rupertwines.com ▪ www.rupertwines.com ▪ S 33° 53' 16.77 E 019° 0' 17.70" (Anthonij Rupert/Cape of Good Hope), S 33° 52' 47. 36" E 019° 0' 10.91" (Terra Del Capo/Protea) ▪ **T +27 (0)21-874-9000/+27 (0)21-874-9041 (tasting)** ▪ F +27 (0)21-874-9111

'Wines of extraordinary quality to be enjoyed when ready for the market.' This, says Anthonij Rupert Wyne MD Gary Baumgarten, is the vision current owner Johann Rupert inherited from his late brother Anthonij over a decade ago, and still espouses at the gracious Franschhoek home-farm, L'Ormarins. Setting for the popular Franschhoek Motor Museum, the property now also houses not one but two elegant cellardoors: one, nearer the entrance, dedicated to the Protea and Terra del Capo ranges, where an antipasti bar showcases the food-friendliness of the Italian varieties, in particular, and a lounge area offers a taste of 'la dolce vita'; the second at the manor house, where antique furniture and art (and glorious mountains) provide the backdrop for the Cape of Good Hope and Anthonij Rupert flagships.

Anthonij Rupert range

★★★★ **Cabernet Franc 08** riper & richer than previous, reigned in by dry tannins. Still polished but quite assertive. Deserves cellar time & decanting. WO Coastal.

★★★★ **Merlot** Muscular **08** is complex & intense, with layers of dark smoky fruit sheathed in firm chalky tannins. Distinguished, will reward cellaring.

★★★★☆ **Optima** Youthful **09** cab, merlot, cab franc blend is tightly coiled, with more restrained fruit & structure in this classic vintage than riper **08**. Shows inherent balance & elegance, with potential for further development.

★★★★☆ **Anthonij Rupert** NEW Classy debut for **07** cab-led Bordeaux blend with cab franc, merlot & petit verdot. New oak provides supportive, not assertive platform for rich cassis & herbaceous flavours. Still an infant but shows inherent pedigree.

Cabernet Sauvignon ★★★★★ **08** raises the bar on **07** (★★★★), with a dense core of lavish dark fruit underpinned by spicy dry tannins. All still tightly buttoned, but with excellent ageing potential. WO Coastal. **Syrah** ★★★★ **08**'s opulent blackcurrant & sweet-spiced fruit equally matched with 100% new oak. Richly textured step up on **07** (★★★★), with power & structure to age. WO Franschhoek. **L'Ormarins Brut Classique** NEW ★★★★ Champagne-method sparkling, **NV** chardonnay & pinot noir (60/40) taut blend shows clean-cut lemon tones. 48 months on lees imparts freshness & elegance.

Cape of Good Hope range

★★★★ **Parel Vallei Farmstead Merlot 09** redolent with eucalyptus, mint & cloves from low-yielding Helderberg vines. Well tailored & sleek, with streamlined tannic structure. New oak melded into opulent fruit.

★★★★ **Van Lill & Visser Chenin Blanc 12** understated, demure fruit from 50 year old Citrusdal bushvines. Structured & silky, threaded with chenin's clean acidity. No **11**.

★★★★ **Altima Sauvignon Blanc** Now bears name of stunningly scenic Rupert farm in Elandskloof. **13** preview shows intensity & refinement of high-altitude fruit, zesty grapefruit leavened by leesy richness & lingering mineral farewell.

Basson Pinotage ⊕ ★★★ Perdeberg grapes in faintly strawberry/acetone **09**. Marked acidity detracts from soft fruit, finish. **Serruria Chardonnay** ★★★★ **12** alluring toasty, lime & honey aromas, more demure on the palate. Svelte undertone to Elandskloof's cool-fruited elegance. **Laing Semillon** ⊕ ★★★★ Judiciously oaked **10** from Citrusdal Mountain raised bar on soft **09** (★★★★) with greater intensity, structure. Yellow peach/fennel hints, fine acid thread, presence & poise at moderate 13% alcohol.

Terra Del Capo range

Sangiovese ✓ ★★★★ Flavoursome & sappy **10** has fennel & savoury tomato nuances. Balanced, with dry food-friendly finish – invite the whole family! WO Coastal. **Arné** ⊕ ★★★★ Successful blend **09** of merlot & sangiovese (50/50) balances forthright dark chocolate notes with gritty black fruit & spice. Last-tasted **07** (★★★★) raised the bar. **Pinot Grigio** 🍷 ★★★★ **13** youthful preview's cool green aromatics & racy acidity, complimented by subtle leesy breadth.

Protea range

Chardonnay ☺ ★★★ Quaffable preview of **13** has clean citrus, pear tones & a brush of oak.

Cabernet Sauvignon ✓ 🗐 ★★★☆ **11** supple, juicy black fruit clothing dry, amenable tannins. Accomplished & accessible. **Merlot** 🗐 ★★★ Food-styled **12** has smoky red fruit & mint in firm, dry tannic embrace. **Shiraz** ✓ 🗐 ★★★★ Balanced **12** is a succulent & characterful quaffer. Savoury & spicy tones supported by a supple structure. WO Coastal, like next. **Reserve** ✓ ★★★★ Appealing aromatic lift to balanced & satisfying **11** blend. Mostly shiraz & mourvèdre, with a splash of viognier. **Chenin Blanc** 🗐 ★★★ Ripe apple & almond flavours on oak-brushed **12**. Plump but balanced by fresh acidity. **Sauvignon Blanc** 🗐 ★★★ **13** tank sample shows brisk herbaceous style. Tad less fruity than previous, still refreshing. — MW

Anura Vineyards

Location: Paarl ▪ Map: Paarl & Wellington ▪ WO: Simonsberg-Paarl/Western Cape/Coastal/Paarl/Darling/Swartland ▪ Est 1990 ▪ 1stB 2001 ▪ Tasting, sales & cellar tours daily 9.30–5 ▪ Closed Good Fri, Dec 25 & Jan 1 ▪ Fee R40 (cheese & wine) ▪ Lilly Pad Restaurant ▪ Tour groups ▪ Farm produce ▪ Conferences ▪ Owner(s) Tymen Bouma ▪ Cellarmaster(s) Tymen Bouma (1990) ▪ Winemaker(s) Johnnie Calitz & Lance Bouma (Jan 2007) ▪ Viticulturist(s) Hannes Kloppers (Oct 1997) ▪ 240ha/120ha (cab, carignan, grenache, malbec, merlot, mourv, nebbiolo, p verdot, ptage, pinot, sangio, shiraz, tempranillo, chard, chenin, nouvelle, pinot gris, sauv, verdelho) ▪ 750t/100,000cs own label 80% red 17% white 2% rosé 1% fortified + 20,000cs for clients ▪ Other export brand: Zee ▪ Brands for clients: Heart & Soul, Joy, Kiss My Springbok, Wine Lover's Collection ▪ IPW ▪ PO Box 244 Klapmuts 7625 ▪ info@anura.co.za, wine@anura.co.za ▪ www.anura.co.za ▪ S 33° 48′ 41.4″ E 018° 53′ 19.8″ ▪ **T** +27 (0)21-875-5360 ▪ F +27 (0)21-875-5657

Diversity is key at the Bouma family's tourist-friendly estate in Klapmuts. It shows in their formidable range of grape varieties and wines, visitor attractions and operations, and their ever-increasing facilities. Soon, a conference centre will be added to the restaurant, smoking house, cheesery, deli and lifestyle tasting venue. In the cellar, the grape sorting system was fine tuned and, beyond, some 8 ha of vineyards, including Italian and Spanish varieties, were planted.

LB Series

★★★★ **Sangiovese** 🖉 Ambitious effort, **10** is fresher, brighter than last-tasted **07**. Thick tannins under cheerful red berry fruit, should soften with time.

★★★★ **Shiraz** ☯ Subtle, smooth & rounded, with floral scents & peppery spices, first-release **09** augurs well. Hints of Rhône with solid New World ripeness.

★★★★ **Cape Blend** NEW 🖉 Debut **10** in prestige series combines pinotage (30%), merlot, malbec & shiraz in appealing, spicy interpretation. Clever balance of power & character, should still improve.

La Traviata ☯ ★★★☆ Oaked **09** based on roussanne, grenache blanc, with chenin & telling 8% viognier. WO Coastal. Discontinued: **Verdelho**.

Reserves & Limited Releases

★★★★ **Malbec Limited Release** 🖉 **10** has last-reviewed **08**'s elegant structure & fruit concentration, with appealing spicy notes & focused finish. Worthy effort.

★★★★ **Merlot Reserve** 🖉 **10** follows previous form, with plush texture & appealing savoury notes in full-bodied, generously ripe fruit. Dark & deep, yet showing subtle floral fragrances.

★★★★ **Syrah Limited Release** 🖉 Meaty butterscotch & white pepper dominate bold nose on **08**, but palate offers enticing scrub, delicate floral & sweet spicy notes over solid tannin backbone. WO Paarl.

★★★★ **Chardonnay Limited Release** 🖉 Barrel-fermented &-matured **12** still struggling with oak, but fruit & mineral notes beginning to emerge. Fresh lemon wrapped in lees creaminess, shows potential.

★★★★ **Sauvignon Blanc Unfiltered Reserve** 🖉 Seriously conceived WO Darling, **12** shows weight & complexity from extensive skin & lees contact. Wild nettle aromas spice up vibrant gooseberry fruit.

★★★★ **Méthode Cap Classique Brut** Oxidative style of **09** chardonnay-pinot blend shows in exaggerated brioche & sherry notes. Long lees-ageing & generous fruit bolster honey-rich palate. WO W Cape.

★★★★ **Cape Vintage Reserve** NEW 🖉 Carefully crafted **10** port-style from Robertson tinta barocca spent 32 months in barrel. Fortified with aged brandy, shows traditional grippy spirit, restrained extraction.

Cabernet Sauvignon Reserve ★★★ **09**'s sappy, leafy intro follows to tarry, ripe black fruit core with bitter twist from hard tannins. Big but unwieldy. **Petit Verdot Limited Release** ★★★★ Improving on **08** (★★★☆), **09** has typical inky depth & spicy black fruit. Muscular but showing restraint. Reflects fine vintage, should soften with time in bottle. **Pinotage Reserve** ⧄ ★★★★ **10** is dense & dark, packed with black berries, spiced with oak vanilla. Brusque tannins should soften & integrate with time. Half notch down on last-tasted **09** (★★★★). **Chenin Blanc Limited Release** ⧄ ★★★★ Heavily wooded, ripe & robust **12** is similar to previous, with peach & melon fruit notes bolstered by rich leesy minerality. Dash viognier. Coastal WO.

Anura range

Merlot ⧄ ★★★ Savoury, meaty aromas on **11**, with earthy liquorice notes on palate. Chewy tannins, less supple than previous. **Pinotage** ⧄ ★★★☆ Solid structure on **12** is masked by sweet spices & wild berry aromatics. More refined than last. **Legato** ✓ ⧄ ★★★☆ Unpretentious merlot-cab blend, **11** is true to form. Bright, supple & appealing, with vibrant fruit. Drink young. **Pinotage-Syrah** 🏠 ⧄ ★★★ Symbiotic pairing in **12** produces cheerfully fruity & juicy Cape Blend. Youthful & approachable, for early drinking. WO W Cape. **Rosé** ⧄ ★★★ Change from previous, **13** shiraz, merlot, pinot noir blend is fresh, crisp & elegant. Just off-dry, with red berry fruit. **Chardonnay** ⧄ ★★★ Pleasant citrus fruit takes centre stage, with whisper of oak lending spice to **12**, from Tradouw Highlands vines. **Sauvignon Blanc** 🏠 ⧄ ★★★★ Weightier **13** shows change in style. Emphatic nutty, khaki bush aromatics dominate, supported by ripe fruit & crisp acid. WO Coastal. **Viognier Barrel Selection** ⧄ ★★★★ Oak reined in a bit on **12**, showing peachy fruit to benefit. Tangy acidic finish on otherwise ripe & rounded profile. Swartland grapes. **Cape Ruby Port** ⧄ ★★★ Current-release **NV** from shiraz shows huge ripeness, modest fortification. Pleasingly plummy, with firm tannic grip.

Frog Hill range

Cabernet Sauvignon-Merlot ☺ ⧄ ★★★☆ Meaty, savoury notes over solid berry fruit on **11**. Drink now.

Pinotage 🏠 ⧄ ★★★ Spicy wild berry fruit on pocket-friendly **12** quaffer. — GdB

Anwilka 🍶 🍷

Location: Somerset West ▪ WO: Western Cape ▪ Est 1997 ▪ 1stB 2005 ▪ Tasting & sales at Klein Constantia ▪ Closed all pub hols ▪ Cellar tours by appt ▪ Owner(s) Zdenek Bakala, Charles Harman, Bruno Prats & Hubert de Boüard ▪ Winemaker(s) Jean du Plessis (Aug 2008) ▪ Viticulturist(s) Piet Neethling, with Johan Wiese (consultant, both 1997) ▪ 48ha/±39ha (cab, merlot, p verdot, shiraz) ▪ 250t/±32,000cs own label 100% red ▪ PO Box 5298 Helderberg 7135 ▪ anwilka@mweb.co.za ▪ www.kleinconstantia.com ▪ **T +27 (0)21-842-3225** ▪ F +27 (0)21-842-3983

Bordeaux luminaries Hubert de Boüard and Bruno Prats were, with Lowell Jooste of Klein Constantia, founders of this ambitious estate in one of Stellenbosch's quieter corners. They remained on board, as minority shareholders and even more importantly as significant advisers, when Anwilka merged with Klein Constantia in 2012. While the administrative base is in far-off Constantia, the Anwilka cellar and vineyards (farmed with a determination to be environmentally responsible) are firmly independent, dedicated to the production of serious red wine.

★★★★☆ **Anwilka 10** slipped by untasted; **11** confirms serious vein noted in **09**. Now 67% shiraz with cab & a drop of petit verdot. Youthful & still showing oak, with lots of ripe fruit translating into power, flavour & firm tannic structure. Deserves good few years in bottle to soften, & gain more harmony & charm.

★★★★ **Petit Frère** ✓ Previously 'Ugaba'. Smoky-perfumed **10** 'Little Brother' basically similar blend to grander sibling. Also big & serious, but easier, sweeter-fruited, less oak, less depth. Give a year or two. — TJ

Arendsig Handcrafted Wines 🍴🎋🏕️📷

Location/map: Robertson ▪ Est/1stB 2004 ▪ Tasting & cellar tours by appt ▪ Tour groups ▪ BYO picnic ▪ Wedding/function venue ▪ Farmhouse (sleeps up to 10 people) ▪ Owner(s) Lourens & Frikkie van der Westhuizen ▪ Cellarmaster(s)/viticulturist(s) Lourens van der Westhuizen (2004) ▪ 95ha/12ha (cab, shiraz, chard, sauv, viog) ▪ 80t/3,000cs own label 50% red 50% white + 100t/3,000cs for clients ▪ Brands for clients: Esona, Mimosa, Star Hill ▪ PO Box 170 Robertson 6705 ▪ info@arendsig.co.za ▪ www.arendsig.co.za ▪ S 33° 55' 37.9" E 020° 0' 47.6" ▪ **T +27 (0)84-200-2163/+27 (0)23-616-2835** ▪ F +27 (0)86-535-0693/+27 (0)23-616-2090

Arendsig co-owner and cellarmaster Lourens van der Westhuizen makes only single-vineyard wines in a boutique cellar on the Robertson family farm, and vinifies on contract for several other small wineries.

■ **Arendskloof** *see Eagle's Cliff Wines-New Cape Wines*
■ **Are We Having Fun Yet** *see Wine Village-Hermanus*

Arniston Bay

Among Stellenbosch Vineyards' top export sellers, these easy-drinkers take their name from a picturesque resort close to Africa's southern tip, known for pristine sandy beaches and rustic white-walled fishermen's cottages.

Bush Vine range

Pinotage 🍷 🖻 ★★★ Burly **11** coffee & berry aromas, dense fruit flavours, finish is tad clunky. This range WO Stellenbosch, others all W Cape. **Chenin Blanc** ✓ 🍷 🖻 ★★★★ Steely, part-oaked **12**'s frisky acidity plumped out by richer nutty apricot flavours; satisfying & well priced.

Arniston Bay range

Shiraz-Pinotage ☺ 🍷 🖻 ★★★ Pre-bottling, **12** lifts the bar with mulberry pie & inviting 'cuppa java' aromas, brisk acidity ups the sippability level. **Chardonnay** ☺ 🍷 🖻 ★★★ Unoaked **13** tank sample fresh & citrus toned, seems shade less flavoursome than previous but might perk up once bottled.

Cabernet Sauvignon 🍷 🖻 ★★★ Fruit-filled **12** preview slightly woody, needs food to counter gruff tannins. **Merlot** 🍷 🖻 ★★ Coriander-dusted plums in light-textured **12**. **Shiraz** 🍷 🖻 ★★★ Tank sample **12** red berry & charry oak combo, acidity cleans & refreshes the palate. **Cabernet Sauvignon-Merlot** 🍷 🖻 ★★★ Unwooded **12** is ripe & rounded, with meaty notes & sappy tail. **Shiraz-Merlot** 🍷 🖻 ★★★ Inky tones on mulberry & apple tart **12**; plush & long, with good tannic grip ex oak-staves. Previewed, rating provisional. **Cabernet Sauvignon-Shiraz** 🍷 🖻 Unrated sample **12** tarry & very tannic. Needs time to settle into **11**'s balanced, succulent profile. **Rosé** 🍷 ★★ Softly sweet **13** is understated flavour wise. **Sauvignon Blanc** 🍷 🖻 ★★★ **13** tank sample with lively lemon candy & grassy flavours. Nice picnic wine. **Sauvignon Blanc-Semillon** 🍷 🖻 ★★ Previewed **13** light blackcurrant & lemon flavours, pleasant quaffing. **Chenin Blanc-Chardonnay** 🍷 🖻 ★★ Muted **13** has some vinosity, undistinguished flavours.

The Shore range

Red ☺ 🍷 ★★★ Easy sippability, salty/fruity contrast on previewed **NV** shiraz, ruby cab, merlot blend, unoaked. **White** ☺ 🍷 ★★★ Melon-toned semi-dry **NV** marries chenin, colombard & muscat for sunset sipping. Tasted ex tank.

Rosé 🍷 🖻 ★★ Previewed **NV** mainly shiraz; offers decent vinosity, just-off-dry enjoyment.

Sparkling range

Méthode Charmat Rosé ⓣ ★★ Pretty packaging reflects in gently frothy, fruitily sweet **NV**. **Sparkling Brut** 🖻 ★★★ Stonefruit, apple & lemon on brisk & fizzy **NV** party wine from 3 varieties.

The Light range

Rosé ⓣ ★☆ **NV** has piquantly sweet berry tone for sunset saluting. **White** 🍷 ★★ Ginger-spiced **NV** offers simple sweet quaffability. **Red** 🍷 ★★ Bready aromas on berry-sweet & friendly **NV**. Low alcohol (5-6%) all this range. — CvZ

Arra Vineyards

Location: Paarl ▪ Map: Paarl & Wellington ▪ WO: Paarl/Coastal ▪ Est 1998 ▪ 1stB 2001 ▪ Tasting & sales Mon-Sat 9-4.30 ▪ Cellarmaster(s) Dee Wentzel (2006) ▪ Viticulturist(s) Johan Southey (2000) ▪ 72ha/30ha (cab, merlot, mourv, ptage, ruby cab, shiraz, viog) ▪ 20,000cs ▪ PO Box 298 Klapmuts 7625 ▪ info@arrawines.com ▪ www.arrawines.com ▪ S 33° 49' 25.9" E 018° 51' 47.7" ▪ **T +27 (0)21-875-5363** ▪ F +27 (0)21-875-5866

Arra's cellarmaster Dee Wentzel concedes the Klapmuts winery has a relatively low profile in the marketplace but says that she and her team are 'very much focused on luring people to the farm.' What to expect when you get there? 'We don't make wines for connoisseurs or critics, but rather for everyday drinking.'

Reserve range

★★★★ **Cabernet Sauvignon** Big & bold **09**, smooth textured but ultimately not unbalanced or overdone. Intense cassis, slight earthy note. No **08**.

★★★★ **Shiraz** Rich, with layers of flavour - red & black fruit, a hint of vanilla, pepper & spice. **09** bright acidity, crunchy tannins. No **08**.

★★★★ **Viognier** ⓣ 🖉 Evident oak spice on **11** (★★★☆), may still meld with peachy, ginger fruit. Medium bodied, smooth & silky, fruitily dry finish. **09** more expressive; **10** not made.

Nobility ⓣ 🖉 ★★★★ Sweetest, most unctuous viognier in range. **11** laced with plentiful spiced crème brulée appeal; richly textured with lingering honeyed tones.

Barrel Select range

★★★★ **Cabernet Sauvignon 08** (★★★☆) not as harmonious as **06**. Already quite evolved, with fruit yielding to a more savoury character. No **07**.

★★★★ **Pinotage** ⓣ One to please even non-pinotage lovers. **08** understated, more savoury spice than sweet red fruits; quite dense but fresh, beautifully polished tannins. Subtly oaked (20% new).

★★★★☆ **Shiraz** ⓝᴇᵂ Finesse & balance characterises **08**, with 3% mourvèdre. Layers of flavour including red berries & spice (coriander seed in particular). Medium body, with fresh acidity & fine tannins.

★★★★☆ **Shiraz-Mourvèdre-Viognier** ⓝᴇᵂ Impresses with its poise & complexity. Aromas of red berries, spice & touch of woodsmoke. Good concentration & fresh acidity on the palate. Start of some developed character lends further interest to early-drinking **08**.

Mourvèdre ⓝᴇᵂ ★★★ Idiosyncratic **08** offers some red cherry but also intense meaty, spicy notes.

Arra Vineyards range

★★★★ **Cabernet Sauvignon-Petit Verdot-Merlot** ⓝᴇᵂ ✓ **10** over-delivers with plenty of dark fruit, attractive oak. Good concentration, bright acidity, firm but fine tannins. Very youthful now, should keep for a good few years.

Cabernet Sauvignon ✓ 🖉 ★★★★ **10** offers real bang for your buck with a brooding nose, pure dark fruit, fresh acidity & fine tannins. Includes dashes of petit verdot, merlot. More substance than **09** (★★★★). **Merlot** ★★★ **10** very ripe to the point of jammy, smooth textured. **Mourvèdre** ⓝᴇᵂ ★★★★ Suitably exotic **10** with dark fruit & fynbos plus attractive hint of vanilla. Good concentration, smooth texture. **Pinotage** ★★★ **10** is lightly fruity but oak dominates. **Shiraz** ★★★ **10** is rich & full but appears a touch sweet, oak to the fore. **Cape Blend** ⓣ 🍽 ★★★ Hearty, country-style **09** headed by well-disguised pinotage with shiraz, cab, merlot. Richly flavoured, chewy tannins. **Shiraz-Mourvèdre** ★★★ Drops carignan in rich & earthy **10**, quite a rustic proposition. Marked by dark fruit, toasty oak & firm tannins. **Shiraz-Cabernet Sauvignon** 🍽 ★★★ Unassuming **11** is medium bodied, with red & black fruit plus a little spice. **Blanc de Noir** 🍽 🖉 ★★★ Shiraz-based **13** blush is light & refreshing, a bit of tannic grip to prevent it from being too facile. **Chenin Blanc** ⓣ ★★★★ Assertive **11** with oxidative, honeyed concentration; grippy close leaves drier sensation than 4.4g/l sugar suggests. WO Coastal. **Viognier** ★★ Partly wooded, modest **12** shows vague peach flavour, firm acidity. **Natural Sweet Red Blend** ⓣ ★★★ **09** spicy shiraz-led septet; ideal candidate for mulled wine. **Natural Sweet Viognier** 🖉 ★★★ Whisper of peach, moderate acidity makes for inoffensive **12** but could do with a bit more verve. — CE

Arumdale Cool Climate Wines

Location/WO: Elgin ▪ Map: Elgin, Walker Bay & Bot River ▪ Est 1962 ▪ 1stB 2003 ▪ Tasting & sales Mon-Fri 10-4 Sat 10-5 Sun 10-4 ▪ Fee R15/5 wines, waived on purchase of 2/more bottles ▪ Closed Easter Fri-Mon, Dec 25/ 26 & Jan 1 ▪ Owner(s) Mark Simpson ▪ Cellarmaster(s) Ian Nieuwoudt (2012) ▪ Winemaker(s)/viticulturist(s) Ian Nieuwoudt ▪ 90ha/10ha (cab, merlot, shiraz, sauv) ▪ 70t/8,000cs own label 80% red 10% white 10% rosé ▪ PO Box 2 Elgin 7180 ▪ royalwine@arumdale.co.za ▪ www.arumdale.co.za, www.robinhoodlegendarywines. co.za ▪ S 34° 9' 14.51" E 019° 1' 48.22" ▪ **T +27 (0)21-859-3430** ▪ F +27 (0)21-859-3430

This Elgin brand has a new home in Grabouw village, where owner Mark Simpson has opened a wine shop and tasting venue to accommodate growing numbers of visitors. The fun and informal second label, Robin Hood Legendary Wine series, is proving popular. We'll taste it next year.

Shiraz ★★★ Meaty sweetness on nose of **07** with some liquorice, fennel & smoke. Stewed black fruit & chewy texture. **Pink Shiraz** 🍽 ★★★☆ Attractive strawberry/raspberry notes on **12**, lowish alcohol (12%) & lively 'pink fizzer' confection. All very delicious & summery. **Special L.Y.C. Sauvignon Blanc** 🍽 ★★★★

Unusual flavours on **12** from 4 months on chardonnay lees - fragrant melons & white peach. Confected fruit, balanced acidity. — CM

Asara Wine Estate & Hotel   🍴🍷☕⛲📷✕♿

Location/map: Stellenbosch ▪ WO: Stellenbosch/Western Cape ▪ Est/1stB 2001 ▪ Tasting Mon-Sat 10-6 Sun 10-4 ▪ Fee R30/3 wines, R50/5 wines ▪ Sales 10-5 ▪ Closed Dec 25 ▪ Tasting centre ▪ Cellar tours by appt ▪ Tour groups ▪ Five star hotel ▪ Raphael's restaurant ▪ Sansibar Cigar & Whisky Bar ▪ Deli ▪ Gift shop ▪ Function & banqueting facilities ▪ Conferences ▪ Weddings ▪ Owner(s) Markus & Christiane Rahmann ▪ Estate manager Pete Gottgens ▪ Cellarmaster(s) Francois Joubert (Sep 2009) ▪ Winemaker(s) Francois Joubert (Sep 2009), with Tanja-Mari Goedhart (Oct 2010) ▪ Viticulturist(s) Allan Cockcroft (2013) ▪ 180ha/102ha (cab, merlot, p verdot, chard, sauv) ▪ 1,000t/80,000cs own label 73% red 25% white 2% rosé ▪ IPW ▪ PO Box 882 Stellenbosch 7599 ▪ info@asarawine.com ▪ www.asarawine.co.za ▪ S 33° 56' 35.00" E 018° 48' 31.00" ▪ **T** +27 (0)21-888-8000 ▪ F +27 (0)21-888-8001

When Markus and Christiane Rahmann bought this historic property – first granted in 1691 – in 2001, they named it Asara, 'meeting point of the African gods Astar (earth), Asis (sun) and Asase (sky)'. Strategically situated at the confluence of two major access roads into Stellenbosch, it was ideal for upmarket hospitality offerings for 'the discerning traveller', wine amongst them. Changes come - like a new sorting table in the cellar, new labels, and tweaks to the ranges - but Avalon, the estate's take on Italy's Amarone, remains constant and a favourite.

Speciality Collection

★★★★ **Bell Tower Estate Wine** ⓘ Was just 'Estate Wine'. Malbec-led blend of 5 Bordeaux red varieties, **07** had 'wet leaf' character when tasted a few years back, but fruit to balance pliable tannins. WO W Cape.

★★★★☆ **Avalon** Striking wine for contemplation from vine/air-dried shiraz & pinotage (increased to 22%). Heady prune perfume on **09**, luscious ripe fruit & a little residual sugar supported by riveting acid, firm build & warming 16.5% alcohol. 3 years in older oak; much longer life ahead.

★★★★ **Carillon** 🈂 Was 'Noble Late Harvest'. Golden botrytis-infused dessert from chenin. Improving on last-tasted **09**, **12** (★★★★☆) lovely peachy purity, juicy flesh enriched but not dimmed by 10 months in older French oak. Low 10% alcohol & whistle-clean finish make for most elegant sipping.

Nouveau 🏠🈂 ★★☆ From gamay noir, more rosé than light red, **13** full of joie de vivre & juicily sweet raspberry flavours. **White Cab** 🈂 ★★ Was 'Cabernet Sauvignon Blanc'. Red grape vinified as white. Light, acidic, off-dry **13**.

Vineyard Collection

★★★★☆ **Petit Verdot** Variety noted for perfume & natural acidity; **09** (★★★★), now bottled, captures a little of the former, more of the latter - to pleasing overall effect, though previous **06** excited more.

Cabernet Sauvignon 🈂 ★★★★ Straightforward **10**'s rather sombre dark fruit leavened by a few grams sugar; good tannin support. Lacks depth of **09** (★★★★). **Merlot** 🈂 ★★★ **10** altogether leaner, less fleshy than previous. Pleasant if fleeting spice, red berries; finishing nip of bitterness. **Shiraz** 🈂 ★★★★ Modernstyle **10** replete with outspoken spice, red berries & smoky oak. Rich, smooth texture framed by gentle tannins. **Cape Fusion** 🈂 ★★★ Sturdy **11** pinotage, shiraz, malbec blend; plummy with smoky oak overtones. **Chardonnay Lightly Wooded** NEW 🈂 ★★★ Toasty oak more evident than 'light' in **12**. Short ageing may harmonise wood with sweetish, lemony flesh. **Sauvignon Blanc** 🈂 ★★★☆ **13** improvement on previous & nicely balanced for immediate drinking. Satisfying tropical fruit purity expanded by lees-ageing. Clean & dry.

Classic Collection

Sauvignon Blanc-Chardonnay ☺🈂 ★★★ Was 'Ivory'. Sauvignon fruit fleshed out with chardonnay & little chenin. **13** tasty & quaffable.

Merlot NEW 🈂 ★★ Tart red plum on lean, brusque **11**. **Shiraz** NEW 🈂 ★★★ Heady scents of red fruit, oak vanilla on **11**. Big 15% alcohol, a few grams sugar. **Merlot Cabernet Sauvignon** ⓘ🏠🈂 ★★★ Was 'Ebony'. Mulberry-laden **10** merlot-cab a bit brash but utterly drinkable. **Pinotage Rosé** 🈂 ★★ Was just 'Rosé'. Tutti-frutti off-dry **13**. **Sauvignon Blanc** NEW 🈂 ★★★ Sprightly **13**, medium-bodied & nicely lingering tropical fruit. — AL

Ashbourne

Location: Hermanus ▪ Map: Elgin, Walker Bay & Bot River ▪ WO: Walker Bay ▪ Est 1996 ▪ 1stB 2001 ▪ Tasting, sales & tours by appt ▪ Owner(s) Anthony Hamilton Russell ▪ Winemaker(s) Hannes Storm (2004) ▪ Viticulturist(s) Johan Montgomery (2005) ▪ 113ha/24.35ha (cabs s/f, malbec, p verdot, ptage, shiraz, sauv, sem) ▪ 20t/ 2,000cs own label 50% red 50% white ▪ PO Box 158 Hermanus 7200 ▪ hrv@hermanus.co.za ▪ S 34° 23' 09.25" E 019° 14' 29.90" ▪ **T +27 (0)28-312-3595** ▪ F +27 (0)28-312-1797

Owner Anthony Hamilton Russell's founding purpose with this Hemel-en-Aarde Valley specialist boutique was to create South African benchmarks which did not copy any international wines. And he wanted to do this with only one red wine and one white. The red, Ashbourne, was initially 100% pinotage but evolved into a pinotage-cab blend, while the white, Sandstone, released after four years in bottle, interleaves mainly sauvignon with chardonnay and semillon. Both have developed a loyal following at home and abroad but remain available in tiny quantities. In 2013, Anthony broke his 'one red, one white' rule with the early-released Ashbourne Sauvignon Blanc-Chardonnay, to 'give the name relevance to a greater community of consumers by being more democratically priced'.

★★★★☆ **Ashbourne** Pinotage (67%) with cab, introverted **08** unfurls in glass to reveal thrillingly restrained cassis & old leather tones; leafy dryness, fine texture & moderate alcohol only add to the appeal. Warrants further cellaring. **07** (★★★★) had equal dabs (9%) shiraz & cab; previous 100% pinotage.

★★★★☆ **Sandstone** ⓣ Masterly **08** blended sauvignon (77%), chardonnay & semillon fermented in clay amphoras. Enticing, with vibrant acid structure & flavour depth. Walker Bay WO.

Ashbourne Sauvignon Blanc-Chardonnay NEW ✓ ⬗ ★★★★ While not displaying siblings' gravitas, **13** seriously conceived & flavourful, 20% unoaked chardonnay enriching vibrant perfumed sauvignon. — CvZ

Ashton Kelder

Location: Ashton ▪ Map: Robertson ▪ WO: Robertson/Western Cape ▪ Est 1962 ▪ 1stB 1970 ▪ Tasting & sales Mon-Fri 8-5 Sat 9-2 (summer) & 10-2 (winter) ▪ Closed Easter Fri/Sat & Dec 25/26 ▪ Cellar tours by appt ▪ Facilities for children ▪ Tour groups ▪ Farm produce ▪ Conferences ▪ Owner(s) 55 shareholders ▪ Cellarmaster(s) Sterik de Wet (Oct 2009) ▪ Winemaker(s) Simon Basson (Nov 2007) & Roy Thorne (Oct 2011) ▪ Viticulturist(s) Hennie Visser (Vinpro) ▪ 1,200ha (cab, ruby cab, shiraz, chard, chenin) ▪ 21,079t/±38,000cs own label 50% red 42% white 6% rosé 2% other; bulk & grape juice concentrate ▪ Other export brands: Berryfields, Mountain Stream ▪ ISO 22000, BWI, HACCP ▪ PO Box 40 Ashton 6715 ▪ info@ashtonkelder.co.za ▪ www.ashtonkelder.co. za ▪ S 33° 50' 12.1" E 020° 1' 48.3" ▪ **T +27 (0)23-615-1135** ▪ F +27 (0)23-615-1284

Ashton Kelder's output includes not only wine (bulk and bottled) but also grape juice concentrate, which enables the 52-year-old Robertson Valley producer to pitch its offering as 'something for every vinotype', from grape juice for kids to Reserve wines for sophisticates. And for employees, ethical performance is being enhanced through WIETA certification for the winery and all 50-plus owner farms.

Reserve range

Chardonnay Limited Release ☺ ⬗ ★★★ Barrel-fermented **12** now bottled & more integrated, offering greater complexity with lemon curd, melon & sweet oak, zesty lime conclusion.

Roodewal ⬗ ★★★★ **11** marries equal cab/merlot, 14% shiraz for mulberry-toned, mineral-seamed & grippy rainy day warmer. Discontinued: **Shiraz Reserve**.

Ashton range

Cabernet Sauvignon-Merlot ☺ ⬗ ★★★ Equal blend **12** shows cab's backbone, merlot's leafiness; pleases with moderate alcohol, sympathetic oaking.

Cabernet Sauvignon ⬗ ★★ Cherry, plum & obvious sweetness on unoaked **12**. **Pinotage** ▦ ⬗ ★★ savoury **12** with charry notes from year in older French barrels. **Shiraz** ▦ ⬗ ★★★ **12** warm country glassful: sweet fruit, big tannins, spirity ±15% alcohol. **Satynrooi** ⓣ ▦ ★★ 'Satin Red' **11** unoaked & uncomplicated for everyday enjoyment. **Satynrosé** ▦ ⬗ ★ Muted Turkish Delight on gently sweet **13** pink from pinotage. **Chardonnay Unwooded** ▦ ⬗ ★★ Zesty **12** has pear, lemon drop & pineapple appeal.

. **Chenin Blanc** 🍶 📷 ★★ Cheerful **13**, lightish & zippy if a tad brief. **Sauvignon Blanc** 🍶 📷 ★★ Early picked **13** shows usual pineapple & green melon plus dusting of pepper. **Satynwit** 🍶 📷 ★★ Bouncy chenin-led **13** blend is tropical & pleasantly grippy, food friendly. **Satynperlé** ⓟ 🍶 📷 ★★ Tiny bubbles provide zing & lift in improved **12** sweet perlé chenin & sauvignon. **Bonica Vin Doux** 📷 ★ Light, sweetish **NV** fizz with tart cranberry, juicy strawberry contrast. **Red Muscadel** 📷 ★★ Fortified dessert drops 'Jerepigo' from name for **11**. Dried apricots, tobacco & toffee in unctuous mouthful. WO W Cape. — DC,JP

Ataraxia Wines

Location: Hermanus ▪ Map: Elgin, Walker Bay & Bot River ▪ WO: Western Cape ▪ Est 2004 ▪ 1stB 2005 ▪ Tasting & sales Mon-Fri 9-4 Sat 10-5 Sun in season only ▪ Fee R15pp for groups of 10 or more, refunded with individual purchase ▪ Closed Easter Fri/Sun, Dec 25 & Jan 1 ▪ Art exhibition ▪ Charcuterie platters available during holiday season ▪ Owner(s) Kevin Grant Wines (Pty) Ltd ▪ Cellarmaster(s)/winemaker(s)/viticulturist(s) Kevin Grant (Sep 2004) ▪ 47ha/2ha (pinot, chard) ▪ 83t/12,000cs own label 40% red 60% white ▪ PO Box 603 Hermanus 7200 ▪ info@ataraxiawines.co.za ▪ www.ataraxiawines.co.za ▪ S 34° 20' 27.0" E 019° 18' 30.8" ▪ **T +27 (0)28-212-2007** ▪ F +27 (0)28-212-1921

Kevin Grant has been a devotee of chardonnay and pinot noir since he started working in Hemel-en-Aarde Valley in the mid-1990s. When he branched out on his own exactly ten years ago, he naturally sought land in the area suitable for both varieties. The land he, with wife Hanli and a few friends, purchased lies at the highest point in the area. The place might generate emotional tranquility (the meaning in Greek of Ataraxia), but Grant himself travels frequently, often to places far from cities and their wine-savvy inhabitants. After a recent show in Polokwane, he was full of enthusiasm. 'Never discount nor underestimate the enthusiasm our rainbow nation instinctively harbours for wine – they just need to be exposed to it.'

★★★★☆ **Serenity 10** in more classic style than fulsome **09** (★★★★); austere yet fresh with deeply ripe & mouthwatering grape tannins; restrained use of new oak. Loads of flavour from unspecified blend; a hint of spice, perhaps, but an overall effect of completeness. Deserves patience. Walker Bay grapes.

★★★★☆ **Chardonnay 12** slightly bigger, more textured richness than usual, in part due to a lower acidity. Compensation comes in the form of more citrus focus, fewer oatmeal notes, aiding precision, freshness & enjoyable longevity. Home grapes plus 15% fruit from Upper Hemel-en-Aarde Valley.

★★★★☆ **Sauvignon Blanc ✓ 13** one of Grant's best. Its racy, rapier-like steeliness perfectly matched by breadth of cool, ripe fruit. Mouthwateringly long. — AL

⬛ **Atkinson Ridge** *see* Amani Vineyards
⬛ **Attie's Long Shadow** *see* Opstal Estate
⬛ **Auberge du Paysan** *see* L'Auberge du Paysan

Auction Crossing Private Cellar

Location: De Doorns ▪ Map: Worcester ▪ WO: Western Cape ▪ Est 2003 ▪ 1stB 2004 ▪ Tasting & sales Mon-Fri 9-5 Sat 9-2 ▪ Closed all pub hols ▪ Cellar tours by appt ▪ Bistro 'Inspirati' ▪ Facilities for children ▪ Tour groups ▪ Gifts ▪ Farm produce ▪ Owner(s) De Villiers Graaff, AJ Reyneke & Leon Dippenaar ▪ Cellarmaster(s)/winemaker(s)/viticulturist(s) Leon Dippenaar (Aug 2004) ▪ ±41ha/2ha (mourv, shiraz, viog) ▪ 10t/4,000cs own label 75% red 25% white ▪ The Pines PO Box 5 Hex River 6855 ▪ auctioncrossing@hexvalley.co.za ▪ www.auctioncrossing.co.za ▪ S 33° 29' 42.8" E 019° 34' 32.7" ▪ **T +27 (0)23-357-9655** ▪ F +27 (0)23-357-9255

The 1938 cellar at this tiny Hex River Valley winery was refurbished (but keeping the traditional open kuipe for fermentation) and saw its first modern vintage in 2004. Part-owner and winemaker Leon Dippenaar takes grapes from different regions, one being Durbanville – De Grendel's De Villiers Graaff is also a co-owner.

Syrah-Viognier ⓟ ★★★★ Co-fermented, aromatic **09** well made & accessible, pleasingly positive spicy finish as tannins tug sweetly ripe dark fruit. **Viognier** 🍶 📷 ★★★ Lightly oaked, flavourful **12** offers pleasantly fruity, spicy savouriness from Durbanville grapes. — IM

Audacia Wines

Location/map/WO: Stellenbosch ▪ Est 1930 ▪ Tasting & sales Mon-Fri 9–4 Sat/Sun 10-3.30 ▪ Fee R20, waived on purchase ▪ Closed Good Fri, Dec 25 & Jan 1 ▪ Root 44 market (food, arts, crafts, jewellery, kiddies area & bar) ▪ Owner(s) Strydom & Harris families ▪ Cellarmaster(s)/winemaker(s)/viticulturist(s) Michael van Niekerk (Aug 2009) ▪ 32ha/20ha (cabs s/f, malbec, merlot, p verdot, roobernet, shiraz) ▪ 120t/18,000cs own label 100% red ▪ IPW ▪ PO Box 12679 Die Boord 7613 ▪ info@audacia.co.za ▪ www.audacia.co.za ▪ S 33° 59' 45.7" E 018° 50' 2.9" ▪ **T +27 (0)21-881-3052** ▪ F +27 (0)21-881-3137

Thanks to Audacia's popular weekend market, local sales from this specialist red wine boutique cellar between Somerset West and Stellenbosch have soared, reports cellarmaster Michael van Niekerk. Last season he produced an unusual rosé from malbec, 'and it's looking good'.

Cabernet Sauvignon ★★★ For early drinking, **12** is ripe & juicy, with a suggestion of pomegranate among its red fruits. **History** Next awaited. **Merlot ★★★** Different batch to last **10**. This is firmer & more savoury, with meaty, spicy & mocha overlays to the fruit. **Shiraz ★★★★** Vintage-aligned **10** bigger, more concentrated & tannic, but shows fine savoury varietal character (roast meat, white pepper), drinks well now, with potential. **Rouge Noble ★★★** 70% malbec in improved **NV** Bordeaux blend. Savoury-seamed fruit displays more intensity, character. **Jeté ★★★** Usual semi-dry styling for latest **NV**, 4 Bordeaux red grapes plus shiraz. Red fruit & moderate tannins for early drinking. Discontinued: **Malbec.** — GM

Aufwaerts Co-operative

Location: Rawsonville ▪ Map: Breedekloof ▪ Tasting by appt ▪ Winemaker(s) Hennie de Villiers ▪ PO Box 51 Rawsonville 6845 ▪ hanepoot39@gmail.com ▪ S 33° 41' 42.4" E 019° 17' 33.7" ▪ **T +27 (0)23-349-1202** ▪ F +27 (0)23-349-1202

A family cooperative, situated on a Breedekloof property in the De Villiers family since the 1800s. Planted with many grape varieties, the estate also features a brandy distillery, declared a National Monument in the 1940s. 'Anybody can visit us by appointment,' says winemaker Hennie de Villiers.

▪▪ **Austin** *see* Noble Hill Wine Estate

Autumn Harvest Crackling

Among South Africa's top sellers, these spritzy lower-alcohol wines are made from widely sourced grapes by Distell.

Crisp Perlé Rosé ⊞ ★★ Coppery semi-sweet blend of red & white wine; newest **NV** fresh &, yes, crisp, thanks to bouncy bubbles. 750ml & 1.5L bottles, as for Red. **Crisp Perlé White ⊞ ★★** Fun all-sorts blend, **NV**, semi-sweet but zingy bubbles impart the advertised crunch. 750ml & 1/1.5L bottles. **Crisp Perlé Red ⊞ ★ NV** uncomplicated sweet-sour quaffer with enlivening prickle of bubbles. — DB, HJ

Avondale

Location/WO: Paarl ▪ Map: Paarl & Wellington ▪ Est 1996 ▪ 1stB 1999 ▪ Tasting & sales Mon-Sat by appt ▪ Fee R50pp ▪ Closed Easter Fri-Mon, Dec 25 & Jan 1 ▪ Cellar tours by appt only ▪ Eco tours Wed-Fri 10-1 by appt: R200pp incl MCC on arrival, tour & tasting in vyds, cellar tour ▪ Art exhibit ▪ Owner(s) Grieve family / The Avondale Trust ▪ Winemaker(s) Corné Marais (Oct 2008), with Ivan September (Jan 2012) ▪ Viticulturist(s) Johnathan Grieve (Jul 1999) ▪ 300ha/100ha (cabs s/f, grenache, merlot, mourv, shiraz, chard, chenin, rouss, sem, viog) ▪ 500t/50,000cs own label 50% red 38% white 2% rosé 10% MCC ▪ EU Organic & USDA NOP organic, LEAF ▪ PO Box 602 Paarl South 7624 ▪ wine@avondalewine.co.za ▪ www.avondalewine.co.za ▪ S 33° 45' 52.9" E 019° 0' 4.7" ▪ **T +27 (0)21-863-1976** ▪ F +27 (0)21-863-1534

For a while now, Avondale GM and viticulturist Johnathan Grieve has advocated an approach to farming which combines organic and biodynamic farming principles with the best that modern science has to offer. It's a philosophy that's evolved since he arrived at the family's Paarl farm in 1999 and realised that it had been thrown out of balance by years of conventional farming. By taking account of everything from the smallest microbes in the soil to planetary influences, he's steadily rejuvenating the property and, as the land regenerates, so the wines are improving and becoming more expressive of their origin, Johnathan believes.

★★★★ **Samsara** 🏵 From shiraz, **07** (★★★★) is already very accessible, fruit still intact but tannins soft Notes of red fruit, smoked meat & fynbos. Not as concentrated as **06**.

★★★★ **Navitas** ⓔ 🏵 Well-assembled, understated **08** is shiraz-led, rest mourvèdre, grenache. Now bottled, it's medium bodied with notes of red fruit & white pepper before a long, dry finish.

★★★★ **La Luna** 🏵 A blend of cab franc, merlot & shiraz, **07** (★★★★) is medium bodied, already quite evolved. Not as well conceived as **06** which was Bordeaux in style.

★★★★☆ **Cyclus** 🏵 📖 Voluptuous, plush-textured **11** is 25% each chardonnay, roussanne, viognier plus some chenin blanc & semillon, native yeast fermented. White & yellow fruit, some leesy character, delicate spice. Very demonstrative for 13.5% alcohol. Even more purity, focus than **10**.

★★★★ **Armilla Méthode Cap Classique Brut** ⓔ 🏵 **NV** sparkling from chardonnay, 10% oaked, 2 years on lees. Rich & full, fine mousse, bright acidity. Latest is more intensely flavoured, precise.

Camissa 🏵 📖 ★★★ Dry rosé from unconventional combo muscat de Frontignan & mourvèdre. Red fruit but also intriguing orange blossom note on **12**. Rich & broad, with zesty acidity. **Anima** 🏵 📖 ★★★★ Unusual **11** naturally barrel-fermented chenin is overtly oxidative, with bruised apple & yeasty notes before a savoury finish. Less fruit expression than **10** (★★★★). — CE

Avondrood Vineyards

Location: Rawsonville ▪ Map: Breedekloof ▪ Est/1stB 2005 ▪ Tasting, sales & cellar tours Mon-Fri 8-12 & 1.30-5 Sat by appt (phone +27 (0)82-578-6841) ▪ Closed most pub hols ▪ Refreshments/food-and-wine tastings by appt or BYO picnic ▪ Conferences ▪ Walks/hikes ▪ Facilities for children ▪ Hewn-stone mountain cottage ▪ Owner(s) Albertus van Rensburg ▪ Winemaker(s) Albertus van Rensburg, with Johannes Damane ▪ Viticulturist(s) Pierre Snyman ▪ 80ha (cab, ptage, shiraz, chard, sauv, viog) ▪ 30t/4,200cs own label 40% red 60% white ▪ PO Box 277 Worcester 6849 ▪ vineyards@avondrood.co.za ▪ www.avondrood.co.za ▪ S 33° 43' 32.9" E 019° 20' 18.7" ▪ **T +27 (0)23-349-1858** ▪ F +27 (0)86-210-5806

The name of this Du Toitskloof mountainside farm was inspired by its beautiful sunsets. 'Every new day brings the promise of a life lived in pure simplicity,' says vine grower and boutique vintner Albertus van Rensburg. 'At Avondrood we're one big family – the van Rensburgs together with the farm people.'

Avontuur Estate

Location: Somerset West ▪ Map: Helderberg ▪ WO: Stellenbosch ▪ Est 1850 ▪ 1stB 1990 ▪ Tasting & sales Mon-Fri 8.30–5 Sat/Sun 9–4 ▪ Fee R20/5 wines ▪ Closed Good Fri, Dec 25 & Jan 1 ▪ Cellar tours by appt ▪ Avontuur Estate Restaurant (see Restaurants section) ▪ Conference venue ▪ Thoroughbred stud ▪ Owner(s) Taberer family ▪ Winemaker(s) / brandy master Jan van Rooyen (Jan 2011) ▪ Viticulturist(s) Pippa Mickleburgh (Sep 1999) ▪ 104ha/48ha (cabs s/f, merlot, p verdot, ptage, pinot, shiraz, chard, chenin, sauv, viog) ▪ 260t/36,000cs own label 60% red 40% white ▪ PO Box 1128 Somerset West 7129 ▪ info@avontuurestate.co.za ▪ www.avontuurestate.co.za ▪ S 34° 1' 33.2" E 018° 49' 23.8" ▪ **T +27 (0)21-855-3450** ▪ F +27 (0)21-855-4600

Elegant thoroughbred horses gaze at visitors and passing travellers from the Avontuur paddocks on the slopes of the Helderberg. This combined winery and racing stud, in prime red-wine country, is replanting, rekitting and reinventing itself under the next-generation Taberer owners and winemaker Jan van Rooyen. Beneficiaries of their efforts include Eastern Cape community Keiskammahoek, who receive a portion of wine sales and proceeds from estate fundraising events.

Avontuur Premiere range

★★★★ **Dominion Royale (Shiraz Reserve)** ⓔ Dense, concentrated & ripe **09** (★★★★★) outperforms **08**, fully deserves Reserve status. Brooding dark power with satin tannins, easily tames new oak regime Appealing wild herb & meaty notes round out substantial body.

Minelli (Pinot Noir Reserve) ★★★ Uncharacteristically deep & savoury **10** atypical but faint floral scents & spicy fruit core deliver on palate. **Baccarat** ⓔ ★★★★ When last tasted, **08** Bordeaux blend was just-dry with ripe fruit & spicy notes, the finish a bit warm from 14.5% alcohol. **Luna de Miel (Chardonnay Reserve)** ⓔ ★★★ Toasty oak dominates **10**, masks well-formed, ripe fruit profile on slender body. Unlike

to evolve. **Sarabande (Sauvignon Blanc Reserve)** ⓐ ★★★☆ With mineral-toned blackcurrant flavours, **10** was fresh & dry, on review looked likely to gain complexity with time.

Avontuur Estate range

★★★★ **Brut Cap Classique** ⓐ Traditional-method sparkling, **NV** from chardonnay. Aromas of ripe apple, pear & spicy gingerbread; creamy mouthfeel, showing yeasty notes & a good dry finish.
Cabernet Sauvignon ★★★☆ Previewed last time, **09** holds course, but adds some tertiary flavours. Rounded body with hint of pickle & sour cherry. **Cabernet Franc** ⓐ ★★★★ Steely varietal grip & layered fruit on **09** reflect stellar vintage. Lean & linear, showing more supple body, tempered alcohol than previous **08** (★★★★). **Pinotage** ⓐ ★★★ **08** sampled previously, raspberry fruit dominated by oak & dry tannin. **Cabernet Sauvignon-Merlot** ▨ ★★★ 50-50 middleweight **11** blend, first since **08**, is supple & juicy, with toasty oak aromas & tarry, dry finish. **Sauvignon Blanc** ▤ ▨ ★★★ Lean, grassy **13** has focused minerality, wild herbaceous & nettle aromas. Firm, taut body with commendable length. **Above Royalty (Noble Late Harvest)** Await new vintage. Discontinued: **Shiraz**.

Vintner's range

> **Red** ☺ ★★★ Blend revised since last edition, **10** still cab-shiraz, partially wooded. Appealing gush of ripe red berry fruit.

Blend ▨ ★★★ Crisply dry & refreshing rosé from chardonnay & pinot, **13** appealingly fragrant fruity notes.
White ▨ ★★ **13** sauvignon-chardonnay blend, bright & fresh, rather brief.

Brandy range `NEW`

★★★★ **10 Year Private Collection** Sweet apricots, nuts, pear & cigar smoke entice on nose. Rich, with gorgeous depth of flavour. Smooth, silky; long sweet marzipan finish. 100% potstill from chenin. — WB, GdB, TJ

Axe Hill

Location/WO: Calitzdorp ▪ Map: Klein Karoo & Garden Route ▪ Est 1993 ▪ 1stB 1997 ▪ Tasting, sales & cellar tours Mon-Sat by appt ▪ Owner(s) Axe Hill Winery (Pty) Ltd ▪ Cellarmaster(s)/winemaker(s) Mike Neebe (Oct 2007) ▪ Viticulturist(s) Johannes Mellet (Aug 2009, consultant) ▪ ±60ha/1.5ha (grenache, souzão, tinta barocca, tinta roriz, touriga nacional, viog) ▪ ±5t/±4,000cs own label 70% red 30% white ▪ Wesoewer Road Calitzdorp 6660 ▪ info@axehill.co.za ▪ www.axehill.co.za ▪ S 33° 30' 54.6" E 021° 41' 23.0" ▪ **T** +27 (0)11-447-4366/+27 (0)44-213-3585 ▪ F +27 (0)11-447-3219

'Adapt our business or drown in wine' is cellarmaster and general manager Mike Neebe's mantra at awarded Calitzdorp boutique cellar Axe Hill, founded as a port-style specialist house by Tony and Lyn Mossop in 1993. 'Port' remains Mike's favourite wine style: 'In spite of rumours of its demise, it is still a product that commands attention when placed on the table – and a bit of sweetness on the side always is an attraction.' But his unfortified wines are also gaining traction in the market. 'We are blessed with unique fruit and remain steadfast in our endeavours to produce wines that characterise our location and climate.' Range expansion continues with 'exciting varietals and ideas' coming soon.

★★★★ **Cape Vintage** Classic port-style back on top form in **11** (★★★★★). Led by touriga (65%) with dashes souzão & tinta, intense black fruit, rich & complex, with fine spice & spirity dry grip; cellar with confidence 6+ years. Also-tasted **10** (★★★★) similar blend, more medicinal, denser. Previously reviewed **09**, with souzão (39%) leading touriga & tinta for 1st time, plump fruit dusted with dried herbs & spices.
Shiraz Await next. **Dry Red** `NEW` ★★ Firm & dry **12** food wine from shiraz, try with richer cassoulets or pork & bean stews. **Distinta** ⓐ ★★★★ 'Different' in name & make-up: **11** vibrant blend shiraz (68%) & tinta, older barrel aged. Floral dark berries, smooth & lipsmackingly dry. **Machado** ★★★★ **12** blend mainly Portuguese varieties, exotic aromas, plush fruit caged by firm tannins, finish is a tad warm. **Cape Ruby** ★★★★ NV port-style from touriga & souzão (82/18), ripe & plummy with tangy farewell, shade less elegant than previous but accessible, tasty. **Cape White** ★★★★ Solera-aged fortified chenin, hence oxidative styling. **NV** mulled honey & sultanas, lovely firm grip & well-judged fortification. — GdB, JP

Ayama Wines

Location: Paarl ▪ Map: Paarl & Wellington ▪ WO: Western Cape/Voor Paardeberg/Paarl/Swartland ▪ Est 2005 ▪ 1stB 2006 ▪ Tasting by appt ▪ Closed all pub hols ▪ Meals/refreshments by appt; or BYO picnic ▪ Walks/hikes ▪

Conservation area ▪ Owner(s) Slent Farms (Pty) Ltd (6 partners) ▪ Cellarmaster(s)/winemaker(s) Michela Sfiligoi (2005) ▪ Viticulturist(s) Attilio Dalpiaz (2005) ▪ 172ha/37ha (cab, merlot, ptage, shiraz, chenin, sauv) ▪ 300t/40,000cs own label 40% red 58% white 2% rosé ▪ WIETA ▪ Suite 106 Private Bag X3041 Paarl 7620 ▪ info@slentfarms.com ▪ www.ayama.co.za ▪ S 33° 37' 22.5" E 018° 49' 19" ▪ **T +27 (0)21-869-8313** ▪ F +27 (0)21-869-8313

On the Perdeberg foothills, Slent Farm is one of the Cape's oldest and home to the Cape Leopard - and, more visibly, Italian family and friends who are passionate about agriculture and wine. Their Ayama ('Someone to Lean On') brand is in the hands of hospitable viti/vini couple Attilio Dalpiaz and Michela Sfiligoi, who can't wait to complete the cellar renovations and begin vinifying onsite.

Leopard range

★★★★ **Shiraz-Pinotage-Mourvèdre** ⊕ 🍴 🎇 Appealing blend with ripe dark berry fruit & soft texture, **10** shows classic Old World touch. Elegant & balanced, eminently drinkable. WO Paarl, like next.
Chardonnay-Chenin Blanc-Viognier ⊕ 🍴 🎇 ★★★★ First tasting, alluringly scented **10** shows richly ripe fruit, thick texture & elegantly balanced acidity.

Ayama Wines range

★★★★ **Méthode Cap Classique Rosé** √ 🎇 Crisp crunch to **10** pink fizz from mainly pinot noir, red berry generosity tempered by light citrus of chardonnay. Brioche & yeast from 2 years in bottle. Dry satisfying tail.
Cabernet Sauvignon ⊕ 🎇 ★★★ Simonsberg-sourced **11** tank sample offers ripe blackcurrant fruit spiced with oak. Thick tannins lend bitter twist at finish. **Merlot** √ 🎇 ★★★★ **12** a step up, herb sprinkle to soft yet intense dark berries. Gentle texture & long finish. Unwooded & WO Voor Paardeberg, as for next two.
Pinotage 🎇 ★★★ Faintest coffee bean note to inky fruited yet succulent **12**, which improves on previous.
Shiraz √ 🎇 ★★★ Vibrant & concentrated yet gentle-textured **12**, harmoniously balanced black berry & plum fruit on long tail. **Baboon's Back Shiraz** ⊕ 🎇 ★★★ Partly oaked **11**, pre-bottling expresses fruit-driven, easy-drinking style. Unpretentiously soft, ripe & eminently moreish. Voor Paardeberg WO. **Slent Shiraz-Pinotage** 🍴 ★★★ Was 'Shiraz-Pinotage'. **12** 55/45 mix is rich, rounded, yielding & refreshing. Light choc-mocha notes add appeal. Easy-drinking & unoaked. **Rosé** ⊕ 🍴 ★★ Spicy, fruity **10** from pinotage previously showed variety's brisk acidity. **Chardonnay** ⊕ 🍴 ★★★ Unoaked **10**, fullish body with intense apricot notes. WO Swartland. **Chenin Blanc** ⊕ 🍴 🎇 ★★★ Dry **12** resolutely fruit-driven, unpretentious & generous. Cheerful, sunny poolside delight. Voor Paardeberg WO. **Sauvignon Blanc** 🍴 🎇 ★★★ Rich & rounded **13** tank sample, lees-ageing adds body to grapefruit, lemon tang. Darling vines. **Viognier** 🍴 🎇 ★★★ Nectarine & citrus on easy-drinking **12** preview. Long, rich leesy finish but succulent too. **Slent Chenin Blanc-Sauvignon Blanc** 🍴 ★★★ Gets 'Slent' prefix in **12**, with rich honeyed fullness to 60/40 blend. Lively & tangy with fig, peach & melon highlights on long finish. **Méthode Cap Classique Brut** ★★★ **09** second edition of bottle-fermented chardonnay, pinot noir fizz. Vibrant apple, lemon & bready richness. Rounded & long with dry leesy tail. **Méthode Cap Classique Blanc de Blancs** ⊕ ★★★ Dry, austere **08** chardonnay sparkler has purity of form, subdued baked apple aromas under mineral-lime lees mantle. —FM

▪ **Azania** see African Terroir

Baarsma Wine Group

Stellenbosch ▪ Closed to public ▪ Owner(s) Baarsma Wine Group BV ▪ MD Chris Rabie ▪ Cellarmaster(s) Hannes Louw (since Jan 2005) ▪ PO Box 7275 Stellenbosch 7599 ▪ info@baarsma.co.za ▪ www.baarsma.co.za ▪ **T +27 (0)21-880-1221** ▪ F +27 (0)21-880-0851

Stellenbosch-based Baarsma SA is a major export marketer of South African wines, shipping more than 1 million cases a year to the major international wine markets. The group's Lyngrove brand is listed separately.

BABISA - Born & Bred in South Africa

Location/WO: Paarl ▪ Est 2008 ▪ 1stB 2007 ▪ Tasting by appt ▪ Tours to estates producing BABISA wines by prior arrangement ▪ Owner(s) BABISA Brand Innovation Holdings Ltd ▪ Cellarmaster(s)/winemaker(s)/viticulturist(s) Various ▪ 10,000cs own label 60% red 30% white 10% rosé ▪ PO Box 52185 Waterfront 8002 ▪ wines@babisa.com ▪ www.babisa.com ▪ **T +27 (0)71-232-8840** ▪ F +27 (0)86-616-2794

'The BABISA Wine Division is in a holding position,' says Paul Burger, CEO of this proudly SA lifestyle brand whose various luxury product segments are being rolled out strategically: 'Timing is very important.' So, red wines are maturing gently, with whites still to be selected, and projected official release date is June.

★★★★ Valerie Reserve ⊕ Serious shiraz-led 6-way blend from Paarl. Lingering **09** repeats previous formula: ripe & heavily oaked, but should evolve. — GdB

Babylon's Peak Private Cellar   🍸🍷☕🎋⛺📷♿

Location: Malmesbury ▪ Map: Swartland ▪ WO: Swartland/Western Cape ▪ Est/1stB 2003 ▪ Tasting, sales & cellar tours by appt ▪ Closed Easter Fri-Mon, Dec 25 & Jan 1 ▪ Pre-booked light refreshments for groups ▪ Olives ▪ BYO picnic ▪ Walking/hiking trails ▪ Conservation area ▪ Self-catering cottage ▪ Dams for fishing ▪ Owner(s) Stephan Basson ▪ Cellarmaster(s)/winemaker(s)/viticulturist(s) Stephan Basson (Jan 2003) ▪ 580ha/230ha (carignan, grenache, mourv, ptage, shiraz, chenin, rouss, viog) ▪ 20,000cs own label 65% red 35% white + 500,000L bulk ▪ PO Box 161 Malmesbury 7299 ▪ info@babylonspeak.co.za ▪ S 33° 33' 40.8" E 018° 48' 38.6" ▪ **T +27 (0)21-300-1052** ▪ F +27 (0)86-518-3773

The name derives from the granite thumb on the eastern slope of the Perdeberg, locally known as Babylonstoren. This large farm has been in the Basson family since 1919, sending grapes to the big houses. In 2003, fourth-generation scion Stephan, with the 'Swartland revolution' happening all around, set out to make wines on his own account, from some of the highest vineyards in the Swartland.

★★★★ Shiraz-Mourvèdre-Grenache ✓ Refined, characterful shiraz-based blend from mature vines. Swartland warmth in spicy, clean leather tones, richness & velvet grip of **10**. Own grapes, but WO W Cape.

★★★★ Chenin Blanc ✓ 🍴 13 full of exuberant youth from venerable 40 year old vines. Generous, juicily fresh green apples, white peaches concentration; lingering, bone-dry. Modest 13% alcohol aids quaffability.

Syrah ⊕ ★★★★ 09 in ripe, bold style, densely layered with savoury liquorice, dark fruits, coffee & tar intensity. **Shiraz-Carignan 🍴 ★★★★ 12** satisfies even without great complexity. Winter-warmer style; generous mix red earth, dark spices, hint of toast; rich texture, chunky, chewy tannins. **11** untasted by us. **Viognier-Roussanne** Await next. Note: 'Coded' range discontinued. — AL

Babylonstoren   🍸🍷☕🏠📷♿

Location: Paarl ▪ Map: Paarl & Wellington ▪ WO: Simonsberg-Paarl/Western Cape ▪ Est 2011 ▪ Tasting & sales daily 10-5 ▪ Tour groups by appt ▪ Gift shop ▪ Hiking/walking trails ▪ Guided garden tours ▪ Hosted wine tasting, cellar tours by appt ▪ Babylonstoren Farm Hotel ▪ Babel Restaurant; Garden glasshouse for teas & light meals ▪ Winemaker(s) Charl Coetzee (Nov 2010), with Wian Mouton (Jan 2011) ▪ Viticulturist(s) Hannes Aucamp (Jan 2010) ▪ 200ha/62ha (cabs s/f, malbec, merlot, mourv, p verdot, pinot, shiraz, chard, chenin, sem, viog) ▪ PO Box 167 Simondium 7670 ▪ cellar@babylonstoren.com ▪ www.babylonstoren.com ▪ S 33° 49' 6.73" E 018° 55' 39.08" ▪ **T +27 (0)21-863-1804** ▪ F +27 (0)21-863-1727

Babylonstoren is the Paarl showpiece estate established by Koos Bekker, CEO of multinational media group Naspers, and wife Karen Roos, complete with boutique hotel, restaurants and formal gardens. All very luxe but the local community hasn't been forgotten. Fees collected at the gate are put towards The Babylonstoren Trust which funds community upliftment projects, in particular helping employees provide a well-rounded education for their children.

★★★★ Shiraz 🈂 Now bottled, **11** is clean & correct with red & black fruit, hint of pepper & attractive oak. Good concentration, bright acidity & firm tannins.

★★★★ Chardonnay 🈂 On a re-taste, **11** shows lime & lemon, discreet vanilla. Clean & fresh with a long pithy finish, it's particularly seamless, graceful - still very tight, it should age well.

Babel 🈂 ★★★★ Bordeaux-style red blend with 24% shiraz, **12** shows dark fruit but also a green edge & lots of toasty oak. A serious effort but perhaps not as fully realised as previewed maiden **11** (★★★★). **Mourvèdre Rosé 🈂 ★★★ 13** attempts elegance but seems particularly light & tart, with red fruit plus hint of fynbos. **Chenin Blanc ✓ 🈂 ★★★★** Unwooded **13** from Helderberg grapes shows peach plus a pleasant burnt matchstick note. Good concentration, fresh acidity & long, dry finish. More refined than **11** (★★★★). **12** sold out untasted. **Viognier 🈂 ★★★★** Carefully considered **12** displays concentrated peach & merest touch of oak. Medium bodied & well balanced. — CE

Backsberg Estate Cellars 🍴🍷🎋📷🎿♿

Location: Paarl ▪ Map: Paarl & Wellington ▪ WO: Paarl/Western Cape/Elgin/Paarl/Elgin ▪ Est 1916 ▪ 1stB 1970 ▪ Tasting & sales Mon-Fri 9–5 Sat/Sun 10–4 ▪ Fee R15 ▪ Open 365 days a year ▪ Cellar tours by appt ▪ Backsberg Restaurant (see Restaurants section) ▪ Facilities for children ▪ Tour groups ▪ Conferences ▪ Weddings & functions ▪ BYO picnic ▪ Hiking ▪ Mountain biking ▪ Bird watching ▪ Environmental tours ▪ Conservation area ▪ Sunday picnic concerts (summer) ▪ Glass blowing workshops ▪ Owner(s) Michael Back ▪ Winemaker(s) Alicia Rechner (Jun 2012) ▪ Viticulturist(s) Clive Trent (Jul 1992) ▪ 130ha (cab, merlot, shiraz, chard) ▪ 900t/ 160,000cs own label 65% red 30% white 5% rosé ▪ PO Box 537 Suider-Paarl 7624 ▪ info@backsberg.co.za ▪ www.backsberg.co.za ▪ S 33° 49' 42.9" E 018° 54' 56.9" ▪ **T +27 (0)21-875-5141** ▪ F +27 (0)21-875-5144

Fourth-generation Simon Back is now running this long-established family winery near Paarl, allowing his father, Michael, to focus his considerable environmental zeal on renewable energy. Abetting Back snr is a new biodiesel plant which, allied with the biomass furnace and continued greening and tree planting projects, will help the farm move closer to going off-grid and becoming energy independent. Harvest 2013 brought its share of challenges for winemaker Alicia Rechner, such as both presses failing within 15 minutes of each other! Backsberg is also one of few local producers with kosher wines in their portfolio.

Flagship - Backsberg Family Reserve range

★★★★ **Red Blend** ⊕ Cab leads the merlot/shiraz chorus in **08** blend. Rich & spicy, with black fruit. Nutty appeal from prominent oak. Big, firm & ripe with long fruity finish. No **06** or **07**.

★★★★ **White Blend** ⊕ 🏠 Chardonnay/roussanne-driven **09**'s waxy overlay complements boldly flavoured yet balanced profile, refreshing acid zing. Drop viognier gives floral lift.

Black Label range

★★★★ **Klein Babylons Toren** ⊕ Classically styled blend of cab & merlot with dab malbec. **07** black fruit with cedar & cigarbox lift. Lithe frame provided by 18 months in small oak. **06** sold untasted.

★★★★ **Elbar** ⊕ Malbec & mourvèdre 70% of **07**'s 7-way blend, tasted from barrel previously. Hedgerow fruit, sprinkle of dried herbs, supple oak add savoury flavours, long silky flourish.

★★★★ **John Martin Sauvignon Blanc** ⊕ 🏠 🔲 **12** (★★★☆) tangy grapefruit succulence less intense than last-tasted **10**. Smoother & more rounded, with good fruit/acid balance.

★★★★ **Hillside Viognier** ⊕ 🏠 Vanilla notes to **09**'s peach/apricot medley. Delicately textured, smooth balanced acidity from 14% roussanne; lingering nutty finish.

Beyond Borders Pinot Noir ⊕ 🏠 🔲 ★★★★ Maiden **10** still young & brash. Raspberry fruit gawky & not mingling with spicy oak mid-2012 but shows promise & oodles of appeal. **Pumphouse Shiraz** ★★★★ Earthy depth & firm frame to richly fruited **09**. Spicy plum succulence lasts seamlessly to long, dry finish. Follows French-styled **08** (★★★★), showing delicacy & refinement. **Brut Méthode Cap Classique** ⊕ ★★★★ Traditional-method sparkling, **08** a blend of chardonnay & pinot; yeasty biscuit aromas, vibrant melon/apple flavours, persistent lemon drop conclusion.

Premium range

★★★★ **Special Late Harvest** ⊕ Litchi floral abundance on **12** (★★★☆), first since **07**. Simple sweet appeal to 70/30 viognier & gewürztraminer mix.

Sauvignon Blanc ☺ 🏠 🔲 ★★★ Fig & gooseberry typicity & tang on juicy, fresh **13**. Crisp & lively with good length & dryness. Light flint at end. Includes Elgin grapes.

Cabernet Sauvignon 🔲 ★★★★ Elegant & light-bodied **10** maintains standard of **09**. Ample fruitcake, cedar & density of flavour. Fresh too. **Merlot** 🔲 ★★★☆ Blackcurrant & tobacco on **12** preview. Dab malbec (10%) adds texture & length. Rich cocoa tang on long, dry tail. **Pinotage** 🔲 ★★★ **12** juicy raspberry appeal. Splash carignan (10%) firms up core & adds length. Cheery simplicity throughout. **Dry Red** 🏠 ★★★ N stalwart matches bar set by previous bottling of unspecified red grape mix. Brambly red fruit appeal galore. **Rosé** 🏠 ★★★ Sweet cranberry texture & flavour on **NV** mix of grenache, shiraz & viognier. Acidity livens sweetness (30g) & dries tail. **Chardonnay** 🏠 🔲 ★★★ Creamy citrus with lively tang on **12** preview, with dab roussanne (5%). Good breadth & body, structured & firm to finish. Elgin & Paarl grapes. **Chenin Blanc** 🏠 🔲 ★★★ **13** tropical peardrop & melon simplicity. Lively & fresh. Pleasant body & length but uncomplicated. WO W Cape.

Kosher range

Merlot 📖 ★★★ Light & fruity mulberry cheer on **13** pre-bottling sample. **Pinotage** ⊕ ★★★ Raspberry & spice appeal, **11** touch short overall. **Chardonnay** 📖 ★★★ Gentle orange blossom & marmalade on **13**, easy & simple. **Brut Méthode Cap Classique** ★★★ Tangy crisp citrus zest & butter on **09** dry sparkler from chardonnay. Lively & fresh, with long creamy finish. **Kiddush Sacramental Wine** 📖 ★★ Syrupy **12** tank sample from shiraz, blueberry & plum simplicity with clove spicing.

Fortified range

Pinneau 📖 ★★★★ Pineau des Charentes-style fortified & oak-matured chenin **10**, appealing roasted hazelnut spice, step up on last-tasted **04** (★★★) from semillon. **Cape Ruby** ⊕ ★★★★ Port-style from cab franc, **06** on review was like drinking brandy-doused fruitcake: full bodied & rich.

Brandy range NEW

★★★★ **Sydney Back 1st Distillation** Dark amber on this 20 year old, with rich prune, caramel & clove on the nose. Richly textured, round & well matured, with marmalade, dark chocolate flavours. Loads of oaky vanilla & mature character, but a touch less fresh than the younger brandies. 100% potstill from chenin, as all.

★★★★ **Sydney Back Special Release** Complex nose of dried fruit & toasty nuts, hint of anise. Dried fruits fill the mouth with apricot, peach & touch of sweet vanilla. Floral notes all the way & hint of orange peel.

Sydney Back Finest Matured ★★★★ Inviting honey, dried apricot & marzipan aromas. Charming & light footed, with vanilla, toasty nuts, sweet tobacco & caramel. 5–8 years oak maturation. — DB, FM, TJ

■ **Badenhorst Family Wines** *see* AA Badenhorst Family Wines

Badgerberg Estate

Location/map: Villiersdorp ▪ WO: Overberg ▪ Est 2000 ▪ 1stB 2009 ▪ Tasting & sales Mon-Thu by appt Fri 3-6 Sat 10-4 (Sep-May) ▪ Light German refreshments, sausages, cheese breads, cold cuts ▪ German Octoberfest & Maibaumfest annually ▪ Owner(s) Heinz & Lynnette Mederer ▪ Winemaker(s) Ryan Puttick ▪ Matthew Krone (MCC consultant) ▪ 35ha/9ha (cab, merlot, shiraz, sauv) ▪ 100t/1,268cs own label 53% red 47% white ▪ PO Box 2605 Somerset West 7129 ▪ info@badgerberg.co.za, lynnettem@badgerberg.co.za ▪ www.badgerberg.co.za ▪ S 33° 57' 07.5" E 19° 19' 29.5" ▪ **T** +27 (0)21-852-1150/+27 (0)83-263-2783 ▪ F +27 (0)86-586-2237

Heinz and Lynnette Mederer's 'retirement project', farming grapes and apples near Villiersdorp, morphed into making Badgerberg wines at Villiersdorp Cellar. Production is snapped up by a thirsty export market, but small quantities are retained for their cellardoor and annual Oktober and Maibaum fests.

Prima ⊕ ★★★ **09** merlot, cab blend oozes red fruit. Bright & uncomplicated, supple fruit flavours balanced by fresh acidity & firm vanilla oak. **Sauvignon Blanc** Await next. **Aquarius Cuvée Brut** ⊕ 📖 ★★★★ Méthode cap classique sparkling from sauvignon, **10** shows variety's grapefruit lift & appley 'seabreeze' character. Lightish, clean & crisp. — FM

Badsberg Wine Cellar

Location: Rawsonville ▪ Map/WO: Breedekloof ▪ Est 1951 ▪ 1stB 1958 ▪ Tasting & sales Mon-Fri 9-5 Sat 10-1 ▪ Fee R20pp for groups of 8+ ▪ Closed all pub hols ▪ Cellar tours Mon-Fri 2-3 (Feb-May only) ▪ Picnics by appt during harvest; or BYO picnic ▪ Facilities for children ▪ Farm produce ▪ Conferences (40 pax) ▪ Conservation area ▪ Soetes & Soup (Jul) & Outdoor festivals (Oct) ▪ Owner(s) 26 members ▪ Cellarmaster(s) Willie Burger (1998) ▪ Winemaker(s) Henri Swiegers (2002) & Nicholas Husselman (2011), with Jaco Booysen (Jan 2007) ▪ Viticulturist(s) Nicholas Husselman (2011) ▪ ±1,500ha/±1,300ha (ptage, shiraz, chenin, cbard) ▪ ±23,000t own label 20% red 65% white 10% rosé 5% fortified ▪ ISO 22000:2009 ▪ PO Box 72 Rawsonville 6845 ▪ enquiries@badsberg. co.za ▪ www.badsberg.co.za ▪ S 33° 39' 40.1" E 019° 16' 9.2" ▪ **T** +27 (0)23-344-3021 ▪ F +27 (0)23-344-3023

This large-scale Breedekloof producer and exporter is focused on processing 'quality grapes effectively to make world-class products for the benefit of all our partners'. Its scenic location in a nature conservancy is consistent with the choice of front-label emblem: the protected March Flower, whose flowering coincides with the ripening of hanepoot, crucial component of the stellar Badslese Natural Sweet.

★★★★★ **Badslese** 🖾 Unwooded Natural Sweet dessert from chenin & muscat d'Alexandrie; only in best years (no **10**, **11**). With muscat portion upped to 30%, now-bottled **12** (★★★★) is pure indulgence: melting quince, melon & grape flavours, as scintillating & precise as **09**, our 2012 White Wine of the Year.

★★★★ **Noble Late Harvest** ⊕ Soft & sweet after-dinner treat in 375ml from (unwooded) chenin; **07** lots of good things - honey, apricot, marmalade - to smell & taste; clean & uplifting.

★★★★ **Red Muscadel** 🖾 Consistent fortified sweetie for year-round enjoyment: fireside in winter; on the rocks in summer. Tealeaf-nuanced **13** delivers signature raisin-sweet but balanced slipperiness.

★★★★ **Red Jerepigo** ⊕ 🖾 Classy fortified pinotage for the sweet-toothed. **11** molasses & caramel overtones, liqueur cherry fruit flavours.

Chenin Blanc ☺ 🗐 🖾 ★★☆ Easy-drinking **13** delightful sunripe guava & melon flavours, with a hint of thatch. **Perlé Muscato** ⟦NEW⟧ ☺ 🗐 🖾 ★★☆ From muscat de Frontignan, charming & lively **13** has gentle bubbles, alluring sweetness, bonus of low alcohol.

Merlot ⊕ 🗐 🖾 ★★☆ Plummy **11**, light textured for refreshing summer sipping. **Pinotage-Mocha Fusion** Next awaited, as for **Noble Late Harvest Limited Edition**. **Belladonna** ✓ 🖾 ★★★ Step-up **11** all-day sipper: moderate alcohol, cranberry zing, black & red berry fusion ex shiraz plus three Bordeaux reds. **Rosé** ⊕ 🗐 🖾 ★★☆ From merlot, **12** pretty sweetish berry-toned party companion. **Chardonnay Sur Lie** ✓ 🖾 ★★★★ **12** punches above its price bracket with complex lemon, fennel & floral bouquet, tangy acidity, engaging lime tail. Less buttery than **11** (★★★★), more satisfying. **Sauvignon Blanc** 🗐 🖾 ★★ Dusty **13** drier, less fruity & expressive than previous. **Vin Doux** ⊕ 🖾 ★★☆ Sweet, frothy & grapey **11** sparkling from muscat d'Alexandrie. **Special Late Harvest** ⊕ 🖾 ★★☆ **11** marries chenin, hanepoot for faintly aromatic, softly sweet Indian-dinner companion. **Hanepoot Jerepigo** ⊕ 🖾 ★★★★ Spirity uplift from grapey-sweet (but not cloying) **11** fortified dessert. **Cape Vintage** ★★★ Smart livery for now-bottled **09** from shiraz, ruby cab. Among the Cape's softer, sweeter port-styles; try with spicy pastries or mushroom soup, say winemakers. — CvZ

⬛ **Bain's Way** see Wellington Wines
⬛ **Bakenskop** see Jonkheer
⬛ **Balance** see Overhex Wines International

Baleia Bay

Location: Riversdale ▪ WO: Cape South Coast ▪ Est 2009 ▪ 1stB 2011 ▪ Sales & cellar tours by appt ▪ Owner(s) Joubert family ▪ Winemaker(s) Piet Kleinhans (consultant) ▪ Viticulturist(s) Jan-Hendrik Joubert (Jan 2009) ▪ 1,000ha/9.5ha (pinot, shiraz, tempranillo, chard, sauv) ▪ 80t/600cs own label 60% red 40% white ▪ PO Box 268 Riversdal 6670 ▪ info@baleiabay.co.za ▪ www.baleiabay.co.za ▪ **T +27 (0)28-713-1367** ▪ F +27 (0)86-560-0367

Baleia Bay is a young winery (first vintage 2011) near the quaintly named hamlet of Vermaaklikeid ('Entertainment'). The Joubert family aim to celebrate the specific limestone-rich terroir of this area close to the Atlantic Ocean with wines of quality. They believe the constant search for new wine areas is what's leading to the exciting happenings and discoveries that enrich our 'rainbow nation'.

Pinot Noir ☺ ★★☆ Billowing oak vanilla, **11** is a real crowd pleaser, unconcentrated but fresh & fruity, an easy-drinker with some style. **Sauvignon Blanc** ☺ 🗐 ★★☆ Revealing its cool provenance, ebullient **12** shouts green fruit & herbaceousness, tangy acidity, touch of minerality & modest 11.5% alcohol.

Chardonnay ★★★ Spirited wooding (100% new) covers **12**'s sweetish ginger-lemon fruit with a duvet of oak, giving a toasty breakfast-in-bed effect which many will find attractive. — GdB, GM

⬛ **Balthazar** see Roodezandt Wines
⬛ **Bandana** see Klein Roosboom
⬛ **Barber's Wood** see Celestina

Barista

Location: Robertson ▪ WO: Western Cape ▪ Est/1stB 2009 ▪ Tasting at Val de Vie ▪ Owner(s) Vinimark ▪ Winemaker(s) Bertus Fourie ▪ 600t/60,000cs own label ▪ PO Box 6223 Paarl 7620 ▪ info@vinimark.co.za ▪ www.baristawine.co.za ▪ **T +27 (0)21-883-8043** ▪ F +27 (0)21-886-4708

The United States, birthplace of Starbucks, is fast becoming a huge market for this coffee-style pinotage, say brand owners Vinimark, adding that South Africans are just as mad for the intricately vinified, mocha-toned wine, which is helping buoy the current double-digit growth in sales.

Pinotage 🗄 🚱 ★★★☆ **12** tones down the overt coffee bean character yet steps up on previous with juicy blueberry & cocoa freshness, smoky mocha tail. — FM

Barnardt Boyes Wines   **[NEW]**

Location: Stellenbosch ▪ WO: Western Cape ▪ Est 2012 ▪ 1stB 2009 ▪ Closed to public ▪ Owner(s) N Barnardt & J Boyes ▪ Winemaker(s) Hendrik Snyman (Jun 2013) ▪ 40,000cs own label 100% red ▪ Other export brands: Le Noe, Carrol Boyes Collection ▪ wim@barnardtboyes.com, neels@barnardtboyes.com ▪ www.barnardtboyes.com ▪ **T** +27 (0)21-883-3447 ▪ F +27 (0)21-883-3491

Stellenbosch negociant business Barnardt Boyes Wines is part of a diverse group of companies, including luxury goods manufacturer Carrol Boyes Functional Art and citrus exporter FruitOne. More specifically, it is a collaboration between FruitOne MD John Boyes (Carrol's brother) and wine industry veteran Neels Barnardt, an old university friend.

Pinotage 🚱 ★★★ Light jammy fruit, **11** easy & uncomplicated, quaffable. **Shiraz-Cabernet Sauvignon** 🚱 ★★ Minty notes to red fruit in fairly firm, warm **10**, early-drinker with winter stews. **Premium Blend** ★★ Char & coffee edge to leafy **09**, mostly from merlot, undemanding dry red. — DC, JP, CvZ, MW

- **Barney Barnato** *see Douglas Wine Cellar*
- **Barn Find** *see Franki's Vineyards*
- **Baroness** *see Oudtshoorn Cellar - SCV*
- **Barony** *see Rosendal Winery*

Barrydale Winery & Distillery   🍷🎋📷

Location: Barrydale ▪ Map: Klein Karoo & Garden Route ▪ WO: Tradouw/Western Cape/Klein Karoo ▪ Est 1941 ▪ 1stB 1976 ▪ Tasting & sales Mon-Fri 9–5 Sat 9–3 ▪ Fee R25 for groups of 5 or more ▪ Closed Easter Fri-Mon, Dec 25/26 & Jan 1 ▪ Book ahead for cellar tours ▪ BYO picnic ▪ Conservation area ▪ Owner(s) Southern Cape Vineyards (SCV) & Oude Molen Distillery ▪ Winemaker(s) / distiller Ferdi Smith ▪ ±102ha (cab, merlot, shiraz, chard, cbard, sauv) ▪ ±997t/10,000cs own label 56% red 43% white 1% rosé + 1,000cs for clients ▪ Other export brand: Joseph Barry ▪ PO Box 59 Barrydale 6750 ▪ sales@barrydalewines.co.za ▪ S 33° 54' 35.83" E 020° 42' 45.20" ▪ **T** +27 (0)28-572-1012 ▪ F +27 (0)28-572-1541

Previously sole proprietor, Southern Cape Vineyards is now joint owner with Elgin-based Oude Molen Distillery of Barrydale Winery & Distillery and its sibling, Ladismith (see entry). Barrydale is home to internationally awarded brandies celebrating English tradesman Joseph Barry's role in fostering 19th-century wine- and brandy-making in Klein Karoo. Once stocks sell out, just three wines, selected annually on grape quality, will be bottled by winemaker Ferdi Smit, who'll also nurture the brandies under the aegis of seasoned MD Andre Simonis.

Merchant's Mark range

Cabernet Sauvignon ⑧ ★★ Dry & medium-bodied **08** soft & approachable for solo sipping. **Merlot** ⑧ ★★ **10** fresh & fruity fun, albeit brief. **Pinot Noir** ⑧ ★★★ **10** first since **05**; dark cherry/earth fragrance & good varietal flavours are easy to like, linger pleasantly. WO W Cape. **Ruby Cabernet** ⑧ 🗄 ★★ Friendly **09** upbeat & rounded quick sip. WO Klein Karoo. **Shiraz** ⑧ ★★ From Klein Karoo vineyards, **08** has black pepper dusting, softer mouthfeel. **Chardonnay** ⑧ 🚱 ★★ **11** ripe apple tones seamed with vanilla & wood char. For fans of an oakier style. **Sauvignon Blanc** ⑧ ★★ Light acid bite to breezy **11**. **Chardonnay-Viognier** ⑧ 🚱 ★★★ Ripe apple & peach complexity, floral lift & smooth vanilla oak raise the bar in **11**. Enjoy chilled. **Brut Rosé** ⑧ 🚱 ★★★★ Cheerful & lively **NV** bottle-fermented sparkling from pinotage & chenin ex Stellenbosch. Fruit & tangy, for early enjoyment.

Decent range

Red ⑧ 🗄 ★★ Uncomplicated fun from **NV** combo red varieties. **White** ⑧ 🗄 ★★ Pot-pourri bouquet on gently sweet **NV** trio white varieties.

Brandy range NEW

★★★★ **Barry & Nephews Muscat** Distinct muscat character, with dried apricot & gentle floral backing, plus vanilla from oak. Lots of dried fruit on palate in balance with oak. Just 3 years maturation, but complex & smooth with a long finish - still hinting at the grape. These all 100% potstill.

Joseph Barry Traditional ★★★☆ 5-year-aged potstill, darkest & most auburn of these three. Hints of apple, pear, some citrus backed by toasty nut, vanilla & butterscotch. Balanced & smooth, with hint of oak on long finish. **Joseph Barry 10 Year Old** ★★★★ Dried fruit, floral wafts with cinnamon on well-matured, rich frame. More forceful, less fruity than Traditional above. Dry, lingering finish. — WB,JP, TJ

Barry Gould Family Wines

Location/WO: Elgin ▪ Map: Elgin, Walker Bay & Bot River ▪ Est 2003 ▪ 1stB 2004 ▪ Tasting, sales & cellar tours by appt ▪ Closed Good Fri, Dec 25 & Jan 1 ▪ Meals/functions by arrangement (up to 20 pax) ▪ Wildekrans Country House (B&B) + self-catering cottage ▪ Child-friendly ▪ Gifts ▪ Farm produce ▪ Conference venue (20 pax) ▪ 4-day fully guided slack-packing trail ▪ Owner(s) Barry Gould & Alison Green ▪ Cellarmaster(s) Barry Gould (2003) ▪ Winemaker(s) Barry Gould (2003), with family (2004) ▪ Viticulturist(s) Grapes bought in from various sources ▪ ±2t/320cs own label 70% red 30% white ▪ PO Box 7 Elgin 7180 ▪ gould.arc@wildekrans.co.za ▪ S 34° 12' 12.7" E 019° 8' 53.6" ▪ **T +27 (0)21-848-9788/+27 (0)82-901-4896** ▪ F +27 (0)21-848-9788

When Barry Gould's day job as an architect got in the way of his winemaking hobby last year, he took stock of the surplus in his cellar and was left reassured he wasn't about to run out any time soon. 'I will resume this harvest,' he says of the 'hands-on, hands-in, hand-made' wines he crafts in Elgin.

A Simple Red Equal cab & merlot. Very dry maraschino cherry-toned **07** barrel sample tad volatile, too unformed to rate. **Chenin Blanc** Await next, like **Sauvignon Blanc**. — DB

■ **Barry & Nephews** see Barrydale Winery & Distillery

Bartinney Private Cellar

Location/map: Stellenbosch ▪ WO: Stellenbosch/Banghoek ▪ Est 2006 ▪ 1stB 2008 ▪ Tasting & sales Mon-Fri 10-4 ▪ Closed all pub hols ▪ Cellar tours by appt ▪ Bartinney Wine Bar Mon-Sat 11-9 (cnr Church & Bird Str, Stellenbosch) ▪ Owner(s) Rose & Michael Jordaan ▪ Winemaker(s) Ronell Wiid (consultant) ▪ Viticulturist(s) Ryno Maree (Oct 2010) ▪ 27ha/±17ha (cab, chard, sauv) ▪ 118t/4,000cs own label 70% red 30% white ▪ BWI champion ▪ Postnet Suite 231 Private Bag X5061 Stellenbosch 7599 ▪ info@bartinney.co.za ▪ www.bartinney.co.za ▪ S 33° 55' 34.66" E 018° 55' 56.79" ▪ **T +27 (0)21-885-1013** ▪ F +27 (0)21-885-2852

Owners Michael and Rose Jordaan are branching out from their boutique wine estate perched atop Helshoogte Pass. Their new venture is a wine bar in the heart of Stellenbosch, forming part of a well-known bakery and deli. For oeno-adviser Ronell Wiid, terroir is everything, and she believes the farm has a unique situation and micro-climate which she strives to capture in every bottle.

★★★★ **Cabernet Sauvignon** ⊕ ⊘ Upfront aromas of blackberries & cassis on **10**. Spiced fruitcake & velvety plummy softness with more than a hint of mint. Well-integrated tannins & oak, should improve.

★★★★☆ **Elevage** ⊕ Not new, but our first taste of outstanding cab-based Bordeaux blend reveals polished black fruit nose, darkly concentrated bitter chocolate edge. **09** minty overtones wrapped around black cherry fruit with plushy tannins & exotic perfumes. A keeper. WO Stellenbosch, like Cab.

★★★★ **Chardonnay** ⊘ Deliciously creamy nose **12** (★★★★☆) with butterscotch, peaches & melons. Rich, rounded flavours of lime cheesecake, ginger biscuits & lemon curd before involved finish. Sure to improve, like **11**.

★★★★☆ **Sauvignon Blanc** ⊘ Masses of interest & appeal in stellar **13**, improving year on year. Restrained elegance takes its time to open up to glorious mouthful of citrus with flinty minerality, zesty acidity & complex finish. Banghoek WO, like Chardonnay. — CM

Barton Vineyards

Location: Bot River ▪ Map: Elgin, Walker Bay & Bot River ▪ WO: Walker Bay ▪ Est 2001 ▪ 1stB 2003 ▪ Tasting, sales & cellar tours Mon-Fri 9–5 Sat 10-4 ▪ Closed Easter Sun, Dec 25 & Jan 1 ▪ Lavender products, olive oil, marinated olives & proteas ▪ Barton Villas (see Accommodation section) ▪ Owner(s) Peter J Neill ▪ Cellarmaster(s)/winemaker(s)/viticulturist(s) PJ Geyer (Oct 2010) ▪ 200ha/30ha (cab, malbec, merlot, mourv-pinot, shiraz, chenin, sauv, sem) ▪ 120t/20,000cs own label 40% red 50% white 10% rosé ▪ IPW ▪ PO Box 100 Bot River 7185 ▪ info@bartonvineyards.co.za ▪ www.bartonvineyards.co.za ▪ S 34° 15' 43.8" E 019° 10' 29.2" ▪ T +27 (0)28-284-9283 ▪ F +27 (0)28-284-9776

French-trained winemaker PJ Geyer brings a wealth of experience to this small-scale family winery between Bot River and popular coastal resort Hermanus. There is a new Bordeaux-style red blend to tempt visitors, as well as a delectable line up of farm produce, luxury 4-star accommodation, and a range of activities for the energetic on a 200 ha working farm, rich in biodiversity.

★★★★ **Shiraz-Cabernet Sauvignon** ⓣ Delicious **10** a little riper, with more truffly, gamey flavours than **09**, & deep, crushed velvet texture. Supple but with sufficient form, freshness for now or years ahead. **Merlot** Next awaited. **Reserve** NEW 🗟 ★★★☆ **11** a merlot-led Bordeaux blend with cab & malbec. Preview shows dark spicy fruit in tight structure. Needs time to reveal inherent quality & harmony. **Shiraz Rosé** ⓣ 🗟 ★★★ Electric pink from shiraz; equally vivid spicy features in refreshing, food-friendly **12**. **Chenin Blanc** ✓ 🗟 ★★★★ Feisty new bottling of **12**. Lovely fruit purity & gentle, leesy breadth, with tangy acidic thread. **Sauvignon Blanc** 🗟 ★★★ Now bottled, **12** shows same wild herb freshness & minerality as last year, now countered by lanolin/oily texture. A seafood partner. **Sauvignon Blanc-Semillon** ✓ 🗟 ★★★☆ **12** step up, now more elegantly restrained than fruit-shy, with richness & texture. Classy table mate, for next 3-6 years. **Blanc** NEW 🗟 ★★ Clean, crisp & waxy **12** is a blend of chenin, sauvignon & semillon. — MW

■ **Basco** see Blomendahl Vineyards

Bayede!

Location: Paarl ▪ Map: Paarl & Wellington ▪ WO: Western Cape/Stellenbosch/Franschhoek/Robertson/Groenekloof ▪ Est 2009 ▪ Tasting & sales in showroom/office at 5 Stasie Street, Southern Paarl Mon-Fri or by appt ▪ Fee R30 ▪ Private VIP tastings at Villa Beanto Winelands Estate by appt only ▪ Closed all pub hols ▪ Tour groups by appt ▪ 60% red 30% white 10% rosé ▪ PO Box 7362 Northern Paarl 7623 ▪ anto@bayede.co.za ▪ www.bayede.co.za ▪ S 33° 45' 54.77" E 018° 57' 41.03" ▪ T +27 (0)21-863-3406/+27 (0)83-650-3585 ▪ F +27 (0)21-863-4884

Named for the traditional greeting reserved for the Zulu King, the Bayede! job-creation initiative includes South Africa's first 'by royal appointment' range of wines, selected by winemaker Altus le Roux and sold in bead-adorned bottles. 'The project puts people to work, shares expertise and resources and, as a result of combined input, produces unique goods,' says Zulu monarch Goodwill Zwelethini.

7 Icon Wines range

★★★★ **HM King Goodwill Cabernet Sauvignon** NEW Generous & forthcoming **08** from Vergelegen, cedar-infused blackberry & firm tannins. Full-bodied yet elegant wine to drink now or keep few years.

★★★★ **HM King Goodwill Pinotage Reserve** ⓣ 🕸 Was 'Pinotage Reserve'. Hinting at blackcurrant & lavender, **10** by Beyerskloof deserves more time to fully integrate. Stellenbosch WO, like Cab & Chenin.

★★★★ **HM King Goodwill Chardonnay** NEW 🕸 Fresh lemon cream & notes of citrus in **12** from Robertson's De Wetshof, rounded & full-bodied, ends clean & dry.

★★★★☆ **HM King Goodwill Chenin Blanc** NEW 🕸 With a hint of crushed leaves, Kleine Zalze's **12** offers peaches & pears before a lees-rich yet savoury palate. Masterfully oaked for depth & structure, ageability. **HM King Goodwill Merlot** NEW 🕸 ★★★☆ Ripe plums & spicy chocolate gaining complexity on palate. Mouthfilling & long lingering **11** from Anthonij Rupert Wyne. **HM King Goodwill Shiraz** NEW By Tokara but not tasted, as for **HM King Goodwill Sauvignon Blanc** ex De Grendel.

King and Queen Range range

King Goodwill Shiraz ⓣ 🕸 ★★★★ Most serious wine in this range, listed as 'Royal Signature' last time. **10** savoury aromas, ripe berry flavours on a peppery, well-managed tannin base. **King Shaka Jubilee** ⓣ ★★★ Bordeaux-style red, mainly cab & merlot, **09** with developed stewed fruit flavours best enjoyed soon. WO Franschhoek. **Queen Thomo Sauvignon Blanc** 🗟 🕸 ★★★★ Gearing up from previous, **12** is unmistakably sauvignon with a full range of greenpepper, nettle & tropical fruit flavours. Balanced & full yet deliciously crisp. **Queen Mantfombi Dry MCC Sparkling Rosé** ⓣ 🕸 ★★★ Fairly refined & understated **11**, pale pink colour, delicate fruit & lively mousse. Ends crisp & dry.

The Prince range

Red ⊕ 🍴 ★★★ Was 'The Prince Red'. Juicy, fruity off-dry cab/shiraz, **11** a real crowd pleaser. **White** ⊕ 🍴 📖 ★★★ Was 'The Prince White'. Fresh, grassy melon fruit on **12**, accessible, easy-drinking chenin & sauvignon.

The Shield range

The Prince Cabernet Sauvignon ⊕ ★★★ Savoury dark chocolate & plums, **11** good with a juicy steak. **The Prince Merlot** 📖 ★★★ Accessible **12** with dusty hay, ripe plum & pleasant savoury notes. Smooth & tasty. **The Prince Pinotage** ⊕ 📖 ★★ Robust **11**, white pepper notes, crisp berry flavours. **The Prince Cabernet Sauvignon-Shiraz-Merlot** ⊕ 📖 ★★★ Shiraz component dominates ripe & approachable **11**, with spicy berry aromas adding to the easy appeal. **The Prince Chenin Blanc** ⊕ 📖 ★★ Lightish, crisp & dry **12**, with herbal flavours. **The Prince Sauvignon Blanc** ⊕ 📖 ★★ Lean & dry **12** needs a food partner. — DB

■ **Bayten** see Buitenverwachting
■ **BC Wines** see Brandvlei Cellar
■ **Beacon Hill** see Jonkheer

Beau Belle

Location/map: Stellenbosch ▪ WO: Stellenbosch/Western Cape ▪ Est 2009 ▪ 1stB 2010 ▪ Tasting, sales & cellar tours by appt Mon-Fri 10-5 Sat 10-3 (first & last Sat of month) ▪ Closed Ash Wed, Easter Fri-Sun, Ascension day, Pentecost, Dec 25/26 & Jan 1 ▪ Meals/refreshments for groups of 10-50 by arrangement ▪ Olive oil ▪ BYO picnic ▪ Mountain biking trail ▪ Weddings ▪ Chapel ▪ Self-catering guest cottage (max 4 people) ▪ Owner(s) Lindeque Family Trust ▪ Directors Tienie & Estelle Lindeque ▪ Cellarmaster(s) Johann Visagie (Apr 2009) ▪ Winemaker(s) Johann Visagie (Mar 2009) ▪ Viticulturist(s) Johann Visagie (Mar 2009) & Tienie Lindeque, advised by Johan Pienaar (consultant) ▪ 36ha/23ha (shiraz) ▪ 243t/6,000cs own label 76% red 24% rosé + 21,000L bulk ▪ PO Box 156 Lynedoch Stellenbosch 7603 ▪ tienie@beaubelle.co.za ▪ www.beaubelle.co.za ▪ S 33° 59' 47.30" E 018° 46' 45.69" ▪ **T +27 (0)21-881-3808/+27 (0)83-522-0100 ▪** F +27 (0)86-670-6720

Since relocating from Gauteng to Stellenbosch's Lynedoch area, former reluctant accountants Tienie and Estelle Lindeque have taken to winefarming like their beloved kayaks to water. With viti/vini adviser Johann Visagie, they're farming organically, niching Beau Belle as a specialist shiraz boutique, and targeting connoisseurs and novices alike with an enlarged portfolio. Cellardoor attractions now include a tasting room and quarterly functions.

Fynbos range

Reserve Shiraz 📖 ★★★★ Was in Beau Belle range. Step-up **11** ideal weekend treat: lightly textured, gently spiced with coffee & oak char ex 19 months mostly older oak, plump with plum & blackberry fruit. **Geneesbos Shiraz** NEW 📖 ★★★★ **11**'s bright red fruit highlighted by toffee notes, reined in by supple tannins courtesy sojourn 2nd fill barrels; a 'damn decent drink'. **Kooigoed Rosé** NEW 🍴 📖 ★★★ Balanced & refreshing **12**, from shiraz, attractively dry with modest alcohol. Good alternative to your regular dry white.

Cooper range NEW

Semi-Sweet Rosé ☺ 🍴 📖 ★★★ Floral & raspberry abundance on pretty sunset pink **NV**; for the sweet-toothed but not cloying. **Sweet Shiraz** ☺ 🍴 📖 ★★★ Well-made, unpretentious **NV** has pleasant tannic grip, coconut & sweet fruit.

Shiraz 🍴 📖 ★★★ Ripe & supple, friendly **NV** slips down easily. WO W Cape.

Beau Belle range
Discontinued: **Shiraz**, **Pink**. — CvZ

Beau Constantia

Location/WO: Constantia ▪ Map: Cape Peninsula ▪ Est 2003 ▪ 1stB 2010 ▪ Tasting & sales Wed-Sun 10-4.30; Mon-Tue 10-4.30 (Sep-Apr) & by appt (May-Aug) ▪ Closed Good Fri & Dec 25/26 ▪ Spa by appt, T +27 (0)21-794-3376 (Anda) ▪ Owner(s) Dormell Properties 139 (Pty) Ltd ▪ Winemaker(s) Justin van Wyk (Sep 2010) ▪ Viticulturist(s) Japie Bronn (Sep 2002) ▪ 22ha/±11ha (cabs s/f, malbec, merlot, p verdot, shiraz, sauv, sem, viog) ▪ 40t/4,000cs own label 80% red 20% white ▪ 1043 Constantia Main Road Constantia 7806 ▪

winesales@beauconstantia.com ▪ www.beauconstantia.com ▪ S 34° 0' 48.57" E 018° 24' 21.67" ▪ **T +27 (0)21-794-8632** ▪ F +27 (0)21-794-0534

This winery (and spa) on the Constantiaberg at the northern end of the Constantia Valley emerged from the ashes of devastating mountain fires in 2000. With an altitude of around 350 metres, the north-facing vineyards are well sited for ripening red-wine varieties; the first fruits of these under the Beau Constantia label, two Bordeaux-style blends named after the owners' children, were launched ten years after the vines' establishment in 2003. But the whites too, especially viognier, have done so well that new plantings are planned.

★★★★ **Lucca** NEW ⊘ More complete of new red pair; 11 well-matched merlot/cab franc (63/37) piqued with mostly new French oak & franc's own leafy spice. Creamy texture carefully shaded by curtain of fine tannin.

★★★★ **Cecily** ▤ ⊘ **12** viognier has a touch more evident oak & body than some vintages, but enough apricot, spice concentration to absorb, with time. Taut core freshness sets this apart from many others.

Pas de Nom Red ✓ ▤ ⊘ ★★★★ **11** quite serious blend petit verdot with 17% each merlot, malbec. Ripe & intense aromas echoed in rich, mouthcoating fruit; firmish grip should benefit from at least two years' cellaring. **Aidan** NEW ▤ ⊘ ★★★☆ Supple, ripe-fruited **11** malbec-led Bordeaux blend. Approachable, satisfying & generously oak-seasoned, if lacking depth for extended ageing. **Pas de Nom White** Await next. — AL

Beau Joubert Vineyards & Winery

Location/map: Stellenbosch ▪ WO: Stellenbosch/Polkadraai Hills ▪ Est 1695 ▪ 1stB 2000 ▪ Tasting & sales Mon-Fri 8-5 Sat by appt ▪ Closed all pub hols ▪ Cellar tours by appt ▪ BYO picnic ▪ Walks/hikes ▪ Bird watching ▪ Self-catering guest cottage ▪ Owner(s) MD Andrew Hilliard ▪ Cellarmaster(s)/winemaker(s) Christian Kuun (Dec 2006) ▪ Viticulturist(s) Ian Engelbrecht (Nov 2010) ▪ 80ha/40ha (cabs s/f, merlot, pinot, shiraz, chenin, sauv) ▪ 280t/40,000cs own label 60% red 35% white 5% rosé + 10,000L for clients ▪ Other export brand: Joubert Brothers ▪ Ranges for customers: Infusino's, Polkadraai Road ▪ PO Box 1114 Stellenbosch 7599 ▪ info@beaujoubert.com ▪ www.beaujoubert.com ▪ S 33° 57' 11.6" E 018° 44' 25.5" ▪ **T +27 (0)21-881-3103** ▪ F +27 (0)21-881-3377

Under stewardship of US entrepreneur Andrew Hilliard, this pretty estate overlooking False Bay from the prestige Polkadraai Hills is expanding at home and abroad, adding and upgrading cellar equipment, and commencing a replanting program that will run over the next 5 years, starting with sauvignon blanc.

Beau Joubert range

★★★★ **Ambassador** ✓ ▤ Preview **10** merlot (69%), cab & dollop shiraz is elegant & understated; bright ripe berries, soft spice & savoury edge adding to the sense of harmony. Worth ageing few years.

Christmas Cabernet ☺ ★★★ Improved NV **(09)** quaffer offers soft, sweet chocolate-wrapped black fruit with easy tannins. Slips down smoothly.

Cabernet Sauvignon ✓ ▤ ★★★★ Pre-bottling, **10** appeals with upfront blackcurrant & fresh herbal notes, balanced by spicy oak grip. Needs year/2 for optimum enjoyment. **Shiraz** ★★★ **10** charms with earthy black fruit, spicy oak flavours, a sprinkle of dry herbs & a firm farewell. **Rosé** ▤ ★★★ **13** from merlot delights with juicy-dry strawberry & candyfloss flavours. **Old Vine Chenin Blanc** ✓ ▤ ★★★★ Lipsmacking **12** has settled nicely & oozes tropical fruit, creamy vanilla oak from barrel-fermented portion. Serious style bodes well for future enjoyment. **Sauvignon Blanc** ▤ ★★★ Balanced & fresh **13** trumps previous with greenpepper & zingy lemon appeal. **Fat Pig** ⊕ ★★★ Light-bodied port-style from pinotage. Sweet fruitcake & cinnamon on previewed **07**, for fireside enjoyment. Polkadraai Hills WO.

Oak Lane range

Shiraz-Cabernet Sauvignon ☺ ▤ ★★★ **12** appealing earthiness & spice, blackcurrant pastilles & dusty notes, silky texture. Easy sipping. **Chenin Blanc-Sauvignon Blanc** ☺ ▤ ★★★ **13** fruity, with smooth mouthfeel & citrus finish for picnic fare.

Pinot Noir In abeyance. **Merlot-Cabernet Sauvignon** ▤ ★★★ Early-drinking **12**, sweet plums, herbs & spice. Smooth, but ends abruptly. — WB

Beaumont Wines

Location: Bot River ▪ Map: Elgin, Walker Bay & Bot River ▪ WO: Bot River/Walker Bay ▪ Est 1750 ▪ 1stB 1994 ▪ Tasting, sales & cellar tours Mon-Fri 9.30–4.30 Sat 10–3 ▪ Fee R25pp for groups of 10+ ▪ Closed Easter Sun, Dec 25 & Jan 1 ▪ Farm produce ▪ Walking/hiking trails ▪ Conservation area ▪ 200-year old watermill ▪ Art/jewellery exhibits ▪ 2 historic self-catering guest cottages ▪ Owner(s) Beaumont family ▪ Cellarmaster(s) Sebastian Beaumont (Jun 2003) ▪ Winemaker(s) Marelise Jansen van Rensburg (Jan 2007) ▪ Viticulturist(s) Sebastian Beaumont (Jun 1999) ▪ 500ha/31ha (mourv, ptage, chenin) ▪ 150t/20,000cs own label 45% red 50% white 5% rosé ▪ BWI, IPW ▪ PO Box 3 Bot River 7185 ▪ info@beaumont.co.za ▪ www.beaumont.co.za ▪ S 34° 13' 27. 2" E 019° 12' 24.9" ▪ **T +27 (0)28-284-9194** ▪ F +27 (0)28-284-9733

The rustic charm of historic Compagnes Drift farm in Bot River, home of Beaumont Wines, has evolved into some savvy winemaking with a good dose of laidback country chic. This wonderful mix is managed courtesy of the personal involvement of the charismatic Beaumont family. From art, jewellery and farm produce, to a lovingly restored Vitruvian watermill, to the boutique cellar handcrafting individual and elegant wines. The latest being an unusual chenin, made like a red wine, dedicated to cellarmaster Sebastian Beaumont's son Leo. Their family crest bears the moto 'Erectus Non Elatus' ('Proud But Not Arrogant'). This, Sebastian notes, echoes the status of the South African wine industry 20 years on since democracy, with wines that show a sense of place, 'reflecting our rich diversity that makes our country special, interesting and challenging'.

Beaumont range

★★★★☆ **Mourvèdre** 🌱 Youthful preview of **11** (★★★★) shade off benchmark **10**. Appears tad weightier & warmer. Firm dry tannins envelop a core of dark berried inky flavours. Only 150 cases made.

★★★★☆ **Ariane** 🌱 Merlot-led Bordeaux blend in **11**. Elegant & restrained, with fine-grained tannins framing sappy cassis & red fruit. Poised & harmonious table mate, will reward cellaring.

★★★★☆ **Vitruvian** Powerful, ripe **09** (★★★★) is a mainly mourvèdre, pinotage & shiraz, with cab franc & petit verdot. Intense, dark fruit masked by brooding tannins. Not as composed as **08**, one to age.

★★★★ **Shiraz-Mourvèdre** 🌱 Youthful **11** barrel sample returns to form. More potential than **10** (★★★★), showing balance & ample ripe spicy fruit. Powerful modern style with creamy texture.

★★★★★ **Hope Marguerite Chenin Blanc** 🌱 Internationally lauded & a SA classic, the farm's top white is from low-yielding old vines. Drier **12**'s cool-fruited focus, tension & freshness has a subtle, rich undertone. Elegant & polished, with modest 12.6% alcohol belying its intensity.

★★★★★ **Chenin Blanc** ✓ 🍴 🌱 Drier styled **13** still exudes all chenin's flavour & charm. Zesty acidity adds verve to creamy texture. Structured & balanced, a shining example of what unoaked chenin can deliver!

★★★★ **Goutte d'Or** 🌱 **12** the farm's first all-chenin Noble Late Harvest since **98**. Unshowy, revealing layers of rich apple pie, marzipan & crème brûlée, offset by tangy freshness. Comfort food in a bottle!

Pinotage 🌱 ★★★★ **11** is a tad riper, richer with more new oak than **12** sibling, although both show similar elegant styling. Structured but lithe, with bright, perfumed berry flavours & clean dry farewell. **Leo's Whole Bunch Chenin Blanc** NEW 🌱 ★★★★ Characterful **11**, vinified in older oak 'like a red wine', combines pithy breadth from skin contact with chenin's baked apple, nutty richness. Limited 1.5L magnum bottling. **Cape Vintage** ★★★ Now bottled, **08** has dried prune & leather nuance from tinta barocca & pinotage. Spirit a tad apart still, but good winter warmer. Walker Bay WO.

Raoul's range

Rosé ☺ 🍴 🌱 ★★★ Was 'Shiraz Rosé'. **13** preview from merlot, tinta barocca & shiraz. Flavoursome cranberry & savoury tones on dry al fresco quaffer. **Jackals River White** ☺ 🍴 🌱 ★★★ Dry **13** tank sample now mainly semillon, with chardonnay & sauvignon. Appealingly drinkable with crisp pear & citrus tone.

Constable House Shiraz-Cabernet Sauvignon 🍴 🌱 ★★★★ **11** bright berry & savoury blend with sappy firm tannins. Balanced & satisfying, with dry finish. Also in 1.5L magnum. **Red Blend** 🍴 🌱 ★★ Was just 'Red'. **11** dry, spicy melange, a touch lean & rustic. — MW

Bein Wine Cellar

Location/map/WO: Stellenbosch ▪ Est 2002 ▪ 1stB 2004 ▪ Tasting, sales & cellar tours Mon-Sat by appt only ▪ Owner(s)/cellarmaster(s)/winemaker(s) Luca & Ingrid Bein ▪ Viticulturist(s) Luca Bein ▪ 3ha/2.2ha (merlot) ▪

16t/2,400cs own label 80% red 20% rosé ▪ IPW ▪ PO Box 3408 Matieland 7602 ▪ lib@beinwine.com ▪ www.
beinwine.com ▪ S 33° 57' 40.0" E 018° 44' 12.0" ▪ **T +27 (0)21-881-3025** ▪ F +27 (0)88-021-881-3025

Former vets, Swiss couple Ingrid and Luca Bein are passionate about their animals (donkeys Poppy and Daisy, dogs and ducks) on their farm in Stellenbosch's
Polkadraai Hills, but even more so about their career change to oenology in one
of the smallest commercial wine ventures in SA. Precision viticulture is the
watchword, identifying and managing micro-terrroirs within their 2.2 ha vineyard, to produce four different styles of their favourite grape, merlot.

★★★★ **Little Merlot** ✓ 🅑 Bright as a button, with supple tannin structure & appealing dark berry, cedar
tone. **12** gets extra panache from some top vineyard fruit. Enjoy over the next 3-5 years.

★★★★☆ **Merlot** 🅑 Graceful & ageworthy, but a shade off **10**, **11** (★★★★) has dashes cab & malbec.
Fresh & spicy, red berry fruit supported by fine-grained tannins & integrated oak.

★★★★☆ **Merlot Reserve** 🅑 Only best vintages & 'best part of our vineyard'. **11** a classic from meticulous
& renowned merlot producers. Elegant, intense, with silky texture & dark perfumed fruit. Lovely structure &
length, deserves cellaring 6-8 years.

Pink Merlot ☺ 🅑 ★★★ **13** crisp & juicy rosé. Subtle brush of hanepoot adds fragrance to dry & refreshing quaffer. —MW

Belfield Wines

Location/WO: Elgin ▪ Map: Elgin, Walker Bay & Bot River ▪ Est 2000 ▪ 1stB 2005 ▪ Tasting, sales & tours by appt
▪ Closed Dec 25 ▪ Owner(s) Mike & Mel Kreft ▪ Cellarmaster(s)/winemaker(s)/viticulturist(s) Mike Kreft ▪ 5.
5ha/2.5ha (cab, merlot, shiraz) ▪ 15t/2,000s own label 100% red ▪ PO Box 191 Elgin 7180 ▪ mike@belfield.
co.za ▪ www.belfield.co.za ▪ S 34° 10' 20.9" E 019° 1' 45.8" ▪ **T +27 (0)21-848-9840/+27 (0)82-575-
1849** ▪ F +27 (0)86-613-3108

It was the pioneering challenge of crafting red wine in Elgin – commonly seen as
a white-wine area – that fired co-owner Mike Kreft's spirit, and his releases to
date certainly have proved doubters wrong. Sample the current releases in the
recently opened tasting venue on Mike and wife Mel's boutique estate.

★★★★ **Magnifica** Flagship named for Queen Protea; 90% cab plus dabs shiraz & merlot in **10**, with
rounded cherry succulence. Like all-cab **08**, tad lighter than concentrated **09** (★★★★★) but good vibrancy &
sleekness from just 20% new oak.

★★★★☆ **Syrah 10** (★★★★) black spicy fruit, violet nuances & harmonious integration with oak. Deliciously fresh yet dry. **09** was shade more substantial & intense.

★★★★ **Aristata** Fruitcake & cocoa nuances on merlot-led **10** Bordeaux-style blend with cabs franc & sauvignon. Inky density & depth to the rounded yet firm palate. Named for an indigenous aloe. —FM

■ **Bellemore** *see Bellevue Estate Stellenbosch*

Bellevue Estate Stellenbosch

Location/map: Stellenbosch ▪ WO: Bottelary/Stellenbosch ▪ Est 1701 ▪ 1stB 1999 ▪ Tasting & sales Mon-Fri
10-4 Sat 10-3 ▪ Closed Good Fri, Dec 25 & Jan 1 ▪ Owner(s) Dirkie Morkel ▪ Winemaker(s) Wilhelm Kritzinger
(Feb 2002) & Anneke Potgieter (Feb 2003) ▪ Viticulturist(s) Dirkie Morkel (Jan 1979) ▪ 291ha/151ha (cabs s/f,
cinsaut, malbec, merlot, p verdot, ptage, pinot, shiraz, chenin, sauv) ▪ ±750t/±20,000cs own label 97% red
3% white; ±40,000cs for clients; balance in bulkwine & grapes ▪ Export brands: Bellemore, Bellemore Family
Selection, Houdamond, Morkel, Tumara ▪ Labels for clients: Cap du Vin, Marks & Spencer, Provoyeur, Pure African, Sizanani, Woolworths ▪ BWI, IPW, WIETA ▪ PO Box 33 Koelenhof 7605 ▪ info@bellevue.co.za ▪ www.
bellevue.co.za ▪ S 33° 52' 48.48" E 018° 45' 50.40" ▪ **T +27 (0)21-865-2055** ▪ F +27 (0)21-865-2899

Planting pinotage back in 1953 was a pioneering move that's still paying dividends at family-owned Bellevue near Stellenbosch, and their version under the
Woolworths branding has really taken off, says winemaker Wilhelm Kritzinger.
Negotiations with a major industry player, that would grow their in-house
brands and benefit the entire Bellevue team, were underway at press time.

PK Morkel range

Petit Verdot 🅟 ★★★ Now bottled, **09** shade less seductive than it was on preview. Full bodied, with subdued
sour cherry fruit, plenty of chocolate & coffee character, drying on finish. **Pinotage** Not tasted. **Tumara** ★★★★

Bordeaux-style red, **06** different bottling to last time, export only. 5-way mix led by cab (69%) is multi-layered, with red & dark fruit fused with earth & cigarbox from 2 years all-new oak. Rung up from **05** (★★★).

Morkel range

Malbec 🦌 ★★★★ In higher league to **09** (★★★), **10** shows fine concentration of red fruit, hints of molasses & mocha in the berried ripeness. Solid tannins set platform for fruitful development. **Pinotage** 🦌 ★★★☆ Full-bore styling, including vanilla from 50% new American oak, & 14.5% alcohol, give **10** body & power but also attractive brambly fruit & a floral/violet lift. **Shiraz** Await next, as for **Atticus Cape Blend** & **Sauvignon Blanc**. **Eselgraf Single Vineyard Chenin Blanc** 🦌 ★★★★ Careful use of oak (only 20% wooded, no new barrels) leaves the fruit intact, creates a showcase for full-bodied **13**'s pear, marzipan & dried apricot flavours. — GM

Bellingham

Location/map: Franschhoek ▪ WO: Coastal/Western Cape/Voor Paardeberg ▪ Est 1693 ▪ 1stB 1947 ▪ Tasting & sales at Bellingham cellardoor, located at Franschhoek Cellar Mon-Fri 9.30-5 (Apr-Sep) & 10-6 (Oct-Mar) Sat 10-3 Sun 11-4 ▪ Closed Good Fri, May 1, Jun 16 & Dec 25 ▪ Cheese lunch daily during tasting hours ▪ Owner(s) DGB (Pty) Ltd ▪ Winemaker(s) Niël Groenewald (Jul 2004), with Mario Damon (Jan 2002) ▪ Viticulturist(s) Stephan Joubert (2006) ▪ 4,000t/560,000cs own label 50% red 49% white 1% rosé ▪ ISO 9001:2000, HACCP, IPW, WIETA ▪ PO Box 52 Franschhoek 7690 ▪ bellingham@dgb.co.za ▪ www.bellinghamwines.com ▪ S 33° 54' 16.4" E 019° 6' 40.7" ▪ **T +27 (0)21-876-2086** ▪ F +27 (0)21-876-4107

A new chapter in the story of an enduring Cape name - founded by French Huguenots as the farm 'Belle en Champ' ('Beautiful Fields') in 1693 - as Bellingham gets its own brand home at the same address as sibling DGB label Franschhoek Cellars. No changes to the ranges, however: Bernard Series still honours maverick vintner Bernard Podlashuk, who revitalised the Bellingham estate and started the brand in the 1940s; Tree Series alludes to the Podlashuks' shady gardens; Insignia recalls the flavours of the farmhouse kitchen; and Ancient Earth acknowledges the foundation of the wine industry – its soils.

The Bernard Series

★★★★ **Basket Press Syrah** 🦌 **11** less powerful & modern than **10** but equally impressive. Smidgen viognier, zesty acidity, well-defined red fruit contribute to refreshing & refined mouthful.

★★★★ **Small Barrel SMV** 🦌 Shiraz (80%), mourvèdre & viognier in **11**, sleek, light-textured with dark & spicy fruit, unobtrusive chocolatey oak sheen. Drinks well but structured to reward cellaring 3+ years.

★★★★ **Old Vine Chenin Blanc** ✓ 🍴 🦌 Old-vine, barrel-fermented **12** as appealing & sumptuous as **11**. White peach & thatch, gravelly grip & tangy lift. Has gravitas, nudges next level.

★★★★ **Whole Bunch Roussanne** ✓ 🍴 🦌 Rare-in-Cape white grape, **12** from Voor Paardeberg restrained but appealing aromas, vibrant silky persistence, food-inviting grip from lees-ageing. Improves on **10** (★★★☆). No **11**.

Bush Vine Pinotage 🦌 ★★★★ Variety's smoke & high tone on step-up **11**. As in **10** (★★★☆), dry tannins give form & length to fruity palate, good oak structure (50% new, as for other reds & chenin) & background spice. **Hand Picked Viognier** 🍴 🦌 ★★★☆ Perfumed **12** has apricot, spice & dried pear nuances, none of variety's blowsiness. Balanced if tad brief. **Whole Bunch Grenache Blanc-Viognier** 🍴 🦌 ★★★☆ Woody aromas & flavours open to reveal **12**'s apricot-scented fruit courtesy 20% viognier, contributing to sweet impression. Similar waxy texture as better **11** (★★★★).

Insignia Series

Mocha Java Merlot 🍴 🦌 ★★★ As advertised, fresh-brewed coffee aroma & red plums, yet little of that welcoming tone on **12** palate. **Citrus Grove Chenin** 🍴 🦌 ★★★ First with a (citrus) scratch-&-sniff on the label though, to us, perfumed **13** preview's aromas are white peaches & flowers; creamy texture ex lees-ageing, zesty lift on finish.

Ancient Earth range

> **Pinotage** ☺ 🍴 🦌 ★★★ Cheerful **12**'s mulberry attraction lifted by acetone whiffs, fruit-sweet musky palate. Balanced, dry. Stock up! **Sauvignon Blanc** ☺ 🍴 🦌 ★★★ Pre-bottling, **13**'s gooseberry & fig nuances perfume its bouquet, flavour its palate. Zippy & attractively priced.

Cabernet Sauvignon 🦌 ★★★ **11** ticks all the cab boxes: cassis fruit, bright acidity, firm tannin; needs a meal to counter its leanness. **Merlot** 🦌 ★★★ Black plums, refreshing acidity & good concentration on **12**

tank sample. **Shiraz** 🍶 🥂 ★★ Now bottled, **11** still shows leaner & savoury styling, with leathery oxidative notes. **Chardonnay** 🍶 🥂 Sample **12** too unformed to rate. WO W Cape.

The Tree Series

Big Oak Red 🍶 🥂 ★★★ Not named for its wooding, which is minimal. Uncomplicated **12** red plum & berry tone, spice from splash malbec, supple tannins. WO Cape, as for all these. **Berry Bush Rosé** 🍶 🥂 ★★ Candyfloss & bubblegum aromas on pale salmon pink, dry **13** from pinotage. **Pear Tree White** 🍶 🥂 ★★★ Eponymous tree planted 1700s a symbol of Bellingham heritage. **13** less expressive than previous, still easy to drink. — CvZ

Bellpost

Location: Vredendal ▪ Map: Olifants River ▪ WO: Western Cape/Olifants River ▪ Est/1stB 2005 ▪ Tasting, sales & cellar tours by appt ▪ Owner(s) Lollies Thiart ▪ Winemaker(s) Koos Thiart (Jan 2005) ▪ Viticulturist(s) Nico Thiart (Jan 2005) ▪ 5ha/2ha (merlot, ruby cab, shiraz, chard, nouvelle, viog) ▪ 12t/1,800cs own label 80% red 20% white ▪ PO Box 39 Vredendal 8160 ▪ bellpost@starmail.co.za ▪ www.bellpost.co.za ▪ S 31° 36' 24.1" E 018° 25' 0.6" ▪ **T +27 (0)27-213-2562, +27 (0)82-619-2428** ▪ F +27 (0)27-213-2562

Owner Lollies Thiart's sons are integral to this West Coast winery between Lutzville and Vredendal. Koos is the part-time winemaker (he's on the red wine team at Namaqua, nearby) and viticulturist Nico steps into the cellar breach when necessary. Sales are looking up, they say, as their label becomes better known.

Merlot ★★★ Mint, capsicum & black tea nuances to firmly structured, somewhat old-fashioned but very sippable & improved **12**. **Ruby Cabernet** ⓘ ★★★ Expressive mulberry-toned **08** takes step up; engaging despite slight bitter edge. Olifants River WO, like next. **Shiraz** ⓘ ★★★★ Smoky bacon character, producer's signature big alcohol on **08** well contained. **Chardonnay** ★★★ Unwooded **12**'s plump fruit veined with lemon acidity; bone-dry & flavoursome for early enjoyment. **C'est la Vie** ★★★ Peachy attraction on chardonnay-led **12** combo from 32% viognier (also barrel fermented), freshness courtesy 25% frisky nouvelle. — HJ, CvZ

■ **Bell Tower** *see* Asara Wine Estate & Hotel

Benguela Cove

Location: Bot River ▪ Map: Elgin, Walker Bay & Bot River ▪ WO: Overberg/Walker Bay ▪ Est 2004 ▪ 1stB 2007 ▪ Tasting Mon-Sat 10-5 (mid Sep-Apr); Fri-Sat 10-5 (May-mid Sep), other days by appt with 24 hrs notice ▪ Fee R30pp, waived on purchase ▪ Sales Mon-Sat 10-5 ▪ Closed Easter Fri/Sun, Dec 25/26 & Jan 1 ▪ BYO picnic ▪ Owner(s) Benguela Cove Investments (Pty) Ltd (Flora Drummond) ▪ Winemaker(s) Kevin Grant (2012 Ataraxia) ▪ Viticulturist(s) Paul Wallace (2011, consultant) ▪ 206ha/66ha (cabs s/f, malbec, merlot, p verdot, pinot, shiraz, chard, sauv, sem, viog) ▪ 600t/4,400cs own label 50% red 50% white ▪ PO Box 112 Onrusrivier 7201 ▪ info@benguelacove.co.za ▪ www.benguelacove.co.za ▪ S 34° 20' 45.0" E 019° 8' 15.7" ▪ **T +27 (0)83-645-6198** ▪ F +27 (0)21-671-5229

Natural farming practices are employed at Benguela Cove residential wine estate near Bot River, not just to create a healthy environment but because it reflects in the grapes. Sea proximity and open slopes create cool growing conditions for good fruit development, and specialist consultants handle the vinifications.

★★★★ **Sauvignon Blanc** ⓘ 🍶 🥂 Ex-tank **12** already shows its class, prominent minerality & a leafy edge, seamed with tangy acidity that awakens the senses. Ex single-vineyard. Could rate better once bottled. **Cabernet Sauvignon** Await next, as for **Rosé**. **Cabernet Franc** ⓘ 🥂 ★★★★ Preview **11** rich & dense, with mocha chocolate & dark plums. Tannins firm & dry, showing some integration but needing time to complete. **Shiraz** ⓘ ★★★★ Rich & ripe, mocha chocolate & vanilla-toned **10** ex barrel is warm hearted, generous; supple tannins allow early enjoyment. Walker Bay WO. — CR

■ **Ben Hur** *see* Blomendahl Vineyards
■ **Berg en Dal** *see* Wine-of-the-Month Club

Bergheim

Location: Paarl ▪ Map: Paarl & Wellington ▪ WO: Paarl/Western Cape/Franschhoek ▪ Est/1stB 2000 ▪ Tasting by appt ▪ Owner(s) Edwin Jordaan ▪ Cellarmaster(s)/winemaker(s) Edwin Jordaan (Jan 2000) ▪ 4-6t/1,000cs own label 66% red 34% white ▪ PO Box 6020 Paarl 7622 ▪ drjordaan@gmail.com ▪ S 33° 45' 20.2" E 018° 57' 42.5" ▪ **T** +27 (0)82-923-3115, +27 (0)21-863-1529 ▪ F +27 (0)21-862-7852

'Business as usual,' says Paarl general practitioner Edwin Jordaan of the past year's micro-scale vinifying, very much a part-time pursuit - he rents cellar space from Mason's Winery. Passionate about food (and cooking), music and wine, his perfect wine moment is sunset on Namibia's Skeleton Coast, glass of bubbly in hand.

Bergheim range

★★★★ **Mignon** Older oak aged **12** is semillon & 45% sauvignon, off Franschhoek vines. Interesting & complex marriage of melon, lime & nettle with more earthy notes. Oily texture & broad, long finish. No **11**.

Pinotage ★★★ Undeniably pinotage, **10**'s smoky banana leaps from the glass. Still feisty, should settle with time in bottle, meantime pair with flavoursome food. **Shiraz** ⓐ ★★★★ **08**'s tannins fully integrated, exuberant fruit & spice. Drink up.

Couple's Wine range

Dry Red Ben ⓐ ★★★★ Same wine as **08** Shiraz. Tall 500ml bottle to partner Celia when couples want different wines. **Dry White Celia** ⓐ ★★★ Friendly alcohol on appley, leafy & bone-dry **10**. 500ml. WO W Cape. — HJ

■ **Berghuis** *see* Group CDV
■ **Bergkelder** *see* Die Bergkelder Wine Centre, Fleur du Cap

---

Bergsig Estate

Location: Wolseley ▪ Map/WO: Breedekloof ▪ Est 1843 ▪ 1stB 1977 ▪ Tasting & sales Mon-Fri 8–5 Sat & pub hols 9–5 ▪ Fee R20 for groups of 10+ ▪ Closed Good Fri, Dec 25 & Jan 1 ▪ Cellar tours by appt ▪ Bergsig Bistro ▪ Facilities for children ▪ Farm produce ▪ Conferences ▪ Self-guided birdwatching route ▪ Conservation area, visits by appt ▪ Lategan family history & historical artefacts on display ▪ Festivals: Cloudy Nouveau (Apr); Soetes & Soup (Jul); Outdoor (Oct) ▪ Owner(s) Lategan family ▪ Cellarmaster(s) De Wet Lategan (Jan 1989) ▪ Winemaker(s) Chris du Toit (Jul 2003) ▪ Viticulturist(s) Louis & Plum Lategan (1991) ▪ ±400ha/253ha (cab, ptage, shiraz, touriga, chard, chenin, sauv) ▪ 3,200t/100,000cs own label 35% red 60% white 4% rosé 1% other + 140,000cs for clients ▪ Other export brand: White River ▪ Brand for clients: Woolworths ▪ BWI, BRC, IPW ▪ PO Box 15 Breërivier 6858 ▪ wine@bergsig.co.za ▪ www.bergsig.co.za ▪ S 33° 31' 9.4" E 019° 11' 38.7" ▪ **T** +27 **(0)23-355-1603** ▪ F +27 (0)23-355-1658

Blessed with immense natural beauty, Bergsig describes itself as 'an innovative family concern with sustainable farming practices and long-term business relationships locally and overseas'. The winery is also blessed with some fully mature vineyards, including a 30-year-old riesling block from which winemakers De Wet Lategan and Chris du Toit have bottled a '12 and '13 (neither tasted). Their plan is to make the noble German grape a permanent part of the portfolio, and annually vinify small quantities in a style dictated by the vintage. 'The '12 is fine, delicate and dry,' they say, 'while '13 is full and slightly sweet, with a touch of botrytis.'

Limited Editions

★★★★ **Cabernet Sauvignon Reserve** ⓐ ▨ Lower yield, longer small-oak ageing for this version. Understated but serious **10**, firm but ripe tannins provide excellent balance. Will reward ageing. **09** held back.

Bergsig Estate range

★★★★ **Icarus** ⓐ ▨ **10** from cab & touriga seduces with sweet blackcurrant & exotic spice profile. Modern & lush, lifted by bright fruit, vibrant acidity, smart oaking. **09** held back.

★★★★ **Chardonnay** ✓ ▨ **12** (★★★★) a touch off **11**, with big toasty oak masking lemon cream & lime fruit. Rich & bold tempered by citrus freshness.

★★★★ **Cape Vintage** ⓐ Succulent, smooth & spicy port-style from tinta. **04** similar to last-tasted **00**, generously flavoured but not sweet, sufficient fire to warm a winter night.

★★★★ **Cape LBV** ✓ **03** (★★★★) port-style from touriga a shade shy of **01**. Charms with molasses, nut & coffee bouquet, dusty oak detracts from chocolate-orange end.

> **White River Chenin Blanc** ☺ 🍖 ▨ ★★★ **12** offers fresh tangy apple, zippy acid & pithy goodbye.

Cabernet Sauvignon ① ⊠ ★★★ **11** dark fruited & youthful, smooth & savoury, firm toasty conclusion. Alcohol is a friendly 12.8%. **Pinotage** ✓ ⊠ ★★★☆ Juicy spicy plum pudding character, **11** has good sweet-sour balance, vanilla oak adds to complexity. For early enjoyment. **Bulldozer Pinotage** Next awaited, as for **Bouquet Light**, **Sauvignon Blanc Brut** & **Special Late Harvest**. **Touriga Nacional** ① ⊠ ★★★ Rare unfortified bottling of port grape. Ripe dark fruit with earthy tones, medium-bodied **11** hints of fynbos & spice, drinks easily. **The Family Friend** ① 🍽 ⊠ ★★★ Merlot & pinotage-driven multi-variety red blend **11** is lightish, succulent & smooth, bright black fruit for fireside enjoyment. **Shiraz Rosé** ① 🍽 ⊠ ★★ Off-dry **12**, lightish, with soft red fruit & spice flavours. **Chenin Blanc** ① 🍽 ⊠ ★★★ Crunchy green apple, crisp acidity, **12** uncomplicated sipping. **Gewürztraminer** ① 🍽 ⊠ ★★★ **12**'s intense litchi & rosepetal fragrance, soft sweetness & light grip as always tick all the right drinkability boxes. **Sauvignon Blanc** 🍽 ⊠ ★★★ Tangy fruit salad & lively acidity, **13** with moderate 12.5% alcohol perfect summer sipping & creamy pasta fare. **Cape Ruby** ① ★★★☆ Unoaked **NV** port-style from tinta, delicious, approachable as this style should be. — WB

Bergwater Winery

Location: Prince Albert ▪ Map: Klein Karoo & Garden Route ▪ WO: Prince Albert Valley/Western Cape/Prince Albert ▪ Est 1999 ▪ 1stB 2003 ▪ Tasting & sales Mon-Thu 8–4.30 Fri 8-4 Sat/Sun 10-3 ▪ Fee R20 ▪ Cellar tours by appt ▪ Meals by prior arrangement ▪ BYO picnic ▪ Gifts ▪ Olives & olive oil ▪ Wedding/conference/function venue (up to 250 pax) ▪ 2 x self-catering guesthouses ▪ Gravel airstrip for light aircraft (phone ahead) ▪ Hiking/mountain biking & 4x4 trail by arrangement ▪ Owner(s) Heimie & Stephan Schoeman ▪ Cellarmaster(s)/winemaker(s) Jacques Kruger (Jan 2013) ▪ 1,500ha/63ha (cab, merlot, shiraz, sauv) ▪ ±400-600t ▪ 80% red 15% white 5% rosé + bulk ▪ PO Box 40 Prince Albert 6930 ▪ wine@bergwater.co.za ▪ www.bergwater.com ▪ S 33° 16' 46.3" E 022° 13' 55.7" ▪ **T** +27 (0)23-541-1703 ▪ F +27 (0)86-541-7335

It's second time around for the Schoemans, owners of this winery near the charming Karoo town of Prince Albert, and their old friend, ex Bernheim winemaker Jacques Kruger: he wasn't available when they needed him first but when their winemaker of a decade left at the beginning of last year, he was.

Reserve range

Cabernet Sauvignon ① 🍽 ★★ Mid-2010, blackcurrant-infused **09** needed time to mellow, should be ready now. **Merlot** ① 🍽 Tank sample **09** on review was fresh & fruit-filled but too young to rate. **Shiraz** ① 🍽 ★★★ Tasted pre-bottling mid-2012, **09** red-fruited & crisp but needed year/2 to show its best. **Royal Reserve** 🍽 ⊠ ★★ **10** equal merlot/cab with 20% shiraz has appealing berry aromas, very ripe palate & firm tannic conclusion. Should mesh in year/2. **Rosé** NEW 🍽 ⊠ ★★★ From merlot, **12** candyfloss & floral appeal, rounding sweetness. **Sauvignon Blanc** 🍽 ⊠ ★★★ Delicate lime & floral **12**, creamy entry but fairly acidic farewell; light body padded by dollop sugar.

Bergwater range

Merlot ① 🍽 ★★ Blackcurrant & vanilla on **08**, chunky, brisk & dry. **Rendezvous Red** ① 🍽 ★★ Plummy **08** merlot & shiraz mix previously noted as harmonious & earthy. **Rendezvous White** 🍽 ⊠ ★★ Shy **12** from sauvignon, toffee apple & sherbet flavours, gently sweet uncomplicated sipper. **Muscat d'Alexandrie** ⊠ ★★ Raisin-toned **12** fortified dessert, for early drinking. WO W Cape & 375 ml, like next. **Tinta Barocca** NEW ⊠ ★★ Port-style **12** from tinta has sweet-sour tang.

Sparkling Wine range

Sparkling Brut Rosé ⊠ ★★★ **12** from merlot, bright & fresh anytime dry sparkling. **Brut Sauvignon Blanc** NEW ⊠ ★★★ Frothy fun in **12** bubbly ex sauvignon. Note: range was 'Pienk Pikkewyn'. — GdB,JP

Bernheim Wines

Location: Paarl ▪ Map: Paarl & Wellington ▪ WO: Paarl/Voor Paardeberg ▪ Est/1stB 2004 ▪ Tasting, sales & tours by appt ▪ Closed all pub hols ▪ Conservation area ▪ Owner(s) Pacas Winery (Pty) Ltd (Pieter Taljaard, Hermann Helmbold, Anelise Taljaard) ▪ Cellarmaster(s)/winemaker(s) Stéfan du Toit (Oct 2008) ▪ Viticulturist(s) Morné van Greunen (Feb 2009) ▪ 133ha/50ha (cabs s/f, merlot, ptage, p verdot, shiraz) ▪ 12,000c own label 95% red 5% rosé & less than 1% port ▪ BWI, IPW ▪ PO Box 7274 Noorder-Paarl 7623 ▪ bernheim@iafrica.com ▪ www.bernheimwines.com ▪ S 33° 35' 22.5" E 018° 52' 45.0" (VP), S 33° 40' 54.73" E 018° 58' 20.92" (P) ▪ **T** +27 (0)21-869-8384 ▪ F +27 (0)21-869-8365

The Bernheim team are looking forward to moving into the new cellar and tasting venue under construction on their Voor Paardeberg farm. Vintage 2013 will be bottled under new labels, so it's fitting that the harvest was a 'huge success'.

JH Pacas & Co range
Cabernet Sauvignon ⊕ ★★★☆ **05** is for lovers of mature cab, with cedar, tobacco & good dark-fruit support, earthy complexity. **Shiraz** ⊕ ★★★☆ **05** long & firm flavours, lavender & red berry hints, 14.5% alcohol hardly noticeable.

Vintners Selection
Cabernet Sauvignon Await next.

Bernheim range
Merlot ⊕ 🍷 🖉 ★★ Savoury **11**, blackcurrant jam & racy acidity. **Merlot-Cabernet Sauvignon** Await next, as for **Classique** & **Dry Red**. **Shiraz-Cabernet Sauvignon** ⊕ 🍷 ★★★ Cheery cranberry & salami combo on **08**. Shiraz edges cab in the blend, adding pepper spice. **Cape Vintage** ⊕ ★★★ 5 barrels of portstyle cab & shiraz, **08** fiery cherry plum & spice.

Casual Collection
Pinotage ⊕ ★★★☆ **10** a step up, offers smoky plum & spice appeal. **Red Select** ⊕ 🍷 ★★★ NV merlot, pinotage & cab blend mirrors its fun label. Light red fruit, cinnamon & a touch of dry tannin. **Pinotage Rosé** ⊕ 🍷 🖉 ★★ **11** dry, with raspberry & spice. — HJ

■ **Berrio** see The Berrio Wines
■ **Berryfields** see Ashton Kelder
■ **Bestvino Cape** see Boutique Baratok

Beyerskloof

Location/map: Stellenbosch ▪ WO: Stellenbosch/Western Cape/Coastal ▪ Est 1988 ▪ 1stB 1989 ▪ Tasting & sales Mon-Fri 8.30-4.30 Sat 10-4.30 ▪ Closed Easter Fri-Mon, Dec 25/26 & Jan 1 ▪ Cellar tours by appt ▪ Red Leaf Restaurant ▪ Farm produce ▪ Conferences (30 pax) ▪ Owner(s) Beyers Truter, Simon Halliday & Jan Morgan ▪ Cellarmaster(s) Beyers Truter (Jan 1988) ▪ Winemaker(s) Anri Truter (Jan 2004) & Travis Langley (Jan 2009), with Buddy Hendricks (Jan 2010) ▪ Viticulturist(s) Johan Pienaar (2000, consultant) ▪ 130ha/94ha (cab, merlot, ptage) ▪ 750t/240,000cs own label 96% red 2% white 2% rosé + 10,000cs for clients ▪ Brands for clients: Pick's Pick, Tesco ▪ WIETA ▪ PO Box 107 Koelenhof 7605 ▪ wine@beyerskloof.co.za ▪ www.beyerskloof.co.za ▪ S 33° 53' 28.0" E 018° 49' 23.6" ▪ **T +27 (0)21-865-2135** ▪ F +27 (0)21-865-2683

The name of Beyers Truter, raconteur and winemaker extraordinary, is synonymous with the highest aspirations of pinotage. He came to prominence during the rise and rise of Kanonkop's fame, but also through his abiding belief in the variety's potential and in his work with bodies and movements promoting it. His community work has been as important, with his foetal alcohol syndrome fund, Faith, his years of service as a Stellenbosch town councillor, and education and social mentorship through, among others, the Cape Winemakers Guild. The estate, now in its 25th year of bottling, has steadily focused attention on pinotage, its innate qualities, its versatility, its connection to the 'rainbow nation'. Basically, says Beyers's winemaker son Anri, 'it's what we do best!'

★★★★ **Pinotage Reserve** Two vintages tasted: **10**'s finely tuned ripeness is concentrated but unheavy, with balanced support, but the finish just a little too sweet. **11** with more forward perfumed spice & livelier; perhaps carries less weight than **10** but may benefit from 3-4 years.

★★★★☆ **Diesel Pinotage** Barrel selection flagship, with all-new French oaking. **10** made Anri Truter Diners Club Young Winemaker of the Year. Combines power with refinement; brooding dark flavours, creamy waves with freshness, structure for long haul. **11** has more aromatics, but the oak still obvious; similarly juicy, the sweet fruit reined in by feisty tannin backing. Age might show it the more interesting of the pair.

★★★★☆ **Field Blend** ⊕ Finely crafted cab-merlot from a very special mixed vineyard. **08** (★★★★) is more subtle, less emphatic than **07**, but offers finesse & herbaceousness, reflecting lighter vintage.

★★★★ **Synergy Cape Blend** As always, pinotage leads **11**, forging a most interesting whole with cab, merlot & a drop of shiraz. Lively tobacco spice, wild scrub, berry fragrance; equally lively juicy acid, grape tannin.

★★★★☆ **Faith** Big & bold - & that's not only the packaging! House favourite pinotage leads cab & merlot in **10**, enriched with 100% new oak. Powerful, with a dense tannic sheath, but balanced. Needs minimum 2 years before opening; should reward much longer.

Cabernet Sauvignon-Merlot ☺ 🍷 ★★★ Unfussy yet satisfying **12**. No dumbing down in its crunchy, fresh cassis, blackberry flavours, sound cab grip & properly dry finish. WO W Cape. **Chenin Blanc-Pinotage** ☺ 🍷 🖾 ★★★ White wine with red fruit juiciness on refreshing **13**. Mainly Swartland chenin.

Pinotage 🍷 ★★★☆ No-frills, fruit-driven & lightly oaked, **12** tells pinotage like it is, juicily quaffable. Impressive volume from widely sourced fruit. **Pinotage Rosé** 🍷 🖾 ★★★ **13** lightish, tangily dry & full of zesty red berries. **Lagare Cape Vintage** ⓕ ★★★★ Port-style fortified from touriga & pinotage. Tuned-down sweetness on foot-stomped **10** suits plummy fruit & appealing brandy-spirit. Discontinued: **Pinotage Rosé Brut.** — AL

Bezalel-Dyasonsklip Wine Cellar

Location: Upington ▪ Map: Northern Cape, Free State & North West ▪ Est 1949 (farm)/1997 (cellar) ▪ 1stB 1998 ▪ Tasting, sales & cellar tours Mon-Fri 9–5 Sat 9–1 ▪ Fee R15pp ▪ Professional tasting by appt ▪ Closed Easter Fri-Sun, May 1, Dec 16/25 & Jan 1 ▪ Green Fig Café - breakfast & light meals ▪ Venue for conferences & weddings up to 250 people ▪ Owner(s) Bezuidenhout family ▪ Cellarmaster(s)/winemaker(s)/viticulturist(s) Inus Bezuidenhout (1989), with Jan-Adriaan Bezuidenhout (2005) ▪ 60ha/44ha (cab, cornifesto, merlot, pinot, ptage, sangio, shiraz, touriga, chard, cbard, gewürz, merbein, sultana) ▪ ±1,000cs own label 100% red ▪ Eurogap certified ▪ PO Dyasonsklip 8805 ▪ info@bezalel.co.za ▪ www.bezalel.co.za ▪ S 28° 36' 28.69" E 021° 6' 19.01" ▪ **T** +27 (0)54-491-1325, +27 (0)83-310-4763 ▪ **F** +27 (0)54-491-1141

The Bezuidenhout family's farm in Upington, on the Northern Cape's recently formed Kokerboom Food & Wine Route, has added a maiden gewürztraminer jerepigo to their range of boutique wines. Father-and-son team Inus and Jan-Adriaan also make potstill brandy and an assortment of liqueurs.

▪ **Big Five** *see* African Terroir
▪ **BIG Flower** *see* Botanica Wines
▪ **Big Six** *see* Old Bridge Wines

Bilton Wines

Location/map/WO: Stellenbosch ▪ Est 1694 ▪ 1stB 1998 ▪ Tasting & sales Mon-Sun 10–5 ▪ Fee R35/6 wines, R50 dark Belgian chocolate & wine pairing (4 wines) ▪ Closed Good Fri, Dec 25/26 & Jan 1 ▪ Cellar tours Mon-Fri by appt ▪ Jungle gym & play area for children ▪ Vineyard walk ▪ Mountain bike route - booking required ▪ Owner(s) Mark Bilton ▪ Winemaker(s) Ruan du Plessis, with Giorgio Dalla Cia (consultant) ▪ Viticulturist(s) Ruan du Plessis (Dec 2004) ▪ 377ha/80ha (cab, merlot, mourv, p verdot, pinot, shiraz, viog) ▪ 100t/16,000cs own label 90% red 10% white ▪ BWI, IPW ▪ PO Box 60 Lynedoch 7603 ▪ info@biltonwines.com ▪ www.biltonwines.com ▪ S 33° 59' 52.9" E 018° 50' 58.3" ▪ **T** +27 (0)21-881-3714 ▪ F +27 (0)21-881-3721

The Bilton family have farmed the prime Helderberg slopes since the late 1950s. Vegetables and fruit gave way to vines, overseen since 1996 by Mark Bilton, great-grandson of Sir Percy, the entrepreneur honoured in the impressive flag-ship wine. A new generation is now involved in the person of Mark's son, Simon.

Private Collection

★★★★ **The Bilton** ⓕ 100% cab, **06** matured 3 years in '500% new oak' produced porty, inky, tannic levia-than, hopefully to emerge with grace.

★★★★☆ **Sir Percy** ⓕ Refined but richly fruited **08** Bordeaux-style red blend maintains the standard of **07**. Dab mourvèdre adds spice to the refined, classic blackberry flavours. Lithe frame & harmonious balance.

★★★★ **Viognier** ⓕ Pricey **08** white flagship was impossibly spicy & intense when last tasted, with ripe peach fruit.

Cellar Selection

★★★★☆ **Cabernet Sauvignon** ⓕ **08** cements this label's claim to higher general rating. Bold, ripe cassis fruit with silky glissade of tannins. Structured & firm but beautifully smooth & rich overall. Light, tasty cocoa note adds complex nuance to the layered palate.

★★★★ **Shiraz** ⓘ Lovely concentration of 08 on par with 07. Intense but seamlessly elegant, ripe blue/black berries & char hint from 80% new oak. Silky smooth texture, long rich tail.

Merlot ⓘ ★★★ Tangy fynbos, herbal edge to 08, lighter than previous but rich dark berry/chocolate mouthfeel pleases.

Bilton range

Matt Black Red Blend ⓘ 🍴 ★★★★ Merlot toned down on 5-way 09 blend, shiraz now leads ample ripe fruity appeal. Rounded, textured palate & structure. **Bonnie Anne** ⓘ 🍴 ▨ ★★☆ 12 from sauvignon blanc soft styled, light, crisp & easy. — FM

■ **Birdfield** *see* Klawer Wine Cellars
■ **Birkenhead Estate & Brewery** *see* Walker Bay Vineyards
■ **Bistro** *see* Zandvliet Wine Estate & Thoroughbred Stud

Bizoe Wines

Location: Somerset West ▪ WO: Western Cape ▪ Est/1stB 2008 ▪ Tasting & sales by appt or during tailor-made tours - booking essential ▪ Fee R1,500pp incl. transport & lunch ▪ Owner(s)/cellarmaster(s)/winemaker(s) Rikus Neethling ▪ Viticulturist(s) Org Viljoen ▪ 2,000cs ▪ Unit 189 Croydon Vineyard Estate Somerset West 7130 ▪ info@bizoe.co.za ▪ www.bizoe.co.za ▪ **T +27 (0)21-843-3307** ▪ F +27 (0)86-653-8186

Asked what his ultimate wine experience is, boutique winemaker and upscale wine-tour leader Rikus Neethling says: 'A bottle of Bizoe Estalét with Estalét.' The Syrah is named after his wife (the white blend after his mother) and the couple were expecting twins at the time of writing. 'I can't wait to raise the next generation of Bizoe winemakers.'

★★★★ **Estalét Syrah** Intriguing 11 (★★★★) from Wolseley grapes shows red fruit & somewhat atypical crushed herb aromas. Lighter bodied & intensely spicy. Lacks density of 10.

Henriëtta Await new vintage. — CE

Blaauwklippen Vineyards

Location/map: Stellenbosch ▪ WO: Stellenbosch/Western Cape ▪ Est 1682 ▪ 1stB 1974 ▪ Tasting & sales Mon-Fri 10-6 (summer)/10-5 (winter) Sat 10-5 Sun/pub hols 10-4 ▪ Tasting fees: R20/3 wines, R30/5 wines, R50/tour & tasting, R80/unique chocolate and (fortified) wine & brandy pairing ▪ Brandy tasting: R10/8 year old, R15/10 year old ▪ Closed Dec 25 & Jan 1 ▪ Food & wine pairing on request ▪ Wine blending on request ▪ Cellar tours by appt only ▪ Family market every Sun 10-3 ▪ Barouche Restaurant (see Restaurants section) ▪ Facilities for children ▪ Pony & carriage rides ▪ Gift shop ▪ Conferences ▪ Weddings/functions ▪ Walks/hikes & mountain biking by appt ▪ Permanent carriage museum ▪ Distillery ▪ Coffee roastery ▪ Owner(s) Blue Lion GmbH ▪ Winemaker(s) / brandy master(s) Rolf Zeitvogel (Sep 2003), with Albert Basson (Jul 2007) ▪ Viticulturist(s) Christo Hamman (Jan 2009) ▪ 180ha/103ha (cabs s/f, malbec, merlot, p verdot, shiraz, zin, viog) ▪ 550t/70,000cs own label 89% red 3% white 6% rosé 2% other & 22,000cs for clients ▪ Brands for clients: Blue Rock (Germany), Eagle Canyon (China) ▪ 650cs (x4-btl) brandy ▪ IPW ▪ PO Box 54 Stellenbosch 7599 ▪ marketing@blaauwklippen.com ▪ www.blaauwklippen.com ▪ S 33° 58' 23.3" E 018° 50' 51.0" ▪ **T +27 (0)21-880-0133** ▪ F +27 (0)21-880-0136

Gale force winds in late 2012 hit these 103ha vineyards adjacent to suburban Stellenbosch hard. Initial estimates were of a 40% - 45% crop loss, while a still-substantial 30% dip was in fact experienced. Looking on the bright side, this popular winery celebrated the 30th staging of their perennially popular - and hotly contested - Blending Competition. Tasting groups nationwide vie fiercely for top honours, which include bragging rights for a year and 'their' commercial bottling of Barouche in limited-release magnum format, with label art by Frans Groenewald. The visitor offering includes weekly markets, high tea, a distillery and restaurant.

Reserve Selection

★★★★ **Shiraz** ⓘ 10 powerful but restrained, with herbal edge to plum, chocolate & charry fruit. Pancetta whiff adds savoury note on soft-textured palate.

★★★★ **Zinfandel** Plush & rounded 11 (★★★★) offers abundant plum, cherry fruit on a lean, focused frame. Spicy but with noticeable alcohol (15.9%). Last-tasted 09 more toned.

Merlot ⓘ ★★★★ Prominent mulberry & cocoa on debut 10. Wood bold too but will soften in time. Dry, chalky texture on serious frame.

Blaauwklippen Vineyard Selection (BVS)

Cabriolet ★★★★ 🖩 Six-way blend in **11** (★★★☆) preview. Intense graphite minerality & black fruit on lean frame. Very dry & a bit austere, unlike last-tasted **07**.

Shiraz ⊕ ★★★★ Last **07** had blackberries & fennel, elegant oak & Rhône-style peppery complexity. Improved on jammy **06** (★★★★). **Zinfandel** ⊘ ★★★★ Distinctive black cherry cinnamon succulence to **10**. Refreshing yet sinewy in its pared-down fruit purity. No **09**. **White Zinfandel** ⊘ ★★★ Cherry blossom & peach abundance to leesy **12** blanc de noir. Sinewy, with faint pink hue, juicy but dry.

Blaauwklippen Blending Competition (BBC)

Barouche ★★★★ Blackcurrant, plum & cinnamon on toned **NV** (**12**) for 30th blending competition. Shiraz leads cab franc, merlot & malbec. Concentrated & deeply fruited to end. Similar spice to previously untasted **07** from the 25th competition. Note: vintages **07** to **NV** (**12**) all available ex farm, all in 1.5L magnum.

Blaauwklippen Cultivar Selection

Cabernet Sauvignon ⊘ ★★★★ **10** step up on last tasted **07** (★★★). Smoky edge to fruitcake flavour. Dry grip & chalky tannin. Structured yet lean. **Malbec** ⊘ ★★★ Red & blue berries with lightly brooding earthiness to **10**. Extracted, tarry hint on lean structure. **Merlot** ⊘ ★★★ **11** retains form of last-tasted **09**. Uncomplicated black fruit with cocoa & herb nuances, dry texture. **Shiraz** ⊘ ★★★★ Lavender perfume to squishy purple fruit on **11**. Dry, with squeeze of tannin & angular frame. Lingering spicy aftertaste. **Rosé** ⊕ ⊘ ★★★ Shiraz & zinfandel combo in off-dry **12** tank sample delivers raspberry/cherry succulence. **Chenin Blanc** 🖩 ★★★ Ripe melon & pineapple see **13** up the ante. Tangy, vibrant & juicy, with a long, clean tail. WO W Cape, like next. **Sauvignon Blanc** 🖩 ⊘ ★★★ Simple grapefruit freshness & acidic zip on **13**. Light end. **Viognier** ⊕ ⊘ ★★★ **12** preview offers lemongrass & peach richness, lees-ageing adds some body & fullness.

Noble Late Harvests

★★★★ **Malbec** Chalky texture & cherry juice appeal to unusual **12** botrytised dessert that improves on **11** (★★★★). Spicy, with cranberry tang & clean, fresh dryness. Sweet yet uncloying.

★★★★ **Viognier** ⊕ Sundried pineapple & peach on rich, honeyed **12** (★★★★), light & tangy, dry-seeming finish. Last was scented **07**.

★★★★ **Zinfandel** Macerated raisin & spicy compote on less sweet **12** (**11** was 316g sugar!). Reticent yet not shy. Good harmony of fruit, sweetness & oak (50% new). Succulent, with long, 'dry' aftertaste.

Aperitif range

★★★★☆ **Before & After** ⊕ Handsome packaging for aptly named berry & spice saturated beauty; cloves, cinnamon, palate silky sweet & very moreish. Fortified to 16% alcohol, brandy-like notes on finish. **NV**.

Brandy range ~~NEW~~

8 Year Potstilled Brandy ★★★ Some rosepetal along with leafy medicinal notes, lacks complexity & balance. 100% potstill from colombard, sauvignon & chenin, as is next. These brandies in notably beautiful packaging. **10 Year Potstilled Brandy** ★★★ Some floral hints, but overt oak, herbal, minty notes. Lacks richness, with the alcohol not well integrated; a little rough. — WB, FM, TJ

■ **Black Box** *see* Wineways Marketing

Black Elephant Vintners

Location/map: Franschhoek ▪ WO: Franschhoek/Wellington ▪ Est 2013 ▪ 1stB 2012 ▪ Tasting, sales & cellar tours by appt ▪ Fee R25, waived on purchase ▪ Owner(s) Kevin Swart, Raymond Ndlovu & Jacques Wentzel ▪ Winemaker(s) Jacques Wentzel (Jan 2013) ▪ 90t/12,000cs own label 30% red 70% white ▪ IPW ▪ PO Box 686 Franschhoek 7690 ▪ sales@bevintners.co.za, jacques@bevintners.co.za, kevin@bevintners.co.za ▪ www.bevintners.co.za ▪ S 33° 55' 15.6" E 019° 7' 39.9" ▪ **T +27 (0)21-876-2904/+27 (0)21-876-2454**

Swapping the 'dog's life' of the financial world for 'the sights, sounds and tastes of Franschhoek and the wine industry', Kevin Swart and Raymond Ndlovu have teamed up with local winemaker Jacques Wentzel in this 'virtual winery', renting cellar space at Bo La Motte to vinify sustainably grown grapes 'scouted from every corner of the valley' using a natural, minimalist approach. 'We want Franschhoek to speak with all its aromas and tastes every time you pull the cork.'

The Back Roads Pinotage ★★★ **12** similar vinification to Syrah results in perfumed, powerful glassful with whoosh of freshness coming through on finish. WO Wellington. **Amistad Syrah** ★★★ Ticks many boxes - fruit-filled, well textured with healthy tannins & better-balanced acidity. **12** old-school vinification: natural ferment, whole berries with some whole bunches, basket press, year mostly older oak. **Two Dogs A Peacock & A Horse Sauvignon Blanc** 🖩 ★★ **13** is tropical & fresh, shows its 14% alcohol in conclusion. —DC, JP

■ **Black Forest** *see Louis*
■ **Black Granite** *see Darling Cellars*
■ **Black Label** *see Backsberg Estate Cellars*

Black Oystercatcher Wines

Location/WO: Elim ▪ Map: Southern Cape ▪ Est 1998 ▪ 1stB 2003 ▪ Tasting, sales & cellar tours Mon-Fri 9-5 Sat/Sun 10-2.30 ▪ Closed Good Fri & Dec 24/25 ▪ Restaurant, function & wedding venue: kitchen open Tue-Sun 11-2.30, booking essential ▪ Facilities for children ▪ Tour groups ▪ Conferences ▪ Conservation area ▪ Cycling route ▪ Annual Sauvignon Blanc & Oyster Festival (Dec); peak season programme ▪ Accommodation ▪ Owner(s)/cellarmaster(s)/viticulturist(s) Dirk Human ▪ Winemaker(s) Dirk Human, with Danel Morkel ▪ 1,550ha/18.5ha (cab, merlot, shiraz, sauv, sem) ▪ ±100t/±18,000cs own label 20% red 60% white 20% rosé ▪ BWI, IPW, WIETA ▪ PO Box 199 Bredasdorp 7280 ▪ venue@blackoystercatcher.co.za, wine@blackoystercatcher.co.za ▪ www.blackoystercatcher.co.za ▪ S 34° 37' 58.0" E 019° 49' 39.9" ▪ **T +27 (0)28-482-1618** ▪ F +27 (0)86-666-7954

The Black Oystercatcher home farm is on the windy Agulhas plain at the southern-most tip of Africa, and a multitude of adaptations have had to be found to meet the often extreme climate conditions and the diverse and distinctive soil types. The property is also in the Nuwejaars Wetland Special Management Area, and conservation runs like a thread through everything its sixth-generation Human family custodians do, from viticulture to the new onsite tourist accommodation.

★★★★ **Triton** 🖩 📷 After shiraz-led **08**, **10** (★★★★) has cab ahead of merlot & shiraz, giving sweet berry & baked stonefruit character overlain with terpenes; overt oak needs time or hearty winter stew. No **09**.

★★★★ **Blanc Fumé** ④ 🖩 📷 Barrel-fermented sauvignon, from special site within a top block. **10** intensely aromatic, vanilla/nut highlights from (600L) cask, glorious rounded mouthfeel ex year lees-ageing.

★★★★ **Sauvignon Blanc** 🖩 📷 After arguably too bracingly fresh **11** (★★★★), **12** more elegant & restrained, showing aperitif-friendly fullness, drinkability. Passionfruit flavour veined with house's minerality.

★★★★☆ **White Pearl** ✓ 🖩 📷 Stately blend semillon (75%) & sauvignon, part barrel fermented. As previous, **10** shows semillon's waxiness, sauvignon's dustiness as well as finely evolved fruit & spices, lovely creamy lees texture, mineral-salty conclusion.

Cabernet Sauvignon-Merlot 🖩 📷 ★★★★ Cab's 57% in **10** shows in blackberry fruit with soft savoury cloak. Juicy, fresh, with chalky tannin. Try with grilled steak & mushroom sauce suggests winemaker. **Rosé** 🖩 📷 ★★★ Bone-dry **13** merlot & cab, candyfloss scents, tutti-frutti flavours, cheerful if brief. —WB, GdB

Black Pearl Vineyards

Location: Paarl ▪ Map: Paarl & Wellington ▪ WO: Paarl/Swartland ▪ Est 1998 ▪ 1stB 2001 ▪ Tasting, sales & tours just about anytime but phone ahead (no credit cards) ▪ Closed Dec 25 ▪ Walks ▪ Lapa & camping facilities ▪ Self-catering cottage ▪ Conservation area ▪ Owner(s) Lance & Mary-Lou Nash ▪ Winemaker(s)/viticulturist(s) Mary-Lou Nash ▪ 240ha/7.2ha (cab, shiraz) ▪ ±5,000cs own label 90% red 10% white ▪ BWI, IPW ▪ PO Box 609 Suider-Paarl 7624 ▪ info@blackpearlwines.com ▪ www.blackpearlwines.com ▪ S 33° 44' 10.5" E 018° 53' 40.8" ▪ **T +27 (0)83-297-9796/+27 (0)83-395-6999** ▪ F +27 (0)86-617-8507

Cape Wine Master Mary-Lou Nash came to wine, and indeed South Africa, purely by chance when, in 1995, she dropped in en route home to the US from an extended stay in Asia, to see her father's newly acquired Paarl farm, Rhenosterkop. She's still there, running her boutique-scale winery in bucolic bliss.

★★★★ **The Mischief Maker Shiraz** 🖩 📷 Was 'Shiraz'. Earthy black fruit & spicy meat on **11** (★★★★) suggest style change. Lighter body than **10** presents juicy ripeness.

★★★★ **Oro** ✓ 🖩 📷 Charming shiraz with 15% cab, **12** combines big, forceful black fruit with supple elegance. Earthy notes, herbaceous spiciness & firm tannins maintain varietal focus. **11** sold out untasted.

Chenin Blanc ✓ 🖩 📷 ★★★★ Second vintage **12** confirms potential: honeyed tropical fruit laced with white nuts. Good concentration & length. WO Swartland. —GdB

■ **Black Tie** *see Wineways Marketing*

Blackwater Wine

Location: Stellenbosch ▪ WO: Swartland/Elgin ▪ Est/1stB 2010 ▪ Closed to public ▪ Owner(s) Blackwater Wines & Vines ▪ Cellarmaster(s)/winemaker(s)/viticulturist(s) Francois Haasbroek (Feb 2010) ▪ (carignan, cinsaut, pinot, shiraz, chenin) ▪ 15t/3,000cs own label 70% red 30% white ▪ 1 Trengrove Avenue Uniepark Stellenbosch 7600 ▪ info@blackwaterwine.com ▪ www.blackwaterwine.com ▪ **T +27 (0)82-329-8849**

If the artistic endeavour involved in winemaking was ever in doubt, then consider Francois Haasbroek's motivation for leaving his position at high-profile Waterford in Stellenbosch and go it alone: 'I wanted 100% creative control. From conception through to execution. For better or for worse.' His wines appear under the Blackwater label and the business is sole-owned. 'Silent partners would certainly help with cashflow but unfortunately silent partners are never completely silent.' His approach is to secure grapes from under-appreciated sites wherever they might be. 'The Western Cape is littered with small blocks planted with the right vines on great sites, whether by accident or design. Unfortunately most of these grapes disappear into big blends. I want to tell their story.'

Omerta Carignan ★★★☆ Promising **12** preview from Swartland vines delivers exotic spicy, peppery & wild herb aromas; light footed & supple. Non-interventionist winemaking, only older oak, as for all. **Prodigium Pinot Noir ★★★★★** Single Elgin vineyard expression, delivers flavour & fullness without extraction. Pre-bottling, **12**'s spicier & less showy than sibling, excellent length, shape & texture. **Cuvee Terra Lux Pinot Noir ★★★☆** Cherries, herbs & violets on firm, unforced **12** from Elgin. Bold frangipani scents, heightened carbonic maceration character. Nicely structured, with long, elegant finish. Follows intensely aromatic **11** from Elgin & Walker Bay fruit. **Cultellus Syrah ★★★☆** Delicate, crystalline expression of Swartland fruit; **11** with gentle tannins, savoury conclusion. **Noir ★★★☆** Rhône blend, shiraz & carignan (85/15) in **11** ex Swartland; shy pepper aromas but steely-fruity juxtaposition on palate. Some bunch fermentation; 27 months in 500/600L 8 year old oak. **10** (★★★★), from Walker Bay & Botriver, harmonises shiraz (70%) & grenache in smaller, newer oak. Generous, plush & deliciously approachable. — GdB, GM, CvZ

BLANKbottle

Location: Somerset West ▪ Map: Helderberg ▪ WO: Western Cape/Stellenbosch/Wellington/Swartland/ Breede River Valley/Bot River/Elgin/Walker Bay ▪ Est 2005 ▪ 1stB 2003 ▪ Tasting & sales Mon-Sat by appt ▪ Sales also via website ▪ Owner(s)/cellarmaster(s)/winemaker(s) Pieter H Walser ▪ Viticulturist(s) Various ▪ 5,000cs own label 70% red 30% white ▪ Lanrust Wine Estate, Winery Road, Somerset West 7129 ▪ pieter@ blankbottle.co.za ▪ www.blankbottle.co.za ▪ S 34° 2' 41.1" E 018° 47' 16.0" ▪ **T +27 (0)21-842-2747/+27 (0)82-872-8658** ▪ F +27 (0)86-503-0974

Brand owner Pieter Walser is an adventurer whose production has evolved from opportunism bought-in batches blended into good-value originals, to an impressive range of area-specific studies. He has made his mark for innovative thinking in an industry awash with marketing gurus, through a combination of intelligent sourcing and blending, striking branding and single-minded independence. Over years his growing e-market following has been treated to many ambitious experiments, each with its own compelling backstory.

BLANKbottle range

★★★★☆ **My Eie Stofpad** ⓟ Focused & eminently satisfying, **11** Stellenbosch cab franc is youthful but promises finer things to come. Complex aromas, velvet texture & lingering finish; a complete package.

★★★★ **The Bomb 11** (★★★★) from Stellenbosch is now a 3-way cab, merlot, shiraz blend. Equally bold, unashamedly ripe & swaggering, but less gravitas than **10** cab-merlot. Needs time.

★★★★ **The Big Spaniard** ⓟ Rhône-style 4-way red blend is serious, full, **09** shows dividends from ripe vintage & longer oaking.

★★★★ **Moment of Silence** ⓦ Rewarding **12** wooded chenin, chardonnay & viognier from Wellington, showing aromatic richness & intensity. Succulent yet crisply balanced, a good fusion food partner.

★★★★ **The White Bomb** NEW NV seriously curvaceous (16% alcohol) bellydancer, exuding fragrant opulence & silky charm. A rich & spicy blend, mainly viognier with chenin, uncloying despite semi-dry styling.

The Misfit Occasional release, like **Batavia, E.K.G., Midnight Call** & **Mnr Professor**. **My Koffer ★★★☆** characterful **12** shows polished leather, fynbos & red fruit coaxed from Breedekloof cinsaut. Smooth textured, contemplative & satisfying. **1st Eulogy** NEW **★★★** Powerful (15% alcohol, but unfortified) tinta barocca from 50 year old Bot River vines, dark & spicy **11**. Brooding & brusque in youth, but has potential. **Fifteen + 1** 📟 ★★★ **11** savoury & juicy allsorts blend of 16 mainly red varieties. **Professor Kukurowitz** 📟 ★★★★ Named for founder of 50 year old chenin block in Wellington. Stewed quince, honey & some minerality on ripe & mouthfilling **12**, older barrel fermented. Ends tad short with an afterglow. **Im Hinterhofkabuff** 📟 ★★★ Literally 'Backyard Shack', German magazine Stern's word for Peter Walser's office! Wood-fermented **12** riesling from Elgin is generous & perfumed. Ripe & sweetish, with fresher clean finish. **Eleventh Hour** 📟 ★★★ **07** rich & unctuous port-style, from Walker Bay tinta barocca. Spirited liquorice & prune flavours, good nightcap. Discontinued: **Nothing To Declare**.

Black & The White Black range
★★★★ **Black** ⊕ Shiraz-based Rhône-style blend from Swartland vineyards. **10** shows meaty herbaceousness & floral hints. Plush, well-rounded plum/damson fruit with solid tannin coating.
★★★★ **The White Black 11** equal chenin, roussannne, clairette, viognier & grenache blanc. Oxidative style with a dry sherry, citrus peel tone & clean, almondy farewell. Trendy & alternative aperitif.

Educational range
Discontinued: **Carignan**, **Cinsaut**, **Grenache**, **Mourvèdre**. — MW

Bloemendal Estate

Location/WO: Durbanville ▪ Map: Durbanville, Philadelphia & Darling ▪ Est 1902 ▪ 1stB 1987 ▪ Tasting & sales Mon-Fri 9–5 Sat 9–4 Sun 11–3 ▪ Bon Amis Bistro: weddings, evening functions & conferences ▪ Owner(s) Spirito Trade 82 (Pty) Ltd ▪ Winemaker(s) Boetman Langevelt, advised by Francois Haasbroek ▪ Vineyard manager(s) / viticulturist Lombard Loubser ▪ 135ha (cab, malbec, merlot, shiraz, chard, sauv, sem) ▪ PO Box 466 Durbanville 7551 ▪ info@bloemendalwines.co.za ▪ www.bloemendalwines.co.za ▪ S 33° 50' 22.1" E 018° 36' 1.4" ▪ **T** +27 (0)21-975-9591 ▪ **F** +27 (0)86-615-7020

Three hundred years old, and producing wine for almost one third of its life, the scenic Bloemendal property's vineyards and cellar are undergoing a makeover under consultant Francois Haasbroek, working with vine man Lombard Loubser, also with Waterford experience under his belt. With existing building blocks and the 2013 harvest to work with, they've created an easy-drinking lifestyle range named after the eponymous 'bloem', alongside more ageworthy offerings.

Bloemendal Estate range
★★★★ **Kanonberg** 📟 Expressive, poised, properly dry Bordeaux white, 70/30 sauvignon & semillon **13**, seriously styled (mostly new-oak ferment) & showing great savoury persistence. Deserves cellaring.
Suider Terras Sauvignon Blanc ★★★★ Restyled & back in form, single-vineyard **13** typical Durbanville 'dust', khaki bush, blackcurrant. Cask ferment adds weight, depth, to textured palate, & rare-in-Cape savoury finish. Improves on last-tasted **11** (★★★★).

Waterlily range 📟
★★★★ **Shiraz** ✓ Spice & red berry entry on appealing **11**, supple & elegant, just the right amount of grip for solo or mealtimes.
Merlot ★★★★ Slight herbaceous lift to violet-toned **11**. Refreshing plummy mouthful, confident & light-footed. **Rosé Syrah** ★★★ With a kiss of pink, **13**'s fruit managed & vinified for rosé - no afterthought, this Light & markedly dry for al fresco entertaining. **Sauvignon Blanc** ★★★★ Sauvignon this estate's calling card. **13** typical dusty fruit profile will please the fans, as will extended farewell, improved texture. — CvZ

Blomendahl Vineyards

Location: Elgin ▪ Map: Elgin, Walker Bay & Bot River ▪ WO: Elgin/Simonsberg-Paarl/Western Cape/Coastal/ Stellenbosch ▪ Est 2003 ▪ 1stB 2006 ▪ Tasting by appt ▪ Owner(s) Blomendahl Trust ▪ Cellarmaster(s), winemaker(s)/viticulturist(s) Franz Josef Blomendahl ▪ 126ha (cab, merlot, ptage, shiraz, chard, chenin) ▪ 480t/70,000cs own label 90% red 10% white ▪ PO Box 52019 Waterfront Cape Town 8002 ▪ info@basco.co.z ▪ www.blomendahl.de ▪ S 34° 13' 12.2" E 019° 2' 28.8" ▪ **T** +27 (0)21-859-2937/+27 (0)72-692-6229 ▪ F +27 (0)21-859-1411

Internationally experienced distiller, negociant and winemaker Franz Jose Blomendahl now has a permanent home for his wines in Elgin. The natural stone cellar and tasting venue completed, he was adding the last touches to the visitor area as the guide went to press, well as building guest accommodation.

Ben Hur range

Shiraz ⊕ ★★ Herbaceous seam to wild berry fruit on medium-bodied **07**. **Quadrega** ⊕ ★★★ Black-fruited **06** trio cab, merlot & shiraz showed sleek oak tannins when last tasted.

Estate Collection

Basco Cabernet Sauvignon ⊕ ★★ Hints of cedar & sweet berries, **10** soft & fruity. WO W Cape. **Basco Merlot** ⊕ ★★★ **07** fruit sweetness held in firm tannic grip when last we tried. Should be ready now. **Môrewag Pinotage** ⊕ ★★★ **06** demure compared with previous, less extracted, with firm tannins. Simonsberg-Paarl WO, as for all Môrewag wines. **Basco Pinotage** ⊕ 🍽 ★★ Acid dominated youthful, magenta-hued, spicy **10** when last tasted. **Blue Bay Shiraz** ⊕ ★★★ Ripe, dark fruit in juicy, accessible **06**. Ex West Coast vines. **Môrewag Rosé** ⊕ 🍽 **09** sweet impression from fruitiness but technically dry & nicely structured. **Basco Rosé** ⊕ 🍽 ★★★ Light pink **10** delighted with off-dry fruity flavours when reviewed. **Basco Chardonnay** ⊕ 🍽 ★★★ Green-apple toned **10** was pleasant summertime sipper mid-2010. Simonsberg-Paarl WO. **Bonny Bay Bushvine Chenin Blanc** ⊕ 🍽 ★★★ Noted previously as tad unexpressive for bushvines, but **09** pleasantly dry food wine. WO Stellenbosch. **Basco Sauvignon Blanc** ⊕ 🍽 ★★★★ **09** attractive stony acidity & minerality when tasted mid-2010. Good table companion. **Môrewag Shiraz** ⊕ ★★★ Natural Sweet **08** had savoury hints last time; sweet, but good grip added balancing savouriness. **Môrewag Cabernet Sauvignon** ⊕ ★★★ Natural Sweet **08** brimmed with fruit, sweetness checked by leafy dry savouriness.

Prime Bin range

Cabernet Sauvignon-Merlot ⊕ ★★★ Mix cab & merlot in black-fruited **06**, was dense & closely knit, should since have softened. **Lady in Red Rosé** ⊕ 🍽 ★★★ Attractively different: more 'light red' than 'rosé', **09** had plenty cab fruit for flavour & structure. Simonsberg-Paarl WO.

Bonolo range

Cabernet Sauvignon Next awaited. — DB

■ **Blouberg** *see* Graça

Blouvlei Wyne

Location: Wellington ▪ Map: Paarl & Wellington ▪ WO: Paarl ▪ Est/1stB 2003 ▪ Tasting, sales & cellar tours Mon-Fri 9-4.30 Sat by appt ▪ Fee R15 ▪ Closed all pub hols ▪ Picnic area by arrangement ▪ Owner(s) BEE Company ▪ Winemaker(s) Abraham Cloete & Chris Roux ▪ Viticulturist(s) Ettienne Barnard (Oct 2010) ▪ ±40ha/28ha (alicante bouschet, cabs s/f, merlot, mourv, p verdot, shiraz, tinta barocca) ▪ ±160t/10,000cs own label 70% red 30% white ▪ IPW ▪ PO Box 817 Wellington 7654 ▪ blouvlei@cknet.co.za ▪ www.montdutoit.co.za ▪ S 33° 39' 31.3" E 019° 2' 2.6" ▪ **T +27 (0)21-873-7745** ▪ F +27 (0)21-864-2737

The easy-drinking wines in this range are made at Mont du Toit in Wellington, whose workers are shareholders in the business. Red wines are the focus, made from grapes at the parent farm - white grapes are brought in from elsewhere.

Red 🍽 ★★★ Light but flavourful **10** cab-based blend. Dry tannins firm up easygoing charm. **Rosé** Not tasted. **Sauvignon Blanc** 🍽 🄸 ★★★ **11** tends to the greener side of the sauvignon spectrum, but has a bit of weight & is crisply & tastily succulent. — TJ

■ **Blue Bay** *see* Blomendahl Vineyards

Blue Crane Vineyards

Location/map/WO: Tulbagh ▪ Est 2001 ▪ 1stB 2004 ▪ Visitors welcome but phone ahead ▪ Owner(s) Fred & Manuela Crabbia ▪ Cellarmaster(s)/winemaker(s) Zia Pienaar ▪ Viticulturist(s) Chris Fox, advised by Andrew Teubes & suppliers ▪ 138ha/6ha (cab, merlot, shiraz, sauv) ▪ 4,000cs own label 75% red 25% white ▪ BWI ▪ PO Box 306 Tulbagh 6820 ▪ info@bluecrane.co.za ▪ www.bluecrane.co.za ▪ S 33° 14' 34.7" E 019° 9' 49.4" ▪ **+27 (0)23-230-0823** ▪ F +27 (0)23-230-0825

Concerted effort at the Crabbia family's Tulbagh estate are bearing fruit. An additional four hectares of olive trees have doubled the size of the grove and their extra virgin oil, bottled under the Blue Crane label, is now commercially available. Young vines planted in 2010 are coming into production this harvest.

Cabernet Sauvignon ★★ **10**, revisited mid-2013, shows power & extraction, fruit in embrace of firm tannins, needing time. **Merlot** ★★★ Modest varietal character on nose, **11** hints of juicy fruit behind strong grape & oak tannins (50% new oak). Allow time. **Shiraz** ★★★★ Now bottled, **10** has mellowed somewhat, tannins creamier & more yielding, appealing vanilla sweetness from American/French oak. **Full Flight** ℗ 🍴 ★★★ Food-friendly combo cab, shiraz & merlot, **08** chunky but well fleshed, blackcurrant flavour & savoury spice. **Sauvignon Blanc** ℗ 🍴 ★★☆ **11** fresh & uncomplicated, lightish grassy body. — CE,CvZ

■ **Blue Rock** *see* Blaauwklippen Vineyards
■ **Bob's Your Uncle** *see* Boer & Brit

Boekenhoutskloof Winery

Location/map: Franschhoek ▪ WO: Franschhoek/Coastal/Western Cape ▪ Est 1994 ▪ 1stB 1996 ▪ Tasting & sales Mon–Fri 9–5 ▪ Closed all pub hols ▪ Owner(s) Boekenhoutskloof Winery (Pty) Ltd ▪ Cellarmaster(s) Marc Kent (1994) ▪ Winemaker(s) Jean Smit, Johan Nesenberend & Elsabé Engelbrecht, with Shaun Meyeridricks ▪ Viticulturist(s) Heini Tait ▪ 71ha/3.71ha (cabs s/f) ▪ 60% red 39% white 1% rosé ▪ BDOCA, BRC, HACCP ▪ PO Box 433 Franschhoek 7690 ▪ info@boekenhoutskloof.co.za ▪ www.boekenhoutskloof.co.za ▪ S 33° 56' 33.0" E 019° 6' 28.0" ▪ **T +27 (0)21-876-3320** ▪ F +27 (0)21-876-3793

At the apex of quality wine production in the Cape, Boekenhoutskloof this year marks the 20th anniversary of its founding by a group of business and advertising executives and impassioned Francophile winemaker Marc Kent. (Rumour has it each of the antique chairs on the label represents a partner.) Since announcing their intentions with a five-star rating in our 2000 edition for the now legendary Syrah 1997, they have led vinicultural and market trends – from their idyllic home at the foot of Franschhoek's mountains to the cutting edge of Swartland's terroir initiatives. The mastery of winemaking plus business acumen are evident in sibling brands Helderberg Wijnmakerij, The Wolftrap and Porcupine Ridge (see entries). Doubtless their upgraded tasting centre will see many celebrations as the precocious teen becomes a twentysomething.

★★★★★ **Cabernet Sauvignon** 🅱 **11** starts with notes of crushed dry cherry, then a fragrant & herbal lift, slowly evolving to dark fruits & earthy hint. All-new oak enhances but never dominates the whole. Apparently fruity & effortless, yet below lurk elegant tannins, needing time. On form after lesser-vintage **10** (★★★★★).

★★★★☆ **Syrah** 🅱 Since inaugural **97**, this has been an industry benchmark. **11**'s fine floral perfume mixed with delicate spice gives way to bright raspberry fruits. Trademark precision, fine acid & good ripe but dry finish. Fruit from Wellington as usual.

★★★★☆ **The Chocolate Block** 🅱 Extremely successful consumer-focused shiraz-based blend. Underneath all that modern livery, **12** impresses with a refined structure, staying fresh & vibrant, in support of billowing red fruit, layers of spice & consummate oak aromas. Mostly Swartland fruit.

★★★★★ **Semillon** 🅱 **11** (★★★★☆), more open & lifted than **10**. Melon, citrus fruit & fine cedar oak aromas confidently lead to a palate with notes of almond paste & citrus pith; finished off with a lingering honey-melon perfume. Dollop of sauvignon adds to the freshness. Great texture, but needs time to meld.

★★★★☆ **Noble Late Harvest** 🅱 Inviting sun-baked peach, tart apricot & delicate caramel whiffs hint at great intensity of **10**. Barrel-fermented & -matured semillon (100% new oak) with trademark refined & restrained palate. Perfectly poised, with cleansing acid. Fine expression of balanced seduction. — JP

Boer & Brit

Location: Paarl ▪ Map: Paarl & Wellington ▪ WO: Western Cape ▪ Est 2010 ▪ 1stB 2008 ▪ Tasting & sales at Bovlei Cellar (see entry) ▪ Owner(s) Stefan Gerber & Alexander Milner ▪ Winemaker(s) Stefan Gerber, Alex Milner (both Jul 2010) & Marco Benjamin (2011) ▪ 30t own label 60% red 40% white ▪ Other export label: Bob's Your Uncle ▪ PO Box 4 Klapmuts 7625 ▪ alex@boerandbrit.com ▪ www.boerandbrit.com ▪ S 33° 38' 18.4" E 019° 54.2" ▪ **T +27 (0)21-807-3331** ▪ F +27 (0)86-531-7137

Stefan Gerber and Alex Milner are direct descendants of two major protagonists in the Anglo-Boer War, hence the name of their maverick winery. Their wines – like their makers – don't take themselves too seriously. Look out for their Boer & Brit brands (The General, The Field Marshal and Gezina) as well as Suikerbossie Ek Wil Jou Hê and Transkaroo-Bring My Huis Toe.

■ **Boland Cellar** *see* Boland Kelder

Boland Kelder

Location/WO: Paarl ▪ Map: Paarl & Wellington ▪ Est/1stB 1947 ▪ Tasting & sales Mon-Fri 9–5 Sat & pub hols 9–1 ▪ Closed Easter Fri-Sun, Ascension day, Sep 24, Dec 25/26 & Jan 1 ▪ Cellar tours by appt ▪ Wynvlieg cellar theatre open for venue hire ▪ Owner(s) 96 producing shareholders ▪ Cellarmaster(s) Bernard Smuts (Feb 2012) ▪ Winemaker(s) JD Rossouw (Sep 2007) & Bernard Smuts (Dec 2001), with Heidi Dietstein (Dec 2009), Handré Barkhuizen (Dec 2009) & Andrie le Roux (Dec 2012) ▪ Viticulturist(s) Jaco Engelbrecht (Feb 2012) ▪ 2,210ha (cab, merlot, ptage, shiraz, chard, chenin, nouvelle, sauv, viog) ▪ 21,976t/240,000cs own label 50% red 40% white 10% rosé + 400,000cs for clients ▪ Other export brands: Lindenhof, Montestell ▪ WIETA ▪ PO Box 7007 Noorder-Paarl 7623 ▪ lizmar@bolandkelder.co.za ▪ www.bolandkelder.co.za, www.bolandcellar.co.za, www.bolandwines.co.za ▪ S 33° 41' 19.6" E 018° 57' 20.1" ▪ T +27 (0)21-862-6190 ▪ F +27 (0)21-862-5379

For more than six decades, grower-owned Paarl winery Boland Kelder has promoted the concept of regional diversity, concentrating on the many meso-climates in their catchment area to produce wines of complexity and character. Innovation and sustainability are other keys to their endeavours, as evidenced by the Flutterby range in lightweight plastic (PET) bottles, now flying on several local airlines and helping reduce the carbon footprint. Further ventures and new product developments in non-traditional markets are promised soon.

Cellar Reserve range

★★★★ **Pinotage** ◪ Showy effort **10** with laudable results. Nose promises much (blackcurrants, cinnamon & clove) whilst palate is shyer, hiding behind sweet tannins. More attractive & pleasing than **09** (★★★☆).

★★★★ **Shiraz** ◪ Spice-packed aromas of liquorice, cinnamon & nutmeg on polished & pleasant **11**. Lovely mouthfeel, clean & freshening acidity, tasty glass of wine for almost any occasion.

Cabernet Sauvignon ⊕ ★★★ **09** showing upfront minty/herbal notes on nose with dry raisined black fruit. Somewhat shy, may speak up given time. **Merlot** ◪ ★★★★ Well-made & interesting **10** shows unusual spice & fynbos notes with some polish & leather. Meaty palate, sweetly fruited with earthy texture. Steps up from **09** (★★★★). **Chardonnay** ◪ ★★★☆ Rich & spicy **11** shows lavish opulence with naartjie peel & caramelised peaches. Quite busy, should come together with time. **Chenin Blanc** ✓ ★★★☆ Attractive & balanced **12** from old Paarl bushvines. Natural barrel ferment produces grapefruit, honey, spiced apples, well integrated oak & acidity.

Five Climates Single Varietal range

Chardonnay ☺ 🖥 ◪ ★★★ **13** bright, fruity little number with fruit salad notes & some oak-staving adding a creamy, toffee apple finish. **Chenin Blanc** ☺ 🖥 ◪ ★★★ Cracking crowd pleaser **13**, zesty, lively yellow & green fruit with enough weight & concentration to please more serious palates. This over-deliverer of note is our deserved 2014 Superquaffer of the Year.

Cabernet Sauvignon 🖥 ◪ ★★★ Forthright & cheery **12** with whiffs of tobacco & cedar spice plus simple & plenteous black berried fruit. **Merlot** ⊕ 🖥 ◪ ★★★ Chocolate/coffee nose **11** gives way to ripe, soft black berries, plums & black cherry yoghurt. Well-managed tannins, mass appeal. **Pinotage** 🖥 ◪ ★★★ Much lighter **11** balances sweet charry notes with juicy succulent fruit. Soft & gentle - one to chill in summertime. **Shiraz** 🖥 ◪ ★★★ Black fruit mouthful on **11** tad less intense than last. Nonetheless, pleasant everyday drinking. **Sauvignon Blanc** 🖥 ◪ ★★☆ Pleasant peppers & fresh hay **13**. A little short on character. **Red Muscadel** ◪ ★★★ Flowery & fragrant **12** fortified dessert has delicate grapey aromas & flavours with nice balance of sugar & alcohol. Tasty winter warmer. **Cape Ruby Port** ⊕ ★★★ Return to form in **09** from shiraz. Plum & tealeaf mouthful of sweetness, spice & fire with chalky texture.

Cappupinoccinotage range

Cappupinoccinotage 🖥 ◪ ★★☆ **12** pinotage delivers on the name with lots of sweet coffee/chocolate notes slightly overwhelming the fruit.

Sixty 40 Blend range

Chenin Blanc-Sauvignon Blanc ☺ 🖥 ◪ ★★★ Off-dry **13** exudes bouncy yellow fruits in happy fresh blend. Crowd-pleasing charmer.

Cabernet Sauvignon-Shiraz 🖥 ◪ ★★ Soft & accessible **12**, sweet black fruit, charry finish.

Flutterby range

Merlot ⊕ 🍽 ⊘ ★★★ Uncomplicated everyday drinker offering charry black fruit in **11**. **Rosé** 🍽 ⊘ ★★ Semi-sweet **12** from cab/shiraz. Confected strawberry jam notes, drink now. **Sauvignon Blanc** 🍽 ⊘ ★★ Quiet & shy **13** lacks real varietal character. In picnic-friendly PET bottles, as in all range. — CM

Bon Cap Organic Winery   🍴🥤⚒📷🎿♿

Location/map: Robertson ▪ WO: Eilandia ▪ Est 2001 ▪ 1stB 2002 ▪ Tasting & sales Mon-Fri 8–5 Sun 10–4 ▪ Closed Sat due to weddings & functions ▪ Bon Rouge Bistro ▪ Facilities for children ▪ Cheese platters ▪ Sunday buffet ▪ Guest house ▪ Owner(s) Roelf & Michelle du Preez/SHZ Winery (Pty) Ltd ▪ Winemaker(s)/viticulturist(s) Roelf du Preez ▪ 460ha/40ha (cab, p verdot, ptage, pinot, shiraz, chard, cbard, sauv, viog) ▪ 295t/42,000cs own label 60% red 35% white 5% rosé ▪ Other export brand: The Greenhouse ▪ Brands for clients: The UK Societies ▪ Certified organic by SGS ▪ PO Box 356 Robertson 6705 ▪ info@boncap.co.za ▪ www.boncaporganic.co.za ▪ S 33° 47' 1.0" E 019° 40' 53.2" ▪ **T +27 (0)23-626-2073** ▪ F +27 (0)23-626-5789

One of the country's largest privately owned organic wineries, Bon Cap welcomes family visits, even families in the making – its wedding venue is now booked 90% of the year. Michelle du Preez, owner with husband Roelf, says: 'It's important that wineries diversify. Our wedding venue provides the ideal opportunity to introduce Bon Cap wines to a 'rainbow' of guests.'

Bon Cap range

★★★★ **Cape Blend** ⊕ 🌿 Unusual combo pinotage, petit verdot, cab works in polished & fresh **07** (★★★★). 1st tasted since **05**. **06** sold out untasted.

The Perfect Blend Await next, as for **Viognier**. **Méthode Cap Classique** 🌿 ★★★★ All-chardonnay dry sparkling in **07**, the bottle-age giving it a honeyed melon-preserve richness, extended finish. **Cape Ruby** ⊕ 🌿 ★★ NV port-style fortified from touriga only available from cellardoor. With garnet hue & savoury tone more 'Late Bottled than fruity 'Ruby'.

The Ruins/The Green House range

★★★★ **Syrah-Cabernet Sauvignon** ⊕ 🍽 🌿 ⊘ Wallet-friendly **11** nod to the Rhône: scrub & black pepper highlights, flexible backbone from majority shiraz. Worthy successor to accomplished & vivacious **10**.

> **Sauvignon Blanc** ☺ 🍽 🌿 ⊘ ★★★ Expressive **13** shows gooseberry & passionfruit perfume, attractive slatey minerality on the extended length.

Pinotage 🍽 🌿 ⊘ ★★★ Berries, a herbal note & savoury oak tones, **12** remains fresh. **Rosé** 🍽 🌿 ⊘ ★★★ Red berries & touch of herbs in dry **13** from pinotage, clean & lively. **Chardonnay-Viognier** 🍽 🌿 ⊘ ★★★ **13**'s 15% viognier emphasises the peachiness, gives an aromatic character to this off-dry easy drinker. **Sparkling Brut** 🌿 ⊘ ★★★ Just-dry **13**'s sauvignon gives a leafy & pear freshness. — CR

Bon Courage Estate   🍴🥤🎿♿

Location/map/WO: Robertson ▪ Est 1927 ▪ 1stB 1983 ▪ Tasting & sales Mon-Fri 8–5 Sat 9–3 ▪ Fee R20pp for groups of 10+ ▪ Closed Good Fri, Dec 25 & Jan 1 ▪ Café Maude T +27 (0)23-626-6806 ▪ Facilities for children ▪ Olive oil ▪ Owner(s) André & Jacques Bruwer ▪ Winemaker(s) Jacques Bruwer ▪ Viticulturist(s) André Bruwer ▪ 150ha (cab, pinot, shiraz, chard) ▪ 40% red 50% white 10% rosé ▪ Export brand: Three Rivers ▪ PO Box 589 Robertson 6705 ▪ wine@boncourage.co.za ▪ www.boncourage.co.za ▪ S 33° 50' 43.8" E 019° 57' 38.0" ▪ **T +27 (0)23-626-4178** ▪ F +27 (0)23-626-3581

October 2013 saw this family winery in Robertson celebrate three decades of autonomy after years of supplying larger brands - and watching them walk off with Young Wine Show acclaim! Versatility and great value remain watchwords with styles ranging from dry to sweet, and bubbly a particular favourite of deep-sea-angling winemaker Jacques Bruwer. It's also a wine style which, along with shiraz, has burnished Bon Courage's reputation in recent years.

Inkará range

★★★★ **Cabernet Sauvignon** ⊘ Brooding aromas of cigarbox, black coffee & savoury olives, balanced tannins & oak, **11** more sweet-sour flavour profile than **10**'s ripe fruit, which makes it good for food partnering.

★★★★ **Shiraz** ⊘ Whole-berry ferment (as for Cab); **11** herbaceous choc-mint tone to red fruit, cradled in soft, sweet new oak (50% American). Ready now to enjoy with rich winter stews.

Pinot Noir ⊕ ⊠ ★★★ Earthy, gamey notes on limited-edition **10**; smooth & supple, very ripe; a crowd-rather than purist-pleasing version of the grape.

Bon Courage Cap Classique range

★★★★ **Jacques Bruére Cuvée Rosé Brut** Salmon-hued sparkling mainly pinot noir (80%), chardonnay. **07** (★★★★☆) laudably fresh, raises the bar with silky mousse, delicate red fruit, persistent savoury-dry conclusion; greater focus than **06**. Portion oaked, 4 years on lees.

★★★★ **Cap Classique Jacques Bruére Brut Reserve Blanc de Blancs** ⊕ Consistently excellent sparkling from chardonnay, **08** as sophisticated & balanced as **07**. Delicious lemon-biscuit snap & persistent creamy finish. 10% oak, 2 years sur lie in bottle.

★★★★☆ **Cap Classique Jacques Bruére Brut Reserve** ⊕ Ever-superb pinot/chardonnay sparkling which, like all-chardonnay version (& **07**) is partly oaked, but spends extra ±36 months in bottle. Exceptional **08** (★★★★★) well worth the effort! Invigorating from start to finish, coiled & engaging, still had much to give mid-2012.

Bon Courage range

★★★★ **Noble Late Harvest** ⊕ ⊠ Elegant botrytised riesling dessert, unoaked. **11** apricot preserve & chocolate-dipped citrus flavour is succulent, super-concentrated, just misses perfect seam of acidity of **10** (★★★★☆).

Chardonnay Unwooded ☺ ▤ ⊠ ★★☆ Sweet yellow fruit, marmalade tang, fair weight & length on **13** version of perennial favourite. **Hillside White** ☺ ▤ ⊠ ★★★ Colombard & chardonnay combo **13** delivers relaxed summer fun with tangerine freshness. **Gewürztraminer Special Late Harvest** ☺ ⊠ ★★★ Enticing bouquet of baked pears & litchi, honey & spice on well-balanced, lightish **13**, delicate sweetness to enjoy solo or with spicy food.

Cabernet Sauvignon ⊕ ⊠ ★★★ Spice highlights on black berry compote, **11** supple & dry, with evident acidity inviting early drinking. **Pinotage** ⊠ ★★★ **11** ripe & savoury with hint of banana, firm flavours better with food than solo. **Shiraz** ⊕ ⊠ ★★★☆ Cream & vanilla invitation on juicy **11**. Fresh & light textured for uncomplicated early enjoyment. **Hillside Red** ⊕ ⊠ ★★★ 60/40 cab/shiraz happy marriage in supple **11**, for youthful enjoyment. **Chardonnay Prestige Cuvée** ▤ ⊠ ★★★☆ Barrel/lees-ageing (8 months older oak) mid-2013 give svelte **12**'s bananas & peaches a toasty overlay, should show more fruit with time. **André's Fame Colombard** ▤ ⊠ ★★ **13**'s pineapple flavour has a slight savouriness, brush of sugar smooths the finish. **Gewürztraminer Dry** NEW ⊠ ★★★ **13**'s floral aromas are delicate, sweet, palate by contrast is bone-dry & firm. **Sauvignon Blanc** ▤ ⊠ ★★★ **13** figs & tinned asparagus, attractive limy freshness, moderate alcohol for patio sipping. **Blush Vin Doux** ⊠ ★★★ Flirtatious **NV** sweet carbonated fizz from red muscadel guaranteed to get the party started - on budget. **Red Muscadel** ⊠ ★★★★ Sunset-hued **13** extremely flavoursome - rum-&-raisin, cranberry, honey & apple jelly - & very sweet; needs crushed ice & twist of citrus. **White Muscadel** ⊠ ★★★ Tinned yellow peaches & honey, **13** lovely sunny ripeness, perfect for those who like their muscadel desserts soft & very sweet. **Cape Vintage** ⊠ ★★★ Tinta (80%) & touriga in port-style **12**, firmish mulberries & plums, lower fortification for lengthy fireside conversations.

Like Father Like Son range

Cabernet Sauvignon-Merlot ▤ ⊠ ★★★ Budget range providing fruity early enjoyment. **12** is leafy & drying, needs a juicy steak. **Pinotage Rosé** ▤ ⊠ ★★ Appealing light blush to **13**, ripe-fruit flavours & balanced sweetness. Pleasant sipper. **Chenin Blanc** ▤ ⊠ ★★ **13** semi-dry picnic white with pineapple & guava flavours. — DC, HJ,JP

Bonfoi Estate

Location/map: Stellenbosch ▪ Est 1699 ▪ 1stB 1974 ▪ Tasting & sales by appt only ▪ Closed all pub hols ▪ BYO picnic ▪ Walks ▪ Conservation area ▪ Owner(s)/winemaker(s)/viticulturist(s) Johannes van der Westhuizen ▪ 200ha/89ha (cabs s/f, merlot, pinots noir/meunier, ptage, shiraz, chard, chenin, sauv, sem) ▪ 800t/2,000cs own label 60% red 40% white ▪ BWI ▪ PO Box 9 Vlottenburg 7604 ▪ bonfoi@mweb.co.za ▪ www.bonfoiwines.co.za ▪ S 33° 56' 29.1" E 018° 46' 29.8" ▪ **T +27 (0)21-881-3774** ▪ F +27 (0)21-881-3807

Boutique winery Bonfoi is situated on a very old estate in Stellenboschkloof, founded in 1699 and in the van der Westhuizen family for several generations now. The name, meaning 'Good Faith' was given by two French ladies who purchased the farm in the 18th century.

Bonne Esperance

Fondly known as 'Bonnies', this KWV entry-level brand was launched in the early 1960s and, after a break, reintroduced locally. It's also available throughout Africa.

Red ★★ Just off-dry light **NV**, easy, ripe & plummy. **White** ★★ Tropical-toned **NV** with litchi highlights, off-dry appeal. WO W Cape for both. — CR

Bonnievale Wines

Location: Bonnievale • Map: Robertson • WO: Bonnievale/Robertson • Est 1951 • 1stB 1977 • Tasting & sales Mon-Fri 8–5 Sat 10–1 • Closed Easter Fri-Mon, Dec 25/26 & Jan 1 • Cheese straws, biltong/droëwors & mini cheese platters • Facilities for children • Tour groups • Conferences (12 pax) • CCC Christmas Market • Owner/s 110 members • Winemaker(s) Esmarie Smuts (Jan 2002), Jolene le Roux (Aug 2007), Marthinus Rademeyer (Dec 2009) & Edwin Mathambo (Dec 2012) • Viticulturist(s) Sakkie Bosman (Nov 2006) • 1,780ha (cab, shiraz, chard, chenin, sauv) • 30,000t/80,000cs own label 30% red 55% white 10% perlé 5% juice + 120,000cs for clients • IPW, WIETA • PO Box 206 Bonnievale 6730 • sales@bonnievalecellar.co.za • www.bonnievalecellar. co.za • S 33° 57' 26.2" E 020° 6' 7.6" • **T +27 (0)23-616-2795/2800/2359** • F +27 (0)23-616-2332

Nip and tuck at one of South Africa's larger wineries sees the old branding replaced with 'Bonnievale Wines', and attractively revamped labelling introduced with a new one-word slogan - 'Unpretentious' - emblazoned on it. The CCC line-up makes way for Riggton White, Red and Semi Sweet (latter two untasted), and, once sold out, the Vertex Reserves will step aside for Barrel Select Cab and Shiraz. Vineyards at black economic empowerment farm Elethu are now online, giving CEO John Barnardt and the team further scope to select the best grapes and 'consistently exceed expectations'.

Vertex Reserve range

Cabernet Sauvignon ★★☆ Now bottled, **10** shows more oak-derived tar & smoke than last time, less plush blackberry fruit. WO Robertson, as next. **Shiraz** ✓ ★★★★ Step-up **11** vibrant red fruit with spice & tobacco from well-absorbed 100% new oak. Modern style deftly executed. Potential to age.

Bonnievale range

Cabernet Sauvignon-Shiraz ☺ 🍽 ★★☆ Shiraz's black pepper & smoky bacon accent cab's dark fruit, creating appealing **12** fireside sipper.

Merlot NEW 🍽 ★★ **12**'s chocolate cherry cake flavour & sweet tannins make it very easy to like. **Shiraz** ⓘ 🍽 ★★ Spices & mulberries, twist of black pepper on lean, food-styled **10** preview. **Cabernet Sauvignon-Merlot** 🍽 ★★ Dark chocolate & red berries in firm, robust **12** food partner. **Chardonnay** 🍽 ★★ **13** preview's stonefruit & citrus daubed with vanilla from light oaking on staves. **Sauvignon Blanc** 🍽 ★★☆ **13** ticks all the sauvignon boxes: leafy, crisp & dry; lightish, too, for all-day enjoyment. **Sauvignon Blanc Brut** ⓘ 🞨 ★★ **NV** party-starting bubbly with frothy mousse, lively acidity. **Cape Ruby** ⓘ ★★ Savoury port-style **10** from tinta still cloaked with oak when tasted, might since have settled.

Riggton range

White 🍽 ★★ Off-dry but crisp **13** from chenin delivers uncomplicated quaffability courtesy peach fruit.

Perlé range

Dusk 🍽 ★ Low alcohol rosé from ruby cab, **NV** with teeny soft bubbles, charming sweetness. **Dawn** 🍽 ★★ Perfumed, sweet spritzy chenin, **NV** with low alcohol for all-day enjoyment. — DB,JP

▪ **Bonny Bay** *see* Blomendahl Vineyards
▪ **Bonolo** *see* Blomendahl Vineyards

Bon Terroir

Location/WO: Stellenbosch • Est 2002 • 1stB 2007 • Closed to public • Owner(s) Agri Marketing Exchange (Pty) Ltd, with shareholder Will-Mag Holdings Ltd • Winemaker(s) Bruwer Raats (2007, consultant) • 15.5ha/4ha (cabs s/f) • 5t/600cs own label 100% red • PO Box 12511 Die Boord 7613 • willie@willmag.co.za • www. bonterroir.co.za • **T +27 (0)82-445-3440** • F +27 (0)86-622-8254

Those founding this tiny Stellenbosch farm revelled in both name and deed in its soil and climatic conditions. These were deemed propitious for reds, so cabernet sauvignon it was. We haven't tasted a new vintage for a few years now, however.

★★★★☆ **Cabernet Sauvignon** ⓅⒶ Modern, big, sweet-fruited **09** (★★★★), showing tobacco & spice from effective oaking, two years back seemed riper, bolder & heavier than **08** - & a touch clumsier. — TJ

Bonview Wines

Location: Somerset West ▪ WO: Western Cape/Stellenbosch ▪ Est 2011 ▪ 1stB 2012 ▪ Closed to public ▪ Owner(s) Teuns Keuzenkamp ▪ 5,700cs own label 95% red 5% white ▪ PO Box 1977 Somerset West 7129 ▪ bonview@telkomsa.net ▪ **T +27 (0)21-887-5812** ▪ F +27 (0)86-224-9348

Negociant business Bonview was established in 2011 to produce wine and grape juice for export. Owner Teuns Keuzenkamp has long-term contracts with various Cape cellars, and targets mainly West Africa and China with 'quality wines that are affordable and attuned to the tastes of everyday wine consumers'.

Pegalle range
Cabernet Sauvignon ⓅⒶ ★★★ **11**'s creamy oak-seamed plum character is quite serious yet very easy to drink. **Merlot** ⓅⒶ ★★ A savoury food wine, **10** has dusty & leafy overtones, firm green olive-like flavours. WO Stellenbosch. **Shiraz** ⓅⒶ ★★★ **11** perfect for times when all you want is a tasty food/solo glass of red with generous fruity flavour - nothing challenging or out there. — HJ, JP

Boplaas Family Vineyards

Location: Calitzdorp ▪ Map: Klein Karoo & Garden Route ▪ WO: Calitzdorp/Western Cape/Coastal/Klein Karoo/ Goudini/Upper Langkloof ▪ Est 1880 ▪ 1stB 1982 ▪ Tasting & sales Mon-Fri 8-5 Sat 9-3 ▪ Fee R20pp ▪ Closed Good Fri & Dec 25 ▪ Cellar tours by appt ▪ Facilities for children ▪ Gifts ▪ Farm produce ▪ Walks/hikes ▪ Conservation area ▪ Ring of Rocks ▪ Owner(s) Carel Nel ▪ Cellarmaster(s) Carel Nel (1982) ▪ Winemaker(s) Margaux Nel (Dec 2006) ▪ Viticulturist(s) Pieter Terblanche ▪ 2,300ha/70ha (cab, ptage, shiraz, tinta, touriga, chard, cbard, sauv) ▪ 55% red 45% white ▪ BWI, IPW ▪ PO Box 156 Calitzdorp 6660 ▪ info@boplaas.co.za ▪ www.boplaas.co. za, www.coolbay.co.za ▪ S 33° 32' 8.0" E 021° 41' 1.9" (Boplaas), S 34° 4' 45.40" E 022° 8' 25.22" (Cool Bay) ▪ **T +27 (0)44-213-3326** ▪ F +27 (0)44-213-3750

Among the pioneers of Cape port-styles in semi-arid Calitzdorp, the Nel family are furthering the Portuguese association with a greater focus on unfortified wines from Portuguese varieties, particularly favourites touriga nacional and tinta barocca. A longer heritage is that of distilling, which dates from 1880, when cellarmaster Carel Nel's great-great grandfather, Daniel, exported brandy to England. More recently, Boplaas was the first to launch an 'estate' brandy after the 1989 change in legislation. Today, Carel takes a holistic view of their business: 'For six generations we have worked hard to build up our wine estate; this has benefited us, the people who work for us and the land on which we farm.'

Heritage Reserve range NEW
★★★★☆ **Muscadel** ✓ ▤ Limited bottling in exceptional years to honour Nel family association with fortified muscadel since mid-1800s. From white muscadel, fragrant **11** honeyed & rich, revels in typical muscat marmalade, jasmine, barley sugar & dried pineapple. Delicious now but will reward lengthy cellaring. WO Goudini.

Family Reserve range
★★★★ **Shiraz** Ⓟ **10**'s (★★★★) bramble berry & spice, fynbos & pepper notes followed by plump sweet fruit, gutsy tannins. Shade off svelte & balanced **09**.

★★★★ **Cabernet Sauvignon-Shiraz** Ⓟ 60/40 duo from Upper Langkloof & home vines, **07** elegant without sacrificing ripeness.

★★★★ **Bobbejaanberg Sauvignon Blanc Reserve** NEW ✓ ▤ High altitude, cool climate & low yield (2 tons/ha courtesy resident baboons) show in pungent, spicy & persistent **13**, off Upper Langkloof vines.

Cabernet Sauvignon Ⓟ ★★★ Cassis, touch of cocoa on **09** medium-bodied & easy-drinking dinner companion. Oak tannins well knit (year French cask) when we tasted mid-2012. WO W Cape for these unless noted. **Ring of Rocks** ★★★★ Merlot joins touriga & cab in **11**, tangy & punchy country-style red with deft oak seasoning. Calitzdorp vines. **Pinot Noir Méthode Cap Classique** Ⓟ ★★★★ Pale pink **09** champagne-method sparkling with bready/honeyed bottle-age notes; lovely pinot noir weight but tad sweeter than usual for this style. Calitzdorp WO.

Boplaas range

★★★★ **Hanepoot Reserve** Fortified dessert from 50+ year old vines planted by Nel patriarch, Oom Danie. 375ml of liquid temptation, poised & persistent, though **13** tad less fresh than last-tasted **11** (★★★★★).

★★★★☆ **Red Muscadel Vintners Reserve** ⓦ Senior citizen **75** suave, engaging, with fully integrated dried fruit flavour, tannin & alcohol.

★★★★☆ **Muscadel Reserve** ⓦ Gingery/grapey **10** fortified dessert is beautifully structured with crisp acid, silky fruit & spicy sweetness (213g/l sugar). Poise in a glass.

★★★★☆ **Cape Vintage Reserve Show Selection Port** Cape benchmark for port-style previously listed as 'Cape Vintage Reserve Port'. Stately new bottling of **10**, Calitzdorp-only touriga (88%), tinta & drop souzão showing huge complexity & persistence, with structure & pedigree to give much pleasure over a decade or more.

★★★★☆ **Cape Tawny Port** ⓦ NV from tinta, touriga, souzão. Nutty & spicy from long ageing in barrel, wonderfully balanced, shows mere hint of sweetness on the aftertaste. WO W Cape.

★★★★☆ **Cape Vintage** ⓦ Ready-to-drink **11** (★★★★) raisined & spiced fruitcake, concentrated bright red fruit, well-judged spirit; polished, though shade less powerful than also-reviewed **10**, proverbial iron fist in a velvet glove. Combo touriga, tinta & souzão.

★★★★ **Cape Tawny Vintners Reserve** Port-style NV from 45+ year old tinta, 15% touriga. Latest billows malt & mead from long barrel-ageing , brandy & dried apricot flavours, rich & endless. 375 ml. WO W Cape.

★★★★☆ **Cape Tawny Port** ⓦ A tinta, touriga, souzão mix (90/8/2), **97** exceptionally classy. Rich & sleek, with superb spirit integration (±19%) from 12 years in old barrels. W Cape WO.

★★★★ **Cape Tawny Show Reserve** ⓦ NV from tinta, touriga, souzão showing nuts & citrus, slightly sweeter than other port-styles in line-up, also richer, creamier.

★★★★ **Chocolate Cape Vintage** ⓦ After hedonistic **09**, port-style tinta (70%), touriga **10** (★★★☆) similar lushness, vivid flavours but tannins still obvious when tasted. Should since have knit. WO W Cape.

★★★★☆ **Cape Tawny Reserve** ⓦ Masterly **95** fortified from tinta (90%) & touriga 'made before Calitzdorp even became a WO district' says cellarmaster Carel Nel. 12 years in cask yield complex, intense medley of nuts, toffee, orange marmalade, lingering dry conclusion. 375ml. WO Klein Karoo.

Chardonnay Unwooded ☺ 🍽 🚱 ★★☆ Light & breezy **13** is citrus toned, balanced & lively for day-long enjoyment.

Cabernet Sauvignon 🍽 ★★☆ **11** convivial, juicy & vibrant, with slight leafy lift. **Merlot** ⓦ 🍽 ★★ Mediumweight **11** sweet plum fruit & charry tannins, for early drinking. **Pinotage** ⓦ 🍽 ★★☆ **11** is accessible, juicy, chocolate-laced, though perhaps shade less textured & complete than previous. **Shiraz** ⓦ ★★★☆ Polished tannins, dense plum centre, earth & floral notes on peppery **08**. **Tinta Barocca** ⓦ ★★★ Lightly wooded **09** is savoury, fresh & friendly. **Tinta Chocolat** 🍽 ★★★ Fashionable 'choc-mocha' overlay to 100% tinta barocca, **12** supple & packed with berries, easy, appealing. WO W Cape. **Touriga Nacional** ⓦ ★★★★ Fragrant (unfortified) **09**, orange peel hint, vibrant red-berry acidity & fair grip. **Sauvignon Blanc** ⓦ 🍽 ★★ Gooseberry & Golden Delicious apple in lightish **12**. **Stoepsit Sauvignon Blanc** NEW 🍽 ★★☆ **13** coincides with 90th vintage of matriarch Rolien Nel, who loves entertaining on her stoep (veranda) with this wine. Light bodied & bone-dry, a good stoep wine! **Viognier** ⓦ ★★★ Apricot & rosepetal on aromatic **10**, attractive, not blowsy; dry & zesty early drinking. **Moscato Light** ⓦ 🍽 ★★ Light (±9% alcohol), grapey & off-dry **12**, perfect foil for Asian cuisine. **Pinot Noir Sparkling** ⓦ ★★ **11** pink & frothy cherry-toned bubbly with sweetish tail. **Hanepoot** ⓦ ★★★ Charming & fragrant fortified dessert, **12** all jasmine & honeysuckle prettiness, easy drinkability assured by tangy acidity. **Red Muscadel Reserve** ⓦ ★★★ Young vines pack quite an aromatic punch! Intense raisin, cinnamon & clove highlights to **11**'s lanolin bouquet, smooth palate. 375ml. **Red Muscadel** ✓ ★★★★ **13** puts up a spirited attack which, with time, should mellow pleasingly. Raisins, Karoo dust & spicy flick in the tail; similar to zesty **12** (★★★★) tank sample but showing greater weight. **Muscadel** ★★★ From white muscat de Frontignan, **13** lives up to nickname for category 'sticky'. Has pleasant raisin & sultana nuances, syrupy consistency. Enjoy over ice-cream in summer or with baked desserts in winter. **Cape Ruby** ★★★☆ Tar & liquorice, dates & Xmas pud on latest port-style NV from touriga, tinta & souzão (70/20/10). Less fleshy than previous bottling but still a delightful digestif. **Cape Pink** ⓦ ★★★ Rosy-hued NV port-style from tinta, touriga, souzão. Tangy, with interesting watermelon nuance **Cape White Port** ⓦ ★★★ NV fortified from chardonnay, with ginger & melon appeal.

Cool Bay range

★★★★ **Sauvignon Blanc Reserve** 🏷 **13** (★★★★), from old Darling bushvines, made for seafood: crisp & dry with characteristic salty edge, good length. As effusive as **12** tank sample but shade less textured.

Sauvignon Blanc ⓐ ★★★ Cool, green **11**, similar pebbly notes to sibling but fruitier.

Brandy range [NEW]

★★★★★ **Potstill 20 Years Brandy** Gold coloured with hint of olive green on rim. Fruitcake, dried apricots, marzipan, sweet prune flavours, mingling with smooth vanilla. Super-complex, elegant & silky palate - both delicate & penetrating - leads to a gorgeous long finish. Just 500 bottles made.

★★★★☆ **Carel Nel 15 Years Reserve Brandy** Rich amber colour with apricot & peardrop, potpourri wafts. Seductive, rich with caramel, almonds & hint of smoke. Full bodied & mouthfilling, well integrated alcohol. Complex, strikes fine balance between rich fruit & oak. Less ethereal than 20YO, touch less drily refined.

★★★★☆ **Potstill 8 Years Brandy** Caramel, sweet & smoky oak, fuller bodied with chocolate, dried peaches, pear & apricot. Silky & complex, still youthful, with a clean vanilla finish. Good example of a fresh young serious potstill. 100% potstill, as is 20YO.

Carel Nel 5 Years Reserve Brandy ★★★☆ Leafy fresh notes with dried apricot & pear aromas. Rich vanilla complexity, yet delicate & smooth, with a floral dry finish. 40% potstill, as is 15 year old. All of these brandies from colombard, all unfiltered & unfined. — WB, GdB,JP, TJ

■ **Borg Family Wines** *see* Painted Wolf Wines
■ **Born & Bred in South Africa** *see* BABISA - Born & Bred in South Africa

---

Boschendal Wines

Location/map: Franschhoek ▪ WO: Western Cape/Coastal/Stellenbosch/Elgin ▪ Est 1685 ▪ 1stB 1975 ▪ Tasting & sales daily 11-5.30 (Oct-Mar) & 11-4.30 (Apr-Sep) ▪ Fee R30pp ▪ Chocolate & wine tasting R60pp booking essential ▪ Closed Good Fri, May 1, Jun 16 & Dec 25 ▪ Cellar tours daily 10.30, 11.30 & 3 ▪ Cheese platters on request ▪ Restaurant ▪ Facilities for children ▪ Tour groups ▪ Gifts ▪ Museum ▪ Owner(s) DGB (Pty) Ltd ▪ Cellarmaster(s) JC Bekker (1986) ▪ Winemaker(s) Lizelle Gerber (whites, 2006) & Bertho van der Westhuizen (reds, 2012), with Lionel Leibrandt (1999) ▪ Viticulturist(s) Stephan Joubert (2006) ▪ 2,240ha/200ha (shiraz, sauv) ▪ 3,100t/500,000cs own label 32% red 43% white 14% rosé 11% sparkling ▪ WIETA ▪ Private Bag X03 Groot Drakenstein 7680 ▪ cellardoor@dgb.co.za ▪ www.boschendalwines.com ▪ S 33° 52' 27.5" E 018° 58' 34.4" ▪ **T** +27 (0)21-870-4200 ▪ F +27 (0)21-874-1531

Established in 1685, Boschendal is one of South Africa's oldest and best-known wine estates and, with the stately Groot Drakenstein peaks as a backdrop, one of the most picturesque. Elegant Cape Dutch architecture, ancient oak trees, tasting facilities, wine bar and Le Pique Nique (sun/starlit picnics on the pavillion lawns) contribute to its evergreen appeal. Renewed focus on méthode cap classique yields a pair of new sparklings this edition: a well-priced non-vintage version of the long-established Grande Cuvée , and a blanc de blancs honouring the property's French Huguenot founder, Jean Le Long.

Cecil John Reserve range

★★★★★ **Shiraz** 🌿 Accomplished flagship. Opulently fruited **11** (★★★★★) spiced with orange zest, cardamom & nutmeg; shows its class in taut tannin frame. With 60% new oak, less seamless than beautifully poised **10**. Both more concentrated than Reserve, should improve 5+ years.

Discontinued: **Sauvignon Blanc**.

Reserve Collection

★★★★☆ **Shiraz** 🌿 **11** (★★★★) departs from 100% new oak regime for previous vintages, only 10% in this. Initially brooding, opens to lilies, red plum fruit, all freshened by zesty acidity, tempered tannins. Less complex than **10**. From Stellenbosch fruit, as are two following.

★★★★ **Grande Reserve** 🌿 Unusual blend petit verdot & shiraz, leafy **11** less ripe, fleshy than **09** but equally composed. Savoury nuances, tobacco & herb tones add complexity, up appeal. No **10**.

★★★★ **Chardonnay** **12** (★★★★★) good lemon fruit intensity on nose & palate, well-judged wooding (third new) though not quite as persistent as **11** (★★★★★), which improved on **09**. **10** untasted.

★★★★ **Sauvignon Blanc** **13** exudes cool green capsicum, fig & nettle, poised & compact with well-judged acidity. Like **12**, has great presence & is a fine-dining companion.

★★★★ **Le Grande Pavillion Méthode Cap Classique Brut Rosé** ✓ 🏵 Pale salmon **NV** sparkling from pinot noir delivers seabreeze freshness, delicate strawberry bubbles, good weight & length for solo sipping.

★★★★ **Grande Cuvée Méthode Cap Classique Brut** NEW ✓ **NV** bottling, creamy & smooth with myriad tiny bubbles, Granny Smith apple bouquet (from chardonnay), genteel toffee apple flavours (from pinot noir). Instant pick-me-up.

★★★★☆ **Grande Cuvée Méthode Cap Classique Brut** Classy **09** chardonnay/pinot noir celebrator has racy bubbles, baked apple & brioche notes from 3 years on lees. Like **08**, rich flavours buoyed by zesty acidity.

★★★★ **Jean Le Long Méthode Cap Classique** NEW Bone-dry & mineral sparkling from chardonnay. 'Oystershell' & biscuit-toned **07** still very fresh; shows little of the creaminess expected from 5 years lees-ageing. For those who prefer a leaner celebration companion or partner for seafood platters. WO Coastal.

★★★★ **Vin d'Or** 🏵 Natural Sweet dessert from riesling, viognier. **12** tank sample back up to speed; apricot, watermelon & peach attractions plus all the vibrancy lacking in chenin/riesling **11** (★★★★).

Elgin Appelation Series NEW

★★★★ **Chardonnay** 🏵 Toast & vanilla overlay, pure lemon core & long, balanced finish the hallmarks of **11**. Deftly oaked (30% new, 11 months), medium bodied (13.7% alcohol), a confident expression.

★★★★☆ **Sauvignon Blanc** 🏵 Accomplished **12** sets a high standard. Slightly herbal nuance with passionfruit & ruby grapefruit fragrances, clever acid-sugar management delivering a smooth, delicate mouthful that is also satisfyingly long & vinous.

Pinot Noir 🏵 ★★★★ **12**'s nose shut down at tasting time, shows faint boiled sweets. Palate more impressive - varietal silkiness, no rough edges but more 'red wine' than 'pinot'. Could show better with year/2.

1685 range

Merlot 🏵 ★★★ Meat & spice on supple, medium-bodied **11**; safe choice for solo sipping or with dinner. WO Coastal. **Shiraz** ✓ 🏵 ★★★★ **11**'s firm tannins, cleansing acidity, commendably dry food-compatible finish; fruity core & vanilla whiffs complete enjoyable glassful. **Shiraz-Cabernet Sauvignon** ✓ 🏵 ★★★☆ Interesting friar's balsam & prune nuances on ripe but dry **11** blend from coastal vineyards. Bold, with athletic tannic grip. **Chardonnay** 🏵 ★★★ Intense buttered toast styling for balanced, creamy **12** stalwart. Fermented/9 months French oak, portion in stainless steel for freshness. **Sauvignon Blanc Grand Vin Blanc** 🏵 ★★★ **13** more pungent & forthcoming than siblings, less elegant. Billows greenpepper & asparagus as it slips down easily if briefly, borne on zippy acidity. WO Coastal. **Chardonnay-Pinot Noir** 🏵 ★★★★ Faintly pink **13**, appealing citrusy chardonnay expression, pleasing weight & hint tannin from 40% pinot.

Boschendal Classics

Lanoy ☺ 🏵 ★★★ A Cape institution, mostly cab, merlot plus undisclosed others. **11** mulberry & leafy notes, generous palate & docile tannins. WO Coastal, like next. **Blanc de Noir** ☺ 🍶 🏵 ★★★ Satisfying, lipsmacking **13** from widely sourced undisclosed varieties. Nicely dry picnic wine.

Chenin Blanc 🍶 🏵 ★★☆ Tank sample **13** uncomplicated, lively summertime sipper, peachy farewell courtesy splash viognier & dab sugar. **Boschen Blanc** 🍶 🏵 ★★★ Characterful **13** preview, combo chenin, chardonnay & sauvignon, fruity & friendly. **Le Bouquet** 🍶 🏵 ★★★ Ex-tank, perennial favourite **13** mainly white muscadel, delivers grapey aromas & genteel sweetness; best well chilled.

The Pavillion range

Shiraz-Cabernet Sauvignon 🍶 🏵 ★★★ Uncomplicated braai companion. Toasty oak, honey & nougat, clean leather, **12** gentle tannins backed by solid core of fruit. **Pavillion Blanc** 🍶 🏵 ★★☆ Muted nettle & gooseberry notes, sippability enhanced by few grams sugar. **13** from unspecified varieties. — CvZ

■ **Boschetto** *see* Stellakaya Winery

Boschheim 🍷

Location/map: Stellenbosch ▪ WO: Stellenbosch/Western Cape/Paarl ▪ 1stB 2003 ▪ Tasting & sales by appt ▪ Owner(s)/winemaker(s) Andy Roediger ▪ 1,800cs own label 85% red 15% white ▪ PO Box 3202 Matieland 7602 ▪ andy@roedigeragencies.co.za ▪ S 33° 55' 54.9" E 018° 50' 10.5" ▪ **T +27 (0)21-887-0010** ▪ F +27 (0)21-886-4731

Involved in international and local wine consulting and winemaking, polymer scientist, phenolic ripeness expert and boutique cellar owner Andy Roediger vinifies for his own label whenever time allows. It's an ever-evolving range, the Cape Wine Master having excellent grape contacts throughout the winelands.

Cabernet Sauvignon ⊕ ★★★☆ **09** savoury & grassy rather than fruity, still withdrawn previously; we noted would benefit from year/2. **Muse** ⊕ ★★★☆ Lots on offer in 100% cab **09**, including cassis & nutmeg spicing, supple tannins. **Mourvèdre** NEW ★★★ Hedgerow fruit & chopped herbs, there's an element of wildness in **12**, forest floor, but its texture is smoothly rounded. From Paarl vines. **Pinot Noir** NEW ★★★☆ Tasted from barrel, **13** shows violets, plush berries, trademark elegance. Has appealing fruity freshness, succulence. WO W Cape. **Elemental Shiraz** Await next. **Ella Marie** ★★★☆ Cab/shiraz mix, touch of mourvèdre, **11** has moist fruitcake richness, supple savoury tannin underpin. Drinks well. — CR

Boschkloof Wines

Location/map: Stellenbosch ▪ WO: Western Cape/Stellenbosch ▪ Est/1stB 1996 ▪ Tasting, sales & cellar tours Mon-Fri 9-5 Sat 10-3 ▪ Fee R30 ▪ Closed Easter Fri-Sun, Dec 25 & Jan 1 ▪ BYO picnic ▪ Owner(s)/cellarmaster(s)/viticulturist(s) Jacques Borman ▪ Winemaker(s) Jacques Borman, with Reenen Borman (Jun 2010) ▪ 30ha/19ha (cabs s/f, merlot, shiraz, chard) ▪ ±80-120t/6-8,000cs own label 90% red 10% white ▪ PO Box 1340 Stellenbosch 7599 ▪ boschkloof@adept.co.za, info@boschkloofwines.com ▪ www.boschkloofwines.com ▪ S 33° 57' 37.0" E 018° 46' 11.8" ▪ **T +27 (0)21-881-3293 (office)/+27 (0)21-881-3268 (cellar)** ▪ F +27 (0)21-881-3032

Shiraz is the not-so-secret passion of Jacques and Reneen Borman at their boutique Stellenbosch property. A highlight in son Reenen's short career to date was enjoying the acclaimed La Chapelle single-vineyard syrah in France. This further entrenched his commitment to Boschkloof's creed – 'Inconcessum persequor' or 'I pursue the unattainable' – and perfecting their modern Rhône-style offering.

★★★★ **Syrah 10**, back on track after **09** (★★★), marries elegance & power without over-extraction. Smoky, peppery & persistent; for serious dinner tables. Smidgen American oak; other reds French only.

★★★★ **Conclusion** Cab franc-led Bordeaux red. Like **09**, **10**'s intensity enhanced by 'bleeding off' 30% of juice; very ripe but 15% alcohol in harmony with brooding fruit & tannins. Broach only in 3+ years. No **07**, **08**.

Cabernet Sauvignon ★★★★ Classically styled **11** delivers cassis fruit, cedar, firm tannins & brisk acidity; built for 5+ years ageing. WO Stellenbosch, as Merlot & Cab-Merlot. **Merlot** ★★★★ **10** high-toned but still very engaging: plum & prune, walnut & chocolate complexity; plush fruit counterpoint for firm oak tannins. **Cabernet Sauvignon-Merlot** ★★★ 60/40 **10** combo shows cab's firm tannins & merlot's succulence, leafy notes. Will improve 3+ years but sweet fruit might tempt you sooner. **Chardonnay** ★★★ Barrel-fermented **12** not quite as vivacious as previous. Oak dominant mid-2013 but might integrate with vibrant lemongrass fruit & acidity over year/2. **Sauvignon Blanc** 🖩 ★★★ Lees-aged **13** attractive blackcurrant, litchi & gooseberry; a softer, less acidic version. — CvZ

Boschrivier De Villiers Family Vineyards

Location: Stanford ▪ Map: Elgin, Walker Bay & Bot River ▪ WO: Klein River ▪ Est 1998 ▪ 1stB 2002 ▪ Tasting & sales Mon-Fri 8-5 Sat 9-5 ▪ Closed Dec 25 ▪ Restaurant ▪ BYO picnic ▪ Gift shop ▪ Farm produce ▪ Conferences (20 pax) ▪ Walking/hiking & 4x4 trails ▪ Self-catering farm house (see Accommodation section) ▪ Owner(s)/viticulturist(s) Theodore de Villiers ▪ Winemaker(s) Mike Dobrovic ▪ 14ha (cab, shiraz) ▪ 7t/ha 928cs own label 100% red ▪ Remhoogte Caledon p/a 70 Fairbairn Street Worcester 6850 ▪ drnjtdevilliers@mweb.co.za ▪ www.boschrivier.co.za ▪ S 34° 31' 19.4" E 019° 37' 51.0" ▪ **T +27 (0)23-347-3313/2 ext 3; +27 (0)76-736-0351** ▪ F +27 (0)23-342-2215

Theo de Villiers, paediatrician and boutique vigneron near Stanford, is proud to employ a multi-ethnic team. 'Wine is part of our culture and personhood. White, coloured and African have cooperated for generations to establish vineyards and make wine. Get the right people and success flows from that.'

★★★★ **Shiraz** 🖾 **11** is rich & concentrated but not at the expense of balance. Dark fruit, attractive oak spice, bright acidity. More convincing than slightly overdone **09** (★★★★). **10** not tasted. — CE

Bosman Family Vineyards

Location: Wellington ▪ Map: Paarl & Wellington ▪ WO: Wellington/Western Cape/Upper Hemel-en-Aarde Valley ▪ Est 1699 ▪ 1stB 2004 ▪ Tasting by appt ▪ Fee R50pp, waived on purchase ▪ Closed Easter Fri-Mon & Dec 20-Jan 6 ▪ Sales Mon-Thu 8-5 Fri 8-4.30 ▪ Cellar tours by appt ▪ Conservation area ▪ Bosman Release Celebration (Nov) ▪ Owner(s) Bosman family & Adama Workers Trust ▪ Cellarmaster(s) Petrus Bosman (Nov 2003) ▪ Winemaker(s) Corlea Fourie (Nov 2006), with Charlene Ferreira (Nov 2006) ▪ Viticulturist(s) Heinie Nel & Pierre Carstens (Jan 2000) ▪ 300ha (47 varieties r/w) ▪ 3,000t/20,000cs own label 70% red 25% white 5%

rosé ▪ Brands for clients: Checkers; Sainsbury Supermarkets; The Cooperative ▪ BBBEE certificate (level 2), BWI, Fairtrade ▪ PO Box 9 Wellington 7654 ▪ info@bosmanwines.com ▪ www.bosmanwines.com ▪ S 33° 37' 34.7" E019° 01' 28.9" ▪ **T +27 (0)21-873-3170** ▪ F +27 (0)21-873-2517

The historic Wellington farm and vine nursery, Lelienfontein, has been home to the Bosman family for eight generations. History has been respected in the 250-year-old cellar, now refurbished, still in use. Wishing to leave a similar legacy to their descendants, they follow ethical methods in producing their wines; for instance, installing solar panels and geysers cut their carbon footprint by 22,000 tons during 2012. Their newer premium Fairtrade range, De Bos Handpicked Vineyards, is now listed separately in this guide.

Unique Innovation range

★★★★ **Adama Red** 🄡 Eclectic blend headed by shiraz & mourvèdre, evident in **10**'s bold spice & roast meat tones. Firm & fresh, with pleasing light feel, given its full body. Well-used mix of American & French oak.

★★★★ **Adama White** 🄡 **12** unsettled & oaky in youth. Full ripe blend of chenin, chardonnay & 3 others is more vinous than fruity, with balanced weight & freshness. Should benefit from year or 2. No **11**. WO W Cape.

Bosman Family Vineyards range

★★★★☆ **Erfenis** ⊕ 🄡 **10** 'Heritage' has complex pinotage, cab franc, petit verdot, shiraz & cinsaut mix - best barrels only. Flirtatious yet serious. Generosity with depth & density. Layered, rounded & succulent.

30 Rosé ⊕ 🍴 🄡 ★★★ Ruby grapefruit & cranberry **10**, mix of 30 different varieties! Dry & zesty. Upper Hemel-en-Aarde Valley WO.

Special Vineyard Selection

★★★★ **Pinotage** ⊕ 🄡 **10** shows return to form after slight dip in **09** (★★★★). Tangy blue & black berry vibrancy with spice highlights. Softly elegant, with smooth, silky mouthfeel. Harmonious & integrated.

Cabernet Sauvignon ⊕ ★★★★ Last-tasted **07** had cassis & fynbos overlay & some elegance. **Optenhorst Chenin Blanc** 🄡 ★★★★ Sunny in its brilliant yellow-gold hue & delicate honeyed tones, old-vine **11** surprises with sizzling freshness, oak enrichment & tangy dry conclusion. Promising future. Step up on **09** (★★★★); **10** untasted. Fairtrade certified as most above. **Dolce Primitivo** Await next. — AL

◼ **Bosman's Hill** see Saxenburg Wine Farm

Botanica Wines   🍷☕⛰📷

Location/map: Stellenbosch ▪ WO: Stellenbosch/Elgin/Citrusdal Mountain ▪ Est/1stB 2008 ▪ Tasting by appt ▪ Wine sales Mon-Fri 8-5 ▪ Farm produce ▪ Conferences ▪ Walks/hikes ▪ Mountain biking trail ▪ Refreshments offered at Sugarbird Manor guesthouse (see Accommodation section) ▪ Owner(s) Virginia C Povall ▪ Winemaker(s) Virginia Povall (Jan 2008) ▪ Viticulturist(s) Francois Viljoen ▪ 21.6ha/5ha (cabs s/f, merlot, p verdot, pinot) ▪ PO Box 12523 Die Boord 7613 ▪ ginny@botanicawines.com ▪ www.botanicawines.com ▪ S 33° 54' 18.5" E 018° 49' 25.4" ▪ **T +27 (0)21-865-2313**

Not only are the Botanica wines particularly elegant, they also boast some of the more original and attractive packaging to be found locally – inspiration for the design coming after Botanica's American owner and winemaker Ginny Povall saw an exhibition of 18th-century British artist Mary Delany's work comprising of botanical cut-paper collages. Ginny, however, is not one to be too sentimental. 'I think South Africans still look at the world with 'colour' too much on their minds. I spent my early adult life in NYC where everyone is from a different culture.' Ginny's approach is simply to get stuck in – her Devon Valley property produces proteas for export and is also the location of a luxury guesthouse. She has bought in grapes until now while waiting for her own vineyards to mature.

The Mary Delany Collection

★★★★☆ **Pinot Noir** ✓ **12** from Elgin back to form after **11** (★★★★). Shows great elegance, delicacy, in its concentration of spicy strawberry fruit, supple structure (no new oak), unflagging savoury conclusion.

★★★★★ **Old Vine Chenin Blanc** ✓ Was just 'Chenin Blanc'. Outstanding varietal expression from ±50 year old bushvines near Clanwilliam. Dry **12** echoes **11** in fine, complex floral, honey & mineral tones, gorgeous citrus freshness. Only 50% oaked, adding to harmony & the promise of much future pleasure.

BIG Flower range

★★★★ **Cabernet Sauvignon** ⓘ Bright character of ripe dark berry fruit, sweet spice & tobacco hint. **09** from Stellenbosch vines is rich, medium bodied yet complex with a dusty, savoury finish.

Merlot ⓘ ★★★★ Intricate aromas of spiced dark berry fruit, **10** rounded mouthfeel & carefully managed tannins. From Devon Valley vines. — WB

Botha Wine Cellar

Location: Worcester ▪ Map/WO: Breedekloof ▪ Est 1949 ▪ 1stB 1974 ▪ Tasting & sales Mon-Fri 9–5 Sat 10–1 ▪ Closed Easter Fri-Sun, Dec 25/26 & Jan 1 ▪ Cellar tours by appt ▪ BYO picnic ▪ Conservation area ▪ Breedekloof Soetes & Soup and Outdoor & Wine festivals ▪ Owner(s) Botha Wynkelder (Edms) Bpk ▪ Cellarmaster(s) Gerrit van Zyl (Nov 2007) ▪ Winemaker(s) Johan Linde & Michiel Visser (Nov 1996/Nov 1999), with Annamarie van Niekerk (Dec 2009) ▪ Viticulturist(s) Jan-Carel Coetzee (Nov 2010) ▪ 1,969ha (cab, merlot, ptage, shiraz, chard, chenin, cbard) ▪ 37,417t/15,000cs own label 75% red 20% white 1% rosé 4% fortified & 1,800cs for clients ▪ ISO 22000:2009 ▪ BWI, IPW, WIETA ▪ PO Box 30 PK Botha 6857 ▪ admin@bothakelder.co.za ▪ www.bothakelder.co.za ▪ S 33° 34' 1.5" E 019° 15' 27.5" ▪ **T +27 (0)23-355-1740** ▪ F +27 (0)23-355-1615

With only 1% of its massive 37,000+ ton harvest going into bottle under an own label, this Breedekloof bulk-wine specialist has the double advantage of unlimited scope for selection and minimal dependence on sales volumes. To help market the Botha-branded portion, a new tasting room manager has been appointed.

Dassie's Reserve range

Dassie's Rood 🍴 🖼 ★★★ Cinsaut with cab & ruby-cab, **11**'s fruit bolstered by pinch of sugar. **Dassie's Rosé** 🍴 🖼 ★★ Floral-scented, semi-sweet **13** retains crisp freshness. **Dassie's Blanc** 🍴 🖼 ★★ Pleasantly crisp & fruity **13**, lightish chenin/colombard blend.

Botha range

★★★★ **Hanepoot Jerepigo** ⓘ 🖼 Stripped-down, focused muscat-raisin fragrance on delicious **12** shows stylish handling. Purity & intensity of fruit allowed to take centre stage. First since **08**.

> **Merlot** ☺ 🖼 ★★★ Pleasantly solid **11** is tinted with oaky mocha, but bright cherry/redcurrant fruit shows through. **Shiraz** ☺ 🖼 ★★★ Improved **11** has better fruit focus, meaty-savoury notes & ripely rounded tannins. **Chenin Blanc** ☺ 🍴 🖼 ★★★ **13** is freshly light, with ripe tropical fruit perked up by dash of sugar. Unseriously refreshing. **Sauvignon Blanc** ☺ 🍴 🖼 ★★★ Wholesome & appealingly aromatic **13** shows ripe stonefruit, well-judged acidity & hints of dusty pebbles.

Cabernet Sauvignon ⓘ ★★★ Tangy stewed prunes & oak spices on drink-now **09**, with hint of rustic farmyard. **Pinotage** 🖼 ★★★ Vanilla-spiced **11** is juicy & fresh easy drinking. **Light White** 🍴 🖼 ★★ Low-alcohol, off-dry **13** is thin with green fruit. **Chardonnay Brut** ⓘ 🖼 ★★★ Nearly-dry **NV** sparkler is fun loving & unfussy. **Red Jerepigo** ⓘ ★★★ Oddly structured pinotage fortified dessert, **08** somewhat 'wild', with green grass notes. **Cape Vintage Reserve** ⓘ ★★★ Barrel-matured **10** port-style offering from shiraz offers spicy brandy spirit & dark baked plum fruit, hint of racy acid. Note: Reserve range discontinued. — GdB

■ **Bottega Family Wines** *see* Idiom Wines

Bottelary Winery

A Perdeberg Winery value-for-money brand, the wines mostly going to China.

> **Merlot** ☺ 🍴 🖼 ★★★ Cheerfully fruity **12** belies entry-level pricing. From Paarl fruit, as all.

Rosé 🍴 🖼 ★★ Sweet **NV**, chenin with muscat & pinotage. Sunny & cheerful. **Chenin Blanc** ⓘ 🍴 🖼 ★★★ Apple & pear freshness in **10** makes for perky summer fare. **Semi-Sweet** ★★ Modestly sweet, fruity **12** chenin. Fresh & light. **Soft Smooth Red** ⓘ 🍴 🖼 ★★ Semi-sweet **11** cinsaut, shiraz, cab mix has berry jam fruitiness. Discontinued: **Velvet Red**, **Classic Red**, **Satin White**. — GdB

Bouchard Finlayson

Location: Hermanus ▪ Map: Elgin, Walker Bay & Bot River ▪ WO: Walker Bay/Overberg/Hemel-en-Aarde Valley/Cape South Coast ▪ Est 1989 ▪ 1stB 1991 ▪ Tasting, sales & cellar tours Mon-Fri 9–5 Sat 10–1 ▪ Fee R40pp for groups of 6+ ▪ Closed all pub hols ▪ Cheese & salami platters ▪ Gift shop ▪ BYO picnic ▪ Conservation area ▪

Nature walks by appt (guided & self-guided) ▪ Owner(s) The Tollman Family Trust ▪ Cellarmaster(s)/viticul-turist(s) Peter Finlayson (1989) ▪ Winemaker(s) Peter Finlayson (1989), with Chris Albrecht (Nov 2010) ▪ 125ha/22ha (barbera, nebbiolo, pinot, sangio, chard, sauv) ▪ 190t/33,000cs own label 25% red 75% white ▪ BWI, IPW ▪ PO Box 303 Hermanus 7200 ▪ info@bouchardfinlayson.co.za ▪ www.bouchardfinlayson.co.za ▪ S 34° 22' 54.0" E 019° 14' 30.9" ▪ **T +27 (0)28-312-3515** ▪ F +27 (0)28-312-2317

To appreciate winemaker and viticulturist Peter Finlayson's deep understanding of the terroir here (which includes the natural fauna and flora), you have to realise he was the pioneer winemaker in the Hemel-en-Aarde Valley (at Hamilton Russell), and he and Burgundian Paul Bouchard started this cellar in 1989. His belief in its suitability for Burgundian grapes has never wavered, hence two highly rated pinot noirs and four chardonnays in the portfolio. Proof that he knows what he's talking about can be seen in Tête de Cuvée's recent track record, the only pinot noir gold at the 2012 Five Nations Challenge and a gold medal at the 2013 Decanter awards. Besides what is done for its own employees, Bouchard Finlayson contributes to the Hermanus Rainbow Trust to assist children with basic education.

★★★★☆ **Galpin Peak Pinot Noir** 🍷 Riper styling in **11** allows the glossy fruit centre stage, with a sup-porting cast of espresso oak-tones, some dried herbs, a whiff of prosciutto. Succulent & harmonious, complex, involving.

★★★★☆ **Tête de Cuvée Galpin Peak Pinot Noir** ⓘ 🍷 Barrel selection & double new oak (75%) of siblings. Now bottled & showing the benefit of the extra year, **10**'s dark fruit & mocha, scrub notes reflect a bold version of pinot noir, but keeps the supple polish of the variety at its best.

★★★★☆ **Hannibal** 🍷 A 6-part marriage of Italian & French varieties, none of them Bordeaux. Always seductive, sangiovese-led **11** (★★★★★) no less so. Black cherry compote, violets & Belgian chocolate spicing, tannins supple & integrated, finishing on an elegant note. Savoury elegance also found on **10**.

★★★★☆ **Kaaimansgat/Crocodile's Lair Chardonnay** From reputed Elandskloof vines. With house-style refinement, **12** has a taut lemony focus, gentle oat biscuit overlay, ends with salty minerality. Complex, holds your attention.

★★★★☆ **Kaaimansgat Chardonnay Limited Edition** ⓘ Citrus rind & buttered toast, **10** has forth-coming perfume but flavours are subtler: crushed almonds, a slatey note. Textured mouthfeel from 60% new oak portion. Masterly construction, layers of interest, speaks in a quiet but authoritative voice.

★★★★ **Missionvale Chardonnay** 🍷 More New World style than other chardonnays from this cellar, **11**'s buttered toast, crushed hazelnuts & citrus preserve richness gives a full-flavoured experience, intense & long.

★★★★ **Sauvignon Blanc Reserve** 🍷 Different styling to its siblings thanks to 14% semillon, **12** has melon & gooseberry flavours & deepening minerality on the finish, leaves the palate clean & refreshed. No **11**.

★★★★ **Sauvignon Blanc** 🍷 Sage & green apple, a seam of passionfruit, **13** has enough personality & tasty freshness to handle a wide variety of dishes, even drink solo.

★★★★ **Blanc de Mer** ✓ 🍷 Riesling-strong with viognier, 3 others, aromatic **12** has wafting floral, peach & ginger scents, becoming more tropical on the palate, tangy-dry. Good enough to drink on its own.

Sans Barrique Chardonnay ★★★★ Showing chardonnay doesn't need oak, **12** has lovely citrus-fresh ripeness, a smooth, sleekly curvaceous body. — CR

Boucheron Wines

Location: Randburg ▪ WO: Stellenbosch ▪ Est 1996 ▪ 1stB 2012 ▪ Closed to public ▪ Owner(s) Fredy Pummer ▪ Cellarmaster(s) Nicholas Ridley (Sep 2011) ▪ 7t/2,288cs ▪ PO Box 870 Strathavon 2031 ▪ info@boucheron.co. za ▪ www.boucheron.co.za ▪ **T +27 (0)11-708-3444** ▪ F +27 (0)11-708-3615

Based in Randburg, Gauteng, Boucheron has grown from a boutique-wine merchant founded by Fredy Pummer in 1996 to a full-fledged producer of over 2,000 cases of fine own-label wines, overseen since 2011 by cellarmaster Nicholas Ridley.

White Merlot ▤ 🍷 ★★ One of tiny handful in this category, previewed pale blush **13** ex Helderberg vines is fresh, uncomplicated & austere, perfect for sushi. — GdB

Boutique Baratok

Location: Paarl ▪ Map: Paarl & Wellington ▪ Est 2012 ▪ Tasting, sales & cellar tours daily ▪ Fee R20pp ▪ Closed on pub hols ▪ Restaurant ▪ Tour groups ▪ Farm produce ▪ Conferences ▪ Owner(s) Alex Boraine & Daniël

Langenhoven ▪ Cellarmaster(s)/winemaker(s)/viticulturist(s) Daniël Langenhoven & Alex Boraine ▪ (cinsaut, grenache, ptage, shiraz, chard, chenin, viog) ▪ 27t/200,000L own label 60% red 40% white; 90,000L for clients + 480,000L bulk ▪ Brands for clients: Bestvino Cape, Roulou, Welgegund ▪ PO Box 668 Wellington 7654 ▪ admin@smlwines.com ▪ www.laskawine.com ▪ S 33° 44' 34.93" E 018° 57' 44.98" ▪ **T +27 (0)84-582-6376/+27 (0)82-375-0519/+27 (0)78-154-8929** ▪ F +27 (0)86-675-4372

Alex Boraine and Daniel Langenhoven, respectively co-owner and cellarmaster of Welgegund Wines, export most of their joint-venture wines, notably to China, though they recently appointed a local agent. The winery name, 'Friends', is from Hungary, source of most of the oak barrels used for maturation.

Bovlei Cellar ♟ ⅃

Location: Wellington ▪ Map: Paarl & Wellington ▪ WO: Western Cape/Wellington ▪ Est 1907 ▪ Tasting & sales Mon-Fri 9–5 Sat & pub hols 9–1 ▪ Closed Easter Fri/Sun, Dec 25/26 & Jan 1 ▪ Owner(s) 32 members ▪ Cellarmaster(s) Gert Boerssen ▪ Winemaker(s) Jacques Theron, Pieter-Niel Rossouw, Fritz Smit & Chris Smit ▪ Viticulturist(s) Marko Roux ▪ 3,130ha ▪ 31,000t/23m L ▪ PO Box 509 Wellington 7654 ▪ sales@wellingtonwines.com ▪ www.wellingtonwines.com ▪ S 33° 38' 18.4" E 019° 1' 54.2" ▪ **T +27 (0)21-873-1582** ▪ F +27 (0)21-864-1483

This venerable winery, founded 1907, recently amalgamated with Wellington Wines (itself a merger of Wellington Cooperative and Wamakersvallei). The belief is more can be offered by pooling resources than competing against each other, including a wide range of products and supply options. The combined entity has access to over 5,000 ha of vineyards, including some sought-after old bushvines.

Vineyard Selected range

★★★★ **Shiraz-Mourvèdre** ⊕ ⊠ Plenty of fruit & body on this New World-styled variation on a Rhône theme. **10** has 71% shiraz, elegantly plumped out by ripe, dark partner.
Cabernet Sauvignon ⊕ ⊠ ★★★★ **10** expresses ripeness in well-weighted & balanced structure. Approachable, unpretentious but satisfying. **Merlot** ⊕ ⊠ ★★★★ Focused, richly fruity **10** offers elegance, balance & good varietal character. Laudable effort at the price. **Pinotage** ⊕ ⊠ ★★★★ Subtlety triumphs over power in this well-restrained interpretation of variety; **10** is light bodied & fragrant. **Shiraz** ⊕ ⊠ ★★★★ **10** top-range release is a cut above previous, showing substance & elegance. Riper & fruitier than Winemakers Selection version.

Mad Hatter's range

Barbera ☺ ▤ ⊠ ★★★ Mainstay grape of Piedmont, North Italy gets a sunny local makeover in **12** easy sipper. Well worth a try. **Carignan** ☺ ▤ ★★★ Charmingly fresh & juicy **12** was aged in 4,000L oak *foudres*. Gush of red berries on light, spicy body.

Malbec ▤ ⊠ ★★★ Bordeaux black grape that Argentina adopted. Local **12** version is light & juicy. **Mourvèdre** ▤ ⊠ ★★★ Local expression of Spanish monastrell, **12** is pleasant quaffing but misses variety's punch & intensity. **Sangiovese** ▤ ⊠ ★★★ Tuscany's noble grape doesn't quite cut it in local **12** effort. **Roussanne-Grenache Blanc** ✓ ▤ ★★★★ Refreshingly different, **12** has lean, stylish body & texture with convincing varietal character.

Winemakers Selection

Cabernet Sauvignon ☺ ⊠ ★★★ Unpretentious but appealing **11** shows ripeness on palate after shy nose. Light in style, but well formed & refreshing. **Merlot** ☺ ⊠ ★★★ Fair depth & complexity on lightly conceived **12**. Pleasing ripe plum fruit, softly rendered tannins. Wellington WO. **Pinotage** ☺ ⊠ ★★★ Light & bright **11** has concentrated berry & pomegranate juiciness. **Shiraz** ☺ ⊠ ★★★ Shy, mild-mannered **11** offers gentle texture & juicy berry fruit, with spicy oak on finish. **Chardonnay** ▤ ⊠ ★★★ Unwooded **12** has aromatic citrus notes, generous body. **Chenin Blanc** ☺ ▤ ⊠ ★★★ Appealing fruit intensity & fresh acidity of **13** a notch above previous. Over-delivers on enjoyment. **Gewürztraminer** ☺ ▤ ⊠ ★★★ Fragrant rosepetal scent & spicy notes on **12** invite exotic food matches. Off-dry, with distinctive litchi fruit. **Sauvignon Blanc** ☺ ▤ ⊠ ★★★ Perky **13** has grassy notes on ripe passionfruit.

Vin Rouge ⊕ ▤ ★★ Ebullient NV poolside quaffer from pinotage in 500ml bottle. **Pinotage Rosé** ⊕ ▤ ★★★ Lightish, off-dry **12** is crisply fruity & cheerful. **Rosé** Untasted. **Vin Blanc** ⊕ ▤ ★★ NV easy picnic-style dry white in 500ml format. **Beaukett** ▤ ★★ Semi-sweet chenin/hanepoot NV cocktail-hour sipper. **Sparkling Pinotage Rosé Secco** ★★ Pleasantly fruity semi-sweet NV fizz. **Sparkling Brut** ⊕

★★★ Light & delightfully unpretentious **NV (12)** chenin-sauvignon with frothy mousse. **Special Late Harvest** Await new vintage. **Hanepoot Jerepiko** Not tasted. **Cape Ruby** ⊕ ★★★ Pleasant if very sweet **NV** fortified winter warmer from classic port varieties. — GdB

■ **Bradgate** see Jordan Wine Estate
■ **Brahms** see Domaine Brahms Wineries

Bramon Wines

Location/WO: Plettenberg Bay ▪ Map: Klein Karoo & Garden Route ▪ Est 2000 ▪ 1stB 2004 ▪ Tasting & sales daily 9–5.30 ▪ Fee R5/tasting glass, waived on wine purchase ▪ Closed Dec 25 ▪ Cellar tours by appt ▪ Restaurant ▪ Facilities for children ▪ Southern Crags Conservancy ▪ Owner(s) Private company ▪ Cellarmaster(s)/winemaker(s) Anton Smal (Feb 2010) ▪ Viticulturist(s) Peter Thorpe (2000) ▪ 10ha/6ha (chard, sauv) ▪ 50t/6,400cs own label 100% white ▪ PO Box 1606 Plettenberg Bay 6602 ▪ accounts@bramonwines.co.za ▪ www.bramonwines.co.za ▪ S 33° 57' 20.30" E 023° 28' 45.02" ▪ **T +27 (0)44-534-8007** ▪ F +27 (0)86-589-6816

Plettenberg Bay winegrowing pioneers Peter Thorpe and his Bramon team doubtless will be popping corks as they celebrate the tenth anniversary of their maiden bottling this year. Best known for sauvignon (still and sparkling), they were launching a new chardonnay méthode cap classique at press time, along with magnum (1.5 L) bottlings both of it and their stellar sauvignon bubbly.

★★★★ **The Crags Sauvignon Blanc** ✓ ▨ **13** tank sample tightly coiled, reflects area's maritime climate with tempered minerality & arresting acidity. Like **12**, needs time to unfurl its herbaceous charms.

★★★★☆ **Méthode Cap Classique** ✓ **08** bone-dry traditional-method sparkler from sauvignon gets better with each new disgorgement. Latest with appealing brioche, baked apple & mineral complexity, salty seabreeze tang & effortless elegance. Misses only an oyster knife. — HJ,CvZ

Brampton

Location/map: Stellenbosch ▪ WO: Coastal/Western Cape ▪ Est/1stB 1996 ▪ Tasting & sales Mon-Sat 10-7.30 ▪ Fee R25/3 wines R50/6 ▪ Closed Good Fri, Dec 25/26 & Jan 1 ▪ Light lunches 11.30-7; snacks & refreshments all day ▪ Owner(s) DGB (Pty) Ltd ▪ Winemaker(s) Bertho van der Westhuizen (Nov 2012) ▪ Viticulturist(s) Stephan Joubert (Nov 2006) ▪ 500t/80,000cs own label 40% red 55% white 5% rosé ▪ WIETA ▪ Private Bag X3 Groot Drakenstein 7680 ▪ brampton@dgb.co.za ▪ www.brampton.co.za ▪ S 33° 56' 17.42" E 018° 51' 38.08" ▪ **T +27 (0)21-883-9097**

Starting life in the Rustenberg cellars, and named for a champion Jersey bull, this DGB brand attracts the creative and 'green' to the Brampton Wine Studio, its recently redesigned and enlarged brand-home in Stellenbosch town centre. Here new winemaker Bertho van der Westhuizen's creations can be sampled with snacks or a light lunch, say managers Yolandi Carstens and Angelo van Dyk.

★★★★ **OVR** ⊕ 🍴 ▨ Sappy **10** now shiraz-led blend. Supple, structured & balanced, with appealing dusty spice undertone. Accessible earlier than **09**, with 3-4 years development.

Cabernet Sauvignon ✓ 🍴 ▨ ★★★★ **11**'s savoury flavours, firm tannins & dry conclusion perfect for solo sipping fireside or with food. **Shiraz** 🍴 ▨ ★★★★ Friendly **11** preview coffee/smoky whiffs, dense red fruit flavours, malleable tannin for now & a few years. **Rosé** 🍴 ▨ ★★★ Lightish (13% alcohol), zesty & softly dry **13** for all-day chilling. **Unoaked Chardonnay** 🍴 ▨ ★★★ Faint lemon, camphor & herb nuances on satisfyingly vinous **13**, pleasant but lacks excitement of previous. WO W Cape, as next. **Sauvignon Blanc** ✓ 🍴 ▨ ★★★★ A step up from **12** (★★★★), **13** tank sample concentrated guava & passionfruit, food-friendly grip, balance & moderate alcohol. Stylish any-occasion white. Discontinued: **Viognier**. — CvZ

Brandvlei Cellar

Location/map/WO: Worcester ▪ Est 1955 ▪ Tasting & sales Mon-Thu 8-5 Fri 8-4.30 Sat 9-1 ▪ Closed all pub hols ▪ Conferences ▪ Owner(s) 19 members ▪ Cellarmaster(s) Jean le Roux (Aug 1995) ▪ Winemaker(s) Willie Biggs (Sep 2009) & Daneel Jacobs (Sep 2007) ▪ Viticulturist(s) Danie Conradie (Sep 2004) ▪ 1,630ha (cab, ptage, chard, chenin, cbard, sauv) ▪ 28,500t 20% red 80% white ▪ PO Box 595 Worcester 6849 ▪ sales@bcwines.co.za ▪ www.bcwines.co.za ▪ S 33° 48' 19.5" E 019° 28' 8.1" ▪ **T +27 (0)23-340-4215** ▪ F +27 (0)23-340-4332

Baking under the Worcester sun, yet cold in winter when snow caps the Jonaskop peak that towers above it, grower-owned Brandvlei Cellar lies in a valley of fine-weather wines. The credo: quality wines that everyone can enjoy and afford. Four-fifths of their production is white wine, including a hanepoot jerepigo whose sweetness owes everything to that summer sun.

BC Wines range

Chardonnay ☺ 🗄 🖉 ★★★ Lightly oaked, **13** raises the bar with spicy lemon biscuit appeal, satisfying weight & length. Good solo or with food. **Chenin Blanc** ☺ 🗄 🖉 ★★★ Forthcoming guava nose, pineapple palate, chalky finish on zingy **13** dry quaffer.

Cabernet Sauvignon 🖉 ★★★ Very firm tannins, prunes & malt on fruit-sweet **12**. To match hearty meat dishes, like all the reds. **Shiraz** NEW 🗄 🖉 ★★ Bready nuances on cranberry-fresh **12**, assertive tannins need food. **Ruby Cabernet-Merlot** 🗄 🖉 ★★ **12** sturdy & fruit-filled; just right for pizzas & pastas. **Shiraz Rosé** 🗄 🖉 ★★ Strawberries-&-cream **13** a gently sweet picnic basket staple. **Bacchanté** 🗄 🖉 ★★ Light NV from gently sweet chenin has very light pear aromas. **Sauvignon Blanc** 🗄 🖉 ★★ Flowers & boiled sweets on easy-sipping **13**. **Hanepoot Jerepigo** ⑦ 🖉 ★★★ **11** fortified dessert is intensely raisined but uncloying. — DB, CvZ

◼ **Bredell's** see JP Bredell Wines

Breëland Winery

Location: Rawsonville ▪ Map: Breedekloof ▪ WO: Slanghoek ▪ Est 1825 ▪ 1stB 2010 ▪ Tasting, sales & cellar tours Mon-Sat by appt ▪ Fee R10pp tour & tasting ▪ Closed Ash Wed, Easter Fri-Mon, Ascension day, Dec 25 & Jan 1 ▪ Pre-booked lunches (5 days prior notice) ▪ BYO picnic ▪ Walks/hikes ▪ Mountain biking & 4x4 trails ▪ Conservation area ▪ Guest accommodation (mountain hut/farm house/camping) ▪ Owner(s) Kosie & Lizelle Marias ▪ Cellarmaster(s) Wickus Erasmus (Dec 2008) ▪ Winemaker(s) Wickus Erasmus (Dec 2008), with Jefry Fry (Jan 2009) ▪ Viticulturist(s) Wickus Erasmus, Kosie Marais ▪ 1,000ha/100ha (cab, cinsaut, ptage, shiraz, chenin, cbard, hanepoot, sauv, sem) ▪ 2,500t/500cs own label 20% red 80% white + 500cs for clients ▪ Brands for clients: Kaap Agri ▪ PO Box 26 Rawsonville 6845 ▪ wine@boegoekloof.co.za ▪ www.buchukloof.co.za ▪ S 33° 39' 2.87" E 019° 13' 40.08" ▪ **T +27 (0)23-344-3129** ▪ F +27 (0)86-562-6056

Blessed with immense unspoilt beauty, Kosie and Lizelle Marais' expansive and rejuvenated farm in Slanghoek Valley is a nature and sports lover's paradise, particularly for triathletes, archery enthusiasts, hikers and mountain bikers. The wines? Cellar chief Wickus Erasmus is especially thrilled with the as yet untasted 2009 sweet hanepoot from young vineyards.

Pinotage ☺ 🗄 🖉 ★★★ Lovely strawberry fruit, hint of vanilla oak on understated (for the variety) **11**. Vibrant, with pleasing tannic tug. **Sauvignon Blanc** NEW ☺ 🗄 🖉 ★★★ Cool & engaging blackcurrant tones, **13** zesty & lightish, nicely balanced for lunchtimes & fun times.

Cabernet Sauvignon Await next. **Chenin Blanc** NEW 🗄 🖉 ★★★ Semi-dry **13**'s peardrops, lemon sherbet & faint barley sugar bouquet, bright acidity hit all the right notes. Discontinued: **Sauvignon Blanc-Chenin Blanc**. — CvZ

Brenaissance

Location/map/WO: Stellenbosch ▪ 1stB 2010 ▪ Tasting Wed-Sun 11-5 ▪ Sales Wed-Sun 11-10 ▪ Pizza & wine pairing ▪ Café Blanc de Noir (see Restaurants section) ▪ Child friendly ▪ Conferences/functions ▪ Wedding chapel ▪ B&B (see Accommodation section) ▪ Boran cattle stud ▪ Owner(s) Tom & Hayley Breytenbach ▪ Winemaker(s) Various ▪ 58.23ha/31.65ha (cabs s/f, malbec, merlot, p verdot, shiraz, chard) ▪ 5,058cs own label 70% red 30% white ▪ Suite 3, Private Bag X4, Die Boord, Stellenbosch 7613 ▪ info@brenaissance.co.za ▪ www.brenaissance.co.za ▪ S 33° 55' 4.31" E 018° 49' 7.82" ▪ **T +27 (0)21-200-2537**

Under owners Tom and Hayley Breytenbach, this Devon Valley property has been transformed almost overnight from an anonymous Stellenbosch grape-growing farm into a wine and lifestyle destination. While the fruit is vinified off-site by winemaker specialists in each variety or style, the Breytenbachs have established a Boran cattle stud as part of their 'diversification and sustainable' agriculture practices on the estate. They also focus on serving food grown and made in the valley at their Café Blanc de Noir. All of this is hinted at in the winery's name: the French word for 'rebirth' preceded by 'B' for Breytenbach.

★★★★ **King of Clubs Cabernet Sauvignon** ① Focused **09** shows complexity: mint, cedar, cassis, black olive, tobacco, cigarbox; ripe & supple tannins for youthful enjoyment or cellaring.

Queen of Hearts Merlot ① ★★★ Plum & meat **10** juxtaposes ripe fruit & green leafy characters. **Jack of Diamonds Shiraz** ① ★★★★ Pepper & liquorice intro to **09**, brooding, tarry & smoky - needs time for dark fruit, muscular tannins to knit & develop. **Full House Bordeaux Style Blend** ① 🎨 ★★★ Herbaceous cabled **10** leaner, more elegant than single-variety reds in range; ready now. **Lord T Secret Blend** ① ★★★★ Engaging **NV**, heady spice & red fruit from 49% shiraz supported by acidity & tannins of malbec (31%), cab. **Knight of White Chardonnay** ① ★★★★ **10** for lovers of oaky style. Vanilla & butterscotch overlay to apple pie flavour; rather broad conclusion, could do with touch more acidity to boost vibrancy. **Lady H Sauvignon Blanc** ① ★★★ Food-friendly **11**, green apple & lime, lively & bright, with firm ripe flavours. — HJ,JP

■ **Brendel Collection** *see* Le Manoir de Brendel

Brenthurst Winery

Location: Paarl ▪ Est 1993 ▪ 1stB 1994 ▪ Open to public only by special appt ▪ Owner(s) José Jordaan ▪ Winemaker(s) Martin Fourie, assisted by José Jordaan ▪ Viticulturist(s) Johan Wiese (1991, consultant) ▪ 5ha (cabs s/f, merlot, p verdot) ▪ 15t ▪ PO Box 6091 Paarl 7622 ▪ martin@amatawines.co.za ▪ **T +27 (0)21-863-1154/1375, +27 (0)83-418-4110** ▪ F +27 (0)21-424-5666

Renewed enthusiasm positively bursts out of this tiny Paarl winery, after advocate, winegrower and keen guitarist José Jordaan's appointment of Martin Fourie as winemaker. 'Inspired by sounds from José Fender Strat,' the duo focussed on a Rhône blend in 2013, awaiting maturation of a 'fantastic' 2012 petit verdot (the farm's own) and shiraz.

■ **Brink Family** *see* Pulpit Rock Winery
■ **Broad Reach** *see* Devonvale Golf & Wine Estate
■ **Broken Rock** *see* Riebeek Cellars
■ **Broken Stone** *see* Slaley

Brothers Wines

Location: Cape Town ▪ WO: Western Cape ▪ Est/1stB 2005 ▪ Closed to public ▪ Owner(s) Greg Castle ▪ Cellarmaster(s)/winemaker(s) Greg Castle (2005) ▪ 10t/1,666cs own label 55% red 45% white ▪ PO Box 21681 Kloof Street Cape Town 8008 ▪ info@brotherswines.co.za ▪ www.brotherswines.com ▪ **T +27 (0)82-600-2555** ▪ F +27 (0)86-528-6081

Capetonian Greg Castle is an advocate of exposing more South Africans to the less snobbish side of wine and breaking down any intimidating perceptions. His focus is thus on domestic sales rather than exports. The Brothers range, named for sons Dylan and Alex, aims to please those simply wanting good value and quality.

Shiraz ★★★★ Hearty **11** flavoursome dark spice, savoury notes & fleshy underbelly. Some frisky tannins need time to calm, soften. Well-judged oak, 25% new. Retasted **09** less dense, but a bit jammy, shorter. No **10**. **Legacy** ① ★★★★ Well-crafted red blend **08** showing fine oak detail (all new for the 33% cab portion, half new for shiraz), plush fruit & supple tannins. For fireside philosophising. **Chardonnay** 🍷 ★★★★ **12** seduces with its rich oatmeal, whipped lemon butter tones; intensified by bright limy freshness, nudge of finishing sweetness. Like Shiraz, from Swartland fruit. **Sauvignon Blanc** ① 🍷 ★★★ Successfully aiming for lower-acid, riper tropical profile, **11** is fattish, well padded, more about mouthfeel than zip & pyrotechnics. — AL

Brunia Wines

Location: Stanford ▪ Map: Southern Cape ▪ WO: Walker Bay ▪ Est 2005 ▪ 1stB 2009 ▪ Tasting & sales by appt Tue-Sun 10-4 & daily during holidays ▪ Closed Dec 25/26 ▪ Light lunches, picnics & tractor rides ▪ Self-guided hiking trails ▪ Mountain biking ▪ Conservation area ▪ Owner(s) W P du Preez ▪ Winemaker(s) Kobie Viljoen (Gabriëlskloof) ▪ Viticulturist(s) Andrew Teubes (consultant) ▪ 417ha/17ha (pinot, shiraz, chard, sauv, sem) ▪ 75t/5,600cs own label 16% red 84% white ▪ PO Box 368 Stanford 7210 ▪ info@bruniawines.co.za ▪ www.bruniawines.co.za ▪ S 34° 28' 9.25" E 019° 39' 42.60" ▪ **T +27 (0)28-341-0432** ▪ F +27 (0)86-669-6064

Problems in the vineyards put paid to owner Willie du Preez's hope of a semillon blend last year, but happily a chardonnay and pinotage will debut this year.

Willie and wife Annetia have opened a wedding venue in 'just the right spot' on their Stanford farm, Cold Mountain, blessed with 300 ha of unspoilt fynbos.

★★★★ **Shiraz** ⊕ Peppery **10** (★★★) generously proportioned but short somewhat on finish & complexity compared with elegant & suave **09**.

Sauvignon Blanc ⊕ 🏠 ★★★★ Lime-scented **11** fine mineral fruit core, chalky finish & a steely dryness that shouts 'oysters!'. **10** (★★★★) flew with/to British Airways & UK's Wine Society. — WB,GdB

Bryan MacRobert Wines 🍷 [NEW]

Location: Malmesbury ▪ Map/WO: Swartland ▪ Est/1stB 2010 ▪ Tasting by appt only ▪ Closed all pub hols ▪ Owner(s) Bryan MacRobert ▪ Cellarmaster(s)/winemaker(s)/viticulturist(s) Bryan MacRobert (Jan 2010) ▪ (cinsaut, mourv, shiraz, chenin) ▪ 10t/1,100cs own label 45% red 45% white 10% rosé + 3,000cs for clients ▪ IPW ▪ c/o Meerhof R46 Riebeek Kasteel ▪ brymac84@gmail.com ▪ S 33° 29' 12.64" E 018° 38' 50.53" ▪ **T +27 (0)71-223-3129**

Bryan MacRobert's wine career may be short but it's full of promise. The first releases under his Tobias label were extremely well received, garnering worldwide acclaim. At the time he was working with Eben Sadie in the Swartland and Priorat, and he's since continued to produce small parcels of fine wine, focusing on old-vine chenin and cinsaut. In 2013 he helped make wine for fellow Swartland Independent member Nativo. The future holds an increase in production with an eye to establishing export markets.

Tobias range

★★★★ **Red Blend** ✓ Limpid, bone-dry savoury flavours, beautifully textured & gossamer fine, define **12** equal shiraz, mourvèdre, cinsaut, older oaked. Deft, assured, moreish. 'Made to be enjoyed' says creator, aptly.

Steen ✓ ★★★☆ Without trying too hard, **12** lightly oxidative chenin gets the basics right, delivering good honey-brushed varietal character & honest drinkability in a quietly delicious & satisfying package. — GdB, GM

▪ **Buckleberry** *see Louis*
▪ **Buddy** *see Overhex Wines International*

Buffalo Creek Wines 🍷🍷

Location: McGregor ▪ Map: Robertson ▪ Est/1stB 2005 ▪ Tasting, sales & cellar tours Mon-Fri 9-6 Sat 9-12.30 Sun by appt only ▪ Closed Easter Sun, Dec 25 & Jan 1 ▪ Owner(s) Leroy & Mark Tolmay ▪ Cellarmaster(s)/winemaker(s) Mark Tolmay (Jun 2005) ▪ 1,328ha/30ha (p verdot, ptage, pinot, merlot, chard, chenin, cbard, sauv) ▪ ±350-380t/500-600cs own label 65% red 25% white 10% rosé ▪ PO Box 124 McGregor 6708 ▪ info@ buffalocreek.co.za ▪ S 34° 0' 2.97" E 019° 53' 11.94" ▪ **T +27 (0)23-625-1727** ▪ F +27 (0)23-625-1727

For two decades, the Tolmay family name has been part of McGregor, where their boutique winery was established nine years ago. 'I discussed exporting when I was overseas recently,' says co-owner Leroy Tolmay, 'but the quantities demanded would mean I'd be sold out in three months. Perhaps in the future...'

Buitenverwachting 🍴🍷☕📷♿

Location: Constantia ▪ Map: Cape Peninsula ▪ WO: Constantia/Western Cape ▪ Est 1796 ▪ 1stB 1985 ▪ Tasting & sales Mon-Fri 9-5 Sat 10-3 ▪ Closed all pub hols ▪ Cellar tours by appt ▪ Buitenverwachting Restaurant (see Restaurants section) ▪ Deli & coffee shop ▪ Picnic area ▪ Conferences ▪ Owner(s) Richard & Sieglinde (Christine) Mueller, Lars Maack ▪ Cellarmaster(s) Hermann Kirschbaum (Jan 1993) ▪ Winemaker(s) Brad Paton (Jan 2005) ▪ Viticulturist(s) Peter Reynolds (Jan 2001) ▪ 147ha/105ha (cab, chard, sauv) ▪ 500t/200,000cs own label 8% red 90% white 2% rosé ▪ PO Box 281 Constantia 7848 ▪ info@buitenverwachting.com ▪ www.buitenverwachting.com ▪ S 34° 2' 30.4" E 018° 25' 1.5" ▪ **T +27 (0)21-794-5190/1** ▪ F +27 (0)21-794-1351

Buitenverwachting now offer a more pronounceable version of the name on their export labels: Bayten. But the wines, it is promised, remain 'beyond expectations' and hence true to the historic meaning. Although their popular commercial Buiten Blanc is produced in volume from bought-in fruit, Buitenverwachting is essentially a family-owned boutique winery diligently striving to produce the best possible quality product from its Constantia soils. The vineyards are now in the fourth year of a major replanting programme, with particular focus on sauvignon (a trio to taste for this edition). The estate is a sustainability pioneer, offering education and health facilities for the staff who live on the farm, and employing renewable energy sources and ecologically sound viticultural practices. Upgrades to the tasting facilities, which now include a coffee shop and deli, are complete.

★★★★ **Cabernet Sauvignon** Strapping tannins on austere **09** mask fruit flavours & need time to soften before broaching. Otherwise in classic mould, with spicy oak & attractive herbal edge to underlying fruit.

★★★★ **Cabernet Franc** ⏱ **09** (★★★★☆) last year showed rich spicy concentration, stern but fine tannins - all soaking up the mostly new French oak. Great young; better with time. **08** perhaps less complex.

★★★★ **Merlot** ⏱ Less flashy than many. **09** ripe spice, dark plum, bitter chocolate features welded & gripped by tight tannin. Well-judged oak; fresh, dry finishing. Should age well. Quieter **08** (★★★★).

★★★★☆ **Christine** Distinctive, classy **09** a masterpiece in seamlessness & balance in refined cab franc, cab, merlot blend. Lovely savoury edge to tightly wound dark fruit, complemented by spicy oak tannins (all-new barrels). Needs cellaring to reveal full charms.

★★★★ **Chardonnay** ✓ Deliciously fresh, creamy & concentrated barrel-fermented **12** (★★★★☆) has better integration of spicy oak & layered citrus fruit than **11**. Fine quality shows on long, flavoursome finish.

★★★★☆ **Husseys Vlei Sauvignon Blanc** Extra dimension in this single-site bottling not immediately apparent, as **12**'s youthfully herbaceous wintergreen tone dissipates to reveal softer side: complex, juicy mélange of rich citrus fruit, sustained by commendable texture & minerality.

★★★★ **Sauvignon Blanc** 🖪 🧱 Immediate, vibrant appeal in excellent **12** (★★★★☆) showing greater poise & grace than **11** in its succulently layered flavours. Small daches of nouvelle & semillon help endow this with enough personality to upstage the others in the trio of sauvignons.

★★★★☆ **3rd Time Lucky** NEW Superb example of Constantia viognier, barrel-fermented & -matured **12** has beautifully integrated oak, with none of variety's blowsiness. Complex, spicy peachiness ends properly dry, firm - & quite delicious.

★★★★ **Méthode Cap Classique Brut** Bottle-fermented bubbly, mostly chardonnay with splash pinot noir, offers easy charm & grace. Enough creamy complexity & dimension to warrant higher rating than last **NV**.

Meifort ✓ ★★★★ Similar blend to Christine's. Impressively rich **09** trumps **08** (★★★★). Excellent value in classic Bordeaux style. Skillful oaking gives structure for food & serious fun. **Blanc de Noir** 🖪 ★★★ Crisply lean, just-dry & structured **12** from Bordeaux varieties. For more thoughtful summer sipping. **Maximus** ★★★★ Softer, more accessible than imposing name suggests. Seriously oaked **11** sauvignon has pretty floral appeal, more depth than maiden **09** (★★★☆), which had some semillon. Ripeness supported by finely judged oak spice. No **10**. **Buiten Blanc** ⏱ 🖪 ★★★★ Ever-popular sauvignon-led blend with chenin, splashes viognier, semillon. **12** brims with delicious fruity acids, extra breadth from minor partners. WO W Cape. **Batavia** ⏱ ★★★☆ Experimental, one-off riesling, oaked viognier, chenin blend. Freshness & silken viscosity on off-dry **09**. **1769** Await next. Discontinued: **G**. — IM

BurCon Wines

Location/map/WO: Robertson ▪ 1stB 2004 ▪ Tasting by appt only Tue-Fri 9-4 Sat/Sun 10-2 ▪ Restaurant ▪ Conferences ▪ Farm produce ▪ Facilities for children & tour groups ▪ Walks/hikes ▪ Mountain biking & guided horseback trails ▪ Owner(s) Frans & Amanda Conradie, Renée Burger ▪ Winemaker(s) Christie Steytler (Feb 2004, Roodezandt) ▪ 234ha/25ha (ptage, shiraz, muscadel) ▪ 16t/2,500cs own label ▪ PO Box 86 Robertson 6705 ▪ info@nerinaguestfarm.com ▪ www.nerinaguestfarm.com ▪ S 33° 50′ 5.2″ E 019° 45′ 55.3″ ▪ **T +27 (0)23-626-2012/+27 (0)82-823-4231** ▪ F +27 (0)23-626-2012

Nerina Guest Farm's BurCon house wines aren't taken too seriously, co-owner Amanda Conradie reports, except perhaps by the bank manager, who, she says, feels ill every time he thinks about them. The unusual brand name commemorates the marriage of a Burger into the Conradie family.

Oompie se Oeps ⏱ 🖪 ★★ Unwooded **NV** pinotage & shiraz (co-planted in error - oops!) plummy fruit & spice. **Miskien Christien** ⏱ ★★★ Rich fortified red muscadel, **09** unctuous & honeyed, in 2L pack. — JP,CvZ

Burgershof

Location/WO: Robertson ▪ Est 1864 ▪ 1stB 2000 ▪ Closed to public ▪ Sales at La Verne, Robertson & Wine Boutique, Ashton ▪ Owner(s) HJ Reynecke ▪ Cellarmaster(s)/winemaker(s)/viticulturist(s) Hennie Reynecke (Jan 1979) ▪ 68ha (cab, merlot, muscadel r/w, ptage, ruby cab, shiraz, chard, chenin, cbard, sauv) ▪ IPW ▪ PO Box 72 Klaasvoogds River 6707 ▪ burgershof@barvallei.co.za ▪ **T +27 (0)23-626-5433** ▪ F +27 (0)23-626-5433

This is a fourth-generation winefarm which has successfully made the transition from traditional Cape specialities (fortified desserts) to modern, market-ready varietal wines - mainly for Dutch supermarket chain Jumbo, but also to be found at local wine shops La Verne (Robertson) and Wine Boutique (Ashton).

Pinotage ☺ 🍴 ★★★ Single vineyard, as are the rest except cab/shiraz. Sappy red berries in **13** preview, nice fresh varietal purity. **Cabernet Sauvignon-Shiraz** ☺ ★★★ Equal blend in **12**, offers plush ripe berries, juicy-fresh drinkability.

Merlot 🍴 📖 ★★ Meaty tones in **12**'s juicy red fruit make it food friendly. **Chardonnay** 🍴 ★★★ Unwooded **13** ex-tank shows melon & gentle peach flavours, softly rounded body, good fresh finish. **Sauvignon Blanc** 🍴 📖 ★★ Crisply dry **13** has light-textured herby styling. — CR

■ **Bush Camp** *see* Landskroon Wines
■ **Bushman's Creek** *see* Wines of Cape Town

Bushmanspad Estate

Location: Bonnievale ▪ Map/WO: Robertson ▪ Est 2000 ▪ 1stB 2006 ▪ Tasting & sales Mon-Fri 8.30–5 ▪ Fee R15/ 6 wines ▪ BYO picnic ▪ Walks/hikes ▪ 4-star B&B/self-catering cottages ▪ Owner(s) Menno Schaafsma ▪ Cellarmaster(s)/winemaker(s)/viticulturist(s) Arthur Basson (Feb 2011) ▪ 52ha (cabs s/f, malbec, merlot, mourv, shiraz, sauv) ▪ 400t own label 80% red 15% white 5% rosé ▪ PO Box 227 Bonnievale 6705 ▪ info@ bushmanspad.co.za ▪ www.bushmanspad.co.za ▪ S 33° 53' 55.0" E 020° 11' 46.7" ▪ **T +27 (0)23-616-2961** ▪ F +27 (0)86-268-3756

Although roadworks made logistics tricky when it came to transporting the picking team from Swellendam to this Bonnievale farm in the folds of the Langeberg on time every day, winemaker Arthur Basson declared harvest 2013 one of the best in a decade and the resultant wines 'lovely'. There's been strong growth in sales following a marketing drive in China.

Bushmanspad range

★★★★ **The Menno** 📖 Shiraz-led mix, only in best years. Berry-rich **12** has a supple texture, its savoury seam adding complexity, flavour, definition, & promising a future. No **10**, **11**.
Cabernet Sauvignon 📖 ★★★ With ripe dark berries, vibrantly juicy **12** has the ideal supple tannins & smooth texture for everyday drinking. **Cabernet Franc** 📖 ★★★ Plush red berries, a whiff of dried herbs, **12**'s firm dry tannin structure shows the potential for ageing a few years. **Malbec** 📖 ★★★ Smoky dark-toned **12** has salty liquorice spicing, attractive succulent smoothness. Drinks easily & well. **Rosé** ⊕ 🍴 ★★★ Attractive strawberry & floral notes on dry, crisp **12**, satisfying summer sipper. **Sauvignon Blanc** 🍴 📖 ★★★★ With lemongrass & some flinty notes, elegant **13** show nice varietal purity, palate appeal.

Red Gold range

Shiraz 📖 ★★★ After impressing with its ripeness & black cherry fruit density, **12** follows through with a smooth, round texture. **Blend** NEW 📖 ★★★ Merlot-led Bordeaux blend, dab of shiraz gives **12** cassis & meaty flavours, & a savoury dryness ideal for rich dishes. — CR

■ **Butcher Shop & Grill** *see* The Butcher Shop & Grill
■ **Buthelezi** *see* Signal Hill Wines
■ **BWC Wines** *see* Catherine Marshall Wines
■ **By Norwegians** *see* Nordic Wines
■ **Cabrière** *see* Haute Cabrière
■ **Café Collection** *see* FirstCape Vineyards

Café Culture

A still and a sparkling wine now make up this KWV 'coffee pinotage' label, noted for its bright and funky packaging.

Pinotage 🍴 📖 ★★ **12** has cappuccino flavours in a fun, smoothly fruity base. **ChocMousse** ★★ Sweet **NV** mocha-toned fizz from pinotage. — CR

Calais Wine Estate

Location: Paarl ▪ Map: Paarl & Wellington ▪ WO: Paarl/Wellington ▪ Est/1stB 2000 ▪ Tasting by appt ▪ Sales daily 8-4 ▪ Guest accommodation ▪ Owner(s) Calais Wine Estate shareholders ▪ Winemaker(s)/viticulturist(s) Helene van der Westhuizen ▪ 23ha (cab, merlot, p verdot, ptage, ruby cab, shiraz, chard, chenin, sauv) ▪ 150t/ 3,000cs own label 90% red 10% white ▪ PO Box 9006 Klein Drakenstein 7628 ▪ info@calais.co.za ▪ www. calais.co.za ▪ S 33° 42' 32.1" E 019° 1' 24.6" ▪ **T +27 (0)21-868-3888** ▪ F +27 (0)21-868-1400

It may date back to 1692, when French Huguenot Jean Manje named this Berg River Valley farm after his home town, but Calais prefers to highlight its 'proactive young management', who are restructuring the portfolio into flagship Klein Valley (inspired by Old World elegance) and Calais (New World fruitiness) ranges.

Klein Valley range [NEW]

St Katerina Barrel Fermented Viognier 📝 ★★★ Attractive, peachy **13** has some richness & texture, sufficient acidity to refresh the creamy finish.

Calais range

Merlot In abeyance, as for **Petit Verdot**, **Pinotage**, **Shiraz** & **Cape Riesling**. **Applause** ★★ **09** raisined & porty blend of cab & shiraz. **Bel Canto** ★★ **10** very ripe & savoury cab-led 4-way blend with firm tannins. **Chardonnay** 🍴 📝 ★★ Unoaked **13** straightforward easy-drinker with tropical pineapple flavour. Wellington WO. **Chenin Blanc** ⊕ ★★ Easy **10** attractive & restrained, but a warming finish. **Sauvignon Blanc** 🍴 📝 ★★ Lightly tropical **13** for uncomplicated quaffing. Wellington WO. Discontinued: **Cabernet Sauvignon**. — IM

Calitzdorp Cellar

Location/WO: Calitzdorp ▪ Map: Klein Karoo & Garden Route ▪ Est 1928 ▪ 1stB 1976 ▪ Tasting & sales Mon-Fri 8-5 Sat 8-1 ▪ Closed Good Fri & Dec 25 ▪ Cellar tours by appt ▪ Tour groups ▪ Farm produce ▪ Picnics/meals by appt; or BYO picnic ▪ Conferences ▪ Succulent garden ▪ Owner(s) 39 members ▪ Cellarmaster(s) Alwyn Burger (1990) ▪ Winemaker(s) Alwyn Burger (1990), with Abraham Pretorius ▪ Viticulturist(s) Johannes Mellet (2005, consultant) ▪ 286ha (13 varieties, r/w) ▪ 5,000t/7,000cs own label 12% red 88% white ▪ IPW ▪ PO Box 193 Calitzdorp 6660 ▪ manager@calitzdorpwine.co.za ▪ www.calitzdorpwine.co.za ▪ S 33° 32' 18.9" E 021° 41' 10.6" ▪ **T +27 (0)44-213-3301** ▪ F +27 (0)44-213-3328

Having helped Calitzdorp Cellar grow into a substantial business pressing 5,000 tons a year, cellarmaster and veteran of 24 harvests here Alwyn Burger is proud that ongoing training for his 'rainbow nation' team is boosting quality substantially. Heavy rain during the 2013 crush meant no sauvignon blanc, their top-selling white. 'A difficult harvest generally but some nice wines nonetheless.'

★★★★ **Hanepoot** Floral fortified dessert **12** (★★★★) with rich bouquet of honey & caramel, unctuous flavours of dried pear. Delicious, though misses cloying tanginess of **10**, tasted out of vintage sequence.

★★★★ **Hanepoot-Muskadel Reserve** ⊕ 📝 Fortified delight from equal portions muscats de Frontignan & d'Alexandrie, **10** pure fruit, great intensity & poise courtesy zesty acidity. Rivals the region's finest.

★★★★ **White Muscadel** One of Klein Karoo's finest, always fragrant & spicy. **12** fortified dessert is exuberant, curvaceous, perfectly balanced. Shows same liquid sunshine character as last-tasted **10**.

★★★★ **Golden Jerepigo** ✓ Usually the 'junior' version of Hanepoot-Muskadel Reserve but latest **NV** very much its equal. Delicious raisins & honey, sweet but firm, some floral scents to pour over ice or share round a fire.

Cape Ruby ☺ ★★★ Latest **NV** port-style is particularly charming & drinkable, as a ruby should be. Chocolates & dates, warm raisiny afterglow. Equal tinta & touriga; also in 375 ml.

Cabernet Sauvignon 📝 ★★ **12** cherry fruit & sweet vanilla overlay from brief oaking (as most reds here). 'Perfect with ostrich' says cellarmaster. **Merlot** ⊕ 📝 ★★ Brief **11** mainly spicy oak aromas, some plums peeping through. **Pinotage** ⊕ 📝 ★★ Unusual (but tasty) curry-spiced strawberry jam character on **11**, soft & juicy. **Shiraz** 🍴 ★★ **12**'s drinkablity upped by sweet rock candy character, tobacco notes & chalky tannins. **Touriga Nacional** ⊕ 📝 ★★★ **10** scented with roses & vanilla, firm tannins cushioned by actual sugar & sweetening effect of high alcohol. **Rosé** 🍴 📝 ★★ Gently sweet **NV** sipper, floral notes from viognier, colour & strawberry taste from splash shiraz. **Chardonnay** ⊕ 🍴 📝 ★★★ Very subdued **11** not quite up to speed of previous. **Sauvignon Blanc** Await next. **Red Muscadel** ★★★★ Enticing raisins & boiled sweets on spicy **NV** fortified dessert with tangy raspberry flavours a shade less long-lingering than previous. **Cape Vintage** ✓ ★★★★ Equal touriga & tinta in port-style **11** marked by lower fortification, higher sugar than previous. Well rounded, tannins & spirit giving form to plum pudding body. — GdB,JP

Callender Peak

Location: Ceres ▪ WO: Western Cape ▪ Est/1stB 2007 ▪ Closed to public ▪ Owner(s) MacDonald & Jeffrey families ▪ Cellarmaster(s)/winemaker(s) Johan Kruger (whites, consultant) & Clive Torr (reds, consultant) ▪ Viticulturist(s) Willem Mouton (1990) ▪ 2ha (cab, merlot, pinot, chard) ▪ 2t/400cs own label 50% red 50% white ▪ clivetorrwines@mweb.co.za ▪ **T +27 (0)82-557-0826**

Extreme vineyards on the higher reaches of the Winterhoek Mountains near Ceres yield a tiny crop of individualistic fruit, vinified on contract. Things don't always go to plan, but when they do, some very interesting wines result.

Callender Peak range

★★★★ **Chardonnay** Heavily oaked & oxidatively styled, with beeswax & marzipan at finish, **11** (★★★☆) is taut & restrained, with underlying citrus, after more forceful **10**.

Cabernet Sauvignon Next awaited. **Merlot** In abeyance, like **Pinot Noir. Sauvignon Blanc** ★★★☆ Wild spicy notes on **12** attest to natural barrel fermentation. Seriously conceived, full & rich, with satisfying fatness. — GdB

Camberley Wines

Location/map/WO: Stellenbosch ▪ Est 1990 ▪ 1stB 1996 ▪ Tasting & sales Mon-Sat & pub hols 9–5 Sun 9-3 ▪ Fee R40 max (depending on wine choice), waived on purchase ▪ Closed Dec 25 & Jan 1 ▪ Cellar tours by appt ▪ Lunch/refreshments by appt; or BYO picnic ▪ Boule court for hire ▪ B&B guest cottage ▪ Owner(s) John & Gaël Nel ▪ Winemaker(s) John Nel ▪ Viticulturist(s) Bennie Booysen ▪ 7ha (cabs s/f, merlot, p verdot, ptage, shiraz, touriga) ▪ ±35t/6,400cs own label 100% red ▪ PO Box 6120 Uniedal 7612 ▪ john@camberley.co.za ▪ www.camberley.co.za ▪ S 33° 55' 8.9" E 018° 55' 58.3" ▪ **T +27 (0)21-885-1176** ▪ F +27 (0)21-885-1822

Ebullient John Nel and family's passionate hobby has evolved into a wine destination well worth a visit for big wines of personality and voluptuous intensity. The spectacularly situated property on Stellenbosch's Helshoogte Pass, overlooking Banhoek Valley, has a welcoming, homely charisma setting it apart. The red-wine (and -bubbly) specialists' newest offering is a cab franc.

Camberley Wines range

★★★★ **Philosophers' Stone 10** cab franc-based Bordeaux blend, with usual big, bold, extracted richness. The high alcohol (nearly 16%!) is kept fresh with poised bright red berry fruit, good dry tannins, integrated oak.

★★★★ **Cabernet Sauvignon-Merlot 10** in bold house style with ripeness in complex layers of dark & red fruit. Bright freshness on the nose & palate harmonises oak, acid & very big alcohol.

★★★★ **Cabernet Franc** NEW **10** has trademark alcoholic kick, but with attractive leafy blackcurrant, layers of tobacco & dark berry leading to plush, powerful end. Decanting or time needed.

Cabernet Sauvignon Reserve Occasional release, as is **Elm Tree Merlot** & **Charisma**. **Pinotage** ★★★☆ **12** youthful, dense & massive, with obvious 15% alcohol. Needs a few years to unravel ripe fruit hinted at by banana loaf notes. **Shiraz** Await next, as for **Sparkling Shiraz** & **Elixir Fortified Red**.

Prohibition range

Red ★★★ NV blend like a light port, with big alcohol, dryish end. **White** Await next. — JP

Cameradi Wines

Location: Wellington ▪ Est 1999 ▪ 1stB 2000 ▪ Closed to public ▪ Owner(s) Stelvest cc (Nic Swingler, Hendrik du Preez & Casper Lategan) ▪ Winemaker(s) Casper Lategan (Jan 1999) ▪ 2t/260cs own label 100% red ▪ 48 Bain Str Wellington 7655 ▪ cas@lategans.co.za ▪ **T +27 (0)21-873-1225** ▪ F +27 (0)21-873-4910

One of the quieter (and smaller) parts of the garagiste winemaker scene... but we hope for more to emerge from the cellar behind co-owner/winemaker Casper Lategan's Wellington house.

Capaia Wine Estate

Location/WO: Philadelphia ▪ Map: Durbanville, Philadelphia & Darling ▪ Est 1997 ▪ 1stB 2003 ▪ Tasting, sales & cellar tours Mon-Fri 8-5 Sat/Sun on request ▪ Closed all pub hols ▪ Tour groups ▪ Mountain bike trail ▪ Mariella's restaurant ▪ Owner(s) Ingrid Baronin von Essen ▪ Cellarmaster(s) Bernabé Strydom (Oct 2006), assisted by Stephan von Neipperg (consultant) ▪ Winemaker(s) Adriaan Burger (Oct 2010) ▪ Viticulturist(s) Schalk du Toit (2009, consultant) ▪ 140ha/60ha (cabs s/f, merlot, p verdot, shiraz, sauv) ▪ 260t/26,000cs own label 85% red 15% white ▪ IPW ▪ PO Box 25 Philadelphia 7304 ▪ info@capaia.co.za ▪ www.capaia.co.za, www.capaia.com ▪ S 33° 42' 45.9" E 018° 34' 6.9" ▪ **T +27 (0)21-972-1081** ▪ F +27 (0)21-972-1894

No expense was spared when establishing this wine estate on the slopes of a Philadelphia hillside where only wheat had grown before. In 2003, Germans Alexander and Ingrid von Essen saw the first vintage off their superb young vineyards, vinified in the magnificent new cellar. Ten years later Ingrid von Essen assumed sole ownership. At press time a fine-dining restaurant, Mariella's, was set to open in the renovated 250-year-old farmhouse.

★★★★ **Merlot-Cabernet Sauvignon** 🕓 🖾 Intense & plush **10**, demure dark fruit, beautifully managed tannins, some spice, textured elegance. Showy yet restrained. Firmer than softly ripe **09** (★★★★).

★★★★ **ONE** 🖾 Flagship from petit verdot & cab with merlot, cab franc & 11% shiraz. Intense black fruit with restrained herbal & tomato notes on **10** (★★★★), savoury, but chunkier, less fresh than **09**.

★★★★ **Sauvignon Blanc** ✓ 🖾 Stylistic variations on the 2 tasted. **13** delivers fresh, limy focus & mineral purity, while **12** (★★★) is more herbaceous & dull, its pulpy textures lacking finesse. — MF

■ **Cap du Vin** *see Bellevue Estate Stellenbosch*
■ **Cape Elephant** *see Lutzville Cape Diamond Vineyards*
■ **Cape Auction** *see Jonkheer*
■ **Cape Avocet** *see Rooiberg Winery*

Cape Chamonix Wine Farm

Location/map/WO: Franschhoek ▪ Est 1991 ▪ 1stB 1992 ▪ Tasting & sales Mon-Sat 9.30-4.30 Sun 9.30-4 ▪ Fee R20 ▪ Closed Dec 25 & Jan 1 ▪ Cellar tours by appt ▪ Restaurant T +27 (0)21-876-2393 ▪ Conservation area ▪ Fully equipped self-catering cottages ▪ Owner(s) Chris Hellinger ▪ Cellarmaster(s)/viticulturist(s) Gottfried Mocke (Sep 2001) ▪ Winemaker(s) Gottfried Mocke (Sep 2001) & Emul Ross (Jun 2011) ▪ 300ha/50ha (cabs s/f, malbec, merlot, p verdot, ptage, pinot, chard, chenin, sauv, sem) ▪ 220-250t/40,000cs own label 60% red 40% white ▪ IPW ▪ PO Box 28 Franschhoek 7690 ▪ marketing@chamonix.co.za ▪ www.chamonix.co.za ▪ S 33° 53' 60.0" E 019° 7' 34.0" ▪ **T +27 (0)21-876-8400** ▪ F +27 (0)21-876-3237

Chamonix was originally part of the La Cotte farm – the first one granted to Huguenot refugees in what was to become known as Franschhoek Valley. This section has belonged to German businessman Chris Hellinger since 1991. The mostly unirrigated vines are on mountain slopes – the altitude no doubt a reason for the quality of fruit vinified by Gottfried Mocke and Emul Ross. But Mocke's tenure since 2002 reveals that hard and intelligent work in vineyard and winery are also vital - the originality of his uniquely vinified pinotage is one example of an approach that has seen Chamonix rising to the highest levels in Cape wine in the past dozen years. Now, he says, upgraded facilities 'allow for gentler bottlings', while there are 'new plantings on promising sites on the farm'.

Reserve range

★★★★★ **Pinot Noir** Restrained, well-delineated **12** (★★★★★) less flamboyant than **11**. Precise raspberry aromas with floral & attractive Asian spice notes. Youthfully tight, needing 5+ years to open & evolve. Natural ferment, integrated oaking (50% new French) give great succulence; a fine soft tannin structure.

★★★★★ **Troika** Depth, class & complexity on **11** (★★★★★) Bordeaux blend, now from 85% cab franc – more than **10**, with dollops cab, merlot. Dark fruit & lead pencil aromas, the palate tightly woven - ripe yet fresh. 60% new oak is present but not intrusive. Beautifully poised & has real interest; with many years to go.

★★★★★ **Chardonnay** Restrained & very fine nose of apple blossom & crushed stones impresses on **12**. Nothing out of place or obvious - an incredibly subtle wine, yet with an extremely long, intense finish. 70% new oak already fully integrated & invisible. As usual, many years maturation will benefit.

★★★★★ **White** 12 (★★★★☆) same 60:40 blend of sauvignon & semillon as 11, 11 months in oak, half new. Restrained notes of vanilla-infused yellow fruit, stone, herbaceousness. Fresh, but still very youthful & tight, with crisp acidity, & needs a few years to start expressing itself fully.

Discontinued: **Sauvignon Blanc**.

Cape Chamonix range

★★★★ **Cabernet Sauvignon** Subtle, youthful 11 still showing primary aromas. Classically moulded as usual, crisp & vibrant, with finely grained, grippy tannin. A little petit verdot adds to the incipient complexity.

★★★★☆ **Greywacke Pinotage** Ripe aromas & a touch of oak on 11. Intense flavours of dark fruit, toasty oak (just 30% new). Like 10 (★★★★★), complex mix of early picked & desiccated grapes - 13% of them pinot.

★★★★ **Chardonnay** Remarkable 12 (★★★★★) a step up on 11. Vanilla, pear & honeysuckle notes predominate, with apricot & minerals on the palate. There's considerable weight & intensity, but lifted by a vibrant acidity. 50% new oak very well integrated.

★★★★ **Sauvignon Blanc** 🏳 Emphatic 13 ex tank offers aromas of nettle, green fig & minerals. Needs a few years to open out - still notably fresh & taut, the acidity accentuated by green-fruit flavours. As with more complex previewed 12 (★★★★☆), includes a small oak-fermented portion.

Rouge 🏳 ★★★★ Finely textured 10 4-way Bordeaux blend shows plummy, savoury fruit with smoky undertones. Approachable now, but no hurry. **Unoaked Chardonnay** NEW 🏳 ★★★☆ Uncomplicated, easygoing 13, pre-bottling is unpretentious but with sufficient intensity & complexity. Fresh, with lingering flavours. **MCC Blanc de Blancs** Await next. Discontinued: **Blanc**. — JPf

Cape Classics

Location: Somerset West ▪ Map: Helderberg ▪ WO: Western Cape ▪ Est 1991 ▪ 1stB 1996 ▪ Tasting by appt only ▪ Owner(s) André Shearer ▪ Winemaker(s) Bruwer Raats (May 2010) ▪ 240,000cs own label 45% red 55% white ▪ PO Box 1695 Somerset West 7129 ▪ info@capeclassics.com ▪ www.capeclassics.com, www.indabawines.com, www.jamjarwines.com ▪ S 34° 4' 5.9" E 018° 53' 38.2" ▪ **T +27 (0)21-847-2400** ▪ F +27 (0)21-847-2414

Founded on export and distribution of premium local wines to the US market, Somerset West-based Cape Classics is also the force behind the successful affordably priced Indaba and Jam Jar wines. The Indaba selections, including a new Bordeaux blend, now appear in new packaging designed to emphasise sustainability and handcrafting, while 'Jam Jar Moscato' has become 'Jam Jar Sweet White' to better link it to its elder sibling and allow for flexibility to explore the sweet side of other varietals'. A desire to nurture the 'rainbow wine nation' underpins Indaba's well-established Scholarship, administered with Stellenbosch University, providing educational support and lifeskills to deserving and financially needy viticulture and oenology students.

Indaba range

Merlot ☺ 🏳 📖 ★★★ Plush, ripe red fruit brings appeal to 12 anytime sipper. Light but supple, with pleasing finish. **Mosaic** NEW ☺ 🏳 📖 ★★★ Cab-led Bordeaux-style blend, debut 12 is fresh & juicy. **Chardonnay** ☺ 🏳 📖 ★★★ Light-bodied 12 is oaked, but tends towards fresh & fruity style. Robertson & Swartland grapes. **Sauvignon Blanc** ☺ 🏳 📖 ★★★ Hint of anise on brisk, taut 13 ex Robertson, with focused green apple fruit & gentle acid grip.

Chenin Blanc 🏳 📖 ★★★ Ripe tropical & stonefruit in easy-drinking, characterful 12. Discontinued: **Shiraz**.

Jam Jar range

Sweet Shiraz 🏳 📖 ★★ Undemanding candy-sweet offering, 13 is true to name. **Sweet White** 🌡 🏳 📖 ★★ Was 'Moscato'. Spicy, low-alcohol 11 non-spritzy muscat for the sweeter tooth. — GdB

■ **Cape Colony** *see* Malanot Wines
■ **Cape Diamond** *see* Lutzville Cape Diamond Vineyards
■ **Cape Discovery** *see* Waterstone Wines
■ **Cape Diversity** *see* Withington

Cape Dreams ♀

Location/map/WO: Robertson ▪ Est/1stB 2009 ▪ Tasting & cellar tours by appt ▪ Owner(s) Bunty Khan ▪ Cellarmaster(s) André van Dyk ▪ 600ha (cab, merlot, ptage, shiraz, chard, chenin, sauv) ▪ 60% red 40% white ▪ ISO 9001, HACCP, BEE, BWI ▪ croftsales@telkomsa.net, info@croftsales.co.za ▪ www.croftsales.co.za ▪ S 33° 46' 35.3" E 019° 45' 42.9" ▪ **T +27 (0)21-531-2016/+27 (0)83-792-7638/+27 (0)71-898-7923**

Wine lover and former marketing and supply chain project manager Bunty Khan dreams of an internationally recognised wine brand which also nurtures aspiring talent, especially among rural youth. Repeat sales overseas and recent expansion into Europe, Russia and Mauritius, plus ongoing local listings at Game and Makro, move her ever closer to the goal.

Reserve range [NEW]

Cabernet Sauvignon 🉑 ★★★ Ripe **11** more fig, prune & Xmas cake than blackcurrant & lead pencil, but powerful tannic grip is unmistakably cab. **Pinotage** 🉑 ★★★★ **11** plump strawberry fruit, creamy oak & banana notes, supple enough to uncork now or keep few years. **Shiraz** 🉑 ★★★★ **11** quite serious: dense fruit, malleable tannins for early enjoyment & brisk acidity for palate refreshment.

Cape Dreams range

Cabernet Sauvignon ☺ 🉑 ★★☆ Food-friendly **12** offers mulberry fruit, creamy texture & long, clean finish. **Shiraz** ☺ 🉑 ★★★ **12** quite the charmer: dark, shapely, wears spicy perfume. Why resist?

Merlot ⏧ 🉑 ★★ Stalky, lightish **11** has dusty plum fruit. **Pinotage** 🉑 ★★★ Smoke & variety's hallmark banana on crisp & dry **12**. **Pinotage Rosé** New bottling not ready, as for **Chenin Blanc**. **Chardonnay** 🍷 🉑 ★★★ Citrus tang makes unwooded **13** refreshing poolside sipper. **Sauvignon Blanc** ⏧ 🉑 ★★ **12** lively if brief appley flavours, hint of sweetness in tail. — CvZ,DB

▪ **Cape Grace** *see* African Pride Wines
▪ **Cape Hill** *see* Stellenrust

Cape Hutton ♀ ♂ 📷

Location/map: Stellenbosch ▪ WO: Stellenbosch/Western Cape ▪ Est 2003 ▪ 1stB 2004 ▪ Tasting, sales & cellar tours by appt 8-4.30 ▪ Weddings/functions ▪ Owner(s)/viticulturist(s) Gerrit & Lesley Wyma ▪ Winemaker(s) Piet Smal (cab), Wynand Hamman (sauv) & Hilko Hegewisch (merlot) ▪ 2ha (merlot) ▪ PO Box 2200 Somerset West 7129 ▪ lesley@capehutton.com ▪ www.capehutton.com ▪ S 33° 58' 27.6" E 018° 51' 10.3" ▪ **T +27 (0)21-880-0527** ▪ F +27 (0)21-880-0666

Founded by oral and maxillofacial surgeon Gerrit Wyma and wife Lesley, Cape Hutton in Blaauwklippen Valley leverages its scenic location and proximity to Stellenbosch to offer weddings and corporate functions in a dedicated venue, as well as varied cellardoor amenities. Vinification is by handpicked winemakers.

★★★★ **Cabernet Sauvignon** ⏧ Smooth, ripe & concentrated **09** reflects good vintage. Elegantly oaked, with subtle spices filling out healthy fruit profile.
Sauvignon Blanc ⏧ 🍷 🉑 ★★★★ **11** intense, complex aromatic profile & steely lees minerality. Fine expression of cool West Coast fruit. Step up from **09** (★★★). **Veri Beri** In abeyance. — GdB

Capelands Estate 🍵 🏛

Location: Somerset West ▪ WO: Stellenbosch ▪ Est 2004 ▪ 1stB 2010 ▪ Closed to public ▪ Tasting at Capelands Restaurant available to patrons ▪ Guest house ▪ Owner(s) Capelands Estate (Pty) Ltd ▪ Cellarmaster(s) Louis Nel (Feb 2010, consultant) ▪ Viticulturist(s) Francois Hanekom (Feb 2009, consultant) ▪ 12.5ha/2.8ha (cab) ▪ 6t/1,333cs own label 100% red ▪ 3 Old Sir Lowry's Pass Road Somerset West 7130 ▪ restaurant@capelands.com ▪ www.capelands.com ▪ **T +27 (0)21-858-1477** ▪ F +27 (0)86-299-3905

Johann Innerhofer, with some 30 years in the international wine trade, and partner Laura Mauri own boutique Somerset West estate Capelands, featuring accommodation, restaurant with stellar wine list and walled vineyard, from which consultant Louis Nel vinifies a single red. 'We're looking for an elegant, delicate wine – I call it a Burgundy-Cabernet,' says Johann.

★★★★☆ **Redstone** Like **10**, 85% cab plus splash malbec in **11** (★★★★), brooding & intensely flavoured, powerful. Very ripe dark fruit, soft acidity & smooth tannins, though not as poised as previous. — CE

■ **Cape Nelson** *see* uniWines Vineyards

Capenheimer

South Africa's original perlé wine, launched 1962. By Distell. 750ml & 1.5L bottles.

Capenheimer ▤ ★★ Lightish, semi-sweet, easy sipping **NV** with a tingle of lively bubbles. — DB, HJ

■ **Cape of Good Hope** *see* Anthonij Rupert Wyne

Cape Point Vineyards

Location: Noordhoek ▪ Map: Cape Peninsula ▪ WO: Cape Point/Western Cape ▪ Est 1996 ▪ 1stB 2000 ▪ Tasting, sales & cellar tours Mon-Sat 11-5 Sun 11-4 ▪ Fee R15-R60 ▪ Closed Good Fri, Dec 25 & Jan 1 ▪ Cheese/antipasti platters available during tasting hours ▪ Weddings & events ▪ Picnics & sundowners ▪ Nature trails & vineyard walks ▪ Facilities for children ▪ Weekly community market Thu evenings in summer/Sun during day in winter ▪ Conservation area ▪ Owner(s) Sybrand van der Spuy ▪ Cellarmaster(s) Duncan Savage (Dec 2002) ▪ Winemaker(s) Duncan Savage (Dec 2002), with Jeremiah Mkhwanazi (Oct 2005) ▪ Viticulturist(s) Duncan Savage (Dec 2002), with Hendri Burger (Sep 2010) ▪ 22ha (chard, sauv, sem) ▪ 16,000cs own label 100% white; Splattered Toad ±50,000cs + 4,000cs for clients ▪ Brands for clients: Foodbarn Restaurant, Woolworths ▪ BWI, IPW, Farming for the Future ▪ PO Box 100 Noordhoek 7985 ▪ info@cape-point.com ▪ www. capepointvineyards.co.za, www.splatteredtoad.co.za ▪ S 34° 5′ 41.82″ E 018° 22′ 17.28″ ▪ **T +27 (0)21-789-0900** ▪ F +27 (0)21-789-0614

Winemaker Duncan Savage has been with this high-flying white-wine specialist producer for more than a decade, and has built an enviable reputation for his terroir-specific range. Loftily perched in splendid isolation on Noordhoek mountain, overlooking one of the Cape's great beaches, the vineyards live a hard life of maritime exposure. The operation moved into its new subterranean cellar, crafted out of an old mine bunker, in the off-season. This represents 'the first time that Noordhoek fruit was vinified in Noordhoek'. Visitors are now offered a tour of the working parts to complement their tasting experience. The estate is closely linked with the village, hosting a weekly community market and staging charity concerts to support the Valley Development Trust's feeding scheme.

Cape Point Vineyards range

★★★★ **Chardonnay** ▨ Barrel-fermented & aged **12** (★★★★★) is finely balanced & weighted, with lovely melange of citrus fruit holding centre-stage. Silky-textured, with hints of lime, baked apples & brioche, promising even greater things with time in bottle. Notch up on **11**.

★★★★☆ **Sauvignon Blanc Reserve** ▨ Gracious expression of variety's potential, **12** oozes class. Barrel ferment elevates rather than flavours, 13% semillon smooths & rounds. Finely integrated, perfectly modulated, fully deserving of reserve status.

★★★★ **Sauvignon Blanc** ▨ Distinctive & classy **12**, now unoaked but with extended lees contact & 4% semillon, harnesses wild nettle aromatics into balanced, harmonious whole.

★★★★★ **CWG Auction Reserve White** After stellar **11**, semillon-led Bordeaux-style **12** (★★★★☆) blend eschews oak props, but delivers at every level. Tiny volumes, slow-fermented in clay amphorae. Profound, complex & beguiling, with layers & textures unfurling into a memorable drinking experience.

★★★★☆ **Isliedh** ▨ Barrel-fermented, sauvignon-led blend with semillon, **12** (★★★★★) version of near-iconic flagship at minimum maintains the standard. Fruit & body easily embrace oak, delivering concentration, subtlety & length with delightful balance & texture. As with **11**, has a rewarding future.

★★★★ **Noble Late Harvest** ▨ Returning to the guide after a break, sauvignon-semillon botrytised **11** shows promise, with dried apricot tang over honeyed sweetness. Rather heavy, ponderous body is bolstered by fine, piercing acidity.

Splattered Toad range

Shiraz ☺ 🍴 📷 ★★★ Light-bodied **12**, now all-shiraz, is a flavoursome quaffer with appealing pepper & wild herb aromas. WO W Cape, like sauvignon. **Sauvignon Blanc** ☺ 🍴 📷 ★★★ Cheerful picnic basket filler, **13** has crisp acidity on green apple fruit, with appealing pinch of sea salt. — GdB

■ **Cape Promise** *see uniWines Vineyards*

Cape Rock Wines   🍴🍷🎋

Location: Vredendal ▪ Map/WO: Olifants River ▪ Est 2001 ▪ 1stB 2002 ▪ Tasting, sales & cellar tours by appt ▪ Closed Good Fri, Dec 25 & Jan 1 ▪ BYO picnic ▪ Owner(s) Willie Brand ▪ Cellarmaster(s) Willie Brand (Jan 2001) ▪ Winemaker(s) Willie Brand (Jan 2001) & Gavin Brand ▪ Viticulturist(s) Jeff Joubert (Jan 2001, consultant) ▪ 62ha/32ha (cab, grenache, merlot, mourv, ptage, roobernet, ruby cab, shiraz, chard, chenin, cbard, rouss, sauv, viog) ▪ 480t/1,200cs own label 50% red 20% white 30% rosé + 32,000L bulk ▪ PO Box 261 Vredendal 8160 ▪ caperockwines@gmail.com ▪ www.caperockwines.co.za ▪ S 31° 37′ 24.0″ E 018° 24′ 52.9″ ▪ **T +27 (0)27-213-2567** ▪ F +27 (0)27-213-5567

The father-and-son team of Willie and Gavin Brand are emerging as leaders of the Olifants River Valley's nascent fine-wine making movement, their increasingly Rhône-influenced varietal bottlings and (somewhat inscrutably named) blends improving by the vintage and packaged to impress. The innovative GRV blend, one of our prestigious Wines of the Year this edition, is a case in point.

★★★★ **SMV** ✓ Well-composed flagship, co-fermented shiraz, mourvèdre & viognier in **12** (★★★★★) goes up a level with restrained tannin & fruit, balanced savouriness despite 15% alcohol. Similar herby berry complexity to elegant **09**, also a step up. No **11**, **10** sold out untasted.

★★★★ **Rosé** [NEW] ✓ 🍴 **13** from 4 Rhône grapes, lightish & bone-dry with food-friendly earthy cherry aromas, chalky tannins & savoury touch.

★★★★ **GRV** ✓ Sophisticated near-equal blend grenache blanc, roussanne & viognier seasoned with smidgen chenin & older oak. **12** leesy, rich & savoury, with fair vivacity; also-tasted **13** (★★★★★) a notch up. Harmonious juxtaposition of floral, nutty & fruity elements, distinctly dry.

Cabernet Sauvignon Await next, as for **SGMV** & **Cape Roca**. **Shiraz** ⊕ 🍴 ★★★☆ **11** spicy & floral, lightly oaked & fruit-filled for early imbibing. — HJ,CvZ

■ **Cape Roots** *see Quest Wines*
■ **Cape Sparrow** *see TCB Wines*
■ **Cape Style** *see Paarl Wine Company*

Cape to Cairo Wines   🍷

Location: Cape Town ▪ Map: Cape Peninsula ▪ WO: Breede River Valley ▪ Est 2007 ▪ 1stB 2008 ▪ Tasting by appt ▪ Owner(s) Trans-Scripto (Pty) Ltd ▪ Winemaker(s) Nico van der Merwe (consultant) & Jolene Calitz-Le Roux ▪ 7,000cs 100% red ▪ PO Box 1358 Cape Town 8000 ▪ info@capetocairo.net ▪ www.capetocairowines.com ▪ S 33° 56′ 29.06″ E 018° 23′ 47.76″ ▪ **T +27 (0)82-579-4849** ▪ F +27 (0)86-660-4323

The Cape Town brand owners aim 'to bring to world markets the taste of The Classic African Adventure'. Each six-bottle case comes with a large map detailing the route from Cape to Cairo, with information on legendary sites inviting wine lovers to dream of Africa as they smell and taste the wine.

Syrah ⊕ ★★★ Accessible **07**'s ripe fruit wrapped in sweet oak, pleasing lingering savouriness. — KM,CvZ

■ **Cape to Cape** *see Nordic Wines*
■ **Cape Tranquility** *see Pulpit Rock Winery*
■ **Cape View** *see Kaapzicht Wine Estate*
■ **Cappupinoccinotage** *see Boland Kelder*
■ **Cap Vino** *see Winkelshoek Wine Cellar*

Carisbrooke Wines   🍷

Location/map/WO: Stellenbosch ▪ Est 1989 ▪ 1stB 1996 ▪ Tasting & sales Mon-Fri 10-2 ▪ Closed all pub hols ▪ Owner(s) Willem Pretorius ▪ Cellarmaster(s)/winemaker(s) Kowie du Toit (1997), Willem Pretorius ▪ Viticulturist(s) Kowie du Toit (1997) ▪ 19ha/6ha (cab, sem) ▪ 50t/800cs own label 100% red ▪ PO Box 25 Vlottenburg 7604 ▪ willem@carisbrooke.co.za ▪ **T +27 (0)21-881-3798** ▪ F +27 (0)21-881-3796/+27 (0)86-518-8767

The brand from lawyer-winegrower Willem Pretorius' Stellenboschkloof farm takes its name from the little train station of Carisbrooke, made famous by Alan Paton's masterpiece Cry, the Beloved Country.

Alan Paton Cabernet Sauvignon ④ 🖾 ★★★★ Seriously styled & elegant **10** savoury, spicy, with fine acid backbone & judicious oaking (75% new). — IM

▪ **Carnival** *see* Orange River Wine Cellars
▪ **Carpe Diem** *see* Diemersfontein Wines
▪ **Carrol Boyes Collection** *see* Barnardt Boyes Wines

Casa Mori

Location/map/WO: Stellenbosch ▪ Est 1995 ▪ 1stB 2009 ▪ Tasting, sales & tours by appt ▪ Meals/refreshments by appt ▪ Farm produce ▪ Conferences/functions ▪ Artichoke festival ▪ Owner(s) Eugene Mori ▪ Cellarmaster(s)/viticulturist(s) Bruno Julian Mori (1997) ▪ Winemaker(s) Bruno Julian Mori (1997), with Mori family ▪ 4.4ha/2.3ha (cab, malbec, sangio, shiraz, viog) ▪ 15t/2,000cs own label 97% red 1% white 2% rosé ▪ Other export label: Mori ▪ PO Box 71 Koelenhof 7605 ▪ mori.wines@gmail.com, casamoricucina@gmail.com ▪ www.casamori.co.za ▪ S 33° 53' 15.28" E 018° 48' 27.64" ▪ **T +27 (0)83-620-0016** ▪ F +27 (0)86-625-0080

At the Mori family's boutique winery in Stellenbosch, wine and food are inseparable, and inspired by Italy. The wine on the table is therefore typically sangiovese-based while home-grown olives, artichokes and an own red-wine vinegar (barrel-aged for over 30 years) are among the usual accompaniments.

Bruno ④ ★★★☆ Unfiltered **NV** combo sangiovese/cab (78/22) elegant & dry, attractive polished leather nuance, firm food-pairing tannins. — CvZ

▪ **Casual Collection** *see* Bernheim Wines

Catch Of The Day

Location: Cape Town ▪ WO: Stellenbosch/Paarl ▪ Closed to public ▪ Owner(s) Cunicsar Vintners cc ▪ Winemaker(s) Warwick Denman ▪ PO Box 26500 Hout Bay 7872 ▪ catchotd@mweb.co.za ▪ www.rainbownationwines.com ▪ **T +27 (0)21-671-6024/+27 (0)79-899-6325** ▪ F +27 (0)86-624-4780

Winemaker Warwick Denman, with seasoning at DeMorgenzon, has joined this Cape Town negociant house for the restaurant trade and is looking out for their next 'catch' – interesting, good-value wines for the table.

Cabernet Sauvignon ④ 🖾 ★★★★ Robust **09**, firm red berry flavours perfect for fireside contemplation. **Shiraz** ④ 🖾 ★★★ Toasty dark berry fruit, satisfying palate weight on easy-drinking **09** pizza partner. WO Paarl. **Merlot-Shiraz** NEW 🖾 Merlot (50%), shiraz plus 3 others in **11** preview. Too unformed to rate, but shows good underlying fruit. **Chenin Blanc** Await next. **Sauvignon Blanc** ④ 🖾 ★★★ Lively **11**, attractive perfumes & crisp apple aftertaste. — CvZ

▪ **Cathedral Cellar** *see* KWV Wines

Catherine Marshall Wines

Location/WO: Elgin ▪ Map: Elgin, Walker Bay & Bot River ▪ Est/1stB 1997 ▪ Tasting, sales & cellar tours by appt ▪ Closed Easter Fri-Sun, Dec 25 & Jan 1 ▪ Meals/refreshments by appt ▪ Owner(s) Cathy Marshall, Greg Mitchell, Jonathan Oxenham & Jeff Jolly ▪ Cellarmaster(s) Catherine Marshall (Oct 1996) ▪ Winemaker(s) Shawn Fortuin (Jan 1996) ▪ Viticulturist(s) Various ▪ 40-50t/8,000cs own label 60% red 37% white 3% fortified ▪ IPW ▪ PO Box 30913 Tokai 7966 ▪ cathy@cmwines.co.za ▪ www.cmwines.co.za ▪ S 34° 12' 12.07" E 019° 02' 35. 10" ▪ **T +27 (0)83-258-1307** ▪ F +27 (0)86-523-7479

A small-scale venture, based at Valley Green farm in Elgin, helmed by equally diminutive but dynamic Catherine Marshall, who handled most of the last harvest solo, after trusty cellar manager Shawn Fortuin was injured. Ever self-effacing, Cathy has been an ardent protagonist of pinot noir for many years, honing her skills with this fickle variety to a fine art. Chenin and merlot have not escaped her attentions either, and she now proudly sources all her grapes from Elgin Valley. Cathy hosts small group tastings and fine-dining experiences to promote her wines and the valley generally, sharing her love of food and travel.

Catherine Marshall Wines range

★★★★☆ **Peter's Vision Merlot Reserve** NEW 🎯 More classically styled than Amatra bottling, with a core of spicy red fruit in a muscular frame. **11** well tailored dry tannins, with inherent balance, fruit intensity & structure to develop for 6-10 years.

★★★★ **Pinot Noir** ⓘ 🍴 **11** a favourite vintage of Cathy Marshall's, notable for its fragrance, fruit purity, delicate freshness, silky mouthfeel & enough of each to charm over several years.

★★★★ **9 Barrels Pinot Noir Reserve** 🎯 Selection of **11** shows understated elegance & supple structure. Beguilingly delicate yet intense. Deserves 3-5 years to really shine.

★★★★ **Sauvignon Blanc** 🍴 Tasted just post-bottling in 2010, **11** captured Elgin's poise, minerality. Weight to balance vivacity without spoiling fruit purity, length. **10** (★★★★) from Durbanville less balanced.

Myriad ★★★ Fortified merlot, **08** dried prune & slightly spirity tone develops a smoother mocha character with decanting. Uncloying cheese partner in 375 ml. Discontinued: **SMG**.

Amatra range NEW

★★★★ **Chenin Blanc Jono's Wave** 🍴 🎯 Classy **12**, 40% older oak fermented. Succulent baked apple, almond & honeycomb threaded with zesty acidity, showcases area's cool fruit intensity. Elegant, with potential.

Merlot ✓ 🍴 🎯 ★★★★ Rung above **11** (★★★★), **12** shimmers with red-berried appeal. Graceful table mate, deftly oaked with lithe tannin structure. — MW

■ **CCC Wines** see Bonnievale Wines

Cecilia Wines 🍴🍷

Location: Klawer ▪ Map/WO: Olifants River ▪ Est 2010 ▪ 1stB 2007 ▪ Tasting by appt ▪ Owner(s) Cerina van Niekerk ▪ Cellarmaster(s)/winemaker(s) Cerina van Niekerk (2007) ▪ 2t/250cs own label 100% red ▪ PO Box 23 Trawal 8147 ▪ cecilia@mylan.co.za ▪ www.ceciliawines.co.za ▪ S 31° 51' 32.16" E 018° 36' 13.37" ▪ **T +27 (0)82-334-9422** ▪ F +27 (0)86-617-0101

Trained concert pianist and Klawer Cellars winemaker Cerina van Niekerk's own brand is named for the patron of music, nobly aiming to interweave wine, music and philanthropy. This edition she debuts her 'work of time': a pinotage seven years in the dreaming, proceeds from which will benefit the local community.

★★★★☆ **Pinotage** NEW ✓ 🍴 🎯 From old hillside vineyard, previewed **12** incredibly complex & flavoursome, shows great restraint; light vanilla overlay on scrub & wet earth aromas, dark berry flavours; bright acidity & deft oak touch (none new) make for satisfying sipping now or 5+ years.

★★★★ **Shiraz-Mourvèdre** ✓ 🍴 🎯 Among the region's most accomplished blends. Pre-bottling, **13** effortless & unforced, elegant & refreshing mouthful with moderate alcohol. Like **11**, lightly brushed with oak to showcase pure fruit. No **12**. — HJ, CvZ

■ **Cecil John** see Boschendal Wines

Cederberg Private Cellar 🍷🎡🏚📷

Location: Citrusdal ▪ Map: Olifants River ▪ WO: Cederberg/Elim ▪ Est 1973 ▪ 1stB 1977 ▪ Tasting Mon-Sat 8-12; 2-4.30 pub hols 9-11.30; 4-5.30 ▪ Fee R20 ▪ Closed Easter Fri/Sun, Dec 25 & Jan 1 ▪ Sales Mon-Sat 8-12.30; 2-5 Sun/pub hols 9-12; 4-6 ▪ BYO picnic ▪ Sanddrif Holiday Resort self-catering cottages; camping ▪ Walks/hikes ▪ Mountain biking ▪ Conservation area ▪ Rock climbing ▪ Sport climbing ▪ Observatory ▪ Owner(s) Nieuwoudt family ▪ Cellarmaster(s) David Nieuwoudt (Jan 1997) ▪ Winemaker(s) David Nieuwoudt (Jan 1997), with Alex Nel & Tammy Turck (Aug 2011) ▪ Viticulturist(s) Ernst Nieuwoudt (Jan 1960) ▪ 5,500ha/60ha (cab, shiraz, bukettraube, chenin, sauv) ▪ 600t/64,000cs own label 40% red 60% white ▪ PO Box 84 Clanwilliam 8135 ▪ info@cederbergwine.com ▪ www.cederbergwine.com ▪ S 32° 30' 12.8" E 019° 15' 27.7" ▪ **T +27 (0)27-482-2827** ▪ F +27 (0)86-531-0491

At around 1,000m above sea level, the vineyards of Cederberg Private Cellar are among the highest in the Western Cape. David Nieuwoudt took over as winemaker in 1997 and in so doing, became the fifth generation of his family to farm this remote land, his great-great-grandfather having originally settled here in 1893. Initially, the undertaking was to grow tobacco and raise cattle, then deciduous fruit. Vines were first planted in 1973, when David's grandfather decided to dabble in winemaking, and in 1977 the first vintage was made (and noted in this guide as 'too small to be certified [but] acclaimed by experts'). In 2008, David purchased land in Elim near Cape Agulhas from which he vinifies under the Ghost Corner label, three stellar wines added and reviewed below.

Five Generations range

★★★★☆ **Cabernet Sauvignon** 🅥 Selection of 12 barrels (all-new French), **11** (★★★★★) is complex & layered, with ripe blackcurrant fruit, scrub, whiff of cherry tobacco. Delicate yet lush & harmonious. Intense fruit concentration & plenty of ripe tannin give body, grip & longevity. Outshines **10** & **09** (★★★★).

★★★★☆ **Chenin Blanc** Barrel-fermented **11** seduces with concentrated flavours of vanilla & cinnamon-dusted baked apples, hints of marmalade. Dollop viognier adds to complexity with delicate floral notes. Dry, but with real opulence & richness, balanced by mouthwatering acidity.

David Nieuwoudt Ghost Corner range

★★★★ **Pinot Noir** NEW 🅥 Debut **12** displays a fine combination of richness & delicacy, with delightful aromas of cherry & spicy oak (20% new French). Concentrated & refined, with a distinct mineral finish.

★★★★★ **Wild Ferment Sauvignon Blanc** NEW 🅥 Dry & uncompromising, this **12** wild yeast barrel-fermented impresses with tightly wound citrus flavours, dusty minerality & creamy vanilla oak. An elegant, serious structure with clarity & unflagging energy, good persistence. Super varietal expression.

★★★★ **Sauvignon Blanc** ⓘ 🅥 This range from Elim. **12** is steely, with a distinct mineral edge, dusty & complex; mouthfilling racy grapefruit & lime flavours. Lush & rounded, great depth on the finish.

★★★★★ **Semillon** ⓘ 🅥 **11** (★★★★★) easily outdoes **10** (★★★★) & **09** with a peacock's tail of aromas: crushed stone, dusty green capsicum, grass with a hint of smoke & seabreeze. Well-judged oak fills out the palate. Elegant & harmonious now & for several years.

★★★★★ **The Bowline** NEW 🅥 Stunning debut for **12**, knockout combo of sauvignon & barrel-fermented semillon with aromas of peach, citrus & candied ginger. Elegant & restrained, luscious texture & long creamy goodbye. Will reward ageing.

Cederberg Private Cellar range

★★★★ **Cabernet Sauvignon** 🅥 **11** shows sweet ripe fruit, tealeaf & vanilla oak (60% new). Supple & mouthfilling, with a firm tannin bite & same build as big brother, a little more approachable in youth.

★★★★★ **CWG Auction Reserve Teen die Hoog Shiraz** **11** follows equally impressive **10** with ripe, succulent concentrated fruit flavours, impressive chewy structure. Rich & full, but well balanced, with superb flavour complexity. Only 3 barrels produced. Will reward the patient.

★★★★ **Shiraz** 🅥 Generous **11** is harmonious & juicy, for lovers of fruit-driven style. Serious & rounded, spicy vanilla oak (French & American) balancing luscious fruit. Ideal for grilled meat dishes.

★★★★ **Chenin Blanc** ✓ 🅥 **13** is serious with intense tropical flavours. Unoaked, bright & focused, mouthwatering succulence & lees-ageing adding breadth.

★★★★ **Sauvignon Blanc** ✓ 🅥 Tangy lime & orchard fruit flavours on captivating **13**. Fruitier than Elim partners. Generously textured & elegant, palate-saturating citrus finish.

★★★★ **Blanc de Blancs 08** (★★★★★) méthode cap classique sparkling from chardonnay (part barrel fermented) in extra-dry style steps up from **07**. Mature biscuit notes from 4 years on lees marries with intense citrus & marzipan flavours; creamy texture, depth & length.

Merlot-Shiraz ✓ 🅥 ★★★★ **11** is fresh & savoury with intense spice-dipped fruit flavours. Oaking rounds off good structure. Food friendly. **Sustainable Rosé** ✓ 🅥 ★★★★ Charming candyfloss pink **13**, from a single-vineyard shiraz, offers perfumed ripe strawberry & spice flavours. Light, dry & fruity - perfect sundowner. **Bukettraube** ✓ 🅥 ★★★★ Back-to-form semi-sweet **13** seduces with fragrant Turkish Delight, but finishes refreshingly crisp. Made for Malay cuisine. — WB

Celestina

Location: Gansbaai • WO: Cape Agulhas • Est 2004 • 1stB 2009 • Closed to public • Owner(s) Caroline Rillema • Winemaker(s) Dirk Human (Black Oystercatcher) • Viticulturist(s) Caroline Rillema & Ray Kilian • 3.4ha/1.85ha (sauv, sem) • 6t/600cs own label 100% white • c/o Caroline's Fine Wine Cellar, Shop 44, Matador Centre, 62 Strand Street, Cape Town 8001 • carowine2@mweb.co.za • **T** +27 (0)21-419-8984 • **F** +27 (0)21-419-8985

Over three decades, Caroline Rillema has built up a classy Cape Town wine merchant business but only more recently realised her dream of owning a vineyard small enough to be managed over weekends. (About her other wish, to be the White

House's wine selector, stay tuned!) She and partner Ray Kilian's sauvignon blanc and semillon, on a slice of land at Baardskeersdersbos near Gansbaai, is vinified by Dirk Human (Black Oystercatcher) and reflects the area's cool elegance.

★★★★ **Sauvignon Blanc-Semillon** 🍽 Flint & zest zing to **12** 60/40 blend. Lightish yet concentrated with no trace of wood despite ferment in older oak barrels. White pepper lift on long clean tail. — FM

Cellar Cask

South Africa's first bag-in-box, launched in 1979, styled by Distell to meet rising demand for Natural Sweet wines with lower alcohol levels.

Select Johannisberger Rosé ★ Friendly strawberry-toned **NV**, dollops ruby cab, shiraz & merlot for colour. Widely sourced, as all these. **Select Johannisberger White** ★ Delicate raisiny fruit flavours for the sweet toothed. **NV** from mainly chenin & colombard. **Select Johannisberger Red** ★ Well-balanced grapey **NV**, chiefly shiraz, merlot & ruby cab. Lightish ±11.5% alcohol, as for all these. — DB, HJ

■ **Cellar Door** see Namaqua Wines
■ **Cellar Road** see Darling Cellars
■ **Centennial** see Group CDV

Chabivin Champagne & MCC House

Location/map: Stellenbosch ▪ WO: Stellenbosch/Breedekloof/Franschhoek/Western Cape ▪ Est 2008 ▪ Tasting & sales Tue-Fri 9-5 Sat/Sun 10-4 ▪ Fee R30/3 MCC, R100/4 Champagnes ▪ Sage Restaurant ▪ Winemaker(s)/ viticulturist(s) Hendrik Snyman ▪ 3ha/0.4ha (pinot, chard) ▪ ±8t/±1,240cs own label 100% MCC ▪ PO Box 12456 Die Boord Stellenbosch 7613 ▪ info@chabivin.co.za ▪ www.chabivin.co.za ▪ S 33° 58' 24.27" E 018° 51' 8.17" ▪ **T** +27 (0)21-880-1643 ▪ F +27 (0)86-540-6237

Jean-Pierre and Brigitte Charbaut of the eponymous Reims champagne house have converted a garden cottage and 'small chaotic forest' in Stellenbosch into a vineyard, maturation cellar, and tasting, lunching and live music venue, dedicated to their local bubblies and imported Champagnes Guy Charbaut.

Diary Series

★★★★ **Mademoiselle Mégane** ⑨ Poised **NV** cap classique from chardonnay, attractive savoury & biscuit tones, steely 'oystershell' minerality from Breedekloof limestone soil.

★★★★ **Adémée** ⑨ **05** traditional-method dry sparkler from Franschhoek semillon, distinctive varietal characteristics of hay, green citrus & lively acidity. Impressive length & texture add to appeal.

Cuvée Jean-Michel ⑨ ★★★★ Classic champagne blend (pinot noir, chardonnay 50/50), but unusual (attractive) pineapple/baked lime hints. **07** tad more evolved than siblings, for earlier drinking. WO W Cape.

Signature Series NEW

★★★★ **Brut Rosé** Pinky gold cap classique from pinot noir, fermented in older oak. **11** captures the grape's richness without overt fruitiness. Tiny tangy bubbles linger mouthwateringly.

Zero Dosage ★★★★ **10** sparkler mainly pinot noir, with 26% chardonnay. Assertively dry, refreshingly brisk bubble showing off bold leesy, bruised apple features. — AL

■ **Chameleon** see Jordan Wine Estate
■ **Chamonix** see Cape Chamonix Wine Farm
■ **Champany Inn** see Simonsig Landgoed
■ **Chandos** see Malanot Wines
■ **Chapel** see Robertson Winery
■ **Chapel Cellar** see Zanddrift Vineyards
■ **Charles Borro** see Govert Wines

Charles Fox Cap Classique Wines

Location/WO: Elgin ▪ Map: Elgin, Walker Bay & Bot River ▪ Est 2007 ▪ 1stB 2010 ▪ Tasting, sales & cellar tours Mon-Thu by appt Fri-Sun 11-4 ▪ Fee R30 ▪ Closed Easter Fri/Sun, July, Dec 25/26 & Jan 1 ▪ Play area for children ▪ Owner(s) Charles & Zelda Fox ▪ Cellarmaster(s) Charles Fox (2010) ▪ Winemaker(s) Nicolas Follet (2010, consultant) ▪ Viticulturist(s) Kevin Watt (2008, consultant) ▪ 33.4ha/6.3ha (pinot meunier, pinot, chard) ▪ 960cs (2010)/3,360cs (2011) own label 100% MCC ▪ PO Box 105 Elgin 7180 ▪ charlesfoxmcc@gmail.

com ▪ www.charlesfox.co.za ▪ S 34° 14' 14.38" E 019° 04' 41.99" ▪ **T +27 (0)21-300-1065** ▪ F +27 (0)86-536-2924

Charles and Zelda Fox left Johannesburg big city life in 2005 for 'a better lifestyle for us and our children'. They found it in Elgin on an old fruit farm they renamed Furneaux (after Charles' mother). They've been guided by 'the soils and climate' (and adviser Kevin Watt) to plant some 6ha of champagne varieties. Cape-based Champenois Nicolas Follet is the consultant winemaker. Watch for a Special Reserve debuting this year, to be followed by a Blanc de Blancs in 2015/6.

★★★★☆ **Brut Rosé Méthode Cap Classique** Master-crafted from pinots noir & meunier (5%), **10** lovely rosepetal & strawberry bouquet, & a voluminous yet amazingly refined mousse which is both fruity & austere, very persistent unaggressively dry finish. Delightful pick-me-up & fine dining partner.

★★★★ **Brut Méthode Cap Classique** Stylish brioche & lemon intro, vibrant mousse & shortbread flavours on **10** happy occasions celebrator. Equal pinot noir & chardonnay, 20% pinot meunier for heft. — GdB, GM, CvZ

■ **Chateau Beau Belle** *see Beau Belle*

Chateau Libertas

The grandfather of South African reds, available since 1932 and still a paragon of value and drinkability. By Distell.

Chateau Libertas ✓ ★★★☆ Reliable & consistent mix of Bordeaux grapes plus shiraz & ruby cab. Standout **12** is serious but still easy to like, offering attractively fresh & spicy dark fruit flavours. — DB, HJ

Chateau Naudé Wine Creation

Location: Stellenbosch ▪ WO: Wellington/Stellenbosch ▪ Est 2006 ▪ 1stB 2007 ▪ Closed to public ▪ Owner(s) Francois Naudé snr, Magda Naudé, Francois Naudé jnr, Melissa Naudé ▪ Cellarmaster(s) Francois Naudé (Jul 2007) ▪ 1,000cs own label 65% red 35% white ▪ 11 Weidenhof Street Stellenbosch 7600 ▪ naude@levindefrancois.co.za ▪ www.levindefrancois.com ▪ **T +27 (0)21-883-8469** ▪ F +27 (0)86-651-3192

Ebullient Francois Naudé snr is an instantly likeable man with a wonderful sense of humour. Being irrepressible by nature, retirement from his regular winemaking job simply meant redeploying his creative oenological talents to start his own family venture - boutique in size, but internationally renowned (exported to eight different countries). Part of the output is sold at a family-staged black-tie auction in the first week in March. Flamboyant as this may sound, Francois is self-effacing ('Wingnut' a reference to the shape of his ears!), driven by an ardent belief in the potential of pinotage, the only variety in his masterly multi-cellar blend, Le Vin de François, this year sourced entirely from Stellenbosch. A new wine, also featuring pinotage, is a champagne-style sparkling. After all, 'Every year is a blessing and warrants a celebration!'

Chateau Naudé Wine Creation range

★★★★☆ **Le Vin de François** All Stellenbosch fruit, from carefully selected barrels, make up the stylish **11** (★★★★★) pinotage. Opulent, complex & intense, with layers of flavour & polished tannins. A gear up on **10** (★★★★) & **09**, & a triumph for the variety.

The Wingnut range

★★★★ **Cabernet Sauvignon 10** a shade off stellar 09 (★★★★☆), but still shows classical elegance & restraint. Bright cassis & herb flavours, underpinned by deft oaking. WO Stellenbosch, as for most in this range.

★★★★ **Méthode Cap Classique Brut Rosé** NEW 📸 Refined & flavoursome **10**, from chardonnay (70) & pinotage, savoury cranberry freshness & fine creamy mousse. Perfect ceviche partner or for any occasion.

Pinotage NEW ★★★ Swaggeringly ripe **11** has a dark liquorice tone. Sweet new oak & alcohol add power. A tad brawny & unbalanced in youth. Needs time & robust fare. **Chardonnay** ⏱ ★★★★ Intense **10**'s upfront lemon cream, oak spice features held by very zesty acid; sweetish close. **Chenin Blanc Barrel Fermented 12** tank sample off Wellington vines too youthful to rate. **White Port** ⏱ ★★★ Fruity, sweetish lightly oaked **10** dessert from chenin.

Nuts About range

Shiraz ★★★ Now bottled, **11** shows tart & tangy acidity offset by a smoky, savoury nuance. Lightish & juicy, for al fresco fare. From Wellington, as next. **Chenin Blanc** ⏣ 🍴 ★★★★ Unshowy yet persuasive **11**, cool clean lines, complementary textural bounce, smooth yet long close. — MW

Chateau VO Extra Fine   NEW

A stalwart of the Cape blended brandy scene, Chateau VO has been bottled as such since the 1920s, having previously been sold wholesale by 19th-century Cape liquor trading company Sedgwick's. It's now handled by Distell subsidiary Henry Tayler & Ries.

Chateau VO Extra Fine ★★★ Decent, straightforward blended brandy designed for mixers. Not short of fruit & floral notes, rich enough, firm & smooth. — WB,TJ

■ **Chatta Box** *see* Distell

Chennells Wines   ❢

Location: Somerset West ▪ Map: Helderberg ▪ WO: Stellenbosch/Western Cape ▪ Est 2004 ▪ 1stB 2008 ▪ Tasting, sales & cellar tours by appt Mon-Sun 9-5 ▪ Closed all pub hols ▪ Owner(s) Jeremy & Colleen Chennells ▪ Cellarmaster(s)/winemaker(s) Jeremy Chennells & Chris Keet (Jul 2009, consultant) ▪ Viticulturist(s) Colleen Chennells & Chris Keet (Jul 2009, consultant) ▪ 5ha/3.2ha (cab, shiraz, viog) ▪ 26t/330cs own label 85% red 15% white ▪ Romond Vineyards, Klein Helderberg Road, Somerset West 7130 ▪ chennell@iafrica.com ▪ S 34° 1' 52.61" E 018° 49' 59.67" ▪ **T +27 (0)21-855-3905** ▪ F +27 (0)21-683-6280

In 2003 Jeremy and Colleen Chennells decided to replace their Somerset West smallholding's fruit trees with vines. The journey of soil analysis and preparation, planting and nurturing of vines and making wines that express their philosophy of vivimus vivamos (whilst we live, let us live), has been 'truly fulfilling'.

Cabernet Sauvignon ⏣ 🥂 ★★★★ Bold & robust **10** aims for seriousness in riper vintage, achieves good concentration of savoury dark berry fruit; supportive tannins & acid but 15% alcohol obvious in youth. **Shiraz** ⏣ 🥂 ★★★ Ripe black berries & spice, some earthiness & tobacco on **10**, otherwise attractive wine somewhat unbalanced by 15% alcohol. WO W Cape. **Viognier** 🥂 ★★☆ 2nd release **12** riper, somewhat fatter though satisfyingly dry. Quiet apricot tones; oak might integrate over short term. — AL

■ **Chris Keet** *see* Keet Wines
■ **Christina Van Loveren** *see* Van Loveren Family Vineyards
■ **Christine-Marié** *see* Niel Joubert Estate
■ **Cilliers Cellars** *see* Stellendrift - SHZ Cilliers/Kuün Wyne
■ **Circle of Life** *see* Waterkloof
■ **Circumstance** *see* Waterkloof

Cirrus Wines   ❢

Location/map/WO: Stellenbosch ▪ Est/1stB 2003 ▪ Tasting & sales at Guardian Peak (see entry) ▪ Owner(s) Jean Engelbrecht & Ray Duncan ▪ Cellarmaster(s)/winemaker(s) Coenie Snyman (Jun 2010) ▪ Viticulturist(s) Dirkie Mouton (Jun 2010) ▪ 30t/3,626cs own label 100% red ▪ IPW ▪ PO Box 473 Stellenbosch 7599 ▪ info@cirruswines.com ▪ www.cirruswines.com ▪ S 34° 0' 44.31" E 018° 50' 33.22" ▪ **T +27 (0)21-881-3899** ▪ F +27 (0)21-881-3000

A transcontinental venture between the owners of California's Silver Oaks Cellars, Ray Duncan and sons David and Tim, and Jean Engelbrecht of Rust en Vrede, aimed at 'capturing the very essence of shiraz influenced by both Stellenbosch and Napa'.

★★★★ **Cirrus Syrah** 🥂 Quality of **10** (★★★★★) notch up on **09**. Genteel plum & cocoa vibrancy. Concentrated, opulent yet spicy & sleek with reined in fine tannin from 18 months new oak. Focused & firm. Offering similar flavours but a tad unyielding now is also-tasted **11**. Long inky finish. — FM

Citrusdal Wines

Location: Citrusdal ▪ Est/1stB 2007 ▪ Closed to public ▪ Owner(s) Charles Back, Mike Paul & other grape farm owners ▪ Cellarmaster(s) Jaco Brand (Nov 2009) ▪ Winemaker(s) Jaco Brand, with Andries de Klerk (both Nov 2009) ▪ Viticulturist(s) Charl du Plessis (Nov 2009) ▪ 550ha (cab, grenache, ptage, shiraz, chard, chenin, pinot grigio, sauv, viog) ▪ 5,000t/50,000cs own label 50% red 45% white 5% rosé + 200,000cs for clients ▪ Brands for clients: Co-op, Fairtrade Original, M&S, Sainsbury's ▪ Fairtrade, HACCP 2004, WIETA ▪ PO Box 41 Citrusdal 7340 ▪ info@citrusdalwines.co.za ▪ www.citrusdalwines.co.za ▪ **T +27 (0)22-921-2233** ▪ F +27 (0)22-921-3937

Citrusdal Wines' Six Hats range is named after the principles (partnership, change, potential, equity, dignity and sustainability) which guide the collaboration between the winery, Fairtrade-certified grape farmers and Fairview's Charles Back to bring ethically traded wines to winelovers locally and overseas.

CK Wines

Location/WO: Stellenbosch ▪ Est 2009 ▪ 1stB 2010 ▪ Tasting by appt ▪ Fee R50 ▪ Owner(s)/cellarmaster(s)/winemaker(s) Christian Kuun ▪ 4,000cs own label 100% red ▪ winemaker@ckwines.co.za, sales@ckwines.co.za ▪ **T +27 (0)82-615-8105** ▪ F +27 (0)86-504-6209

The 'CK' in the branding is Christian Kuun, 'bushveld boykie' from Polokwane, cellarmaster at Stellenbosch's Beau Joubert, self-confessed petrol head ('There are 26 cylinders in my garage!') and boutique vintner, whose after-hours business is booming - and diversifying: a sparkling and high-end white are on the cards, as are 'a few craft beers. We all know winemakers actually drink beer. Lol.'

Sincera ⊕ ★★★★ Appealing rich cocoa & oodles of succulent black fruit on pre-bottling **11**, 100% cab franc. Yielding & plush textured; harmonious oaking with long star anise & liquorice finish. **Integra** ⊕ ★★★★ Switches from varietal cab to 60/40 blend cab & cab franc in **10**, goes up notch on **09** (★★★★). Rich & ripe yet gently soft, heaps of cassis flavour, lovely mouthfeel & balance. Structured & elegantly long. — FM

Claime d'Or

Location: Robertson ▪ WO: Robertson/Western Cape ▪ Est/1stB 2008 ▪ Tasting & sales at Rietvallei Wine Estate (see entry) ▪ Owner(s) Magriet de Wet & Bernardo Rapoport ▪ Cellarmaster(s)/winemaker(s) Kobus Burger (2002, Rietvallei) ▪ Viticulturist(s) Wilhelm Treurnicht (2007, Rietvallei) ▪ 10ha (cabs s/f, sauv) ▪ 30% red 60% white 10% rosé ▪ PO Box 2040 Parklands 2121 ▪ info@claimedorwines.co.za ▪ www.claimedorwines.co.za ▪ **T +27 (0)11-447-8776** ▪ F +27 (0)86-691-7497/+27 (0)11-788-7346

It's no longer a case of 'gold and silver have I none', as history and coin enthusiast Bernardo Rapoport mentions Decanter and Chardonnay du Monde silver medals for the wooded chardonnay from his and Magriet de Wet's Robertson boutique winery. The Solidus range, planned for export, takes its name from the gold coin which was official Roman empire currency.

Claime d'Or range

★★★★ **Cabernet Franc** ▨ **10** unrated preview seems riper, more savoury than perfumed & supple **09**, vibrant & berry-laden **08**.

★★★★ **Cabernet Sauvignon-Cabernet Franc** ▨ Pre-bottling **10** not rated. As with Cab Franc preview, appears more savoury than **09**, which showed suave, smooth black berry fruit & subtle spice.

Pinot Noir NEW ▨ ★★★☆ Attractive, unforced **11** lightly oaked, leaving variety-true sour cherry, earth & forest floor intact. Promising debut from Lutzville grapes. **Shiraz** ▨ ★★★ Super-ripe-picked **11** very sweet fruit & pliant tannins yet surprisingly fresh, perfect for summer evening sipping. **Cabernet Sauvignon Rosé** ⊕ 🍴 ★★★ Floral berry aromas & flavours on dry & savoury **11**. **Chardonnay** ▨ ★★★ Oak driven, as previous, but deftly done & a step up. Vanilla butter richness refreshed by tangy lime acidity. Fans of this style will love **12**. **Sauvignon Blanc** ⊕ 🍴 ★★★★ **11** crisp & gravelly, with long mineral finish. WO W Cape.

Solidus range NEW

Cabernet Sauvignon ✓ ▨ ★★★★ Friendly & supple **12** opens to bright blackberry fruit, lifted by cab's dusty/leafy notes. Elegant dinner companion now & for few years. — HJ,MW

Clairvaux Private Cellar

Location/map/WO: Robertson ▪ Est/1stB 2000 ▪ Tasting & sales Mon-Fri 8-5 ▪ Closed all pub hols ▪ Cellar tours by appt ▪ BYO picnic ▪ Sales (at cellar price) also from La Verne Wine Boutique T +27 (0)23-626-4314 Mon-Fri 9-5.30 Sat 9-5 ▪ Owner(s) Wouter J de Wet snr & jnr ▪ Cellarmaster(s) Jaco van der Merwe (Oct 2011) ▪ Winemaker(s) Jaco van der Merwe (Oct 2011), with Coenraad Groenewald (Jan 2010) ▪ 200ha (cab, merlot, ptage, shiraz, chard, chenin, cbard, muscadel, sauv) ▪ 4,000t/3.2m L bulk ▪ PO Box 179 Robertson 6705 ▪ appelsdrift@lando.co.za ▪ www.clairvauxcellar.co.za ▪ S 33° 48' 13.8" E 019° 52' 21.1" ▪ **T +27 (0)23-626-3842** ▪ F +27 (0)23-626-1925

Jaco van der Merwe's harvest last year gave him a space headache, with grapes of different varieties arriving at the cellar door at the same time. The bulk wine industry is booming, says the cellarmaster, which benefits Clairvaux – just enough is bottled to keep the tasting venue open and the De Wet family owners in wine.

Cabernet Sauvignon ⑨ 🖻 ★★★ A poster for the variety, step-up **10** drinks early & well. **Shiraz** ⑨ 🖻 ★★ Prunes & lilies on quick-sip **10**. **Sauvignon Blanc** 🖻 🖉 ★★ Light in body (12% alcohol) & flavour, **13** has hay & blackcurrant appeal. **Good Night Irene** ⑨ ★★★ Fortified fireside charmer from hanepoot. **10** honey & full-ripe raisins lifted by zesty citrus. **Red Muscadel** ✓ 🖉 ★★★★ Fortified dessert to 'warm dem bones'. Jasmine-scented **12** reminiscent of sweet black tea; tangy lemon & well-integrated spirit cut the sweetness, lift the tail. **Madonna's Kisses Golden Muscadel** 🖉 ★★★ Step-up **11** fortified dessert has winter melon aromas, warm honey & raisin flavours; lively acidity & alcohol. **Port** ✓ ★★★★ Keeps improving: ruby-style **09** shows some complexity, robust cherry flavour with hints of leather & tobacco. Comforting. — DB,CvZ

■ **Clearsprings** *see Trizanne Signature Wines*

Clive Torr Wines

[NEW]

Owner(s)/winemaker(s) Clive Torr ▪ 26 Topaz Street Heldervue Somerset West 7130 ▪ clivetorrwines@mweb.co.za ▪ www.clivetorrwines.co.za ▪ **T +27 (0)82-557-0836** ▪ F +27 (0)86-513-4034

'I'm a micro vinifier,' says Clive Torr, also a Cape Wine Master, wine educator and garagiste mentor. With several listings, past and present, in this guide (Topaz, Conviction, Callender Peak), Clive's new eponymous venture involves limited-edition handmade wines from 'extreme vineyards' in, among others, Koue Bokkeveld and, nearer his Somerset West base, Scarborough. Expect pinot noir, shiraz/syrah and chardonnay to feature in the Francophile porfolio.

Cloof Wine Estate

Location/WO: Darling ▪ Map: Durbanville, Philadelphia & Darling ▪ Est/1stB 1998 ▪ Tasting & sales Mon-Sat 10-4 ▪ Closed Good Fri-Sun, Dec 25 & Jan 1 ▪ Cellar tours by appt ▪ Meals/refreshments Tue-Sat 10-3 ▪ Farm produce ▪ Conservation area ▪ Game & eco drives by appt ▪ Owner(s) Cloof Wine Estate (Pty) Ltd ▪ Winemaker(s) Christopher van Dieren (Jan 2002), with Jody Johannes (Jan 2012) ▪ Viticulturist(s) Peter Duckitt (May 2004) ▪ 1,300ha/166ha (cabs s/f, cinsaut, merlot, ptage, shiraz, chard, chenin, viog) ▪ 600t/100,000cs own label 88% red 12% white ▪ BWI champion ▪ PO Box 269 Darling 7345 ▪ info@cloof.co.za ▪ www.cloof.co.za ▪ S 33° 28' 58.1" E 018° 31' 23.4" ▪ **T +27 (0)22-492-2839** ▪ F +27 (0)22-492-3261

This large Darling property is home to the Rocking the Daisies festival, which entertains more than 15,000 music lovers annually and is regarded as among the best of its kind on the local scene. The event captures Cloof's spirit of fun - as do some of the quirky wine names, but it's an attitude also found in the wines. Sustainability and community improvement are other priorities here, as is keeping a strategic eye on developments in the Asian markets.

Premium range

★★★★☆ **Crucible Shiraz** ⑨ Dark-fruited **06** (★★★★) tasted a few years back less harmonious than **04**.

★★★★ **Lynchpin** 🖉 **10** (★★★★) first since **06**. Austere cab franc (70%) & merlot mix proffers brooding plum, with a tannic frame requiring decanting.

Merlot [NEW] 🖉 ★★★★ **11** opens up with restrained plummy fruit & toasty oak charm. Red fruits slowly unfold, supported by bright acid & austere tannins. Needs time.

Signature range

★★★★ **Duckitt Cabernet Sauvignon-Merlot-Cabernet Franc** ⊕ 09 well crafted, cedar infused from serious oaking. Just off-dry with a lovely freshness. Harmonious tannins should support 6+ years ageing.

Summertime Sauvignon Blanc ☺ 🍴 🖩 ★★★ Previewed 13 offers fresh inviting tropical fruit plus green melon & granadilla. Clean & zingy, with lime pith grip.

Cab Cult Cabernet Sauvignon 🖩 ★★★ Smoky, dark fruited with meaty edge. 11 rather tannic & a touch green. **The Very Posh Pinotage** ⊕ ★★★ 09 offers juicy plums, spice & chocolate notes, mouthfilling & silky with perky smoky end. **Cloof Pinotage** 🖩 ★★★ Was just 'Pinotage'. 11 very fruity with ripe banana, floral & meaty complexity. Flows to earthy & savoury end. Tannic grip a foil for meaty dishes. **The Very Sexy Shiraz** ✓ 🖩 ★★★★ Fruit-forward 11 has juicy palate, black pepper spice & dark berry support. Supple fruit tannins support a satisfying end. **Cellar Blend** ⊕ 🍴 ★★★ All-sorts red blend from press juice in preview 09; dark, brooding berries, chunky solid finish; extracted fruit needs hearty food. **Inkspot Vin Noir** 🍴 🖩 ★★★ Oak spice intro on perennial favourite, pinotage, shiraz, cab, cinsaut combo; 10 offers a mix of berry fruits with an earthy undertow. **The Dark Side Cabernet Sauvignon-Shiraz** 🍴 🖩 ★★★ Cab-led 11 has a herbal edge countering the brooding berry fruit; fleshy & with an appealing rusticity & a tannic finish. **The Very Vivacious Viognier** 🍴 🖩 ★★★ Oak perfume, with dried ginger & attractive yellow peach; hint of honey combines with spice & ripe apple on appealing 12. **40 Days Natural Sweet** ⊕ 🍴 ★★★★ Barrel-aged 09 noted few years ago as rich, but lifted by tangy acidity.

Darling range

Happy Dragon Chenin ☺ 🍴 🖩 ★★★ Honeysuckle intro on still slightly unsettled 13 leads to broad textured palate with limy fresh acid. Good long, dry finish. **Daisy Darling** ☺ 🍴 🖩 ★★★ Combo chenin & sauvignon in 13, delicately perfumed. Modest 12.5% alcohol & nicely dry.

Ruby Darling 🍴 🖩 ★★★ Second bottling of unwooded 11, mostly from pinotage. Easy sipper with good dry grip. **Rosy Darling** 🍴 🖩 ★★ From pinotage, 13 has light peach hue; just-dry with light strawberry playfulness. **Daisy Darling Chardonnay** ⊕ 🍴 🖩 ★★★ Crunchy apple & floral notes & bright acidity on cheeky unwooded 12. — JP

Clos Malverne

Location/map: Stellenbosch ▪ WO: Stellenbosch/Western Cape ▪ Est/1stB 1986 ▪ Tasting & sales Mon-Sat 10-5 Sun 10-4.30 ▪ Fee R25/4 wines ▪ Closed Good Fri, Dec 25 & Jan 1 ▪ Cellar tours Mon-Fri ▪ The Restaurant @ Clos Malverne ▪ Tour groups ▪ Gifts ▪ Farm produce ▪ Conferences ▪ Weddings/functions ▪ Walks/hikes ▪ Wellness Day Spa ▪ Owner(s) Seymour & Sophia Pritchard ▪ Cellarmaster(s)/viticulturist(s) Suzanne Coetzee (Oct 2010) ▪ Winemaker(s) Suzanne Coetzee (Oct 2010), with Mynardt Hitchcock (1999) ▪ 18ha (cab, ptage, sauv) ▪ ±200t/80,000cs own label 50% red 50% white ▪ PO Box 187 Stellenbosch 7599 ▪ info@closmalverne. co.za ▪ www.closmalverne.co.za, www.capeblend.co.za ▪ S 33° 54′ 38.0″ E 018° 48′ 49.2″ ▪ **T +27 (0)21-865-2022** ▪ F +27 (0)21-865-2518

Traditional basket pressing of grapes remains a feature of this winery in Devon Valley, approaching its 30th anniversary and still in the original Pritchard family hands. Back then, the 'Clos' in the name - denoting a (modest) walled vineyard - was consistent with the branding as Stellenbosch's smallest winery. No longer. It's grown to include (among much else) a restaurant with fine valley views and consistent top online rankings for cellardoor experience. Then and now, pinotage and pinotage blends are the speciality, the passion and, in a new release, the 'Spirit'.

★★★★ **Pinotage Reserve** 🖩 Exotic five-spice lift to prune & plum ripeness of 11 (★★★★). Light bodied & gentle, lacks some of the concentration & depth of 10.

★★★★ **Auret** 🖩 Cab (60%), pinotage & merlot in muscular 11 preview. Blueberry & raspberry succulence vies with earthy chocolate. Svelte & seamless, layered & rich but fresh too.

★★★★ **Auret Limited Release** ⊕ Small-production reserve, 08 shows a little more weight, lots more oaky spiciness than regular release. Hard to justify extra cost, but honest effort to raise bar.

Merlot 🖩 ★★★★ 11 is gently mellow, fynbos tinge to ripe mulberry fruit. Medium depth & length with soft suppleness. **Le Café Pinotage** 🖩 ★★★★ Voguishly 'coffee' styled but java element downplayed in 10, giving gentle smoky & dark berry fruit character & making this more appealing than previous. Plush & juicy to dry end.

Cabernet Sauvignon-Merlot ★★★★ **11** step up on **10** (★★★). Body, power & intensity to cassis, tobacco & cocoa. Structured, firm frame. Good concentration on long brooding finish. **Spirit of Malverne Limited Release** NEW ★★★ Bold spicy blueberries on **11** blend of pinotage (50%), cab and shiraz. 70% new oak dominates, making palate a tad astringent & dry. **Cabernet Sauvignon-Shiraz** ★★★★ Cab leads 40% shiraz in **11** that ratchets up a notch on **10** (★★★). Refined yet fresh plum spiciness. Lithe & light to end. **Chardonnay** ★★★ Oak dominates nose & palate of **12**. Creamy vanilla spice, with lime & citrus dialled down. WO W Cape. **Sauvignon Blanc** 🍽 ★★★★ **12** is vibrant & crisp with grapefruit & granadilla tang. Good succulence, with some breadth from lees-ageing. **Sauvignon Blanc Brut Reserve** ★★★ NV low-alcohol sparkler, latest is lean, with variety's lime & lemon tang, lively mousse & good dryness. — FM

Clouds Wine Estate

Location/map: Stellenbosch ▪ WO: Stellenbosch/Walker Bay ▪ Est/1stB 1993 ▪ Tasting & sales Mon-Sat 10-5 ▪ Closed Dec 25 & Jan 1 ▪ Breakfast ▪ Guesthouse & self-catering villas ▪ Conferences ▪ Weddings & functions ▪ Owner(s) Paul Burema & Jolanda van Haperen ▪ Cellarmaster(s) Neil Moorhouse (Jan 2010, Zorgvliet) ▪ Winemaker(s) Neil Moorhouse (Jan 2010, Zorgvliet), with Paul Burema (Jan 2012) ▪ Viticulturist(s) Wynand Pienaar (Aug 2009, consultant) ▪ 4.5ha/2.7ha (cab, pinot, chard, sauv) ▪ 24t/2,500cs own label 40% red 60% white ▪ PO Box 540 Stellenbosch 7599 ▪ info@cloudsestate.co.za ▪ www.cloudsestate.co.za ▪ S 33° 55' 23.9" E 018° 55' 29.7" ▪ **T +27 (0)21-885-1819** ▪ F +27 (0)21-885-2829

Owners Paul Burema and Jolanda van Haperen aren't letting the proverbial grass grow under their feet, having already revamped and modernised the villas at this scenic Helshoogte Pass guest farm and vineyard since acquisition in 2012. Next up is a winery to handle fruit from vines diversified from solely sauvignon blanc.

★★★★ **Sauvignon Blanc** 🍽 Lime & passionfruit zip & zing on **13** (★★★★) pre-bottling sample. Rounded leesy mouthfeel, but less intense than **12**.
Pinot Noir NEW ★★★★ Ethereal delicacy to raspberry, cranberry **13** preview from Walker Bay vines. Light & lacy but focused & intense, with smoky nuance from (older-only) barrels. Deserves time to show best. **Pink Sauvignon Blanc** 🍽 ★★★ Ruby grapefruit tang & hue on **13** tank sample. Uncomplicated but lively & crisp, finishes dry. **Chardonnay** NEW 🍽 ★★★ Tangerine verve on previewed **13**, unoaked, giving fresh grapefruit & lemon succulence free rein. Dry finish, with a light chalky tail. — FM

Clovelly Wines

Location/map/WO: Stellenbosch ▪ Est/1stB 2000 ▪ Tasting, sales & tours strictly by appt ▪ Owner(s) York Partnership t/a Clovelly Wines ▪ Winemaker(s)/viticulturist(s) Jacques Fourie ▪ 4ha/3ha (cab) ▪ 90% red 10% white ▪ Postnet Suite 215 Private Bag X5061 Stellenbosch 7599 ▪ info@clovellywines.com ▪ www.clovellywines.com ▪ S 33° 53' 54.1" E 018° 47' 52.3" ▪ **T +27 (0)82-853-7190** ▪ F +27 (0)21-865-2511

This boutique family farm in Stellenbosch's Devon Valley is triangle shaped - hence the name of The Three Sides Vineyard Blend. But three is also the number of the team at its centre, one of them being the philosophic Jacques Fourie, cellarmaster, reminding himself always that 'winemaking is feelings work'.

Cloverfield Private Cellar

Location/map/WO: Robertson ▪ Est 1945 ▪ 1stB 2002 ▪ Tasting & sales Mon-Fri 9-5 ▪ Closed Easter Fri-Mon, Dec 25 & Jan 1 ▪ Owner(s)/viticulturist(s) Pieter Marais ▪ Cellarmaster(s) Cobus Marais (2002) ▪ Winemaker(s) Cobus Marais (2002), with Gerald Smith (Jun 2009) ▪ ±200ha total (shiraz, chard, chenin, sauv) ▪ 40% red 60% white ▪ PO Box 429 Robertson 6705 ▪ info@cloverfield.co.za ▪ www.cloverfieldwines.com ▪ S 33° 49' 57.3" E 019° 55' 34.1" ▪ **T +27 (0)23-626-4118** ▪ F +27 (0)23-626-3203

Family history has an honoured place - in the winery branding and name of the Shamrock Red - for the much-loved Irish lass who bore Cloverfield patriarch Pietie Marais three sons and brought hope, love as well as luck to the Robertson farm.

Chardonnay Unwooded ☺ 🍽 ★★★ Lemon, quince & pear on fresh & lively ex-tank **13** has satisfying weight, texture. **Sauvignon Blanc** ☺ 🍽 ★★★ Improved **13** aromatic, flavoursome & crisp, lightish alcohol for al fresco entertaining.

Shiraz Preview **12** not rated. **Chardonnay Wooded** ★★★ Subtle vanilla spice on drink-soon **12**, sweet-fruit finish, less focused & concentrated than previous. **Chenin Blanc** ★★ Gently sweet, apple & lemon **13** lightly chilled quaffing fun. **Shamrock Red** ★★ Latest **NV** mainly petit verdot, easy on pocket (as most here) & palate courtesy generous spoon sugar. — DC,MW

■ **Coast** *see PicardiRebel*
■ **Cocoa Hill** *see Dornier Wines*
■ **Coded** *see Babylon's Peak Private Cellar*
■ **Cogmanskloof** *see Zandvliet Wine Estate & Thoroughbred Stud*

Cold Duck (5th Avenue)

Long-established sweet, low-alcohol carbonated sparkling rosé by Distell.

5th Avenue Cold Duck ★★★ Tangy muscat interest in latest **NV**; light, frothy & balanced, uncloying. — DB, HJ

■ **Cold Mountain** *see Brunia Wines*
■ **Collaboration** *see Louis*

Collison's   **NEW**

Recalling brothers John and Francis Collison, English general dealers who distributed and distilled brandy in the Cape Colony, this Distell brandy intends to be funky and fun, and appeal to a young, trendy and inclusively female market.

White Gold ★★★★ Near colourless (useful in cocktails). Light tropical fruity nose, hints of vanilla & roasted nuts. Elegant, youthful with lingering slightly sweet aftertaste. Blended; from chenin & colombard. — WB,TJ

Colmant Cap Classique & Champagne

Location/map: Franschhoek ▪ WO: Western Cape ▪ Est 2005 ▪ 1stB 2006 ▪ Tasting & cellar tours daily by appt ▪ Fee R15 per ½ glass MCC ▪ Sales Mon-Fri 9-4.30 Sat 10.30-1 ▪ Owner(s) Jean-Philippe Colmant ▪ Cellarmaster(s) Jean-Philippe Colmant ▪ Wine consultants Nicolas Follet & Pieter Ferreira ▪ Viticulturist(s) Paul Wallace (consultant) ▪ 5ha/3ha (pinot, chard) ▪ 7,400cs own label 100% MCC ▪ PO Box 602 Franschhoek 7690 ▪ info@colmant.co.za ▪ www.colmant.co.za ▪ S 33° 55' 22.4" E 019° 7' 37.3" ▪ **T +27 (0)21-876-4348/ +27 (0)72-368-4942** ▪ F +27 (0)21-876-3732

It's more than a decade since Jean-Philippe and Isabelle Colmant 'landed in unknown territories from our native Belgium, with luggage, five children and a passion for bubbly...' Now, drawing on grapes from their tiny Franschhoek vineyard and from elsewhere, they have one of the Cape's few wineries devoted to sparkling wine classically made from classic varieties. The wines are mostly kept for unusually long periods on their lees before disgorging, which adds to their finesse and subtle richness of flavour. Widening the range are the slightly sweeter but still serious Sec Reserve, and (untasted) Brut Plaisir intended for 'a younger but discerning market with maximum R100 to spend on a bottle of quality bubbly'.

★★★★ **Brut Rosé** Some red apple & raspberry tartness on charming **NV** (with 75% pinot) which is somewhat more austere & less gushing than many pink bubblies. Dry, with red fruit echoing on a long finish.

★★★★☆ **Brut Reserve** As usual, a little more expressive & generous than the Chardonnay, with 52% pinot giving hints of raspberry. Lightly, silkily rich, fine acidity. **NV** includes 24% wine from earlier vintages, a little oak influence, 32 months on lees. Like next, should repay keeping a few years in bottle.

★★★★☆ **Brut Chardonnay** Biscuity, gently grapey, citrus aromas on latest **NV**. Gorgeously, elegantly severe (though with a plush silk lining), penetrating & vibrantly mineral & dry. Stony, flavourful & long lingering, for those taking bubbles very seriously. Nearly 4 years on lees; 10% reserve wine; a little oak.

★★★★ **Sec Reserve** **NEW** Effectively off-dry **NV** - just sweet enough to lusciously soften the Colmant experience without vulgarising it. Blend as Brut Reserve; 'just' 24 months on lees; 22 grams per litre sugar. — TJ

■ **Compagnies Wijn** *see Oude Compagnies Post Private Cellar*
■ **Condé** *see Stark-Condé Wines*
■ **Confluence** *see Douglas Wine Cellar*

Conradie Family Vineyards

Location/map: Worcester ▪ WO: Nuy/Western Cape ▪ Est/1stB 2004 ▪ Tasting, sales & cellar tours Mon-Fri 9-5 Sat 9-3 Sun 11-2; after-hours by appt ▪ Closed Good Fri, Ascension Day, Dec 25 & Jan 1 ▪ Nuy Vallei Restaurant & Guest House: meals daily 8-5, or by appt ▪ Facilities for children ▪ Tour groups ▪ Gift shop ▪ Farm produce ▪ BYO picnic ▪ Conferences ▪ Walks/hikes ▪ Mountain biking & 4x4 trails ▪ Conservation area ▪ Annual Nuy Valley Feast (May) ▪ Owner(s) Conradie family ▪ Cellarmaster(s) CP Conradie (Jan 2004) ▪ Winemaker(s) CP Conradie (Jan 2004), with Colin Cilliers (Jan 2004) & Ronwan Griffiths (Sep 2009) ▪ Viticulturist(s) Riaan Lambrechts (Aug 2011) ▪ 4,500ha/83ha (cab, ptage, chenin, cbard, crouchen, muscadel w, pinot gris, sauv) ▪ 1,840t total 70t/5,400cs own label 50% red 25% white 25% rosé ▪ BWI ▪ PO Box 5298 Worcester 6851 ▪ wine@ conradievineyards.co.za ▪ www.conradie-vineyards.co.za ▪ S 33° 39' 28.0" E 019° 37' 59.6" ▪ **T +27 (0)23-342-7025** ▪ F +27 (0)86-509-4911

CP Conradie, of the family whose name has long been linked with the Nuy Valley, has had to increase cellar capacity because of the demand he's had locally, and from China and Germany. 'Here in Worcester,' he opines, 'we're becoming better known for producing wines for a little less.'

★★★★ Single Vineyard Barrel Selection Pinotage ✓ 🖾 Now without 'Reserve' in name. Juxtaposition of sweet vanilla & chocolate with savoury bacon & spice in juicy **12**.

Single Vineyard Barrel Selection Cabernet Sauvignon 🖾 **★★★★** Drops 'Reserve' from name. Lightly textured **12** new leather & forest floor whiffs, juicy & refreshing summer or winter red. **Pinotage-Cabernet Sauvignon** 🗄 **★★★** Uncomplicated, nutty **12** has few grams sugar smoothing out the tannins. **Sauvignon Blanc** 🗄 🖾 **★★★** Muted greenpepper & crushed nettle aromas on quiet & well-behaved **13**. WO W Cape. **Sweet Rosaline Perlé Rosé** Await next. Discontinued: **Single Vineyard Chardonnay**. — DB, CvZ

Conspirare 🍴🍷

Location: Stellenbosch ▪ Map: Helderberg ▪ Est/1stB 2002 ▪ Tasting by appt ▪ Owner(s) HB Dowling/LRD Trust ▪ Winemaker(s) Henry Dowling ▪ 24ha (cabs s/f, merlot, shiraz, chenin) ▪ 250t/850cs own label 100% red ▪ PO Box 1210 Stellenbosch 7599 ▪ dowls@mweb.co.za ▪ S 34° 1' 18.4" E 018° 50' 54.6" ▪ **T +27 (0)21-855-0706** ▪ F +27 (0)86-516-3086

Boutique vintner Henry Dowling hasn't vinified his blended red Conspirare in several years, but the 02 is still available from his Helderberg farm.

Constantia de Tulbagh 🍴🍷

Location/map/WO: Tulbagh ▪ Est 1965 ▪ 1stB 2000 ▪ Tasting, sales & tours by appt ▪ Closed all pub hols ▪ Owner(s) Lucas J van Tonder ▪ Cellarmaster(s) Theo Brink (Jan 2008) ▪ Winemaker(s) Theo Brink (Jan 2008), with Niël Russouw (Dec 2011) ▪ Viticulturist(s) Theo Brink (Jan 2008), Niël Russouw (Dec 2011) ▪ 330ha/35ha (cab, merlot, pinot, chenin, riesling, sauv) ▪ 6-10,000cs own label 20% red 80% white ▪ PO Box 79 Tulbagh 6820 ▪ montpellier@montpellier.co.za ▪ www.montpellier.co.za ▪ S 33° 17' 21.3" E 019° 6' 30.7" ▪ **T +27 (0)23-230-0656** ▪ F +27 (0)23-230-1574

Constantia de Tulbagh and neighbour Montpellier, the Tulbagh estates owned by Johannesburg advocate Lucas van Tonder, are farmed more or less as one, says cellarmaster Theo Brink. Constantia's vineyards have been revitalised, and the quality of the grapes is now such that a merlot/cab blend has been vinified.

Cabernet Sauvignon 🖄 **★★★★ 04** last was integrated, with toasty dark berries & yielding tannins. — GdB

Constantia Glen 🍴🍷🍵

Location/WO: Constantia ▪ Map: Cape Peninsula ▪ Est 2000 ▪ 1stB 2005 ▪ Tasting & sales Mon-Fri 10-5 Sat/Sun 10-4 ▪ Fee R40, waived according to purchase ▪ Closed Good Fri & Dec 25 ▪ Cheese & charcuterie platters; various soups during winter ▪ Owner(s) Tumado Investments (Pty) Ltd ▪ Winemaker(s) Justin van Wyk (Dec 2011) ▪ Viticulturist(s) Etienne Southey (Sep 2012, farm manager) & Andrew Teubes (consultant) ▪ 60ha/28.5ha (cabs s/f, malbec, merlot, p verdot, sauv, sem) ▪ 160t/20,000cs own label 70% red 30% white ▪ PO Box 780 Constantia 7848 ▪ wine@constantiaglen.com ▪ www.constantiaglen.com ▪ S 34° 0' 39.6" E 018° 24' 30.6" ▪ **T +27 (0)21-795-6100** ▪ F +27 (0)21-795-6101

Originally part of Simon van der Stel's Constantia farm, the portion now called Constantia Glen was covered by forest or grazed by cattle before the Waibel family joined it to the valley's great tradition of winegrowing in 2000. Thanks to the longer sunlight hours at this northern end of the valley, their favoured Bordeaux grapes, both white and red, flourish. The blends' names, Two, Three and Five, are less complicated: 'Consumers asked for the wine with three or five varieties, which gave us the idea,' explains winemaker Justin van Wyk, 'this also allows us to focus on our brand name.' Dramatically increased export sales and a soon-to-be-enlarged tasting venue mean yet more people get to taste these superb wines.

★★★★☆ **Constantia Glen Five** Sumptuous, sophisticated **09** from 40% petit verdot, rest merlot, cab franc, malbec & cab - all five Bordeaux red varieties, hence the name. Intense dark fruit plus subtle chocolate, moderate acidity & a smooth texture.

★★★★☆ **Constantia Glen Three** **10** (★★★★) is 55% merlot, rest cabs franc & sauvignon. Red & black berries, attractive oak plus a leafy quality. Understated, with juicy upfront fruit before fine tannins. Not quite as characterful as **09**.

★★★★☆ **Sauvignon Blanc** 📚 **12** provides a demanding but ultimately hugely rewarding drinking experience. Flavour spectrum includes lime through green apple to peach & even some white pepper. Bracing acidity & a nicely savoury finish. Contains 10% semillon.

★★★★ **Constantia Glen Two** 📚 **12** (★★★★★) from 71% sauvignon, 29% semillon has good palate weight, coated acidity. Lots going on including notes of peach & tangerine, hint of spice. Better balanced & hence that much more convincing than **11**. — CE

Constantia Mist

Location/WO: Constantia ▪ Map: Cape Peninsula ▪ Est 2004 ▪ 1stB 2009 ▪ Tasting by appt only ▪ Fee R30 ▪ Sales daily 10-5 ▪ Closed Good Fri & Dec 25 ▪ BYO picnic ▪ 4-star guest house (self-catering) ▪ Owner(s) Eagles Nest Property Investments (Pty) Ltd ▪ Cellarmaster(s) John Schooling (2009) ▪ Winemaker(s) Karl Lambour (2009 & 2010 vintages), with Justin van Wyk ▪ Viticulturist(s) Alan Cockroft (2009) ▪ 6.6ha/2.8ha (sauv) ▪ 6t/ha 1,120cs own label 100% white ▪ Postnet Suite 96, Private Bag X16, Constantia 7848 ▪ johns@stagprop.com ▪ www.constantiamist. co.za ▪ S 34° 1' 0.48" E 018° 24' 58.32" ▪ **T +27 (0)21-794-0904** ▪ F +27 (0)21-794-4123

John Schooling caught the wine bug while studying at Stellenbosch University. He bought this tiny Constantia property in the 1990s, and planted only sauvignon blanc, the valley's trademark white grape. After two vintages, work pressure has obliged him to pause production. The 2010 is still available ex farm.

★★★★☆ **Sauvignon Blanc** ⏱ Riper tropical profile on **10** (★★★★). Bone-dry & bracing, with some toasty lees extras, but it lacks the intensity & length of **09**. — AL

Constantia Uitsig

Location/WO: Constantia ▪ Map: Cape Peninsula ▪ Est 1980 ▪ 1stB 1988 ▪ Tasting Mon-Fri 9–5 Sat/Sun & pub hols 10–5 ▪ Fee R25 ▪ Closed Good Fri, Dec 25/26 & Jan 1 ▪ Wine Shop: cheese platters, deli items, gifts ▪ Hanepoot grapes sold annually ▪ Tour groups ▪ Conferences ▪ Horse livery facilities ▪ Cricket oval ▪ La Colombe, Constantia Uitsig Restaurant & River Café (see Restaurants section) ▪ Constantia Uitsig Country Hotel & Spa (see Accommodation section) ▪ Owner(s) Constantia Uitsig Wine Estate (Pty) Limited ▪ Cellarmaster(s) JD Pretorius ▪ Winemaker(s) André Rousseau (2003) & JD Pretorius ▪ Viticulturist(s) André Rousseau (1997) ▪ 60ha/32ha (cabs s/f, merlot, chard, Muscat d'A, sauv, sem) ▪ 120t/20,000cs own label 10% red 90% white ▪ WIETA ▪ PO Box 32 Constantia 7848 ▪ marketingmanager@uitsig.co.za, andre@uitsig.co.za ▪ www. constantia-uitsig.com ▪ S 34° 2' 51.9" E 018° 25' 27.5" ▪ **T +27 (0)21-794-6500** ▪ F +27 (0)21-794-7605

A top-end destination on the wine tourism route, Constantia Uitsig offers not only fine wines, but also a small luxury hotel, a spa and three restaurants. Viticulturist-winemaker André Rousseau's aim is to make wines that match the quality of the food at flagship restaurant La Colombe, which ranks among the world's top 50; and his dreams of producing a premium Bordeaux-style white blend and MCC Blanc de Blancs have been realised. Although he makes his wines at neighbouring Steenberg, Andre's soul remains in the Uitsig vineyards (part of the original 1685 Constantia land grant) where he began sixteen years ago, and where ladybirds bought in by the kilo are released among the vines to help deal with the pests.

★★★★ **Constantia Red** 🌱 Minty hint adds interest to charming cool-climate, merlot-led Bordeaux **11** blend (no **10**). Abundant, accessible, deliciously ripe fruit outlined by integrated, fine oak tannins.

★★★★☆ **Chardonnay** 🌱 Promised return to oaked reserve bottling in **12** (first since **04**) delivers full charm in rich, creamy style, with impeccable balance between spicy oak & sweet fruit. Fresh citrus twist, attractive pithiness & fine acid thread enliven finish.

★★★★ **Sauvignon Blanc** 🍴🌱 Racy **13** shows versatility of combo of both herbaceous green pea & riper melon, with lipsmacking, deliciously rich flavours. Lovely, though a touch off thrilling **12** (★★★★★).

★★★★☆ **Constantia White** 🍴🌱 Serious, earthy **12** blend maintains fine reputation. Barrel-fermented semillon's weight & texture (65%) complement sauvignon's overt fruit flavours & raciness – all in perfect balance throughout persistent finish. No new oak used.

★★★★ **Méthode Cap Classique** 🌱 All-chardonnay sparkling, barrel-fermented **10** back on form after **09** (★★★★); generously rounded, full flavours & long, complex finish. Toasty aromas from 36 months on lees.

★★★★ **Red Muscat d'Alexandrie** Previewed **NV** dessert-style fortified shows overt grape aromas of the variety. Lacks wow-factor of previous, though moreish, sweet impression rendered dry by good spicy tannins.

Chardonnay Unwooded 🍴🌱 ★★★★ Pleasantly youthful **13** has abundant tropical pineapple fruitiness. Easy charm should make delightful summer drink. **Semillon** 🍴🌱 ★★★★★ Convincing, seriously styled **12** needs another year to unwind steely, tightly furled, pithy fruit. Smart oaking & lees-ageing adds breadth to penetrating, persistent finish. Undeniable quality, back on form after lesser **11** (★★★★). — IM

■ **Constitution Road** see Robertson Winery

Conviction 🍸

Location: Somerset West ▪ WO: Elgin ▪ Est/1stB 2009 ▪ Closed to public ▪ Winemaker(s) Clive Torr & David Brown, with Anne Howell ▪ 10ha ▪ 100cs ▪ 26 Topaz Street Heldervue 7130 ▪ clivetorr@bigfoot.com ▪ T +27 (0)82-557-0826

Intended 'to be consumed, not collected', Conviction boutique wines are vinified naturally ('No additives!' emphasises winemaker Clive Torr) at Romond in the Helderberg. The grapes, Clive says, are from Elgin's best site for ripening cab - ripe enough to translate into higher alcohol, in fact. 'It is what it is,' he shrugs.

★★★★ **Cabernet Sauvignon** 🍴🌱 Ultra-ripe **12** with blackcurrant, pencil shavings; supple tannins from all-new oak. Big alcohol less snug than **11** (★★★★★). Intense style will have both fans & detractors. — IM

■ **Cool Bay** see Boplaas Family Vineyards
■ **Cooper** see Beau Belle
■ **Coral Reef** see Wineways Marketing

Corder Family Wines 🍴🍷

Location/WO: Elgin ▪ Map: Elgin, Walker Bay & Bot River ▪ Est 2003 ▪ 1stB 2007 ▪ Tasting & sales Mon-Fri 9-2 Sat/Sun by appt ▪ Closed all pub hols ▪ Owner(s) Ian & Anette Corder ▪ Cellarmaster(s)/winemaker(s) Joris van Almenkerk (Mar 2010) ▪ Viticulturist(s) Kevin Watt (2004) ▪ 40ha/14ha (pinot, shiraz, chard, sauv) ▪ 90t ▪ own label 20% red 80% white ▪ PO Box 169 Elgin 7180 ▪ ian@corderwines.co.za ▪ www.corderwines.co.za ▪ S 34° 12' 8.10" E 019° 0' 47.46" ▪ T +27 (0)21-846-8083 ▪ F +27 (0)21-846-8460

Viticulturist Kevin Watt consults and Joris van Almenkerk of Almenkerk Estate makes the wine, but ultimately boutique vintners Ian and Anette Corder know it's up to them to get the best out of their 14 ha of vineyard. 'We try to take the grapes off as late as possible in keeping with our mantra of "more time on the vine". We want Elgin elegance but also great fruit expression.'

Corder Family Wines range

★★★★ **Cool Climate Chardonnay** 🆕 🍴 **12** is well balanced, entirely enticing with concentrated lemon-lime flavour, tangy acidity & well-judged oak. Delicious now but should also last a good few years.

★★★★☆ **Cool Climate Sauvignon Blanc** ✓ 🍴🌱 Seamless, substantial **12** with peach, some white pepper. Has a richness about it which belies its relatively low 12.5% alcohol. Well balanced, with a coated acidity & savoury finish.

★★★★☆ **Corder Barrel Crafted Viognier** ⏲ 🍴 Peach & hint of spice, **10** (★★★) preview is creamy but lacks intensity & freshness of last **08**.

Corder Special Reserve Shiraz Await new vintage.

Lorry range

Red Lorry Easy Red ⓘ 🍷 🏷 ★★★ From shiraz, this bottling of **NV** big improvement on previous. Uncomplicated but appealing black cherry fruit, good freshness. **Yellow Lorry Sauvignon Blanc** ⓘ 🍷 🏷 ★★ Now bottled, **11** sweet, otherwise simple & short. — CE

■ **Country Cellars** *see* Orange River Wine Cellars
■ **Couple's Wine** *see* Bergheim

Craighall

These easy-drinkers by African Wines & Spirits have been perennial favourites and stalwarts since 1994, and the chardonnay/sauvignon blanc was one of the first such blends in South Africa.

Cabernet Sauvignon-Merlot ⓘ 🍷 ★★ Plummy, fruity **11**, undemanding everyday red. **Sauvignon Blanc** ⓘ 🍷 ★★ Light & dry **12** summer quaffer. WO W Cape for all. **Chardonnay-Sauvignon Blanc** ⓘ 🍷 ★★★ On this label's 20th birthday, **12** still delivers juicy quaffability gussied up with brush of oak. — JP

Cranefields Wine

Location/map: Villiersdorp ▪ WO: Overberg ▪ Est/1st B 1995 ▪ Tasting by appt only ▪ Owner(s) SJ Greve & CJ Roux ▪ Winemaker(s) Riaan Wassüng (Jan 2005, Stellenbosch University Welgevallen Cellar) & Christo Versfeld (Villiersdorp Cellar) ▪ Viticulturist(s) Charl Roux (Feb 1998) ▪ 35ha (cab, merlot, shiraz) ▪ 220t/6,000cs own label 100% red ▪ PO Box 417 Villiersdorp 6846 ▪ info@cranefields.com ▪ www.cranefields.com ▪ S 34° 2' 45.99" E 019° 13' 59.64" ▪ **T +27 (0)28-840-2565** ▪ F +27 (0)28-840-0440

The scenic Overberg Mountains with their varied birdlife inspire these wines, named for South Africa's national bird, the Blue Crane. Vinified by Riaan Wassüng at Welgevallen and Christo Versfeld at Villiersdorp Cellar, the brand continues to do well overseas (Hamburg-based merchant Siegfried Greve is co-owner) while raising funds to help conserve the feathered 'rainbow nation'.

Cabernet Sauvignon ⓘ ★★ **07** true to variety with blackberry fruit, juicy acidity, but straightforward flavours don't linger. **Merlot** ⓘ ★★ **07** food wine has a herbal character with perhaps too much freshness. **Shiraz** ⓘ ★★ Last edition we noted ripe, savoury & very fresh **07** needed drinking soonest. **Red Bishop** ⓘ ★★ Cab-led blend with dollops shiraz & merlot, **07** misses harmony of previous vintage. — CvZ

Creation Wines

Location: Hermanus ▪ Map: Elgin, Walker Bay & Bot River ▪ WO: Walker Bay ▪ Est 2002 ▪ 1stB 2006 ▪ Tasting, sales & cellar tours daily 10-5 ▪ Closed Dec 25 & Jan 1 ▪ Lunch; wine & canapés; secret food & wine pairing; wine & chocolate pairing ▪ Kiddies menu & designated play area ▪ Tour groups ▪ Wine accessories, books & souvenirs on sale ▪ Walking/hiking trails ▪ Conservation area ▪ Art exhibition (paintings & sculptures) ▪ Events: blend your own bottle; barrel/true terroir tasting; vineyard safari on foot; regular musical performances & themed cultural events ▪ Owner(s) Jean-Claude & Carolyn Martin, Jonathan Drake ▪ Cellarmaster(s) Jean-Claude Martin (Jan 2006) ▪ Winemaker(s) Jean-Claude Martin (Jan 2006), with Werner du Plessis (Jan 2012) ▪ Viticulturist(s) Jean-Claude Martin & Peter Davison (consultant), advised by Johan Pienaar (all 2002) ▪ 35ha (cab, grenache, merlot, p verdot, pinot, shiraz, chard, sauv, sem, viog) ▪ 300t/50,000cs own label 65% red 35% white ▪ BWI, IPW ▪ PO Box 1772 Hermanus 7200 ▪ info@creationwines.com ▪ www.creationwines.com ▪ S 34° 19' 51.90" E 019° 19' 33.53" ▪ **T +27 (0)28-212-1107** ▪ F +27 (0)28-212-1127

Husband and wife team of Jean-Claude and Carolyn Martin are in their second decade at the scenic, fynbos and vine bedecked Hemel-en-Aarde estate they created out of virgin sheep pasture. Swiss-born and -trained winemaker JC welcomed countryman and wine aficionado Jonathan Drake on board as an investor, while indefatigable marketer Carolyn reports 27,000 cellardoor visitors in one year, vindicating her belief in tourism as a potentially major contributor to the local and national economy. Adding to the hands-on experience is their presence on YouTube in the form of CreationTV, with online tutorials on food-and-wine pairings, among others. New is a training academy, equipping the next generation in the hospitality sector with marketable wine skills and knowledge.

Premium range

★★★★ **Merlot** 🥂 Chalky texture to fynbos, cocoa-rich **11**. Depth, concentration & body on well-judged oak platform - 35% new. Excellent though not as seamless as **10** (★★★★☆).

★★★★ **Pinot Noir** 🥂 Delicate & ethereal **12** bouquet belies power of deep, smoky cherry, cranberry palate. Layered & silky smooth, as was **11**. Integrated oak platform. Balanced, long finish.

★★★★☆ **Reserve Pinot Noir** 🥂 Forest fruit & loamy notes on lithe, supple yet firmly structured **12** which maintains standard set by **11**. Lacy but with leashed power, depth & concentration. Polished oak, just 25% new. Harmonious, lingering aftertaste.

★★★★ **Syrah** 🥂 Blueberry & plum vibrancy on **11**. Restrained & elegant yet supple & rewarding, as was **10**. Sheen of spice from 25% new oak adds interest & frames pure fruit well.

★★★★ **Merlot-Cabernet Sauvignon-Petit Verdot** 🥂 Thyme & fynbos overlay to pencil shavings, earth & black fruit richness of **11**. Merlot character more prominent than cab, unlike **10**. Poised & balanced, with depth & lengthy dry tail.

★★★★☆ **Syrah-Grenache** ✓ 🥂 Blackcurrant opulence vies with cocoa grip in succulent, spicy **12**, 80/20 blend. Delightful contrast of muscle with silky elegance & depth. Firm yet yielding frame from 14 months oak, 25% new.

★★★★ **Chardonnay** 🥂 Lemon curd & vanilla cream merge deliciously in restrained, classy **12** (★★★★☆). Like **11**, shows Old World style & New World juiciness. Layered palate with oodles of pure fruit that's perfectly countered by oak, just 25% new. Long, rich tail.

★★★★ **Sauvignon Blanc** 🥂 Fresh zesty lime & flint on **13** (★★★★). Grapefruit zing & crunchy dryness on seamless palate. Last-tasted **11** broader, fuller. **12** sold out unreviewed.

★★★★ **Viognier** 🥂 Unwooded **13** shows typical peach vivacity tempered by dry chalky textural note. Seamless & rich, like **11**, not overblown or blowsy. Light & fresh, with elegant long aftertaste.

Sauvignon Blanc-Semillon 🥂 ★★★★ Broad yet crisp & lively **12**. Flinty, pomelo zip yet textured, long. It will reward patience - as with nettly **11**. — FM

Credo

This recently relaunched premium brand is vinified by winemaker Bernard Claassen in conjunction with selected Stellenbosch Vineyards growers, some 3rd generation, to 'express the best that each vintage offers'.

★★★★ **Chenin Blanc** NEW 🥂 Extensive oaking (2 years, 50% new) noticeable on awarded **10** but smartly handled, well integrated. Complex, concentrated Granny Smith/Golden Delicious aromas & flavours.

Shiraz NEW 🥂 ★★★★ Charry oak aromas & flavours, almost jammy fruit on **10** mask 15% alcohol but don't cushion firm tannins & 26 months 80% new oak. Allow few years to settle, integrate. **Shiraz-Merlot-Viognier** NEW 🥂 ★★★★ **10** savoury, with black olive & hint of mint. Not as tannic as red sibling (despite same oaking) but would also benefit from hearty meat dishes or further ageing. **Chardonnay** NEW 🥂 ★★★ Intense lemon flavour well balanced with **12**'s oaky notes, but this rich style perhaps better with (creamy) food than solo. Stellenbosch WO, as for all. Discontinued: **Quattuor**, **Quinque**. — CvZ

Crios Bríde

Location: Stellenbosch ▪ Est/1stB 2007 ▪ Closed to public ▪ Owner(s) Yorke-Smith Family & Martin Bates ▪ Winemaker(s) Carla Pauw (Jan 2007, consultant) ▪ 2,500cs own label 15% red 25% white 60% MCC ▪ PO Box 2290 Dennesig Stellenbosch 7601 ▪ info@criosbride.com ▪ **T +27 (0)21-883-9568** ▪ F +27 (0)88-021-883-9568

Families, especially new offspring, can be unpredictable, and while last edition we delightedly announced the imminent birth of long-gestated (5 years!) MCC triplets for Crios Bríde, we've not actually tasted them yet. We do have their names, though: Ianna, Nimue and Ariane, daughters of Celtic fertility goddess Brighid, whose braided straw girdle gives this Stellenbosch boutique winery its name.

★★★★ **Syrah-Carignan** ⊕ Powerful **07** concentrated molten dark fruit, good structure & ageability.

Chenin Blanc ⊕ ★★★★ Sumptuous & robust **07** ex Swartland vines. **Sauvignon Blanc** ⊕ ★★★★ Last was single-vineyard **08** from Darling, with gentle asparagus tone. **Méthode Cap Classique** ⊕ ★★★★ **07** sparkling from chardonnay & pinot noir, made extra-dry & perfect with oysters. — MW

■ **Cross Collection** *see Dieu Donné Vineyards*

Crows Nest

Location: Paarl ▪ Map: Paarl & Wellington ▪ WO: Coastal ▪ Est/1stB 2002 ▪ Tasting, sales & cellar tours Mon-Fri 10–5 Sat/Sun & pub hols by appt ▪ Fee R25, waived on purchase ▪ Meals by appt; or BYO picnic ▪ Facilities for children ▪ Farm produce ▪ Walking/hiking trails ▪ Conservation area ▪ Owner(s) Marcel & Deidre de Reuck ▪ Winemaker(s) Marcel de Reuck ▪ 33.6ha/11.5ha (cab, shiraz) ▪ 60t/10,000cs own label 90% red 5% white 5% port ▪ PO Box 2571 Paarl 7620 ▪ dereuck@mweb.co.za ▪ www.dereuckwines.co.za ▪ S 33° 40' 33.0" E 018° 54' 25.4" ▪ **T +27 (0)21-869-8712** ▪ F +27 (0)21-869-8714

As expected from one who spent eight years diving off Scotland's oil rigs, Agter Paarl-based boutique vintner Marcel de Reuck's wines are no blushing wallflowers: 'Wine should have a presence, shake you up a bit!'

Torres Claude range

Crow's Nest ⓟ ★★☆ Rhône-inspired **07** blend with forward fruit; rich & densely packed, sweetish finish.

Marcel de Reuck range

Cabernet Sauvignon Next awaited, as for **Syrah**, **Cabernet Sauvignon-Merlot** & **Chardonnay**. — WB

Croydon Vineyard Residential Estate

Location: Somerset West ▪ Map: Helderberg ▪ WO: Stellenbosch ▪ Est/1stB 2004 ▪ Tasting & sales Mon-Fri 10–5 Sat 9–1 ▪ Closed all religious holidays ▪ Cellar tours by appt ▪ Facilities for children ▪ Tour groups ▪ Conferences ▪ Events ▪ Owner(s) Croydon Vineyard Estate Homeowners Association ▪ Cellarmaster(s) Beyers Truter (2004) ▪ Winemaker(s) Corius Visser (2004) ▪ 8ha (cabs s/f, malbec, merlot, ptage, shiraz, chenin) ▪ 65t/4,000cs own label 95% red 5% white ▪ Unit 1 Croydon Vineyard Estate Somerset West 7130 ▪ info@croydon-estate.co.za ▪ www.croydon-estate.co.za ▪ S 34° 2' 23.3" E 018° 45' 5.5" ▪ **T +27 (0)21-843-3610** ▪ F +27 (0)21-843-3609

The names of the wines made at this Helderberg residential estate reflect the character and story of the place. Portion 20 refers to the original farm, where the winery is, while the Title Deed range confirms that the house-owners are also co-owners of the vineyards and cellar. Some, in fact, get involved even before wines reach the bottle - including the occasional bit of grape-crushing by foot.

Title Deed range

★★★★ **Cape Blend** ⓟ Chunky & savoury **11** (★★★☆) preview (rating provisional) foursquare & earthy, lacking promise of **10**. From pinotage & cab supported by merlot, shiraz.

Rosé ▨ ★★★★ Salmon pink **13** has savoury strawberry notes; good intensity yet delicate & polished; dry but not tart, with seductive freshness. From shiraz, as was showier **12** (★★★☆). **Chenin Blanc** ▨ ★★☆ Fresh peardrop aromas mingle with faint vegetal whiffs on overly delicate **13**. Discontinued: **Rhône Blend**.

Croydon Vineyard Residential Estate range

★★★★ **Covenant** ⓟ Intense fruit & new oak on last-tasted **09**. Serious, well made pinotage. Should keep.

Portion 20 ★★★★ Savoury Cape Blend **11** finer than previous; herbal notes from pinotage (40%, with cab, merlot, shiraz) to lift aromas, add spice to rustic charm. — MF

Crystallum

Location: Hermanus ▪ WO: Hemel-en-Aarde Valley/Overberg/Hemel-en-Aarde Ridge ▪ Est 2006 ▪ 1stB 2007 ▪ Closed to public ▪ Owner(s) Crystallum Coastal Vineyards (Pty) Ltd ▪ Winemaker(s) Peter-Allan Finlayson (2006) ▪ 30t/3,700cs own label 60% red 40% white ▪ PO Box 857 Hermanus 7200 ▪ info@crystallumwines.com ▪ www.crystallumwines.com

Behind this small but dynamic winery are two brothers, third generation of Cape winemaking Finlaysons: Andrew, an architect, and Peter-Allan, who left his studies in philosophy and economics to be the winemaker here. Although this adventure began in 2007 with sauvignon blanc, the focus is now solely on the two great Burgundian varieties, chardonnay and pinot noir. And the range is expanding, as they look to explore different sites through these grapes – 'expressing the incredible diversity of site and soils through single vineyard wines'. Vinification is done in a shared winery on an olive farm on the Hemel-en-Aarde Ridge.

★★★★☆ **Cuvée Cinéma Pinot Noir** This H-en-A Ridge **12** perhaps the most refined version here; as perfumed & elegant as ever, with the sweetly dark-fruited notes brighter than Bona Fide's, the texture silk rather than velvet, the colour lighter & redder. Finely balanced, pinioned on graceful acidity.

★★★★☆ **Peter Max Pinot Noir** Like Bona Fide, from H-en-Aarde Valley. Pure sensual, perfumed delight on **12**, though the firm structure - more acid than tannin - ensures that it's also refined, albeit not quite as serious as the other two (drink now while waiting for them). All in delicious harmony; lingering finish.

★★★★☆ **Bona Fide Pinot Noir** NEW Fine **12** less ripely exuberant & opulent than Peter Max; more so than Cinéma. Slight smokiness to berry aromas & flavours. Some power, plenty of substance - grippy acid, subtle tannin, to ensure good few years development. These pinots all modestly oaked; this one 30% new barrels.

★★★★☆ **Clay Shales Chardonnay** **12** less oaky than previous, meaning more subtlety - no less flavour or early complexity (nice hint of butterscotch remains). These chards now matured only in older barrels. Lightly rich & silky, but not heavy; clean & fresh. Some complexity & harmony now - both will grow with few years.

★★★★ **The Agnes Chardonnay** Generous, ripe aromas on **12** with some tropical notes, though less showy on the tasty but elegantly streamlined palate. Ends with subtle lime force. **11** sold out untasted. — TJ

■ **Cubana** see Leeuwenjacht
■ **Culinaria Collection** see Leopard's Leap Family Vineyards
■ **Cutters Cove** see Robert Stanford Estate

Dâbar

Location/WO: Napier ▪ 1stB 2010 ▪ Closed to public ▪ Owner(s) Kevin Snyman & Jannie Gutter ▪ Winemaker(s) Jean Daneel (Jean Daneel Wines) ▪ Viticulturist(s) Dawie le Roux (consultant) ▪ 50% red 50% white ▪ kevinsnyman@telkomsa.net ▪ **T +27 (0)82-926-8459**

Co-owner Kevin Snyman, a tree-crop specialist 'by nature, trying to be a wine specialist', is learning the intricacies of bottling, labelling and marketing these wines made by highly regarded Napier-based winemaker Jean Daneel. Still maturing in barrel at press time is a maiden shiraz from the 2013 vintage.

Pinot Noir NEW ★★★ Spicy pomegranate & rosepetal on gently oaked (50% new), light-footed (±13% alcohol) **11** summer red from block's first crop. **Sauvignon Blanc** ★★★ Khaki bush-toned **11** shows fine acid/fruit balance, lightish alcohol for all-day enjoyment. — WB, GdB

■ **Da Capo Vineyards** see Idiom Wines

Dagbreek

Location: Rawsonville ▪ Map/WO: Breedekloof ▪ Est/1stB 2009 ▪ Tasting, sales & cellar tours Mon-Sat by appt ▪ Closed all pub hols ▪ BYO picnic ▪ Walking/hiking trails ▪ Owner(s) Peet Smith ▪ Cellarmaster(s)/winemaker(s) Peet Smith (2009) ▪ Viticulturist(s) Leon Dippenaar (2009, consultant) ▪ 108ha/48ha under vine ▪ 7t/1,000cs own label 70% red 30% white ▪ WIETA ▪ PO Box 237 Rawsonville 6845 ▪ dagbreek@compnet.co.za ▪ www. dagbreek.co.za ▪ S 33° 39' 56.20" E 019° 18' 26.99" ▪ **T +27 (0)82-820-2256** ▪ F +27 (0)86-529-2865

Third-generation grower on the Breede River near Rawsonville, Peet Smith's boutique-scale portfolio comes with a 'rainbow wine nation' built in: Italian variety nebbiolo, Portuguese touriga nacional and French chenin. 'Our motto, Pleasure Through Quality, is portrayed throughout the cellar and into the bottle.'

Nebbiolo ⊕ ★★★ Inky blueberry **10** has variety's typical bright acidity, still unsettled in youth, needs time or food. **Touriga Nacional** ⊕ ★★★★ **10** black fruit plumped by touch sugar, juicy & flavoursome. **Chenin Blanc Barrel Selection** Previewed **11** barrel sample too young & unformed to rate. — MW

Dalla Cia Wine & Spirit Company

Location/map/WO: Stellenbosch ▪ Est 2004 ▪ Tasting, sales & traditional Italian meals at Pane E Vino Food & Wine Bar, Mon-Fri 10-6 Sat 10-5 ▪ Owner(s)/winemaker(s) Giorgio Dalla Cia ▪ 18,000cs ▪ 7A Lower Dorp Street Bosman's Crossing Stellenbosch ▪ info@dallacia.com ▪ www.dallacia.com ▪ S 33° 56' 25.8" E018° 50' 50.1" ▪ **T +27 (0)21-888-4120** ▪ F +27 (0)21-887-2621

Asked what makes him laugh, Giorgio Dalla Cia replies: 'Looking at the results from some wine competitions.' Long past chasing medals, Giorgio's credentials were well established as longtime winemaker at illustrious Meerlust before starting the Stellenbosch family wine and grappa business (and food, this is an Italian *famiglia*) exactly ten years ago. Grapes are bought in and given the Giorgio treatment, honed over the decades: 'You need attention to detail during winemaking and enough money to invest in high-quality barrels. Innate good taste, the ability to reference the memory of the great wines of France and experience also help.'

Dalla Cia Wine & Spirit Company range

★★★★☆ **Classico Cabernet Sauvignon** 🌱 **11** similar classic styling to ageworthy **10**. Red & black fruit, attractive oak spice. Medium bodied with fresh acidity & nicely grippy tannins.

★★★★ **Pinot Noir** ⓣ Debut **11** serious & demanding. Red & black fruit, slight toasty oak character. Rich but still balanced thanks to fresh acidity. Extremely youthful when tasted, needs time to marry.

★★★★☆ **Giorgio** ⓣ Bordeaux blend, **07** (★★★★★) shows complexity, finesse & balance. Red & black fruit, some herbs & tobacco; same attractive oak as **06**. Great concentration, fine but grippy tannins. Built to last.

Chardonnay 🍽 🌱 ★★★ **12** appears quite stern, with subdued citrus flavour & particularly zesty acidity. Needs a plate of seafood to show best. **Sauvignon Blanc** ⓣ 🍽 ★★★★ **12** whispers rather than shouts class. Lean & fresh, with lime & green apple notes, long savoury finish. More focused than **10** (★★★). **11** sold out untasted.

Grappa-Styles NEW

★★★★☆ **Limited Edition Pinot Noir** The most transparent, water-white of the range, & the closest in delicacy & purity to fine modern Italian examples. Ethereal, subtly complex aromas of fruit, flowers & nuts lead on to energetic, slippery textured & lingering palate.

★★★★ **Pinot-Chardonnay** Fresh aromas of fruit & nuts; some delicacy, focus & refinement evident on a delightfully textured, smooth & balanced palate.

★★★★ **Cabernet Sauvignon-Merlot Premium Selection** Slight straw tinge to this more refined, less aggressive Premium (lightly oak-barrelled) version of the standard Husk Spirit from these varieties. Supple, gently unctuous palate, lingering finish.

Cabernet Sauvignon-Merlot ★★★★ Robust, forward aromas & flavours - 'husky', quiet berry hint. Smooth enough, but with some old-style rusticity. — WB, CE, TJ

Damarakloof

Location/WO: Paarl ▪ Map: Paarl & Wellington ▪ Est/1stB 2006 ▪ Function venue by appt ▪ Owner(s) Agnes de Vos ▪ Winemaker(s) Carla Pauw (Jan 2006) ▪ 19ha (cabs s/f, merlot, chenin) ▪ 10t/1,300cs own label 50% red 50% white ▪ PO Box 38 Elsenburg 7607 ▪ agnesdev@telkomsa.net, carlapauw@gmail.com ▪ S 33° 48' 41.79" E 018° 47' 21.19" ▪ **T +27 (0)21-884-4304** ▪ F +27 (0)21-884-4304

A small but diversified agri-holding (grapes, olives, figs, roses, horses) that has been in Agnes de Vos' family for over a century, Damarakloof near Paarl boasts a 60+ year-old vineyard that was originally a racetrack – then deemed too gravelly for vines. Chenin and a red blend are made in tiny volumes when crops allow.

Racetrack range

Regale ⓣ ★★★★ When last tasted, **08** Bordeaux red returned to classic form after **06** (★★★★☆). Fragrant, refreshingly demure & altogether delightful to drink. No **07**. — DS

▪ **Dam Good** *see* Villiersdorp Cellar
▪ **Danie de Wet** *see* De Wetshof Estate

D'Aria Winery

Location: Durbanville ▪ Map: Durbanville, Philadelphia & Darling ▪ WO: Durbanville/Western Cape ▪ Est/1stB 2007 ▪ Tasting & sales Mon 12-6 Tue-Fri 10-6 (summer) / Mon 11-5 Tue-Fri 9-5 (winter) Sat 10-5 Sun 10-4 ▪ Fee R15 ▪ Closed Dec 25 & Jan 1 ▪ Cheese platters & deli products served in tasting room ▪ Poplars Restaurant ▪ Conferences/functions ▪ Hiking & mountain biking trails ▪ 4-star guest cottages ▪ Music concerts in summer ▪ Owner(s) Barinor Holdings ▪ Brandy master Rudi von Waltsleben (2008) ▪ Winemaker(s) Rudi von Waltsleben (Nov 2007), with Nicola Viljoen (Apr 2010) ▪ Viticulturist(s) Johan von Waltsleben (1998) ▪ 80ha/63ha (cab, merlot, shiraz, sauv) ▪ 400t/160,000cs own label 67% red 30% white 3% rosé + 400cs for clients & ±1,000btls x 500ml brandy ▪ M13 Racecourse Road Durbanville 7550 ▪ tasting@daria.co.za ▪ www. dariawinery.co.za ▪ S 33° 50' 28.6" E 018° 36' 36.2" ▪ **T +27 (0)21-801-6772** ▪ F +27 (0)86-539-4519

Musical themes permeate this winery on the Tygerberg Hills, as cellarmaster Rudi von Waltsleben is both musician and winemaker and sees a connection: 'Music is an expression of emotion, so is winemaking; the creative urge in both is always to do something new and better.' Also new and good is the FAAB project against alcohol abuse begun with the farm and cellar employees.

Reserve Range

★★★★☆ **The Soprano Shiraz** ⚀ Bold, generously oaked (40% new) **09** (★★★★) a dense pliable mouthful. Good fruit but lacks freshness, with a rather cloying finish. Less successful than powerful **08**.

★★★★ **The Songbird Sauvignon Blanc** ▤ **12** (★★★★) tiny 4% oaked portion adds spice, weight, but lacks the steely invigoration of **11**; finishes a bit heavy & sweet.

The Following White Blend ⚀ ▤ ★★★★ Ripe, flavoursome viognier with semillon, sauvignon &, in **11**, oak vanilla. Plush yet lively, roundly dry.

Terra Range

SV Shiraz ☺ ⚠ ★★★ Bright toasty oak, white spice scents on **10**. Big & flavoursome with rounded grip.

Merlot ⚀ ★★★ **10** lighterweight in fruit & structure than **09** - but not alcohol. A few grams sugar lift soft red plum flavours. **Cabernet Sauvignon-Merlot** ⚠ ★★★ Abundance of ripe dark berries on succulent just-dry **11**. Subtle oak is a complementary extra. **Blush** ▤ ⚠ ★★ Peach-pink **13**, fruitily off-dry rosé. **Sauvignon Blanc** ▤ ⚠ ★★★ **12** at the greener end of aroma/flavour spectrum; leesy bounce modifies sharpish acid.

Music Range

Shiraz-Cabernet Sauvignon-Merlot ▤ ⚠ ★★★ Was 'Red'. Uncomplicated **12**'s ripe fruit gives smooth & easy drinking. **Sauvignon Blanc** ▤ ⚠ ★★ Previously 'White'. Gently fresh, quaffable **13**. WO W Cape.

Brandy range [NEW]

The Piccolo 5 Year Potstill Brandy ★★★ Earthy ripe apricots, green herbal notes & a sherry cask edge. Uncomplicated, youthfully rough & fiery. 100% potstill from colombard. — AL

Darling Cellars   🍷 ⚔ 👤 ♿

Location/WO: Darling ▪ Map: Durbanville, Philadelphia & Darling ▪ Est 1948 ▪ 1stB 1996 ▪ Tasting & sales Mon-Thu 9–5 Fri 9-2 Sat 10–2 ▪ Closed Good Fri, Dec 25 & Jan 1 ▪ Cellar tours by appt ▪ Wine & food pairing/sampling, no meals ▪ Facilities for children ▪ Owner(s) 20 shareholders ▪ Cellarmaster(s) Abé Beukes (Dec 1997) & Alastair Rimmer (Jan 2013) ▪ Winemaker(s) Welma Visser & Carel Hugo (Nov 2007/Jun 2009), with Anthony Meduna ▪ Viticulturist(s) Gerhard Rossouw (Mar 2012) ▪ 1,300ha (barbera, cab, carignan, cinsaut, grenache, malbec, merlot, mourv, ptage, shiraz, chard, chenin, riesling, sauv, sem) ▪ 7,500–8,500t/700,000cs own label 70% red 28% white 2% rosé ▪ Other export brands: Alta Casa, Black Granite, Cellar Road, Fountain Crossing, Mamre Road, Victoria Bay ▪ BRC, BWI, WIETA ▪ PO Box 114 Darling 7345 ▪ info@darlingcellars.co.za ▪ www.darlingcellars.co.za ▪ S 33° 26' 25.7" E 018° 31' 25.1" ▪ **T +27 (0)22-492-2276**

Wheatfields are punctuated by gnarled bushvines - a signature sight of the Darling region and a combination that allows for a balanced agricultural harmony that reduces disease. The pay-off line 'True to nature' was obvious to cellarmaster Abé Beukes and the team. Bushvines, they believe, can produce particularly intense flavours and, in combination with the cooling West Coast breezes, produce the characteristic regional expression of elegance with a modern, fruity touch. This large grower-owned cellar has long been a source of great value, but the greater focus on quality is seen as essential to the perception of the brand.

Limited Releases

★★★★☆ **Sir Charles Henry Darling** ✓ ⚠ Cab franc leads cab, merlot & petit verdot in fine flagship. **11** has contained dark berry fruit, whiffs of cedary oak leading to cool entry with good savoury foil to dark berry ripeness. Still young, needing time for tannins to settle.

★★★★☆ **Lime Kilns** ⚀ ⚠ Creamy chardonnay, spicy viognier & rich chenin in **11**. Great balance of fruit & saline support. Poised richness from barrel fermentation & lees-ageing, with fresh acidity.

★★★★ **Blanc de Blancs Brut** ✓ ⚠ With its vibrant mousse, **11** MCC from chardonnay has oystershell & lemon zest intro, brioche complexity & crisp bite with bone-dry follow through.

Cellarmaster's Signature Selection No. 1 Await next, as for **Cellarmaster's Signature Selection No.2.**

Premium range

★★★★☆ **Cabernet Sauvignon** ✓ 🏵 **10** has leafy tobacco top notes typical of cool region, supported by a core of cassis with poised ripe promise. Cool nose continues to fresh palate with attractive savoury thread ending elegant & dry. Back on track after lesser previewed **09** (★★★★).

★★★★ **Shiraz** ✓ 🏵 **10** (★★★★) lacks the intensity & length of **09**. Lighter, with red fruits, bright spice & dry medium finish.

★★★★ **Sauvignon Blanc** 🕓 🏵 Bouncy tropical intro shows off poised granadilla & ruby grapefruit. The rounded palate in modern idiom has fresh citrus finish. **11** less herbal than past regional expressions.

Pinotage 🏵 ★★★★ **11** starts with vibrant cherry lift, has earth, banana loaf & sour plum freshness to support dry firm tannins. Needs food. **Kroon** ✓ 🏵 ★★★★ **10** shiraz & grenache-led 5-way blend. Rich inviting nose, brooding fruit with toasty oak & mulberry core lead to elegant palate with fine dry tannins. Step up on **08** (★★★★). **09** sold out untasted. **Noble Late Harvest** Await next.

Reserve range

Six Tonner Merlot ☺ 🍴 🏵 ★★★ **12** vibrant fresh red fruit with toasty oak support, medium bodied for easy drinking & dry finish. **Old Blocks Pinotage** ☺ 🍴 🏵 ★★★ Perfumed **12** has lifted cherry fruit & ripe banana supported by prune ripeness & caramel oak. Dry, firm & lingering farewell. **Shiraz-Mourvèdre** 🍴 🏵 ★★★ Upfront & fruity, with vivacious mulberry fruit. **12** gets attractive meaty note from 45% mourvèdre. Ends lively & bright. **Quercus Gold Chardonnay** ☺ 🍴 🏵 ★★★ Upfront ripe apple & blossom aromas on appealing **13**; cream-textured follow-through with a rounded, dry end. **Arum Fields Chenin Blanc** ☺ 🍴 🏵 ★★★ Blossoms, poised ripe stonefruit billow from **13**, offering fruity quaffing & a soft landing.

Terra Hutton Cabernet Sauvignon 🍴 🏵 ★★★☆ Smoky tarry top note on **12** leads to savoury herbal end. **Black Granite Shiraz** ✓ 🍴 🏵 ★★★★ Enticing black pepper spice on savoury-styled **12** has tarry undertone leading to vibrant red-fruited finish. **Bush Vine Sauvignon Blanc** ✓ 🍴 🏵 ★★★★ Tropical **13** has blossom complexity leading to vibrant clean & zippy palate with great fruit concentration & gentle acidity.

Growers Signature Selection NEW

The Chairman ☺ 🍴 🏵 ★★★ Shiraz leads the way in vibrant **12** blend with mourvèdre, cinsaut. Some spice, red fruits, baked stone, fresh & savoury. **Cinsaut-Cabernet Sauvignon** ☺ 🍴 🏵 ★★★ Toasty oak on **12**, but lots of easy fruitiness for a daily sipper. **Chenin Blanc** ☺ 🍴 🏵 ★★★ Nectarine blossom, honeysuckle lift flows to soft palate with stonefruit intensity on fleshy **13**. **Mariette** ☺ 🍴 🏵 ★★★ Mostly from chenin & viognier, seductive **13** offers rich aromas & flavours of tinned peaches; full, rounded, but dry.

Classic range

Cabernet Sauvignon-Merlot 🍴 🏵 ★★★☆ Easy oak aromas add to berry fruit on off-dry **12**. **Merlot Rosé** 🕓 🍴 ★★★ Blazing pink off-dry **12** charms with strawberry perfume. **Chenin Blanc-Sauvignon Blanc** 🍴 🏵 ★★★ Quintessential tropical fruit salad on **13** offers easy sipping.

Chocoholic range NEW

Pinotage 🍴 🏵 ★★★ Off-dry **13** - it's all in the name!

Sweet Darling

Red NEW 🍴 🏵 ★★ Fudge & cherry pop on **NV** sweet sipper. **Rosé** 🍴 🏵 ★☆ Boiled sweets in semi-sweet quaffer. Was vintaged, now **NV**. **White** 🍴 🏵 ★★ Lifted floral note on **NV** sweetie. Discontinued: **Pettilant White**. — JP

■ **Darlington** *see* Withington
■ **Daschbosch** *see* uniWines Vineyards
■ **Dassie's Reserve** *see* Botha Wine Cellar

David 🍷

Location: Malmesbury ▪ Map/WO: Swartland ▪ Est/1stB 2010 ▪ Tasting by appt ▪ Owner(s)/winemaker(s)/viticulturist(s) David & Nadia Sadie ▪ (carignan, cinsaut, grenache n/b, shiraz, chard, chenin, clairette, rouss, viog) ▪ 10t/1,100cs own label 50% red 50% white ▪ IPW, Swartland Independent (2011) ▪ wine@davidsadie.co.za ▪ www.davidsadie.co.za ▪ **T +27 (0)72-375-4336** ▪ F +27 (0)86-512-4903

'Hands-on but also hands-off' is how husband and wife David and Nadia Sadie characterise their boutique winery, now headquartered in Swartland capital Malmesbury. 2013 was a big year, the harvest ending just ahead of the birth of their first child, Wilhelm Johann, followed by the launch of red blend Elpidios. David continues to consult at Tulbagh winery Lemberg but his focus is now on this 'remote business making honest, more natural wines, unique to our area'. It's all about 'putting the Swartland above ourselves' for this dynamic yet humble couple: 'There are few things more special than having a fantastic time with a diverse group of people whose only thing in common is the wine.'

★★★★☆ **Elpidios** NEW Mostly shiraz, with carignan, grenache & drop cinsaut debut in soulful, compact **11** from varied soils. Effusively fruity yet crafted to reward cellaring 5+ years. Natural vinification - native yeasts, no additives, long lees-ageing, lower sulphur - sets tone for all.

★★★★☆ **Chenin Blanc** ✓ Personality packed **12** has rock salt nuance to its white & yellow stonefruit, focused acidity, grippy texture. Like well-defined **11**, delicious now & enough structure for several years fruitful ageing. As with all David Sadie's wines, oxidatively styled in older oak.

★★★★★ **Aristargos** ✓ Clairette, chardonnay join chenin, viognier in **12** authoritative blend ex six dryland mountain vineyards (including 50+ year old bushvines). Precise, engaging & with an enduring farewell; quieter yet no less convincing than hedonistic **11** from chenin, roussanne & dash grenache blanc.

Grenache ✓ ★★★★☆ Evocative **12** from Perdeberg vines eloquently speaks of the magic of old vines. Nothing out of place, just pure silky red fruit & super-fine tannins. Vast improvement on funky **11** (★★★). Tiny two-barrel production, like Chenin. — CE,CvZ

David Frost Signature Series �

Champion golfer David Frost gives his name to this range, produced by Perdeberg Winery (see entry). The wines are available in South African retail exclusively through Pick n Pay stores, and exported to China and the US.

Shiraz ☺ 🍾 📖 ★★★ Well-judged middleweight, **12** shows elegant spicy & herbaceous notes, with ripe red berries & bracing tannin. **Classic Red** ☺ 🍾 📖 ★★★ Unchallenging, likeable **12** cab-merlot blend with cinsaut. WO Paarl, as for all.

Chenin Blanc 🍾 📖 ★★★ Fresh, sunny & fruity **13** shows improved flavour concentration, with enticing peach & pear notes. **Soft Smooth Red** 🍾 📖 ★★☆ Prominent crushed berries on slightly sweet **12**. — GdB

David Frost Wines

Location: Paarl ▪ WO: Western Cape ▪ Est 1994 ▪ 1stB 1997 ▪ Closed to public ▪ Owner(s) David Frost ▪ Winemaker(s) Erlank Erasmus (Jan 2010, consultant) ▪ ±13,333cs own label 60% red 40% white ▪ PO Box 68 Main Road Paarl 7620 ▪ erlank@erasmuswine.co.za ▪ www.frostwine.com ▪ T +27 (0)21-872-2429/+27 (0)84-601-8680 ▪ F +27 (0)86-299-1773

Champion golfer David Frost maintains his long association with wine (he financed his earliest golfing efforts picking grapes on his father's farm) with this own-brand, now focused on an accessible and well-priced red and white.

Shiraz ★★★ Citrusdal grapes in appealing & unoaked **12** easy-drinker. Aromas a tad retiring, hint at ripe plums, but palate is refreshing & juicy. **Sauvignon Blanc** NEW ✓ 🍾 ★★★★ Intense tropical & granadilla fruit plays against nice dry finish, lengthy tangy acidic seam extending the flavours. **13** over-delivers. Discontinued: **Cabernet Sauvignon, Merlot, Par Excellence**. — GdB, GM

■ **David Nieuwoudt** see Cederberg Private Cellar

DeanDavid Wines

Location: Riebeek-Kasteel ▪ WO: Swartland ▪ Est/1stB 2003 ▪ Closed to public ▪ Wines available at the Wine Kollective, Riebeek-Kasteel ▪ Owner(s) Dean Thompson, Roger Clayton, Peter Alexander & John Fulford ▪ Cellarmaster(s)/winemaker(s) Dean Thompson & Roger Clayton ▪ 10t/1,000cs own label 80% red 20% white ▪ PO Box 357 Riebeek Kasteel 7307 ▪ dean@unwined.co.za, roger@unwined.co.za ▪ www.unwined.co.za ▪ T +27 (0)71-233-8261 (Dean)/+27 (0)76-826-8500 (Roger)

Of the eponymous pair, Dean Thompson is the part-time winemaking (and marketing-reluctant) son, David his father with a farm outside Riebeek-Kasteel. Roger Clayton joined Dean in the cellar in 2011. The delightfully pure, tiny-volume Syrah is off five 'close to organic' blocks; it's set to be joined by a Chenin.

★★★★ **2 Mile Square Swartland Syrah** Previewed last year, **11** was freshened up in the bottling process; now much improved. Ripely soft, with melting but still-guiding tannin; delicious aromas & flavours. — TJ

▨ **De B** see De Breede Organic Vineyards

De Bos Handpicked Vineyards

These premium Fairtrade wines, available nationwide in Makro stores, are sourced from farms in Upper Hemel-en-Aarde Valley, Wellington and Hermon owned and managed by Bosman Family Vineyards (see entry).

De Bos Handpicked Vineyards range NEW

★★★★ **Chenin Blanc** ✓ 🍶 ▨ Unoaked, dry **12** is slow to unfold then reveals real lees-enriched substance, complex & persistent honeyed fruit. Worth ageing a few years.
Cabernet Sauvignon ✓ ▨ ★★★☆ **11** should satisfy with its uncomplicated dark berry fruit, freshness & classic cab grip. Oak, 30% new, welcomingly modest. **Merlot** ▨ ★★ Simple, off-dry **12** with tart plum fruit.
Pinot Noir ▨ ★★★ Easy-drinking **12** medium bodied & lively with straightforward juicy dark cherry flavours, hint of toasty oak. WO Walker Bay. **Chardonnay** 🍶 ▨ ★★★ Subdued earthy, leesy aromas on unwooded **12** from Walker Bay; pleasingly medium bodied, crisp. **Sauvignon Blanc** 🍶 ▨ ★★★★ Pure yet restrained cool-climate greengage, green apple mellowed by a hint of bottle-age on **12**. Lively yet unaggressive; fruitily sweet finish. WO Walker Bay. — AL

De Breede Organic Vineyards

Location: Worcester ▪ Map/WO: Breedekloof ▪ Est 2006 ▪ 1stB 2009 ▪ Tasting by appt ▪ Owner(s) Tim & Debbie Alcock ▪ Cellarmaster(s)/viticulturist(s) Tim Alcock (2006) ▪ Winemaker(s) Tim Alcock (2006), with Isaac Mabeta (2009) ▪ 26ha/2.5ha (cab, malbec, merlot, p verdot) ▪ 6t/500cs own label 99% red 1% rosé ▪ Certified organic by BCS ▪ PO Box 511 Worcester 6849 ▪ debreedevineyards@burchells.co.za ▪ www.debreedevineyards.co.za ▪ S 33° 37' 10.69" E 019° 22' 44.79" ▪ **T +27 (0)23-342-5388** ▪ F +27 (0)86-684-7778

Owner-winemaker Tim Alcock seeks to express the uniqueness of his boutique-scale Worcester vineyards through minimal intervention in the cellar and organic farming in the vineyards. Working organically means extra hard work, especially struggling against the weeds. Perhaps it's that giving such a characterful, honest, rather rustic charm to the powerfully fruited wines.

De Breede Vineyards range

★★★★ **Syrah** NEW 🏵 Appealing freshness on this bright-fruited **11** - a bit lighter, suppler, less extracted than the others, but still powerful & just as characterful. New oak influence well absorbed by the rich flavours.
Cabernet Sauvignon NEW 🏵 ★★★★ Attractive **11** a touch more refined than the blends, restraining the massive oomph - though still some sweet-fruited power. Nicely structured. **1st XI Merlot** 🏵 Occasional release. **Little Red Rooster** 🏵 ★★☆ Ripe, sweet fruit on **12** merlot-based Bordeaux blend, powerful & heavy. **The Rooster** 🏵 ★★★★ More cab on this very ripe, bold, flavour-packed & rather seductive **11** blend than for the Little Red guy; also some new oak & an extra year. — TJ

▨ **Debutant** see De Kleine Wijn Koöp
▨ **Decent** see Ladismith Winery & Distillery

De Compagnie Wine Estate

Location: Wellington ▪ Map: Paarl & Wellington ▪ Est 2001 ▪ 1stB 2002 ▪ Tasting, sales & distillery tours by appt Mon-Fri 9-4 Sat by appt ▪ Fee R15pp ▪ Closed all pub hols ▪ BYO picnic ▪ Conferences (up to 20 pax) ▪ Die Jonkershuis guesthouse ▪ Owner(s) Johann Loubser & Riana Scheepers ▪ Brandy master Charles Stassen (May 2005) ▪ Viticulturist(s) Charles Stassen (May 2007) ▪ 27ha/12ha (cab, merlot, ptage, shiraz, chenin, sauv) ▪ 25t/430cs own label ▪ PO Box 395 Wellington 7654 ▪ mail@decompagnie.co.za ▪ www.decompagnie.co.za ▪ S 33° 37' 47.01" E 019° 3' 30.72" ▪ **T +27 (0)21-864-1241** ▪ F +27 (0)86-622-6234

Cape history afficionados, lawyer Johann Loubser and Afrikaans novelist wife Riana Scheepers, dedicated their restored 300-year-old Wellington wine farm to traditional brandy production (the rest of their output going to a local winery, hence temporary de-listing from this guide). Vine and wine man Charles Stassen distils just 25T of chenin off old vines in the original 1849 copper potstill for three exclusive brandies. Visitors are warmly welcomed.

Brandy range NEW

★★★★ **10 Year Old Vintage** Amber. Smoother & more refined, with more complex aromas than 5 Year Old - marmalade, dried apricot, Xmas cake, nuts & potpourri. Richer, sweet caramel & creamy vanilla conclusion.

★★★★ **15 Year Old Reserve** Deep amber. More finesse than 10 Year Old, but a touch less fresh. Full nose with dominant oak & an array of aromas, carrying through to palate. Rounded, with big, full finish.

5 Year Old Premium ★★★★ Sweet apricots, mint, nut, vanilla & floral perfume. Delicate, with lovely balance & light smooth finish. 100% potstill from chenin, as are all of these. — WB,TJ

De Doorns Wynkelder (Koöp) Bpk

Location: De Doorns ▪ Map/WO: Worcester ▪ Est 1968 ▪ Tasting & sales Mon-Fri 8–5 Sat 8–12 ▪ Cellarmaster(s) Danie Koen ▪ Winemaker(s) Danie Koen, with Peter James Thomson ▪ PO Box 129 De Doorns 6875 ▪ ddwk@ hexvallei.co.za ▪ www.dedoornscellar.co.za ▪ S 33° 29' 10.3" E 019° 39' 43.2" ▪ **T +27 (0)23-356-2835** ▪ F +27 (0)86-579-1310

Established in Hex River Valley grape farmers in 1968, De Doorns Wynkelder today produces mainly bulk wine under longtime cellarmaster Danie Koen, but also bottles a small range under its own label (including sweet and medium-dry 'sherry'). Tasting is at the Wine & Tourism Centre in De Doorns village.

Cabernet Sauvignon ⓧ ★★★ Sippable 09, gentle spicy notes, fresh berry centre & slight grip. **Roodehof** ⓧ ⚠ ★★ Unoaked & quaffable 10, mainly cab & pinotage, with smoky bacon savouriness. — GdB,CvZ

Definitum Wines

Location: Strand ▪ WO: Stellenbosch ▪ Est/1stB 2009 ▪ Closed to public ▪ Owner(s) Fritz van der Merwe & De Wet Schreiber ▪ 520cs own label 100% red ▪ PO Box 917 Strand 7139 ▪ info@definitum.co.za ▪ www.definitum.co.za

Fritz van der Merwe and De Wet Schreiber first decided to produce wine, later coming to the idea of using less well known varieties. They buy the wine and bottle it themselves. 'We would like winelovers to say we are the definitive – hence the brand name - producer of whatever variety or blend we make,' says Schreiber.

Petit Verdot ⚠ ★★★ Smoky oak mingles with plummy fruit on smooth & juicily off-dry 11. — AL

De Grendel Wines

Location: Durbanville ▪ Map: Durbanville, Philadelphia & Darling ▪ WO: Durbanville/Western Cape/Coastal ▪ Est 1720 ▪ 1stB 2004 ▪ Tasting & sales Mon-Fri 9–5 Sat/Sun 10–4 ▪ Closed Dec 25 ▪ Cellar tours by appt ▪ Conferences ▪ De Grendel Restaurant (see Restaurants section) ▪ Owner(s) Sir David Graaff ▪ Cellarmaster(s) Charles Hopkins (Oct 2005) ▪ Winemaker(s) Elzette du Preez (Jan 2006) ▪ Viticulturist(s) Douglas Muzengeza (2008), & Kudzai Mwerenga (2009) ▪ 800ha/110ha (cabs s/f, malbec, merlot, mourv, p verdot, ptage, pinot noir/gris, shiraz, chard, sauv, sem, viog) ▪ 550t/50,000cs own label 35% red 50% white 15% rosé ▪ 112 Plattekloof Road Panorama 7505 ▪ info@degrendel.co.za ▪ www.degrendel.co.za ▪ S 33° 51' 2.5" E 018° 34' 18.4" ▪ **T +27 (0)21-558-6280** ▪ F +27 (0)21-558-7083

This Durbanville farm has been in the Graaff family, prominent in both South African business and politics, for three generations. The aim is to be an 'island of excellence – the farm has a unique setting on the western side of Tygerberg with no adjacent vineyards – but there's also an awareness that personnel matter. 'It's absolutely our philosophy to make everyone part of development and decision making,' says current owner Sir David Graaff. It was therefore a moment to be particularly proud of when Joseph Phiri won the title of Cellar Worker of the

Year in 2012. 'We put in long, hard hours during harvest but when you're part of a team like the one at De Grendel, it feels more like fun than work,' Joseph says.

★★★★☆ **Shiraz** ✓ 🍷 📖 **11** continues excellent recent form. Great complexity including red & black berries, smoked meat, fynbos. Dense core of fruit, good line of acidity, wonderfully dry on the finish. WO Coastal.

★★★★ **Sauvignon Blanc** ✓ 📖 🍷 Immensely appealing **13**, pure lime fruit plus a slight herbal edge. Rich & smooth (thanks to 100 days on the lees) while zippy acidity ensures balance. Includes 13% semillon.

★★★★☆ **Koetshuis Sauvignon Blanc** 📖 🍷 **13** is complex & complete. Arresting aromas including lime through peach & pear, also a hint of white pepper. Weightless intensity, wonderfully pure & fresh before a gently salty finish. 70% Darling fruit.

★★★★ **Viognier** 📖 🍷 Agreeably understated **13** (★★★★) made in a clean, fresh style (only portion wooded), with subtle peach & pear plus a hint of spice. Not as true to variety as **12**.

Merlot 📖 🍷 ★★★ **11** is innocuous but some will no doubt find it too lean & green. **Op Die Berg Pinot Noir** 📖 🍷 ★★★★ Fine-boned **11** shows subtle dark cherry, attractive oak spice & bright acidity. 90% Ceres grapes, 13 months in barrel, none new. **Rubáiyát** 📖 🍷 ★★★★ Ambitious Bordeaux-style red blend which appears a touch overdone in recent years. Appealing red & black fruit, good freshness on **10** (★★★★) but oak sits apart. Also-tasted **11** (★★★★) rich & full, with sweet dark fruit & lots of toasty oak. WO Coastal. **Rosé** 📖 🍷 ★★☆ Cheerful dry **13** is 50:50 cab & pinotage. Ripe berry fruit, bright acidity. **Pinot Gris** 📖 🍷 ★★★★ **13** light apple & pear notes, touch of spice before super-dry finish. Contains 12% barrel fermented portion. More neutral than **12** (★★★★). **Winifred** ⑨ 📖 🍷 ★★★★ Non-conformist blend, **11** includes 48% chardonnay, roughly equal semillon & viognier. Subtle pear & peach notes, moderate acidity. WO W Cape, as next. **Méthode Cap Classique Brut** 🍷 ★★★★ Well-assembled **11** dry sparkling (70% chardonnay with pinot noir) good fruit & subtle yeasty character, bright acidity & fine, energetic mousse. More precise than **10** (★★★). **Sauvignon Blanc Noble Late Harvest** ⑨ 🍷 ★★★ **12** displays some yellow fruit but rather soft & short. — CE

■ **De Haas** see Hazendal
■ **Dekker's Valley** see Mellasat Vineyards
■ **De Kleine Leeuwen** see Leeuwenberg

De Kleine Wijn Koöp

Location: Stellenbosch ▪ Est/1stB 2011 ▪ Closed to public ▪ Sales via email 9-5 ▪ Owner(s) Rohan Etsebeth & Jan Solms ▪ 400cs own label 100% red ▪ Export brands: Debutant, Steenbok ▪ kantoor@dekleinewijnkoop.co. za ▪ www.dekleinewijnkoop.co.za

The De Kleine Wijn Koöp is owned by Rohan Etsebeth and Jan Solms of Stellenbosch design studio Fanakalo, wine packaging a particular strength. When they come across small and unusual bottlings, they buy these in and dress them in a more 'flip-flops and boardshorts' than 'power suit' fashion.

De Krans   🍷☕🎪📷⛷♿

Location: Calitzdorp ▪ Map: Klein Karoo & Garden Route ▪ WO: Calitzdorp/Western Cape ▪ Est 1964 ▪ 1stB 1977 ▪ Tasting & sales Mon-Fri 8-5 Sat 9-3 ▪ Fee R30pp for groups; individuals free ▪ Closed Easter Fri/Sun & Dec 25 ▪ Pick your own apricots (last week Nov, 1st week Dec) & hanepoot grapes (±10 Feb-10 Mar) ▪ 'Braaivleis' by Vygieshof Home for the Aged available on Wed & Sat during picking season ▪ BYO picnic ▪ Facilities for children school hols ▪ Walking trail ▪ Owner(s) Directors De Krans Directors: MD Boets Nel & directors Stroebel Nel & René Oosthuizen ▪ Winemaker(s) Louis van der Riet (Aug 2012) ▪ Viticulturist(s) Stroebel Nel (Jan 1988) ▪ 78ha/45ha (cab, tempranillo, tinta barocca, touriga nacional, chard, chenin & muscats) ▪ 500t/40-50,000cs own label 50% red 10% white 3% rosé 37% fortifieds ▪ IPW, BWI ▪ PO Box 28 Calitzdorp 6660 ▪ dekrans@mweb.co.za ▪ www. dekrans.co.za ▪ S 33° 32' 6.3" E 021° 41' 9.0" ▪ **T +27 (0)44-213-3314** ▪ F +27 (0)44-213-3562

Calitzdorp's location in the usually hot, dry Succulent Karoo Biome makes it ideal for growing Mediterranean grapes. Capitalising on this geographical windfall, De Krans became one of the family-owned wineries which established Calitzdorp's reputation as South Africa's 'port capital' – before a ban on the use of the word 'port' was activated in 2012. But ever-innovative De Krans is not one to simply jog along, and the Calitzdorp Blend which has long been a dream of MD and winemaker Boets Nel, recently became a reality. This port-grape-only red joins a number unfortified Mediterranean-style wines added to the extensive portfolio over the past few years by Boets and viticulturist brother Stroebel, while continuing to rake in awards for their signature fortifieds.

★★★★ **Touriga Nacional** ✓ Lauded flagship red, **12** preview exudes black plum & orange zest, plush fruit padding to athletic tannin frame. Should improve good few years in bottle.

★★★★ **Tritonia** 🥃 Was 'Calitzdorp Blend', deftly made from touriga (70%), dollops tinta & tempranillo. Appealing Xmas cake notes on revisited **11**, now more integrated, dense black fruit boding well for the future.

★★★★ **Reserve Muscat** ⊕ 🥃 Very appealing fortified dessert from 30 year old vines. **11** offers sweet ginger-spiced flavours, good spirit grip & uncloying farewell. More enjoyment than in **10** (★★★).

★★★★★ **Cape Vintage Reserve** ✓ Standout Cape port-style with brilliant track record. **11** orange rind notes on taut & poised masterpiece from touriga (70%), tinta & soúzão, 19% alcohol. Deliciously silky & accessible, with sufficient substance & grip for 10+ years pleasure-filled cellaring.

★★★★☆ **Cape Vintage** ✓ 🥃 Previewed **12** port-style gloriously fruit-filled yet tightly coiled, with good grip & length auguring well. From 55% touriga, 40% tinta, soupçon soúzão, underlines house's trademark pin-point balance, as did **11** touriga (60%) & tinta combo.

★★★★☆ **Cape Tawny** ✓ 🥃 Latest **NV** port-style takes step up with precise fortification, enlivening tannic nudge & tangy acid bite, plus exceptional flavour array of caramel, spun sugar, marmalade & thatch. Tinta (80%) & touriga, vat-aged average 8 years. WO W Cape.

★★★★ **Cape Ruby** 🥃 As always, irresistible & true to vibrant early-drinking Ruby style. Fresh-baked bread & red fruit attractions on latest **NV** port-style from tinta (60%) with touriga & soúzão.

> **Tempranillo** ☺ 🍴 🥃 ★★★ **12**'s dark fruit perfumed with flowers, spiced with oak vanilla & enlivened by firm tannins for few years ageing or enjoying with heartier tapas. **Tinta Mocha** ☺ 🍴 🥃 ★★★ Tinta barocca given the fashionable 'coffee' styling in **12**. Firm structure, sour cherry flavours, needs robust food.

Cabernet Sauvignon 🍴 ★★★ Work-in-progress **13** has house-style tealeaf nuances, leaner & drier than most reds from De Krans. **Relishing Red** 🍴 ★★★ Cab-led **NV** blend brims with ripe red fruit, few grams sugar make it even more palatable. **Tinta Barocca Rosé** NEW 🍴 🥃 ★★☆ Zippy & dry **13** summer quaffer from tinta has spiced plum & gentle tannin squeeze. **Chardonnay** 🍴 🥃 ★★★ Preview unwooded **13** light lemon sherbet aromas, crisp conclusion for food or solo sipping. **Chenin Blanc** 🍴 🥃 ★★★ Attractive floral & limy notes, creamy texture make for attractive al fresco dry white in **13**. **Moscato Perlé** NEW 🍴 🥃 ★★ Grapey **13**, from two muscats, soft sweetness, low alcohol & gentle bubbles for anytime fun. **White Muscadel Jerepigo** ✓ 🥃 ★★★★★ Following delicious **12** (★★★★), **13** after-dinner delight reaches for the stars with complex aromas (including rosepetal, apricot, ginger, kumquat), seamless & well-judged forti-fication. Bargain-priced charmer. **Original Espresso** 🥃 ★★★☆ Almond, Xmas cake & nut melange on **NV** fortified from tinta & touriga; flavoursome & smooth alternative to coffee at the end of a meal. **The Original Cape Pink** 🥃 ★★★ Pink port-style category pioneer shows unusual curry leaf & green almond aromas, berry flavours on lighter-styled **NV**. Sip fireside, or over ice at the pool. **Cape White** ⊕ 🥃 ★★★ Port-style from chenin, to be served chilled. **NV** is aromatic, with marzipan & orange peel. Excellent alternative to sherry. Discontinued: **Pinotage, Redstone Reserve, Cabernet Sauvignon Rosé, Golden Harvest**. — HJ,CvZ

Delaire Graff Estate 🍴☕🏔📷♿

Location/map: Stellenbosch ▪ WO: Stellenbosch/Western Cape/Banghoek/Swartland/Coastal ▪ Est 1983 ▪ 1stB 1984 ▪ Tasting & sales Mon-Sat 10-5 Sun 10-4 ▪ Fee R30/3 wines, R50/6 wines ▪ Cellar tours by appt (no tours during harvest) ▪ Gifts ▪ Farm produce ▪ Conferences ▪ Walks/hikes ▪ Art collection ▪ Delaire Graff & Indochine Restaurants (see Restaurants section) ▪ 5-star Lodges & Spa (see Accommodation section) ▪ Owner(s) Laurence Graff ▪ Winemaker(s) Morné Vrey (Jul 2009) ▪ Viticulturist(s) Kallie Fernhout (Jun 2010) ▪ 38ha/20ha (cabs s/f, malbec, merlot, p verdot, chard, sauv) ▪ 280t/34,000cs own label 40% red 55% white 5% rosé ▪ WIETA ▪ PO Box 3058 Stellenbosch 7602 ▪ info@delaire.co.za ▪ www.delaire.co.za ▪ S 33° 55' 20.4" E 018° 55' 26.0" ▪ **T +27 (0)21-885-8160** ▪ F +27 (0)21-885-1270

In the 30-odd years since it was founded by John and Erica Platter, there have been various owners and numerous winemakers at this high-flying, high-lying estate on Helshoogte Pass just outside Stellenbosch town (it literally looks down on some very classy neighbours!) But there seems now to be some brilliant stability, since it was bought by jeweller Laurence Graff a decade back and trans-formed into an art-studded restaurant and accommodation showpiece with a winery at its core. Morné Vrey has been in charge of the cellar since 2009, with increasingly deft confidence transforming the grapes from the home vineyards (mostly the Bordeaux black grapes and chardonnay) and from elsewhere into wines of elegance and finesse – with just a hint of diamantine glitter.

★★★★☆ **Cabernet Sauvignon Reserve** 🈯 Finely crafted **11** youthful but not exuberant, tannic & focused. Still quite inaccessible, sweetness & concentration concealed beneath oak. Big 14.5% alcohol well balanced - dimension, substance & intensity are hallmark features. No **10**.

★★★★★ **Laurence Graff Reserve** ⓔ Inky **09** from best barrels of cab. Bright cassis & mulberry aromas; flashy, well integrated oak. Seamless, with refreshing savoury finish. A 'statement' wine without exaggeration.

★★★★☆ **Merlot** ✓ Restrained **10** (★★★★) shows with savoury plum, savoury notes & a brooding intensity. Dense & unshowy, but lacks the depth & detail of more vinous, refined **09**. WO Banghoek.

★★★★ **Shiraz** ✓ 🍴 🈯 Big & juicy **12** with showy raspberry notes. Judicious oaking (older barrels) adds spice & texture to otherwise overly flamboyant wine. Resumes standard after lesser **10** (★★★★). **11** untasted.

★★★★☆ **Botmaskop** 🈯 Bordeaux quintet plus a dollop of shiraz. Concentrated dark fruit aromas on **11** (★★★★★); still a little demure, yet intense & harmonious, with finely etched vinosity. Rather more restrained **10** also tasted: shows ample spice; seamlessly composed, with firm tannins. Still evolving - these will both benefit from time in bottle.

★★★★ **Chardonnay** 🍴 🈯 Pungent & perfumed, more pineapple than citrus on instantly accessible **12**. Some savoury, pithy notes on bone-dry palate, tangy rather than concentrated.

★★★★ **Chenin Blanc** ✓ 🍴 🈯 Tropical, dried apricot & peardrop aromas on **12** (★★★★★). Precise & unshowy yet intense; still with savoury chalky flinty textures; subtly oaked. Finer than **11** - both ex Swartland.

★★★★ **Sauvignon Blanc** ✓ 🍴 🈯 Strikingly perfumed blackcurrant & passionfruit notes with faint cut-grass & floral whiffs on tank sample **13**. Easy-drinking, though, & not complex. Includes fruit from Olifants River.

★★★★☆ **Coastal Cuvée Sauvignon Blanc** ✓ 🍴 🈯 Intense gooseberry & green fig aromas with fainter thatchy whiffs on tank sample **13**, with 5% oaked semillon adding gravitas & plushness. Worthy successor to classically styled **12** - both combining flinty mineral notes with pungent fruit.

★★★★ **White Reserve** Was 'Semillon-Sauvignon Blanc Reserve'. Profound, penetrating **11** (★★★★☆) melds honeyed butterscotch aromas with savoury thatch & cut grass notes. Powerful yet nuanced, with old Franschhoek semillon (30%) adding gravitas to more flamboyant multi-regional sauvignon. Step up on **10**.

★★★★ **Reserve Noble Late Harvest** Was 'Noble Late Harvest Semillon' - last was **08**. That variety just 53% in latest **NV**, with sauvignon from Olifants River. Turbocharged pineapple fruit, gooey yet fresh, massive sugar masked by equally intense acidity. Plush, opulent but short on detail.

★★★★ **Cape Vintage** 🈯 Bright berry fruit, crushed herbs, fynbos notes on **11** from touriga & tinta. Plush rather than overtly sweet, mellow finish. Unevolved despite well integrated alcohol.

Cabernet Franc Rosé ✓ 🍴 🈯 ★★★★ Faint apricot pink **13** tank sample almost creamy; light on detail, savoury & food friendly, but lacking freshness, verve of standout **12** (★★★★). — MF

■ **De Leuwen Jagt** see Leeuwenjacht

Delheim Wines   🍴 🍷 🏕 📷 🍽 ♿

Location/map: Stellenbosch ▪ WO: Simonsberg-Stellenbosch/Stellenbosch/Coastal ▪ Est 1971 ▪ 1stB 1961 ▪ Tasting & sales daily 9-5 ▪ Fee R25 tasting/R35 tasting & cellar tour ▪ Closed Easter Fri/Sun, Dec 25 & Jan 1 ▪ Cellar tours daily at 10.30 & 2.30 ▪ Delheim Restaurant ▪ Facilities for children ▪ Tour groups ▪ Gifts ▪ Farm produce ▪ Conferences ▪ Conservation area ▪ Oakleaf Lodge B&B at Delvera ▪ Events: see website for schedule ▪ Owner(s) Sperling family ▪ Winemaker(s) Reg Holder (Jan 2012) ▪ Viticulturist(s) Etienne Terblanche (Aug 2012) ▪ 375ha/148ha (cab, ptage, shiraz, chard, chenin, riesling, sauv) ▪ 980t/120,000cs own label 50% red 30% white 20% rosé ▪ Brands for clients: Woolworths ▪ BWI champion, Level 1 B-BBEE, WIETA ▪ PO Box 210 Stellenbosch 7599 ▪ delheim@delheim.com ▪ www.delheim.com ▪ S 33° 52' 10.1" E 018° 53' 9.8" ▪ **T +27 (0)21-888-4600** ▪ F +27 (0)21-888-4601

It was Hans and Deli Hoheisen who reintroduced vines to the historic Driesprongh farm on the lower slopes of Stellenbosch's Simonsberg, and in 1949 Delheim ('Deli's home') was born. But it was Spatz Sperling – who arrived from Germany in 1951 to help out – and his family who have built Delheim into today's popular winery. Later, the Vera Cruz farm, some three kilometres away, was added to the estate. Reg Holder took the winemaking job in 2012 and seems to be hinting at a new direction for the wines. In fact there's plenty of tweaking going on, including a more focused range being shaped, and new labels. And in the vineyard, replanting of some vineyards to better express Delheim's terroir.

Vera Cruz Estate range

★★★★☆ **Shiraz** ⏰ **09** (★★★★★) from low-yielding vineyard, tasted last year. Powerful yet well groomed; savoury spicy flavours & supple integration of tannins & oak. Distinguished & ageworthy, as was **08**.

★★★★☆ **Grand Reserve** The effects of all-new oak barrels dominate the youthful flagship **09** - as usual mostly cab with a dab of merlot. But some elegance & good dark-fruited flavour lurks there, shown in a long finish, & this rating reflects hope that harmony will emerge with 5+ more years in bottle.

★★★★☆ **Edelspatz Noble Late Harvest** ⬚ Now bottled, **12** (★★★★★) botrytis dessert from riesling shows beautifully. Rich but elegant & refined, packed with flavour, excitingly balanced. Unoaked & with modest alcohol - more German than French in style. Even better than **10** & **11** (★★★★).

Chardonnay Sur Lie ⬚ ★★★★ Pleasant, straightforward **12** less oaky in youth than previous - in fact, well balanced & fresh, with tangy citrus notes.

Delheim range

★★★★ **Cabernet Sauvignon** ✓ ⬚ Good fruit (with a little petit verdot) on **11**, intense enough to survive obvious oak & provide lengthy - but drying - finish. Otherwise in restrained style. Needs time. No **10** made.

★★★★ **Shiraz** ⬚ **12** (no **11** made) now easier, less tannic, full of juicy berried flavour, but balanced with modest oaking & good grip. Even rather elegantly fresh, despite some power.

Merlot ⬚ ★★★ **12** pre-bottling has ripe fruit & gentle tannins, with big acid. Thickish texture. **Pinotage** ⬚ ★★★ **12** has a winning perfume & warm, friendly fruitiness; easygoing but no pushover, having a good solid structure. Stellenbosch WO. **Unwooded Chardonnay** 🍴 ⬚ ★★★ **13** tasted very young & unready from tank (rating very provisional), but promising some intense pear, citrus aromas & flavours. **Gewürztraminer** 🍴 ⬚ ★★★ As always, off-dry **13** tasted ex-tank billows forth heady rosepetal perfume. Tangy freshness gives a welcome anchor. Discontinued: **Sauvignon Blanc**, **Spatzendreck Late Harvest**.

Lifestyle range

Cabernet Sauvignon-Shiraz 🍴 ⬚ ★★ Tasty, light **12** tasted ex-tank & too young to rate. WO Coastal, like Rosé. **Pinotage Rosé** 🍴 ⬚ ★★ Mildly fruity, just-off-dry **13**. **Chenin Blanc** 🍴 ⬚ Untasted. For export only. **Heerenwijn Sauvignon Blanc** 🍴 ⬚ ★★★ Previously with chenin, now juicy, fruity **13** sauvignon flies cheerfully alone. — TJ

■ **De Liefde** *see* Mountain Ridge Wines

De Meye Wines   🍷 🥂 ☕ 📷 ♿

Location/map/WO: Stellenbosch ▪ Est/1stB 1998 ▪ Tasting & sales Mon-Thu by appt Fri 12-5 Sat/Sun & pub hols 11-4 ▪ Fee R15/5 wines ▪ Closed Good Fri, Dec 25/26 & Jan 1 ▪ Cellar tours Mon-Fri by appt ▪ 'The Table at De Meye' open for lunch Sat-Sun, booking essential T +27 (0)72-696-0530, www.thetablerestaurant.co.za ▪ Farm produce ▪ Owner(s) Jan Myburgh Family Trust ▪ Winemaker(s) Marcus Milner (Sep 1999) & Lofty Ellis (consultant), with Aby Bodlani (Sep 2000) ▪ Viticulturist(s) Philip Myburgh & Johan Pienaar (Jan 2006, consultant) ▪ 100ha/65ha (cabs s/f, merlot, shiraz, chard, chenin) ▪ 300t/36,000cs own label 65% red 25% white 10% rosé ▪ IPW ▪ PO Box 20 Elsenburg 7607 ▪ info@demeye.co.za ▪ www.demeye.co.za ▪ S 33° 49' 0.7" E 018° 49' 48.8" ▪ **T +27 (0)21-884-4131** ▪ F +27 (0)21-884-4154

The Myburgh family estate is one of the most northerly in Stellenbosch and altogether as unpretentious and pleasing as the wines – environmentally responsible too. The care and craft put into them by winemaker Marcus Milner is hinted at by the fact that most of the varietal wines in fact contain splashes of other varieties. All are properly dry – there's no dumbing down with the showy, cheap appeal of sweetness, even with the perennially great-value second tier.

De Meye range

★★★★ **Cabernet Sauvignon** ✓ Blackcurrant & lead pencil aromas lead to dense red berry fruit on **10**. Also apparent are oak vanilla notes, yet to integrate. Not quite the elegance & freshness of standout **09** (★★★★★).

★★★★ **Trutina** ✓ ⬚ Flagship from Bordeaux red varieties plus shiraz. **11** preview faintly herbal, with fresh berry aromas. Shows concentration & focus. Less intense but more polished than **10**.

Merlot ⬚ ★★★ Forest floor notes & faint mulberry whiffs on uncomplicated, soft **11**; warming 14.7% alcohol is evident. **Shiraz** ✓ ⬚ ★★★★ Austere & elegant **11** shows light spicing & lifting herbal hints. Fresh persistent &, like all these reds, genuinely dry. **Shiraz Rosé** ✓ 🍴 ⬚ ★★★★ Faint apricot hue to now-bottled **12**'s still-fresh face; honeysuckle & cherry aromas, zesty, bone-dry savoury flavours. **Chardonnay Unwooded** 🍴 ⬚ ★★★ Faintly honeyed grapefruit aromas on **13** ex tank. Some palate weight, but retiring flavours. **Chenin Blanc** ✓ 🍷 📖 ★★★☆ Intense peardrop & honeysuckle aromas on **13**, Pre-bottling, concentrated & beautifully rounded, finishes bright & fresh.

Little River range

> **Cabernet Sauvignon** ☺ 📖 ★★★ Fine tannins & a hint of sweet cherry fruit on easy-drinking **11**. **Shiraz** ☺ 📖 📷 ★★★ Spicy & lightly aromatic **12**, faint earthy notes to the red fruit, ready to be enjoyed. — MF

▪ **De Mikke Patron** *see* Almenkerk Wine Estate

DeMorgenzon

Location/map: Stellenbosch ▪ WO: Stellenbosch/Western Cape ▪ Est 2003 ▪ 1stB 2005 ▪ Tasting & sales daily 10-5 ▪ Fee R25-R50 ▪ Closed Good Fri, Dec 25/26 & Jan 1 ▪ Cellar tours on request ▪ Conservation area ▪ Owner(s) Wendy & Hylton Appelbaum ▪ Cellarmaster(s) / GM Carl van der Merwe (Jul 2010) ▪ Winemaker(s) Carl van der Merwe (Jul 2010), with Craig Barnard (Dec 2012) ▪ Viticulturist(s) Louis Buys (Sep 2012) & Kevin Watt (consultant) ▪ 91ha/52ha (cab, grenache, merlot, mourv, shiraz, chard, chenin, rouss, sauv, viog) ▪ 252t/30,000cs own label 56% red 33% white 8% rosé 3% other ▪ BWI, IPW ▪ PO Box 1388 Stellenbosch 7599 ▪ info@demorgenzon.co.za ▪ www.demorgenzon.co.za ▪ S 33° 56' 22.99" E 018° 45' 0.17" ▪ **T +27 (0)21-881-3030** ▪ F +27 (0)21-881-3773

This expansive property in the Stellenboschkloof was purchased by Hylton and Wendy Appelbaum in 2003. Since then, the previously Johannesburg-based couple have devoted just some of their impressive energies (both are still involved in business and philanthropic institutions) to having vines replanted across the slopes stretching from 200 to 400 metres above sea level. Believing that biodiversity and an ecologically sensitive environment produce better grapes, the Appelbaums also introduced indigenous flora throughout their 'garden vineyards'. In addition, baroque music is continuously piped to the vines - an unusual concept, but something which they feel positively influences the ripening process. Cellarmaster Carl van der Merwe is equally in tune with the vineyards; since his arrival, the wines have shown greater assurance and personality.

★★★★ **DMZ Syrah** ⏲ 📖 📷 Characterful shiraz in the making, **11** shows pure spice & ripe red fruit, promising complexity to come. Assertive, with a comfortable suppleness waiting to emerge. WO W Cape.

★★★★ **Maestro Red** NEW 📷 Merlot/cab-headed Bordeaux-style blend. **11** modern, ripe-fruited, supported by fresh juicy acids, fine tannin trim. French oak polish (30% new) complements approachability.

★★★★ **DMZ Concerto** 📖 📷 Last was 08. Re-introduced with shiraz-based **12** (★★★) & all exported to Sweden. Suppleness & gentle grip give full rein to rich spiciness. Satisfying & approachable.

★★★★★ **Chenin Blanc Reserve** 📷 Benefit of 40+ year bushvines evident in **12**'s delicacy & concentration. Less oxidative, more (botrytis-free) ripe fruit than **11** (★★★★★), also a touch drier, highlighting the mineral tension. Plenty of savoury richness too. Can be cellared with confidence.

★★★★☆ **Maestro White** 📷 Was 'Concerto White'. **12** (★★★★★), a masterly combination of chenin, roussanne, viognier & chardonnay, is our prestigious 2014 White Wine of the Year. Rich in texture with earthy oxidative tones - lightly oaked, as was **11**. Firm & lively in form; perfectly balanced for delicious current drinking or keeping (if resistible now).

Garden Vineyards Rosé 📖 📷 ★★★☆ No simple summer sipper: older French oak lends gravitas to the charm of **12**. Fresh-fruited, creamy & bone-dry; shiraz, grenache, mourvèdre. **DMZ Chardonnay** Await next, like **DMZ Sauvignon Blanc**. **DMZ Chenin Blanc** NEW 📖 📷 ★★★★ Plump & juicy **12**, with just a hint of oak for extra dimension, adding spicy zest to tail. Approachable but not facile. — AL

▪ **Denneboom** *see* Oude Denneboom
▪ **De Oude Opstal** *see* Stellendrift - SHZ Cilliers/Kuün Wyne

De Redley

WO: Stellenbosch ▪ Est/1stB 2012 ▪ Closed to public ▪ Owner(s) Nicholas Ridley & Fredy Pummer ▪ Cellarmaster(s) Nicholas Ridley (Sep 2011) ▪ Winemaker(s) Piet Bredell ▪ 7t/766cs own label 33% red 66% white ▪ info@deredley.co.za ▪ www.deredley.co.za ▪ **T +27 (0)11-708-3444** ▪ F +27 (0)11-708-3615

Wines are made to spec by Piet Bredell for this Stellenbosch-based boutique winery, under the direction of owners Nicholas Ridley and Fredy Pummer of Boucheron Wines. Volumes are small at this stage but bigger things are planned.

White Merlot 🍷 📖 ★★ Highly unusual style, among tiny handful in SA, previewed **13** blushes palely, shows pared-down, sushi-friendly flavours in a slender body. — GdB

Desert Rose Wines 🍷

Location: Vredendal ▪ Map: Olifants River ▪ WO: Western Cape ▪ Tasting by appt ▪ Owner(s) Alan van Niekerk & Herman Nel ▪ Winemaker(s) Herman Nel ▪ desertrose@nashuaisp.co.za ▪ S 31° 41' 33.1" E 018° 30' 5.9" ▪ **T +27 (0)82-809-2040/+27 (0)82-800-2270** ▪ F +27 (0)27-213-2858

Herman Nel and Alan van Niekerk's boutique winery at Vredendal celebrates the Sting song as well as the flower-like gypsum crystals found on the surrounding plains, each 'rose' as unique as the wines the longtime Namaqua Wines supplier and the nurseryman strive to make, and name after their adored daughters.

Cabernet Sauvignon ⓦ ★★★ Easy-drinking **10** has refreshing acidity, less sweetness than Winemaker's version. **Winemaker's Choice Cabernet Sauvignon** ⓦ ★★★ Interesting salty nuance on blackcurrant-toned **11**, soft & vanilla-scented from 100% new American oak. **Winemaker's Choice Merlot** ⓦ ★★★ Rum & raisin-infused **10** has charry oak notes, cranberry lift for uncomplicated sipping. **Shiraz** ⓦ ★★★ 09 dense & powerful, still tight when last tasted; structured to develop interestingly. **Jada's Rose** ⓦ ★★★☆ 09 happy 60/40 mix cab & shiraz, former's taut grip softened by shiraz's raspberry fruit. **Nicola's Rose** ⓦ ★★★★ Succulent mulberry, savoury nuances on silky **10** dry rosé from cab, merlot & shiraz. — DB,CvZ

De Toren Private Cellar ⓦ🍷📷

Location/map/WO: Stellenbosch ▪ Est 1994 ▪ 1stB 1999 ▪ Tasting, sales & cellar tours by appt ▪ Fee R180, waived on purchase ▪ Donkey walk ▪ Owner(s) Edenhall Trust ▪ Cellarmaster(s) Albie Koch (Oct 1998) ▪ Winemaker(s) Charles Williams (Dec 2008) ▪ Viticulturist(s) Ernest Manuel (Mar 2003, consultant) ▪ 25ha/ ±21ha (cabs s/f, malbec, merlot, p verdot) ▪ 150t/16,000cs own label 100% red ▪ PO Box 48 Vlottenburg 7604 ▪ info@de-toren.com ▪ www.de-toren.com ▪ S 33° 57' 34.5" E 018° 45' 7.5" ▪ **T +27 (0)21-881-3119** ▪ F +27 (0)21-881-3335

When De Toren debuted in this guide's 2001 edition, we noted that Stellenbosch owners Emil and Sonette den Dulk had stumbled upon a little piece of heaven in Polkadraai Hills a decade before. 'Wary about plunging into a crowded field,' we wrote, 'they consulted the experts on the varieties best for their seven different soil types, and then held fire until they found their matching market niche.' Namely, a focus on the 'big five' Bordeaux red varieties, and just one 'super-wine', Fusion V. The then 'new player of genuinely unusual promise' has since convincingly realised that potential, and, while the the portfolio has grown a bit, the focus and philosophy of 'big ideas grounded in minute detail' (from soil analysis and infrared areal imaging to packaging tweaks) remain firmly in place.

★★★★☆ **Fusion V** Flagship cab-based Bordeaux blend **11** trumps **10** (★★★★), offering concentrated, rich fragrant fruit & tightly coiled tannins. Bold, mouthfilling & firmly structured with big 15% alcohol & oaking well hidden. For the long haul; decant if impatient.

★★★★ **Z** Second, earlier-ready 5-way blend, merlot-led. **11** unshowy, bright berry flavours in harmony with precise oaking. Lighter than sibling, with delightful freshness & composure despite big alcohol.

La Jeunesse Délicate NEW ★★★★ Malbec-led, lightly oaked NV 4-way blend is made in a light style for early enjoyment. Soft & moreish, serve slightly chilled. — WB

De Trafford Wines ⓦ🍷

Location/map/WO: Stellenbosch ▪ Est/1stB 1992 ▪ Tasting, sales & tours Fri & Sat 10–1, or otherwise by appt ▪ Fee R50, waived on purchase ▪ Closed all pub hols ▪ Owner(s) David & Rita Trafford ▪ Winemaker(s) David Trafford ▪ Viticulturist(s) Schalk du Toit (consultant) ▪ 200ha/5ha (cabs s/f, merlot, shiraz) ▪ 71t/7,000cs own label 70% red 30% white ▪ PO Box 495 Stellenbosch 7599 ▪ info@detrafford.co.za ▪ www.detrafford.co.za ▪ S 34° 0' 45.1" E 018° 53' 57.8" ▪ **T +27 (0)21-880-1611** ▪ F +27 (0)21-880-1611

It's been 30 years since the first - experimental - vines were planted at Mont Fleur, the Trafford family farm and home to De Trafford Wines, high in the saddle between the Stellenbosch and Helderberg mountains (coincidentally the venue for secret talks between jailed ANC leaders and the ruling National Party, which produced a blueprint for the future 'rainbow nation'). Many of those early plantings' successors were ripped apart in late 2012 by the worst wind in over 100 years, prompting architect, winemaker and co-owner David Trafford to buy in 'some interesting grapes not destined for the regular De Trafford wines'. Vintage dramas inclusive, the focus remains on growing wines on par with the best in the world using traditional methods - right down to hand-bottling the wines.

★★★★☆ **Cabernet Sauvignon** Seamlessly elegant, concentrated **11** abounds with cassis, blackberry & spicy violets, matching stellar **09** & **10**. Complex & layered, with superb definition & structure from 23 months in 40% new oak, it will unfurl for years to come.

★★★★ **Merlot** ⓘ Succulent yet polished **10**, savoury tobacco & ripe plum, tannins still perky but elegant, approachable, already drinks well. Naturally fermented, as all De Trafford wines.

★★★★ **Blueprint Syrah** Pencil shavings & graphite vie with spicy blue & black fruit on deep, broad palate. Integrated oak, all older, gives tobacco nuance. **11** mainly ex neighbour Keermont. Will reward patience.

★★★★☆ **Syrah 393** Powerful, refined & elegant **11**. Plum & blueberry abundance which grows in the mouth. Chalky tannic grip & turned earth, cocoa nuances. Concentration, depth & breadth from focused attention, unfined, unfiltered & hand-bottled. Like **10**, lingering dry, spicy finish.

★★★★☆ **Elevation 393** ⓘ Barrel selection, named for home-vineyard altitude. Cab-led Bordeaux blend & shiraz, each playing their part in **09**. Plush dark berries, whiffs of salty liquorice, scrub, backed by muscular tannins designed for long, slow, bottle evolution.

★★★★ **Chenin Blanc** Natural ferment in barrel makes **12** rich & textured, matching **11**. Ripe pear & apricot with creamy, lees breadth. Balanced & long. Serious yet fresh throughout.

★★★★☆ **Straw Wine** ⓘ Thatchy brûlée & apricot tang on ambrosial **10** (★★★★) from air-dried, barrel-aged (23 months) chenin. Rich, concentrated & rounded but **09** was slightly fresher & more vibrant. 375ml.

Discontinued: **Chenin Blanc Four V**. — FM

Deux Frères Wines　　🍷 🎍 [NEW]

Location/map/WO: Stellenbosch ▪ Est 2008 ▪ 1stB 2012 ▪ Tasting & sales Mon-Fri 10-5 Sat 10-1 ▪ Fee R20 ▪ Closed Easter Fri-Mon, Dec 25 & Jan 1 ▪ BYO picnic ▪ Owner(s) M Wiehe, H Wiehe, S du Toit, R du Toit ▪ Cellarmaster(s)/viticulturist(s) Stephan du Toit (Jan 2008) ▪ 4.2ha/2.1ha (cab, mourv, p verdot, shiraz) ▪ 1,700cs own label 80% red 20% rosé ▪ PO Box 209 Koelenhof 7605 ▪ stephan@dfwines.co.za ▪ www.dfwines.co.za ▪ S 33° 52' 51.16" E 18° 50' 44.93" ▪ T +27 (0)21-889-9865 ▪ F +27 (0)86-621-2425

The two brothers in the artisanal boutique winery's name are Stellenbosch-based Stephan and Retief du Toit, who vinify their young-vine crop in the Croydon cellar near Somerset West. Stephan learnt his trade at L'Avenir, under then winemaker Francois Naudé and owner Marc Wiehe, where the seeds of the dream of owning 'a small piece of land and making wine from it' were born.

★★★★ **Shiraz-Mourvèdre** American oak for shiraz, French for mourvèdre in 70/30 blend. **12** enticing smoky bacon notes & black plum fruit, supple tannins for enjoyment now or keeping few years.

Cabernet Sauvignon-Petit Verdot ★★★★ Cab character leads petit verdot (40%) in promising **11**, older oak matured. Tobacco, wood spice & black cherry fruit gripped by tight tannins. For cellaring 3+ years or food.

Blanc de Noir ▤ ★★★ Floral scents, watermelon tastes, sherbety acidity & lingering dry spicy tail on **13** summer salad accompaniment. — GdB, GM

De Villiers Wines　　🍷

Location: Paarl ▪ Map: Paarl & Wellington ▪ Est/1stB 1996 ▪ Tasting & sales by appt ▪ Owner(s) De Villiers Family Trust ▪ Cellarmaster(s)/winemaker(s)/viticulturist(s) Villiers de Villiers (1996) ▪ 50,000cs own label 80% red 20% white ▪ Other export brand: Heeren van Oranje Nassau ▪ Brands for clients: Huangtai Wines ▪ PO Box 659 Suider-Paarl 7624 ▪ vadev@mweb.co.za ▪ www.devillierswines.com ▪ S 33° 45' 43.3" E 018° 57' 40.8" ▪ T +27 (0)21-863-2175 ▪ F +27 (0)86-653-8988

Continuing their expansion into Asian markets, Paarl-based De Villiers Wines say they have been contracted to produce more than 2 million bottles for a new label, Huangtai Wines, in north-western China. According to cellarmaster Villiers de Villiers, the flagship wines will be pinot noir and eiswein

Devonair

Location/map/WO: Stellenbosch ▪ Est 1994 ▪ 1stB 2000 ▪ Tasting & sales by appt ▪ Closed all pub hols ▪ Conferences ▪ 2 self-catering cottages ▪ Owner(s) Leon & Rina de Wit ▪ Winemaker(s) Ernst Gouws (Mar 2006) ▪ Viticulturist(s) Pierre de Wet (2012) ▪ 2.2ha (cab) ▪ 10t/920cs own label 100% red ▪ PO Box 1274 Stellenbosch 7599 ▪ info@devonair.co.za ▪ www.devonair.co.za ▪ S 33° 53' 44.45" E 018° 48' 27.46" ▪ **T +27 (0)21-865-2190** ▪ F +27 (0)21-865-2327

Specialising in cabernet, Leon and Rita de Wit's Devonair boutique winery in Devon Valley has engaged Stellenbosch University viticulturist Albert Strever to assist winemaker Ernst Gouws in fine-tuning the young vines now coming onstream. Actively involved in the local community, Leon and Rita own the talent showcase, AmaZink Live theatre and restaurant, in nearby Khayamandi.

The Cab ⑨ ★★★★ Medium-bodied **07** shows plush ripe blackberry fruit backed by a fine tannin structure & firm acid balance. **The Cab Family Reserve ⑨ ★★★★** Good fruit in last **06**, cassis & plums, with sturdy oak providing structure, rewarding future. Own, Grangehurst vines. **05** also available from cellardoor. — WB

■ **Devonet** see Clos Malverne

Devon Hill

Location: Stellenbosch ▪ Est 1994 ▪ 1stB 1996 ▪ Closed to public ▪ Owner(s) Geir Tellefsen ▪ Cellarmaster(s)/ winemaker(s)/viticulturist(s) Therese de Beer (Jan 2011, consultant) ▪ 20,000cs own label 80% red 15% white 5% rosé ▪ geir@rosendalwinery.com ▪ **T +27 (0)21-424-4498** ▪ F +27 (0)21-424-1571

Owner Geir Tellefsen is upbeat about this mainly export brand originating from Stellenbosch's Devon Valley and typically including fruit from there. With Scandinavia ticked, Geir's looking to boost the label's presence on local shelves.

★★★★ Bluebird ⑨ 02 well-knit merlot-led (73%) Cape Blend with plummy flavour. Tasted several years back, as for Cab & Pinotage. **Cabernet Sauvignon ⑨ ★★★★** Attractive ripe mulberry, touches tobacco & spice on **05**, pleasing roundness & generosity, tannins under control, add dryness to finish. **Merlot** Await next, as for **Shiraz** & **Sauvignon Blanc**. **Pinotage ⑨ ★★★★** Modern **05** fat & fleshy, oak a sideshow rather than star attraction. 'Ripe' the key word: 15.2% alcohol. — IvH

Devon Rocks

Location/map/WO: Stellenbosch ▪ Est 1998 ▪ 1stB 2003 ▪ Tasting, sales & tours by appt ▪ B&B accommodation ▪ Owner(s) Jürgen & Brita Heinrich ▪ Winemaker(s) Simon Smith (Louisvale) ▪ Viticulturist(s) Gawie du Bois & Paul Wallace (advisers) ▪ 4ha/3.5ha (ptage, shiraz) ▪ 4,400cs 57% red 18% white 25% rosé ▪ PO Box 12483 Die Boord 7613 ▪ info@devonrocks.co.za ▪ www.devonrocks.co.za ▪ S 33° 53' 19.9" E 018° 48' 30.1" ▪ **T +27 (0)21-865-2536** ▪ F +27 (0)21-865-2621

No new wines from Jürgen and Brita Heinrich's small vineyard in Devon Valley, but their Pinotage 05, 07 and 08, and Shiraz Rosé 09 are still available.

Devonvale Golf & Wine Estate

Location/map/WO: Stellenbosch ▪ Est 1997 ▪ 1stB 2004 ▪ Tasting by appt ▪ Fee R25pp ▪ Sales Mon-Sat 11-6 ▪ Chez Shiraz restaurant (see Restaurants section) ▪ Tour groups ▪ Golf ▪ Pro shop ▪ Conferences ▪ Devonvale Golf Lodge (see Accommodation section) ▪ Owner(s) Devonmust (Pty) Ltd ▪ Winemaker(s) Wilhelm Kritzinger (2004, Bellevue Estate) ▪ Viticulturist(s) Ruben Nienaber (2000) ▪ 117ha/26.5ha (shiraz) ▪ 14t/1,900cs own label 100% red ▪ PO Box 77 Koelenhof 7605 ▪ info@devonvale.co.za ▪ www.devonvale.co.za ▪ S 33° 52' 59.6" E 018° 48' 15.0" ▪ **T +27 (0)21-865-2080** ▪ F +27 (0)21-865-2601

Residents of this upmarket Stellenbosch lifestyle estate at harvest time invite family and friends to help bring in the crop from vines fringing some of the fairways, for vinification and bottling at Bellevue. The nautical connotations in the branding are to Devonvale founder and round-the-world yachtsman JJ Provoyeur, and to a particularly favourable angle in sailing.

Owner's Special Reserve range

Shiraz ⊕ ★★★☆ Elegant & rounded **08**, good concentration of plums, savoury edge offset by showy oak.

Broad Reach range

Provoyeur Cabernet Sauvignon ★★★★ **07**, revisited, modern styling with rich cassis & mint. Sweet & spicy oak nuance from staves (as for Shiraz) now integrated, giving sleek polished texture. Gentle alcohol glow; ready to enjoy. **06** (★★★) charry, chunkier. **Provoyeur Shiraz** ★★★ Distinctive savoury, leathery & earthy tone on lighter **07**. **08**, also retasted, riper & fuller. Like Cab, oak has fused with fruit for supple & silky harmony. — MW

DeWaal Wines

Location/map/WO: Stellenbosch ▪ Est 1682 ▪ 1stB 1972 ▪ Tasting & sales Mon-Fri 10–12.30 & 2–4.30 Sat 10–4. 30 (Sep-May only) ▪ Fee R20 ▪ Closed Easter Fri-Mon, Jun 16, Dec 25/26 & Jan 1 ▪ Owner(s) Pieter de Waal ▪ Winemaker(s)/viticulturist(s) Chris de Waal & Daniël de Waal (whites/reds, consultants) ▪ 800t ▪ 50% red 50% white ▪ IPW ▪ PO Box 15 Vlottenburg 7604 ▪ admin@dewaal.co.za ▪ www.dewaal.co.za ▪ S 33° 56' 29.3" E 018° 45' 59.9" ▪ **T +27 (0)21-881-3711** ▪ F +27 (0)21-881-3776

There's a lot of history here. The De Waal family has been involved in Cape wine-growing for nine generations and the lovely home-farm, Uiterwyk, in Stellenboschkloof dates back to 1682. A few years ago Pieter de Waal took owner-ship of the brand, with brothers Chris and Daniël building their own labels, while continuing to make the DeWaal wines. Pinotage remains a great tradition: forbear CT de Waal was the first to successfully vinify the grape (at Welgevallen), and trib-ute to his pioneering work is given in the name of one of the three versions made.

DeWaal range

★★★★ **Cabernet Sauvignon** ⊕ Leafy, herbal **08** (★★★★) from old vineyard in lean, austere style, need-ing food to accompany. Less richness than **07**.

★★★★ **Merlot** ⊕ Full bodied, resolutely dry **09** shows Old-World styling with solid, ripe black fruit.

★★★★ **CT de Waal Pinotage** ⊕ From 50 year old vineyard, gets more serious treatment than standard bottling. Handsome **09** lushly rich but not too ripe; well structured by 60% new oak. No **08**.

★★★★☆ **Top of the Hill Pinotage** 📷 Kingpin of estate's pinotage trio gets grand treatment: tiny yields from 60 year old bushvines judiciously seasoned in all-new oak, yielding a magisterial example of this local vari-ety. Although **11** still youthful, has building blocks of compact fruit & fine acidity for promising future.

★★★★ **Signal Rock** ⊕ Cab-driven **08** Bordeaux-style blend was big & angular when tasted a few years back; tealeaf & forest floor layers over rich blackcurrant fruit.

Pinotage ⊕ 🍴 ★★★ Estate's savoury **10** entry-level pinotage bottling made for early uncomplicated drinking. **Viognier** ⊕ 🍴 📷 ★★★ **11** unusually crisp & zingy for this variety. Bone-dry, lightish & focused.

Young Vines range

Merlot ⊕ 🍴 📷 ★★★ Vivacious, youthful **10** is fresh & simply styled for uncomplicated enjoyment. **Shiraz** ⊕ 🍴 📷 ★★★ Popular mocha-styled **10** perfect for smooth quaffing. **Chenin Blanc** ⊕ 🍴 📷 ★★★ Preview **12** not quite settled when tasted last year, but previous vintages admired for consistency & over-delivery. **Sauvignon Blanc** ⊕ 🍴 📷 ★★★ Fresh, zippy **12** reflects charm of vintage with appealing fruitiness & pleasing harmony. Undemanding **11** (★★★) offers crisp, fruity quaffing. — IM

Dewaldt Heyns Family Wines

Location: Tulbagh/Swartland ▪ WO: Swartland ▪ Est/1stB 2006 ▪ Tasting by appt at Saronsberg ▪ Owner(s) Dewaldt Heyns Family Wines ▪ Cellarmaster(s)/winemaker(s)/viticulturist(s) Dewaldt Heyns ▪ (ptage, shiraz, chenin) ▪ 15t/1,100cs own label 60% red 40% white ▪ dewaldt@saronsberg.com ▪ **T +27 (0)82-441-4117**

Most of the vines on Dewaldt Heyns' father's 80-hectare farm in Swartland's Perdeberg area are old, some around 40 years. It is from a small portion of these and a slightly younger block of shiraz that the celebrated Saronsberg winemaker crafts a minute quantity in his father's honour.

Weathered Hands range

★★★★ **Chenin Blanc** From ±40 year old bushvines on weathered granite, **11** (★★★★☆) like previously tasted **10** is elegant, perfumed, pure; the younger wine slightly richer, with bigger structure but similarly quickened by minerality.

Shiraz ★★★★ Nodding to the Rhône, **09** is concentrated & flavoursome without being heavy, shows greater poise than very ripe but unshowy **08** (★★★☆). Good fruit & fine tannin augur well for ageing. — CE,CvZ

De Wetshof Estate

Location/map/WO: Robertson ▪ Est 1949 ▪ 1stB 1972 ▪ Tasting & sales Mon-Fri 8.30-4.30 Sat 9.30-12.30 ▪ Closed Easter Fri/Sun/Mon, May 1, Dec 25/26 & Jan 1 ▪ Cellar tours by appt Mon-Fri 8.30-4.30 ▪ Conservation area ▪ Owner(s) Danie, Peter & Johann de Wet ▪ Cellarmaster(s) Danie de Wet (Jan 1973) ▪ Winemaker(s) Danie de Wet (Jan 1973), Mervyn Williams (2001) & Peter de Wet (2007) ▪ Viticulturist(s) Rudolf Kriel (2012), advised by Phil Freese & François Viljoen (both 1997) ▪ 600ha/180ha (cab, merlot, pinot, chard, riesling, sauv) ▪ 1,800t 8% red 90% white 1% rosé 1% MCC ▪ ISO 9001:2008, ISO 22000:2005, BBBEE Grade 2, BWI, Enviro Scientific, Integrity & Sustainability, IPW ▪ PO Box 31 Robertson 6705 ▪ info@dewetshof.com ▪ www. dewetshof.com ▪ S 33° 52' 38.0" E 020° 0' 35.1" ▪ **T +27 (0)23-615-1853** ▪ F +27 (0)23-615-1915

Brothers Peter and Johann de Wet fill impressively large shoes: respectively, those of father Danie, winemaker and titan of the local industry, and mother Lesca, whose massive marketing and sales contribution saw this Robertson estate winning the President's Export Achievement Award five times. Chardonnay's always been their calling card, with many honours, but Peter has identified a few special blocks of merlot and cabernet. The resulting Bordeaux blend honours Louis Michel Thibault, 18th century architect of Cape Town's renowned Koopmans De Wet House, upon which the De Wetshof visitor centre is modelled.

De Wetshof Estate range

★★★★ **Naissance Cabernet Sauvignon** ✓ ▨ Moved here from Danie de Wet range, still classically styled & elegant **11** has lead pencil whiffs, taut structure. On song after slightly leafy, austere **10** (★★★☆).

★★★★ **Thibault** ⓣ Impressive Bordeaux red, one of handful made over the years. **09** merlot, cab, petit verdot & cab franc; plush plum & vanilla but still harmonious. Age or decant now to appreciate fully.

★★★★ **Bateleur Chardonnay** ▨ **11** (★★★★☆) notch above tight-wound **09**. Already displays more poise & complexity despite high 14.5% alcohol but needs few years to show at best. **10** sold out untasted.

★★★★☆ **The Site Chardonnay** ✓ ▨ Estate's prosaically named Block 17B birthplace of uncommonly good barrel-fermented chardonnay. **12** same confidence, big buttery personality as **11**. Drinks well now but has concentration & structure to improve over many years.

★★★★ **Riesling** ✓ ▨ Was 'Rhine Riesling'. **12** (★★★★), first since steely **09**, slightly more alcohol & richness, still poised & delicately sweet thanks to lively acidity.

★★★★ **Méthode Cap Classique Pinot Noir Brut** `NEW` Sophisticated **08** owes its elegant fresh bread character to 42 months on fine lees, no dosage after disgorgement. A fine, stately celebratory sparkler.

★★★★ **Méthode Cap Classique Brut** ▨ Champagne-method bubbly from chardonnay (60%) & pinot noir. Latest **NV** half-notch up because of its fine almond-brioche notes, creamy mousse, persistent savoury conclusion. Amazing for just a year's lees-ageing - augurs well for ageing.

★★★★★ **Edeloes** ⓣ Exceptional botrytised dessert, occasional release. Last-tasted **05** (★★★★★) was charming & complex; previous was **00**, very much alive, delicious in fact. 500ml.

Finesse Chardonnay ▨ ★★★★ **12** delivers plenty of flavour, richness at lower alcohol than Bateleur; ups the enjoyment with complex butterscotch & toffee tones, crisp citrus acidity. **10** (★★★) was buttery with a spicy tail, **11** sold out untasted. **Limestone Hill Chardonnay** ▤ ▨ ★★★ Limy fruit compote character leaves suggestion of sweetness on unoaked, lees-aged **13**, perfect foil for oysters. **Bon Vallon Chardonnay** ▨ ★★★★ Charming unwooded work-in-progress **13** revels in tropical fruit, ends with a lovely yeasty note courtesy weekly stirring during lees-ageing. **Sauvignon Blanc** ▨ ★★★☆ This wine's signature lime fruit profile on well-formed **13** preview, along with marzipan & lemon. Dab sugar fluffs out the tail feathers. **12** (★★★★) showed poise & focus. Discontinued: **Chardonnay D'Honneur**.

Danie de Wet range

★★★★ **Chardonnay Sur Lie** ▤ ▨ Unwooded, lees-aged version. **13** continues on same path as effusive **12**: ginger biscuit & citrus whiffs, silky mouthfeel & focused lemon-lime finish.

★★★★ **Cape Muscadel** ⓣ Sweetly simple **07** (★★★), missed complexity of **06** & previous.

Nature In Concert Pinot Noir ★★★★ **10**'s ebullient spice, earth & peppery cherry notes coupled with malleable tannins take it up a notch on choc-mocha **09** (★★★★). Enjoy solo or with food. **Sauvignon Blanc** 🍶 ★★★ Easygoing **13**, pre-bottling tinged with grass & capsicum, accessibly styled with moderate 12.5% alcohol, bright acidity, dry farewell. Discontinued: **Rosé.**

Limelight range

Chardonnay-Pinot Noir 🍶 ★★★ Drink-early, off-dry **13** boasts chardonnay's peachy notes, pinot's weight & depth. — DB,JP

De Wet Winery

Location/map/WO: Worcester ▪ Est 1946 ▪ 1stB 1964 ▪ Tasting & sales Mon-Fri 9-5 Sat 9-12 ▪ Fee R1/wine ▪ Closed all pub hols ▪ Cellar tours by appt ▪ BYO picnic ▪ Owner(s) 60 members ▪ Cellarmaster(s) Piet le Roux (Jan 2000) ▪ Winemaker(s) Tertius Jonck (Sep 2007) & Phillip Vercuiel (Dec 2007) ▪ Viticulturist(s) Hennie Visser (Jul 2008, Vinpro) ▪ 1,000ha (cab, shiraz, chard, chenin, sauv) ▪ 15,500t/30,000cs own label 29% red 36% white 5% rosé 30% fortified + 10m L bulk ▪ ISO 22000, SGS ▪ PO Box 16 De Wet 6853 ▪ admin@dewetcellar.co.za ▪ www.dewetcellar.co.za ▪ S 33° 36' 24.2" E 019° 30' 36.5" ▪ **T +27 (0)23-341-2710** ▪ F +27 (0)23-341-2762

The consumer buying a single bottle of chenin over the counter is as important as the corporate client buying mega-litres from this large Worcester cellar. Top honours at SA's Best Value Winery was welcome news for De Wet, also one of the shareholders in top UK brand FirstCape.

★★★★ **White Muscadel** ✓ **11** fortified sweetie has sunripe sultanas, dried peaches & apples, uncloying tangerine finish.

★★★★ **Cape Vintage** Longer-aged version of **08** port-style tasted last time, as firm & luscious but more complex curry spice, Xmas cake & smoking room aromas. From now-uprooted, ultra-rare pontac.

> **Cabernet Sauvignon** ☺ 🍶 ★★★ Tobacco & raspberry nuanced **12**, with tangy acidity to match richer red meat dishes. **Shiraz** ☺ 🍶 ★★★ Everyday appeal guaranteed by juicy **12**'s satisfying grip, commendably dry tail. **Dry Red** ☺ 🍶 ★★★ **11** equal shiraz/cab combo with lipsmacking berries for anytime sipping. **Chardonnay** ☺ 🍶 ★★★ 6 months new French oak give **12** its buttery aromas & texture, freshness assured by plenty of lemon zest & dried apricot tang.

Pinotage ① 🍶 ★★★ Coffee-toned **12** crisp & dry, exuberantly fruity & very drinkable. **Pinotage Rosé** 🍶 ★★★ Was just 'Rosé'. Soft **NV** perlé pink not overly sweet; enjoy with berry desserts or biltong at sunset. **Chenin Blanc** 🍶 ★★ Faint green apple wafts & pithy grip on reticent **13**. **Petillant Fronté** 🍶 ★★ Floral, sweetish, spritzy **NV** from white muscadel, light 8% alcohol perfect for poolside. **Sauvignon Blanc** 🍶 ★★★ Melon & cut-grass appeal on zesty **13** al fresco sipper. **Cravate** ✓ ★★★★ Among first méthode cap classique sparklings from the region. 100% chardonnay, vibrant **10** raises bar on **09** (★★★★): yeasty notes to lemon meringue taste, creamy mousse & clean citrus farewell. **Hanepoot** ① ★★★★ **10** fortified dessert with heady muscat aroma, lovely nutty tail. More fiery & drier than red & white muscadel stablemates. Delicious now but these known for longevity. **Red Muscadel** ✓ ★★★★ Fortified dessert delivering balanced raisin sweetness & litchi flavours in **12** plus refreshing nutty conclusion. **Cape Ruby** ★★★★ Latest **NV** port-style marries **12** tinta & **09** pontac. Quite robust - emphatic dry-tasting end, leather & tobacco aromas rather than usual mincemeat spices. Enjoy fireside. — DB, CvZ

■ **De Wit Family** *see Signal Gun Wines*

De Zoete Inval Estate

Location: Paarl ▪ Map: Paarl & Wellington ▪ WO: Paarl/Stellenbosch ▪ Est 1878 ▪ 1stB 1976 ▪ Tastings & sales by appt ▪ Owner(s) DZI Agricultural Investments cc (John Robert & Eulalia Frater) ▪ Cellarmaster(s)/winemaker(s) John Robert Frater (1999) ▪ Viticulturist(s) Dirk Blom (2007) ▪ 80ha/20ha (cab, grenache, malbec, mourv, p verdot, shiraz, chard) ▪ 200t/16,000cs own label 50% red 50% white ▪ Other export brands: Eskdale, Safari ▪ PO Box 591 Suider-Paarl 7624 ▪ info@dezoeteinval.co.za ▪ www.dezoeteinval.co.za ▪ S 33° 46' 35.9" E 018° 57' 50.9" ▪ **T +27 (0)21-863-1535/+27 (0)82-731-3898** ▪ F +27 (0)21-863-2158

John Robert and Eulalia Frater are the husband and wife owners of one of South Africa's original farms, granted by the father of SA wine himself, Simon van der

Stel, in 1688. The Fraters' natural and minimal approach includes 'biological' farming and open fermentors, to handle the fruit as gently as possible.

★★★★ **Pinotage Reserve** ⓘ When last tasted, spicy oak dominated **08**, with well-layered plummy fruit, meaty savoury notes. Supple body & texture. Simonsberg vines.

Pinotage Not tasted. **Cabernet Sauvignon-Shiraz** ⓘ ★★★ **09** medicinal, with sweet berry fruit, heavy & full. **Chardonnay** ⓘ ★★ **10** faint wet-wool notes on lean, mineral body. **Chenin Blanc-Viognier-Semillon** ⓘ 🍴 ★★★ Soft & accessible **11**, bursting with peach & spice appeal. Well rounded & a pleasure to drink. Stellenbosch WO. **Vintage Brut** Not tasted. **Cape Vintage** Not tasted. **Sweet Surrender Shiraz** ⓘ ★★★ Fortified campfire warmer, **06** pastille-like blackcurrant flavour & solid spirit grip. — DB

DGB

Wellington ▪ Est 1942 ▪ Closed to public ▪ Owner(s) DGB management, Brait Capital Partners & Kangra ▪ Winemaker(s)/viticulturist(s) see Bellingham & Boschendal ▪ PO Box 246 Wellington 7654 ▪ exports@dgb.co.za ▪ www.dgb.co.za ▪ **T +27 (0)21-864-5300** ▪ F +27 (0)21-864-1287

Well-established merchant house with strong portfolio of premium and own-brand table wines and port- and sherry-styles, including Bellingham, Boschendal, Brampton, Culemborg, Douglas Green, Franschhoek Cellar, Legacy, Millstream, Oude Kaap, Tall Horse, The Bernard Series, The Beachhouse and The Saints, most listed separately.

▪ **D'Hero's** see Govert Wines
▪ **Diamond Collection** see Lutzville Cape Diamond Vineyards
▪ **Diamond Creek** see Wines of Cape Town
▪ **Dido** see The Township Winery

Die Bergkelder Wine Centre   🍷 📷 ♿

Location/map: Stellenbosch ▪ All day tasting & sales Mon-Fri 8–5 Sat 9–2 ▪ Tour fee R25 ▪ Open non-religious pub hols ▪ Tours Mon-Fri 10, 11, 2 & 3; Sat 10, 11 & 12; incl AV presentation; bookings: info@bergkelder.co.za ▪ Tel +27 (0)21-809-8025 ▪ Special group tours, private tastings by appt ▪ Owner(s) Distell ▪ Cellarmaster(s) Andrea Freeborough ▪ Winemaker(s) Pieter Badenhorst (whites) & Wim Truter (reds), with John November ▪ Viticulturist(s) Bennie Liebenberg ▪ 2,500t/428,000cs 45% red 55% white ▪ PO Box 184 Stellenbosch 7599 ▪ info@bergkelder.co.za ▪ www.bergkelder.co.za ▪ S 33° 56' 8.8" E 018° 50' 54.7" ▪ **T +27 (0)21-809-8025** ▪ F +27 (0)21-883-9533

Literally 'Mountain Cellar', after the maturation facilities deep within Stellenbosch's Papegaaiberg, Die Bergkelder is the home of Fleur du Cap, listed separately. FdC wines can be tasted during a cellar tour, while other premium and super-premium wines in the Distell portfolio can be tasted and purchased at Die Bergkelder Wine Centre. The Vinoteque, now in its 30th year, markets fine wines with the option of having purchases stored in perfect cellar conditions. T +27 (0)21-809-8281 • info@vinoteque.co.za • www.vinoteque.co.za.

▪ **Die Laan** see Stellenbosch University Welgevallen Cellar

Die Mas van Kakamas   🍴 ☕ 🎋 ⛺ 📷 🎿

Location/WO: Northern Cape ▪ Map: Northern Cape, Free State & North West ▪ Est/1stB 2005 ▪ Tasting & sales Mon-Fri 8-5 Sat/Sun by appt ▪ Closed Easter Fri-Mon & Dec 25 ▪ 3-hr full farm tour on tractor-pulled wagon during tasting hours ▪ Meals/refreshments by appt; or BYO picnic ▪ Facilities for children ▪ Tour groups ▪ Gift shop ▪ Farm produce ▪ Conferences ▪ Walks/hikes ▪ Mountain biking trail ▪ Conservation area ▪ Camping facilities, 3 self-catering chalets & large lapa/bush pub ▪ Owner(s) Die Mas Boerdery (Pty) Ltd ▪ Cellarmaster(s)/winemaker(s)/viticulturist(s) Danie van der Westhuizen (May 2010) ▪ 1,400ha/80ha (cab, merlot, muscadel r/w, p verdot, pinot, ptage, sangio, shiraz, souzão, tinta, touriga, chard, chenin, cbard, sauv, viog) ▪ 350t/14,000cs own label 50% red 20% white 30% brandy ▪ PO Box 193 Kakamas 8870 ▪ winemaker@diemasvankakamas.co.za ▪ www.diemasvankakamas.co.za ▪ S 28° 45' 48.59" E 020° 38' 26.45" ▪ **T +27 (0)54-431-0245/+27 (0)82-931-5902** ▪ F +27 (0)86-531-9243

The Northern Cape's Orange River is a lush green artery in a parched landscape, and ex-teachers Vlok and Welna Hanekom's 1,400 ha of wine and table grapes, campsites, chalets and other tourist drawcards near Kakamas are sustained by it. Sweet dessert styles predominate but winemaker/viticulturist Danie van der Westhuizen unfortified table wines are improving by the vintage.

Rooi Kalahari range

Cabernet Sauvignon ⊕ ★★★ Approachable & gentle **11** has some blackcurrant appeal matched by firm backbone. Good texture to end. **Merlot** ⊕ ★★★ Soft ripeness on uncomplicated **11**, which ups ante on previous. **Pinotage** 🏵 ★★★ Raspberry, cranberry tang & succulence to uncomplicated **13**. **Shiraz** 🏵 ★★★ Savoury salami notes add interest to **11**'s blue & black fruity mouthful. Backbone supports gentle texture. Long finish. **Droë Rooi Versnit** NEW ★★★ Coffee bean smoky nuance to cab, shiraz-led 3-way NV blend. Plush, velvety feel with ample plum & chocolate flavour. **Rooi Muskadel** NEW 🏵 ★★★ **11** raisined, rich & sweet fortified dessert with floral muscat tones. **Rooi Jerepigo** ⊕ ★★ Ruby cab & shiraz in **12** fortified dessert. Spicy & sweet but tad short. **Cape Ruby** ★★★ Exotic incense nuance to raisined Christmas pudding fruit on **08** port-style fortified. Rich but simple & sweet.

Groen Kalahari range

Chardonnay 🏵 ★★★ Acidity livens the creaminess on barrel-fermented citrussy **12**. Rich & enthusiastic, with oak dominating somewhat. **Sauvignon Blanc** 🏵 ★★★ **13** grapefruit & lemon zest liveliness with light flint tail.

Goue Kalahari range

Hanepoot 🏵 ★★★ **10** packed with sundried sultanas plus interesting pecan nut, almond nuance. Clean dry finish. **Wit Muskadel** NEW 🏵 ★★★ Jasmine & peach syrup appeal to richly sweet, ambrosial **10**. Despite 240 grams sugar, it finishes dry & clean. **Wit Jerepigo** NEW ★★★ Oxidative nutty almond, treacle & sultana bounty on **08**. Spicy spirit lift on rich, uncloying palate. — FM

Diemersdal Estate

Location: Durbanville ▪ Map: Durbanville, Philadelphia & Darling ▪ WO: Durbanville/Western Cape ▪ Est 1698 ▪ 1stB 1976 ▪ Tasting & sales Mon-Fri 9–5 Sat/Sun 9–3 ▪ Closed Easter Fri/Sun, Dec 25 & Jan 1 ▪ Cellar tours by appt ▪ Diemersdal farm eatery (see Restaurants section) ▪ BYO picnic ▪ Walks ▪ Owner(s) Thys Louw & Mari Branders ▪ Winemaker(s) Thys Louw & Mari Branders ▪ Viticulturist(s) Div van Niekerk (1980) ▪ 210ha (cab, grenache, malbec, merlot, mourv, p verdot, ptage, shiraz, chard, sauv) ▪ 2,100t 70% red 30% white ▪ BWI, BRC, HACCIP ▪ PO Box 27 Durbanville 7551 ▪ thys@diemersdal.co.za ▪ www.diemersdal.co.za ▪ S 33° 48' 6.3" E 018° 38' 25. 1" ▪ **T +27 (0)21-976-3361** ▪ F +27 (0)21-976-1810

A farm eatery featuring celebrity chef and Kokkedoor TV show judge Nic van Wyk has opened at the Louw family's Durbanville estate, where there's no guessing the favoured grape variety. In fact the sheer number of sauvignon blancs vinified here itself seems like an extended family, with older (and more serious) siblings MM Louw, Reserve and 8 Rows, youngsters Diemersdal and Matys, plus the techie in the clan, Sauvignon.com. Then there's the West Coast cousin, Sir Lambert, and sundry nearer-by relatives and friends such as Maastricht. Nurturing them all are 6th generation winemaking Louw, Thys, and Mari Branders, who have a sure touch with black grapes, too. So sure, in fact, their MM Louw Estate Red won the 2013 Old Mutual Bordeaux Blend Trophy.

MM Louw range

★★★★☆ **Estate Red** 🏵 Restraint & elegance the hallmarks of Bordeaux blend, always firmly structured for cellaring. **11** more green walnut/cedar than cassis fruit, reflects challenging harvest in its unyielding tannin structure. Needs few years to settle, soften. **10** subtly fruited, very dry.

★★★★☆ **Sauvignon Blanc** 🏵 This version of Diemersdal's speciality variety fermented & aged in mostly new barrels & includes 10% semillon; usually less green & spiky. **12** seamlessly integrates riper papaya fruit & white asparagus with toasty oak. As poised & exquisitely dry as **11**. No **10**.

Reserve range

★★★★ **Pinotage** ✓ 🏵 **12**'s reined-in plum & berry fruit carefully overlain with spicy oak; smooth for solo sipping but sufficient grip for mealtimes. More understated than New-World **11**.

★★★★☆ **Private Collection** 🏵 Old World-inclined, cab-led 5-way Bordeaux blend. Leafy & sanguine **11** (★★★★) fruit-shy with lean tannin structure; similar styling but shade off perfumed **10**.

★★★★ **Chardonnay** ✓ 🈂 **12** less dominated by oak than **11** (★★★★); toasty as opposed to woody, tightly wound lime core, tangy & long conclusion.

★★★★☆ **Sauvignon Blanc** 🈂 From 27 year old vineyard, typically the most tropical of the three 'serious' versions though intensely flavoured **13** also shows a pungent capsicum note; beautifully poised & refreshing has **12**'s fine crystalline tail.

★★★★☆ **8 Rows Sauvignon Blanc** 🈂 Selection from 27 year old vineyard, spends 5 months on lees for additional depth, texture. Brilliant **13** a delicate composition with blackcurrant, focused freshness & 'wet pebble' minerality. **12** was similarly taut & worth seeking out.

Grenache 🈂 ★★★★ High-toned & concentrated **11** shows strawberry jam & antique furniture polish wafts, lengthy dry tail.

Diemersdal Estate range

★★★★ **Pinotage** ✓ 🈂 Traditional style very well done: banana nuances, plums & strawberry core, slight acetone lift in **12**. Fruity, friendly, with **11**'s great grip & refreshing acidity.

★★★★ **Chardonnay Unwooded** 🍶 🈂 Faint lemon & stonefruit appeal, salty finish. **13** (★★★★) not quite the neat parcel **12** was. Just bottled, however, could perk up given time to settle.

> **Sauvignon Blanc** ☺ 🍶 🈂 ★★★ Not as serious as siblings but a most enjoyable everyday drop (plenty to go round, too: 40,000 cases made). **13** cool green fruit, riper tropical notes, zippy acidity.

Merlot 🈂 ★★★ Red pastille fruit, leafy notes on unknit **12**, needs time or country fare. **Shiraz** 🈂 ★★★★ Smoky oak, black pepper introduce handsome **12** cranberry/raspberry glassful. Fleshy & commendably dry, excellent concentration without being overdone. **10** (★★★★) less effusive. **11** sold out untasted. **Sauvignon Rosé** 🍶 🈂 ★★★ **13** colour by cabernet, aroma & flavour by... sauvignon blanc, of course. Grassy, brisk picnic white.

Matys range

> **Cabernet Sauvignon-Merlot** ☺ 🍶 🈂 ★★★ Flamboyant berry fruit checked by slightly tarry oak on unceremonious **12**. These WO W Cape. **Sauvignon Blanc** ☺ 🍶 🈂 ★★★ The entry-level offering; Granny Smith apple tones on wallet-pleasing & sparky **13**. — CvZ

Diemersfontein Wines

Location/WO: Wellington ▪ Map: Paarl & Wellington ▪ Est 2000 ▪ 1stB 2001 ▪ Tasting & sales daily 10–5 ▪ Closed Dec 25 ▪ Cellar tours by appt ▪ Seasons Restaurant ▪ Tour groups ▪ Conferences ▪ Weddings ▪ Walks ▪ 3-star Diemersfontein Country House ▪ Owner(s) David & Susan Sonnenberg ▪ Winemaker(s) Francois Roode (Sep 2003), with Lauren Hulsman (2011) ▪ Viticulturist(s) Waldo Kellerman (Aug 2007) ▪ 180ha/60ha (cabs s/f, grenache, malbec, mourv, p verdot, ptage, roobernet, shiraz, chenin, viog) ▪ 600t/80,000cs own label 90% red 10% white ▪ HACCP ▪ PO Box 41 Wellington 7654 ▪ wine@diemersfontein.co.za ▪ www.diemersfontein. co.za ▪ S 33° 39' 41.1" E 019° 0' 31.1" ▪ **T +27 (0)21-864-5050** ▪ F +27 (0)21-864-2095

When owners David and Susan Sonnenberg returned home from the UK in 2000, the 18th-century Wellington fruit farm that had been in the family since the early 40s was sending grapes to the local cooperative. The couple set about developing the estate, its staff and the local community. Just over a decade after its 'sirens blaring, lights blazing' entrance on the wine scene (as this guide described it at the time), the spread in the shadow of the Hawekwa Mountains is endowed with a full-scale hospitality offering, employee empowerment business Thokozani, and burgeoning reputation as a top-end producer.

Carpe Diem range

★★★★ **Malbec** ✓ 🈂 Blueberry, roasted coffee & nutmeg profile of **11** finds counterpoint & balance in its lithe tannin structure; a beautifully elegant finish.

★★★★☆ **Pinotage** 🈂 Deep, rich & powerful, a super expression of the variety. Stunning **11** packed with ripe dark fruit, heady oak vanilla & warm 14% alcohol, but layered in an oh-so-sleek & polished composition. Perfectly judged 18 months 70% new oak, French & American.

★★★★☆ **Chenin Blanc** ✓ 🈂 Bold & beautiful in New-World style, partly barrel-fermented & oozing tropical fruit in creamy texture. Sample **12** (★★★★), with dollop viognier, not-quite-dry, shade off impressive **11**.

★★★★ **Viognier** ✓ 🈂 Bang for your buck. Peach & apricot flavours glide over fragrant oak (30% barrel-fermented, 30% new) in upfront **12**; luscious, now semi-dry.

Diemersfontein range

★★★★ **Pinotage** 🅚 Choc-mocha **12** (★★★☆) swirls with ripe plum & tobacco; more oaky than sweet-savoury & moreish **11**, needs patience & a plate of food.

> **For The Birds Red** ☺ 🍴 🅚 ★★★ Succulent red Bordeaux-style blend led by merlot in previewed **12**.
> **Chenin Blanc** NEW ☺ 🍴 🅚 ★★★ Bright summer fruit in fresh & appealing **13** sample.

Cabernet Sauvignon 🅚 ★★★ Bright bramble fruit spiced with cedar; firm tannin structure of robust **11** begs for food. **Shiraz** 🅚 ★★★ Juicy mulberry fruit & white pepper spice in **12**, firm tannins need time to soften. **Maiden's Prayer Red** 🍴 ★★★ Merlot-driven **12** Bordeaux-style blend showing lots of tarry oak over sweet dark fruit at preview. **Summer's Lease** ✓ 🅚 ★★★★ Rhône-style red - shiraz, mourvèdre & drop viognier, only seasoned oak. Muscular tannin tightly grips mulberry flesh of **11**, needs time to relax. **For The Birds White** 🍴 🅚 ★★★ Sample **13** chenin/sauvignon blend is perky, with breadth from 10% viognier. Sales benefit BirdLife South Africa, as for red partner. **Maiden's Prayer White** NEW 🍴 🅚 ★★★ Steely grip of previewed **13** chenin/viognier combo softened by 10% viognier. — DS

▧ **Die Tweede Droom** *see Groot Parys Estate*

Dieu Donné Vineyards

Location/map: Franschhoek ▪ Est 1984 ▪ 1stB 1986 ▪ Tasting & sales Mon-Fri 9–4 Sat/Sun 10.30–4 ▪ Fee R15 ▪ Closed Dec 25 & Jan 1 ▪ Cellar tours Mon-Fri by appt ▪ Cheese platters ▪ Gifts ▪ Micro beer brewery ▪ Roca Restaurant ▪ Owner(s) Robert Maingard ▪ Cellarmaster(s)/winemaker(s) Stephan du Toit (May 1996) ▪ Viticulturist(s) Hennie du Toit (Apr 1988) ▪ 40ha (cab, merlot, shiraz, chard, sauv, viog) ▪ ±280t/33,000cs own label 60% red 32% white 3% rosé 5% MCC ▪ PO Box 94 Franschhoek 7690 ▪ info@dieudonnevineyards.com ▪ www.dieudonnevineyards.com ▪ S 33° 53′ 46.9″ E 019° 7′ 45.0″ ▪ **T +27 (0)21-876-2493** ▪ F +27 (0)21-876-2102

A new stop on the Franschhoek Wine Tram route, Dieu Donné is French-Mauritian owned. With longtime winemaker (and Cape Wine Master) Stephan du Toit at the helm, the mountainside winery produces awarded reds, whites and méthode cap classique sparkling (and beer, in an onsite micro brewery).

Diners Club Bartho Eksteen Academy

Location: Paarl ▪ Map: Paarl & Wellington ▪ WO: Paarl/Overberg/Western Cape ▪ Est/1stB 2011 ▪ Tasting, sales & cellar tours by appt ▪ Meals/refreshments by pre-booking ▪ Facilities for children ▪ Farm produce ▪ BYO picnic ▪ Conferences ▪ Walks/hikes ▪ Mountain biking trail ▪ Nature reserve ▪ Owner(s) Bartho & Suné Eksteen ▪ Cellarmaster(s) Bartho Eksteen (Feb 2011) ▪ Winemaker(s) Bartho Eksteen, with Suné Eksteen (both Feb 2011), Pieter Willem Eksteen (Jan 2012) & learners at Hoër Landbouskool Boland ▪ Viticulturist(s) Willie van der Linde (Hoër Landbouskool Boland); Coenie van Dyk & James Downes (bought in grapes) ▪ 20ha (cab, merlot, shiraz, chard, chenin) ▪ 10t/1,800cs own label 40% red 33% white 13% MCC 14% NLH ▪ PO Box 2244 Hermanus 7200 ▪ info@barthoeksteensavvycelebration.co.za ▪ www.barthoeksteensavvycelebration.co.za ▪ S 33° 39′ 11.45″ E 018° 52′ 59.77″ ▪ **T +27 (0)28-312-4612** ▪ F +27 (0)86-554-0896

After winning the Diners Club Winemaker of the Year in 2010, Bartho Eksteen secured a sponsorship from Diners Club to run a three-year winemaking course at his Paarl alma mater, Boland Agricultural High School. Through this endeavour, the Hermanuspietersfontein winemaker hopes secondary level students will also learn about social responsibility, wise alcohol consumption and the role of alcohol in an adult society. Note: wines tasted and rated prior to acquisition of this guide by Diners Club South Africa.

★★★★ **Wijnskool Sauvignon Blanc** ⓐ Intense **11** off Overberg vines. Ripely fragrant; great vigour balanced by attractively oak-enhanced flavours; brisk, bone-dry.

Wijnskool Shiraz ⓐ ★★★★ Rich & spicy **11** last year flaunted its 16 months in 60% new oak but with sufficient supple fruit, substance to harmonise. WO Paarl. **Wijnskool Chenin Blanc** Await next. **Wijnskool Veraison Méthode Cap Classique** ⓐ ★★ Pinky-gold, bone-dry **09** bubbly. WO W Cape. — AL

▧ **Director's Choice** *see Nordic Wines*

Dispore Kamma Boutique Winery ♂♥

Location: Caledon ▪ Map: Elgin, Walker Bay & Bot River ▪ Est/1stB 2002 ▪ Tasting, sales & cellar tours by appt ▪ Owner(s) Philip Mostert & Hannes Coetzee ▪ Winemaker(s) Philip Mostert (Jan 2002), with Hannes Coetzee (Jun 2002) ▪ 150cs own label 100% red ▪ PO Box 272 Caledon 7230 ▪ disporekamma@overnet.co.za ▪ S 34° 13' 40.2" E 019° 25' 10.5" ▪ **T +27 (0)28-212-1096** ▪ F +27 (0)28-214-1077

For Caledon-based general practitioner Philip Mostert and orthopaedic surgeon Hannes Coetzee, vinifying and marketing their shiraz (from Paarl grapes) is an after-hours-only endeavour but a Michelangelo Best Garagiste Wine in their trophy cabinet reflects an aspiration to make 'quality part of our dream'.

Distell

PO Box 184 Stellenbosch 7599 ▪ info@distell.co.za ▪ www.distell.co.za ▪ **T +27 (0)21-809-7000**

From its Stellenbosch headquaters, Distell vinifies some of South Africa's most successful and enduring wine, brandy and sherry-style brands. They include: 4th Street, 5th Avenue Cold Duck, Autumn Harvest Crackling, Capenheimer, Cellar Cask, Chateau Libertas, Chatta Box, Drostdy-Hof, Fleur du Cap, Graça, Grand Mousseux, Grünberger, Ixia, Kellerprinz, Kupferberger Auslese, Libertas, Monis and its trio of sherry-styles, Obikwa, Oom Tas, Overmeer, Place in the Sun, Pongrácz, newcomer RED ESCape, Sedgwick's sherry-style, Ship, Tassenberg, Taverna Rouge, Two Oceans, Virginia and Zonnebloem. Distell also owns the House of JC le Roux, a dedicated sparkling-wine cellar in Devon Valley. Then there are the stand-alone 'estate' labels: Nederburg, Plaisir de Merle and Lomond. Distell is also the co-owner, together with Lusan Holdings, of a handful of top Stellenbosch properties (Alto, Le Bonheur, Neethlingshof, Stellenzicht/ Hill & Dale, Uitkyk/Flat Roof Manor), and, with several local growers, of Durbanville Hills. Distell also has agreements with a few independently owned cellars (Allesverloren, Jacobsdal, Theuniskraal) for which it provides a range of services. Finally, there's the black empowerment venture on Papkuilsfontein farm near Darling, source of Earthbound wines. Brandy labels include Collison's, Klipdrift, Flight of the Fish Eagle, Richelieu, Oude Meester, Van Ryn and Viceroy. See Die Bergkelder for details about the Vinoteque Wine Bank, and separate entries for most of the above brands.

■ **Dixon's Peak** *see* Waverley Hills Organic Wines & Olives
■ **Dolphin Sands** *see* Wines of Cape Town

Domaine Brahms Wineries ♂♥📷

Location/WO: Paarl ▪ Map: Paarl & Wellington ▪ Est 1998 ▪ 1stB 1999 ▪ Tasting & tours (vyd/cellar/wine) by appt ▪ Fee R5/wine ▪ Chapel & wedding/function venue ▪ Owner(s) Johan & Gesie van Deventer ▪ Winemaker(s)/viticulturist(s) Gesie van Deventer (1998) ▪ 12ha (cab, merlot, ptage, shiraz, chenin) ▪ 30,000L 90% red 10% white ▪ PO Box 2136 Windmeul 7630 ▪ brahms@iafrica.com ▪ www.domainebrahms.co.za ▪ S 33° 40' 27.28" E 18° 53' 29.24" ▪ **T +27 (0)21-869-8555** ▪ F +27 (0)86-614-9445

Gesie and Johan van Deventer continue to improve their Paarl property, which includes wedding and conference venues. They've planted more pinotage and chenin, which, like all the vines here, are farmed as sustainably as possible, counting carbon emissions and offsetting them by extensive tree planting.

★★★★ **Shiraz** ⓐ **08** (★★★★) differs from last big & bold **05**: there's more red-fruit tang & chalkiness in the texture, plus a sprinkle of turned earth. Alcohol is big, though, at 15%. No **06**, **07**.

Cabernet Sauvignon Await new, as for **Merlot**, **Pinotage**, **Sonato**, **Chenin Blanc** & **Unwooded Chenin Blanc**. **Quartet** ⓐ ★★★★ **06** ex-cask ripely fruity pinotage (40%) with cab, merlot, shiraz. Succulent but serious, well oaked. — CM

Domaine Coutelier ♥ NEW

Location/map: Stellenbosch ▪ WO: Durbanville ▪ Est/1stB 2012 ▪ Tasting, sales & cellar tours by appt ▪ Closed all pub hols ▪ Owner(s) Quint Cutler ▪ Winemaker(s) Quint Cutler (March 2013), with consultants ▪ Viticulturist(s) Kevin Watt (May 2013, consultant) ▪ 4ha/3.5ha (cab, merlot) ▪ ±21t/2,300cs own label 70% red 10% white 10% rosé 10% MCC ▪ PO Box 346 Stellenbosch 7599 ▪ quint.cutler@gmail.com ▪ www. domainecoutelier.com ▪ S 33° 54' 2.80" E 018° 47'58.46" ▪ **T +27 (0)79-498-0772**

UK-born businessman Quint Cutler and his French wife Floriane had a brief brush with the Stellenbosch winelands back in 2009 - enough to plant the seeds to swap a Paris life for the rural charms of Devon Valley. With support from local wineries, and guidance from Cape Winemakers Guild member Philip Costandius, they made their first wines. Affinity for wines from the Médoc, Burgundy white and Floriane's native Champagne serves as inspiration for the styles they wish to emulate. They also plan to plant some of the first carmenère in South Africa.

The Feast range

★★★★ **Chardonnay** Durbanville fruit shines in classy barrel-fermented (33% new oak) **12**. Lemon & apricot fruit prevails over wood aromas, flavours; buttery & long, very satisfying. — GdB, GM

Domaine des Dieux ♟

Location: Hermanus ▪ Map: Elgin, Walker Bay & Bot River ▪ WO: Hemel-en-Aarde Ridge/Walker Bay/Walker Bay/Elgin ▪ Est 2002 ▪ 1stB 2006 ▪ Tasting & sales at the vineyards Mon-Sun 11-4.30 (Nov-Feb); off-peak periods by appt ▪ Closed Easter Fri/Sun, Dec 25 & Jan 1 ▪ Owner(s) Domaine des Dieux (Pty) Ltd ▪ Winemaker(s) Consultants ▪ Vineyard manager Petrus Bothma ▪ Viticulturist(s) Johan Pienaar ▪ 28ha/20ha (pinot, shiraz & other red varieties, chard, sauv) ▪ 30,000cs own label 25% red 25% white 50% MCC ▪ PO Box 2082 Hermanus 7200 ▪ info@domainedesdieux.co.za ▪ www.domainedesdieux.co.za ▪ S 34° 19' 35.81" E 019° 19' 50.71" ▪ **T +27 (0)28-313-2126/+27 (0)83-536-5916** ▪ F +27 (0)87-230-6286

High is the Hemel-en-Aarde Ridge ward near Hermanus, the Domaine des Dieuxs vineyards benefit from both their elevation and proximity to the ocean. The wines, made by consultants, show cool-climate elegance.

★★★★ **Syrah-Mourvèdre** More shiraz (80%) on **11**, but retains poise & lovely fruit purity. Intense garrigue scrub & spice, surprisingly light footed. Lithe structure & balance, exudes drinkability.

★★★★ **Sauvignon Blanc 11** is tightly coiled, with a flinty herbaceous tone. Some leesy breadth on long, pithy finish. Still quite closed, some time & a lunch date should resolve.

★★★★ **Rose of Sharon MCC Brut Rosé** ⓟ Steely, mineral **08** sparkling is pinot noir-led, chardonnay plumping out austere styling. Oaked portion & 3 years on lees add breadth & creamy length. Some Elgin grapes.

★★★★ **Claudia Brut MCC 08** bubbly from Walker Bay & Elgin chardonnay/pinot (74/26). Revisited, shows lovely refinement & freshness, subtly underscored by extended lees-ageing. Will reward time in the bottle.

Josephine Pinot Noir ★★★★ **11** has appealing red fruit & leather aromas, but less intensity & verve than **10** (★★★★). Brisk chalky farewell. **Chardonnay** ⓟ ★★★★ Spicily oaked, elegant **11** in trim, flinty style. More depth needed to match serious intent. Attractive citrus twist. — MW

Dombeya Wines 🍷🍴🥃♨🏛🍽♿

Location/map: Stellenbosch ▪ WO: Stellenbosch/Western Cape ▪ Est 2005 ▪ 1stB 2006 ▪ Tasting & sales Tue-Fri 9-5 Sat/Sun 10-5 ▪ Closed Mon, Easter Fri-Mon & Dec 25 ▪ Cellar tours on special request only ▪ The Long Table Restaurant & Café: Tue-Sun 9-5; Fri dinner - booking essential ▪ Facilities for children ▪ Self-catering accommodation in The Residence and Cottage (see Accommodation section) ▪ Owner(s) Preston Haskell ▪ Cellarmaster(s) Rianie Strydom (Jan 2005) ▪ Viticulturist(s) Wikus Pretorius (Dec 2005) ▪ 25ha/13.5ha (cabs s/f, merlot, shiraz, chard) ▪ ±80t/15,000cs own label 80% red 20% white ▪ PO Box 12766 Die Boord 7613 ▪ info@ dombeyawines.com ▪ www.dombeyawines.com ▪ S 34°0' 13.9" E 018° 51' 38.4" ▪ **T +27 (0)21-881-3895** ▪ F +27 (0)21-881-3986

Named after a scented indigenous tree, Dombeya has been in the hands of American Preston Haskell since 2002, and operating from a purpose-built cellar under the aegis of Rianie Strydom since 2005. (Sibling brand Haskell Vineyards also vinified there.) Blessed with excellent terroir in Stellenbosch's 'Golden Triangle', the young team's mantra is to over-deliver. Nurturing of winemaking talent, another leitmotif, sees a cellarhand training for a junior winemaking post - with the added incentive of an Australian harvest thrown in for good measure.

★★★★ **Cabernet Sauvignon** Blackcurrant typicity to Helderberg fruit on **09** (★★★★☆) which ups its game a notch on **08**. Lithe & muscular yet yielding & generous as befits the vintage. Focused & polished, with layers of flavour & long cedary tail.

★★★★ **Merlot** Ripe pastille fruit abundance to **09**. Supple cocoa undertone with sleek, fine tannins well balanced courtesy of 14 months French oak, 40% new. Needs more time than bolder **08** (★★★★★).

★★★★ **Boulder Road Shiraz 09** full of inky cherry delights - much like **08**. Chunky dark chocolate texture but leashed power lurks broodingly. Juicy, yet clean, dry sinuous finish.

★★★★ **Altus** Liquorice & earth subtext to **08** Bordeaux-style mix led by cab with merlot/malbec in support. Succulent, but with firm structure & length. Maintains tone & quality of elegant **07**.

★★★★ **Chardonnay 12** delivers limestone & citrus vibrancy within creamy oak frame. Acidity is fresh & lively. Restraint & focus evident - as on **11**. Long, dry aftertaste.

Sauvignon Blanc ✓ 🍴 ★★★★ Bold passionfruit life to fresh **13** which has a dab semillon (10%) added. Weighty intensity on long expressive palate. WO W Cape. — FM

Domein Doornkraal

Location: De Rust ▪ Map: Klein Karoo & Garden Route ▪ Est 1880 ▪ 1stB 1973 ▪ Tasting & sales Mon-Fri 9-5 Sat 9-3 ▪ Closed Easter Fri/Sun & Dec 25 ▪ Light refreshments ▪ Farm produce ▪ Gifts ▪ Conference facility on farm ▪ Self-catering farm cottages & lodge ▪ Owner(s)/winemaker(s) Swepie, Piet & Celia le Roux ▪ Cellarmaster(s) Swepie le Roux (Apr 2011) ▪ Viticulturist(s) Celia le Roux Mostert ▪ 2,000ha/10ha (cab, merlot, muscadel, ptage, chard, chenin, cbard) ▪ 105t/4,000cs own label 15% red 15% white 70% fortified ▪ PO Box 14 De Rust 6650 ▪ wyn@doornkraal.co.za ▪ www.doornkraal.co.za ▪ S 33° 32' 43.5" E 022° 26' 42.6" ▪ **T +27 (0)44-251-6715** ▪ F +27 (0)86-528-5633

Urbane septuagenarian Swepie le Roux and daughter Celia le Roux Mostert now shape respectively the wines and vines at the family's multi-enterprise Klein Karoo farm. Upgrades to their roadside emporium afford a fresh opportunity to taste the 'diverse and moreish' Doornkraal range, plus regional foods and wines.

■ **Donatus** see Dornier Wines

Donkiesbaai 🍷

Location/map: Stellenbosch ▪ WO: Piekenierskloof/Stellenbosch ▪ Est/1stB 2011 ▪ Tasting & sales at Guardian Peak (see entry) ▪ Owner(s) Jean Engelbrecht ▪ Winemaker(s) Coenie Snyman & Philip van Staden (both Jan 2011) ▪ Viticulturist(s) Dirkie Mouton (Jan 2011) ▪ 15t/1,200cs own label 100% white ▪ PO Box 473 Stellenbosch 7599 ▪ info@rustenvrede.com ▪ www.donkiesbaai.com ▪ S 34° 0' 40.19" E 018° 50' 31.99" ▪ **T +27 (0)21-881-3881** ▪ F +27 (0)21-881-3000

Rust en Vrede owner Jean Engelbrecht adroitly combines a number elements and trends - a family heritage backstory, 'proudly Afrikaans' product naming, inspired packaging and, by no means least, outstanding winemaking - in this boutique brand, honouring the West Coast resort (Donkin - 'Donkey' - Bay) where four generations of Engelbrechts have vacationed, glass of cold chenin in hand.

★★★★☆ **Steen** 🍸 Superb **12** maintains **11**'s rich, ripe, peachy style of chenin, with fruit (ex Piekenierskloof) partly fermented in older oak. Oaten wheat notes livened by fresh acidity. Succulent yet dry & spicy. Elegant, with lingering flavour.

★★★★☆ **Hooiwijn** NEW 🍸 Ambrosial straw ('hooi' in Afrikaans) wine from Stellenbosch chenin, barrel fermented & 8 months aged. **12** richly sweet yet focused, poised & livened by vibrant acid. Crisp & dry-seeming finish, the tangy honeyed dried pineapple & apricot flavour lingers long. Just 800 bottles. — FM

■ **Don Morris** see Govert Wines

Doolhof Wine Estate

Location/WO: Wellington ▪ Map: Paarl & Wellington ▪ Est 1995 ▪ 1stB 2003 ▪ Tasting & sales Mon-Sat 10-5 Sun 10-4 ▪ Fee R20/5 wines ▪ Closed Good Fri, Dec 25/26 & Jan 1 ▪ Cellar tours by appt ▪ Light lunches Tue-Sun 11-3; picnics by appt; wine & canapé pairings by pre-booking ▪ Conferences ▪ Walks/hikes ▪ Mountain biking & 4x4 trails ▪ 5-star Grand Dédale Country House ▪ Owner(s) Dennis Kerrison ▪ Cellarmaster(s)/winemaker(s) Friedrich Kühne (Dec 2008), with Rianie Strydom (consultant) ▪ Viticulturist(s) Hendrik Laubscher (Aug 1996) ▪ 380ha/38ha (cabs s/f, malbec, merlot, p verdot, ptage, shiraz, chard, sauv) ▪ 300t/24,000cs own label 73%

red 26% white 1% rosé ▪ BWI, IPW, WIETA ▪ PO Box 157 Wellington 7654 ▪ office@doolhof.com ▪ www.doolhof.com ▪ S 33° 37' 35.6" E 019° 4' 58.7" ▪ **T +27 (0)21-873-6911** ▪ F +27 (0)21-864-2321

Named 'Labyrinth' after its many hills and vales, this historic (1707) Wellington estate was acquired by the Kerrison family in 2003 and transformed into a show-case, with a new modern cellar, refurbished tasting venue and numerous ameni-ties such as the awarded 5 star Grand Dédale Country House. The extensive wine portfolio, also widely hailed, has a new Labyrinth-themed flagship, Theseus.

Signatures of Doolhof range

★★★★ **Cabernet Franc** ⊛ 09 has attractive cedary oak, tart red berry, floral perfume & earthy complex-ity. Juicy, but balanced by vinous & fine tannin grip. Stays fresh though big alcohol & few grams sugar. **Cabernet Sauvignon** ⊛ ★★★ **10** rather lean, with some development evident. Big alcohol & some sweet-ness serve as foil to obvious tannins. **Malbec** ⊛ ★★★☆ Dark fruit supported by dry cocoa notes. **10** has lovely fruit-rich appeal & smoothness. **Merlot** ✓ ★★★☆ Voluptuous chocolate-laden 09 proudly shows off its curves, molten plum flavours. Enough grip for food but drink soon. **Petit Verdot** ⊛ ★★★☆ 09 step up on 08, with poised ripeness balanced by integrated oak spice & red cherry freshness. **Pinotage** ⊛ ★★★☆ 09's ripe charry red & black fruit much like 08. Light bodied but with grip from year French oak, half new. **Shiraz** ⊛ ★★★☆ Good fruit expression & typical varietal black olive & spice, follows to savoury 08's palate with ripe polished end. **Renaissance Cabernet Sauvignon-Merlot** ⊛ ★★★☆ After generous 06 (★★★☆), last-tasted 07 had blackcurrant & cigarbox, ripeness balanced by char from year in 40% new French oak. **Char-donnay Wooded** ⊛ ★★★☆ Barrel-fermented 09 has lovely texture; bruised apple character from bottle-age melds with toasty oak. Ready to enjoy. **Chardonnay Unwooded** ⊛ 🗒 🍸 ★★★☆ Subtle pear & peach aromas on step-up **11** has cream-textured, dry & focused end. Zingy acid makes for ideal food partner. **Sauvignon Blanc** ✓ 🗒 🍸 ★★★☆ Sauvignon at its light (12% alcohol) & lively best, **12** awakens the senses with its grassy tones, flinty core & limy acidity.

Legends of the Labyrinth range

★★★★ **The Minotaur** ✓ Back on track after 08 (★★★☆), showy 09 has curves to spare. Spicy dark fruit & thanks to pinotage, merlot, shiraz & malbec which comprise most of the blend, it is rich, power packed. **Lady in Red** ⊛ 🗒 ★★★☆ Unusual jasmine note few years back to juicy mulberry & mocha on seriously oaked 08, 5-way Bordeaux blend. **Dark Lady of the Labyrinth** ⊛ 🍸 ★★★ **11** from mostly pinotage in mocha/coffee mould, with shy banana-loaf aroma & cherry/chocolate palate. Still very young & needs the new oak to meld. **Lady in White** ⊛ 🗒 ★★★ Chenin, semillon & sauvignon liaison. Lemon butter & nettle, **10** zingy yet also creamy from year in new oak.

Cape range

Boar ☺ 🗒 🍸 ★★★ Merlot with cab, dash 2 others in **12** supplies the plush fruit, appealing juiciness.

Roan ⊛ 🗒 ★★★ As name maybe hints, mostly from shiraz plus other Rhône varieties. **10** has spicy counter to ripe, dark-berried sweetness. Just-dry, like Boar. **Robin** ⊛ 🗒 🍸 ★★★ **11** from shiraz, a dry spicy & plummy quaffer. **Loerie** ⊛ 🗒 🍸 ★★☆ Clean **11** from sauvignon, splash chenin, is light & dry with fruity fresh appeal. Moderate 12% alcohol. **Eagle** ⊛ 🗒 ★★☆ Tropical & tangy **10**, lightish unwooded chardon-nay with splash of chenin. — CR

Doran Vineyards

Location: Paarl ▪ Map: Paarl & Wellington ▪ WO: Voor Paardeberg/Swartland/Western Cape ▪ Est 2010 ▪ 1stB 2012 ▪ Tasting Mon-Fri by appt Sat/Sun & pub hols 10-4 ▪ Closed Good Fri, Dec 25/26 & Jan 1 ▪ Owner(s) Edwin Doran & André Badenhorst ▪ Winemaker(s) Martin Lamprecht ▪ Viticulturist(s) Basson Potgieter ▪ 170ha/50ha (cabs s/f, merlot, ptage, shiraz) ▪ 450t/30,000cs own label ▪ Other export brand: Thorntree ▪ Suite 310 Private Bag X16 Constantia 7848 ▪ andrebad@iafrica.com ▪ www.doranvineyards.co.za ▪ S 33° 35' 15.14" E 018° 52' 06.13" ▪ **T +27 (0)21-869-8328** ▪ F +27 (0)21-869-8329

Asked what his passions beyond wine are, Twickenham-based Edwin Doran replies 'Food and rugby. Or is it rugby and food?' No surprise that the tasting room at the Voor Paardeberg winery he owns with seasoned local wine-man (and fellow food and rugby aficionado) André Badenhorst features an excellent col-lection of rugby, cricket and football paraphernalia autographed by top players.

Doran Vineyards range

★★★★ **Chenin Blanc** Now bottled, **12** delivers on early promise. Peach (& its kernel), some nice yeasty character. Good richness, tangy acidity, savoury finish. Understated but not middle of the road. Swartland WO.
Pinotage NEW ⌘ ★★★ **12** comes in an uncomplicated, fruit-driven style. Red & black cherry, vaguest hint of vanilla, fresh acidity. **Shiraz** ⌘ ★★★ Now bottled, **12** is not unappealing but a bit foursquare, with ultra-ripe dark fruit, moderate acidity & smooth texture. **The Romy D** NEW ⌘ ★★☆ Bordeaux-style red blend **12** is rather slight, insubstantial. Red fruit with a green edge. **Rosie D Pinotage Rosé** NEW ★★ **13** is pleasant enough but unmemorable, slightly sweet-tasting (though technically dry) & lightly fruity.

Horse Mountain range NEW

Pinotage ▤ ★★ Rustic **11** shows earthy notes alongside boiled sweets. **Shiraz** ▤ ★★★ Lightly fruity **11** is undemanding but pleasant. Unwooded, as for next two wines. **Michele** ▤ ⌘ ★★★ Bordeaux-style red **11** is lean but not mean, with red fruit & pleasant tomato cocktail quality about it. **Chenin Blanc-Viognier** ✓ ▤ ⌘ ★★★★ **11** punches above its weight showing plenty of character - peach, vanilla & a waxy note. Rich & full, with soft but sufficient acidity. — CE

Dormershire Estate

Location: Kuils River ▪ Map/WO: Stellenbosch ▪ Est 1996 ▪ 1stB 2001 ▪ Tasting, sales & tours Mon-Fri 8–5 Sat 10–1 ▪ Fee R10pp ▪ Closed all pub hols ▪ Farm market on last Sat of every month ▪ Owner(s) Family Trust ▪ Winemaker(s) Michelle Louw (Apr 2007) ▪ Viticulturist(s) Johan Pienaar (consultant) ▪ 8ha/6ha (cab, shiraz, sauv) ▪ ±50t/8,000cs own label 85% red 10% white 5% rosé ▪ PO Box 491 Bellville 7535 ▪ wine@dormershire.co.za ▪ www.dormershire.com ▪ S 33° 56' 27.0" E 018° 42' 54.7" ▪ **T +27 (0)21-801-4677** ▪ F +27 (0)86-517-0716

An oasis of vines bordered by suburbia, boutique winery Dormershire is well worth a visit, especially on the last Saturday of the month when a market offers a wide range of local produce, arts, crafts and, of course, the estate wines.

Cabernet Sauvignon ⓣ ▤ ★★★★ As expected, juicier & earlier accessible than the Reserve, a savoury note makes **07** a good food match. **Reserve Cabernet Sauvignon** ⓣ ★★★★ Selection of best barrels, 18 months oak (as for all the reds). Despite big alcohol, **07** achieves elegance & poise. **Shiraz** ⓣ ▤ ★★★ **07** toasted bread & spicy cherry flavours, ending dry. Ideal winter casserole red. **Stoep Shiraz** ⓣ ★★★ Wood here a toasty backdrop, **07** earthy & savoury blackberry fruit, pepper seasoning. **Cabernet Sauvignon-Shiraz** ⓣ ★★★★ **07** has this estate's Old World character: peppery/dusty notes, cherry flavours & firm tannins. **Rosé** Await new, as for **Sauvignon Blanc**. **Sweet Red** ⓣ ★★★★ NV jerepiko-style fireside snuggler from shiraz, with intriguing savoury overlay. — DB

Dornier Wines

Location/map: Stellenbosch ▪ WO: Stellenbosch/Western Cape ▪ Est 1995 ▪ 1stB 2002 ▪ Tasting & sales daily 10–5 ▪ Cellar tours by appt ▪ Dornier Bodega Restaurant: lunch daily 12–5 dinner (Oct-Apr) Thu-Sat ▪ Facilities for children ▪ Gift shop ▪ Conference venue ▪ Conservation area ▪ Homestead with 6 bedrooms & large entertainment areas offered ▪ Owner(s) Dornier family ▪ Winemaker(s) Jeanine Faure (Mar 2012) ▪ Viticulturist(s) Theunis Bell (Sep 2009) ▪ 167ha/60ha (cabs s/f, malbec, merlot, p verdot, ptage, shiraz, tempranillo, chenin, sauv, sem) ▪ 270t 80% red 17% white 3% rosé ▪ PO Box 7518 Stellenbosch 7599 ▪ info@dornier.co.za ▪ www.dornier.co.za ▪ S 33° 59' 31.00" E 018° 52' 19.00" ▪ **T +27 (0)21-880-0557** ▪ F +27 (0)21-880-1499

A central feature at the Dornier family's picturesque Stellenbosch property is the visually stunning cellar. The mountain backdrop, coupled with the structure's reflecting pool, further enhances the graceful flow of the design. It's all in full view from the Bodega Restaurant. There is already a 'green' focus here, with recycling, composting and effluent management, and now energy conservation is being put in place. Sadly 2013's malbec grapes were clearly so delicious, all but two short rows in the top vineyard were eaten by baboons.

Founder range NEW

★★★★☆ **CMD** ⌘ Bordeaux blend with malbec taking the lead, **11**'s concentration already shows in the crimson colour. Intense blackcurrants & plums, cedar dusted, still in the prime of youth, tannins a masterly executed bolstering. Expect a glorious future.

Donatus range

★★★★☆ **Red** 📖 Mainly cab, dashes malbec & cab franc, **10**'s flavour array includes cassis, bouillon, creamy café au lait notes. The fresh-fruity juiciness makes it accessible but with an assured future ahead, thanks to its cloaked, sinewy strength.

★★★★ **White** 🕐 📖 Chenin-led oaked blend with semillon. The expected sophistication in **11**, everything expertly matched; oak spice, the quince of chenin, sleek & assured. Nudges the next level. WO W Cape.

Dornier range

★★★★ **Cabernet Sauvignon** 🕐 Complex **07**'s dark plum centre shows dried herb, allspice, even fynbos nuances. Tannins are supple with a backbone for good few more years.

★★★★ **Malbec** NEW 📖 Dusty, chopped herbs, salty liquorice & hedgerow fruit all show how different **11** is, one of a handful of single-varietal bottlings. Fresh & juicy enough to enjoy now, or age a bit.

★★★★ **Pinotage** 📖 Plums & cedar in **11**, showing its youth in the firm but ripe tannins, already accessible but the best is yet to come. Built to last 8+ years, has the muscle tone for it.

★★★★ **Semillon** NEW 📖 Only made in the best years. Barrel fermented/matured 18 months, **11** has a lovely rounded texture, leafy, waxy tones, a savoury thread running through the flavours. Just 160 cases.

Merlot 🕐 ★★★★ Previously **07** had berry-rich, herbal-tinged aromas & flavours; was savoury & firm, with modest fruit intensity. **Tempranillo** NEW 📖 ★★★★ Rare varietal bottling. Morello cherries, dried herbs & smoky spice, **11**'s peppery tannins are designed for rich food, ageing. **Cabernet Sauvignon-Merlot** 📖 ★★★★ Tried & tested combo, merlot giving a juicy liveliness to **11**, cab the structure, & red berry styling coming from both. **Chenin Blanc Bush Vine** Await next. **Froschkoenig Natural Sweet** Await next.

Cocoa Hill range

Sauvignon Blanc 😊 📖 ★★★ With green fig flavours fresh-seamed with minerality, **13** offers a lovely choice for food accompaniment.

Red ★★★ Mainly merlot & shiraz in **11**, with attractive dark-toned ripeness, savoury spice. Ready, & can age a few years. WO W Cape. **Rosé** 📖📖 ★★★ Merlot's fruity-fresh dry **13** has delicate red berry styling. **Chenin Blanc** 📖 ★★★ **13** offers pear-rich fruit salad with a squeeze of lemon. — CR

Douglas Green

Location: Wellington ▪ WO: Western Cape/Wellington/Worcester ▪ Est 1942 ▪ Closed to public ▪ Owner(s) DGB (Pty) Ltd ▪ Cellarmaster(s) Gerhard Carstens, with Liezl Carstens (2000) ▪ Winemaker(s) Jaco Potgieter (oenologist, 2000) ▪ Viticulturist(s) Stephan Joubert (2006) ▪ 50% red 49% white 1% rosé ▪ ISO 9001:2000, Fairtrade, HACCP, IPW, WIETA ▪ PO Box 246 Wellington 7654 ▪ douglasgreen@dgb.co.za ▪ www. douglasgreenwines.com ▪ T +27 (0)21-864-5300 ▪ F +27 (0)21-864-1287

Douglas Green commenced trading from the Stukvat Bottlestore in Main Street, Paarl, in 1938. By 1942 he was making his own wine, negociant style, from grapes carefully sourced around winelands. His approach and philosophy – good wine, at a good price, that people enjoy – remain the foundation of the DGB-owned brand that today bears his name.

Vineyard Creations

Pinotage 😊 🍴 📖 ★★★ Coffee-toned **13** has zesty fruit, soft tannins & a bit of complexity to explore solo or at mealtimes. **Chardonnay** 😊 🍴 📖 ★★★ Pear & faint lemon on oak-brushed **13**, creamy flavours broadened by dab sugar, citrus zest refreshes, readies for next sip. **Sauvignon Blanc** 😊 🍴 📖 ★★★ Fig, nettle & ocean breeze freshness up **13**'s appeal as aperitif or seafood companion.

Cabernet Sauvignon 🕐 🍴 📖 ★★★ **11** subtle but juicy dark fruit in smooth & friendly easy-drinking style. **Merlot** 🕐 🍴 📖 ★★★ **11** smoky nuance to red berries in bright BBQ/pizza partner. **Shiraz** 🕐 🍴 📖 ★★ Brusque **11**'s fruit masked by dusty cinnamon-spiced oak. **Chenin Blanc** 🍴 📖 ★★★ Lovely thatch & beeswax tones, enlivening acidity on **13** deliver easy albeit brief enjoyment.

Diversity range

Cabernet Sauvignon-Merlot 🕐 🍴 📖 ★★★ **10** rich & ripe dark berry fruit in supple accessible style. Balanced, with food-friendly dry finish. **Merlot-Malbec** 🕐 🍴 📖 ★★★ Juicy **11** is bright & spicy, with smooth-textured quaffability. **Pinotage Rosé** 🕐 🍴 📖 ★★★ **10** light & tangy anywhere, anytime pink sipper. **Sauvignon Blanc-Chenin Blanc** 🕐 🍴 📖 ★★★ Previewed **12** lively blend, crisp & juicy yellow peach flavours with enough style to grace the table. **Sunkissed Natural Sweet Rosé** ④ 🍶 ★★ Sweet low-alcohol **NV** sundowner from pinotage & merlot. **Sunkissed Natural Sweet White** ④ 🍶 ★★ **NV** aromatic charmer is smoothly sweet & tangy.

Douglas Green Signature Brands

Ribshack Red ④ 🍶 🥗 ★★★ Savoury, smooth & smoky **10** aptly named, juicy pinotage/shiraz duo, spicy barbecue ribs in a glass! WO Wellington. **St Augustine** ④ ★★ Charry sweet-oak tone to pinotage-led **10**. **The Beachhouse Rosé** ④ 🍶 🥗 ★★ **11** a tutti-frutti sundowner. Light & semi-sweet, from pinotage. WO Wellington. **The Delivery Chenin Blanc** ④ 🍶 ★★★ Genial **10** preview is smooth, with baked apple flavours. **The Beachhouse Sauvignon Blanc** 🍶 🥗 ★★★ Was just 'The Beachhouse'. Step-up **13** (with dash semillon) ticks all the boxes: cool peppery flavours, balanced acidity, fresh sugar-smoothed farewell. **Sprizzo Sweet Rosé** ④ 🍶 🥗 ★★ Sweet, aromatic **NV** is light, fun & fizzy. **Cape Ruby Port** ④ ★★★☆ **NV** blend tinta & souzão with fruitcake sweetness.

Douglas Green Sherry-Styles [NEW]

Dry Fino No. 1 ★★★☆ Pale gold colour, very dry & aromatic, with green olive, savoury & salty nut flavours. Good balancing acidity, with a refreshing lift, spirity grip. Palamino & chenin from Worcester & Robertson, made in a solera, as rest of the range. **Medium Cream No. 2** ★★★★ Pale amber delicately sweet, with layers of dried & candied fruit, nuts & spice. Smooth & silky, slips down easily, but has a refreshing orange zest finish. **Full Cream No. 3** ★★★☆ Smooth winter warmer: rich, with raisin, spiced nut & honey flavours, aromas; full bodied & mouthfilling, but not cloying. — WB, CvZ, CR

Douglas Wine Cellar

Location: Douglas ▪ Map: Northern Cape, Free State & North West ▪ Est 1968 ▪ 1stB 1977 ▪ Tasting & sales Mon-Fri 8–5 ▪ Closed all pub hols ▪ Cellar tours by appt ▪ BYO picnic ▪ Gifts ▪ Owner(s) GWK Ltd ▪ Cellarmaster(s)/winemaker(s) Ian Sieg ▪ Viticulturist(s) Hein Janse van Rensburg ▪ Douglas + Landzicht GWK: 350ha (cab, ruby cab, shiraz, chard, chenin, cbard, muscadels r/w) ▪ 40,000cs own label 20% red 40% white 5% rosé 35% fortified ▪ PO Box 47 Douglas 8730 ▪ wynkelder@gwk.co.za ▪ www.landzicht.co.za ▪ S 29° 3' 57.0" E 023° 46' 7. 8" ▪ T +27 (0)53-298-8314/5 ▪ F +27 (0)53-298-1845

Located in the Northern Cape town of Douglas, near the confluence of South Africa's greatest rivers, the Orange and Vaal, Douglas Cellar is owned by agribusiness GWK (as is sibling Landzicht, listed separately, whose wines are made here). Wine ranges include Confluence and Barney Barnato (a legend of nearishby Kimberley's diamond trade), and are described by viticulturist Hein Janse van Rensburg as 'easily accessible wines that don't intimidate with too much 'posh''.

■ **Down to Earth** *see* Villiera Wines

Dragonridge

Location: Malmesbury ▪ Map/WO: Swartland ▪ Est 2004 ▪ 1stB 2006 ▪ Tasting, sales & cellar tours by appt ▪ Fee R30, waived on purchase ▪ Closed Easter Fri, Dec 25/26 & Jan 1 ▪ Meals by arrangement ▪ Facilities for children ▪ Farm produce ▪ BYO picnic ▪ Weddings/functions ▪ Conferences ▪ Walks/hikes ▪ Mountain biking trail ▪ Conservation area ▪ Guest house ▪ Owner(s) Fynbos Estate (3 partners) ▪ Cellarmaster(s)/winemaker(s) Johan Simons (Jan 2004) ▪ Viticulturist(s) Johan Simons (Jun 1997) ▪ 320ha/13ha (cab, mourv, ptage, sangio, shiraz, chard, chenin, viog) ▪ 35t/1,400cs own label 40% red 40% white 20% rosé ▪ P O Box 526 Malmesbury 7299 ▪ info@fynbosestate.co.za, info@dragonridge.co.za ▪ www.dragonridge.co.za ▪ S 33° 33' 28.9" E 018° 47' 5.6" ▪ T +27 (0)22-487-1153 ▪ F +27 (0)86-611-5125

Fynbos Estate on Perdeberg is an established eco-tourism getaway, with most of the farm formally recognised as a Cape Nature reserve. In these idyllic conditions, winemaker Johan Simons produces his dryland wines with gentle hands, recycling, repairing, reusing; taking the natural options whenever possible.

Sangiovese ④ ★★★ **09** last with same dark cherry, pronounced acid & tarry notes as **08**. **Jack's Red** ④ ★★ Tasted out of vintage sequence, **08** pinotage-led Cape Blend shows squashed berries & tangy acid. **Cosmos** Next awaited, as for **Chenin Blanc** & **Galaxy**. — GdB

Driefontein

Location: Stellenbosch ▪ Map: Helderberg ▪ WO: Elgin/Stellenbosch ▪ Est 2010 ▪ 1stB 2011 ▪ Tasting & sales by appt only ▪ Closed all pub hols ▪ Owner(s) Driefontein (Pty) Ltd ▪ Winemaker(s)/viticulturist(s) Jasper Raats (2010) ▪ 2ha (pinot, sauv) ▪ 10t/600cs own label 70% red 30% white ▪ jasper@longridge.co.za ▪ S 34° 0' 55. 2" E 018° 49' 60.0" ▪ **T +27 (0)76-752-5270** ▪ F +27 (0)21-855-4083

Jasper Raats, who earned a reputation for sauvignon blanc and pinot noir at New Zealand's Koru, has turned his attention to a tiny sauvignon block at Driefontein estate on the Helderberg and pinot in Elgin. 'This has to be one of the coolest sites in Stellenbosch – perfect for achieving ripe sauvignon flavours without losing acidity,' says Jasper, also winemaker at Longridge, where the wines are exclusively available. 'And Elgin's high sunlight hours coupled with relatively low temperatures are just right for top-class pinot.'

Driefontein range

Sauvignon Blanc ★★★☆ More about texture & savouriness than overt fruit, **12** ferment in older oak gives salty tang to persistent pear & honey melon notes. Stylish offering from Stellenbosch vines.

Cuvée range

Pinot Noir ★★★★ Delicate & fresh, fine-boned tannin structure, elegant fruit. Lightly brushed with oak (5 months older barrels) to allow Elgin terroir to shine in **11**. — DC, JP

Driehoek Wines

Location: Citrusdal ▪ Map: Olifants River ▪ WO: Cederberg ▪ Est/1stB 2009 ▪ Sales Mon-Sat ▪ Closed Good Fri & Dec 25 ▪ Facilities for children ▪ Gift shop ▪ BYO picnic ▪ Walking/hiking & mountain biking trails ▪ Horse riding ▪ Bird watching ▪ Fishing ▪ Bushman paintings ▪ Conservation area ▪ Self-catering cottages & camping ▪ Beauty treatments ▪ Owner(s) Du Toit Family ▪ Cellarmaster(s)/winemaker(s) David Nieuwoudt (Jan 2008, Cederberg) ▪ Viticulturist(s) Dawie Burger & Hennie Spamer (both Jun 2006), advised by David Nieuwoudt ▪ 375ha/5ha (pinot, shiraz, sauv) ▪ 2,500cs own label 50% red 50% white ▪ PO Box 89 Clanwilliam 8135 ▪ driehoekcederberg@gmail.com ▪ www.cederberg-accommodation.co.za ▪ S 32° 26' 34.40" E 019° 11' 24.32" ▪ **T +27 (0)27-482-2828** ▪ F +27 (0)86-720-2474

Driehoek is the oldest farm in the mighty Cederberg mountains - the Du Toit family have been here for five generations. The vineyards (amongst the highest in the Cape) are newcomers, however, at less than a decade old. Their grapes are vinified by neighbour David Nieuwoudt at Cederberg Private Cellar.

Driehoek Family Wines range

★★★★☆ **Shiraz** 🍷 **11** (★★★★) has charm but comes close to sweet over-ripeness, though firm acidity aims to add some freshness. Well & unobtrusively oaked. Less intense & interesting than balanced **10**.

★★★★ **Sauvignon Blanc** 🍷 Lots of citrus & tropical aromas & flavours, with some flinty, mineral interest too, on **13**. Firm, fresh & confident, dry & elegant.

Pinot Noir NEW 🍷 ★★★☆ **12** has sweet-fruited red berry aromas & flavours, a little muted by tobacco notes from oaking. No real fruit intensity despite sweet note, but forceful structure, mostly acidity. — TJ

Drostdy-Hof Wines

Location/map: Tulbagh ▪ WO: Western Cape ▪ Est 1804 ▪ Tasting & sales at De Oude Drostdy Mon-Fri 10–5 Sat 10–2 ▪ Fee R20pp ▪ Closed Good Fri, Dec 25 & Jan 1 ▪ Private functions by arrangement ▪ Owner(s) Distell ▪ Cellarmaster(s) Andrea Freeborough ▪ Winemaker(s) Justin Corrans (reds) & Pieter Badenhorst (whites) ▪ Viticulturist(s) Bennie Liebenberg ▪ PO Box 213 Tulbagh 6820 ▪ info@drostdywines.co.za ▪ www.drostdyhof.co. za ▪ S 33° 15' 23.3" E 019° 8' 57.5" ▪ **T +27 (0)23-230-0203** ▪ F +27 (0)23-230-0211

The name of this Distell-owned brand comes from the gabled Oude Drostdy in Tulbagh, designed by the renowned Louis-Michel Thibault as a magistrate's court, and now a national monument, museum and characterful winetasting venue. Value and a convenient range of pack sizes are attributes of the wines.

Winemaker's Collection

★★★★ **Chardonnay-Semillon** ✓ 🍽 Perhaps not quite the complexity & structure of **12**, but previewed **13** (★★★★) still over-delivers with concentrated waxy yellow fruit, lovely lively texture & savoury undertone.

Pinotage ☺ ★★★ Pre-bottling, **13** continues improved form. Crisp, tangy red berries & plums in a gently firm, balanced package.

Cabernet Sauvignon 🗟 ★★★ Fruit-driven **13** ex tank shows good varietal character & concentration, understated oak. Food friendly - try with braised lamb shank. **Merlot** 🗟 ★★★ **13**, sampled from tank, continues previous savoury, lightly fruited style, with black olives & some not-unappealing herbaceous notes. **Shiraz** 🗟 ★★★ Keeps getting better. **13** preview delightful red berry juiciness with nice touch of pepper; surprisingly intense yet fresh, bouncy. **Shiraz-Pinotage** ★★★ Previewed **13** a notch up; bolder, more generous ripe-fruit flavours, smooth & harmonious 60/40 blend. **Chardonnay** 🗟 ★★★ Lively, appealing **13** preview, zesty toasted nut & lemon flavours balanced by some leesy richness. **Sauvignon Blanc** 🗟 ★★ Suggestion of varietal greenpepper & grass, **13** tangy gooseberry on straightforward sweet-sour palate. **Chardonnay-Viognier** ★★★ Aromatic easy-drinking **13**, softly dry vanilla cake flavour; pleasant & characterful. **Adelpracht** ✓ ★★★★ Seductive & delicious Late Harvest-style **12** from chenin. Botrytis, honey & fynbos notes - super complexity within a light, not over-sweet frame. Perfect for mild curries. Discontinued: **Cabernet Sauvignon Rosé**.

Standard range

Claret Select ☺ ★★★ Uncomplicated but tasty off-dry **NV** red, juicy red berries & mild tannins, perfect for pizza.

Shiraz-Merlot 🗟 ★★★ Aka 'Cape Red'. Now bottled, **12** earthy & dry braai wine to be enjoyed soon. **Rosé** 🗟 ★★ Like previous, a happy summer sipper; semi-dry **13** from cab, crisp strawberries-&-cream flavour. **Steen/Chenin Blanc** 🗟 ★★★ Kiwi fruit-scented semi-dry **13**, with splash colombard, as zesty & quaffable as previous. **Premier Grand Cru** 🗟 ★★ Lightish, very basic **NV** 3-way bone-dry white blend. **Stein Select** ★★ Latest **NV** very plain & simple semi-sweet white.

Natural Sweet Light range

Extra Light ★ **NV** no-frills crisp white with low alcohol (9%). **Red** 🗟 ★★ Interesting spicy-tropical contrast in new low-alcohol (7.5%) **NV** bottling. Sweet, simple but nice. **Rosé** 🗟 ★★ Fun low-alcohol **NV** party wine with sweet-sour fruit salad flavours. **White** 🗟 ★★★ Like last, latest **NV** low-alcohol picnic partner full of floral/grapey cheer; tickle of acidity refreshes. — DB, HJ

Druk My Niet Wine Estate

Location/WO: Paarl ▪ Map: Paarl & Wellington ▪ Est 2003 ▪ 1stB 2009 ▪ Tasting, sales & cellar tours by appt ▪ Fee R50pp ▪ Closed all pub hols ▪ Meals/refreshments on request ▪ BYO picnic ▪ Tour groups ▪ Walks/hikes ▪ Mountain biking trail ▪ Conservation area ▪ 3 self-catering cottages (see Accommodation section) ▪ Owner(s) Georg & Dorothee Kirchner, Jens-Peter Stein ▪ Cellarmaster(s)/winemaker(s)/viticulturist(s) Abraham de Klerk (Jun 2008) ▪ 24.5ha/9ha (cabs s/f, malbec, merlot, shiraz, tannat, tempranillo, tinto amerela, chenin, viog) ▪ 60t/3,500cs own label 80% red 20% white ▪ BWI, IPW ▪ PO Box 7383 Paarl 7620 ▪ georg.kirchner@dmnwines.co.za ▪ www. dmnwines.co.za ▪ S 33° 41' 23.26" E 019° 1' 40.23" ▪ **T +27 (0)21-868-2393** ▪ F +27 (0)21-868-2392

The Kirchner and Stein families' 17th century estate in Paarl Valley has been loving restored and refurbished, and now includes an 80-ton boutique cellar and three self-catering cottages. Similar close attention has been paid to the floral kingdom biosphere setting. Winemaking emphasis is firmly on high-end reds and chenin (a limited-release straw wine from the variety, untasted by us, is available).

Flagship range

★★★★☆ **Invictus** 🅥 Merlot-led **10** flagship blend (with cabs sauvignon & franc) in classic, plush Bordeaux style; seamless & understated with pristine dark fruit wrapped around a core of ripe tannins; serious & integrated (60% new oak well judged) with unflagging finish.

★★★★☆ **T3** 🅥 Intriguing red fruit & leafy aromas on creative & unusual **10** tempranillo (42%), tannat & tinta amerela blend. Fruit clarity shines in restrained, elegant style. Ripe berries are balanced by lipsmacking acidity & rounded tannins. Handsome packaging a feature of this range.

★★★★ **C68 Chenin Blanc** 🗟 ★★★ **13**, from vines planted in 1968 is understated, misses the complexity of **12** (★★★★) with lean green-apple & vanilla wafts.

T3 Reserve NEW ★★★ The port-style version of T3, fortified with distillate from T3 husks. Previewed **13** shows sweet red berry fruit still integrating with distinct grappa flavours. Joint venture with Wilderer Private Distillery.

Druk My Niet Collection

★★★★ **Cabernet Sauvignon** ✓ Boldly fruited **10** exhibits generous dark-toned flavours & firm structure. Balanced vanilla oak adds complexity. Needs time to reveal full charm.

★★★★ **Cabernet Franc** ✓ Excellent varietal expression on **10** - dust, leaf, mint, you name it. Elegant, harmonious & touch savoury. Ageing will enhance future drinking pleasure.

Malbec ✓ ★★★★ **10** a better expression than **09** (★★★). Loads of bright cranberry fruit, wild herbs & earthy tones. Good balance & structure with ageing potential. Note: Mapoggo range discontinued. — WB

Dunstone Winery

Location: Wellington ▪ Map: Paarl & Wellington ▪ WO: Wellington/Western Cape ▪ Est/1stB 2006 ▪ Tasting, sales & cellar tours Wed-Sun 10-4, Mon-Tue by appt ▪ Fee R10pp, waived on purchase ▪ Closed Dec 25 & Jan 1 ▪ The Stone Kitchen (see Restaurants section) ▪ Facilities for children ▪ Conferences ▪ Bovlei Valley Retreat luxury B&B guesthouse & self-catering cottage (see Accommodation section) ▪ Owner(s) Abbi & Lee Wallis ▪ Winemaker(s) Lee Wallis & Robert Frith, with Neil Marais (Jun 2011) ▪ Viticulturist(s) Johan Viljoen (Icon Vines & Wines) ▪ 2ha/2.5ha (merlot, shiraz) ▪ 20t/5,000cs own label 90% red 10% rosé ▪ PO Box 901 Wellington 7654 ▪ wine@dunstone.co.za ▪ www.dunstone.co.za ▪ S 33° 38' 5.3" E 019° 3' 36.8" ▪ **T +27 (0)21-873-6770** ▪ F +27 (0)21-873-6770

Dunstone is the name of the UK village where Lee Wallis bought his first house; he and wife Abbi gave the name to their first home. But the Cape proved a strong drawcard and they returned a year after a first visit in 2002, and bought this Wellington property. Their favourite grape, shiraz, was ideal for their soils at the foot of the Bainskloof Pass; it's also the name of the Weimaraner on the label.

Dunstone Winery range

★★★★ **Shiraz** **12** lighter in texture, fresher fruited than **09**. Hint of American oak (but mostly French) lifts bright spicy scents & flavours, adds character. Drinks well now, good for 5+ years. **10** sold out untasted; no **11**.

★★★★ **Sauvignon Blanc** Cool-climate intensity on **13** (★★★★) from high Tradouw Highlands vineyard. Unshowy greengage, apple blossom attractions diminished by sweet/sour tail. **12** better balanced.

> **Shiraz Rosé** ☺ ★★★ Juicy strawberries-&-cream **13**; gentle & fresh; good dry savoury length.

Merlot ★★★ Straightforward, ripe & juicy. Well-harmonised oak/fruit on **11**; shortish finish.

Stones in the Sun range [NEW]

Syrah ★★★ Fresh, medium bodied, with quiet yet tasty spice & red fruit, all lending ready appeal to **11**. Some Swartland fruit. — AL

■ **Du Plevaux** see Imbuko Wines

Du Preez Estate

Location: Rawsonville ▪ Map: Breedekloof ▪ WO: Western Cape/Breedekloof ▪ Est 1916 ▪ 1stB 1998 ▪ Tasting & sales Mon-Fri 8-5 Sat 10-1 ▪ Closed all pub hols ▪ Cellar tours by appt, 2-day prior notice required ▪ BYO picnic ▪ Tour groups (20 pax) ▪ Owner(s) Du Preez family ▪ Cellarmaster(s)/winemaker(s) Lolly Louwrens (Jan 2013) ▪ Viticulturist(s) Jean du Preez ▪ 350ha (merlot, p verdot, ptage, shiraz, chard, chenin, cbard, nouvelle, sauv) ▪ 6,000t ▪ Other export brand: Martinique ▪ IPW ▪ PO Box 12 Route 101 Rawsonville 6845 ▪ info@dupreezestate.co.za ▪ www.dupreezestate.co.za ▪ S 33° 41' 37.1" E 019° 16' 59.6" ▪ **T +27 (0)23-349-1995** ▪ F +27 (0)23-349-1923

Harvest 2013 saw the arrival of veteran Robertson Winery winemaker Lolly Louwrens, 'South Africa's most exciting winemaker', according to tasting room manager Retha van der Merwe. While visitors enjoy the family-owned estate's Breedekloof hospitality, export requests have quadrupled: good news for previously disadvantaged communities that benefit from an allocation of profits.

Hendrik Lodewyk range

★★★★ **Petit Verdot** ✓ Very rich **10** shows lots of variety's extraction & concentration, but also flair & poise. Port-like entry firms up on palate, revealing brooding dark fruit but also the lightness of flowers.

★★★★ **Méthode Cap Classique** ⊕ Elegant & layered sparkler, lemon/lime & nutty aromas mingle with rich brioche flavour. 90% chardonnay, with pinot noir, bottle-aged 48 months, **NV**.

Du Preez Private Cellar range

★★★★ **Maranda Rosé Méthode Cap Classique** ✓ 🈂 Well-crafted/priced NV sparkling from pinot noir as good as previous (which had some chardonnay). Delicate, dry & lightish, keeps balanced red-fruit charm going to the end.

Cabernet Sauvignon ⊕ 🈂 ★★☆ **10** a serious effort with berry & tealeaf tones; dry tannins invite hearty food. **Merlot** 🈂 ★★★☆ **11**'s creamy berry fruit overlain with leafy notes; satisfying concentration & complexity, nicely dry. **Shiraz** ⊕ 🈂 ★★★★ From Breedekloof vines, improved **10** ripe mulberry fruit, soft mouthfeel & mocha nuances. **Polla's Red** ⊕ 🈂 ★★☆ Pinotage dominates in smoky **11** blend, with spice & tannic grip. **Chardonnay** 🍴 🈂 ★★☆ Lime & ripe pineapple, **12** some savoury tones from lees influence, straightforward just-dry white. **Sauvignon Blanc** 🍴 🈂 ★★☆ Begging for tempura-fried seafood, **13** is lean & bone-dry, bracingly fresh from early picking. **Hanepoot** ✓ 🈂 ★★★★ Comforting, full-sweet **11** fortified dessert shows raisins, sundried stonefruit & warming alcohol. For winter nights, or over crushed ice with lime peel, or cellar. Breedekloof WO, like Du Preez Petit Verdot.

Rockfield range

> **Sauvignon Blanc** ☺ 🍴 🈂 ★★★ Friendly fruit salad aroma, pleasantly low in alcohol, juicy & fresh, well-disguised sugar makes **13** slip down easily.

Cabernet Sauvignon Next awaited, like **Shiraz**. **Merlot** 🍴 🈂 ★★★ Plum-perfumed **12** slips down easily with pleasing tannin grip, brisk finish for food, like Private Cellar sibling. — HJ,CvZ

Durbanville Hills   🍴🥂📷🎯♿

Location/WO: Durbanville ▪ Map: Durbanville, Philadelphia & Darling ▪ Est 1998 ▪ 1stB 1999 ▪ Tasting & sales Mon-Fri 9-4.30 Sat 10-3 Sun 11-3 ▪ Fee R40/8 wines incl glass ▪ Closed Good Fri, Dec 25 & Jan 1 ▪ Chocolate & wine pairing; biltong & wine pairing ▪ Tasting room menu available Tue-Sun ▪ Cellar tours Mon-Fri 11 & 3; groups of 10+ to book ahead ▪ The Eatery restaurant Tue-Sun 8.30-3 ▪ Facilities for children & cyclists ▪ Conferences ▪ Weddings/functions ▪ Owner(s) Distell, 9 farmers & workers trust ▪ Cellarmaster(s) Martin Moore (Nov 1998) ▪ Winemaker(s) Wilhelm Coetzee (reds, Sep 2008) & Günther Kellerman (whites, Jul 2003) ▪ Viticulturist(s) Drikus Heyns (consultant) ▪ 770ha (merlot, sauv) ▪ 6,000t/300,000cs own label 40% red 58% white 2% rosé ▪ ISO 9000-1, ISO 14000-1, BWI, BRC, HACCP, IPW, WIETA ▪ PO Box 3276 Durbanville 7551 ▪ info@durbanvillehills.co.za ▪ www.durbanvillehills.co.za ▪ S 33° 49' 29.9" E 018° 33' 56.7" ▪ **T +27 (0)21-558-1300** ▪ F +27 (0)21-559-8169

That cellarmaster Martin Moore has been here from the start in 1998 both underlies and reflects its core feature: consistency of quality, in large enough volumes to maintain listings from Hermanus to Hanoi, year after year. A collaboration between Durbanville farmers and industry giant Distell, farm employees were brought on board with The Durbanville Hills Share Purchase Trust from 2000. The winery's social investment vehicle, it uses wine and olive farming revenues to fund children's education and adult lifeskills programmes. The objective has always been the global market but locals aren't neglected: stylish, recently updated tasting room, restaurant, lounge and picnic facilities allow visitors to share the breath-taking views of Cape Town and Table Mountain across the bay.

The Vineyard Selection

★★★★ **Luipaardsberg Merlot** 🈂 Richest & most structured of cellar's merlot trio, eucalytus-tinged **11** has mineral threads in dry, balanced finish. 16 months French cask, half new. **10** sold out untasted.

★★★★ **Caapmans Cabernet Sauvignon-Merlot** 🈂 Harmonious **11**, 73% cab with merlot & new-oak polish. Toned & athletic, fine grape tannins allow for current drinking but also ageworthy. **10** not tasted.

★★★★ **Biesjes Craal Sauvignon Blanc** 🈂 A sauvignon for every palate from this cellar. Preview **13** for those who like it minerally; steely, with a stony minerality & cool-climate green pea notes. **12** not tasted.

The Rhinofields range

★★★★ **Merlot** 🈂 Usual minty/leafy fragrance but **11** beautifully structured; lovely balance of accessible fruit & supportive tannin. 50% new oak for 14 months well integrated.

★★★★ **Pinotage** 🈂 Full-blooded, ripe **12** is excellent in its opulence, though perhaps not quite as pure fruited as much-liked **11** (★★★★☆).

★★★★☆ **Noble Late Harvest** ⊕ 🈂 This cellar loves sauvignon! **12** a scintillating debut. Honeyed botrytis carefully judged not to swamp untamed 'sauvage' varietal edge; great sugar/acid balance focuses fruit sweetness rather than sugar. Low 9.5% alcohol cherry on top.

Cabernet Sauvignon ★★★☆ Mint & spicy oak launch **10**, but early intensity fades. **Shiraz** ★★★☆ Savoury & succulent **11** has plump mulberry fruit & grippy oak tannins; a fine table accompaniment. **Cape Blend** ★★★☆ Aromatic pinotage leads (60%) with cab giving structure, shiraz flesh; add lugs petit verdot & merlot for satisfying **11** whole. **Chardonnay** ▦ ★★★☆ Golden sheen mirrors ripe tropical/pineapple flavours of **12**; spicy oak (40% new) outpaces juicy fruit though. **Inner Valley Sauvignon Blanc** Next awaited, as for **Outer Valley Sauvignon Blanc**. **Sauvignon Blanc** ▦ ★★★☆ Previewed **13** is clean-cut & steely, lighter than riper fig style of **12** (★★★★) with weight & richness from lees-ageing & balanced alcohol.

The Durbanville Hills range

Cabernet Sauvignon ★★★☆ **11** nicely balanced in retiring style that spotlights simple blackberry profile. **Merlot** ★★★☆ Modest sweet minty flavours in straightforward **11**. **Pinotage** ★★★ Ripe, sweet raspberry/cherry features clipped by **11**'s grippy tannins. **Shiraz** ★★★ Unpretentious **11** brims with smoked meat character framed by firm tannins. **Bastion** ⓘ ★★★☆ Cabernet/shiraz happy partners in **11**. A mouthful of berry-lifted savouriness with supple backing. **Merlot Rosé** ▦ ★★★ Strawberry-toned **13** is juicily smooth & bone-dry. **Chardonnay** ▦ ★★★ Lightly oaked **12**; ripe melon & orange zest flavours focused by dry finish. **Sauvignon Blanc** ▦ ★★★ Open & inviting, **13** satisfies with tropical juiciness & easygoing vivacity. — DS

Dusty Heath Vineyard

Location: Hilton ▪ Est 2009 ▪ Closed to public ▪ Owner(s) Mark & Paula Haldane ▪ Cellarmaster(s) Paula Haldane (Aug 2009) ▪ Winemaker(s) Paula Haldane (Aug 2009), with Maqua Madlala (Aug 2009) ▪ Viticulturist(s) Mark Haldane (Aug 2009) ▪ 20ha/2ha (cabs s/f, merlot, p verdot) ▪ 100% red ▪ dhvineyard@sai.co.za ▪ **T +27 (0)33-383-2001/+27 (0)82-901-4304** ▪ F +27 (0)86-542-8704

Though based in the summer-rainfall Midlands of KwaZulu-Natal, Mark and Paula Haldane always fancied making wine. When some of their neighbours started doing it successfully, they thought why not? Small quantities of 'unstressed "happy sexy wine" in the Bordeaux tradition' is their goal.

▪ **Dusty Rhino** *see* United Nations of Wine

Du'SwaRoo

Location/WO: Calitzdorp ▪ Map: Klein Karoo & Garden Route ▪ Est/1stB 2008 ▪ Tasting & sales by appt Mon-Fri 9-5 Sat 9-1 ▪ Closed all pub hols ▪ Wines also available at Withoek Cellar ▪ Farm produce ▪ Owner(s) Tony Bailey ▪ Cellarmaster(s)/winemaker(s)/viticulturist(s) Tony Bailey (2008) ▪ 0.6ha (shiraz, tinta, touriga) ▪ 200cs own label 80% red 20% port ▪ 1.5ha/20t hanepoot also grown but delivered to Calitzdorp Cellar ▪ PO Box 279 Calitzdorp 6660 ▪ duswaroo@telkomsa.net ▪ www.kleinkaroowines.co.za/cellars/duswaroo.asp ▪ S 33°30' 58.7" E 021°41' 39.5" ▪ **T +27 (0)44-213-3137/+27 (0)83-378-8101** ▪ F +27 (0)44-213-3137

Indomitable Calitzdorp boutique winegrower Tony Bailey says 'each of my wines has come from a vine planted, nurtured and harvested by me'. He's not going to let a disastrous hail storm on 10 February last year get him or his assistant Sydney Cooper down, saying Du'SwaRoo is more of a passion than a business'.

Shiraz ★★ Coconut, cedar oak aromas on dense **10**, with warming 15% alcohol. **Shiraz Winemakers Reserve** Await next, like **Shiloh**. **Sirocco Bin 2** ★★ Adds 'Bin 2' to name. Stewed fruit compote NV (**12**) light but tannic; uncertified. **Quintette Rouge** NEW ★★ Uncertified NV (**12**) mixes Du'SwaRoo & neighbour Withoek grapes in brief 5-way blend. **Mistral** ⓘ ★★ Savoury rosé from shiraz; NV (**11**) bright & friendly al fresco sipper. **Cape Vintage** ⓘ ★★★★ Port-style fortified from 66/34 touriga & tinta. New bottling of **09**, year longer in oak, tealeaf & Christmas cake, plump raisin flavours, nice balance. **Cape Ruby** In abeyance. — GdB, JP

Du Toitskloof Winery   🍷🍴🎋⛲♿

Location: Rawsonville ▪ Map: Breedekloof ▪ WO: Western Cape ▪ Est 1962 ▪ Tasting & sales Mon-Fri 8-5 Sat 9-3.30 ▪ Closed Good Fri, Dec 25 & Jan 1 ▪ Cellar tours by appt ▪ Deli: light meals ▪ Cheese platters ▪ BYO picnic ▪ Owner(s) 22 members ▪ Cellarmaster(s) Shawn Thomson (Oct 1999) ▪ Winemaker(s) Chris Geldenhuys (Mar 2005) & Willie Stofberg (Feb 2011), with Derrick Cupido (Jan 1993) & Jaco le Roux ▪ Viticulturist(s) Leon Dippenaar (Jan 2005, consultant) ▪ 900ha (cab, merlot, ptage, shiraz, chard, chenin, cbard, sauv) ▪ 14,000t/±700,000cs own label 40% red 60% white ▪ Fairtrade ▪ PO Box 55 Rawsonville 6845 ▪ info@dutoitskloof.co.za ▪ www.dutoitskloof.com ▪ S 33° 42' 9.2" E 019° 16' 8.9" ▪ **T +27 (0)23-349-1601** ▪ F +27 (0)23-349-1581

Another sea of good-value smiles for the wines below affirms what we said last year (and budget-minded pundits and punters have been saying for many years now) about this Breedekloof star: Du Toitskloof, you rock! Cellarmaster Shawn Thomson and team's wines really do over-deliver on value and quality, but their 'Mother Nature directly into the bottle' philosophy also translates into satisfying, convivial glassfuls that are refreshingly free of artifice or confection. Our advisory remains: stock up!

Reserve Collection

Nebbiolo ⊕ ★★★☆ Bold, just off-dry **10**, earthy dusty berries & variety's naturally firm tannins, good balance & a spicy nut conclusion. **Dimension Red** ⊕ ⬜ ★★★ Near-equal cab, merlot, shiraz with pinotage. **10** bright, savoury berry fruit with a smooth core, just misses complexity of previous. **Chardonnay-Viognier** ⊕ ★★★★ Pungent floral & peach melba notes, vanilla wafts from barrel fermentation. **11** trumps last-tasted **08** (★★★★) with fine structure & balance.

Du Toitskloof range

> **Cabernet Sauvignon** ☺ 🍴 ★★★ **11** has a firm structure with dark berries, oak spice & herbal touch, but is unassuming & slips down easily. **Merlot** ☺ 🍴 ★★★ **12** offers chocolate & sweet-spiced fruitcake flavours for everyday sipping. **Shiraz** ☺ 🍴 ★★★ Food-friendly preview **10** is uncomplicated & delivers smoky dark berries in a firm structure, harmonious spicy oak. **Pinotage-Merlot-Ruby Cabernet** ☺ 🍴 ★★★ Soft, succulent plum fruit on charming **12**, off-dry with a moreish savoury conclusion. **Cabernet Sauvignon-Shiraz** ☺ 🍴 ★★★ Medley of rich dark berries, smoke & spice on **12**. Supple structure & lingering finish makes this a good everyday quaffer. **Chenin Blanc** ☺ 🍴 ★★★ Off-dry **13** trumps previous with green apple & pineapple perfume; flavourful, with a lemony lift for easygoing fun. **Sauvignon Blanc** ☺ 🍴 ★★★ Ever-dependable **13** oozes tropical fruit & the few grains of sugar makes it extra-drinkable. Will thrill its many fans. **Beaukett** ☺ 🍴 ★★☆ Exuberant **12** a step up, muscat blend with rosepetal & pineapple sweetness. **Sparkling Brut** ☺ ★★★ Crisp, dry, fragrant light-bodied sparkler. Smooth sauvignon-led **NV** offers lemon & zesty lime to set the party mood.

Pinotage ⊕ 🍴 ★★★ **11** a notch up; fresh & well built, juicy plum fruit is nicely balanced for early enjoyment. **Chardonnay** ⊕ 🍴 ★★☆ Back-to-form off-dry **12**'s 50% unwooded portion lets the citrus fruit shine while the oaked fraction creates a delicious creaminess in the wine.

Dessert Wines

> **Hanepoot Jerepigo** ☺ ★★★ Super-sweet fortified after dinner treat, **13** highly perfumed, exudes candied orange, Turkish Delight & a sprinkling of spice. **Cape Ruby** ☺ ★★★ Ripe raisin, plum pudding & hint of tobacco on light-bodied port-style **10** from tinta, souzão, touriga. Not overly sweet.

Noble Late Harvest ⊕ ★★★ Lightish botrytised muscat & chenin. **09** tad off previous, sweet honeyed peach & apricot tone is charming but straightforward. **Red Muscadel** ✓ ★★★★ **13** delights with floral & red fruit aromas, lots of sweet flavour, mouthfilling viscosity, but finish needs a zingier lift for higher rating.

Perlé Wines

Cape Beach Club Rosé 🍴 ★★ **NV** spritzy pink, soft, sweet & fun. **Cape Beach Club Blanc** 🍴 ★★ Easy & light off-dry **NV** with tiny floral bubbles. — WB

DuVon Private Cellar

Location/map: Robertson ▪ Est/1stB 2003 ▪ Tasting, sales & cellar tours by appt ▪ Conferences ▪ Weddings ▪ Guest house ▪ Owner(s) Armand du Toit & Alex von Klopmann ▪ Cellarmaster(s)/winemaker(s)/viticulturist(s) Armand du Toit ▪ 29.5ha/27ha (cab, ruby cab, shiraz, chenin, cbard, sauv) ▪ 400t/1,200cs own label 70% red 30% white ▪ PO Box 348 Robertson 6705 ▪ info@duvon.co.za ▪ www.duvon.co.za ▪ S 33° 48' 46.8" E 019° 47' 4.1" ▪ **T** +27 (0)82-341-1059 ▪ F +27 (0)86-626-1490

Armand du Toit, co-owner and vini/viti man for this small, newish Robertson winery has no plans for expansion, 'not with the market as it is'. What is growing is demand for the wedding venue, but Armand will cap that at 32 ceremonies: 'I don't want to give up all my weekends in Onrus!'

◼ **D' Vine** *see* Swartland Winery
◼ **Dwyka Hills** *see* Eagle's Cliff Wines-New Cape Wines

■ **Dyasonsklip** *see Bezalel-Dyasonsklip Wine Cellar*
■ **Eagle Canyon** *see Blaauwklippen Vineyards*

Eagle's Cliff Wines-New Cape Wines

Location/map: Worcester ▪ WO: Breede River Valley/Western Cape ▪ Est 2000 ▪ Tasting & sales Mon-Fri 8-4.30 ▪ Closed all pub hols ▪ Cheese & meat platters Mon-Fri 10-2 ▪ Facilities for children ▪ Tour groups ▪ Owner(s)/winemaker(s) Christiaan Groenewald ▪ 600ha/80ha ▪ 40% red 60% white ▪ PO Box 898 Worcester 6849 ▪ christiaan@ncw.co.za ▪ www.eaglescliff.co.za ▪ S 33° 50' 25.4" E 019° 25' 7.4" ▪ **T +27 (0)23-340-4112** ▪ F +27 (0)23-340-4132

Owner/winemaker Christiaan Groenewald thinks he's the first in the Worcester district to have bottled pinot noir: 'I planted it for an MCC sparkling which I'll release this year but I'm quite impressed with the single-varietal.' As for reds, he believes Worcester is gaining a reputation for quality at good prices.

Arendskloof range

★★★★ **Syrah-Tannat** ⊕ Unusual & ambitious blend. Noble black plum & prune bouquet, firm tannins (as expected from tannat) on **09**. Hedonistic, well composed despite 15% alcohol.

★★★★ **Pinot Grigio** ✓ ▤ Few pinot grigios reach these quality heights in SA. Lovely non-fruity **13**, good weight & length, savoury tinge for mealtimes. WO W Cape, as all this range unless noted.

Pinot Noir NEW ★★★★ Pioneer of variety in area, **12** off young vines delicate but convincing earth & black cherries, lively acidity & tight but silky tannin. Promising, augurs well as vineyard matures. **Pinotage** ⊕ ★★★★ **08** typical pinotage strawberries, light texture, easy sippability. Toffee bottle-age notes emerging, drink up. WO Breede River Valley. **Chardonnay** ▤ ★★★ Unwooded **13** creamy lemon biscuit flavour, honest & appealing everyday white. **Sauvignon Blanc** ✓ ▤ ★★★★ Step-up **13** flavoursome without overt fruitiness, elegant 'wet pebble' minerality & restraint, upbeat brisk finish, like shyer **12** (★★★☆).

Eagle's Cliff range

Chenin Blanc ☺ ▤ ★★★ Tangy-dry **13**'s white peach & green apple flavours a crunchy complement to lighter picnic fare. **Sauvignon Blanc** ☺ ▤ ★★★ All but escorts you & guests outdoors with al fresco notes of crushed leaves, grasses & slippery riverstones in satisfying **13**.

Pinotage ⊕ ★★★ **11** a little reticent, very dry, but balanced, with ripe strawberry flavour & supple tannin. **Cabernet Sauvignon-Merlot** ⊕ ▤ ★★★ Exuberant **11** 60/40 combo layered with red berries, vanilla & mint, easy to drink. **Shiraz-Pinotage** ⊕ ▤ ★★★ Savoury appeal on 70/30 harmonious mix in **11**. Bright fruit, just the right amount of grip for mealtime enjoyment. **Shiraz Rosé** ⊕ ★★★ Coral-hued **11**, dusty terpene edge, hint of tannin for quaffable semi-dry effect.

Dwyka Hills range

Shiraz ✓ ▤ ★★★★ Up several notches with generous **12**'s plum cake & prune nuances; plush fruit reined in by firm grip. Well priced. Lesser **11** (★★★) had a slightly sweet conclusion. WO W Cape.

Hoeksrivier range NEW

Cabernet Sauvignon ▤ ★★★ Anytime sipper **11** with dusty berries & sweet vanilla. **Chenin Blanc** ▤ ★★★ Keep a chilled bottle of **13**, with apple & spicy clove flavours, on hand for summer fun. **Sauvignon Blanc** ▤ ★★ Lightly herbal **13** is brisk & uncomplicated. — DB, CvZ

Eagles' Nest

Location: Constantia ▪ Map: Cape Peninsula ▪ WO: Constantia/Western Cape ▪ Est 2001 ▪ 1stB 2005 ▪ Tasting & sales daily 10-4.30 ▪ Fee R30pp, waived on purchase of R300+ ▪ Closed Good Fri, Dec 25 & Jan 1 ▪ Light meals ▪ Farm produce ▪ Owner(s) Mylrea family ▪ Winemaker(s) Stuart Botha (2007), with consultant Martin Meinert (2001) ▪ Viticulturist(s) Kobus Jordaan (2008), with consultant Kevin Watt (2001) ▪ 38ha/12ha (merlot, shiraz, viog) ▪ 90t/15,000cs own label 85% red 15% white ▪ PO Box 535 Constantia 7848 ▪ info@eaglesnestwines.com ▪ www.eaglesnestwines.com ▪ S 34° 0' 54.2" E 018° 24' 54.3" ▪ **T +27 (0)21-794-4095** ▪ F +27 (0)21-794-7113

Considering the achievements here, it's hard to believe it started as recently as 2000 - and with a fire. Previously the Constantia property had consisted mainly of a pine forest, and then a devastating fire swept through the area - fortunately sparing the homestead and other buildings. When restoration started, vineyards were considered as a way to combat soil erosion, and advice from Stellenbosch winemaker Martin Meinert and viticulturist Kevin Watt confirmed the soundness of the idea. Director Peter Stewart's love of viognier influenced that choice, in retrospect an inspired one, and the other varieties were chosen to fit the terroir.

★★★★☆ **Merlot** 🍷 A lot of care went into creating this beauty including multiply sourced barrels, & **09** proudly shows it off. Belgian chocolate, lush dark berries, a smoothly succulent palate resting on fine-grained tannins. Impressive.

★★★★★ **Shiraz** 🍷 📖 Multiple award winner. Glossy black cherries, smoked beef & black pepper in seductive **10**, its smoothly polished lines & resonating length hard to resist. French oak 16 months, half new. This is an iron fist in a velvet glove. **09** (★★★★☆) showed more new oak.

★★★★☆ **Viognier** 🍷 📖 A distinctive terroir-specific fruit profile, barrel-fermented **12** displays dried peach & melon aromas, with an intriguing jasmine nuance. There's spice too & lovely biscotti savouriness adding layers to the fruit yet the wine retains its poise, elegance.

Little Eagle ⑦ 🍷 📖 ★★★★ Cab/merlot in **10**, packed with berries but not simple, shows layered spice, chocolate, well supported by ripe tannins. **Sauvignon Blanc** 🍷 📖 ★★★★ Tropical fruit ripeness on **11**, passionfruit & pineapple perfectly balanced by limy acidity, lengthening the flavours. Olifants River & Durbanville grapes. Discontinued: **Verreaux**. — CR

Eaglevlei Wine Estate

Location/map: Stellenbosch ▪ WO: Stellenbosch/Coastal/Hemel-en-Aarde Valley ▪ Est/1stB 1997 ▪ Tasting & sales Tue-Sun 10-5 ▪ Fee R20, waived on purchase ▪ Eaglevlei Restaurant Tue-Thu 8-8 Fri/Sat 8-9 Sun 8-6 ▪ Facilities for children ▪ Tour groups ▪ Conferences ▪ Functions ▪ Owner(s) Rennert van Rensburg ▪ Winemaker(s) Clarise Sciocatti-Langeveldt (Jan 2012), with Carlo Sciocatti ▪ Viticulturist(s) Clarise Sciocatti-Langeveldt (Jan 2012) ▪ 50ha/±8ha (cab, merlot, ptage) ▪ 50t/14,000cs own label 90% red 5% white 5% rosé ▪ PO Box 969 Stellenbosch 7599 ▪ enquiries@eaglevlei.com ▪ www.eaglevlei.com ▪ S 33° 49' 33.5" E 018° 48' 52.2" ▪ **T +27 (0)21-884-4713** ▪ F +27 (0)21-884-4716

A new tasting lounge on the stoep and increased lawn space for children make this family-owned Stellenbosch estate more welcoming than ever. 'A destination for families from all backgrounds,' says winemaker Clarise Sciocatti-Langeveldt. Focused on making good-value wines with minimal intervention, she's delighted that all her reds completed fermentation naturally last year. '2013 was magic!'

★★★★ **Tiervoël** ⑦ 🍷 Charming & well-priced Cape Blend from pinotage & cab. **08** tobacco & dried fruit, big & bold wine with savoury finish, well-managed juicy tannins.

★★★★ **Kroonarend** ⑦ 🍷 Shiraz-mourvèdre blend, splash viognier, leads with dark berry flavours, cloves & pepper unfold in layers in aftertaste of serious **09**, worth laying down. WO Coastal.

Breëkop ☺ 🍷 ★★★ Now bottled, **12** unwooded chardonnay shows lively lime & granadilla notes, light footed but flavourful. Hemel-en-Aarde vines.

Cabernet Sauvignon ⑦ ★★★★ Enticing blackcurrant fruitiness on **07** showed through hefty tannins & oak, needed time to meld when tasted. **Red Affair** ⑦ 🍷 ★★★★ **07** ponderous oak over lively, ripe juicy fruit. Blend cab, merlot, shiraz & pinotage. **Berghaan** ⑦ 🍷 ★★★★ Appealing & serious rosé, near equal pinotage, cab & merlot. Lots going on in **12**, juicy semi-dry earthy/berry flavours, food-friendly savouriness. **Langkuif** Next awaited. **Muscat d' Alexandrie** ⑦ ★★★★ Limited-release fortified dessert. **08** unctuous sweetness & intense muscat fruit, gentle spirit tang. — DB

Earthbound 🍷 [NEW]

Location: Darling ▪ WO: Groenekloof ▪ Est 1998 ▪ 1stB 1999 ▪ Tasting by appt at Trinity Lodge in Darling ▪ Owner(s) Distell, Leopont 98 Properties, Maluti Groenekloof Community Trust, a consortium of Gauteng based black taverners ▪ Winemaker(s) Samuel Viljoen (Sep 2007) ▪ Viticulturist(s) Hannes van Rensburg (1998) ▪ 975ha/373.36ha under vine of which 172ha is organically grown ▪ 73% red 27% white ▪ BWI, Fairtrade, SGS, WIETA ▪ PO Box 184 Stellenbosch 7599 ▪ info@earthboundwines.co.za ▪ www.earthboundwines.co.za ▪ **T +27 (0)21-809-7000** ▪ F +27 (0)21-882-9575

This is the new name for Tukulu, the empowerment project established in 1998, a joint venture between Distell, a consortium of black taverners from Gauteng and a local community trust. Fruit is still sourced from the Darling farm, Papkuilsfontein. The whole range is now certified both organic and Fairtrade.

Cabernet Sauvignon ☺ 🍴 🏺 ⌦ ★★★ Straightforward but satisfying mouthful crunchy cab berries, juicy freshness with a rumble of grainy tannin. All-new oak influence on **12**. **Chenin Blanc** ☺ 🍴 🏺 ⌦ ★★★ Quiet floral, apple blossom character on quaffable **13**. Fuller body, ripe fruity acids & a clean, dry tail.

Pinot Noir 🍴 🏺 ⌦ ★★☆ **12** straightforward fresh, juicy fruit style; just a nip of tannin in tail. **Pinotage** 🍴 🏺 ⌦ ★★★ Modern, boldly oaked style. Underlying juicy red fruit on **12** trimmed by dry tannins. **Sauvignon Blanc** 🏺 ⌦ ★★★ Ripe, tropical tones on **13**; zesty, bone-dry. — AL

■ **Eden Crest** *see* Lourensford Wine Estate
■ **Edenhof** *see* Schalkenbosch Wines

Edgebaston

Location/map: Stellenbosch • WO: Stellenbosch/Coastal/Western Cape • Est/1stB 2004 • Tasting by appt only • Owner(s)/vineyard manager(s) David Finlayson • Cellarmaster(s) David Finlayson (Jan 2004) • Winemaker(s) David Finlayson (Jan 2004), with Franco Lourens (Jun 2013) • 30ha/24ha (cab, shiraz, chard, sauv) • 300t/60,000cs own label 60% red 40% white • PO Box 2033 Dennesig 7601 • david@edgebaston.co.za • www.edgebaston.co.za • S 33° 53' 33.82" E 018° 51' 17.61" • **T** +27 (0)21-889-9570/2, +27 (0)83-263-4353 • F +27 (0)21-889-9572

When David Finlayson purchased this Simonsberg farm outside Stellenbosch it was called Woodlands. He returned it to its original name of Edgebaston, also the area in England his mother, Jill, was born and raised in. The farm buildings are utilitarian, modern and keep getting extended, to accommodate David's ever-growing business. With some of his leftover energy he is a longtime member of the Cape Winemakers Guild, serving a term as chair, thus following in the steps of his father, Walter Finlayson, a founder member of the Guild.

★★★★☆ **David Finlayson 'GS' Cabernet Sauvignon** A tribute to legendary George Spies cabs - adds winemaker's name with **11**. This less approachable, more obviously oaky (100% new) than standard bottling. Abundance of concentrated rich fruit & refreshing mineral lift. Needs time for unyielding grip to harmonise.

★★★★ **Cabernet Sauvignon** Modern, generously built yet cleverly balanced **11**. More fruit-forward than **10** but ripe-toned black berries with cedar trim, still firmly supported by dense, lively grape tannins.

★★★★ **David Finlayson Pinot Noir** ✓ Deliberately follows fruitier, New World style. **12** mirrors pure red berry deliciousness of **11**; tad more structure, but still approachable. Fruit from Stellenbosch, Tulbagh.

★★★★ **Chardonnay** ✓ 🍴 **12** (★★★★★) full of limy vitality underpinned by creamy barrel-ferment character. The whole achieves sense of mouthwatering freshness, complexity held within firm frame. Rewards of further ageing assured. Step up on **11**.

The Pepper Pot ✓ 🍴 ★★★★ Rich, savoury satisfaction aplenty in **12** shiraz-led blend. Generosity of smoky, gamey flavours & deep-pile texture lifted by a rumble of tannin & freshness. WO W Cape, as was **11** (★★★★). **The Berry Box** ✓ 🍴 ★★★★ Full of the eponymous black berries but also bit more tenacious grip in **11** (now merlot-led blend) framing the soft flesh. Good now & few years. **Cast in Stone Sauvignon Blanc** 🍴 ★★★☆ Adds to varietal name in **13**. Tropical tones, a hint of oak spice & mineral backbone happily fuse in easy-drinker. Splash semillon broadens mouthfeel. **The Berry Box White** ✓ 🍴 ★★★☆ **13** appealing fragrant, flavoursome but unshowy sauvignon (74%), semillon, viognier mix. Gently, invitingly fresh; just off-dry. — AL

Eenzaamheid

Location/WO: Paarl • Map: Paarl & Wellington • Est 1693 • 1stB 2010 • Tasting by appt only • Conferences • Owner(s) Christo & Karina Briers-Louw • Winemaker(s) Janno Briers-Louw (Apr 2008) • Viticulturist(s) André Coetzee (Sep 2003) • 1185ha/400ha (cab, cinsaut, ptage, shiraz, chenin) • ±3,000t/1,900cs own label 75% red 25% white • PO Box 22 Klapmuts 7625 • wine@eenzaamheid1.co.za • S 33° 44' 52.67" E 018° 50' 12.06" • **T** +27 (0)82-493-9930 • F +27 (0)86-583-5741

'A small wine business with an intense focus on quality and personal relationships', Eenzaamheid ('Loneliness') is the newish Briers-Louw family winery on their very old Agter Paarl farm. Harnessing the potential of their dryland vines (grapes from which go into several awarded brands), Janno Briers-Louw vinifies on a boutique scale and aims for an Old World style. Caring for the families resident on the property, some 4th generation, is a concerted and ongoing concern.

★★★★ **Chenin Blanc** Barrel-fermented (older oak) **12** is rather lean & tight mid-2013, needs time to unfurl. Citrus, green apple & peach underpinned by fresh acidity. Lower alcohol than **11**.

Pinotage Next awaited. **Pinotage-Cinsaut** NEW ★★★★ Sexy **11** is 90% pinotage. Attractive floral note to go with plenty of red fruit. Sweet & juicy upfront, bright acidity, soft tannins. **Shiraz-Mourvèdre** ⓘ ★★★★ Zesty acidity, robust tannins & hearty alcohol need year/2 to settle & mesh in bold, mulberry-toned **10**. **Cuvée 1693** 🍷 ★★★ Unassuming **NV** is 49% shiraz, rest pinotage, mourvèdre, cab, cinsaut, with plenty of ripe dark fruit, soft tannins. **Shiraz-Mourvèdre-Cinsaut** NEW ★★★★ Dark fruit, pepper & toasty oak (despite little new) on hearty **11**. Good concentration, bright acidity, firm tannins. — CE

Eerste Hoop Wine Cellar

Location: Villiersdorp ▪ Map: Elgin, Walker Bay & Bot River ▪ WO: Western Cape/Theewater ▪ 1stB 2006 ▪ Tasting, sales & cellar tours Mon-Sat by appt ▪ Owner(s) Belgium owners ▪ Cellarmaster(s) Philip Costandius (Mar 2006) ▪ Winemaker(s)/viticulturist(s) Werner Barkhuizen (May 2013) ▪ 24.5ha/11ha (cab, grenache, mourv, pinot, shiraz, chard, chenin, viog) ▪ 95t/14,000cs 55% red 42% white 3% rosé ▪ Brands for clients: Oggendau, Skoon Vallei, Stilfontein ▪ IPW ▪ PO Box 89 Elgin 7180 ▪ wine@eerstehoop.co.za ▪ www.eerstehoop.co.za ▪ S 34° 5' 23.7" E 019° 11' 50.7" ▪ **T** +27 (0)28-841-4190/+27 (0)82-802-5267 ▪ **F** +27 (0)86-625-6028

That the Belgian owners include restaurateur Lode Lemahieu has helped greatly with foreign sales of Eerste Hoop wines to the Netherlands and Belgium, including to his establishments, but the focus is changing to developing local distribution. Experienced Philip Costandius oversees the vineyards and cellar near Villiersdorp with new winemaker and viticulturist Werner Barkhuizen.

Lodewijkx range

White Blend ⓘ ★★★★ **11** wooded chardonnay, chenin, viognier. Nuts, preserved fruit, limy acidity.

Eerste Hoop range

Cabernet Sauvignon ⓘ ★★★★ More so than **08** (★★★★), **09** impresses with rich dark fruit, well-judged oaking, juicy accessibility. Integrated tannins promise a few years ageing. **Shiraz** ⓘ ★★★★ Fruit-rich **09** well bolstered by 18 months in barrel, ends firmly dry. Spice an attractive counterpoint. **Blushing Bride Pinot Noir Rosé** ⓘ 🍷 ★★ Pale blush, muted berries, **11** offers light-textured (12.5% alcohol) dryness. **Wooded Chardonnay** ⓘ ★★★★ **11** reflects bold toast & citrus styling, well served by crisp, livening acidity. **Viognier** ⓘ ★★★ Rosewater, gentle peach, **11** is perked by zesty acidity.

Witklip range

> **Shiraz** ☺ 🍷 ★★★ Fruit-focused lightly oaked **11** has succulent palate appeal.

Chardonnay Not tasted. — CR

◼ **1855** *see* Hermanuspietersfontein Wynkelder

Eikehof Wines

Location/map: Franschhoek ▪ WO: Western Cape/Franschhoek ▪ Est 1903 ▪ 1stB 1992 ▪ Tasting, sales & cellar tours Mon-Sat 10-5 (Sep-Apr) & by appt (May-Aug) ▪ Closed Good Fri, Dec 25 & Jan 1 ▪ Weddings & functions ▪ Owner(s)/cellarmaster(s)/winemaker(s) Francois Malherbe ▪ 29ha/24ha (cab, merlot, pinot, shiraz, chard, sem) ▪ 28t/3,000cs own label 80% red 20% white ▪ PO Box 222 Franschhoek 7690 ▪ eikehof@mweb.co.za ▪ www.eikehof.com ▪ S 33° 52' 53.3" E 019° 3' 52.0" ▪ **T** +27 (0)21-876-2469 ▪ F +27 (0)21-876-2469

This Franschhoek farm with its ancient oak trees has been in the Malherbe family since 1903, cause for a 110th celebration last year. Their current focus is on attracting visitors, with a function room that's the perfect intimate venue for weddings, and a tasting room that opened in time for summer.

Cabernet Sauvignon ★★★ Firmly structured, full-bodied, warm **10** for early drinking with food. Franschhoek WO, like next. **Merlot** 🖉 ★★★ Appealing ripe fruit & spiciness in mouthfilling **11**. **Shiraz** 🖉 ★★ Smoky, savoury **12**'s firm acid structure masks fruit. **Chardonnay** 🍷 🖉 ★★★ Nicely rich yet crisply dry **13** unoaked, uncomplicated & pleasant. **Sauvignon Blanc** NEW 🗎 📷 ★★★ Zippy **13** pleasingly crisp & dry, with some focus & structure. — IM

Eikendal Vineyards

Location: Stellenbosch ▪ Map: Helderberg ▪ WO: Stellenbosch/Western Cape/Stellenbosch/Elgin ▪ Est 1981 ▪ 1stB 1984 ▪ Tasting & sales Mon-Sat 9.30-4.30 (Sep-May)/10-4 (Jun-Aug) Sun 10-4 ▪ Fee R20/5 wines ▪ Closed Good Fri, Dec 25/26 & Jan 1 ▪ Cellar tours Mon-Fri 10 & 2.30 ▪ Restaurant @ Eikendal T +27 (0)21-855-5033: lunch Tue-Sun & dinner Wed ▪ Facilities for children ▪ Tour groups ▪ Gift shop ▪ Conferences ▪ Walks/hikes ▪ Mountain biking trail ▪ Flywaters fly fishing ▪ Cheetah Outreach ▪ Eikendal Lodge (see Accommodation section) ▪ Owner(s) Substantia AG ▪ Winemaker(s)/viticulturist(s) Nico Grobler (2007), with Christo Hanse & Willem van Kerwel (both 2012) ▪ 78ha/±50ha (cabs s/f, malbec, merlot, p verdot, chard) ▪ 250t/70-80,000cs own label 70% red 30% white ▪ IPW ▪ PO Box 2261 Stellenbosch 7601 ▪ info@eikendal.co.za ▪ www.eikendal.com ▪ S 34° 0' 46.7" E 018° 49' 24.5" ▪ **T +27 (0)21-855-1422** ▪ F +27 (0)21-855-1027

The Swiss Saager family bought portions of Longridge and Mietjiesvlei farms, straddling the Eikendal road on the lower slopes of the Helderberg, in 1981. They consolidated the portions and commissioned a new cellar with the aid and advice of Jan Coetzee (Vriesenhof). Abé Beukes (Darling Cellars) made the first vintages, but he was succeeded shortly after by the long-serving Josef Krammer, who was recruited from Villiera and established the estate's reputation for fine Bordeaux-style red wines and chardonnay. Still in the same hands, recent awards locally and around the world herald a return to past glories under current winemaker/viticulturist Nico Grobler. 'Which shows you're never too old to achieve new success.'

Reserve range

★★★★☆ **Classique** 📷 Sublime balance & focus in flagship cabernet-led Bordeaux-style blend. **10** is earthy, dark & supple, richly aromatic. Also-tasted **11** (★★★★★) reflects better vintage, rounder & sleeker, but retaining poise & elegance.

★★★★ **Chardonnay** ✓ 📷 Carefully detailed & focused, **12** (★★★★☆) improves on **11** with fine balance of power & finesse. Carefully considered oak rounds out palate, but should recede with bottle development. An exercise in understated elegance.

Premium range

★★★★☆ **Cabernet Sauvignon** ✓ 📷 Intense, classically shaped **10** follows previous form. Expressive yet finely modulated & refined, with richly ripe fruit. **11**, also reviewed this ed, less assertive, more finely sculpted, with seaweed-iodine minerality.

★★★★ **Merlot** ✓ 📷 **11** signals a further shift to classic Bordeaux styling. All traces of leafy mintiness purged, great depth & intensity of fruit & focus firmly on shape, balance & texture.

★★★★ **Pinotage** 📷 Opulently ripe & muscular, **12** struts its intense wild berry fruit with distinct swagger. Dash of cab tones down the extroverted brashness. **11** sold out untasted.

★★★★ **Charisma** ✓ 📷 Change in direction for **11** red blend, now shiraz-led, with dashes petit verdot & sangiovese, less oak. Stellenbosch vines. Also-assessed **12**, from Swartland & Paarl, follows suit: rich, with fruity appeal, but retaining noble bearing.

★★★★ **Sauvignon Blanc** ✓ 📷 Ex-tank **13** from Elgin, Franschhoek & Lutzville, has some barrel ferment, lees-ageing & dash semillon, showing in rich, lingering mouthfeel. Finely tuned mix of spicy aromas & ripe figs.
Janina Unwooded Chardonnay ✓ 📷 ★★★★ Previewed **13**, with 11% Elgin fruit, shows variety's potential unoaked. Deft clonal blending lends complexity & depth.

Cuvée range

Rouge ☺ 🗎 📷 ★★★ Generously fruity entry-level red, **12** shiraz-led blend with cab & merlot has appealing leafy notes. WO W Cape, like Blanc. **Rosé** ☺ 🗎 📷 ★★★ Pretty salmon-hued **13** from merlot is dry & floral, light & crisp, with appealing raspberry juiciness.

Blanc 🗎 📷 ★★★ **13** is cheerful, light-hearted sauvignon/chardonnay blend. — GdB

■ **Eksteens' Family Vineyards** see Stone Ridge Wines
■ **Elandsberg** see Viljoensdrift Wines & Cruises

Elemental Bob

Location: Hermanus ▪ WO: Hemel-en-Aarde Ridge/Western Cape ▪ Est/1stB 2004 ▪ Closed to public ▪ Owner(s)/winemaker(s) Craig Sheard ▪ 200–300cs own label 75% red 20% white 5% port ▪ elementalbob@gmail.com ▪ T +27 (0)82-265-1071

Spookfontein winemaker Craig Sheard, nicknamed Farmer Bob by his brother, has his own boutique winery based in the Hemel-en-Aarde area, where he makes wine eschewing modern convention. Natural ferments and 'interesting experiments' with less-favoured grapes are what exercises his creative mind.

Wood-Cut Series Limited Edition
My SunShine ⊛ ★★ Idiosyncratic **NV** blend of older-oak-fermented viognier & unwooded sauvignon, offering light, short-lived peachy zest. 'Unfiltered & WILL deposit sediment' notes winemaker.

Sweet Collection Limited Release
My Bauhaus ⊛ ★★★ Ripe choc-fruitcake notes on port-style **11** from Hemel-en-Aarde Ridge shiraz. —FM

■ **Elements** *see* Hartswater Wine Cellar
■ **Elephantasy** *see* Group CDV

Elgin Grove

Location/WO: Elgin ▪ Est 2004 ▪ 1stB 2007 ▪ Closed to public ▪ Owner(s) Nigel McNaught, Abacus Trust & Tony Davis ▪ Winemaker(s) Nigel McNaught ▪ Viticulturist(s) Paul Wallace (2004, consultant) ▪ 20ha/6ha (sauv) ▪ 40t/1,000cs own label 100% white ▪ c/o Stony Brook PO Box 22 Franschhoek 7690 ▪ nigel@stonybrook.co.za ▪ T +27 (0)21-876-2182 ▪ F +27 (0)21-876-2182

The small, steep Elgin Grove sauvignon blanc vineyard produces a wine which co-owner and winemaker Nigel McNaught believes will prove the variety's ability to age, thereby reinforcing its quality image. Vinification is at Stony Brook in Franschhoek, Nigel's other wine property.

Sauvignon Blanc ⊛ 🍴 ★★★★ Minerality & limy acidity follows **11**'s fynbos-spiked perfume. Admirable intensity, flavour length. — CR

Elgin Heights

Location/map: Stellenbosch ▪ WO: Elgin ▪ 1stB 2007 ▪ Tasting & sales by appt ▪ Conference facilities ▪ Owner(s) Ryk Joubert ▪ Winemaker(s) Andries Burger, Kobie Viljoen & Corné Marais (sauv/shiraz/MCC, consultants) ▪ Viticulturist(s) DD Joubert ▪ 111ha/70ha (cab, merlot, shiraz, chard, sauv, viog) ▪ PO Box 52 Vlottenburg 7604 ▪ mwddj@mweb.co.za ▪ www.elginheights.co.za ▪ S 33° 57' 2.60'' E 018° 45' 28.91'' ▪ T +27 (0)84-517-9300 ▪ F +27 (0)86-648-1704

When the Joubert family from Stellenbosch bought the Smarag ('Emerald') farm in Elgin in the mid-1960s, they grew deciduous fruit. Some 30 years later, fifth-generation winefarmer DD Joubert saw how well his neighbours were doing with wine and developed his own extensive vineyards. For the brand, the Jouberts adopted the original farm name, Elgin Heights.

★★★★ **Sauvignon Blanc** ⊛ 🍴 🎨 **11** lives up to previous year's preview with juicy gooseberry, fig flavours, balanced vitality. Easy, characterful drinking.
Shiraz ⊛ 🎨 ★★★★ **10** full of ready, youthful appeal. Crackles with spicy aromas; a touch of sugar emphasises sweet red-fruit flavours; smoothly textured with nip of form-giving tannin. **Chardonnay** ⊛ 🍴 ★★★ Fruit-forward style; **11** pickled limes & peaches, with zippy freshness, pithily dry. **Emerald Méthode Cap Classique Chardonnay** Await next. —AL

Elgin Ridge

Location/WO: Elgin ▪ Map: Elgin, Walker Bay & Bot River ▪ Est 2007 ▪ 1stB 2009 ▪ Tasting, sales & tours by appt Mon-Fri 10-4 Sat/Sun/pub hols by appt only ▪ Food & wine pairing during Elgin Open Gardens weekends 10-4 ▪ Farm produce ▪ BYO picnic ▪ Owner(s) Brian & Marion Smith ▪ Winemaker(s) Niels Verburg (Aug 2009, consultant), with Brian Smith ▪ Viticulturist(s) Kevin Watt (Apr 2007, consultant), with Marion Smith ▪ 10.2ha/4.5ha (pinot, chard, sauv, sem) ▪ 14.5t/2,000cs own label 100% white ▪ Organic certification ▪ PO Box 143 Elgin

7180 ▪ info@elginridge.com ▪ www.elginridge.com ▪ S 34° 12' 10.68" E 019°0' 14.34" ▪ **T +27 (0)21-846-8060** ▪ F +27 (0)21-846-8060

Confident that South Africans of all hues can continue working towards a common goal, Britons Brian and Marion Smith are creating a rainbow of their own with a rosé sparkling and a pinot noir set to join the all-white portfolio. Assisted by Luddite's Niels Verburg, they've carved out a niche as Elgin's only certified organic cellar and are evaluating biodynamics in a 'constant desire to improve our wines'.

282 Sauvignon Blanc ▤ ⚘ ★★★★ Wild yeast ferment & long lees-ageing give **12** lemongrass freshness, good palate weight & impressive length. Discontinued: **282 Chardonnay**. — CR

■ **Elgin Valley Vineyards** *see* Corder Family Wines

Elgin Vintners

Location/WO: Elgin ▪ Map: Elgin, Walker Bay & Bot River ▪ Est 2003 ▪ 1stB 2004 ▪ Tasting & sales by appt ▪ Owner(s) Derek Corder, Max Hahn, Alastair Moodie, James Rawbone-Viljoen, Rob Semple & Paul Wallace ▪ Cellarmaster(s)/winemaker(s) Various (Kevin Grant, Gavin Patterson, Jeff Grier, Nico Grobler, Martin Meinert, Niels Verburg, Joris van Almenkerk) ▪ Viticulturist(s) Paul Wallace ▪ 1,379ha/±102ha (cab, malbec, merlot, pinot, shiraz, chard, riesling, sauv, sem, viog) ▪ 1,100t/16,000cs own label ▪ BWI, IPW ▪ PO Box 121 Elgin 7180 ▪ elginvintners@mweb.co.za ▪ www.elginvintners.co.za ▪ S 34° 10' 09.30" E 19° 00' 29.03" ▪ **T +27 (0)21-859-2779/+27 (0)21-848-9587** ▪ F +27 (0)86-646-3693

There is definitely strength in unity, as this partnership of six Elgin Valley growers has shown. Not just ordinary farmers, but 'otherwise apple farmers going (gr)ape', they devised a successful concept of appointing a specialist winemaker for each of their chosen varieties, sourcing all grapes from the valley. The result is quality wine that reflects the diversity of the terroir and purity of its fruit.

★★★★ **Shiraz** ⓘ ▤ **09** big, but with sense of delicacy. Lots of dark spice, smoked meat appeal, gentle tannins & judicious oaking; all provide delicious drinking now, good potential too. Step up on **08** (★★★★).

★★★★ **Chardonnay** ✓ ▤ **11** (★★★★★) outshines **10** with lush butterscotch, toasted nuts & zesty lime flavours, showing masterly crafting. Youthful, with structure & complexity to age, although already tempting.

★★★★ **Viognier** ▤ Flamboyant **11** (★★★★★) captures more of the essence of viognier's aromatic allure & rich fruit than **10** (★★★★) or **09**. Succulent, leesy breadth & a brush of tannin, all leavened by bright acidity. Svelte & stylish.

★★★★ **The Century** ▨ Unoaked sauvignon (65%) & semillon duo honours Elgin's visionary centenarian, Douglas Moodie. A year on, **11** poised & engaging, with rich, tangy stonefruit more in harmony with alcohol & creamy succulence.

> **Rosé** ☺ ▤ ▨ ★★★ Previewed **13**, from merlot, exudes juicy drinkability. Appealing red berry & savoury tone, finishes clean & dry. Great summer quaffer!

Cabernet Sauvignon ⓘ ★★★ Simple & short fruit on **08**. Balanced freshness, structure for current drinking. **Merlot** ⓘ ★★★★ Appetising **09**, with splash malbec, pleasingly fresh, fruity with lively & succulent grape tannins. Good now, has staying power too. **Pinot Noir** ▤ ▨ ★★★★ Savoury, sweet/sour cherry tones on **11**. Balanced & sappy, with earthy freshness. New oak (30%) adds some muscle tone. **Agama** ⓘ ★★★★ Cab/merlot forge straightforward blend in **08**. Quiet strawberry aromas, flavours in harmony with gentle structure. Not for ageing. **Sauvignon Blanc** ✓ ▤ ▨ ★★★★ **12** a crisp greengage & tropical melange from 3 different vineyards. Leesy breadth & splash of semillon give extra grip. — MW

■ **Embrace** *see* Stellenrust

Emineo Wines

Location: Cape Town ▪ Map: Cape Peninsula ▪ WO: Durbanville/Coastal ▪ Est 2004 ▪ 1stB 2006 ▪ Tasting by appt ▪ Owner(s) Trans-Scripto (Pty) Ltd ▪ Winemaker(s) Nico van der Merwe & Thys Louw ▪ 1,500cs own label 100% red ▪ PO Box 1326 Cape Town 8000 ▪ info@emineo.com ▪ www.emineo.com ▪ S 33° 56' 29.06" E 018° 23' 47.76" ▪ **T +27 (0)82-579-4849** ▪ F +27 (0)86-660-4323

This legally themed brand, with sibling Cape to Cairo, is produced on an occasional basis for Cape Town patent attorney Otto Gerntholtz by Nico van der

Merwe (Saxenburg, Nico van der Merwe Wines) and Thys Louw (Diemersdal). Grapes are sourced from vineyards in Swartland, Durbanville and Stellenbosch.

★★★★ **Liber II JLS** ⊕ Poised **07** cab (65%) with merlot & pinotage. When last tasted, minty chocolate aromas, lively cassis underpinned by acidity & tannin.

★★★★ **Liber III RG** ⊕ **07** big, ebullient shiraz with splash mourvèdre ex Durbanville & Swartland. Seriously styled, with polished oak when tasted some time ago.

Liber I OCG ⊕ ★★★★ On review, **06** 5-way Bordeaux blend mostly cab was soft & approachable. — KM, CvZ

■ **Enon** see Zandvliet Wine Estate & Thoroughbred Stud
■ **Enoteca Bottega** see Idiom Wines

Epicurean Wines

WO: Western Cape ▪ Est 2001 ▪ 1stB 2003 ▪ Closed to public ▪ Owner(s) Global Pact Trading 125 (Pty) Ltd ▪ Cellarmaster(s) Mutle Mogase, Mbhazima Shilowa, Moss Ngoasheng, Ron Gault (Nov 2002) ▪ Winemaker(s) Schalk Willem Joubert (consultant) ▪ 500cs own label 100% red ▪ WIETA ▪ PO Box 280 Parklands 2121 Johannesburg ▪ info@epicureanwine.co.za ▪ www.epicureanwine.co.za ▪ **T +27 (0)11-530-9100** ▪ F +27 (0)11-530-9101

'Epicurean is a product of our love and passion for food, wine and the finer things in life,' says Mbhazima Shilowa, one of four partners behind this venture - committed to producing 'elegant, subtle and refined wines'. Working to achieve this is the winemaking team of Rupert & Rothschild.

★★★★ **Epicurean** ⊕ More lightweight **08** reflects the vintage. Pretty mint-lifted red berry tones are held by a challenging structure. Best opened over next year or two. — AL

Equitania

🍴🎋📷

Location: Somerset West ▪ Map: Helderberg ▪ WO: Stellenbosch ▪ Est 2000 ▪ 1stB 2008 ▪ Tasting & sales by appt ▪ Fee R10 ▪ Closed all pub hols ▪ BYO picnic ▪ Walking/hiking trails ▪ Owner(s) Esme Kruger de Beer ▪ Winemaker(s) PG Slabbert (Stellenbosch Hills) ▪ Viticulturist(s) Gavin Dun (May 2007) ▪ 4.65ha/1.38ha (cabs s/f) ▪ 10.54t/12,000cs own label 100% red ▪ PO Box 5308 Helderberg 7135 ▪ esme14@mweb.co.za ▪ www.equitania.co.za ▪ S 34° 2' 26.15" E 018° 49' 5.51" ▪ **T +27 (0)21-300-1140/1** ▪ F +27 (0)21-300-1092

Equitania, on the outskirts of Somerset West, is the dream home of Esme de Beer, with garden designed by a feng shui master and small vineyard. The resulting wines have been vinified at Stellenbosch Hills since maiden 2008, Esme declaring herself very happy with the efforts of cellarmaster PG Slabbert and his team.

★★★★ **Flag** ✓ Full-bodied but composed **10** Bordeaux red from 57% cab & cab franc. Red & black fruit, subtle 'graphite' hint & crushed herbs. Bright acidity & fine tannins ensure balance.
Fluke 09 sold out untasted. Next awaited. — CE

Ernie Els Wines

🍷☕📷♿

Location/map: Stellenbosch ▪ WO: Stellenbosch/Western Cape ▪ Est 1999 ▪ 1stB 2000 ▪ Tasting, sales & cellar tours Mon-Sat 9-5 ▪ Fee R30/4 wines, R60/8 wines ▪ Closed Easter Fri/Sun, Dec 25 & Jan 1 ▪ Light lunches & cheese platters Tue-Sat ▪ Tour groups ▪ Gift shop ▪ Corporate events & functions ▪ Small conference facilities ▪ Mountain biking trail ▪ Ernie Els' Trophy Room ▪ The Big Easy Restaurant at 95 Dorp Str (see Restaurants section) ▪ Owner(s) Ernie Els ▪ Cellarmaster(s) Louis Strydom (Dec 1999) ▪ Winemaker(s) Louis Strydom (Dec 1999), with Klaas Stoffberg (2009) ▪ Viticulturist(s) Charl van Reenen (2008) ▪ 72ha/45ha (cab, merlot, shiraz) ▪ 250t/18,000cs own label 90% red 10% white + 1,500cs for clients ▪ Brands for clients: SA Rugby ▪ PO Box 7595 Stellenbosch 7599 ▪ info@ernieelswines.com ▪ www.ernieelswines.com ▪ S 34° 0' 52.8" E 018° 50' 53.5" ▪ **T +27 (0)21-881-3588** ▪ F +27 (0)21-881-3688

Four-time major golf championship winner Ernie Els' stylish winery is known for ultra-premium reds, and another one has just been added to the range, namely Proprietor's Cabernet Sauvignon 2011. 'Cab is really a strength of ours but it tends to get camouflaged in a blend. I wanted to highlight the quality of what we get off the Helderberg,' says winemaker and managing director Louis Strydom. He's bullish about the future of the variety and is planting clone 412 from the Médoc, the first new one to be released locally since 1992. 'Cab is king but the average farm can't produce the tonnages to make it economically viable. It's going to become scarce and then supply and demand will do the rest.'

★★★★ **Cabernet Sauvignon** ⓐ **11** very fragrant with notes of red & black berries, fynbos & violets, hint of vanilla. Lots of fruit power, soft tannins, unashamedly modern in style. Follows pure-fruited **10** (★★★★★).

★★★★ **Proprietor's Cabernet Sauvignon** NEW ⓐ Monumental **11** shows staggering depth & richness. Intense cassis & toasty oak, it appeared tight & youthful on tasting & is probably five years off showing anything of its true potential. Very much a statement wine.

★★★★ **Proprietor's Syrah** ⓐ Extremely polished **11** shows ripe berry fruit, vanilla & dried herbs rather than spice. Concentrated & smooth textured. Contains 5% viognier.

★★★★☆ **Ernie Els Signature** ⓐ A Bordeaux blend always made to be big & bold, **10** (★★★★) teeters on the brink of being overdone. Fruit appears very ripe while there's also an unusual tarry note. Sweet & smooth textured, it's love-it-or-hate-it stuff. Lacks composure of **09**.

★★★★ **Big Easy Red** Characterful **11**, red & black fruit, some floral perfume, vanilla & spice. Good concentration, fresh acidity, soft tannins. Like lesser **10** (★★★☆), 6-way blend led by shiraz. WO W Cape.

★★★★☆ **Proprietor's Blend** ⓐ Though not exactly slight, **11** impresses with its poise. A blend of 55% cab, the rest shiraz & 3 Bordeaux reds, it shows red & black berries, attractive crushed herbs. Pure fruited & fresh, with fine tannins.

★★★★☆ **CWG Auction Reserve** ⓐ Faultless **11** is a cab, shiraz, merlot blend. It's undoubtedly forceful but not at the expense of balance. Really layered with notes of red & black berries, dried herbs, attractive oak spice. Intense core of fruit, bright acidity, firm but fine tannins.

Merlot ⓘ ★★★ **11** tends to over-reach itself with jammy fruit, tart acidity & drying finish. Has intensity but at expense of balance. **Big Easy White** ▤ ⓐ ★★★ 100% chenin, **13** is undemanding but appealing with notes of peach & pear. Good concentration, bright acidity. WO W Cape. **Sauvignon Blanc** ▤ ⓐ ★★★ **13** is true-to-type & easy-drinking. Shows green melon with a slight herbal edge, relatively thick texture with coated acidity. Standout **12** (★★★★) offered more complexity. — CE

Ernst Gouws & Co Wines ♥ ⚕ ♿

Location/map: Stellenbosch • WO: Stellenbosch/Western Cape/Swartland/Wellington/Elgin/Coastal • Est/1stB 2003 • Tasting & sales at Koelenhof Winery Mon-Thu 9-5 Fri 9-4 Sat 10-2 • Fee R15pp • Closed Easter Fri/Sun, Ascension day, Dec 25/26 & Jan 1 • Facilities for children • Owner(s) Ernst & Gwenda Gouws • Cellarmaster(s) Ernst Gouws • Winemaker(s) Ernst Gouws snr, with Ezanne Gouws-Du Toit & Ernst Gouws jnr • 72ha total • 60,000cs own label 40% red 60% white • Other export brand: New Gate • IPW • PO Box 7450 Stellenbosch 7599 • ernst@ernstgouws.co.za • www.ernstgouws.co.za • S 33° 50' 3.4" E 018° 47' 52.7" • T +27 (0)21-865-2895 • F +27 (0)21-865-2894

Members of the Gouws family have been active in the Stellenbosch wine business for more than 150 years. Today, Koelenhof-based Ernst and wife Gwenda are the driving force, and following in the footsteps of their father are Ezanne and Ernst jnr, both graduate winemakers from Stellenbosch University.

★★★★☆ **Nineteenfiftytwo** ⓘ ⓐ Stunning debut last ed as 'Depth'. **11** Bordeaux-style white, 65% sauvignon & new-oaked semillon, from Elgin. Mouthfilling yet harmonious & elegant. A showstopper.

Merlot ⓘ ⓐ ★★★★ Ripe black cherry & plum, hints espresso & chocolate, **11** smooth & juicy through to lingering savoury end. **Pinot Noir** ★★★ Ripe & bold **09**, off West Coast vines, reveals earthy dark cherry with savoury mushroom & oaky finish. **Pinotage** NEW ✓ ⓐ ★★★★ Good varietal expression on juicy **12**, with plush dark fruit & fynbos flavours. Fine structure bodes well for future enjoyment with a hearty meat dish. Coastal WO. **Shiraz** ✓ ⓐ ★★★★ Violet & lavender-fragrant **11** from Swartland is fruity, spicy & moreish, with a lingering savoury goodbye. **Chardonnay** ✓ ⓐ ★★★★ From Wellington bushvines, **12** ups the ante on last-tasted **10** (★★★★) exuding nutty, buttery citrus flavours & delicious lemon & vanilla conclusion. **Sauvignon Blanc** Next awaited. Discontinued: **Chenin Blanc**. — WB

Esau Wines 🍶 NEW

Location/WO: Paarl • Est/1stB 2010 • Owner(s) Wim Hugo • Cellarmaster(s) Wim Hugo (2009) • Winemaker(s) Wim Hugo & Jorrie Jordaan (both 2009) • 3t/2,500L 100% red • PO Box 3175 Paarl 7620 • whugo@mbv.co.za • http://urlmin.com/esau • T +27 (0)79-875-4646

Owner and ex-chemical engineer Wim Hugo describes his Paarl enterprise as a 'micro-winery' - small but not garagiste. Focus currently is on reds, from dryland vines on the mountain behind the town, sold into the restaurant trade. Wim believes blends (both grape variety and vintage) provide a better drinking experience but 'once in a while we bottle exceptional cultivar wines'.

Cabernet Sauvignon Reserve ★★★★ Appealing black berry fruit, slight oak vanilla from older wood on intense **12**, from dryland Paarl Mountain vines. Rich, concentrated but not forced; wears 15.5% alcohol lightly. **Château Esau ★★★ NV (10)** shiraz (92%), cab combo. Dense, with fruit-sweet tail perfect for hearty cassoulets & bredies, says Wim Hugo. **Holy Cow ★★★** Easy-drinking **10** Cape Blend led by pinotage (45%) with shiraz, splash cab (from 2011 vintage) adding strawberry fruit gloss & tannin backbone. — CvZ

Escapades Winery

Location/map: Stellenbosch ▪ WO: Coastal ▪ Est/1stB 2006 ▪ Tasting by appt ▪ Owner(s) Evangelos Gerovassiliou, Vassilis Tsaktsarlis & Takis Soldatos ▪ Cellarmaster(s) Vassilis Tsaktsarlis & Evangelos Gerovassiliou (both 2006) ▪ Winemaker(s) Chris Kelly (Oct 2010, consultant) ▪ (cab, malbec, merlot, ptage, shiraz, sauv, sem) ▪ 100t/10,000cs own label 40% red 50% white 10% rosé ▪ PO Box 99 Somerset Mall 7129 ▪ info@escapadewinery.com ▪ www.escapadewinery.com ▪ S 33° 54' 47.7" E 018° 44' 7.7" ▪ **T +27 (0)82-569-3371** ▪ F +27 (0)86-585-6549

The significance of this international venture (escapade?) in the Cape is pointed to by the eminence of the three Greek friends behind it. Highly respected winemakers Evangelos Gerovassiliou and Vassilis Tsaktsarlis take turns in visiting the cellar (where another international figure, New Zealander Chris Kelly, is the permanent presence) and Sweden-based vintner, connoisseur and marketer Takis Soldatos is ever-alert. The wines – from altitude and older vineyards the team have sought out - are as sophisticated and characterful as expected.

★★★★ Semillon-Sauvignon Blanc Food friendly like all these, **13** blend convinces even more than the single varieties. Mixes tropical with citric green; lively & fresh; also breadth, depth, complexity & silky texture. **Cabernet Sauvignon** In abeyance, as for **Merlot** & **Shiraz**. **Pinotage ★★★★** Hard to credit 14.5% alcohol on balanced, fresh & light-seeming **11**, with the variety's tannins well tamed. Characterful & very drinkable; a step-up on last-tried **07 (★★★)**. **Cabernet Sauvignon-Shiraz-Malbec NEW ★★★★** Fresh, attractive **12** flaunts pure fruit. Though big, not intense or dense; gently structured & full of delight. Balanced & immensely drinkable. **Pinotage Rosé ★★★** As usual, just-about-dry **13** from pinotage is prettily pale, softly textured & quietly flavourful. **Sauvignon Blanc 🗃 ★★★★** Aromatic **13** with lots of flavour; enriched & softened by some semillon & a little sugar - but the sweet touch squabbles with acid-drop sourness. **Semillon ★★★★** Understated as usual, easy **13** offers lemon & lanolin & an ingratiating sweet note. Broadening oak element well integrated into deliciousness. — TJ

■ **Eskdale** see De Zoete Inval Estate

Esona Boutique Wine

Location/map: Robertson ▪ Est 2002 ▪ 1stB 2010 ▪ Tasting & sales Mon-Fri 9-5 Sat 9.30-3 ▪ Closed Dec 25 & Jan 1 ▪ Owner(s) Rowan & Caryl Beattie ▪ Winemaker(s)/viticulturist(s) Lourens van der Westhuizen (Jan 2010, Arendsig) ▪ 17ha/9.83ha (pinot, shiraz, chard, chenin, cbard, sauv) ▪ ±250t/6,000cs own label 34% red 66% white ▪ PO Box 2619 Clareinch 7400 ▪ info@esona.co.za ▪ www.esona.co.za ▪ S 33° 54' 16.14" E 020° 0' 38.66" ▪ **T +27 (0)84-622-3687** ▪ F +27 (0)21-787-3792

Family-owned Esona ('The Very One'), on a scenic stretch of the Breede River near Robertson, specialises in limited-release single-vineyard wines, available for tasting and sale in the original cellar, recently renovated to 'take you back to the bygone years of winemaking', says tasting venue manager Melissa Jones.

■ **Essay** see MAN Family Wines
■ **Eternal** see Kumala
■ **Exact Africa** see Stellekaya Winery

Excelsior Estate

Location/map/WO: Robertson ▪ Est 1859 ▪ 1stB 1990 ▪ Tasting & sales Mon-Fri 10-4 Sat 10-3 ▪ Picnics available on request, or BYO picnic ▪ Facilities for children ▪ Conferences ▪ 4-star Excelsior Manor Guesthouse ▪ Owner(s) Freddie & Peter de Wet ▪ Cellarmaster(s) Johan Stemmet (Aug 2003) ▪ Winemaker(s) Johan

Stemmet (Aug 2003), with Kelly Gova (2005) ▪ Viticulturist(s) Freddie de Wet (1970) ▪ 320ha/220ha (cab, merlot, p verdot, shiraz, chard, sauv) ▪ 2,200t/320,000cs own label 75% red 25% white ▪ Other export brand: Stablemate ▪ BRC ▪ PO Box 17 Ashton 6715 ▪ info@excelsior.co.za ▪ www.excelsior.co.za ▪ S 33° 51' 15.1" E 020° 0' 25.6" ▪ **T +27 (0)23-615-1980** ▪ F +27 (0)23-615-2019

As owners of an internationally renowned thoroughbred stud, it's no surprise that the de Wet family of Excelsior should name their (newly repackaged) wines after some of the remarkable horses to grace the estate's paddocks. Those who care for the equines and vines are themselves nurtured, hence for example the full-fledged crèche onsite, two extra teaching posts funded by the family at the local school, and, says co-owner Peter de Wet, a policy of 'training and employing people in better positions/roles than they would have access to in the past'.

★★★★ **Evanthuis Cabernet Sauvignon** Off farm's oldest vines, pays homage to champion Hackney horse imported in 1913. Trim, mocha-toned **10** (★★★★), first since **07**, will appeal to fans of an oakier style.

Cabernet Sauvignon ☺ 🍴 ★★★ **11** is fruit filled, with mint & tealeaf nuances; nice easygoing picnic wine. **Chardonnay** ☺ 🍴 ★★★ **13** tank sample raises the bar with deft part-oaking, giving feisty lemon fruit free rein. **Viognier** ☺ 🍴 ★★★ Perfumed preview **13**, blossoms & stonefruit, satisfying weight & sugar-extended length; for solo sipping or Indian curries.

Merlot 🍴 ★★★ Red berries, sweet coffee the hallmarks of warm-hearted **12**. Also in 1.5L magnums. **Gondolier Merlot Reserve** ⓟ ★★★★ Notch up **10** intense & dense, with polished but rather firm tannins deserving year/2 to soften & let wine show its potential. **Paddock Shiraz** 🍴 ★★ From vines planted on old horse pens, savoury **11** has (saddle?) leather & spice appeal. Good BBQ red. **San Louis Shiraz Reserve** ★★★ Recognises never-say-die Limousin winner. Pepper, blueberry on **10** preview, tad burly with firm tannins, warming 14.5% alcohol. **Purebred Red** ⓟ 🍴 ★★★ Fruity **12** drops viognier, adds 25% each of merlot & cab to base of shiraz; slips down easily with smidgen sugar in tail. **Sauvignon Blanc** 🍴 ★★ Ex-tank **13** faint greengage & kiwi, lightish 12.6% alcohol for lunchtime sipping. **Agricola Sauvignon Blanc** NEW ★★★★ From one of Robertson's highest, coolest blocks, **12** pure fruited, with good grassy nettle definition, bracing freshness calls for seafood. — HJ,JP

Excelsior Vlakteplaas

Location: Oudtshoorn ▪ Map: Klein Karoo & Garden Route ▪ Est 1934 ▪ 1stB 1998 ▪ Tasting & sales by appt only ▪ Closed Easter Fri-Mon, Ascension Day, Dec 16/25/26 & Jan 1 ▪ Owner(s)/winemaker(s) Danie Schoeman 41ha (merlot, ptage, ruby cab, chenin, muscadel r/w) ▪ 490t/2,000cs own label 50% red 50% white ▪ PO Box 112 De Rust 6650 ▪ jjschoeman@telkomsa.net ▪ S 33° 29' 16.74" E 022° 35' 25.50" ▪ **T +27 (0)82-821-3556** ▪ F +27 (0)44-241-2569

Producing mainly bulk wine, Danie Schoeman bottles muscadel under his own label only in even years – a good thing in 2013, as it meant the cellar was available for South African film director Koos Roets to shoot scenes for his adaptation of Pieter Fourie's iconic play, Faan se Trein.

His Master's Choice range
Red Muscadel Await next. **White Muscadel** ⓟ ★★★ Sweet but lively **06** is a barley sugar & orange flavoured treat, especially over crushed ice. — JP,CvZ

Fable Mountain Vineyards

Location/map: Tulbagh ▪ WO: Western Cape/Tulbagh ▪ Est 1989 ▪ 1stB 2009 ▪ Tasting & cellar tours by appt only ▪ Closed Easter Fri-Mon, Dec 25 & Jan 1 ▪ Conservation area ▪ Owner(s) Terroir Selections ▪ Winemaker(s) Rebecca Tanner (Jul 2009) ▪ Viticulturist(s) Paul Nicholls (Jul 2009) ▪ 185ha/30ha (grenache, mourv, syrah, viog) ▪ info@fablewines.com ▪ www.fablewines.com ▪ S 33° 21' 7.9" E 019° 12' 46.1" ▪ **T +27 (0)78-315-3861/+27 (0)73-768-1600** ▪ F +27 (0)86-660-9288

Winemaker Rebecca Tanner and viticulturist Paul Nicholls have been the incumbent winegrowing team at this sustainably farmed and beautiful winery since its earlier incarnation as Tulbagh Mountain Vineyards (TMV), through a change of ownership and name to Fable in 2010, followed recently by rebranding as Fable Mountain Vineyards within the US-owned Terroir Selections portfolio, and tweaking of some wine names and the label design. What hasn't changed are the contents of the bottles: made in the same style, with the same focus on quality, minimal intervention and organic/biodynamic cultivation that first brought the winery to prominence. The last new vines are in the soil, bringing the vineyard footprint to 30 ha, and the team are 'looking forward to a very fruitful year'.

★★★★★ **Syrah** 🅥 Was 'Bobbejaan'. **11** intense black cherry & tobacco aromas, plush fruit tempered by dry tannins. Expressive & elegant despite its ripeness (14.7% alcohol). Profound wine, for contemplation. Like **10**, deserves 5+ years to reveal itself fully. Tulbagh WO.

★★★★☆ **Night Sky** 🅥 Previously 'Lion's Whisker'. Mostly shiraz (60%), dashes mourvèdre & grenache. Vibrant **11**'s (★★★★) chewy tannins need good few years to soften, marry with peppery liquorice fruit. **10** with 20% more shiraz, fleshier, approachable on release.

★★★★★ **Jackal Bird** 🍴 🅥 Stately **12** another assured & accomplished vintage of lightly oaked combo chenin, chardonnay, roussanne, viognier & grenache blanc. Full bodied, yet showing great elegance & balance, persistence. Like **11** (★★★★★) drier, firmer than **10**. All are standouts, well worth cellaring. — GdB,MW

■ **Fair for Life** *see* Re'Mogo Wines
■ **Fairhills** *see* Origin Wine
■ **Fairtrade Original** *see* uniWines Vineyards

Fairvalley Wines   🍷

Location: Paarl ▪ WO: Western Cape ▪ Est 1997 ▪ 1stB 1998 ▪ Tasting by appt only ▪ Fee R25 ▪ Sales at Fairview 9-4.30 daily ▪ Closed Good Fri, Dec 25 & Jan 1 ▪ Owner(s) Fairvalley Farmworkers Association ▪ Cellarmaster(s) Jaco Brand (2010) ▪ Winemaker(s) Jaco Brand, with Andries de Klerk (both 2010) ▪ 30,000cs own label 50% red 50% white ▪ Fairtrade ▪ PO Box 6219 Paarl 7620 ▪ wine@fairvalley.co.za ▪ www.fairvalley.co.za ▪ **T +27 (0)21-863-2450** ▪ F +27 (0)21-863-2591

Established in 1998 and wholly owned by 42 families who work on neighbouring Fairview, this is one of the original farm employee empowerment ventures in South Africa. Fairtrade accredited, and committed to promoting equality and sustainability in the farming community, Fairvalley is setting its sights on the US with a low-key but already well-received relaunch. A local market launch is next.

Pinotage 😊 🍴 🅥 ★★★ A raspberry bomb of a wine, **13** ex barrel has loads of varietal character, well-balanced, well-priced everyday glugger. **Chardonnay** 😊 🍴 🅥 ★★★ From tank, pleasantly fruity & appealing **13** shows bitter lemon, spiced almonds, light oaking. Delicious now & for year/two. **Sauvignon Blanc** 😊 🍴 🅥 ★★★ Sampled prior to bottling, **13** shows ripe fruit salad notes with zippy grapefruit finish. A happy summer wine. Fairtrade certified, as all.

Cabernet Sauvignon 🍴 🅥 **13** preview too unformed to rate. **Chenin Blanc** 🍴 🅥 ★★★ Zesty pineapple fruit on pre-bottling sample of **13**, a mite powdery & confected. — CM

Fairview   🍴🍷☕📷♿

Location: Paarl ▪ Map: Paarl & Wellington ▪ WO: Paarl/Coastal/Darling/Stellenbosch/Swartland/Western Cape ▪ Est 1693 ▪ 1stB 1974 ▪ Tasting & sales Mon-Sun 9-5, last tasting 30min before closing ▪ R25/standard tasting, R60/master tasting ▪ Closed Good Fri, Dec 25 & Jan 1 ▪ The Goatshed Restaurant (see Restaurants section) ▪ Tour groups by appt only ▪ Deli: artisanal cheeses & fresh farm breads ▪ Owner(s) Charles Back ▪ Winemaker(s) Anthony de Jager (Dec 1996), with Stephanie Betts (2010) & Adele Dunbar (2006) ▪ 500ha/ 300ha (cab, carignan, grenache, merlot, mourv, petite sirah, ptage, shiraz, tannat, tempranillo, chenin, sauv, viog) ▪ 2,100t/260cs own label 80% red 15% white 5% rosé ▪ ISO 9001:2001, BWI, BRC, Fairtrade, HACCP, IPW, WIETA ▪ PO Box 583 Suider-Paarl 7624 ▪ info@fairview.co.za ▪ www.fairview.co.za ▪ S 33° 46' 19.16" E 018° 55' 25.26" ▪ **T +27 (0)21-863-2450** ▪ F +27 (0)21-863-2591

The word 'dynamic' is constantly in mind when it comes to this bustling and successful wine and cheese estate in Paarl. Owner Charles Back has created a mini-empire in the shadow of the Taal Monument, recently buying the neighbour farm as the new home for Spice Route. But it is a domain with the watchwords of quality, integrity and value at every level. The many different wine ranges include Goats do Roam, Leeuwenjacht, Spice Route and Land's End, all listed separately in this guide and illustrating Back's love of innovation, inventive use of classic and unusual varieties, and uncanny grasp of what his customers want.

The home-farm continues to reinforce its commitment to the community and all new vintages of their Goats do Roam wines will be Fairtrade.

Fairview range

★★★★ **Cabernet Sauvignon** 🖾 Well-made, polished **11** starts out with minty/eucalyptus hints on nose before blackcurrant elegance kicks in. Fresh & juicy, from Stellenbosch fruit.

★★★★ **Barbera** 🗐 🖾 Polished & sophisticated **11** shows minty hints with whiffs of leather polish, dense black fruit, creamy soft finish. Paarl & Swartland grapes, older American & French oak.

★★★★ **Durif** 🖾 **11** packs quite a punch of black fruit - plums & plumcake - with charry, oaky spice. Upfront tannins need time to integrate but concentrated flavours should ensure happy ending.

★★★★☆ **Primo Pinotage** 🖾 **11** a smooth operator, with particularly floral nose (lilies & violets) before winter berry mix, smoked & cured meats & coriander seeds sweep through to thoroughly satisfying finish. From Paarl fruit, French & American oak this year, 40% new.

★★★★☆ **Eenzaamheid Shiraz** 🖾 The smoky one of the three 'vineyard' shirazes. **11** from Paarl fruit features appetising aromas of smoked meat & sweet charry oak before layers of spiced plumcake & mulled wine sweep the board. Silky tannins round out peppery finish showing plenty more to come.

★★★★☆ **The Beacon Shiraz** 🖾 'The spicy one.' **10** a whirl of exotic excitement, enticing & beguiling with whiffs of chilli-chocolate, black cherries & cloves. 29 months in oak, 40% new, has softened & rounded, giving a full-bodied backbone & excellent charry length.

★★★★☆ **Jakkalsfontein Shiraz** 🖾 'The perfumed one.' **11** from Swartland bushvines woos with aromatic nose of white & black pepper, star anise hints & cloves. Powerful yet elegant, melding black berries with silky tannins, though fraction less concentrated than stellar **09** (★★★★★). No **10**.

★★★★☆ **Cyril Back** 🖾 Stellar shiraz a very fitting tribute to Back patriarch, **09** is also a majestic homage to Hermitage, with intense spice & orange peel notes highlighting soft ripe mouthful of black fruit. More powerful than **07**, tannins still need a further few years. Coastal WO. No **08**.

★★★★☆ **Caldera** 🖾 Grenache-dominated southern Rhône blend, **11** is a blast of red fruit - plums, raspberries, cherries & cranberries. Earthy undertones & whiffs of spice make for excellent food partner. **10** (★★★★) a tad shyer. Coastal WO.

★★★★ **Viognier** 🗐 🖾 Benchmark Cape viognier **12** shows masterly use of subtle oak, giving definition to zesty limes, orange peel & ginger notes. Elegant, restrained food wine, delicate yet confident.

★★★★★ **Nurok White Blend** 🗐 🖾 Effortlessly maintaining standard of maiden **11**, **12** is a symphony of peaches, perfume & poached pears with endlessly evolving length. Viognier dominated, with chenin, roussanne & grenache blanc adding spice, interest & pleasure. Coastal WO.

★★★★ **Méthode Cap Classique Brut** [NEW] 🖾 Unusual **11** dry sparkling from viognier & grenaches noir & blanc continues estate's fascination with Rhône varieties. Baked peaches & marmalade on toast, creamy nutty undertones. 18 months on lees.

★★★★☆ **La Beryl Blanc** 🖾 Breathtaking **12** unwooded straw wine from mainly chenin with 21% muscat carries touch more sweetness than **11** (★★★★★) with elegance & grace. Layers of ripe golden fruit (apricots, peaches, honey) roll around & cascade over the palate into a tumultuous finish.

Pegleg Carignan 🖾 ★★★★ **11** from Swartland bushvines is perfumed & pretty, with black cherry yoghurt character & fragrant spice notes. **Merlot** 🖾 ★★★★ Cherry-choc fruit bomb **11** given backbone by firm spiced oak, well integrated. Crowd pleasing & enjoyable. Stellenbosch WO. **Mourvèdre** 🖾 ★★★☆ Accessible **11** serves up red berries, leather & spice in a chunky, meaty everyday wine of character. **Pinotage** ✓ 🖾 ★★★★ Really attractive & friendly **12**, a Pinotage for the People! Red berry fruit leaps out of the glass, soft juicy texture. **Sangiovese** 🖾 ★★★★ Lipsmacking & savoury **12** from Darling fruit, classic sour cherries, strawberries & earthy undertones. Improves on previous. **Shiraz** 🖾 ★★★★ Sweetly fruited **11** packs in plenty of black cherries, plums, spice & violets for everyday drinking pleasure. Coastal WO. **Tannat** [NEW] 🖾 ★★★ Interesting **11** is intensely perfumed with gritty, grippy tannins. Should be enough ripe jammy fruit for them to soften with time. **Extrano** ⊕ ★★★★ Mediterranean blend of mostly young-vine tempranillo, grenache & carignan, **10** has interesting flavours of peppered steak & black fruit. **Chardonnay** 🗐 🖾 ★★★☆ Was 'Darling Chardonnay'. Touch more oak on **12** (50%, third new) makes for mouthful of creamy yellow fruit still balanced by freshening acidity. Coastal WO. **Darling Chenin Blanc** 🗐 🖾 ★★★★ Zesty citrus is the hallmark of **13**, the lime marmalade & pink grapefruit paired with aromatic spice for rich satisfaction. **Darling Riesling** 🗐 🖾 ★★★★ Intense **13** is firmly off-dry (15.2g/l) to beautifully balance crunchy green appley acidity & perfumed floral notes. **Darling Sauvignon Blanc** 🗐 🖾 ★★★★ Exuberant **13** steps up on **12** (★★★☆) with exotic fruit salad & freshening acidity which never overwhelms, only enhances. Freerun juice only, 3 months fine lees-ageing. **Oom Pagel Semillon** ⊕ 🗐 🖾 ★★★★ Spiced yellow peaches with resinous pine needle character, **11** shows improvement on **10** (★★★☆). Concentrated fruit (pineapples &

apples) handles 100% oak (none new) with style. Darling vines. **Viognier Special Late Harvest** 🍷 🖾 ★★★ Lively purity of fruit on **13** charms & cheers with apricots & peaches freshened by balancing acidity. **La Beryl Rouge** Next awaited. **Sweet Red** 🍷 🖾 ★★★ Port-style **11** now from durif, showing earthy notes with black berries & leather polish. Discontinued: **Pinotage-Viognier**.

La Capra range

> **Malbec** ☺ 🍷 🖾 ★★★ Enticing aromas of plummy black fruit, **12** delivers juicy berried mouthful for everyday enjoyment. WO Paarl. **Pinot Grigio** ☺ 🍷 🖾 ★★★ Name changed from 'Pinot Gris' & **13** coincidentally much improved. Fresh, sappy apples & pears in characterful, daily sipper. Darling fruit. **Viognier** ☺ 🍷 🖾 ★★★ Tinned mandarins & peaches on **13** offers plenty of varietal character for pleasant everyday drinking. Paarl grapes.

Cabernet Sauvignon 🍷 🖾 ★★★ Juicy **12** is a soft, crowd-pleasing mouthful of black berries & currants. Quite appealing all-round. All these WO Coastal unless stated. **Merlot** ✓ 🍷 🖾 ★★★☆ Very lovely flavours of plumcake, cinnamon, cherries on **12**. Plushy & opulent tannins, a thoroughly enjoyable tipple. **Pinotage** 🕙 🍷 🖾 ★★★ Characterful quaffer **11** maintaining standards with sweet cooked cherry jam nose, raspberries & plums. WO W Cape. **Shiraz** 🍷 🖾 ★★★ Fresh, clean, juicy & correct **11** offers shade less intense flavours of pepper, smoked meat, plums than previous. Still good everyday drinking. **Pinotage Rosé** 🍷 🖾 ★★★ Fresh, fruity & uncomplicated dry **13**, strawberries & tomato leaves. **Chardonnay** ✓ 🍷 🖾 ★★★★ Unwooded **13** balances fresh grapefruit & crunchy apple flavours with creamy almond notes from 6 months lees-maturation. Paarl WO. **Chenin Blanc** 🍷 🖾 ★★★ Tutti-frutti **13** is perfectly pleasant everyday mouthful of tropical fruit with lively acidity. WO Paarl. **Sauvignon Blanc** 🍷 🖾 ★★★ Clean & fresh **13**, tropical fruits for summer stoep wine. WO W Cape. Discontinued: **Hanepoot Straw Wine**. — CM

False Bay Vineyards   🍷

Location: Somerset West ▪ WO: Western Cape ▪ Est/1stB 2000 ▪ Tasting at Waterkloof ▪ Owner(s) Paul Boutinot ▪ Cellarmaster(s) Nadia Barnard (Jan 2013) ▪ Winemaker(s) Nadia Barnard (Jan 2004), with Jacques van der Vyver (Jan 2012) ▪ 160,000cs own label 30% red 65% white 5% rosé ▪ PO Box 2093 Somerset West 7129 ▪ info@ waterkloofwines.co.za ▪ www.falsebayvineyards.co.za ▪ **T** +27 (0)21-858-1292 ▪ **F** +27 (0)21-858-1293

The False Bay and Peacock Ridge ranges are the 'pocket-friendly' offerings of the Helderberg-based Waterkloof project of British wine merchant Paul Boutinot. Though they are made at that estate to take advantage of additional winemaking capacity, grapes are sourced from across the Cape winelands.

False Bay Vineyards range

> **Sauvignon Blanc** ☺ 🍷 🖾 ★★★ **12** has peach & pear, is juicy, clean & fresh. Very approachable.

Pinotage ✓ 🍷 🖾 ★★★★ Pretty **12** shows red cherry, floral aromas. Medium bodied but well defined with fresh acidity & fine tannins. **Shiraz** 🕙 🖾 ★★★ Very ripe & fruity **11** much less elegant than previous vintage & a little hollow; neatly built - if a tad astringent. **Rosé** 🍷 🖾 ★★ **12** offers vague red fruit & little else. **Chardonnay** ✓ 🍷 🖾 ★★★★ Unwooded **12** pretty citrus blossom on the nose while the palate has good weight offset by bright acidity. **Chenin Blanc** 🍷 🖾 ★★★ **12** is honest, unpretentious with concentrated breakfast punch flavour, bright acidity.

Peacock Ridge range

Cabernet Sauvignon NEW 🍷 🖾 ★★★ Dense, pleasantly rustic **11** shows ultra-ripe dark fruit, plenty of tannic grip. Cries out for a big steak. **Merlot** 🕙 🍷 🖾 ★★★★ Lovely sweet, pure fruit on **11**, mingling with subtle oak influence & a nice herbal twist. Rather elegant; fresh & dry. **Shiraz** 🍷 🖾 ★★★ **12** has appealing black cherry fruit but not much grunt otherwise. **Chenin Blanc** 🍷 🖾 ★★★ Vague white peach, some yeasty character on wild-yeast-fermented **12**. **Sauvignon Blanc** 🍷 🖾 ★★★ Unimposing **12** is broad & soft with yellow apple flavour. — CE

🔳 **Fantail** *see* Morgenhof Wine Estate
🔳 **Far & Near** *see* L'Avenir Vineyards

Faraway House Wine Estate   👤 🍷

Location/map: Villiersdorp ▪ WO: Overberg ▪ Est 2002 ▪ 1stB 2008 ▪ Tasting by appt ▪ Closed Easter Fri-Mon, Ascension day, Pentecost & Dec 25/26 ▪ Owner(s) Faraway House Estate (Pty) Ltd ▪ Winemaker(s) Nicolas

Follet & David Ciry ▪ Viticulturist(s) Willem Pelser ▪ 90ha/9ha (merlot, ptage, shiraz, chard, sauv) ▪ 30t/4,000cs own label 80% red 15% white 5% rosé ▪ PO Box 403 Villiersdorp 6848 ▪ sales@farawayhouse.co.za ▪ www. farawayhouse.co.za ▪ S 33° 56' 24.63" E 019° 19' 39.41" ▪ T +27 (0)72-342-5052 ▪ F +27 (0)28-840-2740

Extensive Faraway farm, mostly given over to indigenous flora, lives up to its name, lying high above Theewaterskloof Dam near Villiersdorp. Only a small portion is planted with vines and an even smaller quantity of grapes vinified for the estate label, the remainder sold off to high-profile wineries.

Shiraz ⓪ ★★★★ **10** very ripe olive & leather aromas; tightly gripped by assertive grape tannins; lightish, very fresh feel. **Quadrille** ⓪ ★★★ Merlot-led **10** red blend; ultra ripe, intensely fresh contrast, touch bitter. **09** (★★★★) was better. **Classic** ⓪ ★★★★ **10** similar shiraz, cab, merlot mix as flavoursome **09** (★★★★); bright red fruit, smoked meat, spice, clamped by firm tannins; briskly dry. — AL

■ **Farm Animals** *see* Osbloed Wines

Fat Bastard

What started out as an experimental chardonnay tasted in a dank cellar by two friends, UK wine brand creator Guy Anderson and French winemaker Thierry Boudinaud, who pronounced it a 'fat bastard', has become a successful range on both sides of the Atlantic. In South Africa, it's made by Robertson Winery.

Cabernet Sauvignon ▨ ★★★ Already creamy from French/American oak, **10**'s crowd appeal boosted by few grams sugar & sweet-tasting alcohol. **Pinotage** NEW ✓ ▨ ★★★★ Characterful **11** ticks same drinkability boxes as Cab with more classic styling: lively acidity, pleasantly firm grip. **Shiraz** ▨ ★★★ Some tealeaf & coconut notes on sweet-sour **12**. WO W Cape, rest Robertson. **Chardonnay** ▨ ★★★ Appropriately corpulent thanks to spoon sugar & buttery marmalade flavours, aromas; **12** well-executed oaky style. **Sauvignon Blanc** ▨ ★★★ Total contrast to Chardonnay, despite small oaked portion: **12** austere, bone-dry & lightish. — HJ,CvZ

Feiteiras Vineyards

Location/WO: Bot River ▪ Map: Elgin, Walker Bay & Bot River ▪ Est 2003 ▪ 1stB 2004 ▪ Tasting & sales by appt ▪ Owner(s) De Andrade family ▪ Cellarmaster(s)/winemaker(s) Marelise Jansen van Rensburg (Beaumont) & Jose de Andrade ▪ Viticulturist(s) Manuel de Andrade ▪ 16.2ha/4.2ha (cab, merlot, mourv, shiraz, verdelho) ▪ 1,200cs own label 60% red 30% white 10% rosé ▪ PO Box 234 Bot River 7185 ▪ feiteiraswine@icon.co.za ▪ www. feiteiraswine.co.za ▪ S 34° 14' 3.6" E 019° 12' 33.3" ▪ T +27 (0)82-453-1597 ▪ F +27 (0)28-284-9525

Brothers Manuel and Jose de Andrade brought traditional Portuguese winemaking – including a rare pole-operated basket press – to their Bot River farm a decade ago. They since moved operations up the road to Beaumont, where Marelise Jansen van Rensburg crafts the wine under Jose's guidance.

Cabernet Sauvignon ⓪ ▨ ★★★★ Preview **11** robust & brambly, food-friendly tannins add succulence. **Troca Tintas** ✓ ▨ ★★★★ Effortless & enjoyable **12** preview is a step up, shiraz more prominent (with cab & dashes merlot & petit verdot), well-defined savoury black fruit. Like previous, perfect for espetada or spicy trinchado. **Côr de Rosa** ⓪ ▤ ★★★ Strawberry-pink, bone-dry rosé from merlot; **11** grip from seasoned casks fills out the cherry fruit. **Casa Merlot Rosé** ⓪ ▤ ★★★ The unwooded edition of cellar's rosé duo; **12** coral hue, lovely dry red-berry zing. **Verdelho** ▤ ★★★★ Rare-in-Cape white grape, unwooded **13** tank sample picked early for freshness but doesn't sacrifice flavour - alluring lime, pineapple, honeysuckle, all in a fragrant, light, dry body. **Vinho Forte Tinto** ⓪ ★★★★ Unusual fortified mourvèdre. **06** lush, earthy chocolate features & warm 19% alcohol bite. 375ml, like Branco. **Vinho Forte Branco** ⓪ ★★★★ Fortified verdelho, **06** clean nutty toffee note to spiritous aftertaste. — DC

Felicité

Easygoing wines that all pass through clever winemaking hands in the Newton Johnson winery, although the chardonnay and rosé are vinified at Stettyn Cellar. Success with the wines had put pressure on the limited space in the premium NJ cellar - but the pinot, cornerstone of the brand, is fully vinified there.

Pinot Noir ▤ ▨ ★★★★ **12** from Robertson (mostly) & Hemel-en-Aarde grapes. Back on form with plenty of easy, elegant charm, & genuine pinot character. The right amount of structure to support the sweet fruit. **Dry Rosé** Await next, like **No Oak Chardonnay**. — TJ

■ **Ferling Noble** *see* Rooiberg Winery

Fernskloof Wines   ！🎋 ⛺ 📷 🏃

Location: Prince Albert ▪ Map: Klein Karoo & Garden Route ▪ WO: Prince Albert Valley ▪ Est 2009 ▪ 1stB 2010 ▪ Tasting & sales Mon-Fri 9-5 Sat 10-5 Sun by appt 10-5 ▪ Closed Good Fri, Ascension Day & Dec 25 ▪ Facilities for children ▪ BYO picnic ▪ Walks/hikes ▪ 10km mountain running trail ▪ Conservation area ▪ Angeliersbosch guest house (up to 8 guests) ▪ Owner(s) Le Grange family ▪ Cellarmaster(s)/winemaker(s) Diederik le Grange (2010) ▪ Viticulturist(s) Diederik le Grange (2009) ▪ 1,026ha/8ha (cab, merlot, ptage, shiraz, chard) ▪ 40t/1,900cs own label 42% red 29% white 29% rosé ▪ BWI, SGS ▪ PO Box 41 Prince Albert 6930 ▪ diederiklg@hotmail.com ▪ www.facebook.com/FernskloofWines ▪ S 33° 16' 23.77" E 022° 10' 55.60" ▪ **T +27 (0)23-541-1702** ▪ F +27 (0)23-541-1702

Describing Fernskloof in the Groot Karoo's Prince Albert Valley as 'an organic boutique winery in an area still relatively new to winemaking', co-owner Diederik le Grange tells us his wines are now available in Gauteng, he's 'stuck out my neck and started participating in wine festivals alongside the "big dogs"', the first fully organic vintages are in bottle, and a mountain running trail is open on the farm.

> **Cabernet Sauvignon** ☺ ★★★ Now bottled, older oak brushed **11** is lean but well formed with moderate alcohol, refreshing berry acidity, dry conclusion. Amicable dinner companion now or over year/2.

Pinotage In abeyance, like **Shiraz**. **Red** NEW ★★☆ Merlot (71%) & cab in **11** easy-drinker with dark berry & liquorice highlights. **Pinotage-Shiraz** NEW ★★☆ **11** rounded but brief, coffee-toffee oak & chewy tannins to enjoy with braai meats. **Barrel Fermented Pinotage Rosé** Next awaited. **Chardonnay** ✓ 🏵 ★★★★ Has gained complexity, integration since previewed last time, **12** lightish for chilled summer enjoyment, brief oaking adds slight buttery overlay to apple-lemon refreshment. — GdB,JP

■ **5th Avenue Cold Duck** *see* Cold Duck (5th Avenue)
■ **Finch Mountain** *see* Rooiberg Winery
■ **Find Art Collection** *see* Druk My Niet Wine Estate
■ **Firefly** *see* Stellar Winery

FirstCape Vineyards   🍶

Location: Paarl ▪ Est 2002 ▪ Closed to public ▪ Owner(s) De Wet, Goudini, Aan de Doorns, Badsberg & Stettyn wineries ▪ Winemaker(s) David Smit ▪ WIETA accredited ▪ PO Box 62 Simondium 7670 ▪ david@firstcape.com ▪ www.firstcape.com ▪ **T +27 (0)21-874-8340** ▪ F +27 (0)21-874-8344

Formed in 2002, this joint venture between five Breede Valley cellars and British marketer Brand Phoenix retains its position as the biggest-selling South African brand in the UK wine market overall. All bottling is now done offshore in the UK and Germany. The export-only wines are available as FirstCape (Entry, Limited Release, First Selection, Winemaker's Selection, Sparkling), low-alcohol (5.5%) Café Collection and Discovery Series (including some low-alcohol bottlings).

■ **First Dawn** *see* Nwanedi Estate
■ **First Sighting** *see* Strandveld Wines

Fish Hoek Wines   🍶

Location: Somerset West ▪ Map: Helderberg ▪ WO: Western Cape ▪ Tasting, sales & cellar tours at Flagstone Winery (see entry) ▪ Owner(s) Accolade Wines South Africa ▪ Winemaker(s) Karen Bruwer (Feb 2013) & Bruce Jack (1998) ▪ 50% red 50% white ▪ PO Box 769 Stellenbosch 7599 ▪ flagstone@accolade-wines.com ▪ S 34° 5' 26.38" E 018° 48' 30.04" ▪ **T +27 (0)21-852-5052** ▪ F +27 (0)21-852-5085

Fish Hoek, an Accolade Wines South Africa's mid-tier brand, continues to find new friends, particularly in Asia where their good value and accessibility are enjoyed. It's hoped the radical new pack design will maintain the upward curve, described by winemaker Bruce Jack as one of the most robust and stable in the group.

Pinotage ☺ 🍴 ★★★ Juicy, friendly quaffer **12** is light-bodied mouthful of black fruit for characterful everyday drinking. **Chenin Blanc** ☺ 🍴 ★★★ Lively **13** tank sample grapefruit & green gooseberries, should settle into reliable everyday drop.

Merlot 🍴 ★★★ Characterful everyday red, **12** with coffee, chocolate & dark plums, all with slightly stalky background. **Shiraz** ✓ 🍴 ★★★★ Cheerful, correct **12** with classic pepper/spice. Sweet-fruited cherry palate makes for cut-above everyday quaffing. **Pinotage Rosé** 🍴 ★★★ **13** sample shows confected strawberries & bubblegum in off-dry summer sipper. **Sauvignon Blanc** 🍴 ★★★ Guava & grapefruit on **13** preview. Snappy acidity, but tad dilute. — CM

■ **Five Climates** see Boland Kelder
■ **Five Generations** see Cederberg Private Cellar
■ **Five's Reserve** see Van Loveren Family Vineyards

Flagstone Winery   🍷 ♿

Location: Somerset West ▪ Map: Helderberg ▪ WO: Western Cape/Breedekloof/Elgin/Cape South Coast/Tulbagh ▪ Est 1998 ▪ 1stB 1999 ▪ Tasting & sales Mon-Fri 10-4 Sat 10-3 ▪ Fee R20, waived on purchase ▪ Closed Dec 25-Jan 2 ▪ Cellar tours by appt ▪ Owner(s) Accolade Wines South Africa ▪ Winemaker(s) Gerhard Swart (Sep 2008) & Bruce Jack (1998), with Gerald Cakijana (Jan 2000) ▪ Viticulturist(s) Chris Keet (consultant) ▪ 70% red 30% white ▪ PO Box 769 Stellenbosch 7599 ▪ flagstone@accolade-wines.com ▪ www.flagstonewines.com ▪ S 34° 5' 26.38" E 018° 48' 30.04" ▪ **T +27 (0)21-852-5052** ▪ F +27 (0)21-852-5085

'Flagstone wines are all about integrity,' says winemaker and founder Bruce Jack of this quality-focused arm of international wine company, Accolade Wines. 'We look for unique terroir in diverse regions and match it to specific varieties. That's the Flagstone way.' And one that is successful both locally and internationally, backed up by Bruce's renowned marketing savvy and creative quirkiness, and consultant Chris Keet's vine savvy. Settled near the Cheetah Outreach project in Somerset West, the winery plans to launch a new wine, sales of which will help support these magnificent creatures. Meanwhile they continue to fund a primary school in Stellenbosch, opening two new classrooms last year and expanding the facilities to accommodate over 200 children.

Flagstone range

★★★★☆ **Music Room Cabernet Sauvignon** Darkly concentrated **10** oozes class & grace, with spiced black plums, dried meat overtones, refreshing acidity & clean tomato-leaf finish. Carries its 15% alcohol lightly. Seamless wine, sure to improve over good few years.

★★★★ **Fiona Pinot Noir** ⊛ 🍴 Previewed **10** sweet, funky aromas with some eucalyptus, well-hung meat & spice. Soft raspberry & red cherry fruit with plenty of spicy oak. Should improve over next 2 years. No **09**.

★★★★☆ **Writer's Block Pinotage** 🍴 Smoky dark-berried notes on well-integrated **11** from Breedekloof vines. Layers of baked meats, cranberries, liquorice & spice all offset by balancing acidity & slightly charry tannins. Poised & assured pinotage.

★★★★ **Dark Horse Shiraz** 🍴 **10** (★★★★★) shows less overt fruit than **09** but packs a powerful yet controlled punch of spice, dark chocolate, cherries & smooth, plushy tannins. Sensuous texture suggests more to come.

★★★★ **Dragon Tree** Enticing **10** Cape Blend of mainly cab with shiraz & pinotage shows biltong notes (coriander & pepper) swathed in dark-berried fruit. Savoury length makes for superior everyday indulgence.

★★★★ **Free Run Sauvignon Blanc** ⊛ 🍴 🎋 2 years in bottle has allowed **11** (★★★★★), last a preview, to open up from **10** with lively herbaceous notes & lime marmalade on the nose. Well-judged acidity, serenely poised & confident rather than strident & brash.

★★★★ **Word of Mouth Viognier** 🍴 Focused & concentrated **12** retains desired elegance & freshness. Spice notes (ginger & coriander) from 40% barrel-fermented portion, hint of cream, apricots & lime cordial tail.

★★★★★ **Treaty Tree Reserve White Blend** 🍴 Following **10**'s success, **11** sauvignon (75%) & semillon presents similar intensity of fruit, elegance of manner & promise of longevity. Naartjies, limes, fresh herbs, beeswax & lanolin combine to form layers of excitement & pleasure.

Longitude ✓ 🍴 ★★★★ Rich & satisfying **12** value-for-money cab, shiraz, malbec blend. Lacks integration of **11** (★★★★) but still a delicious drop. **Noon Gun** ✓ 🍴 ★★★★ **13** tank sample of always-enjoyable unwooded sauvignon, chenin, viognier blend shows tangerines & fresh limes in lively all-day, everyday drink.

Last Word ⏱ 🍷 ★★★☆ Port-style fortified from Tulbagh shiraz, **06** hedonistic, slippery & sweetly delicious.

Time Manner Place range NEW

★★★★☆ **Pinotage** Impressive debut **10** from Breedekloof fruit. Weighty yet elegant aromas of savoury, peppery roasted meat flow into layers of black fruit, some smoke, dark berries & leather on palate. Already integrated 15% alcohol & sturdy tannins, this looks good for another decade.

Stumble Vineyards range

Malbec 🍷 ★★★★ Big-step-up **12** offers pleasing flavours of black stewed fruit, spice, lovely texture & lots of varietal interest. **Merlot** 🍷 ★★★ Coffee notes abound on **12**, allied to chocolate & cherry, with spicy finish. Easy-drinking everyday wine. **Cape Blend** ★★★ **12** blend of pinotage, shiraz & 3 others shows smoky coffee notes & baked fruit. Touch of sugar makes for early-drinking pleasure. **White Pinotage** NEW ★★★ Interesting & unusual conversation-piece **12**, just off-dry with pleasant aniseed twist. **Verdelho** NEW 🍷 ★★★ Rare-in-SA white grape. Light citrus **12** with slightly bitter peach stone overtones.

Poetry range

> **Sauvignon Blanc** ☺ 🍷 ★★★ Improved **12** gives real drinking enjoyment. Nettles & greenpeppers, well-managed acidity, just-dry sugar adds to good palate weight.

Merlot ★★★ Crowd-pleasing **12** melds dark chocolate & black plums with herbaceous grassy hints.

Rustler range

Pinotage 🍷 🖊 ★★★★ Appealing **12** offers real interest & satisfaction. Mixed berries, chewy tannins, leathery/meaty notes. **Chenin Blanc** 🍷 ★★★ Cheery **12** slightly misses mark of previous but offers bright citrus notes & lively acidity. **Sauvignon Blanc** NEW 🍷 **13** tank sample too unformed to rate.

Whispering Jack range

Chardonnay 🍷 ★★★☆ Very accessible & friendly **12** just off-dry, lightly wooded, with flavours of tropical fruit & ripe citrus. — CM

Flat Roof Manor

These are the trendy counterpoint to the more serious Uitkyk Estate offerings. The flat roof in the branding is real - it's on the elegant Georgian manor house at the Uitkyk property outside Stellenbosch.

> **Pinot Grigio** ☺ 🍷 🖊 ★★★ **13** is a semi-dry, beautiful example of what pinot grigio can be. Pleasant gooseberry nuance calls out for outside dining.

Merlot 🍷 🖊 ★★★ With splash malbec, **12** offers mocha, prunes & spices in unpretentious everyday red. **Shiraz-Mourvèdre-Viognier** ✓ 🍷 🖊 ★★★☆ Robust & hearty barbecue pal, **11** is packed with spicy & leathery raspberry fruit. WO W Cape, like Pinot Grigio, rest Stellenbosch. **Pinot Rosé Light** 🍷 🖊 ★★ Mainly pinotage with pinot gris/grigio in **13** low-alcohol, off-dry lunchtime pleaser. **Sauvignon Blanc Light** 🍷 🖊 ★★ Herbal & perfumed guava notes with big acid grip in **13**. Serve chilled. — DB

Fleur du Cap 🍷🍷

Location: Stellenbosch ▪ WO: Western Cape/Stellenbosch ▪ Est 1968 ▪ 1stB 1969 ▪ Tasting, sales & tours at Die Bergkelder Wine Centre (see entry) ▪ Owner(s) Distell ▪ Cellarmaster(s) Andrea Freeborough (Aug 2005) ▪ Winemaker(s) Justin Corrans (Aug 2005, reds) & Pieter Badenhorst (Dec 2006, whites), with Christoff de Wet (Sep 2010) & Sanelisiwe (Praisy) Dlamini (Jan 2011) ▪ Viticulturist(s) Bennie Liebenberg (Apr 2001) ▪ ±17,000t/±290,000cs own label 47% red 53% white ▪ ISO 14001, ISO 9001, BRC, HACCP, IFS ▪ info@ fleurducap.co.za ▪ www.fleurducap.co.za ▪ **T +27 (0)21-809-8025** ▪ F +27 (0)21-887-9081

Distell-owned Die Bergkelder ('Mountain Cellar') has been home to the prestige Fleur du Cap brand since its opening in 1968. Grapes, in significant volumes, are sourced from the far corners of the winelands, offering Andrea Freeborough and her team an enviable choice of components. Die Bergkelder Wine Centre centre in Stellenbosch (see entry), including the labyrinthine cellar burrowed into the Papegaaiberg hillside, offers visitors insights into South Africa's winemaking past. The Unfiltered Collection represents their no-holds-barred efforts to produce the best possible wines, using innovative and artisanal techniques.

Unfiltered Collection

★★★★☆ **Cabernet Sauvignon** 🍾 Seriously conceived & stylishly executed, **11** Stellenbosch-sourced flag bearer delivers noble black fruit, with leafy notes & firm but supple tannin. Quintessential cab, showing potential for graceful ageing.

★★★★ **Merlot** 🍾 Classy, liquorice-scented **11** is smooth & seamless, showing plum pudding dark fruit with rich savoury undertones. Substantial & satisfying. Stellenbosch fruit.

★★★★ **Chardonnay** 🍷 🍾 Elegant classical form of **12** (★★★★★) trumps already fine **11**, allowing lime & chalky notes to subdue hefty oak. Mouth-caressing texture coaxes the palate to lingering finish. Robertson & Stellenbosch fruit.

★★★★☆ **Sauvignon Blanc Limited Release** Strikingly direct, unmistakably Darling, **13** showpiece delivers emphatic varietal punch. Finely balanced, with poise, power & length, ticks all the boxes.

★★★★ **Semillon** 🍷 🍾 Steely minerality of Agulhas fruit dominates **12**, with stony-dusty notes mingled with aromatic lanolin & anise. Solid, confident fruit copes easily with barrel-ageing (older oak).

★★★★ **Viognier** 🍷 🍾 Typical brisk peach fruit on **12**, ex Agulhas vines still masked by oak spices. Rich & leesy, showing charm of natural winemaking techniques. Needs time in glass to open fully.

★★★★ **Sauvignon Blanc-Chardonnay-Semillon-Viognier** NEW 🍷 🍾 Intriguing oak-matured blend joins elite range of varietal bottlings, offering forthright glimpses of components, but still harmonising in bold, complex **12** debut.

Fleur du Cap Bergkelder Selection

★★★★☆ **Laszlo** 🍇 Signature blend a homage to legendary cellarmaster Dr Julius Laszlo. Powerful Bordeaux quartet: merlot, cab, petit verdot, malbec. **08** (★★★★★) judiciously oaked, has layers of rich black & blueberry fruit on lattice of fine, powdery tannins. Complex, strikingly elegant. No **07**. **06** 18% shiraz & less oak.

★★★★★ **Noble Late Harvest** 🍾 Rich & unctuous, with aristocratic bearing, mostly chenin, unwooded super-sweet dessert wine has a lofty track record to follow. Intense & lingering, with piercing acidity to balance sugar, **12** maintains standard after brilliant **11** (& **10**, **09**, **08**, **07**, **06**).

Cabernet Sauvignon 🍾 ★★★ **11** from Stellenbosch vines is plummy, generous & appealing. Good honest red for early drinking. **Merlot** 🍾 ★★★ Unpretentious **11** shows green leaf, minty notes over light red-berry fruit, spiced with oak vanilla. **Pinotage** 🍾 ★★★ Spicy sweet cranberry juice on **11**, with smoky oak, chewy tannins. **Shiraz** 🍾 ★★★ **11**, ex Stellenbosch, Agulhas vines shows smoky meat aromas with satisfying plum pudding fruitiness on middleweight structure. **Chardonnay** 🍷 🍾 ★★★ Oaky & predictable, **12** loses fruit definition to overt spiciness. **Chenin Blanc** ✓ 🍷 🍾 ★★★★ Appealingly familiar varietal definition on **13** from Darling & Elgin fruit. Touch of oak flavours ripe tropical fruit. **Sauvignon Blanc** 🍷 🍾 ★★★ Competently structured **13** offers plenty of upfront aromatic appeal, with fresh, crisp acid zing. **Natural Light** 🍾 ★★ Off-dry **13**, chenin-based low alcohol, fruity easy-sipper. — GdB

Flight of the Fish Eagle   NEW

Named after one of Africa's best-loved raptors (for its evocative call), this Distell brandy is, says brand manager Simphiwe Pato, 'perfect for first-time brandy drinkers'. A significant ad and events campaign pitches it at South Africa's young high flyers, particularly the emerging black market.

★★★★ **Natural Brandy** Pale gold colour belies the intense red berry fruit, orange, honey; delicate traces almond & vanilla. Refined, with a long finish. Modern style; 100% potstill from chenin & colombard. — WB, TJ

■ **Flutterby** see Boland Kelder
■ **Foodbarn** see Cape Point Vineyards

Foothills Vineyards   🍷 ☕ ⛰ 📷 NEW

Location/WO: Stellenbosch ▪ Map: Helderberg ▪ Est 2008 ▪ 1stB 2012 ▪ Tasting & sales by appt ▪ Fee R25 ▪ Meals/refreshments by appt ▪ Olive oil ▪ Conferences ▪ Luxury guesthouse (B&B) ▪ Owner(s) Glenn Hesse & Jim Featherby ▪ Winemaker(s) Neil Moorhouse (consultant) ▪ Viticulturist(s) Bennie Booysen (consultant) ▪ 9ha/19ha (shiraz, sauv, sem, viog) ▪ 4,000cs own label 15% red 80% white 5% rosé ▪ IPW ▪ PO Box 647 Somerset Mall 7137 ▪ steve@foothillsvineyards.co.za ▪ www.kleinwelmoed.co.za, www.foothillsvineyards. co.za ▪ S 34° 0' 58.86" E 018° 47' 43.08" ▪ **T +27 (0)21-842-0045** ▪ F +27 (0)21-842-2775

Owners Glenn Hesse and Tim Featherby have established a boutique winery and luxury guesthouse on previously rundown Klein Welmoed farm in the Helderberg foothills. 'The area is historically known to produce great wines,' they point out, determined to do the same by engaging consultants Nei Moorhouse and Bennie Booysen to take care of the winegrowing while the rest of the 'dedicated and passionate' team grows the brand at home and abroad.

The Partners ☺ 🍴 ◻ ★★★ Sauvignon (70%) with dollops semillon & viognier in food-styled **13** preview, good vinosity & weight from 6 months lees-ageing.

Syrah 🍴 ◻ ★★★ White pepper & violet nuanced **12** tank sample still tight, needs time to fully reveal underlying minerality. Very young vines show potential. **Dry Rosé** 🍴 ◻ ★★★ Mainly shiraz, dash viognier **13** ex tank delicate, bone-dry strawberries & cherries for Mediterranean food partnering. **Sauvignon Blanc** 🍴 ◻ ★★★ Pre-bottling, **13** cool fig & nettle notes, zesty & commendably dry but tad brief. — DC,CvZ

■ **Foot of Africa** *see* Kleine Zalze Wines
■ **Footprint** *see* African Pride Wines
■ **Forresters** *see* Ken Forrester Wines
■ **Fortress Hill** *see* Fort Simon Wine Estate

Fort Simon Wine Estate

Location/map/WO: Stellenbosch ▪ Est 1997 ▪ 1stB 1998 ▪ Tasting & sales Mon-Fri 9.30–5 Sat 10–2 ▪ Fee R20, 5wines ▪ Closed all pub hols ▪ Cellar tours by appt ▪ Cheese platters ▪ Farm produce ▪ Venue for after-hours functions/weddings & conferences (120 guests) ▪ Owner(s) Renier, Petrus & Michéle Uys ▪ Winemaker(s) Stander Maass (Sep 2006) ▪ Viticulturist(s) Renier Uys ▪ 80ha (cabs s/f, malbec, merlot, p verdot, ptage, shiraz, chard, chenin, sauv, viog) ▪ 800t/80,000cs own label 60% red 30% white 10% rosé ▪ PO Box 43 Sanlamhof 7532 ▪ accounts@fortsimon.com ▪ www.fortsimon.co.za ▪ S 33° 55' 9.5" E 018° 45' 19.4" ▪ **T +27 (0)21 906-0304** ▪ F +27 (0)21-903-8034

Forts are usually intended to repel or intimidate strangers but not at this Bottelary Hills cellar modelled on the magnificently eccentric Duwisib Castle in Namibia. The Uys family added a functions and wedding venue to attract more visitors to their late father Simon's crenellated creation.

Platinum Collection

★★★★ **Viognier** Vibrant & alive **12** (★★★) has ample nectarine & peach, with light nuttiness on dry finish but shade less impressive than **09**.

★★★★ **Viognier Noble Late Harvest** 🅢 ◻ Older-oak-fermented **10** matches intensity of last-tasted **07**. Concentrated but still light on its feet. Long, appealing finish & peach brûlée aftertaste. 375ml.

Fort Simon Estate range

★★★★ **Chenin Blanc** ◻ Peardrop & apricot vie with lime zest on vibrant, focused **12**. Fresh & lively, light oak sheen adding creamy length. Follows rich & concentrated **10**.

★★★★ **Sauvignon Blanc** 🅢 ◻ Lemon curd & grass on lively pre-bottling sample of **12** (★★★★). Fresh, zesty & rounded though acidity not as smooth as **10**.

Cabernet Sauvignon 🅢 ★★★★ Tad off well-structured **07** (★★★★), **08** offers rich black fruit & vanilla flavours. **Merlot** ★★★★ Textured, seamless fruitcake generosity typical of the grape on **11**. Spicy & delicious to light, easy finish. **Pinotage** ★★★☆ Cocoa depth to ripe blackberry on **09**. Medium bodied but softly textured with a rich, long finish. **Shiraz** ★★★★ Easy plum affability to **09**, reminiscent of **08**. Uncomplicated with soft texture throughout. Succulent but short. **Rosé** 🅢 ★★★ Previewed from tank, **11** oozes pinotage ripe strawberries. Easy dry summer sipper. **Chardonnay** Next awaited.

Fortress Hill range

Merlot ★★★★ **11** ramps up a notch with pillowy cocoa & fruitcake appeal. Crowd-pleasing texture, length & lightness. **Shiraz** 🅢 ★★★ Savoury leather & spice on **09** uncomplicated easy-drinker, black berries in abundance, gentle mouthfeel. **Sauvignon Blanc** 🅢 ★★★ Preview of **12** tangy & vibrant with lime zest pungency. Mouthfilling & juicy, lipsmackingly high acidity. — FM

■ **Fountain Crossing** *see* Darling Cellars
■ **Four Cousins** *see* Van Loveren Family Vineyards

Four Fields Vineyards

Location/WO: Durbanville ▪ Est/1st B 2004 ▪ Closed to public ▪ Sales mainly via Wine Concepts, Cape Town ▪ Owner(s) 8 shareholders ▪ Cellarmaster(s)/winemaker(s) Chris Kühn (Sep 2004) ▪ 5t 100% red ▪ 49 Arabella Drive Augusta Place Sunningdale 7441 ▪ dockuhn@gmail.com ▪ **T** +27 **(0)**83-929-9199

Rising costs have caused Chris Kuhn to mothball his micro cellar and tasting venue in Durbanville, but the retired insurance man intends to continue his life-long love of wine by vinifying in rented premises. Meanwhile his new step-up Bordeaux red is available from Wine Concepts, Cape Town, and selected outlets.

Cabernet Sauvignon-Cabernet Franc ✓ ★★★★ Improved **09** shows supple black fruit with commend-able spicy complexity. Hint of earthiness & sour cherry on finish. **Chardonnay** ⊕ 📖 ★ Barrel-aged **08** had overt oak patina when last tasted. — GdB

4G Wines

Location: Stellenbosch ▪ Est 2009 ▪ 1stB 2010 ▪ Closed to public ▪ Owner(s) Private shareholders ▪ Winemaker(s) Mia Fischer, Giorgio Dalla Cia, Denis Dubourdieu, Valérie Lavigne, with Annalie van Dyk ▪ 20t ▪ own label 100% red ▪ Other export brands: G, The Echo of G ▪ info@4g-wines.com ▪ www.4g-wines.com

Based near Stellenbosch, and sourcing from a variety of carefully selected sites, 4G Wines is all about building a South African 'first growth', says director Philipp Axt, adding that this is not about flattering shareholders' or customers' egos. 'Our ambition is rather to create a delicate, delicious and inimitable wine [by] combining European winemaking expertise, craftsmanship and innovative tech-nologies with South Africa's outstanding natural assets and winemaking skills.' To this end, French consultants Denis Dubourdieu and Valérie Lavigne are on board, along with Giorgio Dalla Cia, creator of the iconic Meerlust Rubicon.

Four Paws Wines

Location/map: Franschhoek ▪ WO: Franschhoek/Western Cape/Piekenierskloof ▪ Est 2005 ▪ 1stB 2006 ▪ Tast-ing by appt at La Vigne, Robertsvlei Road, Franschhoek (contact Anne +27 (0)83-447-1376/Gerda +27 (0)82-375-0524) ▪ Owner(s) Rob Meihuizen, Gerda Willers & Anne Jakubiec ▪ Winemaker(s) Gerda Willers (2005) ▪ Viticulturist(s) Gerda Willers ▪ 60t/12,000cs own label 70% red 30% white ▪ PO Box 69 Simondium 7670 ▪ anne@southerntrade.co.za ▪ www.fourpawswines.com ▪ S 33° 53' 28.0" E 019° 5' 0.5" ▪ **T** +27 **(0)**21-874-1033 ▪ F +27 (0)21-874-2110

A trio of cat lovers with day jobs in the wine trade established Four Paws Wines in 2006 to offer value-for-money wines for those who drink what they like (not what they're told). 'Authentic, small, warm and personal' is their approach, and they think Picatso is, um, the cat's whiskers for winning a Michelangelo trophy.

★★★★ **Picatso** ⊕ Feline theme given cubist edge. **11** naturally dried viognier 8 months in seasoned oak; voluptuous, luxurious & moreish. Pity, only 560L in 375ml format.

Pinotage Next awaited, like **Chardonnay. Pablo** ✓ 📖 ★★★★ Ripe-fruited vintage blend is 50% shiraz (with 4 Rhône/Bordeaux reds) in **11**. Smooth & svelte - like Pablo, a Brown Point Siamese. Piekenierskloof & Franschhoek vines. **Sauvignon Blanc** 📖 ★★★ Piekenierskloof fruit for **12**, uncharacteristically subdued citrus hints fused with tropical fruit, might gain verve with time. **Calico** ⊕ 📖 ★★★ Retasted last edition, **11** a fruit cup of flavours driven by chenin & semillon, ended bone-dry. WO Franschhoek. — GM

Four Secrets `NEW`

The 'mystery' behind this Stellenbosch Vineyards brand is that the wines are blends sourced over four vintages from the same vineyards in the Helderberg.

Shiraz 📖 ★★★ Attractive sweet rum-&-raisin aromas, contrasting firm tannins & bold flavours in block-buster **NV** tank sample. **Sparkling Shiraz** 📖 ★★★ Among tiny handful of shiraz sparklers in SA. Characterful carbonated **NV** has firm, ever so slightly sweet lavender & blackberry bubbles. Try with smoked salmon, say winemakers. — CvZ

4th Street

'Unashamedly uncomplicated, easy-drinking and flirtatious' is Distell's slogan for these budget-priced low-alcohol Natural Sweet wines.

Natural Sweet Red 🍷 ★★ Unchallenging **NV** full of raisiny sweetness, countered by a hint of dry tannin. **Natural Sweet Rosé** 🍷 ★★ Light & frivolous **NV** with ripe but fresh berry taste. **Natural Sweet White** 🍷 ★★★ Floral **NV**'s grapey flavours well balanced by crisp acidity. — DB, HJ

■ **Fowl Play** *see* TCB Wines

Fraai Uitzicht 1798

Location/map: Robertson ▪ WO: Klaasvoogds ▪ 1stB 2000 ▪ Tasting & sales daily 10-6 ▪ Closed Easter Fri/Sun, Dec 25/31 & Jan 1 ▪ Restaurant (see Restaurants section) ▪ 4-star guesthouse (see Accommodation section) ▪ Owner(s) Karl Uwe Papesch ▪ Winemaker(s) Karl Uwe Papesch (2005) ▪ Viticulturist(s) Michael Marson ▪ 175ha/13ha (grenache, merlot, mourv, shiraz, viog) ▪ 1,000cs own label 100% red ▪ PO Box 97 Robertson 6705 ▪ info@fraaiuitzicht.com ▪ www.fraaiuitzicht.com ▪ S 33° 47' 43.0" E 020° 0' 18.2" ▪ **T +27 (0)23-626-6156** ▪ F +27 (0)86-662-5265

This historic cellar, one of the oldest in Robertson Valley, is best known for its handcrafted Merlot. But winemaker Karl Uwe Papesch is delighted that his maiden Syrah has been 'very well received' as he continues working towards a Rhône-style blend from the 'sunny vineyards' of the Klaasvoogds wine ward.

Merlot ⓘ ★★★ Perfumed **10** seriously styled, smooth tannins & dark cherry fruit for elegant enjoyment. **Prima** ⓘ ★★★★ 100% merlot aged 2 years in French oak. Generous **08** fresh & balanced, satisfying. **Syrah** [NEW] ★★★ Soft & pliable **11** hint milk chocolate on plum/prune base; charming rainy day companion. — JP,DB

Francois La Garde

Location/map: Stellenbosch ▪ WO: Franschhoek ▪ Est 2004 ▪ Tasting by appt ▪ Owner(s) PL Matthée ▪ Cellarmaster(s)/winemaker(s) Piet Matthée (Jan 2009) ▪ 15t/2,000cs own label 100% white ▪ PO Box 12366 Die Boord 7613 ▪ admin@technofill.co.za ▪ www.francois-lagarde.co.za ▪ **T +27 (0)21-887-3674** ▪ F +27 (0)21-887-5274

Bubbly lover Piet Matthée says he's fulfilling the dream of an ancestor (after whom this specialist label is named) to make champagne-method wine. And he's responding to his own passion too, while he also runs a specialist bottling and labelling company. Vinification is carried out at Zorgvliet in Stellenbosch.

String of Pearls range

★★★★ **Brut Méthode Cap Classique** Faintly smoky biscuity aromas on classic **08** bubbly from pinot noir & chardonnay, with long ageing on lees. Baked apple, clove & bready notes. Elegant, markedly dry & restrained. **Reinette Rosé MCC** ⓘ ★★★ Coppery salmon pink **08** dry bubbly from mourvèdre, with a fine mousse but slightly dank, smoky notes, finishing fresh & limy. **Blanc de Blancs** Await next. — MF

Franki's Vineyards

Location: Malmesbury ▪ Map/WO: Swartland ▪ Est 2004 ▪ 1stB 2007 ▪ Tasting, sales & cellar tours by appt Mon-Fri 8-5 ▪ Closed all pub hols ▪ Meals by arrangement ▪ Tour groups ▪ BYO picnic ▪ Conferences ▪ Walks/hikes ▪ Conservation area ▪ Classic car museum ▪ Franki's Guest Lodge (10 bedrooms) & Solitude @ Franki's B&B (4 bedrooms) ▪ Owner(s) Franco Afrique Technologies (Pty) Ltd ▪ Winemaker(s) Erica Joubert (Jan 2004), with Nicci Hanekom (Jan 2004) ▪ 700ha/22ha (grenache, mourv, viog) ▪ 174t/450cs own label 100% red ▪ PO Box 972 Malmesbury 7299 ▪ erica.joubert@cropspec.co.za ▪ www.frankisvineyards.co.za ▪ S 33° 20' 59.5" E 018° 32' 12.4" ▪ **T +27 (0)22-482-2837/+27 (0)82-888-3702** ▪ F +27 (0)86-660-3677

Founded ten years ago, Franki's produces only 12 barrels a year from their grenache, mourvèdre and viognier vines, says Erica Joubert, winemaker since inception. 'Old school meets new techniques' and 'natural ferments with an open mind' are her guiding principles.

Barn Find range

Grenache 🌿 ★★★ Naturally fermented (as is blend) **12** pale ruby in colour, opens to reveal spice & understated black cherry flavours. **Joubert Red Blend** 🌿 ★★★★ Mourvèdre (75%) with grenache, older oak matured. Dusty hay & savoury dark prunes on notch-up **12**, pleasantly dry food wine. Only 250 cases. — DB

Franschhoek Cellar

Location/map: Franschhoek ▪ WO: Western Cape/Franschhoek/Coastal ▪ Est 1945 ▪ Tasting & sales Mon-Fri 9.30-5 (Apr-Sep) & 10-6 (Oct-Mar) Sat 10-3 Sun 11-4 ▪ Wine tasting, 6 wines with 6 cheeses, 6 wines with assorted chocolates ▪ Closed Good Fri, May 1, Jun 16 & Dec 25 ▪ Cheese lunch daily during tasting hours ▪ BYO picnic ▪ Farm produce ▪ Owner(s) DGB (Pty) Ltd ▪ Winemaker(s) Richard Duckitt (Dec 2005) ▪ Viticulturist(s) Stephan Joubert (Nov 2006) ▪ 300ha (cab, merlot, shiraz, chard, chenin, sauv, sem) ▪ 30,000t 49% red 50% white 1% rosé ▪ ISO 9001:2001, IPW, IPW ▪ PO Box 52 Franschhoek 7690 ▪ fhcellardoor@dgb.co.za ▪ www.franschhoek-cellar.co.za ▪ S 33° 54' 16.4" E 019° 6' 40.7" ▪ **T +27 (0)21-876-2086** ▪ F +27 (0)21-876-4107

Picturesque Franschhoek is steeped in history, dating back to its French Hugue-not founders in the 1680s. Various landmarks around the area honour the pio-neers and the village's rich cultural heritage. Franschhoek Cellar shows its loyalty and support by naming the wines under The Village Walk range after some of these historic locations and using mostly locally sourced grapes.

Franschhoek Vineyards range

Shiraz ⏻ 🍴 ▥ ★★★★ Last edition **10** was very good but introverted, needed time for tight core of pep-pery fruit to unfurl. **Semillon** 🍴 ▥ ★★★ Part natural ferment in 10% new oak for **12**, slightly less sumptu-ous than **11** (★★★★), offers subdued lemongrass tones, enlivening lemon acidity. WO Franschhoek.

The Village Walk range

Old Museum Merlot ☺ 🍴 ▥ ★★★ Sugared plums & chocolate notes on fruity, supple **11**, now bot-tled & a real crowd pleaser, with lingering farewell. **Stone Bridge Pinotage** ☺ 🍴 ▥ ★★★ Friendly **11** fresh bread aroma, supple plum & mulberry fruit, good dry finish. Perfect solo or with spicy lamb.

The Churchyard Cabernet Sauvignon 🍴 ▥ ★★★ Lovely deep hue, familiar varietal aromas of cassis & tobacco, & firm but amenable tannins on **11**, a preview last time. **Baker Station Shiraz** 🍴 ▥ ★★☆ Now bottled, savoury **11**'s liquorice & olive tapenade flavours checked by strong tannins. For hearty stews, not for keeping. **Clubhouse Rosé** 🍴 ▥ ★★★ Strawberries-&-cream **12**, just off-dry & good match for smoked meat platters. WO Coastal. **Our Town Hall Chardonnay** 🍴 ▥ Preview of unwooded **13** too young to rate. Engaging pear & orange aromas, zingy lemon flavours promise well. **La Cotte Mill Chenin Blanc** 🍴 ▥ ★★★★ Previewed **13**'s thatch & floral notes still cloaked with fermentation character mid-2013 but crisp & crunchy apple fruit, lively balance, pithy texture bode well. **Statue de Femme Sauvignon Blanc** 🍴 ▥ ★★★ Effusive fruit plus hint earthiness on tank sample **13**; balanced & long, with brisk acidity. — CvZ

Freedom Hill Wines

Location: Paarl ▪ Map: Paarl & Wellington ▪ WO: Paarl/Stellenbosch ▪ Est 1997 ▪ 1stB 2000 ▪ Tasting Mon-Fri 10.30-5 Sat/Sun 12-3 Sun by appt in winter ▪ Closed Easter Fri/Sun & Dec 25 ▪ Wedding & function venue ▪ Owner(s) Francois Klomp ▪ Cellarmaster(s)/winemaker(s) Kowie du Toit (Feb 2007) ▪ Viticulturist(s) Paul Wallace & Bruce Mcreadie ▪ 82ha/19ha (cab, pinotage, shiraz) ▪ ±70t/12,000cs own label 100% red ▪ PO Box 6126 Paarl 7620 ▪ info@freedomhill.co.za, chanine@freedomhill.co.za ▪ www.freedomhill.co.za ▪ S 33° 49' 48.33" E 019° 0' 35.90" ▪ **T +27 (0)21-867-0085** ▪ F +27 (0)86-244-9748

New growth at this southern Paarl winery overlooking the former Victor Verster Prison (now Drakenstein) from where Nelson Mandela took his first free steps after years of incarceration. Owner Francois Klomp's daughter Chanine is ring-ing in the changes, revamping the gardens, turning the restaurant into a wed-ding and function venue while also handling management and marketing.

Freedom Hill range

Pinotage Cellar Selection ▥ ★★★ Was just 'Pinotage'. Spicy oak frames generous raspberry succulence on **12**. A cheery quaffer. **Shiraz Cellar Selection** ★★★☆ Now bottled & renamed (from just 'Shiraz'), **10** is nicely chunky with oodles of spices. Medium bodied, lightly tannic from 20% new oak. **Cape Blend** ▥ ★★★ Tobacco leaf & cedar liven this **12** mix of cab & pinotage. Spicy grip to light-bodied palate. **Shiraz-Cabernet Sauvignon** ⏻ ▥ ★★★ Two-third shiraz edges cab in **10** blend. Black cherry simplicity cloaked in oak veneer. Uncomplicated easy-drinker. **Chardonnay** ⏻ ▥ ★★★ Toasty, buttery peaches & cream on oaked **10** from Stellenbosch grapes. Poised & rounded, with good length & harmony. **Chenin Blanc** Next awaited, as for **Sauvignon Blanc**.

Freedom Walk 1335/88 range

Pinotage ⊕ ⊘ ★★★ Savoury **10** displays smoky, meaty edge on light tarry body. **Shiraz** ⊕ ★★★ Liquorice & cocoa depth to juicy black fruit, **10** straightforward but ripe & approachable. **Cape Blend** ⊕ ★★★ Cab/pinotage **09** will appeal to fans of oak, its fragrance & spice pervades the chalky blackcurrant. — FM

■ **Freedom Walk** *see* Freedom Hill Wines
■ **French Connection** *see* Lynx Wines
■ **Fridham Gaard** *see* Migliarina Wines
■ **Friesland** *see* Kaapzicht Wine Estate
■ **Frisky Zebras** *see* United Nations of Wine
■ **Frog Hill** *see* Anura Vineyards
■ **Frogner** *see* Nordic Wines
■ **Frost Vineyards** *see* David Frost Wines

Fryer's Cove Vineyards

Location: Doring Bay ▪ Map: Olifants River ▪ WO: Bamboes Bay/Western Cape ▪ Est 1999 ▪ 1stB 2002 ▪ Tasting, sales & cellar tours Mon-Fri 8-5 Sat 10-5 ▪ Fee R5 ▪ Closed Christian hols ▪ Pre-booked cheese platters & picnics; or BYO picnic ▪ Restaurant ▪ Farm produce ▪ West Coast walking trail ▪ Owner(s) Jan Ponk Trust, JH Laubscher Family Trust & Wynand Hamman ▪ Cellarmaster(s) Wynand Hamman (Apr 1999) ▪ Viticulturist(s) Jan van Zyl (Apr 1999) ▪ 10ha/6ha (pinot, sauv) ▪ 50t/6,000cs own label 20% red 80% white ▪ PO Box 93 Vredendal 8160 ▪ janponk1@kingsley.co.za, fryerscove@mylan.co.za ▪ www.fryerscove.co.za ▪ S 31° 45′ 53.1″ E 018° 13′ 55.8″ ▪ **T +27 (0)27-213-2312 (office)/+27 (0)27-215-1092 (tasting)** ▪ F +27 (0)27-213-2212

The realisation of viticulturist Jan 'Ponk' van Zyl and brother-in-law winemaker Wynand Hamman's dream – a green-as-it-gets ocean-cooled winery with maritime vineyards a mere 600 m from the Atlantic shoreline – is one they are sharing with the people of West Coast fishing village Doring Bay. 'They are proud to send tourists to "their" winery,' says marketer Alberta van der Mescht, and equally pleased to recommend the delicious seafood from the winery's on-site kitchen, run in conjunction with the local community. Visitors can also taste the maiden shiraz, made from bought-in grapes and available only from the cellardoor.

★★★★☆ **Bamboes Bay Sauvignon Blanc** ✓ 🍴 Consistently impressive wine adds 'Bamboes Bay' to its name. Both **13** & **12** (★★★★) tasted, both showing pedigree with typical passionfruit & blackcurrant, 'oystershell' minerality, **12** perhaps not as convincingly. Both shade off standout **11** (★★★★★).

★★★★ **Bay To Bay Sauvignon Blanc** 🍴 Satisfying weight, lengthy farewell on extremely herbaceous **12** (★★★☆). Some Lutzville Valley grapes versus Lamberts Bay's less pyrotechnic contribution to **11**.

The Jetty Sauvignon Blanc NEW ☺ 🍴 ★★★ Green asparagus, pea & fig on just off-dry **12** from own vineyards. Delicious now but no rush - winemaker believes it shows better with some bottle-age.

Pinot Noir Await next. — HJ, CvZ

■ **Fugue** *see* Anatu Wines
■ **Fynbos** *see* Beau Belle

Gabriëlskloof

Location/WO: Bot River ▪ Map: Elgin, Walker Bay & Bot River ▪ Est 2002 ▪ 1stB 2007 ▪ Tasting & sales Mon-Fri 9-5 Sat 11-3 ▪ Fee R15, waived on purchase ▪ Closed Dec 24/25 ▪ Cellar tours by appt ▪ Restaurant (see Restaurants section) ▪ Deli ▪ Child-friendly; dogs welcome ▪ Weddings (very limited availability) ▪ Annual market (Dec 14-15) ▪ Owner(s) Bernhard Heyns & shareholders Johan Heyns, Barry Anderson & Wally Clarke ▪ Winemaker(s) Kobie Viljoen (Jun 2008), with Christiaan van der Merwe (Jan 2011) ▪ Viticulturist(s) Barry Anderson (2001) ▪ 150ha/68ha (cabs s/f, malbec, merlot, mourv, p verdot, pinot, shiraz, sauv, sem, viog) ▪ BWI ▪ PO Box 499 Kleinmond 7195 ▪ info@gabrielskloof.co.za ▪ www.gabrielskloof.co.za ▪ S 34° 14′ 19.89″ ▪ **T +27 (0)28-284-9865** ▪ F +27 (0)28-284-9864

The revitalisation of what was a neglected sheep and wheat farm before it was rescued in 2002 by Bernhard Heyns and partners continues apace. The social upliftment focus of its staff includes educational workshops, like one on personal finances, and loyal farm and cellar personnel are being rewarded with purpose-built houses in nearby Bot River. On the sales front, Gabriëlskloof wines have been exported to China for the first time.

Reserve range

★★★★ **Swartriver Shiraz** Back on track after 09 (★★★☆), showing spicy dark fruit layers, streamlined **10** has peppery dryness, ideal for rich food, game dishes. Shows more than a nod to the Old World.

★★★★☆ **Five Arches** Flagship 5-part Bordeaux red blend. Intriguing juxtaposition of savoury tones with fruit ripeness in **10**, black plums & graphite, pepper grindings, with a polished smoothness, harmonious tannins. There's a long future ahead, all of it good.

★★★★ **Viognier** 🖉 Tamed version of the variety, thanks to earlier picking, oak treatment. **12** has gentle peach pip flavours, crushed almonds, a delicious tangy edge giving elegant vibrancy, length.

★★★★ **Magdalena** 🖉 Wooded semillon/sauvignon blend. **12** is carefully made to showcase leafy citrus-toned fruit, a savoury biscuit overlay & lovely zesty elegance. Promises food compatibility.

Premium range

Shiraz ✓ ★★★☆ Dabs mourvèdre, viognier, **11**'s plush dark tones have a creamy, peppery richness, with enough backbone for ageing. **The Blend** ★★★☆ Similar blend to Five Arches, half the oaking, **11** has Xmas cake richness, is supple, smooth & harmonious, finishing dry. **Rosebud** 🗃 🖉 ★★★ Back in guide after a break, viognier/shiraz rosé, aromatic **13** has off-dry red berry flavours. **Sauvignon Blanc** 🗃 🖉 ★★★★ Lemongrass & gooseberries on taut **13** tank sample, bursting with freshness, pure, clean & bone dry. — CR

Galleon Wines

Location/WO: Durbanville ▪ Est 2003 ▪ 1stB 2004 ▪ Tasting by appt at Diemersdal ▪ Owner(s) BK Investments/Andries Brink Trust/Thys Louw ▪ Winemaker(s) Thys Louw & Mari Branders ▪ Viticulturist(s) Div van Niekerk ▪ 1,700cs own label 50% red 50% white ▪ PO Box 62 Durbanville 7551 ▪ info@galleonwines.co.za ▪ www.galleonwines.co.za ▪ T +27 (0)21-976-8129 ▪ F +27 (0)86-664-4202

Diemersdal's winemaker Thys Louw is intimately involved in this Durbanville boutique label; the estate provides it with grapes, cellar facilities and tasting room. The wallet-friendly wines engender conviviality no matter the occasion. A legacy the remaining partners are determined to build on to honour founder, retired cardiologist Andries Brink, who passed away in 2012.

Cabernet Sauvignon ⓣ ★★★ 09's subtle oaking supports ripe mulberry aromas & savoury overlay. **Shiraz** Await next, as for **Chardonnay**. **Sauvignon Blanc** 🗃 ★★★ Honeyed bottle-age adds to appeal of herbal & tropical **12**, reined-in acidity for softer glassful. **Isaac Pinotage** NEW 🖉 ★★★ Appealing mix of modern 'mocha' oak styling & traditional plum fruit; **11** delicious in & with hearty lamb or oxtail stews. Discontinued: **Cabernet Sauvignon Reserve**. — CvZ

Garden Route Wines

🍷 ♿

Location: Calitzdorp ▪ Map: Klein Karoo & Garden Route ▪ WO: Outeniqua ▪ Est/1stB 2008 ▪ Tasting & sales at De Krans (see entry) ▪ Wines also available at Outeniqua Wine Emporium, Waboomskraal on N12 between George & Oudtshoorn ▪ Owner(s) Boets Nel ▪ Cellarmaster(s) Boets Nel (2008) ▪ Viticulturist(s) Jean Fourie (Jan 2011) ▪ 9ha (shiraz, chard, sauv) ▪ 80t/±3,000cs own label 40% red 60% white ▪ PO Box 28 Calitzdorp 6660 ▪ dekrans@mweb.co.za ▪ S 33° 32' 6.3" E 021° 41' 9.0" ▪ T +27 (0)44-213-3314/+27 (0)23-541-1702 ▪ F +27 (0)44-213-3562/+27 (0)23-541-1702

Inland De Krans' champion port maker Boets Nel revels in working with grapes from a small mountain vineyard in the Outeniqua wine ward on the Cape south coast's famed Garden Route. The 'outstanding cool climate' slow-ripens whites mid-March and shiraz mid-April for 'terroir-specific wines' (available at De Krans and Outeniqua Wine Emporium on the N12).

Shiraz 🗃 🖉 ★★★★ **12** shows cool origin in restrained pepper & tealeaf bouquet, light red-fruit palate. Refreshing & refined solo sipper or dinner companion. **Sauvignon Blanc** ✓ 🗃 🖉 ★★★★ **13** less fruity than **12** (★★★☆), shows more balance, wet pebble minerality & rapier acidity extend the finish. Should improve in bottle but we doubt it'll get the chance! — HJ,CvZ

■ **Gecko Ridge** *see Long Mountain Wine Company*

Genevieve Méthode Cap Classique

Location: Elgin ▪ WO: Overberg ▪ Est 2009 ▪ 1stB 2008 ▪ Tasting by appt ▪ Owner(s) Melissa Nelsen ▪ Viticulturist(s) Leon Engelke (2008) ▪ 16t/1,650cs own label 100% MCC ▪ PO Box 122 Elgin 7180 ▪ melissa@genevievemcc.co.za ▪ www.genevievemcc.co.za ▪ **T +27 (0)83-302-6562**

Melissa Genevieve Nelsen's bubbly inspiration comes from her grandmother who was inclined to broach a bottle no matter how minor the occasion. Based in Elgin, Melissa's grapes come from near Bot River and are vinified in Paarl.

★★★★ **Genevieve** ⊛ Debut **10** sparkling from chardonnay is fruit driven, as expected from blanc de blancs, the small oak-fermented portion almost invisible among crisp, bright appley bubbles. — HJ,JP

- ◼ **Ghost Corner** see Cederberg Private Cellar
- ◼ **Giant Periwinkle** see The Giant Periwinkle
- ◼ **Giant's Peak** see Wine-of-the-Month Club

Gilga Wines

Location/map: Stellenbosch ▪ WO: Western Cape ▪ Est/1stB 2002 ▪ Tasting & sales by appt ▪ Owner(s) John Rowan ▪ Cellarmaster(s)/viticulturist(s) Stefan Gerber (Jun 2010, consultant) ▪ Winemaker(s) Stefan Gerber (Jun 2010, consultant), with Marco Benjamin (Dec 2010, consultant) ▪ 4ha/3.5ha (grenache, mourv, shiraz, tempranillo) ▪ 10t/1,100cs own label 100% red ▪ PO Box 871 Stellenbosch 7599 ▪ info@gilga.co.za, stefan@boerandbrit.com ▪ www.gilga.co.za ▪ S 33° 56' 46.1" E 018° 47' 20.6" ▪ **T +27 (0)84-515-6677** ▪ F +27 (0)86-531-7137

Gilga is named after the courtesan always overlooked by King Amurabi until she accidentally discovered wine. Consultant winemaker Stefan Gerber, also involved at Boer & Brit, announces a new white blend, Zagros, and the return of red blend Amurabi, to join the established Syrah, none tasted this edition.

- ◼ **Gilysipao** see Orange River Wine Cellars
- ◼ **Girlfriends Wine** see Val du Charron
- ◼ **Give Me A Chance** see Alluvia Winery & Private Residence Club
- ◼ **Glass Collection** see Glenelly Cellars

Glen Carlou

Location: Paarl ▪ Map: Paarl & Wellington ▪ WO: Paarl/Coastal/Robertson/Durbanville ▪ Est 1985 ▪ 1stB 1988 ▪ Tasting & sales Mon–Fri 8.30–5 Sat/Sun 10–4 ▪ Fee R25–R50 ▪ Closed Good Fri, Dec 25 & Jan 1 ▪ Cellar tours by appt ▪ Restaurant @ Glen Carlou (see Restaurants section) ▪ Facilities for children ▪ Tour groups ▪ Gifts ▪ Honey ▪ Conferences ▪ Conservation area ▪ Hess Art Collection Museum ▪ Owner(s) Hess Family Wine Estates Ltd (Switzerland) ▪ Cellarmaster(s)/winemaker(s) Arco Laarman (Jan 2000) ▪ Viticulturist(s) Marius Cloete (2000) ▪ 145ha/68ha (cabs s/f, malbec, mourv, p verdot, pinot, shiraz, chard) ▪ ±700t/100,000cs own label ▪ PO Box 23 Klapmuts 7625 ▪ welcome@glencarlou.co.za ▪ www.glencarlou.co.za ▪ S 33° 48' 44.85" E 018° 54' 12.88" ▪ **T +27 (0)21-875-5528** ▪ F +27 (0)21-875-5314

Since Donald Hess's Hess Family Wine Estates Ltd bought out the Finlaysons, founders of this Paarl farm, it has become a destination venue; apart from the wine, there's the Hess Art Museum, a restaurant, tapas bar and a speciality shop, where wine paraphernalia and wines from the other Hess Estates may be purchased. In their commitment to the environment, the team established a fynbos garden, set among giant boulders and filled with endemic indigenous plants, through which visitors are encouraged to wander. Grape varieties too are chosen for their suitability to the farm's warmer climate. Cellarmaster Arco Laarman particularly likes petit verdot and his new three-way blend 'shows how these tannic varieties can partner well in the correct climate with no new oak.'

Prestige range

★★★★☆ **Gravel Quarry Cabernet Sauvignon** ⊛ Handsome & powerful, farm's top cab in pure-fruited bramble form in **09**. Classy blackcurrant flavours are melded with the pliable tannin frame, giving great grip.

★★★★ **Petit Verdot Blend** NEW Unusual petit verdot, tannat, petite sirah mix (57/37/6) shows sensitive approach to warm-climate fruit. **09** ripe & full bodied, balanced by freshness & fine tannins. Only older oak.

★★★★☆ **Quartz Stone Chardonnay** 🌱 Grapes from single, old vineyard, vinified in oak (90% new) & concrete 'eggs', forge the tightest of cellar's three distinctive chardonnays. **12** is bold, but also shows polish, refinement in its citrus vitality, broad undertones. A keeper.

★★★★ **The Welder** 🌱 Concentrated, silky chenin Natural Sweet a mouthful of light-bodied refreshment. **12** returns to sizzling form after lesser **11** (★★★★), with pinpoint sugar/acid balance, low 10.5% alcohol.

Cellar Reserve range

★★★★ **Pinot Noir Reserve** 🕐 🌱 Serious package; dense **11** has forest floor & farmyard richness, with firm grippy tannins. 11 months in all-new casks. Needs 2-5 years to develop.

★★★★ **Méthode Cap Classique** 🕐 Exclusive bottling by Bon Courage in Robertson under Glen Carlou finery. Evolved **06** sparkling shows broad lines, for current drinking. Barrel-fermented, 4 years on lees.

Tannat NEW 🌱 ★★★★ From grape originating in Madiran in S-W France, noted for forbidding tannins. **10** has earthy, bitter chocolate character, its powerful, sturdy build alleviated by freshness, bone-dry finish.

Classic range

★★★★ **Cabernet Sauvignon** 🌱 Mint & blackcurrants identify **11** as modern & perfectly ripe cab with sound structure. Oak, none new, a harmonising factor.

★★★★ **Grand Classique** 🌱 Elegant **10** cab-led Bordeaux quintet. Bright fruit packed into supple, chewy texture framed by balanced freshness & lively tannins. Attractive package with good ageing potential.

★★★★ **Chardonnay** 🍴 🌱 **12** celebrates 25 vintages of this New World-style, well-oaked white. Firmer, fresher than **11** but with creamy, nutty underbelly waiting to advance complexity over several years.

★★★★ **Unwooded Chardonnay** ✓ 🍴 🌱 Previewed last year, **12** has grown in character. Sophisticated yet approachable; layers of texture with citrus, nut. Ferment in concrete 'eggs', with extended lees-ageing.

Merlot 🌱 ★★★★ With class & charm, **11** displays subtly oak-spiced mulberry fragrance, smooth juiciness with nip of forming tannin. Impresses more than **10** (★★★★). **Pinot Noir** 🍴 🌱 ★★★ Modest earthy features on **12**; full bodied, with a suggestion of alcohol glow (14.5%) in tail. **Syrah** 🌱 ★★★★ First since **07**, **10** has reserved, ripe, dark plum tones clamped down by grippy tannins. Balanced oak, freshness. Needs year or 2 to relax. **Zinfandel** 🕐 ★★★★ **09** has sultry, spice-infused raspberry flavours in generous mouthful. **Sauvignon Blanc** 🍴 🌱 ★★★ Brisk & full of juicy fruit, **13** concludes with mouthwatering freshness. WO Durbanville.

Contemporary range

Tortoise Hill White ☺ 🍴 🌱 ★★★ **13** full of zesty pineapple, citrus refreshment. Dry chenin/chardonnay blend; digestible 12.5% alcohol. Coastal WO, like next.

Tortoise Hill Red 🍴 🌱 ★★★ Bright cab fruits, also some firm grip on **12** blend with merlot. — AL

Glenelly Cellars

Location/map/WO: Stellenbosch ▪ Est/1stB 2003 ▪ Tasting & sales Mon-Fri 10-4.30 Sat 10-4 ▪ Closed Easter Fri/Sun, Dec 25/26 & Jan 1 ▪ Cellar tours by appt ▪ Gift shop ▪ Glass museum ▪ Owner(s) May-Eliane de Lencquesaing ▪ Cellarmaster(s) Luke O'Cuinneagain (Jan 2008) ▪ Winemaker(s) Luke O'Cuinneagain (Jan 2008), with Jerome Likwa (Jan 2008) ▪ Viticulturist(s) Heinrich Louw (2003) ▪ 128ha/65ha (cabs s/f, merlot, p verdot, shiraz, chard) ▪ 500t/55,334cs own label 95% red 5% white ▪ PO Box 1079 Stellenbosch 7599 ▪ info@glenelly.co.za ▪ www.glenellyestate.com ▪ S 33° 55' 6.1" E 018° 52' 45.1" ▪ **T** +27 (0)21-809-6440 ▪ F +27 (0)21-809-6448

Repeated South African success in winning the Pichon Lalande Trophy at the International Wine & Spirit Competition was an initial attraction for Madame May-Eliane de Lencquesaing, then owner of that Bordeaux classed growth, to invest in the Cape. After she bought Glenelly on Stellenbosch's Simonsberg, a redevelopment of the old fruit farm to vineyards was undertaken and a cellar built. All her projects have been carried out along environmentally friendly lines - the cellar, for example, has heat- and water-saving systems. The French owner also shows keen interest in local community and social development, with a focus on housing, training and, especially, education of employees' children.

Glenelly range

★★★★☆ **Lady May** 🕐 🌱 Graceful & stylish, cab with a dash of petit verdot, all **10**'s components - berry fruit, new oak, fine tannins, fresh acid, & 14.7% alcohol - melded into seamless class. Exceptional **09** (★★★★★).

★★★★☆ **Grand Vin de Glenelly** Elegant & accessible shiraz/Bordeaux blend. **09** with polished, dark berry fruit laced with spice & supple tannins. **08** (★★★★) was lighter. Earlier drinking than Lady May.

★★★★ **Grand Vin de Glenelly Chardonnay** ✓ 🖩 Naturally fermented **12** wonderful delicacy as well as layers of concentration in its subtle citrus, nutty oatmeal features. Sensitively oaked, poised, fresh & charming.

The Glass Collection

Cabernet Sauvignon 🖩 🖩 ★★★★ **11** doesn't shy away from cab's traditional firm build but this marches in tandem with flavoursome ripe fruit. Enhanced by year in 30% new French oak. **Merlot** ✓ 🖩 🖩 ★★★★ Gentle in structure, with velvety tannins, **11** has fresh minty fruit that's attractively ripe & lingering. **Shiraz** 🖩 ★★★★ **10** more peppery than rich **09**, roasted nut & spicy warmth, dense tannins need time. **Chardonnay Unwooded** ✓ 🖩 🖩 ★★★★ Was 'Chardonnay'. **12** full of character. Extended lees-ageing adds mouthfeel & nutty dimension to citrus freshness. Moderate 12.5% alcohol. — AL

Glen Erskine Estate   🍴🍷🎋

Location/WO: Elgin ▪ Map: Elgin, Walker Bay & Bot River ▪ Est 2005 ▪ 1stB 2009 ▪ Tasting, sales & cellar tours by appt ▪ Closed Easter Fri/Sun, Dec 25 & Jan 1 ▪ BYO picnic ▪ Owner(s) Reine & Annelien Dalton ▪ Cellarmaster(s)/winemaker(s) Annelien Dalton ▪ Viticulturist(s) Reine Dalton ▪ 14.6ha/3.04ha (sauv, sem, viog) ▪ 21t/840cs own label 100% white + 250cs for clients ▪ Ranges for customers: Kievits Kroon ▪ PO Box 111 Elgin 7180 ▪ annelien.dalton@gmail.com, reinedalton@gmail.com ▪ S 34° 10' 34.94" E 019° 2' 12.75" ▪ **T +27 (0)21-848-9632** ▪ F +27 (0)86-547-4473

Replanting their Elgin apple farm in 2005, Reine and Annelien Dalton decided to turn over a tiny portion to vines. Their approach to marketing is also to keep things small and personal, build relationships with visitors and sell as much wine as possible from the cellardoor. It is in the cellar that visitors are introduced to the wines.

Sauvignon Blanc 🖩 ★★★★ Heady greengage & grassy freshness on **12**. Small portion of oaked semillon rounds the more bracing edges. **Reserve Viognier** NEW 🖩 ★★★★ Individual orange & peach character plus evident oak vanilla on **12**. Quite robust, with intense flavours, pithy firm finish. Includes 12% semillon. **Reserve Sauvignon Blanc-Semillon** 🖩 ★★★★ Varieties added to 'Reserve' name in **12**. Gentle yet compelling blend; the 33% semillon portion oaked, adding breadth & texture to the cool-climate elegance. — AL

Glen Heatlie   🍴🍷

Location: Worcester ▪ Est 2006 ▪ Tasting by appt only ▪ Owner(s) Orange Grove Trust ▪ Winemaker(s) Joan-Marie Heatlie ▪ Viticulturist(s) Charlie Heatlie ▪ 3,100ha/45ha (cab, merlot, shiraz, chenin, chard, cbard, sauv, sem) ▪ Orange Grove PO Box 18 De Wet 6853 ▪ joan@glenheatlie.co.za ▪ **T +27 (0)82-364-4702** ▪ F +27 (0)23-341-2708

Now assistant winemaker at Solms-Delta in Franschhoek, Joan-Marie Heatlie will continue to vinify small parcels on her family's farm near Worcester in her spare time. Her Syrah '12 will be released this year (nothing made in 2013).

Glenview Wines

Location: Cape Town ▪ WO: Coastal ▪ Est/1stB 1998 ▪ Closed to public ▪ Owner(s) Robin Marks ▪ Winemaker(s) Frank Meaker (Nov 2010, consultant) ▪ 14,000cs own label 50% red 50% white ▪ PO Box 32234 Camps Bay 8040 ▪ bayexport@kingsley.co.za ▪ **T +27 (0)21-438-1080** ▪ F +27 (0)21-511-2545

Camps Bay-based Robin Marks' online wine business is driven by his belief in over-delivering on quality and friendly consumer-driven service. Supporting hopes of major supermarket listings is a new label design, 'more modern, eye-catching; it's important in a very competitive market'.

Chenin Blanc ☺ 🖩 🖩 ★★★ Jovial **13** is fresh & fruity, with pineapple tang, pleasant good-value quaffer.

Merlot 🖩 🖩 ★★ Tannins are smooth, flavours are ripe, down-to-earth **12** is ready for drinking solo or with your favourite pizza/pasta. **Sauvignon Blanc** 🖩 🖩 ★★★ Combo flowers & tropical fruit in **13**, nice vein of freshness though flavours don't hang about. — GM

GlenWood

Location/map: Franschhoek = WO: Franschhoek/Coastal = Est/1stB 2002 = Tasting & sales Mon-Fri 11-4 Sat/Sun (Sep-Apr only) 11-3 = Closed Easter Fri/Sun, Dec 25 & Jan 1 = Tasting R30/R50 incl cellar tour = Tours daily at 11 = Le Bon Vivant@GlenWood = Hikes = Owner(s) Alastair G Wood = Cellarmaster(s)/viticulturist(s) DP Burger (Apr 1991) = Winemaker(s) DP Burger (Apr 1991), with Justin Jacobs (Jan 2011) = 49ha/30ha (merlot, shiraz, chard, sauv, sem) = 150t/16,000cs own label 50% red 50% white = BWI, IPW = PO Box 204 Franschhoek 7690 = info@glenwoodvineyards.co.za = www.glenwoodvineyards.co.za = S 33° 54' 56.7" E 019° 4' 57.0" = **T +27 (0)21-876-2044** = F +27 (0)21-876-3338

Owner Alastair Wood left a career in business consulting to set up his picturesque estate at Robertsvlei in Franschhoek Valley, with its characterful boutique winery and Le Bon Vivant restaurant. Under longtime winemaker, DP Burger, they have built a reputation for standout chardonnay and consistent quality throughout the range.

Grand Duc range NEW

★★★★☆ **Syrah** This range only in exceptional vintages, which **11** clearly is. Bunch pressing, wild yeast fermentation & 100% new oak yield supremely elegant, layered wine. Richly textured, smoothly concentrated fruit flavours mingle with well-judged wood to unflagging finish. Some Stellenbosch fruit. For the long haul.

★★★★☆ **Chardonnay** Range motto 'Pursuit of Perfection' shows in outstanding **11**, vinified as above & showing fine, intense citrus, nut & vanilla flavours in a crisp, elegant structure & long, succulent finish. For luxury crayfish dishes, now & for many years.

GlenWood range

★★★★ **Merlot** ✓ Smooth **11** is complex & harmonious, with chocolate-dipped ripe plums. Rich fruit flavours are tempered by spicy tannins. Balanced, with good ageing potential.

★★★★☆ **Chardonnay Vigneron's Selection** 🖺 Barrel-fermented **12** seduces with multidimensional aromas of citrus, pear, white flowers & roasted nuts. Wonderfully sumptuous, without being weighty, reflecting the judicious oaking regime (13 months). Will reward those who wait.

★★★★ **Unwooded Chardonnay** 🕭 🖾 **12** is a breath of fresh air with vibrant clean citrus & apple flavours. Poised & intense, there's a spicy/creamy element in the finish which is very moreish.

★★★★ **Semillon Vigneron's Selection** Wild yeast fermented **12** offers lingering wafts of peach, nut, spice & flowers. Rich & silky, with a fruit-filled toasty conclusion inviting ageing.

Shiraz Next awaited, as for **Syrah Vigneron's Selection**. **Merlot-Shiraz** ✓ ★★★★ Medium-bodied, friendly **11** trumps previous with balanced sweet fruit & soft vanilla notes. WO Coastal. **Sauvignon Blanc** ★★★★ Exuberant **13** a step up from **11** (★★★) with vibrant tropical fruit flavours; crisp yet mouthfilling, zesty lemon finish, modest 12.5% alcohol. **12** sold out untasted. — WB

Goats do Roam Wine Company

Location: Paarl = WO: Coastal/Western Cape = Est/1stB 1998 = Tasting & sales at Fairview = Owner(s) Charles Back = Winemaker(s) Anthony de Jager, with Stephanie Betts = PO Box 583 Suider-Paarl 7624 = info@goatsdoroam.com = www.fairview.co.za = **T +27 (0)21-863-2450** = F +27 (0)21-863-2591

The well-established, well-made Goats do Roam range of over-delivering blends continues to play on the synergy between the goats, grapes and cheese (much of it from goats' milk) at Charles Back's busy Fairview property in Paarl. Last year saw the first Fairtrade wine under this label, and more is on the way soon.

★★★★ **Goat Roti** ✓ 🖺 🖾 Smooth, spicy **11**, meaty undertones & baked plums from shiraz given lift & lightness by fragrant viognier. Elegant over-deliverer.

Goats do Roam Red 🖺 🖾 ★★★★ Appetising, perfumed **12** from Rhône varieties makes for silky smooth, fruit-packed mouthful. Robust, rustic, food friendly. WO W Cape. **The Goatfather** 🖺 🖾 ★★★☆ Italianesque blend of sangiovese, cab, barbera & touch of nebbiolo, **12** shows densely raisined fruit & lively acidity. **Goats do Roam Rosé** ✓ 🖺 🖾 ★★★★ Pretty & attractive cherry notes on the nose of **13** give way to lipsmacking mouthful of berry fruit. Dry & delicious. **Goats do Roam White** 🖺 🖾 ★★★ Rhône blend of viognier, roussanne & grenache blanc **13** tank sample is perfumed peaches with fresh acidity. Lively & interesting. — CM

Goede Hoop Estate

Location/map: Stellenbosch ▪ WO: Bottelary ▪ Est 1928 ▪ 1stB 1974 ▪ Tasting, sales & cellar tours Mon-Fri 9-4 Sat 10–1 ▪ Closed Easter Fri-Sun, Dec 24/25/26/31 & Jan 1 ▪ Pieter's private cellar: monthly 4-course gourmet meal with wine R305pp, booking essential (12 seats only) ▪ BYO picnic ▪ Mountain biking trail ▪ Owner(s) Pieter Bestbier ▪ Winemaker(s) Albert Ahrens (Jun 2009, consultant), with Janette Hartshorne (Jan 2012) ▪ Viticulturist(s) Altus van Lill (May 2011) ▪ 122ha/71ha (cab, merlot, ptage, shiraz, chenin, sauv) ▪ ±600t/20,000cs own label 91% red 9% white & ±200,000L bulk ▪ PO Box 25 Kuils River 7579 ▪ goede@adept.co.za ▪ www.goedehoop.co.za ▪ S 33° 54' 32.0" E 018° 45' 14.0" ▪ **T +27 (0)21-903-6286** ▪ F +27 (0)21-906-1553

This venerable family estate spreads its vineyards on a horseshoe of slopes in Stellenbosch's Bottelary Hills. Albert Ahrens - perhaps spurred on by previous Swartland experience - gives the wines an unpretentious elegance, balance and eminent drinkability. The Heritage label is a joint venture between Albert and Goede Hoop's owner Pieter Bestbier (third generation here). Expected in 2013 was the return of a chardonnay, and a new look for the good-value Domaine range.

Heritage Wines

★★★★ Estate Wine ⓟ **10** harmoniously blends merlot, pinotage, cab, shiraz, malbec & cinsaut! Subtly oaked & just 13% alcohol, with a light, bright herbal elegance & charm. Delicious young - but there's no hurry.

★★★★ Estate Straw Wine ⓟ **10** from air-dried chenin. Hugely sweet & concentrated, with healthy ripe fruit flavours. To be enjoyed in small helpings.

Goede Hoop Estate range

Cabernet Sauvignon ⓟ **★★★★** Light-feeling & rather elegant **09**, with intelligently modest use of oak. No great intensity, but balanced & harmonious. **Merlot ★★★** Pleasing **11** in established house-style of restraint, charm & seriousness with a light touch. Easy enjoyment the achieved goal. **Pinotage ✓ 🖉 ★★★★** Nicely perfumed, tasty **10** is bigger, sweeter & richer than most of these reds, but still balanced & very drinkable. **Shiraz** ⓟ **★★★★** Spicy, smoked meat intro to **09**. Some richness & a savoury tannic bite, but the customary welcome light touch. **Chardonnay** ⓟ In abeyance. **Sauvignon Blanc 🖉 ★★★ 12** more neutral & less pungent than previous **10**. Unassuming & pleasant enough. **Shiraz LBV Port** Await next.

Domaine range

Red ☺ 🍴 **★★★** Forward, ripe, vibrant aromas & flavours on sweet-fruited, juicy but grippy & bone-dry **12** cab-shiraz blend. **White** ☺ 🍴 **★★★** Easy, lightly pleasant & dry **12** mixes sauvignon & chenin. — TJ

Goedvertrouw Estate

Location: Bot River ▪ Map: Elgin, Walker Bay & Bot River ▪ WO: Overberg ▪ Est 1990 ▪ 1stB 1991 ▪ Tasting & sales by appt ▪ Home-cooked meals & accommodation by appt ▪ Play area for children ▪ Walks ▪ Farm produce ▪ Small conferences ▪ Conservation area ▪ Small art gallery ▪ Owner(s)/winemaker(s)/viticulturist(s) Elreda Pillmann ▪ 8ha (cab, pinot, chard, sauv) ▪ 70% red 30% white ▪ PO Box 37 Bot River 7185 ▪ goedvertrouwwineestate@telkomsa. net ▪ S 34° 9' 56.7" E 019° 13' 24.1" ▪ **T +27 (0)28-284-9769** ▪ F +27 (0)28-284-9769

If you think cellardoors are becoming too homogenised, program your GPS for Elreda Pillmann's farm, a few kilometres from Bot River on the Van der Stel Pass. The delightful tannie Elreda is a force of nature, making wine, fund-raising for Tommy Prins Foundation, featuring in Elgin Open Gardens Week and Bot River Pink Weekend, running a B&B, and cooking 'boeremeals' for visitors!

Cabernet Sauvignon ⓟ **★★★ 06** yeasty aromas, pure fruit & ripe tannin when last tasted. Should be harmonious now. **Pinot Noir** ⓟ **★★** Earthy strawberry notes & hint of vanilla on light-hearted **09**. **Chardonnay** ⓟ **★★★** Orange peel & biscuit tones waft out of nicely round **06**. **Sauvignon Blanc** ⓟ **★★★** Previewed **08** finished satisfyingly dry previously. — WB

Goedverwacht Wine Estate

Location: Bonnievale ▪ Map/WO: Robertson ▪ Est 1960's ▪ 1stB 1994 ▪ Tasting, sales & cellar tours Mon-Fri 8. 30-4.30 Sat 10-1 ▪ Closed Easter Fri/Sun, Dec 25/26 & Jan 1 ▪ Mediterranean or quiche & salad platter; picnic basket for 2 (incl sparkling wine) - 2 days prior booking essential ▪ BYO picnic ▪ Tour groups ▪ Conservation area ▪ Owner(s) Jan du Toit & Sons (Pty) Ltd ▪ Winemaker(s) Henry Conradie (Aug 2005), with Charles Petrus Adam (Jan 2003) ▪ Viticulturist(s) Jan du Toit, advised by Francois Viljoen ▪ 220ha/130ha (cab, merlot, shiraz, chard, cbard, sauv) ▪ 1,600t/1m L 43% red 50% white 7% rosé ▪ Other export brands: Ama Ulibo, Misty Kloof's, Mzansi's, Soek die Geluk ▪ Brands for clients: Vinimark Trading ▪ BEE, BWI, IPW ▪ PO Box 128 Bonnievale 6730 ▪ goedverwachtestate@lando.co.za, info.goedverwacht@breede.co.za ▪ www.goedverwacht.co.za ▪ S 33° 55' 11.3" E 020° 0' 19.1" ▪ **T +27 (0)23-616-3430** ▪ F +27 (0)23-616-2073

Winemaker Henry Conradie is proud they were one of the top five wineries in the 2013 Best Value Guide, particularly as they were the smallest contender in the line-up and the only estate. How to celebrate? 'On the stoep at Vleesbaai with a potjie simmering on the coals and a bottle of shiraz!'

Maxim range

★★★★ **Cabernet Sauvignon** 🤎 Polished, modern take on variety. **11** similar leafy notes to elegant **10** (★★★☆) but greater presence & more complexity (chocolate, coffee, liquorice) from 100% new French oak.
Chardonnay ⑤ 🤎 ★★★☆ Vanilla biscuit wafts, coconut & butter richness give **11** California styling. Bold, could easily pair with spicy dishes.

Goedverwacht range

> **Triangle** ☺ 🍽 🤎 ★★★ Only older wood for cab-led Bordeaux red. Step-up & well-balanced **11** savoury, exudes leafy black fruit. **The Good Earth Sauvignon Blanc** ☺ 🍽 🤎 ★★★ Modest alcohol & few grams smoothing sugar make nettle & capsicum **13** perfect for solo or (sea)food.

An Acre of Stone Shiraz 🍽 🤎 ★★★ **12**'s big (±15% alcohol), punchy black olive & raspberry flavours need toning down - try venison roast. **Shiraz Rosé** 🍽 🤎 ★★★ Cherry, plum appeal on **13** easy semi-dry lunchtime sipper. **Great Expectations Chardonnay** 🍽 🤎 ★★☆ Oaky (100% new wood) style **13**'s warm buttery flavours need either equally rich or contrastingly light, acidic food. Discontinued: **Pink Shiraz Rosé, Crane White Sauvignon Blanc**.

Crane range

Red Merlot 🍽 🤎 ★★ Unpretentious fireside sipper, **13** with charry cherry flavours. Oak-staved, unlike barrel-matured reds above. **White Colombar** 🍽 🤎 ★★ **13** brisk & tropical; wallet-pleasing uncomplicated enjoyment. **Rosé Brut Sparkling** 🤎 ★★☆ Gently sweet fizz from shiraz with maraschino cherry taste in **12**. **Brut Sparkling** Await new. — DC,JP

■ **Golden Chalice** *see* Southern Sky Wines
■ **Golden Triangle** *see* Stellenzicht Vineyards
■ **Golden Vine** *see* Waterstone Wines

Goudini Wines

Location: Rawsonville ▪ Map: Breedekloof ▪ WO: Goudini/Western Cape ▪ Est 1948 ▪ Tasting & sales Mon-Fri 9–5 Sat 9–2 ▪ Closed Good Fri, Dec 25/26 & Jan 1 ▪ Cellar tours by appt ▪ Bistro: light meals during tasting hours ▪ Fully licensed bar ▪ Conferences ▪ Owner(s) 40 members ▪ Cellarmaster(s) Hennie Hugo (Dec 1984) ▪ Winemaker(s) Hendrik Myburgh (Nov 2001), with Tinus le Roux (Jan 2010) & Marius Prins (Jul 2013) ▪ Viticulturist(s) Hendrik Myburgh (Nov 2001) ▪ 1,000ha (merlot, ruby cab, shiraz, chard, chenin, sauv) ▪ 22,000t/66,000cs own label 45% red 45% white 10% rosé + 14,000cs for clients ▪ PO Box 132 Rawsonville 6845 ▪ info@goudiniwine.co.za ▪ www.goudiniwine.co.za ▪ S 33° 41' 37.8" E 019° 19' 9.5" ▪ **T +27 (0)23-349-1090** ▪ F +27 (0)23-349-1988

Selected from the 20,000+ tons produced by its 40 grower-owners, Breedekloof's Goudini Wines' own brand previously focused on easy-drinkers. More recently the Goudini range became a touch more serious, and now the new Reserve wines go up a notch. Some are named for the ancient desert plant Welwitchia mirabilis, and coincide with the launch of a new book, Uncrowned Monarch of the Namib, and the centenary of Cape Town's renowned Kirstenbosch Botanical Gardens.

Reserve range NEW

★★★★☆ **Gevonden Hendrik de Wet Cape Hanepoot** Marvellous fortified dessert wine from single-vineyard believed planted ca 1880. Unoaked **13** luxurious apricot, raisin, nut aromas; smooth & very sweet but balanced by pinpoint acidity; lovely barley sugar conclusion. Cellarworthy 4,060 bottles, 375 ml.
Mirabilis Primus-Capio ★★★☆ Cab-led (80%) Bordeaux blend, **11** meaty with high-toned red fruit, oaky sheen & long fresh finish, supple tannins. Only 1,620 bottles made. Widely sourced grapes; future releases will include more home fruit, as next. **Mirabilis Regis-Filia** ★★★☆ Chardonnay from Stellenbosch, showing

obvious oak vanilla, cinnamon & slight oxidative note on **11** followed by intense ripe tangerine flavours, creamy mid-palate & fresh conclusion. 1,560 bottles.

Goudini range

Ruby Cabernet-Merlot ☺ 🍴 🌿 ★★★ Plum & icing sugar attractions on **12**, fruity yet commendably dry & measured (13.5% alcohol). Fire- or pool-side quaffer. **Chenin Blanc** ☺ 🍴 🌿 ★★★ Thatch, flowers & honey notes on cheery & satisfying **13**, mere touch sugar ups the crowd appeal. **Sauvignon Blanc** ☺ 🍴 🌿 ★★★ 13's fresh-mown lawn, capsicum & zesty acidity - all summer sipper boxes ticked.

Pinotage ⊕ 🍴 🌿 ★★★ Fresh & juicy **11**, with lightly spiced redcurrant for easy drinking. **Shiraz** ⊕ 🍴 🌿 ★★ Sweet oak spices on bright & tangy **11**. **Rosé** 🍴 🌿 ★★ Previously dry, now semi-sweet, **13** strawberry toned & delicate, to be serve well chilled. **Unwooded Chardonnay** Await next. **Brut Sparkling** 🌿 ★★★ NV from sauvignon; waxy rather than typical grassy tone, dry finish makes it a foodie. **Natural Sweet** 🍴 🌿 ★★ Latest is **NV**, lightish, pleasant pineapple flavoured & softly sweet. **Hanepoot** ★★★ Delicious **10** fortified dessert is unctuous, packed with grapey & nutty flavours, then a wave of lime comes along & freshens the palate for the next sip.

Umfiki range

Cabernet Sauvignon 🍴 🌿 ★★ There's beef & cranberry sauce flavour right in your glass, in light & zesty **NV**. Who needs dinner? **Merlot** 🍴 🌿 ★★★ NV uncomplicatedly tasty with plum & cherry charm. Discontinued: **Dry White**, **Semi Sweet Chenin Blanc**, **Sauvignon Blanc**. — CvZ

■ **Goue Kalahari** see Die Mas van Kakamas
■ **Gouverneurs** see Groot Constantia Estate

Govert Wines

Location: Stellenbosch ▪ Est 2002 ▪ 1stB 2007 ▪ Closed to public ▪ Owner(s) Teuns Keuzenkamp ▪ 180,000cs own label 80% red 5% white 15% rosé ▪ PO Box 1977 Somerset West 7129 ▪ info@govertwines.com ▪ www.govertwines.com ▪ **T +27 (0)21-887-5812** ▪ F +27 (0)86-224-9348

The Stellenbosch-based Keuzenkamp family source export wines from around the Cape winelands for clients and their own labels, Loyal Brothers, Charles Borro, D'Heros, Don Morris and Ruby Ridge.

■ **Gower Family Wines** see Ross Gower Wines

Graça

Inspired by Portugal's vinho verde wines, these popular easy-drinkers are made by Distell from widely sourced vineyards.

Rosé 🍴 🌿 ★★ Sweetly pleasant, latest NV shade less balanced & easy to quaff, same moderate ±11% alcohol though. **Graça** 🍴 🌿 ★★★ Semi-dry (unlike traditional vinho verde), seafood-friendly **NV** from sauvignon, colombard & chenin. — DB, HJ

Graceland Vineyards

🍴 🍷

Location/map/WO: Stellenbosch ▪ Est/1stB 1998 ▪ Tasting & sales Mon-Fri by appt ▪ Fee R30 ▪ Closed all pub hols ▪ Owner(s) Paul & Susan McNaughton ▪ Cellarmaster(s)/winemaker(s)/viticulturist(s) Susan McNaughton (2001) ▪ 18ha/10ha (cab, merlot, shiraz) ▪ 55t/8,000cs own label 100% red ▪ Suite 144 Private Bag X4 Die Boord 7613 ▪ graceland@iafrica.com ▪ www.gracelandvineyards.com ▪ S 33° 59' 37.5" E 018° 50' 3.1" ▪ **T +27 (0)21-881-3121** ▪ F +27 (0)86-556-4600

It's more than 15 years since Paul McNaughton and winemaking wife Susan first bottled (and beautifully packaged) wine from this small but ambitious estate in Stellenbosch's 'Golden Triangle' of eminent vineyards. The focus is on handcrafted, sumptuous reds - generous, modern wines with oodles of personality.

★★★★ **Cabernet Sauvignon** 🌿 Poised ripeness & seductive aromas balanced by tart cherry & appealing wet tobacco on **11**; juicy fruit mingles with dry powdery tannins & melds with obvious big alcohol.

★★★★ **Strawberry Fields** 🌿 **11** mostly shiraz (66%), plus cab & splash merlot. Ripe berry aromas over shy cedary oak open to very ripe fruit & spice. Unashamedly modern, with firm & plush tannic structure.

★★★★ **Three Graces** 🖉 Barrel selection of best cab, merlot & shiraz, **11** - like others in the range - ripe & bold fruited, but shows tad more finesse with savoury undertone adding complexity. Rewards decanting. **Merlot** ★★★★ Rich plummy nose with fine gravelly edge evolves to dark berry & ripe plums. **11** shows better balance & rounder palate than **09** (★★★★). Good grippy end bodes well for cellaring. **Shiraz** ★★★★ Black pepper, spice & mulberry fruit on **11**; warmth from 15% alcohol, bold fruit, tarry edge & a gawky, sweet send-off. **Colour Field** NEW 🖉 ★★★ Mostly merlot in **11**, made for earlier drinking, with cocoa & strawberry fruit; light feeling & dry, yet plush & powerful (15% alcohol). — JP

Graham Beck Wines   🍷🍴♿

Location/map: Robertson ▪ WO: Western Cape/Robertson/Coastal/Stellenbosch/Paarl/Groenekloof ▪ Est 1983 ▪ 1stB 1991 ▪ Tasting & sales Mon-Fri 9–5 Sat/Sun 10–4 ▪ Tasting fees: classic is complimentary; deluxe R50, waived on purchase of R200+; MCC R75 ▪ Closed Good Fri & Dec 25 ▪ Owner(s) Graham Beck Enterprises ▪ Cellarmaster(s) Pieter Ferreira (Aug 1990) & Erika Obermeyer (Jan 2005) ▪ Winemaker(s) Pierre de Klerk (Oct 2010) ▪ Viticulturist(s) Dérick Hamman & Pieter Fouché ▪ 246ha under vine (cabs s/f, grenache, merlot, p verdot, ptage, pinot, shiraz, chard, sauv); Robertson 150ha/Stellenbosch 96ha ▪ 2,800t/540,000cs own label ▪ ISO 14001, BWI champion, IPW, SABS 1841, WIETA ▪ PO Box 724 Robertson 6705 ▪ cellar@grahambeckwines. co.za, market@grahambeckwines.co.za ▪ www.grahambeckwines.com ▪ S 33° 48' 14.95" E 019° 48' 1.41" ▪ **T +27 (0)23-626-1214; marketing offices: +27 (0)21-874-1258** ▪ F +27 (0)23-626-5164; marketing offices: +27 (0)21-874-1712

Very few wineries worldwide have a resident conservation manager, so the presence of loquacious and enthusiastic Mossie Basson on the team speaks volumes about the premium placed on custodianship by top-ranking Graham Beck Wines. It's an ethos dating from the earliest days, when the late Graham Beck bought a beautiful but semi-arid stretch of Robertson scrubland upon which to develop a world-class winery, and almost immediately set aside a large portion of it as a private nature reserve. Though today sourcing widely, the original Madeba wine and thoroughbred estate remains the Graham Beck nerve centre, and the brand home of The Game Reserve, a feel-good, do-good range inspired by naturalist Sir David Attenborough's trenchant words: 'People are not going to care about animal conservation unless they think that animals are worthwhile.'

Ad Honorem range

★★★★ **Coffeestone Cabernet Sauvignon** 🖉 Classy mint & redcurrant-toned **11** (★★★★☆), with spice highlights, powdery tannin & protracted elegant farewell. Very fine, almost regal Stellenbosch cab, will reward cellaring. Improves on denser **09**. No **10**.

★★★★☆ **The Ridge Syrah** 🖉 Barrel selection from Robertson single-vineyard, spice & violet-perfumed **11** (★★★★) less well-integrated than elegant & streamlined **09**. No **10**.

★★★★☆ **The Joshua** 🖉 Co-fermented shiraz, 5% viognier seriously wooded (90% new oak, some American) in **11** (★★★). Aromatic & dense, with big 14.7% alcohol. Misses the generous fruit & muscular structure that underpinned **09**. No **10**. WO Coastal.

★★★★★ **Ad Honorem** ⊕ 🍽 Oak-spicy **09** (★★★★★) *grand vin* is opulent & tarry, with impressive focused dark fruit, weight & length. Has greater shiraz component than noble & silky **07** cab-shiraz blend (72:28).

★★★★ **Bowed Head Chenin Blanc** 🖉 Orange blossom & baked apple on extroverted **12**. Expansive oak aromas & flavours, slippery palate, loads of fruit concentration from ripe Paarl dryland vineyards.

★★★★★ **Pheasants' Run Sauvignon Blanc** 🍽 Much-lauded label, from Groenekloof-only grapes in **13** (★★★★★) & showing intense cool khaki bush & blackcurrant aromas, figgy flavours. Not quite as attention-grabbing as **12**, but vivacious, finely crafted. Enough grip & structure for few years cellaring.

★★★★ **Rhona Muscadel** 🖉 Fragrant & luxurious fortified dessert from Robertson & Montagu, rounded in older oak. **12** (★★★★) full of grapey sunshine, slightly more spiritous than elegant **11**.

Discontinued: **The William**.

Méthode Cap Classique Sparkling range

★★★★ **Brut Rosé** ✓ Stylish **09** bubbly from Robertson pinot noir (82%) & chardonnay, co-fermented ('a first for South Africa'). New disgorgement (after 36 months) more savoury, with long, fine chalky finish.

★★★★ **Brut Rosé** 🖉 Red berries & savoury nuances on latest **NV** bubbly; drop more chardonnay than pinot than previous strawberry & cream infusion. Tangy, dry & balanced but less complex.

★★★★☆ **Cuvée Clive** Flag bearer of the accomplished MCC sparklings. New bottling of **07** majestic & profoundly mineral, with elegant lemon persistence & freshness, creamy texture courtesy lengthy lees-ageing. Robertson chardonnay (81%) & pinot noir.

★★★★ **Brut Blanc de Blancs** From Robertson chardonnay. Small portion oaked base-wine adds breadth & depth to new disgorgement of **09** (★★★★☆). Gorgeous fynbos-scented bubbles tinged with brioche, lemon & pear. Improves on **09** version reviewed last time & **08** with extra persistence.

Brut 🗟 ★★★ The house's mainstay **NV**, 50/50 chardonnay/pinot in latest bottling. Approachable aperitif style, with lemon & quince tang, few grams sugar smoothing the tad brief finish. **Brut Zero** ★★★★ With just 1 g/l sugar, this ultra-dry version gets its richness & character from 5 years ageing on lees, 25% wooded base wine, 20% pinot noir. Preserved lemon & lime on coiled, flinty **08**, from Robertson. **Bliss Demi Sec** 🗟 ★★★ Latest **NV** equal chardonnay, pinot noir enriched by 40 g/l sugar. Fragrant & smooth enjoyment for the sweet-toothed.

The Game Reserve range

★★★★ **Cabernet Sauvignon** 🗟 Now bottled, **11** confirms class shown last edition, cab's opulence & leafiness managed with aplomb. Tannins prominent previously have softened. Rung above herbal **10** (★★★).

Merlot 🗟 🗟 ★★★ Minty **11** back on track, likeable, easy to sip, with balanced savoury conclusion. WO Coastal. **Pinotage** 🗟 🗟 ★★★☆ **12** brushed with older oak, slips down easily & charms with complex bouquet cherry, mocha, rose & earth. **Shiraz** 🗟 ★★★ From Stellenbosch, two vintages tasted: meaty **11** lean & sappy; **10** (★★★★) modern, with juicy fruit contained by polished tannin structure. Less new oak (25%) than gutsy **09**. **Rosé** 🗟 🗟 ★★★ Aperitif-style **13** semi-dry, flavoursome & lightish. WO Robertson. **Chardonnay** 🗟 🗟 ★★★ **12** ex Robertson has vanilla, lemon butter & dried apricot flavours, crowd-pleasing fruit/oak sweetness. **Chenin Blanc** 🗟 ★★★★ Step-up **13** filled with baked apple & stonefruit flavour, lifted by fresh acidity, satisfying vinosity & dry conclusion. Lightly oaked; from Paarl fruit. **Sauvignon Blanc** 🗟 🗟 ★★★ Provisional rating for muted but crisp **13** tank sample. WO Coastal. **Viognier** 🗟 🗟 ★★★ Faint lime & green melon on aromatically restrained (for variety) **13**, with warm 14.4% alcohol farewell. WO Robertson.

Everyday Favourites range

Railroad Red ☺ 🗟 🗟 ★★★ Mainly shiraz with 5 others, **11** bouncy, balanced & convivial red.

Pinno 🗟 🗟 ★★☆ 100% pinotage; **12** budget quaffer is fruity & fresh, with light tannin & hint greenness. **Waterside Unoaked Chardonnay** 🗟 🗟 ★★★ **13** faint peardrop tone & light body for poolside enjoyment. WO Robertson. — DC, IM, CvZ, MW

■ **Grand Duc** see GlenWood

Grande Provence Heritage Wine Estate 🍴🥂⚓📷♿

Location/map: Franschhoek ▪ WO: Western Cape/Franschhoek ▪ Est 1694 ▪ 1stB 2004 ▪ Tasting & sales Mon-Sun 10-6 ▪ Fee R40/4 wines, R50/7 wines, R80/food & wine pairing ▪ Group tastings in cathedral extension of art gallery (seat up to 120 pax); winemaker tastings in private tasting room (up to 12 pax) ▪ Cellar tours Mon-Fri 11 & 3 Sat/Sun by appt ▪ The Restaurant at Grande Provence (see Restaurants section) ▪ Tour groups ▪ Gift shop ▪ Farm produce ▪ Conferences ▪ Art gallery ▪ Harvest festival ▪ The Owner's Cottage & La Provençale at Grande Provence (see Accommodation section) ▪ Owner(s) Dutch & Belgium consortium ▪ Cellarmaster(s)/winemaker(s)/viticulturist(s) Karl Lambour (May 2012) ▪ 32ha/22ha (cab, merlot, chard, sauv) ▪ 120t/10,000cs own label 60% red 40% white ▪ PO Box 102 Franschhoek 7690 ▪ reservations@grandeprovence.co.za ▪ www.grandeprovence.co.za ▪ S 33° 53' 57.6" E 19° 06' 10.5" ▪ **T +27 (0)21-876-8600** ▪ F +27 (0)21-876-8601

The estate dates back to a land grant to a French Huguenot in 1694 (the grand manor house is from the following century). After many vicissitudes, 310 years later Grande Provence was acquired by a consortium of Dutch and Belgian business people, who confirmed it as a place offering more than wine – luxury accommodation, fine dining and an art gallery, among others. Widely experienced Karl Lambour arrived in 2012 to take charge of the vineyards and cellar.

Premier range

★★★★ **Shiraz** Densely packed, flavoursome **09** (★★★★) in rich, modern house style. Mainly new oak balanced by powerful fruit; soft tannins allow for early drinking. From Stellenbosch grapes, as was finer **08**.

★★★★ **The Grande Provence** Blockbuster **09** from merlot & cab shows intense mint, oak & red fruit. Showy, forward & big (15.4% alcohol) - subtlety not the point, but all-new oak matched by ripe fullness.

★★★★ **Chardonnay** ⊕ 🏠 Big, ripe, rich & buttery **11** with lots of oak on show. Full body, with gentle acidity, good lingering flavours. Franschhoek WO.

★★★★ **Chenin Blanc-Viognier** 🏠 Fragrant **12** (★★★★) has viognier's peach & orange blossom, chenin adds freshness, restraint. Clean & vibrant, but alcohol glow on finish. Last-tasted **10** more elegant.

Cabernet Sauvignon ★★★ Red-fruited **10**'s aromas dominated by oak in youth & the palate a bit unyielding but promising sufficient fruit. These all from Franschhoek grapes (but certified W Cape) unless indicated.
Pinot Noir ★★★★ Soft-spoken **12** shows raspberries & some spicy notes; palate subtle with vibrant acidity but lacks real depth & complexity. **Sauvignon Blanc** ⊕ 🏠 ★★★★ Unpretentious but rather smart **12**, balanced & fresh, with typical aromas of cut grass & green fruit. Durbanville grapes. **Muscat d'Alexandrie** NEW ★★☆ Clean & fragrant **12** fortified dessert, but sweet & cloying due to low acidity. — JPf

Grand Mousseux

Enduring (launched 1929) budget-priced carbonated sparkling brand by Distell.
Vin Doux ★★ Bubbly that's launched a million brides, **NV** explosively fizzy, sweet, serve well chilled. — DB, HJ

Grangehurst

Location/WO: Stellenbosch ▪ Map: Helderberg ▪ Est/1stB 1992 ▪ Tasting & sales Mon-Fri 9–4 Sat/Sun 10-3 (plse phone to confirm) ▪ Fee charged for group tastings depends on wines being presented ▪ Closed Easter Fri-Mon, Dec 25/26 & Jan 1 ▪ Self-catering guest cottages ▪ Owner(s) Grangehurst Winery (Pty) Ltd ▪ Cellarmaster(s) Jeremy Walker (Jan 1992) ▪ Winemaker(s) Jeremy Walker (Jan 1992), with Gladys Brown (Jan 2002) ▪ ±13ha/6ha own (cab) + 8ha bought in grapes (merlot, p verdot, ptage, shiraz) ▪ 80t/9,000cs own label 90% red 10% rosé + 2,000cs for clients ▪ Brands for clients: Woolworths ▪ PO Box 206 Stellenbosch 7599 ▪ winery@grangehurst.co.za ▪ www.grangehurst.co.za ▪ S 34° 01′ 02.9″ E 018° 49′ 50.5″ ▪ **T +27 (0)21-855-3625** ▪ F +27 (0)21-855-2143

'Handcrafted, traditional, unhurried' is the mantra of Jeremy and Mandy Walker's boutique winery on Stellenbosch's Helderberg. One that is maintained thanks to the limited quantities of classically styled reds, released only when they've had time to settle into themselves. Current releases are ready to enjoy but should in most cases give pleasure for many years yet. Only cabernet sauvignon is grown on the property, other grapes being sourced elsewhere in Stellenbosch. All are reds, apart from the Cape Rosé, which started life as the family house wine and, Jeremy suggests, fills the gap when 'you are in the mood for neither white nor red wine'.

Grangehurst range

★★★★ **Cabernet Sauvignon Reserve** ⊕ After charming **05**, classic **06** (★★★★☆) showed bold ripe tannins, delicate blackcurrant fruit with extended finish. Tasted some years back.

★★★★☆ **Pinotage** ⊕ Mature **05** full of fresh charm. Refined though rather exotic perfume - more in pinot noir vein, as is light-textured, smooth-tannined, lively palate. Includes 14% cab. No **04**.

★★★★ **CWG Auction Reserve** NEW **07** cab-led with petit verdot & merlot. Cedary oak fragrance remains a strong influence. Fresh, black berry fruit peeps through dense, fine tannin. Needs time.

★★★★ **Cabernet Sauvignon-Merlot** More mature than most new releases, **06** still displays youthful cedary, cassis fragrance. Tannins also finely & firmly in control on this elegant, focused cab-dominated blend.

★★★★☆ **Grangehurst** ⊕ Cab-led **06** with merlot, petit verdot. House-style restraint, also some pleasing early maturity. Gentle meaty, iron features highlighted by balanced freshness, rounded savoury tannins.

★★★★ **Nikela** Just a whisper of pinotage's raspberry & tannin bite on elegantly rich & savoury **06**, with cab a dominant presence. Also shiraz & a little merlot. Fresh & firm with good further potential.

★★★★☆ **Shiraz-Cabernet Sauvignon Reserve** ⊕ Complex cassis, red pepper, spice, leather & earthy notes on **05** (★★★★) after finer **03**. Tasted a few years back.

★★★★ **Cape Rosé Blend** ⊕ 🏠 'Between light red & rosé' says winemaker Jeremy Walker of **11**, soft yet refreshing, lingering multi-variety blend. Part oaking adds to red-wine feel, not obscuring red fruit. — AL

◼ **Greendale** *see* Withington
◼ **Green Drake** *see* Stellar Winery
◼ **Green Shebeen** *see* Org de Rac
◼ **Grimont** *see* Tulbagh Winery

■ **Groblershoop** *see* Orange River Wine Cellars
■ **Groen Kalahari** *see* Die Mas van Kakamas

Groenland ▮🏕📷&

Location/map/WO: Stellenbosch ▪ Est 1932 ▪ 1stB 1997 ▪ Tasting & sales Mon-Fri 10–4 Sat 10–1 ▪ Fee R10pp for groups of 6+, waived on purchase ▪ Closed Easter Fri/Sun & Dec 25 ▪ Cellar tours by appt ▪ Gift shop ▪ BYO picnic by appt ▪ Conference/function venue (20-60 pax) ▪ Owner(s) Kosie Steenkamp ▪ Cellarmaster(s) Kosie Steenkamp (Feb 1975) ▪ Winemaker(s) Kosie Steenkamp (Feb 1975), with Piet Steenkamp (Jan 2001) ▪ Viticulturist(s) Piet Steenkamp (Jan 2001) ▪ 190ha/154ha (cab, merlot, ptage, shiraz, chard, chenin, sauv) ▪ 1,500t/±13,000cs own label 75% red 25% white ▪ BEE level 3, BWI, IPW ▪ PO Box 4 Kuils River 7579 ▪ steenkamp@groenland.co.za ▪ www.groenland.co.za ▪ S 33° 53' 48.9" E 018° 44' 5.3" ▪ **T +27 (0)21-903-8203** ▪ F +27 (0)21-903-0250/+27 (0)86-571-4969

The Steenkamp family's farm on Stellenbosch's Bottelary Road is a cheerful place to be, with good old-fashioned hospitality from the affable Kosie and his son, fellow winemaker Piet. They like people, wine and good humour, and shun pretension. Only a small selection of their harvest is bottled under their own label.

Premium range

★★★★ **Merlot** ⌘ **10** (★★★☆) has minty, dusty-oak notes meshed with exuberant red berry fruit after fine **09**. Restrained extraction shows in supple, juicy body.

★★★★ **Antoinette Marié** Classy & elegant, **09** equal blend of shiraz, cab & merlot is spiced up by all-new oaking. Solid dark fruit has savoury aromatic notes, following to long farewell.

Cabernet Sauvignon ⓘ ★★★★ **08** has developed handsomely after a year in bottle. Plush, dark fruit with supportive structure. Integrated new oak adds creamy texture, tempting enjoyment earlier than more restrained **07** (★★★☆). **Shiraz** ★★★☆ Medium bodied but generously ripe, **09** has prominent oak-vanilla spiciness on juicy cherry fruit.

Classic range

Cabernet Sauvignon ⓘ ★★★☆ **07** juicy & elegant, slightly dusty tones. Balanced & supple supportive structure. **Shiraz** ⓘ ★★★☆ Tighter **07** shows restraint & cool tones with savoury, dusty overlay; food style. **Antoinette Marié** ⓘ ★★★★ **08** half shiraz & equal cab/merlot; ripe, with juicy exuberance, pliable tannins, so easy to drink! **Sauvignon Blanc** ✓ 🍴 ★★★★ Spicy, substantial **13** has intriguing aromatic scents woven with dusty, grassy & gooseberry elements. Crisply tart finish.

Landskap range NEW

Chenin Blanc ☺ 🍴 ⌘ ★★★ Cheerful & generously fruity **13** outperforms its modest status. Lovely crisp tropical fruit.

Shiraz-Merlot 🍴 ★★★ Jammy baked berry fruit on **12** entry-level braai partner. — GdB

Groot Constantia Estate ▮▯🍷☕📷🎿&

Location/WO: Constantia ▪ Map: Cape Peninsula ▪ Est 1685 ▪ 1stB 1688 ▪ Tasting & sales daily 9–6 ▪ Fee R30 incl glass, R40 tasting & tour ▪ Closed Good Fri & Dec 25 ▪ Cellar tours 10-4 on the hour, every hour ▪ Simon's at Groot Constantia Restaurant; Jonkershuis Constantia Restaurant (see Restaurants section) ▪ Facilities for children ▪ Tour groups ▪ Gifts ▪ Conferences ▪ Walks/hikes ▪ Conservation area ▪ Iziko Museum, manor house, historic buildings & orientation centre ▪ Owner(s) Groot Constantia Trust NPC RF ▪ Estate manager Floricius Beukes ▪ Winemaker(s) Boela Gerber (Jan 2001), with Daniel Keulder (Sep 2009) ▪ Viticulturist(s) Andrew Teubes (2009) ▪ 170ha/±90ha (cab, merlot, ptage, shiraz, chard, muscat, sauv, sem) ▪ 483t/68,000cs ▪ Private Bag X1 Constantia 7848 ▪ enquiries@grootconstantia.co.za ▪ www.grootconstantia.co.za ▪ S 34° 1' 36.5" E 018° 25' 27.3" ▪ **T +27 (0)21-794-5128** ▪ F +27 (0)21-794-1999

This most historically significant farm produced its first wines in the 17th century, when it was the home of Governor Simon van der Stel, the founding father of the Cape's wine industry. His stately Cape Dutch residence is a national treasure and tourist must-see. The property has a chequered past, alternating between the fame of its great sweet wines under Hendrik Cloete and the ravages of oidium and phylloxera, destructive neglect and family infighting. Since 1976 it has been run by a Government-appointed board of trustees. The estate has re-established itself as a premium producer under longtime cellar chief Boela Gerber, with extensive vineyard renewal and a wide range of visitor attractions, including new tasting facilities for small groups in the production cellar itself.

Gouverneurs range

★★★★☆ **Reserve Red** Ⓢ 🀫 Steely minerality on **10** 4-way Bordeaux-type blend indicates classical styling. Refined & complex, with dark depths & aromatic lightness, challenging the senses. Fine effort in difficult vintage, rewarding attention to detail.

★★★★☆ **Reserve White** Ⓢ 🀫 Brazenly oaky **11** semillon-dominated Bordeaux-style blend has impressive creamy/chalky texture, bold floral-tinged passionfruit & persistent dry finish. Should benefit from ageing.

Groot Constantia range

★★★★ **Cabernet Sauvignon** 🀫 Taut, herbaceous aromas on **11**, mingled with truffle & tarry blackcurrant. Lean & lithe, demanding close attention, but offering precise varietal profile. **10** (★★★★) was lighter.

★★★★ **Merlot** 🀫 Classy, Old-World styling on **11** (★★★★★) avoids clichés, with noble austerity, intriguing minerality & dark pure fruit. Lengthy finish plays on inky, raw-meat savoury elements. Shows potential to age with grace, as did marginally lighter **10**.

★★★★☆ **Pinotage** 🀫 Substantial & stylish **11** (★★★★) offers juicy berry compote on plush, smooth-textured body. Precise & balanced, with oak seamlessly integrated. First since excellent **08**.

★★★★ **Shiraz** 🀫 Hints of smoked bacon on **11**, less focused than **10** (★★★★★), but still showing muscle tempered with subtle liquorice, white pepper & violet aromas.

★★★★☆ **Chardonnay** 🀫 Big-bodied but consummately balanced, **12** combines serious oak regime with well-rounded, focused lemon-butter fruit. Beautiful varietal expression of weight, texture & finesse; power in a velvet glove.

★★★★☆ **Sauvignon Blanc** Ⓢ 🀫 Hot-off-the-press **12** (★★★★) needs time to settle, but already showing forceful pungent nettles on solid structured platform. Less subtle complexity than **11**.

★★★★ **Méthode Cap Classique** Rung above **08**, elegant all-chardonnay **09** (★★★★★) shows added complexity from 8 months in oak & extended lees-ageing. Crisp apple cider & shortbread combine in lean, taut yet creamy house style.

★★★★☆ **Grand Constance** 🀫 Nostalgic natural sweet showpiece from red & white muscat de Frontignan, **10** emerges from 2 years-plus in barrel exuding fragrant charm. Intense, pervasive & floral, but consummately elegant in pretty onion-skin livery.

Constantia Rood 🀫 ★★★ **11** all-sorts blend is unpretentious but satisfyingly plump & fruity. Wild berries with a gentle oak mantle. **Blanc de Noir** Ⓢ 🀫 ★★★ **12** dry blush from merlot & cab shows good fruit intensity, appealing crispness. Fresh & cheerful. **Semillon-Sauvignon Blanc** Ⓢ 🀫 ★★★★ Unoaked **11** Bordeaux-style blend has more immediate appeal than serious big brother. Light & fresh faced. **Cape Ruby** 🀫 ★★★★ Carefully-crafted touriga fortified, **11** emphasises up-front fruit in true ruby fashion, with solid tannic grip. — GdB

■ **Grootdrink** see Orange River Wine Cellars
■ **Groot Eiland** see uniWines Vineyards

Groote Post Vineyards

Location: Darling ▪ Map: Durbanville, Philadelphia & Darling ▪ WO: Darling/Coastal ▪ 1stB 1999 ▪ Tasting, sales & cellar tours Mon-Fri 9–5 Sat/Sun & pub hols 10–4 ▪ Fee R20 for groups of 10+ ▪ Closed Good Fri, Dec 25 & Jan 1 ▪ Hilda's Kitchen open for lunch Wed-Sun, booking essential ▪ Facilities for children ▪ BYO picnic ▪ Conferences ▪ Walks/hikes ▪ Conservation area & bird hide ▪ Owner(s) Peter & Nicholas Pentz ▪ Winemaker(s) Lukas Wentzel (Nov 2000) ▪ Viticulturist(s) Jannie de Clerk (1999), advised by Johan Pienaar ▪ 4,000ha/107ha (cabs s/f, merlot, pinot, shiraz, chard, chenin, riesling, sauv, sem) ▪ 580t/64,000cs own label ▪ Brands for clients: Woolworths ▪ PO Box 103 Darling 7345 ▪ wine@grootepost.co.za ▪ www.grootepost.com ▪ S 33° 29′ 0.5″ E 018° 24′ 35.0″ ▪ **T +27 (0)22-492-2825** ▪ F +27 (0)22-492-2693

At 4,000 hectares, the Pentz family farm is one of the largest in the winelands. Once home to a famous dairy herd, earning for co-owner and patriarch Peter Pentz the SA Farmer of the Year title in 1998, it has now become a destination in itself with game drives, bird viewing, eco-hikes and of course wine. Darling is justifiably renowned for cool-climate sauvignon blanc, and Groote Post has capitalised on the conducive climate for its other wines too. Not least are the well-priced wines specially crafted to suit Peter's taste, the 'Old Man's Blend' range.

Reserve range

★★★★ **Kapokberg Pinot Noir** ⓥ Previously 'Pinot Noir'. Last was **09** but **12** worth the wait. Raspberries & black cherries reflect perfectly ripe fruit, deft oaking adds cedar spicing, a stiffening to the plushness.

★★★★ **Chardonnay** ⓥ 'Wooded Chardonnay' last ed. Signature roasted almonds & stonefruit in **12**, the flavours given lift & vibrancy by the tangy freshness. Seamless & delicious, reflecting good fruit well handled.

★★★★ **Sauvignon Blanc** ✓ ⓥ Selection of top vineyard blocks. Improving on **11** with its leafy notes, deep-packed green melon & greengage, **12** (★★★★★) is threaded through with limy acidity. Reveals not only concentration but its ability to age. Drink till ±2018.

Groote Post range

★★★★☆ **Shiraz** ✓ ⓥ Scrub, prosciutto, campfire smoke, black pepper, dark wild fruit, **12** ticks all the boxes. This is textbook shiraz, perfectly ripe & silky smooth. Will hold till ±2018 but why postpone the pleasure?

★★★★ **Unwooded Chardonnay** ✓ ⓥ Catering for a growing market, **12** shows chardonnay can stand proud without oak. Melon & yellow peach backed by zesty freshness, flavours remain long after glass is empty.

★★★★ **Chenin Blanc** 🗒 🗒 Nice combo of ripeness & elegance in **13** (★★★★), white peach, fresh & streamlined body, but lacks the punch of **12**.

★★★★ **Riesling** ✓ 🗒 Pineapple & ginger in **13**, pure & focused but lacks **12**'s (★★★★☆) intensity. The svelte body perfectly fits the wine style, while brisk acidity offsets 18 g/l sweetness.

★★★★ **Sauvignon Blanc** ✓ 🗒 ⓥ Showcasing the terroir, vivid capsicum & lime abounds in **13**, the lipsmacking tangy freshness has you reaching for a second glass.

Merlot ⓘ ⓥ ★★★ Grippier than previous, but fruit is there in **11**'s blackberry & cedar profile. Could age 3-4 years, still in its youthful prime. **Noble Late Harvest** Await new vintage.

The Old Man's Blend range

★★★★ **The Old Man's Blend White** ✓ 🗒 ⓥ Successful sauvignon-led, chenin, semillon combo. Designed for enjoyment rather than show, **13** has gooseberry piquancy, zesty freshness.

The Old Man's Blend Red ✓ 🗒 ⓥ ★★★★ Merlot leads 4-part blend & gives lightly oaked **12** a smoky, berry-rich succulence, spot on for an early drinking wine. WO Coastal, like White. **The Old Man's Sparkle Brut Rosé Méthode Cap Classique** ⓥ ★★★☆ Switch to 70% chardonnay brings **NV**'s citrus to the fore, pinot noir's red berries subservient. Enhances freshness & appeal. — CR

■ **Groot Geluk** *see* Villiera Wines

Groot Parys Estate 🍷

Location/WO: Paarl ▪ Map: Paarl & Wellington ▪ Est 1699 ▪ 1stB 1709 ▪ Tasting & sales by appt ▪ Owner(s) Eric Verhaak, Mariëtte Ras & Peter Ras ▪ Viticulturist(s) Gawie Kriel (consultant) ▪ 81ha/45ha (ptage, ruby cab, chard, chenin, cbard) ▪ 105t 90% white 10% rosé ▪ CERES internationally certified organic ▪ PO Box 82 Huguenot 7645 ▪ grootparys@wam.co.za ▪ www.grootparys.co.za ▪ S 33° 44' 48.0" E 018° 58' 41.6" ▪ **T +27 (0)72-480-9550**

Chenin blanc and organic farming are Groot Parys' Dutch co-owner, Mariëtte Ras', twin passions. Last year she travelled to Lesotho to vinify the maiden vintage off chenin vines planted in partnership with the Thamea family. This prompted her quip: 'Could Platter's in the not too distant future become an African wineguide?'

Die Tweede Droom range

★★★★ **Chenin Blanc Vatgegis** 🌿 Drier than **11** (★★★★), seasoned-oak-fermented (natural yeasts) **12** shows lemon & quince complexity, freshness; needs year/2 for obvious wood to integrate.

★★★★ **Straw Wine** 🌿 Characterful dessert from air-dried chenin, **12** similar to unctuous **11**, integrated all-new oak, endless orange marmalade farewell.

> **Pinotage** NEW ☺ 🌿 ★★★ Cheerful **13** winery's first red. Crafted for early consumption: lightly wooded & fruity, to enjoy slightly chilled.

Rosé Vatgegis NEW 🌿 ★★★★ Older-barrel-fermented **12** from ruby cab, dry & savoury; interesting & quite serious. Should keep few years. **Chardonnay Vatgegis** 🌿 Await new, as for **Chenin Blanc Unwooded Wild Yeast**. **Chenin Blanc Dopkontak** ✓ 🌿 ★★★★ Extended skin/lees contact & natural yeasts give **12** a fino sherry nuttiness, pleasant grip. As tangy as **11** (★★★★); fermented in 2nd fill oak as previous 'new'. Worth seeking out. **Chenin Blanc Iced** NEW 🌿 ★★★★ From air-dried & frozen grapes fermented in 2nd fill oak. **13**, with icing sugar flavour, not as sweet or complex as sibling dessert above. **Chenin Blanc Sparkling** NEW 🌿 ★★★ Characterful bottle-fermented dry bubbly, among few oaked versions. **12**

bursts with Granny Smith apple aromas, flavours & acidity, though ends a tad short. Discontinued: **Chardonnay Unwooded**.

Groot Parys range
Rosé Unwooded 🌸 Await new, like **Chenin Blanc Unwooded**. — CvZ

Group CDV

Location: Somerset West • WO: Swartland/Western Cape • Est/1stB 2006 • Closed to public • Owner(s) Groupe LFE BV Netherlands • Cellarmaster(s) Nicky Versfeld (consultant) • 1,200,000cs own label 60% red 35% white 5% rosé • Fairtrade • PO Box 88 Somerset Mall 7137 • rob@groupelfe.co.za • www.groupelfe.co.za • **T +27 (0)21-850-0160** • F +27 (0)21-851-3578

Selling well over a million cases, mainly to Europe, Group CDV (Cape Dutch Vignerons) is first and foremost a negociant. Owned by Groupe LFE of the Netherlands, it also offers services to those seeking value-for-money South African wines. In addition to those listed below, also available are the export-only Kaapse Geskenk and Songloed ranges. MD Rob Coppoolse's favourite is Klein Kasteelberg Chardonnay. 'It goes so well with the summer on the veranda!'

Centennial 5 Barrel Reserve range
Shiraz ⓟ ★★★ Vibrant **08** red berries & savoury nuances; ripe creamy tannins for early enjoyment.

Groupe LFE South Africa range
Grâce Blanche Natural Sweet 🍴 🗎 ★★ Delicate **13** balanced sweetness, low alcohol for all-day quaffing. WO W Cape.

Klein Centennial range
Pinotage 🍴 🗎 ★★★ Pre-bottling, mulberry & strawberry attraction on commendably dry & sociable **13**. These all WO W Cape. **Shiraz Rosé** NEW 🍴 🗎 ★ Boiled sweet note on lightish, dry **13**, tasted ex tank. **Chenin Blanc-Viognier** NEW 🍴 🗎 ★★★ Provisionally rated preview **13** has chenin's spice & floral notes, none of viognier's blowsiness. Fresh, promises easy-drinking satisfaction once bottled.

Klein Kasteelberg Private Bin range
Merlot 🍴 🗎 ★★★ Greater depth of aroma & flavour in this export-only line-up than sibling KK range. **12** exudes plums, mulberries, firmer tannins need food. **Pinotage** 🍴 🗎 ★★ Faint varietal banana, strawberry on lightly fruited, dry **12** quaffer. **Shiraz Rosé** ⓟ 🍴 🗎 Await next. **Chardonnay** 🍴 🗎 ★★ Unwooded **13** pleasant, albeit more 'dry white' than 'chardonnay'. **Secco** ⓟ 🗎 ★★★ Bouncy peach-toned **NV**, dry & lightly spritzy.

Klein Kasteelberg range
Merlot 🍴 🗎 ★★ **12** uncomplicated dry red to enjoy with friends at the braai. **Pinotage** 🍴 🗎 ★★ **12** doesn't shout the variety but is easy to drink. **Shiraz Rosé** ⓟ 🍴 🗎 ★★ Fresh & dry **10** with candyfloss flavour. **Chardonnay** 🍴 🗎 ★★ Faint citrus notes on very lightly flavoured unwooded **13**. **Chenin Blanc** ⓟ 🍴 🗎 ★★★ **10** softly dry & fresh cling peach-toned thirst quencher.

Nuwe Wynplaas range NEW
Cabernet Sauvignon 🍴 🗎 ★★★ Juicy **12** has cranberry flavours, firm tannins to pair with steak. **Merlot** 🍴 🗎 ★★★ Juicy fruit firmly gripped by tannins, **12** for country fare. **Chardonnay** 🍴 🗎 ★★ **13** fresh but lightly flavoured. — CvZ

Grünberger

Introduced more than 60 years ago, the flattish, rounded 'bocksbeutel' flagon, first of its kind in South Africa, remains a feature of this Natural Sweet range by Distell.

Freudenlese ☺ ★★★ Sweet, fragrant mix sauvignon, white muscadel & gewürztraminer, **13** generous honeyed flavours, low ±7% alcohol. Perfect korma wine.

Spritziger ★★ Spritzy **13** gently sweet but sassy party-goer. **Spritziger Rosé** ★★ Ruby cab supplies the blush for lightish, slightly spritzy **13**, creamily sweet & candyflossy. **Rosenlese** ★★ Pleasant sweet rosé with arresting coral colour from cab, **13** light (±7% alcohol), delicate strawberries-&-cream flavour. — DB, HJ

Grundheim Wines   ♟♦&

Location: Oudtshoorn ▪ Map: Klein Karoo & Garden Route ▪ WO: Klein Karoo/Western Cape ▪ Est/1stB 1995 ▪ Tasting & sales Mon-Fri 9-5 Sat 9-1 ▪ Fee R20 for groups of 10+ ▪ Closed Easter Fri/Sun, Dec 25 & Jan 1 ▪ Owner(s) Danie Grundling ▪ Winemaker(s) Dys Grundling (1997) ▪ 25ha (cinsaut, muscadel r/w, ruby cab, tinta, touriga, cbard, hanepoot, palomino) ▪ 360t/10,000L own label 100% fortified ▪ PO Box 400 Oudtshoorn 6620 ▪ grundheim@absamail.co.za ▪ S 33° 37' 40.1" E 022° 3' 54.6" ▪ **T +27 (0)44-272-6927** ▪ F +27 (0)86-616-6311

Aside from fortified dessert wines and brandy, the Grundling family makes a speciality of witblits, South Africa's fiery eau de vie, with a range which includes buchu- and chilli-infused varieties. If names like 'Bite' and 'Firehose' aren't sufficient warning, the labels additionally portray owner Danie Grundling's Withond (Bull Terrier): 'Once it bites, it doesn't let go,' explains the lady of the house.

Grund heim Wines range

★★★★ **Rosyntjiewyn** ⓦ ⓥ Jerepiko-style dessert, **11** (★★★) is 100% touriga & very sweet; though checked by firm tannin, misses crispness & alcohol punch of previous **NV**, which included pinotage.

★★★★ **Late Bottled Vintage** ⓦ Commendable & complex winter-warming port-style from touriga & tinta. **09** (★★★★), first since **05** (only touriga), is richly fruity & textured. WO W Cape, as Rosyntjiewyn.

Red Muscadel ⓦ ⓥ ★★ Rosepetal-nuanced **11** fortified firesider is extremely sweet, doesn't linger. **White Muscadel** ⓦ ⓥ ★★★ Clean & pure flavours of fresh grapes & orange rind on satisfying **12** fortified sweetie. **Rooi Jerepiko** NEW ⓥ ★★★ Equal touriga, pinotage **NV** has appealing chocolate-coated Xmas cake richness, very sweet though, needs more fiery grip. **Cape Ruby Port** ⓦ ★★★ Easy-drinking **NV** from touriga, spiced plum jam, balanced finish. **Cape Vintage Port** ⓦ ★★★★ Bit soft for style, but **09** good dense fruit from touriga, layered with chocolate. **White Port** ⓦ ★★★ Fortified chenin aged year in old brandy barrels. **10** fynbos & almond notes, with honey-slathered yellow plum & pear, lovely sweet/savoury contrast in the tail.

Brandy range NEW

Potstill Brandy ★★★ Firm & powerful with floral & dried fruit notes, hint of smoke & caramel. Leanish style, quite fiery for 9 year old. Dry, savoury oaky finish. 100% potstill from colombard & chenin. — WB, CR, TJ, CvZ

■ **Grysberg** *see* Wandsbeck Wyne Koöp Bpk
■ **G Spot** *see* United Nations of Wine

Guardian Peak Wines   ♟♦🍴

Location/map: Stellenbosch ▪ WO: Western Cape/Stellenbosch/Wellington/Stellenbosch ▪ Est 1998 ▪ 1stB 2000 ▪ Tasting & sales Mon-Sun 9-5 ▪ Closed Easter Fri/Sun, Dec 25 & Jan 1 ▪ Guardian Peak Winery & Grill (see Restaurants section) ▪ Owner(s) Jean Engelbrecht ▪ Winemaker(s) Philip van Staden (Jan 2009) ▪ Viticulturist(s) Dirkie Mouton (Jun 2010) ▪ 50,000cs own label 100% red ▪ Brands for clients: Pick's Pick ▪ IPW ▪ PO Box 473 Stellenbosch 7599 ▪ info@guardianpeak.com ▪ www.guardianpeak.com ▪ S 34° 0' 40.19" E 018° 50' 31. 99" ▪ **T +27 (0)21-881-3899** ▪ F +27 (0)21-881-3388

Owner Jean Engelbrecht (also proprietor of highly regarded Rust en Vrede nearby) has entered into long-term contracts with grape growers to ensure longevity and consistency, and allow his winery (and restaurant) to truly reflect a sense of place. Said 'place' being the beautiful and prestigious 'Golden Triangle' presided over by Guardian Peak, the highest point on Stellenbosch Mountain, now more prominently displayed on the redesigned labels.

★★★★ **Lapa Cabernet Sauvignon** ⓥ **11** (★★★★) steps up a gear on **10** in its restrained cassis cocoa richness with light brush of fynbos. Satin smooth yet tautly structured, the palate is layered, textured & beautifully integrated. WO Stellenbosch.

★★★★ **Frontier** ⓥ Switches to 100% cab in previewed **12**, with silky cassis fruit framed by ripe tannins. **11** was a cab, shiraz merlot mix. Both lithe & supple with cedar spice & layers of interest.

★★★★ **SMG 11** has black cherry vibrancy from unoaked grenache while shiraz still leads mourvèdre, as in **10**. Ripe yet layered. Ample spice & lightly tannic tail. WO Stellenbosch.

★★★★ **Tannat-Malbec** ⓥ Cheery blueberry anise appeal to **10** (★★★★). Friendly, ripe & juicy, it's light bodied, ending on a gentle note. **09** more firm. Dual Wellington/Stellenbosch WO.

Merlot ⓥ ★★★★ Hedgerow fruit & compote spice on velvety **12**. Concentration & depth combine with a gentle tannic squeeze from combo French/American oak. **Shiraz** 🍴 ⓥ ★★★★ Plush & yielding spicy blue & plum fruit on **12**. Light & fresh with medium density. Succulent tail. **Sauvignon Blanc** NEW 🔲 🖩 ★★★★ Zesty **13** is more crisp & fresh than **12**. Both are lengthy & succulent while the older wine is rounder. — FM

■ **Gugu** *see* Belbon Hills Private Cellar
■ **Guinea Fowl** *see* Saxenburg Wine Farm
■ **Guru** *see* Hoopenburg Wines
■ **Gwendolyn** *see* Saxenburg Wine Farm
■ **Hagelsberg** *see* Middelvlei Estate

Halala Afrika Wines

These are export wines of highly rated Stellenbosch producer Rudera, intended for early and easy drinking. The name means 'Celebrate Africa'.

Merlot NEW ★★ Savoury & earthy rather than fruity, **12** noticeably dry. WO W Cape, as all. **Shiraz** 🔲 ★★☆ Smoky bacon & spice on **11** youthfully unsettled tank sample, needs short time to settle. **Chenin Blanc** 🔲 ★★★ **13** preview ripe apple & primary guava, fresh & fruity with gentle acidity. — JP

Location: Hermanus • Map: Elgin, Walker Bay & Bot River • WO: Hemel-en-Aarde Valley • Est 1975 • 1stB 1981 • Tasting & sales Mon-Fri 9–5 Sat 9–1 • Closed Easter Fri/Mon, Dec 26 & Jan 1 • Tours by appt • Fynbos reserve & 2 wetlands • Owner(s) Anthony Hamilton Russell • Winemaker(s) Hannes Storm (2004) • Viticulturist(s) Johan Montgomery (2005) • 170ha/52ha (pinot, chard) • 18,704cs own label 50% red 50% white • BWI Champion • PO Box 158 Hermanus 7200 • hrv@hermanus.co.za • www.hamiltonrussellvineyards.com • S 34° 23' 23.0" E 019° 14' 30.6" • **T +27 (0)28-312-3595** • F +27 (0)28-312-1797

Hamilton Russell Vineyards

Hemel-en-Aarde Valley pioneer and 2nd generation family estate, Hamilton Russell Vineyards specialises in pinot noir and chardonnay, enjoying an enviable, enduring international reputation for quality and unusually classic styling given its New World origin. With 22 years at the helm, owner and globetrotter Anthony Hamilton Russell is well qualified to comment on the state of the local industry and the perception of its wine in foreign markets. He's adamant that the best South African wines have never been better value in a world context, sadly because 'Country of Origin South Africa' carries an unwarranted discount. This extends to his own wines, which offer particular value for those who enjoy top Burgundy but not that French region's price premium.

★★★★ **Pinot Noir** 🖩 Pair of vintages tasted, both ±30% new oak, 8-10 months, with hallmark understated authority, restraint. **12** (★★★★★) riper & generous, raspberry & strawberry fruit, fine seam of acidity & tannin; **11** more delicate but with same silken conclusion. Delicious now, worth cellaring good few years.
★★★★★ **Chardonnay** 🖩 Perennial star in SA's chardonnay firmament, always paying homage to Montrachet with its sleek lines, layered complexity. Poised **12** worthy follow-up to stately **11**. Taut & pure, with deft oak framing lime-lemon fruit. 7% fermented in clay amphoras & tank. Will richly reward cellaring. — CvZ

Hannay Wines

Location/WO: Elgin • Map: Elgin, Walker Bay & Bot River • Est/1stB 2011 • Tasting & sales Mon-Fri 9–5 Sat/Sun/after hours by appt only • Fee R10 pp for groups of 10+ • Closed Easter Fri-Mon & Dec 25 • Cellar tours by appt • BYO picnic • Light/buffet lunches & picnics by appt • Owner(s) Malcolm J Dicey • Cellarmaster(s) Catherine Marshall (Jan 2011, consultant) • Winemaker(s) Catherine Marshall (Jan 2011, consultant), with Shawn Fortuin (Jan 2011, consultant) • Viticulturist(s) Kevin Watt (2012, consultant) • 72ha/15ha under vine • 150t mostly sold to other cellars, own label 50% red 50% white • IPW • PO Box 36 Elgin 7680 • info@valleygreen.co.za, elzaan@valleygreen.co.za • S 34° 12' 12.07" E 19° 02' 35.10" • **T +27 (0)21-848-9770** • F +27 (0)86-718-2203

Another fledgling producer in the burgeoning Elgin Wine Route, owner Malcolm Dicey teamed up with respected winemaking consultant Catherine Marshall (see separate entry) to guide him through the opening phases. His experience in growing table grapes in the Hex River valley is now being tweaked to address the complexities of fine wine.

Cabernet Franc ⊕ ⍉ ★★★ Soundly crafted **11** has pleasant body & shape, but lacks varietal definition. Spicy berry juice with firm tannin cloak. **Sauvignon Blanc** ⊕ ⍰ ⍉ ★★★★ Promising 2nd release **12** still unsettled mid-2012 but showing substance & complexity, & a lingering finish. —GdB

■ **Harmonie Wine Cellar** *see* Snowfield Boutique Winery
■ **Harmony Tree** *see* United Nations of Wine

Harrison Hope

Location: Queenstown ▪ Est 2000 ▪ 1stB 2009 ▪ Tasting & tours by appt ▪ Accommodation ▪ Owner(s) Ronnie & Janet Vehorn ▪ Cellarmaster(s)/winemaker(s)/viticulturist(s) Ronnie Vehorn ▪ 2ha (merlot, ptage, chard) ▪ 2,000cs own label ▪ PO Box 1394 Queenstown 5320 ▪ rvehorn@gmail.com ▪ www.harrisonhope.com ▪ S 32° 10′ 01.11″ E 026° 50′ 28.28″ ▪ **T +27 (0)40-842-9444/+27 (0)82-808-5284** ▪ F +27 (0)40-842-9200

Harrison Hope is owned by American couple Ronnie and Janet Vehorn, who arrived in the Eastern Cape in 1988 to do missionary work. Their small vineyard near the village of Whittlesea represents missionary work of another kind: generating economic and skills development for the local community. A recipient of their Mentorship In Wine Excellence program, started in 2012, is 25-year-old local Monwabisi Feni, who has just completed his first year.

Hartenberg Estate

Location/map/WO: Stellenbosch ▪ Est/1stB 1978 ▪ Tasting & sales Mon-Fri 9–5/9-5.30 (Nov-Easter) Sat 9–4 Sun (Dec-Easter only) 10-4 ▪ Closed Good Fri, Dec 25 & Jan 1 ▪ Tasting fee for groups, refunded with purchase ▪ Cellar tours by appt ▪ Picnics & lunches 12-2.15: daily seasonal blackboard menus ▪ Light snacks, specialised food & wine pairings, charcuterie and cheese platters served throughout the day ▪ Facilities for children ▪ Farm produce ▪ Conference facility by appt only ▪ Walking/hiking trail ▪ Bird watching ▪ Bottelary Renosterveld Conservancy ▪ Owner(s) Hartenberg Holdings ▪ Cellarmaster(s) Carl Schultz (Nov 1993) ▪ Winemaker(s) Patrick Ngamane (Jan 2001), with Oscar Robyn (Nov 2003) ▪ Viticulturist(s) Wilhelm Joubert (May 2006) ▪ 187ha/ 85ha (cab, merlot, shiraz, chard, riesling, sauv) ▪ 550t/60,000cs own label 80% red 20% white ▪ BWI, IPW ▪ PO Box 12756 Die Boord 7613 ▪ info@hartenbergestate.com ▪ www.hartenbergestate.com ▪ S 33° 53′ 52.5″ E 018° 47′ 30.4″ ▪ **T +27 (0)21-865-2541** ▪ F +27 (0)21-865-2153

Cellarmaster Carl Schultz will have to have to get used the term 'veteran' winemaker after celebrating 20 years with this renowned Bottelary Hills property last year. Under Carl's quiet, calm leadership the estate's offering has become shiraz focused, with five distinct and classy varietal iterations, plus a blend and CWG Auction bottlings in the line-up now. Yet there's enough novelty to maintain winelovers' attention - see the new rieslings below - and, with the annual Riesling Rocks and Shiraz & Charcuterie festivals, enough pizzazz and a warm country welcome to keep visitors returning to the cellardoor.

Ultra Premium range

★★★★☆ **Gravel Hill Shiraz** Powerful yet polished & taut **09** reflects top vintage & gravelly site. Leashed black fruit whispers rather than shouts. Light, powdery violet subtext to refined, concentrated palate. Genteel backbone & length from 22 months all-new French oak. Effortlessly refined.

Super Premium range

★★★★☆ **The Stork Shiraz** ⍉ Cherry fruitcake boldness of **10** more than matches outspoken **09**. Clay soils influence gregarious nature of ripe richness & succulent palate. Oak (20 months all new French) is integrated & balanced. Lingering dry finish.

★★★★☆ **The Mackenzie** ⍉ Cab leads trio merlot & petit verdot in refined **10** red Bordeaux-style blend. As elegant, poised & balanced as **09**. Cassis, star anise & cocoa mingle harmoniously on effortlessly svelte layered & structured palate. Years of enjoyment ahead.

★★★★☆ **The Eleanor Chardonnay** ⍉ Harmony oozes from every pore of smart barrel-fermented **10**. Marmalade, cream, vanilla & hazelnut with light orange freshness adding life. Fruit, acid & wood tango confidently on a structured palate, as in **09**.

CWG Auction Reserves

★★★★☆ **Cabernet Sauvignon** NEW 🏵 Hedgerow fruits & fynbos edge to svelte **10**. Smooth & silky, with polish & refinement as befits best cab vineyard fruit. Broad, deep & complex, with layers of rich spice & fruitcake flavour. As supple as a gymnast, it'll reward patience.

★★★★☆ **Shiraz** 🏵 Blueberry muffin & plum pudding impact on sultry **10**. Bold, powerful & yet restrained with depth & concentration. Firm frame but sleek & supple despite 21 months oaking, 80% new French. A triumphant expression of the farm's trademark grape.

Premium range

★★★★ **Cabernet Sauvignon** ✓ 🏵 Brooding yet succulent thyme-brushed cassis on **10**. Cigar leaf & liquorice twist on layered yet firm palate. Nothing is overplayed - including 60% new oak.

★★★★ **Merlot** ✓ 🏵 **10** elegant yet powerful cocoa & juicy red fruit appeal. Plush suppleness, with gentle caress of silky tannin from 18 months oak, 50% new. Matches **09** in deep, dark concentrated finish.

★★★★ **Shiraz** ✓ 🏵 Cranberry & plum spice on **10**, which happily holds its own against stellar stablemates. Toned yet ripe & refined, with light lavender nuance.

★★★★ **Chardonnay** ✓ 🏵 **11** seamlessly merges tangerine vibrancy with vanilla cream from barrel ferment. Textured & rich yet lean & focused throughout. A peaches & cream delight with a dry finish.

★★★★ **Riesling** 🏵 Flinty lime zest typicity of **12** is toned by gentle sweetness of 10% botrytis portion. Pure & intense, with nectarine freshness. Never loses poise or focus. Lingering.

★★★★ **Riesling Noble Late Harvest** NEW ✓ 🏵 Confident debut for **10**, with oily tang typical of riesling. Brûlée & marmalade richness balanced by fresh lime acidity. Toned sweetness doesn't cloy in long aftertaste.

Doorkeeper Shiraz ✓ 🏵 ★★★★ Entry-level **11**'s savoury, tangy black berries are lighter than big siblings' but enough backbone to last. **Cabernet Sauvignon-Shiraz** ✓ 🏵 ★★★★ Fynbos & cigarbox edge to **11**. Peppery lift on juicy palate. Supportive oak adds body, length. **Occasional Riesling** NEW 🏵 ★★★★ Waxy lime typicity on maiden **12**. Kiss of botrytis apparent in gentle peach notes. Juicy & lively yet lean, poised & dry. **Sauvignon Blanc** 🏵 ★★★★ Taut granadilla & white pepper zip on pared-down **12**. Lees influence adds creamy body, weight & length. — FM

Hartswater Wine Cellar

Location: Hartswater ▪ Map: Northern Cape, Free State & North West ▪ WO: Northern Cape ▪ Tasting & sales Mon-Fri 8.30-1, 2-5 ▪ Sales also from outlet in Hartswater; orders delivered to liquor stores in Northern Cape (350km radius), Free State & North West ▪ Cellar tours by appt ▪ Owner(s) Orange River Wine Cellars ▪ Winemaker(s) Deon Truter ▪ 800t ▪ PO Box 2335 Hartswater 8570 ▪ deon@wynkelder.co.za ▪ S 27° 55' 2.2" E 024° 49' 38.2" ▪ **T +27 (0)53-474-0700** ▪ F +27 (0)53-474-0975

Under the aegis of Orange River Wine Cellars, this far-flung winery in the Hartswater irrigation region of the Northern Cape produces uncomplicated, mostly sweet easy-drinkers with whimsical elemental names for its own brand.

Elements range

Earth 🍷 ★★ Juicy, fruity, light-bodied & near-dry **NV** red from ruby cab. **Fire** 🍷 ★★ Fully sweet **NV** rosé from ruby cab. **Wind** 🍷 ★★ Acrid edge to near-dry **NV** from colombard. **Rain** 🍷 ★★ Semi-sweet **NV** from colombard with modest 10% alcohol. **Thunder** 🍷 ★★ Semi-sweet **NV** version of Earth.

Overvaal range

Red Jerepico 🕐 ★★★ Extremely sweet **NV** ruby cab fortified dessert is rescued by firm spirit grip. **White Jerepico** 🕐 🍷 ★★ Fleshy raisin sweetness, **NV** fortified from fernão pires. — GdB

Haskell Vineyards

Location/map/WO: Stellenbosch ▪ Est 2002 ▪ 1stB 2008 ▪ Tasting & sales Tue-Fri 9-5 Sat/Sun 10-5 ▪ Fee R40 - only for tasting on weekends ▪ Closed Mon, Easter Fri-Mon & Dec 25 ▪ Cellar tours on special request only ▪ The Long Table Restaurant & Café Tue-Sun 9-5; light dinners Fri (Sep-Mar) - booking essential ▪ Facilities for children ▪ Self-catering accommodation in The Residence and Cottage (see Accommodation section) ▪ Owner(s) Preston Haskell ▪ Cellarmaster(s) Rianie Strydom (Jan 2005) ▪ Viticulturist(s) Wikus Pretorius (Dec 2005) ▪ 25ha/13.5ha (cabs s/f, merlot, shiraz, chard) ▪ ±80t/3,600cs own label 80% red 20% white ▪ PO Box 12766 Die Boord 7613 ▪ info@haskellvineyards.com ▪ www.haskellvineyards.com ▪ S 34° 0' 13.9" E 018° 51' 38.4" ▪ **T +27 (0)21-881-3895** ▪ F +27 (0)21-881-3986

Haskell Vineyards CEO Grant Dodd and cellarmaster Rianie Strydom are 100% comfortable benchmarking multiple vintages of the stellar Haskell IV blended red against top international examples - with local media vindicating their faith when awarding it top scores. Their confidence echoes that of American owner Preston Haskell, who bought this premium property in Stellenbosch's renowned 'Golden Triangle' more than a decade ago, investing considerably in replanting and rejuvenation. Confidence is about attitude, so much so that 'interesting wines - not just our own' are on offer in the tasting room, shared with sibling brand Dombeya (listed separately).

★★★★★ **Pillars Syrah** ⊕ Sensuous, textured & concentrated **10** (★★★★☆) follows brilliant **08** (no **09**). Intense, brooding yet silky & expressive refined black fruit. Perfumed & complex, with restraint in oaking evident. Glorious long finish.

★★★★☆ **Aeon Syrah** ⊕ Expressive floral & spice abundance, **10** (★★★★) ample vibrant black fruit intensity & concentration but oak is tad prominent, needs time to knit. **08** more heady. **09** not made.

★★★★ **Haskell IV** ⊕ Cab leads merlot, petit verdot & cab franc in sophisticated Bordeaux-style blend. **08** (★★★★★) steps up from **07**. Rich, full, lithe & concentrated, with depth & intensity. Firm yet yielding structure.

★★★★☆ **Anvil Chardonnay** Seamlessly svelte & elegant **12** offers lime & lemon curd vibrancy as it glissades on polished oak stage. Integration & harmony as good as **11**. Refined & silky, with a light zesty twist in the long, full finish.

Haskell II Occasional release. — FM

Hathersage

Location: Somerset West ▪ Map: Helderberg ▪ WO: Stellenbosch ▪ 1stB 2007 ▪ Tasting & sales by appt Mon-Fri 9-4 ▪ Closed all pub hols ▪ Tour groups ▪ Conference & wedding/function venue with catering (10-150 pax) ▪ Conservation area ▪ Owner(s) Stephan Holdings cc & Stephan Brothers (Pty) Ltd ▪ Winemaker(s) Michael Liedtke (Jan 2010, consultant) ▪ 40ha/12ha (cabs s/f, merlot, p verdot, shiraz, chard, sauv, sem) ▪ 52t/3,036cs own label 43% red 57% white ▪ PO Box 2517 Somerset West 7129 ▪ info@hathersage.co.za ▪ www. hathersage.co.za ▪ S 34° 4' 54.42" E 018° 51' 55.32" ▪ **T +27 (0)21-851-1644/+27 (0)21-851-5076** ▪ F +27 (0)21-851-8382

A lot more than winegrowing happens now (market days, weddings, conferences) on what winemaker Michael Liedtke describes as 'the last green belt almost in the centre of Somerset West'. But vines and wine go back the longest way, here on the Lourens River banks, with historic Schapenberg rising above.

★★★★ **Cabernet Sauvignon** Finely textured **10** (★★★★) with well-managed tannins. Lifted spice despite herbal notes - no doubt abetted by 15% merlot. Firmer, more restrained than delicately perfumed **09**.

★★★★ **Merlot** Light herbal tealeaf aromas on deep crimson **11** (★★★★). Well-expressed fruit & savoury, lightly grippy tannins giving some austerity on the finish. Less serious than **09** barrel sample.

Special Edition Red Blend 🍽 Await next. **Mouille Grange** [NEW] ★★☆ Cab-based **10** Bordeaux red shows delicate green-edged spice. Insubstantial but elegant, some grip. **Chardonnay** ★★☆ Subtly oaked, modest **12** has faint brioche & light citrus notes. **Sauvignon Blanc** 🍽 ★★★ Floral, cut grass & honeysuckle whiffs on **12**; lacks opulence of more tropical **11** (★★★★). Both with a splash of semillon. **Semillon** ✓ ★★★★ Restrained, faint lanolin aromas on **12** with 15% sauvignon. Thatchy, not green, though some savoury fern-leaf notes. More detail, dimension than previous. **Special Edition White Reserve** ★★★ Adds 'Special Edition' to name in **12** sauvignon-semillon blend. Faintly peachy, fresh & zesty. Not charmless but needs a year or so to emerge. — MF

Haute Cabrière

Location/map: Franschhoek ▪ WO: Western Cape/Franschhoek ▪ Est 1982 ▪ 1stB 1984 ▪ Tasting & sales Mon-Fri 9-5 Sat/pub hols 10-4 Sun 11-4 ▪ Fees: classic selection R30pp/5 wines, premium selection R40pp/6 wines, exclusive cap classique R60pp/5 MCC ▪ Public cellar tour/tasting Mon-Fri 11 & 3 and cellarmaster's tour/tasting Sat at 11 R60pp; private tasting/tour (pre-booked) R70pp ▪ Closed Good Fri, Dec 25/26 & Jan 1 ▪ Haute Cabrière Restaurant (see Restaurants section) ▪ Tour groups ▪ Owner(s) Clos Cabrière Ltd ▪ Cellarmaster(s) / Winegrower(s) Achim von Arnim (1984), with Takuan von Arnim (2005) ▪ Viticulturist(s) Nikey van Zyl (Aug 2011) ▪ 30ha (pinot, chard) ▪ 40% red 60% white ▪ PO Box 245 Franschhoek 7690 ▪ marketing@cabriere.co.za ▪ www.cabriere.co.za ▪ S 33° 54' 51.8" E 019° 8' 8.2" ▪ **T +27 (0)21-876-8500** ▪ F +27 (0)21-876-8501

This Franschoek family estate was the first in the Cape to specialise in sparkling wines and, although there are a handful of other wines now also made, there has been no deviation from the restriction in the vineyards to growing just chardonnay and pinot noir. It's clearly something of an obsession handed down from father (Achim von Arnim) to son (Takuan) – both of whom insist they are winegrowers, perhaps cellarmasters, but not winemakers. Terroir and vines are what count most: 'sun, soil, vine, man' is the mantra mounted on a sundial-supporting pillar at the entrance to the tasting room.

Haute Cabrière range

Pinot Noir ★★★ Perfumed & elegant **10**, quietly satisfying & supple flavours, accessible & probably best enjoyed early. Franschhoek WO. **Unwooded Pinot Noir** ⊕ 🍽 ★★★ Rounded, easy-drinking **11** not completely dry; cherry fruit, slight spice. **Chardonnay-Pinot Noir** ✓ 🍽 ★★★★ Faintly pink-hued light **13**, fresh & elegant with savoury, faintly tannic sweet-sour edge.

Pierre Jourdan range

★★★★ **Blanc de Blancs** Crafted chardonnay MCC with delicate lime-citrus aromas, subtle biscuit notes. Latest **NV** 24-36 months on lees, mousse a little exuberant but offering lime-edged creaminess, persistence.
★★★★ **Cuvée Reserve** Luminous green gold, latest chardonnay **NV** 5 years on lees. Faint camphor whiffs, lacking the baked bread richness of previous, more complex release.

> **Tranquille** ☺ 🍽 ★★★ Pale mauve-edged, pinot-chardonnay rosé. Current **NV** fresh, with bright cherry aromas leading to tangy textured finish. Nearly dry.

Cuvée Belle Rose ★★★ Latest burnished bronze **NV** MCC from pinot noir has fine brioche mousse, but herbal, brambly finish. **Brut** ★★★ Fragrant & faintly honeyed MCC with light cherry notes, biscuit whiffs on latest **NV** from chardonnay & pinot. **Brut Sauvage** ★★★ Bone-dry **NV** from chardonnay & pinot; delicate sherry-like whiffs, but restrained & lacking verve. **Ratafia** ★★★★ Chardonnay fortified with house's own brandy. Honeyed grapefruit aromas, light sweet-sour freshness. Current **NV** harmonious, finer & more perfumed than previous. 375 ml. — MF,MW

Haut Espoir ▮ 🍷 📷 🚻 ♿

Location/map/WO: Franschhoek ▪ Est 1999 ▪ 1stB 2004 ▪ Tastings, sales & cellar tours by appt ▪ Closed all pub hols ▪ Fynbos walks ▪ Conservation area ▪ Owner(s) Armstrong family ▪ Cellarmaster(s)/winemaker(s)/viticulturist(s) Rob Armstrong ▪ ±23ha/12ha (cab, merlot, p verdot, shiraz) ▪ 70t/10,000cs own label 70% red 30% white ▪ BWI ▪ PO Box 681 Franschhoek 7690 ▪ wine@hautespoir.co.za ▪ www.hautespoir.co.za ▪ S 33° 56' 23.6" E 019° 6' 20.9" ▪ **T +27 (0)21-876-4000** ▪ F +27 (0)21-876-4038

One of the prime movers behind a conservancy in Franschhoek (along with neighbour Boekenhoutskloof), Haut Espoir cellarmaster Rob Armstrong loves living close to nature. The Scherpenheuwel farm is already managed eco-sensitively, and biodynamic certification is the next goal because of Rob's belief in the benefits for soil, vine, wine and man.

★★★★ **Chardonnay** ⊕ Wild yeast (40%), barrel fermented **08** broad, balanced & complex, spicy end when last tasted. Citrus gleamed through serious oaking (11 months Hungarian & French).
Cabernet Sauvignon ⊕ ★★★★ Previously **05**'s oak provided backbone for pure, ripe & rich black fruits. **Petit Verdot** Next awaited, as for **Shiraz Rosé**. **Shiraz** ⊕ ★★★★ Last-tasted **06** full bodied & concentrated compared with restrained **05** (★★★). Ripe berry & sweet spice flavours, part carbonic maceration. **Gentle Giant** ⊕ ★★★★ Improved **07** merlot-dominated combo previously showed bright sweet ripe berries, spicy oak, good intensity. **Semillon Reserve** ⊕ ★★★ Shy, crisp **07** last showed typical lanolin & fynbos notes. Lightly oaked; modest 12.5% alcohol. — FM

Havana Hills 🍷

Location: Philadelphia ▪ WO: Philadelphia/Coastal ▪ Est 1999 ▪ 1stB 2000 ▪ Closed to public ▪ Owner(s) Kobus du Plessis ▪ Winemaker(s) Piet Kleinhans (Sep 2008), Joseph Gertse (Jan 2000) & Mike Dobrovic (consultant) ▪ Viticulturist(s) Rudi Benn (Jan 2001) ▪ 260ha/60ha (barbera, cabs s/f, merlot, mourv, sangio, shiraz, sauv) ▪ 70,000cs own label 50% red 20% white 30% rosé ▪ Fairtrade, IPW, WIETA ▪ PO Box 451 Melkbosstrand 7437 ▪ sales@havanahills.co.za ▪ www.havanahills.co.za ▪ **T +27 (0)21-972-1110** ▪ F +27 (0)21-972-1105

At the turn of the millennium, Cape businessman Kobus du Plessis discovered almost 300 ha of wheatlands between Melkbosstrand and Philadelphia which he thought would be ideal for high-quality wine production. Today, there are some 60 ha under vineyard and Mike Dobrovic, who previously enjoyed a successful career at Mulderbosch, is consultant. The always deep-feeling Dobrovic is glad to report that new houses with full amenities have recently been built for all the staff, while training on such topics as ecology and environmental awareness are given regularly. Particularly noteworthy is a course in growing vegetables for home consumption, free seed, water and compost available on request.

Kobus range

★★★★☆ **Red** Bordeaux-style **08** (★★★★) is 59% cab, rest merlot, cab franc, already seems quite mature. Brooding nose with forest floor to go with dark berries. Sweet fruited, with moderate acidity & soft tannins. Coastal WO. Lacks majesty of last-tasted **05**.

★★★★ **Chardonnay 12** very youthful on preview. Lime, burnt matchstick, prominent oak (100% new, 8 months). Pleasantly lean with bright acidity & pithy finish. No **11**.

Havana Hills range

★★★★ **Du Plessis Reserve** ⓘ Lovely mix plush berries, pepper & prosciutto reflects **07** blend shiraz, cab, merlot, with fruit deepening on palate. Silky seduction, already drinking well & will do till ±2018. **Cabernet Sauvignon** Next awaited, as for **Petit Verdot**. **Merlot** ⓘ ★★★ Creamy berries with vanilla & spice infusion, **08** instantly appeals, has softly smooth drinkability. **Shiraz** ⓘ ★★★ Juicy dark berries, touch of dried herbs, **10** is gentle, restrained & tasty. **Cabernet Sauvignon-Barbera** ⓘ ★★★☆ This **09** blend shows something different, blackcurrants with a dusty, herbal note, a lively sleekness. **Sauvignon Blanc** 🍷 🥦 ★★★★ Dramatic **13** offers massive intensity of flavour - lots of herbal bite to go with green melon. Thick texture (technically off-dry) but also racy acidity, low alcohol of 11%. Even more over the top than **12** (★★★☆). **Chardonnay-Pinot Noir** NEW 🍷 ★★★ **12** thankfully not too anodyne. Citrus, red fruit, hint of spice. Rich but balanced by tangy acidity. Coastal WO.

Lime Road range

Shiraz ⓘ ★★★ **10** luscious, with black plums, campfire smoke, nice fresh finish. **Cabernet Sauvignon-Merlot-Cabernet Franc** ★★★ Crowd-pleasing **10** has plenty of sweet fruit, no real tannic grip. **Cabernet Sauvignon Rosé** Next awaited. **Sauvignon Blanc** 🍷 🥦 ★★★ **13** nice flavour profile (green melon, hint of grapefruit) but touch sweet, needs more punch. Discontinued: **Merlot Rosé**. — CE

■ **Haven Point** *see* Overhex Wines International
■ **Hawk's Head** *see* Southern Sky Wines

Hawksmoor at Matjieskuil

Location: Paarl ▪ Map: Paarl & Wellington ▪ WO: Paarl/Coastal ▪ Est 1692 ▪ 1stB 2005 ▪ Tasting by appt 10-4 daily ▪ Fee R20, waived on purchase ▪ Sales by appt Mon-Sat ▪ Specialise in group tastings (10-20 people), can provide lunch in the Cape Dutch manor house - prior arrangement essential ▪ Closed Easter Fri-Sun, Dec 25/31 & Jan 1 ▪ Luxury guest house ▪ Owner(s) Brameld Haigh ▪ Winemaker(s) Various ▪ Viticulturist(s) Paul Wallace (2004) ▪ Farm manager Jan Lategan ▪ ±23ha (cab f, mourv, ptage, shiraz, chenin) ▪ ±130t/1,000cs own label 65% red 25% white 10% rosé ▪ PO Box 9 Elsenburg 7607 ▪ wines@hawksmoor.co.za ▪ www.hawksmoor.co.za ▪ S 33° 48' 47.4" E 018° 46' 14.1" ▪ **T** +27 (0)21-884-4587 ▪ F +27 (0)21-884-4465

Grape farming started in the 18th century at Matjieskuil, but the Hawksmoor branding is much more recent, the maiden bottling being 2005. Buildings have been returned to their former glory and serve as a luxury guesthouse. The wines are made offsite by various winemakers, but all from Matjieskuil grapes. Proclivity for experimentation sees a blush wooded chenin debut this edition, and marketing wise, a wine club with redeemable 'Hawksmoor Points' is in the works.

Limited Releases

Mourvèdre ⓘ 🍷 ★★★★ Appealing soft damson fruit, spicy aromas on **08**. **Pinotage** ✓ 🍷 ★★★★ **09** lovely fresh aromas of banana, red berries & cherries, with earthy complexity. Easy & fresh, good poise & balance. First tasted since savoury **06** (★★★). **Vanbrugh** ⓘ 🍷 ★★★ From pinotage, **07** was shy & restrained, with muted berry fruit encased by rigid tannins. **Shiraz** 🍷 ★★★★ Black olives, brine & smoked meats on **09**, with earthy undertone & restrained fruit support. Judicious oaking & lively acid. **Barrel 69** Await next, as for **Saint Alfege's** & **Algernon Stitch**. **Cape Blend** NEW 🍷 ★★★★ Earthy & meaty notes on **09** mourvèdre, shiraz, pinotage combo; tart red fruit & brightly woven acidity. Lightly oaked & fresh. **French Blend With A Cape Twist NEW** ✓ 🍷 ★★★☆ Smoked bacon intro on **09** from shiraz, mourvèdre & pinotage. Spice & delicate red fruit following to dry food-friendly palate, with moderate 13% alcohol (like most of these). **Magdalen** 🕙 🍷 📷 ★★★ Previewed last time as 'Mourvèdre Rosé', **12** had clean entry with good berry richness & delicate lingering dry end. **Rosé** 🕙 🍷 ★★★ Pleasantly plump **09** from mourvèdre & sauvignon, restrained strawberry notes. Coastal WO. **Edward Goodge** 🕙 🍷 ★★☆ **09** chenin was oaky & oxidative. **Paradox NEW** ✓ 🍷 ★★★☆ Previewed **12**, from chenin aged in barrels previously for shiraz, giving onion-skin hue. Light dried peach & delicate berry tones lead to lingering & dry finish. Interesting wine.

Classic range

Hawksmoor Pinotage 🕙 🍷 ★★★ Was just 'Pinotage'. Accessible **06** plummy, rich & earthy. **Serliana** 🕙 🍷 ★★★ Was 'Chenin Blanc'. **12** adds honeysuckle finesse to dried pear & stonefruit complexity. Light & dry, with crisp acidity. — JP

Hazendal

Location/map/WO: Stellenbosch ▪ Est 1699 ▪ 1stB 1950 ▪ Tasting, sales & Hermitage Restaurant Tue-Sun 9-4.30 ▪ Fee R10/5 wines ▪ Closed Good Fri & Jan 1 ▪ Cellar tours Tue-Fri 11-3 ▪ Facilities for children ▪ Tour groups ▪ Gifts ▪ Cheese platters ▪ Conferences ▪ Mountain biking trail ▪ Russian Arts & Culture Museum ▪ Owner(s) Voloshin & Schumacher families ▪ Winemaker(s) Ronell Wiid (Jan 1998) ▪ 140ha/40ha (cab, merlot, pinot, shiraz, chenin, sauv) ▪ 200t/30,000cs own label 50% red 50% white ▪ PO Box 336 Stellenbosch 7599 ▪ info@hazendal.co.za ▪ www.hazendal.co.za ▪ S 33° 54' 2.7" E 018° 43' 9.1" ▪ **T +27 (0)21-903-5035** ▪ F +27 (0)21-903-0057

Tourist-friendly Hazendal in Stellenbosch's Bottelary ward is owned by the Voloshin and Schumacher families. Since acquiring the estate, they have restored and augmented the facilities, including a restaurant, Russian arts and culture museum, conference venue and mountain biking trail.

Hazendal range

Merlot 🕙 ★★★★ Satisfyingly full & intense, **09** improves on **07** (★★★★) with savoury hints & black fruit on substantial tannins. **Pinotage** Await next, as for **Marvol Pinotage**, **Shiraz**, **Shiraz-Cabernet Sauvignon**, **Sauvignon Blanc** & **The Last Straw**. **Bushvine Chenin Blanc** 🕙 ★★★★ Dense, ripe **10** unwooded, from 30 year old vines. Over-delivers at price. **White Nights Brut Cap Classique** 🕙 ★★★★ Champagne-method sparkling **NV** (**07**) 80% chardonnay, with pinot, in classy livery. Discontinued: **Reserve Red**, **Chenin Blanc Wooded**.

De Haas range

Red 🕙 🍷 ★★★ Base-level line of price-friendly quaffers. Meaty-spicy **NV** fresh & undemanding. **Rosé** 🕙 ★★★ Berry flavoured, salmon hued, semi-dry; **NV** with substance. **White** 🕙 🍷 ★★★ **NV** white from chenin-sauvignon high on drinkability. — GdB

■ **HB Vineyards** *see* Hout Bay Vineyards
■ **Heart & Soul** *see* Anura Vineyards
■ **Heeren van Oranje Nassau** *see* De Villiers Wines

Helderberg Wijnmakerij

Location/WO: Stellenbosch ▪ Map: Helderberg ▪ Est 2010 ▪ 1stB 2009 ▪ Tasting & sales Mon-Fri 9-5 ▪ Closed weekends & all pub hols ▪ Owner(s) Boekenhoutskloof Winery (Pty) Ltd ▪ Winemaker(s) Heinrich Hugo (Sep 2010) ▪ 75% red 25% white ▪ BRC, HACCP ▪ PO Box 1037 Stellenbosch 7130 ▪ info@helderbergwijnmakerij.com ▪ www.helderbergwijnmakerij.com ▪ S 34° 1' 45.67" E 018° 48' 19.39" ▪ **T +27 (0)21-842-2371** ▪ F +27 (0)21-842-2373

Owned by Boekenhoutskloof, this property, taking its name from a famous sub-region (and mountain!) in Stellenbosch, offers just a pair of varietal wines. Fun packaging and fine crafting have rejuvenated and transformed the wines. Like siblings The Wolftrap and Porcupine Ridge, they offer good value.

> **Cabernet Sauvignon** 😊 🍷 📷 ★★★ **12** has good typicity: tobacco, cassis & earth, wrapped up in dry youthful tannins, with leafy lift. Fresh & dry. **Sauvignon Blanc** 😊 🍷 📷 ★★★ **13** explodes with upfront passionfruit & crunchy pineapple; vibrancy & zest wonderfully toned by dry finish. — JP

■ **Hendrik Lodewyk** *see* Du Preez Estate

Henry Tayler & Ries   ♀ 🍵

Location: Cape Town ▪ Tasting, sales & distillery tours by appt ▪ Meals/refreshments by arrangement ▪ Owner(s) Henry Tayler & Ries Ltd ▪ 242,000 x 750ml ▪ msingh@htr.co.za ▪ www.htr.co.za ▪ **T +27 (0)21-555-7028**

A subsidiary of Distell, liquor wholesaler Henry Tayler & Ries handles brandies from two Breede River Valley distilleries (in Goudini and Worcester). Its labels Chateau VO, Limosin Extra Fine and Olof Bergh Solera are listed separately.

■ **Hercules Paragon** *see* Simonsvlei International

Hermanuspietersfontein Wynkelder   🍴♀🍵⌂📷&

Location: Hermanus ▪ Map: Elgin, Walker Bay & Bot River ▪ WO: Sunday's Glen/Western Cape/Walker Bay ▪ Est 2005 ▪ 1stB 2006 ▪ Tasting & sales Mon-Fri 9-5 Sat 9-4 Sun (15 Dec-15 Jan) 10.30-3 ▪ Closed Easter Fri/Sun, Dec 25/26 & Jan 1 ▪ Cellar tours on request ▪ Food & wine market Sat 9-1 ▪ Self-catering cottages ▪ Owner(s) /shareholders The Pretorius Family Trust, Bartho Eksteen, Gerrie Heyneke ▪ Winemaker(s) Bartho Eksteen, with Kim McFarlane (Feb 2006) ▪ Viticulturist(s) Lochner Bester (Nov 2012) ▪ 320ha/±62.2ha (cabs s/f, grenache, malbec, merlot, mourv, p verdot, shiraz, nouvelle, sauv, sem, viog) ▪ 265t/20,000cs own label 50% red 40% white 10% rosé ▪ BWI champion ▪ Hemel en Aarde Village, Suite 47, Private Bag X15, Hermanus 7200 ▪ kelder@hpf1855.co.za ▪ www.hpf1855.co.za ▪ S 34° 24' 38.7" E 019° 11' 51.7" ▪ **T +27 (0)28-316-1875** ▪ F +27 (0)28-316-1293

It's nearly a decade since the establishment of this 'proudly local' winery at the entrance to Hemel-en-Aarde Valley and the resort town of Hermanus, founded in 1855 as Hermanuspietersfontein. The grapes are drawn mainly from the large Stanford farm (a Biodiversity & Wine Initiative Champion since 2007) of Johan and Mariette Pretorius. They, and others, are shareholder partners in the winery with winemaker Bartho Eksteen. The farm's different soils and elevations allow varieties as diverse as sauvignon blanc and mourvèdre to thrive. If Bartho is best known for his love of and expertise with sauvignon blanc – he won the 2010 Diners Club Winemaker of the Year award for his No 5 2009 - he has a sure touch with all wines across the range.

Flagship Wines

★★★★ **Die Arnoldus** From vintage with big reputation, cab-led Bordeaux quintet 09 (★★★★☆) in classic style. Aromatic mix cedar spice, fresh cassis; plush, meaty substance to finely knit, insistent frame. All well able to handle 2 years in new oak, & further lengthy ageing. WO W Cape, as next.

★★★★ **Die Martha** 🌿 Full-bodied **10** shiraz, mourvèdre, viognier blend shows spicy, meaty perfume, savoury flavours. Supple texture; sound fresh backbone reigns in ripe, rich finish.

★★★★☆ **CWG Auction Reserve Vloekskoot Sauvignon Blanc** NEW 🌿 **12** aged a year in 500L older oak. The tightest, most rapier-fresh of the whites for this edition, with mere glimpses of allspice, chalky features. Needs time to settle.

★★★★☆ **Die Bartho** 🏠 🌿 Mix oak-fermented sauvignon (65%) & semillon, with splash nouvelle, all then a year in large oak. **12** more sombre-toned than **11**. Bracing acid tension cloaks textural richness which time should expose.

Classic Wines

★★★★ **Swartskaap** 🌿 Retasted, **10** (★★★★) from cab franc shows very quiet spice, leafy features; light texture & fruit; firm dry tannin trim. Good food partner & for current drinking. **09** more concentrated.

★★★★ **Kleinboet** 🌿 Cab-led Bordeaux quintet. **10** (★★★★) light in hue, also lighter fruit & build. But balanced, with pretty spice cassis flavours, dry finish. To drink while **09** (★★★★★) & **08** mature.

★★★★ **Sauvignon Blanc No 5** 🏠 🌿 Distinctive, oaked sauvignon. Hint allspice to expressive aromas on **12**. Slightly awkward sweet fruit & bracing acid are less attractive; but may resolve with further ageing.

★★★★ **Sauvignon Blanc No 3 Bergblokke** 🏠 🌿 **13** at greener end of spectrum but greengage & Granny Smith apple notes are fragrant & offer plenty of succulence on lees-enriched palate. Lightish, with mouthwateringly fresh finish.

★★★★ **Sauvignon Blanc No 7** 🏠 🌿 Vigorous, intense & assertively bone-dry, **13**'s lees-enriched core allows for full varietal repertoire to emerge after few months. Tasted just post-bottling, as was No 3.

★★★★☆ **Sauvignon Blanc No 2** ⊕ 🌿 Tantalising dessert sauvignon, **12** shows great balance of botrytis & varietal character. Full of long-lingering flavour, fruity acid tension; low 8% alcohol. 375 ml bottles.

Makes an impact on you, not the environment.

The new Mercedes-Benz E-Class Hybrid, the world's most efficient luxury sedan.

The new E-Class E300 Hybrid turns power and sophistication into a cleaner, greener experience. By reducing fuel consumption by up to 28% while producing up to 23% fewer CO_2 emissions, it changes the way the world sees you.
For more information visit www.mercedes-benz.co.za/e-class

Vehicle specifications may vary for the South African market.

A Daimler Brand

Mercedes-Benz
The best or nothing.

Located on Audacia wine farm, conveniently just off the R44 between Stellenbosch and Somerset West, ROOT44 is a young but already hugely popular all-weather family-friendly country market, open each weekend and offering everything from antiques, apparel, jewellery, homeware, arts and crafts to organic fresh produce, food of many different styles, local craft beers and, of course, wine. Pictured at the Audacia boutique red wine stall are co-owners **Trevor Strydom** (left) and **Richard Downing**.

Celebrity chef and restaurateur **Reuben Riffel** was recently made brand ambassador for Fairtrade in South Africa, and is responsible for increasing awareness of Fairtrade in the country with special emphasis on the hospitality industry. He has started by adding Fairtrade products to his menus, including De Bos, a wine brand owned by the families living on the home-farm of Bosman Family Vineyards in Wellington.

Catching up with friends over dinner is pleasant. Getting a concierge to recommend and book you a restaurant, now that's Prestige.

Give your banking the Prestige treatment. Experience our other offerings including:

- The VIP treatment you deserve
- Gain exclusive access to the Bidvest Airport lounge
- Valet airport parking at a discounted rate
- Free take me home cab service

For more information visit www.standardbank.co.za/prestige

Standard Bank

Moving Forward™

New to Platter's tasting team this year, sommeliers **David Clarke** (left) and **Gregory Mutambe** arrived in the Cape winelands along very divergent paths: Melbourne-raised David, who is as partial to craft beer as he is wine, via Australia and London; and pinot noir enthusiast Gregory via the country of his birth, Zimbabwe, where he worked as a cellar hand, and Johannesburg. David is on hand to advise guests at Burrata in Woodstock and Gregory oversees the award-winning winelist at Azure Restaurant at the 12 Apostles Hotel and Spa in Camps Bay.

Some choose not to follow their passion. Our track record is proof that we do.

Our passion. Your investment's success.

Right now, we're BUBBLING over with pride!

FIVE of Ultra Liquors own MCCs have been selected for the Best Value Guide 2014... talk about Ultra Sparkling Results!

TABLE BAY
CAPE OF GOOD HOPE
Methode Cap Classique
BRUT
SOUTH AFRICA

TABLE BAY
CAPE OF GOOD HOPE
MCC
BLANC de BLANCS

SECRET CELLAR
MCC
Brut

RT CEL
MCC

SECRET CELLAR
MCC
Brut Rosé

ULTRA Liquors

Distell's Zonnebloem brand has its home in one of South Africa's most significant historic cellars, Adam Tas. Cellarmaster **Deon Boshoff**, appointed at just 32, is a role model for aspirant winemakers and tangible proof that talent, focus and dedication can combine to transcend old school barriers to getting ahead. Deon Leads a team dominated by women - white-wine maker **Elize Coetzee** (left), viticulturist **Annelie Viljoen** (centre) and red-winemaker **Bonny van Niekerk** (right) - and is happy to admit that they add nuance to the wines because of the way they think and approach winemaking.

J.

Joostenberg

Family traditions, good food & wine, happy times & lots of laughter.
Some things never change...

Tel: 021 8844 141 | bistro@joostenberg.co.za
Joostenberg Bistro, Deli, Events Venue, Wines & Pork Butchery
Klein Joostenberg R304 Muldersvlei 7606
www.joostenberg.co.za

REAL AFRICA REAL CLOSE TO CAPE TOWN

DAY TRIP SAFARIS

Welcome drink • 2-3 hour Big-5 Game Drive
Visit adjacent ARC (Animal Rescue Centre)
Lunch in an African Boma restaurant
Browse our African curio shop • Hotel pick-up & transfer

THOSE WHO NEVER STAND STILL. BELONG

DINERS CLUB WINEMAKER OF THE YEAR 2013

CONGRATULATIONS TO THE WINNING WINEMAKERS WHO
PROVED ONCE AGAIN THAT REWARDS BELONG TO THOSE
WHO ARE ALWAYS LEARNING, ALWAYS EXPLORING,
ALWAYS ARRIVING.

FOR THE FULL STORY VISIT CONNOISSEURS.DINERSCLUB.CO.ZA

 Diners Club SA   @DinersClubSA   Diners Club South Africa

A UNIQUE
CELEBRATION OF THE
GREAT MAKERS OF WINES

Now in its 33rd year, the Diners Club Winemaker of the Year Award has become the highlight of the local wine calendar. Keenly anticipated by winemakers eager to leave an enduring mark, the award celebrates the work, the dedication and the genius of the makers of great wines.

The 2012 Diners Club Winemaker of the Year is Razvan Macici, Nederburgs Cellarmaster extraordinaire and deserved winner of the award.

Proving that the journey of a great winemaker can be as rich and as complex as the wines he creates, Razvan Macici began his journey of wine as a child in the vineyards of Dealu Mare, Romania. His father was a prominent Romanian winemaker and the young Macici followed suit.

Razvan rapidly made a name for himself and in 2001 was approached by Nederburg, seeking to reclaim its status as one of the countrys leading names in wine.

As Nederburg Cellarmaster, Razvan has shown remarkable versatility. Equally adept at making red, white and dessert wines he has won kudos for wines across the range.

However, it was his delectable dessert wines that drew the highest praise from the Diners Club Winemaker of the Year judges.

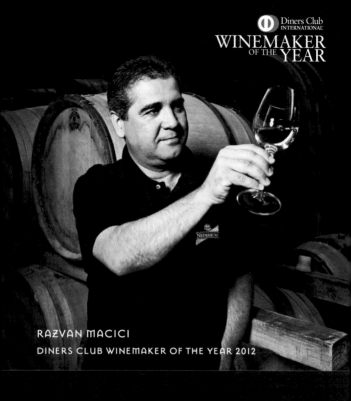

RAZVAN MACICI
DINERS CLUB WINEMAKER OF THE YEAR 2012

Who will be the Winemaker of the Year for 2013?
This year the category is Non-Bordeaux Red
Blends and there has been a gratifying number
of winemakers entering in the hope of lifting the
prestigious award.

The Diners Club Winemaker of the Year Awards are a
vital part of our wine landscape, and as long as there
are great winemakers eager to bottle their talent,
we can be sure South African wines will continue to
grow in stature.

To learn more about Diners Club Winemaker of the
Year, go online to connoisseurs.dinersclub.co.za

Diners Club Connoisseurs is a meeting place, where
like-minded people can converse, learn, share and
cultivate their passion for the   ner things in life.

cuvée

RESTAURANT | van niekerk room

SIMONSIG   Wine Estate's Finest

Cuvée, our signature restaurant, will have you captivated with its quirky mix of nostalgia and Cape Dutch modernism.

Enjoy genuine hospitality and uncomplicated dishes with a sustainable conscience from our locally inspired, seasonal menu, either inside or on the terrace, with a perfect view of the majestic Simonsberg Mountain.

Tel: +27 (0) 21 888 4932
E-mail: cuvee@simonsig.co.za

Tasting & Tours
Taste and learn more about our award winning wines from our knowledgeable team at our tasting room, set amidst the tranquil gardens on the estate.

GPS: 33º 52' 14.19 S
and 18º 49' 34.92 E
www.simonsig.co.za

Skoonma ★★★ **12** shiraz-based blend; uncomplicated ripe fruit, sturdy grip. Less characterful, approachable than previous. WO W Cape. **Bloos** ★★★★ Aromatic, dry **13** rosé from Bordeaux red varieties. Oak, lees-ageing enhance mouthfeel without dimming plentiful berry fruit. Walker Bay WO.

Lifestyle Wines
1855 Posmeester ★★★ Veritable fruit-basket of 9 varieties, mainly merlot, cab, shiraz in rounded, richly flavoured **12**. Unchallenging enjoyment. WO W Cape. — AL

Hermit on the Hill Wines

Location: Durbanville ▪ WO: Durbanville/Stellenbosch/Coastal/Wellington/Paarl/Swartland ▪ Est/1stB 2000 ▪ Tasting & sales by appt ▪ Owner(s)/cellarmaster(s) Pieter de Waal ▪ Winemaker(s) Pieter & Lohra de Waal ▪ bastardo, cinsaut, gamay, grenache n/b, malbec, mourv, shiraz, chard, rouss, sauv, viog ▪ 15t/1,600cs own label 60% red 40% white ▪ PO Box 995 Bellville 7535 ▪ pieter@dw.co.za ▪ www.hermitonthehill.co.za ▪ **T** +27 (0)83-357-3864 ▪ F +27 (0)21-948-3441

Bored with same old same old? Boutique vintners Pieter and Lohra de Waal's wines are specifically intended to be 'off the beaten track' for those who 'dare to be different'. The couple have moved vinification back to Durbanville, and now share and work closely with Nomada's Riaan Oosthuizen. Tasting venue? 'Nope. Though we have presented some lovely long-table tastings at home, with Lohra doing capas (Cape-styled tapas) and me presenting the tasting and talk.'

★★★★ **Aurora Grenache** ⓘ From Durbanville grapes, **10** is particularly pretty, with red fruit & fynbos character. Medium bodied with fresh acidity.

★★★★☆ **Stellenbosch Syrah** Classically styled **09** shows dark fruit, pepper & spice. Plenty of stuffing but not weighty, bright acidity & fine tannins. As ever with this producer, doesn't trade off sweetness or oak. Grapes from Lievland in Stellenbosch. No **08**.

★★★★ **Aurora Syrah** ⓘ Made by De Waal's wife Lohra from Durbanville grapes, **09** is medium bodied with pure red fruit, spice & driving acidity. An elegant offering with great persistence on the finish.

★★★★ **The Second Crusade** ⓘ Shiraz, the Hermit's signature red grape, combo with third each grenache, mourvèdre. Naturally fermented **08** shows red fruit, floral fragrance; fresh, with fine tannins.

★★★★ **Aurora Chardonnay** NEW Unfussy but satisfying **12** is medium bodied yet broad, with stonefruit & a hint of spice, more savoury than sweet. Durbanville grapes, older-oaked 9 months.

★★★★ **Aurora Blanc** ⓘ De Waal's favoured white grape is sauvignon. This the tank-fermented version, aged older barrels 9 months. Durbanville grapes, **10** complex & unusual, broad structure, spicy but balanced.

★★★★ **The Infidel** Unconventional, thought-provoking **12** (★★★★☆) from Stellenbosch sauvignon, naturally fermented/9 months older oak. Green melon, blackcurrant, subtle leesy character, some herbal bite on the finish. Rich & full, smooth textured. No **11**. **10**, also ex Stellenbosch but more traditional.

★★★★☆ **The White Knight** ⓘ **11** (★★★☆) blend of 90% sauvignon & semillon. Yellow fruit, creamy texture, gentle acidity. More commercial styling by winemaker's own admission after standout **09**. No **10**.

Wellington Grenache ⓘ ★★★ Dark cherry & mint on rustic **09**, finish is somewhat astringent. **Knights in Tights** NEW ★★★★ From Swartland mourvèdre, rosé-like lightness in **13** preview. Impresses with good concentration, tangy acidity - red cherry, strawberry & spice. **Paarl Syrah** ⓘ ★★★★ **09** is shiraz & 8% mourvèdre; rich & broad with ultra-ripe fruit, moderate acidity & relatively soft tannins. **The Red Knight** ⓘ ★★★ Was 'Aurora GSM' last edition, since renamed. 55% grenache & shiraz, made quirky by dash malbec, **10** rich & broad with soft acidity, firm tannins. Durbanville grapes. **The Souvenir Viognier** NEW ★★★★ **12** more about mouthfeel than any primary fruit (though there are subtle citrus & peach), medium bodied with bright acidity, very dry finish. WO Stellenbosch. — CE

Herold Wines

Location: George ▪ Map: Klein Karoo & Garden Route ▪ WO: Outeniqua ▪ Est 1999 ▪ 1stB 2003 ▪ Tasting, sales & cellar tours Mon-Sat 10-4 ▪ Fee R15, waived on purchase ▪ Closed Easter Sun, Dec 25 & Jan 1 ▪ Light refreshments/cheese platters during opening hours ▪ Picnic baskets/farm lunches with 2 days prior notice ▪ Facilities for children ▪ Tour groups ▪ Gifts ▪ Farm produce ▪ Walks/hikes ▪ Mountain biking ▪ Conservation area ▪ Self-catering cottages ▪ Owner(s) Nico & Maureen Fourie ▪ Winemaker(s)/viticulturist(s) Nico Fourie (Jul 2011) ▪ 324ha/6ha (cab, merlot, pinot, shiraz, chard, sauv) ▪ 35t/3,400cs own label 55% red 25% white 20% rosé ▪ PO Box 10 Herold 6615 ▪ info@heroldwines.co.za ▪ www.heroldwines.co.za ▪ S 33° 51' 49.4" E 022° 28' 9.9" ▪ **T** +27 (0)72-833-8223 ▪ F +27 (0)86-698-6607

It's challenging growing wine in the Outeniqua Mountains along the coastal Garden Route, where floods, fungus and feathered friends can wreak havoc. Hence Herold's newish hands-on owners Nico and Maureen Fourie's delight at last year's healthy 35-ton crop. Most rewarding are tastings for people popping in: 'a kaleidoscope with one thing in common: wine'.

Cabernet Sauvignon Await next. **Merlot** 🍴 ★★★ High-toned **12** has zesty acidity, light tannin frame for early imbibing with food. **Pinot Noir 'Screwcap'** 🍴 🖾 ★★★☆ Shy floral & meaty scents, redcurrant fruit on tangy, easy **12**. Brushed with oak, genteel alcohol for lunch. **Pinot Noir** Next awaited. **Red Men** In abeyance. **Skaam Skaap** 🍴 ★★★ Characterful dry rosé from oaked chardonnay & pinot noir, smidgen sauvignon. Appealing green apple bouquet & crunch, satisfying grip & dry conclusion on previewed **13**. **Sauvignon Blanc** 🍴 ★★★ Shy on nose, **12** comes alive on palate with sweet but zesty gooseberry & lemon, grain sugar gives padding for solo sipping. — GdB,JP

Heron Ridge

Location: Somerset West ▪ Map: Helderberg ▪ WO: Stellenbosch ▪ Est 1997 ▪ 1stB 2001 ▪ Tasting, sales & cellar tours by appt ▪ Fee R20 ▪ Closed all pub hols ▪ Cheese lunches on Saturdays by appt ▪ Owner(s) Orpen family ▪ Cellarmaster(s)/winemaker(s) Pippa Orpen (May 2006) ▪ Viticulturist(s) Paul Wallace (Sep 1999, consultant) ▪ 4.29ha/4ha (cab, shiraz) ▪ 20t/300cs own label 100% red ▪ PO Box 5181 Helderberg 7135 ▪ orps@xsinet.co.za ▪ www.heronridge.co.za ▪ S 34° 2' 45.6" E 018° 47' 58.1" ▪ **T +27 (0)21-842-2501** ▪ F +27 (0)86-613-6960

The joys and challenges of natural winemaking are captured in two harvest incidents shared by Jane Orpen, Helderberg family boutique co-owner and mother of winemaker Pippa: 'We stopped adding yeast and were delighted that fermentation happened spontaneously... The bunches became the nesting places for a million shongololos (millipedes). Many hours were spent dipping the bunches in a sulphur solution and more than half were discarded!'

Family Reserve range

Shiraz ⓕ ★★★☆ **06** is full bodied, slightly rough around the edges but not without charm. Red & black fruit, vanilla, hint of spice. Contains 13% cab.

Heron Ridge range

Shiraz ⓕ ★★★★ **07** raised the bar on **06** (★★★☆), showed attractive rusticity & real liveliness, interest when last tasted. 30% oak well integrated. **The Flight** ⓕ ★★★★ Spicy, well-built **06** shiraz/cab had peppery red fruit, slightly drying tannins & good savouriness. — CE

Het Vlock Casteel

Location: Riebeek-Kasteel ▪ Map/WO: Swartland ▪ Est/1stB 2005 ▪ Tasting & sales Mon-Fri 9-5 Sat 9-2 ▪ Closed Good Fri & Dec 25 ▪ Tour groups ▪ Gift shop ▪ Farm produce: olives, olive oil, jams, chutneys etc - sampling available ▪ Conferences ▪ Café Merlot functions: by appt only ▪ Owner(s) Johan Louw Vlok ▪ Winemaker(s) Alecia Boshoff ▪ Viticulturist(s) Johan Vlok snr & Johan Vlok jnr ▪ 100ha (cab, merlot, ptage, shiraz, chard) ▪ 1,300t/14,000cs own label 100% red ▪ PO Box 8 Riebeek-Kasteel 7307 ▪ info@hetvlockcasteel.co.za ▪ www.hetvlockcasteel.co.za ▪ S 33° 23' 22.74" E 018° 53' 40.75" ▪ **T +27 (0)82-567-9132** ▪ F +27 (0)86-720-6281

The Vlok family, wine and table grape farmers near Riebeek-Kasteel since 1958, named their boutique brand after the Castle of Good Hope. Vinified to spec by Riebeek Cellars, the wines are just one of a cornucopia of products and amenities on offer at their castle-like visitor venue, including functions at Café Merlot.

Cabernet Sauvignon ⓕ ★★★ Accessible & juicy **09**, soft blackberry flavours, smooth savoury conclusion. **Merlot** ⓕ ★★★ Similar mocha chocolate character to previous, **09** bit firmer, peppery, still a satisfying everyday red. **Shiraz** ⓕ ★★★ Earthy, toasty & savoury notes balanced by juicy plums in **09** steakhouse wine. **Sauvignon Blanc** Await next. — DB

■ **Hex River Crossing Private Cellar** see Auction Crossing Private Cellar
■ **Heyden's Courage** see Welmoed

Hidden Valley Wines

Location/map/WO: Stellenbosch ▪ Est/1stB 1995 ▪ Tasting, sales & cellar tours Mon-Fri 9-6 (summer) & 9-5 (winter) Sat/Sun 9-5 ▪ Fee R30pp ▪ Closed Dec 25/26 & Jan 1 ▪ Overture Restaurant ▪ Cheese/chocolate platters ▪ Picnics, to be pre-booked ▪ Table olives & olive oil ▪ Tour groups ▪ Conferences ▪ Weddings/functions ▪ Walks/hikes ▪ Conservation area ▪ Owner(s) David Hidden ▪ Winemaker(s) Emma Moffat (May 2010) ▪ Viticulturist(s) Johan 'Grobbie' Grobbelaar (Feb 1999) ▪ STB: 28ha/15ha (cab, merlot, p verdot, shiraz, tannat, sauv, viog); ELIM: 56ha/13ha (cab, p verdot, shiraz, sauv, sem) ▪ 200t/12,000cs own label 60% red 40% white ▪ BWI ▪ PO Box 12577 Die Boord 7613 ▪ info@hiddenvalleywines.com ▪ www.hiddenvalleywines.com ▪ S 34° 1' 15.3" E 018° 51' 13.9" ▪ **T +27 (0)21-880-2646** ▪ F +27 (0)21-880-2645

High on the northern slopes of the Helderberg, Dave Hidden's pride and joy gazes out over the breathtaking beauty of its surroundings. The showpiece winery is also home to celebrated Overture restaurant, and tasting room hospitality now includes soup in winter, cheese in summer and chocolate paired with wine.

★★★★ **Pinotage** 🌐 🍴 No mistaking the variety. Smoky, meaty, bold **11** shows complex layers of spices, ripe fruit & preserves. Clean & precise fruit with a hint of dark chocolate on the finish. No **10**.

★★★★☆ **Hidden Gems** ✓ 🖼 Overtly New World **11**, from cab & petit verdot, satisfies on many levels: succulent, bright dark fruit, well-judged oaking & exhilarating length. Great depth & intensity, yet light on its feet & perfectly balanced. No **09**, **10** sold out untasted.

★★★★ **Hidden Secret** ✓ 🖼 Dark, brooding **11** from shiraz & tannat bursts with black cherry fruit & Rhône-like spiciness, fynbos & whiff of roasted nuts. Rounded, smooth & satisfying. Perfect for a Sunday roast.

★★★★ **Sauvignon Blanc** ✓ 🍴 🖼 Floral **13** honeysuckle, lemon & lime flavours, reflecting different picking times. Impressive, with smooth acidity & mouthwatering citrus goodbye.

Barbera Await new vintage. — WB

High Constantia Wine Cellar

Location: Constantia ▪ Map: Cape Peninsula ▪ Est 1693 ▪ 1stB 2000 ▪ Tasting, sales & cellar tours Mon-Fri 8-5 Sat 10-1 ▪ Fee R50 ▪ Closed Easter Sun, Dec 25 & Jan 1 ▪ BYO picnic ▪ Meals pre-arranged with private chef, Marc Wassung ▪ Owner(s) David van Niekerk ▪ Cellarmaster(s)/viticulturist(s) David van Niekerk (Jan 1999) ▪ Winemaker(s) David van Niekerk (Jan 1999) & Roger Arendse (Jan 2001) ▪ 14.5ha (cabs s/f, malbec, merlot, pinot, chard, sauv) ▪ 70t/11,000cs own label 52% red 15% white 3% rosé 30% MCC + 3,800cs for clients ▪ Brands for clients: Terra Madre ▪ Groot Constantia Rd Constantia 7800 ▪ david@highconstantia.co.za ▪ www.highconstantia.co.za ▪ S 34° 1' 31.3" E 018° 25' 36.1" ▪ **T +27 (0)21-794-7171/+27 (0)83-300-2064** ▪ F +27 (0)21-794-7999

High Constantia was once an aristocrat of the Cape's wine culture. Under owner/winegrower Sebastiaan van Renen, the property competed with its illustrious neighbour Groot Constantia for the favour of Europe's mid-19th century royal courts. Present owner David van Niekerk is reviving the glory days with new plantings and wines vinified in a cellar 'reminiscent of High Constantia's original home for wine' and sold under the High Constantia and Silverhurst labels.

Highgate Wine Estate

Location: Howick ▪ Map: KwaZulu-Natal ▪ Est/1stB 2010 ▪ Tasting & sales daily 9-5 ▪ Closed Dec 25 & Jan 1 ▪ Facilities for children ▪ Coffee shop (see www.pigglywiggly.co.za) ▪ Country shops catering for all ages ▪ Owner(s) Rudi & Cindy Kassier ▪ Winemaker(s)/viticulturist(s) Rudi Kassier ▪ 57ha/3ha (cab, merlot, ptage, shiraz, chard) ▪ 2.5t/840cs own label 50% red 50% white ▪ PO Box 1025 Howick 3290 ▪ rudi@pigglywiggly.co.za ▪ www.highgatewineestate.co.za ▪ S 29° 27' 29.92" E 030° 8' 8.66" ▪ **T +27 (0)82-895-1667/+27 (0)33-234-2911** ▪ F +27 (0)86-535-3187

Among a tiny handful of vintners bringing wine culture to KZN-Natal province, Rudi and Cindy Kassier's Highgate brand has a very charming home: Piggly Wiggly Country Village on the Midlands Meander. The wine-passionate fresh produce growers to took the opportunity to plant a small vineyard as part of a 2005 trial, and their flagship is a wooded chardonnay under the Lions River label. Taste (and buy) it at the excellent Meander Fine Wines outlet on the property.

Highlands Road Estate

Location/WO: Elgin ▪ Map: Elgin, Walker Bay & Bot River ▪ Est 2005 ▪ 1stB 2007 ▪ Tasting, sales & cellar tours Wed-Sun 9-5 ▪ Breakfast & light lunches ▪ Facilities for children ▪ Kayaking ▪ Fly fishing ▪ Boule ▪ Owner(s) Michael White ▪ Viticulturist(s) Paul Wallace ▪ 28ha/10ha (pinot, shiraz, chard, sauv, sem) ▪ 30t/4,500cs own label 35% red 65% white ▪ PO Box 94 Elgin 7180 ▪ info@highlandsroadestate.co.za ▪ www. highlandsroadestate.co.za ▪ S 34° 14' 4.4" E 019° 4' 14.3" ▪ **T +27 (0)71-271-0161**

Changes at this boutique Elgin farm see Michael White taking over his former partners' ownership stakes. Though the focus remains on sauvignon blanc and pinot noir, varieties suited to Elgin's cooler climate, 'each year throws up something new', hence their maiden port-style - under a rather un-Scottish name!

Pinot Noir 🖩 ★★ **11** very ripe, with sweetish, alcohol-laden tail. **Ruadh** 🖩 ★★☆ Ripe fruit jam on **11** merlot/shiraz blend. Modest juiciness subdued by dry tannins. **Rosé** Await next, as for **Slainte MCC Bubbly** & **Sauvignon Blanc Sweet**. **Sauvignon Blanc** 🖩 ★★ **12** very ripe & honeyed. Modest vigour, big 15.5% alcohol. **Sine Cera** 🖩 ★★☆ Partially oaked semillon adds light waxy/honeyed interest to otherwise uncomplicated **12**. Equal partner with sauvignon. **Tinta Amarela** NEW 🖩 ★★ Port-style **11**, sweet & noticeably spirity. — AL

Hildenbrand Wine, Olive & Art Estate

Location/WO: Wellington ▪ Map: Paarl & Wellington ▪ Est 1991 ▪ 1stB 1999 ▪ Tasting & sales Mon-Sat 10-4 Sun 9-12 by appt ▪ Wine tasting R10pp/wine; olive & oil tasting R10pp ▪ Closed Easter Sat/Sun, Dec 24/25 & Jan 1 ▪ Restaurant ▪ Klein Rhebokskloof Country & Guest House ▪ Art by Adri Swart ▪ Owner(s)/cellarmaster(s) Reni Hildenbrand ▪ Winemaker(s) Reni Hildenbrand, with Marinus Bredell ▪ ±4,500cs ▪ PO Box 270 Wellington 7654 ▪ info@wine-estate-hildenbrand.co.za ▪ www.wine-estate-hildenbrand.co.za ▪ S 33° 39' 33.3" E 019° 1' 46.3" ▪ **T +27 (0)82-656-6007**

Her role as an international olive and olive oil judge keeps Wellington boutique winery owner Reni Hildenbrand busy in winter (hence no time to submit wines for tasting). She has a new agent in the Philippines, while at home her new Belgian cattle dog Maximilian is settling in nicely.

★★★★ **Shiraz** ⊕ Big wine though not bold, more understated in last **07**. Cracked pepper, black cherry & warm spice meld in ripe palate.
Cabernet Sauvignon Barrique ⊕ ★★★☆ Plush blueberry texture to **07**'s muscular frame noted previously. Savoury, ripe, dry tannins from 17 months French oak, just 25% new. **Cabernet Sauvignon Unwooded** Await next, as for **Malbec**, **Shiraz Rosé**, **Chenin Blanc**, **Semillon**, **Lady Jemaina Cuvée** & **Bonnie & Claire**. **Chardonnay Barrique** ⊕ ★★★★ **10** nutty tangerine vibrancy, creamy rich vanilla from older oak & lees-ageing. **Chardonnay Unwooded** ⊕ ★★★ Floral highlights on **12** preview. Hints of honey & kerosene with soft yellow/green fruit. Individual & interesting wine. **Emma & Asa** ⊕ ★★★ Named for farm's two goats, **09** blend of chenin, semillon & chardonnay. All barrel fermented, rich honey/muesli notes, fresh acidity, good match for goats' cheese! **Sleepless Nights Semillon Noble Late Harvest** ⊕ ★★★ **07** laudable effort, the name tells it all! Less sweet, hint of estate's distinctive grassiness. — CM

Hill & Dale

Easy-drinking wines vinified from grapes off selected Stellenbosch vineyards at Stellenzicht (see that entry for tasting/sales information).

Merlot 🖾 ★★ Some perfume, distinct herbaceous edge & astringent tannins in **12** preview. **Pinotage** 🖾 ★★ Even with splash shiraz, **12** shows pinotage's big tannins & acidity. Time or food recommended. **Shiraz** ⊕ 🖾 ★★★ Good typicity on **11**, with notes of black cherry, some floral fragrance & a hint of pepper. Medium body, fresh acidity. **Cabernet Sauvignon-Shiraz** 🖾 ★★★ Balanced **11**, with dash cab franc, harmonious blend; satisfying main course of red/black fruit & some leafiness on the side. **Dry Rosé Merlot** 🖩 🖾 ★★★ Dry as advertised, pleasant & eminently drinkable **13**, leafy red berries, 'absolute winner with sushi' say H&D team. **Chardonnay** Next awaited. **Pinot Grigio** 🖩 🖾 ★★☆ Spring flowers & herbs, pleasing soft texture but **13**, as previous, basically a no-frills dry white. **Sauvignon Blanc** ✓ 🖩 🖾 ★★★★ Improved substance, concentration & weight send **13** up a notch, yellow apple & citrus fruit in poised, moreish mouthful. — DC

Hillcrest Estate

Location/WO: Durbanville ▪ Map: Durbanville, Philadelphia & Darling ▪ Est/1stB 2002 ▪ Tasting & sales daily 9–5 ▪ Fee R10, waived on purchase ▪ Closed Good Fri, Dec 25 & Jan 1 ▪ Cellar tours by appt ▪ Restaurant (T +27 (0)21-975-2346) open daily for breakfast & lunch ▪ Wedding/function venue ▪ Farm produce ▪ Walking/hiking & mountain biking trails ▪ Conservation area ▪ Owner(s) PD Inglis, R Haw & G du Toit ▪ Winemaker(s) Graeme Read (Jan 2003) ▪ Viticulturist(s) G du Toit ▪ 25ha (cabs s/f, malbec, merlot, p verdot, chard, sauv) ▪ 60t/±6,000cs own label 45% red 55% white ▪ Private Bag X3 Durbanville 7551 ▪ cellardoor@hillcrestfarm.co.za ▪ www.hillcrestfarm.co.za ▪ S 33° 49' 38.2" E 018° 35' 25.9" ▪ **T +27 (0)21-970-5800** ▪ F +27 (0)21-975-2195

The vineyards, their soils and management are paramount to Graeme Read, the self-taught, talented winemaker here. He revels in the cool climate and special terroir, which, together with his fine-tuning, make the wines of this small-scale Durbanville winery so distinctively elegant. The Metamorphic Collection, featuring the Hornfels blend, alludes to the farm's interesting and ancient geology. This premier range gets a remarkable new prestige sauvignon, vinified by the still-enthusiastic and spry Graeme in his tenth harvest at Hillcrest.

Metamorphic Collection

★★★★ **Quarry 11** solely from merlot (previous had a little petit verdot). Well-integrated, seriously structured & ripely fruited style, though a less convincing vintage for this tricky variety.

★★★★☆ **Hornfels** Immaculately constructed, seamless **11** 5-way Bordeaux blend (cab franc-led) deserves its Trophy Show Gold, after a dip in **10** (★★★★). Structured for cellaring, though the layered, rich dark fruit is accessible now, mineral edge adds to intriguingly complex finish. Named for vineyard's geology.

★★★★☆ **Relief** NEW Austere **12** from sauvignon as earthy & stony as geological range name implies. Its full potency not immediately obvious in youth, though it promises to develop into a stunner, with plenty of depth, breadth & focus to sustain it. Bone-dry; just 13% alcohol.

Hillcrest Estate range

Cabernet Sauvignon Rosé ☺ ▦ ★★★ Engaging **13**, ex tank firmly structured though nicely balanced; dry, crisp & flavourful.

Cabernet Franc ★★★★ More substantial **12** preview a step-up on lighter **11** (★★★☆). Properly ripe & elegant, with none of variety's more herbal tones. Judicious oaking supports rich fruit. Like Malbec & Petit Verdot only available from cellar. **Malbec** ★★★★ Firmly structured, spicy **12** barrel sample's lightness & elegance (13% alcohol) bestowed by cool-climate vineyards. A convincing step up from boisterous **11** (★★★). **Petit Verdot** ★★★★ Previewed **12** lightly tart, requiring dimension from usual blend partners to give completeness, despite its pure-fruited charm. **Robbenzicht** NEW ✓ ★★★☆ Delightfully pure-fruited, elegant **11** merlot-led blend, both cabs adding supporting structure. A joy to drink. **Sauvignon Blanc** ✓ ▦ ★★★★☆ Pristine, brilliant, steely **12** needs time to reveal depth & unfurl compact fruit core. Lean, cool-climate pungency & focus aided by dash semillon & lees-ageing for weight & texture. **11** (★★★☆) was lighter. — IM

Hillock Wines

Location: Ladismith ▪ Map: Klein Karoo & Garden Route ▪ WO: Klein Karoo/Western Cape/Darling ▪ Est 2010 ▪ 1stB 2011 ▪ Tasting, sales & cellar tours daily 10–5 ▪ Closed Dec 25 ▪ Light lunches & refreshments 10–5 daily; or BYO picnic ▪ Tour groups ▪ Gifts ▪ Farm produce ▪ Guided hikes & vineyard tours ▪ Mountain biking ▪ 4-star guest house (sleeps 20), Mymering Estate www.mymering.com ▪ Owner(s) Andy & Penny Hillock ▪ Winemaker(s) Mynhardt van der Merwe (Jan 2013) ▪ Viticulturist(s) Riaan Steyn ▪ 400ha/50ha (shiraz, chard, chenin) ▪ 24t/3,600cs own label 50% red 50% white ▪ PO Box 278 Ladismith 6655 ▪ penny@mymering.com ▪ www.hillockwines.com ▪ S 33° 29' 55.24" E 021° 10' 18.65" ▪ **T +27 (0)28-551-1548** ▪ F +27 (0)28-551-1313

Expect a warm welcome at this boutique winery on Mymering Guest Farm outside Ladismith, not least from rescued boerbul Harry, whose name graces the new Bordeaux blend. Winemaker Mynhardt van der Merwe's diverse team 'works everyday with pride' to help co-owner Andy Hillock, a retired surgeon and aviation enthusiast, fulfil his lifelong winefarming dream.

★★★★ **Black Poodle Reserve Sauvignon Blanc** Top dog **12** is heady, intense; mouthfilling flavours of baked apple & passionfruit, poised acidity & enduring length make an elegant glassful.

Mile High ☺ 🍴 ★★★ Easy-drinking **NV** blend pinotage & cab plus cab franc (ex Stellenbosch) & shiraz. Every pilot's wine range has to have one!

Shiraz ✓ 🍴 ★★★★ Red fruit & faint lily fragrance on restrained **12**. Deft oak touch (22% new) & plenty of finesse raise the bar. Elegant dinner companion. **Big Harry** [NEW] 🍴 ★★★★ Cab (56%) & merlot combo, Creamy tailed **12** ripe & as friendly as eponymous farm Boerbul. **Blanc de Noir** [NEW] 🍴 ★★☆ Pale copper hue, faint berry aromas & flavours on quaffable **13** from shiraz; gram sugar to flatter prosciutto or goat's cheese quiche. **Black Poodle Reserve Chardonnay** 🍴 ★★★ Replaces 'Chardonnay'. Restrained oaking (25% new) gives appealing light vanilla overlay to citrus-melon fruit on elegant **13**. **Chenin Blanc** 🍴 ★★ Muted thatch & wet earth notes on **13**, slight sweetness countered by brisk acidity, passionfruit pithiness. **Sauvignon Blanc** 🍴 ★★★★ Off Darling vines, **13**'s gooseberry tones broadened by brief lees-ageing; crisp Granny Smith apple acidity & savoury note allow creative summer food matching. **Barrel Roll** ⊕ 🍴 ★★★ **12** blend of cask-fermented chenin & chardonnay, & unwooded sauvignon; appealing yeastiness & tropical fruit, zippy acidity extending the farewell. — HJ,CvZ

▪ **Hilltop** see Rosendal Winery

Hilton Vineyards

Location: Stellenbosch ▪ WO: Western Cape ▪ Est 2003 ▪ Closed to public ▪ Owner(s) Richard Hilton ▪ Cellarmaster(s)/winemaker(s) Richard Hilton (2003) & Riaan Wassüng (2005) ▪ Viticulturist(s) Tjuks Roos & Richard Rose ▪ (shiraz, viog) ▪ 21t/2,600cs own label 35% red 65% white ▪ richard@hiltonvineyards.co.za ▪ www.hiltonvineyards.co.za ▪ **T +27 (0)21-855-5244** ▪ F +27 (0)86-618-4089

Previously 'Pax Verbatim', boutique vintner and tour company owner Richard Hilton's wine brand focuses on small parcels of Rhône grapes syrah/shiraz and viognier, sourced from two favoured growers in Helderberg and Elgin, and vinified in Stellenbosch's historic Welgevallen cellar. Production is increasing, as are exports, and Richard makes time to support worthy initiatives like the Pebbles Project and Cape Leopard Association. The 'Dalmatian' in his first five star wine recognises the possible origin of its tiny but crucial viognier component.

★★★★ **Blazing Hill Syrah** Vibrant mouthful of soft black fruit (plums & cherries) on **10** matched with tarry tannins & classic perfume notes. Elegant cool-climate feel.

★★★★★ **The Dalmatian Syrah** [NEW] Classic aromas of violets & spice on maiden **10** from Helderberg fruit with 5% viognier seasoning from Elgin. Beautifully integrated mouthful of spicy oak, well-managed alcohol, sweet black cherries & leather lead to lengthy finish.

★★★★ **Rockwater Fountain Viognier** 🍴 Powdery texture & restrained quintessential aromas of apricots & lilies on **12** (★★★★). Not quite the intensity & focus of **11**. — CM

▪ **Hippo Creek** see PicardiRebel
▪ **His Master's Choice** see Excelsior Vlakteplaas

Hofstraat Kelder

Location: Malmesbury ▪ Map/WO: Swartland ▪ Est 2002 ▪ 1stB 2003 ▪ Tasting, sales & tours by appt ▪ Owner(s)/cellarmaster(s)/winemaker(s) Wim Smit, Jack de Clercq & Jerry Finley ▪ 2.5t/250cs own label 100% red ▪ PO Box 1172 Malmesbury 7299 ▪ renosterbos@cornergate.com ▪ S 33° 26' 56.1" E 018° 44' 1.8" ▪ **T +27 (0)83-270-2352** ▪ F +27 (0)22-487-3202

Working from their recently completed cellar in Malmesbury, wine friends Wim Smit, Jack de Clercq and Jerry Finley have raised production by 30% - to 250 cases! The scale might be micro but the passion is huge, Wim confiding his one-item bucket list is drinking a bottle of Château Pétrus, and perfect wine experience 'when people phone or email to say how much they're enjoying our wine'.

Renosterbos range

★★★★ **Barbera** Rare varietal bottling will please its fans but **12** (★★★★) misses the focus & purity of **11**. Offers violets, dusty black cherries & meaty flavours with firm, grainy tannins & spicy grip. **Cabernet Sauvignon** Next awaited, like **Merlot**. **Pinotage** ★★★★ Fresh & fruity **12** brims with bright plum, spicy fynbos & hint of coffee. Good acid balance with savoury finish. **Shiraz** ★★★ Dense & dark-fruited **12** with fynbos & lavender perfume, bold structure needs hearty meat fare or time to reveal charm. — WB

Holden Manz Wine Estate

Location/map: Franschhoek ▪ WO: Franschhoek/Elgin ▪ Est 2010 ▪ 1stB 2005 ▪ Tasting, sales & cellar tours daily 10-5 ▪ Fee R30 ▪ Franschhoek Kitchen (see Restaurants section) ▪ Spa ▪ Picnic area ▪ Holden Manz Country House (see Accommodation section) ▪ Owner(s) Gerard Holden & Migo Manz ▪ Winemaker(s) Schalk Opperman (Sep 2011) ▪ Viticulturist(s) Tertius Oosthuizen (Sep 2010) ▪ 20ha/16ha (cabs s/f, merlot, shiraz) ▪ 110t/13,332cs own label 85% red 3.85% white 6.65% rosé 4.5% port ▪ IPW ▪ PO Box 620 Franschhoek 7690 ▪ info@holdenmanz.com ▪ www.holdenmanz.com ▪ S 33° 56' 6.3" E 019° 7' 8.3" ▪ T +27 (0)21-876-2738 ▪ F +27 (0)21-876-4624

Named after owners Gerard Holden and Migo Manz, this Franschhoek property was originally developed into a wine farm in 1999. Today it is also a lifestyle destination, boasting five-star guest house and spa, restaurant, picnics by the Franschhoek River, with an art collection housed in the town. A red-wine-only farm, fruit for the first white, a chardonnay, was sourced from Elgin.

Avant Garde range

Big G ▨ ★★★★ Like last, **10** equal cab & cab franc blend. Opens with smoky/spicy blackberry (partly from 80% new oak), concludes with a chocolaty herbal flourish in which fruit/acid are finely poised. **Chardonnay** **NEW** ▨ ★★★☆ Elegant debut for barrel-fermented **12** from Elgin, deftly & attractively interweaving bright lemon freshness with richer tones of marmalade, caramel & toffee. Lingering flavours augur well. **Good Sport Cape Vintage** ▨ ★★★ Following on from **09**, **10** from shiraz has serious port-style intention, needs time for spirit to meld with pleasant nutty dark berry flavours.

Modern range **NEW**

Vernissage ▨ ★★★ Cab/shiraz blend gives plum pudding ripeness & spice in **12**, warm & comfortable fireside red. **Rosé** ▤ ★★★★ Same serious styling as previous, with food in mind, **13** attracts with light salmon hue, creamy ripe fruit, full heady finish. Nudges next level.

Contemporary range

Cabernet Sauvignon ① ▨ ★★★★ Dark brooding **10** has generous fruit concentration, with ultra-ripeness well contained. Textured & ready. **Merlot** Next awaited, as for **Shiraz**. — DB,HJ

Hoopenburg Wines

Location/map: Stellenbosch ▪ WO: Stellenbosch/Coastal/Western Cape ▪ Est/1stB 1992 ▪ Tasting, sales & cellar tours Mon-Fri 8.30-4 ▪ Fee R20/6-8 wines ▪ Closed all pub hols ▪ BYO picnic ▪ Conferences ▪ Guest house T +27 (0)21-884-4534 ▪ Owner(s) Gregor Schmitz ▪ Cellarmaster(s) Anton Beukes (Aug 2009) ▪ Viticulturist(s) Gert Snyders ▪ 70ha/30ha (cab, merlot, shiraz, chard) ▪ 180t/40,000cs own label 80% red 18% white 2% MCC ▪ PO Box 1233 Stellenbosch 7599 ▪ info@hoopenburg.com ▪ www.hoopenburgwines.co.za ▪ S 33° 49' 33.4" E 018° 49' 9.3" ▪ T +27 (0)21-884-4221 ▪ F +27 (0)21-884-4904

'Unbelievable growth in sales' tops the list of good news from the Schmitz family's Stellenbosch estate, where former cellarhand Gert Snyders, empowered by (among others) an exchange programme with French producers, last year 'handled the entire winemaking process, with good results to look forward to'. GM/cellarmaster Anton Beukes notes with some puzzlement that sauvignon is flying out of the cellar. 'Don't understand. Previously it never moved.'

Integer range

★★★★ **Cabernet Sauvignon** Agreeably dry & savoury **10** in classic style: plenty of blackcurrant fruit in harmony with firm, integrated tannins. Restrained oaking part of the sleek & stylish effect.

★★★★ **Syrah-Mourvèdre-Carignan** Mourvèdre restrains exuberant shiraz in well-contained, structured & balanced **10**. Savoury, spicy with ripe red fruit. **09** (★★★★☆) was a standout. WO Coastal.

★★★★ **Chardonnay** Crowd-pleasing **12** rich & creamily oaked. Tasted alongside **10** & **11**, this the best of trio: richer flavours, better balanced, though all have somewhat stern finish.

Syrah ★★★★ Statement **10** exuberant & bold. Richly heady, spicy pepper & layered dark fruit flavours, plenty of oak but not let down by heavy-handedness of **09** (★★★☆). **Méthode Cap Classique Brut** ★★★☆ Pale gold, developed **NV** (mostly **11**) from chardonnay. Well structured & bone-dry, though lacks some of the complexity & charm of last bottling.

Hoopenburg Bush Vine range

Chenin Blanc NEW ☺ ★★☆ Zippily dry, crisp & harmonious **13** offers plenty of flavour. WO W Cape.

Cabernet Sauvignon ★★★ Herbal edge to aromatic **11**, drying tannins overshadow lighter fruit while acidity yields pleasant sweet-sour finish. **Merlot** ★★★ **10**, now bottled, still showing ingratiatingly sweet, the baked fruit checked by savoury oak tannins & ample acidity. **Pinot Noir** ⓧ ▤ ★★★ Elgin fruit adds restraint to ripe, smooth **10**, gently supported by oak. Easy charm, balance; for early drinking. **Pinotage** ⓧ ★★★ Mocha **11** in popular easy-drinking Starbucks style; ample fruit offers pleasant dab sweetness. **Shiraz** ★★★ Plushly ripe, smoky **09** won't disappoint with juicy dark fruit, chocolate & satisfyingly firm, savoury tannins. Coastal WO. **Shiraz-Cabernet Sauvignon** ⓧ ★★ Savoury, uncomplicated, meaty **08**. **Shiraz Rosé** ▤ ★★ Adds variety to name for dry, straightforward **12**. **Chardonnay** ★★☆ Confected, lightly oaked **12** for uncomplicated quaffing. **Sauvignon Blanc** ▤ ★★☆ Rather coarsely textured **13** from Durbanville grapes, for early drinking.

Guru range

Merlot ★★ Overly ripe, semi-dry **10**. WO W Cape, as next. **Cabernet Sauvignon-Merlot** ★★ Soft, ripe but dry, lightly oaked **10**. **Sauvignon Blanc** ▤ ★★ Undemanding tropical **13** quaffer. Coastal WO. — IM

Hornbill Garagiste Winery

Location: Hermanus ▪ Map: Elgin, Walker Bay & Bot River ▪ WO: Western Cape/Overberg ▪ Est 2004 ▪ 1stB 2005 ▪ Tasting, sales & tours Mon-Fri 9-5 Sat 9-2 ▪ Closed Easter Fri/Sun, Dec 25 & Jan 1 ▪ Gifts ▪ Art gallery & ceramic studio ▪ Self-catering accommodation ▪ Restaurant ▪ Owner(s) John Dry ▪ Winemaker(s) John Dry (2004) ▪ 6t/800Cs own label 100% red ▪ PO Box 4 Hermanus 7200 ▪ hornbill@intekom.co.za ▪ www.hornbillhouse.co.za ▪ S 34° 24' 46.3" E 019° 11' 54.4" ▪ **T +27 (0)28-316-2696** ▪ F +27 (0)28-316-3794

Owner/winemaker John Dry attributes all success at this ceramic studio, gallery and garagiste winery in Hermanus to the 'very close involvement of family and friends'. Supporting his quest 'to compete at the highest level', they have now even bought him his first new French oak barrels (in return for wine, naturally!).

Hornbill range

★★★★ **Pinotage** NEW ✓ ▤ New addition brims with earthy farmyard wafts, spicy plums & juicy dark berries. **10** full, rounded & complex with extended plummy finish. Upper Hemel-en-Aarde vines, as for blend.

★★★★ **Cape Blend** NEW ✓ ▤ Unusual, charming blend cab franc (47%), pinotage, shiraz, filled with new leather & bright berries. The fresh cranberry note, undimmed by new oak, makes **10** end on a highlight.

Discontinued: **Reinet, Milan.**

The Naked Vine Collection

Discontinued: **Rapture Cabernet Sauvignon, Mystique Merlot, Persuasion Pinotage, Epiphany Cape Blend.** — DB

▪ **Horse Mountain** see Doran Vineyards
▪ **Horses of the Apocalypse** see Osbloed Wines
▪ **Houdamond** see Bellevue Estate Stellenbosch

House of Mandela

WO: Western Cape/Stellenbosch/Coastal/Elgin ▪ Est/1stB 2009 ▪ Closed to public ▪ Owner(s) Makaziwe Mandela & Tukwini Mandela ▪ Cellarmaster(s) Charles Back & Erlank Erasmus ▪ Winemaker(s)/viticulturist(s) Various ▪ 60% red 40% white ▪ info@houseofmandela.com ▪ www.houseofmandela.com

The negociant wine business owned by Makaziwe and Tukwini Mandela, children of South Africa's celebrated past president and Nobel laureate Nelson Mandela, shows its respect for ancestry in the brand names chosen. While the flagship Royal Reserves were sourced from various producers a few years ago, the earlier-drinking Vusani and Thembu portfolios have been created with the help of Fairview's Charles Back and consultant Erlank Erasmus.

Royal Reserve range

★★★★☆ **Cabernet Sauvignon** ⓧ Harmonious **08** from Stellenbosch fruit has classic cassis, lead pencil, fine tannins; silky precision. These tasted a few years back.

★★★★ **Shiraz** ⓧ Ex Paarl single-vineyard, **07**'s brooding black fruit gripped by powerful savoury tannins.

★★★★ **Chardonnay** ⓘ Oaking on **09** from Elgin gives vanilla glow to apple blossom & citrus; creamy core.

Vusani Series [NEW]

Cabernet Sauvignon ⓥ ★★★ Uncomplicated **11** firm yet comfortable with slight mint aroma. Stellenbosch WO, as next. **Merlot** ⓥ ★★★ **11** plummy with fruit-sweet core; slips down easily. **Pinotage** ⓥ ★★★ Succulent **11** leads this pack of everyday sippers with black plum & mulberry charm. WO Coastal, like next. **Shiraz** ⓥ ★★★ Plush red fruit on round & soft **10**, lifted by light black pepper notes.

Thembu Collection

> **Sauvignon Blanc** ☺ ▤ ★★★ Al fresco companion **13** is fresh & zippy, has melon, grass & tropical attractions. Fairtrade certified, as all these.

Cabernet Sauvignon ⓘ ▤ ⓥ ★★★ **12**'s smooth entry & pleasantly firm finish makes for easy sipping. **Pinotage** [NEW] ▤ ★★ Deep, purple-hued **12** has coffee & charry oak flair. **Shiraz** ⓘ ▤ ⓥ ★★★ Coffee-infused **12** crisp & refreshing - like a shot of java. **Chardonnay** [NEW] ▤ ★★ Appealing lemon whiffs on zesty unwooded **12**. **Chenin Blanc** [NEW] ▤ ★★ Faintly thatchy **13** is very understated. Labels for these early drinkers inspired by colourful 'dashiki' shirt made famous by Nelson Mandela. — CvZ

Hout Bay Vineyards

Location: Hout Bay ▪ Map: Cape Peninsula ▪ WO: Hout Bay/Western Cape ▪ Est 2001 ▪ 1stB 2004 ▪ Tasting, sales & cellar tours by appt ▪ Fee R30 ▪ Facilities for children ▪ Owner(s) Peter & Catharine Roeloffze ▪ Cellarmaster(s)/winemaker(s)/viticulturist(s) Peter & Catharine Roeloffze (both Jan 2004) ▪ 1.5ha/1.1ha (pinots meunier/noir, merlot, shiraz, chard, sauv, viog) ▪ 15t/4,000cs own label 44% red 24% white 14% rosé 18% MCC ▪ Other export brand: HB Vineyards ▪ PO Box 26659 Hout Bay 7872 ▪ cathy@4mb.co.za ▪ www.houtbayvineyards.co.za ▪ S 34° 1' 31.0" E 018° 22' 31.0" ▪ **T +27 (0)83-790-2372** ▪ F +27 (0)86-514-9861

Cathy and Peter Roeloffze learned the hard way about viticulture and winemaking – from the initial backbreaking (and pioneering) work of planting vines (each one tied to its own pole) on steep rocky slopes not far from picturesque Hout Bay. Birds and wind didn't help. The family vineyards being limited, grapes are also brought in - mostly from the area, but from further afield too.

★★★★ **Petrus** Overt woodsmoke aroma on shiraz-led **11** Rhône blend (**10** was Bordeaux style); very ripe, dense dark fruit checked by supple tannins & oaky bite. Wellington & Swartland fruit. Tasted ex-tank. **Cabernet Sauvignon** ⓘ ★★★★ Youthful **10** seriously styled, tight tannins interwoven with seductively ripe, rich, spicy fruit. **Merlot** ⓘ ★★★★ Deliciously ripe, opulent **10** reined in by fine tannin structure & savoury acid thread. This & above two WO W Cape. **Shiraz** ★★★ Smoky, spicy **11** (previewed) offers very ripe, meaty dark fruit combined with edgy acidity & firm oaky finish. **Blush** ★★★ Lightly burnished, satisfyingly dry **13** tank sample blend pinots noir & meunier, chardonnay & viognier; lightish alcohol for lunchtime sipping. **Sauvignon Blanc** ★★★★ Pre-bottling, **13** needs time to settle; ripe fig flavours as juicy as **12** (★★★★) though perhaps less vibrancy & depth. **Klasiek by Catherine** ⓘ ★★★★ Rich, fine flavours in bone-dry **09** chardonnay, pinot MCC sparkling; harmonious & vibrant, with more character than **08** (★★★☆). Discontinued: **Black Swan Vintage Port**. — IM

Howard Booysen Boutique Wines

Location/WO: Stellenbosch ▪ Est 2009 ▪ 1stB 2010 ▪ Sales by appt ▪ Owner(s) Howard Booysen ▪ Cellarmaster(s)/winemaker(s)/viticulturist(s) Howard Booysen (Nov 2009) ▪ (cinsaut, riesling) ▪ 3,500cs own label 33.3% red 66.7% white ▪ howard@howardbooysenwines.com ▪ www.howardbooysenwines.com ▪ **T +27 (0)72-414-5458**

The first Protégé of the Cape Winemakers Guild, with mentorships at prestigious Guild member estates, Howard Booysen launched his own brand with an impressive German-inspired semi-sweet Riesling 2010. It has since been joined by an Australian-style steelier version, under a Pegasus sub-label, and a cinsaut.

Pegasus range

Riesling ⓘ ⓥ ★★★★ Pineapple & spice, limy tang on near-dry **11**, satisfying flavour, intensity & length; enjoy well chilled. From Stellenbosch grapes.

Howard Booysen range
Cinsaut Await next, as for **Riesling**. — CvZ

■ **Huangtai Wines** *see* De Villiers Wines

Hughes Family Wines

Location: Malmesbury ▪ Map/WO: Swartland ▪ Est 2000 ▪ 1stB 2004 ▪ Tasting by appt ▪ Owner(s) Billy & Penny Hughes ▪ Cellarmaster(s)/winemaker(s) Billy Hughes ▪ Viticulturist(s) Kevin Watt (Jul 2005, consultant) ▪ 52ha/27ha (grenache n/b, merlot, mourv, ptage, tempranillo, shiraz, chenin, rouss, viog) ▪ 180t total 25t/3,600cs own label 85% red 15% white ▪ Organic ▪ 6 Riverstone Road Tierboskloof Hout Bay 7806 ▪ penny@nativo.co.za ▪ www.nativo.co.za ▪ S 33° 20' 37.71" E 018° 43' 45.09" ▪ **T +27 (0)21-790-4824** ▪ F +27 (0)86-549-1080

Argentinian-born Billy Hughes' interest in winefarming began when he accompanied his agricultural engineer father on his trips in Mendoza. Interest became reality in 1990, after Billy and wife Penny settled here. As a member of the Swartland Independent group, Billy makes his wine in as natural a way as possible, just as his vineyards near Malmesbury are farmed organically.

Nativo range
★★★★ **Red Blend** ⓔ Soft spice intro on shiraz-based blend with mourvèdre, grenache, pinotage & merlot. Finely balanced **10** offers complexity, harmony & medium-bodied drinkability. Pure-fruited elegance.
★★★★ **White Blend** ✓ 🍽 Unshowy, satisfying **12**. Natural ferment in older oak melds chenin & viognier into appealing peachy, floral harmony. Gently rich & refreshing; memorable fruity length. — AL

■ **Hugh Masekela** *see* Veenwouden Private Cellar

Huguenot Wine Farmers

Wellington ▪ Closed to public ▪ Owner(s) Kosie Botha ▪ Cellarmaster(s) Bill Matthee (1984) ▪ Trade enquiries Gert Brynard ▪ PO Box 275 Wellington 7654 ▪ jcb@mynet.co.za ▪ **T +27 (0)21-864-1293** ▪ F +27 (0)21-873-2075

Privately owned wholesalers, blending, marketing and distributing a wide range of wines, liqueurs and spirits. Own wine brands include Huguenot and Zellerhof.

Huis van Chevallerie

Location: Malmesbury ▪ Map/WO: Swartland ▪ Est 2005 ▪ 1stB 2011 ▪ Tasting by appt only ▪ Closed most pub hols ▪ Owner(s) Chevallerie Family Trust ▪ Cellarmaster(s)/winemaker(s)/viticulturist(s) Christa von La Chevallerie ▪ 110ha/20ha (ptage, chenin) ▪ 100% sparkling wine ▪ PO Box 185 Malmesbury 7299 ▪ info@chevallerie.co.za ▪ www.chevallerie.co.za ▪ **T +27 (0)72-237-1166**

Making winzersekt, Germany's 'winegrower's bubbly', and travels in Italy's and France's sparkling wine regions ignited Christa von La Chevallerie's passion for the style. Now, on family farm Nuwedam in Swartland, she's crafted her first champagne-method sparkler from chenin and named it 'Filia' ('Daughter'). She's bottled almost as many 1.5L magnums as 750 ml, noting 'I know way too many winelovers for whom a standard bottle of bubbly would never suffice!'

Filia ✓ ★★★★ Aiming to offer 'joy in blissful abundance', **11** zero dosage sparkling from Swartland chenin carefully, thoughtfully made. Appealingly robust, nascent brioche on palate, finishes crisp & tart. Really zingy bone-dry bubbles guaranteed to bring promised joy. — GdB, GM

Hunneyball Wines

Location: Stellenbosch ▪ WO: Western Cape ▪ Est 2012 ▪ 1stB 2011 ▪ Closed to public ▪ Winemaker(s) Jim & Marie Hunneyball ▪ 0.75t ▪ 100% red ▪ PO Box 6089 Stellenbosch 7612 ▪ jim.hunneyball@gmail.com ▪ **T +27 (0)76-284-6951**

Businessman and IT specialist Jim Hunneyball and wife Marie returned to South Africa from Sweden in 2007. A deepening love for wine inspired them to try their hand at making it. The 'ambitious garagistes' first shiraz is now bottled and awaiting release, and more serious offerings are contemplated. 'Wish us luck.'

Cabernet Sauvignon ⓐ ★★★ Unfettered by new oak, **11**'s walnutty blackcurrant comes powering through. Textbook cab, big, forthright, will have you reaching for braai tongs. Swartland vines. — HJ,JP

■ **Hunterspeak** *see* Niel Joubert Estate
■ **Hunting Family** *see* Slaley
■ **Hunting Owl** *see* African Terroir

Idiom Wines

Location: Sir Lowry's Pass ▪ Map: Helderberg ▪ WO: Stellenbosch ▪ Est 1999/1stB 2003 ▪ Tasting & sales: see website - new visitor centre to open in 2014; see also Whalehaven entry ▪ Vineyard tours by appt (Sir Lowry's Pass) ▪ Owner(s) Bottega family ▪ Winemaker(s) Reino Thiart ▪ Vineyard manager(s) Tim Clark ▪ 35ha (barbera, cabs s/f, merlot, mourv, nebbiolo, p verdot, ptage, sangio, shiraz, zin, sauv, sem, viog) ▪ 85% red 15% white ▪ PO Box 3802 Somerset West 7129 ▪ wine@idiom.co.za ▪ www.idiom.co.za, www.bottegafamilywine.co.za ▪ S 34° 6' 14.1" E 018° 56' 12.4" ▪ **T +27 (0)21-858-1088 (vyds)/+27 (0)21-852-3590 (sales)/+27 (0)28-316-1633 (tasting: Whalehaven)** ▪ F +27 (0)21-858-1089 (vyds)/+27 (0)21-851-5891 (sales)/+27 (0)28-316-1640 (winery)

The 'feature visitor centre' under construction on the Helderberg for Idiom boutique brand is set to open midyear, offering (among splendid views and much else) comparative tastings of Idiom's Italian styles with top examples from the Bottega family owners' imported Vinotria Italian Fine Wine portfolio. Also new are a white Bordeaux blend, malbec plantings, and a Heritage Series aimed at making Italian varietal wines more accessible.

Idiom range

★★★★ **Zinfandel** ⓐ Wild strawberry, spice & dried herbs on elegant & varietally expressive **10**. Like **07**, firm acid & grippy savoury finish for mealtimes. No **08**, **09**.

★★★★ **Merlot-Pinotage-Cabernet Sauvignon-Petit Verdot** ⓐ After accomplished **07** (★★★★★), exuberant **08** wide array of aroma & flavour: plums, red cherry, fynbos & toasty oak. Rich & full, good intensity before savoury finish.

★★★★ **Viognier** Full-bodied yet still elegant **11**, with rich floral perfume, voluptuous peach melba & subtle vanilla complexity.

900 Series Cabernet Franc ⓐ ★★★ Attractive red fruit on last **06**; overwhelming oak may since have integrated. **900 Series Barbera** ★★★★ **09** trumps **08** (★★★★) with concentrated red & black fruit, smooth tannins, super acidity. Rich & bold - made for food & ageing. **900 Series Mourvèdre** ⓐ ★★ Ultra-ripe, meaty **08** last appeared excessively weighty, tired. **Nebbiolo** ★★★★ Ripe, juicy black fruit, fynbos & fennel flavours on **10**. Robust but restrained, with good structure, built to last. For food & Nabucco at full volume. Improves on last-tasted **08** (★★★★), listed as '900 Series Nebbiolo'. **900 Series Sangiovese** ★★★ Was 'Sangiovese'. **10** ripe & plush plummy fruit with firm tannin backbone; perfect for hearty Italian fare. **Cabernet Sauvignon-Merlot-Cabernet Franc-Petit Verdot** ⓐ ★★★ Fragrant, medium-bodied **08** pulls back from ultra-ripeness of previous but seems tad developed, not for further keeping. **SMV** ★★★ Shiraz (52%) with mourvèdre, splash viognier. **08** oozes bright red fruit & sweet spice flavours, some savouriness & loads of oak. More character than previous. **Shiraz-Mourvèdre-Viognier** ⓐ ★★★ Soft & accessible **08**, juicy fruit compote & hints of flowers & spice. **Sauvignon Blanc-Semillon** NEW ★★★★ Juicy citrus, dill & spicy vanilla on **12**. Bright, firm & pithy, but fleeting dry finish.

Enoteca Bottega range

Super Rosso ⓐ 🍽 ★★★ Pizza-friendly **09** from 83% sangiovese, rest cab & merlot is fruit driven yet not overly sweet. Follows powerful cab-led **05** (★★★★). **Rosso** ⓐ 🍽 ★★ **10** from 4 Italian varieties not as interesting as might be hoped for. **Bianco di Stellenbosch** ⓐ ★★★ Fresh & fruity **12** from pinot gris/grigio billows floral & ripe stonefruit perfume. Light, balanced & perfect for a summer seafood braai. — WB

■ **Ilula Gepa** *see* Stellar Winery

Imbuko Wines

Location: Wellington ▪ Map: Paarl & Wellington ▪ WO: Western Cape/Wellington ▪ Est/1stB 2004 ▪ Tasting Mon-Fri 9-4 Sat by appt ▪ Fee R15/5 wines ▪ Closed all pub hols; Dec 25-Jan 1 ▪ Sales 8-5 ▪ Meals/refreshments by appt (48hr notice) ▪ Olives, olive oil, pinotage/merlot/shiraz jams, pinotage relish ▪ Owner(s) Imbuko Wines (Pty) Ltd ▪ Cellarmaster(s) Theunis van Zyl (2004) ▪ Viticulturist(s) Jan-Louw du Plessis ▪ 60ha

(cab, cinsaut, merlot, ptage, shiraz, chenin, sauv, viog) ▪ 570t/120,000cs own label 60% red 40% white ▪ Other export brands: Makulu, Releaf Organic & Rebourne Fairtrade, Van Zijls Family Vintners ▪ Fairtrade, IPW, ISO, Organic ▪ PO Box 810 Wellington 7654 ▪ crm@imbuko.co.za ▪ www.imbuko.co.za ▪ S 33° 40' 30.84" E 019° 01' 18.87" ▪ **T** +27 (0)21-873-7350 ▪ F +27 (0)21-873-7351

At the Du Plessis family's farm, home of Imbuko Wines, visitors can stock up not just on wine but also jams and relishes from wine grapes, and on olives and olive oils. But if they can't make it to Wellington, the Shortwood and Imbuko brands are now available from Blue Bottle Liquors, Food Lover's Market and Tops@Spar.

Du Plevaux range

Pinotage ☺ 🍷 ★★★ Sugared strawberries, supple tannins & bright acidity on refreshing **11**. 'Try with chocolate soufflé' says team. **Sauvignon Blanc** ☺ 🍷 ★★★ Full-bodied **13** with lengthy, lipsmacking tropical flavours.

Shiraz 🍷 ★★ Liquorice notes on sweet-sour **11**; somewhat stalky finish. **Chenin Blanc-Viognier** NEW 🍷 ★★☆ Chenin's thatch & flowers spiced with 5% viognier in flavoursome, fresh **13**. WO Wellington, as entire range.

Imbuko range

Cabernet Sauvignon 🍴 🍷 ★★ Ripe & foursquare **12**, a flavoursome red for country foods. **Iswithi Pinotage** ⊕ 🍴 🍷 ★★ **12** sweet & soft for spicy food. **Chardonnay** Await next. **Sauvignon Blanc** 🍴 🍷 ★★ Melon-toned **13** light-footed & very zesty.

Pomüla NEW

Moscato Spumante ☺ 🍴 🍷 ★★★ Exuberant grapey flavours laced with minuscule bubbles, low-alcohol **NV** perlé from muscadel to be served well chilled.

Shortwood range

Rosé ⊕ 🍴 ★★ Spice & boiled sweets on leafy **12** pink sipper. **White** ⊕ 🍴 🍷 ★★ Citrus blossom on **12** crisp summer celebrator. **Red** ⊕ 🍴 ★★ Though sweet, **NV** on release not as friendly as expected. — CvZ

Imoya   NEW

One of the new-age Cape brandies introduced into the newly resurgent premium brandy market of the 1990s, Imoya ('The Ancient Wind of Africa') reflected a broadening of approach by brandy producer KWV, long renowned for its award-winning eponymous range. The newcomer, designed to appeal to modern tastes and a growing, discerning African market, made its mark in 2000 as the International Wine & Spirit Competition's World's Best Brandy.

★★★★ **Imoya Fine Potstill** Modern, beautifully presented brandy. Fresh fruity aromas & flavours. Elegant, rich balance, subtle texture with nutty, spicy oak in support, lifted by a fresh, spirity finish. — WB,TJ

▪ **Indaba** see Cape Classics
▪ **Infiniti** see Kumkani
▪ **Infusino's** see Beau Joubert Vineyards & Winery
▪ **Ingenuity** see Nederburg Wines
▪ **Inglewood** see Neil Ellis Wines
▪ **Inkará** see Bon Courage Estate
▪ **Insignia Series** see Bellingham
▪ **Integer** see Hoopenburg Wines

Intellego Wines

Location: Malmesbury ▪ Est/1stB 2009 ▪ Closed to public ▪ Owner(s)/winemaker(s) Jurgen Gouws ▪ 1,000cs own label 40% red 60% white ▪ jurgen@intellegowines.co.za ▪ **T** +27 (0)82-392-3258

Intellego ('Understand') brand owner Jurgen Gouws hopes consumers 'get' his handcrafted bottlings. Assistant winemaker at Lammershoek, where he makes his small runs, Jurgen's committed to the natural wine ideals of Swartland Independent, handcrafting 'real' wines true to their origins - and full of life.

■ **Interlude** see Nwanedi Estate

Iona Vineyards

Location/WO: Elgin ▪ Map: Elgin, Walker Bay & Bot River ▪ Est 1997 ▪ 1stB 2001 ▪ Tasting, sales & tours Mon-Fri 8–5 Sat by appt ▪ Closed all pub hols ▪ Walks/hikes ▪ Mountain biking ▪ Conservation area ▪ Owner(s) Andrew & Rozanne Gunn, Workers Trust ▪ Winemaker(s) Werner Muller (May 2011), with Thapelo Hlasa (Jun 1997) ▪ Viticulturist(s) Kevin Watt (Jan 2002, consultant) ▪ 100ha/40ha (cab, merlot, mourv, p verdot, pinot, shiraz, chard, sauv) ▪ 250t/24,000cs own label 25% red 75% white ▪ BWI ▪ PO Box 527 Grabouw 7160 ▪ orders@iona. co.za ▪ www.iona.co.za ▪ S 34° 16' 42.2" E 019° 4' 58.2" ▪ **T** +27 (0)28-284-9678 ▪ F +27 (0)28-284-9078

On one of the remotest Elgin farms, the cows and ducks are part of the ongoing conversion to biodynamic farming. Iona Vineyards' co-owners Andrew and Rosy Gunn are pursing this method in their goal to reflect terroir, and the range has been streamlined accordingly. 'We employ as many people already working and living on the farm to fill positions traditionally filled by graduate students,' say the Gunns. 'The staff are shareholders in Iona, making their contribution meaningful to both us and them'.

★★★★☆ **Pinot Noir Limited Release** Delicacy of silken feel, intensity & length of flavour (ripe cherries, hint of forest floor) - all pinpoint the freshness of **11**; all impart charm & personality. Precociously delicious, but there should be further rewards for the patient.

★★★★☆ **One Man Band** Impenetrable **08** an eclectic, seamless blend of shiraz, merlot, cab franc, petit verdot & mourvèdre. Big, spicy tannins & fragrant sweet dark fruit in polished, booming balancing act.

★★★★☆ **Chardonnay** All the hallmarks of quality Elgin chardonnay on **12** - focused, intense & complex, a mineral thread adding structure & length to zesty citrus core. Oak an unobtrusive enhancement. **10** (★★★★) was less concentrated. **11** untasted.

★★★★☆ **Sauvignon Blanc** Slightly riper profile in pure, cool-climate-fruited **12**; a hint of oaked semillon adds a further dimension. Lipsmacking vibrancy, thrilling minerality. Impressive ageing potential.

Viognier Occasional release. Discontinued: **Syrah**, **The Gunnar**. — AL

■ **Isis** see Schalkenbosch Wines
■ **Island View** see Orange River Wine Cellars
■ **Ithemba** see Stellar Winery
■ **Iwayini** see Maiden Wine Cellars
■ **Ixia** see Distell

Izak van der Vyver Wines

Location/WO: Elgin ▪ 1stB 2002 ▪ Closed to public ▪ Owner(s) Izak van der Vyver ▪ Cellarmaster(s) Andries Burger (Paul Cluver Wines) ▪ Winemaker(s) Izak van der Vyver (Jan 2002) ▪ 1.4t/±166cs own label ▪ PO Box 42 Grabouw 7160 ▪ drs@telkomsa.net ▪ **T** +27 (0)21-859-2508 ▪ F +27 (0)21-859-3607

Living among Elgin's cool vineyards, general practitioner Izak van der Vyver couldn't resist having a go at producing his own wine. In the cellar of his friends the Cluvers, he has vinified two rows of sauvignon from a local farm since 2002.

Sauvignon Blanc ★★★★ Powerful riverstone & gunflint notes energise the grapefruit profile of super **11**, fuller & better balanced than tense **10** (★★★★). — AL

■ **Jabari** see Vrede Wines

Jacaranda Wine & Guest Farm

Location/WO: Wellington ▪ Map: Paarl & Wellington ▪ Est/1stB 2009 ▪ Tasting & sales Mon-Sat 10-5 ▪ Fee R20/4 wines, served with olives & bread ▪ Closed Easter Fri/Sun, Dec 25 & Jan 1 ▪ Mediterranean/cheese platters & picnic baskets by appt ▪ B&B: 2 cottage units ▪ Owner(s) René & Birgit Reiser ▪ Cellarmaster(s)/viticulturist(s) René Reiser (Jun 2009) ▪ Winemaker(s) René Reiser (Jun 2009) & Jean-Paul Schmitt (2013) ▪ 4.5ha/4ha (cab, merlot, shiraz, chenin, viog) ▪ 9t/1,500cs own label 50% red 40% white 10% rosé ▪ PO Box 121 Wellington 7654 ▪ jacarandawines@gmail.com ▪ www.jacarandawines.co.za ▪ S 33° 36' 49.2" E 019° 0' 16.1" ▪ **T** +27 (0)21-864-1235

Much emotion last harvest as estate wine was made for the first time in many years in the recommissioned cellar by boutique vintners René and Birgit Reiser, guided by Alsace winemaker and long-term friend, Jean-Paul Schmitt. Rejuvenating the vineyards and making the wine as naturally as possible continue to be the focus.

Cuvée Rouge ☺ 🍴 🍷 ★★★ Friendly red quaffer from Bordeaux varieties, mainly cab/merlot, **11** offers juicy black cherries & dark chocolate.

SMV 🍷 ★★★ Mainly shiraz, splashes mourvèdre & viognier. **11**, now bottled, pleasant mouthful of black fruit (cherry & currant). Still tight mid-2013, tad short. **Pinotage Rosé** 🍴 🍷 ★★★ Jammy strawberries & fresh herbs on **12** cheery summer quaffer, a preview last time. Bouncy acidity & appetisingly dry finish. **Chenin Blanc** 🍴 🍷 ★★★ Baked pineapples, meringue & cream on **12** as dash of lightly-oaked chardonnay shows presence in satisfying food wine. — CM

■ **Jacksons** see Stanford Hills Winery

Jacobsdal

Location/map/WO: Stellenbosch ▪ Est 1916 ▪ 1stB 1974 ▪ Tasting on the farm by appt only ▪ Tasting & sales also at Die Bergkelder (see entry) ▪ Owner(s) Dumas Ondernemings (Pty) Ltd ▪ Cellarmaster(s) Cornelis Dumas ▪ Winemaker(s)/viticulturist(s) Cornelis Dumas, with Hannes Dumas ▪ 100ha (cab, ptage, chenin, sauv) ▪ 600t/26,000cs own label 100% red ▪ PO Box 11 Kuils River 7579 ▪ info@jacobsdal.co.za ▪ www.jacobsdal.co. za ▪ S 33° 58' 4.9" E 018° 43' 34.6" ▪ **T +27 (0)21-881-3336** ▪ F +27 (0)21-881-3337

Wines at the Dumas family's Stellenbosch farm really are made with minimal intervention - no commercial yeast has ever been used, leading researchers to believe a unique yeast strain has developed which imparts a particular set of flavour characteristics to the must.

Cabernet Sauvignon ★★★ Improved **10**, generous red & dark fruit flavours followed by dark chocolate & a pleasing wood spice from 25% new French barrels. **Pinotage** ★★★ Savoury tone to the chocolaty red/dark fruit of **11**, tannins are well integrated & there's an interesting chicory note in the conclusion. — GM

■ **Jacoline Haasbroek Wines** see My Wyn

Jacques Smit Wines

Location/WO: Wellington ▪ Map: Paarl & Wellington ▪ Est/1stB 2003 ▪ Tasting, sales & tours by appt ▪ Closed Easter Fri/Sun/Mon, Dec 25/26 & Jan 1 ▪ Facilities for children ▪ Owner(s) Jacques & Marina Smit ▪ Cellarmaster(s)/winemaker(s)/viticulturist(s) Jacques Smit ▪ 60ha/32ha (cab, roobernet, shiraz, chenin, Cape riesling) ▪ 300t total 100% red ▪ Welvanpas PO Box 137 Wellington 7654 ▪ info@vines2wine.com ▪ www.vines2wine.com ▪ S 33° 39' 2.2" E 019° 1' 9.0" ▪ **T +27 (0)21-873-1265** ▪ F +27 (0)21-873-2143

Raising their profile, artisanal winemaker Jacques Smit's vineyards, cellar and vine nursery are now a stop on the popular Wellington Wine Walk as well as appearing on the Walk On Foot programme during the Wellington Wine Harvest Festival.

Limited Releases
Cabernet Sauvignon ⦿ ★★★★ Juicy & appealing **07** easygoing mealtime companion. **Shiraz** ⦿ ★★★★ Lively & intense palate hide **05**'s heavy 16% alcohol. **Vine Valley** ⦿ ★★★★ Boldly fruited **06** blend, cab (67%) & shiraz nicely integrated, pleasing firm handshake. **Chenin Blanc** Await next. **Cape Ruby Roobernet Port** ⦿ ★★★★ Exuberantly fruity **07** given ageability by firm tannins. Also in 375 ml. — MW

Jakkalsvlei Private Cellar

Location: Herbertsdale ▪ Map: Klein Karoo & Garden Route ▪ Est 1987 ▪ 1stB 2008 ▪ Tasting & sales Mon-Fri 9 30-5 Sat 9.30-3 ▪ Closed Sun ▪ Cheese platters ▪ Deli ▪ BYO picnic ▪ Walks/hikes ▪ Mountain biking ▪ Owner(s) cellarmaster(s)/viticulturist(s) JG Jonker ▪ 80ha/26ha (cab, merlot, muscadel r, ptage, chenin, hanepoot sauv) ▪ 350t/12,000cs own label 40% red 20% white 20% rosé 20% dessert + 150,000L bulk ▪ PO Box 79 Herbertsdale 6505 ▪ info@jakkalsvlei.co.za ▪ www.jakkalsvlei.co.za ▪ S 33° 59' 15.31" E 021° 43' 9.33" ▪ **T +27 (0)28-735-2061** ▪ F +27 (0)86-593-0123

Named for the many foxes, jackal and wild cats in the mountains above the farm, Jakkalsvlei near Herbertsdale has been in Jonker family hands for several decades. Making bulk wines is also well established but boutique vinification, by Jantjie Jonker, is much more recent. Watch for his creations at wine shops on the Garden Route or 'come and explore this unique, off-the-beaten-track wine farm'.

Jakob's Vineyards

Location: Hermanus ▪ Map: Elgin, Walker Bay & Bot River ▪ WO: Walker Bay ▪ Est 2002 ▪ 1stB 2006 ▪ Tasting by appt ▪ Owner(s) André & Yvonne de Lange ▪ Winemaker(s) Peter-Allan Finlayson (2010, consultant) ▪ Viticulturist(s) Johan Pienaar (Jun 2003, consultant) ▪ Farm manager Peter Davison ▪ 5ha/2ha (cabs s/f, merlot) ▪ 10t/±1,000cs own label 100% red ▪ PO Box 15885 Vlaeberg 8018 ▪ wine@jakobsvineyards.co.za ▪ www.jakobsvineyards.co.za ▪ **T +27 (0)82-371-5686** ▪ F +27 (0)86-589-4619

André and Yvonne de Lange - he an attorney, she a scientist, then living in Johannesburg - bought this tiny farm in 2002 and now have two hectares of Hemel-en-Aarde vines producing their likeable blend. The 'master plan' is to fully integrate the farm 'into the greater ecological landscape of which it forms part'.

Bordeaux Blend ★★★☆ Cabs sauvignon & franc & merlot (50/38/12) in **09** show a leafy nuance to creamy plum fruit, well-judged oak polish, big but balanced ±15% alcohol. — DC,CvZ

■ **Jardin** see Jordan Wine Estate

Jason's Hill Private Cellar

Location: Rawsonville ▪ Map: Breedekloof ▪ WO: Slanghoek/Breedekloof ▪ Est/1stB 2001 ▪ Tasting & sales Mon-Fri 8–5 Sat 10-3 ▪ Closed Easter Fri-Sun, Dec 25 & Jan 1 ▪ Cellar tours by appt ▪ Bistro Mon-Sat 10-3 (also available for functions) ▪ Shop ▪ Facilities for children ▪ Spa ▪ Weddings/functions ▪ 6.5km hiking trail ▪ Owner(s) Du Toit family ▪ Cellarmaster(s) Ivy du Toit (Jan 2001) ▪ Viticulturist(s) Alister Oates (Jan 2004) ▪ 100ha ▪ 1,200t 45% red 50% white 5% rosé ▪ PO Box 14 Rawsonville 6845 ▪ info@jasonshill.co.za; ivy@jasonshill.co.za ▪ www.jasonshill.com ▪ S 33° 39' 52.3" E 019° 13' 40.6" ▪ **T +27 (0)23-344-3256** ▪ F +27 (0)86-523-6655

The du Toit family are proud to have been making wine here since 1844. Latest scion Ivy, current cellarmaster, views the Slanghoek Valley as a region with the ideal climate suited to the production of quality wines. She was Woman Winemaker of the Year in 2004, so speaks from experience.

Cabernet Sauvignon ★★★ 09 ready to enjoy; soft fruit, deep cassis, fresh herbal whiff co-mingle with meaty entry. **Merlot ★★★** Plummy, toasty oak aromas. **10** is softly approachable, with good textured juicy fruit & a zippy end. **Pinotage ★★★** Lovely lifted nose on **10** has floral, earth & raspberry appeal. Smoky & savoury, balancing juicy fruit. **Shiraz ★★★** Dark cherry on ripe, fruity **10**. Big alcohol adds bite to the finish. **Classic Red ★★★ 10** ripe & smoky with same alcoholic glow as others in the range, off-dry conclusion. WO Breedekloof. **Chardonnay** Await next, as for **Chenin Blanc**, **Sauvignon Blanc**, **Viognier** & **Sparkling Rosé**. — JP

■ **JC Kannemeyer** see Wolfkloof
■ **JC le Roux** see The House of JC le Roux

Jean Daneel Wines

Location: Napier ▪ Map: Southern Cape ▪ WO: Western Cape/Napier ▪ Est/1stB 1997 ▪ Tasting, sales & cellar tours by appt ▪ Closed Dec 25 & Jan 1 ▪ Restaurant & deli ▪ Owner(s) Jean & René Daneel ▪ Winemaker(s) Jean-Pierre Daneel ▪ 50t 40% red 60% white ▪ PO Box 200 Napier 7270 ▪ info@jdwines.co.za ▪ www.jdwines.co.za ▪ S 34° 28' 38.11" E 019° 54' 15.47" ▪ **T +27 (0)28-423-3724** ▪ F +27 (0)28-423-3197

Veteran winemaker Jean Daneel had award-winning stints at top cellars Buitenverwachting and Morgenhof but always wanted to do his own thing. After a few itinerant years he and food-and-deco-passionate wife René found their niche in Southern Cape hamlet Napier, turning it into a must-stop restaurant and larder destination for fresh bread, a meal or even a chandelier! Son Jean-Pierre has his hand on the winemaking tiller and is proud of the new Le Grand Jardin label, named by his father who, gazing over their small home-vineyard one evening, glass in hand, 'realised that it was really only a big garden'. A

sauvignon is set to join the line-up while the patriarch gets busy with chisels and woodworking tools, making tables and even wooden platters for René's shop(s).

Signature Series

★★★★☆ **Red** Standout blend of mainly merlot & cab with 21% shiraz, lengthy (33 months) barrel maturation. 09's heady aromatic assault has tobacco spicing, its bold fruit a tarry liquorice & bouillon overlay, opulence effortlessly countered by firm acid, silky tannins, bone-dry finish.

★★★★★ **Chenin Blanc** Just-dry **12** harmonious marriage Rubenesque fruit & judicious oak (year 20% new). Exudes fresh orange & marmalade, shows great vibrancy & freshness. Like aromatic **11**, combines elegance & richness in stylish, ageworthy package.

Directors Signature Red Occasional release, as for **Directors Signature Chenin Blanc**.

Le Grand Jardin NEW

Red ★★★ These are the Daneels' first, limited-edition offerings from home vines. Drink-young **09** shiraz (75%) & merlot, fullish, soft & smooth cherry fruit, dusty oak & grip. **Chenin Blanc** 🥂 ★★★ Interesting notes of smoky cinders & brimstone to unoaked **12**'s appealing tropical fruit. Good aperitif style. **White** ★★★ Equal chenin & sauvignon in **10**, aged in older barrels hence buttery oak spice to full, satisfying body.

JD Initial Series

Red Await next, as for **White**. — WB, GdB

■ **Jemma** *see* Painted Wolf Wines

Jeu

Location/WO: Stellenbosch ▪ Est/1stB 2010 ▪ Closed to public ▪ Owner(s)/winemaker(s) Nadia Barnard ▪ jeuwines@gmail.com ▪ T +27 (0)83-324-8466

Nadia Barnard, cellarmaster at Waterkloof, decided the first wine under her own label should be a port in honour of her gran, who taught her to love fortified wines. Friend Margaux Nel of Boplaas also offered inspiration, and grapes were sourced from a member of another famous port-making family, Albert Bredell.

Jeu ⊕ ★★★ **10** port-style from tinta is delicious but not usual affable Ruby style: chunky mouthful, lots of extracted dark choc & spicy plumcake, almost salty flavours, very low sugar. Give time to blossom. — WB, IM

JH Meyer Signature Wines

Location: Riebeek-Kasteel ▪ WO: Elgin ▪ Est/1stB 2011 ▪ Private tastings on request ▪ Owner(s) Johan Meyer ▪ Cellarmaster(s)/winemaker(s)/viticulturist(s) Johan Meyer (2011) ▪ 3t/400cs own label 50% red 50% white ▪ PO Box 396 Riebeek-Kasteel 7307 ▪ jhmeyerwines@gmail.com ▪ www.jhmeyerwines.co.za ▪ T +27 (0)72-045-9592

Johan Meyer's day job is vinifying for others, but a love for Burgundy varieties chardonnay and pinot noir compelled him to make his own wine. Access to two additional blocks has seen output double (to 400 cases!), and a single-vineyard range is in prospect. 'NO yeast, NO enzymes, NO additives, NO fining and NO filtration!' defines the approach to his 'very sexy fermented grape juice in a bottle'.

★★★★ **Chardonnay** 🥂 Understated but fascinating **12** with citrus & some funky, savoury flavours. Medium bodied, with a core of pure fruit & really bright acidity before a super-dry finish.

Pinot Noir 🥂 ★★★ Non-conformist but likeable **12** shows raspberry & intense spice thanks to 100% bunch ferment. Light body, with pleasantly sour acidity. — CE

■ **JH Pacas & Co** *see* Bernheim Wines
■ **JJ Handmade Wines** *see* Stellenrust
■ **Johan de Wet Wines** *see* Lorraine Private Cellar
■ **John B** *see* Rietvallei Wine Estate

Jonkheer

Location: Bonnievale ▪ Map: Robertson ▪ WO: Western Cape/Robertson ▪ Est 1912 ▪ 1stB 1956 ▪ Tasting & cellar tours by appt ▪ Wine sales Mon-Fri 8-5 at Jonkheer offices in Main Str ▪ Closed all pub hols ▪ 4 self-catering guest houses ▪ Klasi Lifestyle Centre ▪ Owner(s) Andries Jonker & Dirk Du Plessis Jonker ▪ Cellarmaster(s)

winemaker(s) Erhard Roothman (Feb 1971) ▪ Viticulturist(s) Andries Jonker (1984) ▪ 300ha/130ha (cab, merlot, muscadel r/w, ptage, chard, pinot grigio, sauv) ▪ 1,500t/34,000cs own label 25% red 65% white 10% rosé ▪ PO Box 13 Bonnievale 6730 ▪ info@jonkheer.co.za ▪ www.jonkheer.net ▪ S 33° 56' 54.9" E 020° 2' 48.4" ▪ T +27 (0)23-616-2137/8/9 ▪ F +27 (0)23-616-3146

The hub of this family winery is at their Klasi Lifestyle Centre in Bonnievale town, where wine and furniture find an easy home together. Last year was a 'good one', most of the harvest being pre-sold. Relationships built over the past eight years are bearing fruit, with Far East exports continuing to grow. Co-owner Dirk Jonker says one of his dreams is still to play golf at St Andrews.

Jonkheer range

★★★★ **Muscatheer** ⓘ From 30+ year old muscat de Frontignan bushvines. **05** (★★★☆) first since maiden **00**, shade less elegant.

Pinotage ⓘ ★ Rustic **10** dark fruited & high toned. **Shiraz Family Reserve** ⓘ ★★ Smoke & juicy fruit on oak & mocha **10** get-together-with-friends red. **Chardonnay Family Reserve** ★★★ Step-up **12** appealing melon & lime, orange marmalade bouquet; buttery palate nicely balanced by savoury tone. **Buccanheer Touriga Nacional** ⓘ ★★★★ Individual & attractive lighter styled fortified dessert, **04** marries port, sherry & jerepiko characters. Last-tasted **02** (★★★★) offered Xmas-cake flavours. Robertson WO, like Muscatheer.

Bakenskop range

Cabernet Sauvignon ⓘ 🍷 ★ Sour cherries & bold tannins on light-bodied **11**. **Merlot** ⓘ 🍷 ★★ **11** earth & hay notes, dab chocolate in a lightish package. **Pinotage** ⓘ 🍷 🍇 ★★★★ Quintessential pinotage, **11** fleshy banana & strawberry fruit, slippery as Teflon. **Shiraz** ⓘ 🍷 ★ Smoky-savoury **11** for game dishes, reflects estate's moderate alcohol levels. **Chardonnay** 🍷 ★★ Unwooded **13** fresh & uncomplicated food partner. **Sauvignon Blanc** 🍷 ★★ Light styled for al fresco sipping, **13** has crisp Granny Smith apple acidity. **Es la Vida Blanca** ⓘ 🍷 ★★ NV off-dry party starter from muscadel, with low alcohol & slight sparkle. **Es La Vida Rosa** ⓘ 🍷 ★★ Pretty pink, off-dry **NV** with tingly bubbles for anytime sipping. **Red Muscadel** 🍷 ★★★ Light-textured **12** fortified intended as 'welcome drink or nightcap after a heavy meal'. **White Muscadel** 🍷 ★★★ **12** fortified dessert with interesting saline/iodine nuance, pleasant grip & dried fruit flavours.

Beacon Hill range

Sauvignon Blanc ⓘ ★★ Export only. Uncomplicated **12** greenpepper & tropical nuances, for early sipping.

Cape Auction range

Red ⓘ 🍷 ★★ Plummy **NV** crowd pleaser. **Rosé** ⓘ ★★ Muscatty **NV** rosé for the sweet-toothed. **White** ⓘ 🍷 ★★ **NV** with soft quaffability. **Late Harvest** ⓘ ★★ Affable chenin/semillon **NV** duo. — DB,CvZ

Joostenberg Wines 🍷🥂📷🎋&

Location: Paarl ▪ Map: Paarl & Wellington ▪ WO: Paarl/Western Cape ▪ Est/1stB 1999 ▪ Sales daily 10–5 at the Deli on Klein Joostenberg Farm ▪ Tasting & cellar tours by appt ▪ Closed Dec 25 & Jan 1 ▪ Joostenberg Bistro (see Restaurants section) ▪ Facilities for children ▪ Tour groups ▪ Gifts ▪ Farm produce ▪ Honey shop ▪ Conferences ▪ Ludwigs rose nursery & Van den Berg garden centre ▪ Owner(s) Philip & Tyrrel Myburgh ▪ Cellarmaster(s)/viticulturist(s) Tyrrel Myburgh (1999) ▪ Winemaker(s) MC Stander (2012) ▪ 31ha (cab, merlot, mourv, shiraz, touriga nacional, chenin, rouss, viog) ▪ 120t/16,000cs own label 35% red 50% white 15% NLH ▪ PO Box 82 Elsenburg 7607 ▪ winery@joostenberg.co.za ▪ www.joostenberg.co.za ▪ S 33° 49' 34.8" E 018° 47' 45.5" ▪ T +27 (0)21-884-4141 ▪ F +27 (0)21-884-4135

The Joostenberg farm, between Paarl and Stellenbosch, has been in the Myburgh family since 1877. The current generation display the same tenacious character and generosity of spirit in the running of their small-scale winery and popular delicatessen/bistro, as their ancestors did. Despite suffering both wind and fire damage during the last vintage, they remained optimistic, experiencing a good harvest, of mainly organically grown grapes. The star of their show is however their delicious desert wine from chenin!

Joostenberg range

★★★★ **Syrah** ⓘ 🍷 **10**, first since **07**, delights with floral/red fruit fragrance; more spicy flavour buzz borne on supple, luscious mouthfeel. Too good not to drink now & in next few years.

★★★★ **Bakermat** ⓘ 🍷 Cab-led blend with shiraz, merlot, touriga forged in dark-fruited, very fresh **10** (★★★★). Tastily savoury if rather straightforward & brief. **09** full bodied, great balance.

★★★★ **Fairhead** 🍴 Chenin-led blend with viognier & roussanne, retains refined freshness of **10** but has less fruit depth in **11** (★★★★), with a gentle aromatic citrus tone.

★★★★ **Family Blend White** 🍴 🌦 **13** tank sample, too young to rate, now from chenin & viognier. **12** sample, also with roussanne, delighted with a gentle fruity tang & creamy texture.

★★★★ **Chenin Blanc Noble Late Harvest** Alluring cornucopia of flavours & aromas on **12**. Almonds, butterscotch, dried pineapple & buchu coaxed from low-yielding vines & naturally fermented in old oak. Richness deftly offset by tangy acidity, an elegant dessert partner.

Family Blend Red 🍴 🌦 ★★★☆ **12**'s eclectic blend is shiraz-led, with savoury, gamey flavours. Juicy & approachable, one to chill or for the fireside. **Family Blend Rosé** NEW 🍴 🌦 ★★★ **13** dry, tangy, savoury al fresco wine from shiraz with merlot.

Little J range

Shiraz Await next, as for **Chenin Blanc. Rosé** ⏲ 🍴 🗒 ★★★ **11** basketful fresh ripe strawberries, with dusting of fruit-lifting sugar. WO W Cape. — MW

Jordan Wine Estate

Location/map/WO: Stellenbosch ▪ Est 1982 ▪ 1stB 1993 ▪ Tasting & sales daily 9.30–4.30 ▪ Fee R35pp, waived on purchase ▪ Closed Easter Fri-Mon, Dec 25 & Jan 1 ▪ Cellar tours by appt Mon-Fri 9.30-4.30 ▪ Jordan Restaurant ▪ Jordan Deli ▪ Conferences (60 pax) ▪ Walks/hikes ▪ Mountain biking ▪ Conservation area ▪ Visits to old prospector's mine shafts ▪ Fly fishing (catch & release) R100/adult & R50/child under 12, booking essential ▪ Owner(s) Jordan family ▪ Cellarmaster(s) Gary & Kathy Jordan (1993) ▪ Winemaker(s) Sjaak Nelson (Jan 2002) ▪ Viticulturist(s) Gary Jordan (1983) ▪ 160ha/105ha (cab, merlot, syrah, chard, chenin, riesling, sauv) ▪ 850-950t/100,000cs own label 45% red 54% white 1% rosé ▪ Other export brand: Jardin ▪ Brands for clients: Pick's Pick, Woolworths ▪ BWI ▪ PO Box 12592 Die Boord Stellenbosch 7613 ▪ info@jordanwines.com ▪ www.jordanwines.com ▪ S 33° 56' 33.7" E 018° 44' 41.3" ▪ **T +27 (0)21-881-3441** ▪ F +27 (0)21-881-3426

Vinified by husband-and-wife winemaking team Gary and Kathy Jordan, the large wine portfolio designed to use all the fruit on the Jordan family estate in Stellenboschkloof has been thoughtfully separated into ranges at different price points and wine styles. A closer analysis reveals specialisation: counting in wines specially made for Woolworths, there are six chardonnays, and six Bordeaux-style blends, reflecting the terroir diversity to be found here. Some wine names are personal: Cobblers Hill refers to the family's previous footwear business; Gary's geology training shows in Outlier Sauvignon Blanc (the vineyard is on a geological outlier with a 360-degree view) and Prospector Syrah is named for a 2010 thwarted tin mining application. The awards and accolades continue to stream in, and they've decided to plant tempranillo and grenache on the warmer slopes of their recently purchased extra 20 hectares.

Jordan Estate range

★★★★ **Cabernet Sauvignon** 🍴 📓 Opulent cassis & smoky liquorice, savoury spice, richly layered **10** grabs your attention with its vanilla-toned silkiness, curvaceous body. A lesson in cab's feminine side!

★★★★ **Merlot** 🍴 📓 Cocoa-rich chocolate & cassis, some white pepper notes, cedar, there's lots going on in **11**. Expensively oaked but absorbed by the fruit, this wine will get even better over time.

★★★★ **Cobblers Hill** 📓 Single-vineyard, barrel-selected Bordeaux blend aims for harmony & cracks it. Hugely complex **10** has blackcurrant compote at core, Belgian chocolate, cedar, bouillon whiffs. Silky succulence & incredible length complete the seduction.

★★★★☆ **Sophia** 📓 Blend of best Cobblers Hill barrels & reserve cab, & gets 26 months in all-new French barrels. Cigarbox, plums & blackcurrants, beef extract, **10** is multi-layered, master-crafted, polished, poised & seamless.

★★★★ **Chardonnay Barrel Fermented** 🍴 📓 Showy, with citrus preserve & buttered toast but still drinkable, **12** is for chardonnay lovers. Oaked, & a clever touch of tank-fermented wine freshens the palate.

★★★★★ **CWG Auction Reserve Chardonnay** 🍴 📓 Grape selection from Nine Yards vineyard, wild ferment & new French barrels creates a sophisticated wine. Pear & citrus, pine nuts, **12** (★★★★★) is laced with brightening acidity extending its length. Like **11**, a delicacy, finesse that beguiles.

★★★★☆ **Nine Yards Chardonnay** 🍴 📓 Vineyard selection & always impressive, **12** spent 18 months in 92% new Burgundian oak, portion wild yeast ferment. The result is layers of flavour, quince preserve, crushed hazelnuts, limy acidity, but the finish is savoury, toasty, needs time.

★★★★ **Chenin Blanc Barrel Fermented** ✓ 🍷🍽🖾 Achieving perfect pitch with the fruit/oak balance, **12** has the variety's melon & quince styling, dusted with crushed almonds. Elegant, mouthwatering zestiness.

★★★★ **The Outlier Sauvignon Blanc** ✓ 🍷🖾 Different take on sauvignon, partial barrel ferment deftly done. 2012's fruit shines through, slight savoury shading expands the food matching repertoire. Will age well.

★★★★ **Sauvignon Blanc** ✓ 🍷🖾 Cellar's usual fruit purity on **13**, gooseberries & lime, while a taut, focused minerality carries the wine to a refreshing conclusion.

★★★★☆ **Mellifera** 🖾 Natural Sweet-style dessert (all previous were Noble Late Harvest). From riesling, which fits sweet wines like a glove, **12** has vivid floral & preserved pineapple aromas, & a remarkable palate elegance & finesse, the sweetness counterpointed by racy acidity. Low 9.8% alcohol.

The Prospector Syrah ⊕ 🍷 ★★★★ Plump hedgerow fruit lightly dusted with pepper, preview **10**'s silky elegance makes it a pleasure to drink. **Unoaked Chardonnay** 🍷🖾 ★★★ Appealing citrus & peach flavours backed by crisp freshness gives **13** lively drinkability. **The Real McCoy Riesling** 🍷🖾 ★★★★ Pineapple perfume & flavours in an off-dry elegant form, what could be nicer than **12**, chilled, on a warm summer's day?

Bradgate range

Syrah ☺ 🍷🖾 ★★★ Smoky, fruitcake-toned **12** has the 'drink me' smooth succulence you'd expect from an early-drinking shiraz. **Cabernet Sauvignon-Merlot** ☺ 🍷🖾 ★★★ Full ripe blackcurrants give **11** an attractively juicy palate, supple tannins add to the enjoyment.

Sauvignon Blanc-Chenin Blanc ⊕ 🍷🖾 ★★★ Leafy note in **12**'s appley freshness shows sauvignon's effect, zesty & bright. Riper styling in **11** (★★★), apple & melon, a savoury thread from long lees-ageing, extra year in bottle.

Chameleon range

Cabernet Sauvignon-Merlot ☺ 🍷🖾 ★★★ Lovely blackcurrant ripeness in **11**, the tannins integrated, giving immediate drinking pleasure. **Rosé** ☺ 🍷🖾 ★★★ Merlot & shiraz give dry **12** fresh red berries, a herbal touch. Add friendly alcohol (12.5%) & it's a great food wine.

Merlot No Added Sulphur 🍷🖾 ★★★ A herbal note in unoaked **12** tones down the minty berry fruit, finishing smooth but dry. Best served with food. **Sauvignon Blanc-Chardonnay** ⊕ 🍷🖾 ★★★ Previewed **12** holds true to its drinkability aim with summer fruits, vibrant limy freshness. — CR

■ **Joseph Barry** see Barrydale Winery & Distillery
■ **Joubert Brothers** see Beau Joubert Vineyards & Winery

Joubert-Tradauw Wingerde & Kelder 🍴🍷⛰📷🎿♿

Location: Barrydale ▪ Map: Klein Karoo & Garden Route ▪ WO: Tradouw ▪ Est/1stB 1999 ▪ Tasting, sales & cellar tours Mon-Fri 9-5 Sat 10-2 ▪ Closed Easter Fri/Sun & Dec 25 ▪ R62 Deli Mon-Fri 9-3 Sat 10-1 breakfasts, lunches & Klein Karoo tapas ▪ Walks/hikes ▪ Mountain biking ▪ Conservation area ▪ Lentelus B&B (www.lentelus.co.za) ▪ Owner(s) Lentelus Family Trust ▪ Cellarmaster(s)/winemaker(s)/viticulturist(s) Meyer Joubert (1999) ▪ 1,100ha/30ha (cab, merlot, shiraz, chard) ▪ 5,000cs own label 70% red 30% white ▪ PO Box 15 Barrydale 6750 ▪ info@joubert-tradauw.co.za ▪ www.joubert-tradauw.com ▪ S 33° 55′ 26.4″ E 020° 35′ 40.6″ ▪ **T** +27 (0)28-572-1619 ▪ F +27 (0)86-555-3558

It is just over six decades since Schalk-Willem Joubert, grandfather of current co-owner and cellarmaster Meyer, left Wellington to farm in the beautiful but then remote Tradouw Valley. Today Route 62 which runs by the cellar is one of the most popular wine meanders, something Meyer foresaw when he made his first wine at the estate some 15 years ago and named it 'R62'.

★★★★ **Syrah** 🖾 Revisited as bottled wine, smoky & savoury **11** (★★★★) has carefully crafted tannin structure to restrain opulent fruit, fine varietal black pepper & lily aromas. Follows **08** (no **09**, **10**).

R62 ⊕ 🖾 ★★★ Characterful '2nd red', recently 100% cab. **10** farmyard notes to pleasant leafy, very dry body. Drink soon with country fare. **Chardonnay Barrel Fermented** 🖾 ★★★★ Elegant & balanced **12**, oak nicely integrated with green apple flavour, some almond complexity, chalky dry finish. Better managed than **11** (★★★) where obvious wood influence masked orange & mandarin fruit. — HJ,CvZ

Journey's End Vineyards

Location: Sir Lowry's Pass ▪ Map: Helderberg ▪ WO: Stellenbosch ▪ Est 1995 ▪ 1stB 2001 ▪ Tasting, sales & cellar tours by appt Mon-Fri 9-5 Sat 9-1 ▪ Fee R50pp (incl cellar tour) ▪ Closed Easter Fri-Mon, Dec 25 & Jan 1 ▪ Cheese platters & snacks by appt; or BYO picnic ▪ Conferences (20 pax) ▪ Walks/hikes ▪ Horse riding ▪ Mountain biking ▪ Conservation area ▪ Owner(s) Gabb family ▪ Cellarmaster(s)/winemaker(s) Leon Esterhuizen (Jun 2006) ▪ Viticulturist(s) Lodewyk Retief (Jun 2011) ▪ 50ha/30ha (cabs s/f, merlot, mourv, shiraz, chard, pinot gris, sauv, sem, viog) ▪ 200t/30,000cs own label 70% red 30% white ▪ IPW, WIETA ▪ PO Box 3040 Somerset West 7129 ▪ info@journeysend.co.za ▪ www.journeysend.co.za ▪ S 34° 6' 35.11" E 018° 54' 54.06" ▪ T +27 (0)21-858-1929 ▪ F +27 (0)86-540-1929

A car, defunct church organ and gas bomb hurled into the air by a 13-ton mediaeval trebuchet – no, not the start of a siege, but the launch of the Trebuchet Syrah, part of the new Gabb Family Vineyards range. The feat raised funds to purchase a new organ for the Acton Round Church in Shropshire, England, from where Rollo Gabb hails. The trebuchet, built by Rollo and a friend, will be shipped to Journey's End in Sir Lowry's Pass, installed and utilised for monthly 'barrel chucking' events to raise funds for the local community. The farm has gone up a gear this year.

Reserve range

★★★★☆ **Cape Doctor Cabernet Sauvignon** Polished & suave **08** (★★★★) has layers of cool-fruited mint & cassis in sleek & streamlined balance, for earlier accessibility than more structured **07**.

★★★★ **Destination Chardonnay** ⓣ Bold mouthful of ripe fruit, oak, alcohol & sweetish finish, **11** not to be taken lightly - & preferably taken with food. Drinkable now, can go few years.

Journey's End range

★★★★ **Merlot** ✓ **09** step up on **08** (★★★). Understated, with a core of minted red fruit & integrated oak. Lithe, elegant structure, restrained in cool vintage. Deserves time.

★★★★ **Chardonnay** ✓ 🍴 📷 **12** New World style, with more plush, creamy oak (60% new) than Haystack version. Ample fruit balanced by tangy freshness. Succulent & satisfying.

Cabernet Sauvignon ✓ ★★★★ **08** fruitier, with appealing cassis & cool mint, than **07** (★★★★), but has less depth & complexity. Balanced for early enjoyment. **Shiraz** ✓ ★★★★ Dark spicy fruit on riper **08** absorbs oak (18 months 34% new). Full bodied, with rich & robust drinkability.

Cellar range

The Pastor's Blend 🍴 📷 ★★★ **10** supple & savoury Bordeaux-style red, structured for earlier enjoyment. **Haystack Chardonnay** ✓ 🍴 ★★★★ **12** shows creamy oatmeal & peach flavours, zested with fresh lime. Balanced & juicy. **Weather Station Sauvignon Blanc** 🍴 📷 ★★★ Riper, plump & peachy **13** shows sustained pithy grip, for food pairing. — MW

▪ **Joy** *see Anura Vineyards*

JP Bredell Wines

Location: Somerset West ▪ Map: Helderberg ▪ 1stB 1991 ▪ Tasting & sales by appt ▪ Owner(s) Helderzicht Trust ▪ Cellarmaster(s)/viticulturist(s) Anton Bredell ▪ Winemaker(s) Denzil Tromp ▪ 50ha/13ha (cab, merlot, ptage, pinot) ▪ 10,000cs own label 60% red 40% port ▪ PO Box 5266 Helderberg 7135 ▪ info@bredellwines.co.za ▪ www.bredellwines.co.za ▪ S 34° 1' 29.04" E 018° 46' 18.72" ▪ T +27 (0)82-783-4413

This winery was one of those responsible for the 1990s new wave of Portuguese-style port. There have been no new releases for a few years (and clearly some big changes), and only small quantities of the wines reviewed previously available.

Bredell's range

★★★★ **De Rigueur** ⓣ **08** cab-led blend tasted a few years back.

★★★★ **Late Bottled Vintage** ⓣ **04** port-style from tinta, souzão, touriga last was still seductive.

★★★★★ **Cape Vintage Reserve** ⓣ **07** Last-tasted port-style **07** usual splendid blend tinta, touriga, souzão. Intriguing & complex; fiery in richly fruity-spicy & balanced style.

Cape Vintage ⓣ Await next, as for **Cape Tawny Port**. — JP

▪ **JP le Hanie Wines** *see Vredevol Private Wine Cellar*

Julien Schaal

Location: Elgin ▪ WO: Hemel-en-Aarde Valley/Elgin ▪ Est 2004 ▪ 1stB 2005 ▪ Sales from Paul Cluver Estate ▪ Tasting by appt only ▪ Owner(s)/winemaker(s) Julien Schaal ▪ 28t/4,000cs own label 15% red 85% white ▪ c/o PO Box 48 Grabouw 7160 ▪ julien@vins-schaal.com ▪ www.vins-schaal.com ▪ T +33 (0)6-10-89-72-14

Julien Schaal wanted to make wine in South Africa since his first visit as a cellarhand in 2002. His dream was realised in 2004. He's now based at Paul Cluver in Elgin and visits five times a year. As with his French wines, he aims to reflect origin in his local pair: 'Altitude and cool nights are key factors in achieving full ripeness without losing acidity in my Elgin Chardonnay, while Hemel-en-Aarde's red clay soil and sea breezes off Walker Bay are major influences on my Syrah.'

★★★★☆ **Mountain Vineyards Syrah** 🈂 Schaal's wines benefit enormously from his sensitive handling but also from a few years ageing. Delicacy, perfume, freshness are all to be found in youthful **12**, all serving to enhance the convincing & persistent varietal notes of lilies, roast meat & spice.

★★★★☆ **Mountain Vineyards Chardonnay** 🈂 **12** still needs to settle but does suggest future complexity in its companionable refined lime, oatmeal & spicy oak notes. Precise, pure & alive with a lightness of touch that belies its intensity. Another WO Elgin winner. — AL

Juno Wine Company

Location: Paarl ▪ Map: Paarl & Wellington ▪ WO: Western Cape/Coastal ▪ Est/1stB 2004 ▪ Tasting & sales at 191 Main Str Paarl Mon-Fri 7.30–6.30 Sat 9–2 ▪ Open most pub hols ▪ Café Juno ▪ Winemaker(s) Stephanie Betts & Adele Dunbar ▪ 70% red 30% white ▪ PO Box 68 Main Road Paarl 7622 ▪ info@junowines.com ▪ www.junowines.com ▪ S 33° 44' 36.9" E 018° 57' 46.1" ▪ T +27 (0)21-872-0697 ▪ F +27 (0)21-872-1863

Named for the Roman goddess Juno, this fun and funky Paarl-based brand celebrates women everywhere through their sassy labels and smart, modern styling. The wines are made by the women winemakers from the Fairview team, while the all-female office crew handles increasing overseas and local sales.

Shiraz ☺ 🍴 🈂 ★★★ Quaffable **11** invites you in with freshly picked plums & raspberries with some black pepper & touch of mint. Medium-bodied, effortless goes-with-anything red. **Sauvignon Blanc** ☺ 🍴 🈂 ★★★ **13** an easy-drinker with plenty to offer: green asparagus & lime, hint of guava, grassy/savoury flavour, dry floral finish.

Cabernet Sauvignon ⓘ 🍴 🈂 ★★★★ Complex blackcurrant, spice & plum pudding combo, **10** textured, dry but concentrated, structure to last a few years. **Shiraz-Mourvèdre-Viognier** 🍴 🈂 ★★★ Sweet/savoury Black Forest cake & black olive tapanade contrast works well in **12**, lively, versatile blend from Coastal vines. — DC

▪ **Kaap Agri** *see* Breëland Winery
▪ **Kaapdal** *see* Robertson Wide River Export Company
▪ **Kaaps Geskenk** *see* Group CDV

Kaapzicht Wine Estate

Location/map/WO: Stellenbosch ▪ Est 1946 ▪ 1stB 1984 ▪ Tasting & sales Mon-Fri 9–4.30 Sat 10–1 ▪ Fee R20pp, waived on purchase ▪ Closed Easter Fri/Sun, Dec 25 & Jan 1 ▪ Cellar tours by appt ▪ Conference/function/wedding & braai venues ▪ Walks/hikes ▪ Mountain biking trail ▪ Conservation area ▪ 2 self-catering cottages ▪ Owner(s) Steytdal Farm (Pty) Ltd/Steytler Family Trusts ▪ Cellarmaster(s) Danie Steytler snr (Jan 1979) ▪ Winemaker(s) Danie Steytler jnr (Feb 2009) ▪ Viticulturist(s) George Steytler (Jan 1984) & Schalk du Toit (Jun 2003) ▪ 190ha/162ha (cabs s/f, cincaut, malbec, merlot, p verdot, ptage, shiraz, chard, chenin, hanepoot, rouss, sauv, sem, verdelho) ▪ 1,100t/60,000cs own label 70% red 30% white + 20,000cs for clients ▪ Other export brands: Cape View, Friesland ▪ Brands for clients: Escapades, Handmade, K&V Harmony ▪ IPW ▪ PO Box 35 Koelenhof 7605 ▪ carin@kaapzicht.co.za ▪ www.kaapzicht.co.za ▪ S 33° 54' 47.7" E 018° 44' 7.7" ▪ T +27 (0)21-906-1620/1 ▪ F +27 (0)21-906-1622

From the Bottelary Hills is the wonderful view over Cape Town and its mountain that gives Kaapzicht its name. The large estate itself (only a third of the harvest is bottled here, the rest sold off) is a real family one, and has been so since the Steytlers arrived in 1946. Brothers Danie and George own it and have overall

responsibility for, respectively, the cellar and the vines. Wives Yngvild and Mandy take care of export markets and look after the entertainment and guest venues. Danie jnr has been winemaker since 2009 (and wife Carin handles national sales). The wines themselves, mostly reds and off unirrigated vineyards (an increasingly rare thing in Stellenbosch), at the top level combine classic dryness (not all that common either) with modern flamboyance, power and flair.

Steytler range

★★★★☆ **Pinotage** Massive, somewhat rustic **10**, with huge oak (100% new French, 2 years) dominating finely managed fruit. In youth still with arresting tannins, though spice & brooding intensity emerging, some chocolate & raspberry notes. No **09** made.

★★★★☆ **Pentagon** ⚠ Sinewy **10** cab-based blend with merlot & malbec. Restrained, despite overt oak. Cassis notes predominate, though faint tobacco whiffs hint at forthcoming complexity. Good integration of components & the lime-edged sweet fruit lift it above chunkier **08** (★★★★). Ageworthy. No **09**.

★★★★☆ **Vision** ⚠ Mammoth & multi-layered **10** from cab with 37% pinotage, 10% merlot. Finely honed sweet fruit seamlessly dovetailed with vanilla-toned French oak (all new, 2 years). Polish is evident despite youthful exuberance, but fruit nuance still some way off - needs time. No **09**.

★★★★☆ **CWG Auction Reserve Cape Blend** Robust & unashamedly brash **10** - similar blend, vinification to Vision. Chunky oak still sitting firmly on bright plum, raspberry fruit. Less plush with **09** though promising similar harmony, vinosity & integration.

Kaapzicht range

★★★★ **Merlot** ✓ ☺ Savoury & herbal, with earthy mulberry & tobacco aromas dominating **10** (★★★★), slighter than **08** but bulked-up by oak & dry tannin. No **09**.

★★★★ **Pinotage** ✓ Supple **10** (★★★★☆) with sensitive oaking allowing restrained strawberry fruit to show. Plusher & better integrated than previous **09**. Surprisingly forward & accessible but not dumbed-down.

★★★★ **Shiraz** ✓ More edifice than fruit on **10** (★★★★); foursquare, mouthpuckering & a little green. Lacks the restraint, spice & detail of previous **08**.

> **Kaleidoscope** ☺ 🍴 ★★★ Concentrated easy-drinking, just-off-dry **11** cab. Fresh, fragrant & will keep a few years. **Chenin Blanc** ☺ 🍴 ⚠ ★★★ Light melon & peardrop notes on fresh, dry & simply pleasing **13**. **Combination** ☺ 🍴 ⚠ ★★★ Sauvignon-dominated blend with chenin. Attractively crisp **13** has tropical & citrus notes & a hint of grapefruit pith.

Cabernet Sauvignon ✓ ★★★★ Treacly & dense **10** with sweet blackcurrant spice. Brooding tarry notes, a bit chunky & youthfully gawky but purer, more harmonious than last-made **08** (★★★★). **Estate Red** ⚡ ⚠ ★★★★ Bright red fruit on accessible **10** from shiraz & cab, but lacks the harmony of **09** (★★★★). **Bin-3** ✓ ★★★★ Traditionally styled rustic red **10** lacks fruit & sweetness of standout **09** (★★★★). Herbal merlot (58%) dominates the blend. **Sauvignon Blanc** ✓ 🍴 ⚠ ★★★★ Intense gooseberry tropical notes introduce limy, zesty & food-friendly **13**. **Ice** NEW ★★★ Raisiny, sweet-sour & tangy **09** riesling-based 'icewine' dessert from frozen grapes, naturally barrel fermented. **Hanepoot Jerepigo** ⚡ ★★★ Overdone **08**, gooey but spice still evident. **Tawny Cape Ruby** ⚡ ★★★★ Fresh **06** previewed some years ago as 'Tawny Port'. Discontinued: **Chardonnay**, **Natural Sweet**.

Brandy range NEW

★★★★ **10 Year Potstill** Complex, well-aged nose of dried fruit, almond & toasty oak. Layers of flavour, rich texture, smoothly harmonious; good length. 100% potstill from colombard, chenin, crouchen. — WB, MF, TJ

▪ **Kakamas** see Orange River Wine Cellars
▪ **Kango** see Mooiuitsig Wine Cellars

Kanonkop Estate

Location/map: Stellenbosch ▪ WO: Simonsberg–Stellenbosch/Stellenbosch ▪ Est 1910 ▪ 1stB 1973 ▪ Tasting & sales Mon–Fri 9–5 Sat 9–2 pub hols 10–4 ▪ Fee R10 ▪ Closed Good Fri, Dec 25 & Jan 1 ▪ Cheese platters in summer; traditional snoek barbecues by appt (min 15 people); or BYO picnic ▪ Conservation area ▪ Art gallery ▪ Owner(s) Johann & Paul Krige ▪ Cellarmaster(s) Abrie Beeslaar (Jan 2002) ▪ Winemaker(s) Abrie Beeslaar (Jan 2002), with Jeremy Arries (2007) & Frikkie Elias (1992) ▪ Viticulturist(s) Koos du Toit (Jan 2004) ▪ 120ha/100ha (cabs s/f, merlot, ptage) ▪ 1,200t/170,000cs own label 98% red 2% rosé ▪ WIETA ▪ PO Box 19 Elsenburg 7607 ▪ wine@kanonkop.co.za ▪ www.kanonkop.co.za ▪ S 33° 51' 18.4" E 018° 51' 36.1" ▪ **T +27 (0)21-884-4656** ▪ F +27 (0)21-884-4719

Undertaking a self-imposed performance analysis, Kanonkop co-owner and CEO Johann Krige says 'less work and more strategic thinking' would make him more productive. He's being unduly hard on himself. Kanonkop is probably the property most regarded as South Africa's equivalent to a 'first growth' and that comes from careful custodianship of every aspect of the brand. At one end of the scale, various processes from the vineyard to the cellar are being mechanised (a new bottling plant going in last year) to optimise quality and, at the other, a re-corking service for loyal customers whose wines show too much ullage. 'Constant tiny improvements but never reinventing the wheel.'

★★★★ **Cabernet Sauvignon 10** very youthful, still way off showing at its best. Cranberry & cassis, subtle leafy note, hint of vanilla. Medium bodied with bright acidity before a pleasantly austere finish.

★★★★☆ **Pinotage** ⓥ Classic **11** shows perfectly ripe dark fruit & attractive oak spice (80% new wood). Rich & intense but balanced. Bright acidity, nicely grippy tannins. A wine of real distinction, as was standout **10** (★★★★★).

★★★★☆ **Paul Sauer** Thrilling return to form for iconic Bordeaux blend cab (68%) & equal merlot, cab franc. After slightly under-done **09** (★★★★), **10** red & black fruit, incense on the nose, plenty of reined-in power on the palate. Great fruit definition, bright acidity, firm but fine tannins. 100% new oak, 26 months. Promises to give much pleasure in the future.

Kadette Dry Red ★★★ Anytime, anywhere **11** is pinotage led, with red fruit, hint of banana & spice. Thinner than previous vintages. WO Stellenbosch, like next. **Kadette Pinotage Dry Rosé** ⓥ ★★★ **12** light & breezy, with red cherry flavour & bright acidity. Also-tasted **13** (★★★★) more weight, with strawberry plus subtle spicy, earthy notes. 'For funky styled food.' — CE

Kanu Private Cellar & Vineyards

Location/map: Stellenbosch ▪ WO: Western Cape/Stellenbosch ▪ Est/1stB 1998 ▪ Tasting & sales Mon-Fri 9.30–4.30 ▪ Fee R35pp ▪ Closed all pub hols ▪ Owner(s) Ben Truter Trust ▪ Cellarmaster(s)/winemaker(s) Johan Grimbeek (Jan 2002) ▪ Viticulturist(s) Wynand Pienaar (2011) ▪ 48ha/26ha (cab, merlot, chard, sauv) ▪ 200t/60,000cs own label 50% red 45% white 5% rosé + 8,000cs for clients ▪ BWI ▪ PO Box 548 Stellenbosch 7599 ▪ info@kanu.co.za ▪ www.kanu.co.za ▪ S 33° 53' 23.35" E 018° 49' 8.44" ▪ **T** +27 (0)21-865-2488 ▪ F +27 (0)21-865-2351

This marque started life as 'Goedgeloof' off Stellenbosch's Polkadraai Road in the late 90s. Then owned by diversified corporate Hydro Holdings, which had bought sister property Mulderbosch, and driven by star winemaker Teddy Hall, it was rebranded 'Kanu' – a mythical African bird symbolising the promise of a bountiful harvest. A decade later Ben Truter acquired the brand, moved operations to the old Mulderbosch property and, with longtime cellarmaster Johan Grimbeek, set about revitalising Kanu as a family business offering consistent quality and value.

Premium range

★★★★ **KCB Chenin Blanc** ✓ 🍽 ⓥ **11** bursts with flavour; fleshy summer fruit, vanilla buff of oak (French & American, 9 months, 41% new) & tangerine twist to off-dry tail. WO Stellenbosch. **10** sold out untasted.

★★★★ **Kia-Ora Noble Late Harvest** ✓ ⓥ Botrytised chenin dessert; full-blooded **10** loaded with candied peel & piquant kumquat, refined in all-new oak (16 months) & balanced by vivacious acid.

Cabernet Sauvignon ★★★ Tarry notes to **12**, oak masks fruit mid-2013. **Merlot** ⓥ ★★★ Scented berry tone to sweet finish, **12** warm & rounded but short of verve. **Shiraz** ★★★ **08** is bold, ripe & spicy; 68% new wood well absorbed into sturdy body. **Keystone** ★★★★ Clean-cut Bordeaux-style red blend. **08**'s alluring minty cassis charm restrained by tight structure & oak; needs time to shine. **GSM** ★★★★ **10** grenache-led blend, with shiraz & mourvèdre. Supple structure, savoury red fruit shining through spicy oak mid-2013. **Chardonnay-Pinot Noir** NEW 🍽 ⓥ ★★ **12** semi-dry rosé with candyfloss charm. **Chardonnay Barrel Fermented** ⓕ ⓥ ★★★★ Elegant **11** has lovely fruit purity & length. Deft oaking adds rich brioche tone zested with lemon/lime freshness. **Chardonnay Unwooded** Await next release. **Sauvignon Blanc** 🍽 ★★★ **12** a pick-me-up. Grassy green crispness will kick-start a summer lunch. WO Stellenbosch. **Viognier** ⓥ ★★★★ **12** ups ante on **11** (★★★). It's like liquid confectionery; waves of apricot & marmalade jostle with oak in luscious off-dry send-off. Not subtle, but delicious.

Prime range

Rockwood ⓐ 🍽 ★★★ Round, ripe & accessible red quaffer. **08** shiraz spices up Bordeaux mix. **Chenin Blanc** ⓐ 🍽 ★★★ Plump apple-toned **12** lacks aromatic verve of previous. Stellenbosch WO. **Natural Sweet Shiraz** 🔲 ★★ **12** elevated from Pouring range; warming, sweetly spiced berry tone.

Méthode Cap Classique range

Giselle New vintage not available.

Pouring range

Rifle Range Red ⓐ 🍽 🔲 ★★★ NV shiraz-led blend hits straight to the mark for supple, juicy fruited drinking pleasure. **Merlot Rosé** 🍽 ★★ Crisply off-dry **NV** is plump, with strawberry charm. **Classic Dry White** ⓐ 🍽 🔲 ★★★ NV chenin/sauvignon's crunchy acidity tempers warm tropical tone. **Semi-Sweet White** ⓐ 🍽 ★★★ Lively **NV** blend. Tangy, with a brush of oak & botrytis. Delightful quaffer & fusion food partner. —DS

■ **Kap Hase** *see* Migliarina Wines
■ **Karoo Classique** *see* Karusa Vineyards

Karusa Vineyards

Location: Oudtshoorn ▪ Map: Klein Karoo & Garden Route ▪ WO: Klein Karoo/Western Cape ▪ Est/1stB 2004 ▪ Tasting & sales Mon-Fri 9.30-4 Sat 10–2.30 ▪ Closed Good Fri & Dec 25 ▪ Karoo Tapas Restaurant & Deli ▪ Microbrewery ▪ Conferences (30-40 pax) ▪ Owner(s) Karusa Partnership ▪ Cellarmaster(s) Jacques Conradie (2004) ▪ 8ha (grenache, mourv, muscadel r, ptage, shiraz, touriga nacional, chard, sauv, viog) ▪ 50-70t/5,000cs own label 30% red 50% white 5% rosé 15% other ▪ PO Box 1061 Oudtshoorn 6620 ▪ info@karusa.co.za ▪ www.karusa.co.za ▪ S 33° 28' 36.0" E 022° 14' 33.2" ▪ **T +27 (0)44-272-8717** ▪ F +27 (0)86-600-3167

A must-stop destination for Klein Karoo sightseers and winelovers – it's en route to the Cango Caves – this family winery offers a wide range of products, the most recent being beer from its microbrewery. Partner/cellarmaster Jacques Conradie offers an invitation: 'Relax with an ice-cold sauvignon in one hand and a complex amber ale in the other, as you look out over the Swartberg range, pausing to snack on ostrich carpaccio from the deli.'

Reserve Collection

The 5th Element Syrah-Viognier ★★★★ Only a soupçon viognier in step-up **11**. Herbal notes enliven smoky bacon aroma & dense black fruit; tannins, oak (30% new) & 13.5% alcohol amenable for solo sipping or dining. **Earth's Art Chardonnay-Viognier** 🍽 ★★★ Chardonnay's citrus tones in the lead, 20% viognier adds spice & richness to **12** unusual & distinctive oaked blend.

Terroir Specific Collection

The Ancients Pinot Noir NEW ✓ 🍽 ★★★★ Pinotphiles on a budget should stock up on **12**. Appeals with cherry fruit, moderate 13% alcohol, gentle brush of tannin - & reasonable price. **Double Black Petite Sirah** NEW 🍽 ★★★ Living up to name, inky **12** offers brooding fruit & black olives, commanding structure & tannins need few years to meld, soften. **One Tree Hill Pinotage** ✓ 🍽 ★★★★ Super expression of the variety, **12** exuberant dark fruit & spice, vanilla from American oak (60% new), reined in by zesty acidity, fine & long tannins. Several rungs above light & easy **11** (★★★). **Terre Noire Syrah** 🍽 ★★★★ Tad less new oak than sibling, 100% shiraz. Fascinating combo Karoo scrub, lilies & peaches; commendable dryness; persistent bitter-choc finish: improved **12** ticks all the boxes. **Aloe Ridge Unwooded Chardonnay** Await next. **Southern Slope Sauvignon Blanc** ✓ 🍽 ★★★★ Characterful aperitif style. **12** unfurls to gooseberry, blackcurrant, passionfruit & flowers; brisk acidity & lengthy farewell. **Stonerock Viognier** 🍽 ★★★ Oak-fermented **12** typical heady viognier peach & jasmine; creamy oak-sweet goodbye invites spicy accompaniment.

Lifestyle Collection

Shiraz-Cabernet Sauvignon ⓐ 🍽 ★★★ Savoury plum pudding laced with pepper & spice, **11** is ripe & pleasantly light hearted. WO W Cape. **Muscat Rosé** ⓐ 🍽 ★★★ Off-dry **12** candyfloss & ripe strawberries, zesty & refreshing. **Muscat Blanc** ⓐ 🍽 ★★★ White muscadel's grapey perfume & spice suffuse charming **12**'s gently sweet apricot flavour. **Chenin Blanc-Sauvignon Blanc** ⓐ 🍽 ★★★★ Chenin leads in **12**, provides good ripe body; sauvignon adds pebbly minerality & complexity - more satisfying than previous.

Karoo Classique Collection

Pinot Noir Rosé ★★★ Strong brioche & strawberry, some evolution on bottle-fermented dry bubbly. Now **NV**, less fresh but as well flavoured as vintage-dated previous. **Chardonnay Brut** NEW ★★★ Attractive yeasty saline notes on **NV** dry celebratory fizz from chardonnay. Lively mousse & tangy acidity - no wallflower!

Liqueur Collection

Soleil de Karusa White Muscadel NEW ★★★ Dessert in a glass. **13**'s raisins overlain with watermelon, honey & molasses; gentle acidity & syrupy sweetness. **Soleil de Karusa Red Muscadel** ★★★★ **NV** fortified sweetie, aged in large old barrels, has tealeaf & blueberry jam attractions, fiery conclusion to chilly winter days & evenings. 375 ml, as all these. **Soleil de Karusa Cape Vintage** ★★ Port-style from touriga. Meaty **12**'s jammy palate needs more spirity zing. For for keeping. **Soleil de Karusa Cape White** ★★★ Intriguing **NV** port-style from viognier goes up a notch with bold grapey aromas & flavours, icing sugar & almond nuances, ginger-spiced farewell. — HJ,CvZ

Katbakkies Wine

Location/map/WO: Stellenbosch ▪ Est/1stB 1999 ▪ Tasting & sales Mon-Sat by appt ▪ Closed all pub hols ▪ Owner(s) Andries van der Walt ▪ Cellarmaster(s) Andries van der Walt (1999) ▪ Winemaker(s) Teddy Hall (2002, consultant) & Andries van der Walt (1999) ▪ 29ha/10ha (cab, merlot, syrah) ▪ 1,000cs own label 40% red 60% white ▪ PO Box 305 Stellenbosch 7599 ▪ info@katbakkies.co.za ▪ www.katbakkies.co.za ▪ S 33° 55' 37.4" E 018° 49' 14.6" ▪ **T +27 (0)82-882-9022** ▪ F +27 (0)86-557-0597

It was a Rustenberg '63 cabernet that finally inspired architect Andries van der Walt to start his own winery. The name is that of his Cederberg farm, where ravenous baboons deny a viable yield off the vines. Andries turned to Stellenbosch for fruit, and with plans to build house and cellar in Devon Valley.

★★★★ **Cabernet Sauvignon** Ⓕ Classic, understated character on mature **05**. Pleasing, but on the austere side. All these wines tasted a few years back.

★★★★ **Syrah Reserve** Ⓕ Dense, complex **04**; firm structure, bold but balanced.

★★★★ **Chenin Blanc** Ⓕ **09** (★★★★) more obviously off-dry than **08**; good depth of flavour, but the soft sweetness slightly awkwardly jostling some hard acidity. Pleasant enough, however.

★★★★ **Viognier** Ⓕ **08** elegant & fresh when tasted, off-dry sugar level giving richness. **07** clumsy (★★).

Syrah Ⓕ ★★★★ Last tasted was suave, spicy & unshowily fruity **08**. **Perpendiculum Viognier** ★★★ Quiet varietal character on **NV** blend of vintages 05 to 09, & quietly attractive, just off-dry. — AL

■ **KC** *see* Klein Constantia Estate

Keermont Vineyards

Location/map/WO: Stellenbosch ▪ Est 2005 ▪ 1stB 2007 ▪ Tasting, sales & cellar tours by appt ▪ Owner(s) Wraith family ▪ Winemaker(s)/viticulturist(s) Alex Starey (Jan 2005) ▪ 156ha/27ha (cab, merlot, syrah, chenin) ▪ 65t/3,000cs own label 65% red 33% white 2% sticky white ▪ BWI, IPW ▪ PO Box 713 Stellenbosch 7599 ▪ info@keermont.co.za ▪ www.keermont.co.za ▪ S 34°0' 27.0" E 018° 53' 39.0" ▪ **T +27 (0)21-880-0397** ▪ F +27 (0)21-880-0566

Nature and all things natural are major themes at this property straddling the Helderberg and Stellenbosch mountains. Indigenous vegetation, eradicated of aliens, beautifies much of it, with less than 30 hectares of scattered high-altitude vineyards. Riverside, a chenin vineyard planted in 1971 and Uitkyk, sauvignon planted in 1988, are the oldest; the rest joined since 2005. Owner Mark Wraith and his family, as well as winemaker Alex Starey, believe in non-interventionist winemaking, allowing spontaneous fermentation, with no fining or filtration.

★★★★ **Syrah** Power a given in **11**'s 15.5% alcohol, but there's nothing loud or showy in its rich spice & roast meat tones. Tannins are supple yet telling, oaking (5% new) an enhancement. Better food partner than solo.

★★★★ **Keermont** Complexity & freshness in **11** Bordeaux trio with shiraz despite 15.5% alcohol. Polished, well integrated & firmly built; ageing potential to around 2019. Super **09** (★★★★★); **10** untasted.

★★★★ **Terrasse** Near-equal blend barrel-fermented chenin, sauvignon, chardonnay plus apricoty viognier. **12** bolder, a bit less steely cored than **11**. Savoury, gentle grippy finish nicely offsets opulence.

Fleurfontein Await next. — AL

Keet Wines

Location/WO: Stellenbosch ▪ Est 2008 ▪ 1stB 2010 ▪ Tasting by appt ▪ Owner(s) Christopher Keet ▪ Cellar-master(s)/winemaker(s)/viticulturist(s) Christopher Keet (Oct 2008) ▪ 10t/1,000cs own label 100% red ▪ PO Box 5508 Helderberg 7135 ▪ chris@keetwines.co.za ▪ www.keetwines.co.za ▪ **T +27 (0)82-853-1707** ▪ F +27 (0)86-544-3347

Chris Keet works flexibly as he establishes his brand: sourcing grapes across Stellenbosch and making wine in rented space on the Polkadraai Hills, from where he also works as a consultant. Unsurprisingly, the wine under his own name shows the understated elegance he's long been associated with. Unusually for a top Bordeaux blend, he uses little new oak - it's a part of the unshowy Keet style.

★★★★☆ **First Verse** ⚓ 🌿 Leafy fragrance & hint of cedar a lovely intro to unusually dry & restrained 5-way Bordeaux red **10** (★★★★★). Light-stepping, balanced elegance belies powerful alcohol, but flavour length reveals subtle fruit intensity, untrammelled by oak. Drinks well but will mature, like maiden **09**. — TJ

▪ **Keimoes** see Orange River Wine Cellars
▪ **Keizer's Creek** see Roodezandt Wines

Kellerprinz

Budget-priced white for the sweet toothed, in 2L bottle, by Distell.

Late Harvest ★☆ Fresh, lively semi-sweet **NV** white with pear & peach flavours. — DB, HJ

▪ **Kelvin Grove** see Simonsvlei International

Ken Forrester Wines

Location: Stellenbosch ▪ Map: Helderberg ▪ WO: Western Cape/Stellenbosch ▪ Est/1stB 1994 ▪ Tasting & sales on home farm, cnr R44 & Winery Rd: Mon-Fri 9-5 Sat 9.30-3.30 (Sep-May) & 9.30-1.30 (Jun-Aug) ▪ Fee R30 KF & Petit range/R50 Icon range ▪ Closed Good Fri, Dec 25 & Jan 1 ▪ Sundays & after hours tasting available at 96 Winery Rd Restaurant (see Restaurants section) ▪ Owner(s) Ken & Teresa Forrester ▪ Cellarmaster(s) Ken Forrester (1994) ▪ Winemaker(s) Ken Forrester (1994) & Martin Meinert ▪ Viticulturist(s) Pieter Rossouw (Oct 2009) ▪ (grenache, merlot, mourv, shiraz, chenin, sauv) ▪ 950t/140,000cs own label 35% red 65% white ▪ Other export brand: Work-horse (Marks & Spencer) ▪ Brands for clients: Woolworths ▪ ISO 9001:2000, BWI, HACCP, SEDEX, WIETA ▪ PO Box 1253 Stellenbosch 7599 ▪ info@kenforresterwines.com ▪ www.kenforresterwines.com ▪ S 34° 1' 31.06" E 018° 49' 05.92" ▪ **T +27 (0)21-855-2374** ▪ F +27 (0)21-855-2373

Talk about making a virtue out of necessity. Vintner and restaurateur Ken Forrester (with longtime collaborator Martin Meinert) has taken widely planted but commercially challenged chenin blanc and made it key to his offering. The ultra-premium FMC is highly respected, but he provides versions of the grape which represent great quality relative to price at all market levels. Next on his list is to gain a similar sort of public acceptance for his Rhône-style reds. 'The greatest single problem we face in South Africa is that we harvest in the peak of summer whereas the rest of the world harvests in autumn,' he says. 'We are undoubtedly a Mediterranean climate and hence we should be using Mediterranean varieties such as grenache and mourvèdre – they're late ripening and with the aid of a little irrigation can survive our harsh summers.' For top examples featuring these grapes, look no further than Three Halves, in particular.

Icon range

★★★★☆ **The Gypsy** Exquisite **10** is 64% old-vine grenache from Piekenierskloof, 30% shiraz & mourvèdre. Red & black berries plus some floral fragrance. Excellent purity, fresh acidity & fine, spicy tannins. Perhaps more medium bodied than **09** (★★★★★) but complex & wonderfully composed.

★★★★ **Three Halves** With mourvèdre in the ascendancy, rest grenache, shiraz, **09** (★★★★★) has more grunt than its counterpart above but pure & focused even so. More black berries than red, spice plus an earthy quality. Even better realised than **07**. No **08**.

★★★★☆ **The FMC** 🗄 'Forrester Meinert Chenin' naturally fermented in new oak. Magnificent **11** all about controlled power. Rich & full but tension provided by wonderful line of acidity. Hugely complex: honeysuckle,

peach, pineapple, wax, fresh bread, spice, the list goes on. Starts sweet, ends savoury, has real sense of deliciousness about it. Stellenbosch WO, like next three.

★★★★ **FMC Première Sélection Moelleux** ⊕ 'Mellow' made weather permitting. **10** chenin has real peaches & custard character about it. Sweeter (sugar at 19 g/l vs 15 for FMC), moderate acidity, creamy texture.

★★★★☆ **'T' Noble Late Harvest** Barrel-fermented botrytised chenin named for Mrs Forrester. **10** (★★★★) is thick but not unctuous, shows apricot plus vanilla & a slight nutty quality which adds interest. Tangy acidity lends balance. Excellent yet not quite as poised as **09**.

Sparklehorse NEW ★★★ A first for this producer, méthode cap classique sparkling from chenin, **11** is redolent of apple, & great fun. Appletiser for grown-ups.

Ken Forrester range

★★★★ **Old Vine Reserve Chenin Blanc** ✓ 🍴 **12** shows yellow fruit, some leesy complexity, hint of vanilla. Closed on tasting but typically lasts a good few years. Part barrel ferment. Name changed from 'Reserve' - vineyards in question all over 30 years.

Merlot Next awaited. **Renegade** 🍴 ★★★★ Cleverly assembled **09** is 46% grenache, rest shiraz, mourvèdre. Red fruit, spice, touch of earthiness. More intensity than **08** (★★★★). WO W Cape, others in this range WO Stellenbosch. **Sauvignon Blanc** 🍴 📷 ★★★☆ On preview, **13** is lightly fruity with bright acidity. Lime, apple & white pepper before a long, dry finish.

Petit range

Sauvignon Blanc ☺ 🍴 📷 ★★★ **13** over-delivers with intense pear & white peach, some texture & zippy acidity. Smiley face indeed. Stellenbosch WO.

Pinotage 🍴 📷 ★★★☆ Moreish **12** is unwooded & all the better for it. Mulberry, red & black cherry, some fynbos. Juicy & fresh with fine tannins. **Cabernet Sauvignon-Merlot** 🍴 📷 ★★★ **12** appears lush & dense, no doubt aided by good whack of sugar. Ultra-ripe dark fruit, some fragrance, soft tannins. **Rosé** 🍴 📷 ★★ From Stellenbosch grenache, **13** shows vague strawberry character, is sweet & soft. **Chenin Blanc** ✓ 🍴 📷 ★★★☆ Hugely appealing **13** (unwooded) with concentrated peach & pear, coated acidity, good length. Go-to summer drinking. **Semi-Sweet** 🍴 📷 ★★★ **13** from chenin. Peach & spanspek, bright acidity prevents it from being overwhelmingly sweet. — CE

■ **Kevin Arnold** see Waterford Estate
■ **Kievits Kroon** see Glen Erskine Estate

Kingna Distillery ¶♦🍴🏠📷 NEW

Location/WO: Montagu ▪ Map: Klein Karoo & Garden Route ▪ Est 2007 ▪ 1stB 2012 ▪ Tasting, sales & distillery tours Mon-Fri 10-5 Sat/Sun 10-3 ▪ Closed Easter Sat/Sun, Dec 25/26 & Jan 1 ▪ Tour groups ▪ BYO picnic ▪ Conferences ▪ Weddings/functions ▪ Hiking & mountain biking trails ▪ Self-catering chalets ▪ Owner(s) Norbert Engel ▪ Brandy master Ruan Hunlun (Jan 2005, consultant) ▪ 1,000ha/8ha (chenin, cbard) ▪ 140t/9,000L ▪ PO Box 395 Montagu 6720 ▪ ruan@kingna.co.za ▪ www.kingna.co.za ▪ S 33° 49' 45.87" E 20° 15' 39.10" ▪ **T +27 (0)23-614-2721** ▪ F +27 (0)23-614-2721

Norbert Engel's long-dreamt-of brandy distillery on his Montagu farm, named after a local river, allows brandy master Ruan Hunlun to introduce blended brandy-and-cola lovers to an alternative that is 'smooth, refined but affordable'. The 2,000L still's output, oak-matured five years, goes to Europe; farm hikers, holidaymakers and wedding parties; and restored Dutch ship Oosterschelde.

Potstill Brandy ★★★ Smooth textured, light, 'feminine' & elegant, with fresh apricot, fynbos, clove & floral perfume; oak rather obvious. 100% potstill from colombar. — WB,TJ

Kingsriver Estate ¶♦🍵🏠📷

Location/WO: McGregor ▪ Map: Robertson ▪ Est 2003 ▪ 1stB 2005 ▪ Tasting & sales Mon-Sat 8-9 Sun 8-5 ▪ Cellar tours daily 8-5 ▪ Tour groups ▪ Farm produce ▪ BYO picnic ▪ Hiking trails ▪ Conferences ▪ 4-star Kingsriver Country House & Restaurant ▪ Owner(s) De Clercq Family Trust ▪ Cellarmaster(s) Ruud de Clercq & Patrick Julius ▪ Winemaker(s) Ruud de Clercq (2005) ▪ Viticulturist(s) Patrick Julius (2005) ▪ 348ha/38ha (cab, ptage, ruby cab, shiraz, tannat, chard, chenin, cbard) ▪ 190t/10,000cs own label 80% red 20% white ▪ Other export label: Mzansi ▪ PO Box 203 McGregor 6708 ▪ kingsriver-office@breede.co.za ▪ www.kingsriver-estate.com ▪ S 33° 55' 19.5" E 019° 49' 45.5" ▪ **T +27 (0)23-625-1040** ▪ F +27 (0)23-625-1045

Biodynamic farming at the de Clercq family's wine and hospitality estate near McGregor is yielding better-tasting grapes and a diversity of wild yeasts, enthuse cellarmasters Ruud de Clercq and Patrick Julius. 'Difficult!' conditions prompt the imminent return of the Mzansi budget range and Ruud to wryly name 'finding the right bank' as the only item in his bucket list.

Ruby Cabernet Await next, as for **Sauvignon Blanc**. **Shiraz** ⓘ ★★★ Slightly warming **07** Aussie-style bluegum & charry oak, smoke & nutty nuances for added appeal. **Chardonnay** ⓘ ★★ Ripe tangerine fruit, vanilla highlights on crisp **10** crowd pleaser. — JP,CvZ

Kirabo Private Cellar

Location: Rawsonville ▪ Map: Breedekloof ▪ Est 2002 ▪ 1stB 2003 ▪ Tasting, sales & cellar/vineyard tours Mon-Fri 8.30-5 Sat by appt ▪ Closed all pub hols ▪ Meals by appt only ▪ Facilities for children ▪ Tour groups ▪ Gift shop ▪ Farm produce ▪ BYO picnic ▪ Walking/hiking/4x4 trails ▪ Weddings/functions ▪ Conservation area ▪ Owner(s) Pieter & Karen le Roux ▪ Cellarmaster(s) Pieter le Roux (2002) ▪ Winemaker(s) Pieter & Karen le Roux (2002) ▪ Viticulturist(s) Pieter le Roux ▪ 1,000t/6,000L total ▪ 10t own label 100% red ▪ IPW ▪ PO Box 96 Rawsonville 6845 ▪ info@kirabocellar.co.za ▪ www.kirabocellar.co.za ▪ S 33° 42' 36.68" E 019° 21' 27.55" ▪ **T +27 (0)23-349-6764** ▪ F +27 (0)23-349-6764

To matriarch Karen le Roux, the file of elephants tramping across Kirabo's labels represents the succession of Le Roux generations – now up to six – inhabiting and tending the family's Rawsonville farm. Kirabo means 'a gift from God', gathered in and handed on in the bottles from this boutique reds-only cellar.

▪ Kiss My Springbok *see Anura Vineyards*

Klawer Wine Cellars

Location: Klawer ▪ Map/WO: Olifants River ▪ Est 1956 ▪ Tasting & sales Mon-Fri 8-5 Sat 9-1 ▪ Fee R5 pp for groups of 5+ ▪ Closed all pub hols ▪ Facilities for children ▪ BYO picnic ▪ Conferences (office hours only) ▪ Owner(s) 92 members ▪ Cellarmaster(s) Pieter van Aarde (Nov 2011) ▪ Winemaker(s) Roelof van Schalkwyk & Cerina van Niekerk, with Christo Beukes & Bennie Avenant ▪ Viticulturist(s) MG van der Westhuizen ▪ 2,095ha (cab, merlot, ptage, ruby cab, shiraz, chard, chenin, cbard, hanepoot, muscadel, sauv, viog) ▪ 43,000t/60,000cs own label 40% red 40% white 5% rosé 15% other ▪ Other export brand: Travino ▪ ISO 22000:2009, Organic, DLG, IPW ▪ PO Box 8 Klawer 8145 ▪ klawerwyn@kingsley.co.za ▪ www.klawerwine.co.za ▪ S 31° 47' 34.9" E 018° 37' 36.1" ▪ **T +27 (0)27-216-1530** ▪ F +27 (0)27-216-1561

At hospitable grower-owned Klawer in big-sky Olifants River, things are moving along 'nicely', says cellarmaster Pieter van Aarde. The harvest was 7% up, with white grapes, especially, brought in early owing to really hot weather. They sent 'a whole lot' of wine to Russia and are eyeing the Chinese market with interest.

Merlot ☺ 🍴 ★★★ Step-up **12** is easy to like: soft red fruit, dusty/leafy notes, pliable tannins. **Grenache Blanc de Noir** ☺ 🍴 ★★☆ **13** semi-sweet poolside sipper with perky strawberry & bubblegum appeal. **Chardonnay** ☺ 🍴 ★★★ Ripe citrus & pine nut combo, **12** appetising savouriness for al fresco sipping.

Cabernet Sauvignon ⓘ 🍴 ★★★★ **11** notch up from last-tasted **08** (★★★). Dry & refreshing, with elegant tannins, smoky overtones. **Pinotage** 🍴 ★★★ **12** tad over-ripe, less convincing than previous which had generous flavour, moderate alcohol & freshness. **Shiraz** 🍴 ★★ Toast, vanilla & butterscotch bouquet belie **11**'s austere mouthful. **Shiraz-Merlot** 🍴 ★★★ Everyday sippability assured by **10**'s black fruit charm, supple structure. **Chenin Blanc** 🍴 ★★ **13** shows stonefruit, zippy acidity & pithy grip but farewell is brief. **Sauvignon Blanc** 🍴 ★★★ **13** pungent grass & khaki bush notes, satisfying vinosity & length. **Viognier** ✓ 🍴 ★★★★ Peach & apricot **12**, round & quite rich. Showcase for variety's aromatic charms; one to watch. **Michelle Sparkling** 🍴 🥂 ★★★ Unassuming **13** pink sparkler with pretty muscat & jasmine aromas, light body; chill well to fluff out its sweet tail. **Hanepoot** Next awaited. **Red Muscadel** ✓ 🍴 ★★★★ Delicious full-sweet fortified dessert **13** first reviewed since **09**. Complex tealeaf & barley sugar aromas, berry & molasses flavours; deft tannin/spirit grip. **White Muscadel** ⓘ ★★★☆ **08** fortified dessert a real treat - perfect with crème brûlée. **Travino Matador** ⓘ ★★ Port-style fortified from ruby cab technically very sweet but well-judged spirit makes **09** seem dry. — HJ, CvZ

▪ Klein Centennial *see Group CDV*

Klein Constantia Estate   🍷📷♿

Location: Constantia ▪ Map: Cape Peninsula ▪ WO: Western Cape/Constantia ▪ Est 1823 ▪ 1stB 1824 ▪ Tasting & sales Mon-Fri 9–5 Sat 10-5 (summer)/10-4.30 (winter) Sun 10-4 (summer only) ▪ Fee R30 ▪ Closed some pub hols ▪ Gift shop ▪ Estate honey for sale ▪ Collection of original Constantia bottles on display ▪ Owner(s) Zdenek Bakala, Charles Harman, Bruno Prats & Hubert de Boüard ▪ Winemaker(s) Matthew Day (2009) ▪ Brandy masters Matthew Day & Giorgio Dalla Cia (Dalla Cia) ▪ Viticulturist(s) Stiaan Cloete (Jul 2008) ▪ 146ha/82ha (cabs s/f, malbec, merlot, p verdot, shiraz, chard, muscat de F, riesling, sauv, sem) ▪ 500t/80,000cs own label 30% red 70% white ▪ BWI champion ▪ PO Box 375 Constantia 7848 ▪ info@kleinconstantia.com ▪ www.kleinconstantia.com ▪ S 34° 2' 19.0" E 018° 24' 46.5" ▪ **T +27 (0)21-794-5188** ▪ F +27 (0)21-794-2464

Klein Constantia, historic 'grande dame' of the Constantia Valley, is receiving a new lease of life under MD Hans Astrom and his team. (Helderberg sibling winery Anwilka run and listed separately). The rich cultural heritage of the estate is rooted in the surrounding community and much effort is made to maintain a balance between both, to build and grow for the future. Latest onsite projects include soil erosion prevention, critical on the steep Constantiaberg slopes, and investment in new cellar kit under aegis of winemaker Matt Day to ensure internationally hailed (and Fifty Shades of Grey-referenced) Vin de Constance continues to receive state-of-art cosseting. Naturally the other wines receive no less attention, from the new prestige Estate Red to the accessible-to-all KC range.

Estate Wines

★★★★☆ **Estate Red Blend** NEW 5-way cab-dominated blend with 13% shiraz, **11** is elegantly composed, with clean, fresh blackcurrants & blackberries showcased with tobacco & cedar spice. Darkly brooding core with gritty, well-integrated tannins & lengthy finish.

★★★★ **Riesling** 🗄 Fragrant, floral **12** exudes lime cordial & exotic musk. Tightly wound flavours of creamy stonefruit, needs & deserves time. Ex older & younger vines, briefly lees-aged. On form after **11** (★★★★).

★★★★★ **Perdeblokke Sauvignon Blanc** Intriguing complexity forming on delicious **12** with groomed layers (lemon curd, tinned litchis, pink grapefruit), tight acidity & steely freshness. Mouthfilling mid-palate & elegant length suggest a great future, as did **09**. **11** untasted. **10** (★★★★) youthfully muscular - a sleeper?

★★★★ **Sauvignon Blanc** ⏱🗄 **12** delicate yet focused, with bright stonefruit & some minerality. Dab of semillon adds waxy breadth. Returning to form after riper-styled **11** (★★★★). Constantia WO.

★★★★☆ **Brut Méthode Cap Classique** 🥂 Very fine **10** (★★★★★) sparkling sings & dances elegance, a rock salt note giving way to toasted almond, buttered croissant & lemon curd. Cask-aged chardonnay, 2 years on lees. Released in 3 stages, next with extra year sur lie. **09** gained extra vivacity from fine vintage.

★★★★☆ **Vin de Constance** Iconic dessert from unbotrytised muscat de Frontignan. Rich & satisfying **08** offers fragrant aromas of candied orange peel, faint scent of fynbos. Warm alcohol asserts on entry, then unctuous flavours of toffee apples & glazed pineapples. 54 months 60% new oak, French & Hungarian.

Marlbrook Await new vintage, as for **Madame Marlbrook**. Discontinued: **Cabernet Sauvignon**.

KC range

Cabernet Sauvignon-Merlot 🗄 ★★★☆ Attractive cherry/choc notes on **11** with some cassis, all surrounded by fine cab tannins. Superior everyday sipper. **Rosé** Next awaited. **Sauvignon Blanc** ⏱🗄 ★★★☆ **12** widely sourced grapes give fruitier style but retain crisp balance for summer refreshment.

Grappa-Styles NEW

Spirit of Constance ★★★ Made from Vin de Constance husks, with powerfully grapey, floral scents insisting on its muscat origin. Soft, smooth, monolithic palate; lots of flavour but little finesse or delicacy. — WB, CM, TJ

◼ **Kleindal** *see* Robertson Wide River Export Company

Klein DasBosch   🍴☕

Location/map: Stellenbosch ▪ Tasting & sales at Mont Marie Restaurant, Blaauwklippen Road, T +27 (0)21-880-0777 - please call first as tasting hours are subject to change ▪ Owner(s) James Wellwood Basson ▪ Marketing director Nikki Basson-Herbst ▪ Admin manager Annalette Reynolds ▪ Viti/vini consultant Jan Coetzee (1997) ▪ Winemaker(s) Jan Coetzee (1994) ▪ ±25ha ▪ 90% red 10% white ▪ PO Box 12320 Stellenbosch 7613 ▪ dasbosch@telkomsa.net ▪ www.kleindasbosch.co.za, www.montmarie.co.za ▪ S 33° 58' 56.0" E 018° 51' 44.5" ▪ **T +27 (0)21-880-0128/+27 (0)83-406-8836** ▪ F +27 (0)21-880-0999

Much expanded label vinified at Vriesenhof by Jan Coetzee for neighbour James 'Whitey' Basson, CEO of retailing empire Shoprite/Checkers. The wines can be tasted and purchased at the new Mont Marie Restaurant on Blaauwklippen Road, Stellenbosch. Please confirm hours of tastings as they are subject to change. A small selection also appears on a few other local restaurant lists and wine shops.

Kleine Draken

Location/WO: Paarl ▪ Map: Paarl & Wellington ▪ Est 1983 ▪ 1stB 1988 ▪ Tasting & sales Mon-Fri 8–4 ▪ Closed all pub hols & Jewish holy days ▪ Cellar tours by appt ▪ Pre-booked kosher picnics available ▪ Owner(s) Cape Gate (Pty) Ltd ▪ Winemaker(s) Jean van Rooyen (Dec 2007) ▪ Viticulturist(s) Frank Pietersen (1984) ▪ 12.5ha/5ha under vine ▪ 55t/20,000cs own label 50% red 47% white 3% rosé ▪ IPW, OU certified ▪ PO Box 2674 Paarl 7620 ▪ zandwijk@capegate.co.za ▪ www.kosherwines.co.za ▪ S 33° 46′ 33.3″ ▪ E 018° 56′ 50.4″ ▪ **T +27 (0)21-863-2368** ▪ F +27 (0)21-863-1884

Still the sole kosher-only winery in South Africa, Kleine Draken aims to produce 'good-quality, value-for-money Orthodox Union-certified wines under the supervision of the Cape Town Beth Din'. Replanting at home-farm Zandwijk on Paarl Mountain continues, winemaker Jean van Rooyen says, adding that his wines are also vegan friendly as no animal products are used, and some are low alcohol.

Cabernet Sauvignon ▨ ★★★ Dry cassis & berry pastille on **11**, continues form of last **09**. Well knit & seamless, with oak & fruit in harmony. **Merlot** ▨ ★★☆ Cheery red berry firmness on **12**, a touch lean but up on previous. **Dry Red** ⊕ ★★ Mature, merlot-led **06**, savoury, with bitter hint. **Rosé** ⊕ ▤ ▨ ★★ Light semi-sweet **10**, blend of red & white varieties. **Chardonnay** ▤ ▨ ★★ **12** a step up, easy citrus typicity, some creaminess from light oaking. **Sauvignon Blanc** ▤ ▨ ★★ Animated **12** ups the ante on previous. Good zesty quaffer. **Vin Doux** Next awaited. **Natural Sweet Red** ★★★ Easy lollipop sweetness on low-alcohol **NV** cinsaut/merlot mix. **Natural Sweet White** ★★ Simple floral & banana aromas to low-alcohol **NV** from riesling. **Kiddush** ⊕ ▤ ★★ Light (9% alcohol) **NV** wine for sacramental purposes. Ruby hued & syrupy sweet. — FM

■ **Kleine Parys** see Klein Parys Vineyards
■ **Kleine Rust** see Stellenrust

Kleine Zalze Wines

Location/map: Stellenbosch ▪ WO: Coastal/Western Cape/Stellenbosch ▪ Est 1695 ▪ 1stB 1997 ▪ Tasting & sales Mon-Sat 9-6 Sun 11-6 ▪ Fee R20/5 wines ▪ Closed Good Fri, Dec 25 & Jan 1 ▪ Terroir Restaurant (see Restaurants section) ▪ Kleine Zalze Lodge ▪ De Zalze Golf Course ▪ Conference/function venue ▪ Owner(s) Kobus Basson & Rolf Schulz ▪ Cellarmaster(s) Johan Joubert (Nov 2002) ▪ Winemaker(s) RJ Botha (Dec 2012), with Zara Conradie (Feb 2008) ▪ Viticulturist(s) Henning Retief (May 2006) ▪ 90ha/84ha (cab, merlot, shiraz, chenin, sauv) ▪ 2,300t/ 400,000cs own label 40% red 50% white 10% rosé ▪ PO Box 12837 Die Boord 7613 ▪ quality@kleinezalze.co.za ▪ www.kleinezalze.co.za ▪ S 33° 58′ 14.1″ ▪ E 018° 50′ 8.9″ ▪ **T +27 (0)21-880-0717** ▪ F +27 (0)21-880-0716

The Kleine Zalze property near Stellenbosch has a history dating back 300 years, but it is in its latest incarnation, including a luxury housing estate, golf course and leading restaurant, Terroir, that it has come into its own. So has - emphatically - the eponymous winery on the premises, and trophies and awards continue to crowd the cabinet space. Ranges are clearly defined and offer good value at each level. Cellarmaster Johan Joubert is at the top of his game and must be a very busy man, but in addition to his daily duties he finds the time to produce something special for the Cape Winemakers Guild. A quiet sense of confidence about the project and these wines ensure an ever-growing challenge to the top ranks of commercially successful wineries in South Africa.

Family Reserve range

★★★★☆ **Cabernet Sauvignon** 09 in trademark sweet-fruited & ripe mode, from home-farm vineyard that gives layers of cherry tobacco, cassis & milk chocolate. This svelte fruit balanced by fine gravelly tannins, dry finish & lively acidity. Unashamedly bold, but pulls it off. 08 (★★★★) reflected lesser vintage.

★★★★ **Pinotage** ⊕ Bold, alluring 09 a few years back had structure to contain - just - its 15+% alcohol.

★★★★ **Shiraz** Smoky black pepper spice intro on 09 explodes with ultra-ripe cherry cola & plush vanilla. A big wine with warm alcohol, walking the tightrope of ripeness. Will need another year to settle.

★★★★★ **Chenin Blanc** NEW From 3 Helderberg sites, **12** has very fine aromas! Clean & shy, with restrained promise – crisp apple, blossoms follow to serious palate with savoury entry, focused texture & complex dried fruits (peaches, pineapple). Supportive rather than obtrusive oaking. Ends rich & dry.

★★★★★ **Sauvignon Blanc** **12**'s shy, tight gooseberry aromas evolve to layers of lemon & lime, green melon, fig - mixing pyrazines & poised ripeness. Lovely concentration, ripe citrus acidity. Ends with good focused dry intensity. WO W Cape as was **11** (★★★★★) previewed last year; others in range all Stellenbosch.

Vineyard Selection

★★★★ **Cabernet Sauvignon Barrel Matured** ⓧ Oaky gloss over tobacco, gravel, dark brooding cassis on ex-barrel **10**. Ripe & full bodied, with grippy tannin - a serious offering. WO Stellenbosch.

★★★★ **Chardonnay Barrel Fermented** ▨ Oaky cloak hides subtle dried mango, brioche & ripe apple. Lemon pie part of creamy all-round appeal on **12**. Soft citrus acidity balances sweet-fruited richness.

★★★★ **Chenin Blanc Barrel Fermented** ▨ Multi-layered, with stonefruit & apple complexity, well-oaked **12** refreshing acid cut to oak richness. WO Stellenbosch. Others in range W Cape or Coastal unless noted.

Pinot Noir ▨ ★★★☆ Red cherry fruits on **11**, less refined than **10** (★★★★). A little sugar, warm alcohol & unintegrated acidity detract. **Shiraz Barrel Matured** ⓧ ★★★★ Bold richness helped by oak & few grams sugar, yet **10** cask sample is fresh & vibrant. 15.4% alcohol held by red berry zippiness. Less gawky than **09** (★★★★). WO Stellenbosch. **Shiraz-Mourvèdre-Viognier** ★★★☆ Dusty oak, shy spice & fine red/black berry combo on off-dry **11** needs time for grippy tannins & tangy, vibrant acid to meld. 80% shiraz.

Cellar Selection

> **Merlot** ☺ 🍽 ▨ ★★★ Fresh & bright **12** with tart bramble & red cherry fruit – sour plums jumping from the glass. Easy, fruity pleasure. **Pinotage** ☺ 🍽 ▨ ★★★ Fresh hay, vanilla, ripe red berry, some toasty banana loaf on pleasing **11**, rounded & fruity in style. Just-dry. **Gamay Noir Rosé** ☺ 🍽 ★★★ Lovely bronzed onion skin colour. Ripe berry fruit fragrance. Fresh entry on previewed **13** stays focused, with dry-seeming end. **Chardonnay** ☺ 🍽 ★★★ Tasted ex tank, unwooded **13** starts with peardrop, stonefruit & a hint of lemon curd; clean, soft & refreshing sipping. **Sauvignon Blanc** ☺ 🍽 ★★★ Delicate fig, tropical notes on **13** combo from 5 different regions. Palate offers good acid & fine lingering granadilla tartness.

Cabernet Sauvignon 🍽 ★★★ Fresh cherry & dry tobacco. **11** is earthy, fruity & lively with grippy tannins to balance hint of sweetness. **Gamay Noir** 🍽 ★★★ Previewed **13**, fruity & grapey. Unwooded & best chilled. **Cabernet Sauvignon-Merlot** ⓧ 🍽 ★★★ Just-dry **10** fresh, with nice tannic grip. **Chenin Blanc Bush Vines** ✓ 🍽 ★★★★ **13** continues value benchmark. From untrellised vines, combining botrytised richer fruit with drier, savoury components. This & below ranges all WO Coastal or W Cape.

Foot of Africa range

Shiraz-Viognier 🍽 ★★ Fresh **12**, spicy with firm finish. These for export only; WO W Cape. **Chenin Blanc** 🍽 ★★☆ Easy tutti-frutti & dry **13** for daily sipping.

Zalze range

Pinotage ⓧ 🍽 ★★★ **10** sweet fruited & ripe, usual light oak seasoning. **Shiraz-Mourvèdre-Viognier** 🍽 ★★★ **12**'s vibrant fruit flows to fresh bite & gentle tannin grip. These for export only. **Shiraz-Grenache-Viognier** ⓧ 🍽 ★★★ Shiraz-dominated blend has wet stone earthiness, complemented by bright fruit. Off-dry **11** ends fresh & fruity. **Cabernet Sauvignon-Shiraz Rosé** 🍽 ★★ Light pink **13** fruity, dryish & awkward. **Bush Vine Chenin Blanc** 🍽 ★★★ Fresh upfront & youthful **13** has lovely apple crisp freshness, honey blossom, with savoury interest. — JP

Kleinfontein

Location/WO: Wellington ▪ Est 1995 ▪ 1stB 2003 ▪ Closed to public ▪ Guesthouse ▪ Owner(s) Tim & Caroline Holdcroft ▪ Winemaker(s) Charles Stassen (May 2004) ▪ Viticulturist(s) Tim Holdcroft (Aug 1998) ▪ 12ha/1ha (cab, merlot) ▪ 5-8t/840cs own label 65% red 35% rosé ▪ IPW ▪ PO Box 578 Wellington 7654 ▪ kleinfon@ iafrica.com ▪ www.kleinfontein.com ▪ **T +27 (0)21-864-1202** ▪ F +27 (0)86-587-2675

Named for the spring running through it, Tim and Caroline Holdcroft's Kleinfontein guest farm and vineyard offers relaxed comforts in Wellington's Bovlei Valley. The indigenous garden attracts some 60 different bird species, while the organic garden provides seasonal produce to enjoy with these housewines.

★★★★ **Eminence 11** (★★★★) merlot & cab combo, as previously tasted **07**, overt mint tones suffuse chocolate & red fruit, tad less pleasing but not without charm.

Cabernet Sauvignon ★★ Usual minty note in **10**, with cooked black fruit & soft tannins. **Merlot** ★★★ Smoky, charry tones to **09** surrounding spiced plums & supple tannins for everyday drinking. **Rosé** 🍴 ★★ From merlot, **12** is lightish, sweet fruited & just off-dry. — CM

Klein Gustrouw Estate

Location: Stellenbosch ▪ WO: Jonkershoek Valley ▪ Est 1817 ▪ 1stB 1993 ▪ Closed to public ▪ Owner(s) Klein Gustrouw (Pty) Ltd ▪ Winemaker(s) Warren Ellis (2006) ▪ Viticulturist(s) Pieter Smit (consultant) ▪ ±23ha/ ±14ha under vine ▪ 70% red 30% white ▪ PO Box 6168 Uniedal 7612 ▪ info@kleingustrouw.co.za ▪ **T +27 (0)21-882-8152/+27 (0)82-445-4074** ▪ F +27 (0)86-609-7229

Businessman Jannie Mouton bought this old estate in Stellenbosch's Jonkershoek in 2007, his new broom much in evidence. The 1817 manor was restored, and a major replanting of vineyards inaugurated. In 2012 came the first new crop; meanwhile, grapes from elsewhere in Jonkershoek have been brought in.

Reserve 📷 ★★★★ **11** blend of cab, cab franc & shiraz shows aromas of red fruit, blackcurrant & chocolate. Fresher & better defined than **10** (★★★★), with a dry, firm, concentrated palate - fine-grained tannins needing time. **Sauvignon Blanc** 🕐 🍴 📷 ★★★★ Previewed **12** with expressive tropical & grassy aromas. Mineral palate with vibrant acidity. **11** untasted, **09** (★★★★) was more complex. — JPf

Kleinhoekkloof

Location: Ashton ▪ Map: Robertson ▪ Est 2004 ▪ 1stB 2006 ▪ Phone ahead for opening hours ▪ Owner(s) Raudan Trust ▪ Cellarmaster(s)/winemaker(s) Theunis de Jongh (2011) ▪ Viticulturist(s) Loure van Zyl (Mar 2004, consultant) ▪ 114ha/11.8ha (merlot, p verdot, pinot, shiraz, sauv, viog) ▪ 110t/2,400cs own label 45% red 40% white 15% rosé ▪ Other export brand: Mountain Eye ▪ PO Box 95134 Waterkloof 0145 ▪ theunis@khk.co.za ▪ www. kleinhoekkloof.co.za ▪ S 33° 46' 51.87'' E 020° 03' 17.30'' ▪ **T +27 (0)23-615-2121** ▪ F +27 (0)86-677-5399

The De Jongh family farm high in the Wildepaardekloof near Ashton is so remote, you have to traverse two others to reach it. Water comes straight from a source even higher up in the mountains, and the location has a built-in 'vine cooler': the late-afternoon wind which blows without fail. These favourable conditions facilitate an organic approach to winegrowing.

■ **Klein Kasteelberg** *see* Group CDV
■ **Kleinood** *see* Tamboerskloof Wine – Kleinood Farm

Klein Optenhorst

Location/WO: Wellington ▪ Map: Paarl & Wellington ▪ Est/1stB 2001 ▪ Tasting & sales by appt ▪ Owner(s) Naas Ferreira ▪ Cellarmaster(s)/winemaker(s) Pieter Ferreira (2009, consultant) ▪ Viticulturist(s) Naas Ferreira (2001) ▪ 0.25ha (pinot) ▪ ±2t/164cs own label 100% rosé ▪ PO Box 681 Wellington 7654 ▪ kleinoptenhorstwines@gmail.com ▪ www.kleinoptenhorst.com ▪ S 33° 37' 48.60'' E 019° 3' 19.54'' ▪ **T +27 (0)21-864-1210**

Sparkling supremo and consultant winemaker Pieter Ferreira, who at Graham Beck oversees many thousands of cases a year, and owner-viticulturist Naas Ferreira coaxed just 634 bottles - fewer than last time! - of champagne-method bubbly from the 2011 crop off Naas' tiny parcel of mature pinot noir in Wellington.

★★★★ **Pinot Noir Méthode Cap Classique** Delicate, perfumed bubbles rise to next level in **11**. Spring flowers & Turkish Delight are giddy, fun, but there's also seriousness here, for making lasting memories. — HJ

Klein Parys Vineyards

Location: Paarl ▪ Map: Paarl & Wellington ▪ WO: Paarl/Western Cape ▪ Est 1692 ▪ 1stB 2002 ▪ Tasting, sales & cellar tours Mon-Fri 10-5 Sat 10-3 ▪ Fee R20/4 wines ▪ Closed Good Fri, Dec 25 & Jan 1 ▪ Facilities for children ▪ Conferences ▪ Weddings/functions ▪ Owner(s) Kosie Möller ▪ Cellarmaster(s)/winemaker(s) Kosie Möller (2002) ▪ 56ha/45ha (cab, shiraz, chard, chenin) ▪ 1,800t/500,000cs own label 48% red 48% white 4% sparkling + 1m cs for clients ▪ Brands for clients: Millers Mile ▪ PO Box 1362 Suider-Paarl 7624 ▪ logistics@kparys.

co.za ▪ www.kleinparysvineyards.co.za ▪ S 33° 45' 0.2" E 018° 58' 48.6" ▪ T +27 (0)21-872-9848 ▪ F +27 (0)21-872-8527

Situated on one of Paarl's oldest farms, winemaker/entrepreneur Kosie Möller's already sizeable business is expanding, with the international client base widened, the tasting room area enlarged to accommodate bigger tour groups and functions, and plans in place to enter the local market 'systematically'.

Family Selection

★★★★ **Jacob Selection** ⓐ Attractive **09** combo mainly pinotage, shiraz, cab franc & petit verdot. **Beatrix Selection** ⓐ ★★★ Last tasted was very ripe shiraz-dominated **07**. **Niclas Selection** Next awaited. **Charl Sias Selection** NEW ★★★★ Unusual bottle-fermented sparkling from chardonnay, nouvelle, viognier & sauvignon. Full-bodied & ripe **10** is technically bone-dry but leaves sweet impression from 14.5% alcohol.

Kleine Parys Selection

Cabernet Sauvignon 🍷 ★★★ Aromatic **12** in appealingly accessible & popular style, ripe fruit & chocolate supported by savoury tannins. **Merlot** Next awaited, as for **Pinotage Coffee Style**, **Méthode Cap Classique** & **Red Muscadel**. **Pinotage** 🍷 ★★★ Spicy vanilla oak plays supporting role to earthy, dark cherry fruit in ripely juicy yet elegant **12**. **Shiraz** 🍷 ★★★ Smoky, spicy **12**'s savoury red fruit carried by firm acidity. **Chardonnay** 🍷 ★★★ Butterscotch-toned (though unoaked) **13** has dollop aromatic viognier & racy acidity. **Chenin Blanc** ⓐ 🍷 ★★★ Lees-ageing broadens dry but fruity/tropical **12** sipper with modest alcohol. **Sauvignon Blanc** 🍷 ★★★ Crisply quaffable tropical **13** dry & nicely light for summer. WO W Cape. Discontinued: **Cuvée Brut**.

Tooverberg range

Contour Merlot ⓐ 🍷 ★★★ Smooth, easy **11** red with sufficient savoury grip from 15% cab. WO W Cape, as rest of range. **Pinotage** ⓐ 🍷 ★★★ Popular chocolate-mocha styled **12** more subtle than most. **Cabernet Sauvignon-Shiraz** ⓐ 🍷 🥂 ★★★ Fruity grip in decent, lightly oaked **12** blend. **Chenin Blanc** ⓐ 🍷 ★★★ Tropical, sweetly fruity **12** has plenty of character & lovely balance. **Chenin Blanc-Chardonnay** ⓐ 🍷 ★★ **12** very simple easy-drinking quaffer. — IM

Klein Roosboom 🍷🍽🎋📷♿

Location/WO: Durbanville ▪ Map: Durbanville, Philadelphia & Darling ▪ Est 1984 ▪ 1stB 2007 ▪ Tasting, sales & cellar tours Tue-Fri 10-5 Sat/Sun 10-3 ▪ Fee R15, waived on purchase ▪ Closed Good Fri, Dec 25/26 & Jan 1 ▪ Cheese platters Sat/Sun; soup & bread in winter ▪ Café Ruby ▪ Facilities for children ▪ Tour groups ▪ Rubies & Roses: gifts, interior, deli & more ▪ BYO picnic ▪ Owner(s) Jean de Villiers Trust ▪ Cellarmaster(s)/winemaker(s) Karin de Villiers (2007) ▪ Viticulturist(s) Jean de Villiers (1984) ▪ 260ha/130ha (cab, merlot, shiraz, chard, sauv) ▪ 3,000cs own label 40% red 60% white ▪ Postnet Suite #3 Private Bag X19 Durbanville 7551 ▪ cellar@kleinroosboom.co.za ▪ www.kleinroosboom.co.za ▪ S 33° 49' 6.24" E 018° 34' 25.86" ▪ T +27 (0)82-784-5102 ▪ F +27 (0)21-975-7417

This Durbanville boutique winery is all about family: parents Jean and Karin de Villiers handle viticulture and winemaking, daughter Marné runs the craft shop and Café Ruby restaurant, grandma Janét gives her name to the new shiraz, and Isak Wessels, raised on the farm, runs the tasting venue, featuring a recent conversion that allows visitors to wine-taste inside an old cement fermenter.

Cabernet Sauvignon ★★★ **11** has dark fruit & firm dry tannins, all tightly buttoned. **Merlot** ★★★ **10** dark fruit & mint cloaked in oak char & brisk acidity mid-2013. Needs time. **Janét** NEW ★★★ From shiraz, **12** richer & more balanced than brusque **11**. Ample mint/eucalyptus flavours & integrated oak. Medium bodied & succulent, with brisk finish. **My Way** NEW ★★★★ **11** bright & sappy cab/merlot duo, still tightly coiled, with clean mint & dark berried tone. Food styled, good for few years. **Sauvignon Blanc** 🍷 ★★ **13** ripe & tropical style, with pithy core & warm farewell. **Marné Brut Méthode Cap Classique** Await next, as for **Bandana Blanc**. — MW

Klipdrift   **[NEW]**

This brandy and South African cultural icon originated in 1938 as the home brew of winegrower and distiller Kosie Marais on his Robertson farm Klipdrift. Man and brand are entertainingly presented at the town's trendy Klipdrift House and showcase boutique distillery, owned by Distell. Long popular with cola as a mixer ('Klippies and Coke'), the original, best-selling Export has been joined by a premium version and the much-awarded Gold.

★★★★☆ **Gold** Seduces with complex aromas of dried apricot, raisin, orange peel & sweet spice. Finely textured, well rounded, with greater complexity than others. Vanilla & cinnamon come into greater focus just before long, fruit-filled finish. 100% potstill brandies of between 3 & 20 years age.

Export ★★★★ The famous 'Klippies', a standard blended brandy (30% potstill), but one of the best of its type. Rich ripe aromas with dried apricot, prune & toasty nut. Smooth & full bodied & a satisfying finish. From chenin and colombard, as are all in this range. **Premium** ★★★★ Blend of 5-year-matured potstill with 70% unmatured spirit. Richer & fuller than Export, with greater maturity bringing sweet tobacco & spice from oak. Powerful, but not too harsh to sip neat. — WB,TJ

■ **Kloof Street** *see* Mullineux Family Wines

Kloovenburg Wine & Olives

Location: Riebeek-Kasteel ▪ Map/WO: Swartland ▪ Est 1704 ▪ 1stB 1998 ▪ Tasting & sales Mon-Fri 9-4.30 Sat 9-2 Sun at Kloovenburg Pastorie Guesthouse 10.30-2 ▪ Fee R10 wine/olive tasting ▪ Closed Easter Fri-Mon, Dec 25/26 & Jan 1 ▪ Cellar tours during tasting hours ▪ Tour groups ▪ Gift shop ▪ Farm produce/olive products ▪ BYO picnic ▪ Walks/hikes ▪ Conservation area ▪ Christmas Market (Dec) ▪ Owner(s) Pieter du Toit ▪ Cellarmaster(s)/winemaker(s) Pieter du Toit (Jan 1998) ▪ Viticulturist(s) Kobus van Graan (Jan 1998, consultant) ▪ 300ha/130ha (cab, merlot, shiraz, chard, sauv) ▪ 229t/24,000cs own label 55% red 40% white 4% rosé 1% sparkling ▪ PO Box 2 Riebeek-Kasteel 7307 ▪ info@kloovenburg.com ▪ www.kloovenburg.com ▪ S 33° 23' 36.3" E 018° 53' 27.5" ▪ **T +27 (0)22-448-1635** ▪ F +27 (0)22-448-1035

'Family' is core to owner Pieter du Toit's Riebeek-Kasteel wine and olive estate, named 'The Place in the Ravine'. First settled in 1704, wine hadn't been made on the property for four decades until Pieter, wife Annalene (who founded the olive business that quickly outgrew its farm kitchen origins) and their children footstomped 200 bottles of shiraz in 1997, going to market with the 1998 harvest.

★★★★ **Cabernet Sauvignon** ✓ 🍷 Best of these reds. Classic styling for **11**, lovely composition of bright blackcurrant fruit & supple, yielding tannins - a complex pleasure.

Merlot ✓ 🍷 ★★★★ **11** back on track in dry muscular form; floral violet tones to meaty mouthful, satisfying spicy lift. **Shiraz** 🍷 ★★★★ Very ripe **11** brims with mulberry fruit, but like **10** lacks intensity & complexity of earlier vintages. **Eight Feet** 🍷 ★★★★ Children's feet crushed the farm's first vintage. **11** now 100% shiraz, (**10** had cab as equal partner); hugely fruity, ripe blueberry pastilles linger. **Shiraz Rosé** 🏠 🍷 ★★☆ Savoury **13** has food-friendly grip in bone-dry tail. **Barrel Fermented Chardonnay** ✓ 🍷 ★★★★ Previewed **13**, after 5 months in French oak, shows spicy interest to citrus flavours. Oak-sweet finish needs time to meld. **Naturally Fermented Chardonnay** 🍷 ★★★★ **12** as big, bold as off-dry **11** (★★★★☆) but far better balance to weighty fruit, oak (9 months) & alcohol (14.5%); now dry. **Unwooded Chardonnay** 🏠 🍷 ★★★★ Piercing lemon/lime fruit of mediumweight preview **13** promises much once bottled. **Sauvignon Blanc** 🏠 🍷 ★★★ Plump **13** is tropical rather than grassy; still roundly dry & persistent. **White From Red Brut** ⓣ ★★☆ Coppery off-dry pink **NV** sparkling. Quiet fruit lifted by vivacious bubble. — DS

Knorhoek Wines

Location/map: Stellenbosch ▪ WO: Simonsberg-Stellenbosch ▪ Est 1827 ▪ 1stB 1997 ▪ Tasting, sales & cellar tours daily 10-5 ▪ Fee R20/5 wines ▪ Closed Dec 25 ▪ Towerbosch Restaurant Wed-Sun 11.30-3.30 (Sat/Sun booking essential T +27 (0)21-865-2958) ▪ Facilities for children ▪ Tour groups ▪ Gift shop ▪ Weddings/conferences ▪ Hiking trail ▪ Horse riding ▪ Conservation area ▪ 3-star guesthouse & self-catering cottages ▪ Owner(s) Hansie & James van Niekerk ▪ Cellarmaster(s)/winemaker(s) Arno Albertyn (April 2005) ▪ Viticulturist(s) James van Niekerk (1977) ▪ ±80ha (cabs s/f, merlot, ptage, shiraz, chenin, sauv) ▪ 640t/20,000cs own label 51% red 42% white 4.65% rosé 2.35% sparkling & 184,500L bulk ▪ BWI ▪ PO Box 2 Koelenhof 7605 ▪

office@knorhoek.co.za, cellar@knorhoek.co.za, towerbosch@knorhoek.co.za ▪ www.knorhoek.co.za ▪ S 33° 52' 44.8" E 018° 52' 19.1" ▪ **T +27 (0)21-865-2114** ▪ F +27 (0)21-865-2627

So successful has the wedding and function business become on this picturesque Simonsberg family farm, that functions are now run in-house with the aid of four chefs. That, and the other attractions and facilities have made Knorhoek a popular destination. The wines fit right in, with their spread of varieties and styles to suit the fine food, and a value range to sip around the tree-shaded lake.

Pantère Range

★★★★☆ **Cabernet Sauvignon** NEW ✓ 🍇 Still far off its peak, dark fruited **11**'s meaty cocoa flavours already give lots of pleasure but this wine has been built for the long haul. Carefully made, its firm backbone has been crafted with the aid of 24 months new oak.

★★★★ **Bordeaux Blend** 'Pantère' previously. **09** cab-led & serious, 24 months in French barrels, half new. Glossy fruit beautifully retained, tannins already integrated but this has been built to go the distance. No **08**.

★★★★ **Chenin Blanc** ✓ 🍇 Was 'Chenin Blanc Barrel Fermented' in Knorhoek range. Individual **12** (★★★★★) improves on **11** by successfully combining old-vine fruit, oak & sweetness. The result is an opulent beauty packed with peach & apricot flavours, full bodied yet delicious, thanks to a seam of livening acidity.

Knorhoek range

★★★★ **Cabernet Sauvignon** ⊕ 🍇 Meaty, spicy, rich dark fruit, there's heaps to like in **10** (★★★★☆), especially a superb balance. Tops **07**. Serious attention, 19 months all-new French oak, has paid off, drinks beautifully & could age 8+ years but doubt you'd wait. **08, 09** sold out untasted.

★★★★ **Cabernet Franc** ⊕ Plums & a typical herbal nuance, dash white pepper, **09** is a fine example of the variety. Textured tannins are amenable, perfectly judged. Enjoy now till ±2018. **07, 08** sold out untasted.

★★★★ **HVN Cape Ruby** ⊕ In tribute to the patriarch, Hannes van Niekerk. NV port from cab; mixed spice & fruitcake flavours, smooth, richly sweet. Enough acid grip to whet the appetite for a second glass. 375ml.

Konfetti Rosé Sparkling ☺ 🍇 ★★★ NV party fare with its lowish alcohol, sweet red berries.

Merlot NEW ✓ 🍇 ★★★★ Molten plums & dark chocolate, **11**'s deftly built structure (21 months oak) is for ageing, but leaves its appeal intact. **Pinotage** ⊕ ★★★ Dark tones in **09**, mulberries & smoked meat but palate is juicy, vibrant, all light & laughter. Good oak foundation. **Shiraz** ✓ 🍇 ★★★★ Dark fruit interwoven with prosciutto & sweet spice, yet delicious **11** has enough tannin backing for further cellaring. **Chenin Blanc** ⊕ 🍶 🍇 ★★★★ Pre-bottled **12** retains house-style elegance. Ripe melon & passionfruit, lovely underlying minerality on palate, long finish. **Sauvignon Blanc** ⊕ 🍶 🍇 ★★★ Tasted as sample, nice leafy/lemongrass freshness & purity in **12**, perky acidity extends the flavours. Good food partner.

Two Cubs range

Cabernet Franc-Merlot-Cabernet Sauvignon ☺ 🍶 🍇 ★★★ Was 'Red Blend'. Cab franc's dominance gives **11** its herbaceous nuances, brambleberry plushness. Juicy & silky smooth. **Rosé** ☺ 🍶 🍇 ★★★ Light-textured, dry **13**'s bright pinotage berries provide charm, flavour. **Chenin Blanc** NEW ☺ 🍶 🍇 ★★★ Melon, hint of honey, **12** is smoothly rounded, flavourful. **Sauvignon Blanc** NEW ☺ 🍶 🍇 ★★★ Sleek, bone-dry **12** has mellow grassy tones.

Pinotage NEW 🍶 🍇 ★★★ Smoky dark fruit backed by a firm oak foundation, **11** has ageing potential, needs a year to settle. **White Blend** ⊕ 🍶 🍇 ★★★ Ex-tank, light-textured **12** is spot on as a quaffer: crunchy summer fruits, tangy acidity, flavourful length. Sauvignon with chenin. — CR

■ **Kobus** see Havana Hills
■ **Koelenbosch** see Koelenhof Winery

Koelenhof Winery   🍷🍴📷🎣♿

Location/map/WO: Stellenbosch ▪ Est 1941 ▪ 1stB 1970's ▪ Tasting & sales Mon-Thu 9-5 Fri 9-4 Sat 10-2 ▪ Closed Easter Fri/Sun, Ascension day, Dec 25/26 & Jan 1 ▪ Cellar tours by appt ▪ Facilities for children ▪ Gift shop ▪ Farm produce ▪ BYO picnic ▪ Conference/function venue ▪ Owner(s) 67 shareholders ▪ GM Andrew de Vries (2006) ▪ Winemaker(s) Martin Stevens (Nov 2003) & Wilhelm de Vries (2002), with Erika van Zyl (Jun 2011) ▪ Viticulturist(s) Wilhelm de Vries (2010) ▪ 16,500t/22,000cs own label 45% red 45% white 8% rosé 2% fortified + 2,000cs for clients & 100,000 litres bulk ▪ Other export brand: Simonsbosch ▪ IPW ▪ PO Box 1 Koelenhof

7605 ▪ koelwyn@mweb.co.za ▪ www.koelenhof.co.za ▪ S 33° 50' 5.2" E 018° 47' 52.7" ▪ **T +27 (0)21-865-2020/1** ▪ F +27 (0)21-865-2796

This Stellenbosch cellar's farmer-owners broke a record last year, delivering 16,500 tons to the presses. All to the good, says winemaker Martin Stevens, since the Chinese market is growing, necessitating more trips each year to visit their agent (and more hours labouring over his Mandarin lessons).

Koelenbosch range

Merlot ✓ 🖾 ★★★ Two vintages tasted: **11** lighter toned, purer & more elegant, with raspberry, redcurrant & sweet oak. **10** (★★★) slightly overripe & extracted, blackcurrant & chocolate, lots more tannin & alcohol. **Pinotage** 🖾 ★★★ Like previous, **11** a robust barbecue mate with fresh, bright raspberry fruit & big strong tannins. **Sangiovese** 🖾 ★★ More tannic version of the Italian variety in **12**, more pizza/pasta partner than solo wine. Appealing jammy fruit & vanilla. **Shiraz** 🖾 ★★☆ Pair of vintages tasted, both big & powerful (14.5+ alcohol) with chewy, fresh, food-seeking tannins. **11** minty plums & oak char; slightly better **10** (★★★) more intensity & definition, brooding black fruit. **Nineteenfortyone** 🖾 ★★★ Honours cellar's founding date, equal cab, shiraz, merlot in **11**. Lovely berry compote aromas with oak spicing, good structure, finish needs bit more finesse for higher rating. **Pinotage Rosé** ⏱ 🗄 🖾 ★ Light-textured & dry **11**. **Chenin Blanc Wooded** 🗄 🖾 ★★★ Has more to say in **12**. Evident sweet oak but enough fruit to balance, misses previous vintage's easy, gentle texture though. **Sauvignon Blanc** 🗄 🖾 ★★ Lightish **13** unconcentrated but fresh, floral, comfortably dry. **Méthode Cap Classique** NEW ★★☆ Food-styled bubbly from chardonnay. 2 years on lees yield powerful & very dry **08**, with toasted croissant overtones & sour pink apple flavour.

Koelenhof range

Koelenberg 🖾 ★★ Ripe, slightly sweet merlot & pinotage blend, **11** black fruit on palate with hint of clove. **Pinotage Rosé** ⏱ 🖾 ★★ **12** candyfloss-light & semi-sweet. Frivolous summer fun. **Koelenhoffer** 🗄 🖾 ★★ As previous from sauvignon, but **13** is more aromatic, grass & guava pungency, pithy interest on off-dry finish. **Koelnektar** 🖾 ★★ Delicate semi-sweet **12** from gewürztraminer, splash muscat d'Alexandrie, with fleeting litchi, rose & honey flavours. **Pinotage Rosé Vin-sec** 🖾 ★★ **12** light, berry-fragrant pink bubbly, off-dry & racy-fresh. **Sauvignon Blanc Vin-sec** ⏱ 🗄 🖾 ★★☆ Sweet but lively fizz, light & tropical-toned **11** a spring celebration. **Hanepoot** ★★★ Fortified dessert returns to the guide with fragrant & floral **12**, generous & sweet but attractively firm wild honey flavour. **Pinorto** 🖾 ★★★ Was 'Pino Porto', remains a port-style fortified from pinotage. **11** quite decadent, with marked choc-cherry sweetness. — DC

Koelfontein

Location/WO: Ceres ▪ Map: Tulbagh ▪ Est 1832 ▪ 1stB 2002 ▪ Tasting & sales Mon-Fri 9-4 Sat 10-1 ▪ Closed all pub hols ▪ Farm produce ▪ BYO picnic ▪ Walks/hikes ▪ Conservation area ▪ Die Kloof self-catering historic house (sleeps 6) ▪ Die Snystoor function venue ▪ Owner(s) Handri Conradie ▪ Winemaker(s) Dewaldt Heyns (2004) ▪ Viticulturist(s) Hennie van Noordwyk ▪ 950ha/±6ha (shiraz, chard) ▪ ±24t/2,400cs own label 50% red 50% white ▪ BWI ▪ PO Box 4 Prince Alfred's Hamlet 6840 ▪ wine@koelfontein.co.za ▪ www.koelfontein.co.za ▪ S 33° 15' 54.70" E 019° 19' 29.28" ▪ **T +27 (0)23-313-3304/3538** ▪ F +27 (0)23-313-3137

Seven generations of Conradies have lived on this fruit and wine farm along the high-lying Gydo Pass near Ceres. Vineyards account for a tiny portion of the irrigated farmland. Grapes for brandy distillation gave way to noble varieties in the 1990s. Today, vinification is by Dewaldt Heyns at Saronsberg in Tulbagh.

★★★★ **Chardonnay** ✓ With intense lime & passionfruit, **11** (★★★★★) parades its cool-climate conditions, while the hazelnut spicing from new barrel fermentation/maturation adds to the whole delicious experience. More tightly focused & polished than **10**.

Shiraz ⏱ ★★★★ Complex bouquet smoked meat, roasted nuts & hint truffle, **09** rich but unheavy, with integrated tannins. More elegant expression than dense yet well-judged **08** (★★★★). — CR

▪ **Koffieklip** *see* Koopmanskloof Wingerde
▪ **Kogmans Kloof** *see* Zandvliet Wine Estate & Thoroughbred Stud

Koopmanskloof Wingerde

Location/WO: Stellenbosch ▪ Est 1801 ▪ 1stB 1970 ▪ Private Nature Reserve with self-catering Berghuis, accommodate 30 people with overnight facilities for 16 ▪ Owner(s) Managed by Koopmanskloof Wingerde

(Pty) Ltd ▪ Winemaker(s) Stephan Smit ▪ Viticulturist(s) Louwtjie Vlok ▪ 480ha (cab, carignan, merlot, ptage, roobernet, ruby cab, shiraz, chard, chenin, sauv, sem) ▪ ±3,700t/±2.5m L 50% red 50% white ▪ Other brands: Vredehoek, One World ▪ BWI, Fairtrade, IPW, WIETA ▪ PO Box 19 Koelenhof 7605 ▪ info@koopmanskloof.co.za ▪ www.koopmanskloof.co.za ▪ **T** +27 (0)21-865-2355 ▪ **F** +27 (0)86-560-7145

With the produce of six farms – one owned, managed and run by employees – in Stellenbosch's Bottelary, winemaker Stephan Smit has a lot to work with. All efforts are empathetically and ethically nature driven, and the wines certified Fairtrade. A 100-ha nature reserve is modern-era founder Stevie Smit's legacy.

Koopmanskloof range

Cabernet Sauvignon 🍴 🈁 ★★★ Gentle Christmas cake spice & ripe appeal to light-bodied, easy-drinking & succulent **12**. Cab for beginners. **Motherblocks Carignan** ⊕ 🍴 🈁 ★★★ Dry but ripe **11**, sweet maraschino cherry & clove taste, lightish & fresh body. **Pinotage** ⊕ 🍴 🈁 ★★ Youthful **10** offers oaky sweet-fruited freshness. **Shiraz** 🈁 ★★★ **12** improves in its smoky plum generosity. Nice integrated oak that lends a firm edge to ripeness. **Cabernet Sauvignon-Shiraz** 🍴 🈁 ★★★ Depth of flavour sees **12** step up. Tasty black cherry & clove appeal. Earthy aftertaste. **Pinotage Rosé** 🍴 🈁 ★★ Strawberry & candyfloss charm on dry yet juicy **13**. **Shiraz Rosé** ⊕ 🍴 🈁 ★★★ Cherry Fizz Pop vibrancy to flavourful **12**, with food-friendly weighty dry finish. **Chardonnay** 🍴 🈁 ★★★ Undemanding **13**, light & zesty citrus with lively palate. **Chenin Blanc** 🍴 🈁 ★★ **13** simple charmer with crisp tropical tang that finishes dry. **Bushvine Chenin Blanc** 🍴 🈁 ★★★ Bold pineapple & peach on structured **12**. Good balance of fruit & acid. Medium bodied with a light tail. **Sauvignon Blanc** 🍴 🈁 ★★★ Fig & flint effortlessness to **13**, tangy & light easy-drinker. **Sauvignon Blanc-Semillon** ⊕ 🍴 🈁 ★★★ **11** 70/30 blend, grapefruit crispness & honeyed undertone, pleasant structure & length.

Koffieklip range

Pinotage ⊕ 🍴 🈁 ★★★ Smoky mocha appeal to **10**, quite chunky in texture, for hearty country fare.

Vredelust range NEW

Merlot ★★★ **12** shows fynbos overlay to cocoa & black fruit. Gentle body, length & concentration. Merlot for non-red wine drinkers. — FM

Kranskop Wines 🍷🎋

Location/map: Robertson ▪ WO: Klaasvoogds ▪ Est 2001 ▪ 1stB 2003 ▪ Tasting, sales & tours Mon-Fri 10-4.30 Sat & pub hols 10-2 ▪ Closed Easter Sun & Dec 25 ▪ BYO picnic ▪ Owner(s)/viticulturist(s) Newald Marais ▪ Cellarmaster(s)/winemaker(s) Newald Marais (2008) ▪ 43ha/30ha (cab, merlot, pinot, shiraz, tannat, chard, sauv, viog) ▪ 240t/3,000cs own label 75% red 25% white ▪ BWI, IPW ▪ PO Box 49 Klaasvoogds 6707 ▪ newald@kranskopwines.co.za ▪ www.kranskopwines.co.za ▪ S 33° 47' 53.1" E 019° 59' 56.6" ▪ **T** +27 (0)23-626-3200 ▪ F +27 (0)23-626-3200

Softly spoken Newald Marais is where he's wanted to be since 14 (and after 30 years as corporate cellarmaster): with hands in the soil 'where it all begins', personally sharing his passion with people wanting a wine experience, not a brand. Longtime employee James Meyer's equal enthusiasm prompted the following visitor's book entry: What a fantastic example of a 'rainbow nation'!

★★★★ **Viognier** ✓ 🈁 Lightly wooded **12** shows a deft touch in the way the oak melds with the dried fruit richness & gives a savoury tone, extending the elegant finish. Can be enjoyed before, during &/or after dinner.

Cabernet Sauvignon ☺ 🈁 ★★★ Modern **10** juicy & generous, year oak (45% new) adds layers of spice & polished grip for food compatibility.

Merlot 🈁 ★★★ Smoky bacon & tobacco nuances on savoury **10**, tangy cherry fruit & lively acidity. **Pinot Noir** NEW 🈁 ★★ **11** charms with floral & forest floor notes, concludes fairly firmly. **Shiraz** 🈁 ★★★ Piquant **10** folds black pepper spicing, dark berry fruit & coconut oak into an attractive package. **Chardonnay** ✓ 🈁 ★★★★ Partly barrel-fermented **12** continues bold-but-balanced styling, the obvious buttery oak in step with the lemon pie flavours & creamy feel. **Sauvignon Blanc** 🈁 ★★★ Diverging from previous release, **12** seems more serious, food styled. Smoke & flint appeal, weight & depth from lees-ageing. **Viognier Noble Late Harvest** NEW 🈁 ★★★★ Light (10% alcohol) & characterful after-dinner treat; **11** older oak fermented; peach, dried pear & honey persisting through to the lovely sticky end. — DB,JP

■ **Krone** see Twee Jonge Gezellen Estate-The House of Krone

Kronendal Boutique Winery

Location/WO: Durbanville ▪ Map: Durbanville, Philadelphia & Darling ▪ Est 2003 ▪ 1stB 2006 ▪ Tasting & sales Mon-Fri by appt Sat 11-3 ▪ Fee R30/6 wines ▪ Closed Easter Fri/Sun, Ascension Day, Dec 25/26 & Jan 1 ▪ Cellar tours by appt ▪ Cheese platters ▪ Conference facilities ▪ Art ▪ Seasonal 'langtafel' lunches ▪ Owner(s) Pieter & Magdaleen Kroon ▪ Winemaker(s) Magdaleen Kroon ▪ 2ha/0.6ha (mourv, shiraz, tempranillo, viog) ▪ 4t/520cs own label 100% red ▪ PO Box 4433 Durbanville 7551 ▪ info@kronendalwine.co.za ▪ http://kronendal.belmet.co.za ▪ S 33° 48' 30.78" E 018° 36' 50.82" ▪ **T +27 (0)82-499-0198** ▪ F +27 (0)86-603-1170

Less than one hectare of Pieter and Magdaleen Kroon's property is devoted to vines: 'Boutique size means I can do everything from pruning to winemaking on my own, though I also need all the equipment required for a larger concern,' Magdaleen says. Rhône varieties are not the commonest grapes in Durbanville, but suit her preference for red wines from that cooler climate.

★★★★☆ **Mirari ✓ 10** (★★★★) not quite up to **09**, but still attractive syrah-based blend with mourvèdre & viognier dash. Fresh, light texture, fine tannins with wild scrub & cherry features. Balance belies 15%+ alcohol. Discontinued: **Impromptu**. — AL

Kumala

Location: Somerset West ▪ Map: Helderberg ▪ WO: Western Cape/Worcester ▪ Tasting, sales & cellar tours at Flagstone Winery (see entry) ▪ Owner(s) Accolade Wines South Africa ▪ Winemaker(s) Ben Jordaan (Jul 2002), Bruce Jack (Feb 2008) & Karen Bruwer (Oct 2008) ▪ 50% red 50% white ▪ PO Box 769 Stellenbosch 7599 ▪ flagstone@accolade-wines.com ▪ www.kumala.co.za ▪ S 34° 5' 26.38" E 018° 48' 30.04" ▪ **T +27 (0)21-852-5052** ▪ F +27 (0)21-852-5085

The big-selling Kumala brand is owned by multinational Accolade Wines, and produced from various Western Cape sources. Several of the previously export-only labels have been launched on local markets. Public tasting and sales are offered at sibling label Flagstone Winery's cellardoor at Somerset West.

Zenith range

Merlot-Cabernet Sauvignon-Shiraz ☺ 🍴 🚫 ★★★ **12** 4-way blend (splash of ruby-cab) shows blackcurrant, rhubarb & oak vanilla on spare frame. Pleasant quaffing. **Chenin Blanc-Chardonnay** ☺ 🍴 🚫 ★★★ **13** 70-30 blend is fresh & fruity, light & unfussy.

Rosé 🍴 🚫 ★★★ Off-dry **13** from pinotage reflects variety's wild berry jam character.

Reserve range

Shiraz ⊕ 🍴 🚫 ★★★ Export-only **11** from Swartland grapes, pleasing cherry fruit on spicy oak. **Chenin Blanc** ⊕ 🍴 🚫 ★★★ Lean, mildly fruity, light-bodied **11** has pinch of oak dust.

Core range

Cabernet Sauvignon-Shiraz ☺ 🍴 🚫 ★★★ Juicy, ripe red fruit on **12**, spiced with oak. Youthful appeal suggests early drinking. **Sauvignon Blanc-Semillon** ☺ 🍴 ★★★ Dry, lean & light **12** offers wild nettle aromas, softer acidity.

Shiraz 🍴 🚫 ★★ **12** light & unfussy, with hint of sweetish fruit. **Merlot-Pinotage** 🍴 🚫 ★★★ Export-only, berry-rich **12** has sweet vanilla tones on sunny, juicy fruit core. Smooth, simple drinking pleasure. **Pinotage-Shiraz** 🍴 🚫 ★★★ Export-only blend, **12** is sweetly fruity with vanilla lift. **Shiraz-Mourvèdre** ⊕ 🍴 🚫 ★★★ **11** shows distinctive peppery spice with smoky oak notes on light, juicy structure. Uncomplicated, easy drinking. **Merlot-Ruby Cabernet** 🍴 🚫 ★★★ Fruity, easygoing sipper, **12** has appealingly honest fruit core. **Dry Red** 🍴 🚫 ★★ Ruby cab & cinsaut in **NV** lightweight. **Rosé** 🍴 🚫 ★★★ Off-dry **12** export label. Berry juice with rosepetal scent. **Chardonnay** 🍴 🚫 ★★★ Vanilla oak spices up modest but pleasant **12**. **Chardonnay-Semillon** 🍴 🚫 ★★ **12** has touch of oak flavour & lemon-butter. Export only. **Colombard-Chardonnay** ⊕ 🍴 🚫 ★★★ Appealing mineral leanness of **11** lifted by lemon acidity. Worcester WO. **Chenin Blanc-Chardonnay** 🍴 🚫 ★★★ Lean **13** has waxy lanolin notes. Fresh & dry, easy to drink. **Sauvignon Blanc-Colombard** 🍴 🚫 ★★ Waxy, nutty notes on easy-drinking **12**. Light & dry. **Chenin Blanc-Viognier** 🍴 🚫 ★★★ **12** export-only, possibly best of bewildering array of blends. Ripe pineapple & yellow peach notes, generous body. **Dry White** 🍴 🚫 ★★ NV chenin-colombard,

near-dry, brightly fruity & crisp. **Medium Sweet White** 🖺 ★★ Unappealing colombard-based **NV**. **Medium Sweet Red** 🖺 ★★ Ruby cab & cinsaut **NV**'s sweet berry juiciness may have entry-level appeal.

Eternal range

Merlot-Cabernet Sauvignon-Shiraz ⓘ 🖺 ★★★ Sampled from tank, nuanced blend with dab viognier. **11** rich blackberry & cinnamon, fleshy yet supple & gentle. **Chenin Blanc-Chardonnay-Semillon** 🖺 🖺 ★★★ Export-only, crisply dry **13** has easygoing appeal. — GdB

🔳 **Kumkani** see Thandi Wines

Kupferberger Auslese

Liquid history, this 1952 Distell stalwart was among the first to benefit from cold and controlled fermentation of white wines.

Kupferberger Auslese 🖺 ★ Latest **NV** plain & simple, sweetness less balanced than previous. — DB, HJ

🔳 **K&V Harmony** see Kaapzicht Wine Estate

KWV

Location: Paarl ▪ Map: Paarl & Wellington ▪ KWV Wine Emporium: Kohler Street, T +27 (0)21-807-3007/8 F +27 (0)21-807-3119, friederm@kwv.co.za, www.kwvwineemporium.co.za ▪ Tasting & sales Mon-Sat 9-4. 30 Sun 11-4 ▪ Several food & wine pairings available ▪ Cellar tours: Eng Mon-Sat 10, 10.30 & 2.15; Ger 10.15; Sun Eng 11 ▪ Tour groups by appt ▪ Closed Good Fri, Dec 25 & Jan 1 ▪ KWV Sensorium: 57 Main Road, T +27 (0)21-807-3094, sensorium@kwv.co.za, www.kwvsensorium.co.za ▪ Tasting, sales & art museum Mon-Fri 9-4.30 Sat 9-2 ▪ Art & wine pairing ▪ Owner(s) KWV (Pty) Ltd ▪ Chief winemaker Johann Fourie ▪ Winemaker(s) Anneke du Plessis, Izelle van Blerk, Louwritz Louw & Kobus van der Merwe ▪ Viticulturist(s) Marco Ventrella & De Wet Hugo ▪ PO Box 528 Suider-Paarl 7624 ▪ customer@kwv.co.za ▪ www.kwv.co.za ▪ S 33°45' 46.87" E 018°57' 59.92" (Emporium), S 33°45' 43.26" E 018°57' 44.06" (Sensorium) ▪ **T +27 (0)21-807-3911 (office)** ▪ F +27 (0)21-807-3000

Founded in 1918 as the Ko-operatiewe Wijnbouwers Vereniging van Zuid-Afrika with statutory control over the Cape wine industry, KWV has evolved into a public, independently owned commercial wine and spirits giant. Its long-standing international reputation for fine wines, fortifieds and brandies is matched by modern wine tourism initiatives, particularly at stately La Concorde HQ in Paarl. The Sensorium, pairing a major SA artwork collection with fine-wine tastings, is a venue for collaborations with SA creatives (foodies, designers, musicians). The Emporium wine shop has moved here from the sprawling cellar complex nearby. KWV's products are listed separately under KWV Wines (including Cathedral Cellar), individual wine brands (Bonne Esperance, Café Culture, Laborie, Pearly Bay and Roodeberg), KWV Sherry-Styles, KWV Brandies and Imoya.

KWV Brandies   [NEW]

Their international reputation is as burnished as the massive copper pot and six-column stills that, together with several thousand barrels of maturing elixir, impress visitors to KWV's dedicated House of Brandy in Worcester. The 10, 15 and 20 Year Old have each shone as the International Wine & Spirit Competition's World's Best Brandy. As has the 15 Year Old at the 2013 International Spirits Challenge, says spirits manager Lourens Stander, filling former longstanding brandy master Kobus Gelderblom's sizable shoes.

★★★★ **5 Year Old Superior** Dark amber colour; notes of sweet caramel, fruit, nuts & vanilla. Excellent balance, clean & lightly fiery on sweet-tinged finish. Blended; could compete with pure potstills on turf!

★★★★☆ **10 Year Old Vintage** Enticing nose of apricot, raisin, red berry fruit & spice on vintage style. Full bodied & well rounded, with more complexity, power & oak than 5YO, but perhaps less charm. Long-lingering, fruity, slightly sweet finish.

★★★★★ **15 Year Old Alambic** Attractive honey, soft spice & dried fruit with floral backing & some fine oak. Smooth, fine texture & good balance; great complexity from a range of citrus & rich fruitcake flavours. Mellow & mature, with everlasting finish. 100% potstill, as next.

★★★★★ **20 Year Old** Exquisite aromas - sandalwood, apricot, scented flowers, hints spice & oxidative maturity. Rich & full, yet super-refined & delicate. A touch less forceful than 15YO, but more grace. Beautifully balanced, with supreme oak support. Long, mellow, mature notes carry to slightly sweet finish. Thrilling!

3 Year Old Finest Blend ★★★★ Less aggressive than many young blended brandies - sippable neat. Fruity apricot nose with caramel, roasted nuts, dark molasses, tealeaves. Sufficiently complex, balanced. — WB,TJ

KWV Sherry-Styles **NEW**

There's renewed focus on fortifieds at KWV, says chief winemaker Johann Fourie. Besides the Cape Tawny and Red Muscadel for which KWV has long been known (see under KWV Wines), these include the two sherries nurtured by team member Anneke du Plessis. Having traditionally bought in wine, chenin is now vinified especially for fortification and flor development in a dedicated cellar.

★★★★ **Cape Medium Cream** Golden brown, with candied apricot, orange peel & caramelised nuts. Balanced, fresh yet savoury, gentle spirity warmth. Chenin & colombard, year in barrel, 4-6 in solera, as next.

★★★★ **Cape Full Cream** Pale amber hue. Stewed fruit, a delightful floral note. Layered nuts & rich caramel, complex, elegant. Although sweet, uncloying finish is savoury & dry, lifted by a spirity glow. — WB,CR

KWV Wines

The major wine changes made at this large, historic (1918) winery have taken place under the guidance of Australian cellarmaster Richard Rowe, whose mantra is drinkability. This translates into making more elegant, balanced and fresher wines of quality, as well as closely evaluating range compositions. The Mentors range in particular, with its own dedicated production cellar, has reaped the benefit of vineyard selection where particular parcels have been chosen because of what they can bring to the wines. This strategy has resulted in an unprecedented number of awards in the past three years. Handing the reins over to chief winemaker Johann Fourie while he takes on a consultancy role, Richard is leaving the business in the experienced hands of a well-knit team.

The Mentors range

★★★★ **Petit Verdot** 🍴 🖵 Glossy dark berries & violets, dried herbs, **11**'s succulent palate has an attractive fruit freshness, supple tannins. No **10**.

★★★★ **Pinotage** 🍴 🖵 From dryland bushvines, which accounts for **11**'s upfront raspberry/strawberry fruit, well matched by vanilla-coated tannins. Has a fleshy roundness that's very easy to like.

★★★★ **Shiraz** 🍴 🖵 Ripe & expressive, with 70% new French/American barrels, **11**'s fleshy vanilla-spiced berries easily absorb the tannins. Whiff of scrub, a cocoa note add complexity, surpass **10** (★★★★).

★★★★☆ **Orchestra** 🍴 🖵 Aptly named because of the harmony of all the players, **11** is a classic cab-led Bordeaux blend, modern, succulent, with pure fruit expression, supple tannins. Misleadingly accessible, there's enough deep muscle tone for a distinguished future.

★★★★ **Canvas** 🍴 🖵 Shiraz-led in **11**, components chosen for their contribution to the 'canvas'. Dark toned & ripe, there's fruitcake & smoky spice, cocoa. Juicy, & just enough tannin to give definition.

★★★★ **Chardonnay** 🍴 🖵 Barrel ferment/maturation 9 months, 80% wild yeast, **12** offers yellow peach & citrus, buttered toast. Laced with livening acidity, adds length & longevity, a tangy end note. WO Elgin.

★★★★ **Chenin Blanc** 🍴 🖵 Attention paid in its creation, different yeasts & oaking, including a tank fermented portion, shows in the **12** (★★★★☆) melon/quince preserve & aromatic almond richness. A lemon seam freshens the flavours, promising a future. Last was pungent **08**.

★★★★ **Sauvignon Blanc Darling** **NEW** 🍴 🖵 Nice counterpoint to the Stellenbosch version, **12** bursts with flavour, gooseberries & lime, intense & pure, with a zesty freshness that lasts & lasts.

★★★★ **Sauvignon Blanc Stellenbosch** **NEW** 🍴 🖵 From a high-lying vineyard, **12**'s grapefruit styling is matched by an elegant structure, the balancing acidity giving it cool-climate poise, streamlined & delicious.

★★★★ **Semillon** 🍴 🖵 Partial barrel fermentation gives gentle palate creaminess to **12**, a nutty overlay, but the essence is a leafy, lime-zest freshness, focused & fine boned. WO Lutzville.

★★★★★ **Noble Late Harvest** **NEW** 🍴 🖵 From Walker Bay sauvignon blanc, **12** offers mango & pear, orange blossom, full-sweet but you'd never say so, the acidity keeping it tangy fresh, tightly focused. A triumph of intensity & concentration, with its own individual style.

Cabernet Franc Await next, as for **Grenache Blanc**, **Viognier** & **Sauvignon Blanc-Semillon**. Discontinued: **Sauvignon Blanc**.

Cathedral Cellar range

★★★★ **Cabernet Sauvignon** Piquant blackberry juiciness, oak's cinnamon & nutmeg notes adding layered appeal. So accessible **11**'s underlying structure misleads, but it's all there, back on track after **10** (★★★★).

★★★★ **Triptych** 🏵 Cab & petit verdot/shiraz, **11** is fruit rich, the blackberry focus given deft tannin support. Cedar & white pepper, a hint of tapenade, there's lots going on, but also a good future ahead.

★★★★ **Chardonnay** 🏵 Admirable restraint but no lack of character, **12** would convert any anti-oak drinker. Here it's subtle, a gentle lemon cream biscuit effect, leaving zesty citrus freshness on the palate.

★★★★★ **Chenin Blanc** ✓ 🏵 Reflecting utmost care (3 tranches for final blend), **12** (★★★★★) showcases perfectly balanced fruit & oak in its quince/crushed almonds, thatch/honeycomb array of flavours. Lemon acidity provides a delicious underpin. Not as complex as **11**.

★★★★ **Sauvignon Blanc** 🏵 A floral nuance on **13** add an extra dimension to the gooseberries & lime freshness, but at core is slatey minerality, taking over in the flavours & finish, pure & long. **12** sold out untasted.

★★★★ **Méthode Cap Classique Brut** ✓ Mainly chardonnay in **10**, giving the lemon zest freshness but pinot noir & 2 years lees-ageing show in the creamy biscuity palate. Very fine bubbles, youthful, can age.

Merlot Await next. **Pinotage** 🏵 ★★★★ Intense blueberries but **11** has a serious side, a firm tannin foundation balances the fruit vibrancy, promises a good future. **Shiraz** 🏵 ★★★★ Expressive red berries & sweet spice in **11**, succulent & smooth, drinking beautifully, with some ageing potential built in.

Reserve Collection

★★★★ **Sauvignon Blanc** ✓ 🏵 Grapefruit & minerality but **13** also has cool-climate berries, this is a layered, complex wine, holds your attention to the last lime-fresh drop. **12** sold out untasted.

Cabernet Sauvignon Await next. **Shiraz** Await next. **Chardonnay** 🏵 ★★★★ Nice combo peach & citrus, **12**'s flavours are enriched by enough nutty oak to provide a savoury match for food.

Concordia range

White ☺ 🏵 ★★★ Sauvignon/chenin in **13**, going for freshness. Peardrops & litchi, just off-dry, its acidity provides a tangy counterpoint.

Red 🏵 ★★ Soft & easy **12** blend has meat extract tones, juicy berry core.

Classic Collection

★★★★★ **Cape Tawny** ✓ Not just sweetly rich, 8-10 years in barrel has given **NV** much more complexity than the last bottling. Caramelised nuts, dried fruit, especially citrus, & a creamy mocha chocolate tone. Spirit provides a touch of warmth, fits perfectly.

Merlot ☺ 🏵 ★★★ Red berry array in attractive **12**, supported by supple tannins, smooth & round, a touch of sweetness fitting the style. **Chardonnay** ☺ 🏵 ★★★ Light oaking adds a biscuit seam to **13**'s just off-dry citrus flavours, nicely rounded, finishing fresh. **Sauvignon Blanc** ☺ 🏵 ★★★ Crunchy green apples & a hint of lime make **13** food friendly, the ideal summertime wine, crisply dry.

Cabernet Sauvignon 🏵 ★★★ Cassis & black pepper, **12** can age, already drinks well. **Pinotage** 🏵 ★★★ Blueberries & spice, **12** goes down easily, helped by a dab of sugar. **Shiraz** 🏵 ★★★ With juicy appeal, **12**'s smoky red fruit is pepper seasoned. **Shiraz Rosè** ⊕ 🏵 ★★★ **12** juicy mouthful spice, wild strawberries; tangily fresh, just off-dry. **Chenin Blanc** 🏵 ★★★ Litchi & melon-toned dry **13** has piquant freshness, light-textured appeal. **Sparkling Rosé** ★★ Fresh red berries in pretty **NV** sweetish sparkler. **Sparkling Cuvée Brut** 🏵 ★★ Lemon drops, hint of melon, off-dry gently fruity **NV** bubbly. **Sparkling Demi-Sec** 🏵 ★★ Sweet & fruity **NV** fizz with a nice tangy freshness. **Red Muscadel** ★★★ Raisin-rich **NV** with smooth mouthfilling sweetness, only lightly oaked to allow the fruit centre stage. **Cape Ruby** ★★★ Blend of 4 varieties, port-style **NV** has fruit preserve & caramelised nut flavours, rich, sweet & full-bodied. Note: Contemporary Collection discontinued. — CR

Kyburg Wine Estate　🍷 ⚰

ocation/map: Stellenbosch ▪ WO: Devon Valley/Stellenbosch ▪ Est 1998 ▪ 1stB 2006 ▪ Tasting & sales by appt ▪ Closed Easter Sun, Dec 25/26 & Jan 1 ▪ Self-catering guesthouse (exclusive use - rental min 2 weeks) ▪ wner(s) Fred & Rosmarie Ruest ▪ Cellarmaster(s)/winemaker(s) Jacques Fourie (Jan 2006, consultant) & hris Keet (2013, consultant) ▪ Viticulturist(s) Frans Snyman (Jul 2006, consultant) ▪ 28ha/18ha (cab, merlot,

shiraz) ▪ 150-160t/7,500cs own label 100% red + 2,500cs for clients ▪ Brands for clients: Pick Up 53 ▪ PO Box 12799 Die Boord 7613 ▪ info@kyburgwine.com ▪ www.kyburgwine.com ▪ S 33° 54' 59.3" E 018° 49' 28.4" ▪ **T +27 (0)21-865-2876**

This Devon Valley property vinifies only one third of its crop. 'We sell the balance to other well-known private producers,' says co-owner Fred Ruest. Modern viticultural techniques, as well as infrared imagery, ensure the fruit matches not only Fred's standards but also those of the producers who buy from him.

Cabernet Sauvignon ⊕ ★★★☆ Bright cassis flavours, fruit richness in balance with generous tannic base on **09**. Like **08** (★★★★) had development potential. These all tasted a year or two back **Merlot** ⊕ ★★★☆ **09** showed rich, ripe fruit with sweet length & firm tannin support. **Shiraz** ⊕ ★★★☆ Spicy whiff livens up slightly jammy notes on **09**. Tasty, if simple. **08** (★★★★) more complex. **33 Latitude** ⊕ ★★★☆ Fruity, savoury mix of cab with shiraz, merlot on **09**. Soft core with grippy tannin contrast. — AL

■ **La Bonne Vigne** *see* Wonderfontein

Laborie Wine Farm

Location: Paarl ▪ Map: Paarl & Wellington ▪ WO: Western Cape ▪ Est 1691 ▪ Tasting & sales Mon-Sat 9-5 Sun 11-5 ▪ Fee R20/5 wines R30/farm tour & tasting ▪ Chocolate & wine pairing R35 ▪ Olive & wine pairing R30 ▪ Closed all Christian pub hols ▪ Tours for large groups by appt ▪ Harvest Restaurant (see Restaurants section) ▪ Carols by Candlelight ▪ Conferences ▪ Weddings/functions ▪ Laborie Guest House (see Accommodation section) ▪ Owner(s) KWV (Pty) Ltd ▪ Winemaker(s) Johan Fourie & Kobus van der Merwe ▪ Viticulturist(s) Marco Ventrella, with De Wet Hugo ▪ Brandy master Pieter de Bod (Nov 2011) ▪ (ptage, pinots noir/meunier, shiraz, chard, chenin, sauv) ▪ BWI, IPW, WIETA ▪ PO Box 528 Suider Paarl 7624 ▪ info@laboriewines.co.za ▪ www.laboriewines.co.za ▪ S 33° 45' 55.2" E 018° 57' 27.6" ▪ **T +27 (0)21-807-3390** ▪ F +27 (0)21-863-1955

On the edge of bustling Paarl, KWV-owned showcase Laborie is an island of tranquility. Vineyards stretch up Paarl mountain, the historic buildings have been tastefully restored and visitors are offered a wide range of experiences. The wine range is equally comprehensive and includes some specialities, such as MCC sparkling, shiraz and the unique Pineau de Laborie, sweet pinotage fortified with pinotage brandy. Newest offering is a low-alcohol range, Lazy Days.

Laborie range

★★★★ **Jean Taillefert** 🏠 Fruit-rich **11** shiraz is vanilla-spiced from combo French & American barrels, 60% new. Lovely texture, silky smooth & just enough grip to hold it all together, promise a future.

★★★★ **Méthode Cap Classique Blanc de Blancs** ✓ Lemony fresh **10**'s oatmeal richness on the palate reveals the bubbly's balance; long enough lees-aged for added flavour, yet allowing the chardonnay fruit to shine through. No **09**.

★★★★ **Pineau de Laborie** 🖼 NV dessert, pinotage providing both fortifying spirit & base wine. Violets & blueberries, with a lovely fresh seam in the fruitcake richness. Captures the variety in a deliciously sweet way.

Cabernet Sauvignon ✓ 🏠 ★★★☆ Moist fruitcake richness on **12** supported by sturdy tannins, ideal for food matching, some cellaring. Drink now till ±2016. **Merlot** ✓ 🏠 ★★★☆ Macerated plums, lightly spiced there's lots to like in **12**: a curvaceous body, juicy drinkability, nice grippy finish. **Shiraz** ✓ 🏠 ★★★☆ Spicy, fruity & soft-textured **12** would win any popularity contest with its generous flavour breadth, succulent appeal. **Limited Collection Shiraz** ⊕ ★★★☆ **09** youthful, gawky tasted mid-2011. Perhaps now its pretty oak-laced spice, red fruits, gentle texture offering pleasure. **Merlot-Cabernet Sauvignon** ✓ 🏠 ★★★★ Lead pencils & savoury meaty notes, **12** has enough tannin/fruit balance to provide drinking pleasure as well as a future. **Chardonnay** ✓ 🏠 🖼 ★★★☆ Partial oaking adds savoury shading to **12**'s citrus preserve flavours, smoothly round, zesty & long. **Limited Collection Chardonnay** ⊕ ★★★★ Richer, bolder style though moderate alcohol, on **11**. Forthcoming lemon butter scents, flavours, with balanced freshening acid. **Sauvignon Blanc** ✓ 🏠 🖼 ★★★☆ Expressive grapefruit & greengage in **13**, its leafy freshness leaving the palate invigorated, ready for food. **Méthode Cap Classique Brut Rosé** 🖼 ★★★★ From pinot noir, chardonnay & pinotage, dry & bright-hued **10** offers red berry piquancy, tasty bubbles in celebratory mode. **Méthode Cap Classique Brut** ★★★★ Equal chardonnay/pinot noir in **10** sparkler, shows biscuit, citrus & red berry tones, lacks the stylishness of **08** (★★★★).

Lazy Days range NEW

> **Chenin Blanc** ☺ 🍴 ★★★ Aptly named, **12**'s light tropical sweetness is ideal summer fare. **Shiraz** ☺ 🍴 ★★★ Curvy (15 g/l sugar), juicy **12** offers dark berries, liquorice & lowish alcohol.

Rosé 🍴 ★★ **12** semi-sweet easy drinker, light (9% alcohol) & fruity-fresh.

Brandy range NEW

★★★★ **Alambic** Light amber, with a delightfully fresh nose of honey, fruit, flowers & vanilla. Has finesse & delicacy, though well rounded; fine oak influence. Finish is long & dry. — WB, CR, TJ

La Bri Estate

Location/map/WO: Franschhoek ▪ Est 1694 ▪ Tasting, sales & cellar tours Mon-Fri 10-5 Sat 10.30-4 ▪ Fee R30pp, waived on purchase ▪ Closed Easter Fri/Mon, Dec 25/26 & Jan 1 ▪ Chocolate & wine pairing ▪ Cheese platters ▪ Bicycle friendly ▪ Old wine cellar open by appt ▪ Weddings & functions ▪ Owner(s) Robin Hamilton ▪ Winemaker(s) Irene Waller (Oct 2010), with Glen Isaacs (Jun 2009) ▪ Viticulturist(s) Gerard Olivier (Oct 2010) ▪ ±20ha/±15ha (cabs s/f, merlot, p verdot, shiraz, chard, viog) ▪ 97t/7,500cs own label 80% red 20% white ▪ PO Box 180 Franschhoek 7690 ▪ info@labri.co.za ▪ www.labri.co.za ▪ S 33° 55' 18.3" E 019° 7' 1.5" ▪ **T +27 (0)21-876-2593** ▪ F +27 (0)86-275-9753

This is, says owner Robin Hamilton with simple eloquence, 'a small, quiet, very beautiful place'. It is also the name-bearing part of the first farm allocated to the refugee Huguenots in what was to become known as the Franschhoek Valley. Three centuries on, Irene Waller is building a fine reputation, not least through many competition successes, for crafted, eminently drinkable wines.

★★★★ **Affinity** 🔲 Made only in special years. **11** Bordeaux blend led by cab & merlot. Classic notes of ripe blackcurrant & liquorice; ripe & firm with detectable but balanced oaking. More intense than last **09** (★★★★).
Cabernet Sauvignon Await next. **Merlot** 🔲 ★★★★ Inviting blackberries, earth & dark chocolate, **11** classic merlot ripe & plush feel, structured & focused. **Syrah** 🔲 ★★★★ Voluptuous, as usual, with spice, dark fruit & a floral note from splash viognier. **11** intelligently oaked & structured, but warmish finish from big (14. 9%) alcohol. **Chardonnay** 🔲 ★★★★ Easygoing & well-constructed **12**, hints of lemon curd & nuts in welcomely dry palate with uplifting freshness; oak is integrated & supportive of fruit. **Viognier** ⊕ 🔲 ★★ **11** rich ripe peach, oily texture, low acidity. — JPf

▪ **La Capra** *see* Fairview
▪ **La Cave** *see* Wellington Wines
▪ **Lace** *see* Almenkerk Wine Estate

La Chataigne

Location/map/WO: Franschhoek ▪ Est 1972 ▪ 1stB 2003 ▪ Tasting & sales Mon-Sun 10-4 ▪ Closed all pub hols ▪ 3 guest cottages ▪ Owner(s) Parkfelt family ▪ Winemaker(s) Gerda Willers (2003, consultant) ▪ 27ha/17ha (cab, merlot, ptage, shiraz, chenin, sauv, sem) ▪ 200t/4,000cs own label 25% red 65% white 10% rosé ▪ PO Box 301 Franschhoek 7690 ▪ office@lachat.co.za ▪ www.lachat.co.za ▪ S 33° 52' 43.8" E 019° 3' 34.1" ▪ **T +27 (0)21-876-3220** ▪ F +27 (0)86-545-1039

Old-vine chenin and semillon have pride of place for Richard Parkfelt and family at 'The Chestnut' estate near Franschhoek. Their wines are boutique styled, with handwritten labels and limited bottlings reflecting passion and dedication. Fine guest cottages against a picturesque backdrop allow visitors to linger longer.

Marron ⊕ ★★★★ Aromatic tarry notes blend attractively with stewed wild fruit on **09** mix merlot, cab & pinotage. Full bodied, with meaty backdrop. **Rosé** 🍴 ★★★ Light strawberry hued **12** has floral lift before dry, fuller end. From merlot & shiraz. **Kastanje** √ 🍴 ★★★★ From low-yielding chenin with dash semillon, unoaked. Dried fruit on **12** leads to concentrated palate, with good pithy citrus texture & dry finish. **Sauvignon Blanc** 🍴 ★★★★ Grapefruit & elderberry unfold on lightish **12**, with good dry, zingy & assertive food-friendly focus. **Semillon** NEW ★★★ **12** entices with citrus spritz over almond paste & richer oak-derived sweetness. Year older barrels underscores serious intent. — JP

La Chaumiere Estate

Location/map/WO: Franschhoek ▪ Est 2001 ▪ 1stB 2003 ▪ Tasting & cellar tours by appt ▪ Sales from local outlets ▪ Owner(s) Michael Pawlowski ▪ Winemaker(s)/viticulturist(s) Wynand Pienaar ▪ 4ha (cab, pinot, shiraz, chard) ▪ 18t/1,800cs own label ▪ PO Box 601 Franschhoek 7690 ▪ wynlpers@iafrica.com ▪ S 33° 54' 34.0" E 019° 6' 54.9" ▪ **T** +27 (0)21-876-4830/31 ▪ **F** +27 (0)21-876-2135

This small riverside vineyard is owned by Cape Town steelman Michael Pawlowski (also owner of nearby luxury Franschhoek guest house La Clé des Montagnes). Winemaker/viticulturist Wynand Pienaar was able to increase production last year, doubling the amount of pinot, bottling a 2011 cabernet and disgorging another batch of méthode cap classique.

★★★★ **Pinot Noir** Like debut **11**, **12** convinces with typical maraschino cherry & wild fruit tones, 30% new French oak supports underlying savouriness & fine tannin structure. Unlike **11**, alcohol is a reined-in 13.5%. **Cabernet Sauvignon** NEW ★★★ Pre-bottling, **12** a 'big wine' (as winemaker notes) but smooth, tannins soft but active & drying, unusual cherry tobacco fruit tone. Has potential. **Shiraz** ★★★★ **12** preview shows ripe red fruit, light cinnamon & white pepper perfume, better managed alcohol. **Chardonnay** ✓ ★★★★ Winery's original label returns to the guide in fine style after a break. **12** delicious kumquat & peach aromas, full almond & honey finish in which oaking is well absorbed. **MCC Chardonnay** ⓐ ★★★ **10** traditionally made sparkler offers sweet apple fruit, racy freshness but limited complexity. Might perk up as it ages. —GM

La Couronne Wines

Location/map: Franschhoek ▪ WO: Franschhoek/Western Cape ▪ Chocolate & wine tasting/sales Mon-Sat 11–4 ▪ Closed Christian religious hols ▪ Restaurant ▪ Traditional braai & picnics to be booked in advance ▪ Facilities for children ▪ Tour groups ▪ Weddings ▪ Conferences ▪ Le Chais Villa (6 en-suite rooms) ▪ Winemaker(s) Rudi Zandberg ▪ 21ha (cabs s/f, malbec, merlot, p verdot, ptage, shiraz, chard, sauv, viog) ▪ 160t/±25,000cs own label 60% red 40% white ▪ eldorette@lacouronnewines.co.za ▪ www.lacouronnewines.co.za ▪ S 33° 55' 8.9" E 019° 6' 40.9" ▪ **T** +27 (0)21-876-3939/+27 (0)82-495-8579

Named for Cardinal de Richelieu's 17th century warship 'The Crown', boutique winery La Couronne in Franschhoek Valley continues its revival with further tasting venue upgrades, a new restaurant opening as the guide went to press, new labels, and additions to the wine range.

Malbec NEW ⓐ ★★★ **11** opens with sour cherry & earthy undertone. Youthful, needs time to settle. **Merlot** ⓐ ★★★ Plummy choc-minty **12** is ripe, with long sweetish end. **Pinotage** NEW ⓐ ★★★ Coconut & cherry combo, **11** made in voguish coffee/mocha style. WO W Cape. **Shiraz** ★★★★ **11** first since fine **06** (★★★★) in lighter vein, with bright spice, lifted fruit & oak support ending dry. **Portside Red** ▤ ★★ Unwooded **11** from Bordeaux varieties, year on is sweet fruited, with a green edge. **Merlot Rosé** ▤ ★★★ **12** light bronze in colour, offers dry, crisp non-fruity sipping. **Chardonnay Unwooded** ▤ ★★ **12** shy-fruited & unformed. WO Darling. **Starboard White Sauvignon Blanc** ▤ ★★ Bone-dry & ultra-light **12**, for early drinking. **Muscadel** Await next. —JP

Ladera Artisan Wines

Location: Wolseley ▪ Map: Breedekloof ▪ WO: Coastal/Western Cape ▪ Est/1stB 2009 ▪ Tasting, sales & cellar tours Mon-Sat by appt ▪ Picnics & longtable lunches in the fruit orchards by prior booking ▪ Owner(s) Charles Ochse ▪ Cellarmaster(s)/winemaker(s) Charles Ochse (2003) ▪ 6-8t/800cs own label 51% red 33% white 16% rosé ▪ PO Box 193 Wolseley 6830 ▪ info@ladera.co.za ▪ www.laderawines.co.za ▪ S 33° 28' 20.66" E 019° 11' 27.45" ▪ **T** +27 (0)72-536-0055

Winemaker Charles Ochse recalls his schooldays running through vineyards 'chasing thieving birds away'. After 17 crushes locally and abroad, he now heads up the family fruit farm in Wolseley and handcrafts Ladera ('Hillside') wines after hours.

★★★★ **Zahir Syrah** ⓐ Complex, ripe & rich mouthful of blue & black berries, naturally fermented, older oak-aged **10** soft yet structured, layered & silky; lovely mouthfeel & long finish. Alcohol down from **09**'s 15%+. **Wild Child Chardonnay** ▤ ★★★ **11** offers up a creamy, nutty, oxidative & idiosyncratic mouthful. Oak is prominent & masks muted tangerine fruit. WO W Cape. —FM

Ladismith Winery & Distillery

Location: Ladismith ▪ Map: Klein Karoo & Garden Route ▪ WO: Klein Karoo/Western Cape ▪ Est 1941 ▪ 1stB 1988 ▪ Tasting & sales Mon-Fri 9–5 Sat 9–3 ▪ Fee R25 for groups of 5 or more ▪ Closed Easter Fri-Mon, Dec 25/ 26 & Jan 1 ▪ Book ahead for cellar tours ▪ Restaurant ▪ Owner(s) Southern Cape Vineyards (SCV) & Oude Molen Distillery ▪ Distiller Bertie Burger ▪ Winemaker(s) Jandre Human ▪ 600ha/520ha (cab, merlot, ptage, ruby cab, shiraz, chard, chenin, cbard, viog) ▪ 4,800t/20,000cs own label 20.25% red 79.75% white ▪ Other export brand: Cape ▪ PO Box 56 Ladismith 6655 ▪ info@scv.co.za ▪ www.ladismithwines.co.za ▪ S 33° 29' 49.38" E 021° 15' 59.40" ▪ T +27 (0)28-551-1042 ▪ F +27 (0)28-551-1930

Klein Karoo-based Southern Cape Vineyards (SCV), previously sole proprietors of this wine and brandy house (and its siblings Oudtshoorn Cellar and separately listed Barrydale Cellar), are now equal owners with Elgin's Oude Molen Distillery. In a major upgrade, several million rands' worth of assets have been acquired from Oudtshoorn and installed here. (Oudtshoorn itself is temporarily closed pending discussions with grape growers, after the sale of the wholesale business to Bonnievale-based producing wholesaler Mooiuitsig.) New winemaker Jandre Human (ex Overhex) once stocks have sold out will focus on three wines, selected on vintage performance, and on brandy-quality wines for nurturing by distiller Bertie Burger.

Towerkop range

Cabernet Sauvignon ⓘ ★★★ Characterful **11** preview has juicy & clean fruit flavour. **Merlot** ⓘ ★★★ Plummy **10** unfettered by oak, pleasant to sip. **Pinotage** ⓘ 🍷 ★★★ **11** laudably restrained aroma, unoaked to let pristine fruit shine through. **Ruby Cabernet** ⓘ 🍷 ★★ Unoaked **11** tank sample bursts with berries; supple & juicy for effortless enjoyment. **Shiraz** ⓘ ★★★ Spice, smoke & plum attractions on friendly unoaked **11**, fresh & charming anytime red. WO W Cape. **Touriga Nacional** ⓘ ★★ (Unfortified) **09** slight malty overtone to jammy fruit. **Rosé** ⓘ 🍷 ★★★ Candyfloss **12**, off-dry shiraz, pleasant chilled summer sipping. **Chardonnay** ⓘ 🍷 ★★ Unwooded **11** preview shy lemon/nut aromas, insubstantial flavours. **Chenin Blanc** ⓘ 🍷 ★★ Work-in-progress **11** Karoo scrub & nuts, bracing acidity from early picked grapes. **Sauvignon Blanc** ⓘ 🍷 ★★ Pre-bottling, **11** cool green varietal fruit, lowish 12% alcohol. **Chardonnay-Sauvignon Blanc** ⓘ 🍷 ★★★ Lipsmacking **10** in early-drinking style; chardonnay's citrus palate weight balanced by sauvignon's zestiness. **Aristaat** ⓘ 🍷 ★★ Sweetish white named for rare protea; drink-soon **10** features dash muscadel. **Towersoet** ⓘ 🍷 ★★★★ Fortified dessert from muscat d'Alexandrie. **09** bottled sunshine: ripe & juicy grape flavours, lovely clean fresh finish, whereas **07** (★★★) was cloying. WO W Cape. **Amalienstein Muscadel** ⓘ 🍷 ★★★★ Delightful **10** fortified after-dinner treat again raises the bar. Bursts with enough lemon, lime, nutty complexity to brighten any dull winter's day. More depth & verve than last-tasted **06** (★★★).

Brandy range [NEW]

★★★★ **Klein Karoo Pot Still Brandy** Clean aromas with abundant floral notes mixed with dried fruit. In a lightish, elegant style, with muted fire, unobtrusive oak element & a long, dry finish. — WB, JP, TJ

▪ **Lady Anne Barnard** *see African Pride Wines*
▪ **Lady Somerset** *see Somerset Wines*

La Ferme Derik

Location: Paarl ▪ Map: Paarl & Wellington ▪ WO: Paarl/Western Cape ▪ Est 1695 ▪ 1stB 1895 ▪ Tasting, sales & cellar tours by appt ▪ Function venue for 160 guests ▪ Guest house ▪ Owner(s) Hardus Otto ▪ Winemaker(s)/ viticulturist(s) Eurica Scholtz ▪ 7ha (shiraz, grenache b/n, rouss, viog) + 45ha export table grapes & macadamia nuts ▪ 35t 10% red 90% white ▪ PO Box 2008 Windmeul 7630 ▪ functions@lafermederik.com ▪ www. lafermederik.com ▪ S 33° 40' 33.348" E 18° 55' 56.964" ▪ T +27 (0)21-869-8380/+27 (0)82-953-0185 ▪ F +27 (0)21-869-8433

Eurica Scholtz makes the wine on this Paarl property, where the main focus of activity is the farming of table grapes but conference, function and accommodation facilities are also available. She studied winemaking part-time, the small annual production intended to 'add to the package of what we offer'.

Adagio Await next, as for **Grenache Rosé** & **Vlinnay**. **Chénine** ⓘ ★★★★ **09** a blend of old-vine chenin & viognier (80/20). Intense peach & apricot, rich & full with soft acidity. **Concerto 'Les Quatre Saisons'** ⓘ

★★★★ 5-way white blend in **09** with sauvignon in lead (48%). Step up on **08** (★★★) with good fruit integrity, full body & balanced zesty acidity. **Vivace** ⊕ ★★★★ Blend of chenin (52%) & 4 other whites. **09** better concentration, more layers of flavour than maiden **08** (★★★). — CE

Laibach Vineyards

Location/map: Stellenbosch ▪ WO: Simonsberg–Stellenbosch/Western Cape/Stellenbosch ▪ Est 1994 ▪ 1stB 1997 ▪ Tasting & sales Mon-Fri 10–5 Sat 10–1 (Nov-Apr) pub hols 10–1 ▪ Fee R10/4 wines ▪ Closed Easter Fri/Sun, Dec 25/26 & Jan 1 ▪ Cellar tours by appt ▪ Laibach Vineyards Lodge (see Accommodation section) ▪ Owner(s) Petra Laibach-Kühner & Rudolf Kühner ▪ Cellarmaster(s)/winemaker(s) Francois van Zyl (Jan 2000) ▪ Viticulturist(s) / MD Michael Malherbe (Jun 1994) ▪ 50ha/37ha (cabs s/f, malbec, merlot, p verdot, ptage, chard, chenin, viog) ▪ 300t/48,000cs own label 70% red 30% white + 9,000cs for Woolworths ▪ BWI, Organic ▪ PO Box 7109 Stellenbosch 7599 ▪ info@laibachwines.com ▪ www.laibachwines.com ▪ S 33° 50' 43.3" E 018° 51' 44.2" ▪ **T +27 (0)21-884-4511** ▪ F +27 (0)21-884-4848

Ladybirds - in the vineyards, on the front labels and on the shelves - have helped create a following for this focused organic Simonsberg-Stellenbosch winery, in the German Laibach family for two decades. Appropriate then that they won the 2013 Green Wine Awards with winemaker Francois van Zyl's favourite grape - merlot. Newly installed and long-anticipated irrigation for young vines made life a lot easier last year. Good conditions meant that grapes reaching the cellar were deliciously ripe, aiding their vinification - kept as natural as possible.

★★★★ **Merlot 11** retains form of **10** with spicy mulberry & cherry vibrancy. Lithe & sleekly supple but concentrated & focused. Ceres grapes again added, hence WO Western Cape.

★★★★☆ **Claypot Merlot** ⊠ Serious, broodingly elegant **11** picks up where **10** ended. Hedgerow fruit with cocoa & graphite below. Fine tannins from 12 months all-new oak - & 14 months more in old vats. Sleek but taut, with a long rich tail.

★★★★ **Pinotage** ✓ ⊠ Raspberry & forest fruit generosity of juicy **12** speaks of grape's pinot noir parentage. Firm frame yet light suppleness throughout, like **11**. Stellenbosch WO, like Chenin.

★★★★☆ **Friedrich Laibach** Integration & harmony the watchwords for this **11** Bordeaux red blend of cab & merlot with 1% cab franc. Light oak juxtaposed with dark concentration of ripe, juicy berries. Tobacco & cedar reminiscent of equally elegant **09**. No **10**.

★★★★ **Red Ladybird** ⊕ ▤ ♨ ⊠ Cab, cab franc & merlot lead classy **11** 5-way Bordeaux blend. Elegant, with layered complexity, ripeness & sleekly statuesque body. Velvety mouthfeel & rewarding conclusion. **Widow's Block Cabernet Sauvignon** Occasional release. **Chenin Blanc** ▤ ⊠ ★★★★ Bold guava & pear on **13**. Refreshing acidity on broad palate. Lighter than **11** (★★★★), but venerable Bottelary vines add to mid-palate presence. **12** sold out untasted. **White Ladybird** ⊕ ▤ ♨ ⊠ ★★★★ Smart tangerine tang cloaked in oak sheen on **12**. Rich, ripe & mouthfilling, with lively zestiness. 86% chardonnay, with viognier & chenin. Discontinued: **Cabernet Sauvignon**. — FM

La Kavayan

Location/WO: Stellenbosch ▪ Est 1999 ▪ 1stB 2001 ▪ Closed to public ▪ Owner(s) Gabriël Kriel & Theo Beukes ▪ Winemaker(s) PG Slabbert (2001, consultant) ▪ Viticulturist(s) Gabriël Kriel ▪ 4ha (cab, shiraz) ▪ ±10,000L own label 100% red ▪ PO Box 321 Stellenbosch 7599 ▪ diana@lakavayan.co.za, theo@minpro.co.za ▪ **T +27 (0)83-601-9030/+27 (0)21-881-3246/3289** ▪ F +27 (0)21-881-3211

These two red wines are produced by long-time contract winemaker PG Slabbert for Stellenbosch boutique winery La Kavayan, owned by friends Theo Beukes and Gabriël Kriel. Their quest is for 'wines of timeless quality', and they exercise 'patience and attention to detail', content to 'leave the rest to Mother Nature'.

Cabernet Sauvignon ⊕ ★★★☆ Classic violet & blackcurrant scents, supple tannins on medium-bodied **09**. **Cabernet Sauvignon-Shiraz** ⊕ ★★★☆ Commendably savoury & dry **09** back on track with red/black fruit complexity, more presence than **08**. — CvZ

▪ **LAM** see Lammershoek Winery

Lammershoek Winery

Location: Malmesbury • Map/WO: Swartland • Est 1999 • 1stB 2000 • Tasting, sales & cellar tours by appt • Light lunch platters by appt (R100pp incl wine tasting); or BYO picnic • Owner(s) Paul & Anna Kretzel, Stephan family • Cellarmaster(s)/viticulturist(s) Craig Hawkins (Oct 2009) • Winemaker(s) Craig Hawkins (Oct 2009), with Jurgen Gouws (Jan 2011) • 210ha/70ha (carignan, grenache, merlot, mourv, ptage, shiraz, tinta barocca, zin, chard, chenin, hárslevelü, sauv, viog) • 195t/25,000cs own label 55% red 40% white 5% rosé • PO Box 597 Malmesbury 7299 • info@lammershoek.co.za • www.lammershoek.co.za • S 33° 31' 30.2" E 018° 48' 21. 1" • T +27 (0)22-482-2835 • F +27 (0)22-487-2702

This large family-run farm on Swartland's Perdeberg is blessed with many old vines, and viticulturist-winemaker Craig Hawkins aims to reflect their essence and that of his land. 'Wines that are unpretentious, unassuming and pure, or basically simple.' Simple in that sense, perhaps, but full of vitality. 'It's the hardest thing to capture,' Hawkins says, 'but is achieved through farming and winemaking without chemicals, except for a little sulphur.' Lammershoek is now fully certified as organic, and gaining increasing international recognition as an important source of fully 'natural' wines, from vine to bottle - a rare thing anywhere, certainly in the Cape. The LAM and Lammershoek wines are treated similarly, but the former are drawn from younger vineyards, the latter from the farm's top sites.

Lammershoek range

★★★★ **Syrah** ⊕ ⊠ Delicacy, freshness & lightness of touch, flavour intensity define new-style **10**. Alluring spice, red earth perfume, more complex sanguine/iron flavours focused by supple yet lively structure.

★★★★☆ **Roulette** ⊕ ⊠ Complex mix game, red earth, dark fruit on generous **10** from shiraz with grenache, carignan, mourvèdre. Mouthfilling flavour, focusing mineral vitality & buzz of fine tannin. Older oak.

★★★★☆ **Chenin Blanc** ⊕ ⊠ Large old-oak maturation gives 'old gold' tinge to 'natural', ethereal **11**. Delicious, creamy oxidative texture, vitality & near-endless length. 12% alcohol; a few grams sugar.

★★★★☆ **Roulette Blanc** ✓ Usual chardonnay, chenin base with clairette, viognier. Fine example of oxidative style, with lifted fresh contrast. Sumptuous **11**'s notes of grapefruit, honey & nuts energised by mineral thread; fantailing finish. Sulphur the only addition. Matured in older oak & concrete.

LAM range

★★★★ **Pinotage** ✓ ⊠ Fruit the main feature in **12**; gloriously perfumed cherries supported by lively freshness; minimal tannin yet still confidently structured for few years' ageing. Modest alcohol, bone-dry.

★★★★ **Syrah** ✓ ⊠ **12** the least exuberant fruit of the LAMs; delicate yet assured feel, with lovely savoury edge. Good now, further rewards promised with few years cellaring. Like all these, no new oak - of course!

Syrah Rosé ✓ ⊠ ★★★★ More serious than most (but plenty of enjoyment too), with natural ferment in old oak casks, year on lees. **12**, redolent of scented scrub, wild peaches; refreshing & tangily dry. Under 11% alcohol. **White** ✓ ⊠ ★★★★ **12** drops Chenin Blanc-Viognier from name, but same blend as **11** (★★★★). Swartland's warmth, flavour intensity & persistence but feather-light 10.5% alcohol. Alive, firmly dry. — AL

La Motte

Location/map: Franschhoek • WO: Western Cape/Franschhoek • Est 1969 • 1stB 1984 • Tasting & sales Mon-Sat 9-5 • Fee R30 • Themed tastings R200pp, booking essential • Closed Easter Fri/Sun & Dec 25 • Pierneef à La Motte (see Restaurants section) • Facilities for children • Tour groups (max 16), booking essential • Farm shop: lavender, vegetables, bread • Walking trail Mon-Sat 9-2 R50pp (duration 2-3hrs, not recommended for children under 10) • Historic walk Wed 10-11 R50pp • 35ha conservation area • Museum Tue-Sun 9-5: Rupert family, history of La Motte, Cape Dutch architecture, life/art of JH Pierneef & other SA artists • Monthly classical music concerts • Owner(s) Hanneli Rupert-Koegelenberg • Cellarmaster(s) Edmund Terblanche (Dec 2000) • Winemaker(s) Michael Langenhoven (Dec 2006) • Viticulturist(s) Pietie le Roux (May 1986) • 170ha/75ha (merlot, pinot, shiraz, chard, sauv) • 1,200t/120,000cs own label 30% red 69.6% white 0.4% sparkling + 30,000cs for clients • Other export brand: Schoone Gevel • Brands for clients: Woolworths • ISO 14001:2003, BWI champion, EU & NOP organic certification, Farming for the Future: Woolworths, Global GAP, HACCP, IPW, WIETA • PO Box 685 Franschhoek 7690 • cellar@la-motte.co.za • www.la-motte.com • S 33° 52' 49.9" E 019° 4' 28.3" • T +27 (0)21-876-8000 • F +27 (0)21-876-3446

Purchased by the late Anton Rupert in 1970, this property dating from the early 1700s is now owned and run by his daughter, Hanneli Rupert-Koegelenberg, with

her husband, Hein Koegelenberg, as CEO. The arts and culture are given as much prominence here as the wines: the restored buildings now house, among others, a museum where many Pierneef artworks may be seen, and a restaurant which focuses on recipes brought over by early settlers, while classical music concerts are held in the historic cellar. These and many other attractions have twice earned La Motte Great Wine Capitals of the World's Best of Wine Tourism awards for South Africa. Cellarmaster Edmund Terblanche crafts wines in an elegant, classic style that complement their gracious surroundings.

Pierneef Collection

★★★★★ **Shiraz-Viognier** 🆚 Refined, perfect partnership in classic-style flagship. **11** (★★★★☆) a touch less powerful than elegant, polished **10**, may mature sooner, but equally persuasive in its delicate perfume, crushed velvet feel, enlivening freshness.

★★★★ **Shiraz-Grenache** ⑨ **08** few years back showed piquant spice & gamey tannin grip.

Sauvignon Blanc (Organically Grown) 🌿 Await next.

Classic Collection

★★★★ **Cabernet Sauvignon** 🆚 Strong presence marks **11**, a perfect introduction for a newcomer to cab. Expressive & crunchy blackberry fruit amply fills its vibrant fine tannin frame. Polished in 50% new French oak.

★★★★☆ **Shiraz** ✓ 🆚 No holding back of fruity exuberance in **11**; happy melange juicy red fruits, spices, hint of game - all delivered with elegance, freshness & promise of future, more complex delights. Youthfully enjoyable too. Back on track after slightly lesser **10** (★★★★).

★★★★ **Chardonnay** ✓ 🍽 🆚 **12** (★★★★☆) beautifully structured, balanced. Tangy fruity acids focus richer nutty, limy notes, enhanced by moderate 13% alcohol & oaking (30% new). Franschhoek grapes, like **11**.

★★★★ **Méthode Cap Classique** Refreshing & truly dry **10**. From Franschhoek pinot (68%) & chardonnay with pinkish-straw colour & appley, raspberry features. Further bready complexity promised after few years.

Straw Wine NEW 🆚 ★★★ NV dessert but from barrel each 2011, 2012 air-dried viognier. Light body & lightish fruit; soft but not too sweet.

La Motte Collection

★★★★ **Millennium** ✓ 🆚 Merlot's (60%) flesh gently fills out tailored **11**. Cab franc adds spice, petit verdot & malbec some mineral tautness into whole of quiet charm. Smooth, fruity **10** (★★★★).

Sauvignon Blanc ✓ 🍽 🆚 ★★★☆ Unaggressively refreshing **13**; lengthy apple, greengage flavours to dry finish. — AL

Landau du Val 🍷

Location/map: Franschhoek ▪ Tasting by appt ▪ Sales at La Cotte Wine Sales, Franschhoek ▪ Owner(s) Basil & Jane Landau ▪ Winemaker(s) Wynand Grobler ▪ Viticulturist(s) Martin du Plessis & Pietie le Roux (consultant) ▪ 15ha under vine ▪ La Brie Robertsvlei Road Franschhoek 7690 ▪ basillandau@mweb.co.za ▪ S 33° 55' 34.3" E 019° 6' 34.1" ▪ **T +27 (0)82-410-1130** ▪ F +27 (0)21-876-3369

The prime vineyard of unirrigated, bushvine semillon on Basil and Jane Landau's Franschhoek farm, La Brie, was planted in 1905, making it easily one of the Cape's most ancient. Recognising the advantage of bottle age for semillon, they are holding back the release of the 2012 Private Selection until some time in 2014.

■ **Land of Hope** *see* The Winery of Good Hope

Land's End

As implied, these Fairview and Hidden Valley joint-venture wines come from the the southern tip of Africa and its cool, windy Agulhas plain. See Fairview entry.

★★★★ **Syrah** 🍽 🆚 Fynbos & a salty sea breeze note complement bright dark berries on **11**, from vineyards 8km from the ocean. Restrained, fruit mingling with spicy oak. Will reward few years ageing.

Rosé In abeyance. **Sauvignon Blanc** ⑨ 🍽 🆚 ★★★☆ **12**'s upfront tropical aroma let down a bit by fruit-shy palate & zingy acidity. Not the solid body of last **10** (★★★★). Elim grapes, as Syrah. — WB

Landskroon Wines

Location: Paarl ▪ Map: Paarl & Wellington ▪ WO: Paarl/Western Cape ▪ Est 1874 ▪ 1stB 1974 ▪ Tasting & sales Mon-Fri 8.30–5 Sat (Oct-May) 9.30–1 ▪ Closed Good Fri, Dec 25 & Jan 1 ▪ Fee R10/5 wines, waived on purchase of 6btls ▪ Cellar tours by appt Mon-Fri 9-4 ▪ BYO picnic ▪ Play area for children ▪ Permanent display of Stone Age artefacts ▪ Self-catering cottage ▪ Owner(s) Paul & Hugo de Villiers Family Trusts ▪ Cellarmaster(s) Paul de Villiers (Jan 1980) ▪ Winemaker(s) Abraham van Heerden (Sep 2007) ▪ Viticulturist(s) Hugo de Villiers jnr (1995) ▪ 330ha/200ha (cab, cinsaut, merlot, ptage, shiraz, souzão, tinta amerela, tinta barocca, touriga nacional, chenin, chard, sauv, viog) ▪ 1,200t 74% red 19% white 7% port ▪ IPW ▪ PO Box 519 Suider-Paarl 7624 ▪ huguette@landskroonwines.com ▪ www.landskroonwines.com ▪ S 33° 45' 38.2" E 018° 55' 0.8" ▪ **T +27 (0)21-863-1039** ▪ F +27 (0)21-863-2810

To say Landskroon is well-established is putting it mildly: the Paarl estate has been home to wine production since the 17th century. As a family concern, it currently involves five members of the de Villiers clan, the fifth generation at the helm. Fittingly, the style is never flashy or mercurial - constant and reliable, rather, with marginal tweaks now and then (like the recent label and tasting room revamps). And there's always quality and value aplenty.

Paul de Villiers range

★★★★ **Cabernet Sauvignon** ✓ 🌿 Cedar & vanilla perfume cloaks dark, black berry appeal. **11** abounds with rich polished confidence. Acid & tannin nicely balanced, but will benefit from a year or two in bottle.

★★★★ **Reserve** ✓ 🌿 Flagship blend shiraz & merlot plus dollops cab & touriga. **11** has cedar oak welcome, leading to bright fruited, medium body with fine balanced tannins. Needs a year or so to settle.

Shiraz 🌿 ★★★☆ An oft-awarded label, **11** in usual winning rich & soft style with cherry cola appeal & black pepper spice follow-through.

Landskroon range

★★★★ **Cape Vintage** ✓ 🌿 Much-awarded fortified **10** from tintas barocca & amarela, souzão, touriga. Brooding dark fruit complements toffee note & balanced sweetness. Brandy spirit needs time to settle.

Cabernet Sauvignon ☺ 🌿 ★★★ **12** offers redcurrant, mulberry & cedary oak with fruit-sweet palate ending just dry. Ripeness well harnessed. **Merlot** 🌿 ★★★ Pretty, red-fruited & fresh **12** for easy sipping, has oak support. **Pinotage** ☺ 🌿 ★★★ Lifted banana note, berried **12** has tannic grip to balance. **Shiraz** ☺ 🌿 ★★★ **11**'s brooding fruit has smoke & spice edge leading to a palate with vibrant acid foil to curb American oak sweetness. **Blanc de Noir Pinotage Off-Dry** ☺ 🍴 🌿 ★★★ **13** pale onionskin hue & balanced, fruity appeal. **Chardonnay** ☺ 🍴 🌿 ★★★ Crisp apple intro on unwooded **13**; nicely judged ripeness balanced by citrus freshness & pleasant dry end. **Chenin Blanc Dry** ☺ 🍴 🌿 ★★★ Clean-fruited with finely balanced peach & citrus contrast, **13** offers fresh, crisp & dry summery refreshment. **Chenin Blanc Off-Dry** ☺ 🍴 🌿 ★★★ Light & fruity, with fresh peach, hay & blossom lift. **13** fruitier than sibling, but same balanced freshness.

Cinsaut 🌿 ★★ Light fruity **12** is unwooded. **Cabernet Franc-Merlot** ⓔ 🌿 ★★★ Wood spice & floral aromas on appealing, balanced **11**, plus splash shiraz. **Cinsaut-Shiraz** 🌿 ★★ Undemanding **11**, fruity & easy. **Paul Hugo Red** 🍴 🌿 ★★ **12** is a fruity blend cab franc, shiraz & merlot. **Bush Camp Our Daily Red** ⓔ ★★★ Red berry & spicy **09** is easy, soft & fruity. **Bush Camp Blanc de Noir** ⓔ 🍴 ★★ Off-dry but fresh **11**, with berry twist. **Bush Camp The Sundowner** ⓔ 🍴 🌿 ★★★ Pleasing sweet-fruited chenin has good texture with cleansing acidity on well balanced **11**. **Sauvignon Blanc** 🌿 ★★★ Tropical-styled **13**, light & easygoing. WO W Cape. **Paul Hugo White** ⓔ 🍴 🌿 ★★☆ **12** mostly chenin. Easy, crisp & charming. — JP

Landzicht GWK Wines

Location: Jacobsdal ▪ Map: Northern Cape, Free State & North West ▪ WO: Northern Cape/Douglas ▪ Est 1976 ▪ 1stB ca 1980 ▪ Tasting & sales Mon-Fri 8-5 ▪ Closed all pub hols ▪ Tours - bottling plant ▪ Meals/refreshments by appt ▪ Owner(s) GWK Ltd ▪ Winemaker(s) Ian Sieg ▪ Viticulturist(s) Hein Janse van Rensburg ▪ Production: see under Douglas Wine Cellar ▪ PO Box 94 Jacobsdal 8710 ▪ landzicht@gwk.co.za ▪ www.landzicht.co.za ▪ S 29° 8' 35.5" E 024° 46' 42.8" ▪ **T +27 (0)53-591-0164** ▪ F +27 (0)53-591-0145

Owned by agribusiness GWK, and sibling to Douglas Wine Cellar, where vinification takes place, Landzicht (in the words of new viticulturist Hein Janse van Rensburg) is 'an undiscovered gem close to the diamond city of Kimberley,

producing extraordinary value for money wines true to their terroir'. Believing 'quality out of quantity' is the future, Hein and team are looking to add more varietal reds and create a region-specific, sustainably farmed line-up.

Merlot NEW ☺ ★★★ Uncomplicated quaffing delivered by honest & brightly fruited **12**. WO Douglas.

Cabernet Sauvignon ★★ 11 friendly braai companion with redcurrant notes. **Cabernet Sauvignon Reserve** Next awaited, as for **White Muscadel & Red Jerepigo**. **Chenin Blanc ★★ 12** winter melon toned & gently sweet. WO Douglas. **Blanc de Blanc ★** A colombard & muscat d'Alexandrie mix, **12** is light bodied & lightly flavoured. **Rosenblümchen ★★** Faint raisin appeal on shy but fresh **NV** Natural Sweet rosé. **Blümchen ★** Aromatic sweet-&-sour low-alcohol **NV** white. **Nagmaalwyn** NEW **★★** Sweet, rose-scented **NV** sacramental wine from red muscadel. **Hanepoot ★★** Was 'Sweet Hanepoot' but remains just that: sweet fortified muscat d'Alexandrie, **12** with honey & lemon flavours. **Red Muscadel ★★★** Honest, well-made fortified oozing strawberries & cherries. **12** carefully balances 16.7% alcohol with slippery sweetness, slight herbal lift. **Ruby Port ★★** Fiery **11** port-style from pinotage will put a rosy glow on any stormy night. WO Douglas. **Oak Matured** NEW **★★** Sherry-style **NV** mainly chenin, splash muscadel, fleeting sweet choc-raisin flavours. — DC, JP

▪ **Langeberg Wineries** *see* Wonderfontein
▪ **Langtafel** *see* Mooiplaas Estate & Private Nature Reserve

Langverwacht Wynkelder   🍷🏷

Location: Bonnievale ▪ Map/WO: Robertson ▪ Est 1954 ▪ Tasting, sales & tours Mon-Fri 8-5 ▪ Closed all pub hols ▪ Owner(s) 25 members ▪ Cellarmaster(s) Johan Gerber (Dec 1986) ▪ Winemaker(s) Theunis Botha (Dec 2005) ▪ Viticulturist(s) Hennie Visser (Jul 2008) ▪ 640ha (cab, ruby cab, shiraz, chenin, chard, cbard, sauv) ▪ 13,500t/8,000cs own label 64% red 36% white ▪ IPW ▪ PO Box 87 Bonnievale 6730 ▪ info@langverwachtwines.co.za ▪ S 33° 57' 32.8" E 020° 1' 35.3" ▪ **T +27 (0)23-616-2815** ▪ F +27 (0)23-616-3059

Top quality at an affordable price is one of the mantras of the team led by cellarmaster Johan Gerber, veteran of 28 vintages at this Bonnievale winery. Another focus, Johan says, is to keep the 25 owner-growers on the farm and in production, in spite of financial obstacles over which they have no control. 'In production' they certainly were in 2013, with tonnage through the cellar topping out at 13,500.

Colombar ☺🏷📖 ★★★ Step-up **13** tank sample boasts pineapple, citrus & Granny Smith apple complexity, good intensity.

Cabernet Sauvignon 🏷📖 ★★ **13** preview sweet fruited, tangy, for quaffing fun. **Ruby Cabernet** 🌱 🏷📖 ★★★ Unwooded **10** chocolate & raspberry toned pizza pal. **Shiraz** 🏷📖 ★★ Sample **11**'s rich fruit core lifted by stalky tannins. **4 Barrels Shiraz** NEW 📖 ★★★ Mocha, cherry cola & spice on **11** crowd pleaser. Aged (14 months) in barrels; other reds oak-staved. **Chardonnay** 🌱 🏷📖 ★★★ Wallet-friendly & easygoing **12**, nice touch of lime marmalade & litchi complexity, delicious creamy conclusion. **Chenin Blanc** 🏷📖 ★★ Dried peach **13**, moderate 12.5% alcohol for lunchtime sipping. **Sauvignon Blanc** 🏷 📖 ★★ Unusual sweet-sour apricot character, **13** lightish & uncomplicated sipper. — JP,HJ

Lanner Hill   🍷

Location: Darling ▪ Map: Durbanville, Philadelphia & Darling ▪ WO: Darling/Coastal ▪ Est 1999 ▪ 1stB 2002 ▪ Tasting by appt ▪ Sales Mon-Fri 9-3 via email/phone; from farm by appt only ▪ Owner(s) David & Nicola Tullie ▪ Winemaker(s) Nicky Versfeld (2002) ▪ Viticulturist(s) David Tullie ▪ 91ha/51ha (cab, merlot, p verdot, shiraz, sauv, sem, viog) ▪ 450-500t/1,000cs own label ▪ PO Box 220 Darling 7345 ▪ tulliefamilyvineyards@gmail.com ▪ S 18° 22' 8.18" E 033° 23' 34.05" ▪ **T +27 (0)22-492-3662/+27 (0)82-882-2260 (marketing & sales)** ▪ F +27 (0)22-492-3664

The Lanner Hill brand is a partnership between seasoned winemaker and Cape Winemakers Guild member, Nicky Versveld, and the Tullie family. It is also the name of the family farm, now open for visits by appointment in Darling's cool Groenekloof ward that has become synonymous with top sauvignons.

★★★★ **Sauvignon Blanc** 🏷📖 Like **11** preview, **13** flies the Darling flag, ticking all the variety's boxes. Lovely fruit purity & racy acidity end with a clean-cut flinty farewell. **12** sold out untasted.

★★★★☆ **CWG Auction Reserve Double Barrel White** NEW **12** rich & complex oaked semillon, combines creamy textured richness & fruit intensity. Mouthfilling layers of flavour, with pervasive thread of acidity. Poised yet restrained, with good potential to develop. WO Coastal.

★★★★ **The Yair** ⊕ Elegant **09** Bordeaux styled white (52% sauvignon, with semillon) exuded tropical & greenpepper flavours previously.

Merlot NEW ▦ ★★★★ **11** shows cool provenance. Red fruit & mint, deftly oaked. Bright & sappy, with serious underlying structure. — MW

Lanzerac

Location/map/WO: Stellenbosch ▪ Est 1692 ▪ 1stB 1957 ▪ Tasting & sales daily 9.30–4.30 ▪ Fee R30 ▪ Cellar tours at 11 & 3 ▪ Closed Good Fri & Dec 25 ▪ Cheese platters; wine & chocolate tasting ▪ 5-star Lanzerac Hotel, Spa & Restaurants (see Accommodation & Restaurants sections) ▪ Conferences ▪ Weddings/functions ▪ Owner(s) Lanzerac Estate Investments ▪ Winemaker(s) Wynand Lategan (Jan 2005) ▪ Viticulturist(s) Danie Malherbe (2008) ▪ 150ha/46ha (cab, merlot, ptage, chard) ▪ 500t/24-26,000cs own label 55% red 30% white 15% rosé ▪ BWI ▪ PO Box 6233 Uniedal 7612 ▪ winesales@lanzerac.co.za ▪ www.lanzeracwines.co.za ▪ S 33° 56' 14.7" E 018° 53' 35.5" ▪ **T +27 (0)21-886-5641** ▪ F +27 (0)21-887-6998

The gateway to Stellenbosch's beautiful Jonkershoek Valley, this historic estate was the source of the first commercial pinotage (vintage 1959) and has since continued to champion the variety. Lanzerac's fine Cape Dutch homestead and buildings house a luxury hotel with spa and restaurants in a quintessential winelands setting. The property was recently sold to a British consortium who are intent on 'building it up so it can take its rightful place in the wine industry.'

Heritage range

★★★★ **Pionier Pinotage** 🎨 Tribute to world's first commercial pinotage release, Lanzerac **59**, bottled 1961. Naturally fermented **10** (★★★★☆) from single-vineyard ups ante on **09** with excellent balance & structure. Mouthfilling & complex, with precise oaking & length. Will reward the patient.

★★★★☆ **Le Général** ⊕ Understated **09** cab-led Cape Blend with shiraz, pinotage & malbec offers concentrated dark berry, vanilla & milk chocolate flavours. Well structured, complex with supportive oaking & a delicious spicy lift. Built to last.

★★★★☆ **Mrs English** ⊕ 🎨 Stellar debut in **11** for barrel-selected chardonnay. Complex aromas of citrus, melon, white flowers & spice; dense yet silk textured, no excess weight. Unflagging vanilla cream on the finish.

Premium range

★★★★ **Cabernet Sauvignon** 🎨 Classic & restrained, **11** offers melange of cedar & dark chocolate over bright black fruit. Complex, smooth fruit & fine tannin balance bode well for the future.

★★★★ **Merlot** Christmas cake, fresh plums & savoury olives on preview **11**. Juicy, with a vibrant seam of acidity, balanced by well-judged aromatic oak. Good varietal character.

★★★★ **Pinotage** 🎨 Crimson-coloured fruity **11** shows bright red berries in an elegant & understated body. Well balanced, with a fragrant spicy plum pudding conclusion.

★★★★ **Chardonnay** ✓ Ex-tank **12** has balance & poise. Delicate floral hints mingle with vanilla, lemon & buttered toast from barrel fermentation. Layered & intense fruit flavours augur well for future enjoyment.

★★★★ **Sauvignon Blanc** ✓ ▦ 🎨 Bright & crisp **13** tank sample back to form after **11** (★★★★), with full-flavoured grassy, lemony freshness, depth & elegance. The zesty finish will complement rich fish dishes.

Alma Mater range NEW

Red ☺ ▦ ★★★ Fruity & spicy shiraz/cab combo **12** is smooth & savoury with a hint of oak for fresh early-drinking fun. **Rosé** ☺ ▦ 🎨 ★★★ Cherries & spice on fruity off-dry **13** from shiraz & malbec. Bright, crunchy berry fruit - perfect for summer. **White** ☺ ▦ 🎨 ★★★ Chenin & dollop pinot blanc combine in floral & tropical-fruited **13** party delight. Easy, juicy, with a citrus lift.

Lanzerac range
Discontinued: **Rosé**. — WB

La Petite Ferme Winery

Location/map: Franschhoek ▪ WO: Franschhoek/Western Cape ▪ Est 1972 ▪ 1stB 1996 ▪ Tasting daily from 11 by appt ▪ Fee R50pp (complimentary if you book lunch) ▪ Sales daily 8.30-5 ▪ Cellar tours from 11-12.30 ▪ Res-

taurant & guest suites ▪ Gift shop ▪ Walking/hiking trails ▪ Owner(s) Dendy Young family ▪ Cellarmaster(s)/winemaker(s) Mark Dendy Young (1996) ▪ Viticulturist(s) John Dendy Young ▪ 16ha/14ha (cabs s/f, merlot, shiraz, chard, sauv, viog) ▪ 60-70t/12,000cs own label 40% red 50% white 10% rosé ▪ PO Box 55 Franschhoek 7690 ▪ jomark@mweb.co.za ▪ www.lapetiteferme.co.za ▪ S 33° 55' 6.43" E 019° 8' 10.32" ▪ **T +27 (0)21-876-3016** ▪ F +27 (0)86-720-6284

The Dendy Young family's ever-popular restaurant, guest farm and boutique winery on Franschhoek Pass commands splendid vistas over Franschhoek town and valley. Enjoy a tasting and cellar tour before you take your seat at the lunch table, where the range features prominently on the wine list.

La Petite Ferme range

★★★★ **The Verdict** ✓ Cabernet franc-based blend (with merlot & cab), preview **12** bodes well. Harmony reigns with cassis, spice & a light leafiness. Alcohol (15.5%) well hidden on firm frame.

★★★★ **Barrel Fermented Chardonnay** 🍷 Exotic & creamy **12** bursts with apple pie & lemon curd, toasted nuts highlights from well-judged oak & lees-ageing. Refreshing citrus finish.

★★★★ **Viognier** 🍷 Fragrant peach blossom appeal on **13** (★★★★). Creamy, round, with hints of marzipan from part oaking complements the tropical fruit finish. Last **11** was a poster for the variety.

> **Baboon Rock Unwooded Chardonnay Wild Yeast Fermented** ☺ 🍷 ★★★ Named after the baboon troop that invade the vineyard, **13** is unoaked, fresh with floral appeal for easy sipping. WO W Cape.

Cabernet Sauvignon ✓ ★★★★ Brooding aromas of black fruits, dark chocolate & oak on **12**. Lush, ripe & broad with intense fruit concentration. A sprinkling of dried herbs adds complexity. Gear up on last-tasted **09** (★★★★). **Cabernet Franc** In abeyance. **Merlot** ★★★★ **12** rich fruitcake, nutmeg & mint flavours. Playful, balanced & structured, with lingering mocha finish. **Shiraz** ✓ ★★★★ **11**, a step up from **10** (★★★★) offers savoury olive, ripe mulberry, violet & dusting of white pepper. Vibrant, rich & ample smooth oak influence for a long life. **Sauvignon Blanc** 🍷 ★★★★ Tropical aromas with green fruit streaks, **13** light bodied & tangy, with a lemony zestiness, perfect for seafood.

Maison range

> **Rouge** ☺ ★★★ Gluggable cab/merlot blend **11** is harmonious & bright, with some grip. For everyday drinking. WO W Cape, like Blanc. **Rosé** ☺ 🍷 ★★★ Candyfloss & strawberries on summery sipper, **13** from merlot is gentle & fruity with crisp acidity. **Blanc** ☺ 🍷 ★★★ Picnic special **13** from chenin ticks all drinkability boxes: fruit-forward, crisp & delicious. — WB

La Petite Provence Wine Company   🍷

Location/WO: Franschhoek ▪ Est 2001 ▪ 1stB 2005 ▪ Tasting & sales Mon-Sat by appt ▪ Owner(s) La Petite Provence Wine Trust ▪ Winemaker(s) Johan van Rensburg (2003, La Provence) ▪ 3.5ha (cab, merlot) ▪ 30t/900cs own label 90% red 10% rosé ▪ 2 Cabernet Drive, La Petite Provence, Franschhoek 7690 ▪ info@lapetiteprovence.co.za ▪ www.lapetiteprovence.co.za ▪ **T +27 (0)21-876-4178/+27 (0)21-876-3860**

This small-scale Franschhoek business makes most of its wine for the residents, mainly summer visitors, of La Petite Provence Residential Estate, whose cab and merlot grapes are used in production. The balance has been exported to an agent in China, where more consignments, reports director Haydn Parry, went last year.

Cabernet Sauvignon ★★★ **11** juicy cassis & mint, with supple structure & clean, dry finish. This & all below, unoaked. **Merlot** ★★★ **11** succulent, smoky berry fruit in firm, dry tannin frame. **Mélange** ★★★ Balanced, red-fruited quaffer in **11**. Mainly merlot with cab. — MW

La Petite Vigne

Location/map: Franschhoek ▪ WO: Franschhoek/Western Cape ▪ 1stB 2012 ▪ Tasting & tours by appt only ▪ Owner(s) Kema Consulting (Kevin & Mandie Swart) ▪ Cellarmaster(s) Kevin Swart (Jan 2012) ▪ Winemaker(s) Kevin Swart (Jan 2012), with Gary Swart & Jospeh Ratabana (both Jan 2012) ▪ Viticulturist(s) Jacques Wentzel (Jan 2012, consultant) ▪ 3.3ha/2.5ha (cab) ▪ 20t/3,400cs own label 35% red 35% white 30% rosé ▪ PO Box 686 Franschhoek 7690 ▪ kevin@lapetitevigne.co.za ▪ S 33° 54' 9.00 E 019° 7' 14.00" ▪ **T +27 (0)21-876-2903/+27 (0)83-655-6611**

Kevin Swart is expanding the range (a Syrah and MCC arrive this year) at his small family winery in Franschhoek, and also gaining painful experience. The

first vintage (2012) was relatively easy, he says, but the second 'reminded us how challenging and exhausting winemaking can be... Awesome!'

La Petite Vigne range

Cabernet Sauvignon Await next. **Deep Red Rosé** 🍷 ★★★ Supple, juicily fruity **13** pink from cab, aged in older oak, leaves barely-dry, smooth impression.

Timothy White range

The Sauvignon Blanc 🍷 ★★★ Pale **13** attractively herbaceous & uncomplicated, with zesty acid edge. **The Viognier** NEW 🍷 ★★★ Peachy **12** appealingly dry & with just 13% alcohol; brisk lemony acidity defines finish. WO W Cape. — IM

■ **La Place** *see* Stellar Winery
■ **Last Chance** *see* Zoetendal Wines

Lateganskop Winery   🍴🍷

Location: Wolseley ▪ Map/WO: Breedekloof ▪ Est 1969 ▪ 1stB 2004 ▪ Tasting & sales Mon-Fri 8–12 & 1–5 ▪ Closed Easter Fri-Mon, Dec 25/26 & Jan 1 ▪ Cellar tours by appt ▪ Owner(s) 5 members ▪ Cellarmaster(s) Heinrich Lategan (Oct 2008) ▪ Winemaker(s) Heinrich Lategan, with Kean Oosthuizen (May 2011) ▪ 238ha (cab, ptage, chard, chenin, sauv, sem) ▪ 2,900t/600cs own label 70% red 30% white & ±2m L bulk ▪ PO Box 44 Breërivier 6858 ▪ lateganskop@breede.co.za ▪ S 33° 30' 57.27" E 019° 11' 13.65" ▪ **T +27 (0)23-355-1719** ▪ F +27 (0)86-637-6603

The Lategan family have been vinegrowing in the scenic Wolseley area for more than 100 years. Oupa Willie, who reached a remarkable 102, built a cellar in 1969, founding a legacy that continues today, most of the wine sold in bulk but a small portion bottled under the own Lateganskop and Twin's Peak labels.

Lateganskop Winery range

The Zahir 🔶 📖 ★★★ Fresh & appealing Cape Blend, equal cab & pinotage, **10** chocolate & ripe berry fruit.

Twin's Peak range

Pinotage 🔶 📖 ★★★ Some caramel mingles with savoury & red berries on medium-bodied **10**. **Chenin Blanc** Await next, as for **Chardonnay-Viognier** & **Hanepoot Jerepigo**. **Sauvignon Blanc** 🔶 🍷 📖 ★★ Fresh & pleasant **12** summer tipple. — JP

La Terre La Mer   🍷

Location: East London ▪ WO: Swartland ▪ Est/1stB 2008 ▪ Closed to public ▪ Owner(s) Deon le Roux, Charles Benn, Mark Wiehahn, Stef Kriel & Adrian Toma ▪ Cellarmaster(s) Partners & Peter Turck (2008, consultant) ▪ Winemaker(s) Peter Turck (2008, consultant), with Deon le Roux, Charles Benn, Mark Wiehahn, Stef & Fiona Kriel, Adrian Toma (all Jan 2008) ▪ Viticulturist(s) Various ▪ 2.5t/300cs own label 100% red ▪ 6 Princess Drive, Bonza Bay, East London 5241 ▪ dleroux@iafrica.com ▪ **T +27 (0)83-701-3148** ▪ F +27 (0)43-735-2494

Guided by winemaker Peter Turck, and empowered by a Stellenbosch University garagiste course, six wine enthusiasts are vinifying from a facility overlooking East London's Quinera Lagoon. Their maiden shiraz, still available at press time, is to be followed by a Swartland-sourced shiraz-mourvèdre blend.

Shiraz 🔶 ★★★ Step up **10** ripe red-fruit compote, leather & smoke, rounded, fuller, good length & texture. Swartland grapes, as for unrated preview **11**, light & juicy, still unformed. — IM

Lathithá Wines   🍷

Location: Cape Town ▪ WO: Western Cape ▪ Tasting by appt only ▪ Owner(s) Sheila Hlanjwa ▪ Winemaker(s) Rolf Zeitvogel & Albert Basson (both Blaauwklippen) ▪ Viticulturist(s) Christo Hamman (Blaauwklippen) ▪ 100ha (cabs s/f, malbec, merlot, shiraz, zin, viog) ▪ Washington Shopping Centre Langa 7455 ▪ info@ lathithawines.co.za ▪ www.lathithawines.co.za ▪ **T +27 (0)21-556-6029** ▪ F +27 (0)21-695-1953

Lathitha Wines is an empowerment project spearheaded by Sheila Hlanjwa, introduced to wine through a wine marketing course at Stellenbosch University. The name is derived from a Xhosa expression meaning 'sunrise', and the initiative is intended to introduce local communities to wine.

Red ⊕ 🍷 ★ Dense tannin overrode shy chocolate notes on **09** last edition. **Rosé** ⊕ 🍷 ★★ Last was **09**, with fruitily sweet wild strawberry flavours. — CR

L'Auberge du Paysan

Location/WO: Stellenbosch ▪ Closed to public ▪ Owner(s) Michael Kovensky ▪ PO Box 36825 Chempet 7442 ▪ kovensky@aroma.co.za ▪ **T +27 (0)21-529-3990** ▪ F +27 (0)21-555-3033

The country inn is closed but the vines on this small property at the edge of Raithby mission village, off Winery Road, are still producing and the grapes vinified for owner Michael Kovensky by neighbouring farmer Tjuks Roos.

Merlot ★★★ Previewed **12** shows improved fruit intensity & structure, with still-tough tannins. Should improve when settled. **Pinotage** Next awaited. — GdB

L'Avenir Vineyards

Location/map: Stellenbosch ▪ WO: Stellenbosch/Western Cape ▪ Est/1stB 1992 ▪ Tasting & sales Mon-Fri 9–5 Sat 10–4 ▪ Fee R20 ▪ Closed Easter Fri/Sun, Dec 25 & Jan 1 ▪ Cellar tours by appt ▪ BYO picnic ▪ Child friendly ▪ Luxury 4-star Country Lodge ▪ Owner(s) Advini ▪ Winemaker(s) Dirk Coetzee (Aug 2009), with Mattheus Thabo (Jan 2007) ▪ Viticulturist(s) Leigh Diedericks, with Johan Pienaar ▪ 64.9ha/27.26ha (cabs s/f, merlot, ptage, chenin, sauv) ▪ 250t/41,000cs own label 44% red 38% white 18% rosé ▪ IPW ▪ PO Box 7267 Stellenbosch 7599 ▪ info@lavenir.co.za ▪ www.larochewines.com, www.lavenir-lodge.com ▪ S 33° 53' 18.7" E 018° 50' 59.1" ▪ **T +27 (0)21-889-5001** ▪ F +27 (0)21-889-5258

This Stellenbosch winery has always retained a French accent, most obviously in its name, meaning 'the future'. If the first (Mauritian) owner was French-speaking but not French, Michel Laroche added that touch when he purchased the farm in 2005. A 2010 merger with French company Jeanjean formed a new group, Advini, the third-largest French wine producer - and now owner of L'Avenir. The wines, by Dirk Coetzee and Mattheus Thabo, have their own classic French slant: from the French classic varieties to South Africa's pinotage (together with chenin, long a signature grape here) the style is invariably one of elegance and restraint.

Single Block range

★★★★☆ **Pinotage** 📷 Range name changes from 'Icon'; its wines drop 'Grand Vin'. This always a particularly sophisticated pinotage. Unshowy yet with core intensity & concentration in fine-textured **10**. Subtle oaking enhances overall polish. To drink now would deny greater pleasure around 2016-2020.

★★★★☆ **Chenin Blanc** ⊕ 🍷 📷 Sophisticated, complex **11**. Glimpses of lees, minerals, chalk, lemon blossom & oak spice woven into creamy yet fresh mouthfeel. Dry & very long. For contemplation & ageing.

Provenance range

★★★★ **Cabernet Sauvignon** ⊕ 📷 Range name was 'Platinum'. Classic freshly ripe blackberry, blackcurrant features on **11**; typically firm yet amiable tannin backing. Deliciousness increased by moderate alcohol.

★★★★ **Pinotage** ✓ **11** takes a while to open up, but has unshowy appeal in its ripe damson, dark cherry features. Freshness & build allow for current enjoyment, but should keep. **10** (★★★★) more austere.

★★★★ **Stellenbosch Classic** ⊕ 🍷 📷 Sternish cab-based **10** (★★★★); merlot & cab franc (25%/5%) add some flesh; but with noticeable acid & rigid tannins it lacks the charm of **08**; no **09**.

★★★★ **Chenin Blanc** 🍷 📷 A little more richness, power in **12** (★★★★) than **11**, maybe due to 6 months oak (previously unwooded). Honeyed attractions, balanced acid still allow characterful drinking.

★★★★ **Brut Rosé Méthode Cap Classique** ⊕ 📷 **10** bubbly switches from chenin to chardonnay as pinotage partner. Pretty colour, packaging. Subtle red fruits, biscuity tones, fine bead & refreshing 'brut' dryness.

Merlot ☺ 🍷 📷 ★★★ Riper dark plum, meaty fruit flavours trimmed by freshness & rounded grip provide general satisfaction in **12**.

Discontinued: **Chardonnay**.

Far & Near range

Pinotage-Merlot ☺ 🍷 📷 ★★★ Fruit-focused **12** encapsulates best of both partners. Fresh, succulent, with a mere squeeze of tannin. Satisfying, moreish. **Rosé de Pinotage** ☺ 🍷 📷 ★★★ Lots of eye appeal in twinkling pink **13**. And a wealth of juicy raspberries, redcurrants; perkily fresh & dry.

Pinotage Export only, not tasted, as for **Chenin Blanc**. Range name changes from 'Classic'. All these WO W Cape. **Sauvignon Blanc** ✓ 🍴 🖫 ★★★★ 'Crispy white' advises **13** label; gently but refreshingly so. Apple blossom, Pink Lady apple scents enhance overall charm. — AL

La Vierge Private Cellar

Location: Hermanus ▪ Map: Elgin, Walker Bay & Bot River ▪ WO: Hemel-en-Aarde Ridge ▪ Est 1997 ▪ 1stB 2006 ▪ Tasting & sales daily 10–5 ▪ Closed Good Fri & Dec 25 ▪ Cellar tours by appt ▪ La Vierge Restaurant & Champagne Verandah ▪ Tour groups by appt ▪ Owner(s) La Vierge Wines (Pty) Ltd & Viking Pony Properties 355 (Pty) Ltd ▪ Winemaker(s) Gerhard Smith (Nov 2012), with Jan Fortuin (Jun 2009) ▪ Viticulturist(s) Petrus Bothma (2008) ▪ 90ha/40ha (pinot, sangio, shiraz, chard, riesling, sauv, sem) ▪ 75t ▪ 50% red 50% white ▪ PO Box 1580 Hermanus 7200 ▪ info@lavierge.co.za ▪ www.lavierge.co.za ▪ S 34° 22' 22.3" E 019° 14' 29.4" ▪ **T** +27 (0)28-313-0130 ▪ F +27 (0)28-312-1388

With some of the most original and evocative labels on the market, sourced from myths, legends, history and biblical stories, La Vierge ('The Virgin', because this Hemel-en-Aarde farm was virgin land) has added another wine to the range. Well-priced Seduction Pinot Noir has the label to match its name and is aimed at a younger market. That's two Pinots they offer, in an area with a particular focus on the variety. And fittingly, new winemaker Gerhard Smith has just returned from 9 years in New Zealand, where he won awards for his pinot.

La Vierge range

★★★★ **La Vierge Noir Pinot Noir** The expected varietal elegance in **12** yet packed with flavour. Offers raspberries, cherries & a lovely oak savouriness, succulent & streamlined to the end.

La Vierge Collection

★★★★ **Original Sin Sauvignon Blanc** ☺ Classic styling in **11** thanks to cool growing conditions, good handling; minerality & earth, elegant & tight focus, with an extended finish. Some own H-&-A Valley grapes. **Seduction Pinot Noir** NEW 🍴 ★★★ Fruit-driven **12** charms with its raspberry-infused succulence, the touch of oak only apparent on the dry finish. **Anthelia Shiraz** ✓ ★★★★ Smoky plums are woven throughout **11**'s light-textured juicy palate, giving delicious drinkability. Not for long ageing. **Nymphomane Cabernet Sauvignon-Cabernet Franc-Malbec-Merlot** ★★★★ **11** shows its ripeness in creamy black plums, meat extract, while deft oaking gives black pepper spice, supple tannins. **Satyricon Sangiovese-Nebbiolo** ✓ ★★★★ Italy's classic varieties give **11** a food-friendly dry finish but in addition offer juicy black cherries & savoury spice. **Jezebelle Chardonnay** ★★★★ Sleekly built, partly unoaked **12**'s lime & white peach flavours, crisp acidity offer a flavour-packed refreshing dining companion. **Last Temptation Riesling** ★★★ Offering a svelte food-styled dry version of riesling, **11**'s gently spiced floral tones end on a mineral note.

Special Vintage Releases

Discontinued: **The Affair**, **Redemption Sauvignon Blanc**. — CR

Lazanou Organic Vineyards

Location/WO: Wellington ▪ Map: Paarl & Wellington ▪ Est 2002 ▪ 1stB 2006 ▪ Tasting & sales by appt ▪ Open days with wine & food pairing - booking required ▪ Tour groups ▪ Farm produce ▪ Owner(s) Josef Lazarus & Candice Stephanou ▪ Winemaker(s) Rolanie Lotz (Jan 2011, consultant) ▪ Viticulturist(s) Johan Wiese (Jan 2006, consultant) ▪ 8.48ha/5.54ha (mourv, shiraz, chard, chenin, viog) ▪ 50t/6,000cs own label 50% red 50% white ▪ Organic certification by SGS ▪ PO Box 834 Wellington 7654 ▪ wine@lazanou.co.za ▪ www.lazanou.co.za ▪ S 33° 35' 59.58" E 018° 59' 36.12" ▪ **T** +27 (0)83-265-6341 ▪ F +27 (0)86-670-9213

The organic ethos at this tiny family estate near Wellington goes way beyond the vineyards, encompassing home-grown food and harmony with nature at all levels (and a Jersey cow named Gertrude). Their popular Open Day food-and-wine pairing events allow visitors to partake of their bounty in al fresco splendour.

Syrah 🌿 ★★★★★ Single-vineyard **11** outclasses **09** (★★★★) with understated elegance, succulent pure fruit, delicate spice & precise oaking. Rich & flavoursome, with a lovely moreish smoothness. **Syrah-Mourvèdre** 🌿 ★★★★ Back to form, **11** bright sweet-ripe berries, a firm backbone of oak & espresso lift. Needs time to reveal full charm. **Chardonnay** 🌿 Await next. **Chenin Blanc** 🌿 ★★★★ Creamy, understated **13** trumps **11** (★★★★), tropical fruit & hint of vanilla oak, well structured with lees-ageing adding complexity. Impressive texture & structure for ageing. **12** sold out untasted. **Viognier** 🍴 🌿 ★★★ **13** lacks

gravitas of previous, faint wafts of peach blossom, hint of vanilla. Soft & easy conclusion. **Chenin Blanc-Chardonnay-Viognier** ✿ ★★★ Shy peach & stonefruit perfume on unoaked **13**, light fruit flavours & subdued farewell. — WB

▪ **Lazy Days** *see Laborie Wine Farm*
▪ **LB** *see Anura Vineyards*
▪ **Leatherwood** *see Prospect1870*
▪ **Le Bistro** *see Zandvliet Wine Estate & Thoroughbred Stud*

Le Bonheur Wine Estate

Location/map/WO: Stellenbosch ▪ Est 1790s ▪ 1stB 1972 ▪ Tasting & sales Mon-Fri 9–5 Sat/Sun 10–4 ▪ Fee R15/5 wines ▪ Closed Good Fri, Dec 25 & Jan 1 ▪ Conferences ▪ Foreign film festival, every last Fri of the month - booking essential ▪ Owner(s) Lusan Premium Wines ▪ Cellarmaster(s)/winemaker(s)/viticulturist(s) Sakkie Kotzé (Oct 1993) ▪ 163ha/75ha (cab, merlot, chard, sauv) ▪ 560t/60,000cs own label 30% red 65% white 5% rosé ▪ PO Box 104 Stellenbosch 7599 ▪ info@lebonheur.co.za ▪ www.lebonheur.co.za ▪ S 33° 50′ 1.0″ E 018° 52′ 21.4″ ▪ **T +27 (0)21-875-5478** ▪ F +27 (0)21-875-5624

Part of the original Natte Valleij land grant, this estate on the northern slopes of Stellenbosch's Klapmuts Hill was hived off in 1820. Until 1970 it was known as Oude Weltevreden, then became Le Bonheur ('Happiness') under part-ownership of Bergkelder. It's now in the Lusan portfolio. In one of the Cape's longer tenures, Sakkie Kotzé has been managing cellar and vineyards for 20+ years. The natural Le Bonheur style, he says, is 'wines with soft, ripe tannins that can age for years'.

★★★★ **Cabernet Sauvignon** ⏻ **09** firmly fruit, soundly dry to please the classically inclined drinker. Lovely ripe & fresh cab fruit too, ending on a savoury note. 18 months in oak give a complementary polish.

★★★★ **Prima** ⏻ Unshowy, elegantly fresh **08** Bordeaux red. Merlot-led but shows cab's strong, informing tannins. Drinkable but should improve for good few years.

★★★★ **Tricorne** ⏻ Cab, cab franc, shiraz blend in slightly plusher mode for this winery. **09**'s bright, mint, spicy features enliven soft, fleshy core, add sweet-fruited length to dry hilka. Tasty if fairly straightforward.

★★★★ **Single Vineyard Sauvignon Blanc** NEW ▤ ▨ **12** more flinty, citrus vigour than standard bottling; firm mineral palate broadened by 6 months on lees. Concentrated, with ripe length & moderate alcohol.

Pinot Noir Rosé ⏻ ▨ ★★★ Salmon-hued **11** with gently refreshing strawberries-&-cream flavours, unaggressively dry. **Chardonnay** ▨ ★★★★ Previewed **13** follows in fruit-forward style of last-tasted **11**. Juicy pineapple/lemon features; judicious oak spice. Promises enjoyable, easy drinking. **Sauvignon Blanc** ▤ ★★★★ **12** returns to form. Gently fresh, with ripe, lees-enriched tropical fruit & limy, flinty overtones. — AL

▪ **Leeumasker** *see Maske Wines*

Leeuwenberg

WO: Darling/Bot River/Coastal/Paarl/Western Cape ▪ Est/1stB 2010 ▪ Tasting only in Wiesbaden, Germany Mon-Fri 11-7 Sat 10-6 ▪ Closed all pub hols ▪ Owner(s) Tanja Kastien-Hilka ▪ Winemaker(s) Frank Kastien & Kobie Viljoen ▪ 2,500cs own label 70% red 30% white ▪ PO Box 50723 West Beach 7449 ▪ sales@ leeuwenbergwines.com ▪ www.leeuwenbergwines.com ▪ **T +49 (0)611-308-6778**

The mainly exported Leeuwenberg wines since founding in 2010 have been sourced from around the winelands by Tanja Kastien-Hilka and her team with a focus on the German market, aiming to offer both value and interest.

Flagship range

Barrel Selection Pinotage NEW ★★★★ **12** has sweetish charm from both oak & ultra-ripe fruit, the rich profile including milk chocolate & cherry cola. Paarl WO. **Two Barrels Shiraz** ▨ ★★★★ Previewed **11** from Bot River is very showy, 15% cab adding structure. Needs time for the oak dominance to settle & integrate. Not as accomplished as **10** (★★★★). **Cellar Blend** NEW ★★★ Bordeaux mix cab, merlot & cab franc is ripe fruited but also big on grip & freshness, **09** for country casseroles. **Raphael Cape Blend** ▤ ★★★ **12** combo pinotage, cab, shiraz & petit verdot shows rich fruit-forwardness, leading to oaky palate, all very boldly styled. Coastal WO. **Sauvignon Blanc** Next awaited.

Drie Kleine Leeuwen range

Shiraz-Cabernet Sauvignon NEW ★★★ Herbal twist to **11**, savoury rather than fruity. WO W Cape. **Pinotage Rosé** NEW ▤ ★★ Reddish pink colour, with tart red berry fruit on dry **12**. **Chardonnay**

Unwooded 📖 ★★★ Ripe peach aromas & stonefruit lead to soft palate of **12**, with easy appeal. Range last listed as 'De Kleine Leeuwen'. Discontinued: **Shiraz, Cape Blend**. — JP

Leeuwenjacht

Location: Paarl ▪ WO: Western Cape/Coastal ▪ Est 1692 ▪ 1stB 1989 ▪ Closed to public ▪ Winemaker(s) Adele Dunbar ▪ 20,000cs own label + 5,000cs for clients ▪ Brands for clients: Cubana ▪ PO Box 583 Suider-Paarl 7624 ▪ info@fairview.co.za ▪ www.deleeuwenjagtwines.co.za ▪ **T +27 (0)21-863-2450** ▪ F +27 (0)21-863-2591

This brand of entry-level wines, much favoured and supported by restaurants around the country, is made by Fairview's Adele Dunbar, using classic varieties and combinations to make it accessible and friendly.

Leeuwenrood ☺ 📖 🍷 ★★★ **11** unwooded blend of shiraz, cab & merlot mixes jammy black & red fruits with cough drop finish in fresh, zippy quaffer. Coastal WO.

Rosé 📖 🍷 ★★★ Hints of liquorice & aniseed on spicy **13** preview with strawberry fruit. Clean, fresh & dry, cries out for summer food. **Leeuwenblanc** 📖 ★★★ Peach blossom notes from chenin & viognier in **12**, slightly less concentration than previous but fresh, clean & appetising. **Nuance** 📖 🍷 ★★★ Unusual combo muscadel & sauvignon, **13** ex tank aromatic & off-dry everyday drinker. — CM

Leeuwenkuil Family Vineyards

Location: Paarl/Swartland/Stellenbosch ▪ WO: Coastal/Swartland ▪ Est 2008 ▪ 1stB 2011 ▪ Closed to public ▪ Owner(s) Willie & Emma Dreyer ▪ MD Kobus de Kock ▪ Cellarmaster(s) Pieter Carstens (Aug 2008) ▪ Winemaker(s) Gustav Fouche & Johan Gerber (both Dec 2012), Corrien Geleijnse & Bernard Allison (both Jan 2012), with Jehan de Jongh (Aug 2008) ▪ Viticulturist(s) Koos van der Merwe (Dec 2008) & Claude Uren (Jan 2012) ▪ 4,550ha ▪ 32,500t/24m L ▪ 70% red 30% white ▪ WIETA ▪ PO Box 249 Koelenhof 7605 ▪ kobus@leeuwenkuilfv.co.za ▪ **T +27 (0)21-865-2455** ▪ F +27 (0)21-865-2780

Grapes from Willie and Emma Dreyer's vast vineyard holdings in Swartland and Paarl have been channelled anonymously into many vaunted brands over the years. They then founded their own Leeuwenkuil label, named for the historic home-farm. The wines may represent a mere drop in overall production but it's clearly a thoughtfully made, rather tasty and even impressive drop.

★★★★ **Family Reserve White** ✓ 📖 Like previous, richly fruited **12** is half chenin plus 4 others. Smart aromatics include nuts & orange rind, leading to savoury & textured palate, integrated oak. Ends just-dry.

Shiraz ☺ 📖 ★★★ Unoaked **12** has light coriander & nutmeg spice, mingled with ripe mulberry fruit, leading to soft-fruited, easy-drinking palate. **Chenin Blanc** ☺ 📖 ★★★ Pretty stonefruit & ripe apple allure on **13**, clean & fresh, happy sipping for friends or food. These two both WO Swartland.

Family Reserve Red 🥇 📖 🍷 ★★★★ Savoury, spicy shiraz-based blend. **11** deftly executed, & showing potential in the way older oak forms a supple framework on which to hang fresh, vibrant smoke-laced fruit. **Rosé** NEW 📖 ★★ Fresh **13** from cab & merlot, green-fruit flavours, light & near-dry. — JP

Le Fût

Location/WO: Paarl ▪ Map: Paarl & Wellington ▪ Est 2004 ▪ 1stB 2005 ▪ Tasting by appt ▪ Conference/function/wedding venue ▪ Owner(s) Trevor & Joan Ernstzen ▪ Winemaker(s) Trevor Ernstzen (Nov 2004) ▪ Viticulturist(s) Joan Ernstzen (Nov 2004) ▪ ±17ha/9ha (shiraz, chenin, cbard, riesling) ▪ 80t/600cs own label 100% red ▪ PO Box 156 Paarl 7622 ▪ wine@lefut.co.za ▪ www.lefut.co.za ▪ S 33° 44' 34.38" E 019° 0' 39.90" ▪ **T +27 (0)83-561-1555** ▪ F +27 (0)86-675-5114

Le Fût, Trevor and Joan Ernstzen's Paarl winery, this year celebrates 10 years of being nano (just 600 cases a year) and proudly artisanal. So: Congratulations! However, given Trevor's bucket list - making full-grain beer and charcuterie - we might be toasting a much diversified home of handcrafting a decade from now...

Shiraz Reserve 🥇 ★★★ Development shows on interesting **07**. Not heavy (though big 15% alcohol) though shy on fruit, with more savoury, smoky & earthy notes to follow. — JP

■ **Legends of the Labyrinth** see Doolhof Wine Estate

Le Grand Chasseur Wine Estate

Location/map: Robertson ▪ Est 1881 ▪ 1stB 1999 ▪ Tasting by appt ▪ Closed all pub hols ▪ Owner(s) Albertus de Wet ▪ Cellarmaster(s)/winemaker(s) Carel Botha (Jan 2011) ▪ Viticulturist(s) Francois Viljoen (Jan 1998, consultant) ▪ ±1,300ha/300ha (cab, merlot, ptage, ruby cab, shiraz, chard, chenin, cbard, muscadel w, nouvelle, sauv) ▪ ±4,500t ▪ IPW ▪ PO Box 439 Robertson 6705 ▪ cellar@lgc.co.za, sales@lgc.co.za ▪ www.lgc.co.za ▪ S 33° 48' 26.8" E 019° 52' 40.1" ▪ **T +27 (0)23-626-1048** ▪ F +27 (0)23-626-1048

Named after the splendid African Fish Eagles which frequent this stretch of the Breede River, the de Wet family winery near Robertson is benefiting from increased sales into Canada. There have been considerable replantings, so production two years hence is something cellarmaster Carel Botha is relishing.

▪ **Leipoldt 1880** see Wineways Marketing

Leipzig Winery

Map: Worcester ▪ Est/1stB 2013 ▪ Tasting, sales & cellar tours Sat/Sun 10-3; or by appt ▪ Closed Ash Wednesday, Easter Monday, Dec 25 & Jan 1 ▪ Raven-ous restaurant Sat/Sun 11.30-2 ▪ Facilities for children ▪ Tour groups ▪ Conferences ▪ Weddings/functions ▪ Walks/hikes ▪ Mountain biking trail ▪ Guided tours by appt: historic buildings & art ▪ Leipzig Country House ▪ Owner(s) Francois & Lida Smit ▪ Cellarmaster(s)/winemaker(s) Mark Carmichael Green (Feb 2013, consultant) ▪ 10ha/4.5ha (sauv) ▪ 26t/2,917cs own label 49% red 51% white ▪ PO Box 5104 Worcester 6849 ▪ winery@leipzigcountryhouse.co.za ▪ www.leipzigcountryhouse.co.za ▪ S33° 38' 29.90" E 019° 38' 9.44" ▪ **T +27 (0)23-347-8422** ▪ F +27 (0)86-295-5116

New to this guide but not to the wine world, Leipzig farm and luxury accommodation in Nuy Valley near Worcester has a winemaking history dating from the 1890s to 1963. British royalty even enjoyed their blend, White Leipzig, post WWII. Winemaking has been revived by owners Francois and Lida Smit, guided by consultant Mark Carmichael-Green. Adding a touch of nostalgia is the new-generation White Leipzig, a viognier, chardonnay, chenin and sauvignon blend.

Le Joubert

Location/WO: Paarl ▪ Map: Paarl & Wellington ▪ Est 1693 ▪ 1stB 2007 ▪ Tasting & sales by appt ▪ Owner(s) Dawie & Alison Joubert ▪ Cellarmaster(s)/winemaker(s) Dawie Joubert ▪ 25ha/4ha (cab, p verdot) ▪ 20t/2,000cs own label 90% red 10% white ▪ PO Box 2963 Paarl 7620 ▪ alison@lejoubert.com ▪ www.lejoubert.com, www.lejoubert.co.za ▪ S 33° 43' 29.02" E 018° 57' 16.61" ▪ **T +27 (0)21-870-1070/+27 (0)82-552-3671** ▪ F +27 (0)87-803-7886

A boutique red-wine label owned by Dawie and Alison Joubert, and the latest passion for the ex-Gauteng motor trade entrepreneur, car-and-racing mad Dawie. Self taught, he makes the kind of traditional robust reds he enjoys. Sample them at the private tasting venue in the Jouberts' new residence on their Paarl estate.

1070 ⓕ ★★★☆ Named for days between harvest & release. Cab-led **09** deft marriage showy cassis & new oak, good grip, ageworthy. **1070s** ⓕ ★★★☆ Shiraz-led with 4 Bordeaux varieties. **09** spice-laden rich fruitcake, mocha chocolate. Savoury foundation & length from new oak. **Brillianté** ⓕ Await next. **Viognier** ⓕ ★★☆ Pear & barley sugar, wooded **10** shows maturity, honeyed tones. Enjoy soon. — CR

Le Lude Méthode Cap Classique

Location: Franschhoek ▪ Est 2009 ▪ 1stB 2012 ▪ Tasting by appt only ▪ Owner(s) Nic & Ferda Barrow ▪ Winemaker(s) Paul Gerber (May 2010) ▪ Viticulturist(s) Eben Archer (2011, consultant) & Alain Deloire (2011, consultant/research) ▪ 6.2ha/3.4ha (pinot noir/meunier, chard) ▪ 50t/5,200cs own label 100% MCC ▪ PO Box 578 Franschhoek 7609 ▪ paulgerberwyn@gmail.com ▪ www.lelude.co.za ▪ **T +27 (0)82-321-0820** ▪ F +27 (0)44-279-1793

In 2009, Nic and Ferda Barrow, who own a portfolio of hotels and country houses, decided to build a specialist méthode cap classique cellar in Franschhoek to express their passion for wine. Paul Gerber was later appointed winemaker after internships at bubbly houses both here and abroad. The approach is traditional – some of the secondary fermentation on cork rather than crown-cap, higher

volumes than usual of reserve wines and a minimum maturation period of 36 months - maiden vintage 2012 is set for release next year.

Le Manoir de Brendel

Location/map/WO: Franschhoek ▪ Est/1stB 2003 ▪ Tasting daily 12-4 ▪ Fee R40pp, waived on purchase ▪ Sales daily 7.30-4.30 ▪ Closed Good Fri, Dec 25/26 & Jan 1; also closed when booked for weddings/conferences ▪ Group lunches on request, book ahead ▪ Facilities for children ▪ Gift shop ▪ Conferences: day package (60 pax)/ overnight package incl 9 rooms ▪ Walks ▪ Weddings (up to 60 pax) with chapel & wooden terrace on the river ▪ 5-star guest house (10 suites) ▪ Spa, booking essential ▪ Owner(s) Christian & Maren Brendel ▪ Winemaker(s) Cerina de Jongh & Gerda Willers ▪ Viticulturist(s) Paul Wallace (consultant) ▪ 30ha/±23ha (cab, merlot, ptage, shiraz, chard, chenin, sauv, sem) ▪ ±150t ▪ PO Box 117 La Motte Franschhoek 7691 ▪ lmb@brendel.co.za ▪ www.le-manoir-de-brendel.com ▪ S 33° 52' 52.8" E 019° 3' 42.2" ▪ **T +27 (0)21-876-4525** ▪ F +27 (0)21-876-4524

Christian Brendel, co-owner of luxury Franschhoek tourism and wine venue Le Manoir de Brendel, says winemaking is a hobby which enables him and spouse Maren to bypass commercial considerations and mature their wines in bottle for three or more years. Understandably, the couple enjoy very much sitting incognito near restaurant guests extolling the quality of their wines.

Le Manoir de Brendel Collection
Shiraz Await next.

Brendel Collection
Cabernet Sauvignon ⓦ ★★★ Mature **07** rhubarb & prune notes, firm tannin structure for food pairing. **Merlot** ⓦ ★★★ Tobacco, dried tomato & fruit-sweet edge to **06**, was nearing drink-by date when last reviewed. **Pinotage** ⓦ ★★★ Sweet fruit, spicy aromas & typical acetone whiffs on ready **08**; handles 15% alcohol with aplomb. **Shiraz** ⓦ ★★★ Engaging sweet-sour yin-yang on meaty **06**; soft textured, slips down easily. — GdB,FM

Lemberg Wine Estate

Location/map/WO: Tulbagh ▪ Est 1978 ▪ Tasting, sales & cellar tours Mon-Fri 9-5 Sat/Sun 10-3 ▪ Fee R15 waived on purchase ▪ Closed Easter Fri/Sat/Mon, Dec 25 & Jan 1 ▪ Meals, cheese platters & picnics by appt - book prior to visit ▪ BYO picnic ▪ Table olives & olive oil ▪ Function venue (40-60 pax) ▪ 3 self-catering guest cottages (sleeps 2, 4 & 6 respectively) ▪ Fly fishing (equipment available) ▪ Sunset rowboat trips by prior arrangement ▪ Owner(s) Henk du Bruyn ▪ Winemaker(s) David Sadie (Feb 2011), with Sheree Nothnagel (Jan 2013) ▪ Viticulturist(s) David Sadie (Feb 2011), Sheree Nothnagel (Jan 2013) & consultants ▪ 21ha/9ha (grenache, ptage, pinot, shiraz, hárslevelü, sauv, viog) ▪ 80t/9,000cs own label 60% red 30% white 9% rosé 1% vine dried sauv ▪ IPW, Envirowines (2012) ▪ PO Box 221 Tulbagh 6820 ▪ suzette@lemberg.co.za ▪ www.lemberg.co.za ▪ S 33° 18' 8.27" E 019° 6' 23.06" ▪ **T +27 (0)21-300-1130** ▪ F +27 (0)21-300-1131

There's a strong impetus by owner Henk de Bruyn and rising-star winemaker David Sadie to rejuvenate and improve the once-flagging fortunes at this small Tulbagh estate. The cellar and tasting facilities have been extensively remodelled, and vineyards replaced or nursed back to health. Now in their third new-era vintage, results are beginning to show in the fast-improving range. This edition sees the return of former owner Janey Muller's legacy: a varietal hárslevelü.

Yellow Label range
★★★★ **Hárslevelü** NEW Rare-in-SA white grape, long associated with Hungarian sweet white, here made dry & in unashamedly oxidative style, with oaky spice, roasted nuts & sherry-like notes on full-bodied **12**.

★★★★ **Lady** NEW Innovative mix of oxidatively made (in older wood) viognier (57%), hárslevelü & semillon, plus tank-fermented sauvignon. Conversation-starting **12** succulent & poised, with subtle gingery spicing.

★★★★☆ **Surin** ▨ Standout dessert from vine-dried sauvignon, older oak fermented. **12** (★★★★) barrel sample oozes honeyed raisins, baked apples, glacé pineapples, the decadent richness well refreshed by lively acidity, though overall a touch more unctuous than elegant, spicy **11**.

Pinot Noir ▨ ★★★ Genteel **12** lightly perfumed with violets & red berries, gently dusted with oak for easy enjoyment. **Spencer** ▨ ★★★ From pinotage. New oak portion, no whole-berry fermentation distinguishes this from White label offering. Subtle **11** opens in the glass to layered fruit, serious structure.

White Label range NEW

Syrah ☺ ★★★ **12** goes up a notch with savoury tones of roast beef & stewed prunes, firm tannins to match hearty winter stews.

Pinotage ▨ ★★★☆ Dark coffee & tobacco nuances on bright & fresh **11**. Drinks well now but with sufficient savoury, pliable tannins to improve few years. **Cape Blend** ★★★ Supple shiraz-led **12**, with pinotage & splash pinot noir, offers earthy mulberry flavours. **Syrah Blanc de Noir** ▤ ▨ **13** tank sample too young to rate, shows appealing light texture. **Sauvignon Blanc** ▤ ▨ Partly wooded **13** preview too unformed to rate. Follows impressive **12** (★★★★) from 33 year old vines. — GdB,MW

■ **Le Noe** *see Barnardt Boyes Wines*

Leopard Frog Vineyards

Location/WO: Stellenbosch ▪ Closed to public ▪ Owner(s) Dogwood Trust ▪ Cellarmaster(s)/winemaker(s) David John Bate (Jun 2005) ▪ 1,500cs own label 60% red 40% white ▪ Fairtrade ▪ 8 Royal Ascot Lane Sandown Sandton 2196 ▪ info@leopard-frog.com ▪ www.leopard-frog.com ▪ **T +27 (0)11-884-3304** ▪ F +27 (0)11-883-0426

Fairtrade-accredited David Bate's output may be 'ridiculously small', but his creativity in crafting innovative and interesting wines (and labels) is boundless. The Canadian's bottlings are also unusual in being marketed with a range of branded chocolates and cigars 'for wine enthusiasts who appreciate bespoke experiences'.

Proprietor's Limited Releases

Aphrodite Africa Await new vintage, as for **Midnight Maasai Shiraz**, **Spellbinding Chenin Blanc** & **Singularity**. **Tantra** ⊕ ★★★ Cab franc's perfume & supple structure temper oak on Bordeaux red blend. Lower-key **06** lacks gravitas & fruit of **05** (★★★★). **Tribe** ★★★ **07** pinotage & its parents pinot noir & cinsaut. Silk-textured & balanced, with earthy red fruit. For current enjoyment. **Kiss & Tell** ⊕ ★★★ **06** ripe & savoury shiraz-led blend with shade less fruit-filled intrigue. For early drinking. **Tao** ⊕ ★★★ **09** quirky blend, mainly zinfandel with sangiovese & barbera. Supple, with bright savoury red fruit & lively drinkability. **Ingénue** ⊕ ▨ ★★★ **11** savoury, tangy cab rosé. Feisty oak (all new) requires food. **Titillation** NEW ▨ ★★★ Limited-release **NV** champagne-method pink sparkling from, highly unusually, pinotage. Vivacious berry/cherry tone with enough fruit to soften bone-dry 'brut nature' styling & crisp, short finish. **Tryst MCC Blanc de Blancs Brut** ⊕ ★★★ Lengthy lees-aged **08** chardonnay méthode cap classique bubbly is dry, smooth & waxy. — MW

Leopard's Leap Family Vineyards

Location/map: Franschhoek ▪ WO: Western Cape ▪ Est 2000 ▪ Tasting & sales Tue-Sat 9-5 Sun 11-5 ▪ Fee R25/5 wines ▪ Hands-on cooking classes ▪ Shop: lifestyle gifts, wine accessories, tableware, linen ware, kitchen utensils & equipment, food literature ▪ Rotisserie lunches Wed-Sun 11.30-3 ▪ Child friendly ▪ Owner(s) Hanneli Rupert-Koegelenberg & Hein Koegelenberg ▪ Cellarmaster(s) Eugene van Zyl (Nov 2002) ▪ 600,000cs own label 60% red 39% white 1% rosé ▪ PO Box 1 La Motte 7691 ▪ info@leopards-leap.com ▪ www.leopards-leap.com ▪ **T +27 (0)21-876-8002** ▪ F +27 (0)21-876-4156

Launched in 2000 as the in-house range of Rupert-family-aligned wine services group Historic Wines of the Cape, Leopard's Leap was for export to the UK. Now under the aegis of Hanneli Rupert-Koegelenberg and husband Hein, it reaches more than forty countries – most recently China – from its chic Franschhoek base. The new for-food Culinaria Collection expands the portfolio, and underscores the brand philosophy that quality and affordability aren't mutually exclusive.

Culinaria Collection NEW

★★★★ **Grand Vin** ✓ Merlot-led Bordeaux blend lives up to its name. **10** lilting tobacco & forest floor aromas herald plush, velvety red berry fruit. Year 40% new oak seamlessly integrated. Ready to drink.

★★★★ **Shiraz-Grenache** ✓ ▨ Handsome package matched by content; **10** earthy, smoky allure, generous dark fruit flavours & super balance in a grippy finish. With 10% cinsaut.

Pinot Noir-Chardonnay ▨ ★★★ Onion skin blush, brimming red berry fruit in undemanding, charming dry **12** rosé. **Muscat de Frontignan** ★★★ Enticing saffron hue, **13** pleasant red fruit flavour but needs more

verve to balance 85 g/l residual sugar. **Chenin Blanc-Grenache Blanc** ✓ 📖 ★★★★ Blend of Perdeberg grapes, barrel fermented; **12** has earthy grip & quince flavour balanced by perky fruit acidity. **Méthode Cap Classique** 📖 ★★★★ Lively dry **NV** bubbly from 55% chardonnay with pinots noir & meunier, 2 years on lees. Tart, appley flavour stimulates the appetite.

Family Collection
Shiraz-Mourvèdre-Viognier ✓ 📖 ★★★★ Exotic tang of viognier pervades sultry **11** & fills the already ample choc-mocha palate. 2 years in oak reflect wine's serious intent. Discontinued: **Chenin Blanc**.

Classic range

> **Cabernet Sauvignon** ☺ 🍴 ★★★ Open styling of cassis-laden **11** delicious in youth. Like all reds, manageable 13.5% alcohol. **Merlot** ☺ 🍴 📖 ★★★ Floral/violet charm to plummy, meaty depth of flavour in firm, oaky **11**. **Cabernet Sauvignon-Merlot** ☺ 🍴 ★★★ Velvety 2:1 blend, **11** glossy red fruit woven with svelte tannins. **Chardonnay** ☺ 🍴 📖 ★★★ Unwooded **13** lemon-&-lime flavour with herby grip. **Chenin Blanc** ☺ 🍴 📖 ★★★ Boisterous tropical fruit of **13** brought to order in tasty dry tail. **Sauvignon Blanc** ☺ 🍴 📖 ★★★ Grassy/melon **13** profile tightened by lipsmacking citrus tang.

Shiraz 🍴 ★★★ Smoky, leather-toned berry fruit gripped by firm tannins; **11** better with food than solo.

Lookout range
Cabernet Sauvignon-Shiraz-Cinsaut 🍴 📖 ★★ Down-to-earth berry fruit in chunky **12**. **Pinotage Rosé** 🍴 📖 ★★ Just-dry **13** a tad less generous than usual, still zippy. **Semi Sweet** 🍴 📖 ★★ From chenin, **13**'s candyfloss appeal is balanced by fresh acid. **Chenin Blanc-Chardonnay** 🍴 📖 ★★ Zesty fillip to summer sunshine richness of **13**, ends just-dry. — DS

Le Pommier Wines

Location/map: Stellenbosch ▪ WO: Banghoek/Stellenbosch ▪ Est/1stB 2003 ▪ Private tastings by appt; wine sales during restaurant hours ▪ Facilities for children ▪ Petting zoo ▪ Picnics ▪ Le Pommier Restaurant ▪ Spa ▪ Accommodation ▪ Owner(s) Marietjie van der Merwe ▪ Winemaker(s) Neil Moorhouse ▪ Viticulturist(s) Hannes Jansen van Vuuren ▪ 16ha/4.8ha (malbec, sauv) ▪ 4,000cs own label 45% red 55% white ▪ PO Box 1595 Stellenbosch 7599 ▪ info@lepommier.co.za ▪ www.lepommier.co.za ▪ S 33° 55' 8.58" E 018° 55' 43.14" ▪ T +27 (0)21-885-1269/+27 (0)21-885-1561 ▪ F +27 (0)21-885-1274

Like many other properties at the top of Stellenbosch's Helshoogte this was originally an apple farm, hence the name. Today it boasts a spa, wine lounge, country lodge, restaurant and a petting zoo. The wine range is made by Zorgvliet.

★★★★★ **Five-Three-Five** 🥂 🍴 From single-vineyard planted at altitude of 535 m. Sweet tropical **11** (★★★★) last year lacked some of the verve of **10**, though natural ferment imparted lovely mouthfilling texture. **Cabernet Sauvignon Reserve** Next awaited, as for **Jonathan's Malbec, Rosé** & **Natural Sweet Sauvignon Blanc**. **Chenin Blanc** 🥂 🍴 ★★★★ Flavoursome **10** tasted some years ago had frisky acidity enlivened by ripe tropical flavours. **Sauvignon Blanc** 🥂 🍴 ★★★ Easy, fresh, uncomplicated tank sample **11**. Discontinued: **Shiraz**. — AL

Le Riche Wines

Location/WO: Stellenbosch ▪ Map: Helderberg ▪ Est 1996 ▪ 1stB 1997 ▪ Tasting, sales & cellar tours Mon-Fri 8. 30-4.30 Sat by appt ▪ Closed all pub hols ▪ Owner(s) Etienne le Riche ▪ Cellarmaster(s) Etienne le Riche (Jan 1997) ▪ Winemaker(s) Christo le Riche (Jan 2010), with Mark Daniels (Sep 2000) ▪ 70t/9,000cs own label 90% red 10% white ▪ PO Box 6295 Stellenbosch 7612 ▪ wine@leriche.co.za ▪ www.leriche.co.za ▪ S 34° 0'52. 87" E 018° 48' 9.06" ▪ T +27 (0)21-842-3472 (cellar)/+27 (0)79-542-2343 (sales/marketing) ▪ F +27 (0)21-842-3472

Winemaker Etienne le Riche established his own label after moving from Rustenberg in the mid-1990s, and set up shop in an old cellar in Jonkershoek Valley. Now, at last, he has his own purpose-built winery in the Firgrove/Raithby area of Stellenbosch, on a smallholding he recently acquired. The grapes continue to be sourced around Stellenbosch, however. Of course, the fine new cellar has traditional cement fermenters (plus modern tweaks). But now son Christo is in charge of winemaking (daughter Yvonne is also fully involved) – his first vintage was 2010, evidencing a turn to riper power. There's also a re-born wine,

cleverly called Richesse, bearing the first of the redesigned labels. Plenty that's new, then. But, says Etienne with a smile, 'there's really no change...'.

★★★★☆ **Cabernet Sauvignon Reserve** Undoubtedly impressive, flattering & powerful **10**, though without the harmonious elegance of some earlier vintages - big, balanced 15% alcohol relevant here. Ripe, intense flavours - more loganberry than blackcurrant. Gorgeously melting but firm tannins.

★★★★☆ **Etienne le Riche CWG Auction Reserve Cabernet Sauvignon** Single-vineyard bottling. Lusciously ripe **10** more oaky in youth than other Reserve, & a little more intense, muscular, burly & less prettily charming. Power (15+% alcohol) & firm structure well balanced by fruit. Impressive now, should mature well.

★★★★ **Cabernet Sauvignon** Wonderfully attractive aromas, as on all these reds. **10**'s rich, ripe flavours supported by structure to offer satisfying drinking now & for years to come, though not too concentrated.

★★★★ **Richesse** Was 'Cab-Merlot' - same blend, same dabs cab franc & petit verdot. Stylish **11**'s ripe, fruity aromas lead to gently balanced, plush, plump palate. Swops intensity, elegance for upfront charm.

★★★★ **Chardonnay** 🩹 Elegant, supple, finely balanced **12** starts with nutty highnotes, finishes with limy length. Oaking modest & subtle. A sophisticated blonde charmer to be taken anywhere. — TJ

- ▪ **Les Coteaux** *see* Mont du Toit Kelder
- ▪ **Les Fleurs** *see* Southern Sky Wines
- ▪ **Le Vin de François** *see* Chateau Naudé Wine Creation
- ▪ **L'Huguenot** *see* Leopard's Leap Family Vineyards

Libby's Pride Wines

Location: Wellington ▪ WO: Western Cape ▪ Tasting, sales & tours by appt ▪ Owner(s) Elizabeth Petersen ▪ Winemaker(s) Hennie Huskisson (Linton Park Wines) ▪ 750t/40,000cs own label 75% red 25% white ▪ info@libbyspridewines.com ▪ www.libbyspridewines.com ▪ **T +27 (0)82-745-5550** ▪ F +27 (0)86-215-1811

Elizabeth Petersen's motto is 'Never think your dream is beyond your reach'. With star sign Leo, which she associates with strength and pride, she's intent on developing Libby's Pride into South Africa's most successful black-woman-owned wine business. In this endeavour she's partnered by Linton Park Wines.

Cabernet Sauvignon Await next, as for **Merlot**, **Shiraz**, **Signature Red** & **Chardonnay**. **Sauvignon Blanc** ⑨ 🩹 ★★ Shy, lightish **12**, faint grass & greenpepper, perky finish. — WB

- ▪ **Libertas** *see* Distell

Lievland Estate

Location/map/WO: Stellenbosch ▪ Est/1stB 1982 ▪ Tasting, sales & cellar tours by appt T +27 (0)71-325-5382 ▪ Closed Dec 25 ▪ Summer picnic baskets by arrangement ▪ B&B accommodation ▪ Owner(s) Susan Colley ▪ Winemaker(s) Kowie du Toit (2004) ▪ Viticulturist(s) Conrad Schutte (2010, Vinpro) ▪ 50ha (cab, merlot, shiraz) ▪ 250t/10,000cs own label 95% red 5% white ▪ PO Box 66 Klapmuts 7625 ▪ lievland@icon.co.za ▪ www.lievland.co.za ▪ S 33° 50' 29.5" E 018° 52' 34.8" ▪ **T +27 (0)21-875-5226** ▪ F +27 (0)86-628-1917

Part of the reputed Simonsberg terroir since 1715, Lievland's recent more settled phase has brought 'significantly' increased wine sales, especially of the Lievlander value red and the sauvignon. Their flagship remains the shiraz, and the focus on informal winetastings - beside the fire, out on the patio or the lawns.

Merlot NEW ☺ 🩹 ★★★ 15 months oak still prominent on **11** but ripe berry fruit has herbal freshness to balance, & a lively acid cleanout invites the next sip. **Lievlander** ☺ 🩹 ★★★ Equal parts shiraz & cab on early-drinking **09**, good dollop oak still showing mid-2013 but will meld with juicy berry fruit in year or so.

Shiraz 🩹 ★★★ First since **06**, savoury **11** offers fynbos & coriander spice. Textured, medium bodied, with bright cranberry crunch. **Sauvignon Blanc** 🩹 ★★★ Fresh cut grass & tropical melange for easy quaffing in **13** & a year or two. — JP

- ▪ **Like Father Like Son** *see* Bon Courage Estate

L'illa

Location: Hermanus ▪ WO: Eilandia ▪ Est/1stB 2006 ▪ Tasting & sales at Newton Johnson Vineyards ▪ Owner(s)/winemaker(s) Gordon & Nadia Newton Johnson ▪ Viticulturist(s) AA Cilliers (Jan 1973) ▪ (chenin) ▪ 220cs own

label 100% white ▪ PO Box 225 Hermanus 7200 ▪ gordon@newtonjohnson.com, nadia@newtonjohnson.com ▪ www.newtonjohnson.com ▪ **T** +27 (0)28-312-3862 ▪ F +27 (0)86-638-9673

The name (pronounced leeya) means 'island' in Catalan, and alludes to the wine's origin in Robertson's Eilandia ward and to the farm there, also Eilandia, of the Cilliers family for six generations. Nadia Cilliers married into the Newton Johnson clan in the Hemel-en-Aarde and makes the wine in the eponymous cellar.

★★★★ **Noble Late Harvest** Off 40 year old chenin vines, **12** has discreet but real charm. Delicate honeyed raisin notes supported by fine acidity, giving gently sweet brightness & depth, if no real intensity. 375 ml. — TJ

■ **Limelight** *see* De Wetshof Estate
■ **Lime Road** *see* Havana Hills

Limosin   `NEW`

Part of the Cape brandy scene for many decades, Limosin boasts maturation in barrels from the Limousin oak forests of France. It's distributed by Henry Tayler & Ries, a subsidiary of Distell.

Limosin Extra Fine ★★★ Uncomplex blended brandy, best for cocktails or with mixer. Caramel obvious on fruity nose. Rather sweet, with a dark, dense, spirity finish. — WB,TJ

■ **Lindenhof** *see* Boland Kelder

Lindhorst Wines

Location: Paarl ▪ Map: Paarl & Wellington ▪ WO: Paarl/Coastal/Durbanville ▪ Est 1996 ▪ 1stB 2002 ▪ Tasting, sales & cellar tours by appt 11–5 daily ▪ Closed Dec 25 ▪ Meals by special request only ▪ Self-catering cottage ▪ Owner(s) Mark & Belinda Lindhorst ▪ Winemaker(s) Mark Lindhorst, advised by Philip Costandius (Aug 2009, consultant) ▪ Viticulturist(s) Mark Lindhorst, advised by Kevin Watt (Jan 2001, consultant) ▪ 65ha/18ha (cab, merlot, mourv, ptage, pinot, shiraz, viog) ▪ 140t/8,000cs own label 100% red ▪ PO Box 1398 Southern Paarl 7624 ▪ mark@lindhorstwines.com ▪ www.lindhorstwines.com ▪ S 33° 47' 46.0" E 018° 56' 59.0" ▪ **T** +27 (0)21-863-0990 ▪ F +27 (0)21-863-3694

'Lindhorst is all about the personal touch,' says Mark Lindhorst of the boutique winery he and wife Belinda own just outside Paarl. Tastings are generally conducted by a family member, and most sales are made through a database of loyal fans, built up from the many shows Mark personally attends around the country.

Cabernet Sauvignon ⊕ ★★★ Uncomplicated **07** shows dark fruit, fresh acidity, firm tannins; last year needed time to lose slightly hard edges. **Merlot** ⊕ ★★★ Rich & full **07** exhibits dark fruit & chocolate flavours; broad structured & smooth textured but lacks a little freshness. **Pinotage** ⊕ ★★★★ Succulent yet complex, **07** had liquorice, graphite nuances alongside brambleberry fruit when last tasted. **Shiraz** ⊕ ★★★★ Big & bold **07** shows red & black fruit, some spice before long, savoury finish. Appears quite evolved already so drink up. **Partner's Choice** ⊕ ★★★★ **07** equal cab & shiraz, 2% pinotage. Red & black fruit, dusty oak on the nose, fresh acidity, fine tannins. **Max's Tribute** ⊕ ★★★ **07** blend of 74% shiraz, rest mourvèdre, viognier. Rich & broad, already quite developed with lots of savoury character. WO Coastal. **Statement** Await next. **Sauvignon Blanc** ⊕ 🍴 ★★★★ From Durbanville grapes, **12** displays classic cool-climate grassiness, greenpepper. Fresh but not hard acidity. — DC

Lingen   🍾🍷

Location: Stellenbosch ▪ WO: Jonkershoek Valley ▪ Est 2003 ▪ 1stB 2008 ▪ Tasting & sales at Stark-Condé Wines (see entry) ▪ Owner(s) JD Krige Family Trust ▪ Cellarmaster(s)/winemaker(s) José Conde (Jan 2003) ▪ Viticulturist(s) Pieter Smit (Jan 2003, consultant) ▪ 7ha/2ha (cab, p verdot, shiraz) ▪ 14t/508cs own label 100% red ▪ PO Box 389 Stellenbosch 7599 ▪ info@stark-conde.co.za ▪ www.stark-conde.co.za ▪ **T** +27 (0)21-861-7700/+27 (0)21-887-3665 ▪ F +27 (0)21-887-4340

It's just over a decade since the Krige family established a 2ha vineyard in their 'vilafonte' soils, different to those of Stellenbosch's Jonkershoek Valley neighbour Stark-Condé where the boutique-scale Lingen blend is made and marketed. Vintner José Conde sees it as somewhat softer than his own wines; it's no less classy.

★★★★ **Lingen** Equal cab/shiraz blend with 22% petit verdot, half fermented with natural yeasts. **11** is lithe & supple, with soft red/black berry fruit in an elegant structure. — DS

Linton Park Wines 🍷🍴🌲📷

Location: Wellington ▪ Map: Paarl & Wellington ▪ WO: Wellington/Paarl/Western Cape ▪ Est 1995 ▪ 1stB 1998 ▪ Tasting, sales & cellar tours between 9-4 by appt ▪ Fee R50pp ▪ Closed all pub hols ▪ BYO picnic ▪ Walks/hikes ▪ 4x4 & mountain biking trails ▪ Annual harvest festival Mar/Apr ▪ Owner(s) Camellia PLC UK ▪ Cellarmaster(s) Hennie Huskisson (2007) ▪ Winemaker(s) JG Auret (2007) ▪ Viticulturist(s) Rudolf Jansen van Vuuren (2012) ▪ 210ha/84ha (cab, merlot, pinot, shiraz, chard, sauv, viog) ▪ 650t/120,000cs own label 50% red 40% white 10% rosé ▪ Fairtrade ▪ PO Box 1234 Wellington 7654 ▪ sales@lintonparkwines.co.za, info@lintonparkwines.co.za ▪ www.lintonparkwines.co.za ▪ S 33° 36' 40.1" E 019° 2' 15.0" ▪ **T +27 (0)21-873-1625** ▪ F +27 (0)21-873-0851

A venerable document - the original 1699 land grant by Willem Adriaan van der Stel - is proudly on display in the Cape Dutch manor house on the Wellington home-farm Slangrivier, owned by UK-based diversified group Camellia. The Louis Fourie 1699 range of occasional releases honours the original farmer, Louis Fleurij.

Reserve range

★★★★ **Cabernet Sauvignon** ⓣ Rich & full-bodied **08** last was dominated by blackcurrant, dark cherry & chocolate. Expressive fruit, firm centre of supple tannin, savoury tail. WO Paarl.

★★★★ **Merlot** ⬜ **10** continues form of last-reviewed **05**. Earthy chocolate tones with graphite & tar grip. Firm dry tannin on a somewhat lean body indicative of 24 months in French/American oak, third new.

★★★★ **Shiraz** 08 (★★★☆) dips on **07**. Spicy plum succulence doesn't match the oak tannin (24 months, third new) which results in a lean, dry astringency. Medium bodied.

Linton Park range

Cabernet Sauvignon ⬜ ★★★ Violet whiffs, cassis & blue fruit entry of **11** promises much. Oak then takes over, drying the mouth. **Café Cabernet** ⓣ ⬜ ★★★ Fashionable coffee/mocha tone to **11**, structure, texture & flavour all oak derived. Mediumweight & pleasant. **Merlot** ⓣ ★★★☆ Dark & ripe spicy fruitcake & plums, **09** juicy fruit mingles with supple tannins, dry savoury conclusion. **Shiraz** ★★★★ Vibrant black cherry/berry spice to juicy **10**. Toned & savoury, with dry tannin twist from year oaking, 33% new. **De Slange Rivier** ⓣ ⬜ ★★★★ Big & bold smoky entry for **10** Bordeaux red blend, concentrated deep dark fruit & liquorice. Ripe tannins add texture & length. **Chardonnay** ⬜ ★★★★ **12** recalls last-tasted **09** (★★★★) in its vanilla, peaches & cream appeal. Rounded, with fresh acidity to balance 12 months in oak. **Private Bin 177 Sauvignon Blanc** ⬜ ★★★ Sharp tartness to lemon curd flavour of **13**. Simple & easy. WO W Cape.

Louis Fourie 1699 range

Cabernet Sauvignon ⓣ 🍱 ⬜ ★★★ Inky blackcurrant softness on **11**, rounded & medium bodied with light chalky grip. WO Paarl, like Chardonnay. **Merlot** Occasional release, like **Shiraz**, **Chenin Blanc** & **Sauvignon Blanc**. **Chardonnay** 🍱 ★★★ Tension of opposites between tangy orange juiciness & creamy vanilla nuttiness of oak on **13**. Medium structure & length. — FM

▪ **Lion Creek** see Napier Winery
▪ **Lion Ridge** see Valley Vineyards Wine Company
▪ **Lion's Drift** see Silkbush Mountain Vineyards
▪ **Lion's Pride** see Stellenrust
▪ **Lions River Vineyards** see Highgate Wine Estate
▪ **Liquor City** see Orange River Wine Cellars
▪ **Lisha Nelson Signature Wines** see Nelson Family Vineyards

Lismore Estate Vineyards 🍷🍴📷🎿

Location: Greyton ▪ Map: Southern Cape ▪ Est 2003 ▪ 1stB 2006 ▪ Tasting & sales by appt ▪ Facilities for children ▪ Tour groups ▪ Walking/hiking & mountain biking trails ▪ Owner(s)/winemaker(s) Samantha O'Keefe ▪ Viticulturist(s) Andrew Teubes (consultant) ▪ 232ha/12ha (shiraz, chard, sauv, viog) ▪ 45t/6,000cs own label 20% red 80% white ▪ PO Box 76 Greyton 7233 ▪ wine@lismore.co.za ▪ www.lismore.co.za ▪ S 34° 4' 25.23" E 019° 17' 16.83" ▪ **T +27 (0)82-343-7913**

'I am so blessed. It's been a fantastic year for me!' says boutique winemaker Samantha O'Keefe, owner of Lismore Estate outside Greyton. Increased

production has seen her successfully expand local sales. 'I've been here for 10 years now. I want to continue to make and sell beautiful wine and just "be"...'

■ **Literature Wine** *see Nordic Wines*

Lithos Wines

Location: Sir Lowry's Pass ▪ Map: Helderberg ▪ WO: Stellenbosch/Elgin/Stellenbosch ▪ Est/1stB 2012 ▪ Tasting, sales & cellar tours Mon-Fri 8-5 by appt Sat/Sun by appt ▪ Fee R20, waived on purchase ▪ Closed all pub hols ▪ Owner(s) Sean & Lorraine Emery ▪ Winemaker(s)/viticulturist(s) Timothy Hoek (Jan 2012) ▪ 16ha/2ha (ptage, shiraz) ▪ 13.5t/2,000cs own label 75% red 25% rosé ▪ Postal Suite 346 Private Bag X15 Somerset West 7129 ▪ winemaker@lithos.co.za ▪ www.lithos.co.za ▪ S 34° 6' 12.66" E 018° 55' 15.28" ▪ **T +27 (0)21-858-1851** ▪ F +27 (0)860-552-5521

When venture capitalist Sean Emery and wife Lorraine purchased a few hectares of 'sad-looking' Sir Lowry's Pass vines and a cellar with three 'dubious quality' barrels, making their own wine seemed a doubtful and brave endeavour. But, along with winemaker/viticulturist Tim Hoek (ex Jordan) and much tenacious hard work, they believe their small quantities of handcrafted wine will be worth it all.

Cape Blend ★★★ Confident & promising start with shiraz/pinotage combo, supported by two cabs. Some Elgin vines. **12** fine structure of tangy dark fruit & fragrant oak (none new), intense albeit unlingering blackberry flavours. **Blanc de Noir** ▦ ★★ A savoury mealtime or picnic companion, **13** blush mainly from pinotage is light & slightly herbal, with dry spicy grip. — DC, JP

Litigo Wines [NEW]

WO: Hemel-en-Aarde Valley/Hemel-en-Aarde Ridge ▪ Est 2011 ▪ 1stB 2012 ▪ Closed to public ▪ Owner(s) Eben van Wyk ▪ Winemaker(s) Eben van Wyk & Peter-Allan Finlayson (both 2011) ▪ òt/105cs own label 100% red ▪ Postnet Suite 134, Private Bag X1005, Claremont 7735 ▪ info@litigowines.com ▪ www.litigowines.com ▪ **T +27 (0)82-803-4503** ▪ F +27 (0)21-683-5952

Eben van Wyk is an intellectual property lawyer whose love of wine has led him to help a few winemakers with problems in his field. His wine is masterminded by Peter-Allan Finlayson of Crystallum, though Eben gets his own hands dirty during harvest and keeps an eye and a tastebud on his barrels through the year.

★★★★☆ **Pinot Noir** Fragrant, pure-fruited **12** is engagingly lovely even in youth - though should develop a few years, as the soft, lingering sensuality is built on a firm, elegant structure of acidity & gentle tannin. — TJ

■ **Little J** *see Joostenberg Wines*
■ **Little River** *see De Meye Wines*
■ **Live-A-Little** *see Stellar Winery*
■ **Living Rock** *see Withington*
■ **Lodewijkx** *see Eerste Hoop Wine Cellar*

L'Olivier Wine & Olive Estate

Location/map: Stellenbosch ▪ Tasting & sales by appt only ▪ Fee R50 ▪ Accommodation in Manor House/Villa (sleep 8) & two cottages (sleep 6) ▪ Owner(s) Theuns Kuhn ▪ Viticulturist(s) Leander Koekemoer ▪ 22ha (cab, chard, sauv) ▪ ±120t/2,914cs own label 30% red 70% white ▪ Stellenboschkloof Road Stellenbosch 7600 ▪ info@lolivierestate.com ▪ www.lolivierestate.com ▪ S 33° 55' 37" E 018° 46' 54" ▪ **T +27 (0)21-881-3218** ▪ F +27 (0)86-519-0615

Elevation and a secluded valley situation overlooking False Bay mean that olives as well as vines flourish at this family-owned Stellenboschkloof property. No wonder staffers consider the oil and wine without equal, or 'Non Pareil' (the brand name on the labels). Accommodation on the estate is popular with weekenders and holidaymakers who relish the hikes and horse rides on offer.

Lomond

Location: Gansbaai ▪ Map: Southern Cape ▪ WO: Cape Agulhas ▪ Est 1999 ▪ 1stB 2005 ▪ Tasting & sales at Farm 215 Mon-Sun 9-4 by appt ▪ Closed all pub hols ▪ Guest accommodation, restaurant, conferences, hiking trail, conserva-

tion area (www.farm215.co.za) ▪ Owner(s) Lomond Properties, Distell & workers trust ▪ Cellarmaster(s)/ winemaker(s) Kobus Gerber (2004) ▪ Viticulturist(s) Wayne Gabb (1999) ▪ 1,100ha/120ha (merlot, syrah, nouvelle, sauv) ▪ 750t 40% red 60% white ▪ ISO 9002, BWI ▪ PO Box 184 Stellenbosch 7599 ▪ lomond@capelegends. co.za ▪ www.lomond.co.za ▪ S 34° 34' 12" E 019° 26' 24.00" ▪ **T** +27 (0)21-809-8330 ▪ **F** +27 (0)21-882-9575

Floral and avian names reflect the commitment to sustainable farming on this large property: 1,100ha in the Uilenkraal River Valley near fishing hamlet Gansbaai on Walker Bay. Member of the Biodiversity & Wine Initiative and Walker Bay Fynbos Conservancy, the Lomond joint venture (between Lomond Properties, Stellenbosch drinks giant Distell and a worker's trust) uses the cool coastal climate of the vaunted Cape Agulhas wine area and 120 ha of vines (selectively established on previously virgin land marked by an array of soil types) for wines that show impressive, occasionally profound, site and varietal expression.

★★★★ **Syrah** ✓ 🍷 Generously fruited **10**'s berry & rhubarb appeal balanced by lively acidity, complemented by lengthy & precise finish. Cosseted by smooth tannins & well-judged oak.

★★★★☆ **Conebush Syrah** 🍷 From a single-vineyard, **10** is scented with flowers, cranberry & redcurrant; spiced with cinnamon & vanilla; characterised by restraint & fine chalky tannins.

★★★★ **Pincushion Sauvignon Blanc** 🍴 Classy **12** is vibrant & poised (as always); though shade off **11**'s (★★★★★) elegance & length, shows similar presence & unusual, engaging aromas of quince & flowers.

★★★★ **Sugarbush Sauvignon Blanc** 🍴 **12** ticks all the boxes: ripe layered palate; fullish body & zesty lime finish. Easy-drinking appeal enhanced by pinch sugar. Juicy & delicious.

★★★★☆ **Buzzard's Trail** ✓ 🍴 🍷 Was 'SSV', still is appealing blend sauvignon (80%), barrelled semillon & splash viognier. Summer table companion **13**'s (★★★★) fresh white peach & lime contrast with salted tropical fruit; delightfully firm chalky texture. Touch less sauvignon, more semillon in compelling debut **12**.

★★★★ **Snowbush** 🍴 **12** (★★★★☆) continues upward trajectory of **11** & **10** (★★★★). Sauvignon with wooded semillon, nouvelle, dash viognier. Buttery & full, nicely rounded & creamy, ends with enticing grassy notes & lemon zest.

Merlot 🍷 ★★★ Pleasant mealtime sipping delivered by characteristic meaty, plummy **10**. **Pinot Noir** NEW 🍷 ★★★ Barrel sample **12** fruity & juicy, with smoky oak & pomegranate complexity, attractively lean palate. **Cat's Tail Syrah** 🍷 ★★★★☆ Returns to guide after **06** (★★★☆) with highly aromatic **11**, showing bouillon & liquorice; big bodied, intense & lavishly fruity, with plush texture & long finish. Delicious now but will reward cellaring, as most Lomond wines. **Sauvignon Blanc** ✓ 🍴 🍷 ★★★★ Vivacious **13** goes up a step with composure & flavour intensity. More serious than **12** (★★★★). — WB, GdB

Londinium Wines NEW

Location: Somerset West ▪ WO: Stellenbosch ▪ Owner(s) Alan & Christine Bent ▪ Cellarmaster(s) Alan Bent ▪ Winemaker(s) Bruno Julian Mori ▪ 200cs own label 100% red ▪ PO Box 3747 Somerset West 7129 ▪ wineandwhales@telkomsa.net ▪ **T** +27 (0)21-852-6545

After 25 years in New Zealand and two in the United Kingdom, Alan Bent has returned to home town Somerset West to begin a new life as a wine tour guide (Wine & Whales) and boutique winemaker. His first commercial bushvine shiraz received the nod from some serious UK palates last year, but he's quick to share the kudos with his 'instructor', Casa Mori's Julian Mori.

The Dog's Bollocks Bush Vine Shiraz ★★★ From Stellenbosch vines, **10** is high toned, with rum-&-raisin notes & curry leaf spicing, intense sweet-sour twist. For early drinking. — CvZ

Longbarn Winery

Location/WO: Wellington ▪ Map: Paarl & Wellington ▪ Est/1stB 2006 ▪ Cellar tours by appt ▪ Owner(s) David & Sue Power ▪ Winemaker(s) David Power (Feb 2006) ▪ Viticulturist(s) David Power (Sep 2003) ▪ 69ha/4ha (pinot, sauv) ▪ 7t/280cs own label 100% white ▪ PO Box 1295 Wellington 7654 ▪ david@longbarn.co.za ▪ www.longbarn.co.za ▪ S 33° 34' 13.6" E 019° 3' 53.6" ▪ **T** +27 (0)21-873-6396 ▪ **F** +27 (0)86-611-1534

David and Sue Power's Georgian-era barn has been refurbished and kitted out as the cellar on this serenely rural property in Wellington's Agter Groenberg. Only a fraction of the harvest is vinified here, in decidedly garagiste scale and style.

Pinot Noir Next awaited. **Sauvignon Blanc** ⊕ 🍴 ★★★★☆ Commendable body & vibrant fruit on **12** preview bolstered by bracing acidity, showing this micro-vineyard's potential. — GdB

Long Beach

Attractively packaged brand by Robertson Winery for Vinimark, exported to Europe, Asia and the rest of Africa.

■ **Longmarket** *see* Woolworths

Long Mountain Wine Company

Location: Cape Town ▪ WO: Western Cape/Breede River Valley ▪ Est/1stB 1994 ▪ Closed to public ▪ Owner(s) Pernod Ricard ▪ Cellarmaster(s)/winemaker(s)/viticulturist(s) Emile Gentis (Oct 2006) & Morne van Rooyen (Jan 2013) ▪ 200,000cs own label 55% red 40% white 5% rosé ▪ 2nd Floor, The Square, Cape Quarters, 27 Somerset Road, Cape Town 8005 ▪ emile.gentis@pernod-ricard.com, morne.vanrooyen@pernod-ricard.com ▪ www.longmountain.co.za ▪ **T +27 (0)21-405-8800** ▪ F +27 (0)86-504-2052

For international drinks giant Pernod Ricard, owner of the Long Mountain and Gecko Ridge brands, sub-Saharan Africa is 'the final frontier' and it's being tackled with great energy under the aegis of wine production manager Emile Gentis, who emphasises not just the opportunities for growth in these new markets, but also Pernod Ricard's ethical and responsible track record in promoting and selling alcohol. An example is the partnership with Massmart (Makro) aimed at reducing underage drinking, drink-driving, and strengthening and expanding codes of conduct. 'Our mission is to build strong brands whilst being committed to social responsibility and the promotion of responsible drinking.'

Long Mountain range

Cabernet Sauvignon 🖻 🍷 ★★ Trailing red fruit & smoke, **12** slides down easily on a light cushion of sweetness. **Merlot** NEW 🖻 🍷 ★★ **12** preview's tart plum bite nicely padded by blackberry plushness. WO Breede River Valley. **Pinotage** 🖻 🍷 ★☆ 'Barista'styling for **12**, with coffee/mocha percolating through the fruit. **Pinotage Reserve** 🍷 ★ Sweet-sour **10**'s choc-mocha & plum-cherry appeal let down slightly by obtrusive woody notes. **Ruby Cabernet** 🖻 🍷 ★ Unwooded **12** for sipping around the campfire. **Shiraz Reserve** 🍷 ★ Like Reserve sibling, matured in older barrels (versus oak-chips for rest of range), giving charry tone to **11** subtle blueberry. **Rosé** NEW 🖻 🍷 ★★ Salmon pink **13** tank sample from pinotage, soft sweetish strawberries-&-cream. Serve well chilled. WO Breede River Valley, like next two. **Chardonnay** 🖻 🍷 Unwooded **13** tank sample too unformed to rate. **Chenin Blanc** 🖻 🍷 ★★ Ethereal **13** faint guava aroma, apple pith texture. **Sauvignon Blanc** 🖻 🍷 ★★ **13** crisp & light bodied for al fresco sipping.

Gecko Ridge range

Cabernet Sauvignon ☺ 🖻 🍷 ★★★ Delightful **12** quaffer, cherry tobacco & raspberry notes, bright acidity & gentle brush of tannin. **Chenin Blanc** ☺ ★★★ Bone-dry **13** delicately balanced summer white.

Pinotage ★★ Easy-drinking **12**'s fruity appeal enlivened by clean leather, balsamic notes. **Chardonnay** 🍷 ★★ Pineappley **13** in the riper spectrum, slight vanilla tone from oak staving. — DC, JP

Longridge Wine Estate

Location: Stellenbosch ▪ Map: Helderberg ▪ WO: Stellenbosch/Western Cape ▪ Est 1841 ▪ 1stB 1992 ▪ Tasting & sales Mon-Sat 10-5 ▪ Closed Easter weekend & Dec 25 ▪ Cellar tours by appt ▪ Longridge Restaurant T +27 (0)21-855-4082 ▪ Conferences ▪ Owner(s) Van der Laan family ▪ Cellarmaster(s) Jasper Raats ▪ Winemaker(s) Jasper Raats, with Hendrien de Munck ▪ Viticulturist(s) Albert le Roux & Jasper Raats ▪ 38ha (cab, merlot, pinot, chard, chenin) ▪ 255t/27,200cs own label 53% red 45% white 2% MCC ▪ PO Box 2023 Dennesig 7601 ▪ info@longridge.co.za ▪ www.longridge.co.za ▪ S 34° 0' 55.2" E 018° 49' 60.0" ▪ **T +27 (0)21-855-2005** ▪ F +27 (0)21-855-4083

Although first registered in 1841, the commercial production of wine on this Helderberg property began only in 1992. Initially under company ownership, it has been family run since 2007. Committed to a social responsibility programme, the estate has joined forces with The Dream Tree School which caters for children with autism and associated neuro-developmental disorders. It also supports The Health Teachers, which provides training in hygiene, health and prevention of illnesses in the townships.

★★★★ **Pinotage** Perfumed & fresh, **10** also appeals with light feel, spicy fruit & complementary lively tannins. **09** sold out untasted.

★★★★ **Chardonnay** In typical house style, **10** rich in golden lights, roast hazelnut tones. Springs to life via citrusy zest, clean lingering tail. 2 years oak well-absorbed. Last tasted was silky **08** (★★★★★).

★★★★ **Chenin Blanc** ⓘ **11** (★★★☆) full-bodied, seeming sweetness from oak vanilla, alcohol, but in fact bone-dry. Lacks concentration, potential of **10**.

★★★★ **Sauvignon Blanc** ⓘ Cool, clean lines focus attractive dried fig bouquet on **10**. Fresh acid is assimilated well with the rich flavours; most pleasurable drinking. **09** (★★★★) was less balanced. WO W Cape.

★★★★ **Edelgoud** ⓘ A first in South Africa, Noble Late Harvest from verdelho? **11** a marriage of variety's spiced yellow peach & a deft brush of botrytis. Lightish body, crisply fresh & juicy.

Cabernet Sauvignon ★★★☆ **10** pleasant, though light fruit gives tannins a rather unbalanced assertiveness. Lacks usual gravitas, for earlier drinking. **09** untasted. **Cabernet Franc** Await next. **Merlot** ★★★☆ Youthful **11** too unknit for current enjoyment, but properly ripe dark plum tones & fleshiness hold promise for a few years time. **10** & **09** sold out untasted. **Shiraz** ⓘ ★★★★ Crushed velvet feel highlights concentrated flavours on well-structured, long **08**. Smart oak polish, rather than the dryness of **07** (★★★★). Like all below, WO W Cape. **Rouge** 🗒 ★★★ Uncomplicated, unoaked mix shiraz/merlot. **12** juicy, soundly dry. **Blanc** ⓘ 🗒 ★★★ **12** interesting 6-way blend, harmonious & flavoursome. **Brut** ⓘ ★★★★ Méthode cap classique sparkling. Last year, a new disgorgement of **08**, year longer on lees. Touch more creamy & developed chardonnay toasty notes. Smoothly dry. — AL

◾ **Lookout** *see* Leopard's Leap Family Vineyards
◾ **Lord Somerset** *see* Somerset Wines

Lord's Wines

Location: McGregor ▪ Map: Robertson ▪ WO: McGregor/Robertson ▪ Est 2005 ▪ 1stB 2006 ▪ Cellar: Tasting, sales & cellar tours Mon-Fri 9-5 Sat/Sun by appt ▪ Lord's Wine Shop, Robertson: tasting & sales Mon-Fri 9-5 Sat/Sun 10-4; toffee & wine pairing R20, barrel tasting ▪ Closed Good Fri, Dec 25 & Jan 1 ▪ Tour groups by appt ▪ Farm produce ▪ Owner(s) 12 shareholders ▪ Cellarmaster(s)/winemaker(s) Ilse van Dijk (Nov 2010) ▪ Viticulturist(s) Jacie Oosthuizen (Jan 2003) ▪ 33ha/13ha (pinot, shiraz, chard, chenin, sauv) ▪ 90t/13,200cs own label 50% red 45% white 5% rosé ▪ PO Box 165 McGregor 6708 ▪ ilse@lordswinery.com, sales@lordswinery.com ▪ www.lordswinery.com ▪ S 33° 59' 20.98" E 019° 44' 28.39" ▪ T +27 (0)23-625-1265

At 500m above sea level, winemaker Ilse van Dijk says, Lord's is one of the highest – and coolest – spots in Robertson and thus suited to pinot noir. So expect to see more of this Michelangelo gold-winning variety in the future, possibly even blended with chardonnay soon.

Pinot Noir 🗒 ★★★ Attractive, variety-true **11** similar earthy sour cherry notes & restrained oaking as previous, but big alcohol out of sync with elegant persona. **Shiraz** 🗒 ★★★ Savoury **11** has meaty, smoky appeal, fresh sweet-sour flavours. Only older oak for this & Pinot Noir. **The Wicked Maiden Pinot Noir Rosé** 🗒 🗒 **13** preview too young to rate conclusively. WO Robertson. **Chardonnay Barrel Fermented** 🗒 ★★★ New oak dominant from 100% to 45%, but mid-2013 wood still the dominant theme in **12**, some banana/apricot fruit peeping through the rich, soft styling. **Sauvignon Blanc** 🗒 🗒 ★★★ Step-up **12** still fresh & lively, with passionfruit & flowers to enjoy. Delicious now, will reward cellaring says winemaker. **Méthode Cap Classique Brut** NEW ★★★ Traditional-method dry bubbly from 70% chardonnay, pinot, with apricot tang to **11**'s yeasty richness. Mouthfilling & long. **Nectar Natural Sweet** ★★ Light-bodied **12** from rare white grape nouvelle, shade sweeter, less vibrant than last. Discontinued: **All Rounder Chardonnay**, **First Innings Chenin Blanc**. —

◾ **L'Ormarins** *see* Anthonij Rupert Wyne
◾ **Lorna Hughes** *see* Stonehill

Lorraine Private Cellar

Location: Rawsonville ▪ Map: Breedekloof ▪ WO: Goudini ▪ Est 1996 ▪ 1stB 2002 ▪ Tasting, sales & cellar tours Mon-Fri 8-1 ▪ Closed all pub hols ▪ Outdoor wine tasting & picnic by appt R200pp; or BYO picnic ▪ Tour groups ▪ Walks/ hikes ▪ Conservation area ▪ Owner(s) Lorraine Trust (Johan & Lori Ann de Wet) ▪ Cellarmaster(s)/winemaker(s) Johan de Wet (Jan 2002) ▪ Viticulturist(s) Leon Dippenaar (2003, consultant) ▪ ±417ha/155ha (cab f, merlot, p verdot, ptage, ruby cab, shiraz, chard, chenin, nouvelle, sauv, viog) ▪ 2,000t total 50t/±8,400cs own label 45% red 50% white 5% rosé ▪ Fairtrade ▪ PO Box 2 Rawsonville 6845 ▪ info@lorraine.co.za ▪ www.lorraine.co.za ▪ S 33° 42' 43.14" E 019° 15' 40.83" ▪ T +27 (0)23-349-1224 ▪ F +27 (0)86-664-2279

Cellarmaster Johan de Wet is deeply attached to this land, where his family has been growing wine for five generations. Small wonder: the farm is situated in a fertile valley with clear rivers, diverse soils, late sunrises and long afternoon shadows cast by the Du Toitskloof Mountains - perfect conditions for vines.

Shiraz ⓘ ★★★☆ When last tasted 04 was opulent, velvety & seductive. **Cape Harmony** Next awaited, as for **Love Of My Life Pinotage Rosé**, **Chardonnay** & **Viognier**. **Sauvignon Blanc** ⓘ ★★★ 11 bright & tangy, gooseberry twist to gentle tropical flavours. Crisp & summery, solo or with a light meal. — MW

■ **Lorry** see Corder Family Wines
■ **Lo Splendore del Sole** see African Terroir

Lothian Vineyards

Location/WO: Elgin ▪ Map: Elgin, Walker Bay & Bot River ▪ Est 2004 ▪ 1stB 2010 ▪ Tasting first weekend in every month, or by appt ▪ Honey ▪ Conferences/functions ▪ Conservation area ▪ Luxury guesthouse (7 double en-suite bedrooms) ▪ Owner(s) Wilson family ▪ Winemaker(s) Stefan Gerber, with Marco Benjamin (both 2010) ▪ Viticulturist(s) Kevin Watt (Mar 2009) ▪ 46ha/13ha (pinot, chard, riesling, sauv, viog) ▪ 60t 25% red 75% white ▪ IPW ▪ 68 Reservoir Rd Somerset West 7130 ▪ info@lothianvineyards.com ▪ www.lothianvineyards.com ▪ S 34° 11' 31.49" E 018° 58' 57.78" ▪ **T +27 (0)21-859-9901** ▪ F +27 (0)86-718-1672

The Scottish grandmother of the Wilson brothers behind Lothian Vineyards used to own Rust en Vrede in the 50s and 60s, so it was only natural that they wanted to continue the family involvement in winemaking. An old protea farm on the banks of the Palmiet River in Elgin was acquired in 2004 and transformed into a model viticultural property with a focus on chardonnay and pinot noir.

Vineyard Selections [NEW]
★★★★ **Pinot Noir** ✓ Perfumed 11 complex earth, truffle & spice, some floral notes. As engaging on the palate, with berry fruit, smooth tannins & fine, persistent finish. 30% new oak, 11 months.
Chardonnay 🗎 ★★★★ Two vintages tasted: 12 only just trumped by 11's (★★★★) balanced richness & complexity. The younger wine shows tad less fruit & more oak, but also a lovely acid seam & freshness. 15% new oak for both. **Riesling** 🗎 ⊘ ★★★ Developed terpene nuances on lime & litchi fruit, 11 good fresh dry finish. Enjoy this summer. — GdB, GM

Louiesenhof Wines

Location/map/WO: Stellenbosch ▪ Est 1991 ▪ 1stB 1995 ▪ Tasting & sales Mon-Fri 9–5 Sat/Sun 10-5 ▪ Fee R10pp ▪ Closed Good Fri, Ascension day & Dec 25 ▪ Bistro open daily 10-3, group bookings advised ▪ Play area for children ▪ Tour groups ▪ Gift shop ▪ Farm produce ▪ Conferences (20 pax) ▪ Conservation area ▪ Hiking & MTB trails ▪ Antique brandy kettle on display ▪ B&B guesthouse ▪ Owner(s) WS Smit Watergang Trust ▪ Cellarmaster(s) WS Smit ▪ Brandy master(s) Stefan Smit & Jos le Roux (both 1991) ▪ Winemaker(s) Jos le Roux ▪ Viticulturist(s) Stefan Smit (1991) ▪ 135ha (cabs s/f, merlot, ptage, shiraz, chard, chenin, pinot grigio, sauv) ▪ 900-1,000t/675,000L ▪ BWI, IPW, WIETA ▪ Koelenhof Road (R304) Stellenbosch 7601 ▪ info@louiesenhof.co.za ▪ www.louiesenhof.co.za ▪ S 33° 53' 34.7" E 018° 49' 35.3" ▪ **T +27 (0)21-865-2632 (office)/+27 (0)21-889-5550 (cellar)** ▪ F +27 (0)21-865-2613

Stephan Smit, the prime mover here, learnt eco-values in his early studies in Germany, inspiring a 'bio-organic wine' way back in 1991. Respect for the environment persists, as evidenced by the fact that Louiesenhof supports the Bottelary Hills Conservancy and strives to make wines 'in harmony with nature'.

Premier Collection
Shiraz ⊘ ★★★★ 11 now bottled & settled into a more balanced wine. The lovely dark-fruited nose has a green edge, following to rich full-bodied end. **Cabernet Sauvignon-Cabernet Franc** ⊘ ★★★ Now bottled, 11 has fresh cab franc appeal balancing liquorice, smoke & Xmas cake aromas. Full bodied, with grippy tannin to finish. **Chardonnay Sur-Lie** [NEW] ⊘ ★★★★ Dark golden colour on 11 alludes to rich honey & seductive oak aromas. Almonds, sun-baked hay lead to creamy marzipan send-off.

Louiesenhof Wines range
Pinotage ⓘ 🗎 ⊘ ★★★ Attractive smoke & flint harmonises with clean berry aromas & firm tannins on 10, good match for spicy food. **Cape Blend** ⓘ 🗎 ⊘ ★★★ Cab franc & pinotage combo on ultra-ripe, awkwardly balanced 10. **Perroquet Merlot Pétillant Rosé** ⓘ 🗎 ★★ 08 off-dry quaffer. **Chardonnay**

Sur-Lie ⊕ 🍴 📖 ★★★ Charry wood cloaks peachy nose on **11** & really defines the wine with oaky sweetness (though dry). **Sauvignon Blanc** ⊕ 📖 ★★★ **11** with unlingering tropical flavours. **Sweet Red** ⊕ ★★ Individual **NV** fortified dessert. **Perroquet Cape Tawny** ⊕ ★★★★ **NV** rustic glow-inducing port-style from tinta, with savoury touches. **Roobernet Cape Ruby** ⊕ ★★★ Youthful **10** fortified has spicy, medicinal notes. Pleasantly dry, dusty, with typical sweetness.

Brandy range NEW!

3 Year Old Blended Brandy ★★★ 100% potstill, from colombard (like next). Fresh & fruity, a touch sweet, with little oak influence. Ideal for mixing or cocktails. **Marbonne 16 Year Brandy** ★★★ Less fresh than younger one, earthy, oaky notes along with fruit & spice. Fairly rich & smooth, if not harmonious. — WB, JP, TJ

Louis

Location: Stellenbosch • WO: Stellenbosch/Darling • Est/1stB 2007 • Closed to public • Owner(s) Louis Nel • Cellarmaster(s)/winemaker(s) Louis Nel (Jan 2007) • 15t/3,000cs own label 50% red 50% white + 1,200cs for clients • Brands for clients: Collaboration (Overture restaurant) • 9 Forest Street Stellenbosch 7600 • louis@louiswines.com • www.louiswines.com • **T +27 (0)82-775-8726**

Cape Winemakers Guild member Louis Nel likens his negociant-style wine venture to a Jack Russell dog, small, energetic and nimble. His creativity and sales of the 3,000 cases of his own wines bears this out. Mentored by one of the industry's greats, Neil Ellis, Louis sagely notes that 'the causality of greatness is often an illusion' and continues to focus on getting the basics right.

Louis range

★★★★ **Cabernet Sauvignon** ⊕ **08** (★★★★☆) raises the bar on **07**. Sweet reward from reprieved vineyard, the silky texture tempts earlier enjoyment but complexity & fruit depth deserve good few years cellaring.

★★★★ **Sauvignon Blanc** ✓ 📖 **13** continues to showcase the quality & intensity of sauvignon from Darling. Flinty & crisply tropical, with structure & length. Good solo or with food.

Cabernet Sauvignon-Merlot 📖 ★★★★ **12** has a core of dark fruit still tightly wrapped in fine-grained chalky tannins. Leaner & less approachable in youth than **08** (★★★★). 2009-2011 skipped.

Black Forest range

Black Forest ⊕ ★★★☆ **11** aptly named shiraz (85%) merlot blend. Ripe & juicy, with creamy textured savouriness that melts into subtle mocha flavours.

Buckleberry range

Buckleberry ⊕ 📖 ★★★ Quintessential sauvignon, vivacious, tangy & fresh **12** has a melange of crisp tropical flavours. Balanced & friendly, ready to entertain. — MW

■ **Louis Fourie** *see Linton Park Wines*

Louisvale Wines   🍷🍴🎋♿

Location/map: Stellenbosch • WO: Stellenbosch/Coastal • Est/1stB 1989 • Tasting, sales & cellar tours Mon-Fri 10-5 • Fee R20 • Closed all pub hols • BYO picnic • Owner(s) Louisvale Wines (Pty) Ltd • Directors Altmann Allers, Hendrik Kluever, Johann Kirsten & Zane Meyer • Winemaker(s)/viticulturist(s) Simon Smith (Jul 1997) • 34ha/23ha (cab, merlot, chard) • 220t/16,000cs own label 50% red 50% white • PO Box 542 Stellenbosch 7599 • winery@louisvale.com • www.louisvale.com • S 33° 54' 32.3" E 018° 48' 24.3" • **T +27 (0)21-865-2422** • F +27 (0)21-865-2633

The focus on chardonnay at this Devon Valley farm goes back to its founding in 1989. It's still the only white grape planted, with different clones and blocks for long-time winemaker-viticulturist Simon Smith to work with, while some red grapes are brought in. In 2010 new owners arrived – a quartet of business friends.

Louisvale Wines range

Dominique 📖 ★★★★ **12** cab-based blend with merlot & cab franc shows some toasty oak notes along with red & black fruit. All in order - but unexciting. WO Coastal. **Chardonnay** 📖 ★★★★ **12** with 50% new oak slightly richer than Chavant but similar fruit profile & lift. Attractive hazelnut tones add some complexity. **Chavant** 📖 ★★★★ Light-bodied **12** chardonnay shows a little unobtrusive oak beside the yellow apple & pear aromas. The palate is crisp & clean with some length. **Chardonnay Unwooded** 🍴 📖 ★★★★ **13** redolent of stonefruit, lemon curd, green melon & fig. Zesty drinking. Also-tasted **12** (★★★) shows riper

fruits, the palate enriched by 5g/l sugar, making it less lifted. These both with food-friendly 13% alcohol & WO Coastal. **Chardonnay-Pinot Noir** NEW 🍷 🖾 ★★★ **13** an uncomplicated crowd pleaser with some freshness & notes of red apples & cream soda. Moderate 12.5% alcohol.

Stone Road range

Cabernet Sauvignon 🍷 🖾 ★★ Slightly green but easy-drinking **12**. **Merlot** 🍷 🖾 ★★★ Soft, plush **12** with chocolate & blackberry tones. These reds lightly oaked. **Sauvignon Blanc** 🍷 🖾 ★★★ **13** is rather shy at first, but refreshing & crisp, with typical green, grapefruity hints. — JPf

---

Lourensford Wine Estate

Location: Somerset West ▪ Map: Helderberg ▪ WO: Stellenbosch/Western Cape ▪ Est 1999 ▪ 1stB 2003 ▪ Tasting, sales & cellar tours daily 9-5 ▪ Fee R30 ▪ Closed Good Fri & Dec 25 ▪ Millhouse Kitchen ▪ Tour groups ▪ Art exhibition ▪ A-Place Interior ▪ Coffee Roastery ▪ Cheesery ▪ Function hall ▪ Conservation area ▪ Owner(s) Christo Wiese ▪ Winemaker(s) Hannes Nel (Nov 2002), with Timothy Witbooi (May 2005) ▪ Viticulturist(s) Francois Viljoen ▪ 4,000ha/152ha (cab, merlot, shiraz, chard, sauv, viog) ▪ 1,200t/240,000cs own label 40% red 58% white 2% rosé ▪ Brands for clients: Eden Crest (Checkers), Matumi (UK), Pracht Gaarden (Belgium), River Crossing (UK & Ireland) ▪ BRC, BWI champion, HACCP ▪ PO Box 16 Somerset West 7129 ▪ info@lourensford.co.za ▪ www.lourensford.com ▪ S 34° 4' 3.7" E 018° 53' 44.2" ▪ **T +27 (0)21-847-2300** ▪ F +27 (0)21-847-0910

On the edge of Somerset West lies businessman Christo Wiese's vast, multi-faceted estate, reaching far up the slopes of the majestic mountain amphitheatre. The property boasts one of the largest and most technologically advanced wineries in the country, together with a small village of craft-orientated enterprises, eateries and galleries, as well as its imposing venue, The Laurent. The estate regularly hosts cycling and trail-running events, and its outdoor concert venue on the polo fields showcases world-famous performers. The team is at the forefront of conservation in the area, resuscitating the ailing upper reaches of the Lourensford River and confronting alien invasions in their fynbos reserves.

Winemaker's Selection range

★★★★☆ **Merlot** NEW 🖾 What a debut! Aromas of bright cherry, forest berries, aniseed & savoury oak (all-new) pad the firm tannin backbone on **11**. A benchmark example of the variety. Rich, satisfying & full of promise for years of enjoyment.

★★★★☆ **Syrah** ✓ 🖾 Fruit-packed **11** is super concentrated with an interplay of mulberry, spice & velvety tannins with savoury/earthy nuances & dry tannic grip. Complex, made with flair. No **10**.

★★★★☆ **Reserve Red Blend** ⑲ Excellent debut **09** shows plush berry fruit, wood spice & floral aromas from cab (64%), shiraz & smidgen viognier. Elegant, with a firm structure, beautiful balance & length. Decant to reveal all its charms or, better, wait a few years - built for the long haul.

★★★★☆ **Chardonnay** ✓ 🖾 Captivating apple & floral nose on back-to-form **12** - like an early morning walk though an orchard. A rich & textured expression of the variety. Creamy, rounded & seamless without being heavy, like lesser **11**.

★★★★ **Sauvignon Blanc** ✓ 🖾 **12**'s cool, fragrant white peach, gooseberry, lime fruit & oak spice from barrel fermentation provides good structure. Dry, full & complex. Deserves time to reach potential.

★★★★ **Viognier** ✓ 🖾 **12** seduces with fragrant spicy peach, clove & jasmine flavours enriched by creamy subtle vanilla oak (some Hungarian). Vivacious, curvy & exotic.

★★★★☆ **Reserve White Blend** ⑲ 🖾 **11** is back to form after **10** (★★★★). A blend of best barrel-fermented (older wood) sauvignon, chardonnay & viognier. Rounded, with superb balance & poise, supported by subtle vanilla oak. Cellar or decant to reveal full potential.

★★★★☆ **Semillon Noble Late Harvest** ⑲ Unctuous botrytis dessert, **09** previously delighted with typical dried peach aroma, long juicy orange marmalade finish well balanced by fine acidity.

Lourensford range

★★★★☆ **Shiraz** ⑲ 🍷 🖾 Medium-bodied **10** (★★★★) a shade off super **08**. Offers fragrant fruit, smoky & herbal notes, but lacks body. Needs time & food. **09** sold out untasted.

★★★★ **Sauvignon Blanc** ✓ 🍷 🖾 **12** (★★★★) lacks concentration of **11**, offers upfront lime & gooseberry fruit. Needs time for bracing acidity to integrate.

★★★★ **Méthode Cap Classique Rosé** NEW 🖾 Salmon-hued, crisp & dry **10** bubbly from pinot noir (7% oaked), delicate raspberry flavours & appealing biscuit overlay. Good depth & elegance, creamy notes to finish.

★★★★☆ **Méthode Cap Classique** Exuberant **09** bottle-fermented sparkling from chardonnay (7% oaked) & pinot noir. Fine, lazy mousse blossoms in the mouth with crisp appley brioche flavour & creamy texture from 48 months lees-ageing. Classy, with richness & finesse. A special treat!

Cabernet Sauvignon ✓ 🗏 ⬜ ★★★★ **11** blackcurrant & floral note, juicy, with soft oak influence, firm grainy, peppery finish. Shorter oaking in older barrels for this range. **Merlot** ✓ 🗏 ⬜ ★★★★ Deep ruby **11**, offers plum pudding, pepper & smoke. Good ripeness, but tannins need time to meld. Food friendly. Earlier drinking than big brother. **Shiraz-Mourvèdre-Viognier** ✓ 🗏 ⬜ ★★★★ Smoky, spicy notes & wild berry fruit, firm structure & earthy finish on **11**. Delightful floral note from viognier. **Chardonnay** ✓ 🗏 ⬜ ★★★☆ **12** bright Granny Smith apple, lime fruit, creamy lemon biscuit due to part natural barrel ferment & ageing.

River Garden range

★★★★ **Cabernet Sauvignon-Merlot** 🗏 ⬜ **11** (★★★) shy of serious **10**, with medium-bodied fruity black berries mingling with oak spice for an easy sip. WO W Cape, as next.

Chardonnay ☺ 🗏 ⬜ ★★★ Lightly oaked **13** shows attractive candied pineapple flavours, rounded & smooth for everyday enjoyment.

Shiraz-Cabernet Sauvignon 🗏 ⬜ ★★★ Uncomplicated **11** upstaged by last-tasted **10** (★★★★), chunky ripe plums & brush of oak lending structure. For easy quaffing. **Rosé** ⓣ 🗏 ⬜ ★★★ Off-dry **12** from shiraz, mourvèdre & merlot offers sweet strawberries & spice. Lively, light & friendly anytime rosé. **Sauvignon Blanc** ⓣ 🗏 ⬜ ★★★ **12** with fresh greenpepper & greengage tone. Dry, zingy & summery. —WB

Lovane Boutique Wine Estate

Location/map/WO: Stellenbosch ▪ Est 2003 ▪ 1stB 2006 ▪ Tasting, sales & cellar tours Mon-Sun 10-5 ▪ Tasting fee R20, waived on purchase ▪ Closed all pub hols ▪ Conferences ▪ Lovane Guesthouse (see Accommodation section) ▪ Owner(s)/viticulturist(s) Philip & Gail Gous ▪ Winemaker(s) Philip Gous, with Gail Gous (both 2006) ▪ 3.6ha/2.5ha (cabs s/f, p verdot) ▪ 20t/2,800cs own label 90% red 5% white 5% rosé ▪ PO Box 91 Vlottenburg 7604 ▪ info@lovane.co.za ▪ www.lovane.co.za ▪ S 33° 57' 09.74" E 018° 48' 02.38" ▪ **T +27 (0)21-881-3827** ▪ F +27 (0)21-881-3546

The Gous family planted this 2.5ha of then virgin earth between established Stellenbosch heavyweights Overgaauw and Neethlingshof just over ten years ago. Cabernet-led winemaking followed in 2006, along with a 4-star guest house and chic conference amenities. The rhythm is now set: all reds are bunch-pressed and matured at least three years in oak.

★★★★☆ **Isikhati 09** (★★★★) cab-led blend, with telling input from petit verdot & cab franc; developed leafy features, tannins softened. 42 months cask. Less sprightly & refreshing than **07**. No **08**. **Cabernet Sauvignon Umbhidi Wholeberry** Next awaited, as for **Summer Mist** & **Sweet 77**. **Cabernet Sauvignon Iziko** ⓣ ★★ 'Fireplace' moniker suggests a warm hearth beside which to drink chunky **08**. **Cabernet Sauvignon Umgidi** ⓣ ★★★ Dense tannic structure of **07** calls for food accompaniment, as its name 'Feast' proposes. **Cabernet Sauvignon Tamkulu** ⓣ ★★★☆ 'Grandfather' dedicated to owner Gail Gous' parent. **08** filled with cassis character, but nicely within itself. **Cabernet Sauvignon Berries Only** ★★★★ Perfumed **09** now all cab (previously with petit verdot) & more lissom than cellarmates; ready for enjoyment after 3.5 years mainly older oak. **Cabernet Franc Iliwa** ⓣ ★★★★ Meaning 'rock' or 'cliff', just 344 bottles from 500 vines. **08** packed with sappy fruit flavour - & 15% alcohol. Gear up on **06** (★★★★). No **07**. **Petit Verdot Umama** ⓣ ★★★★ **08**'s pleasantly taut & lean profile will be appreciated by New-World-weary palates. **Unfiltered Blanc de Noir** ★★★ Firm berry fruit & dry tail of **13** call for sushi. **Méthode Cap Classique** ★★★ Latest **NV** bottling is white from chardonnay after diversion to pink (**09**); warm brioche styling gets unusual mineral fillip from 10% riesling. —DS

▪ **Loyal Brothers** see Govert Wines
▪ **Luca & Ingrid Bein** see Bein Wine Cellar

Luddite Wines

Location: Bot River ▪ Map: Elgin, Walker Bay & Bot River ▪ WO: Cape South Coast ▪ Est/1stB 2000 ▪ Tasting & sales Mon-Fri 9-4 Sat/Sun by appt ▪ Closed Dec 25 & Jan 1 ▪ Cellar tours by appt ▪ Farm produce ▪ Walks/hikes ▪ Conservation area ▪ Owner(s) Niels Verburg & Hillie Meyer ▪ Cellarmaster(s)/winemaker(s) Niels Verburg (2000) ▪ Viticulturist(s) Penny Verburg (2000) ▪ 17ha/5.8ha (cab, mourv, shiraz, chenin) ▪ 30t/3,500cs own label 100% red + 4,000cs for clients ▪ Brands for clients: Elgin Vintners, Oneiric, Ridgelands ▪ PO Box 656 Bot

River 7185 ▪ luddite@telkomsa.net ▪ www.luddite.co.za ▪ S 34° 12' 50.5" E 019° 12' 24.1" ▪ **T +27 (0)28-284-9308/+27 (0)83-444-3537** ▪ F +27 (0)28-284-9045

Wine made traditionally - without machinery and mechanisation - has been the Luddite way since winemaker Niels Verburg, viticulturist wife Penny and investor Hillie Meyer started out in Bot River 14 years ago. Farm produce, notably much-in-demand charcuterie from free-ranging pigs has since been added, and an own cellar built, from where the first (stellar-quality) home-farm-vinified releases are now emerging. Yet Luddism has remained a constant throughout, so it's no surprise that their first white wine is an old-school chenin blanc, from venerable 30 to 60-year-old vines, fermented on its own yeasts in older oak.

★★★★☆ **Shiraz** Seductive spicy berry compote of **09** follows **08**. Complex, layered, refined & elegant. Powerful & generous yet focused, restrained. Maiden vinification in home cellar of all Bot River fruit. Just 30% new oak used in 24 month maturation.

★★★★★ **CWG Auction Reserve Just Alice Shiraz-Mourvèdre** As with **09**, splash mourvèdre (8%) adds spicy lift to black fruit, cocoa depth & inky complexity of shiraz in **10**. Supple & lithe, with refined ripe plum core. Concentrated, rich & rewarding; long maturation in 100% new French oak.

★★★★★ **Saboteur** NEW Leashed power on **09** shiraz, cab, mourvèdre blend. Textured mouthful of ripe, succulent, rounded black fruit. Firm oak backbone (100% new) yet silky, fine tannins & spicy nutmeg lift on a long tail. One for the long haul.

Chenin Blanc NEW ★★★★ Pineapple & creamy citrus zest on expressive, broad, rich **12**, naturally fermented in older oak. Tangy acidity with leesy, long finish. — FM

LuKa Wine Estate

Location/WO: Plettenberg Bay ▪ Map: Klein Karoo & Garden Route ▪ Est 2008 ▪ 1stB 2011 ▪ Tasting in Dec, Mar/Apr or by appt ▪ Owner(s) Hennie & Anita Kritzinger ▪ Cellarmaster(s)/winemaker(s) Anton Smal (Bramon Wines) ▪ Viticulturist(s) Hennie Kritzinger ▪ ±7ha/1.5ha (sauv) ▪ ±3t/422cs own label 100% white ▪ PO Box 2519 Plettenberg Bay 6600 ▪ henita@telkomsa.net ▪ henita@lukawines.co.za ▪ S 34° 2' 28.14" E 023° 15' 57.56" ▪ **T +27 (0)82-457-8110/+27 (0)82-332-3299** ▪ F +27 (0)44-533-6782

With a ready market of upscale holidaymakers and a conducive maritime climate, small-scale winegrowing around the resort town of Plettenberg Bay is taking off via a handful of intrepid pioneers like Hennie and Anita Kritzinger, whose retirement venture is gaining devotees and visitors to the on-site tasting venue.

Sauvignon Blanc ▦ ★★★ Ex-tank **13**, crisp, cool & composed, ideal partner for seafood platters. — HJ,CvZ

Lula Wines

The Xhosa name of this Rudera export brand means 'easy', and the wines are intended to be effortless. The shiraz moved one UK fan to verse: 'A ripe and fruity body for when I unwind/ That's my Lula, she's really such a find.'

Merlot NEW ▨ ★★ **12** super-dry, with savoury & earthy tones rather than fruit. WO W Cape, like all. **Syrah** ▨ ★★★ Was 'Shiraz'. Previewed **11** shows smoked bacon & spice; very young, needs time to unfold. **Chenin Blanc** ▨ ★★★ Ripe apple & fermentation guava on fresh & fruity **13**, ends dry with soft acid. — JP

Lusan Premium Wines

Closed to public ▪ imstrydom@distell.co.za ▪ **T +27 (0)21-883-8988** ▪ F +27 (0)21-883-8941

Umbrella organisation for Alto, Le Bonheur, Neethlingshof, Stellenzicht (and its value brand Hill & Dale) and Uitkyk (including Flat Roof Manor). See entries.

▪ **Luscious Hippos** *see* United Nations of Wine

Lutzville Cape Diamond Vineyards

Location: Lutzville ▪ Map: Olifants River ▪ WO: Lutzville/Olifants River ▪ Est 1961 ▪ 1stB 1980 ▪ Tasting, sales & cellar tours Mon-Fri 9-5 Sat 9-2 ▪ Closed Sun, Easter Sat, Dec 25 & Jan 1 ▪ Coffee shop Mon-Fri 9-4 Sat 10-1 ▪ Function/conference venue ▪ Owner(s) Lutzville Wingerde Beperk ▪ Cellarmaster(s) Gideon Theron (Nov 2005) ▪ Winemaker(s) Jaco van Niekerk (Sep 2009), Brenda Thiart (Nov 2011) & Hugo Lambrechts (Oct 2012)

▪ Viticulturist(s) Gideon Engelbrecht (Sep 2009) ▪ 2,100ha (cab, merlot, ptage, pinot, ruby cab, shiraz, chard, chenin, cbard, nouvelle, sauv, sem, viog) ▪ ±46,000t/400,000cs own label 11% red 89% white ▪ BRC ▪ PO Box 50 Lutzville 8165 ▪ info@lutzvillevineyards.com ▪ www.lutzvillevineyards.com ▪ S 31° 33′ 35.9″ E 018° 21′ 0.2″ ▪ **T +27 (0)27-217-1516** ▪ F +27 (0)27-217-1435

A harvest of more than 46,000 tons and juice from neighbouring cellars meant that the equivalent of 50,000 tons was processed last year by this West Coast winery. Accompanying demand-fuelled growth in bulk wine sales has been a shift to better prices for what cellarmaster Gideon Theron describes as 'the heart of the cellar', its chenin and colombard wines. They're now being taken off the lees sooner; 'that single action has improved the taste profile of our wines'.

Francois Le Vaillant range NEW

★★★★☆ **Noble Late Harvest** 🖉 From chenin, hedonistic **12** has distinctive dried apricot & citrus peel flavour, mouthwatering acidity to balance syrupy sweetness (276g/l), reboot the palate. Worthy addition to the botrytis dessert category.

Pinotage 🖉 ★★★☆ Seriously styled & oaked **12** shows variety's typical strawberry, banana & tar, slightly astringent conclusion.

The Diamond Collection

★★★★ **Oaked Chenin Blanc** ✓ 🖿 🖉 Was just 'Chenin Blanc'. An undiscovered gem, barrel-aged **12** has similar nut & cream appeal, elegance as **11**; appetising & extended quince farewell. Nudges next level.

★★★★ **Semillon** 🖿 🖉 Now bottled, **10** confirms team's assertion that their top whites can age with benefit. Still restrained but more interesting, with richness & length.

Cabernet Sauvignon ⏲ 🖉 ★★★★ Last edition **10** displayed fine balance of oak & fruit, healthy tannins for few years keeping. Fruit selection & barrel maturation (as opposed to oak-staves) for reds, chardonnay & chenin distinguish this from Lutzville range. **Shiraz** 🖉 ★★★ **11** quite taut & savoury, with strong tannins. **Ebenaezer** ✓ 🖉 ★★★★ Expressive 4-way blend, equal parts merlot, ruby cab, cab, 10% shiraz. Now bottled, **11** harmonious, with plush fruit cosseted by 100% new oak. **Chardonnay** Await next. **Sauvignon Blanc** ✓ 🖿 🖉 ★★★★ Bottled since last edition, **12** pungent tinned pea, grass & nettle complexity, assertive acidity now integrated, wine nicely poised & satisfying - at only 11% alcohol.

Lutzville range

> **Pinotage** ☺ 🖉 ★★★ Easygoing **12** has bramble & strawberry flavours, friendly tannins to enjoy with the BBQ. **Shiraz** ☺ 🖉 ★★★ Spicy **12** anytime red; contrasts sweet fruit with pleasing dry end. **Sauvignon Blanc** ☺ 🖿 🖉 ★★★ Leafy blackcurrant & grassy aromas, **13** eager to please... & does.

Cabernet Sauvignon 🖉 ★★★ Mint & vanilla overlay on sweet-sour **12**. **Merlot** 🖉 ★★ Meaty **12** has sharp acidity. **Shiraz Rosé** Not tasted. **Chardonnay** 🖿 🖉 ★★★ Savoury & zingy unwooded version, **13** preview raises the bar with vibrant lime notes, sleek texture. **Chenin Blanc** 🖉 ★★★ Touch richness from lees-ageing & slight sweetness rounds out peach-toned **13**. **Viognier** NEW 🖿 🖉 ★★★ Baked apple **12** aged in French oak, 50% new, gives good grippy finish. **White Muscadel** ⏲ ★★★★ **10** rich & full but light-footed. Uncloying, delightful step up on last-tasted **07** (★★★). This range was 'Cape Diamond'.

Cape Elephant

Ruby Cabernet ⏲ 🖉 ★★★ Typical thatch & mulberry appeal on appealing **12**, house red for those on a budget. **Natural Sweet Red** 🖉 ★★ Latest **NV** has a weak black tea nuance. WO Olifants River. These all low alcohol (±8.5%), unashamedly sweet, except for ruby cab. **Natural Sweet Rosé** 🖉 ★★ Pretty ruby grapefruit smell/taste on colombard-led **13** preview. **Natural Sweet White** 🖉 **13** preview too unformed to rate. — HJ,CvZ

Lyngrove

Location: Somerset West ▪ Map: Helderberg ▪ WO: Stellenbosch ▪ Est/1stB 2000 ▪ Tasting & sales Mon-Fri by appt Sat/Sun 9-3 breakfast & wine tasting ▪ Guesthouse ▪ Conferences (12 pax) ▪ Hiking trail (5km) ▪ Owner(s) Baarsma's Holdings B.V. ▪ Winemaker(s) Hannes Louw & Danielle le Roux (Jun 2006) ▪ Viticulturist(s) André van den Berg ▪ 76ha (cab, merlot, p verdot, ptage, shiraz, chard, chenin, sauv) ▪ 100,000cs own label 70% red 20% white 10% rosé ▪ WIETA ▪ PO Box 7275 Stellenbosch 7599 ▪ wine@lyngrove.co.za ▪ www.lyngrove.co.za ▪ S 34° 1′ 8.7″ E 018° 48′ 10.2″ ▪ **T +27 (0)21-880-1221** ▪ F +27 (0)21-880-0851

Part of export-focused Baarsma SA, Lyngrove has vineyards and a 5-star country house in the Helderberg foothills between Somerset West and Stellenbosch. Untimely hail hit early last year, while rain mid-harvest made picking tricky, but the team say they still captured Lyngrove's 'character and soul' in bottle.

Platinum range

★★★★ **Latitude** Changing blend: equal parts cab & pinotage with dollop shiraz in shapely **11** (★★★☆). Juicy fruitcake notes with light squeeze of tannin. Last **08** was mainly cab with merlot.

Pinotage ★★★☆ **11** with blueberry ripeness & American oak adding distinct cinnamon spice on gentle textured palate. **10**'s (★★★★) wooding was subtler. **Shiraz** ★★★☆ Plum concentration on **10**, lightish yet integrated & harmonious. Nicely layered, oak supporting the fruit.

Reserve range

Shiraz-Pinotage ★★★☆ Hedgerow fruit & earth flavour marry with firm frame on **10**. Mocha & fynbos notes add complexity, along with a dry tail. **Chardonnay** ★★★☆ **11** ticks the boxes of ripe peaches & cream with rich oak backing. Integrated & approachable style.

Lyngrove Collection

Cabernet Sauvignon ★★★☆ Blackberry & cigarbox appeal on rung-up **11**. Smooth & ripe yet structured, with light chalky grip. **Merlot** ★★★ Gentle, appealing everything to plummy **11**: length, fruit, ripeness & structure. **Pinotage** ★★☆ **12** offers cheery raspberry nose but dry, meaty palate. **Shiraz** ★★★ **11** black cherry spice & complex, textured palate framed by nice oak. Balanced & long. **Chenin Blanc** ★★★ Pear & pineapple zip on rounded yet vibrant **13**. Fresh acidity & lees flesh out the palate & add texture & length. **Sauvignon Blanc** ★★★ Nettle & grapefruit tang on zesty & fresh **13**. Lively acidity & twist of white pepper on long dry finish. — FM

Lynx Wines

Location/map/WO: Franschhoek ▪ Est/1stB 2002 ▪ Tasting, sales & cellar tours Mon-Fri 10–5 Sat/Sun & pub hols by appt ▪ Fee R30 (tasting & tour) ▪ BYO picnic ▪ Owner(s) Vista Hermosa (Pty) Ltd ▪ Cellarmaster(s) Dieter Sellmeyer (Jan 2002) ▪ Winemaker(s) Dieter Sellmeyer (Jan 2002), with Helgard van Schalkwyk (Nov 2010) ▪ Viticulturist(s) Kevin Watt ▪ 26ha/11ha (cabs s/f, grenache, merlot, shiraz, viog) ▪ 90t/9,000cs own label 50% red 15% white 35% rosé ▪ IPW ▪ PO Box 566 Franschhoek 7690 ▪ winemaker@lynxwines.co.za ▪ www.lynxwines.co.za ▪ S 33° 51' 46.1" E 019° 2' 14.6" ▪ **T +27 (0)21-867-0406** ▪ F +27 (0)21-867-0397

This family-owned boutique in Franschhoek counts the Royal Navy among its customers. 'When HMS Dauntless docked in Cape Town on her way to the Falklands for a few weeks, Lynx combat helicopters literally dropped in to buy a few cases,' says family head and cellarmaster Dieter Sellmeyer. More significantly, the holding company has been restructured to give farmworkers more decision-making power. 'Not earth-shattering in the greater scheme of things, but certainly meaningful for the individuals involved.'

Premium range

★★★★ **Cabernet Sauvignon** **11** (★★★☆) in a plusher style with softer tannins than **10**. Ultra-ripe dark fruit with a hint of tealeaf, vanilla. Very much in the easy modern idiom.

★★★★ **Cabernet Franc** Understated **11** (★★★☆) not as rich, complex as **10**. Red fruit, some herbal character, modest oaking make for appealing, if low-key, drinking.

★★★★ **Shiraz** **11** (★★★☆) is soft & accessible, lacks concentration, structure of **10**. Overtly fruity, for earlier drinking.

★★★★ **Xanache** Bordeaux red blend **11** (★★★☆) displays ultra-ripe fruit, soft acidity, smooth tannins. Not as convincing as **10**.

★★★★☆ **The Lynx** Flagship **10** Bordeaux blend (equal cab & cab franc, 24% merlot) in another league. Medium body with bright acidity & deft oaking; great composure & a pleasantly austere finish.

★★★★ **Viognier** Subtle & complex **12**, with peach, some floral perfume & oak spice (50% wooded). Lovely juicy fruit but also bright acidity ensuring that there's nothing overdone about it.

Grenache ★★★☆ Vibrant ruby, with upfront soft red berries & spice, **10** light bodied yet serious, with a fresh oaky grip. **Merlot** ★★★ Ripe dark fruit & soft tannins mark **11**. Medium bodied & easy to like, & should probably be drunk young. **SMV** ★★★☆ Mainly shiraz, seasonings of mourvèdre & viognier. Dark fruit, dried herbs on above-average **11**. Good fruit expression, fresh acidity & pleasantly firm tannic grip. **Sweet Lynx** Await new vintage.

Classic range
Vino Tinto ⊕ ▤ ▨ ★★★ 6-way red blend **11** displays red & black fruit, some spice but appears slightly tired. **Blanc de Noir** ▤ ▨ ★★★★ From merlot, **13** has more character than most in the category. Pretty coral colour, concentrated red fruit, a touch of spice, bright acidity. **Viognier Tardio** **12** not tasted.

French Connection range
The French Connection ⊕ ▤ ▨ ★★ Shiraz, dash viognier, **11** lacks concentration, oak sits apart. — CE

■ **Maankloof** *see* Mountain River Wines

Maastricht Estate

Location/WO: Durbanville ▪ Est 1702 ▪ 1stB 2009 ▪ Closed to public ▪ Owner(s) Wheaty Louw ▪ Cellarmaster(s) Thys Louw & Mari Branders (both Jan 2009) ▪ Viticulturist(s) Wheaty Louw (1986) & Thys Louw jnr ▪ 105ha (cab, ptage, shiraz, sauv) ▪ ±1,100t/3,000cs own label 40% red 60% white ▪ wine@maastricht.co.za ▪ **T +27 (0)21-976-1995** ▪ F +27 (0)86-521-9062

After hatching in 2009 under the wings of the redoubtable Diemersdal cellar team of Thys Louw and Mari Branders, Durbanville boutique winery Maastricht is taking flight with another Thys Louw - a cousin, dubbed Thys jnr - at the controls. The sauvignon below is the recently graduated and Napa-honed youngster's debut for the family label, joined this edition by a maiden pinot noir and, soon, an own cellar.

★★★★ **Pinotage** ▨ Judicious oaking (50% new) on perfumed **12** (★★★★) allows violets, lavender & variety's strawberry fruit to take centre stage. Shade off seamless **11**, ends slightly astringent.
★★★★ **Shiraz** ✓ ▨ Like **11**, modern **12** shows variety-true red fruit, wild scrub & lilies. Intense & soulful, savoury finish is satisfying & mealtime compatible.
Cabernet Sauvignon ⊕ ▨ ★★★ Not-for-the-faint-hearted **11** dense black fruit, strong tannins, oak-sweet & warming finish from 14.7% alcohol. **Pinot Noir** ⟨NEW⟩ ▨ ★★★ Showing more body & ripeness than expected from cool Durbanville, **12** is raspberry toned, pleasantly firm. Moderate alcohol - & price! Definitely worth a try. **Sauvignon Blanc** ✓ ▤ ▨ ★★★★ Water-white **13**, capsicum & ruby grapefruit flavours, pleasant vinosity, not-too-brisk acidity is enjoyable solo or with food. — CvZ

■ **Mad Hatter's** *see* Bovlei Cellar

Maiden Wine Cellars

Location: Gordon's Bay ▪ Est 1995 ▪ 1stB 1999 ▪ Tasting/tours by appt; also tailor-made wine tours (max 6 people) ▪ Owner(s) Danie Hattingh ▪ 3,000cs own label 100% red ▪ PO Box 185 Gordon's Bay 7151 ▪ mwines@mweb.co.za ▪ www.maidenwines.co.za ▪ **T +27 (0)82-554-9395** ▪ F +27 (0)86-688-1177

Exporter Danie Hattingh was 'cautiously optimistic' that harvest 2013 was going to be even better than 1999, his best yet, and upbeat about a strong show of interest from the Angolan market. Although getting sales to China off the ground proved to be a difficult task he was making progress, particularly with his Iwayini label.

Main Street Winery

Location: Paarl ▪ WO: Swartland ▪ Est/1stB 1999 ▪ Tasting & tours by appt ▪ Owner(s)/winemaker(s) Marais de Villiers ▪ 200cs own label 100% red ▪ PO Box 2709 Paarl 7620 ▪ mainstreet@mweb.co.za ▪ **T +27 (0)21-872-3006** ▪ F +27 (0)21-872-3006

Marais de Villiers, part-time micro-scale winemaker, spends the rest of his time consulting in the industry, supplying, commissioning and repairing wine production equipment. He also mentors and advises fellow garagistes.

Grenache-Shiraz ⊕ ★★ **11** preview cloaked with tannins, very ripe fruit peeping though. — GdB

Maison

Location/map/WO: Franschhoek ▪ Est 2005 ▪ 1stB 2008 ▪ Tasting & sales Wed-Sun 10-5 ▪ Closed Dec 25 ▪ The Kitchen @ Maison (fusion bistro, lunch 12-5) ▪ Owner(s) Chris Weylandt & Kim Smith ▪ Winemaker(s)/viticulturist(s) Antwan Bondesio ▪ 11ha/4.5ha (shiraz, chard, chenin, viog) ▪ 50% red 50% white ▪ PO Box 587

Franschhoek 7690 ▪ sales@maisonestate.co.za ▪ www.maisonestate.co.za ▪ S 33° 53' 09.7" E 019° 4' 39.80" ▪ **T** +27 (0)21-876-2116 ▪ F +27 (0)21-876-2116

Interior/homeware gurus Chris Weylandt and Kim Smith's chic Franschhoek estate's name aptly translates as 'Home', recalling travels and comforting memories of good wine and food shared with friends. Their own-brand wines, though often generous in alcohol, enjoy an elegance that make them fine partners for the wide range of home-grown and -made goods at Maison's new Deli.

★★★★ **Shiraz** 🖫 **11** back on elegant, spicy form after jammy **10** (★★★☆). Still youthful, but charms with pure sweet fruit (3% viognier co-fermented), gentle extraction & lively bearing. Big but not intrusive alcohol.

★★★★ **Single Vineyard Chenin Blanc Reserve** NEW 🖫 Same vines as unwooded version, **12**'s spicy barrel ferment (30% new) evident but structure, lees-enrichment & freshness to integrate & develop.

★★★★ **Single Vineyard Chenin Blanc** 🖫 Most attractive unwooded **12** combines honeyed/citrus elegance with lees richness in perfectly proportioned whole. Lovely now, good potential.

★★★★ **Straw Wine** ⑴ Stellar debut; **11** packed with lush, honeyed tropical fruit & warm brioche richness, plump mouthful held in check by brisk acid. From chenin, fermented in older oak. 500ml.

Blanc de Noir Not tasted. **Chardonnay** 🖫 ★★★☆ **12** richer, creamy style neatly offset by natural fresh feel, zesty citrus tail. Well-judged oak (30% new). Should further improve with year/2. **Viognier** 🖫 ★★★☆ **12** in characterful footsteps of **11**; ripe & fragrant, oak-enhanced richness & dry tapered length. Bring on fusion dishes! **Cape Ruby** ⑴ ★★★☆ Shiraz-based port-style **11** offers sweet spice & fruitcake. Wild, forest-floor earthiness & youthful spirit dictate some time in bottle. 500ml. — AL

■ **Maison De Cygne** *see* Oude Compagnies Post Private Cellar

Maison de Teijger

Location: Durbanville ▪ WO: Durbanville/Walker Bay/Paarl/Coastal/Bottelary/Elgin ▪ Est/1stB 2004 ▪ Closed to public ▪ Owner(s)/cellarmaster(s) Charl van Teijlingen ▪ Winemaker(s) Charl van Teijlingen, with Danél, Matthew & Elda-Marie van Teijlingen (all 2004) ▪ 6-9t/650-800cs own label 100% red ▪ PO Box 2703 Durbanville 7550 ▪ charlvt@kingsley.co.za ▪ **T** +27 (0)83-456-9410 ▪ F +27 (0)21-975-0806

Working since 2004 in his De Tyger Street home's double-garage with a few tons of classic red varieties winkled from prime vineyards, Durbanville garagiste Charl van Teijlingen, wife Danél and children Matthew and Elda-Marie market their vinifications off-site through group tastings such as wine clubs.

Pinot Noir range

Walker Bay ⑴ ★★★☆ Part of 6-bottle tasting pack from 4 farms, culminating in Coastal blend below. **11** has a tart bite to end but is most balanced of the range. PN 777B clone. **Durbanville Gold Screwcap** ⑴ ★★★ Easy-drinking **11** from BK5 clone, high-toned with green tea notes & sweetish follow-through. **Durbanville Gold Foil** Next awaited. **Durbanville Black Foil** ⑴ ★★★☆ French clone mix, this version has richer body but a tighter structure, with more focus on fruit giving **11** a sweetish feel. **Paarl** ⑴ ★★★ Darkest in colour, a ripe, soft & fruity **11** from PN 52C and PN 459B clones. **Coastal** ⑴ ★★★ **11** half Walker Bay plus combo of regions above, ditto for clones. Cherry mixed with spicy lift follows to sweetish rich palate. **Elgin** NEW 🗖 ★★★★ Last in regional selection now tasted, has lifted red cherry on **11** ex Elgin & from clone D115. Bright food-craving acidity refreshes.

Stellenbosch range

Petit Verdot ☺ ★★★ Brooding fruit, tart & rich, following to bold tarry palate with good acid cleanout. **11** fine varietal exposition.

Cabernet Sauvignon Next awaited, as **Cabernet Franc**, **Malbec**, **Merlot** & **Voorhout Bordeaux Blend**.

Durbanville range

Malbec NEW ☺ ★★★ Earthy, with strong coconut overlay, fresh **11** needs to shake oak dominance.

Cabernet Sauvignon (Fermicru XL) Next awaited, as for **Cabernet Sauvignon (NT 112)**, **Cabernet Franc**, **Malbec Diemersdal**, **Malbec Bloemendal**, **Merlot Klein Roosboom**, **Merlot Meerendal**, **Petit Verdot** & **Voorhout Bordeaux Blend**. — JP

■ **Makulu** *see* Imbuko Wines
■ **Malagas Wine Company** *see* Sijnn

■ **Malan de Versailles** *see* Versailles

Malan Family Vintners

Malan Family Vintners is an exclusive range developed by the Malan brothers of Simonsig Landgoed for export to Kenya and other East African countries.

Cape Rouge ⊕ 🍴 🏾 **★★ NV** shiraz with splash petit verdot. Juicy & easy quaffer. WO Stellenbosch, as next. **Cape Blanc** ⊕ 🍴 🏾 **★★☆** Pleasantly light **NV** sauvignon spiced with muscat. — GdB

Malanot Wines

Location/map: Stellenbosch ▪ WO: Western Cape ▪ Est/1stB 2006 ▪ Tasting & sales by appt ▪ Cellar tours by appt & during harvest only ▪ Owner(s) Malanot cc ▪ Cellarmaster(s)/winemaker(s)/viticulturist(s) Marius Malan (Jan 2006) ▪ 3ha/1.5ha (cab) ▪ 60t/10,000cs own label 50% red 50% white + 2,000cs for clients ▪ Brands for clients: Selma ▪ PO Box 22 Lynedoch 7603 ▪ info@malanotwines.co.za ▪ www.malanotwines.co.za ▪ S 33° 59' 57.8" E 018° 49' 55.2" ▪ **T +27 (0)72-124-7462**

'Wine is in my blood,' says Marius Malan, referring to his family's grape-growing heritage in the Perdeberg area. With his own brands and business based in Stellenbosch, he consults to various clients keen to share his philosophy of making wine as naturally as possible, letting the fruit reflect the terroir.

Malanot Wines range

★★★★ Family Reserve ⊕ From shiraz, aromatic nose of cinnamon, allspice & cloves, **10** is concentrated, elegant, with black cherries/cream balancing well-integrated oak (60% new French) & refreshing acidity.
★★★★ Cherry Blossom ✓ Plenty of promise on dense & intense cab-based Bordeaux blend **11**. Masses of spicy appeal - liquorice & aniseed predominate - with black plums, cherry tobacco & gritty tannic finish.
Vino Café Pinotage Await next, as for **Bush Pig**. **Flower Pot ★★★☆** Plenty of expressive fruit on pleasing **13**, partly oaked blend chenin & 20% chardonnay: peaches, spiced apple crumble. Tad more acidity would add vibrancy.

Vior range

Shiraz ☺ **★★★** Harmonious **11** improves on previous with pleasant black fruit, peppery hints & clean fresh finish. Some good quaffing here.

Cabernet Sauvignon ★★☆ Black fruit & dark chocolate with a caramel core on **11**. **Pinot Noir** Await next.
Pinotage ★★★★ Well-made **12** shouts its varietal characteristics to the skies! Perfume, spice, smoked meat, black & red fruit. **Red Blend** ✓ **★★★★** Bright & cheery **11** from cab & merlot delights & entices with aromas of cherry tobacco, dark chocolate & spice. Thoroughly enjoyable. **Chardonnay** Await next.

Cape Colony range NEW

Malbec ★★☆ Over-ripe & slightly unfocused **09** shows some dark chocolate & black fruit.

Chandos range

Pinotage Export only. Await next, as for **Red Blend** & **Red Blend BIB**. — CM

■ **Malgas** *see* Sijnn
■ **Mamre Road** *see* Darling Cellars

MAN Family Wines

Location: Stellenbosch/Paarl ▪ WO: Coastal/Paarl/Western Cape ▪ Est 2001 ▪ Tasting & sales by appt ▪ Owner(s) MAN Vintners (Pty) Ltd ▪ Cellarmaster(s) Tyrrel Myburgh (2001) ▪ Winemaker(s) Francois Bezuidenhout (Jul 2011) ▪ 350,000cs own label 60% red 39% white 1% rosé ▪ PO Box 389 Stellenbosch 7599 ▪ info@manwines.com ▪ www.manwines.com ▪ **T +27 (0)21-861-7759** ▪ F +27 (0)21-887-4340

MAN was named after Marie, Anette and Nicky, wives to the friends who started the winery - José Conde of Stark-Condé, and brothers Tyrrel and Philip Myburgh of Joostenberg. In a major rebranding, the name changes to 'MAN Family Wines' to emphasise the familial nature of the business; redesigned labels show vineyard scenes in Agter Paarl, source of most of the grapes; and Afrikaans names strengthen the brand's South African heritage and give 'a deeper backstory'.

Tormentoso range

Cabernet Sauvignon 🏠 🍷 ★★★★ Somewhat old-fashioned **11** with dark fruit, slight herbal edge, toasty oak. Medium bodied, with fresh acidity & good tannic grip. Grapes from Paarl & Stellenbosch, rest of range Paarl. **Mourvèdre** ① 🏠 🍷 ★★★ Dark fruit, fynbos & some earthy character on **12**, with 15% shiraz. Rustic in style, ideal with country cooking. **11** sold out unrated. **Bush Vine Pinotage** 🍷 ★★★ **11** is soft, easy & entirely likeable with cherries, plums & milk chocolate. Rich & broad with just enough acidity. **Syrah-Mourvèdre** 🏠 🍷 ★★★ Dark & brooding **11** has earthy, malty notes to go with dark fruit. Rich & full, not for the faint hearted. **Old Vine Chenin Blanc** 🏠 🍷 ★★★ Part-oaked **12** has plenty of concentrated stonefruit & fresh acidity but arguably lacks a little nuance.

Essay range

Shiraz-Cinsault-Mourvèdre-Viognier ① 🏠 🍷 ★★★ Eminently likeable **10** is medium bodied, with red & black fruit, hint of spice, bright acidity & fine tannins. Light the barbecue already. **Chenin Blanc-Viognier** ① 🏠 🍷 ★★★ Citrus, peach & slight leesy note on **11**, uncomplicated summer aperitif. WO W Cape for these.

MAN Family Wines range

Ou Kalant Cabernet Sauvignon 🏠 🍷 ★★★ 'Old Rascal' is modest but likeable, shows red fruit, fresh acidity, fine tannins. **12** includes 15% merlot. Lightly wooded & not super-dry, as for all reds in this range. **Jan Fiskaal Merlot** 🏠 🍷 ★★★ Name refers to the fiscal shrike, a common sight in the vineyards. Red-fruited **11** is accessible but lacks real oomph. **Bosstok Pinotage** 🏠 🍷 ★★★ 'Bushvine', source of gluggable **11**. Shows plummy fruit, brush of vanilla. WO Paarl. **Skaapveld Shiraz** 🏠 🍷 ★★★ Name references grazing land adjoining many Agter Paarl vineyards. No mess, no fuss **11** red fruit, fresh acidity, crunchy tannins. **Hanekraai Rosé** 🏠 🍷 ★★ 'Rooster's Crow' **13** is entirely straightforward, sweet & soft. **Padstal Chardonnay** 🏠 🍷 ★★★ 'Farmstall'. Understated **12** shows lemon-lime & subtle vanilla, seems rather lean despite some sugar. **Free-run Steen Chenin Blanc** 🏠 🍷 ★★★ **13** is clean & crisp with notes of guava & pear. **Warrelwind Sauvignon Blanc** 🏠 🍷 ★★★ 'Whirlwind'. Lime, fynbos & gravel road dustiness on **13**. Appears sweet on entry before pithy finish. WO W Cape. Discontinued: **Cuvée V Chenin Blanc**. — CE

Manley Private Cellar

Location/map: Tulbagh ▪ WO: Tulbagh/Coastal ▪ Est/1stB 2002 ▪ Tasting & sales Mon-Fri 9–5 Sat 10-3 ▪ Fee R25, waived on purchase ▪ Cellar tours by appt ▪ Closed Good Fri & Dec 25 ▪ Luxury B&B ▪ Restaurant ▪ Wedding & conference facilities ▪ Chapel ▪ Walks ▪ Owner(s) Manley Wine Lodge (Pty) Ltd ▪ Winemaker(s)/viticulturist(s) Stefan Hartmann ▪ 38ha/7ha (cab, merlot, ptage, shiraz) ▪ PO Box 318 Tulbagh 6820 ▪ bookings@ manleywinelodge.co.za ▪ www.manleywinelodge.co.za ▪ S 33° 16' 15.8" E 019° 8' 43.8" ▪ **T +27 (0)23-230-0582** ▪ F +27 (0)23-230-0057

Winemaker Stefan Hartmann refers to a 'hands-on approach to the whole cycle' on this small Tulbagh winery and tourist destination, best exemplified by his taking on the role of viticulturist. Towards the end of the cycle, the Manley marketing thrust aims at converting every person in SA's 'rainbow nation' into a drinker of wine as first choice.

Cabernet Sauvignon ★★★ After well-judged 09 (★★★★), **10** seems over-ripe, lacking verve. **Merlot** ★★★ Plum fruit & oak char on **10**, tight tannins need time to relax & soften. **Pinotage** ★★★ Unlike previous, **11** has distinct pinotage character, drinkability upped by crowd-pleasing vanilla from American oak. **Shiraz** ★★★ Fruit-filled **10** has meaty Marmite overlay, freshness & balance. Tasty & versatile enough to make it your housewine. **Thatch House Red** ① 🏠 ★★★ Shiraz-led blend with cab & merlot, **09** interesting star anise fragrance, soft fruity body. **Semillon-Sauvignon Blanc** ① ★★★ Variation on **10** blend tasted mid-2011. This has 64% semillon, better balance & length, satisfying vinosity. Fine mealtime companion. WO Coastal. — CE,CvZ

■ **Manor House** *see* Nederburg Wines
■ **MAN Vintners** *see* MAN Family Wines
■ **Mapoggo** *see* Druk My Niet Wine Estate
■ **Marcel de Reuck** *see* Crows Nest

Marianne Wine Estate

Location/map: Stellenbosch • WO: Simonsberg-Paarl/Western Cape • Est/1stB 2004 • Tasting, sales & cellar tours Mon-Sun 9–10 • Fee R20/5 wines, waived on purchase • Olivello Restaurant • Tour groups • Panoramic tasting deck • Gift shop • Deli • Conference facilities • 1hr 'grape to wine' tour • 4-star accommodation • Owner(s) Dauriac family • Wine consultant Francois Haasbroek (Dec 2012) • Viticulturist(s) Schalk Pienaar (Jan 2013) • 36ha/±18ha (cab, merlot, ptage, shiraz, sauv) • 100t/16,000cs own label 90% red 5% white 5% rosé • PO Box 7300 Stellenbosch 7599 • info@mariannewinefarm.co.za • www.mariannewinefarm.co.za • S 33°49' 57.6" E 018°53' 37.4" • **T +27 (0)21-875-5040**

It's a decade since Bordeaux's Dauriac family put down New World roots on the Simonsberg to craft timeless wines with a modern – rich, big – profile. That's about as long as these boutique reds need to open up and display their full potential, as a recent vertical tasting showed. Luckily for visitors to the rejuvenated cellardoor, mature back vintages are still available.

★★★★ **Merlot** Opulent meaty succulence of **10** well contained within a firm structure; smooth texture, with fine tannins for graceful ageing. **09** & **08** for sale at the tasting room.

★★★★ **Floreal** Flagship blend merlot, cab & shiraz is densely packed but relatively understated in context of house style. **10** firm tannins grip intense, deep-piled cassis fruit, need time to relax. **04 - 09** all available.

Selena NEW ☺ ★★★ Attractive **11**, four-way red blend with pinotage, proffers red & black berry fruit supportively oaked.

Cabernet Sauvignon ⓟ ★★★★ Dramatic **09** has plenty of fruit weight & power but also balance thanks to fresh acidity, firm tannins. **08** (★★), **07** & **06** available. **Pinotage** Next awaited. **Shiraz** ★★★☆ Whiffs of white pepper tether huge dark-fruit concentration of **10**, but somewhat weighty, in search of elegance. **09, 08** & **07** also for sale. **Desirade** ⓟ ★★★★ Silky merlot-led **05** with 19% cab; fleshy sweet plum, fine grip. **04** also available. **Cape Blend** ★★★ Approachable **10** including pinotage is medium bodied, with juicy plum fruit, moderate acidity & soft tannins. **09** & **08** still selling. **Rosé** ⓟ 🍷 ★★ Red fruit & dried herbs on dry, undemanding **11**. WO Western Cape. **Sauvignon Blanc** 🍷 ★★★ Wooded **12** is round & developed, with noticeable leesy character. — DS

■ **Marimba** see Southern Sky Wines

Marklew Family Wines

Location/map: Stellenbosch • Est 1970 • 1stB 2003 • Tasting, sales & tours by appt • Tour groups (max 20) • Private/business functions for small groups • Walks • Mountain biking • Conservation area • Owner(s) Marklew family (Edward Dudley, Edward William, Lyn & Haidee) • Winemaker(s) Duan Brits (Sep 2012) • Viticulturist(s) Billy Marklew (Jun 2001), with Duan Brits (Sep 2012) • 58ha/45ha (cabs s/f, merlot, ptage, shiraz, chard, sauv) • ±300t/5,000cs own label 80% red 20% white • BWI, IPW • PO Box 17 Elsenburg 7607 • wine@marklew.co.za • www.marklew.co.za • S 33°50' 35.7" E 018°51' 50.3" • **T +27 (0)21-884-4412** • F +27 (0)21-884-4412

Bill and Haidee Marklew restored the original, disused 180-year-old wine cellar on this prime Simonsberg, Stellenbosch, farm when their parents retired in 2001 after four decades of grape growing. Winemaker Duan Brits, who helped vinify the boutique's maiden 2003, has returned to continue the classic-yet-modern style. The range was sold out at press time, and new vintages were unready for tasting.

■ **Marlbrook** see Klein Constantia Estate
■ **Martinique** see Du Preez Estate

Mary Le Bow Trust

Location: Somerset West • WO: Western Cape • 1stB 2005 • Wine sales Mon-Fri 8.30-4 • Owner(s) Frater family • Winemaker(s) Bruce Jack • 516cs own label 100% red • PO Box 3636 Somerset West 7129 • info@thedrift.co.za • **T +27 (0)86-150-2025** • F +27 (0)86-563-9533

Grapes for this wine come from a farm near Ashton owned by the Frater family and the winemaker is Bruce Jack of Flagstone fame – the late James Frater and Jack having been good friends. James's mother Angela has distant ancestors buried in the crypt of London's St Mary le Bow Church, giving rise to the name.

★★★★ **Mary le Bow** Powerful **11** (★★★★) roughly equal cab & shiraz, 23% petit verdot. Dark fruit, smoked meat & fynbos; lacks finesse of **09** & seems to be tending to an ever more imposing style. No **10**. —CE

Maske Wines

Location: Wellington ▪ Map: Paarl & Wellington ▪ WO: Coastal/Western Cape ▪ Est/1stB 2000 ▪ Tasting & sales Mon-Sun by appt ▪ Closed Ash Wed, Easter Fri/Sun & Dec 25 ▪ BYO picnic ▪ Owner(s) Erich & Janine Maske ▪ Winemaker(s)/viticulturist(s) Outsourced ▪ 7ha/5ha (cab, merlot, chenin) ▪ 80% red 20% white, blends outsourced ▪ Klein Waterval PO Box 206 Wellington 7654 ▪ laureat@iafrica.com ▪ www.maskewines.co.za ▪ S 33° 40' 4.2" E 019° 2' 37.3" ▪ **T +27 (0)21-873-3407** ▪ F +27 (0)21-873-3408

Wellington-based Erich and Janine Maske say their winery has grown from a hobby into a promising export business, though the emphasis remains on 'quality of life' and 'common ground we have with people from all over the world'. Like their friends who visited a tattoo parlour and gave name to a new red blend.

Leeumasker range
Cape Blend ⊕ ▤ ★★★★ Pinotage with cab, shiraz & minor others, previewed **11** offers flowers & black cherries, ripe but balanced fruity flavours.

Maske range
Cabernet Sauvignon Await new, as for **Merlot** & **Chenin Blanc**. **Tattoo** NEW ★★★ **11** shiraz/cab combo (67/33) very ripe & fruit-sweet, slips down easily. WO W Cape. — CvZ

▪ **Mason's Hill** *see* The Mason's Winery
▪ **Maties** *see* Stellenbosch University Welgevallen Cellar
▪ **Matumi** *see* Lourensford Wine Estate

Matzikama Organic Cellar

Location: Vredendal ▪ Map: Olifants River ▪ Est/1stB 2001 ▪ Tasting by appt ▪ Owner(s)/winemaker(s)/viticulturist(s) Klaas Coetzee ▪ 12ha/2.5ha (cab, shiraz) ▪ 24t 100% red ▪ PO Box 387 Vredendal 8160 ▪ klaas@matzikamawyn.co.za ▪ www.matzikamawyn.co.za ▪ S 31° 36' 34.37" E 018° 44' 11.32" ▪ **T +27 (0)82-801-3737**

His day job as winemaker at the West Coast's Stellar Winery provides Klaas Coetzee with plenty of experience but little time for his own Matzikama brand. He intends, perhaps this year, to use the wine from tannat vines planted in 2012 'to bottle a bit, perhaps a shiraz/tannat blend'.

McGregor Wines

Location: McGregor ▪ Map: Robertson ▪ WO: McGregor/Robertson ▪ Est 1948 ▪ 1stB 1978 ▪ Tasting & sales Mon-Fri 8-5 Sat 10-3 ▪ Closed Good Fri, Dec 25/26 & Jan 1 ▪ Cellar tours by appt ▪ BYO picnic ▪ Owner(s) 27 members ▪ Winemaker(s) Elmo du Plessis ▪ 12,000t 22% red 78% white ▪ IPW ▪ PO Box 519 McGregor 6708 ▪ info@mcgregorwinery.co.za ▪ www.mcgregorwinery.co.za ▪ S 33° 56' 5.4" E 019° 50' 56.3" ▪ **T +27 (0)23-625-1741/1109** ▪ F +27 (0)23-625-1829

The valed-in village of McGregor may be situated at the end of a road that leads nowhere, 'but it's a good tarred road!' chuckles Valinda Oosthuizen of McGregor Wines, playing along with their slogan of being geographically down-tempo and therefore offering the mellowest wines around. Valinda particularly treasures the many friendships formed every Pensioners' Day, held monthly.

Winemaker's Reserve range
Cabernet Sauvignon ⊕ ★★★★ When last tasted, **08**'s dark fruit interwoven with leather & vanilla from year older oak worked well, though alcohol gave a slightly hot finish.

McGregor range

Pinotage ☺ ▤ ▨ ★★★ Spicy & juicy **12** is a natural born quaffer, unwooded & commendably dry.
Chenin Blanc ☺ ▤ ▨ ★★★ Fruit salad & flowers to take to your **13** al fresco music concert. **Red Muscadel** ☺ ▤ ▨ ★★★ **13** cheerful fortified sipper for winter or summer, nice spicy grip & upbeat raisin farewell.

Ruby Cabernet 🍷 📖 ★★ Unoaked **12** not its ebullient fruity self, more reserved, herbal. **Shiraz** 🍷 📖 ★ **11** brisk acidity to lift rich meat dishes. **Cabernet Sauvignon-Merlot** 🕐 🍷 📖 ★★★ Juicy & savoury **11** somewhat leaner than last time, easily remedied with rich country stews. **Pinotage Rosé** 🍷 📖 ★★ Semi-dry **12** undemanding, with rock candy & cream flavour. **Chardonnay** 🍷 📖 ★★★ Offering tangy apricot taste, **12** is delicate & uncomplicated, needs drinking soon. **Colombard** 🍷 📖 ★★★ Round & sweetish, **13** offers typical guavas in a light, carefree body. **Sauvignon Blanc** 🍷 📖 ★★ Pleasantly airy & floral, **13** slight creaminess to soften the bone-dry finish. **White Muscadel** 🕐 ★★★ **08** packed with flavour richness, like drinking liquidised sultanas. **Cape Ruby** 🕐 📖 ★ **10** port-style from ruby cab, shade less characterful than previous. WO Robertson. — HJ,JP

MC Square

Location: Somerset West ▪ WO: Stellenbosch ▪ Est/1stB 1996 ▪ Closed to public ▪ Owner(s)/winemaker(s)/viticulturist(s) Jean-Luc Sweerts ▪ 200cs MCC Brut & 800cs Sophiatown ▪ PO Box 436 Somerset West 7129 ▪ mcsquare@iafrica.com ▪ **T +27 (0)83-303-5467**

DRC-born, Somerset West-based boutique vigneron Jean-Luc Sweerts' winery name is a shortening of 'méthode cap classique', so it's appropriate that he's added a 10-year-old NV bubbly named La Vie en Rosé to his range. We're looking forward to taste it next time.

★★★★ **Sophiatown** 🕐 Classically styled **05** cab; dry, elegant & serious, but not for keeping.

★★★★☆ **Cuvée Brut Méthode Cap Classique** 🕐 Classic & expressive **NV (06)** sparkling from pinot noir, chardonnay, pinot meunier. Persistent pinpoint bubbles & complex perfume.

Isand Iwana Await next, as for **Cuvée Chardonnay**. — IM

▪ **Meander** see uniWines Vineyards
▪ **Meditation** see Nwanedi Estate

Meerendal Wine Estate 🍷🍴☕🏕📷🚴♿

Location/WO: Durbanville ▪ Map: Durbanville, Philadelphia & Darling ▪ Est 1702 ▪ 1stB 1969 ▪ Tasting & sales Mon-Sun 9-6 ▪ Closed Good Fri, Dec 25 & Jan 1 ▪ Cellar tours by appt ▪ Meerendal Bistro Restaurant & Deli open daily ▪ Barn & Lawn function venue ▪ Facilities for children ▪ Tour groups ▪ Farm produce ▪ Conferences ▪ Weddings/functions ▪ Walks/hikes ▪ Mountain biking ▪ Conservation area ▪ The Meerendal Boutique Hotel ▪ Owner(s) Coertze family ▪ Cellarmaster(s) Liza Goodwin (Sep 2006) ▪ Viticulturist(s) Victor Rossouw (Feb 2007) ▪ 220ha/70ha (merlot, ptage, pinot, shiraz, chard, sauv) ▪ 650t/50,000cs own label 75% red 20% white 5% rosé ▪ IPW ▪ Private Bag X1702 Durbanville 7551 ▪ info@meerendal.co.za ▪ www.meerendal.co.za ▪ S 33° 47' 55.8" E 018° 37' 26.2" ▪ **T +27 (0)21-975-1655** ▪ F +27 (0)21-975-1657

The dates 1702 and 1969 (founding and first bottled vintage) speak of heritage and tradition but any recent visitor to Durbanville's Meerendal will hardly recognise the estate for all the recent stylish revitalisation. Most visibly, the palm-flanked Cape Dutch homestead has been converted into a boutique hotel, and in line with the slogan 'Home of Food & Wine', there's a restaurant and deli plus many other cellardoor amenities. Pinotage roots run deep, thus gratifying to see winemaker Liza Goodwin's namesake Cape Blend debuting this edition.

Prestige range

★★★★ **Heritage Block Pinotage** 🕐 Accomplished version from 1955-planted bushvines. Elegant **10** (★★★★★) pays homage to Old World restraint with fairly moderate alcohol & proper dryness, while offering vibrant strawberry fruit. No **08**, **09**. Flavours on **07** were muted by firm tannins.

★★★★ **Liza** NEW Cape Blend of pinotage & 15% piquant shiraz. Moderate 13.2% alcohol, refreshing acidity contribute to elegant debut in mulberry-toned **11**. Polished tannins from older oak, refined conclusion.

★★★★ **Blanc de Blancs Méthode Cap Classique** 🕐 Well-structured **07** sparkling, typical yeast & green apple notes; 6 months lees-ageing for broader flavours.

★★★★☆ **Natural Sweet** 🕐 From naturally fermented chenin, older oak. **09** (★★★★) had just enough acid to balance overly ripe marzipan flavours. Medalled **06** was also from chenin.

Merlot Reserve Await new. **Bin159 Shiraz** 🕐 ★★★★ Blockbuster-style **07** baked mulberry & fruitcake flavours, mouthfilling tannins. **Bin 242 Sauvignon Blanc** 🕐 ★★★★ Last tasted was subtle & rich **07**, more complex than **06** (★★★★).

Meerendal range

★★★★ **Pinotage** 🀫 **11** 'older style' with leather, sugar plum whiffs but oh-so familiar & comfortable. As pliable as soft & juicy **10**.

Pinotage Rosé ☺ 🍴 🀫 ★★☆ **13** ticks all the summer fun boxes: pretty hue, moderate alcohol, teasing sweetness.

Cabernet Sauvignon ⓔ 🀫 ★★★ **10**'s supple tannins almost overwhelmed by plush & sweet fruit. **Merlot** 🀫 ★★★☆ Creamy oak, subtle plummy notes & supple tannins on well-made **11**. For food or solo. **Pinot Noir** ⓔ 🀫 ★★★☆ Raspberry/cherry-infused **11** bright & finely structured, with meaty conclusion. **Shiraz** ★★★☆ Ripe fruit interwoven with charry oak & fresh acidity. Like all reds in this range, **10** shows supple tannins for early approachability. Just misses the poise of standout **09** (★★★★). **Chardonnay Wooded** ⓔ ★★★ Half-oaked **08** has breadth from lees-ageing, matched by pronounced citrus-apple acidity. **Chardonnay Unwooded** ✓ 🍴 🀫 ★★★☆ Inviting lemon cream whiffs, pinpoint acidity, lovely dryness on elegant **13**; well priced & worth seeking out. **Sauvignon Blanc** 🍴 🀫 ★★★☆ Consistent & flavour packed. **13** nettle, grass & fig highlights; bright, long farewell. Discontinued: **Cabernet Sauvignon-Merlot**. — CvZ

Meerhof Family Vineyards 🍴🍷

Location: Riebeek-Kasteel ▪ Map: Swartland ▪ WO: Western Cape/Coastal ▪ Est/1stB 2000 ▪ Tasting & sales by appt only ▪ Owner(s) Cobus Kotze ▪ Winemaker(s)/viticulturist(s) Johan Meyer ▪ 150ha/17ha (cab, merlot, mourv, ptage, shiraz, chenin) ▪ 2,400cs own label 55% red 45% white ▪ PO Box 1229 Malmesbury 7299 ▪ meerhof@wcaccess.co.za ▪ www.meerhof.co.za ▪ S 33° 24' 19.8" E 018° 52' 15.0" ▪ T +27 (0)82-572-5940 ▪ F +27 (0)86-683-8132

Newer vintages are being held back for further maturation, says owner Cobus Kotze, but the intention is to continue producing wine using the facilities at Riebeek-Kasteel's Meerhof cellar, also used by other small-scale vintners.

★★★★ **Drège** ⓔ Shiraz-headed **08** offers appealing spicy, truffly notes, savoury persistence. Light touch from deftly handled tannins, tangy mineral thread prolong drinking pleasure. Merlot & cab are other partners. **Salomon** Await next, as for **Saffronne Blanc de Noir**. **Syrah** ⓔ ★★★★ Delicate **08** presents full, pure dark spice, truffle flavours. Fresh core, comfortably padded tannins. Includes splashes mourvèdre, viognier. Previous was **06** (★★★★). **Antebellum Chenin Blanc** ⓔ ★★★★ **12** almost ethereal floral/earthy notes; fresh with underlying lees-enriched breadth. Should develop well. Paarl grapes, natural ferment, mainly older oak. — AL

■ **Meerkat** *see* Welbedacht Wine Estate

Meerlust Estate 🍴🍷

Location/map/WO: Stellenbosch ▪ Est 1693 ▪ 1stB 1975 ▪ Tasting & sales Mon-Fri 9–5 Sat 10–2 ▪ Fee R30 ▪ Closed all pub hols ▪ Cellar tours by appt ▪ Owner(s) Hannes Myburgh ▪ Cellarmaster(s) Chris Williams (Jan 2004) ▪ Winemaker(s) Altus Treurnicht (assistant, 2008) ▪ Viticulturist(s) Roelie Joubert (2001) ▪ 400ha/ 106ha (cabs s/f, merlot, p verdot, pinot, chard) ▪ 500t/50,000cs own label 90% red 10% white ▪ PO Box 7121 Stellenbosch 7599 ▪ info@meerlust.co.za ▪ www.meerlust.co.za ▪ S 34° 1' 1.7" E 018° 45' 24.7" ▪ T +27 (0)21-843-3587 ▪ F +27 (0)21-843-3274

This beautiful Stellenbosch estate has belonged to the Myburgh family since 1757 and the gabled old manor house is (rather a rare thing, this) the home of current owner Hannes Myburgh – full of his artworks and older treasures. In the 1950s winemaking was reborn here, and Meerlust's reputation has long been high. Winemaker Chris Williams has brought new energy and added lustre since moving into the top cellar job a decade back, and his wines show a fine balance between modern stylistics and classic ideals. But Williams is always quick to credit the sterling vineyard work of Roelie Joubert, and indeed to recognise the contribution of the whole team. There's a genuine, pervading concern for the social fabric, for the whole Meerlust community, which adds greatly to the place.

★★★★☆ **Cabernet Sauvignon** ⓔ 🀫 Impressive **10** in more austere style than last expressive vintage. Seamlessly integrated tannins conceal dense, nicely ripe blackcurrant fruit. Needs time to realise potential.

★★★★☆ **Merlot** Polished, classy **10** lifted by 11% notably aromatic cab franc. Rich, suavely textured dark plum fruit underpinned by fine acid thread & spicy, mostly new oak. A mineral centre contributes to the complete, harmonious whole.

★★★★☆ **Pinot Noir** Initially reticent, youthful **12** from 26-year-old vines takes time to reveal its utterly compelling, silken charm. Earthy core with profound, pure red fruit structured by supple tannins & fine, savoury acidity in seamless whole.

★★★★☆ **Rubicon** Sensational **09**, indisputably great vintage of venerable cab-dominated (70%) Bordeaux blend. Indulgently plush, with dark fruit that easily absorbs & integrates the oak influence (65% new barrels) to produce an impressively complex, densely structured & promising masterpiece.

★★★★ **Red** Label used for 'declassified' Rubicon, in lesser years. Drinkable, plummy, fresh & fleshy **11** merlot-dominated & accessible, but lighter than flagship - for earlier drinking.

★★★★ **Chardonnay** Light, creamy **11** less concentrated & complex than **10** (★★★★☆); tricky vintage well put together to deliver appealing signature of citrus twist for appetising though earlier enjoyment. — IM

Meinert Wines

Location/map: Stellenbosch ▪ WO: Devon Valley/Elgin ▪ Est 1987 ▪ 1stB 1997 ▪ Tasting Mon-Sat strictly by appt only ▪ Closed all pub hols ▪ Owner(s) Martin Meinert ▪ Cellarmaster(s)/winemaker(s) Martin Meinert (Nov 1997) ▪ Viticulturist(s) Henk Marconi (Jan 1991) ▪ 16ha/12ha (cabs s/f, merlot, p verdot, ptage, sem) ▪ 90t/14,000cs own label 50% red 50% white ▪ PO Box 7221 Stellenbosch 7599 ▪ info@meinertwines.com ▪ www.meinertwines.com ▪ S 33° 54' 1.8" E 018° 48' 50.2" ▪ **T +27 (0)21-865-2363** ▪ F +27 (0)21-865-2414

Martin Meinert is well into his second quarter-century as owner of this family farm and boutique winery in Stellenbosch's Devon Valley. The first plot he bought in 1987 was known simply as 'Remainder of Farm 78'! Ten years later he gave up his prestigious security as Vergelegen winemaker (he'd helped plan both vineyards and cellar there) to realise his 'dream of a small private vineyard and winery'. Wines which had been sold off in bulk now appeared under his own label. Development continues (a new straw wine, and a red under the La Barry label, named for his white wine-loving wife Leigh Ann Barry) but core values remain – restraint, dry elegance, and Martin's belief in 'the pleasure of wines that can age'.

Meinert Wines range

★★★★ **Cabernet Sauvignon** ⊛ 🍾 Always serious & strongly built. **08** (★★★★) was on the sombre side; **09** has much more life, juicy bright fruit. Well balanced & approachable, but will benefit from ageing.

★★★★☆ **Synchronicity 09** again shows classic approach to grapes from a warmer climate: alcoholic power, but also balance & drinkability; fruit & structure in partnership but neither overt. From cab & merlot, plus pinotage, cab franc. Rich, concentrated, succulent & savoury. Still very young, but not impossible now.

★★★★☆ **Semillon Straw Wine** NEW **12** from vine-dried grapes off the estate's only white-wine vineyard. Delicious aromatic & flavour complexity to the sweet succulence; concentrated, but not heavy: tangy, lemony acidity ensures elegance & lively freshness. Natural ferment & maturation in older oak.

Merlot 🍾 ★★★☆ **10** has plenty of flavour, but also a lean sternness most asserted in its tannic grip & partly derived from 2 years in (older) oak. Has 14% cab. **Printer's Ink Pinotage** 🍾 ★★★☆ Attractive **10** includes some merlot, but the perfume & sweet-berried fruit is all pinotage's - while the serious but moderate tannin structure is perhaps shared! Needs time. **La Barry Red** NEW 🍾 ★★★ Attractive, simple, slightly awkward merlot-based **11** blend is ripely smooth & fruity, but also has some lean, green elements. **La Barry Sauvignon Blanc** ⊛ 🍾 ★★★★ Preview **12**'s exuberant, ripe aromas & flavour continued through to a succulent, lingering finish. **11** (★★★★) greener. From Elgin.

Family Collection

★★★★ **Chardonnay** 🍾 **12** less oaky in youth than previous (here the wood is nicely supportive), but similar oatmeal & citrus notes. Mouthfilling, fresh & lively, with a lingering limy finish. WO Elgin, like Riesling. **The Italian Job** ⊛ 🍾 ★★★ Merlot blanc de noir (well, pale coppery pink) in **11**. Puzzling: unfruity & indeterminate, but well structured; oaked but soft, just-dry. **Riesling** NEW 🍾 ★★★☆ Rather more hearty than delicate, **12** has very attractive, varietally true aromas & flavours. Balanced & easy, just off-dry - nicely so. — TJ

■ **Melck's** see Muratie Wine Estate

Melkboomsdrift Wines

Location: Lutzville ▪ Map: Olifants River ▪ Tasting & sales Mon-Fri 9-5 ▪ Melkboomsdrift Lodge serving farm breakfasts, with dinner & picnic baskets on request; also self-catering option ▪ Conference venue (20 max) ▪ Owner(s)/cellarmaster(s)/winemaker(s) Hilsa van den Heever ▪ Viticulturist(s) Jeff Joubert ▪ (cab, merlot, ptage, shiraz) ▪ PO Box 1124 Vredendal 8160 ▪ info@melkboomsdrift.co.za ▪ S 31° 36' 15.24" E 018° 24' 19.86" ▪ **T +27 (0)27-217-2624** ▪ F +27 (0)27-217-2535

For a more personal encounter with the wines of the West Coast, traditionally associated with large wineries, visit Hilsa van den Heever at her Melkboomsdrift lodge and conference venue on the Olifants River. Here Hilsa vinifies a boutique range of red wines which, if all goes to plan, will be available for sampling at a new tasting area on the riverbank, conveniently near her planned new campsite.

Mellasat Vineyards

Location/WO: Paarl ▪ Map: Paarl & Wellington ▪ Est 1996 ▪ 1stB 1999 ▪ Tasting & sales Mon-Sat 9.30-5.30 Sun & pub hols 10-4 ▪ Closed Good Fri, Dec 25 & Jan 1 ▪ Cellar tours by appt ▪ Light lunches for groups/tours or private dinner functions by appt; pop-up seasonal restaurant & other food-based events ▪ Tour groups ▪ Conferences ▪ Paarl Ommiberg Festival ▪ Owner(s) Stephen Richardson ▪ Cellarmaster(s)/winemaker(s) Stephen Richardson (Jan 1999) ▪ Viticulturist(s) Poena Malherbe (Sep 1996) ▪ 13ha/8ha (cab, ptage, shiraz, tempranillo, chard, chenin, viog) ▪ 50t/7,000cs own label 40% red 50% white 10% rosé ▪ IPW ▪ PO Box 7169 Paarl 7623 ▪ mellasat@mweb. co.za ▪ www.mellasat.com ▪ S 33° 44' 30.0" E 019° 2' 31.0" ▪ **T +27 (0)21-862-4525** ▪ F +27 (0)21-862-4525

In owner Stephen Richardson's own words, 'A family run boutique wine producer with an emphasis on innovation'; latest innovation is the Pop-up Restaurant, which only pops up one weekend per season. The rest of the time, its kitchen provides catering for wine-tasting groups and tailor-made functions.

Premium Exclusives NEW

★★★★ **Viognier** ⚗ Barrel-fermented/matured in Romanian oak, **12** oozes peach blossom & vanilla perfume. Mouthfilling & firm with rich fruit flavours & delicious persistent nutty farewell.

Mellasat Premium range

'Sigma' White Pinotage ⚗ ★★★★ Pinotage vinified in Romanian oak barrels as white wine, **12** is fruity & spicy, full-flavoured & creamy. **Chardonnay** ⚗ ★★★★ Barrel-fermented **12**, creamy caramel biscuit, citrus flavour & vibrant acidity, rounded & full. Perfect for seafood. **Tuin Wyn** Next awaited. Discontinued: **'M'**.

Dekker's Valley range

Shiraz ☺ 🍽 ⚗ ★★★ Toasty oak, mulberry & mocha finish on cheerful **11**. **Revelation** ☺ 🍽 ⚗ ★★★ Cab, shiraz, pinotage blend, **10** now bottled, is fresh & vividly fruity, with supple tannins. Easy winter sipper. **Chenin Blanc** ☺ 🍽 ⚗ ★★★ Preview **13** trumps previous with bright, juicy apple, melon & guava notes. Moreish, with perky acidity.

Shiraz Rosé 🍽 ⚗ ★★ Previewed dry **13** is pale pink, crisp & fruity for summer sunsets. — WB

◼ **Mentors** *see* KWV Wines
◼ **Merchant's Mark** *see* Barrydale Winery & Distillery

Merwida Winery

Location: Rawsonville ▪ Map/WO: Breedekloof ▪ Est 1963 ▪ 1stB 1975 ▪ Tasting & sales Mon-Fri 9-12.30; 1. 30-5 Sat 9-1 ▪ Closed Easter Fri-Mon, Dec 25-Jan 1 ▪ Merwida Country Manor T +27 (0)23-349-1435 ▪ Owner(s) Schalk & Pierre van der Merwe ▪ Cellarmaster(s)/viticulturist(s) Magnus Kriel ▪ Winemaker(s) Magnus Kriel (Dec 2000), with Sarel van Staden (Aug 1982) ▪ 630ha (cab, merlot, shiraz, chard, chenin, sauv, sem, viog) ▪ 15,000t 40% red 60% white ▪ ISO 22000, BWI, Fairtrade, WIETA ▪ PO Box 4 Rawsonville 6845 ▪ wines@merwida.com ▪ www.merwida.com ▪ S 33° 41' 24.9" E 019° 20' 31.1" ▪ **T +27 (0)23-349-1144** ▪ F +27 (0)23-349-1953/+27 (0)86-538-1953

This Breedekloof family cellar, which offers value-for-money Fairtrade-accredited wines, experienced a bumper crop of 'outstanding' quality last harvest, says winemaker Magnus Kriel, who has great expectations for the Sauvignon in

particular. It's a best seller, along with the Barbera and Cabernet, which 'usually run out at the exact same time' according to marketing manager Monique Smith.

★★★★ **Barbera** ✓ 🖾 Becoming consistently excellent expression of the Italian variety. **11**, like previous, tangy fruit in foreground, supportive oaking, earthy complexity & lifted acidity. Perfect food wine.

★★★★ **Chardonnay** ✓ 🗒 🖾 Citrus & peach with subtle supporting vanilla notes. **13** (★★★☆) not quite the structure of **11**, more fruit driven, still pleasant, fresh & clean. **12** sold out untasted.

> **Pinotage Rosé** NEW ☺ 🗒 🖾 ★★★ The whole confectionery store - from candyfloss to winegums! **13** just off-dry, soft & creamy, very easy to sip. Step up from discontinued Merlot-based version.

Cabernet Sauvignon 🖾 ★★★ Delicate & light **11**, gentle tealeaf, cedar & mint layers to red fruit, will benefit from short-term ageing. **Pinotage Limited Edition** ⏲ ★★★ **09** fleshy & succulent, toasty vanilla & dark ripe fruit with cedar trim. **Sauvignon Blanc** ✓ 🗒 🖾 ★★★★ Going up a notch on **12** (★★★), handsomely packaged **13** shows excellent structure & balance. Guava, pineapple & lime with savoury intensity & length. Delicious now, will benefit from short-term bottle-ageing. **Cuvée Brut** Next awaited. **White Muscadel** ✓ 🗒 🖾 ★★★★ Unctuously sweet **13** not showing flair of earlier **11** (★★★★). (No **12**.) Sultana, honey & rosepetals warmed by alcohol. Might show better with time. Fairtrade certified, as most of these. Discontinued: **Merlot Rosé**. — HJ

■ **Metamorphic** *see Hillcrest Estate*

Metzer Wines

Location: Somerset West ▪ WO: Stellenbosch ▪ Est/1stB 2004 ▪ Tasting by appt ▪ Owner(s)/winemaker(s) Wade Metzer & Barry Holfeld ▪ 16t/2,400cs 100% red ▪ PO Box 35398 Northcliff 2115 ▪ metzerwines@gmail. com ▪ www.metzerwines.com, www.kitchensinkwines.co.za ▪ **T +27 (0)82-774-4121**

Somerset West-based Wade Metzer understands wine micro-biology even more than most Elsenburg graduates – and has a Swiss diploma to prove it. Science proves a good basis for his aim to craft wines expressing their origin, using simple, non-interventionist principles. Shiraz has been a focus as it responds so 'articulately' to different terroirs. Then comes innovative naming and packaging.

★★★★ **Vitamin B Syrah** ⏲ 🖾 Clean black fruit, herbal & savoury notes on velvety **09** tasted a few years back.

★★★★ **Syrah** ⏲ 🖾 **09** (★★★★☆) offered perfumes of dark berries, flowers & spice a few editions back. Strikingly pure, vibrant & juicy fruit around a core of tannin. Helderberg grapes; **07** was from Swartland.

★★★★ **The Kitchen Sink Syrah** ⏲ **10** (★★★★) showed big, ripe fruity aromas & some sweet flavours on firm base, but a little more awkward & oaky than maiden **05**, with drying tannins.

Vitamin B Blanc ⏲ 🖾 ★★★★ Pleasingly gentle, easygoing charm on lightly, unobtrusively oaked **11** blend of chenin with chardonnay plus a touch of viognier to add a floral note. Fairly rich, with good texture. — TJ

M'hudi Wines

Location/map: Stellenbosch ▪ WO: Stellenbosch/Paarl ▪ Est 2005 ▪ Tasting by appt Mon-Fri 10-5 Sat 10-3 ▪ Conferences (up to 70 pax) ▪ Owner(s) Rangaka family ▪ Winemaker(s) Outsourced ▪ 22ha ▪ 70,000cs own label 80% red 10% white 10% rosé & sparkling ▪ WIETA ▪ PO Box 30 Koelenhof 7605 ▪ info@mhudi.com ▪ www.mhudi.com ▪ S 33° 50' 32.3" E 018° 45' 13.9" ▪ **T +27 (0)21-988-6960**

The Rangaka family leapt into the world of wine despite knowing nothing about it. They moved across the country, bought a derelict Stellenbosch farm and started the first wine estate to be owned and managed by a black family in modern South Africa. M'hudi ('Harvester') is now part of giant Bidvest Food Services, and looking forward 'to become a nationally recognisable brand in the on-trade'.

Platinum range NEW

★★★★ **Shiraz** ✓ Generously flavoured, harmonious **11** shows Perdeberg Winery origins (like all in this range) in plush, dense, dark fruit & ripe tannins exerting perfectly integrated savoury grip. Temptingly moreish.

★★★★ **Cabernet Sauvignon** ✓ Well-made **11** generous rendition of cab: lithely textured tannins support lush blackcurrant fruit, delivering great value & a properly dry finish.

★★★★ **Pinotage** ✓ Vibrant, plush harmonious **11** made to charm with juicy, succulent red fruit & hint mocha for unpretentious enjoyment.

M'hudi Wines range

Merlot ★★★ Earthy, lightly herbal **11**'s mocha plum flavours focused by acidity; made exclusively for Marks & Spencer, UK. **Pinotage** ★★★ Roasted coffee & oodles of bright red fruit in balanced, supple-tannined **11**. This range made at Villiera. **Chenin Blanc** ★★★ Tropical **12** has earthy touch & appeal-ing freshness, oaking provides breadth & texture. Discontinued: **Sauvignon Blanc**. — IM

Mia *see Nordic Wines*

Micu Narunsky Wines

Location: Somerset West ▪ Map: Helderberg ▪ WO: Coastal/Swartland/Stellenbosch ▪ Est 2005 ▪ 1stB 2006 ▪ Tasting by appt ▪ Owner(s)/cellarmaster(s)/viticulturist(s) Micu Narunsky ▪ Winemaker(s) Micu Narunsky, advised by Francois Naudé ▪ 4.8t/450cs own label 85% red 15% white ▪ PO Box 427 Somerset Mall 7137 ▪ micunarunsky@gmail.com ▪ www.micunarunsky.com ▪ S 34° 1' 52.20" E 018° 50' 46.73" ▪ **T +27 (0)73-600-3031 / +27 (0)21-855-2520**

This is Micu Narunsky's passion - less 'business' than following an 'inner instinct'. The Israeli-born jazz musician fell in love with wine while living in France before coming to South Africa. He is Anatu's winemaker, but makes his own range in rented space in Stellenbosch - near where his grandfather once made brandy.

★★★★ **lemanjá** Attractively rustic, powerful **10** touriga-led red (with 30% tinta) shows violets, bergamot & black fruit. 15% alcohol noticeable but integrated in a rich, firm palate. Stellenbosch, Swartland grapes.

Olodum ★★★ Mirror image of lemanjá: tinta leading, 17% touriga in powerful, firm-tannined **10** preview from Swartland. Less precise than **09**, its ripe, dark fruit with slight overripe undertones. These reds unusually dry. **La Complicité** ★★★★ Fresh & friendly, lightly oaked **11** reaches higher than usual for colombard. Oak well meshed with fruit; palate full but fresh. WO Stellenbosch. Last tasted was **06** (★★★) from muscat. — JPf

Middelvlei Estate

Location/map: Stellenbosch ▪ WO: Devon Valley/Western Cape ▪ Est 1941 ▪ 1stB 1973 ▪ Tasting & sales daily 10–4.30 ▪ Fee R15pp ▪ Closed Good Fri, Dec 25 & Jan 1 ▪ Cellar tours by appt ▪ Traditional lunchtime braai 7 days a week; evenings by prior arrangement for groups of 15+ ▪ Facilities for children ▪ Conferences ▪ Walk-ing/hiking & mountain biking trails ▪ Cottage (2 pax) ▪ Owner(s) Momberg family ▪ Cellarmaster(s)/winemaker(s)/viticulturist(s) Tinnie Momberg (Feb 1992) ▪ 160ha/110ha (cab, merlot, ptage, shiraz, chard, sauv) ▪ 650t/60,000cs own label 95% red 5% white ▪ Other export brands: Hagelsberg, Red Falcon ▪ IPW, WIETA ▪ PO Box 66 Stellenbosch 7599 ▪ info@middelvlei.co.za ▪ www.middelvlei.co.za ▪ S 33° 55' 41.2" E 018° 49' 55.9" ▪ **T +27 (0)21-883-2565** ▪ F +27 (0)21-883-9546

Two Momberg brothers bought this expansive farm in Stellenbosch's Devon Valley in 1919. It remains a Momberg family farm, run by another pair of brothers, Tinnie and Ben (with father Stiljan - who was sole owner since 1963 - a continuing influ-ence). Tradition doesn't preclude innovation, as the eclectic flagship blend, Momberg, makes clear; but the focus in vineyards and cellar remains firmly red.

★★★★ **Shiraz** Satisfyingly dry, savoury **10** appeals with succulent fruit flavours, checked by spicy tannins. Usual quality, harmony & complexity from reliable shiraz producer.

★★★★ **Momberg** Plush, full-bodied **11** shows a touch more elegance, accessibility & light-footedness than last - perhaps from reduced new-oak usage. Richly spicy shiraz leads blend with pinotage, merlot, cab.

Cabernet Sauvignon ★★★★ Elegant feel to **10** despite alcohol near 15% - bone-dry & balanced. Rich red fruits meld well with textured tannins. **Merlot** ★★★ Well-made **11** in bold, alcoholic, popular mocha style; succulence & sweet richness will appeal, as will smooth tannins. **Free Run Pinotage** ★★★★ Was just 'Pinotage'. Pleasurable **12** a well-balanced step up on last-tasted **09** (★★★★), in a more serious style. Richly sweet fruit underpinned by new oak, leading to a savoury finish. **Pinotage-Merlot** ★★★ Lush fruit on decently structured **12**, lively acidity gives pleasing freshness & structure for early drinking. **Chardonnay** ★★★ Peachy, lively, unwooded **13** in light, dry, creamy style for easy enjoyment. WO W Cape. — IM

Migliarina Wines

Location: Stellenbosch ▪ WO: Stellenbosch/Elgin ▪ Est 2001 ▪ 1stB 2002 ▪ Closed to public ▪ Owner(s)/winemaker(s) Carsten Migliarina ▪ 2,400cs own label 65% red 35% white + 320cs for clients ▪ Brands for cli-

ents: Kap Hase, Fridham Gaard ▪ PO Box 673 Stellenbosch 7599 ▪ carsten@migliarina.co.za ▪ www.migliarina.co.za ▪ **T +27 (0)72-233-4138**

Stellenbosch boutique vintner Carsten Migliarina always knew he wanted to make wine; his first was as a teenager using table grapes. The journey since has included wine courses, contract cellar work and stints as a sommelier locally and abroad. He exports and hasn't stopped looking for new wines to make.

★★★★ **Shiraz** ⓣ With dark plums at core, **09** reflects quite savoury styling, scrub & black pepper, further confirmed by the oak-influenced dry palate, finish. Drink now till 2017.

Chardonnay ✓ ★★★★ Citrus enriched by oak, **12** improves on **11** (★★★★) with its layers of flavour, yet remains smoothly elegant, polished. WO Elgin. — CR

■ **Miko** see Mont Rochelle Hotel & Mountain Vineyards

Miles Mossop Wines

Location: Stellenbosch ▪ WO: Stellenbosch/Coastal ▪ Est/1stB 2004 ▪ Closed to public ▪ Owner(s)/winemaker(s)/viticulturist(s) Miles Mossop ▪ 15t/2,000cs own label 47% red 48% white 5% NLH ▪ PO Box 7339 Stellenbosch 7599 ▪ miles@milesmossopwines.com ▪ www.milesmossopwines.com ▪ **T +27 (0)82-413-4335** ▪ F +27 (0)21-808-5911

Miles Mossop is now established as one of the top winemakers in South Africa. It's evident in the wines he makes at Tokara and in his own range - named for his three children. The late Tony Mossop was a famous wine judge and journalist and the same vinous element flows in the blood of Miles, his son. What makes the latter's winemaking so acute is his reliance on his gut-feel and his ability to take what nature offers and deliver wines of great polish as well as integrity.

★★★★★ **Max** ⓣ **09** blend of half cab with petit verdot, merlot % malbec. Like **08** (★★★★★), modern & plush in the best possible sense. Textured, with silky tannins & fine dry end. Deserves time before broaching.

★★★★★ **Saskia** ⓣ ⓢ Stunning new-generation blend from chenin, viognier & splashes clairette & verdelho ex Stellenbosch, Swartland & Paarl. **11** (★★★★★), with attractive toasty intro, yet more voluptuous opulence than **10**, delivers promised richness with great finesse (despite 15% alcohol), ending drier than previous.

★★★★☆ **Kika** ⓢ Gorgeous Noble Late Harvest dessert from chenin, named after youngest Mossop clan member. **12** lovely piquant apricot invitation shows ripeness yet is clean, poised & pure. Many layers of flavour – great acid cleanout aids lingering end. Touch of oak well integrated. — JP

■ **Millberg** see Tulbagh Winery
■ **Millers Mile** see Klein Parys Vineyards
■ **Millstone** see Stettyn Cellar

Mimosa Boutique Wines

Location: Montagu ▪ Map: Klein Karoo & Garden Route ▪ WO: Robertson ▪ Est 2004 ▪ 1stB 2003 ▪ Tasting & sales daily 9-5 ▪ Facilities for children ▪ Tour groups ▪ Conservation area ▪ 4-star Mimosa Lodge: 23 rooms, conference centre, pool, boules pitch, wine cellar, tasting room & Ma Cuisine restaurant ▪ Owner(s) Bernhard Hess ▪ Cellarmaster(s)/winemaker(s)/viticulturist(s) Lourens van der Westhuizen (consultant) ▪ 5ha/3ha (cab, shiraz, chard, sauv) ▪ 20t/2,480cs own label 70% red 30% white ▪ PO Box 323 Montagu 6720 ▪ bernhard@mimosa.co.za ▪ www.mimosawines.co.za ▪ S 33° 47' 27.59" E 020° 6' 44.55" ▪ **T +27 (0)23-614-2351** ▪ F +27 (0)86-535-0720

At Montagu's Mimosa Lodge the freshest seasonal ingredients are deliciously prepared by Swiss-born chef patron Bernhard Hess, who also handcrafts wines with consultant winemaker Lourens van der Westhuizen of Arendsig to complement the menu. Now, for postprandial sipping, there are Mimosa 3 Year Old blended and 5 Year Old potstill brandies.

Cabernet Sauvignon Await next, as for **Shiraz** & **Sauvignon Blanc**. **Hess Reserve** ⓣ ★★★★ Elegant Bordeaux blend **10** from Somerset West vines, harmonious & fresh marriage of sweet fruit & oak. **Chardonnay** ★★★★ Barrel-fermented **12** a real crowd pleaser, packed with pineapple fruit & fragrance, buttery oak & sugar. Not classic, but many will love its oh-so-easy opulence. — CvZ,MW

Miravel

Location: Somerset West ▪ Map: Helderberg ▪ WO: Stellenbosch ▪ Est 2002 ▪ 1stB 2005 ▪ Tasting & sales Mon-Sat & pub hols by appt ▪ Closed Ash Wed, Easter Fri-Mon, Ascension Day, Pentecost, Dec 25/26 & Jan 1 ▪ Meals & cheese platters by prior arrangement ▪ Self-catering Fynbos Cottage ▪ Owner(s) Maarten van Beuningen ▪ Winemaker(s) Gerda Willers (whites) & Arno Cloete (reds) ▪ Viticulturist(s) Francois Hanekom (Apr 2007) & Paul Wallace (Jun 2004, consultant) ▪ 39ha/27ha (cab, merlot, p verdot, ptage, chenin, sauv) ▪ 125t/1,500cs (sauv) & 2,250L (cab, merlot, p verdot, ptage) own label 35% red 65% white ▪ PO Box 5144 Helderberg 7135 ▪ maarten@miravel.co.za ▪ www.miravel.co.za ▪ S 34° 1′ 58.7″ E 018° 46′ 46.9″ ▪ T +27 (0)21-842-3154 ▪ F +27 (0)21-842-3154

When Maarten and Janine van Beuningen decamped from Zimbabwe to this 27 hectare Helderberg vineyard, they didn't know much about growing or making wine. A decade later, their grapes are sought after by high-end cellars and their rebranded, handcrafted, own-label wines are growing in stature.

Cabernet Sauvignon In abeyance. **Ella Family Reserve Cabernet Sauvignon** ✷ ★★★★ 'Cabernet' now on revamped **10** label: farm's best grapes, named for granddaughter. Demure cassis fruit tightly woven with fine tannins, will reward patience. 44% new casks, 2 years, whereas **08** (★★★★) saw no new wood. No **09**. **Merlot** ✷ ★★★★ Game & iron aromas lead out smooth **10**, uncomplicated & finely balanced. **Pinotage** NEW ✷ ★★★★ Typical plum/prune cake character of variety, sweet-tasting 14.7% alcohol boost in **10**. **1952 Family Blend** NEW ★★★★ 2:1 cab/merlot blend with petit verdot, seasoned in older oak (like Merlot, Pinotage); **10** a brooding smoky mouthful, medium in weight with savoury tang. **Sauvignon Blanc** ★★★ Generous rather than steely; tropical **12** has fresh racy finish. — DS

▪ **Mischief Maker** see Valley Vineyards Wine Company
▪ **Miss Molly** see Môreson
▪ **Misty Kloof's** see Goedverwacht Wine Estate

Mitre's Edge

Location/map: Stellenbosch ▪ WO: Simonsberg-Paarl ▪ Est 1999 ▪ 1stB 2004 ▪ Tasting & sales by appt Mon-Fri 9-5 Sat 9-1 ▪ Cellar tours by appt ▪ Guest house B&B ▪ Olive oil ▪ Owner(s) Bernard & Lola Nicholls ▪ Winemaker(s) Lola Nicholls (2004), with Bernard Nicholls ▪ Viticulturist(s) Danie Kritzinger (consultant) ▪ Vineyard manager Bertus de Clerk ▪ 28ha/18ha (cabs s/f, malbec, merlot, p verdot, shiraz, chenin, viog) ▪ 150t/2,000cs own label 95% red 5% rosé ▪ PO Box 12290 Die Boord 7613 ▪ info@mitres-edge.co.za ▪ www.mitres-edge.co.za ▪ S 33° 49′ 47.3″ E 018° 52′ 34.4″ ▪ T +27 (0)21-875-5960 ▪ F +27 (0)21-875-5965

A family-run business encompassing wine, accommodation and olive oil production, every family member, friend, employee, consultant and client quickly becomes part of the Mitre's Edge 'family' – in true rainbow spirit. Ensuring the spirit is affordable for all is the idiosyncratic nvME (numerous varietals Mitre's Edge) with a screwcap for easy access.

Flagship range
Cabernet Sauvignon ✦ ★★★★ Stern tannin softened by cushion of sweetness (sugar & fruit) in appealing, well-composed **08**. **Merlot** Await new vintage.

Mitre's Edge range
Shiraz ✦ ★★★ **08** plush & fruit-filled but tad spiritous from big alcohol. **NVME Classic Red** NEW ★★★ Crunchy red fruit & tea leaf tannins in cab-led **NV** blend, billed as a 'braai aperitif'. **Rosé** Not tasted. — CvZ

Mofam Wines

Location/WO: Elgin ▪ Map: Elgin, Walker Bay & Bot River ▪ Est 2005 ▪ 1stB 2010 ▪ Tasting daily 8-5 ▪ Closed Dec 25 ▪ Flavours Restaurant (see Restaurants section) ▪ Facilities for children ▪ Tour groups ▪ Conferences ▪ Walks/hikes ▪ Mountain biking trail ▪ Conservation area ▪ Mofam River Lodge 4-star B&B & self-catering chalets ▪ Owner(s) Derek & Sharon Moore ▪ Cellarmaster(s) Justin Hoy (Dec 2009, consultant) ▪ Winemaker(s) Justin Hoy (Dec 2009, consultant), with Paul Lötter (Mar 2012) ▪ Viticulturist(s) Johan Wiese & Paul Wallace (Jan 2005, consultants) ▪ 260ha/20ha (pinot, shiraz, sauv, viog) ▪ 80t/1,872cs own label 25% red 56% white 19% rosé ▪ Global Gap ▪ PO Box 192 Elgin 7180 ▪ admin@mofam.co.za ▪ www.mofam.co.za ▪ S 34° 13′ 42.06″ E 18° 59′ 18.30″ ▪ T +27 (0)21-846-8345 ▪ F +27 (0)86-295-0084

Derek and Sharon Moore, passionate Elgin vinegrowers and conservationists, recently launched a boutique wine range off their own vineyards to complement the offerings for guests visiting Mofam River Lodge. Each wine is named for a family member - Shaz for Sharon, Zar for Zaren.

Zar Pinot Noir ⊛ ▤ ★★☆ Food-styled **11** is dark hued & funky, beefy alcohol noticeable in very firm finish. **Shaz Sauvignon Blanc** ⊛ ▤ ★★★★ **11** Elgin's green-spectrum notes of nettle, fig & apple; broad & balanced, not too crisp. Bottle-age honey appearing when tasted last year. — HJ,JP

MolenVliet Wine & Guest Estate

Location/map/WO: Stellenbosch ▪ Est/1stB 2005 ▪ Tasting & sales by appt ▪ Fee R50 ▪ Wedding/conference venue ▪ Self-catering accommodation/B&B ▪ Owner(s) Ockie & Susan Oosthuizen ▪ Winemaker(s) Jan Coetzee (2007, consultant) ▪ Viticulturist(s) Calvin Booysen (2005) ▪ 14ha/8ha (cab, merlot, shiraz) ▪ 13t/±2,500cs own label 100% red ▪ PO Box 6288 Uniedal 7612 ▪ info@molenvliet.co.za ▪ www.molenvliet.co.za ▪ S 33° 54' 52.9" E 018° 56' 30.6" ▪ **T +27 (0)21-885-1597** ▪ F +27 (0)21-885-1684

Wine aside, the main attraction at this winelands lifestyle venue in Banhoek Valley is the wedding and conference facility, which consumes a significant portion of the output. Owners Ockie and Susan Oosthuizen have fashioned a beautiful place to complement their Limpopo lodge and central Stellenbosch guest house.

★★★★ **Cabernet Sauvignon** ⊛ Despite 16% alcohol, **07** achieved fine rounded balance previously.

★★★★ **Shiraz** ⊛ **07** rich, bold & complex. Silky texture & lingering vanilla chocolate flavours.

★★★★ **Proprietors Blend** ⊛ **05** classy Bordeaux red with enticing blackcurrant & mineral bouquet.

★★★★ **Diagonal Reserve** ⊛ Full-bodied shiraz/cab-led **07**, upfront & perfumed with black fruit.

★★★★ **Meraz** ⊛ Merlot & shiraz in equal proportion, finely structured **07** debut tasted for 2011 guide.

Proprietors Selection ⊛ ★★★ **05** Bordeaux red on review offered herbal hints, mulberry flavours. —GdB

Momento Wines

WO: Swartland ▪ 1stB 2012 ▪ Private tastings on request ▪ Winemaker(s)/viticulturist(s) Marelise Jansen van Rensburg ▪ 2t/130cs own label 100% red ▪ marelise@momentowines.co.za ▪ www.momentowines.co.za ▪ **T +27 (0)82-968-8588**

For her own-brand wines, well-travelled Marelise Jansen van Rensburg sources grapes from vineyards she discovers, sometimes in unexpected places, and vinifies at Beaumont in Bot River, where she has worked for seven years. Her focus is on winelovers who are thirsty for the new and the interesting out of the Cape. 'People who want to learn, explore, and appreciate purity and elegance in a wine.' Her approach: 'As little as possible fiddling by the winemaker.'

★★★★ **Grenache** A beautiful interpretation of Swartland grenache noir, **11** is elegant & subtle, scents of frangipani lifting the savoury plum fruit; light, ultra-fine texture & juicy fruit acids contribute to a very special showcase for the 50+ year old bushvines so attractively depicted on the label. — DC, JP

▪ **Moments Collection** see Teddy Hall Wines
▪ **Monfort** see Ultra Liquors

Monis Wines

Location: Paarl ▪ WO: Stellenbosch/Breede River Valley/Calitzdorp ▪ Est 1906 ▪ Closed to public ▪ Owner(s) Distell ▪ Cellarmaster(s)/winemaker(s) Dirkie Christowitz (Aug 1979) ▪ 52,000cs 100% fortified ▪ PO Box 266 Paarl 7620 ▪ dchristowitz@distell.co.za ▪ www.moniswines.co.za ▪ **T +27 (0)21-860-1601** ▪ F +27 (0)21-872-2790

This fortifieds-only cellar is based in Paarl, but draws fruit from areas renowned for each style: muscadel from Breede River, Portuguese varieties for the port-styles from Calitzdorp and Paarl, and chenin for the sherries from Stellenbosch. The fortifying brandy spirit is from parent group Distell's own distilleries.

Monis Wines

★★★★☆ **Wood Matured Muscadel** ⊛ Flame-licked **04** 500ml of irresistible dried orange zest, spicy muscat complexity. Rich, silky sweetness disciplined by 5 years older oak, tangy acid. Breede River fruit.

★★★★ **Tawny Port** ⊛ Gorgeous **96** ex Paarlberg tinta & cinsaut still selling.

Vintage Port ⓟ ★★★☆ From Calitzdorp grapes. Dried fruit, leather & touriga's fragrance enhance **06**, with its warming spirity tail. Slightly more concentration would lead to higher rating.

Monis Sherry-Styles NEW

★★★★ **Full Cream** 🍷 Rich, with nuances of dried fruit, melon preserve, roasted hazelnuts giving complexity. Not overly sweet, with a nutty, savoury finish. Perfect for melon & ham.

Pale Dry 🍷 ★★★★ Crunchy apple plus nuts & tealeaves, zesty palate is clean & refreshing. Satisfyingly dry, savoury finish; enjoy chilled. From chenin, matured under flor for 3 years in 59 year old solera barrels, fractional blend of vintages, as for all these. **Medium Cream** 🍷 ★★★★ Brightly fruited nose is fresh, with hints of sweet candied fruit & roasted almonds. Smooth, long on flavour & intensity, yet still delicate & light. For solo sipping or soups. — WB, AL, CR

Mon Rêve Estate

Location: Paarl ▪ Map: Paarl & Wellington ▪ WO: Simonsberg-Paarl ▪ Est 2009 ▪ 1stB 2011 ▪ Tasting, sales & cellar tours by appt ▪ Fee R15pp, waived on purchase ▪ Closed Easter Fri/Sun, May 1, Dec 25 & Jan 1 ▪ Facilities for children ▪ BYO picnic ▪ Owner(s) Guillaume & Heidi Masson ▪ Cellarmaster(s)/winemaker(s)/viticulturist(s) Marius Malan (Jan 2012) ▪ 12ha/±6ha (cab, merlot, shiraz, muscat d'A) ▪ 8,000L own label 94% red 6% white + 12,000L for clients ▪ PO Box 438 Paarden Eiland 7420 ▪ heidim@naturalstonewarehouse.com ▪ S 33° 49' 4.98" E 018° 54' 47.21" ▪ **T +27 (0)82-379-9937** ▪ F +27 (0)21-511-0880

Appaloosa horses with their distinctive markings so evocative of the American West graze serenely in the paddocks of this Simonsberg-Paarl winery, where Heidi and Guillaume Masson escape the demands of their Cape-based tiling business by 'living the dream: farming grapes, making wine and riding horses'.

Cabernet Sauvignon ⓟ ★★★ Youthful **10** is ripe & bold, sweet red-fruit flavours still masked by firm oaking. Needs time. **Single Vineyard Merlot** ⓟ ★★★ Very ripe **10** oozes dark fruit flavours with hint of cured meat smokiness & warm finish. **Appaloosa** ⓟ ★★★ **10** from merlot, cab & splash of shiraz is bold with rich meaty red-berry fruit & firm finish. **Muscat d'Alexandrie** ⓟ ★★★☆ Grapey **10** fortified dessert is pretty & unctuous, slightly cloying, needs bit more zing in tail. — FM

Mons Ruber Wine Estate

Location/WO: Oudtshoorn ▪ Map: Klein Karoo & Garden Route ▪ Est ca 1850 ▪ 1stB 1985 wine/1995 brandy ▪ Tasting & sales Mon-Fri 9–5 Sat 9–1 ▪ Closed all pub hols ▪ Farm produce ▪ Hiking trail in proclaimed conservation area ▪ BYO picnic ▪ Owner(s) Radé & Erhard Meyer ▪ Winemaker(s) Radé Meyer ▪ Brandy master Radé Meyer (1990) ▪ Viticulturist(s) Radé Meyer (1990) & Johannes Mellet (consultant) ▪ ±1,800ha/38ha (cab, cinsaut, muscadel r/w, chard, chenin, hanepoot, palomino) ▪ ±500t/20,000cs own label 50% red 50% white & ±178cs brandy ▪ PO Box 1585 Oudtshoorn 6620 ▪ monsruber@gmail.com ▪ S 33° 32' 1.0" E 022° 28' 38.9" ▪ **T +27 (0)44-251-6550** ▪ F +27 (0)86-566-6550

Family-owned Mons Ruber, named after the distinctive red hills in this part of Klein Karoo, was among the first to re-apply for a distilling licence in the 1990s after long prohibition of private production. Co-owner, winemaker and brandy master Radé Meyer uses an original wood-fired copper potstill. There's history too in the tasting room, a 19th-century toll house turned watering hole, visited by at least one poet (CJ Langenhoven) and one princess (later Queen Elizabeth II).

Brandy range NEW

★★★★ **Estate Potstill Brandy** Muscat d'Alexandrie origin shows subtly on bright, grapey, floral fragrance. Easy, smooth & balanced, with effective oak maturation. Old-style label gives **03** vintage.

Buchu Brandy 🍷 ★★★ A quirky, light yellow medicinal brandy, infused (very noticeably) with round-leaf buchu plant. Fiery finish. From cinsaut. — WB, TJ

Montagu Wine & Spirits Co

Location: Montagu ▪ Map: Klein Karoo & Garden Route ▪ WO: Klein Karoo/Montagu ▪ Est 1941 ▪ Tasting & sales Mon-Fri 9-5 Sat 9-1 ▪ Owner(s) 79 shareholders ▪ Winemaker(s) Christiaan van Tonder (Rietrivier) & Chris Crafford (Uitvlucht) ▪ 553ha ▪ 10,000t/30,000cs 28% red 22% white 50% muscadel ▪ PO Box 332 Montagu 6720 ▪ admin@mwsc.co.za ▪ www.mwsc.co.za ▪ S 33° 46' 59.8" E 020° 7' 53.6" ▪ **T +27 (0)23-614-1340** ▪ +27 (0)86-556-1340

'Nothing has changed,' reports marketer Gerda de Waal happily. Christiaan van Tonder and Chris Crafford still oversee winemaking at, respectively, the Rietrivier and Uitvlucht cellars, which joined forces in 2010 to create Montagu Wine & Spirits Co with some 80 shareholders. Mainly bulk wine producers, they also bottle small batches of own-brand wine. Tastings at Uitvlucht in Montagu.

Chenin Blanc ☺ 🍴 ★★★ Improved **13** pear toned, light & refreshing, tangy-dry for summer salads.

Pinotage ⊕ ★★★ Step-up **09** fresh & engaging: mulberry & vanilla appeal, deepening tar nuance. **Rouge** 🍴 🗵 ★★ Pinotage & merlot combo in **12**, sweet fruit & actual gram sugar contrast with firm grip of tannin. **Rosé** NEW 🍴 🗵 ★★ Budget-priced pink from muscat de Frontignan, **12** fragrant & sweet if short. **Chardonnay** ⊕ 🍴 ★★ Tank sample **12** lightish, with understated tangy lemon taste. **Sauvignon Blanc** ⊕ 🍴 🗵 ★★ Demure **12**, faint blackcurrant taste, acidic bite. **Red Muscadel** ⊕ ★★★ **11** fortified with raisined sultana character & fiery spirit. **White Muscadel** ⊕ 🗵 ★★ Shy fortified dessert **11** has Golden Syrup sweetness & warm tail. **Jerepico Red** ⊕ 🍴 ★★★ Fortified dessert from muscadel, now **NV** & improved: fragrant tealeaf, candyfloss & strawberry complexity, warming spirit glow. **Jerepico Reserve** ★★★ Roasted nuts, toffee & raisin appeal on fortified **NV** from red muscadel, best enjoyed soon. **Jerepico White** ⊕ 🍴 🗵 ★★★ Fortified sweetie from muscadel, **NV** rich but uncloying raisin sweetness, hint of apricot in firm, moreish conclusion. **Cape Ruby** ✓ 🗵 ★★★★ Port-style **11** from touriga continues upward path. Well expressed choc-toffee aromas, prune & plum flavours, pleasant (& correct) tannic bite & fiery heart. Discontinued: **Rietrivier Muscadel White**, **Vintage Port Revolution**. — GdB,JP

Montagu Wine Cellar 🍷 ♿

Location/WO: Montagu ▪ Map: Klein Karoo & Garden Route ▪ Est 1941 ▪ 1stB 1975 ▪ Tasting & sales Mon-Fri 8–5 ▪ Closed all pub hols ▪ Farm produce ▪ Owner(s) 54 members ▪ Executive manager Jacques Jordaan (2013) ▪ Winemaker(s) Hermias Vollgraaff (Aug 2013) & Aldert Nieuwoudt (Nov 2011) ▪ Viticulturist(s) Johannes Mellet (2005, consultant) ▪ 620ha (11 varieties r/w) ▪ 16,000t/11,000cs own label 12% red 82% white 6% muscadel ▪ IPW ▪ PO Box 29 Montagu 6720 ▪ sales@montaguwines.co.za ▪ www.montaguwines.co.za ▪ S 33° 46' 37.3" E 020° 7' 58.4" ▪ **T +27 (0)23-614-1125** ▪ F +27 (0)23-614-1793

Record grape intakes year on year for this grower-owned winery, it seems. Following 2012's 25% increase, came 2013's nearly 1,000T more, requiring assistance from McGregor's Jacques Jordaan and probably new grape delivery and run-off water treatment facilities, says winemaker Aldert Nieuwoudt, now reporting to Hermias Vollgraaff.

Cabernet Sauvignon ⊕ 🍴 ★★★ Straightforward **08** was tad oaky when reviewed, may since have settled. **Merlot-Ruby Cabernet** Await new vintage. **Chenin Blanc** 🍴 🗵 ★★ **13** tropical fruit & lively freshness, cheerful budget-priced quaffer. **Colombard** ⊕ 🍴 🗵 ★★★ Tank sample **12** fresh & pleasantly fruity, light & refreshing. **Sauvignon Blanc** NEW 🍴 ★ **13** lightly flavoured, slightly chalky conclusion. **Late Harvest** ⊕ ★★★ Improved **12** preview has pineapple & melon complexity, lipsmacking balance. **Red Muscadel** 🍴 🗵 ★★★ Step-up **12** fortified dessert is pretty & floral, with enough spirit grip to counter unctuous raisin sweetness. **White Muscadel** ⊕ 🍴 ★★★ Ex-tank **11** fortified pudding wine, lovely grapey flavour, light lime lift. — GdB,JP

■ Montagu Wine Company *see* Montagu Wine & Spirits Co

■ Mont Destin 🍷♿📷

Location/map: Stellenbosch ▪ WO: Simonsberg-Paarl/Paarl/Coastal ▪ Est/1stB 1998 ▪ Tasting, sales & cellar tours by appt ▪ Closed all pub hols ▪ Open air wine bath ▪ Owner(s) Ernest & Samantha Bürgin ▪ Winemaker(s) Samantha Bürgin (May 1996) ▪ Viticulturist(s) Bertus de Clerk (2006, consultant) ▪ 10ha/7ha (cab, cinsaut, grenache, mourv, shiraz, viog) ▪ 15t/2,000cs own label 100% red ▪ IPW ▪ PO Box 1237 Stellenbosch 7599 ▪ info@montdestin.co.za ▪ www.montdestin.co.za ▪ S 33° 49' 58.9" E 018° 53' 27.8" ▪ **T +27 (0)21-875-5870** ▪ F +27 (0)21-875-5870

Halfway between Stellenbosch and Paarl, and noted for its Luis Barragan architecture, Mont Destin boutique cellar is owned by Ernest and Samantha Bürgin, who makes the wine. Specialising in Rhône varieties, made in small quantities, the flagship Destiny Shiraz in particular gives new meaning to the term 'handcrafted': a 2-3 barrel selection, each bottle hand labelled, numbered and waxed, all with family participation. A unique feature available to visitors is al fresco bathing in wine.

★★★★★ **Destiny Shiraz** Showing its class, 09's deeply layered plums, Provençal herbs & prosciutto complexity involves & seduces. But the main attraction is the structure, such sinuous lines that the deeper muscle tone is overlooked. A 'must have'. 07 too was elegant & serious. Simonsberg-Paarl WO. No 08.

★★★★☆ **Passioné** ② Shiraz with cinsaut, grenache, lacks 09's complexity. The fleshy ripeness is mirrored by dried herb, earthy notes, while firm tannins need rich dishes. Will age well. WO Paarl.

11 Barrels 🔲 ② ★★★★ Shiraz-led Rhône mix brings out dark tones, cocoa, pepper & wild fruit in 12. Nicely dry, would suit charcuterie. WO Coastal. — CR

Mont du Toit Kelder

Location: Wellington ▪ Map: Paarl & Wellington ▪ WO: Paarl/Wellington ▪ Est 1996 ▪ 1stB 1998 ▪ Tasting, sales & cellar tours Mon–Fri 9-4.30 Sat by appt ▪ Fee R15/R35 ▪ Closed all pub hols ▪ Hiking trails ▪ BYO picnic, picnic area by arrangement ▪ Guest cottages ▪ Owner(s) Stephan du Toit ▪ Cellarmaster(s) Bernd Philippi & Loftie Ellis (1997, consultants) ▪ Winemaker(s) Chris Roux (2012), with Abraham Cloete (Jan 2005) ▪ Viticulturist(s) Ettienne Barnard (Oct 2010) ▪ ±40ha/±28ha (alicante bouschet, cabs s/f, merlot, mourv, p verdot, shiraz, tinta barocca) ▪ ±165t/±16,000cs own label 100% red & ±2,000cs for clients ▪ IPW ▪ PO Box 704 Wellington 7654 ▪ kelder@montdutoit.co.za ▪ www.montdutoit.co.za ▪ S 33° 39' 27.72" E 019° 1' 45.81" ▪ **T +27 (0)21-873-7745** ▪ F +27 (0)21-864-2737

Du Toits have been winefarming in the Cape since 1691, when a French Huguenot du Toit planted vines in the area now known as Wellington. Since 1996, Johannesburg-based advocate Stephan du Toit's love for classic red wine has been expressed by continuing the tradition in his farm at the foot of the Hawequa Mountain (silhouetted on his labels). Well-known German vintner Bernd Phillipi has been advising here, since he first helped to plan the vineyards and cellar.

Mont du Toit Kelder range

★★★★ **Mont du Toit** ⓟ 07 red has 6 varieties supporting cab - even more than brooding 06 (★★★★☆). An interesting, if chunky, package of ripe richness, sweet dark fruit; austere dryness a little awkward.

★★★★ **Le Sommet** Powerfully built, austere 06 (first since 03) another secret blend. Mature, should keep a few more years, but drying tannins (clearly partly from oak) likely to outlast the dark, sweet-edged fruit.

Hawequas ✓ ★★★★ Mature, serious-minded & even rather severe 5-way red blend, 08 is dark-fruited with savoury, oak-tobacco notes. For export.

Les Coteaux range

★★★★ **Cabernet Sauvignon** ✓ 11 in established handsome, serious, classic style. Big, with plenty of flavour, but restrained thanks to dryness, balance & unshowy fruit. Should mature well, like most of these.

★★★★ **Cabernet Franc** 11 has developed & settled since tasted last year ex barrel. A little lighter & juicier than the others, though as serious-minded; dry-leaf fragrance & red fruit. Modestly, intelligently oaked.

★★★★☆ **Sélection** ✓ Characterful, interesting, mature 08 (★★★★) a cab-based blend, as was 07. Bright, tasty fruit, with tobacco & dried-herb notes. This wine more elegant than austere, carrying its big alcohol well.

Merlot ★★★ Previewed last edition, 11 now has pleasant, light flavours, but fruit outgunned by dry tannin structure. **Shiraz** ★★★★ The big, dry tannins noted last year on previewed 11 now settled, though still a bit severely dry. But generally pleasing & balanced, if not concentrated. Wellington WO, like Cab Franc. — TJ

◼ **Montebello** see Wine-of-the-Month Club

Monterosso Estate

Location/map/WO: Stellenbosch ▪ Est/1stB 2000 ▪ Tasting, sales & cellar tours by appt only ▪ Owner(s) Francesco & Orneglio De Franchi ▪ Cellarmaster(s)/winemaker(s) Orneglio De Franchi (Jan 2000) ▪ Viticulturist(s) Francesco De Franchi & Orneglio De Franchi (both Jan 2000) ▪ 83ha/60ha (cab, merlot, ptage, sangio, shiraz, chard, chenin, riesling, sauv, sem) ▪ 540t/760cs own label 60% red 40% white ▪ PO Box 5 Stellenbosch 7599 ▪ defranchivin@mweb. co.za, monterosso@mweb.co.za ▪ www.monterosso.co.za ▪ S 33° 54' 6.8" E 018° 50' 10.4" ▪ **T +27 (0)21-889-7081/+27 (0)21-889-5021** ▪ F +27 (0)21-889-7081/+27 (0)21-889-5021

In a nostalgic nod to his birthplace on Italy's Liguria coastline, De Franchi family patriarch Socrate named his Stellenbosch grape and olive farm Monterosso. Sons Orneglio and Francesco keep il Tricolore flying high, unprecedented demand obliging them to bottle and label all last year's wines simultaneously.

Sangiovese Socrate ★★★☆ **11** a step up. Fruitcake generosity cloaked in spicy, dry oak frame. Lithe & supple yet substantial. **Cabernet Sauvignon-Merlot** ★★★ Cheery, light-bodied friendly appeal to 55/45 mix. Tobacco & dark fruit make **12** a good braai, pizza partner. **Chenin Blanc Old Bush Vine** ★★★ Lively acidity on **13** gives refreshing lift to pear & green peach tang. Crisp, dry finish a touch short. **Sauvignon Blanc** ★★★ Flinty lemon zest on **13** a notch up. Nice rounded fullness & dry tail. —FM

■ **Montestell** *see Boland Kelder*

Montpellier

Location/map/WO: Tulbagh ▪ Est 1714 ▪ Tasting, sales & tours Mon–Fri 9–12 & 2–5 Sat 9–12 ▪ Closed all pub hols ▪ Pre-booked cheese platters & light meals available during tasting hours ▪ Tour groups - gazebo with pizza oven ▪ Olives ▪ Walking/hiking trails ▪ Conservation area: Renosterbos ▪ Guesthouse/B&B/self-catering ▪ Weddings ▪ Owner(s) Lucas J van Tonder ▪ Cellarmaster(s) Theo Brink (Jan 2008) ▪ Winemaker(s)/viticulturist(s) Theo Brink (Jan 2008), with Niël Russouw (Dec 2011) ▪ 482ha/60ha (cab, merlot, p verdot, pinot, shiraz, chard, chenin, gewürz, viog) ▪ 300t/4,400cs own label 48% red 27% white 25% MCC + 150,000 litres in bulk ▪ PO Box 79 Tulbagh 6820 ▪ montpellier@montpellier.co.za ▪ www.montpellier.co.za ▪ S 33° 16' 30.4" E 019° 6' 40.0" ▪ **T +27 (0)23-230-0656** ▪ F +27 (0)23-230-1574

A landmark year for this Tulbagh wine farm – farming began here 300 years ago. A huge celebratory dinner is planned, with chandelier-lit long tables set in the maturation cellar, its hay-bale insulation now extended into the MCC cellar and the courtyard. 'Bonne chance!' to owner Lucas van Tonder, cellarmaster Theo Brink and their team.

> **Theo's Synchrony** ☺ ★★★ 50/50 gewürztraminer & chenin. **12** beguilingly off-dry & delicate. Enjoy all summer long, well chilled.

Cabernet Sauvignon ⓟ ★★★ Touch mint, dark berries on sweet-fruited **10** early drinker. **Shiraz** Await next. **Spyseniersberg** ⓟ ★★★ Spicy black fruit on **10** Bordeaux blend cab, merlot & petit verdot; leaner than other reds but more refreshing. **Chardonnay** ★★★ Fermented & briefly aged in older oak, **12** buttery orange notes, pleasing rounded acidity. **Chenin Blanc** ★★ Nice nutty nuance & food-friendly grip on **12**. **Gewürztraminer** ⓟ ★★ Litchi, rosepetal - textbook varietal aromas on **10**; year older oak appears to highlight grape's bitter lift. **Sauvignon Blanc** In abeyance. **Viognier** ✓ ★★★ As a finished wine, **11** surpasses last edition's promise. Understated & elegant, subtle oak from 15 months older French cask, waxy peach attraction. **Méthode Cap Classique** ★★★ Traditional-method sparkling was **NV** from pinot noir, now vintage dated & chardonnay based (54%). Celebration tipple **10** shows pinot's meaty side, explosive bone-dry mousse. **Port** ⓟ ★★ Dusty plum-pudding **NV** fireside fortifier from shiraz. — CvZ,CE

Mont Rochelle Hotel & Mountain Vineyards

Location/map: Franschhoek ▪ WO: Franschhoek/Western Cape ▪ Est 1994 ▪ 1stB 1996 ▪ Tasting & sales 10–7 daily ▪ Fee R20 ▪ Closed Dec 25 ▪ Cellar tours Mon–Fri 11, 12.30 & 3 Sat/Sun/pub hols 11 & 3 ▪ Mange Tout & Country Kitchen (see Restaurants section) ▪ Mont Rochelle Hotel (see Accommodation section) ▪ Conferences/functions ▪ Picnics ▪ Walking/hiking trails ▪ Educational wine tastings ▪ Full moon hikes in summer ▪ Owner(s) Erwin Schnitzler & Rwayitare family ▪ Cellarmaster(s)/winemaker(s)/viticulturist(s) Neil Strydom (Nov 2012) ▪ 33ha/16ha (cab, merlot, shiraz, chard, sauv, sem) ▪ 100t/12,000cs own label 60% red 35% white 5% MCC ▪ PO Box 334 Franschhoek 7690 ▪ wine@montrochelle.co.za ▪ www.montrochelle.co.za ▪ S 33° 54' 52.1" E 019° 6' 21.9" ▪ **T +27 (0)21-876-2770** ▪ F +27 (0)21-876-2362

Set in the mountains above Franschhoek, elegant Mont Rochelle continues to offer fine dining and hospitality while the wine side undergoes a nip and tuck in the hands of new winemaker Neil Strydom. He has some exciting plans, including MCC sparkling. The Chardonnay Sur Lie, meanwhile, still honours late owner Miko Rwayitare, first black African to solely own a Cape wine farm.

Miko Premier range

★★★★☆ **Chardonnay Sur Lie** ⓟ Flagship white honours late owner. Cooler **09** (★★★★) when last tasted was intense, youthful, needed time. Shade off previous elegant **06**.
Cabernet Sauvignon Await next.

Mont Rochelle range

★★★★ **Barrel Fermented Chardonnay** ⊕ Vivacious **10** is elegantly balanced, with a good marriage of oak, pear, butterscotch & lime. Natural ferment adds richness to lively clean-cut citrus tone. No **09**.
Cabernet Sauvignon ⊕ ★★★★ Richly textured **07** retains supple elegance, with alcohol integrated into juicy fruit & structure. **Merlot** ⊕ ★★★ Character change in **06** to minty & leafy. Creamy oak pacifies edginess, but best with a meal. **Syrah** ⊕ ★★★★ Robust **07** is concentrated & juicy. Generous savoury fruit & firm structure absorb alcohol. **Artemis** ⊕ ★★★ **08** is mostly a Bordeaux blend, splashes shiraz & mourvèdre. Fruit-filled, supple structure for satisfying food-friendly enjoyment. **Rosé** 🗔 ★★ Shiraz-based **11** is savoury & light. Pithy dry exit invites food. **Unwooded Chardonnay** ⊕ 🗔 ★★★ **11** delightfully fresh summer quaffer. Gentle pear/melon flavours given a zesty citrus tweak. Walker Bay grapes. **Sauvignon Blanc** Await next. — MW

■ **Moody Lagoon** *see Benguela Cove*
■ **Mooiberg** *see Zidela Wines*

Mooi Bly Winery

Location/WO: Paarl ▪ Map: Paarl & Wellington ▪ Est/1stB 2005 ▪ Tasting, sales & cellar tours by appt ▪ Fee R50pp ▪ Closed Dec 25 & Jan 1 ▪ BYO picnic ▪ Walks (see Accommodation section) ▪ Owner(s) Wouters family ▪ Cellarmaster(s)/winemaker(s) Erik Schouteden (Jan 2005) ▪ Viticulturist(s) Erik Schouteden (Feb 2001) ▪ 32ha/18ha (cab, malbec, shiraz, tannat, chard, chenin) ▪ 70t/6,000cs own label 50% red 50% white ▪ PO Box 801 Huguenot 7645 ▪ wine@mooibly.com ▪ www.mooibly.com ▪ S 33° 41' 7.0" E 019° 1' 21.9" ▪ T +27 (0)21-868-2808 ▪ F +27 (0)21-868-2808

Originally from Belgium, the Wouters family settled in Paarl and gained not only a son-in-law but a winemaker in Erik Schouteden, who was instrumental in planting tannat. One of the rarer varieties in the winelands, it and malbec set Mooi Bly apart, especially since both clearly are suited to the soils and climate.

Selection range

★★★★ **Malbec** Creamy salty liquorice, loads of spice threaded through the black plums yet **09** is polished, sleekly muscular, retains an elegant drinkability. Cellar with confidence.
Tannat ★★★★ Rarely bottled variety. Underbrush & smoked beef, smooth-textured **09**'s tannins are well integrated. Match with venison.

Cultivar range

Cabernet Sauvignon ★★★ **09** shows lead pencils, smoky plums & enough well-crafted tannins for some ageing. Nudges next level. **Shiraz** Await next release. **Chardonnay** New vintage not available. **Chenin Blanc** ✓ 🗔 🖾 ★★★★ From old bushvines. Thatch, beeswax & gentle melon perfume in **12**, backed by limy acidity. Friendly 12.5% alcohol. — CR

Mooiplaas Estate & Private Nature Reserve

Location/map: Stellenbosch ▪ WO: Stellenbosch/Western Cape/Coastal ▪ Est 1806 ▪ 1stB 1995 ▪ Tasting & sales Mon-Fri 9–4.30 Sat 10–4 ▪ Fee R20 (incl. glass), waived on purchase ▪ Closed Easter Fri/Sun/Mon, Dec 25/26 & Jan 1 ▪ Gourmet picnic hampers & cheese platters ▪ Langtafel (30 seater) luncheons or dinners every 6-8 weeks in the manor house (a National Monument); Taste Experience presented by Dirk Roos in the 'voorkamer' (10-18 guests); booking essential ▪ Guest accommodation ▪ Walks/hikes ▪ Mountain biking ▪ Horse riding, riding lessons & trail rides ▪ 60ha private nature reserve ▪ Owner(s) Mooiplaas Trust ▪ Cellarmaster(s) Louis Roos (1983) ▪ Winemaker(s) Louis Roos (1983), with Mathilda Viljoen (Jan 2011) ▪ Viticulturist(s) Tielman Roos (1981), with Anton Bothma ▪ 250ha/100ha (cabs s/f, p verdot, ptage, pinot, chard, chenin, sauv) ▪ 750t/50,000cs own label 57% red 41% white 2% rosé ▪ Other export brand: The Collection ▪ BWI, IPW ▪ PO Box 104 Koelenhof 7605 ▪ info@mooiplaas.co.za ▪ www.mooiplaas.co.za ▪ S 33° 55' 16.3" E 018° 44' 21.4" ▪ T +27 (0)21-903-6273/4 ▪ F +27 (0)21-903-3474

At family-owned Stellenbosch estate Mooiplaas, it all begins at the convivial langtafel – literally 'long dining table' – which is why the elegant, gabled manor house is regularly opened for luncheons and dinners. Visitors arrive as guests but leave as members of the Roos clan. 'Wonderful things happen when strangers sit around a table, break bread and drink wine. This is how we build our rainbow nation,' says regular host, co-owner and cellarmaster Dirk Roos.

The Mercia Collection

★★★★ **Watershed Shiraz** Polished, perfumed & noble **09**. Less earthy, tannic than **08**, more approachable now but has potential to improve good few years.

★★★★ **Rosalind** ⓣ Satisfying **07** cab-led Bordeaux blend with cab franc & merlot. Smooth, rounded, classic - maybe even old-fashioned - glass of SA red.

★★★★ **Houmoed Bushvine Chenin Blanc** 🖾 Barrel-fermented/aged version, **12** (★★★☆) with vanilla touch from slightly longer oaking; powerful dry finish, good integration & weight but shade off **11**.

Duel Méthode Cap Classique ⓣ ★★★☆ **NV** champagne-method sparkling ex pinot noir & chardonnay bursts with strawberry sherbet appeal, creamy but dry end.

Classic range

★★★★ **Chenin Blanc Bush Vine** ✓ 🖾 Old-vine, lees-aged (unwooded) treasure. **12** similar to steely **11**: bone-dry, persistent, for contemplation. **10**, with 15% botrytis, was more voluptuous.

Cabernet Sauvignon ⓣ ★★★★ Classic cab markers on **06**: cassis, pencil shavings & old leather; taut tannins & properly dry mineral farewell. Better balance than **05** (★★★). **Pinotage** 🖾 ★★★★ Estate's mainstay grape - back to 100% in **12** - unoaked; offers mulberry fruitiness, variety's signature banana notes. **Sauvignon Blanc** ★★★ Muted, water-white **13** tank sample has faint khaki bush nose, satisfying vinosity. Coastal WO. Discontinued: **Cabernet Franc**, **Merlot**, **Shiraz**.

Langtafel range

White ☺ 🍴 🖾 ★★★ Fresh & zesty sauvignon-led **13** combo with semillon, chenin, packed with flavour. Perfect for patio entertaining. WO W Cape, as all these.

Red 🍴 🖾 ★★★ Early-drinking unwooded **12**, plummy & creamy courtesy 55% merlot; two cabs add freshness, firmness. **Rosé** 🍴 ★★ Boiled sweets & strawberries on lightish & bone-dry **13** pink. — CvZ

Mooiuitsig Wine Cellars

Location: Bonnievale ▪ Map: Robertson ▪ Est 1947 ▪ Sales Mon-Thu 8-5 Fri 8-1.30 ▪ Tours by appt ▪ Stay-overs at De Rust Lodge info@outdoorarena.co.za; T +27 (0)23-616-2444 ▪ Owner(s) Jonker family ▪ Winemaker(s) Nico van der Westhuizen & Jean Aubrey, with Lazarus Kholomba ▪ Viticulturist(s) Casper Matthee ▪ 150ha total ▪ 2,900t ▪ PO Box 15 Bonnievale 6730 ▪ info@mooiuitsig.co.za ▪ www.mooiuitsig.co.za ▪ S 33° 56' 59.0" E 020° 2' 36.1" ▪ **T +27 (0)23-616-2143** ▪ F +27 (0)23-616-2675

The Jonker family's drinks enterprise near Bonnievale recently acquired the Kango brand from Southern Cape Vineyards, widening an already substantial portfolio. Mooiuitsig has its own distribution network and even retail outlets, and caters comprehensively to South Africa's enduring off-dry palate.

▪ **Mooiuitzicht** *see* Mooiuitsig Wine Cellars
▪ **Moonlight Organics** *see* Stellar Winery

Moordenaarskop

Location: Sir Lowry's Pass ▪ Map: Helderberg ▪ WO: Stellenbosch ▪ Est 1999 ▪ 1stB 2002 ▪ Tasting, sales & cellar tours by appt ▪ Owner(s)/cellarmaster(s)/winemaker(s)/viticulturist(s) Graham Smith ▪ 0.33ha (cab) ▪ 2t/ 240cs own label 100% red ▪ PO Box 2889 Somerset West 7129 ▪ mwsmiths@mweb.co.za ▪ S 34° 5' 55.3" E 018° 54' 53.7" ▪ **T +27 (0)21-858-1202** ▪ F +27 (0)86-672-6797

The rather grim name (it means Murderer's Peak) is that of the mountain behind garagiste Graham Smith's tiny Helderberg property. 'We decided we'd call it Moordenaarsdop (Murderer's Drink) in a bad year,' he quips. He's just had one of those, but at least has bottled a small quantity of his Cabernet.

Cabernet Sauvignon Reserve Await next. **Cabernet Sauvignon** ★★★ Savoury, earthy **10**'s tannins mask meaty red berry fruit, needing time to soften. — IM

Môreson

Location/map: Franschhoek ▪ WO: Franschhoek/Coastal ▪ Est 1983 ▪ 1stB 1994 ▪ Tasting, sales & cellar tours daily 9.30-5 ▪ Fee R30 ▪ Closed Dec 25 ▪ Bread & Wine Restaurant daily 12-3 & The Farm Grocer (for lighter meals) daily 9.30-4.30 ▪ Charcuterie produced by Neil Jewell ▪ Exotic Plant Company ▪ Wine blending &

breadmaking ▪ Owner(s) Richard Friedman ▪ Winemaker(s) Clayton Reabow (May 2007), with Marozanne Grobbelaar (Nov 2008) ▪ Viticulturist(s) James McNaught Davis ▪ 35ha/±18ha (chard, chenin) ▪ ±120t 30% red 45% white 25% MCC ▪ Euro Gap, IPW ▪ PO Box 114 Franschhoek 7690 ▪ sales@moreson.co.za ▪ www. moreson.co.za ▪ S 33° 53' 11.9" E 019° 3' 30.6" ▪ **T +27 (0)21-876-3055** ▪ F +27 (0)21-876-2348

The 'Morning Sun' rose for owner Richard Friedman when he took over this Franschhoek vineyard from his parents twenty years ago. Wines had been vinified by the local cooperative but Richard built a cellar and surged to prominence with a solo, debut 1994 harvest. He's since built an impressive wine and hospitality offering including a restaurant showcasing chef Neil Jewell's singular charcuterie. Aviator and adventurer, Richard's penchant is for intriguing wine names; the game is on to guess their meaning!

Môreson range

★★★★ **Pinotage** Now-bottled **11** showing lavish dark fruit, sweet-tasting viscous texture boosted by 14% alcohol. Year oak, third new. WO Coastal.

★★★★ **Mata Mata** Merlot & cab franc-led Bordeaux quartet retains elegance & lower alcohol in warm **10** vintage. Good fruit weight in firm framework of supple oak & tannin.

★★★★☆ **Mercator Premium Chardonnay** ⬚ Was 'Premium Chardonnay'. Rich but restrained **12** flagship has tangy lime & nectarine infused with creamy toasted nut flavours from barrel fermentation & year ageing, 50% new.

★★★★ **Knoputibak** NEW Delicious & complex ensemble chardonnay & 10% semillon; **12** densely fruited, generous oak brought to order by citrus tang.

Cabernet Franc ★★★★ Leafy, tad herbaceous **10** has intriguing perfume; balanced, with development potential. WO Coastal. **Magia** Await new vintage, as for **Pink Brut Rosé**, **Sauvignon Blanc**, **Gala Cuvée Cape** & **One Méthode Cap Classique**. **The Fudge** NEW ★★★★ Intricate vinification for vine-dried chardonnay, naturally fermented, then year in barrel (none new). **12**'s ample sweetness (171 g/l sugar) seamlessly absorbed into tropical fruit-toned mouthful. **Dr Reason Why** NEW ✓ 🍴 ★★★☆ **12** unwooded chardonnay from 3 parcels vinified differently (all with wild yeasts), then blended to give breadth to citrus core. **Solitaire Blanc de Blancs Méthode Cap Classique** ⬚ ★★★☆ Multi-vintage blend, reserve wines add complexity to fresh apple-toned style. Latest **NV** in the groove, 18 months on lees. Discontinued: **Chenin Blanc**.

Miss Molly range

In My Bed Cabernet Sauvignon-Merlot Await new vintage, as for **Hoity Toity Chenin Blanc-Viognier**, **Kitchen Thief Sauvignon Blanc**, **Bubbly** & new **Petite Rosé** sparkling. —DS

■ **Môrewag** see Blomendahl Vineyards

Morgenhof Wine Estate   🍷🍵⌂📷🎿♿

Location/map: Stellenbosch ▪ WO: Simonsberg-Stellenbosch/Stellenbosch ▪ Est 1692 ▪ 1stB 1984 ▪ Tasting & sales Mon-Fri 9-5.30 (Nov-Apr) & 9-4.30 (May-Oct); Sat/Sun 10-5 (Nov-Apr) & 10-3 (May-Oct) ▪ Fee R25 pp ▪ Closed Good Fri, Dec 25 & Jan 1 ▪ Cellar tours/viewing of underground barrel cellar on request ▪ Cheese platters ▪ Morgenhof Restaurant (see Restaurants section) ▪ Facilities for children ▪ Gift shop ▪ Conferences ▪ Weddings/functions ▪ Heli-pad ▪ Conservation area ▪ Morgenhof Manor House (see Accommodation section) ▪ Owner(s) Anne Cointreau ▪ Winemaker(s) Andries de Klerk (Jan 2012) ▪ Viticulturist(s) Pieter Haasbroek (Apr 1998) ▪ 212ha/74ha (cabs s/f, malbec, merlot, chenin) ▪ 410t/70,000cs own label 60% red 38% white 2% rosé ▪ BWI, IPW ▪ PO Box 365 Stellenbosch 7599 ▪ info@morgenhof.com ▪ www.morgenhof.com ▪ S 33° 53' 38.5" E 018° 51' 39.2" ▪ **T +27 (0)21-889-5510** ▪ F +27 (0)21-889-5266

As befits a property dating back to 1692, and under French ownership since 1993 (owner Anne Cointreau is from the famous French cognac and liqueurs family), classic traditions are often invoked here. Such as the generally restrained style of the winemaking, but also such factors as the lack of irrigation in the vineyards on the lower slopes of Stellenbosch's Simonsberg – where a diversity of aspects and soils (the latter on display at the tasting centre) allow for careful matching of variety to site. Conservation responsibilities are not forgotten, with 22 of the estate's 212 hectares under natural fynbos.

Morgenhof Estate range

★★★★ **Cabernet Sauvignon** Youthful, unevolved **11** shows espresso, toasty oak & dark fruit. Classically structured, with a rich flavourful palate & fine tannins, leading to long finish. Needs 5+ years to develop.

★★★★ **Merlot** Attractive, youthful **10** (ex barrel) in house's classic style. Smart oaking does not intrude on the fruit & the palate is concentrated, with lots of energy & uplift; fine tannin & a dry finish.

★★★★ **The Morgenhof Estate** Retasted **06** still has noticeable acidity but it's now better integrated. Delicious aromas still, & the palate with a firm tannin grip to support the fruit flavours.

★★★★ **Chenin Blanc** Restrainedly oaked **12** off old vines shows subtle aromas of peach & nectarine. The palate is creamy & attractive with good, intense flavours, but lacking the vibrancy of a serious acidity.

★★★★ **Brut Reserve** Fresh **08** MCC bubbly from chardonnay & pinot with green apple, peach & delicate floral notes. Not very complex, but attractively tight, with a steely edge.

★★★★ **Cape LBV 04** Late Bottled Vintage spent 6 years in oak barrels. Rich, full & intensely flavoured, with grippy tannins to balance the sweetness. From touriga.

Merlot-Cabernet Franc ★★★ Retasted **08** shows meaty, herbaceous aromas. The finish remains slightly acidic, rustic. **Chardonnay** ★★★ Modestly oaked, fairly evolved **12** has notes of ripe apple, dried fruit. The palate is warming & could do with a little more freshness. **Sauvignon Blanc** ★★★☆ Fresh, tropical & forward **12** tasted last year pre-bottling. Now a pleasing but uncomplex mix of herbal & tropical aromas & flavours. **Noble Late Harvest** Occasional release.

Fantail range

Cabernet Franc-Cabernet Sauvignon ☺ ★★★ Enjoyable **11**'s crisp red & black fruits have slight herbaceous undertones from 85% cab franc. Firm tannins balanced by sweet fruit.

Pinotage ★★★ Previewed last year, softly textured **11**'s attractive aromas lead to slightly warming palate. This & wines below WO Stellenbosch. **Pinotage Rosé** ★★★ Easygoing, red-fruited **12** off-dry but nicely balanced. **Sauvignon Blanc-Chenin Blanc** ★★ Name change reflects blend on undemanding, off-dry **12**. — JPf

Morgenster Estate

Location: Somerset West ▪ Map: Helderberg ▪ WO: Stellenbosch ▪ Est 1993 ▪ 1stB 1998 ▪ Tasting & sales Mon-Fri 10-5 Sat/Sun 10-4 ▪ Tasting fee R25 wine/R20 olive oil & olive products ▪ Closed Good Fri & Dec 25 ▪ Owner(s) Giulio Bertrand ▪ Cellarmaster(s)/winemaker(s) Henry Kotzé (Oct 2009) ▪ Viticulturist(s) Bob Hobson (Aug 2008) ▪ 200ha/30ha (cabs s/f, merlot, nebbiolo, p verdot, sangio) ▪ ±200t own label 90% red 5% white 5% rosé ▪ BWI, IPW ▪ PO Box 1616 Somerset West 7129 ▪ info@morgenster.co.za ▪ www.morgenster.co.za ▪ S 34° 5' 2.9" E 018° 53' 7.8" ▪ **T +27 (0)21-852-1738** ▪ F +27 (0)21-852-1141

Retirement is a relative term for Giulio Bertrand, who purchased Morgenster on the slopes of the Schapenberg as a retirement home in 1992. Since then he has overseen the planting of vineyards and imported the best varieties of olive tree for his now renowned oil - also establishing a nursery for the benefit of other oil producers. With Pierre Lurton of Châteaux Cheval Blanc and Yquem as consultant and Henry Kotzé as winemaker, Bordeaux-style blends as well as Italy-inspired sangiovese and nebbiolo are produced. (Unusually, parcels of each vintage are held back, enabling Morgenster to offer a selection of vintages bottle-aged at the estate under ideal conditions.) Busier-than-ever Bertrand is now establishing fine dining and luxury accommodation on his much-loved estate.

Morgenster Estate range

★★★★☆ **Morgenster** Carefully judged merlot (48%), with cab, cab franc & petit verdot blend brings out best in lighter **10**. Less plush than usual, with lively freshness & a fine, succulent grip. Oak subtle enhancement. As drinkable as a good young wine should be; has room to improve in medium term.

★★★★☆ **Lourens River Valley** **10** from half cab franc with merlot, cab & petit verdot. Elegant & charming; shows restrained dark berry, spice fragrance, complexity. Sweet flesh contained by natural freshness, fine polished tannins. Balanced to age.

White ★★★★ Increased semillon in **12** (53% versus 45% in **11**) balances sauvignon, lends better weight, texture, though still elegant style. Mostly older oak.

Italian Collection

Nabucco ★★★★ Intense, pure tarry, tobacco aromas introduce youthful **11**. Light textured, fresh & with finishing austerity associated with nebbiolo. One of best to date. **10** (★★★★) had splashes merlot & cab.

Tosca ★★★★ **11** more authentic sangiovese character than fleshier **10** (★★★★); cab, merlot quietly supportive. Pleasantly fresh feel highlighting sour cherry features. Careful oak spicing enhances appeal.

Caruso ★★★☆ Coral pink **13** rosé from sangiovese more vinous than fruity; softish but firm, bone-dry finish assures good companionship with food.

Nu Series 1 NEW

★★★★ **Merlot** ✓ From young vines (as all these) in approachable yet classic style. Medium-bodied **12** offers generous dark fruits, fresh, ripe grape tannins & good length on dry finish. Harmonised in older oak.

Cabernet Sauvignon ★★★☆ Slight minty edge to **12**. Lightish fruit braced by slightly firmer grip than implied by back label's suggestion of approachable styling. — AL

■ **Mori Wines** *see* Casa Mori

■ **Morkel** *see* Bellevue Estate Stellenbosch

Mostertsdrift Noble Wines

Location/map/WO: Stellenbosch ▪ Est/1stB 2001 ▪ Tasting, sales & cellar tours by appt ▪ Fee R10pp for groups ▪ Meals for groups by prior arrangement ▪ Facilities for children ▪ Conference venue ▪ Owner(s) André Mostert & Anna-Mareè Uys (Mostert) ▪ Cellarmaster(s)/winemaker(s) Anna-Mareè Uys (Jan 2001) ▪ Viticulturist(s) Nico Mostert (Jan 2001) ▪ 13ha/±8ha (cab, merlot, pinot, chard, hanepoot) ▪ ±80-100t/3,986cs own label 70% red 10% white 20% rosé + 15,000L bulk ▪ PO Box 2061 Dennesig Stellenbosch 7601 ▪ winemaker@mostertsdrift.co.za ▪ www.mostertsdrift.co.za ▪ S 33° 53' 31.7" E 018° 50' 17.6" ▪ **T +27 (0)73-194-9221** ▪ F +27 (0)86-516-1730

Passionate hockey player, coach and umpire Anna-Mareè Uys, with brother André Mostert and their father Nico in the vineyards, runs the hospitable family winery on the northern edge of Stellenbosch with little pomp but lots of enthusiasm, spreading the message and bringing wine to people, people to wine.

Cabernet Sauvignon ⑨ ★★★ Previously, **07** was more accessible than preceding vintage, with nutty complexity & creamy mouthfeel. **AnéRouge** ⑨ ★★★ Mainly cab, rest merlot. Last-tasted **07**'s well managed ripe fruit delivered balance & soft appeal. **Cape Blend** ⑨ ▤ ★★★ Overtly fruity **08** shows some development, good ripeness. Mainly merlot & pinotage (50/30), rest cab. **Merlot Rosé** Tank sample **13** too unformed to rate. **Chardonnay** ★★★ Unwooded **13** preview still showing fermentation aromas, but fresh & fruit rich, with appealingly rounded body. **White Muscadel** ⑨ Await next. — GdB

Mount Abora Vineyards

Location: Riebeek-Kasteel ▪ Map/WO: Swartland ▪ Est/1stB 2012 ▪ Tasting & sales by appt ▪ Owner(s) Vinotage (Pty) Ltd ▪ Winemaker(s) Johan Meyer ▪ 6,000cs own label 60% red 40% white ▪ PO Box 396 Riebeek Kasteel 7307 ▪ wine@abora.co.za ▪ www.abora.co.za, www.cinsaut.co.za ▪ S 33° 24' 19.8" E 018° 52' 15.0" ▪ **T +27 (0)82-413-6719/+27 (0)72-045-9592**

Named after the imaginary landmark in Coleridge's poem 'Kubla Khan', the Mount Abora wines - crafted within Swartland Independent guidelines, and embodying the excitement surrounding Swartland as a region, have gained an enthusiastic following since debut in 2012. Newer vintages of Saffraan Cinsaut, Koggelbos Chenin and maiden vintage of Mount Abora The Abyssinian missed the deadline (the '11 Koggelbos Chenin still available at press time). Vinification is by rising star Johan Meyer at (for the time being) Meerhof custom crush cellar.

★★★★ **Koggelbos Chenin Blanc** ⑨ Epitomises serious new-generation Swartland chenin in complex, rich-yet-fresh **11**. Flavours are fruity (lemon, lime & tangerine) but retain a vibrant mineral core. — JP,CvZ

■ **Mountain Eye** *see* Kleinhoekkloof

Mountain Oaks Organic Winery

Location: Rawsonville ▪ Map: Breedekloof ▪ WO: Slanghoek ▪ Est/1stB 2003 ▪ Tasting, sales & cellar tours by appt ▪ Farm tours & talks on organic farming by appt ▪ Farm produce ▪ Owner(s) Stevens family ▪ Viticulturist(s)

Mark Stevens (2000) ▪ 200ha/16ha (cabs s/f, ptage, shiraz, chard, chenin) ▪ 20-30t own label 70% red 20% white 10% rosé ▪ SGS organic certification ▪ PO Box 68 Rawsonville 6845 ▪ eikenbosch@iafrica.com ▪ S 33° 38' 16.1" E 019° 13' 36.0" ▪ **T +27 (0)23-344-3107** ▪ F +27 (0)86-613-6687

It was the wish to farm organically that led the Stevens family to the Slanghoek Valley, where the project was eased by 'little pollution, abundant water, cold winters, high rainfall and fairly cool summer evenings'. Today the farm is certified organic, and tours and talks on organic farming are offered by appointment.

★★★★ **Pinotage** ⒷⒺ After juicy **10**, pre-bottling sample **11** (★★★★) had ripe raspberry scent & delicious flavours, but perhaps not the depth for its ambitious structure. Drying tannin might resolve in time. **Eikenbosch Red** ⒷⒺ ★★★ Lively, pleasant **10** cab/cab franc blend balances ripe flavours with more spicy, savoury character. Firmly structured. **Le Jardin Rouge** ⒷⒺ ★★ Pleasant but porty **11** blend ex tank showed more structure than fruit a few years back. **Le Jardin Rosé** Ⓔ Await next, as for **Chardonnay Reserve**, **Eikenbosch White** & **Le Jardin**. — TJ

Mountain Ridge Wines ▮⏣⛊

Location: Wolseley ▪ Map: Breedekloof ▪ WO: Western Cape ▪ Est 1949 ▪ 1stB 1976 ▪ Tasting & sales Mon-Fri 8-5 ▪ Closed all pub hols ▪ BYO picnic ▪ Owner(s) 20 members ▪ Cellarmaster(s) Paul Malan (Oct 2010) ▪ Winemaker(s) Christo Stemmet (Jan 2010) ▪ Viticulturist(s) Pierre Snyman (consultant) ▪ 400ha (cab, shiraz, chenin, cbard) ▪ 9,000t/8,000cs own label 48% red 37% white 15% rosé ▪ IPW ▪ PO Box 108 Wolseley 6830 ▪ sales@mountainridge.co.za ▪ www.mountainridge.co.za ▪ S 33° 28' 42.8" E 019° 12' 16.2" ▪ **T +27 (0)23-231-1070** ▪ F +27 (0)23-231-1102

Their focus having shifted from bulk wine production to vinifying for the own quality-driven range, the grower-owners of Mountain Ridge are attracting more visitors to their cellardoor on the R303 between Worcester and Wolseley via the Ramkiekie Farmer's Market, held on the last Saturday of each month.

★★★★ **Shiraz Reserve** ⒷⓏ Big, dramatic **10** continues improved form of **09**, integrates rich dark berries with elegant tannins, French oak adds boldness. From Hemel-en-Aarde vines. **Cabernet Sauvignon Reserve** ⒷⓏ ★★★★ **10**, from Stellenbosch grapes, firm tannins supporting ripe blackberry flavours. Could age elegantly. **Shiraz Rosé** Await next, as for **Sauvignon Blanc**. — DB

Mountain River Wines

Location: Paarl ▪ WO: Western Cape ▪ Est 1993 ▪ 1stB 1998 ▪ Closed to public ▪ Owner(s) De Villiers Brits ▪ Cellarmaster(s) De Villiers Brits, with consultants ▪ 1.2ha (shiraz) ▪ 60,000cs own label 60% red 40% white ▪ 146 Main Road Paarl 7646 ▪ dev@mountainriverwines.co.za, mattie@mountainriverwines.co.za ▪ www.mountainriverwines.co.za ▪ **T +27 (0)21-872-3245/6/7** ▪ F +27 (0)21-872-3255

Owner/winemaster De Villiers Brits' negociant business, with its 'proudly South African' branding, has seen increased sales of bulk wine over the past year, most of it destined for Europe. His market in Russia continues to grow, with the Ukuzala range (there's that ZA identifier again!) sold there exclusively.

Mountain River range

Pinotage Next awaited, as for **Pinotage-Shiraz**. **Chardonnay** NEW ★★★★ Medium-bodied **12**, zesty lime a tad overshadowed by spicy oak but enough flavour & life to knit & drink well for few years.

Maankloof range

Sauvignon Blanc ☺Ⓩ ★★★ **13** is fresh, herbaceous & crisp. Light summer style.

Cabernet Sauvignon Next awaited, like **Shiraz**. **Pinotage** ★★★ **12** has bright & sappy mulberry flavours. Unoaked & friendly. **Chenin Blanc** ⒷⒹⓏ ★★★ Tank sample **12** is zingy, well balanced; attractive thatch/hay characters, satisfying dryness, just 12% alcohol.

Ukuzala range

Dry Red ★★ **12** pale, crisp & lightly fruited. **Dry White** Ⓑ ★★ Lemon & thatch tones on **11**, from chenin & colombard.

Zaràfa range

> **Sauvignon Blanc** ☺ ★★★ **13** light, fresh herbaceous tone to bright seafood BBQ partner.

Cabernet Sauvignon ⊕ ⬚ ★★ Fruit-filled **11** with good grip, moderate 13.5% alcohol. **Pinotage** ⬚ ★★★ Unwooded & amiable **12** has a lively & juicy mulberry tone. **Shiraz** ⊕ ⬚ ★★ **12** faint red fruits, fresh acidity, gruff end when reviewed. **Rosé** NEW ★★ **13** crisp & friendly dry summer quaffer. — MW

🔲 **Mountain Shadows** see Wineways Marketing
🔲 **Mountainside** see Ruitersvlei Wines
🔲 **Mountain Stream** see Ashton Kelder
🔲 **Mountain View** see Farm 1120

Mount Babylon Vineyards   🔳🍷

Location: Hermanus ▪ Map: Elgin, Walker Bay & Bot River ▪ Est 2002 ▪ 1stB 2007 ▪ Tasting, sales & cellar tours by appt ▪ Cheese platters ▪ Owner(s) Johan Holtzhausen ▪ Winemaker(s) Jean-Claude Martin (2008, consultant) & Johan Holtzhausen ▪ Viticulturist(s) Johan Pienaar (2002, consultant) ▪ 65ha/7ha (malbec, shiraz, viog) ▪ ±38t/±400cs own label 90% red 10% white ▪ PO Box 7370 Stellenbosch 7599 ▪ info@mountbabylon. co.za ▪ www.mountbabylon.co.za ▪ S 34° 19' 44.0" E 019° 19' 34.3" ▪ **T +27 (0)21-855-2768/+27 (0)84-511-8180** ▪ F +27 (0)21-855-2768

Johan Holtzhausen owns this small family concern, a pioneer in the Hemel-en-Aarde Ridge ward. As a corporate financier, he says, winemaking was 'a dream realised when I bought our own little "Heaven on Earth"' of vines, fynbos and birdsong. Since then (is he surprised?), 'passion has often ruled common sense!'

★★★★ **SMV** ⊕ Bright & refreshing **07** (★★★★) had mocha, chocolate aromas; harmonious but lacking complexity of maiden **06** (from shiraz, with malbec, viognier). Like next, tasted a few years back.

★★★★ **Pioneer Brut Reserve** ⊕ Polished **07** a rare 100% shiraz blanc de noir MCC sparkling. Apricot-tinged, with berry hints, intriguing nuttiness & herbal persistence. — TJ

Mount Pleasant Vineyards

Location/WO: Darling ▪ Est 2009 ▪ 1stB 2011 ▪ Closed to public ▪ Owner(s) Pascale Palmer & the Legner family ▪ Winemaker(s) Wim Smit (Dec 2010, Hofstraat) ▪ Viticulturist(s) Alfred Legner (Jun 2006) ▪ 0.2ha/0.1ha (shiraz) ▪ 2t/ha 66cs own label 100% red ▪ 11 High Street, Darling 7345 ▪ info@darlingmusic.org ▪ **T +27 (0)72-015-1653**

Alfred Legner, former London banker now tending a small vineyard in West Coast cultural hotspot Darling, had a tinier than usual crop in 2013. But 'the quality was good', and his shiraz, made by Hofstraat Kelder, continues seeking 'elegance' to 'overcome perceptions of the area as producing only big wines'.

Mount Pleasant Vineyards range NEW
Darling Pascale's Shiraz ★★★★ Named for Mount Pleasant co-owner Pascale Palmer. Leafy nuance to **11**'s black cherry & spicy red fruit. Showy, with tight tannins, deserves time or a good meal. — GdB, GM

Mount Rozier Estate   🍷🔺📷

Location: Sir Lowry's Pass ▪ Map: Helderberg ▪ WO: Stellenbosch ▪ Est/1stB 2011 ▪ Tasting & cellar tours by appt only ▪ Wine sales Mon-Fri ▪ The Peacock Cottage; Mount Rozier wedding & conference venue T +27 (0)73-338-7032, shelleyr@journeysend.co.za ▪ Owner(s) Gabb family ▪ Winemaker(s) Leon Esterhuizen ▪ Viticulturist(s) Lodewyk Retief ▪ 40ha/30ha (cab, malbec, merlot, p verdot, shiraz, chard, pinot gris) ▪ 200t/25-30,000cs own label 100% red ▪ IPW, WIETA ▪ PO Box 3040 Somerset West 7129 ▪ wines@mountrozier.co.za ▪ www.mountrozier.co.za ▪ S 34° 6' 21.22" E 018° 54' 35.80" ▪ **T +27 (0)21-858-1929** ▪ F +27 (0)86-540-1929

Following the purchase by Journey's End Vineyards of Mount Rozier in 2012, the relaunched brand has been enjoying success in the UK and US multiple retail sector. A replanting programme including malbec and petit verdot is underway. Clearing 15 ha of alien vegetation from these Shapenberg foothills was part of a five-year plan to elevate their status from BWI member to Champion.

Tobacco Street Shiraz ☺ ★★★ A real charmer, **11** gets sweetness from oak & very ripe spicy blackberry fruit. Misses some freshness but oh-so-easy to like. **Peacock Chardonnay** ☺ ★★★ Another crowd pleaser, bringing oak-derived buttery & sweet creamy tones to the table in **12**. Not multi-dimensional, but tasty & well priced. **The Garland Sauvignon Blanc** ☺ 🖩 ★★★ Showing good intensity in a fragrant body, **12** appeals to the 'green' averse with tropical, apple & pear flavours.

Myrtle Grove Cabernet Sauvignon ✓ 🖩 ★★★★ Attractive, aromatic **11**, sweet green herbs & fresh redcurrants, well-judged oak creates sympathetic structure to nicely medium-weighted wine. Nudges next level. **The Beekeeper Merlot** ⦿ 🖩 ★★☆ Olive & meaty savouriness in **10**, light textured, touch sweetness helps smooth tad lean tannins. — DC

Mount Vernon Estate

Location: Paarl ▪ Map: Paarl & Wellington ▪ WO: Simonsberg-Paarl/Western Cape ▪ Est 1996 ▪ 1stB 2005 ▪ Tasting, sales & cellar tours Mon-Fri 10-5 Sat 10-3 ▪ Owner(s) David & Debbie Hooper ▪ Cellarmaster(s) Debbie Hooper (Jan 2003) ▪ Winemaker(s) Debbie Hooper (Jan 2003), with Philip du Toit (Jan 2005) ▪ Viticulturist(s) Philip du Toit (Jun 1997) ▪ 110ha/27.5ha (cab, malbec, merlot, p verdot, ptage, shiraz, chard) ▪ 210-225t/2,000cs own label 80% red 15% white 5% rosé ▪ PO Box 348 Klapmuts 7625 ▪ john@mountvernon.co.za ▪ www.mountvernon.co.za ▪ S 33° 48' 57.8" E 018° 52' 51.9" ▪ **T +27 (0)21-875-5073** ▪ F +27 (0)86-618-9821

This property in the Simonsberg-Paarl ward is owned by the Hooper family, who run liquor distributors E Snell. The name was inspired by George Washington's home in Virginia, but also reflects the middle name of every Hooper male, given in memory of Vernon Edward Hooper - the crest on the elegant labels is his rank insignia as a sergeant major in World War II.

Mount Vernon range

★★★★ **Malbec** 🔲 Slightly earthy aromas on **10** (★★★☆); fresher mint, spice flavours, mineral lift just cover 15% alcohol warmth. **09** had greater character & presence.

Cabernet Sauvignon 🔲 ★★ **10** very different from impressive **09** (★★★★). Forceful mint & cassis character, with persistent alcohol (15%) glow. **Chardonnay Single Vineyard** ⦿ 🖩 ★★★ As in **10**, oaky **11** drowns out brave attempt by ripe & willing citrus fruit. May integrate better with time.

Three Peaks range

Sauvignon Blanc ☺ 🖩 🔲 ★★★ Mellow tropical tones on **12**. Lightish body & savouriness enhance quaffability. WO W Cape.

Pinotage 🖩 🔲 ★★ Sweet-fruited **12** oaky & very ripe. **Cantata** 🖩 🔲 ★★★ Mint-laced but not unripe **11**, 5-way blend headed by cab. Fruit driven & lively, with a brush of fine tannin trimming sweetish tail. **Jean Pierre's Lunchtime Rosé** ⦿ 🖩 🔲 ★★☆ **12** merlot-led blend in dry strawberry juice style. — AL

Mulderbosch Vineyards

Location/map: Stellenbosch ▪ WO: Stellenbosch/Western Cape/Coastal ▪ Est 1989 ▪ 1stB 1991 ▪ Tasting & sales Tue-Sun & pub hols 10-6 ▪ Fee R35 ▪ Closed Mon, Easter Fri-Mon, Dec 25 & Jan 1 ▪ Pizzas & cheese boards, cappuccinos, artisanal beer, juice ▪ Olive oil ▪ Bocce ball courts (Italian boules) ▪ Conservation area ▪ Owner(s) Terroir Capital ▪ Winemaker(s) Adam Mason (Dec 2011), with Mick Craven (Jan 2013) ▪ Viticulturist(s) Adam Mason (Jun 2013) ▪ 80ha/45.2ha (cabs s/f, merlot, p verdot, shiraz, chard, chenin, sauv, viog) ▪ BWI ▪ PO Box 12817 Die Boord Stellenbosch 7613 ▪ info@mulderbosch.co.za ▪ www.mulderbosch.co.za ▪ S 33° 56' 56.00" E 018° 45' 57.00" ▪ **T +27 (0)21-881-8140** ▪ F +27 (0)21-881-3514

It was thanks to Mulderbosch's agent in the US and their success there that Charles Banks, via his California-based investment group, Terroir Capital, purchased the winery in late 2010. As part of the deal, Mulderbosch moved to the Polkadraai premises of what had been its sibling brand, Kanu, as these offered bigger facilities and more land. Buildings and vineyards both have undergone a major makeover, though contract growers remain significant suppliers of fruit. Chenin is a key focus, with three premium site-specific labels from various areas in Stellenbosch joining the range in 2014: 'Sonop on shale, Rustenhof on decomposed granite and Eikenhof on very sandy soil,' explains cellarmaster Adam

Mason. Things that haven't changed are the distinctive Mulderbosch 'cigar band' label and the brand's popularity in the US.

Mulderbosch Vineyards range

★★★★☆ **Faithful Hound** 🍷 Bordeaux quintet, with cab franc in the lead. Like any quality wine, **11** tastes good in youth but its layered tobacco, spice, ripe dark berries & savoury tail, braced by fine tannin, suggest more complexity over next 5 to 7 years. Smartly oaked, 60% new.

★★★★ **Chardonnay** 🍷 Unchallenging yet satisfying **12** (★★★★). Unobtrusive oak adds interesting nuance to nutty, citrus juiciness; zesty acid but finishes tad sweet. **11** more impressive.

★★★★☆ **Chardonnay Barrel Fermented** 🍷 Elegant & complex, **12** shows seamless integration between mineral, limy fruit & oak (50% new, 18 months). Expansive mouthfeel, good length though still tight core of flavour. Will reward cellaring. No **11**.

★★★★ **Sauvignon Blanc Noble Late Harvest** 🍷 Yellow-gold **11**. Botrytis & oak nicely judged not to swamp sauvignon (& a little chenin) fruit. Lightish body; sweetness cut by tangy acid. No **10**. WO W Cape.

Cabernet Sauvignon Rosé 🍽 🍷 ★★★ Colour & scents of fresh strawberries immediate attractions on nearly dry **13**. Tangy, juicy flavours no let-down either. WO Coastal. **Chenin Blanc Steen op Hout** 🍽 🍷 ★★★★ **12**, tasted as 'Chenin Blanc' tank sample last year, now complex, concentrated with deep yellow peach, lees features. Mouthfilling & rich, balanced by tangy acidity. Step up on **11** (★★★★). W Cape WO, like next. **Sauvignon Blanc** 🍽 🍷 ★★★☆ Graceful **12** has blossomed since last year's preview. Gentle vigour with splash semillon adding weight to granadilla, winter melon flavours; rounded finish.

1000 Miles range NEW

★★★★★ **Sauvignon Blanc** 🍽 🍷 Serious, delicious **12** has distinctive blackcurrant, granadilla character. Confidently firm with crystalline acid & ripe substance, it should age well & fully integrate the 15 months French oak. Elgin, Stellenbosch & Darling grapes.

Sonop Single Vineyard Chenin Blanc 🍽 🍷 ★★★★ Most elegant, focused of single-vineyard trio. From Bottelary. **13**, like others, tasted pre-bottling, rating provisional; lovely floral & fresh apples expression; delicate, with poised freshness. 15 months matured French oak, 20% new, as all. **Rustenhof Single Vineyard Chenin Blanc** 🍽 🍷 ★★★★ From Faure, **13** in riper, more juicy style (& extra 1% alcohol at 14.7%) but still with fine-tuned fruit tones - tropical, red apple - poise & great length. **Eikenhof Single Vineyard Chenin Blanc** 🍽 🍷 ★★★★ From Polkadraai, retiring & very delicate **13**, more minerality than obvious fruit but similar concentration, length to others. Probably the slowest to evolve. — AL

Mullineux Family Wines 🍷🍷

Location: Riebeek-Kasteel ▪ Map/WO: Swartland ▪ Est 2007 ▪ 1stB 2008 ▪ Tasting, sales & tours by appt Mon-Sun; Sat (Oct-May) 10-3 ▪ Closed Easter Sun, Dec 25 & Jan 1 ▪ Owner(s) Mullineux Family Wines (Pty) Ltd ▪ Cellarmaster(s) Chris & Andrea Mullineux (May 2007) ▪ Winemaker(s) Chris & Andrea Mullineux (May 2007), with Tremayne Smith ▪ Viticulturist(s) Chris & Andrea Mullineux (May 2007), Rosa Kruger (consultant) ▪ 18ha (carignan, cinsaut, mourv, shiraz, chenin, clairette, viog) ▪ 90t/9,000cs own label 50% red 40% white 10% dessert ▪ PO Box 369 Riebeek-Kasteel 7307 ▪ info@mullineuxwines.com ▪ www.mullineuxwines.com ▪ S 33° 23' 1.16" E 18° 53' 46.65" ▪ T +27 (0)22-448-1183 ▪ F +27 (0)86-720-1541

In the village of Riebeek-Kasteel, Chris and Andrea Mullineux have established what they describe as a 'wholesome' boutique cellar (we describe it as our prestigious and hugely deserving 'Winery of the Year' for 2014). The benefits of their endeavours include no less than eleven 5 star ratings to date and international acclaim, which has helped revolutionise their favoured Swartland wine district and focus attention on the South African wine category. The talented young couple, both qualified oenologists (Andrea now a member of the elite Cape Winemakers Guild) and parents of JZ and Philippa, remain refreshingly unassuming. They focus on site-specific wines and blends, showcasing the effects of terroir and impeccable viticulture. Two new members have joined their team, consultant Rosa Kruger, with extensive knowledge of old vines, and Tremayne Smith, assistant winemaker, having helped with the recent 'fast and furious' crush. Their latest project involves Devil's Peak Brewery, where there is a mystery chenin/beer beverage brewing. As Andrea notes: 'We feel proud to be part of that generation where there are no boundaries and the sky is the limit.'

Terroir Specific range

★★★★☆ **Granite Syrah** 🗾 Fascinating demonstration of the effect of two soil types on Swartland shiraz. Identical vinification for this & schist-grown version. Impressive **11** (★★★★★) is muscular & tightly coiled, with brooding dark fruit & minerality. Structure & class to age for 10+ years, like **10**.

★★★★★ **Schist Syrah** 🗾 Shows more elegant poise & harmony in youth, with fragrant red fruit & white pepper. **11** lithe, supple tannins & silkier texture than Granite bottling, but with inherent fruit purity & structure to age with distinction.

★★★★★ **Schist Chenin Blanc** NEW 🗾 Elegant debut from 35 year old vineyards for third in this terroir trio. **12** refined, mineral undertone to almond & citrus peel freshness. Understated but focused, with older oak in seamless balance. Natural ferment, as for all wines from Mullineux.

Mullineux Family Wines range

★★★★★ **Syrah** **11** (★★★★☆) a combination of soil types & vineyards, reveals a bouquet of flavours, although a tad less intense than **10**, last edition's Red Wine of the Year. Nonetheless retains understated elegance & streamlined balance for savouring over the next decade.

★★★★☆ **White Blend** 🗾 Chenin-led **12**, with clairette & viognier exudes richness, flavour & freshness. A Cape benchmark for this genre, with beguiling intensity woven into a silky texture & lingering farewell. Deserves cellaring but has balance for earlier enjoyment.

★★★★★ **Straw Wine** 🗾 One of South Africa's icon dessert wines, **12** is the epitome of liquid, viscous decadence! A thrilling balance of sweetness (282 g/l sugar) & tangy acidity, with complex layers of dried fruit & nougat. From air-dried chenin grapes, naturally fermented over 9 months.

Kloof Street range

★★★★ **Swartland Rouge** ✓ 🗾 **12** shiraz-led second label, with cinsaut & carignan, has a Rhône-style spicy melange of flavours & supple structure. Bright, balanced & eminently drinkable, but classy.

★★★★ **Chenin Blanc** 🗄 🗾 **13** (★★★★) is restrained & leaner than vibrantly tropical **12**. Clean stonefruit flavours & some minerality, tightly buttoned & crisp. From low-yielding old vines. — MW

Muratie Wine Estate

Location/map: Stellenbosch ▪ WO: Stellenbosch/Simonsberg–Stellenbosch/Western Cape ▪ Est 1685 ▪ 1stB ca 1920 ▪ Tasting & sales daily 10–5 ▪ Fee R25/5 wines R35/port & chocolate ▪ Closed Good Fri, Dec 25/26 & Jan 1 ▪ Cellar tours by appt ▪ Light lunches daily 12-3 ▪ Cheese platters ▪ Conference/function venue ▪ Art gallery ▪ Guest cottage ▪ Harvest festival with live music ▪ Owner(s) Melck Family Trust ▪ Cellarmaster(s)/winemaker(s) Francois Conradie (Dec 2005) ▪ Viticulturist(s) Francois Conradie (1995), assisted by Paul Wallace ▪ 110ha/ 42ha (cab, merlot, pinot, shiraz, chard, hanepoot, port) ▪ 300t/40,000cs own label 60% red 14% white 6% rosé 20% other ▪ BWI, IPW ▪ PO Box 133 Koelenhof 7605 ▪ info@muratie.co.za ▪ www.muratie.co.za ▪ S 33° 52' 14.8" E 018° 52' 35.1" ▪ **T +27 (0)21-865-2330/2336** ▪ F +27 (0)21-865-2790

Visiting Stellenbosch family farm Muratie is like stepping back into history, from the gnarled oaks to the old winemaking equipment that greets you on arrival; the rickety cobwebbed tasting room with stained glass windows; the renovated fermenters, with tartrate-encrusted walls, where lunches are held; the antique carpets and furniture; and original art. History is also commemorated in the naming of the wines, all the important figures are there, with their colourful stories on the back labels. But there's nothing old-fashioned about the cellar practices or wine quality, as the line-up below shows: fashionable blends and styles, classic varieties plus warming fortified wines.

Apex range

★★★★ **Ronnie Melck Shiraz Family Selection** ⒸⒻ Premium low-yield grapes for this. **08** (★★★★★) greater complexity & structure than **07**. Bold & intense aromas, core of cassis & mulberry. WO Simonsberg-Stellenbosch, as for Lady Alice.

Flagship range

★★★★☆ **Ansela van de Caab** 🗾 Lots of care taken in cab-led Bordeaux blend, as **10** shows. Blended wine aged further 6 months to meld, getting 24 months in total. Deep layers of creamy dark fruit, cigarbox spicing &, despite current appeal, the build to last 10 years.

★★★★ **Laurens Campher** ✓ 🗾 Changing chenin-led oaked blend, **12** shows preserved melon & ginger with beeswax nuances, the bright acidity keeping its fresh, vibrantly long & eminently ageworthy. Lots to like.

Premium range

★★★★ **George Paul Canitz Pinot Noir** 🎐 Lovely bright fruit in **11**, red cherries, raspberries throughout, give a necessary succulence & counterpoint to the firm tannin backbone. Drink now till ±2020.

★★★★☆ **Ronnie Melck Shiraz** ⚡ 🎐 Honours family patriarch & industry luminary who loved shiraz. Dense & dark toned, **10** is a force to be reckoned with (as was its namesake), seriously made to develop over next 10 years. Start drinking after year or 2.

★★★★ **Isabella Chardonnay** ✓ 🎐 Boldly styled **12** has perfumed richness, tropical fruit, dried peach, even clementine preserve, but the palate's savoury, nutty tones confirm pleasurable food compatibility.

★★★★ **Lady Alice Méthode Cap Classique** ✓ ⊚ Name change from '1763'. Lovely biscuit overlay to **10** sparkling's red berry perfume & flavours, given further focus by the vibrant limy acidity, extended length. Mainly pinot noir, with chardonnay.

Alberta Annemarie Merlot 🎐 ★★★☆ Plump dark berries match **10**'s oak, creating a harmonious drink, the variety's freshness adding a lift.

Fortified Wines

★★★★ **Amber Forever** 🎐 Fortified dessert from muscat d'Alexandrie. Powerfully expressive **12** (★★★★★) gets a lead on **10** with jasmine & exotic spice, sultanas, ginger biscuit, all captured within sumptuous richness. No **11**. WO Western Cape.

★★★★ **Cape Ruby** ⚡ Deep rich fruitcake & brandy, this port-style **NV**'s perfume is already seductive & the flavours don't disappoint either. Nutty, a savoury underpin, finishing with a livening alcohol grip.

★★★★ **Ben Prins Cape Vintage** ⚡ Cocoa dusting on **09**'s deep fruitcake richness, with spirit adding grip to the sweetness. Classic styling, from Portuguese port varieties.

Discontinued: Late Bottled Vintage.

Melck's range

Shiraz-Cabernet Sauvignon ☺ 🍴 🎐 ★★★ Plumply ripe **12** is designed to please with its juicy plum flavours, touch of oak. WO Western Cape, as all these. **Cabernet Franc Rosé** ☺ 🍴 🎐 ★★★ Good typicity on **13**, cranberries, touch of herbs, light & dry. **Sauvignon Blanc** ☺ 🍴 🎐 ★★★ Guava & passionfruit in zinging fresh **13**. Friendly 12.5% alcohol. — CR

Mvemve Raats ♟

Location/map/WO: Stellenbosch ▪ Est/1stB 2004 ▪ Tasting & sales by appt ▪ Closed all pub hols ▪ Owner(s) Bruwer Raats & Mzokhona Mvemve ▪ Cellarmaster(s)/viticulturist(s) Bruwer Raats & Mzokhona Mvemve (both Jan 2004) ▪ Winemaker(s) Bruwer Raats & Mzokhona Mvemve (both Jan 2004), with Gavin Bruwer Slabbert (Feb 2010) ▪ (cabs s/f, malbec, merlot, p verdot) ▪ 10t/900cs own label 100% red ▪ PO Box 2068 Dennesig Stellenbosch 7601 ▪ braats@mweb.co.za ▪ www.raats.co.za ▪ S 33° 58' 16.6" E 018° 44' 55.3" ▪ **T** +27 (0)21-881-3078 ▪ F +27 (0)21-881-3078

Accolades and international honours continue to fall the way of this collaboration of two good friends. Mzokhona Mvemve and Bruwer Raats (of Raats Family Wines) source the grapes for their wine from carefully selected Stellenbosch vineyards and each variety is vinified separately before the all-important blending begins. Quality is paramount and vintages may be skipped (as happened in 2010) if the wine isn't up to the stellar standards of their 'blend of stars'.

★★★★☆ **MR De Compostella** 🎐 Returns to cab franc dominance (52%) in superb 5-way Bordeaux red blend, but **11** follows standout **09** (★★★★★) in style. Polished & elegant dense black fruit with whiffs of violets, cedar, cassis, beautifully handled tannins & promising, gritty length. Shyer, & earlier released than normal, deserves more time. No **10**. — CM

▪ **Mwitu** *see* African Terroir
▪ **My Best Friend** *see* Zandvliet Wine Estate & Thoroughbred Stud

My Wyn

Location/map/WO: Franschhoek ▪ Est/1stB 2001 ▪ Tasting, sales & cellar tours Mon-Fri 10-1 Oct-Apr; after hours, weekends & pub hols by appt or as indicated on the gate ▪ Fee R50pp, waived on purchase ▪ Sunset MCC tastings on koppie (15min walk, weather permitting) by appt only ▪ Cheese platters by prior booking ▪ Owner(s) Jacoline Haasbroek ▪ Winemaker(s) Jacoline Haasbroek (2001) ▪ 1,250cs own label 40% red 20%

white 20% port 20% MCC ▪ IPW ▪ PO Box 112 Franschhoek 7690 ▪ tastewine@telkomsa.net ▪ www. mywynfranschhoek.co.za ▪ S 33° 53' 29.3" E 019° 8' 3.6" ▪ **T** +27 (0)21-876-2518/+27 (0)83-302-5556 ▪ F +27 (0)86-608-0233

My Wyn ('My Wine') is the brand of boutique vintner Jacoline Haasbroek, who vinifies in a tiny, hospitable Franschhoek mountainside cellar. ('Handy, helpful' husband Johan advises other growers.) Energetic Jacoline made follow-up vintages of all wines listed below, though regretfully they were not received in time for tasting. 'Next year I'll be more organised!'

My Wyn range
Cabernet Franc Not tasted, as for **Merlot**, **Petit Verdot**, **Shiraz**, **Semillon**, **Viognier**, **Sauviognier**, **Méthode Cap Classique** & **Amber**. **Robyn** ⊕ ★★★ Shiraz fortified with 3 year old postill brandy for pleasant fireside sipping. **09** Xmas pud & dark chocolate; lighter than most port-styles. — WB,IM

▪ **Mzansi** see Kingsriver Estate
▪ **Mzanzi** see Kingsriver Estate
▪ **Mzanzi's** see Goedverwacht Wine Estate

Mzoli's Wines

Location: Cape Town ▪ Map: Cape Peninsula ▪ WO: Darling ▪ Meals & tasting daily 11-8 ▪ Owner(s) Mzoli Ngcawuzele ▪ NY 115 Shop No 3 Gugulethu 7750 ▪ mzoli@darlingwine.co.za ▪ www.mzoliwine.co.za ▪ S 33° 58' 34.9" E 018° 34' 11.1" ▪ **T** +27 (0)21-638-1355/+27 (0)82-487-0980

The shisa nyama ('buy and barbecue') offered at Mzoli's Place in Cape Town's Gugulethu has become a must-see attraction for tourists and locals alike, often featured in guide books, websites and travel shows. The man behind it is Mzoli Ngcawuzele, also co-founder of the Gugulethu Wine Festival (and writer of our Foreword this year), whose own wines are geared at unpretentious enjoyment.

Mandisi Merlot ⊕ ★★★ Light smoke & mulberry, **11** medium depth but attractively soft, approachable. **Madala** ⊕ ★★★★ 'The Elder' most serious wine in meat-friendly range. Cab & merlot in **11**, layers of black berry, spice & liquorice. Good grip; long, velvety finish. **Unathi** ⊕ ★★★ Herbal edge to black cherry succulence of **09**, different blend to cinsaut & ruby cab tasted previously. **One One Five Rosé** Await next. — FM

Nabygelegen Private Cellar

Location: Wellington ▪ Map: Paarl & Wellington ▪ WO: Wellington/Coastal/Western Cape ▪ Est 2001 ▪ 1stB 2002 ▪ Tasting, sales & cellar tours Mon-Fri 10-5 Sat 10-1 ▪ Closed all pub hols ▪ Tour groups ▪ Conferences/ functions ▪ Small weddings ▪ Walks/hikes ▪ Mountain biking trail ▪ Self-catering luxury accommodation ▪ Owner(s) James McKenzie ▪ Cellarmaster(s) James McKenzie (Jan 2002) ▪ Winemaker(s) Charles Stassen (consultant), with Maria Bosman (Jan 2002) ▪ Viticulturist(s) Johan Wiese (May 2001, consultant) ▪ 35ha/ 17ha (cab, merlot, p verdot, tempranillo, chenin, sauv) ▪ 180t/24,000cs own label 50% red 50% white ▪ PO Box 302 Wellington 7654 ▪ marketing@nabygelegen.co.za ▪ www.nabygelegen.co.za ▪ S 33° 37' 54.7" E 019° 3' 51.2" ▪ **T** +27 (0)21-873-7534 ▪ F +27 (0)86-561-7761

Owner James McKenzie's venerable farm in Wellington has produced wines fit for a queen (served at a Jubilee banquet for Commonwealth leaders), with some of the grapes coming from long-term leased vineyards at high altitude. Visitors can expect enthusiastic welcomes from James' pack of friendly pooches.

Nabygelegen Private Cellar range
★★★★ **Merlot** 🖉 Forthright minty choc chip notes on **12** before sweep of ripe black fruit (plums & cherry yoghurt) heads through to vanilla finish. Well-structured wine, plenty of drinking pleasure.
★★★★☆ **1712** 🖉 **07** roughly equal merlot & cab, soupçon petit verdot shows concentrated dark fruit, fresh acidity, firm but fine tannins. 30% new oak a subtle presence. More like **05** than lighter **06** (★★★★).

> **Sauvignon Blanc** ☺ 🍴 🖉 ★★★ Step-up **13** has nice gooseberry intensity with green fig finish. Lovely everyday drinking. **Lady Anna** ☺ 🍴 🖉 ★★★ Chenin-dominated blend with sauvignon & semillon, unwooded. Citrusy zinger **13**, grapefruit, naartjie peel & lime for delicious stoep wine.

Scaramanga 🖉 ★★★★ Unusual blend cab & merlot with malbec & tempranillo takes definite step up in **12** on **11** (★★★★), with bags of juicy fruit nicely supported by handsome tannins. Black berries & currants, some

American oak adding coconut interest. **Chenin Blanc** 🈐 🈲 ★★★★ Barrel-fermented **13** packed with fresh fruit (crunchy apples & pears), disguises hefty alcohol (14.5%) with layers of concentrated flavour & lively acidity. Ideally needs food. Discontinued: **Petit Verdot**.

Snow Mountain range

★★★★ **Syrah** Cool-climate class on **11** as white & black pepper burst forth overlaying mixed black & red berried fruit. Fresh & delicious. WO Coastal as are all unless noted.

> **Chardonnay-Pinot Noir** NEW ☺ 🈐 🈲 ★★★ Easy-drinking summer sipper **13** has clean citrus lines & hint of spice. Crisp & dry, 5% pinot.

Pinot Noir ⓣ ★★★ A good summer red, **11** soft crushed berries & floral notes, hint of spice & easy tannins. WO W Cape. **Chardonnay** 🈐 🈲 ★★★★ Cool, calm & collected **12** shows fresh crunchy fruit as apples, peaches & some floral notes meld effortlessly with spice. Discontinued: **Merlot Rosé**. — CM

◾ **Naked Truth** see PicardiRebel
◾ **Naked Vine Collection** see Hornbill Garagiste Winery

Namaqua Wines

Location: Vredendal ▪ Map/WO: Olifants River ▪ Est/1stB 2002 ▪ Tasting & sales Mon-Fri 8–5 Sat 9–3 ▪ Closed Easter Fri-Mon, Ascension day & Dec 25/26 ▪ Cellar tours Mon-Fri 10 & 3, book ahead ▪ Die Keldery Restaurant T +27 (0)27-213-3699/8 Mon-Fri 8–5 & dinner Thu-Fri 7-10 Sat 9-3 Sun buffet 11-3 booking required ▪ Facilities for children ▪ Conferences ▪ Owner(s) 200 members ▪ Production manager Len Knoetze ▪ Winemaker(s) Driaan van der Merwe, Dewald Huisamen, Alwyn Maass, Roelf Retief, Koos Thiart, Johan Weideman, Reinier van Greunen & Jaco Theron ▪ Viticulturist(s) Marina Cornellisen ▪ 4,990ha ▪ 113,692t/9.3m cs 20% red 80% white ▪ PO Box 75 Vredendal 8160 ▪ info@namaquawines.com ▪ www.namaquawines.com ▪ S 31° 42' 34.9" E 018° 30' 15.6" ▪ **T +27 (0)27-213-1080** ▪ F +27 (0)27-213-3476

This large West Coast winery, supplied by 200 owner-growers and producing over 9-million cases a year, last year crushed a bumper 113,692 tons at their Vredendal and Spruitdrift cellars. Though known for their ubiquitous 5L packs ('We Box The Best!'), they've shown they're serious contenders with an internationally awarded Pinotage and excellent Cabernet. Not resting on their laurels, they intend developing their range even further, until the name Namaqua is 'on everyone's lips.'

Spencer Bay Winemakers Reserve range

★★★★ **Cabernet Sauvignon** ⓣ Smoky **09** maintains pace set by warm-hearted **08**; firm tannic grip & bright acidity reins in concentrated fruit.

★★★★ **Pinotage** ⓣ **08**'s improved form matched by **09** & Decanter gold-winning **10**. Both structured for 3+ years cellaring, with mulberry centre & acetone hint.

Shiraz ⓣ ★★★★ **09** a steps up on smooth **08** (★★★★). Powerful (14.8% alcohol) without being warming; satisfying weight & length. **The Blend** ⓣ ★★★★ Cab dominates confident **09** 5-way Bordeaux-style red. Commendably dry, unheavy (13.7% alcohol), amenably firm. Improves on ripe, plummy **08** (★★★★).

Namaqua range

★★★★ **Noble Late Harvest** ⓣ **10** older-oak-matured botrytis dessert from semillon. Slippery & sweet (265g/l sugar) but elegant & engaging.

★★★★ **Red Muscadel** 🈐 Winter enjoyment guaranteed by delicately balanced fortified dessert. Latest **NV** shade less rich than previous much-awarded bottling but still excellent.

> **Sauvignon Blanc** ☺ 🈐 ★★★ **13** ticks all the sippability boxes: engaging passionfruit aromas & flavours, zesty acidity, wallet-friendly price. **Sauvignon Blanc-Semillon** NEW ☺ 🈐 ★★★ **12** worth seeking out. Vivacious sauvignon (70%) green fruit & zip padded out by older-oak-aged semillon.

Cabernet Sauvignon ⓣ 🈐 ★★ Peppery **11** has gentle acidic bite, light oak detail for early drinking, as all these reds. **Merlot** ⓣ 🈐 ★★★ Affable **11** ruby hued, plum toned, gently tannic. **Pinotage** ⓣ 🈐 ★★ Old-style **10** fleeting earth & plum flavours. **Shiraz** ⓣ 🈐 ★★★ Clove- & mulberry-infused **11** big on taste, structure. **Chenin Blanc-Sauvignon Blanc** NEW ✓ 🈐 ★★★★ Exceptional value from **12** lightly oaked 60/40 combo. Quince & pineapple complexity on nose & palate, zingy acidity pleasant counterpoint to ripe fruit. **Guinevere Méthode Cap Classique** ⓣ ★★★ Lively **06** dry sparkling. Savoury note & pink hue from pinot noir

(60%), appley flavours ex chardonnay. **White Muscadel** 🍷 ★★★ Luscious **NV** pudding wine, flowers & caramel, rich & slippery. **Hanepoot Jerepigo** ✓ 🍷 ★★★★ Profusion of papaya & orange marmalade on latest bar-raising **NV** fortified dessert. Ebullient & tangy, perfect anytime tipple - just add fire or ice!

Cellar Door range
Discontinued: **Merlot**. — HJ, CvZ

Napier Winery

Location: Wellington ▪ Map: Paarl & Wellington ▪ WO: Wellington/Western Cape/Coastal ▪ Est 1989 ▪ Tasting, sales & cellar tours Mon-Fri 8–5 Sat 10–3 ▪ Fee R10 ▪ Closed Easter Fri-Sun, Dec 25/26 & Jan 1 ▪ Tapas platters, preferably pre-booked ▪ Conferences ▪ Owner(s) Michael & Catherine Loubser ▪ Cellarmaster(s)/winemaker(s)/viticulturist(s) Leon Bester (Apr 2000) ▪ 135ha/±89ha under vine ▪ 70% red 30% white ▪ Other export brand: Sir George ▪ PO Box 638 Wellington 7654 ▪ info@napierwinery.co.za ▪ www.napierwinery.co.za ▪ S 33° 38' 37.0" E 019° 2' 24.8" ▪ **T +27 (0)21-873-7829** ▪ F +27 (0)21-864-2728

A family-owned farm in Wellington where the Napier-labelled wines, with the exception of flagship Red Medallion, have single-vineyard status. Second range, well-priced Lion Creek, is named after the Leeuwens River on the property.

Napier range
★★★★ **Cabernet Sauvignon** NEW Single-vineyard **11** is packed with flavour, blackcurrants & dark plums, a cedar overlay from 90% new oak. Handsome, impressive, has a sturdy structure built to last.

★★★★ **Red Medallion** Bordeaux blend, cab/cab franc-led. Mixed berries, sprinkle of herbs, cigarbox spicing, **08**'s lovely succulence balances the tannin's deep muscle tone. Nudges next level.

★★★★ **St Catherine** Single-vineyard chardonnay. Getting the balance right between fruit & oak, **11** shows creamy white peach & oatmeal, nothing overt, well meshed. Nicely defined mineral-fresh finish.

Greenstone ✓ ★★★½ Single-vineyard chenin. Elegant **12** offers thatch & minerality, with a fine bead of acidity keeping it fresh & pure.

Lion Creek range

Cabernet Sauvignon ☺ 🍷 ★★★ Just enough tannin grip for food, but fruit is **11**'s main attraction, juicy blackcurrants, lightly spiced. **Cabernet Sauvignon-Shiraz** ☺ 🍷 ★★★ Scrub & liquorice in **11**'s cassis flavours attests to shiraz's influence, smoothly rounded, appealing. WO W Cape.

Sauvignon Blanc-Chenin Blanc ⑂ 🍷 ★★★ Summer fruits in **12** preview, tangy & vibrant, awaken the taste buds. Nice leafy note from sauvignon. WO Coastal. Discontinued: **Chenin Blanc**. — CR

▪ **Nativo** see Hughes Family Wines

Natte Valleij Wines

Location/map: Stellenbosch ▪ Est 1715 ▪ Tasting, sales & cellar tours Mon-Fri 10-4 Sat 10-3 ▪ Closed all pub hols ▪ Facilities for children ▪ Conference/indaba venue ▪ Art gallery & art classes ▪ Artifacts & various paintings ▪ Natte Valleij B&B/self-catering cottages (see Accommodation section) ▪ Owner(s) Milner family ▪ Winemaker(s) Alexander Milner (2005), with Marcus Milner (2010) ▪ 28ha total ▪ 15t/2,000cs own label 100% red ▪ PO Box 4 Klapmuts 7625 ▪ alex@boerandbrit.com ▪ www.nattevalleij.co.za ▪ S 33° 50' 3.6" E 018° 52' 43.2" ▪ **T +27 (0)21-875-5171**

Natte Valleij is one of Stellenbosch's oldest and most atmospheric farms, home to the Milner family since the 1960s. Brothers Marcus (also winemaker at De Meye Wines) and Alexander (the Brit in Boer & Brit) handcraft small parcels of suitably characterful wine under the estate and Swallow labels. Alexander's reply to our question - How was last harvest? - hints at the not-too-terribly-serious approach here: 'Nothing a few cold beers couldn't sort out'.

▪ **Natural Star** see Stellar Winery

Naughton's Flight

Location: Constantia ▪ WO: Stellenbosch/Coastal ▪ 1stB 2003 ▪ Closed to public ▪ Owner(s) Francis Naughton ▪ Winemaker(s) Ronell Wiid (consultant) ▪ (carignan, mourv, shiraz, viog) ▪ ±20,000 btls ▪ 25 Willow Rd Constantia 7806 ▪ naughts@mweb.co.za ▪ **T +27 (0)21-794-3928** ▪ F +27 (0)21-794-3928

Francis Naughton worked for many years for SFW (now Distell) following his 'flight' from his native Ireland (he retains plenty of the accent and a bit of the blarney he brought with him). With him from the start has been Ronell Wiid in the cellar, making small volumes of these wines.

Shiraz ★★★★ Nicely maturing **08** in the customary style, stressing the leathery, savoury side rather than the fruity - but there's a good touch of red berry succulence on the lean but balanced, structured palate. Stellenbosch grapes. **Tribua ⏂ ★★★☆ 09** from shiraz & mourvèdre, viognier. Engaging, ripe flavours: sweet fruit in modestly oaked, dry, firm package. WO Coastal. **Viognier** Next awaited. **Délice ⏂ ★★★ 09**, from rack-dried shiraz, deliciously grapey. Sweet, clean & fresh; only 11% alcohol. Tasted a few years back. — TJ

■ **Naughty Girl** *see* Alvi's Drift Private Cellar

Nederburg Wines

Location: Paarl ▪ Map: Paarl & Wellington ▪ WO: Western Cape/Coastal/Groenekloof/Paarl/Philadelphia/Stellenbosch ▪ Est 1791 ▪ 1stB ca 1940 ▪ Tasting & sales Mon-Fri 8–5 Sat 10–2 (May-Sep)/10–4 (Oct-Apr) Sun 11–4 (Oct-Apr) ▪ Various tasting fees, waived on purchase of R100+ ▪ Closed Good Fri, Dec 25 & Jan 1 ▪ Cellar tours Mon-Fri 10.30 & 3 Sat 11 Sun 11 (Oct-Apr) ▪ Large groups/foreign language tours by appt only ▪ Visitors' centre: wine tasting, cheese & wine pairing ▪ Historic Manor House (national monument) now featuring The Red Table restaurant, open Tue-Sun T +27 (0)21-877-5155 ▪ Tour groups ▪ Gifts ▪ Conferences ▪ Museum ▪ Conservation area ▪ Owner(s) Distell ▪ Cellarmaster(s) Razvan Macici (2001) ▪ Winemaker(s) Wilhelm Pienaar (reds, 2009) & Wim Truter (whites, 2012), with Samuel Viljoen (reds) & Danie Morkel (whites) ▪ Viticulturist(s) Unathi Matshongo & Henk van Graan ▪ 1,100ha (cab, carignan, grenache, malbec, merlot, p verdot, ptage, shiraz, tannat, tempranillo, chard, riesling, sauv, sem) ▪ 18,000t/2.8m cs own label ▪ ISO 0001:2008, ISO 14001:2004, BWI, HACCP, IPW, BRC, SGS organic certification ▪ Private Bag X3006 Paarl 7620 ▪ nedwines@distell.co.za ▪ www.nederburg.co.za ▪ S 33° 43' 15.4" E 019° 0' 9.4" ▪ **T +27 (0)21-862-3104** ▪ F +27 (0)21-862-4887

For a large-volume winery which emphatically aims to cater for all sectors of the market, the very great amount of awards that Nederburg reaps is quite simply astonishing. One accolade which must have mattered more than most, however, was when Romanian-born cellarmaster Razvan Macici took the title of Diners Club Winemaker of the Year, his Private Bin Eminence 2007 winning in the featured category of sweet wines. Ever innovative, Macici and team are extending the flagship Ingenuity tier for the first time since debut in 2007, the newest iteration being a Spanish blend of tempranillo and graciano. Other new lines are Fairtrade-accredited Fair Selection, and 56Hundred, recalling the 5,600 guilders paid for the Paarl home-farm by founder Philippus Wolvaart in 1791.

Ingenuity range

★★★★☆ Red 🂠 Sangiovese & barbera, a dab nebbiolo, the local version of the best of Italy. Powerful, richly fruited **10** boasts black cherries & earthy truffles, cigarbox, toned polished tannins for 8+ years ageing. Perfect for a hearty meat dish & Pavarotti singing!

★★★★★ White 🂠 Splendid 8-part sauvignon-led blend which includes aromatic varieties, some oaking. Following **11**, equally superb **12** offers intense floral & fruity notes, spice & vibrant freshness, depth & impeccable balance. Will age gracefully.

Heritage Heroes range

★★★★ The Brew Master ✓ 🂠 Saluting Nederburg founder Johann Graue, **10** cab-led 4-way Bordeaux blend has engaging blackcurrant ripeness & smoke, with firm well-proportioned build. Tannin grip adds texture. Will age well. WO Coastal for all these unless noted.

★★★★☆ The Motorcycle Marvel ✓ Rhône-style red from grenache, carignan, shiraz & dollops of mourvèdre & cinsaut gives **10** concentrated earthy hedgerow fruit, black pepper & cloves. Spice & smooth tannins rounds off this flavour drama. Very impressive.

★★★★ The Anchorman ✓ 🗄 🂠 Combo oak & tank, **12** brilliantly captures chenin's character: focused & pure crunchy apple & just-ripe melon, sprinklings hay & almond; restrained & harmonious.

★★★★ The Beautiful Lady NEW ✓ 🂠 A walk in a rose garden! Semi-sweet **12** gewürztraminer oozes alluring Turkish Delight, litchi & pineapple, tempered by lively acidity. Perfect for spicy fare. WO Stellenbosch.

★★★★☆ The Young Airhawk ✓ 🗄 🂠 Bright & energetic sauvignon, with oaking adding savoury element to **12**. Variety-true, with tightly wound citrus & spicy orchard fruit flavours of noteworthy complexity, depth & clarity. A long lime zest finish completes the picture.

Manor House range

★★★★ **Cabernet Sauvignon** ✓ Succulent ripe blackcurrant & plummy fruit on generous **11**, perfectly matched with the firm vanilla oaking. Made to drink on release, & to cellar few years. Paarl WO.

★★★★ **Shiraz** ✓ 🏵 Scrub & hedgerow fruit mingle with cinnamon & clove spice in **11**, underpinned by a peppery texture. Perfect for hearty meat casseroles. Promises well. WO Philadelphia.

★★★★ **Fairtrade Shiraz-Mourvèdre** ✓ 🏵 Attractive spicing in **11**'s dense, earthy red & black berries from mix of barrels: dried herbs, allspice, fynbos. Best with food, yet supple enough for solo. Groenekloof WO.

★★★★ **Sauvignon Blanc** ✓ 🏵 Gooseberries with whiffs of greenpepper, fresh thyme, the **13** is appealing, racy & inviting, with a lemon twist goodbye. WO Coastal.

Two Centuries range

★★★★ **Cabernet Sauvignon** ⏱ Flagship cab available cellardoor only. Selection best Paarl vineyards, 2 years new French oak. Improving on **07**, showing great fruit concentration, layered complexity, **08** (★★★★☆) is one to keep, watch unfold, but already drinks well.

Private Bin range for Nederburg Auction

★★★★☆ **Pinotage Private Bin R172** 🏵 Seductive **10** is suave, dense with a creamy complex core of vanilla-wrapped dark fruit, polished elegance. Broad & rich, finishing long with a lingering sweetness. A firm spine from all-new barrels ensures 8+ year rewarding future. WO Groenekloof.

★★★★ **Chardonnay Private Bin D270** Expertly combining oak & fruit, **12** (★★★★☆) trumps **11**. Bright, creamy citrus, camomile & nectarine tango on silky platform of oak. Harmonious & beautifully balanced, made for the long haul. Coastal WO.

★★★★★ **Eminence** 🏵 Natural Sweet white from Paarl muscat de Frontignan. Richer of the sweeties & flamboyantly ripe, **12** has candied pineapple, apricot & ginger. Pure & focused, round & unctuous, tangy-sweet & very long with liquid silk texture & balance. Same finesse as **10**, which **11** (★★★★☆) just missed.

★★★★★ **Edelkeur** 🏵 The first Cape Noble Late Harvest, always chenin. Densely packed melon, apricot fruit & herb-tinged honey, but magically light on its feet due to brisk acidity. The finish on **12** is extremely long, with terrific lift & grip. Rung up on **11** (★★★★☆). Low alcohol, 375 ml only, Like Eminence.

Winemaster's Reserve range

★★★★ **Edelrood (Cabernet Sauvignon-Merlot)** ✓ 🏵 Bordeaux-style red **11** brims with ripe berry perfume, silk texture & mellifluous, perfectly judged oaking. Buy loads & keep some for later enjoyment.

★★★★ **Special Late Harvest** ✓ 🏵 Ex-tank **13** from chenin misses the intensity of **12** (★★★★☆). Sweet & fragrant, with apricot & pineapple flavours, lemon blossom wafts & a tangy farewell.

★★★★★ **Noble Late Harvest** ✓ 🏵 Cellar's expertise demonstrated in its only botrytis dessert freely available. **12** chenin & muscat de Frontignan follows spectacular **11** & is a major mouthful of gingered apricot & honey; tangy & richly aromatic. Perfect with dessert.

Cabernet Sauvignon Rosé ☺ 🍴 🏵 ★★★ Raspberry pink **13**, crackling red berries & crisp dry finish.

Cabernet Sauvignon ✓ 🏵 ★★★★ Richly fruited preview **12** showcases cab's blackcurrants & oak's spice, supple tannins are a hidden support. **Merlot** ✓ 🏵 ★★★☆ Dark chocolate notes & perfumed violets in **12** combine with the vibrant & delicious red berries, but all in harmony for a smooth sip. **Pinotage** ✓ 🏵 ★★★☆ 2 vintages tasted: **11** is succulent & appealing, with a ripe tannin core. **12** similar, with a fresh berry lift to finish. Perfect braai wines! **Shiraz** ✓ 🏵 ★★★★ Both vintages reviewed are templates for shiraz: **11** filled with rich, dark hedgerow fruit & loads of smoky spice, supple & smooth. Ditto **12**, with crunchy cranberry finish. Both over-deliver on price. **Baronne (Cabernet Sauvignon-Shiraz)** ✓ 🏵 ★★★★ A longtime favourite. Well-matched varieties, **12**'s lush spicy berries are backed by velvety harmonious tannins. Slips down easily. **Chardonnay** ✓ 🍴 🏵 ★★★☆ Citrus with tropical fruit nuances, **12** has a soft, creamy & mouthfilling richness, contrasted by the zesty lemon spritz at the end - very moreish. **Pinot Grigio** ✓ 🍴 🏵 ★★★★ A floral perfume explosion greets you on pre-bottled **13**. Semi-dry, with delicate hints of apple & citrus & refreshing finish. WO Coastal. **Riesling** ✓ 🍴 🏵 ★★★★ Appealing off-dry **13** offers candied ginger & pineapple, wafts of jasmine & stylish delicacy. Light, with a crispy lift. **Sauvignon Blanc** ✓ 🍴 🏵 ★★★★ Crisp & bursting with greenpepper & passionfruit, **13** seduces with zesty mouthwatering lift. Discontinued: **Chenin Blanc**.

56Hundred range [NEW]

Cabernet Sauvignon ☺ 🍴 🏵 ★★★ Chocolate-smothered dark berries in **12** marry well with supple, easy tannins for al fresco enjoyment. Soft & fleshy, with a lingering dry finish. **Chenin Blanc** ☺ 🍴 🏵 ★★★ Just-off-dry **13** tank sample offers a bite from a ripe, fresh Granny Smith apple. Friendly 12% alcohol.

Fair Selection `NEW`

Pinotage 🥃 ★★★ **11** offers engaging ripe plum, dried herbs & seasoned oak flavours. WO Groenekloof, Fairtrade accredited & export only (as next). **Sauvignon Blanc** 🍷🥃 ★★★☆ Tropical fruit flavours are wrapped around a zingy coil of mouthwatering acidity on balanced **13** - for poolside summer fun.

Foundation Collection

Cabernet Sauvignon ☺ 🍷 🥃 ★★★ Oak-spiced **12**'s lush black fruit shows just-picked freshness, smooth tannins for early drinking. **Merlot** ☺ 🍷 🥃 ★★★ Juicy & fruity **12** attracts with red berries, smooth oak spice & a savoury note. Ideal quaffing fun. **Pinotage** ☺ 🍷 🥃 ★★★ **12** offers coffee-dipped blueberries with a firm tannin structure as support. Drinking well now, can age a few years. **Shiraz** ☺ 🍷 🥃 ★★★ Violets & dark plums abound on spicy **12**. With ripe tannins to balance, it's accessible, unassuming & food friendly. **Duet (Shiraz-Pinotage)** ☺ 🍷 🥃 ★★★ With 60% dominance, shiraz rules in **12**. Chocolate-rich dark fruit is tempered by pinotage's fresh juicy texture. For picnic pleasure. **Shiraz-Viognier** ☺ 🍷 🥃 ★★★ Firm & fragrant **12** is packed with rich, dark berry fruit & lavender wafts, with a savoury, lipsmacking conclusion. **Rosé** ☺ 🍷 🥃 ★★☆ Nicely packaged **13** appeals with semi-sweet red berry flavours. **Chardonnay** ☺ 🍷 🥃 ★★★ Stonefruit & buttered toast in previewed **13**, fresh, with a hint of oak spice on the finish, rounding off early-drinking fun. **Stein** ☺ 🍷 🥃 ★★★ **13** chenin semi-sweet is pure drinking pleasure - luscious & fresh from the peach orchard. Made for spicy fare. **Sauvignon Blanc** ☺ 🍷 🥃 ★★★ Gooseberry- & lime-laced **13** is intensely flavoured & entices with mouthwatering bright acidity. For summer salads & seafood. **Chardonnay-Viognier** ☺ 🍷 ★★★ Tank sample **13** ups ante with peach melba flavours & brush of spicy oak. For early pleasure. **Sauvignon Blanc-Chardonnay** ☺ 🍷 🥃 ★★★ Medium-bodied **13** shows savoury oak-sprinkled citrus & baked apple flavours & crisp acidity. Versatile & food friendly. **Lyric (Sauvignon Blanc-Chenin Blanc-Chardonnay)** ☺ 🍷 🥃 ★★★ Sauvignon leads the **13** blend with herbal tones & off-dry tropical flavours, finishing with a tangy lime twist. Friendly 12% alcohol. **Première Cuvée Brut** ☺ 🥃 ★★★ NV dry sparkling from Cape riesling & chenin, dabs chardonnay & colombard is frothy, zesty & fun to get the party started.

Cabernet Sauvignon-Shiraz Next awaited.

Brandy range `NEW`

★★★★ **Solera Potstilled Brandy** Lightish gold colour good intro to lightly elegant style of this 100% potstill brandy, aged up to 12 years in solera. Smooth, balanced, serene & complete; fine fruity flavours. — WB, TJ

Neethlingshof Estate

Location/map/WO: Stellenbosch ▪ Est 1692 ▪ 1stB 1880 ▪ Tasting & sales Mon-Fri 9–5 Sat/Sun 10-4 ▪ Fee R30pp ▪ Closed Good Fri & Dec 25 ▪ Public cellar tours daily at 10; private cellar tours by appt ▪ 'Flash Food & Slow Wine' pairing R60pp - booking recommended for 6+ ▪ Jungle gym ▪ Tour groups ▪ Conferences ▪ Conservation area ▪ Annual music concert in conjunction with Die Woordfees (Mar) ▪ Lord Neethling Restaurant & Palm Terrace ▪ Owner(s) Lusan Premium Wines ▪ Cellarmaster(s) De Wet Viljoen (Jun 2003) ▪ Winemaker(s) Monique Fourie ▪ Viticulturist(s) Hannes van Zyl & Nico Nortje ▪ 273ha/95ha (cabs s/f, malbec, merlot, p verdot, ptage, shiraz, chard, chenin, gewürz, riesling, sauv, viog) ▪ 1,400t/100,000cs own label 55% red 45% white ▪ BWI Champion, WIETA ▪ PO Box 104 Stellenbosch 7599 ▪ info@neethlingshof.co.za ▪ www. neethlingshof.co.za ▪ S 33° 56' 28.2" E 018° 48' 6.7" ▪ **T +27 (0)21-883-8988** ▪ F +27 (0)21-883-8941

Colourful characters have shaped the history of this Lusan-owned Stellenbosch estate over past three centuries, including Maria Magdalena Marais, after whom their delectable desert wine is named, and her son-in-law, the dapper Johannes Henoch Neethling, dubbed 'Lord Neethling'. An eco-sustainable replanting program has focused on identifying ideal cultivar-specific terroirs, and on preserving 42% of the estate for indigenous vegetation and conservation. Hence their deserved Biodiversity & Wine Institute (BWI) Champion status.

Short Story Collection

★★★★ **Owl Post Pinotage** ✓ 🥃 In dark & brooding mode, **11** denser fruit than **10** (★★★★). Savoury, leathery tone with firm structure & weight, despite moderate alcohol. Deserves some ageing.

★★★★☆ **Caracal** ✓ 🍷 🥃 Now a cab-led blend, with merlot, malbec & cab franc. **11** classic cassis, cedar & inky nuance with complementary oaking. Still quite tight, but lithe structure & balance to age elegantly. Step up on **10** (★★★★).

★★★★ **Six Flowers** ✓ 📖 📾 Now bottled, **12** confirms the quality of preview. A chardonnay, chenin-led sextet with sauvignon & aromatic understudies. Engaging, with supple structure & creamy oak-infused texture.

★★★★☆ **Maria** ✓ 📾 **13** preview of one of the Cape's consistently fine botrytised rieslings, with a splash of sauvignon. A symphony of citrus & glacé pineapple flavours, unctuous texture & beautifully balanced tangy acidity. Delicious intensity!

Neethlingshof range

★★★★ **Sauvignon Blanc Single Vineyard** ✓ 📖 📾 **13** exudes sauvignon's vibrant freshness, with clean flinty tone & loads of stonefruit. More intense & structured than sibling, with long mineral finish.

Chardonnay Unwooded ☺ 📖 📾 ★★★ **13** balanced & creamy quaffer. Ripe pear & citrus tone lifted by crisp acidity.

Cabernet Sauvignon ★★★ Powerful, ripe **08** still in a brusque tannic grip. **Malbec** 📖 📾 ★★★★ **12** preview shows ample brambleberry fruit & sweet vanilla tone from oak. Supple & creamy structure for amiable drinkability. **Merlot** 📾 ★★★ Riper **10** has bright red berry & mint flavours, just a tad brisk in youth. Some time & a meal will restore harmony. **Pinotage** 📾 ★★★ Generous dark fruit, earthy & tobacco aromas on **12**. Firm fleshed & toned, with integrated oak & tannins. **Shiraz** ★★★ **08** is ripe & rounded with opulent dark fruit. Oak's sweet, spicy tone & balance are appealing now & for the next few years. **Cabernet Sauvignon-Merlot** ✓ 📾 ★★★★ Mediumweight **11** is fresh & balanced. Lovely cassis & mint tone, neatly structured. **Chenin Blanc** ✓ 📖 📾 ★★★★ **13** exudes Golden Delicious apple flavours & freshness, with a thread of minerality. Balanced & engaging. **Gewürztraminer** ✓ 📖 📾 ★★★★ **13** captures the essence of gewürztraminer, with appealing litchi & rosepetal aromas & charm. Genteel yet intense; just off-dry, but a fresher step up on **12** (★★★). **Sauvignon Blanc** ✓ 📖 📾 ★★★★ Ripe & tropical **13** is packed with flavour. Medium bodied with crisp balance, ready to enjoy. — MW

Neil Ellis Meyer-Näkel 🍷🍴

Location: Stellenbosch ▪ WO: Western Cape/Jonkershoek Valley ▪ Est/1stB 1998 ▪ Tasting & sales at Neil Ellis Wines ▪ Owner(s) Neil Ellis Meyer-Näkel (Pty) Ltd ▪ Winemaker(s) Werner Näkel & Warren Ellis (2006) ▪ Viticulturist(s) Pieter Smit & Warren Ellis ▪ 7,000cs own label 100% red ▪ PO Box 917 Stellenbosch 7599 ▪ tasting@neilellis.com ▪ www.neilellis.com ▪ **T +27 (0)21-887-0649** ▪ F +27 (0)21-887-0647

An established friendship between two top-ranking winemakers, Neil Ellis, based in Stellenbosch and Werner Näkel, from Germany, has developed into a small-scale but significant venture. The launch of their Zwalu ('New Beginning') blend coincided with the emergence of the 'rainbow nation' from the apartheid era.

★★★★ **Zwalu** ✹ 📾 Equal blend of Jonkershoek grapes (cab, cab franc & shiraz) achieves elegance even in warmer **10** vintage. More open textured & earlier maturing than **09**, still supple & satisfying.

Z 📖 📾 ★★★★ Gentle cassis fruit pads out dry amenable tannins, **11** poised, mediumweight & suave. — MW

Neil Ellis Wines 🍷🍴☕🍫♿

Location/map: Stellenbosch ▪ WO: Stellenbosch/Jonkershoek Valley/Western Cape/Piekenierskloof/Elgin/Groenekloof ▪ Est 1986 ▪ 1stB 1984 ▪ Tasting & sales Mon-Fri 9.30-4.30 Sat & pub hols 10-5 ▪ Fee R25 Premium range/R35 Vineyard Selection range ▪ Closed Good Fri, Dec 25/26 & Jan 1 ▪ Antipasto platters ▪ Tour groups ▪ Owner(s) Neil Ellis Wines (Pty) Ltd ▪ Winemaker(s)/viticulturist(s) Warren Ellis (2006) ▪ 100,000cs own label 50% red 50% white ▪ Brands for clients: Woolworths ▪ WIETA ▪ PO Box 917 Stellenbosch 7599 ▪ info@neilellis.com ▪ www.neilellis.com ▪ S 33° 55' 34.92" E 018° 53' 32.46" ▪ **T +27 (0)21-887-0649** ▪ F +27 (0)21-887-0647

This is a well-established family business with a local and international reputation for exceptional quality, elegance and value. It's run by the formidable Ellis father and son team. Neil, unassuming doyen with more than 30 influential years in the industry, still plays a mentoring role and is involved in the strategic and tactical decision making. Son Warren, with an MSc in viticulture, is responsible for the vines and winemaking. This allows Neil to pursue his creative side, returning to his pioneering negociant roots, seeking out parcels of interesting vines to make exceptional wines. Like the new Rhodanos ('Rhône') and other stylistic blends planned, with a view to rationalising their range.

Vineyard Selection

★★★★☆ **Cabernet Sauvignon** ✓ 🏵 Stellar Jonkershoek Valley quality evident even in warmer vintage. **10** (★★★★★) reveals rich cassis fruit earlier than tighter-knit **09** but shows the same inherent elegance, structure & complexity. Much pleasure for the patient.

★★★★☆ **Grenache** 🏵 Alluringly fragrant & expressive **11** is from low-yield old Piekenierskloof vines. Composed yet intense, shows real presence. Lovely fruit purity woven into a silky & seamless structure. One to savour over the next 4-6 years.

★★★★ **Pinotage** 🏵 Savoury polished leather tone to brooding & spicy **11** from Jonkershoek. Firm but pliable tannins & a creamy texture. Already shows balance & track-record-bestowed ageworthiness.

★★★★☆ **Rodanos** NEW Shiraz (79%) & grenache blend shows nobility, & touch aloofness in youth. Restrained layers of garrigue scrub, pepper & cedar, streamlined by fine tannic structure. Complex & contemplative, **09** will reward long-term cellaring.

★★★★ **Amica** NEW 🏵 **12** natural fermentation in oak adds richness & texture to sauvignon from Jonkershoek. Lovely palate weight & length, infused with clean stonefruit flavours. Unshowy but stylish.

Syrah Await next. Discontinued: **Sauvignon Blanc**.

Premium range

★★★★ **Cabernet Sauvignon** ✓ 🖿 🏵 Riper in **11** than previous. Generous dark fruit with sleek polished texture. Approachable now but with backbone for 3-5 years ageing. WO Stellenbosch, as for next.

★★★★ **Cabernet Sauvignon-Merlot** ✓ 🖿 🏵 **11** shows classic lead pencil & cassis aroma. Fruit still enveloped in dry food-friendly tannins. Elegantly reserved, 4-6 years development potential.

★★★★ **Aenigma Red** ✓ 🖿 🏵 **11**'s eclectic 7-way mix (mainly shiraz & cab 58/22) is a symphony of spicy & savoury flavours. Harmonious & appealingly drinkable without being simple. WO W Cape. No **10**.

★★★★ **Stellenbosch Chardonnay** ✓ 🏵 Now bottled, **12** (★★★★☆) shows more vitality & fruit purity. Rich texture still vibrantly fresh courtesy partial malo. Long mineral farewell. **11** was unrated preview; **10**, also ex tank, similar exhilarating verve.

★★★★☆ **Groenekloof Sauvignon Blanc** 🖿 🏵 **12** (★★★★), now in bottle, shows more of Groenekloof's flinty herbaceous character, clean-cut freshness & tangy length. Classy flag bearer for terroir & variety, although a shade off **10**. **11** was an unrated preview.

Pinotage ⓘ 🖿 ★★★★ **09** sweet-fruited elegance with supple structure & balance. Streamlined, for satisfying drinkability. Stellenbosch WO. **Shiraz** 🖿 🏵 ★★★★ Elgin's cooler provenance shines in lighter-styled & elegant **11**. White pepper & sappy red fruits, lithe & balanced. **Aenigma White** 🖿 🏵 ★★★★ 'Mystery' revealed as viognier-led duo with chenin. **12** aromatic succulence with a fresh juicy twist. Enjoy solo or with fusion fare. **11** (★★★★) from chardonnay. WO W Cape.

Inglewood range

Red Next awaited, as for **White**. — MW

Nelson Family Vineyards   🍷⛓📷🏃♿

Location: Paarl ▪ Map: Paarl & Wellington ▪ WO: Paarl/Western Cape ▪ Tasting, sales & cellar tours by appt only ▪ Closed all pub hols ▪ Facilities for children ▪ Tour groups ▪ Conferences ▪ Weddings ▪ Walks/hikes ▪ Mountain biking trails ▪ Guest accommodation ▪ Owner(s) Alan Nelson ▪ Cellarmaster(s) Lisha Nelson (Nov 2007) ▪ Winemaker(s) Lisha Nelson (Nov 2007), with Solly Hendriks (Apr 2011) ▪ Viticulturist(s) Petrus de Villiers ▪ 142ha/46ha (cabs s/f, merlot, p verdot, ptage, shiraz, chard, chenin, sauv, sem) ▪ 210t/9,340cs own label 30% red 60% white 10% rosé ▪ IPW ▪ PO Box 2009 Windmeul 7630 ▪ lisha@nelsonscreek.co.za ▪ www. nelsonscreek.co.za ▪ S 33° 39' 31.2" E 018° 56' 17.3" ▪ **T +27 (0)21-869-8453** ▪ F +27 (0)21-869-8424

Family matters a great deal to this pastoral Paarl property, with most members actively involved and the wines made by daughter Lisha, so last year the name was changed (from 'Nelson Wine Estate') to reflect this kinship. Exports continue to grow, particularly to the UK, and onsite weddings and functions remain popular.

Lisha Nelson Signature Wines

★★★★☆ **Cabernet Franc** 🏵 Pungent varietal aromas of tomato leaves & geraniums on **10** before generous mouthful of intense black berries, plushy plum fruit backed up with still-taut tannins. 21 months new French oak need time to settle.

★★★★ **Dad's Blend** Cab franc-dominated **09** Bordeaux blend with tomato leaf giving way to blackcurrants, capsicum, hint of coffee.

Nelson Estate range

> **Sauvignon Blanc** ☺ 🍴 🌢 ★★★ Gooseberries & guavas burst forth on exuberant **13**, only just dry but sugar balanced by fresh acidity & depth of fruit. WO W Cape.

Shiraz ⊕ ★★★★ Spicy coconut & juicy plum, **08** smoky hint, firm dry tannin from 18 months new oak. **Cabernet Sauvignon-Merlot** ⊕ ★★★★ When tasted, deliciously ritne **08** had berry compote & cigarbox tones, was velvety, genteel & lingering. **Rosé** 🍴 🌢 ★★★ Just-dry **13** from equal parts cab & shiraz. Ripe cherries with soft cheese notes. **Chardonnay** Next awaited.

Nelson's Creek range

Shiraz ⊕ 🍴 🌢 ★★★★ Stewed plums & black cherries, step-up **11** with plenty of rustic appeal. **Chenin Blanc** ⊕ 🍴 🌢 ★★★ Whiffs of pineapple & tropical fruit, **12** off-dry, with tinned grapefruit conclusion. **Pinotage Rosé** 🍴 🌢 ★★ **13** cheery Natural Sweet-style quaffer with fresh acidity. — CM

New Beginnings Wines

Location: Cape Town ▪ WO: Paarl/Stellenbosch/Coastal ▪ Est 1996 ▪ 1stB 1999 ▪ Closed to public ▪ Owner(s) Klein Begin Farming Association ▪ Brand manager FMS Food & Beverages SA cc ▪ 13ha/10ha (cab, ptage, shiraz, chard, chenin) ▪ 20,000cs own label 70% red 25% white 5% rosé ▪ PO Box 51869 Waterfront 8002 ▪ info@fms-wine-marketing.co.za ▪ www.fms-wine-marketing.co.za ▪ **T +27 (0)21-426-5037** ▪ F +27 (0)21-413-0825

This small cooperative belongs to empowered vineyard staff who are being nurtured by wine exporters FMS under CEO Anton Blignault. The relationship between them is 'built on mutual trust and respect, coupled with an intense desire to succeed and leave a legacy for our children'. Exports are growing, and the Pinotage and Chardonnay especially popular in Japan, Poland, and Germany.

> **Chardonnay** ☺ 🍴 🌢 ★★★ Ripe pear & citrus flavours on friendly, easy unwooded **12**. WO Coastal.

Cabernet Sauvignon ★★★ Cassis & leather tone to brusque, structured **10** barbecue mate. Stellenbosch WO, like Pinotage. **Pinotage** 🌢 ★★ Frisky **10** is both ripe & tart. Rustic, outdoors styling. **Shiraz** ⊕ 🌢 ★★★ Anytime sipping delivered by quince & blackberry toned, lightish **11**. **Pinotage Rosé** ⊕ Next awaited. **Shiraz Rosé** ⊕ 🍴 🌢 ★★★ **11** crisp & tangy quaffer with savoury cranberry tone. **Chenin Blanc** ⊕ 🍴 ★★★ Plump & effortless **10** has waxy apple & almond flavours. — MW

- ■ **New Cape Wines** *see* Eagle's Cliff Wines-New Cape Wines
- ■ **New Gate** *see* Ernst Gouws & Co Wines
- ■ **New Mountain View Partnership** *see* Santa Cecilia

Newstead Lund Family Vineyards

Location/WO: Plettenberg Bay ▪ Map: Klein Karoo & Garden Route ▪ Est 2008 ▪ 1stB 2012 ▪ Tasting & sales by appt ▪ Closed Dec 25 ▪ Cheese platters, deli, seasonal kitchen by appt ▪ Tour groups ▪ Gift shop ▪ Farm produce ▪ Walks ▪ Mountain biking trail ▪ Owner(s) Doug & Sue Lund ▪ Cellarmaster(s)/winemaker(s) Anton Smal (Jan 2011, consultant) ▪ Viticulturist(s) Doug Lund & Gift Lwazi ▪ 11ha/5ha (pinot, chard, sauv) ▪ 24t/4,500cs own label 80% white 20% MCC ▪ PO Box 295 The Crags 6602 ▪ info@newsteadwines.com ▪ www.newsteadwines.com ▪ S 33° 57' 7.24" E 023° 28' 18.66" ▪ **T +27 (0)84-586-1600** ▪ F +27 (0)44-534-8387

Ex-international polo player Doug Lund and wife Sue were among the pioneers of the Plettenberg Bay wine district when they first planted vines in 2006. New Zealand was their inspiration to make wine and choose sauvignon, chardonnay and pinot noir, there being significant similarities in geography and climate. Vinification of the much-pampered grapes is by ex-Villiera Anton Smal.

Chardonnay 🍴 ★★★ Previewed **13** 2nd crop off young vineyard. Fruity & fresh, given extra weight, breadth by 4 months lees-ageing & 10% wooded portion from **12** vintage. **Sauvignon Blanc** 🍴 ★★★★ **13** revealing more on the nose than palate: fresh pea & asparagus, slight sweaty nuance, brisk acidity & pithy grip. Previewed, so rating is provisional. — HJ,CvZ

Newton Johnson Vineyards

Location: Hermanus ▪ Map: Elgin, Walker Bay & Bot River ▪ WO: Upper Hemel-en-Aarde Valley/Walker Bay/
Cape South Coast/Elgin ▪ Est 1996 ▪ 1stB 1997 ▪ Tasting & sales Mon-Fri 9–4 Sat 10–2 ▪ Closed all pub hols ▪
Newton Johnson Restaurant: lunch 12-3 Wed-Sun (Apr-Nov)/Tue-Sun (Dec-Mar) & dinner Fri-Sat 6-9 ▪
Owner(s) Dave & Felicity Johnson ▪ Cellarmaster(s)/viticulturist(s) Gordon Newton Johnson (Jan 2001) ▪
Winemaker(s) Gordon Newton Johnson (Jan 2001) & Nadia Newton Johnson (Aug 2006) ▪ 140ha/18ha (gre-
nache, mourv, pinot, shiraz, chard, sauv) ▪ 240t/20,000cs own label 50% red 50% white ▪ PO Box 225
Hermanus 7200 ▪ wine@newtonjohnson.com ▪ www.newtonjohnson.com ▪ S 34° 22' 9.7" E 019° 15' 33.3" ▪
T +27 (0)28-312-3862 ▪ F +27 (0)86-638-9673

Dave Johnson and wife Felicity (née Newton) have been some 40 years concerned
in wine, and founded this estate in the Hemel-en-Aarde area in the mid 1990s –
when only the earliest pioneers were already here. Two generations are now
fully involved (and the next one no doubt learning) making this a quintessential
family operation. Thoughtful, intelligent work in the expanding vineyards and
winery (where natural processes rule: gravity rather than mechanical pumping,
no yeast inoculation, for example) have brought an ever-growing reputation for
quality. The passion for pinot noir has now led to the release of the three single-
vineyard wines going into the Family Vineyards blend – giving, they say, 'a sense
of place and perspective to the variations in the granitic soils of our vineyards'.

★★★★ **Elgin Pinot Noir** ✪ Lovely, fresh-fruited & perfumed aromas on **11** lead to slightly less substantial, lighter palate. But well balanced, with understated firm structure.

★★★★★ **Family Vineyards Pinot Noir** 🌿 As with **11**, **12** combines fruit from estate's best sites. As
always, a triumph of subtle insistence, the fresh, pure fruit integrated with succulent acidity, subtler tannins &
sensitive oaking in an elegant whole. This perhaps the tightest, brightest, most finely articulated yet.

★★★★☆ **Block 6 Pinot Noir** NEW From the estate's oldest pinot block; the family's favourite component in
the blended wine. **12** the lightest of these, with the prettiest aromas but perhaps less persistent intensity than
Windansea. Supple, elegant, smooth & silky.

★★★★☆ **Mrs. M Pinot Noir** NEW From a vineyard dedicated to the late Moya McDowall. **12** not the
brightest or most harmonious of the pinots, but with deep, dark-fruited, spicy-earthy notes. Looser weave. Like
all these pinots, fermented with natural yeast; matured 12 months in oak, 30% new.

★★★★★ **Windansea Pinot Noir** NEW Our prestigious Red Wine of the Year, rich, fragrant, warmly sensuous **12** has particularly impressive structure (notably a succulent, mineral acidity) supporting the spicy red &
black berry fruit. Lively, long-lingering; very satisfying.

★★★★ **Walker Bay Pinot Noir** NEW Mostly off younger vines & flatter slopes, but **12** very attractive. Fresh
clean aromas of berries, tinged with earthiness. Gentle balance, with bright acidity & understated tannins.

★★★★ **Full Stop Rock** Savoury, handsome **10** from syrah with dollops mourvèdre & grenache. Less generous than some similar blends, but with a lean, muscular elegance. Some sweet fruit, but finishing dry.

★★★★ **Southend Chardonnay** Adds originating farm name on **12**. Forward, varietal citrus aromas lead
to balanced, concentrated palate with some weight; fruity sweetness cut by lively acidity. Orange-zesty end.

★★★★☆ **Family Vineyards Chardonnay** **12** (★★★★★) more restrained & youthfully complex than
Southend version. Supple, silky charm bound up with a quiet, limy intensity & a quickening acidity. Oaking modest (just 25% new) & unobtrusive - as is the 12.9% alcohol. Assertive in only the most subtle way! Improves on
11 & tough-vintage **10** (★★★★).

★★★★ **Sauvignon Blanc** 🗃 🌿 Bright, attractive **13** is forceful, succulent & flavoursome, nicely poised
between greener & riper aromas & flavours. A little oaked Elgin semillon adds breadth & texture.

★★★★ **Resonance** 🌿 **12** (★★★★★) has 16% oaked Elgin semillon with sauvignon - more than the varietally named wine, showing in waxy, earthy notes & a light tannic grip. Sauvignon's blackcurrant hints especially
pleasing. Perhaps less youthfully charming than **11**, but deeper. Should develop over a few years.

Discontinued: **Grenache Blend**. — TJ

■ **Nicholas L Jonker** see Jonkheer

Nick & Forti's Wines

Location: Tulbagh ▪ WO: Coastal ▪ Est/1stB 2004 ▪ Tasting at Saronsberg Cellar (see entry) ▪ Owner(s)
Fortunato Mazzone & Saronsberg ▪ Winemaker(s) Dewaldt Heyns (2004) ▪ 4,000cs own label 85% red 15%

white ▪ Box 25032 Monument Park Pretoria 0105 ▪ ritrovo@mweb.co.za ▪ www.saronsberg.com ▪ **T +27 (0)12-460-4367** ▪ F +27 (0)12-460-5173

Started ten years ago as a celebration of 'life, friendship and superb wine', the venture between restaurateur Fortunato 'Forti' Mazzone and Saronsberg winery owner Nick van Huyssteen continues to flourish. The range, made by Dewaldt Heyns at Saronsberg, is available at the winery as well as Forti's Pretoria restaurant, Ritrovo, his stores and the selected outlets and restaurants he supplies.

Shiraz 🔲 ★★★★ Satisfying if fairly straightforward **11** has good ripe red fruit & spice. Comfortably padded, with balanced freshness. **Epicentre** 🔲 ★★★★ Quiet ripe red fruit on cab-led Bordeaux quintet. **11** plush & ready, with gentle grip & sweet-fruited tail. **Viognier** 🎯 ★★★★ Peach pip & shortbread, rich consistency & resonating savoury length on **09**. Rung up on **08** (★★★★), with peach & pine nut opulence. — AL

Nico van der Merwe Wines

Location/map: Stellenbosch ▪ WO: Stellenbosch/Western Cape ▪ Est/1stB 1999 ▪ Tasting & sales by appt only ▪ Owner(s) Nico & Petra van der Merwe ▪ Cellarmaster(s)/winemaker(s) Nico van der Merwe ▪ 50t/4,000cs own label 80% red 20% white ▪ PO Box 12200 Stellenbosch 7613 ▪ nvdmwines@vodamail.co.za ▪ S 33° 57' 48.2" E 018° 43' 51.8" ▪ **T +27 (0)21-881-3063** ▪ F +27 (0)21-881-3063

Nico van der Merwe, longtime cellarmaster at Saxenburg, has produced his own premium label since 1999 but the past few years have seen his ambition of owning his own winery slowly come together. Winemaking philosophy is based on traditional methods, hands-on involvement - and an aversion to screwcaps. The tiny Mas Nicolas spread in Stellenbosch's Polkadraai is up and running, and the tasting venue almost complete (but receiving visitors by appointment). Its affable owner dreams of taking a six-month break to study bread baking in Europe.

Nicolas van der Merwe range

★★★★☆ **Red** ✓ Deliciously plump Bordeaux-style **08** exudes pure red berry & spice. Elegant, with a sumptuous mouthfeel, intense fruit concentration & super balance. Finishes with a lovely vanilla spice grip.

★★★★☆ **Mas Nicolas Cape** Cab & shiraz (70/30) from same vineyards since maiden **99**. Following superlative **07** (★★★★★), elegant **08** has great depth & earthy notes. Layers of black berry & plum fruit with great intensity, concentration & finesse. Perfectly judged oak adds to length & power.

★★★★ **White** ✓ Vibrant aromas of green apple, dusty lemon & lime on **12**, from sauvignon & semillon. Displays vibrancy & fine minerality. Expect more complex fruit flavours with ageing. WO W Cape.

Syrah 🎯 ★★★★☆ Big, muscular (15.5% alcohol) **07** set new standard for label last edition. Larger-than-life fruit demanded attention, needed time - contrast with open-textured **06** (★★★★). **Méthode Cap Classique Brut** Next awaited.

Robert Alexander range

Merlot ✓ ★★★★ Rich berry fruit on **12** a shade off **09** (★★★★). Medium bodied, with good balance & supple fruit structure & concentration & enduring finish, belies modest pitch of range. **10** & **11** sold out untasted.

Shiraz 🎯 ★★★★ Improving on **08** (★★★★), **09** shows ripe black fruits, richness & depth. Lush, harmonious & moreish, with good balance & length. **Cape Elements** ★★★ Was 'Shiraz-Cinsaut-Grenache'. New-wave blend of warm-climate varieties, **10** is fresh, juicy & bright with dark berry & spice flavours. Delightful all-year appeal. WO W Cape. — WB

Nico Vermeulen Wines

Location: Paarl ▪ WO: Coastal ▪ Est/1stB 2003 ▪ Closed to public ▪ Owner(s)/viticulturist(s) Nico Vermeulen ▪ Winemaker(s) Nico Vermeulen, with Judy & Izelle Vermeulen ▪ 3,000cs own label & 240,000L bulk export ▪ 3 Pieter Hugo Str Courtrai Suider-Paarl 7646 ▪ nicovermeulen@webmail.co.za ▪ **T +27 (0)21-863-2048/+27 (0)82-553-2024** ▪ F +27 (0)21-863-2048

'I'm very pleased with the 2013 vintage,' says winemaker Nico Vermeulen, who has scaled right back on bulk-wine exports from his Paarl base to focus on marketing his own wine brand in the South African market, as well as Germany.

★★★★ **The Right Red** Shiraz from Stellenbosch & Paarl perfect for hearty meals. Preview **10** plush & juicy, bold & tannic but, like **08**, not for long keeping. No **09**.

The Right Two Reds Await next, as for **The Right Two Whites**. **The Right White** 🏠 🍷 ★★★★ Sauvignon from Durbanville coated with honeyed bottle-age, layered with asparagus in **12**, liveliness abetted by grapefruit acidity & a lees-age-induced pithiness. Amenable solo or with food. — DB

Niel Joubert Estate   🍷🍷

Location: Paarl ▪ Map: Paarl & Wellington ▪ WO: Western Cape/Paarl ▪ Est 1898 ▪ 1stB 1996 ▪ Tasting & sales Mon-Fri 9-4 by appt ▪ Closed all pub hols ▪ Owner(s) Joubert family ▪ Cellarmaster(s) Ernst Leicht ▪ Winemaker(s) Ernst Leicht, with Niel Joubert jnr (May 2011) ▪ Viticulturist(s) Daan Joubert ▪ 1,000ha/300ha (cab, merlot, ptage, shiraz, chard, chenin, sauv) ▪ 1,953t/±160,000cs own label 49% red 50% white 1% rosé ▪ Other export brand: Hunterspeak ▪ Global Gap, IPW ▪ PO Box 17 Klapmuts 7625 ▪ wine@nieljoubert.co.za ▪ www.nieljoubert.co.za ▪ S 33° 49' 54.7"   E 018° 54' 3.2" ▪ **T +27 (0)21-875-5936** ▪ F +27 (0)86-599-0725

Klein Simonsvlei estate near Klapmuts has been home to the Joubert family since 1898, producing wine continuously under four successive generations. Current co-custodian Mari Joubert, with Pebbles Project, has set up an entirely self-funded pre-school and care centre school for employees' children. Fans of Byter ('Biter'), patriarch Niel Joubert's late, lamented and misnamed dog, will be delighted that the old pushover will be memorialised in future labellings of the estate chenin.

Christine-Marié range

★★★★ **Shiraz** 🏠 Tasted out of sequence, **07** matches **08**'s form, still exudes youthful charm. Classy middleweight shows restraint but expresses meaty, peppery cherry juice with silky tannins.

Cabernet Sauvignon 🏠 ★★★★ Refined, elegant flagship label, **09** retasted this edition delivers on preview's promise. Shows poise, balance & structure, with enticing blackcurrant fruit. Step up from last-tasted **06** (★★★★). **Merlot** ⏸ 🏠 ★★★★ Bold cherry & brambles, **06** dark earthy grip & concentration, big alcohol (15%) but soft appeal. **Chardonnay** ⏸ 🏠 ★★★★ Tangerine blast on smoky vanilla **08**, lavishly oaked (18 months 2nd fill), rich & delicious. WO Paarl, like next. **Viognier** ⏸ 🏠 ★★★★ **08** is redolent of peaches & cream. Rounded & full, restrained but firm toasty oak from (older) barrels. **Méthode Cap Classique** ⏸ ★★★★ Opulent & appealing **09** dry bubbly from chardonnay, harbours powerful yeasty influence. Rich, creamy & persistently dry, with chalky lime finish. Improves on **08** (★★★★). **First Kiss Fortified Chenin Blanc** 🏠 ★★★★ Quirky **09** spent 18 months in oak. Has caramel-like dessert appeal, with ginger & honey notes.

Niel Joubert Estate range

Chardonnay ☺ 🏠 ★★★ Previewed last edition, **12** retains appeal, with oak spice & lively acidity settled into citrus fruit. **Sauvignon Blanc** ☺ 🏠 ★★★ **13** perfect for summer picnic hampers. Crisp, fresh & light.

Cabernet Sauvignon 🏠 ★★★ Light & pleasantly fruity **11** has dusty oak spicing. **Merlot** 🏠 ★★ **11** light & juicy, with mocha notes. **Pinotage** 🏠 ★★★ Strident wild berry fruit on **11**. **Shiraz** 🏠 ★★★ Hint of minty vanilla on **10** bolsters cherry fruit. Better shape & structure than previous. **Rosé** 🏠 ★★★ Pleasantly fresh **12** pink from pinotage is dry & berry fruity. **Chenin Blanc** 🏠 ★★★ **13** is light & crisp, for uncomplicated everyday quaffing. — GdB

■ **Niels Verburg** *see* Luddite Wines

Nietgegund

Location/WO: Stellenbosch ▪ Est 2004 ▪ 1stB 2008 ▪ Closed to public ▪ Owner(s) Nietgegund Boerdery (Edms) Bpk ▪ Winemaker(s) Ronell Wiid (Jan 2013, consultant) ▪ Viticulturist(s) Francois Hanekom (Sep 2006, consultant) ▪ 3.4ha/1ha (cab, merlot, shiraz) ▪ 4t/100cs own label 100% red ▪ IPW ▪ PO Box 12684 Die Boord 7613 ▪ jan@dreyer.za.net ▪ **T +27 (0)21-880-0738**

When in 2001 Stellenbosch lawyer Jan Dreyer bought a Blaauwklippen property amidst several red-wine luminaries he couldn't not plant a hectare of merlot, shiraz and a small parcel of cab. The latter is managed according to the guyot system and vine man Francois Hanekom is eagerly awaiting the first crop. Niche wines that make and keep friends remain the focus.

Pro Amico ⏸ ★★★★ Merlot spiced by 10% shiraz; serious intent evident in firm structure & judicious oaking (30% new). **10** provisionally rated preview needed time to settle last edition. — WB,IM

Nietvoorbij Wine Cellar

Location/map: Stellenbosch ▪ Est 1963 ▪ 1stB 1992 ▪ Tasting & sales Mon-Fri 9–4 ▪ Closed Sat/Sun & all pub hols ▪ Conferences ▪ Owner(s) Agricultural Research Council ▪ Acting winemaker Craig Paulsen ▪ Vineyard manager(s) Guillaume Kotzè (Apr 2002) ▪ 32ha (cabs s/f, malbec, merlot, ptage, shiraz, chard, sauv, viog) ▪ 75t/6,000s own label 56% red 40% white 4% port ▪ Private Bag X5026 Stellenbosch 7599 ▪ cellar@arc.agric. za, winesales@arc.agric.za ▪ www.arc.agric.za ▪ S 33° 54' 43.5" E 018° 51' 48.9" ▪ **T +27 (0)21-809-3091/ 3084** ▪ F +27 (0)86-623-4014

Charmingly set on an avenue of oaks, Nietvoorbij Cellar is owned by the Agricultural Research Council. During harvest many hundreds of tiny experimental batches are vinified here for clients by acting winemaker and Elsenburg graduate Craig Paulsen. The knowledge gained is used to develop an increasing range of good-quality (often good-value) wines for the Nietvoorbij commercial label.

Nieuwedrift Vineyards

Location: Piketberg ▪ Map/WO: Swartland ▪ Est/1stB 2002 ▪ Tasting, sales & cellar tours Mon-Fri 9–1 & 2–6 Sat 9–2 ▪ Closed Easter Fri/Sun, Dec 25/26 & Jan 1 ▪ Meals on request; or BYO picnic ▪ Facilities for children ▪ Tour groups ▪ Conferences ▪ Owner(s)/viticulturist(s) Johan Mostert ▪ Cellarmaster(s) Johan Mostert (Jan 2002) ▪ 151ha/31ha (shiraz, chard, chenin, cbard) ▪ 410t total 10t/1,316cs own label 28% red 40% white 16% rosé 16% MCC ▪ PO Box 492 Piketberg 7320 ▪ nieuwedrift@patat.za.net ▪ S 32° 58' 28.1" E 018° 45' 10.6" ▪ **T +27 (0)22-913-1966/+27 (0)82-824-8104** ▪ F +27 (0)88-022-913-1966

Johan Mostert's remote vineyards, tucked into a bend of the Berg River near Piketberg, are really a sideline to his wheat farming business, but he takes them seriously. He vinifies a small portion of his crop under his own label, and is impressed by the increasingly rainbow-hued flow of visitors to his tasting room.

Blanc de Noir ☺ 🍾 ★★★ Tank sample **13** is invitingly fresh, dry & fruity; alcohol is modest, too.

Shiraz ★★★★ **11**, though with extended barrel time, shows same cheerful juicy red berries & sweet spices as previous. **Chenin Blanc** ✓ 🍾 ★★★★ Previewed & provisionally rated **13** still showing bottle shock, but promising better things. Wild yeast ferment & lees-ageing (no wood) show in creamy texture. **Méthode Cap Classique** ⊕ ★★★ Longer lees-ageing for 2nd disgorgement of **10** sparkling brings added body & texture. Resolutely dry, with oaky nuttiness. — GdB

Nitida Cellars

Location: Durbanville ▪ Map: Durbanville, Philadelphia & Darling ▪ WO: Durbanville/Coastal ▪ Est/1stB 1995 ▪ Tasting & sales Mon-Fri 9–5 Sat 9.30–3 Sun 11-3 ▪ Closed Good Fri, Dec 25 & Jan 1 ▪ Cassia Restaurant (see Restaurants section) ▪ Tables at Nitida T +27 (0)21-975-9537, www.tablesatnitida.co.za ▪ Conference & function venue at Cassia T +27 (0)21-976-0640 ▪ Facilities for children ▪ Mountain biking: Vellerdrome track for novice riders; part of Hillcrest/Majik forest trail (www.tygerbergmtb.co.za) ▪ Conservation area ▪ Annual festivals: Season of Sauvignon (Oct); Feast of the Grape (Mar); Soup, Sip & Bread (June) ▪ Owner(s) Bernhard & Peta Veller ▪ Cellarmaster(s) Bernhard Veller ▪ Winemaker(s) Brendan Butler (2013) ▪ Viticulturist(s) Bernhard Veller & Brendan Butler ▪ 35ha/ 16ha (cabs s/f, p verdot, riesling, sauv, sem) ▪ 150t/18,000cs own label 30% red 70% white + 3,000cs for clients ▪ Brands for clients: Woolworths, Checkers ▪ PO Box 1423 Durbanville 7551 ▪ info@nitida.co.za ▪ www.nitida.co.za ▪ S 33° 50' 3.8" E 018° 35' 37.0" ▪ **T +27 (0)21-976-1467** ▪ F +27 (0)21-976-5631

Bought by engineer Bernhard Veller and wife Peta as a residence, the run-down Durbanville sheep farm has been transformed into a prime family-oriented wine destination, with nature playing a major role in the process. Accolades such as Top Producer at the Michelangelo Awards and Diners Club Young Winemaker of the Year show they are clearly doing many things right, though Bernhard claims the secret of their success is to make wines they love to drink, and bottle only the best. His membership of the prestigious Cape Winemakers Guild since 2005 is further confirmation of that. Current news is the appointment of winemaker Brendan Butler, and the 2013 crush of their first pinot noir.

★★★★ **Cabernet Sauvignon** ✓ 🖼 Cassis & maraschino cherries, there's intense plush fruit in **11**, tailored tannins & a long cocoa-infused finish. Delicious, good enough to drink on its own.

★★★★☆ **Calligraphy** Merlot-dominated Bordeaux blend in **11**, offering fruitcake richness, cigarbox spicing & even cocoa, all built on a good tannin foundation. Promises well for future development.

★★★★ **Riesling** ✓ 🍽 Balanced between Old World & New, **13**'s floral, pineapple & ginger perfume draws you in to a palate laced with racy acidity, anchoring the flavours. Promises excellent ageing potential.

★★★★ **Sauvignon Blanc** ✓ 🍽 A treat as always, with a dab of semillon **13** has nice greengage & fennel notes, following the 'green but ripe' style of the area. Backed by limy acidity, giving resonating length.

★★★★ **Club Select Sauvignon Blanc** 🍽 Special selection to highlight cool terroir, which **13** reveals in its minerality, lime essence note. Elegant, flavour packed & briskly fresh, will age beautifully.

★★★★★ **Coronata Integration** ✓ 🍽 Name promises perfect partnership sauvignon/semillon & its merging with oak. Difficult to pin down, complex **12** has lime & shortbread, fennel, green fig, but what is beyond dispute is its elegant core of minerality. Done with grace & style.

Pinotage 🍽 ★★★ Last vintage made here, **12**'s gentle oak allows the vivid blueberry fruit centre stage, gives smooth, easy drinking. **Shiraz** ★★★★ **11** ticks all the shiraz boxes: glossy dark fruit, meaty/smoky spice, a whiff of scrub & smooth-textured accessibility. **Chardonnay** 🍽 ★★★★ Lemon-fresh perfume with peach creeping into **13**'s flavours, giving lovely palate appeal, zesty liveliness. Lightly oaked. **Semillon** Await next. **Matriarch in Red** ★★★ Rare traditional-method sparkling from oaked shiraz. Smoky dark plums with a herbal thread in **11**, finishing nicely dry. **The Matriarch** ★★★★ Aperitif style méthode cap classique sparkling, classic chardonnay/pinot noir blend. Dry, youthfully fresh **12** has a light biscuit overlay. Lively mousse. WO Coastal. **Modjadji Semillon Noble Late Harvest** New vintage not available. — CR

■ **Nixan Wines** see Blue Crane Vineyards

Noble Hill Wine Estate

🍴🥢☕📷🎿♿

Location: Paarl ▪ Map: Paarl & Wellington ▪ WO: Simonsberg-Paarl/Western Cape/Coastal ▪ Est/1stB 2001 ▪ Tasting & sales daily 10–5 ▪ Fee R30, waived on purchase ▪ Cellar tours by appt during tasting hours ▪ cosecha Restaurant (see Restaurants section) ▪ Picnic baskets ▪ Facilities for children ▪ Farm-produced extra virgin olive oil ▪ Conservation area ▪ Owner(s) Noble Hill Trust ▪ Winemaker(s) Bernard le Roux (May 2010) ▪ Viticulturist(s) Rodney Zimba (2001) & Johan Viljoen (consultant) ▪ 50ha/30ha (cabs s/f, merlot, mourv, p verdot, shiraz, sauv, viog) ▪ PO Box 111 Simondium 7670 ▪ info@noblehill.com ▪ www.noblehill.com ▪ S 33° 49' 38.0" E 018° 56' 12.1" ▪ **T +27 (0)21-874-3844**

This American family-owned winery in the Simonsberg-Paarl foothills continues to add new features to its already considerable visitor offerings: new wines (though untasted by us - the first 1,200 bottles of blanc de blancs bubbly sold out in a flash), and the growing Bloem ('Flower') brand, now also available in New York and Tokyo, reflecting their pride in the Western Cape's floral diversity. Still fermenting are ideas for a beer-and-wine garden, Brewdité.

Noble Hill range

★★★★ **Cabernet Sauvignon** Powerful pure blackberry fruit on cedary **09**. Light tannic squeeze from 18 months new French oak. Gentle texture yet structured & long, with a liquorice twist at the end.

★★★★ **Merlot** Black fruit intensity tempered by cocoa depth on **10**. Lithe & light yet shows some power & fine focus. Luscious breadth with graphite tail. Same oaking as Cab.

★★★★ **Estate Blend** Was '1674'. Maintaining standard of **09**, **10** 3-way cab, merlot & petit verdot blend a sexy melange of berries & spice; depth, breadth & succulence well framed by integrated oak, 30% new.

★★★★ **Syrah-Mourvèdre-Viognier 09** (★★★★) less impressive than rich **08**. Chalky feel to Rhône-style spice & black fruit. Lighter & less dense, concentrated.

Syrah ★★★★ **09** ups ante on previous in its juicy plum, blueberry vivacity. Earthy concentration with spice lift in the conclusion. **Bloem Red** ✓ 🍽 ★★★★ Chocolate & cherry generosity on **12** shiraz, mourvèdre mix. Dry, fruity & lively, with medium body & heaps of interest. WO W Cape, as for Sauvignon & Bloem White. **Mourvèdre Rosé** 🍽 ★★★★ Fresh **13** cranberry zip & crunchy apple tang with broad mouthfeel. Clean, dry finish. Ideal for food. **Chardonnay** ★★★★ **12** lemon cream richness with elegant vanilla from lees & 9 months in oak, 40% new. **Sauvignon Blanc** 🍽 ★★★★ Nettle & granadilla tang on zesty **13**. Crisp, clean & refreshing, delightfully rounded. **The Longest Day Sauvignon Blanc** Next awaited. **Viognier** ★★★ Toasty vanilla cream richness on **12**, light nectarine zip, partial natural ferment in older oak. WO Coastal. **Bloem White** 🍽 ★★★ Sprightly granadilla entry to **13** chenin, viognier. Lively & clean, with white pepper twist & appealing mouthfeel.

Austin range
Cabernet Sauvignon-Merlot Next awaited. — FM

Noble Savage

The fun Noble Savage wines from Bartinney Private Cellar aim to offer good
value with, as their marketing strapline has it, a 'sexy blend of mischief'.
Winemaker Ronell Wiid recommends enjoying them at Bartinney's new wine bar
in the heart of Stellenbosch, as they're not for tasting at the home-farm.

★★★★ **Cabernet Sauvignon-Merlot** ⑨ 🍴 📖 Sweet jammy black fruit on **10** edged with some
meaty savouriness, liquorice/anise & elegant length. Banghoek WO, as all.

Sauvignon Blanc ☺ 🍴 📖 ★★★ Lively & feisty **13** with pungent grapefruit flavours packing a punch.
Well-managed acidity balances delicious summer wine. WO W Cape.

Cabernet Sauvignon Rosé ⑨ 🍴 📖 ★★★ **12** preview shows plenty of pomegranate intensity & slight
medicinal note, but appealing, cherry menthol fruit & fresh finish. Stellenbosch WO. — CM

Nomada Wines

Location/WO: Durbanville ▪ Map: Durbanville, Philadelphia & Darling ▪ Est/1stB 2007 ▪ Tasting Tue-Sun 10-4 ▪
Owner(s) Riaan & Gina Oosthuizen ▪ Winemaker(s)/viticulturist(s) Riaan Oosthuizen (2007) ▪ 66ha/7ha (cabs
s/f, merlot, chenin, sauv) ▪ 55t total 10t/2,000cs own label 40% red 60% white + 6,000cs for clients ▪ Brands
for clients: Klein Roosboom Wines, Red White Pink Wines, Schaap Wines (Netherlands), Signal Gun Wines ▪
PO Box 5145 Tygervalley 7536 ▪ nomadawines@gmail.com ▪ S 33° 50' 15.70" E 018° 36' 23.88" ▪ **T +27
(0)83-280-7690**

Owned by husband-and-wife team Riaan and Gina Oosthuizen, Nomada Wines
have opened a tasting venue on Morgenster farm in Durbanville. The boutique
vintners also rent cellar space here – a real creative hub during harvest, as Riaan
also vinifies on contract for several other small wineries.

Georgina ⑨ ★★★★ Bordeaux-style red blend is robust in youth but more balanced & riper in **10**, with firm
tannin structure. Ageworthy table mate. **Sauvignon Blanc** 🍴 ★★★ Feisty, food-styled **13** shows
Durbanville's signature dusty nuance. Crunchy apple & grapefruit leavened by leesy breadth. **Rustica** 🍴 ★★
13 sauvignon (93%) & dash viognier, with brisk green & dried fruit, still melding at press time. — MW

■ **Non Pareil** see L'Olivier Wine & Olive Estate

Nordic Wines

Location: Robertson ▪ WO: Stellenbosch/Swartland ▪ Est 2007 ▪ 1stB 2010 ▪ Closed to public ▪ Wine orders
Mon-Fri 9-5 from export offices: Nordic Wines, Robertson ▪ Owner(s) Wiggo Andersen & Peter Tillman ▪
Winemaker(s)/viticulturist(s) consulting ▪ Other export brands: By Norwegians, Cape to Cape, Frogner, Literature Wine, Mia, Selma, Wedgewood ▪ PO Box 896 Robertson 6705 ▪ info@nordicwines.co.za, peter@
nordicwines.co.za, alison@nordicwines.co.za ▪ www.nordicwines.co.za ▪ **T +27 (0)23-626-1413/+27
(0)83-283-5354** ▪ F +27 (0)23-626-1031

Sourcing wines locally for export mainly to Scandinavia is the chief focus of co-
owners Wiggo Andersen and Peter Tillman, and recently they secured a bottling
for a well-known Norwegian singer. A percentage of the Norwegian sales of this
special wine will be used in South Africa for a charity she has chosen that specifically empowers disadvantaged women and children. Note: entry last listed as
'Wedgewood Wines'.

Director's Choice range
Cabernet Sauvignon-Merlot ⑨ 🍴 ★★★ Understated **09** appealing combo of cedar & savoury ripe
berry. **Malbec-Pinotage** Await next. **Chenin Blanc** ⑨ 🍴 ★★★ Thatch & peach nuances, tangy lime-
apricot tail on juicy **10**, from venerable Malmesbury vines. — DB

■ **Nuts About** see Chateau Naudé Wine Creation
■ **Nuwehoop** see uniWines Vineyards

Nuweland Wynkelder

Location: Malmesbury ▪ WO: Swartland/Coastal/Malmesbury ▪ Est 2007 ▪ 1stB 2008 ▪ Vygevallei farm stall & Nuweland wine house (R27): Tasting & sales Mon-Sat 10-6 Sun 10-4 ▪ Closed Dec 25 & Jan 1 ▪ Restaurant ▪ Facilities for children ▪ Tour groups ▪ Gifts ▪ Art ▪ Farm produce ▪ Conferences ▪ Cellar tours by appt only ▪ Owner(s) Juan Louw ▪ Winemaker(s)/viticulturist(s) Juan Louw (Jan 2007) ▪ 300ha/96ha (cab, merlot, ptage, tinta barocca, chenin, sauv) ▪ 560t/1,500cs own label 45% red 35% white 20% dessert ▪ PO Box 283 Malmesbury 7299 ▪ juan@nuweland.za.net ▪ www.nuweland.za.net ▪ S 33° 24' 03.87" E 018° 16' 41.73" ▪ **T +27 (0)78-111-7913**

Owner/winemaker Juan Louw's boundless enthusiasm has resulted in the creation of an eclectic range of whites, reds and sweeties, all handcrafted by him, 90% of which are only available ex-cellar in minuscule quantities. His personality is indelibly stamped on the wines, and he justifies the large range by claiming that he wants to make wines to suit everyone's individual tastes. And he can't resist vinifying small parcels from neighbouring farms, when he spots something particularly interesting or old. The range represents a journey of discovery for people who aren't yet aware of what the Swartland has to offer.

Premium range

★★★★☆ **Straw Wine** From muscat d'Alexandrie, new bottling **08** is apricot-hued & -flavoured, 5 year barrel ageing giving it distinctive savouriness, upping the ante from original bottling. Tealeaves, nuts, even citrus peel & tangy sweet from good acidity.

★★★★ **Muscat d'Alexandrie** Fortified dessert wine from air-dried grapes. Now 4 years in barrel, gives **09** lovely raisiny richness, the oak a minor influence. Very sweet, mouthfilling, drink it chilled.

★★★★☆ **Muscat de Frontignan** Red & white muscadel mix fortified dessert. New bottling **09** has tangerine marmalade fruit intensified by a honeycomb tone. Taking it to a new level from original bottling is 4 years in barrel, imparting a salted nuts savoury thread, anchoring the richness. Coastal WO.

18 Mei Grenache Noir ⓥ ★★★ **10** delivered on preview promise previously. Picked 18 May, very late for Swartland harvest. Ripe & smoky notes with firm & savoury support. **Makstok Pinotage** ★★★★ Bushvine fruit, naturally bunch-fermented. Plums & blueberries, elegant **12** showcases the variety well, with juicy fruit purity on the palate, plumped up by a touch of sugar. Tannins nicely in support. **Van Reenen Ruby Cabernet** NEW ★★★★ Cedar-nuanced intense berries, but **12**'s tannins too sturdy to show the wine's full potential. Keep 2-3 years, drink till 2020. **Haasbek Tinta Barocca** ★★★ Fennel & ginger-scented **11** retaste is fruitier on the palate, redcurrants, supported by zesty acidity, sturdy tannins. **Juan II** ★★★★ Shiraz-led 13-part (!) red blend. Peppery, smoky fruit, some floral notes, sleek, characterful **12** has friendly fresh tones. **Bosstok Rosé** NEW ★★★ Light, dry cinsaut-led **12** has a herbal edge to the red berries. **Bosstok Steen Chenin Blanc** ⓥ ▤ ★★★ From 30 year old bushvines; **11** distinctly different, off-dry & rich. **Gesuierde Sauvignon Blanc** Next awaited. **Sauvignon Blanc** ⓥ ▤ ★★★★ Wonderful food wine ('Snoek braai!' says winemaker). **11** especially given maximum sun exposure to ensure concentrated tropical fruit richness; both soft & dry. WO Coastal. **Wilna** NEW ★★★★ Sauvignon-led 7-part oaked blend. **12**'s thatch & oatmeal, preserved orange suggests richness, but the palate is dry & light.

Louw range

Rooipad Cabernet Sauvignon ★★★★ From ultra-low-yielding vineyard, **11** retaste has cassis & campfire smoke flavours & lipsmacking juicy freshness that makes it appealingly accessible. **Droëland Merlot** NEW ★★★ Cassis & creamy mocha/vanilla spicing, curvaceous **12** has just enough tannin grip for ageing, or partnering rich casseroles. **Oustok Cinsaut Rosé** NEW Not tasted. **Semi-Soet Merlot Rosé** NEW ★★★ Previewed **13**'s grapey, candied fruit flavours fit the sweetness. Soft, smooth, easy. Malmesbury WO. **Semi-Soet Bukettraube** NEW ★★ Muscat-like & grapey, there's a nice tang in **13**'s sweetness. **Rolbos Chardonnay** NEW ★★ Melon-toned **13** is light textured, freshly dry. Only 35 cases. Malmesbury WO. **Probus Viognier** NEW ★★★ Guava roll & peach, dab of ginger in aromatic, lightish (12% alcohol) **13**. Tastes off-dry because of the fruitiness, but is dry. **Ruby Cabernet Jerepigo** NEW ★★★★ With vanilla-coated pruney fruit, dark-hued **13** preview aims to please, its sweetness benefiting from the tannin grip at the end. **Bukettraube Jerepigo** NEW Peach-coloured fortified NV tank sample, not yet harmonious, the oak standing apart from the stewed fruit sweetness. Too unfinished to rate. — CR

■ **Nuwe Wynplaas** *see Group CDV*

Nuy Wine Cellar 🍴🌳📷♿

Location/map: Worcester ▪ WO: Nuy ▪ Est 1963 ▪ Tasting & sales Mon-Fri 9–4.30 Sat 9–12.30 ▪ Closed Good Fri, Dec 25/26 & Jan 1 ▪ BYO picnic ▪ Mountain biking ▪ Owner(s) 19 members ▪ Cellarmaster(s) Christo Pienaar (Sep 2003) ▪ Winemaker(s) Charl Myburgh (Dec 2012) ▪ Viticulturist(s) Pierre Snyman (Vinpro) ▪ 580ha (cab, merlot, muscadel, ptage, shiraz, chard, chenin, cbard, nouvelle, sauv) ▪ 16,600t/10,000cs own label ▪ PO Box 5225 Worcester 6849 ▪ wines@nuywinery.co.za ▪ www.nuywinery.co.za ▪ S 33° 39' 8.7" E 019° 38' 30.9" ▪ **T +27 (0)23-347-0272** ▪ F +27 (0)23-347-4994

Grower-owned Nuy Cellar, famous for its delicious and long-lived fortifieds (and good-value easy-drinkers), celebrated its 50th anniversary last year by bottling a special barrel-matured version of its best-known wine, the Red Muscadel. A birthday gift from Mother Nature was a record harvest of almost 17,000 tons.

★★★★ **Barrel Selection Cabernet Sauvignon** ⊛ After 08 (★★★★☆) trumped 07 (★★★), elegant **10** affirms improved form of this reserve label (**09** not reviewed). Gentle spice & cedar from 2 years in oak, intense blackcurrant flavour, dry & savoury aftertaste. Modest 13% alcohol adds to appeal.

★★★★ **Barrel Selection Syrah** ⊛ Bright & poised **10**, well crafted to showcase succulent fruit, judiciously oaked (2 years). Shade more powerful than **08** but no less elegant. **09** not tasted.

★★★★ **Red Muscadel** ⊛ 🏵 **12** fortified dessert on track after slight wobble in **11** (★★★★). Full-sweet but uncloying, spiced raisin richness & uplifting conclusion. Delicious on release, these age beautifully too.

★★★★☆ **Red Muscadel Limited Release** NEW ✓ Only 1,500 bottles of this fortified & barrel-matured **NV** nectar released to mark Nuy's 50th anniversary. Enticing Indian spices, tobacco & tealeaves followed by an ambrosial raisin mouthful. Rich & refined, with subtle tannic grip. Do try to cellar some.

★★★★ **White Muscadel** ✓ 🏵 Irresistible **12** (★★★★☆) steps up with greater orange marmalade, sweet tea complexity, similar gingery honeyed raisins as **10**, buoyed by tangy acidity & integrated spirit. Total bargain.

> **Pinotage** NEW ☺ 🏵 ★★★ Tasty **12** dusty/smoky plum flavour, firm tannins & commendable dryness. Priced to go - order now! **Chardonnay** ☺ 🏵 ★★★ **12**'s beguiling sweet vanilla from year in barrel uplifted zingy grapefruit flavour & lemon acidity. **Colombar Semi-Sweet** ☺ 🏵 ★★★ Peachy **13** gently sweet, delicate & poised summer sipper. **Sauvignon Blanc Sparkling Vin Sec** ☺ ★★★ Gooseberry-toned, off-dry **13** bright & cheerful addition to the picnic basket.

Cabernet Sauvignon 🏵 ★★ Attractive bready, cherry notes on big, powerful **12** braai wine. **Pinotage Barrel Selection** NEW 🏵 ★★★ Quintessential pinotage mulberry & plum notes, slight farmyard nuance on **10**. Leaner style but pleasant, satisfying. **Rouge de Nuy** Await next. **Chenin Blanc** 🏵 ★★ Just-bottled **13** slightly sweaty, tart. Rating provisional. **Blanc de Blanc** NEW ★★★ 100% chenin in latest **NV** (**13**) party-size 3L box, tropical smells & tastes, zippy tail fluffed out by touch of sweetness. **Sauvignon Blanc** 🏵 ★★ Recently bottled, nettly **13** should perk up by summer & join the beach party. **Chant de Nuit** 🏵 ★★ Fragrant **NV** dry white with distinctive pineapple aroma from splash Ferdinand de Lesseps. Discontinued: **Colombar Dry**. — DB,CvZ

◼ **Oak Lane** *see* Beau Joubert Vineyards & Winery

Oak Valley Wines 🍷☕🏔📷♿

Location/WO: Elgin ▪ Map: Elgin, Walker Bay & Bot River ▪ Est 1898 ▪ 1stB 2003 ▪ Tasting & sales Mon-Fri 9–5 Sat/Sun 10-4 ▪ Closed Easter Fri-Sun, Dec 25/26 & Jan 1 ▪ The Pool Room @ Oak Valley (see Restaurants section) ▪ Deli (artisanal breads, homegrown free-range meats & charcuterie) ▪ Self-catering 1-bedroom cottage ▪ Walks/hikes ▪ Mountain biking trail ▪ Conservation area ▪ Owner(s) AG Rawbone-Viljoen Trust ▪ Winemaker(s) Pieter Visser ▪ Viticulturist(s) Pieter Visser, assisted by Kevin Watt ▪ 30ha (merlot, p verdot, pinot, shiraz, chard, sauv, sem) ▪ ±150t/±24,000cs own label 50% red 50% white ▪ BWI champion, GlobalGap, IPW, WIETA ▪ PO Box 30 Elgin 7180 ▪ wines@oak-valley.co.za ▪ www.oak-valley.co.za ▪ S 34° 9' 24. 4" E 019° 2' 55.5" ▪ **T +27 (0)21-859-4110** ▪ F +27 (0)21-859-3405

This large family estate in Elgin was founded in 1898 by Sir Antonie Viljoen. There were vines in the earlier years, but for much of the twentieth century the farming focus was on flowers, fruit and livestock. New vineyards were planted in the 1980s, however, but it was not until the 2003 vintage that current owner Anthony Rawbone-Viljoen released wines under the Oak Valley label (made by Pieter Visser in the cellar of neighbouring Paul Cluver). A fine reputation was soon established. Son Christopher joined the team a few years back as Marketing

Manager, a significant function for a large farming operation as well as the range of activities that make the estate an important part of Elgin's appeal to tourists.

★★★★ **Pinot Noir** 🍷 Maraschino cherry fruit aromas on **12** promise perhaps more than the palate delivers. Light spice notes, a touch savoury, a touch gamey. Fine texture, restrained oaking & modest 13% alcohol.

★★★★ **Shiraz** 🕐 🍷 Intense cerise, almost opaque barrel sample **11**. Raspberry, red fruit whiffs, plush tannins, full yet unflamboyant. Lovely wood integration, fine peppery hints on finish.

★★★★ **The Oak Valley Blend** 🕐 Ripe, sweet merlot spiced with cab & cab franc & whiff of French oak combine in polished **07**. Firm but not harsh or inaccessible. Tasted a few years back, as was The OV.

★★★★☆ **Chardonnay** 🍷 **12** has notes of grapefruit pith & pineapple - also caramel butterscotch, hinting at the 35% new oak. The palate has a fine elegance, rounded rather than plush, almost ethereal.

★★★★☆ **The OV** 🕐 🍷 Distinctive 81/19 sauvignon/semillon blend, compatibly oaked. **09** bounded back after **08** (★★★★). Persuasive citrus, honey-rich complexity with precise mineral lines. Tasted a few years back.

Sauvignon Blanc ✓ 🍷 ★★★★ Smoky, mineral gunflint & faintly herbal character on **12**, a splash of oaked semillon adding to the complexity. Elegant, persistent & zesty. — MF

Obikwa

Distell good-value brand named for the indigenous Obikwa people and sold in more than 40 countries. Widely sourced, and made for early enjoyment.

> **Pinotage Rosé** ☺ 🍷 ★★☆ Slightly sweet poolside pink with boiled sweet & pot-pourri flavours, mouthwatering **13** will also please as light lunch partner. **Chardonnay** ☺ 🍷 ★★☆ Richer, bigger than white siblings, step-up **13** successfully integrates light oak with orange, peach blossoms & some vanilla. **Moscato** ☺ 🍷 ★★☆ Delicious floral, grapey **13** sweet but fresh & mouthwatering, serve ice-cold.

Cabernet Sauvignon 🍷 ★★★ Perhaps most polished of the reds, **13** elegant & light, broadened by pinch sugar (as most here). Shows variety's dusty notes, with clean red fruit & mint. **Merlot** 🍷 ★★☆ Herbaceous **12** tealeaf & savoury vegetable stock character, mediumweight & friendly, with moderate alcohol (as all). **Pinotage** 🍷 ★★★ Brooding **13** good varietal typicity in wild berry spice & tar; quite serious for entry level: has some structure, firm tannins, savouriness. **Shiraz** 🍷 ★★★ Party wine **13** with black pepper & earthy notes, fruity flavours of blackcurrant & bramble. **Pinotage-Cabernet Sauvignon** Next awaited. **Chenin Blanc** 🍷 ★★ Missing charm of previous, **13** tad leaner, showing more green fruit, firm acid on clean, fresh palate. **Pinot Grigio** 🍷 ★★☆ From tank, lightish **13** semi-dry sipper with savoury/lemon nuance. **Sauvignon Blanc** 🍷 ★★ Straightforward crisp, dry **13** with zippy acidity & lemon/lime flavour. **Classic Dry White** 🍷 ★★ All sunshine & friendly appeal on nose, **13**'s summer fruit medley becomes shade less generous on palate. **Cuvée Brut** 🍷 ★★★ Everyday **13** fizz from chenin, dash colombard. Just-dry, lively if coarse guava & pear-toned bubbles. **Natural Sweet Red** 🍷 ★★ Uncomplicated low-alcohol **NV** sweet red with sweet tea & candied red fruit notes. **Natural Sweet White** 🍷 ★★ NV sweet, low-alcohol party wine for the sweet-toothed. W Cape WO for all the above. — DB, HJ

■ **Ocean Basket** *see Simonsvlei International*
■ **Oddbins** *see Shoprite Checkers*
■ **Oggendau** *see Eerste Hoop Wine Cellar*

Old Bridge Wines

St Francis Bay ▪ Closed to public ▪ Owner(s) Paulinas Dal Mountain Vineyards (Pty) Ltd ▪ 40,000cs 60% red 40% white ▪ PO Box 557 De Rust 6312 ▪ rickety@iafrica.com ▪ **T +27 (0)82-777-1519**

Export-focused producer and negociant sourcing wines for various brands, including private labels for specialised corporate clients. The wines include limited-edition African Gold Collection mainly for US, Europe and Asia; Big Six Collection, boxed sets for local game lodges/retreats and export; and Old Bridge.

■ **Old Brown** *see Sedgwick's Old Brown*

Oldenburg Vineyards

Location/map/WO: Stellenbosch ▪ Est 1960s ▪ 1stB 2007 ▪ Tasting & sales Mon-Fri 10-4.30 Sat & pub hols 10-4 (Nov-Apr)/by appt (May-Oct) ▪ Fee R30 ▪ Closed Good Fri, Dec 25/26 & Jan 1 ▪ Refreshments for sale (cheese platters, biltong, etc.) ▪ Owner(s) Adrian Vanderspuy ▪ Winemaker(s) Simon Thompson (May 2004) ▪ Viticul-

turist(s) Simon Thompson (May 2004), with Paul Wallace (consultant) ▪ 50ha/30ha (cabs s/f, merlot, shiraz, chard, chenin) ▪ 227t/8,000cs own label 57% red 43% white ▪ PO Box 2246 Dennesig 7601 ▪ cellardoor@ oldenburgvineyards.com ▪ www.oldenburgvineyards.com ▪ S 33° 55' 7.61" E 018° 56' 8.75" ▪ **T +27 (0)21-885-1618** ▪ F +27 (0)21-885-2665

Adrian Vanderspuy was born in Stellenbosch's Banhoek Valley and after a long sojourn overseas bought Oldenburg farm there in 2003: 'It was a chance to participate in two very positive stories, the rise of South Africa and its wine industry's renaissance.' The fruits of optimism can be tasted in vinified form at the estate, soon to offer accommodation, and bought via a new online shop and Wine Club.

★★★★ **Cabernet Sauvignon** Unshowy, brooding **10** shows ripe raisin & cassis notes. Savoury, dusty tannins on a palate showing elegance despite the 15% alcohol - but lacks the restraint of more savoury **09**.

★★★★ **Cabernet Sauvignon Barrel Selection** NEW Restrained & perfumed **09**, with delicacy rather than intensity the hallmark of this selection. House-style big alcohol (15%) & all-new oak well managed.

★★★★☆ **Merlot** Firm tannins & shy fruit on unflamboyant but not evanescent **11** (★★★★), without the plush, overt sweet mulberry notes of **10**. It hides the 15% alcohol well, but dries out on the finish.

★★★★ **Chenin Blanc** 🏠 Ripe & rich, brash & showy **12** has plush, generous fruit pushing the limit of ripeness; palate has sweet-sour grippiness, but lacks the mineral spark of more restrained **11** (★★★★☆).

Cabernet Franc ★★★★ Super-ripe & plush **10**, with faint herbal notes, plummy fruit & powdery tannins. Brash, but lacking intensity. **Syrah** ★★★ Concentrated & lush, raisiny, dried compote notes on **10** balanced by dense, savoury oak tannins. Just off-dry. **Rhodium Red Blend** NEW ★★★★ Herbal & dense **10** from merlot & cab franc with a little malbec. Some harmony, despite firm tannins, light fruit & youthful inaccessibility. **Chardonnay** 🏠 🎨 ★★★★ Pineapple & tropical whiffs plus plush caramel oaky notes. 50% new wood also adds a slightly astringent edge to limy, mineral finish in **12**. — MF

Old Vines Cellars

Location: Cape Town ▪ WO: Coastal/Stellenbosch ▪ Est/1stB 1995 ▪ Closed to public ▪ Owner(s) Irina von Holdt & Françoise Botha ▪ Winemaker(s) Irina von Holdt ▪ 20,000cs own label 40% red 60% white + 8,000cs for clients ▪ 50 Liesbeek Rd Rosebank 7700 ▪ info@oldvines.co.za ▪ www.oldvines.co.za ▪ **T +27 (0)21-685-6428** ▪ F +27 (0)21-685-6446

'Driven by women power and a deep love of chenin', is how matriarch Irina von Holdt describes her small-scale wine venture, which she runs with her daughter Françoise. Irina was one of the earliest protagonists of quality chenin in South Africa and she continues to chart a steady course for her business, based in Cape Town. She is now exploring the Chinese market, aware of the big 'rainbow nation' outside our borders and of chenin's compatibility with Asian cuisine.

Old Vines range

★★★★ **Barrel Reserve Chenin Blanc** 🄯 🎨 Tiny yield from 63 year old vines, now-bottled **10** layered complexity & genteel Old World restraint. Contemplative food wine with silky texture & dried peach tone.

★★★★ **Chenin Blanc** ✓ 🎨 Ageworthy unwooded version from Stellenbosch vines. Persistent, gentle glacé pineapple, quince & almond flavours unfurl & develop on **12** (★★★★☆), a rich silky texture threaded with vibrant acidity. Elegantly understated, more intensity & length than previewed **11**.

Baron von Holdt In abeyance, like **Vintage Brut**.

Spring Valley range

Merlot ☺ 🍽 ★★★ Tank sample **12** plump & friendly, succulent red berries & hint of mint. Appealing drinkability. **Chenin Blanc-Sauvignon Blanc** ☺ 🍽 ★★★ **13** ex tank crunchy apple, stonefruit & herbaceous tone. Lively, crisp balance for carefree summer quaffing.

Pinotage NEW 🍽 ★★★ **11** has a light & sappy mulberry tone. Delightful undemanding quaffer. **Shiraz-Merlot** 🍽 ★★★ **12** preview is juicy but firm, savoury & food friendly. **Sauvignon Blanc** ✓ 🍽 ★★★★ Bright & crisp **13** preview exudes fresh-cut grass & passionfruit flavours, with creamy lees texture. — MW

Olifantsberg Family Vineyards

Location: Worcester ▪ Map/WO: Breedekloof ▪ Est 2003 ▪ 1stB 2005 ▪ Tasting & sales Mon-Fri by appt ▪ Owner(s) Paul J Leeuwerik ▪ Cellarmaster(s)/winemaker(s)/viticulturist(s) Jacques du Plessis (Nov 2009) ▪

95ha/10ha (carignan, grenache n/b, mourv, ptage, shiraz, chard, chenin, rouss) ▪ 35t/±4,667cs own label 75% red 25% white ▪ PO Box 942 Worcester 6849 ▪ duplessis.je@gmail.com ▪ www.olifantsberg.com ▪ S 33° 35' 42.76" E 019° 21' 42.39" ▪ **T +27 (0)23-342-0401** ▪ F +27 (0)23-342-0401

Stirrings here in Breedekloof of next-generation viticulture, with Rhône red/ white varieties coming into play, new high-slopes vines planted (mindful of conservation needs), and organic practices augering well. Production is small, but new vineyards are coming onstream, as is a new fermentation cellar.

> **Cabernet Sauvignon** ☺ ★★★ Blackcurrant fruit emerging valiantly from mantle of oak on **10** may yet find centre-stage. Juicy & ripe.

Pinotage ⓐ ★★★★ Approachable **11** exudes plummy mulberry varietal charm. Firm but supple structure with sweet-fruited length. **Syrah** ★★★★ Meaty, leathery **11** has pleasant pepper spiciness on full, ripe fruit. Fullish body cloaked in thick tannins. **Chardonnay** In abeyance. **Chenin Blanc-Chardonnay** ★★★ Wild meaty coriander notes & hint of oak on plump, ripe **12**. — GdB

Olof Bergh Solera   `[NEW]`

Olof Bergh brandy is a local rarity, being matured using the solera method of racking brandies from different distillations down tiers of barrels, for a final product of greater character and age than the usual blended brandy. Its 'home' distillery is in Goudini, and it's handled by Distell subsidiary Henry Tayler & Ries.

Olof Bergh Solera Brandy ★★★ Blended brandy, sippable but best for cocktails & mixers. Straightforward, with nice fruity fragrance to sniff & some caramel & oak vanilla coming through. Clean, dry finish. — WB,TJ

Olsen Wines

Location/WO: Paarl ▪ Map: Paarl & Wellington ▪ Est/1stB 2002 ▪ Tasting by appt only ▪ Fee R25pp ▪ Light meals for groups of ±10 by appt ▪ Farm-style jams ▪ Owner(s) Greg & Kimberly Olsen ▪ Cellarmaster(s)/viticulturist(s) Armand Botha (2000) & Kimberly Olsen ▪ Winemaker(s) Armand Botha (2007) & Loftie Ellis ▪ 30ha ▪ 1,000cs own label 90% red 10% white ▪ Europgap registered ▪ PO Box 9052 Huguenot 7645 ▪ olsenwines@ mweb.co.za ▪ www.olsenprivatevineyards.co.za ▪ S 33° 44' 4.7" E 019° 3' 5.0" ▪ **T +27 (0)21-862-3653** ▪ F +27 (0)21-862-2589

New labels will adorn the '10 releases from the Paarl estate of arguably the Cape's lowest-profile celebrity: third private citizen in space Greg Olsen. A huge fan of South Africa's 'rainbow grape', Greg even took some pinotage on his ride of a lifetime, and he and wife Kimberly planted the variety on their land in Montana.

Pinotage ⓐ ★★★ Owner's favourite variety in ripe spicy style, **09** nicely structured by half new oak - slightly bitter finish, though marginally less so than also-tasted **08**. **Chardonnay** ⓐ 🍽 ★★★ Butterscotch & marzipan on oak-fermented (all new) **11**; pleasantly light yet mouthfilling. **Chenin Blanc** ⓐ ★★★ Fresh **10** has chenin's trademark savoury acidity to lift & carry tropical flavours. — IM

Onderkloof

Location: Somerset West ▪ Map: Helderberg ▪ WO: Stellenbosch/Walker Bay/Western Cape ▪ Est 1998 ▪ 1stB 1999 ▪ Tasting, sales & cellar tours by appt ▪ Conservation area ▪ Self-catering cottages ▪ Owner(s) Beat Musfeld ▪ Winemaker(s) Yves Musfeld (Jan 2012) ▪ Viticulturist(s) Botha Marais (Aug 2012) ▪ 64ha/12ha (ptage, shiraz, chenin, muscat d'A, sauv) ▪ 75t ▪ PO Box 90 Sir Lowry's Pass 7133 ▪ info@onderkloof.com ▪ www.onderkloof.com ▪ S 34° 6' 37.9" E 018° 53' 49.2" ▪ **T +27 (0)21-858-1538**

A seat on one of the Cape's best-known hills (breezy Schapenberg, shared by such luminaries as Vergelegen) marks Beat Musfeld's Helderberg estate as special. Beat has entrusted son Yves with revitalising the vineyards and upholding the focus on tourism as essential building blocks to future success.

> **Sauvignon Blanc** ☺ 🍽 ★★★ Fresh, fruity & tropical exposition, **13** clean focused palate, ends with a dry & zippy pounce. **Floreal Blanc de Blanc** ☺ 🍽 ★★★ **13**, medley of hanepoot & chenin, offers seductive grapey/spice aromas with cleansing acid, fresh off-dry end. WO W Cape.

Cabernet Sauvignon ⓘ ★★★☆ Violet-toned **06** wild berry fruit, unknit tannins when tasted a few years back. **Pinotage** ⓘ ★★★☆ From low-cropped bushvines, **07** offered black plum & cherry flavours when last tasted. **Shiraz** Await next. **Chardonnay** ⓘ 🍴 ★★★☆ Ripe yellow stonefruit aromas lead to rounded soft-styled **12** with elegant dry finish. Light oak nicely harmonises whole. WO Walker Bay. **Chenin Blanc** NEW 🍴 ★★★ Spicy dried peach aromas on **12** lead to dry, yeasty palate. — JP

■ **Ondine** *see* Ormonde Private Cellar

Oneiric Wines 🍴🍸🎋📷

Location: Elgin ▪ Map: Elgin, Walker Bay & Bot River ▪ Est 2007 ▪ 1stB 2009 ▪ Tasting & sales by appt only ▪ BYO picnic ▪ Gift shop ▪ Walks/hikes ▪ Conservation area ▪ Owner(s) Pascall family ▪ Winemaker(s) Niels Verburg (2013, consultant) & Jean Smit (2009, consultant) ▪ Viticulturist(s) Paul Wallace (Aug 2007, consultant) ▪ 64ha/8ha (cab, merlot, syrah, chard, sauv) ▪ ±90t/5,000cs own label 65% red 35% white ▪ shan@oneiric.co.za ▪ www.oneiric.co.za ▪ S 34° 14' 31.0" E 019° 03' 05.8" ▪ **T +27 (0)71-481-9560**

Oneiric, 'of or pertaining to dreams', describes Matt and Jennifer Pascall and family's aspiration to bottle wines from their Elgin property on the border of the Kogelberg Biosphere under an own brand. An own cellar has been built, and the adjacent Button Barn allows visitors 'to not only taste our wines while browsing our gift shop filled with arts and crafts but also to sit back, put their feet up and marvel at the beauty that is Oneiric wine farm', says MD Shan Pascall.

■ **One World** *see* Koopmanskloof Wingerde

Oom Tas

Distell big-volume white depicts winefarmer 'Uncle Tas' beaming from retro label.
Oom Tas 🍴 ★★ Amber hue implies sweetness but simple fruity **NV** is bone-dry. 1,2, 5L bottles. — DB, HJ

■ **Opener's** *see* Waterstone Wines

Opstal Estate 🍴☕📷🚴♿

Location: Rawsonville ▪ Map: Breedekloof ▪ WO: Slanghoek/Breedekloof ▪ Est 1847 ▪ 1stB 1978 ▪ Tasting, sales & cellar tours Mon-Fri 9–5 Sat 10–2 Sun by appt ▪ Closed Easter Fri-Mon, Dec 25/26 & Jan 1 ▪ Restaurant Wed-Sun 9–5 ▪ Facilities for children ▪ Tour groups ▪ Gift shop ▪ Farm produce ▪ Conferences ▪ Conservation area ▪ Mountain biking trail ▪ Monthly music/theatre shows with dinner (Jul-Nov) ▪ Quarterly farmers market ▪ Owner(s) Stanley Louw ▪ Winemaker(s) Attie Louw (Sep 2010) ▪ Viticulturist(s) Gerhard Theron (Jan 2002) ▪ 419ha/101ha (cab, ptage, shiraz, chard, chenin, muscat d' A, sauv, sem, viog) ▪ 1,500t/12,000cs own label 20% red 65% white 10% rosé 5% dessert ▪ BWI, IPW ▪ PO Box 27 Rawsonville 6845 ▪ wine@opstal.co.za ▪ www.opstal.co.za ▪ S 33° 38' 19.8" E 019° 13' 40.8" ▪ **T +27 (0)23-344-3001** ▪ F +27 (0)23-344-3002

No shortage of history here, as 6th and 7th generation Louws are currently involved on the improbably scenic family farm. Attie Louw is a vibrant young winemaker eager to share knowledge, and passionate about better expressing the Slanghoek Valley terroir. We think that the first Heritage wine launched is a firm indicator that Attie and his team are on the right track.

Heritage range NEW

★★★★★ **Carl Everson Chenin Blanc** 🍷 Fine regional expression from 33 year old home vineyard, naturally vinified **12** is the debut wine in Opstal's Heritage range. And what a debut! Complex layers of white & green fruit, honey - loads of flavour, the dry end belying the rich palate. Only older oak used on this serious offering.

Opstal Estate range

★★★★ **Hanepoot** 🍷 Great typicity of raisin, spice & fragrant lift, following to sundrenched viscosity. **12** partly barrel-aged fortified dessert has wonderful cleansing acidity to balance the sweet richness.
Cabernet Sauvignon ⓘ 🍴 🍷 ★★★★ Taut, structured **11** has fresh lift to bright cherry. Red-fruited with light juicy appeal & dry firm end. **Syrah-Viognier Blush** 🍴 🍷 ★★★ Strawberry & musk on co-fermented **13** lead to bright juicy palate, barely pink in hue & just off-dry. **Sauvignon Blanc** 🍴 🍷 ★★★ White fruit & blossoms invite on **13**, adds a touch of oak gravitas on end. **The Mill Iron** 🍴 🍷 ★★ Potpourri-scented **13**, fresh off-dry sipper from viognier, muscat d'Alexandrie & colombard. **Sauvignon Blanc Sparkling Sec** 🍷

★★★ Fresh & fruity celebratory off-dry sparkler. **NV** from sauvignon. **Chardonnay Barrel Dessert** ⊕ 🖫
★★★★ Fruity green fig intro to charming **11** fortified dessert, oak in judicious support of viscous freshness.

Sixpence range

Cabernet Sauvignon-Merlot ☺ 🖬 🖫 ★★★ Breezy, red-fruited sipper from cab, merlot & splash pinotage. **12** ends just-dry. Breedekloof WO, like next. **Sauvignon Blanc-Semillon** ☺ 🖬 🖫 ★★★ Like sibling, offers oodles of value. **13** from 16 year old semillon, offering hay & dry grassy foil to tropical zest of sauvignon. — JP

■ **Oracle** see Distell

Orangerie Wines

Location: Malmesbury ▪ Map: Swartland ▪ Est 1707 ▪ 1stB 2009 ▪ Tasting, sales & cellar tours by appt only ▪ Paardeberg Conservation Area ▪ Owner(s)/viticulturist(s) Loffie & Pieter Euvrard ▪ Winemaker(s) Pieter Euvrard (2009) ▪ 200ha/70ha (cab, malbec, merlot, mourv, ptage, shiraz, chard, chenin, rouss, sauv, verdelho, viog) ▪ 15t/ 600cs own label 60% red 40% white ▪ PO Box 92 Malmesbury 7299 ▪ orangeriewines@yahoo.com ▪ www. orangeriewines.co.za ▪ S 33° 32' 20.8" E 018° 49' 55.6" ▪ **T +27 (0)22-482-2169** ▪ F +27 (0)22-487-3046

As well as supplying grapes to others from this venerable Perdeberg farm, Pieter Euvrard makes some wines in his own tiny cellar that meet the 'natural wine' standards of the Swartland Independent organisation. There have been new plantings of scarce varieties - for himself and others, and more will follow.

Orange River Wine Cellars

Location: Upington ▪ Map: Northern Cape, Free State & North West ▪ WO: Northern Cape/Koekenaap ▪ Est 1965 ▪ 1stB 1968 ▪ Tasting & sales Mon–Fri 8–4.30 Sat 8.30–12 ▪ Fee R10/5 wines ▪ Closed all pub hols ▪ Cellar tours Mon– Fri 9, 11 & 3 (Jan-Mar) ▪ Owner(s) ±890 shareholders ▪ Cellarmaster(s) Gert Visser ▪ Cellar managers Bolla Louw (Kakamas), Johan Dippenaar (Keimoes), Johan Esterhuizen (Upington), Jim de Kock (Grootdrink), Riaan Liebenberg (Groblershoop), with winemakers (in same cellar order) George Kruger/Heinrich Coetzee/Andre Smit; Rianco van Rooyen/Mariken Jordaan; Jopie Faul/Cobus Viviers/Philane Gumede; Rudi de Wet/Tinus Kotze; Marco Pentz ▪ Viticulturist(s) Henning Burger (viticultural services manager), with (in same cellar order) Stoney Steenkamp, Chris Kalp, Dirk Sutherland, Ockert Vermeulen ▪ 4,200ha (ptage, ruby cab, shiraz, chard, chenin, cbard, Muscat varieties) ▪ 141,000t/20m L own label 20% red 40% white 20% rosé 20% other + 30m L for clients/bulk ▪ Other export labels: Island View, Gilysipao, Star Tree ▪ Ranges for customers: Country Cellars & Carnival (Spar); Seasons Collection (Liquor City) ▪ ISO 9001:2008 & 2011, PAS 22000:2010, FSSC 20000, PAS 220:2008, BRC, IPW, HACCP, WIETA ▪ PO Box 544 Upington 8800 ▪ info@orangeriverwines.com ▪ www.orangeriverwines.com ▪ S 28° 26' 33.0" E 021° 12' 30.6" ▪ **T +27 (0)54-337-8800** ▪ F +27 (0)54-332-4408

Winning top honours as South Africa's overall Best Value winery in 2012 was the crowning glory for this operation which stretches for 400km along the banks of the mighty Orange River in the Northern Cape. Leaving large shoes to fill, industry stalwart Matthee van Schalkwyk bade this huge five-cellar winery farewell after 45 years. His pride in having been part of its growth from humble beginnings to 140,000 ton annual production with wineries at Grootdrink, Groblershoop, Keimoes, Kakamas and the HQ in Upington was tangible. Markets now include Asia and the United States, while sales into Africa continue to grow apace - not that anything else is hurried in this land of long red Kalahari dunes.

Reserve range

★★★★ **Straw Wine** Air-dried & barrel-fermented dessert, delicious debut **10** from colombard followed by **12** (★★★) ex chenin, all pineapple & peach sunripe sweetness & charm, though acid a bit disjointed this time.
Lyra ★★★★ The juicy mix of petit verdot, merlot & cab on **10** raises the bar. Good grip & depth to fruitcake flavour. **Chenin Blanc de Barrique** Next awaited.

Orange River Wine Cellars range

★★★★ **Red Muscadel** ✓ 🖬 🖫 Tawny hue seduces, along with grapey, floral scent & raisined flavour on **12** - as did **11**. Harmonious fortification & ripe typicity of muscat. Honeyed memory lingers.
★★★★ **White Muscadel** 🖬 🖫 **12** (★★★) butterscotch & praline bounty joined by rich sweetness. Seamless fortification yet not as lingering as **11**, with rich aftertaste.

Rosé ☺ 🍴 ★★☆ Tangy liquid Turkish Delight appeal to lightish, off-dry **13** quaffer. **Chenin Blanc** ☺ 🍴 ★★☆ **13** a light but crisp melon & mandarin quaffer. Tangy & fresh. **Colombard** ☺ 🍴 ★★☆ Off-dry simplicity to melon-fruited **13**. A summer staple. **Sauvignon Blanc** ☺ ★★☆ Vibrant grapefruit zest on **13** from Koekenaap vines. Uncomplicated & crisp. **Sparkling Rosé** ☺ ★★★ Floral perfume & flavour on **13** fizz. Straightforward & lively with fresh raspberry appeal.

Cabernet Sauvignon 🔲 ★★★ Good pepper edge to gentle, tasty fruitcake spice on **12**. Fresh & light but structured. Appealing length of flavour. **Pinotage** ★★★ Vibrant raspberry appeal to ripe **12**. Tangy & succulent if a little short on the finish. Enjoy young. **Ruby Cabernet** ★★★ **12** shows fynbos nuance to ripe black fruit & liquorice flavours. Light coffee sheen too. Juicy & easy-drinking. **Shiraz** ★★★ **12**'s friendly blueberry & plum spice softness & keeps up trend of previous. Structured appeal. Nice quaffer. **Chardonnay** ★★★ Vanilla oak veneer lightly coats peach & orange fruit on **12**. Light body & depth. Pleasant creamy texture. **Sparkling Brut** ★★★ Lemon sherbet crunch to **13** sparkler from chenin. Clean dry finish. **Sparkling Doux** NEW ★★☆ Fruity muscat simplicity on **13** white bubbles. Light, fresh & clean. **Nouveau Blanc Natural Sweet** NEW 🍴 ★★ Lime tang to fresh apple crispness of light-bodied **13** debutant. **Soet Hanepoot** 🍴 ★★★☆ Typical rich barley sugar muscat sweetness on **NV** offering. Lingering aftertaste with clean, dry-seeming finish. **Red Jerepigo** ★★★ Spicy fire & fynbos sheen on **NV** sweet fortified. Abundant cherry & prune flavour but spirit is noticeable. **White Jerepigo** 🍴 ★★★☆ **NV** up a notch on previous. Sweet yet uncloying glucosal grape flavour. Balanced & long. **Cape Ruby** NEW 🍴 ★★★ Fruitcake & plum spice on sweet port-style **12**. Mild-mannered & gentle, with light body & length. Discontinued: **Shiraz-Cabernet Sauvignon**. — FM

■ **Oranjeland** *see* Zidela Wines
■ **Oranjerivier Wynkelders** *see* Orange River Wine Cellars

Org de Rac

Location: Piketberg ▪ Map/WO: Swartland ▪ Est 2001 ▪ 1stB 2005 ▪ Tasting, sales & tours Mon-Fri 9–5 Sat 9–1 ▪ Closed Good Fri, Dec 25 & Jan 1 ▪ Meals/refreshments/cheese platters by prior arrangement; or BYO picnic ▪ Tour groups ▪ Weddings/functions/conferences ▪ Walks/hikes ▪ Mountain biking ▪ Conservation area ▪ Game viewing ▪ Owner(s) Nico Bacon ▪ Winemaker(s) Gilmar Boshoff (Jan 2011) ▪ Viticulturist(s) Wesley du Plessis (Jun 2010) ▪ 50ha (cab, grenache, merlot, mourv, shiraz, chard, chenin, rouss, verdelho) ▪ 400t/50,000cs own label 85% red 10% white 5% rosé ▪ Other export brand: Abbotsville ▪ Brands for clients: Imbuko Wines ▪ SGS (Organic) ▪ PO Box 268 Piketberg 7320 ▪ wine@orgderac.co.za ▪ www.orgderac.co.za ▪ S 32° 57' 44.3" E 018° 44' 57.4" ▪ **T +27 (0)22-913-2397/3924** ▪ F +27 (0)22-913-3923

An abiding conviction in better health – for people, soils, plants, the birds and bees and the Jungian inter-connectedness of it all – informs everything at Piketberg's Org de Rac. The soils were vine virgins when planted in 2001. Now the self-styled 'green heartbeat' of the Swartland has lavender, rosemary, olives – with oil from all – as organic and natural as the wine.

Reserve range

★★★★ **Cabernet Sauvignon** ✓ 🌿🔲 Opulent blackcurrant fruit dominates spicy oak in **11**, wrapped in assertive tannin cloak. Should soften & integrate with time. Previewed last edition, now bottled, as next two.
★★★★ **Shiraz** ✓ 🌿🔲 Generously fruit driven, with faint smoky meat notes, **11** is plump & ripe, with soft texture & lingering finish. Time in bottle shows in improved integration & suppleness.
Merlot 🌿🔲 ★★★☆ **11** fulfils last year's promise with soft tannins, juicy berry fruit & pleasant savoury notes. Gently assertive & elegant.

Org de Rac range

★★★★ **Merlot** 🌿🔲 **11** (★★★) mint & savoury notes over plummy fruit, not as complex as **10**. Previewed last edition, now bottled, as Cab & Shiraz.
★★★★ **La Verne Méthode Cap Classique** NEW 🌿🔲 Commendable all-chardonnay sparkling, showing rich, leesy brioche with baked apple fruit. **11** lively mousse, refreshing acidity & lingering creamy finish.
Cabernet Sauvignon 🌿🔲 ★★★ **11** offers dusty, leafy berry fruit on lean body. **Shiraz** 🌿🔲 ★★★ Honest, juicy & undemanding, **11** lightish body & well-defined fruitiness with spicy oak. **Merlot Rosé** 🍷 🍴🌿 ★★ Lightish dry **12** perky picnic pink with cranberry charm. **Lightly Wooded Chardonnay** 🌿🔲 ★★★ Was 'Wooded Chardonnay'. Overt toasty oak masks fruit on **13**, belying new name. **Unwooded Chardonnay** NEW 🍴🌿🔲 ★★★ Appealingly bright, cheerful **13** plays down fruit, but offers refreshing lime-mineral notes.

Green Shebeen range
Cabernet Sauvignon ⑭ ❀ ★★ Easy-drinking **11**, ex-cask offers mix of black berries & spice. **The Blend** ⑭ ❀ ★★★ NV amiable cab/merlot packed with juicy fruit & easy tannins. **Rosé** ⑭ ▤ ❀ ★ Fetching pink **12** from undisclosed varieties, dry faintly berried flavour. **Chardonnay** ⑭ ▤ ❀ ★ **12** unoaked poolside dry white. Discontinued: **Merlot.** — GdB

Origin Wine

Location/map: Stellenbosch ▪ Est/1stB 2002 ▪ Tasting strictly by appt ▪ Owner(s) Bernard Fontannaz ▪ Cellarmaster(s) Hermias Hugo (2011) ▪ Winemaker(s) Seugnét Rossouw (2007), with Siphiso Mbele & Terence Capes ▪ 10m cs ▪ 50% red 40% white 10% rosé ▪ BRC, DLG, Fairtrade, HACCP, IFS, WIETA ▪ PO Box 7177 Stellenbosch 7599 ▪ info@originwine.co.za ▪ www.originwine.co.za, www.fairhills.co.za, www.stormhoek. co.za, www.streetart.co.za ▪ S 33° 52' 39.07" E 018° 48' 35.50" ▪ **T +27 (0)861-ORIGIN/+27 (0)21-865-8100** ▪ F +27 (0)21-865-2348

Headquartered on Stellenbosch's Bottelary Road, this largely export winery continues to uplift - staff and quality alike. Among its array of labels catering to a variety of local and international markets, the Fairhills range remains one of the world's largest Fairtrade brands. Upskilling employees, and improving their living and working conditions remain core focuses under CEO Bernard Fontannaz, a believer in moving forward and pushing the boundaries of possibility.

Ormonde Private Cellar

Location: Darling ▪ Map: Durbanville, Philadelphia & Darling ▪ WO: Darling/Coastal ▪ 1stB 1999 ▪ Tasting & sales Mon-Fri 9-4 Sat & pub hols 9-3 ▪ Closed Good Fri, Dec 25/26 & Jan 1 ▪ Vineyard tours by appt ▪ Chocolate & wine tasting R50pp by appt ▪ Cheese & wine tasting R55pp by appt - tasting fee applies to Ormonde range only ▪ Picnic baskets by appt or BYO ▪ Facilities for children ▪ Walks ▪ Owner(s) Basson family ▪ Winemaker(s) Michiel du Toit ▪ Viticulturist(s) Theo Basson ▪ ±300ha (cabs s/f, merlot, mourv, p verdot, pinot, shiraz, chard, chenin, sauv, sem) ▪ 1,000t/70,000cs own label 40% red 60% white ▪ BWI ▪ PO Box 201 Darling 7345 ▪ info@ormonde.co.za ▪ www. ormonde.co.za ▪ S 33° 22' 20.2" E 018° 21' 23.6" ▪ **T +27 (0)22-492-3540** ▪ F +27 (0)22-492-3470

Not resting on its laurels as a pioneer here - current MD Theo Basson's father Nico established Darling as a quality wine area in the 1970s - there have been wine additions to the Ormonde and Ondine ranges, as well as a new range launch, Alexanderfontein Chip Off The Old Block, incorporating vineyard selections. The line-up now includes four lines, offering varieties and blends at different price points, all aimed at over-delivering on value. Patriarch Nico would approve.

Ormonde range
★★★★☆ **Vernon Basson** ⑭ Last tasted **07** (★★★★) blend, cab franc's leafiness accentuated by lighter vintage, cab ensuring class & balance. Follows richer debut **06**, with dash merlot.
★★★★ **Shiraz** NEW With layered black plums & cocoa meatiness throughout, barrel-selection **09**'s oak foundation adds a serious note to the plush palate, assures future development.
★★★★ **Chardonnay** ⑭ Lime & oatmeal are **09**'s primary flavours but there are many nuances, including orange peel, honey. Elegant, complex but unshowy, still in the prime of youth.
★★★★ **Sauvignon Blanc** NEW ⊘ Standout in the cellar's sauvignon line-up, **12**'s 'oystershell' minerality, lemongrass finish & overall sleek refinement are the product of rigorous vineyard selection.
Cabernet Sauvignon NEW ★★★★ Broad spectrum of perfumes, flavours in youthful **08**: berry richness, fynbos whiffs & supple tannins. All-new oak. **Pinot Noir** NEW ⊘ ★★★★ More serious than its sibling, barrel-selected **10**'s meaty tones add depth to the red fruit, extend the savoury finish. **Theodore Eksteen** ⑭ ★★★★ Nothing shy about **08** shiraz & grenache blend; ripe (15.5% alcohol), fruit driven, spice rich, especially aniseed, & all-new oak. Discontinued: **Proprietor's Blend**.

Ondine range

> **Pinot Noir** NEW ☺ ⊘ ★★★ **10**'s juicy red berries elegantly packaged with enough gentle oak to add a bit of grip, creating an appealing mouthful.

Cabernet Franc ✓ ★★★★ **09** improves on **08** (★★★★) with its blackcurrant & violet perfume drawing you in to a juicy, silk-textured palate, masterly oak balance, great length. **Malbec** NEW ⊘ ★★★ Sappy wild berries, whiffs of underbrush, **10** is a slender but true rendition of the variety. **Merlot** ⑭ ★★★ Last-reviewed **08**

was dusty & lean, showed hints of strawberry & prunes. Somewhat sharp & dry. **Chardonnay** ☑ ★★★☆ Mellow citrus gently perfumed with biscuity oak, becoming more focused as **11**'s crisp acidity enlivens the palate. **Chenin Blanc** ⊕ ☑ ★★★ Melon & white peach in attractive **10**, perked up by brisk acidity. Good food match. **Sauvignon Blanc** ☑ ★★★☆ Minerality interwoven with fig leaf, lemongrass, there's purity & focus in **11**; intensity backed by taut acidity. Ageworthy. **Semillon** ⊕ ☑ ★★★☆ Freshness is the key in **10**, grassy, quite sauvignon like, with fine acidity. Discontinued: **Cabernet Sauvignon**, **Shiraz**.

Alexanderfontein range

> **Cabernet Sauvignon** ☺ ▤ ☑ ★★★ Freshness is the keynote in **12**, just-picked blackcurrants & plums, a vibrant juiciness. Coastal WO, as all these unless noted.

Merlot ▤ ☑ ★★★ Smoky plums, some underlying chocolate notes & a nice grip make **11** a good food companion. **Shiraz** ▤ ☑ ★★★ Mulberries & black plums, no shortage of fruit in **10**, also shows in palate succulence. Nice dry finish from oak. WO Darling. **Chardonnay** ⊕ ▤ ☑ ★★☆ Light-textured peach styling in unwooded **12**, perked by fresh finish. **Chenin Blanc** ⊕ ▤ ★★★ Perfumed with green apples, hint of passionfruit, **12**'s crispness makes it a good food wine. **Sauvignon Blanc** ✓ ▤ ☑ ★★★☆ Appealing combo fynbos & litchi in sleekly powerful **13**. Twist of lime on the tangy finish, intense & long.

Alexanderfontein Chip Off The Old Block range NEW

> **Cabernet Sauvignon** ☺ ★★★ Plum & chocolate richness in **09**, counterbalanced by a succulent freshness which livens the palate.

Merlot ✓ ☑ ★★★☆ Molten black plums & dark chocolate throughout, smoothly curvaceous **10** has heaps of appetite appeal. **Shiraz** ✓ ★★★☆ Glossy dark plums & sweet spice, whiffs of dried herbs, **09** completes the seduction with its smoothly rounded texture. **Sauvignon Blanc** ✓ ☑ ★★★☆ With citrus & gooseberry freshness, **13**'s zesty elegance focuses the flavours, would make a perfect seafood companion. — CR

Osbloed Wines

Location: Somerset West ▪ Map: Helderberg ▪ WO: Coastal/Durbanville/Stellenbosch/Elgin ▪ Est 2009 ▪ 1stB 2010 ▪ Tasting, sales & cellar tours daily - please call ahead ▪ Tasting fee R20, waived on purchase ▪ Owner(s) Bertus van Niekerk & Selma Albasini ▪ Cellarmaster(s) Bertus van Niekerk (Jan 2010) ▪ Winemaker(s) Bertus van Niekerk (Jan 2010), with Selma Albasini (2010) & Hendrik van Niekerk (2011) ▪ 600cs own label 75% red 25% white ▪ 33 Eagle Crescent Somerset West 7130 ▪ bertus@osbloed.com ▪ www.osbloed.com ▪ S 34° 5′ 26. 22″ E 018° 51′ 55.87″ ▪ **T +27 (0)83-400-2999**

Former clergyman and self-proclaimed 'lovable anarchist' Bertus van Niekerk ranges far and wide for his garagiste wines. No longer making a single barrel, this year he'll be in leased cellar space with 20! Unconventional as ever, he parlays his love for cinsaut into more than one wine, including a blend with pinot noir and pinotage in a mother, (father) and child reunion.

Icon range NEW

★★★★ **Wonderbare Raadsman** Intriguing, rewarding blend of pinotage & parents cinsaut & pinot noir. **12** advent noted for ethereal delicacy: forest fruit & smoke tendrils vie with sinewy depths & leashed power.

Farm Animals range

Osbloed ▤ ★★★★ Textured five-way Bordeaux/shiraz blend from Philadelphia grapes. **12** ups game on **10** (★★★★). Serious & brooding, dark fynbos-tinged tobacco & hedgerow fruit. Rich & ripe yet restrained. **Hanekam** NEW ▤ ☑ ★★★☆ Equal cinsaut & grenache. Light grip & cocoa brush to bright cranberry vibrancy & succulence, **12** delightful lingering fruited tail. **Blommetjie** NEW ▤ ★★★★ Rich yet soft peach spice on **12** chenin, semillon & sauvignon. Sumptuous & broad, chenin portion fermented in acacia barrels.

Horses of the Apocalypse range

Black Horse Cabernet Sauvignon ★★★★ Durbanville fruit sees **12** juicily gentle cassis mouthful ramp up a notch. Firm, structured yet svelte & sexy. **Red Horse Cinsaut Noir** ★★★★ Raspberry cheer & spice on uncomplicated, light-bodied **12**. Swansong of now-uprooted 60 year old Stellenbosch vines. **White Horse Chardonnay** ⊕ ★★★★ Gutsy & big **11** is packed with citrus. Lively & yet also restrained, with not overplayed oak. Good mouthfeel throughout. **Pale Horse Riesling** ★★★★ Highly unusual oxidative oak maturation, giving bruised apple & pear notes on **12** from Elgin. Idiosyncratic yet broad & rich, clean dry finish. — FM

Oude Compagnies Post Private Cellar

Location/map/WO: Tulbagh ▪ Est 1996 ▪ 1stB 2003 ▪ Tasting, sales & cellar tours by appt ▪ Walking trail (flower season Sep-Oct) ▪ Hiking trail 1-2 days (sleepover on Obiqua mountain in own tent) ▪ Mountain bike (difficult) & 15km off-road motorbike trails ▪ Owner(s) Jerry Swanepoel Family Trust ▪ Cellarmaster(s) Jerry Swanepoel ▪ Winemaker(s) Jerry Swanepoel, with Ervin Koen (Jul 2011) ▪ Viticulturist(s) Marius Robert (consultant) ▪ 235ha/18ha (cab, grenache, merlot, mourv, ptage, shiraz) ▪ 70t/10,000cs own label 90% red 10% rosé + 20,000L bulk ▪ Other export brand: Buchu Berg ▪ PO Box 11 Tulbagh 6820 ▪ swanepoel@intekom.co.za ▪ S 33° 14' 56.9" E 019° 6' 49.1" ▪ **T +27 (0)23-230-0840** ▪ F +27 (0)23-230-0840

Like the Tulbagh mountains, boutique vintner Jerry Swanepoel's wines are built to last, with robust tannins and bold (though not alcoholic) flavours in youth. In that sense his line-up is a true reflection of the area, known for hearty reds. His newest release is also arguably the most accessible - a blend originally for a German visitor, now available locally and named, serendipitously, after a mountain.

Compagnies Wijn range

Buchu Berg NEW ☺ ★★★ Personable blend shiraz (70%), mourvèdre. Maiden **NV** bright & engaging with spicy appeal, house's solid tannins.

Cabernet Sauvignon ★★ Variety's signature blackcurrant & leafy/herbaceous notes on burly **12** preview. **Merlot** ★★★ Opaque **10** barrel sample packed with plum fruit, savoury slightly wild notes & firm tannins. Needs a tomato pasta. **Mourvèdre** ⓟ ★★★ **10** cherry cola flavour & hint of spice, amiable get-together-with-friends wine. **Pinotage** ⓟ ★★ **09** plump & juicy with some funky hints. **Pinotage Grand Reserve** ★★★ Pre-bottling **09**'s dark mulberry fruit, concentration & purity diminished by strong tannin; cellar 3+ years or pair with country fare. **Shiraz** ★★★ Previewed **09** characterful if oaky dinner companion. Intriguing cigarbox/Turkish Delight aromas, refreshing (red) fruity flavours, acidity. **Caap Ensemble** ⓟ ★★★ Cape Blend of merlot, cab & dash pinotage; **09** oak still integrating when last tasted. **Cabernet Sauvignon-Merlot** Await next, as for **Ruby Blanc**. **Merlot-Mourvèdre** ⓟ ★★ Equal partnership **08** warm fruit & vanilla charm, for early drinking. — CE,CvZ

Oude Denneboom

Location: Paarl ▪ Map: Paarl & Wellington ▪ WO: Voor Paardeberg ▪ 1stB 2003 ▪ Tasting by appt ▪ 4-star self-catering cottages ▪ Private game reserve ▪ Owner(s) Niel de Waal ▪ Cellarmaster(s)/viticulturist(s) Willem de Waal ▪ 199ha/±55ha (cab, mourv, ptage, shiraz, chenin, nouvelle, viog) ▪ 500t/1,000cs own label 70% red 30% white ▪ Global GAP ▪ PO Box 2087 Windmeul 7630 ▪ info@oudedenneboom.co.za ▪ www.oudedenneboom.co.za ▪ S 33° 37' 47.28" E 018° 51' 55.08" ▪ **T +27 (0)21-869-8072** ▪ F +27 (0)86-552-2695

De Waals have long been established in the Cape winelands, but no doubt Voor Paardeberg's Niel de Waal is the first to have a private game reserve along with vines. The animals to be found on his tranquil estate are more than hinted at in the names of the wines.

Black Harrier Shiraz ⓟ ★★★★ **08** higher flier than **07** (★★★☆). Fleshy plum, blueberry & nutmeg spice on lissome, velvety frame. Succulent & ripe. Like next, tasted a few years back. **Eland** ⓟ ★★★★ Shoulder above maiden **07** (★★★), **08** blend of shiraz, mourvèdre, grenache full of cherry, blackberry & pepper. Velvet texture, superb wood integration. **Grysbok Chenin Blanc** Await next, as for **Steenbok**. — FM

Oude Meester   NEW

Venerable Oude Meester brandy was launched in 1946, heralding the arrival of Distillers Corporation (now Distell) as one of the country's leading wine and spirit producer-wholesalers. Oude Meester VSOB was joined in 2006 by Demant to celebrate the diamond jubilee. Recent additions, offering fans extra-long barrel-aged premium brandies are the Reserve and Souverein.

★★★★☆ **Demant** ✓ Fine value offered with this 5-10 year matured potstill brandy. Stressing a fresh, lighter elegance rather than full richness, like all in this range. Satisfying blend of maturing floral notes along with fruitier youthful ones.

★★★★★ **Souverein** A fairly recent label & amongst the elite of the Cape's older potstill brandies - minimum 18 years in oak. Lightish amber colour to yellow rim. Thrilling floral & spice notes, more delicate than Reserve, even more complex. Not a roughness or jagged edge. Serene, silken, very long.

★★★★☆ **Reserve 12 Year Old** Molten gold colour. Aromas suggest some development - nutty & spicy along with fruit & honeysuckle. Fuller, richer than Demant, as elegant & dry, with restrained oak backing. Complex, lingering, mellow finish.

VSOB ★★★☆ Standard blended brandy, first step of a ladder of quality in this range. Good fruity nose & palate, a little dry oak, some sweet forcefulness. Great for mixing, but not impossible to sip solo. — WB,TJ

Oude Molen Distillery **NEW**

Location: Elgin ▪ Map: Elgin, Walker Bay & Bot River ▪ Tasting, sales & distillery tours Mon-Fri 9-4 Sat/Sun & pub hols by appt ▪ Fee R50pp (incl tour & tasting) ▪ Closed Dec 25 & Jan 1 ▪ Tour groups ▪ Gift shop ▪ Conferences ▪ 4x4 trail ▪ Mountain biking ▪ Brandy master Kobus Gelderblom (Jun 2013, consultant) ▪ PO Box 494 Grabouw 7160 ▪ sc@oudemolen.co.za ▪ www.oudemolen.co.za ▪ S 34° 8' 27.77" E 019° 1' 15.64" ▪ **T +27 (0)21-859-2519** ▪ F +27 (0)21-859-3192

The distillery of French-born René Santhagens, early 20th-century initiator of the Cape's strict Cognac production methods, Oude Molen was originally in Stellenbosch. It's now in Elgin, with a stylish brand-home offering various visitor amenities. The old Big Bertha and Long Tom potstills and award-winning brandies were nurtured since 2006 by master distiller Dave Acker, and since his retirement they've been in the skilled hands of production manager Eddie Beukes, master blender Andy Neill, advised by former KWV chief distiller Kobus Gelderblom.

★★★★☆ **René Single Cask** All potstill, minimum 6 year maturation. Label shows cask & bottle numbers (about 600 bottles in each). More refined than Solera; a touch little less showy on the nose, but loads of fruit & flowers, with hints of prune & caramel. Rich, but some real finesse, & a long, soft finish.

★★★★ **VOV Rare Vintage Selection** 14 years matured pure potstill. Lightish colour, medium rich; shows more oak & more sweetness than others in range. Lovely aromas & flavours: fruit, flowers, nuts, vanilla.

100 Reserve ★★★★ 100 months in oak, that is, after double distillation in potstill. Attractive, even charming, with dried fruit notes & a touch of oak vanilla. Smooth & light, just a little fiery but sippable even without a mixer. **Solera Grand Reserve** ★★★★ 100% potstill matured for consistency in a solera system. Nutty sherry notes, some jasmine fragrance as part of a pleasing complexity. Smooth & subtly persistent. — WB,TJ

■ **Oude Rust** see Mooiuitsig Wine Cellars
■ **Out of Africa** see African Terroir

Overgaauw Wine Estate

Location/map: Stellenbosch ▪ WO: Western Cape/Stellenbosch ▪ Est 1905 ▪ 1stB 1970 ▪ Tasting & sales Mon-Fri 9-5 Sat 10-2 ▪ Closed Easter Fri-Mon, Dec 25/26 & Jan 1 ▪ Owner(s) Braam van Velden ▪ Winemaker(s) David van Velden (Jan 2003) ▪ Viticulturist(s) Braam & David van Velden; Vinpro ▪ 100ha/60ha (cabs s/f, merlot, ptage, touriga, chard, chenin, sauv, sylvaner) ▪ 60% red 40% white ▪ Other export brand: Sandrivier ▪ HACCP, IPW ▪ PO Box 3 Vlottenburg 7604 ▪ info@overgaauw.co.za ▪ www.overgaauw.co.za ▪ S 33° 56' 52.1" E 018° 47' 33.4" ▪ **T +27 (0)21-881-3815** ▪ F +27 (0)21-881-3436

Photograph portraits of four generations of winemaking van Veldens appear on each Overgaauw backlabel (including young David, the current winemaker), testifying to the long history of this family estate in the Stellenboschkloof. More than a century, in fact, although the first own-label wine was in 1970. The family have been amongst the pioneers in many significant areas of Cape wine – including the use of portuguese port varieties, the making of Bordeaux blends and of wines from chardonnay and sylvaner, and the Cape's first varietal merlot bottling (vintage 1982). The latest thing they're proud of is the new crèche at Overgaauw for the children of farm employees in the valley.

Overgaauw Estate range

★★★★ **Cabernet Sauvignon** Ⓥ Ripe, full-flavoured **11** is fragrant & succulent as well as burly. Promising - the big tannins & new-oak influence should greatly benefit from some years in bottle. WO Stellenbosch.

★★★★ **Tria Corda** ⑪ **11** first since classic **09** (★★★★☆). Big, ripe & bold blend cab, merlot & touch cab franc, with attractive fruit aromas & flavours, probably intense enough to cope in time with all the tannic power.

★★★★ **Cape Vintage** ⑫ The oldest current release in the winelands? **93** from sextet port varieties, smooth, warmingly ready with mature polished bouquet & fruity richness.

Merlot 🌿 ★★★ Sweet, light, dark fruit on **11** a little defeated by prominent acidity & tobacco notes from oak. Might perhaps achieve harmony in time. **Touriga Nacional** NEW 🌿 ★★★★ Unpretentious, but tasty & juicy, lightly oaked **12** replaces previous blend with cab. Ripe & friendly, but good grip keeps it from triviality. These mostly WO W Cape. **Chardonnay** 🌿 ★★★★ Pleasant **12**, citrus & tropical aromas & flavour augmented by oak needing year or 2 to harmonise. Rounded & easy - creamy more than vibrant. **Sauvignon Blanc** 🍷 🌿 ★★★★ As usual tasted ex-tank, promising & forcefully fruited **13** neatly blends tropical & green characters. **Sylvaner** ⑫ 🍷 🌿 ★★★ Unusually expressive spicy baked apple aromas, flavours on pre-bottling **12** tasted last year; long, fruitily dry. Discontinued: **Touriga Nacional-Cabernet Sauvignon**.

Shepherd's Cottage range

Cabernet Sauvignon-Merlot 🍷 🌿 ★★☆ Despite some fruit & sugar sweetness, **11** is more lean & bony than generously fleshy. Discontinued: **Chenin Blanc-Chardonnay**. — TJ

Overhex Wines International

Location/map: Worcester ▪ WO: Western Cape ▪ Est/1stB 2006 ▪ Tasting & sales Mon-Thu 8–5 Fri 8-4 Sat/Sun 9-4 ▪ Closed Easter Fri-Tue & Dec 23-Jan 8 ▪ Cellar tours by appt ▪ Bistro Wed-Sun 10-4 ▪ Facilities for children ▪ Tour groups ▪ Conferences ▪ Owner(s) G van der Wath & JC Martin ▪ Cellarmaster(s) Jandre Human (Aug 2009) ▪ Winemaker(s) Willie Malan (2002) & Ben Snyman (Dec 2010), with Dirk Rust (Jan 2012) ▪ Viticulturist(s) Pierre Snyman & Dirk Bosman (both Vinpro) ▪ 9,000t ▪ 45% red 50% white 5% rosé ▪ ISO 22000, Fairtrade, WIETA ▪ PO Box 139 Worcester 6849 ▪ marketing@overhex.com ▪ www.overhex.com ▪ S 33° 39' 28.6" E 019° 30' 55.8" ▪ **T +27 (0)23-347-5012** ▪ F +27 (0)23-347-1057

Owned by Creation Wines' JC Martin and former lawyer Gerhard van der Wath, Overhex's wines are easy on palate and pocket, and its brand home at Worcester welcoming and family friendly. Advocacy of ethical practice sees grapes for the Haven Point range sourced from a Fairtrade-accredited Swartland farm, and priority given to staff empowerment through ongoing education.

Balance Winemaker's Selection

Pinotage ☺ 🍷 🌿 ★★★ Improved **12** has smoky mulberry-blueberry allure, good concentration & pleasing tannic conclusion. You could keep it few years, but we bet you won't! **Chardonnay** ☺ 🍷 🌿 ★★★ Barrel-fermented **13** has immediate vanilla & lemon cream appeal, amicable acidity to pair with butter chicken or crayfish.

Cabernet Sauvignon NEW 🍷 🌿 ★★★ Nutty **12**'s juicy palate wrapped by firm tannins to accompany hearty venison stews. All reds aged year in French oak, portion new for some. **Merlot** 🍷 🌿 ★★★ Well-made, fruity **12**, stewed plums laced with cardamom & sweet oak. For convivial occasions. **Shiraz** 🍷 🌿 ★★ Braai mate **12**, mocha berry flavours & firm tannins. **Chenin Blanc** 🍷 🌿 ★★★ Bright & breezy **13** ticks all the boxes: aromatic, juicy & well priced. **Sauvignon Blanc** 🍷 🌿 ★★★ Greenpepper & pineapple nuances, good length on **13** crowd pleaser. For those who don't like their sauvignons too racy.

Balance Best Blends

Pinotage-Shiraz ☺ 🍷 ★★★ Soft, fruity & cheery, **12** slips down easily. **Sauvignon Blanc-Semillon** ☺ 🍷 🌿 ★★★ Crisp & zingy 80/20 marriage in **13** has sauvignon's ruby grapefruit taste, lovely pithy texture from lees-ageing.

Cabernet Sauvignon-Merlot 🍷 🌿 ★★ **12**'s classic leafy & cassis aromas let down by too-robust tannins. Briefly oak-staved, like all red siblings. **Shiraz-Merlot** 🍷 🌿 ★★ Fruit-forward **12** has smoky bacon whiffs, sour cherry tastes; ends slightly gruff. **Shiraz Rosé** 🍷 🌿 ★★★ Faint berry & straw notes on lightish, dry **13**. **Semi-Sweet Muscat** 🍷 🌿 ★★★ **13** changes from 'Muscat d'Alexandrie', delivers balanced sweetness, slight hanepoot spice; take to an Indian dinner. **Chenin Blanc-Colombar** 🍷 🌿 ★★☆ Typical colombard guava on **13**, pithy & lively, balanced sweet-sour flavours. Discontinued: **Pinot Gris-Sauvignon Blanc**.

Balance Buddy range

Sweet Rosé 🏠 📷 ★★ Pinotage & chenin tango in **NV** simple, juicy party pink. **Sweet White** 🏠 📷 ★★★ These all drop 'Natural' from name. Passionfruit-infused **NV** drier-tasting than advertised - not necessarily a bad thing. From chenin & hanepoot. Low alcohol, as for all these. **Sweet Red** 🏠 📷 ★★★ Thatch & freshly baked bread notes, gently sweet **NV** from ruby cab, cinsaut.

Balance Sparklings

Sweet Temptation Sparkling Selling but not tasted, like **Boldly Brut Sparkling** & **Lusciously Fruity Sparkling**.

iSpy range NEW

> **Shiraz** ☺ 🏠 📷 ★★★ Dark chocolate & toasty mocha invitation, plums & cherries, supple tannins on easygoing **12**. Well priced & characterful, as all these. **Cape Blend** ☺ 🏠 📷 ★★★ Friendly 5-way dinner companion **12** has pinotage's (52%) banana overlay, effusive berry palate & nicely firm farewell. **Chenin Blanc** ☺ 🏠 📷 ★★★ Lees-aged **13**, peach & tropical notes, creamy palate for spicy Asian food. **Moscato** ☺ ★★★ **13**'s muscat & rosepetal aromas spiced up with honey to charm & beguile, solo or with food.

Haven Point Fairtrade range

Shiraz 🏠 📷 Available but not tasted by us, as **Viognier-Shiraz** & **Pinot Gris**. — DB, CvZ

Overmeer Cellars

Since 1996, no-frills range by Distell. Modest alcohol levels and 3/5L packs for all.

Selected Red ★ Medium-bodied, slightly herby pizza/pasta wine from pinotage, ruby cab & cinsaut. **NV**. **Rosé** ★ Copper-hued **NV**, straightforward, overtly sweet strawberry flavour. **Premier Grand Cru** ★ Uncomplicated **NV** dry white from chenin, colombard & Cape riesling. **Stein** ★★ Pleasant, undemanding semisweet white, **NV**, juicy & rounded. **Late Harvest** ★★ Fresh, tropical **NV** with balanced sweetness, ends clean. — DB, HJ

■ **Overvaal** *see* Hartswater Wine Cellar

Paardebosch Wines   🍴 🎋 📷

Location: Malmesbury ▪ Map/WO: Swartland ▪ Est/1stB 2011 ▪ Tasting & cellar tours Mon-Sat by appt ▪ Sales Wed & Fri 10-4 ▪ Closed all pub hols ▪ BYO picnic ▪ Walks/hikes ▪ Owner(s) Wiggo Anderson & Des Kruger ▪ Cellarmaster(s)/winemaker(s) Marius Malan (2011, consultant) ▪ Viticulturist(s) Christopher Lawak (2005) ▪ 45/da 22ha (malbec, ptage, chenin, sem) ▪ 25t/2,500cs own label 15% red 85% white + 4,400cs for clients ▪ redlex@ cybersmart.co.za ▪ S 33° 32' 41.41" E 018° 49' 36.14" ▪ **T +27 (0)82-565-4218/+27 (0)23-626-1413**

Co-owner Des Kruger describes the winemaking venture that's been restarted on venerable Paardebosch farm in Siebritskloof after a century's break as 'embryonic and experimental'. Marius Malan, previously of Slaley in Stellenbosch, is the consultant winemaker and he's having a blast getting to know the impact of Swartland terroir. It's not just about wine, however, as the business has a specific ethos: 'We want to be fair and equitable to all those engaged in our venture.'

★★★★ **Phoenix White Blend** 🍐 Impressive fusion semillon (60%), chenin, both barrel fermented. **11** similar nutty oxidative notes to Shani but greater focus, textural qualities.

Malbec NEW ★★ Burly **11** has ultra-ripe dark fruit, some spice but is short of freshness & grip. **Pinotage** NEW ★★★ **11** charmingly rustic, soft & easy. Red fruit plus some earthy, malty notes. **Shani Chenin Blanc** 🍐 🏠 ★★★★ Barrel-fermented **11**'s sweet baked apple, caramel & toffee oxidative bouquet belies its tangy-dry, sherry-like palate. Quirky & individual meal companion. — CE

PaardenKloof   🍷

Location/WO: Bot River ▪ Map: Elgin, Walker Bay & Bot River ▪ Est 2003 ▪ 1stB 2007 ▪ Tasting & tours by appt ▪ Sales Mon-Fri 9-12 ▪ Winemaker(s) Kobie Viljoen (cab/shiraz) & Adam Mason (sauv/pinot) ▪ Vineyard manager Michael Edon ▪ Viticulturist(s) Kevin Watt (Dec 2006) ▪ 23.6ha (cab, pinot, shiraz, sauv) ▪ BWI, IPW ▪ PO Box 381 Bot River 7185 ▪ info@paardenkloof.co.za ▪ www.paardenkloof.co.za ▪ S 34° 17' 44.1" E 019° 14' 5.4" ▪ **T +27 (0)28-284-9824** ▪ F +27 (0)28-284-9419

More than 80% of the 1,430ha of fynbos-rich PaardenKloof ('Valley of the Horses') property near Bot River is actively conserved but ±23ha of vineyard were established from 2004 and now the resulting wines are coming to market. Labels bear renditions of the work of Peter E Clarke, one of South Africa's great artists who found inspiration in Tesselaarsdal, a little village near the farm. A portion of sales go towards a foundation for young artists from underprivileged communities.

Peter Clarke Collection

Die Lang Pad Shiraz NEW ★★★ Black cherry jam & malty aromas, similar very concentrated flavours, obvious 15% alcohol on hearty **08**. Crafted for easy, early sipping with only 20% new oak & hint of sweetness.

Gaiety Sauvignon Blanc 🗒 ★★★ A year in bottle hasn't dimmed **12**'s gunsmoke whiffs, attractive gravelly minerality. From young vines, is lightly flavoured so acidity is apparent. — CvZ

Packwood Wines

Location: Knysna ▪ Map: Klein Karoo & Garden Route ▪ WO: Plettenberg Bay ▪ Est 2006 ▪ 1stB 2009 ▪ Tasting & sales Mon-Fri 11-3 ▪ Closed all pub hols ▪ Cheese & wine lunch - book ahead ▪ Small tour groups by appt ▪ Farm produce ▪ Hikes ▪ Mountain biking trail ▪ 4-star country house & self-catering cottages ▪ Owner(s) Peter & Vicky Gent ▪ Winemaker(s) Teddy Hall (Mar 2009, consultant) ▪ Viticulturist(s) Vicky Gent (Jan 2006) ▪ 380ha/3.5ha (pinot, chard, sauv) ▪ 5t/10,000cs own label 30% red 70% white ▪ PO Box 622 Knysna 6570 ▪ vicky@packwood.co.za ▪ www.packwood.co.za ▪ S 34° 0' 18.77" E 023° 13' 43.33" ▪ **T +27 (0)44-532-7614**

Packwood, on the periphery of Knysna Forest, is a country estate owned by Peter and Vicky Gent originally from England, complete with luxury accommodation, dairy herd and small vineyard. 'Best harvest yet,' says Vicky of last year. 'Finally we get to make a still pinot noir and chardonnay.'

★★★★ **Sauvignon Blanc** 🗒 Compelling **12** is rich & full (despite only ±12% alcohol), with green melon & papaya before some paprika bite on the finish. Full of verve thanks to tangy acidity.

Gent Méthode Cap Classique ⓧ ★★☆ NV rosé sparkling from pinot noir rather rustic, with earthy & spicy notes to go with red fruit. — CE

■ **Paddagang** *see Tulbagh Winery*

Painted Wolf Wines

Location: Paarl ▪ Map: Paarl & Wellington ▪ WO: Coastal/Swartland/Paarl/Stellenbosch ▪ Est/1stB 2007 ▪ Tasting & sales by appt Mon-Sun 10-5 ▪ Fee R25 ▪ Closed Easter Fri-Mon, Dec 25 & Jan 1 ▪ Lunch by appt (parties of 6 or less) ▪ Owner(s) Jeremy & Emma Borg, & 16 'pack members' ▪ Cellarmaster(s) Rolanie Lotz & Johan Gerber (consultants) ▪ Winemaker(s) Jeremy Borg ▪ ±65ha/40ha (grenache, merlot, mourv, ptage, shiraz, chenin, sauv, viog) ▪ 80t/40,000cs own label 75% red 20% white 5% rosé ▪ Other export brand: Jemma ▪ PO Box 1489 Suider Paarl 7624 ▪ sales@paintedwolfwines.com ▪ www.paintedwolfwines.com ▪ S 33° 46' 14.8" E 018° 57' 14.6" ▪ **T +27 (0)21-863-2492**

This Paarl-based, multi-membered enterprise goes from strength to strength. The aim is simple: produce interesting wines of quality, offering value, and in the spirit of suitability and fun. The African wild dog theme that inspires their name is central to the ethos of how grapes are sourced, wines are made and marketing approached. Conservation is extremely important to Jeremy Borg and his team, and this focus on a good cause helps fuels the endeavour - and supports one of the continent's most remarkable wild creatures.

The Black Pack range

★★★★ **Pictus III** 🗒 Was 'Pictus Red'. Flagship blend of Swartland shiraz, mourvèdre & grenache. **11** combines power & charm in rich-fruited & polished style. New oak (70%) is evident, but seductive.

Merlot Await next, like **Shiraz**. **Stellenbosch Pinotage** ✓ 🗒 ★★★★ Lovely nose, showing fresh banana loaf, brooding fruit; seriously oaked **11** has better balance & composure of fruit & oak than **10** (★★★★). **The Chase** NEW 🗒 ★★★★ Previewed **12** merlot-led blend with 25% cab. A harmonious combo, with restrained fruit but oaky cloak still evident. Fine tannins bode well for future evolution. Genuinely dry end.

Chenin Blanc 🗒 ★★★★ Drops 'Wild Yeast Fermented' from name. Soft creamy allure on **12** leads to broad, well structured follow-through, with balanced spice & oak support. Sweetish send-off (technically dry).

Roussanne ✓ 🖫 ★★★★ **12** shy peach, dried apricot & lovely composure - floral but also nutty, following to distinct wet stone & pith, yet juicy & rich. Better than **11** (★★★★). Older large oak well integrated. WO Paarl.

The Pack range

★★★★ **Guillermo Swartland Pinotage** 🖫 🖫 Intense aromas of red sweets, some coconut & wood. **11** has fragrant abundance, fruity entry, plush & composed, juicy & warm. With dollops shiraz & grenache.

Rosalind Paarl Pinotage Rosé ☺ 🖫 🖫 ★★★ Onionskin-hued **13** has delicate dried strawberry/ spice combo, with dry, crisp & savoury length.

Penny Swartland Viognier 🖫 🖫 ★★★★ **13** tasted ex-barrel has clever use of older oak in support of exuberant fruit flavours, with delicate aromas & great textured mouthfeel. More pizazz than **10** (★★★★).

Cape 'Hunting' Blends range

★★★★ **Lekanyane** 🖫 🖫 Lightly oaked, off-dry **12** (★★★☆) from chenin with viognier. Ripe stonefruit, intense & almost syrupy. Exudes bold fragrance, but lacks balancing acid of **11**. WO Swartland.

Madach 🖫 🖫 ★★★★ 'Peloton' for export. Plums & ripe berry allure on **11** from mix shiraz, pinotage & other varieties. Savoury & juicy, showing toasty oak; dry finish.

The Den Comfort Wines range

Cabernet Sauvignon 🖫 🖫 ★★★ Ripe & easy-drinking, lightly oaked **12** charms with milk chocolate, mulberry & red cherry freshness. **Pinotage** 🖫 🖫 ★★★ Red cherry notes, a little shy to start, but fresh; **12** bright, fruity & bouncy on the palate - ending dry, with acid lift. **Chenin Blanc** 🖫 🖫 ★★★★ Previewed **13** has honeysuckle, ripe apples & spice, supported by good balancing acid & gentle oaking adding some grip. **Sauvignon Blanc** 🖫 ★★★★ **13** tasted ex-tank expresses grass, paprika & spicy notes. Fine crisp palate follows with tropical & dusty flavours. — JP

▪ **Palesa** see uniWines Vineyards
▪ **Pantére** see Knorhoek Wines
▪ **Papillon** see Van Loveren Family Vineyards

Paradisum

NEW

Peter-Allan Finlayson of Crystallum (see entry) first thought of this as a Swartland project, but grenache from his Hemel-en-Aarde home base (where he makes the wine) joins the blend from the 2012 vintage. Always keen to try new projects, Peter-Allan wanted, he says 'to work with Swartland fruit and also try out some different techniques – like whole-bunch fermentation, some of it in small barrels'.

★★★★ **Paradisum** Gently perfumed, complex aromas on **11** from shiraz, 20% mourvèdre; palate a touch less charming - rather elegant, yes, with fresh acidity, subtle oak & restrained, firm grip, but less generosity. — TJ

▪ **Paradyskloof** see Vriesenhof Vineyards
▪ **Parker Family** see Altydgedacht Estate
▪ **Parlotones** see Woolworths

Passages Wine

WO: Stellenbosch/Coastal ▪ 1stB 2006 ▪ Closed to public ▪ Owner(s) Ronald T Gault & Charlayne Hunter-Gault ▪ Cellarmaster(s)/winemaker(s) Ernst Gouws (2007, consultant) ▪ (cab, merlot, ptage, chard) ▪ ±10,000cs own label 70% red 30% white ▪ gaultronald@gmail.com ▪ www.passageswine.com

Former banker Ron Gault and journalist wife Charlayne Hunter-Gault arrived in South Africa at the birth of the democratic era, and put down permanent roots. Commenting on this edition's 'Rainbow Wine Nation' theme, they say: 'We have drunk from the waters and wines of the world, settling in South Africa, where its people have enhanced our taste for all things good. Each of our wines highlights the uniqueness of our South African experience with friends, food and drink. Our Passages wine speaks to our embrace of new beginnings - people, places and things - and our desire to share the joy of our ongoing journey to the horizon.'

Merlot ⊕ 🖫 ★★★★ Cocoa & mulberry appeal on **11**, displaying length, depth & breadth. Light chalk texture & mouthfeel add interest. **Pinotage** ★★★☆ **12** as friendly as **11**: instant mocha blueberry attraction, juicy & fresh, light body & medium length. Coastal WO. **Cabernet Sauvignon-Merlot** ⊕ ★★★ Black

cherry succulence vies with cocoa depth, **09** medium body & length, light tannic grip. **Chardonnay** ⏱ 🍷
★★★☆ Rich creamy peach & citrus wrapped in light oak, **11** soft & approachable yet juicy & fresh. — FM

Paul Cluver Estate Wines

Location/WO: Elgin • Map: Elgin, Walker Bay & Bot River • Est 1896 • 1stB 1997 • Tasting & sales Mon-Fri 9–4
Sat 9–2 • Fee R50 for groups - limited to 10 pax per group • Closed Easter weekend, Dec 25/26 & Jan 1 • Conservation area (part of Kogelberg Biosphere UNESCO heritage site) • Mountain biking track open to public, fee
payable • Open air amphitheatre hosting concerts Dec-Mar • Owner(s) Cluver family • Cellarmaster(s)/
winemaker(s) Andries Burger (Nov 1996) • Viticulturist(s) Craig Harris (Jan 2010) & Kevin Watt (Mar 2005,
consultant) • 2,400ha/90ha (pinot, chard, gewürz, riesling, sauv) • 300t/40,000cs own label 20% red 80%
white • Brands for clients: Woolworths, ScruCap • BWI Champion • PO Box 48 Grabouw 7160 • info@cluver.
com • www.cluver.com • S 34° 10' 6.2" E 019° 5' 8.1" • **T** +27 (0)21-844-0605 • F +27 (0)21-844-0150

The Cluver family farm, De Rust, dating back to 1896, is situated within the
Kogelberg Biosphere in Elgin Valley, one of South Africa's cooler wine districts.
Visionary Paul Cluver snr pioneered commercial winefarming here in the late
1980s and became a leader in environmental and social sustainability, initiating
the Thandi project, one of the first black economic empowerment ventures.
'This is my home,' he notes, ' I have no other. I am passionately committed to
making this land work for the benefit of all of us.' The younger generation, who
subscribe to the same principles, took over in 2003 (four of the five siblings are
involved here) and continue to build the reputation of the thriving and diverse
business (eco-tourism and amphitheatre concerts included). Son-in-law and
winemaker Andries Burger now collaborates with Burgundian guru Martin
Prieur to fine-tune their acclaimed chardonnay and pinot noir.

Paul Cluver Estate Wines range

★★★★ **Close Encounter Riesling** ✓ 🍴 ▤ 🖺 **12** sweeter of the rieslings (34.7 g/l sugar) retains classic
tangy balance notwithstanding rich passionfruit flavours. Appealing low 8% alcohol & lingering clean farewell.

★★★★ **Sauvignon Blanc** ✓ 🍴 ▤ 🖺 **12** is light footed yet intense, fresh & vibrant. Stonefruit & minerality
focused by acidity, with a splash of oaked semillon & lees to enrich the mid-palate.

★★★★☆ **Riesling Noble Late Harvest** 🖺 Slimline elegant packaging & appealingly low 9% alcohol
belie the riveting freshness & intensity of dried apricot, lime & botrytis flavours on scintillating **12** icon dessert
wine, partly wooded. **11** (★★★★★) was last edition's White Wine of the Year.

CWG Auction Reserves

★★★★☆ **Pinot Noir** 🖺 Much more understated than exuberant **10**, **11** (★★★★) has a core of tightly buttoned perfumed fruit from cool, high-lying vineyards. A fine tannin structure, with bright acidity & touch of
minerality reflect inherent pedigree. Restrained & elegant, one for the cellar.

★★★★☆ **Wagon Trail Chardonnay** 🖺 Older vineyards reward with fine-tuned balance of fruit intensity,
purity & freshness. Deft oaking adds hazelnut & brioche richness to limy tone. **12** youthful & elegant, with
potential to develop for good few years. No **11**.

Paul Cluver range

★★★★ **Pinot Noir** ▤ 🖺 **11** (★★★☆) less fruit intensity & radiance than **10**. Still refined & smooth textured, with earthy, savoury nuance.

★★★★☆ **Seven Flags Pinot Noir** 🖺 Polished **11** (★★★★) makes a confident statement, but is less
intense than **09** & **10**. Barrel selection & judicious 25% new oak highlight single clone's savoury red fruit, from
farm's best vineyard. Appealing balance in youth, but will develop & reward cellaring.

★★★★ **Chardonnay** ▤ 🖺 **12** has a clean-cut steeliness with zesty acidity streamlining cool citrus tone.
Less new oak than previous & only partial malo (20%). Restrained & food-styled wine, deserves time.

★★★★ **Gewürztraminer** ✓ ▤ 🖺 Vivacious **12** is fresh, light & fragrant. Delicate rosepetal & spice flavours focused by crisp acidity. Semi-dry & quite delicious!

★★★★ **Dry Encounter Riesling** ✓ ▤ 🖺 **12** renamed from just 'Riesling' for lower sugar (8.6 g/l) being
drier than Close Encounter, though not lacking sprightly balance. Delicate but penetrating lime, turpene & nutty
impression, with good length. — MW

■ **Paul de Villiers** *see* Landskroon Wines
■ **Paulina's Reserve** *see* Rickety Bridge Winery

Paul Wallace Wines

Location/WO: Elgin ▪ Map: Elgin, Walker Bay & Bot River ▪ Est/1stB 2004 ▪ Tasting by appt from Jan 2014 ▪ Owner(s)/viticulturist(s) Paul Wallace ▪ Winemaker(s) Paul Wallace, with Martin Meinert ▪ 25ha/10.5ha (malbec, pinot, sauv) ▪ 80t/1,000cs own label 100% red ▪ BWI, IPW ▪ PO Box 141 Elgin 7180 ▪ wallovale@ mweb.co.za ▪ www.wallovale.co.za ▪ S 34° 12' 58.67" E 19° 03' 32.18 ▪ **T +27 (0)21-848-9744/+27 (0)83-255-1884/+27 (0)82-572-1406** ▪ F +27 (0)86-646-3694

'Dark in colour, well muscled, intense and full of character.' Thus Elgin-based Paul Wallace sums up both his wine and Jake, his canine shadow after whom it's named. Viticulturist Paul knew of a malbec vineyard with a fine crop that wasn't going to be harvested. Believing the variety underrated, he 'gave it a bash'.

★★★★ **Black Dog Malbec** ⓟ Dark-hued **09** more closed, concentrated than **08**. Has all basics in place; ripe, mineral-laced black cherry fruit, rich texture, freshness & French oak for great future. — AL

▪ **Pax Verbatim Vineyards** *see* Hilton Vineyards
▪ **Peacock Ridge** *see* False Bay Vineyards
▪ **Pearlstone** *see* Rhebokskloof Wine Estate

Pearly Bay

Named for a pearly white beach on the Southern Cape coast, this KWV range is unpretentious, modestly priced and styled to encourage novices to enjoy wine.

Dry Red 🗄 ★★ Ripe & fruity **NV**, smoothly accessible. **Sweet Rosé** 🗄 ★★ Pale pink **NV** has sweet cherry-toned appeal. **Rosé** ⓟ 🗄 🗷 ★★ Attractive wild strawberries & cream flavours; **NV** semi-sweet & quaffable. **Sweet White** 🗄 ★★ Apple & litchi flavoured **NV** offers easy drinking. **Dry White** 🗄 🗷 ★★ Pear drops with a tang, in light-textured off-dry **NV**. **Celebration Sparkling Rosé 8%** ★★ Gently fruity **NV** party fare fizz. Low alcohol & sweet, as next. **Celebration White 8%** ★★ Tangy-fresh grapey aromatic **NV** sparkler. — CR

▪ **Pecan Stream** *see* Waterford Estate
▪ **Pegalle** *see* Bonview Wines
▪ **Pella** *see* Super Single Vineyards
▪ **Pepin Condé** *see* Stark-Condé Wines

Perdeberg Winery

Location/WO: Paarl ▪ Map: Paarl & Wellington ▪ Est 1941 ▪ 1stB 1942 ▪ Tasting & sales Mon-Fri 8–5 Sat 9.30–2 ▪ Closed Easter Fri-Mon, Dec 25/26 & Jan 1 ▪ Cellar tours Mon-Fri by appt ▪ Meals, pre-booked week in advance, for groups of 10+ ▪ BYO picnic ▪ Annual October festival ▪ Owner(s) 30 members ▪ Cellarmaster(s) Albertus Louw (Oct 2008) ▪ Winemaker(s) Riaan Möller (Dec 2006) & Carla Herbst (Jun 2008) ▪ Viticulturist(s) Jaco Engelbrecht (Nov 2011) ▪ 6,000ha/2,564ha (cab, cincaut, merlot, ptage, shiraz, chenin, sauv) ▪ 18,000t/300,000cs own label 63% red 37% white ▪ BWI, HACCP, IPW, WIETA ▪ PO Box 214 Paarl 7620 ▪ info@perdeberg.co.za ▪ www.perdeberg.co.za ▪ S 33° 39' 30.00" E 018° 49' 37.00" ▪ **T +27 (0)21-869-8244** ▪ F +27 (0)21-869-8245

Originally one of the ubiquitous large co-ops that dotted the winelands, this unpretentious producer in the recently fashionable Voor Paardeberg region consistently delivers some of the best value in the industry. Although their vast tracts of vineyards cover most major varieties, they remain synonymous with fine chenin. Wines are released under their own two-tiered labels as well as customer, partnership and themed ranges: Waka Waka, David Frost Signature, Bottelary and Saam (see separate entries).

Dryland Collection [NEW]

★★★★ **Cabernet Sauvignon** ✓ Characterful newcomer, seriously conceived. **11** shows fine fruit focus on noble structure. Still taut & nervous, with piercing acid, but should settle in time.

★★★★ **Pinotage** ✓ Stylish, restrained **11** shows variety's gentle side but still presents luscious ripe berry fruit. Spicy & elegant.

★★★★ **Josephs Legacy** ✓ Impressive top-end newcomer, **10** petit verdot with shiraz & cab, matured in 100% new oak, shows class. Inky mineral core with ripe black fruit & supple texture.

★★★★ Shiraz Vanilla-scented **11** generous & harmonious; savoury, meaty notes laced with dried prunes, ripe tannins exerting satisfying grip on middleweight body.

Barrel Fermented Chenin Blanc ✓ ★★★★ Overt oak on **11** still masks sweetly ripe tropical fruit notes. Laudable effort, should mellow with time in bottle.

Reserve range

★★★★ Pinotage From old bushvines. Fruit just one of **10**'s attractions: crushed berry vibrancy supported by balanced oaking.

★★★★ Chenin Blanc ✓ Rich & ripe, with waxy texture, **12** shows impressive fruit concentration through still-dominant oak. Should settle into elegant balance in 1-2 years.

★★★★ Chardonnay-Viognier Heavily wooded **11** (★★★★) 70/30 blend from Agter Paarl vines has ripe fruit struggling to emerge. Needs time to settle. **10** bolder, smoother.

★★★★☆ Weisser Riesling ✓ Impressive Natural Sweet with whopping 176 g/l sugar shows this noble variety to benefit. Piercing acid scythes through layers of honeyed raisin essence. **11** from Paarl grapes (previous ex Durbanville), vinified in seasoned barrels.

Shiraz ★★★☆ Smoky, aromatic **10** offers generous body & structure, but remains supple & approachable. Unpretentious but carefully shaped. **Méthode Cap Classique Brut** Await new vintage. Discontinued: **Cabernet Sauvignon, Sauvignon Blanc**.

Popular range

Cabernet Sauvignon ☺ ★★★ 12 shows convincing inky mineral core with generous black fruit & dash of oak spice. Satisfying everyday drinking. **Pinotage ☺ ★★★** Reined-in wild berries on **12**, with typical spicy aromas. Succulent, fresh & vibrant anytime quaffer. **Shiraz ☺ ★★★** Meaty **12** delivers satisfying body & youthful, well-defined character. Lovely casual drinking. **Chenin Blanc ☺ ★★★** Perennial over-performer delivers again in **13**, with cheerfully ripe fruit, solid body & tingling acid. **Sauvignon Blanc ☺ ★★★** Bright, perky **13** shows satisfying passionfruit on crisp acidity. Pocket friendly yet classy. **Sparkling Chenin Blanc ☺ ★★★** Real chenin fruit appeal on crisp **13** carbonated bubbly.

Merlot ★★★ Forthright **12** offers everyday drinking pleasure without frills. Ripe red berries with a hint of oak spice. **Cabernet Sauvignon-Merlot ★★★ 12** is pleasantly juicy with hints of spice & currants. **Rosé** Await next release. **Sparkling Rosé ★★** Bright & cheerful sweetish chenin-based carbonated NV with low alcohol. **Soft Smooth Red ★★★ 12** shiraz, cinsaut, cab mix with a hint of sweetness. — GdB

▇ Pernod Ricard *see* Long Mountain Wine Company

Peter Bayly Wines

Location/WO: Calitzdorp ▪ Map: Klein Karoo & Garden Route ▪ Est 2002 ▪ 1stB 2004 ▪ Tasting, sales & tours by appt ▪ Owner(s) Peter Bayly Wines (Pty) Ltd ▪ Winemaker(s)/viticulturist(s) Peter Bayly ▪ 6.6ha/1.2ha (tinta, touriga, souzão) ▪ ±8t/±1,320cs own label ▪ PO Box 187 Calitzdorp 6660 ▪ info@baylys.co.za ▪ www.peterbayly.co.za ▪ S 33° 26' 54.62" E 021° 47' 33.92" ▪ **T +27 (0)44-213-3702** ▪ F +27 (0)86-513-2727

In secluded Groenfontein Valley near Calitzdorp, Peter and Yvonne Bayly are fulfilling their dream of 'living free range', handcrafting port-style wines and a country red from Portuguese varieties planted in ancient red soils.

★★★★ Cape Vintage Port-style **09** mostly touriga (45%), roughly equal tinta & souzão. Choc/savoury flavours, balanced fortification & sugar; tad firmer than **07**, inviting cellaring - though hard to resist. No **08**.

III ★★ Rustic red, **11** older-oak-matured touriga with dashes tinta & souzão. **Cape Late Bottled Vintage ★★★** Ripe plum & malty berry compote, **08** chiefly souzão (58%) & tinta, dash touriga. Soft & accessible, as per style. **Cape White ★★** NV port-style from chenin, with sherry-like nutty marzipan tone. Versatile: sip solo or over ice, or mix things up! — GdB,CvZ

Peter Falke Wines

Location/map: Stellenbosch ▪ WO: Stellenbosch/Coastal ▪ 1stB 2003 ▪ Tasting & sales Tue-Sun 11-7 Mon by appt ▪ Fee R40 ▪ Closed Good Fri, Dec 25/26 & Jan 1 ▪ Cellar tours by appt 11-4 ▪ Cheese platters & refreshments ▪ Owner(s) Franz-Peter Falke ▪ Winemaker(s) Rianie Strydom (2012, consultant) ▪ Viticulturist(s) / GM Werner Schrenk (Jan 2009) ▪ 20ha/±6ha (cab, shiraz) ▪ 100t/12,000cs own label 65% red 25% white 10%

rosé ▪ PO Box 12605 Stellenbosch 7613 ▪ info@peterfalkewines.com ▪ www.peterfalkewines.com ▪ S 34° 0' 2.1" E 018° 50' 19.3" ▪ **T +27 (0)21-881-3677** ▪ F +27 (0)21-881-3667

Owned by Germany-based sports-footwear king Franz-Peter Falke, the focus is on terroir-driven wines in Stellenbosch's predominantly red-wine 'Golden Triangle' area. But there is much else to attract visitors, like trendy items for sale plus an ultra-modern tasting room inspired by the five senses.

Signature range

★★★★ **Signature Blend** ⓟ Cab franc dominant, with merlot, cab, **09** (★★★★☆) improves on **08** with its ripeness manifest in molten berries, plums, fruitcake spicing. Delicious drinkability is ensured by a fleshy palate, polished tannins.

Syrah ⓟ ★★★★ Admirable fruit focus in **09** masks the 15.2% alcohol. Tannins are integrated, the wine ready to enjoy, drink now till ±2016.

PF range

Pinot Noir ★★★★ Nice combination raspberries & savoury spice in **12**, with the variety's customary succulent elegance & length. **Ruby Blend** NEW ★★★☆ Cab/shiraz combo **11** shows sumptuous spice-laden plums, supple tannins, a welcoming flavourful palate. **Blanc de Noir** ★★★ Red berry perfume & flavours to the fore in **13**, a merlot/pinotage blend. Light (13% alcohol) & tasty. **Sauvignon Blanc** ✓ ★★★★ With 'drink me' written all over it, **13**'s peardrop & touch of fynbos is underpinned by lipsmacking limy freshness. Coastal WO. — CR

■ **Petit** *see Ken Forrester Wines*

Pfeifer's Boutique Wines

Location: Somerset West ▪ Map: Helderberg ▪ Est 2000 ▪ 1stB 2003 ▪ Tasting & sales by appt ▪ Closed Easter Fri/ Sun, Dec 25 & Jan 1 ▪ Owner(s) Pascal & Maya Pfeifer ▪ Winemaker(s)/viticulturist(s) Pascal Pfeifer (Jun 2006) ▪ 1.675ha/1.4ha (shiraz) ▪ 14-16t/±150cs own label 100% red ▪ IPW member ▪ PO Box 5238 Helderberg 7135 ▪ enquiries@pfeifersvineyard.co.za ▪ www.pfeifersvineyard.co.za ▪ S 34° 01' 10.98" E 018° 47' 17.06" ▪ **T +27 (0)21-842-3396** ▪ F +27 (0)86-616-8850

Co-owner and winegrower Pascal Pfeifer advises that vintages 2005 to 2007, the last Caelum Syrah made, are still available from his family's Helderberg farm.

■ **Phambili** *see Wellington Wines*
■ **Philip Jonker** *see Weltevrede Estate*

Philip Jordaan Wines

WO: Western Cape ▪ Est/1stB 1998 ▪ For wine orders call T +27 (0)82-573-0620 ▪ Owner(s)/cellarmaster(s)/ winemaker(s) Philip Jordaan ▪ Viticulturist(s) Leon Dippenaar ▪ P/Bag X15 Hermanus 7640 ▪ jordaanphilip1@ telkomsa.net ▪ **T +27 (0)82-573-0620**

The eponymous cellarmaster-owner of this venture was also cellarmaster for 26 years at a somewhat larger venture - Du Toitskloof. There he acquired his taste for cabernet franc. With talk of more vintages of it in barrel, we are hopeful.

Limited Edition Cabernet Franc ⓟ ★★★★ Elegant, supple & mature **06** with savoury, lean red fruit, tasted a few years back. — IM

Phizante Kraal

Location/WO: Durbanville ▪ Map: Durbanville, Philadelphia & Darling ▪ 1stB 2005 ▪ Tasting & sales Mon-Fri 9-4 Sat 10-2 ▪ Fee R15 ▪ Owner(s) André & Ronelle Brink ▪ Winemaker(s) Thys Louw (Jan 2005, Diemersdal) ▪ Viticulturist(s) André Brink ▪ 50ha (cab, shiraz, chenin, sauv) ▪ 2,000cs own label ▪ PO Box 8 Durbanville 7551 ▪ info@phesantekraal.co.za ▪ www.phizantekraal.co.za ▪ S 33° 47' 7.66" E 018° 40' 15.6" ▪ **T +27 (0)21-976-2114** ▪ F +27 (0)21-976-2113

Small changes and improvements continue at the Durbanville boutique winery owned by André and Ronelle Brink, who sell most of their grapes but keep back slightly more each year for their Diemersdal-vinified own label. When renovations are complete, the farm will boast a new function space and tasting venue.

★★★★☆ **Sauvignon Blanc** ✓ 🍴 🖼 Distinctive & different **13** has aromas of fynbos, pine needles, lemongrass with delicious green apples, guavas, hints of hay. Layered finish keeps you coming back for more, beautiful structure, elegant wine.

Shiraz ☺ 🖼 ★★★ Sturdy **10** has all the classic pepper, spice, smoked meat flavours with sour cherry & chocolate notes. Integrated appeal.

Cabernet Sauvignon ⓘ ★★☆ **09** sweet black & red fruit, a little coarse on the finish. **Chenin Blanc** 🍴 🖼 ★★★ Pineapples & limes on shy **13**, with nicely managed alcohol & slightly bitter stonefruit finish. — CM

PicardiRebel

Est 1994 ▪ PO Box 1868 Cape Town 8000 ▪ **T +27 (0)21-469-3301** ▪ F +27 (0)21-469-3434

The PicardiRebel nationwide chain of drinks stores offers budget-wine shoppers a number of good-value options under house brands and occasional labels Coast, Hippo Creek, Naked Truth and Simply Red/White.

Pick n Pay

WO: Robertson ▪ Enquiries Neil Cooke ▪ Pick 'n Pay Corporate Brands PO Box 1960 Bedfordview 2008 ▪ ncooke@pnp.co.za ▪ www.picknpay.co.za ▪ **T +27 (0)11-856-7000** ▪ F +27 (0)86-616-5949

An upgrade of this national supermarket chain's in-house portfolio under the auspices of Pick n Pay Corporate Brands' Neil Cooke has included a switch to full-colour branding for the boxed wines, and the enlargement of the 750ml bottled range (untasted this edition) with four sparklings and, due to customer demand, a new Light addition to the single-variety wines. The boxed range, made by Robertson Winery, is variously available in 500ml, 3L and 5L packs.

Smooth Dry Red ★★ Latest **NV** lives up to its name: smooth, dry, red, also fresh & fruity. **Rosé** Next awaited. **Dry White** ★★ Clean-cut everyday **NV** white with potpourri hints. **Extra Light Dry White** ★★ Latest low-alcohol & frisky **NV** is back up to speed of previous. **Stein** ★★ Faintly floral, gently sweet **NV** for comfortable sipping. **Johannisberger Sweet White** ★★ Delicate, frangipani-scented **NV** tad flabby. **Late Harvest** ★★ Flowers & peaches on creamy **NV**. **Natural Sweet Rosé** ★★ Sweet but not syrupy, Day-Glo pink **NV** party starter. **Johannisberger Sweet Red** ★ **NV**'s combo sweet red fruit & dusty tannin up for a braai. — HJ,CvZ

▪ **Pick's Pick** see The Butcher Shop & Grill
▪ **Piekeniers** see Tierhoek
▪ **Pienk Pikkewyn** see Bergwater Winery
▪ **Pierneef Collection** see La Motte
▪ **Pierre Jourdan** see Haute Cabrière
▪ **PK Morkel** see Bellevue Estate Stellenbosch

Place in the Sun

Location/WO: Stellenbosch ▪ Est/1stB 2010 ▪ Closed to public ▪ Owner(s) Distell ▪ Cellarmaster(s)/winemaker(s) Deon Boshoff (2010) ▪ Viticulturist(s) Annelie Viljoen (2010) ▪ 1,000t ▪ ISO 9001 & ISO 14001 (pending), Fairtrade, IPW ▪ PO Box 184 Stellenbosch 7599 ▪ dboshoff@distell.co.za ▪ www.placeinthesun.co.za ▪ **T +27 (0)21-809-7000**

This Distell-owned brand is Fairtrade accredited and among the first to earn the Ethical Seal guaranteeing equitable labour practice. A portion of the wines' purchase price is directed towards workers' social development. Winemaker Deon Boshoff, appointed cellarmaster of Distell's Adam Tas aged only 32, is himself the son of farm employees and learned his trade on a bursary open to the community.

Cabernet Sauvignon 🍴 🖼 ★★★ **12** shows good cab fruit but also the variety's solid tannin structure. Better with a hearty stew. **Merlot** 🍴 🖼 ★★★ Shade less ripe & generous than previous, **12** is leafy, firm, needs a food accompaniment. **Shiraz** 🍴 🖼 ★★★ Like previous, **12** is more about leathery spice & less about fruit mid-2013. Might simply need time to reveal all its charms. **Chardonnay** NEW Not tasted. **Sauvignon Blanc** 🍴 🖼 ★★★★ **13**'s crisp, herby greenpepper styling is very attractive, will have you heading straight for the seafood counter. — DB, HJ

Plaisir de Merle

Location: Paarl ▪ Map: Franschhoek ▪ WO: Western Cape/Paarl/Simonsberg-Paarl/Coastal ▪ Est 1993 ▪ 1stB 1994 ▪ Tasting, sales & cellar tours Mon-Fri 9–5 Sat 10–4 (Nov–Mar) & 10–2 (Apr–Oct) Sun by special request for groups of 15+ ▪ Tasting fees: standard R40/sweet sensation R70/flavour R70/exclusive R100 ▪ Closed Easter Fri/Sun & Dec 25 ▪ Cheese platters available during trading hours R80 ▪ Children welcome ▪ Gifts ▪ Conservation area ▪ Manor House (sleeps 8) can be booked for functions, conferences & weddings ▪ Owner(s) Distell ▪ Cellarmaster(s) Niel Bester (1993) ▪ Viticulturist(s) Hannes van Rensburg & Freddie le Roux (both 1993) ▪ 974ha/400ha (cabs s/f, malbec, merlot, p verdot, pinot, shiraz, chard, sauv) ▪ 800t/80,000cs own label 80% red 20% white ▪ ISO 9001:2008, ISO 14001:2004, BRC, BWI, SGS, WIETA ▪ PO Box 121 Simondium 7670 ▪ info@plaisirdemerle.co.za ▪ www.plaisirdemerle.co.za ▪ S 33° 51' 0.0" E 018° 56' 36.2" ▪ **T +27 (0)21-874-1071** ▪ F +27 (0)21-874-1689

This Simonsberg-Paarl farm has been in the stable of Distell (then Stellenbosch Farmers' Winery) since 1964, with winemaker Niel Bester in charge of the cellar since the maiden Plaisir de Merle-branded vintage of 1993. Fruit from the extensive vineyards, which includes some of the Cape's more unusual varieties, is also delivered to other cellars under Distell ownership.

★★★★ **Cabernet Sauvignon** 10 (★★★★) quite subdued, though nicely structured to highlight simple, already evolving flavours. Best drink before more ageworthy **09**. WO Paarl, like Merlot.

★★★★ **Shiraz** Coconut & minty spice winning over sweet, slightly jammy red fruit when **10** (★★★★) tasted mid-2013. More awkward than the affable **09**. WO Simonsberg-Paarl, like Grand Plaisir.

★★★★ **Grand Plaisir** ⓥ Cab-based Bordeaux sextet with shiraz. Maturing savoury features on **08**; charry oak hints too. Good flavour concentration, rounded tannins & fresh core allow for current drinking.

★★★★ **Chardonnay** ⓥ **12** returns to calm, assured style after less substantial **11** (★★★☆). Good varietal definition; pickled limes, oatmeal tones, lees-enriched substance & mineral lift. Convincingly dry & long.

★★★★ **Sauvignon Blanc** ▤ ⓥ Youthful **13** delivers unusually exuberant fruity acids. More typical ripe apple, greengage purity prolonged on refreshing, dry finish. Nearly half Darling fruit.

Merlot ▤ ⓥ ★★★ Modest, rather plain fruit shielded further by quite dense feel & evident dry oak tannins on **11**. May reach degree of harmony in year or 2. **Petit Plaisir** ▤ ⓥ ★★★ Shiraz (65%) brings much that benefits **11** including savouriness, crushed velvet texture. Cab, merlot partners freshen & lift. Includes Swartland fruit. **Grand Brut Méthode Cap Classique** NEW ⓥ ★★ **10** fizz from pinot & chardonnay. Earthy notes, brisk bubble. Discontinued: **Cabernet Franc, Malbec.** — AL

Plettenvale Wines

Location/WO: Plettenberg Bay ▪ Map: Klein Karoo & Garden Route ▪ Est 2008 ▪ 1stB 2011 ▪ Tasting & sales by appt ▪ Self-catering cottages ▪ Owner(s) Gloria Strack van Schyndel ▪ Winemaker(s) Anton Smal (consultant) ▪ Viticulturist(s) Paul Wallace (Nov 2007, consultant) ▪ 5.3ha/2.3ha (pinot, shiraz, chard) ▪ PO Box 2103 Plettenberg Bay 6600 ▪ info@plettenvalewines.co.za ▪ www.plettenvalewines.co.za ▪ **T +27 (0)44-533-9146** ▪ F +27 (0)44-533-9146

Plettenberg Bay may be one of SA's fastest-populating appellations, but vintning here is not for the faint hearted. Gloria Strack van Schyndel's later-in-life, family-run wine venture, on land reclaimed from alien vegetation, lost 70% of her maiden 2011 crop to marauding birds. Happily last season was free of 'the little buggers' and this, plus the fillips of her own micro cellar, several new wines (some yet untasted) and the maiden cap classique selling out, made 2013 'great!'

Dry Rosé ▤ ★★★ Pre-bottling **13** partridge-eye pink combo pinot noir & chardonnay, pleasingly dry & chalky al fresco sipper. **Chardonnay** NEW ▤ ★★★ Promising unwooded **13** work-in-progress shows orange blossom nuances, taut acidity & savoury conclusion for food. **Brut Rosé Methode Cap Classique** NEW ★★★ Preview of **12** traditional-method bubbly has weight & appealing baked apple of pinot (32%), chardonnay's zingy acidity. Enjoy with fruity desserts or sunsets. — HJ,CvZ

▪ **Poetry** see Flagstone Winery
▪ **Poker Hill** see Somerbosch Wines
▪ **Polkadraai Road** see Beau Joubert Vineyards & Winery
▪ **Polo Club** see Val de Vie Wines
▪ **Pomüla** see Imbuko Wines

Pongrácz

Specialist méthode cap classique bubbly brand named after Desiderius Pongrácz, Dachshund-loving aristocrat who fled the Hungarian uprising, settled in Stellenbosch in 1958 and went on to become chief viticultural adviser to Distillers Corporation, Distell's precursor.

★★★★ Desiderius First since **03**, prestige cuvée **08** (★★★★★) from chardonnay (70%) & pinot noir shows aristocratic class of namesake. Delightful brioche with lemon shortbread borne on fine mousse, crisp, nutty finish.

Brut Rosé ★★★★ Charming dry pinot noir-chardonnay **NV** bubbly with lively mousse & creamy texture. Strawberry shortbread in a rose-tinted glass. WO W Cape, as for all. **Brut ★★★★** Lean & focused **NV** sparkler from pinot noir & chardonnay with appealing bakery aromas & green apple finish. — GdB

■ **Porcelain Mountain** *see* Porseleinberg

Porcupine Ridge

This was the first 'value' range made by Boekenhoutskloof (under whose entry it was previously listed), but continues to build its reputation. The Rhône-inspired offerings, sourced in Swartland and Piekenierskloof, are the more interesting in the line-up, yet all these wines constantly over-perform in terms of price.

Merlot ☺ 🏠 🖾 **★★★** Bright, clean-fruited **12** proffers herbal-spice combo with cranberry crunch. Dry & fresh to finish. **Syrah-Viognier** ☺ 🏠 🖾 **★★★** Tart-fruited intro on **12** has savoury black olive & brine notes. Palate is vibrant & zippy, with food-friendly fresh end. Like Syrah, from Swartland. **Sauvignon Blanc** ☺ 🏠 🖾 **★★★** Shy, with herbal hint & jasmine, **13** has flavoursome, light & dry frame.

Cabernet Sauvignon ✓ 🏠 🖾 **★★★★** Leafy notes on **12** add to youthful restraint, with light redcurrant freshness, ending dry & firm. Over-delivers at price. **Syrah** ✓ 🏠 🖾 **★★★★ 12** has complex layers of vibrant fruit & spice with smoky overtones, all supported by peppery savoury membrane. Punches way above its weight. **Viognier-Grenache Blanc** ✓ 🏠 🖾 **★★★★** Apricot kernel, spice & poised floral interest on **12** - less complete than standout **11** (★★★★) yet over-performs handsomely. Subtly oaked & dry. — JP

Porseleinberg

Location: Malmesbury ▪ Est 2009 ▪ 1stB 2011 ▪ Closed to public ▪ Owner(s) Boekenhoutskloof Winery Pty Ltd ▪ Winemaker(s)/viticulturist(s) Callie Louw (Jun 2009) ▪ 85ha/30ha (shiraz) ▪ 6t/600cs own label 100% red ▪ Organic EU Control Union ▪ PO Box 433 Franschhoek 7690 ▪ callie@porseleinberg.com ▪ www.porseleinberg.com ▪ T +27 (0)79-884-2309 ▪ F +27 (0)86-566-9332

This ambitious Swartland farm is owned by Boekenhoutskloof, which will take most of the fruit coming off the vineyards. These continue to expand, on soils previously unused for vines - something that helps the organic, even biodynamic, farming practices of Callie Louw. Certain blocks, though, go into the wine made here by Callie (nothing new tasted as they're holding back the 2011).

■ **Porter Mill Station** *see* Tulbagh Winery
■ **Porterville Cellars** *see* Tulbagh Winery

Post House Vineyards

Location: Somerset West ▪ Map: Helderberg ▪ WO: Stellenbosch ▪ Est/1stB 1997 ▪ Tasting, sales & cellar tours Mon-Fri 9-5 Sat by appt ▪ Fee R30 ▪ Closed all pub hols ▪ BYO picnic ▪ Guest house ▪ Owner(s) Nicholas Gebers ▪ Cellarmaster(s) Nick Gebers ▪ Winemaker(s) Nick Gebers, with Pippa Orpen ▪ 70ha/39ha (cab, merlot, p verdot, ptage, shiraz, chenin, sauv) ▪ 200t/16,000cs own label 65% red 35% white ▪ PO Box 5635 Helderberg 7135 ▪ info@posthousewines.co.za ▪ www.posthousewines.co.za ▪ S 34° 1' 8.1" E 018° 48' 41.6" ▪ T +27 (0)21-842-2409 ▪ F +27 (0)21-842-2409

Having set up home in an old post office building next to the Helderberg village of Raithby, boutique owner/winemaker Nick Gebers chose a philatelic theme for his wines. From the appropriately inky Penny Black to the whimsical Missing Virgin, each carries a historical explanation and a yarn to entertain you while you sip.

★★★★ **Missing Virgin** Dense, impossibly concentrated pinotage & petit verdot blend, **11** follows previous form. Opaque black, with unyielding tannins, berry syrup fruit. May soften with extended cellaring.

★★★★ **Blueish Black** Shiraz, pinotage, cab & merlot blend. 2 vintages tasted: **11** shows ripe primary fruit core with spicy nuances. Wild whiffs on thinner **12** (★★★).

★★★★☆ **Penny Black** 5-way shiraz/Bordeaux blend with dash of chenin, **10** (★★★★) is massively dense, packed with fruit (& alcohol), plum pudding spiciness with inky iodine notes. Weighty & serious, though less complex than impressive **09**.

★★★★☆ **Stamp Of Chenin** Exuberantly spicy, with wild aromatic notes & tropical fruit salad, barrel-fermented **12** (★★★★) is not for the faint-hearted. Rich & complex, but not quite up to **11**.

★★★★☆ **Treskilling Yellow** Naturally barrel-fermented botrytised chenin, more focused **12** preview improves on **10** (★★★★) with rich dried apricot & mulled honey notes lending varietal form. Loads of exotic botrytis character, intriguingly complex spiciness & elegantly clean finish. No **09**, **11**.

Cabernet Sauvignon ★★★★ **10** foursquare fruit-driven powerhouse with high-toned medicinal whiff. **Merlot** ★★★★ **10** shows plush ripe fruit with faint medicinal hints. Ripe & robust, for the longer haul. **Shiraz** Next awaited, as for **Sauvignon Blanc**. **Blueish White** ★★★ **12** sauvignon blend with chenin is light & refreshing, with mineral leanness. Wisps of green apple fruit. — GdB

▪ **Post Tree** see Valley Vineyards Wine Company
▪ **Pot Luck Club** see Almenkerk Wine Estate
▪ **Pracht Gaarden** see Lourensford Wine Estate
▪ **Princess** see Alluvia Winery & Private Residence Club
▪ **Private Collection** see Saxenburg Wine Farm
▪ **Prohibition** see Camberley Wines
▪ **Protea** see Anthonij Rupert Wyne
▪ **Provenance** see Saronsberg
▪ **Provoyeur** see Devonvale Golf & Wine Estate

Pulpit Rock Winery

Location: Riebeek West ▪ Map/WO: Swartland ▪ Est 2003 ▪ 1stB 2004 ▪ Tasting & sales Mon-Fri 9–5 Sat 10–2 ▪ Closed Easter Fri-Sun, Dec 25/26 & Jan 1 ▪ Cellar tours by appt ▪ BYO picnic ▪ Walks/hikes ▪ Mountain biking trail ▪ Annual olive festival (May) ▪ Self-catering accommodation ▪ Owner(s) Brink family ▪ Winemaker(s) Riaan van der Spuy (Dec 2011) ▪ Viticulturist(s) Marco Roux (Dec 2008, consultant) ▪ 600ha/450ha (ptage, shiraz, chard, chenin) ▪ 650t/30,000cs own label 70% red 29% white 1% rosé + 200,000L bulk ▪ Other export brand: Cape Tranquility ▪ PO Box 1 Riebeek West 7306 ▪ info@pulpitrock.co.za ▪ www.pulpitrock.co.za ▪ S 33° 20' 47.4" E 018° 51' 14.1" ▪ **T +27 (0)22-461-2025** ▪ F +27 (0)22-461-2028

Lying on the foothills of the Swartland's Kasteelberg, Pulpit Rock takes its name from a distinctive craggy outcrop on that mountain. The Brink family have grown grapes here for over half a century, but made their own wine first in 2004. Their style is fruit driven, something they believe is dictated by the soil and climate, whose diversity also gives a unique character.

Reserve range

★★★★ **Pinotage** 🖉 The Swartland does pinotage as well as more-popular shiraz. Youthful **12** (★★★★☆) no exception, & has a real sense of place. Pure, unshowy perfume; big but beautifully proportioned, even if the oak (80% new) needs time to integrate - it should be worth the wait. Follows sturdy **10**.

★★★★ **Chardonnay** 🖉 **12** (★★★★) flourishes all-new French oak, ripe citrus fruit. Opulent & creamy, with nudge of alcoholic bitterness in tail. Tasted just post-bottling, may settle; but without focus of last **09**.

Cabernet Sauvignon 🖉 ★★★ Vanilla, cassis on uncomplicated **12**; full-bodied with firm acid. **Merlot** ⊕ ★★★ **09** juicy dark fruit, fresh acidity, pleasing tannic grip; well balanced & appealing. **Shiraz** 🖉 ★★★ Oak (60% new) & 15.5% alcohol currently lend awkward feel to **12**. Some attractive red fruit & spice make a case for short-term ageing - but monitor. **09** was last tasted.

Brink Family range

Pinotage ☺ 🖉 ★★★ Hearty **11**; ripe yet unshowy with appropriate roundly firm grip. **Chardonnay** ☺ 🖫 🖉 ★★★ Plentiful bright, ripe citrus features in flavoursome, lively, lightly oaked **13**. Straightforward but satisfying. **Chenin Blanc** ☺ 🖫 🖉 ★★★ Chenin in quaffable, charming style. **13**, with gentle yet persuasive fresh tropical fruit, is bouncy & juicy; time on lees adds to concentration, length.

Cabernet Sauvignon 🔲 ★★ Earthy & austere, **11**'s tannins overpower light, sweetish fruit. **Merlot** 🔲 ★★ **11** is simple, tart, sweetish. **Shiraz** ✓ 🔲 ★★★★ Warm red earth, spice & dark fruit a tempting mélange on **11**. Warmingly smooth, balanced. **Pinotage Rosé** 🔲 🔲 ★★ Dry **13** with honest raspberry, redcurrant flavours.

Swartland Stories NEW

> **Chenin Blanc-Viognier** ☺ 🔲 🔲 ★★★ Swartland sun shines through this **13**; 10% viognier adds gentle spice. Easygoing, just-off-dry.

Shiraz-Pinotage 🔲 🔲 ★★★ Full-bodied, flavoursome **11** has gentle tannins, but also an alcohol kick. — AL

◼ **Pure African** *see* Bellevue Estate Stellenbosch

Quando Vineyards & Winery

Location: Bonnievale ▪ Map/WO: Robertson ▪ Est/1stB 2001 ▪ Tasting & sales by appt ▪ Closed all pub hols ▪ Owner(s) F M Bruwer cc ▪ Cellarmaster(s)/winemaker(s) Fanus Bruwer (Jan 1991) ▪ Viticulturist(s) Martin Bruwer (Jan 1991) ▪ 190ha/80ha (mourv, chenin, sauv) ▪ 6,000cs own label 10% red 90% white ▪ PO Box 82 Bonnievale 6730 ▪ info@quando.co.za ▪ www.quando.co.za ▪ S 33° 56′ 9.6″ E 020° 1′ 28.8″ ▪ **T +27 (0)23-616-2752** ▪ F +27 (0)23-616-2752

'When are you going to make your own wine?' friends kept asking Robertson brothers Fanus and Martin Bruwer. When they did eventually oblige, both thought the Italian song 'Quando, Quando, Quando?' ('When?') was the perfect brand name. Ongoing success resulted in a cellar upgrade before the 2013 harvest, but for Fanus, the real heroes of Quando are the vineyard and cellar teams, 'who know their jobs inside out but are never mentioned anywhere'.

★★★★ **Chenin Blanc-Viognier** 🔲 Dried pear & flowers on unwooded **13**, (★★★★) unusual blend from 30 year old chenin, 14% viognier. As delicious & vibrant as **11** but shade less opulent. **12** sold out untasted.

> **Mourvèdre Rosé** ☺ 🔲 🔲 ★★★ Lively strawberry-toned **13**, dry & zesty crowd pleaser.

Pinot Noir 🔲 🔲 ★★★ Raspberry & whiff tobacco, ripe red cherry appeal on charming if robust **12**. Ex elevated Langeberg vines, takes step up. **Sauvignon Blanc** ✓ 🔲 🔲 ★★★★ Riverine home-farm vineyard delivers characterful **13**, with grapefruit, peach & saline attractions. Exceptional value. **Natural Sweet Sauvignon Blanc** 🔲 ★★★ All raisins & ripe peaches, **12** attractively balanced, bonus of light alcohol. — DB, JP

◼ **Quay 5** *see* Two Oceans
◼ **Queen** *see* Alluvia Winery & Private Residence Club

Quest Wines

Location: Worcester ▪ WO: Western Cape ▪ Est 2006 ▪ 1stB 2010 ▪ Closed to public ▪ Owner(s) Anja van Rijswijk & Hendrik Myburgh ▪ Cellarmaster(s)/winemaker(s) Hendrik Myburgh (2006) ▪ 2,000cs own label 100% red ▪ 12 Otto du Plessis Street Worcester 6850 ▪ admin@questwines.co.za ▪ www.questwines.co.za ▪ **T +27 (0)23-342-5856** ▪ F +27 (0)23-342-5856

Worcester-based Anja van Rijswijk and Hendrik Myburgh concentrate on supplying restaurants with good-quality, affordable housewines, a growing business arena. No new vintages this year from winemaker Hendrik, who sources the wines more widely to keep up with demand.

Cape Roots range
Cabernet Sauvignon 🔲 🔲 ★★ **11** more 'dry red' than 'cab' but soft & juicy. **Merlot** 🔲 🔲 ★★★ Cheerful, light, well-formed **10** picnic sipper with hint of liquorice. — CM

Quinta do Sul

Location: Calitzdorp ▪ Map: Klein Karoo & Garden Route ▪ WO: Klein Karoo ▪ Est 2005 ▪ 1stB 2008 ▪ Visits by appt ▪ Owner(s) Alwyn Liebenberg ▪ Cellarmaster(s)/winemaker(s) Alwyn Liebenberg (Jun 2005) ▪ 10ha/2. 5ha (shiraz, souzão, tannat, tinta amerela/barocca/roriz, touriga) ▪ 5t/580cs own label ▪ 54 Siffie Crescent Vermont 7201 ▪ alwyn@thegoosewines.com ▪ www.quintadosul.co.za ▪ **T +27 (0)82-610-2279**

Boutique vintner Alwyn Liebenberg (also winemaker at The Goose) sees a bright future in the niche port-style market, citing 'excellent sales and listings in the top restaurants' for his Vintage Port. Alwyn's expertise comes from stints in the Douro and at Boplaas; his grapes from the small family vineyard in Calitzdorp.

★★★★ **Vintage Port** Ⓤ Traditional port grapes plus shiraz, tannat. Very ripe & fruit-sweet **09** is plump & pliable, more Ruby in style, with less spirit attack & tannic grip than Vintage. — CvZ

Quoin Rock Winery

Location/map: Stellenbosch ▪ WO: Simonsberg–Stellenbosch/Cape South Coast ▪ Est 1998 ▪ 1stB 2001 ▪ Tasting & sales daily 9-5 (summer) & 10-4 (winter) ▪ Fee R20 ▪ Closed Easter Fri/Sun, Dec 25/26 & Jan 1 ▪ Cheese platters ▪ Owner(s) Quoin Rock Wines (Pty) Ltd ▪ Winemaker(s) Narina Cloete (Jun 2010) ▪ Viticulturist(s) Nico Walters (Sep 2012) ▪ 193ha/15ha (cabs s/f, merlot, mourv, shiraz, sauv, viog) ▪ 200t/22,000cs own label 55% red 35% white 7% MCC 3% dessert ▪ PO Box 1193 Stellenbosch 7599 ▪ tasting@quoinrock.co.za ▪ www.quoinrock.com ▪ S 33° 52' 42.5" E 018° 52' 2.3" ▪ **T +27 (0)21-888-4740** ▪ F +27 (0)21-888-4744

Since its ownership passed to a wineloving Ukranian businessman, the necessary changes to position Stellenbosch's Quoin Rock at the top end of the local wine industry - and a globally recognised producer - have begun. Some repairs, refurbishing and landscaping have already taken place, with more to come. Overseeing the rejuvenation, including social development, sustainability and ecotourism, is general manager Thys Lombard, ex Tokara and with wide local and international business experience, with an executive team of winemaker Narina Cloete and viticulturist Nico Walters.

★★★★☆ **Syrah** ✓ ▨ Plush dark wild fruit, deep layers of spice, some scrub & dried herb nuances, muscular, handsome **11** has rejected the pretty side of shiraz, gone for character, structure & the longer haul. With 13% mourvèdre.

★★★★ **The Centaur** Ⓤ Great care in shiraz-led **09**: whole-berry natural ferment, long skin contact, new oak maturation, result is crimson-hued brambleberries & black pepper, fine-grained tannins. Drink till ±2020.

★★★★ **Chardonnay** ✓ ▨ With cool-climate fruit (WO Cape South Coast), bunch pressing, wild yeast barrel ferment, 11 months on the lees, **12** (★★★★★) is a silky, svelte, melon & peach flavoured beauty, improves on **11**. Oak's gentle hazelnut shading leaves the fruit intact.

★★★★☆ **The Nicobar Reserve Sauvignon Blanc** ▨ Distinctive wooded sauvignon only in the best years. With a lime pickle & pine nut intro, **12** draws you in to a vital, zesty palate, lip-smacking freshness. Threaded throughout & taking a bow on the finish is a lovely pure minerality.

★★★★☆ **Cape South Coast Sauvignon Blanc** ▨ With 'Cape Agulhas' prefix previously. Wet pebbles, oyster shells, there's no mistaking **12**'s cool-climate provenance. Alluring purity & finesse, Old World elegance. Something special. Requires quiet contemplation, don't rush it.

★★★★ **The Oculus** Ⓤ ▨ Sauvignon with a twist, wild ferment & ageing in French oak, portion viognier. Savoury peach overlay to **10**'s leafy minerality adds intrigue, creativity, heaps of flavour. No **08**, **09**.

★★★★ **Cape South Coast Cap Classique** Ⓤ ▨ With a touch of pinotage to pinot noir & chardonnay, latest **NV** gains more red berry profile but the elegance, finely crafted bubbles & refined palate remain intact, memorable.

★★★★☆ **Vine Dried Sauvignon Blanc** ▨ Marmalade, pineapple & apricot flavours in barrel-fermented/aged **12**, lovely fruit purity showing in its perfume & mouthfilling sweet richness. Acidity adds a lift but ultimately the wine forces you to submit to the whole heady experience.

Merlot Await new release. **The Mendi** New vintage not available. — CR

Raats Family Wines

Location/map: Stellenbosch ▪ WO: Stellenbosch/Coastal ▪ Est/1stB 2000 ▪ Tasting & sales by appt only ▪ Closed all pub hols ▪ Owner(s) Bruwer Raats ▪ Cellarmaster(s) Bruwer Raats (Jan 2000) ▪ Winemaker(s) Gavin Bruwer Slabbert (Feb 2010) ▪ Viticulturist(s) Bruwer Raats (Jan 2000) & Gavin Bruwer Slabbert (Feb 2010) ▪ 30ha (cab f, chenin) ▪ 150t/20,000cs own label 30% red 70% white ▪ PO Box 2068 Dennesig Stellenbosch 7601 ▪ braats@mweb.co.za ▪ www.raats.co.za ▪ S 33° 58' 16.6" E 018° 44' 55.3" ▪ **T +27 (0)21-881-3078** ▪ F +27 (0)21-881-3078

In pursuit of only the very best chenin, Bruwer Raats seeks out specific soil combinations ('my chenin soil!') planted with older vines. Three different vineyards

of this soil dotted around Stellenbosch are under long-term contract and provide the grapes for his top wine, a perennial high-flyer in many international competitions and tastings. Continuing his fascination with the Loire, his other focus is cabernet franc, either singly or as the dominating grape in Bordeaux blends, both under the Raats label and for Mvemve Raats (listed separately), his winemaking collaboration with friend Mzokhona Mvemve.

★★★★☆ **Cabernet Franc** 🖫 Vibrant & delicious **11** (★★★★★) has pronounced aromas of black fruit with classic tomato leaf twist. Ripe black berries & savoury black olive hints with polish & leather, integrated tannins & lengthy finish. **10** also elegant.

★★★★ **Dolomite Cabernet Franc** ✓ 🖫 🖫 Over-delivering **11**, cherries, pepper & smoky notes before sweep of meaty red fruit - cranberries, ripe plums. Not as typical as **10**, but deliciously different.

★★★★ **Red Jasper** 🖫 Seriously beautiful Bordeaux blend **11** (★★★★★) steps up on **10** with classic black fruit, cassis, perfume, fresh acidity & good length. Cab franc-dominated but less than previous.

★★★★☆ **Old Vine Chenin Blanc** 🖫 Back on top form after **11** (★★★★), **12** exudes elegance & charm. Baked apple Danish & almond pear tart flavours supported by freshening acidity draw you through to a tantalising finish. Utterly compelling wine from old Stellenbosch vines (45+ years), only 20% oaked.

Original Chenin Blanc 🖫 🖫 ★★★★ Unwooded **13** improves deliciously on **12** (★★★★) with fresh flavours of yellow peaches & perfumed pears, bouncy acidity & lengthy finish. A cut above your everyday sipper. Coastal WO. — CM

■ **Racetrack** see Damarakloof
■ **Radford Dale** see The Winery of Good Hope

Rainbow's End Wine Estate   🍷🎍📷

Location/map: Stellenbosch ▪ WO: Banghoek ▪ Est 1978 ▪ 1stB 2002 ▪ Tasting, sales & tours by appt ▪ Fee R25, waived on purchase of 4+ btls ▪ Closed Dec 25 & Jan 1 ▪ Sales also via website, delivery free of charge ▪ BYO picnic ▪ Conservation area ▪ Owner(s) Malan family ▪ Cellarmaster(s) Anton Malan (Nov 2000) ▪ Winemaker(s) Anton Malan (Nov 2000) & Francois Malan (Jan 2005) ▪ Viticulturist(s) Francois Malan (Jan 2005) ▪ 52ha/21.6ha (cabs s/f, malbec, merlot, p verdot, shiraz) ▪ 120t/8,200cs own label 90% red 10% rosé ▪ IPW, GlobalGap (CMI) ▪ PO Box 2253 Dennesig 7601 ▪ info@rainbowsend.co.za ▪ www.rainbowsend.co.za ▪ S 33° 56′ 25.8″ E 018° 56′ 42.6″ ▪ **T** +27 (0)21-885-1719/+27 (0)83-411-0170/+27 (0)82-404-1085 ▪ F +27 (0)21-885-1722

Huge anticipation in the Malan family on Banhoek's highest slopes for the launch, after 9 vintages, of their first Bordeaux-style red blend. Anton (winemaker/marketer) and Francois (viticulturist) say the 5-way blend is a block, row and barrel selection, from mature vines, and should be on the market early this year. In a 'green' development, 15,000 proteas are being planted, and vat-cellar humidifiers installed 'by us personally, as for all the cellar equipment'.

★★★★ **Cabernet Sauvignon** 🖫 **11**'s deep sweet cassis & earthy herbal notes mingle with vanilla oak flavours, leading to a lively liqueur-like finish. Good balance & structure bodes well for a long life.

★★★★ **Cabernet Franc** 🖫 Full ripeness & a melange of herbal, peppery, cassis & mint chocolate notes. **11** full body, firm oaky grip & satisfying tang. Excellent expression of the variety.

★★★★ **Limited Release Cabernet Franc** ✓ 🖫 From single vineyard & clone, **11** (★★★★★) dazzles with creamy milk chocolate & sour dark cherries in a firmly structured mouthful of herb-tinged fruit. Elegance & poise reign, with unflagging spicy herbal conclusion. Built for the long haul. A leap up from **10**.

★★★★ **Merlot** 🖫 Full bodied, with spicy rich plumcake fragrance. Ripe & serious, with silky mouthfeel & firm grip as the flavours linger on & on. **11** good varietal expression.

★★★★☆ **Shiraz** **NEW** ✓ 🖫 Dark & brooding **11** is spicy with concentrated, chewy berry fruit notes. Firmly structured, yet a regal elegance with dustings of cedar oak & spice. Fruit is still tight, but promises later reward.

Rosé ☺ 🖫 ★★★ Feisty pink from all varieties on farm, **12** dry, with appealing bright berries in a light body - for summer fun.

Mystical Corner 🖫 🖫 ★★★ 5-way malbec-led red blend **12** is supple with juicy black fruit, rounded tannins in support. Unassuming & harmonious. Discontinued: **Shiraz Single Vineyard**. — WB

Raka   🍷🍴📷♿

Location: Stanford ▪ Map: Elgin, Walker Bay & Bot River ▪ WO: Klein River/Western Cape/Coastal/Cape South Coast ▪ Est/1stB 2002 ▪ Tasting & sales Mon-Fri 9-5 Sat 10-2.30 ▪ Tasting fee: 4 wines on daily tasting list free, other wines R10/wine ▪ Closed Sun, Good Fri & Dec 25 ▪ Cellar tours & large groups by appt ▪ BYO picnic ▪ Conservation area ▪ Owner(s) Piet Dreyer ▪ Winemaker(s) Josef Dreyer (Jan 2007) ▪ Viticulturist(s) Pieter Dreyer (Jan 2007) ▪ 350t/30,000cs own label 75% red 17% white 8% rosé ▪ BWI, IPW ▪ PO Box 124 Caledon 7230 ▪ info@rakawine.co.za ▪ www.rakawine.co.za ▪ S 34° 23' 56.1" E 019° 37' 26.7" ▪ **T +27 (0)28-341-0676** ▪ F +27 (0)86-606-5462

Out on a limb in every sense, the ebullient Piet Dreyer, squid fisherman extraordinary, burst onto the wine scene a little over a decade ago to considerable acclaim. His unabashed enthusiasm and desire to learn quickly triumphed over his lack of experience. The remote, family-run winery and vineyards near Stanford produced controversial but highly rated wines from the start, and this has continued unabated, with its persistent nautical references. Although more noted as a red-wine specialist, the whites' star is ascending. Expect a warm welcome in their charming, quirky tasting room.

★★★★ **Cabernet Sauvignon** ⓟ **10** has trademark ripe dark berry fruit, concentrated flavours & gentle oak spice. Elegant, with a super balance, freshness & structure.

★★★★☆ **Cabernet Franc** ✓ 🖉 **11** follows on stellar **09** (★★★★★) with class, elegant perfume, concentrated berry flavours, herbal edge & dusty tannins. Oak is in perfect harmony with the fresh & intense fruit, balanced by a fine acid structure.

★★★★ **Malbec** ⓟ **09** starts very shy (some cellar time wanted?). Fine lavender & sea breeze notes lead to firm but fine tannin structure & good mouthfeel.

★★★★ **Mourvèdre** ✓ 🖉 Meaty, fragrant coriander spice allures on **11**. Firmly structured & made for food, the sweet-savoury marriage is harmonious & moreish. A lifting sour cherry finish delights.

★★★★ **Petit Verdot** ⓟ Deep ruby-hued **10** offered intense dark cherry & blackcurrant with great fruit purity previously. Rich, complex savoury support & refreshing acidity. Should be drinking well.

★★★★☆ **Biography Shiraz** ⓟ Flagship offers a kaleidoscope of black berry, violet, vanilla & white pepper aromas & flavours in **10** (★★★★★). The lush texture, seamless & complex structure adds to elegance & refinement. Excellent expression of the variety, like more delicate **09**.

★★★★ **Quinary** ✓ Five-way Bordeaux-style red shows silky, harmonious berry & vanilla flavours in **09**. Good balance, with mouthfilling savoury fruit & velvety tannins.

★★★★ **Figurehead Cape Blend** ✓ Five Bordeaux varieties & a dollop of pinotage, **09** is now settled & balanced. Big & bold, with with smooth & appealing spicy fruit flavours.

Sangiovese ☺ 🖉 ★★★ Ripe, easy & sweet **12** shows fragrant mulberry compote, earthy tones & firm dry tannins. Pass the pizza. WO W Cape. **Spliced** ☺ 🍴 🖉 ★★★ Friendly all-sorts red blend from Robertson grapes, **10** is juicy, spicy with a moreish dry & savoury grip. Still ticks every drinkability box. WO W Cape. **Rosé Dry** ☺ 🍴 🖉 ★★★ **13** from 7 red varieties is fragrant & spicy, with juicy strawberry flavours & dry finish. Playful & summer fun. **Sauvignon Blanc** ☺ 🍴 🖉 ★★★ **13** offers ripe tropical fruit flavours, concentrated & juicy with an upbeat conclusion.

Barrel Select Merlot ✓ 🖉 ★★★☆ Spicy sweet plum fruit on **11** is fresh & blends well with firm tannin core, needs time to bloom. **Pinotage** ✓ 🖉 ★★★☆ Good oak balance supports ripe juicy plum fruit concentration. **11** offers a savoury, earthy handshake. **Chenin Blanc** ✓ 🍴 🖉 ★★★☆ Delicious **12**, now bottled, juicy & fruity with apple pie & light vanilla flavours. Mouthfilling, rounded, with a good zesty finish. Coastal WO. **Shannonea Dry White Blend** ✓ 🍴 🖉 ★★★★ **12** from sauvignon & viognier, now bottled, brims with heady fruit & floral perfume, to the rounded mouthfeel & textured food-friendly end. Cape South Coast WO. — WB

Rall Wines   🍷

Location: Swartland ▪ WO: Swartland/Coastal ▪ Est/1stB 2008 ▪ Tasting, sales & cellar tours by appt ▪ Owner(s)/winemaker(s)/viticulturist(s) Donovan Rall ▪ 10t/1,000cs own label 50% red 50% white ▪ info@ rallwines.co.za ▪ www.rallwines.co.za ▪ **T +27 (0)72-182-7571**

Donovan Rall started out studying Psychology at the University of Stellenbosch but then the wine bug bit and he switched to Oenology & Viticulture. He finished his studies in 2005 and made his first own-label wine in 2008. Asked to name SA's

most exciting winemaker, he replies 'It's still [Sadie Family's] Eben Sadie, isn't it?' But he himself is one of the more prominent members of a group of young winemakers energising the local wine scene.

★★★★★ **Rall Red** Pretty **11** with red & black berries, fynbos & white pepper. Good fruit purity, relatively soft acidity & tannins. Blend of 80% shiraz, 20% grenache. Not the same depth as **10** (★★★★★).

★★★★★ **Rall White** Less fireworks, more refinement on **12**. A naturally fermented, older-oaked blend of 50% chenin, rest verdelho, chardonnay, viognier from Swartland & Stellenbosch. Subtle white & yellow fruit but also yeasty, earthy notes before a briny finish. Something to savour. — CE

■ **Ralph Parker** *see* Altydgedacht Estate
■ **Raoul's** *see* Beaumont Wines

Rare Earth Wines   **NEW**

Location/WO: Plettenberg Bay ▪ Est 2009 ▪ 1stB 2012 ▪ Closed to public ▪ Guest house (Rare Earth Retreats www.rare-earthretreats.co.za) ▪ Owner(s) John Legh ▪ Cellarmaster(s)/winemaker(s) Anton Smal (2012, consultant) ▪ Viticulturist(s) Doug Lund (2009, consultant) ▪ 16.23ha/3.99ha (pinot, chard, sauv) ▪ 27t/1,110cs own label 100% white ▪ PO Box 295 The Crags 6602 ▪ dltadmin@iafrica.com ▪ **T +27 (0)44-534-8387** ▪ F +27 (0)44-534-8387

In the Tsitsikamma foothills on Plettenberg Bay's wine route, John 'Chick' Legh's polo estate is home to two Rare Earth Retreats: the Redford Farm Country House and Rondebosch Wine Estate, with self-catering cottage and almost 4 ha of vines. Sauvignon blanc, chardonnay and pinot noir are 'lovingly grown' here for the Rare Earth Wines vinified by consultant winemaker Anton Smal.

Sauvignon Blanc ▦ ★★★★ Previewed **13** stonefruit & flowers, brisk acidity cushioned by leesy richness & riper passionfruit flavours. Big boned for Plettenberg (13.8% alcohol) but still balanced. — HJ,CvZ

■ **Ready Steady** *see* Southern Sky Wines
■ **Rebourne Fairtrade** *see* Imbuko Wines
■ **Rebus** *see* Romond Vineyards
■ **Red Chair** *see* Rooiberg Winery

RED ESCape   **NEW**

Billed as 'a virtual product by Stellenzicht', RED ESCape is positioned as an antidote to the demands of 24 x 7 connectedness, the unserious packaging promising a convivial, any-occasion red 'filled with LOLs and good friends'.

Red Blend ▦ ▨ ★★ Several grains sugar notwithstanding, **11** shiraz & pinotage comes across as firm, even stern, more food wine than solo boot-me-up. Try with cherry-choc mousse, says winemaker. — DC, JP

■ **Red Gold** *see* Bushmanspad Estate

Red Tape

Location: Somerset West ▪ WO: Stellenbosch/Elgin ▪ Est 2007 ▪ 1stB 2010 ▪ Sales by prior arrangement ▪ Owner(s) Tanja Beutler ▪ 650cs own label 100% red ▪ PO Box 804 Somerset Mall 7137 ▪ tanja@hiddengems.co.za ▪ **T +27 (0)21-855-4275** ▪ F +27 (0)86-612-6118

With over 20 years of wine selling, marketing and garagiste fostering, brand owner Tanja Beutler knows a thing or two about bureaucracy, and her merlots are intended as a tonic against such absurdities as government's toll-free hotline for entrepreneurs to negotiate... governmental red tape!

★★★★★ **Merlot** ▨ Powerful yet lithe & unintimidating **10** continues trend of **09**. Silky rich black fruit & fine ripe tannins, admirable restraint in oaking. Dry, with a light spice sheen at end.

Merlot **NEW** ▨ ★★★★ Earthy forest floor fruits on approachable **NV** blend (**11 & 12**) from Elgin. Succulent plum spice, cocoa tail. — FM

■ **Red White Pink** *see* Nomada Wines

Reiersvlei

Location: Prince Albert ▪ Map: Klein Karoo & Garden Route ▪ WO: Prince Albert Valley ▪ Est 1999 ▪ 1stB 2010 ▪ Tasting, sales & cellar tours Tue-Fri 10-3 Sat 10-2; or by arrangement ▪ Closed Sun-Mon, Easter Fri-Mon, Dec 25/26 & Jan 1 ▪ Light refreshments for group tastings, booking essential ▪ Owner(s) Reiersvlei Investments CC (Russell & Elize Inggs) ▪ Cellarmaster(s)/winemaker(s)/viticulturist(s) Russell Inggs (Sep 2007) ▪ 113ha/9ha (cab, p verdot, ptage, red muscadel, shiraz, tinta, touriga, sauv) ▪ 70t/3,600cs own label 90% red 10% white ▪ PO Box 33 Prince Albert 6930 ▪ reier@absamail.co.za ▪ S 33° 16' 50" E 022° 14' 38" ▪ **T +27 (0)23-541-1983/1556** ▪ F +27 (0)23-541-1983

Named after its resident grey herons, this young and growing wine farm is one of the highest in SA (average altitude 860m). 'Proudly Great Karoo' is how prime mover Russell Inggs sums up the demographic makeup of the team and the mini-mum-interference approach for achieving 'an honest reflection of our terroir'.

Pinotage Await next, as for **Tinta Barocca** & **Cape Blend Reserve**. **Shiraz** ★★ Big but balanced 15.6% alco-hol on **11** country food partner. **Touriga Nacional** ★★★ Friendly **11** has spice & orange peel lift, noticeable but well-behaved tannins, juicy conclusion masking high alcohol. **Sauvignon Blanc** ★★★ Early picked **12**, lightish for al fresco sipping, needs food to counter high acidity. **Red Muscadel** ★★★ 'Jerepigo' dropped from name since we previewed **12** fortified dessert last time. Sweet toffee apple flavour enlivened by tangy acid & gentle tannic grip. **Cape Vintage Port** Ⓟ ★★ Charming cherry notes on rustic **10** from shiraz. — HJ,CvZ

■ **Releaf Organic** *see Imbuko Wines*

Remhoogte Wine Estate

Location/map: Stellenbosch ▪ WO: Simonsberg–Stellenbosch ▪ Est 1994 ▪ 1stB 1995 ▪ Tasting & sales Mon-Fri 9–5 Sat 10-4 ▪ Closed Easter Fri-Sun, Dec 25/26 & Jan 1 ▪ Cellar tours by appt ▪ Picnic baskets - booking required ▪ Functions ▪ Walking/hiking trails ▪ Game ▪ Guest cottage ▪ Owner(s) Murray Boustred Trust ▪ Cellar-master(s) Chris Boustred (Jan 2011) ▪ Winemaker(s)/viticulturist(s) Chris Boustred (Jan 2007) ▪ 55ha/30ha (cab, merlot, ptage, shiraz, chenin) ▪ 170t/16,000cs own label 80% red 20% white ▪ BWI, IPW ▪ PO Box 2032 Dennesig 7601 ▪ info@remhoogte.co.za ▪ www.remhoogte.co.za ▪ S 33° 53' 4.2" E 018° 51' 4.6" ▪ **T +27 (0)21-889-5005** ▪ F +27 (0)21-889-6907

It's 20 years since Murray Boustred moved with his wife and young family from Johannesburg to this Simonsberg farm, with its title deeds dating back to 1812. At the time it was in a run down state but under the Boustreds old vineyards have been revived and new ones planted. The farm's Dutch name refers to the days of oxwagons applying the brakes as they descended into Stellenbosch. Another member of the family has joined Remhoogte, great grandfather Sir Thomas Cullinan, whose name is honoured on the flagship red blend.

Reserve range

★★★★☆ **Sir Thomas Cullinan** NEW 🍇 Flagship named after (winemaker) Chris & (marketer) Rob Boustred's great grandfather. Intention is to keep it merlot based - 85% in refined maiden **10**, its dark-fruited, rare-meat plushness confidently reined in by cab's taut fresh grip. Satisfying savoury conclusion.

★★★★☆ **Honeybunch Chenin Blanc** ✓ 🍇 Harvested only from morning side of single, old vineyard; natural ferment, year in mainly older oak creates stylish **12** individual. Appealingly restrained yet concentrated, honeyed fruit wrapped in gently fresh, silky folds. Memorably long.

Estate range

★★★★ **Terroir Cabernet Sauvignon** ✓ 🍇 Adds 'Terroir' to name. **11** in classic style (but 15.2% alco-hol!). Impressively plush with brooding dark fruit, dusty oak, controlled by cab's fine grip. Sensitively oaked, like whole range.

★★★★ **Aspect Merlot** NEW 🍇 Attractive **11** from farm's highest, best site; deeply fragrant with comple-mentary dark plum flesh, measured ripe tannin. Would convert the most hardened sceptic.

★★★★ **Estate Blend** Ⓟ Powerful **07** (★★★★) even more demanding than bold **06**. Merlot, shiraz, cab, pinotage deliver plush black fruit concentration, well-rounded mouthfeel; tannins a satisfyingly dry finish.

Bushvine Pinotage 🍇 ★★★☆ Was just 'Pinotage'. **11** quite wild yet not unattractive. Ripe yet fresh rasp-berry, cherry succulence well able to soak up 30% new oak. Full bodied; nicely judged tannins. **09** (★★★★) more polished. **Valentino Syrah** 🍇 ★★★★ Elegant **11** quality climb. Complex vinification in larger French

oak, natural ferment. Pure & delicate with lingering white spice, fine tannin trim. More persistent than **10** (★★★☆).

Lifestyle range

★★★★ **Chenin Blanc** ✓ A breakfast table of features lends distinction to **12**: oats, honey, gentle toast (from 'declassified' Honeybunch barrels). Concentrated, firm & dry; much more serious than an easy sipper.
Aigle Noir ✓ ★★★★ Well-fruited blend, **11** cab-led with shiraz, merlot & drop pinotage. Supple & juicy; offers satisfaction now & for few more years.

Remhoogte Wine Estate range
Discontinued: **Merlot, Merlot Reserve, Woodbrook Cabernet Sauvignon-Shiraz.** — AL

Re'Mogo Wines

Location/map: Stellenbosch ▪ Est 2004 ▪ Tasting & sales Mon-Fri & pub hols 9-3 Sat 9-12 by appt only ▪ Owner(s) Re'Mogo Holdings Trust & Re'Mogo Holdings (Pty) Ltd ▪ Winemaker(s) Klaas Coetzee (Stellar Winery) ▪ 50% red 50% white ▪ Khayamandi Tourism Centre, George Blake Street, Stellenbosch/PO Box 7462 Stellenbosch 7599 ▪ remogo.holdings@gmail.com ▪ www.remogo.co.za ▪ S 33° 55' 9.47" E 018° 51' 7.90" ▪ **T +27 (0)82-638-6774/+27 (0)82-253-5126/+27 (0)72-249-7999** ▪ F +27 (0)86-610-7047

Stellenbosch empowerment brand Re'Mogo ('Standing Together') have shown their Fair for Life-accredited organic wines – including single-variety bottlings, blends and sparkling – everywhere from Soweto and Lagos to Brazil, Germany and China, where they now have a permanent representative, resulting in steady growth, according to international trade manager Thamsanqa Hombana.

■ **Renosterbos** see Hofstraat Kelder

Restless River

Location: Hermanus ▪ Map: Elgin, Walker Bay & Bot River ▪ WO: Upper Hemel-en-Aarde Valley/Walker Bay ▪ Est 1999 ▪ 1stB 2005 ▪ Tasting, sales & tours daily by appt ▪ Closed all pub hols ▪ Charcuterie, cheese platters & refreshments - booking essential ▪ BYO picnic ▪ Owner(s) Craig & Anne Wessels ▪ Winemaker(s) Craig Wessels (Jan 2005) ▪ Viticulturist(s) Anne Wessels (Nov 2004) & Craig Wessels ▪ 20ha/6ha (cab, chard) ▪ 10t/1,000cs own label 55% red 45% white ▪ PO Box 1739 Hermanus 7200 ▪ anne@restlessriver.com ▪ www.restlessriver.com ▪ S 34° 21' 26.11" E 19° 16' 32.80" ▪ **T +27 (0)28-313-2881/+27 (0)82-650-3544**

It's a near-miracle to make a cabernet in cool Hemel-en-Aarde – let alone as fine a one as Craig and Anne Wessels coax from their small vineyard. The grapes, perhaps lingering on the vines till autumn, are treated with infinite care, and as little intervention as possible in the cellar: natural ferment, no additives, no pumps. Chardonnay is commoner, but theirs gets the same intricate attention.

★★★★☆ **Cabernet Sauvignon** Classy & stylish **09** perhaps even more impressive than **07**, which was released after lesser **08** (★★★☆). There's vivacity & depth & rich, dark fruit (cherries, berries, plums), with a fine tannin structure, & a robust but balanced 14.3 alcohol. Sensitively oaked, just 30% new.

★★★★ **Chardonnay 10** (★★★★☆) as characterful as **09** but more refined, with aromas of vanilla-infused apple & pears, & smoky undertones. Plenty of power & ripeness on the subtly oaked palate, with a mouthfilling viscosity - but no sense of overweight, thanks to a good balancing acidity. WO Walker Bay. — JPf

Retief Wines

Location/WO: Paarl ▪ Map: Paarl & Wellington ▪ Est 1747 ▪ 1stB 2004 ▪ Tasting & sales by appt ▪ Closed all pub hols ▪ Owner(s) Pearl Mountain Wines (Pty) Ltd ▪ Winemaker(s) Robert Frater (2004, De Zoete Inval) ▪ Viticulturist(s) Graham Retief ▪ 11.28ha (cab, merlot, shiraz, chard, chenin, sauv) ▪ 67t/7,500L 100% red ▪ PO Box 709 Northern Paarl 7623 ▪ retief@new.co.za ▪ S 33° 41' 44.4" E 018° 57' 11.1" ▪ **T 021-872-9088** ▪ F 021-872-9983

Graham Retief, prime mover of boutique Retief Wines, based on a mainly table grape farm in Paarl, says he was persuaded just before harvest last year to sell all the wine to a very persistent Chinese visitor who arrived unannounced waving Platter's Guide. 'I resisted to the tune of 100 cases, for our regulars,' he chuckles.

Above the Mist range
Cabernet Sauvignon ⊕ ★★★ Honest, well-oaked **07** showing classic blackcurrant & cedar tones. **Merlot** ⊕ ★★★ Whiffs coffee & chocolate on fleshy **07**.

Retief range
Wagon Trail Not ready at press time, like **Above the Mist** & **Yes It's Red**. — CvZ

■ **Reuben's** *see* The Goose Wines
■ **Revelation** *see* Osbloed Wines

Reverie **NEW**

WO: Swartland ▪ Est 2011 ▪ 1stB 2012 ▪ Tasting & sales by appt ▪ Closed all pub hols ▪ Owner(s) Jacques de Klerk ▪ Cellarmaster(s)/viticulturist(s) Jacques de Klerk (Nov 2011) ▪ Winemaker(s) Jacques de Klerk (Nov 2011), with Amelie de Klerk (Nov 2011) ▪ (chenin) ▪ 2t/60cs own label 100% white ▪ 5 Birkenhead Road Somerset West 7130 ▪ reveriechenin@gmail.com ▪ **T +27 (0)82-783-7647**

Owner of this boutique label from the Swartland, Jacques de Klerk (also The Winery of Good Hope winemaker), describes Reverie as a 'liquid art project' striving to reflect a seldom-seen side of chenin blanc. 'Old vines give the wine substance, early harvesting its finesse, and the Paardeberg granitic soils its soul.'

★★★★ **Chenin Blanc** 🍴 🍷 No blockbuster or 'statement' (& better for it), barrelled **12** gentle whisper of oak & oxidativeness; rich, full & leesy, ripe tropical fruit in creamy textured finish. Unfined/filtered. — GdB, GM

Reyneke Wines

Location/map: Stellenbosch ▪ WO: Stellenbosch/Western Cape ▪ Est 1863 ▪ 1stB 1998 ▪ Tasting, sales & cellar tours Mon-Fri 10-5 Sat & pub hols by appt ▪ Paintings by Mila Posthumus on display ▪ Owner(s) Reyneke Wines (Pty) Ltd ▪ Cellarmaster(s) Rudiger Gretschel ▪ Winemaker(s) Rudiger Gretschel & Ryan Mostert (Jan 2011) ▪ Viticulturist(s) Johan Reyneke ▪ 40ha/32ha (cabs s/f, merlot, ptage, shiraz, chenin, sauv) ▪ 160t/30,000cs own label 70% red 30% white + 2,000cs for clients ▪ Brands for clients: Woolworths ▪ CERES (organic), Demeter (biodynamic), FFF (Woolworths), IPW, WIETA ▪ PO Box 61 Vlottenburg 7604 ▪ wine@reynekewines.co.za ▪ www.reynekewines.co.za ▪ S 33° 57' 27.7" E 018° 45' 7.0" ▪ **T +27 (0)21-881-3517/3451** ▪ F +27 (0)21-881-3285

Johan Reyneke long since shifted his Stellenbosch family farm towards organic practices and then further - it is registered as biodynamic, a rare distinction in the Cape. Johan's passionate concern for his vines and the well-being of the land is matched in the cellar by the brilliance of Rudiger Gretschel, chief guru at wine company Vinimark (which has an interest in the Reyneke brand). Together they are building this into unquestionably one of the Cape's top estates. But people are also respected here - the farm's workers, Johan says, are its cornerstone, hence the name of a wine whose profits go to a project benefiting them and their families. 'Quality with integrity' is the Reyneke mantra, and there's a purity and freshness allied with growing finesse in the wines that speaks volumes for both.

Biodynamic range
★★★★ **Pinotage** ⊚ 🍷 Inviting perfumed aromas introduce **11**. Serious though supple tannins need time to integrate, but there's enough bright fruit for them to do so. Light touch of bitterness on finish does no harm.
★★★★ **Syrah** ✓ ⊚ 🍷 Fragrance & lifted sweet red fruit on **11** (★★★★★) are the charming elements flirting with the serious, even elegantly austere structure - firm tannins & acid all in balance. No new oak. Possibly less easy, generous than **10**, but finer.
★★★★ **Cornerstone** ⊚ 🍷 **11** (★★★★★) blend of cab, merlot & cab franc integrates full-fruited deliciousness with firm structure & oak support to make a balanced, lively, rather elegant whole. Like **10**, best left a few years for increased harmony.
★★★★☆ **Reserve Red** ⊚ 🍷 **10** a remarkable, interesting wine - a spine-tingling blend of syrah/shiraz (whose pure-fruited flavours dominate) with 40% cab to enrich the superb tannic structure & add to the emerging complexity. Freshness & lightness belie 14.5% alcohol. Almost irresistibly compelling now, but will develop.
★★★★☆ **Chenin Blanc** ✓ ⊚ 🍷 Bright & fresh, subtle & supple, **12** (★★★★★) another exercise in lightly oaked elegance. Combines richness with a long dry finish, full fruit (melon, dried peach, apple, etc) with earthy notes & a mineral core. Deeply pleasing texture. Like **11**, from old, low-yielding vines.

★★★★☆ **Reserve White** ⊙ ▨ From new-barrelled sauvignon blanc & a bit of magic. 2 vintages tasted, oak still apparent on both, but will integrate in a few years. Youthful **11** (★★★★★) a touch sterner, with notable acid, fruit still enmeshed in emerging complexity. Exquisitely balanced **12** riper, easy in youth, with more delicate, floral, blackcurrant, citrus character. Notably fine textures, dry richness, long-lingering finishes on both.

★★★★ **Sauvignon Blanc** ⚘ ▨ Delicate floral, citrus aromas on **12**, leading to acid-drop green bite on good finish. Balanced, with typically lovely textures. Includes Voor-Paardeberg grapes. **11** (★★★★★) more exciting.

Organic range

Shiraz-Cabernet Sauvignon ⚘ Await next. **Chenin Blanc-Sauvignon Blanc-Chardonnay** ✓ ▤ ⚘ ▨ ★★★★ Name change reflects varietal proportions on **12**. Fresh & fruity, full-flavoured & round, with a slightly sour green bite. WO W Cape. — TJ

Rhebokskloof Wine Estate

Location: Paarl ▪ Map: Paarl & Wellington ▪ WO: Coastal/Paarl ▪ 1stB 1975 ▪ Tasting & sales Mon-Fri 9-5 Sat/Sun 10-3 ▪ Fee R15/5 wines ▪ Cellar tours by appt ▪ Rhebokskloof Restaurant open daily for b'fast & lunch; dinner Wed, Fri & Sat ▪ Facilities for children ▪ Tour groups ▪ Gifts ▪ Weddings, functions & conferences ▪ Walks/hikes ▪ Live concerts ▪ Owner(s) Siebrits & Albie Laker, ASLA Group ▪ Cellarmaster(s) Francois Naudé (Nov 2012) ▪ Winemaker(s) Rolanie Lotz (Jan 2007) ▪ Viticulturist(s) Karin Louw (Jan 2007) ▪ 180ha/30ha (grenache, mourv, ptage, shiraz, chard, viog) ▪ 250t/40,000cs own label 80% red 15% white 5% rosé + 3,000cs for buyers own brands ▪ PO Box 2637 Paarl 7620 ▪ info@rhebokskloof.co.za ▪ www.rhebokskloof.co.za ▪ S 33° 41' 6.1" E 018° 55' 56.6" ▪ **T +27 (0)21-869-8386** ▪ F +27 (0)21-869-8386

Owners and winemakers have come and gone at this centuries-old Paarl estate since its wines first appeared in this guide in 1991. Current proprietors Siebrits and Albie Laker of civils group ASLA are determined for Rhebokskloof to be a Top 10 South African winery, and extensive replanting and repositioning of the wine, hospitality and tourism businesses has begun. To this end, celebrated Francois Naudé (L'Avenir, Chateau Naudé) joined as cellarmaster from harvest 2013.

Mountain Vineyards Reserve range

★★★★ **Black Marble Hill Syrah** ▨ Serious (20 months all-new oak), handcrafted flagship in striking etched black glass bottle. Smoky **11** concentrated yet not weighty; savoury tang lifts controlled tannins.

Sandstone Grove Chardonnay ▨ ★★★★ **12** reticent at first, then opens to reveal fine citrus fruit melded with buttery oak (year, 30% new), full but not blowsy. From home grapes, like Syrah.

Rhebokskloof range

Pinotage ▨ ★★★★ **11** more affable & brightly fruity, less reliant on wood than several other reds in this stable. WO Paarl. **Shiraz** ✓ ▨ ★★★★ New bottling of **10** eschews dollops grenache & mourvèdre in last edition's offering; clean mulberry fruit in harmony with oak, 30% new. **Mourvèdre-Grenache-Shiraz** ⊕ ▨ ★★★★ Smidgen American oak adds sweetness to mulberry/cranberry fruit in **10**. **Viognier-Shiraz** `NEW` ▤ ▨ ★★ Unusual rosé; **12**'s 2% shiraz gives pink colour & moderates viognier's tropical tones. From home grapes. **Chardonnay** ▨ ★★★ Food-styled **12** without previous dash viognier. Already firm citrus tones get further stiffening from 20% new oak. **Viognier** ▨ ★★★ Plump, sweet peach/pine fruit, yet **12** restrained for the variety; attractive drinking. WO Paarl. **Chardonnay Méthode Cap Classique** ⊕ ★★★★ Inviting toffee apple & toasty brioche, fine mousse & creamy finish lift the bar in **07**. Discontinued: **Tamay Sparkling**.

Pearlstone range

Pinotage ▤ ▨ ★★★ Near-tropical banana/clove **11** finishes with bitter lift. **Shiraz** ▤ ▨ ★★★ Smoky pepper attraction; **11**'s red berry fruit tethered by firm tannins. **Cabernet Sauvignon-Merlot** ▤ ▨ ★★★ Cassis fruit of **11** not quite up to liberal 16 months seasoned oak. **Rosé** ⊕ ▤ ▨ ★★ Drops 'Merlot' from name, now shiraz-based; **11** easy off-dry pink sipper. **Bosstok Chenin Blanc** ▤ ▨ ★★★ 'Chenin Blanc' previously. Vibrant melon fruit of **13** lifts thatchy edge. Perdeberg bushvines. **Sauvignon Blanc** ▤ ▨ ★★ Green apple & grass-nuanced **13** a pleasant pick-me-up. **Sparkling Rosé** ⊕ ★★★ Drop shiraz provides rosy hue to viognier-led carbonated **NV** fizz. — DS

■ **Rhino** see The Rhino of Linton Park
■ **Rhinofields** see Durbanville Hills

Richard Kershaw Wines

Location/WO: Elgin ▪ Est/1stB 2012 ▪ Tasting by appt ▪ Owner(s) Richard Kershaw ▪ Cellarmaster(s) Richard Kershaw (2012) ▪ 20t/±2,500cs own label 52% red 48% white ▪ PO Box 77 Grabouw 7160 ▪ richard@rikipedia.co ▪ www.rikipedia.co ▪ **T +27 (0)21-300-1629 (VoIP)/+27 (0)21-848-9114** ▪ F +27 (0)86-637-6202

Owner and winemaker Richard Kershaw established his boutique winery 'to create clonally selected, site-specific, cool-climate wine paradigms' from noble grapes capable of producing world-class examples. He chose Elgin Valley for its 'higher altitude, ocean proximity, specific cloud cover sequencing, high cold-units and a large diurnal range', believing these factors would allow his preferred chardonnay and shiraz to show a sense of place. The first winemaker in South Africa to qualify as a Master of Wine, Richard modestly insists he's still learning: '2013 brought the ability to hone down particular skills wrought in 2012'. His 'Richard's' range is made exclusively for UK retailer Naked Wines.

Clonal Selections NEW

★★★★★ **Elgin Chardonnay** Refined understatement in stellar **12**, reflecting minimal but careful crafting (of Dijon clones CY95, CY96 & CY76), allowing fine acidity, minerality & judicious oak (40% new) to perfectly frame & support citrus & white peach fruit. Precise & classy. Delicious now & for many years. — DC, JP

Richelieu   NEW

This South African-owned brand straddles both Cognac and the Cape. The product of a French company founded in 1962 by the late Anton Rupert of Distillers Corporation (now Distell) to produce a richer, sweeter brandy akin to cognac, the brand now comprises three brandies: Richelieu XO Cognac Fine Champagne is Cognac-grown, distilled and matured for 25+ years (entitling it to be labelled 'cognac'); and Richelieu International and new 10 Year Old, which are local.

★★★★ **10 Year Vintage Brandy** At least ten years maturation on both the potstill (30%) & spirit content. Elegant but rich; harmonious & dry, with integrated vanilla oak colouring the apricot & prune complexity.

Richelieu International ★★★ Grapey, fruity aromas on this blended brandy - a mixer will tame its rather sweet aggression. — WB, TJ

Rickety Bridge Winery   

Location/map: Franschhoek ▪ WO: Franschhoek/Western Cape/Paarl/Coastal ▪ Est 1990 ▪ Tasting, sales & cellar tours Mon-Sat 9-7 (Dec-Mar)/9-5 (Apr-Nov) Sun 10-5 ▪ Closed Dec 25 & Jan 1 ▪ Fee R20, waived on purchase ▪ Paulina's at Rickety Bridge (see Restaurants section) ▪ Facilities for children ▪ Gift shop ▪ Conferences ▪ Weddings ▪ Rickety Bridge Manor House (see Accommodation section) ▪ Owner(s) DS Sarnia (Pty) Ltd ▪ Cellarmaster(s) Wynand Grobler (Nov 2007) ▪ Winemaker(s) Wynand Grobler (Nov 2007), with Danie de Bruyn (Jan 2011) ▪ 91ha/39ha (cab, merlot, shiraz, chard, chenin, sauv, sem) ▪ 195t/28,000cs own label 45% red 45% white 10% rosé ▪ PO Box 455 Franschhoek 7690 ▪ info@ricketybridge.com ▪ www.ricketybridge.com ▪ S 33° 53' 58.5" E 019° 5' 27.6" ▪ **T +27 (0)21-876-2129** ▪ F +27 (0)21-876-3486

A venerable Franschhoek property granted to the widow Paulina de Villiers in 1797, Rickety Bridge in recent years has been transformed under the aegis of British owner Duncan Spence. Luxury accommodation and varied, family-welcoming cellardoor facilities have been created (look out for new deli and wine-and-canapé tastings), and the wine team under Wynand Grobler have steadily ratcheted up the bar. Debuting this edition are a blanc de blancs bubbly and jazzed-up livery for Mediterranean blend The Foundation Stone.

Icon Wines

★★★★☆ **The Bridge** Flagship from 100% cab, naturally fermented, seriously oaked (100% new, 25 months). **09** (bottle 166 of 2,000 tasted) restrained & subtle cassis fruit, firm structure; like elegant **08** shows wonderful integration of cool fruit & fine wood tannin.

Paulina's Reserve range

★★★★ **Cabernet Sauvignon 10** iron fist in velvet glove: dense texture & firm tannic structure swathed in cool mint & blackberry fruit. Similar to **09** (★★★★★) yet on review not showing as much charm. WO Paarl.

★★★★ **Sauvignon Blanc** ✓ 🍴 Opposite to prevailing green, spiky styles: 30% barrel-fermented for broadness, softer white-asparagus & tinned pea tones. **12** tasty mouthful, very satisfying. WO W Cape, as next.
Chenin Blanc ✓ 🍴 ★★★★ Quietly beguiles with subtle honey & flowers, bright dry finish; large-format oak (100% new) smartly used to provide weight, depth & vanilla patina. **12** more convincing than **11** (★★★★).
Semillon ★★★★ Unlike genteel **09**, **10** struts its oak ferment/ageing (20% new) in overt vanilla & butterscotch, oak-sweet farewell to lemongrass fruit.

Rickety Bridge range

★★★★ **Merlot** Seduction in a glass, **10**'s antique furniture polish nuances, luxurious plum & boozy cherry tastes, seamless tannins as delicious as svelte, step-up **09**. Unless noted, these WO W Cape.

★★★★ **Shiraz** **11**'s savoury body contains black pepper, garrigue scrub & red fruit layers. Tight, will be better after year/2 cellaring, yet no less admirable than supple & sweet-fruited **10**, **09**.

Pinotage 🈯 ★★★ Opaque **12** perfumed with violets & strawberries, belying strong tannic underpin. **The Foundation Stone** ★★★★ Widely sourced fruit for **11**, savoury shiraz-led 6-way blend, now more fetchingly packaged. Characterful dinner companion with fynbos notes. For current enjoyment. **Rosé** ★★★ Mainly shiraz & merlot, **13** tank sample faint raspberry & bubblegum, distinctly dry tail for food. **Chardonnay** ✓ ★★★★ Continues improving with effortless **12**, smooth creaminess from well-applied oak (10% new), perfectly offsetting citrus acidity. WO Franschhoek, as for MCCs & Natural Sweet. **Chenin Blanc** 🍴 ★★★ Honeyed oats, nutmeg & cinnamon on previewed **13** very inviting. Satisfying if brief; might settle & grow after bottling. **Sauvignon Blanc** ★★★ Tank sample forthcoming & complex khaki bush, grass & passionfruit notes, pleasant gravelly texture. **13** goes up a rung. **Méthode Cap Classique Brut Rosé** ⓐ ★★★★ Smouldering magnetism to **10**; onion skin hue, languid bubble & smooth yeasty mousse. Oaked 6 months then 18 months on lees. **Méthode Cap Classique Blanc de Blancs** NEW ★★★★ Food-friendly **09** sparkling from chardonnay exudes smoky, yeasty aromas (courtesy 30% oaked portion, 30 months on lees), lipsmacking dry finish. **Natural Sweet Chenin Blanc** 🍴 🈯 ★★★★ Improved **12** complete opposite of last **10**. Discreet white peach & almond notes, similarly delicate flavours; light & fresh. — CvZ

Rico Suter Private Cellar

Location: Worcester ▪ Map/WO: Breedekloof ▪ Est/1stB 2004 ▪ Tasting, sales & tours by appt ▪ Cheese platters & homemade bread ▪ Tour groups ▪ Olive oil & table olives ▪ BYO picnic ▪ Walking/hiking & mountain biking trails ▪ Bird watching ▪ Guesthouse (bookings: erika@ricosuterwines.com) ▪ Owner(s) Suter Family Trust ▪ Cellarmaster(s) Rico Suter, advised by Carlo Suter ▪ Winemaker(s) Rico Suter ▪ Viticulturist(s) Bruno Suter (2004) ▪ 750ha/45ha (cab, cinsaut, p verdot, ptage, shiraz, sauv, viog) ▪ 8-15t/ha 8,850L own label 95% red 5% white ▪ PO Box 38 Breerivier 6858 ▪ ricosuterwines@breede.co.za ▪ S 33° 31' 39.00" E 019° 15' 13.00" ▪ **T +27 (0)23-355-1822** ▪ F +27 (0)86-642-6591

At this beautifully situated Swiss family estate in Breedekloof, co-owner/winemaker Rico Suter is pleased to have son Carlo back with him semi-permanently, especially as they had a very good harvest. 'Times are tough,' Rico notes, 'but we're trying to add China to our overseas clients.'

★★★★ **L'Amitié** ⓐ Individual & complex **06** combo cinsaut, shiraz, petit verdot, viognier. Silky mouthfeel, floral notes, emphatic dry exit.

★★★★ **Cabernet Sauvignon-Syrah** ⓐ **06** earthy wafts, ripe black berries, soft & seductively juicy centre contrasts with elegant dry end.

Cabernet Sauvignon ⓐ ★★★ **05** succulent & plummy, with savoury flavours. **Petit Verdot** ⓐ Broad shouldered **04**, savoury tones & chocolate/mocha overlay, good tannic support. **Pinotage** ⓐ 🈯 **12** preview (first since **08**) exudes scented fruit pastille charm. Smooth textured & supple. **Syrah** Await next, as for **Cabernet Sauvignon-Petit Verdot**, **Sauvignon Blanc**, **Viognier-Chenin Blanc**. — MW

Ridgeback

Location: Paarl ▪ Map: Paarl & Wellington ▪ WO: Paarl/Western Cape ▪ Est 1997 ▪ 1stB 2001 ▪ Tasting & sales Mon-Sat 10-5 (summer)/10-4 (winter) Sun 10-4 ▪ Fee R25/5 wines, R50/10 wines ▪ Closed Good Fri, Dec 25 & Jan 1 ▪ Cellar tours by appt ▪ The Deck Restaurant Tue-Sun 9.30-3 ▪ 4-star/5-room Ridgeback Guest House ▪ Hiking trails ▪ Children's play area ▪ Owner(s) Kilimanjaro Investments ▪ Cellarmaster(s)/winemaker(s) Toit Wessels (Jan 2007) ▪ Viticulturist(s) Toit Wessels (Mar 2000) ▪ 65ha/35ha (cabs s/f, grenache, merlot, mourv, p verdot, shiraz, sauv, viog) ▪ 225t/30,000cs own label 60% red 35% white 5% rosé ▪ BWI ▪ PO Box 2076

Windmeul Paarl 7630 ▪ tasting@ridgeback.co.za ▪ www.ridgebackwines.co.za ▪ S 33° 40' 24.9" E 018° 54' 53.5" ▪ **T** +27 (0)21-869-8068 ▪ F +27 (0)21-869-8146

Jerry Parker, who bought this Paarl property in 1997, had retired from farming tobacco in Malawi and Zimbabwe - which accounts for the winery name and branding associated with Rhodesian Ridgeback dogs. Toit Wessels was first the viticulturist, but later took over winemaking duties as well, producing a range noted for its fine quality:price ratio. He's also proud of the closeness of the whole team, which, he says, was very evident during 'the record breaking harvest for 2013, when everyone worked tirelessly towards the common good'.

★★★★ **Cabernet Sauvignon** ✓ ⧄ Forthcoming, ample sweet black fruit pastille aromas & flavours in **11**, well integrated, with supple & cedary oak tannins; the result is an accessible & flavoursome whole. No **10**.

★★★★ **Shiraz** ✓ Complex, judiciously oaked **09** fresh & ripe, layered dark red fruit restrained by svelte tannins. Plush dark chocolate tones complement rich spiciness; yields full-flavoured finish.

★★★★ **Journey** ✓ ⧄ Fragrant, spicy **12** (first tasted since **06**) trimly elegant cab franc-led blend with merlot, cab & petit verdot. Vibrant red fruit structured & seasoned by older oak; complex & accessible.

★★★★ **Chenin Blanc** ✓ ⧄ Barrel-fermented, lees-enriched, balanced **13** from bushvines focuses on mouthfeel; gets greater richness & complexity from tiny addition of natural sweet wine prior to bottling.

★★★★ **Viognier** ⧄ Richly floral, classy, polished **12** maintains usual charm with peachy fruit & spiciness from serious oaking. Harmonious & flavourful, though a touch more acid would add welcome verve.

Vansha Red ☺ ⊞ ⧄ ★★★ Emphasis on spiciness & accessibility in **12** juicy shiraz-led blend. Older oak imparts agreeable grip to ripe fruit. **Vansha White** ☺ ⊞ ⧄ ★★★ **13** sauvignon's inviting freshness blends well with oaked chenin's fullness & viognier's easy, fragrantly spicy charm. WO W Cape.

Cabernet Franc Await next. **Merlot** ⧄ ★★★★ Ripe, savoury **11** has appealing sour cherry edge to plum fruit, well seasoned by spicy oak; touch less convincing than **09** (★★★★). No **10**. **SGMV** ✓ ⧄ ★★★★ Softly spicy, savoury shiraz-based **12** in deftly oaked blend with succulent grenache, mourvèdre & splash viognier. **His Master's Choice** ✓ ★★★★ Harmonious, seamless **08** blend led by shiraz, with mourvèdre & dollop viognier; pliable tannins & oak structure complex, spicy, succulent fruit. Step up from **06** (★★★☆). **Shiraz Rosé** ⊞ ⧄ ★★★ Strawberry-toned **13** delightfully fresh, dry & savoury. **Sauvignon Blanc** ⊞ ⧄ ★★★★ Tropical-toned, harmonious **13**; staggered harvesting merges zippy acid with fruity ripeness, wrapped around mineral core. **Natural Sweet Viognier** Await next. Discontinued: **Cape Ruby**. — IM

■ **Ridgelands** *see* Luddite Wines

Riebeek Cellars

Location: Riebeek-Kasteel ▪ Map/WO: Swartland ▪ Est 1941 ▪ Tasting & sales Mon-Fri 9-5 Sat 9-4 Sun 10.30-4 (wine boutique) ▪ Closed Good Fri, Dec 25 & Jan 1 ▪ Cellar tours by appt ▪ BYO picnic ▪ Owner(s) ±40 shareholders ▪ Cellarmaster(s) Zakkie Bester (Dec 1999) ▪ Winemaker(s) Eric Saayman & Alecia Boshoff (Jan 1997/Dec 2004), with Daniel Slabber (May 2013) ▪ Viticulturist(s) Tharien Hansen (Jul 2013) ▪ 1,200ha (cab, carignan, merlot, mourv, ptage, shiraz, tinta amerela, chard, chenin, sauv, viog) ▪ 17,000t/300,000cs own label 50% red 40% white 10% rosé & ±80,000cs for clients ▪ Brands for clients: Broken Rock, Rocheburg, Royal, Steenbok ▪ BWI, Fairtrade, HACCP, WIETA ▪ PO Box 13 Riebeek Kasteel 7307 ▪ info@riebeekcellars.co.za ▪ www.riebeekcellars.com ▪ S 33° 22' 58.0" E 018° 54' 54.5" ▪ **T** +27 (0)22-448-1213 ▪ F +27 (0)22-448-1281

While tiny producers in this part of the Swartland take the headlines, large wineries like Riebeek Cellars play a vital part in the scheme of things – not only in supplying grapes to some well-known Cape brands, but also in offering affordable good value, with easygoing, often slightly sweet and simply fruity wines. Not that ambition is lacking, as shown in the more serious-minded A Few Good Men wines and the Kasteelberg range, which, the winemakers say, 'gives us the opportunity to slow down the process'. Unsurprisingly perhaps – given that this is the Swartland – shiraz and chenin are generally the standouts.

A Few Good Men range

Merlot ☺ ⧄ ★★★ Ripe, mellow berry & spicy tobacco notes on firmly structured, balanced & savoury **10**. **Chardonnay** ☺ ⧄ ★★★ More character & weight on neatly oaked **10** than on standard version, with pickled lime presence.

Cabernet Sauvignon ⊕ 🗟 ★★★ Classic, pleasing fruit profile on **11**. Drier, more structure than standard version. **Pinotage** ⊕ 🗟 ★★★ Spicy, smoky oak notes add complexity to heavy textured **11**, but tannins are too much in youth for the modest sweet fruit. **Shiraz** ⊕ 🗟 ★★★★ Less oak (& power) than Kasteelberg version means lovely berry fruit shows more. Satisfying grip takes **10**'s charm to a good dry finish.

Kasteelberg range

Shiraz ⊕ 🗟 ★★★★ Ripely powerful **10**, high alcohol balanced by rich fruit & savoury tannins. Generous oaking adds spicy tobacco notes. **Chenin Blanc** ⊕ 🗟 ★★★★ Good fruit flavour on **10** with vanilla & nut from well-integrated oak. Not intense, but a fresh dry elegance & charm. **Viognier** Await next. **Kasteelberg Méthode Cap Classique** ⊕ ★★★ NV white sparkler tasted some years back; apple zip & baked bread richness. **Soet Steen** ⊕ 🗟 ★★★★ From brandy-fortified chenin, **NV** (**10**) old-oaked jerepigo very sweet but piercingly balanced, good flavour. 500ml.

Riebeeck Collection

> **Cabernet Sauvignon** ☺ 🍴 🗟 ★★★ Pleasantly fruity but not too overt **12** is firm & engaging, fairly dry. **Merlot** ☺ 🍴 🗟 ★★★ Softly but effectively structured **12**, subtly oaked so as not to spoil the gentle fruit. **Shiraz** ☺ 🍴 🗟 ★★★ Pick of the bunch – nicely supple & balanced, savoury but sweet-fruited **12**. **Pinotage Rosé** ☺ 🍴 🗟 ★★★ Light flavours & berry fragrance on fresh, charming & just-dry **13**. **Chardonnay** ☺ 🍴 🗟 ★★★ Dry, light-footed **12** though biggish alcohol adds weight & warmth to pithy unwooded citrus notes. **Chenin Blanc** ☺ 🍴 🗟 ★★★ Typically easygoing **13**, modestly flavoursome with good fresh grip.

Pinotage 🍴 🗟 ★★ Mildly perfumed **12** a bit sweeter, thicker textured than others. **Cabernet Sauvignon-Merlot** ⊕ 🍴 🗟 ★★★ Successful **11** blend, the pretty, sweet fruitiness well contained. **Shiraz-Cinsaut** Await next. **Sauvignon Blanc** 🍴 🗟 ★★ A herbaceous tingle on mild **13**. **Pieter Cruythoff Brut** 🗟 ★★★ Short-lived bubbles, notes of apples & berries on crisp **NV** from chardonnay & pinot. **Cape Ruby Port** ⊕ 🗟 ★★★ Friendly, fruity **NV** has gentle toffee notes leading to lingering, fiery end. Mostly touriga. Discontinued: **Viognier**.

Montino range

Petillant Natural Sweet Rosé 🍴 🗟 ★ Sweet, pale, insipid **NV**. Low alcohol, as for all these. **Petillant Light** 🍴 ★★ Semi-sweet, grapey **NV** perlé white. **Petillant Natural Sweet Red-Rosso** NEW ★ Vague traces of flavour on spritzy **NV** - try chilled. — TJ

■ **Rietrivier** *see Montagu Wine & Spirits Co*

Rietvallei Wine Estate 🍴🍷☕📷♿

Location/map: Robertson ▪ WO: Robertson/Western Cape ▪ Est 1864 ▪ 1stB 1975 ▪ Tasting & sales Mon-Fri 8. 30–5 Sat 10–2 ▪ R25pp for groups of 15+ ▪ Closed Easter Fri/Sun, Dec 25 & Jan 1 ▪ Cellar tours by appt ▪ Cheese platters, book ahead for groups of 6+ ▪ Farm produce ▪ Conservation area ▪ Owner(s) Kobus Burger ▪ Cellarmaster(s)/winemaker(s) Kobus Burger (2003) ▪ Viticulturist(s) Wilhelm Treurnicht ▪ 215ha/130ha (cab, ref muscadel, shiraz, chard, sauv) ▪ 2,500t/110,000cs own label 40% red 50% white 5% rosé 5% fortified + 950,000L bulk ▪ Other brands: John B, Stonedale ▪ PO Box 386 Robertson 6705 ▪ info@rietvallei.co.za ▪ www. rietvallei.co.za ▪ S 33° 49' 25.7" E 019° 58' 39.4" ▪ **T +27 (0)23-626-3596** ▪ F +27 (0)23-626-4514

Celebrating 150 years of Burger family ownership this year, Rietvallei is one of the oldest wine farms in Robertson. The estate was bought in 1864 by Alewyn Burger for his son Jacobus Francois who, at age 70, planted a muscadel vineyard still very much in production (see below). Muscadel was also the first wine bottled under the estate label, released in 1975. The maiden estate white wine debuted in 1987, a wooded chardonnay. Exactly 25 vintages on, Rietvallei Special Select Chardonnay was placed 4th overall in the Chardonnay du Monde competition, a particularly proud moment for 6th generation winemaker Kobus.

Special Select range

★★★★ **Estéanna Red** 🗟 Bordeaux blend cab & cab franc (60/38), petit verdot in **10** (★★★). Preview very ripe, with strong grape & wood tannins (100% new oak) needing time, unlike early-approachable **09**.

★★★★ **Estéanna White** 🗟 Flagship barrel-fermented white led by sauvignon & chardonnay, dashes chenin & viognier. Aromatic **12** tank sample similar fruit-filled roundedness as **11**. Could age interestingly.

★★★★☆ **Muscadel 1908** ⏲ 🍇 Gorgeous fortified dessert from 105 year old red muscat de Frontignan vines. **11** amazingly nuanced perfume - tealeaf, cranberry, lime, strawberry - all in a light almost delicate body that endures forever. Special wine for special occasions. **08** more unctuous but still balanced. No **09**, **10**.

Shiraz ⏲ 🍇 ★★★★ Welcoming spice & red berries on concentrated & generous yet still refreshing **10**, plush fruit laps up 100% new oak. **Chardonnay** 🍇 ★★★☆ 70% new oak for decadent, full-bore **12**, toasty oak overlay to lemon & baked apple fruit, chalky citrus uplift to palate. Big, showy wine, will hopefully integrate with time. **Sauvignon Blanc** 🍇 ★★★☆ Now bottled, **12** combines 50% Durbanville fruit with own grapes. Bone-dry, with sweet fig & tropical complexity, poised acidity, lengthy conclusion.

Classic Estate range

Chenin Blanc ☺ 🍶 🍇 ★★★ Previously unwooded, **13** with naturally barrel-fermented component. Honey, baked apple & almond tart richness countered by crisp acidity. Moderate 13% alcohol.

Cabernet Sauvignon 🍇 ★★★ Cedar & tobacco on **11** preview, tightly knit, reined-in flavours (& alcohol - 13.5%); well-composed dinner companion. **Pinot Noir** ⏲ 🍇 ★★★ Cherry perfumed maiden **10** tad brusque & very dry last time, needed time to settle & develop. **Shiraz-Petit Verdot-Viognier** ✓ 🍇 ★★★☆ Improved **11** spicy, juicy & vibrant, with lovely intensity, pliable tannins. Very good now with structure to improve. **Natural Chardonnay** ⏲ 🍶 ★★★ Appealing lime-lemon freshness on unwooded **12**, extra weight & depth from 4 months lees-ageing. **Sauvignon Blanc** ⏲ 🍶 🍇 ★★★ Picked at three different ripeness levels, **12** youthful & bit introverted mid-2012. Might have perked up by now. **Red Muscadel** 🍶 🍇 ★★★★ For summer or winter, just add ice or fire; **12** sweet fortified treat with molasses, cinnamon & Christmas cake flavours.

The Innings range

Cabernet Sauvignon 🍶 🍇 ★★★★ These a joint venture with cricketers Jacques Kallis & Mark Boucher. **11** hits the sweet spot with intense fruit, refreshing acidity, savoury grip & balanced 13.5% alcohol. **Sauvignon Blanc** ⏲ 🍶 ★★★ **12** lean (courtesy early picking), flinty & ultra-brisk. — HJ,MW

◼ **Rijckholt** see Zandvliet Wine Estate & Thoroughbred Stud
◼ **Rijckshof** see Oudtshoorn Cellar - SCV

Rijk's

Location/map: Tulbagh ▪ WO: Tulbagh/Coastal ▪ Est 1996 ▪ 1stB 2000 ▪ Tasting & sales Mon-Fri 10–4 Sat 10–2 ▪ Fee R10/wine, waived on purchase ▪ Closed Easter Fri-Mon, Dec 25 & Jan 1 ▪ Cellar tours by appt ▪ Rijk's Guest House ▪ Conferences ▪ Owner(s)/viticulturist(s) Neville Dorrington ▪ Winemaker(s) Pierre Wahl (Jan 2002) ▪ 135ha/36ha (carignan, grenache noir, mourv, ptage, shiraz, tinta amarela, chard, chenin, viog) ▪ 210t/ 24,000cs own label 75% red 25% white ▪ IPW ▪ PO Box 400 Tulbagh 6820 ▪ wine@rijks.co.za ▪ www.rijks.co.za ▪ S 33° 16' 1.5" E 019° 8' 42.0" ▪ **T +27 (0)23-230-1622** ▪ F +27 (0)23-230-1650

Rijk's owner Neville Dorrington originally made his money manufacturing luxury leather goods but chose to abandon Cape Town for some country living in 1996. Opting for unfashionable Tulbagh, he bought a large plot of virgin land and though advised to plant fruit, set about establishing vineyard. Today the property specialises in chenin, pinotage and shiraz and Dorrington, along with winemaker Pierre Wahl, have pretty much confounded conventional wisdom making seriously good versions of all three varieties.

Estate range

★★★★ **Shiraz** ⏲ Very ripe **07** retained composure thanks to crisp acidity, savoury oak & dash viognier; ±15% alcohol not a detraction.

★★★★ **The Master** ⏲ Dark-fruited & opulent **07** shiraz-led (50%) with dashes mourvèdre, pinotage. New oak hid ±15% alcohol & tight tannin previously noted may have relaxed now.

Reserve range

★★★★☆ **Pinotage** Distinguished from Private Cellar & Touch of Oak versions by more new oak. Classy **09** (★★★★★) true to variety, with plush dark fruit, whiff banana, tightly coiled structure & measured tannins. Like **08**, juicy & well composed, with enough substance to reward extended cellaring.

★★★★ **Shiraz** ⏲ Silky **09** another well-crafted & satisfying offering from the maestro of the riper end of the spectrum, handled 66% new French oak very well.

★★★★ **Chenin Blanc** ⏲ 08's (★★★★★) fine expression of Tulbagh fruit raised bar on **07**. Mouthcoating honey, candied lime & butterscotch, creamy persistence.

Discontinued: **Chardonnay**.

Private Cellar range

★★★★ **Pinotage** Raspberry-toned **09** dusted with spice, sweet impression from American oak portion lifted by firm tannins. Less powerful than Reserve, less elegant than much-awarded **08** (★★★★★).

★★★★ **Shiraz** Commanding **08** (★★★★★) improves on excellent **07**. Ripe yet unshowy, with similar vibrancy & malleable tannins but a greater presence.

★★★★ **Chenin Blanc** ⏲ Consistently excellent barrel fermented/aged version, from **09** off own vines. Extravagantly flavoured, lemony & slightly sweet from big alcohol & grain sugar.

Discontinued: **The Crossing**, **Bravado**, **Chardonnay**, **Fascination**.

Touch of Oak range

★★★★ **Pinotage** **11** more 'red wine' than 'pinotage', flavoursome & satisfyingly glassful all the same. Coastal WO, like Chenin. These for enjoying in youth.

★★★★☆ **Chenin Blanc** **11** back on track: starts rich & creamy then reveals a steely, almost challenging fruit core, demanding cellaring or decanting now. **10** (★★★★), was a touch off flamboyant **09**.

Shiraz ⏲ ★★★ Deft dab of oak, medium body & olive-like savoury flavours in last tasted **10**. — CE,CvZ

■ **Rijk's Estate** *see Rijk's*

Rivendell

Location/WO: Bot River ▪ Map: Elgin, Walker Bay & Bot River ▪ Est 2008 ▪ 1stB 2011 ▪ Tasting & sales daily 8-5 ▪ Bistro open daily 8-5; Fri eve by prior booking; cater for functions of various sizes ▪ Picnics in summer, to be pre-booked ▪ Facilities for children ▪ Tour groups ▪ Venue for weddings & seminars with fully equipped kitchen (94 pax inside) ▪ Walks/hikes ▪ Owner(s) Whales & Castle Investments (Pty) Ltd, with shareholders Heimo & Maria Thalhammer ▪ Winemaker(s) Kobie Viljoen (Mar 2010, Gabriëlskloof) & PJ Geyer (Feb 2013, Barton) ▪ Viticulturist(s) Schalk du Toit (Mar 2008, consultant) ▪ ±8ha/±4ha (shiraz, sauv) ▪ 32t/1,000cs own label 33% red 67% white ▪ PO Box 181 Onrusrivier 7201 ▪ office@rivendell-estate.co.za ▪ www.rivendell-estate.co.za ▪ S 34° 18' 5.22" E 019° 8' 32.23" ▪ **T** +27 (0)28-284-9185/9597 ▪ **F** +27 (0)28-284-9597

Rivendell boutique winery in up-and-coming Bot River boasts a picturesque function venue and home-styled bistro set among the vines. The new selection of organic Zotter chocolates imported from Austria form interesting pairings with the wines (red and white made at Gabriëlskloof, rosé at Barton).

★★★★ **Shiraz** NEW ▨ **11** sashays confidently onto scene with juicy black & red fruit, soft tannins, spicy tail. Looks set to be trumped over time by also-tasted **12** preview, with excellent depth of fruit & firm tannins.

★★★★ **Sauvignon Blanc** ▤ ▨ Very delicious **13** (★★★★★) continuing upward quality curve from **12** preview & **11** (★★★★), showing plenty of grassy herbaceous notes, well-managed acidity & classic black-currant finish. Powdery texture & fine structure suggest it's a keeper.

Rosé NEW ▨ ★★★★ From shiraz, **13** is a zippy little number with strawberry, cranberry & spice. Dry & appetizing, good food partner. — CM

■ **River Crossing** *see Lourensford Wine Estate*
■ **River Garden** *see Lourensford Wine Estate*
■ **River Grandeur** *see Viljoensdrift Wines & Cruises*
■ **Riverscape** *see Viljoensdrift Wines & Cruises*
■ **Robert Alexander** *see Nico van der Merwe Wines*

Robertson Wide River Export Company

Joint venture between Robertson Winery and Vinimark, handling all Robertson Winery exports under brand names such as Robertson Winery, Kaapdal, Kleindal, Silversands and Veldt. See Vinimark for contact details.

Robertson Winery

Location/map/WO: Robertson ▪ Est 1941 ▪ 1stB 1987 ▪ Tasting & sales Mon-Fri 9-5.30 Sat/Sun 9-3 pub hols 9-5 ▪ Closed Good Fri, Dec 25 & Jan 1 ▪ Cellar tours by appt ▪ Conferences ▪ Small wine museum ▪ Owner(s) 43

members ▪ Cellarmaster(s) Bowen Botha (Jan 1982) ▪ Winemaker(s) Francois Weich (Sep 1997), Jacques Roux (Jan 2001), Thys Loubser & Olivia Poonah (both Jan 2012) ▪ Viticulturist(s) Briaan Stipp (May 2005) ▪ 2,200ha (cab, shiraz, chard, chenin, sauv) ▪ 37,200t ±27m L for clients ▪ ISO 22000, WIETA ▪ PO Box 37 Robertson 6705 ▪ info@robertsonwine.co.za ▪ www.robertsonwinery.co.za ▪ S 33° 48′ 36.8″ E 019° 52′ 51.4″ ▪ **T** +27 (0)23-626-3059 ▪ F +27 (0)23-626-2926

Labelling itself as 'progressive, competitive and dynamic', grower-owned Robertson Winery is one of South Africa's largest producers, and it continues to set inhouse records: last year's 37,200-ton crush was the biggest since founding in 1941. Future harvests will benefit from expanded investment in red-wine production facilities – a growth area for the winery - planned for this year. For 'always-welcome' visitors, the adjacent cellardoor in downtown Robertson has been remodelled to include a dedicated venue for chocolate-and-wine pairings.

Constitution Road range

★★★★☆ **No. 1 Constitution Road Shiraz** 🌐 Serious flagship from single-vineyard. Bold **10**'s plush fruit soaks up 100% new oak, counters 14.7% alcohol for balance, sophistication of **08**. Sweet vanilla detail enlivened by spice, smoke; similar nuances found on unashamedly 'New World' **09** (★★★★).

Vineyard Selection range

★★★★ **Retreat Sauvignon Blanc** 🍷 Tasted pre-botting as usual, **13** heady grass & fig aromas followed by well-defined palate, showing satisfying weight & length at moderate 13% alcohol. **Prospect Hill Cabernet Sauvignon** 🌐 ★★★★ Classic cab cassis & lead pencil bouquet, but **11** is atypically soft & broad; still delivers elegant, tasty glassful. **Phanto Ridge Pinotage** 🌐 ★★★★ Returns to guide with **11**, interesting mouthful banana, smoke & mulberry; not-overdone 13.8% alcohol & deft oaking (older barrels) ensure current drinkability, provide platform for improvement 3+ years. **Wolfkloof Shiraz** ★★★★ **11** work-in-progress very smart indeed: modern & intense but no rough edges; handles 100% new oak, big 14.7% alcohol with aplomb & delivers greater complexity than spicy **08**. **10**, **09** sold out untasted. **Kings River Chardonnay** Await next.

Winery range

★★★★☆ **Red Muscadel** ⓕ Fortified style not noted for elegance but this **NV** bottling shows great refinement & delicacy. Red fruit, some raisin, spice & nuts in a medium body, with fresh acidity & well-handled fortification; subtle & poised conclusion.

Pinot Noir ☺ 🍴 🌐 ★★★ Unoaked **12** now bottled; still showcases appealing strawberry aromas/flavours, gentle spice & savoury tail for food. Serve slightly chilled in summer. **Pinotage** ☺ 🍴 🌐 ★★★ **12** rings all the pinotage bells: banana & smoke aromas, mulberry palate, zesty farewell; at only 13% alcohol you can enjoy a second glass. **Ruby Cabernet** ☺ 🍴 🌐 ★★★ **13** fruit-packed, with mere suggestion of tannin; just add friends. **Shiraz** ☺ 🍴 🌐 ★★★ **12** brisk & engaging, unpretentious bistro red with white pepper top notes. **Chenin Blanc** ☺ 🍴 🌐 ★★★ Oak-touched **13** is off-dry, with lovely quince grip & pleasing green-fruit tang. **Beaukett** ☺ 🍴 🌐 ★★★ **13** as advertised: posy of roses & litchis, sweet but zingy combo muscat (70%) & colombard.

Cabernet Sauvignon 🍴 🌐 ★★ Sweet-sour fruit, softly dry palate on easygoing **12**. As for most reds in range, oak-staved in tank. **Merlot** 🍴 🌐 ★★ Fairly intense choc-plum, slight leafy character on lively **13** tank sample. **Cabernet Sauvignon-Shiraz** 🍴 🌐 ★★★ Cab's dark fruit & acidity, shiraz's spice in **12** blend provide uncomplicated drinking. **Chardonnay** 🍴 🌐 ★★★ Oak & texturing lees noticeable on **13**, wins you over with vanilla-infused yellow stonefruit & dusting of sugar. **Pinot Grigio** 🍴 🌐 ★★☆ Seafood companion **13** zippy lemon-lime delight, slippery texture from nearly 14% alcohol. **Sauvignon Blanc** 🍴 🌐 ★★ **13** simple but lively, some grapefruit aromas/flavours. **Viognier** 🍴 🌐 ★★★ Unwooded **13** quintessentially viognier peach & apricot scents, spice & fair grip on palate for food or solo. **Méthode Cap Classique** ⓕ ★★★ **07** dry sparkling from chardonnay & pinot noir is subtle & fresh, with a savoury conclusion. **Gewürztraminer Special Late Harvest** 🍴 🌐 ★★★☆ Light bodied but rich & delicious **12** luxuriates in unabashed gewurz charm: litchi, Turkish Delight, sun-kissed raisins & long, balanced finish. **Cape Ruby** Await new release. Discontinued: **White Muscadel**.

Chapel range

Cabernet Sauvignon-Merlot ★★ Was 'Red'. Choc-infused **13** for get-togethers with friends. Lightly oaked, previewed. These variously available in 500ml, 750ml & 1.5L. **White** Await next. **Extra Light** [NEW] 🍴 ★★ **NV** delivers plenty of lemon refreshment at 10% alcohol. Drink soon. **Semi-Sweet** ⓕ ★★☆

Sweetish **NV** lifted by zesty acidity, appealing baked fruit aromas. **Natural Sweet** ★★ Low-alcohol **NV** rosé's light, sweet red fruit complemented by crisp nip in tail. Chill & enjoy.

Natural Sweet range

Red ★★ Lightly fruity, low-alcohol quaffing fun for the sweet-toothed. Latest **NV** brushed with oak. Available in 750ml, 1.5L as are some of the others. **Rosé** ★★ Latest Bollywood pink **NV** with cherry perfume & measured sweetness. **White** ★★ Gently sweet **NV** tastes like papaya & pineapple.

Two-Litre Certified Cultivar Cask range

Ruby Cabernet ☺ 𝄞 ★★★ Fruity & crisp party red **13** glides down effortlessly. **Shiraz** ☺ 𝄞 ★★★ Licorice, spice & all things nice... on friendly **12** sipper. **Chenin Blanc** ☺ 𝄞 ★★★ Floral **13** briefly oaked for a bit of weight, texture; versatile picnic white.

Cabernet Sauvignon 𝄞 ★★ Black tea nuances, dusty oak on dry **12** BBQ sipper. **Merlot** 𝄞 ★★ Previewed **13** choc-plums & slight leafiness, brisk acidity for tomato pasta. **Chardonnay** 𝄞 ★★★ Apricot & peach nuance, vanilla daub on affable **13**; hint of oak, spoonful of sugar for extra appeal. **Sauvignon Blanc** 𝄞 ★★★ Grapefruit flavour in tangy & very drinkable **13**.

Three-Litre Cultivar Slimline range

Shiraz ☺ 𝄞 ★★★ **12**'s rhubarb & white pepper notes, perky acidity is appealing & food friendly.

Cabernet Sauvignon 𝄞 ★★ **12** sufficient fruit, dry impression for mealtimes. Oak-staved in tank, as most reds in this range. **Merlot** 𝄞 ★★ Early drinking **13** has soft red-berry appeal, slightly leafy tannins. **Chardonnay** 𝄞 ★★★ Kiss of oak, smidgen sugar on crowd-pleasing, peachy **13**. **Sauvignon Blanc** 𝄞 ★★ Muted **13** has faint grapefruit tones, perky tail. **Sauvignon Blanc Extra Light** 𝄞 ★★ Friendly 9% alcohol, soft peachy & appley **13**. **Natural Sweet White** NEW ★★ Bright tropical appeal on softly sweet **NV** sipper.

Three-Litre Blended range

Smooth Dry Red ★★ Very drinkable **NV** with mouthfilling red fruit. **Crisp Dry White** 𝄞 ★★ **NV** clean-cut glassful of potpourri-scented fruit. **Refreshing Extra Light** ★★ Much improved **NV** with Granny Smith nose/palate. **Johannisberger Semi-Sweet White** ★★ As always frangipani redolence; latest **NV** needs more zip. **Natural Sweet Red (Slimline Packed)** ★★ Uncloying but sweet & light **NV** very drinkable. **Natural Sweet Rosé (Slimline Packed)** ★★ **NV** lifted by thatch notes, sweet but not cloying. **Johannisberger Semi-Sweet Red** ★ Unexpected but pleasant toasted bread character on sweetish **NV**.

Combibloc range

Cabernet Sauvignon NEW 𝄞 ★★ **12**'s sweet-sour acid lift, dry finish perfect for meaty dinners. As for most reds in range, oak-staved in tank. **Smooth Dry Red** ★★ Balanced, pocket-friendly **NV** cheer. **Chardonnay** NEW Not ready at tasting time. **Sauvignon blanc** NEW 𝄞 ★★ Bouncy acidity, faint grapefruit flavour in **13** al fresco white. **Crisp Dry White** ★★ Lemon, mint & faintly floral **NV** book club favourite. **Crisp Extra Light** ★★ Latest **NV** raises the bar with rousing apple freshness. **Selected Stein** ★★ Simple enjoyment from **NV**'s peach & pear flavours. **Fruity Late Harvest** ★★ Semi-sweet **NV** has peaches & cream whiffs. **Natural Sweet Rosé** ★★ Cherry cordial & dried grass combo in shocking pink **NV**. **Natural Sweet White** ★★ Latest **NV** offers sweet melon & pineapple for chilled summer tippling. **Smooth Sweet Red** ★★ Sweetness in latest **NV** cut by frisky acidity.

Light Cultivar range

Extra Light Merlot ▤ 𝄞 ★ Wood-touched **12** lightish & noticeably dry, needs food. **Pinotage Rosé** Await next, as for **Light Chenin Blanc**. **Extra Light Sauvignon Blanc** ▤ 𝄞 ★★ Cheerful Golden Delicious apple & yellow peach flavours on **13** slimmer's friend.

Sparkling Wines NEW

Sweet Red ☺ ★★★ Sweet **NV**, exuberant red fruit, hint of tannin amid the froth. **Brut** ☺ ★★★ Vibrant dry mousse, appealing pear flavour, appetising acidity make a good **NV** celebrator.

Sweet Rosé ★★ **NV** tastes like strawberry juice spiked with cheery bubbles. **Sweet White** ★★ Fizzy fun in floral & fruity **NV**. — HJ,CvZ

Robert Stanford Estate

Location: Stanford ▪ Map: Elgin, Walker Bay & Bot River ▪ WO: Walker Bay ▪ Est 1855 ▪ 1stB 2008 ▪ Tasting & sales Fri-Mon 10-3.30 ▪ Closed Good Fri, Dec 25 & Jan 1 ▪ Madre's Kitchen Thu-Mon 8-4 ▪ Facilities for children ▪ Gift shop ▪ Farm produce ▪ Conservation area ▪ Art studio ▪ Tractor tours/vineyard walks by appt ▪ Owner(s) Kleinrivier Beleggings (Pty) Ltd ▪ Winemaker(s) Johan Joubert (Sep 2007, Kleine Zalze) & Van Zyl du Toit (Allée Bleue) ▪ Viticulturist(s) Jan Malan (Jan 2003) ▪ 176ha/60ha (pinot, shiraz, chenin, sauv) ▪ 320t/2,500cs own label 40% red 30% white 15% rosé 15% MCC ▪ BWI champion ▪ wines@robertstanfordestate.co.za ▪ www.robertstanfordestate.co.za, www.madreskitchenstanford.co.za ▪ S 34° 25' 49.41" E 019° 27' 49.98" ▪ **T +27 (0)28-341-0647** ▪ F +27 (0)86-655-6944

A process of rejuvenation has seen much of the energy and entrepreneurship displayed by 19th century owner Robert Stanford restored to one of Walker Bay's most historic properties. The new spirit is reflected in the varied visitor offering, which includes a country-style restaurant, art studio and the Klein River Conservancy.

Sir Robert Stanford Estate range

★★★★ **Shiraz** ⓦ Potentially boisterous blackberry fruit of **10** cajoled into order by layers of warm spice; lovely composure & unwavering length of flavour swaddle 14.9% alcohol.

★★★★☆ **The Hansom** ⓦ Bold cab-led **10** (★★★★) blend is piled high with bramble fruit, but derailed by weighty 15.3% alcohol, whereas understated **09**'s notable alcohol & smidgen sugar didn't jar.

★★★★ **Sauvignon Blanc** ⓦ Natural acidity of cooler clime enlivens **12**'s riper fig profile; great persistence, like **10**. No **11**.

Rosé ⓦ ★★★ Strawberry freshness in brisk dry **12**. **Chenin Blanc** Await new vintage.

Cutters Cove

Shiraz-Viognier ⓦ ★★★ **09** brims with succulent cherry/mulberry fruit bursting to be enjoyed. Lipsmacking & delicious. **Chenin Blanc** ⓦ 🗔 ★★ Crisp tropical tones to gluggable **12**. — DS

■ **Robin Hood Legendary Wine Series** *see* Arumdale Cool Climate Wines
■ **Rocheburg** *see* Riebeek Cellars
■ **Rockfield** *see* Du Preez Estate

Romond Vineyards

Location: Somerset West ▪ Map: Helderberg ▪ WO: Stellenbosch ▪ Est 1993 ▪ 1stB 2003 ▪ Tasting, sales & tours by appt Mon-Sat 10-5.30 Sun 11-5.30 ▪ Fee R30, waived on purchase ▪ Closed Easter Fri-Sun, Dec 25/26 & Jan 1 ▪ Olive oil ▪ The Vintner's Loft self-catering apartment ▪ Owner(s) André & Rhona Liebenberg ▪ Winemaker(s) André Liebenberg ▪ Viticulturist(s) Francois Hanekom (May 2007) ▪ 11.5ha/9.5ha (cabs s/f, merlot, ptage) ▪ PO Box 5634 Helderberg 7135 ▪ info@romond.co.za ▪ www.romondvineyards.co.za ▪ S 34° 1' 52.61" E 018° 49' 59.67" ▪ **T +27 (0)21-855-4566** ▪ F +27 (0)21-855-0428

Wildlife is rife on André and Rhona Liebenberg's boutique Helderberg property with duiker and grysbok being regular visitors to nibble on the grapes - but the appearance of a young Cape leopard was the surprising highlight of last year! The wines continue to win fans and André is considering expanding the range.

Rebus range

★★★★ **Fanfaronne** ⓦ Fragrant **09** (★★★★☆) best yet; complex, classic cab franc leads Bordeaux blend with cab, merlot. Savoury fruit balances firmly structured tannins. Step up from **07** (labelled as 'Rebus'); no **08**.

Pinotage ⓦ ★★★★ **09** fruity but serious, balanced & juicy, with delicious grip to finish. Like Impromptu, tasted a few years back. **Impromptu** ⓦ ★★★★ Dry rosé from merlot. **10** more complex & vibrant than previous, with mouthfilling ripe cherries, rosepetal & spice. Range listed as 'Romond Vineyards' last time. — IM

Roodeberg

One of the best-known and most enduring (1949) South African reds, KWV's Roodeberg for a long time was export only, which increased its local desirability. Designed for drinking, older bottles from private cellars prove its ageing ability. Recent addition Dr Charles Niehaus honours the creator.

Dr Charles Niehaus ★★★★ Shiraz/cab-led **11** has smoky, spiced dark fruit & good tannin backing. Nicely smooth & approachable, some ageing ability. WO Coastal. **Roodeberg Red** Await new vintage. — CR

Roodezandt Wines   🍷 ✕ 🍴 ♿

Location/map/WO: Robertson ▪ Est 1953 ▪ Tasting & sales Mon-Fri 9-5 ▪ Cellar tours by appt Mon-Fri 8-12 & 2-5 ▪ Closed all pub hols ▪ Sales (at cellar price) also from La Verne Wine Boutique Mon-Fri 9-5.30 Sat 9-5 ▪ Facilities for children ▪ Owner(s) 60 members ▪ Cellarmaster(s) Christie Steytler (May 1980) ▪ Winemaker(s) Jean du Plessis (2012), with Tiaan Blom (Oct 2005) ▪ Viticulturist(s) Jaco Lategan (Dec 2006) ▪ 1,800ha (cab, merlot, ptage, ruby cab, shiraz, chard, chenin, cbard, muscadel w, sauv) ▪ 30,000t/23m L bulk ▪ BSCI, HACCP, IPW, WIETA ▪ PO Box 164 Robertson 6705 ▪ info@roodezandt.co.za ▪ www.roodezandt.co.za ▪ S 33° 48' 33.2" E 019° 52' 47.3" ▪ **T +27 (0)23-626-1160** ▪ F +27 (0)23-626-5074

Long a fixture in wine town Robertson's main road, Roodezandt Wines has maintained long-term relationships with growers and buyers of bulk wine (local and overseas premium brand owners). Slow, steady growth was recently bolstered by WIETA accreditation (recognising ethical trading), increased storage space and fresh faces (winemaker Jean du Plessis).

Balthazar range

★★★★ **Chardonnay Brut Méthode Cap Classique** Ⓟ Elegant top-label sparkling. Vintage-dated **09** maintains standard set by **NV (07)**, with appealing marzipan notes, toned yet generous body, nutty conclusion. Discontinued: **Classic Cabernet Sauvignon**.

Roodezandt range

Cabernet Sauvignon ☺ 🍴 ★★☆ New bottling of **11** aged year (previous 7 months). Soft & spicy crowd pleaser. **Chenin Blanc** ☺ 🍴 ★★☆ Chill-and-enjoy **13** softly peachy.

Syrah Ⓟ ★★☆ Was 'Shiraz'. Spicy tomato & pepper-dusted red berries on plump **11**. **Sauvignon Blanc** 🍴 ★★ **13** floral toned, soft fruitiness for casual quaffing. **Special Late Harvest** Ⓟ 🍴 ★★☆ Floral **11** lively, fruity chenin, hanepoot duo. **Red Muscadel** ✓ 🍴 ★★★★ Apricot & raisin profusion on sweet, comforting **12** (★★★). Extra zing on **11** extends its length. Enjoy either over ice in summer, fireside in winter.

Keizer's Creek range

The Red 🍴 ★★ Unwooded **NV** mainly cab; savoury pizza or pasta buddy. — DB,JP

Rooiberg Winery   🍷 🍽 📷 ✕ ♿

Location/map/WO: Robertson ▪ Est 1964 ▪ 1stB 1974 ▪ Tasting & sales Mon-Fri 9–5.30 Sat 9-4 ▪ Fee R10pp for tour groups ▪ Closed Good Fri, Dec 25 & Jan 1 ▪ Bodega de Vinho restaurant & bakery Mon-Fri 8–5.30 Sat 8-4 ▪ Facilities for children ▪ Tour groups ▪ Gift shop ▪ Rooiberg Conservancy ▪ Owner(s) 30 members ▪ Cellarmaster(s) André van Dyk (Oct 2002) ▪ Winemaker(s) André Scriven (Jan 2008), with Pieter Rossouw (Jan 2013) ▪ Viticulturist(s) Hennie Visser (2007, Vinpro consultant) ▪ 667ha (cab, merlot, ptage, ruby cab, shiraz, chard, chenin, cbard, sauv) ▪ 12,000t/400,000cs own label 40% red 60% white ▪ Other export brands: African Dawn, Amandalia, Cape Avocet, Finch Mountain, Table View, Tembana Valley, Zebra Collection ▪ Brands for clients: AlexKia, Cape Dreams, Ferling Noble, Woolworths ▪ ISO 9001:2000, BWI, HACCP, IPW, SGS Organic ▪ PO Box 358 Robertson 6705 ▪ info@rooiberg.co.za ▪ www.rooiberg.co.za ▪ S 33° 46' 35.3" E 019° 45' 42.9" ▪ **T +27 (0)23-626-1663** ▪ F +27 (0)23-626-3295

There's a sense of purpose at this large grower-owned Robertson cellar - turning 50 this year - its versatility described by CEO Johan du Preez as 'bulk and bottle, multi-brand and multi-country'. The last refers to the more than 20 international markets where bulk sales and bottled wines find buyers, including China and Russia. At home, private label customers include the Protea hotel group and retailer Woolworths, for whom the team recently produced a quantity of organic wine.

Reserve range

★★★★ **Pinotage** ✓ Full-bore **12** as hedonistic as opulent & seductive **11**. Violet & banana (typical for variety), strawberry fruit, creamy conclusion; 100% new oak & 14.8% alcohol expertly handled.

★★★★ **Shiraz** ✓ Stylish **12** & supple **11** (both tasted this edition) less brooding than **10** yet as vibrant & refreshing despite fruit concentration. Elegant dinner companions now & within ±5 years.

Cabernet Sauvignon ✓ 🍇 ★★★★ Always one of the region's more accomplished & appealing. Smooth vanilla-infused **12**'s plush fruit & 100% new oak delicious now but will reward few years cellaring. **Merlot** 🍇 ★★★ **12** black plum & tobacco from 100% new oak, cranberry freshness, but tannins are gruff. **Cape Blend** ⊕ 🍇 ★★★☆ **11** older barrels provide supportive backbone, subtle spice; strawberry tone supplied by 50% pinotage, supple tannins & freshness by shiraz (30%) & cab. **Chardonnay** 🍇 ★★★★ Lime marmalade fruit just peeks through all-new wood's vanilla, cream & butter mid-2013; brief spell in bottle should bring integration, reveal **12**'s charms.

Rooiberg range

> **Cabernet Sauvignon** ☺ 🍇 ★★★ Mulberries & cream, previewed **12**'s long clean flavours ideal for mealtimes (main courses & desserts). **Cabernet Sauvignon-Merlot (Roodewyn)** ☺ 🍴 🍇 ★★☆ Milk chocolate & plums on **12** cheery BBQ mate. **Mountain Red** ☺ 🍴 🍇 ★★★ Unwooded **12** light bodied & savoury allsorts blend for anywhere, anytime. **Blanc Natural Sweet** ☺ 🍴 🍇 ★★★ Now bottled, **12** white muscadel/colombard duo is sweet but clean & full of joie de vivre.

Merlot 🍇 ★★ Bold tannins detract somewhat from **12**'s mocha-plum appeal. **Pinotage** 🍇 ★★★ Preview **12** juicy & soft for early enjoyment. **Shiraz** 🍇 ★★★ Step-up **12** exudes spicy dark fruit, savoury bacon whiffs; brisk acidity for refreshing summer sipping. **Pinotage Rosé** 🍴 🍇 ★★★ Pretty pink hue, strawberry attraction in just-off-dry **13** preview. **Chardonnay** 🍴 🍇 ★★★ Picnic basket staple, **13** long & lemony, roundly dry finish. Unwooded. **Chenin Blanc** 🍴 🍇 ★★★ Thatch & floral notes on brisk & easy-drinking **13**. **Colombar** 🍴 🍇 ★★★ Shy on nose, **13** more expressive fruit salad palate, softly sweet. **Sauvignon Blanc** 🍴 🍇 ★★★ Tropical **13** understated but lively & dry. **Chenin Blanc-Sauvignon Blanc** 🍴 🍇 ★★ Cheerful, semi-dry **13** light hearted (12% alcohol) & lightly fruited. **Flamingo Sparkling** ★★★ Latest **NV** celebratory pink fizz raises the bar with balanced peachy/berry sweetness. **Brut Sparkling** ★★ Improved **NV** sparkler, clean grapey fun, softly dry. **Vin Doux Sparkling** 🍴 🍇 ★★ Not over-sweet **NV**, frothy bubbles to perk you up. **Red Natural Sweet** 🍴 🍇 ★★ **12** dusty raisin notes, bitter touch to sweet tail. **Rosé Natural Sweet** 🍴 🍇 ★★ Genteel **13** sweetie, lightish to enjoy all night long. **Red Muscadel** 🍇 ★★★★ Jasmine-scented fortified **12** as seamless as **11** (★★★★) but more elegant & complex. Sip fireside, or pour over ice-cream for aromatic summer treat. **Cape Vintage** 🍇 ★★★ **12** port-style from pinotage offers plum pudding & mulberry tart richness, enough grip & structure for cellaring few years.

Red Chair range [NEW]

Pinotage 🍴 🍇 ★★★ Easygoing **12** is crowd pleasing & purse friendly. **Sauvignon Blanc Light** 🍴 🍇 ★★ Appealing grassy intro to **13**, pleasantly light & lean. — DB,CvZ

■ **Rooi Kalahari** *see* Die Mas van Kakamas

Rosendal Winery

Location/map: Robertson ▪ WO: Western Cape ▪ 1stB 2003 ▪ Tasting, sales & cellar tours Mon-Sat 8-5 Sun 9-1 ▪ Fee only charged for groups of 10+ ▪ Wine & Lindt chocolate tastings ▪ Restaurant & guesthouse ▪ Spa & wellness centre ▪ Conferences ▪ Owner(s) Geir Tellefsen & Sissel Anderssen ▪ Cellarmaster(s)/winemaker(s) Therese de Beer (Jan 2012) ▪ 18ha ▪ 80% red 15% white 5% rosé ▪ PO Box 3 Suite 128 Roggebaai 8012 ▪ info@rosendalwinery.com ▪ www.rosendalwinery.com ▪ S 33° 48' 7.8" E 019° 59' 19.0" ▪ **T +27 (0)21-424-4498 (sales)/+27 (0)23-626-1570 (farm)** ▪ F +27 (0)21-424-1570

This mainly direct-to-customer wine business based in Robertson Valley vinifies a range of wines to please the palates of its 10,000 customers in southern Africa and Scandinavia. To please the 'rainbow nation', it participates in outreach initiatives including a 200-pupil farm school and a fundraising partnership with the Amy Biehl Foundation and Pick n Pay.

Reserve Limited range

★★★★ **Black Eagle** ⊕ First since **04**, Stellenbosch-sourced **07** (★★★★) is shiraz (40%) & 3 Bordeaux reds. Savoury & earthy flavours in more Old than New World style, with juicy balance.

Blue Mountain Next awaited. **Cape Francolin** ⊕ ★★★★ **09** cab-led Bordeaux blend from Durbanville grapes, lightly textured, touch leafy but juicy & satisfying. **Classic Cuvée** ⊕ ★★★ Stellenbosch fruit stars in savoury **09** merlot/cab-led Bordeaux red. **Leopard's Eye** [NEW] ★★★ Tinta amarela & shiraz cosseted by older oak in spicy & bright **10**. Lipsmacking, with lively tannins to match with rare beef.

Barony range

Heidi Shiraz NEW ★★★ Partial wild ferment, older oak for promising **11**. Plush palate followed by raisined, tad bitter tail; interesting counterpoint to rich meat stews. **Cecile Sauvignon Blanc** ⓣ 🔲 ★★★ Intense asparagus & tinned pea bouquet, soft acidity & creamy texture on **11** from Hermanus vineyards.

Hilltop range

Cabernet Sauvignon Reserve Next awaited. **Merlot Reserve** NEW ★★★☆ Amiable **11** has no rough edges, only supple tannins, plum & mulberry flavours, nutmeg seasoning for delicious imbibing. **Sauvignon Blanc** ★★★ Pungent white asparagus, zesty acidity & satisfying vinosity on characterful **12**. Enjoy soon.

Rosendal range

Chardonnay New bottling not ready, as for **Riesling**. **Sauvignon Blanc** ⓣ 🔲 ★★★ **11** attractively un-fruity & food friendly, silk texture from extended ageing on lees. — CvZ

Ross Gower Wines

Location/WO: Elgin • Map: Elgin, Walker Bay & Bot River • Est 2003 • 1stB 2004 • Tasting & sales by appt • Glen Stuart self-catering cottages • Conservation area • Owner(s) Gower family • Winemaker(s) James Gower (2007), assisted by Mike Dobrovic • Viticulturist(s) James Gower • 83ha/±7ha (shiraz, sauv) • 20,000cs own label 5% red 10% white 85% MCC • PO Box 161 Elgin 7180 • info@rossgowerwines.co.za • www.rgw.co.za • S 34° 14' 17.7" E 019° 7' 3.7" • **T +27 (0)21-844-0197** • F +27 (0)86-611-2179

This small Elgin-based family enterprise is run by indefatigable mother, Sally Gower, and winemaking son James, after founder and father Ross passed away. Co-rejuvenator of Klein Constantia in the 1980s, Ross's energetic and creative spirit is kept very much alive here, with renewed emphasis on bubblies. Seasoned Mike Dobrovic advises and assists.

Cabernet Sauvignon ⓣ 🔲 ★★★★ When last tasted, **07** showed brooding cassis & liquorice with a tinge of greenpepper & firm structure. **Merlot** Next awaited. **Shiraz** ⓣ 🔲 ★★★★ On review, **08** combined savoury white pepper nuance & red berry juiciness in supple & accessible styling. **Rosé** 🔲 ★★★ **12** appealing sunset quaffer from shiraz & sauvignon with tangy cranberry tone. Briskly semi-dry. **Rhine Riesling** ⓣ 🔲 ★★★★ Perfumed **10** crisply off-dry, genteel, shows varietal's delicate sweet/sour balance & potential to develop. **Sauvignon Blanc** 🔲 ★★★★ Initially restrained & flinty, **12** develops in intensity & texture. Some minerality, with clean-cut acidity & length. **10** & **11** sold out untasted. **Pinot Noir Méthode Cap Classique Brut** ⓣ ★★★★ Fruity champagne-method sparkling **08**, a dapper & appealing aperitif or food partner. **Chardonnay Méthode Cap Classique** NEW ★★★★ Bottle-fermented bubbly in fresh & fruity style. **11** cream-textured quaffability for any occasion. — MW

■ **Rouana** *see* Simonsig Landgoed
■ **Roulou** *see* Boutique Baratok
■ **Rowlands** *see* Southern Sky Wines
■ **Royal** *see* Riebeek Cellars
■ **Royle** *see* Arra Vineyards
■ **Ruby Ridge** *see* Govert Wines

Rudera Wines

Location/map: Stellenbosch • WO: Stellenbosch/Elgin • Est 1999 • 1stB 2000 • Tasting by appt only • Owner(s) Riana Hall • Cellarmaster(s) Chris Keet (2011, consultant) • 15ha/10ha (cab, shiraz, chenin) • ±120t/15,000cs own label 40% red 60% white • IPW • info@rudera.co.za • www.rudera.co.za • S 33° 56' 26.5" E 018° 54' 14.3" • **T +27 (0)21-852-1380** • F +27 (0)21-852-1380

Rudera as a brand has had a nomadic past but is now grounded in a venerable property in the Jonkershoek Valley Stellenbosch. Initially it was at the forefront of developing chenin into a highly reputed grape, but also established a reputation for cabernet and shiraz/syrah. Rudera has always maintained quality and classic styling, and there's a sense that it's now settled and, with the excellent Chris Keet (Keet Wines) as mentor/consultant, increasingly worth watching for top-end reds as well as chenin.

★★★★☆ **Cabernet Sauvignon** **11** starts with cedar perfume, hints of cocoa; slowly unpacking layered red fruits, with fine-grained grape tannin & judicious oak (22 months, 50% new) celebrating restrained fruit. Wonderfully dry end to a classy & refined whole.

★★★★☆ **Platinum Cabernet Sauvignon** ① Last tasted was intense, concentrated, velvety **07**.

★★★★ **Syrah** ② Bright-fruited **11** (★★★★☆) from Simonsberg grapes, vibrant & more tightly knit than **10**. Perfumed, well composed red berry fruit slowly comes alive. Fine tannins mesh on very dry finish. Needs a year-plus for 11 months in oak to integrate.

★★★★ **De Tradisie Chenin Blanc** ① **10**'s ripe yellow stonefruit & crisp apple lead to textured mouthfeel with good weight - only just dry but balanced by clean freshness. Obvious oak should integrate.

★★★★☆ **Robusto Chenin Blanc** ② Muted white peach & floral notes in creamy oak cloak (8 months, mostly older barrels). **11** fruit & toasty vanilla in lovely balanced dance, fine acidity serves as perfect foil to off-dry sweetness & rich fruit weight.

★★★★☆ **Noble Late Harvest** ① Oak-matured **10** dessert from chenin with smatterings chardonnay, viognier & sauvignon. Excellently balanced, with right hint of honeyed botrytis adding complexity to luscious ripe peach & tart apricot.

Platinum Chenin Blanc ① ★★★☆ Some years back, **09** ex Elgin had taut flinty palate, good length. — JP

■ **Rudi Schultz Wines** see Schultz Family Wines

Ruitersvlei Wines 🍴🍷🚚🏕📷🛗

Location: Paarl ▪ Map: Paarl & Wellington ▪ WO: Paarl/Western Cape ▪ Tasting & sales Mon-Fri 9-5 Sat 9-1 ▪ Restaurant ▪ Weddings & conferences ▪ 8 guest rooms ▪ Owner(s) Rara Avis Property Investments (Pty) Ltd ▪ Winemaker(s) Hein Hesebeck (Dec 2012) ▪ Viticulturist(s) Kobus Mostert (Nov 2001) ▪ 120ha ▪ PO Box 532 Suider-Paarl 7624 ▪ marketing@ruitersvlei.co.za ▪ S 33° 45' 10.8" E 018° 54' 28.0" ▪ **T +27 (0)21-863-1517** ▪ F +27 (0)21-863-1443

Rejuvenation here on Paarl Mountain, as a new winemaker (the widely seasoned Hein Hesebeck) takes the reins and vinifies wine for bottling and sale under the Ruitersvlei label for the first time since 2010. The cellardoor and other visitor facilities are being enlarged and upgraded, and vineyard replanting is poised to begin. New freehold housing and a school are being built on the property, and employees will share in the profits from the wine and hospitality businesses.

Ruitersvlei range

Cabernet Sauvignon 🍴 ★★★☆ Plummy & spicy aromas, **11** contrasting dry palate with tannins asking for steak on the braai. WO W Cape, as next. **Merlot** NEW ★★★ Youthfully unsettled when tasted, **11** good heart of fruit which should show better as tannins settle, relax. **Pinotage** Await next, also **Shiraz**, **Private Collection** & **Chenin Blanc**. **Sauvignon Blanc** ★★ **13** light bodied & savoury, with salty acidity & earthy tones.

Mountainside range

Red Await next. **Bloom** NEW 🍴 ② ★★ **13** semi-dry pinotage rosé with musky cherry notes. Enjoy well chilled. **White** 🍴 ② ★★ Light, uncomplicated & semi-dry **13**, with yellow peach flavour. Colombard & chenin, as next. **Dew** NEW 🍴 ② ★★ Airy **13**, lemon drops & gentle sweetness. — CvZ,MW

■ **Runner Duck** see Vergenoegd Wine Estate
■ **Running Duck** see Stellar Winery

Rupert & Rothschild Vignerons 🍴🍷🛗

Location: Paarl ▪ Map: Paarl & Wellington ▪ WO: Western Cape ▪ Est 1997 ▪ 1stB 1998 ▪ Tasting, sales & cellar tours Mon-Sat 9-4.30 ▪ Closed Ash Wed, Easter Fri-Mon, Dec 25 & Jan 1 ▪ Owner(s) Rupert family & Baron Benjamin de Rothschild ▪ Winemaker(s) Yvonne Lester (Sep 2001) & Clive Radloff (Jun 1997) ▪ 90ha (cabs s/f, merlot, p verdot) ▪ 1,000t/162,000cs own label 95% red 5% white ▪ ISO 14001, HACCP, IPW ▪ PO Box 412 Franschhoek Valley 7690 ▪ info@rupert-rothschildvignerons.com ▪ www.rupert-rothschildvignerons.com ▪ S 33° 50' 14.5" E 018° 56' 51.1" ▪ **T +27 (0)21-874-1648** ▪ F +27 (0)21-874-1802

This winery at the foot of the Simonsberg was jointly founded in 1997 by the late South African businessman Dr Anton Rupert and the late Baron Edmond de Rothschild of Château Clarke in Bordeaux. Today, the Rupert family and Baron Benjamin de Rothschild continue the families' partnership. With the two other Franschhoek-based Rupert properties, Rupert & Rothschild established the

Dennegeur community initiative for their staff. This project gives families who have lived in Franschhoek Valley for decades the opportunity to own their own homes. It also involves a sustainable farming venture, with organic vegetables, which helps empower employees through extra earnings. The wines, ever more classic in style, are now made under the leadership of Yvonne Lester.

★★★★☆ **Baron Edmond** 🈂 Generously scented merlot-cab blend plus a little cab franc, with dark, ripe fruit & spicy cedarwood, **11** immediately impresses. Medium bodied & beautifully balanced, if slightly less intense than **10**. Worth cellaring until around 2020. Stellenbosch & Darling fruit, as is Classique.

★★★★ **Classique** **11**'s charm hinges on its ripe, fresh fruit, supple feel & fine tannin extraction. Classic dryness, modest 13% alcohol. Merlot & cab partners joined by motley crew of 7 other varieties!

★★★★ **Baroness Nadine** 🈂 Richness and mineral freshness sing in unison on **11** (★★★★★) - the one giving breadth, the other lightness & length to characteristic limey, hazelnut features. Particularly elegant vintage from Elgin, Barrydale & Robertson vineyards. **10** a lighter year. — AL

■ **Rupert Wines** see Anthonij Rupert Wyne

Russo Family Vintners   🍷🍾

Location: Durbanville ▪ Map: Durbanville, Philadelphia & Darling ▪ Est 2004 ▪ 1stB 2007 ▪ Tasting, sales & tours Mon-Fri 9-4 Sat by appt ▪ Closed all pub hols ▪ Owner(s) Henk & Terèsa Rossouw ▪ Winemaker(s) Terèsa Rossouw (2007) ▪ 6.5ha/4ha (cabs s/f, malbec, merlot, p verdot) ▪ 35t/800cs own label 100% red ▪ PO Box 4402 Tyger Valley 7536 ▪ teresa@russowines.co.za ▪ www.russowines.co.za ▪ S 33° 48' 37.9" E 018° 37' 04.3" ▪ T +27 (0)21-979-1960 ▪ F +27 (0)21-979-1996

Terèsa and Henk Rossouw bought a Durbanville smallholding in 2004, and feel inspired by one of the Cape's first winemakers, Pierre Rousseau, who arrived in 1688. The potential for fine red wine from Bordeaux grapes was early identified. Now the whole family (including dog) is involved, and caught up in the dream.

★★★★ **Russo** ⏱ Opulent but elegant & well structured **07** tasted a few years back. — JP

Rustenberg Wines   🍷🍾📷♿

Location/map: Stellenbosch ▪ WO: Stellenbosch/Simonsberg-Stellenbosch/Coastal/Western Cape ▪ Est 1682 ▪ 1stB 1892 ▪ Tasting & sales Mon-Fri 9-4.30 Sat 10-4 Sun 10-3 ▪ Closed Good Fri, Dec 25 & Jan 1 ▪ Garden ▪ Weddings ▪ Owner(s) Simon Barlow ▪ Cellarmaster(s) Murray Barlow (Nov 2011) ▪ Winemaker(s) Randolph Christians (Nov 1995), with Gareth le Grange (2003) & Craig Christians (Jun 2012) ▪ Viticulturist(s) Simon Barlow (Aug 1987) ▪ 1,200ha/±154ha (cabs s/f, grenache n/b, malbec, merlot, mourv, p verdot, shiraz, chard, rouss, sauv, sem) ▪ ±1,050t/154,000cs own label 51% red 47% white 2% other ▪ BWI, IPW ▪ PO Box 33 Stellenbosch 7599 ▪ wine@rustenberg.co.za ▪ www.rustenberg.co.za ▪ S 33° 53' 44.8" E 018° 53' 33.6" ▪ T +27 (0)21-809-1200 ▪ F +27 (0)21-809-1219

This beautiful estate on the lower slopes of Stellenbosch's Simonsberg is one of the great names in Cape wine history, though it was split in two in 1810. It seems that, remarkably, wine has been bottled here continuously since Schoongezicht farm was bought in 1892 by John X. Merriman, the Cape's last prime minister. That farm and Rustenberg itself were both acquired by industrialist Peter Barlow in the 1940s and reunited. It remains in the hands of the Barlow family, with owner Simon Barlow as fully involved as ever – particularly on the viticultural side, and with Peter's grandson, Murray, now in charge of the cellar and intent on keeping in step with modern styles while preserving the estate's rich heritage.

Site Specific range

★★★★☆ **Peter Barlow** ⏱ 100% cab from Rustenberg's finest red vineyard. **08** a few years back had restrained power & regal bearing. Gorgeous fruit still masked by polished oak. Should reward ageing.

★★★★☆ **Buzzard Kloof Syrah** ⏱ 🈂 Was just 'Syrah'. Youthful, opaque **10** needing time to show full potential. Seamless integration, dense fruit masked in youth by tannins. Powerful but neatly contained.

★★★★☆ **Five Soldiers** 📖 🈂 Supremely elegant & complex single-vineyard **11** exhibits all prerequisites for world-class chardonnay: oak plays supporting role to intense, layered citrus core, bound by intricate minerality & precise acidity.

Regional range

★★★★ **John X Merriman** 🏚 🔲 Lighter, savoury **11** (★★★☆) blend of all the Bordeaux red varieties suffers dip in this vintage; would need the greater fruit density of **10** to provide flesh & cope with firm tannins.

★★★★ **RM Nicholson** ⏲ 🏚 **10** cab, shiraz, merlot-led blend with pure fruit & hint of oaky vanilla tasted ex barrel few years back. Balanced, firm & rich.

★★★★ **Stellenbosch Chardonnay** 🏚 🔲 Creamy, refined **12** heralded by fine oak which helps frame vibrant, rich fruit. Complexity aided by natural ferment, while lively acidity pulls through to sustain finish.

★★★★ **Sauvignon Blanc** 🏚 🔲 Appealing, very drinkable **12** (★★★☆) more ripely tropical than herbaceous, beautifully balanced but less depth & focus than **11**.

★★★★☆ **Straw Wine** 🏚 🔲 Delicately sweet, honeyed **11** from air-dried chenin, viognier & crouchen in lighter dessert style, making food-pairing easy. Thread of bright acidity sustains delightful savoury finish. Coastal WO.

Merlot ⏲ 🏚 🔲 ★★★★ Maiden **10** previewed few years back poised & well-structured, with delicious concluding fruit acid grip. **Stellenbosch Shiraz** NEW 🔲 ★★★★ Perfumed, supple **11** elegant & charming, designed for early drinking. Full marks for balance & accessibility. **Stellenbosch Roussanne** 🏚 🔲 ★★★★ Peachy **12** dips after **11** (★★★★), but has its bold charms: sweet fruit enveloped by oak & attractive spiciness. Overly firm finish & contrasting sweet, warm impression from big 15% alcohol. Simonsberg-Stellenbosch WO, as for Buzzard Kloof Syrah, Peter Barlow & John X Merriman. Discontinued: **Unwooded Chardonnay**.

Ida's / Est.1682 range

Red 🏚 🔲 ★★★ Accessible, pleasantly savoury shiraz & cab-led **12** blend for early drinking. **White** 🏚 🔲 ★★★ Friendly, tropical **12** sauvignon-led 6-way blend in simple quaffing style. WO W Cape. — IM

Rust en Vrede Estate

Location/map/WO: Stellenbosch ▪ Est 1694 ▪ 1stB 1979 ▪ Tasting, sales & cellar tours Mon-Sat 9–5 ▪ Fee R40/4 wines & R70/6 wines, waived on purchase ▪ Closed Easter Fri/Sun, Dec 25 & Jan 1 ▪ Rust en Vrede Restaurant (see Restaurants section) ▪ Gift shop ▪ Owner(s) Jean Engelbrecht ▪ Cellarmaster(s) Coenie Snyman (Dec 2006) ▪ Winemaker(s) Coenie Snyman (Dec 2006), with Roelof Lotriet (Nov 2011) ▪ Viticulturist(s) Dirkie Mouton (Jun 2010) ▪ 50ha/45ha (cab, merlot, shiraz) ▪ ±300t/40,000cs own label 100% red ▪ IPW ▪ PO Box 473 Stellenbosch 7599 ▪ info@rustenvrede.com ▪ www.rustenvrede.com ▪ S 33° 59' 54.0" E 018° 51' 22.5" ▪ **T +27 (0)21-881-3881** ▪ F +27 (0)21-881-3000

True to form, owner Jean Engelbrecht continues to build on - and not simply maintain - the already excellent reputation of this historic Stellenbosch property. A fifth appearance in the influential Wine Spectator's World Top 100 is justification for his conviction that the Helderberg soils are perfect for shiraz, cabernet and merlot, and the estate blend the best possible reflection of the harmony of site and grape. The property's substantial status rests in the capable hands of former Diners Club Winemaker of the Year Coenie Snyman, one of just four custodians of its wines over the more than three decades of Engelbrecht family piloting. And with the elegant restaurant serving equally refined fare, the future seems assured.

★★★★ **Cabernet Sauvignon** 🔲 Herbal tone to **11**, with ripe cassis checked by dry, firm tannins from 18 months French oak. Structured yet not lean or austere. Keeps standard set by **09**. **10** (★★★☆) needed time.

★★★★☆ **Single Vineyard Cabernet Sauvignon** NEW Confident debut for refined **10**. Whispers of cassis & blackcurrant alongside pencil shavings while oak (100% new) is a tad prominent still. Seductive & complex with layers of interest. Needs time.

★★★★ **Merlot** 🔲 Light violet whiff to elegant & refined mulberry palate on **12**. Concentrated deep layers of fruit, like **11** (★★★★) with similar cocoa nuances & sleek, long body.

★★★★ **Shiraz** 🔲 Spicy seduction of inky blue plums appeals on **11**, reminiscent of **10**'s (★★★★) effortless stature. Harmony of oak, fruit & acid indicates good restraint. Silky aftertaste.

★★★★☆ **Single Vineyard Syrah** 🔲 **11** (★★★★★) is big & powerful yet simultaneously velvety, plush & yielding. All is amplified - including alcohol (15.7%) - but tightly controlled. Ripe, richly fruited, spicy & dense yet already deliciously drinkable. Lingers long. Improves on **10**.

★★★★☆ **1694 Classification** ⏲ Pricy shiraz-cab blend honouring date property was granted. Massive & unabashed **09**, with dense raisiny fruit, weighty & plush. Tobacco & wood-shaving whiffs (customary new oak, mostly French here), sumptuous textures, fruit & generous alcohol.

★★★★☆ **Estate** Regular house style on **10** 3-way combo of cab, shiraz & merlot: generous in its hedge-row fruit tempered by savoury oak, heft & persistence. Firm yet toned structure cradles ripe lavishness. Will reward patience. — FM

■ **Rusthof** *see* Mooiuitsig Wine Cellars
■ **Rustler** *see* Flagstone Winery
■ **Ruyter's Bin** *see* Stellenrust

Saam Mountain Vineyards

Location/WO: Paarl ▪ Tasting & sales at Perdeberg Winery ▪ Owner(s) 31 shareholders ▪ Cellarmaster(s) Albertus Louw (Oct 2008) ▪ Winemaker(s) Riaan Möller (Dec 2006) & Carla Herbst (Jun 2008) ▪ PO Box 214 Paarl 7620 ▪ info@perdeberg.co.za ▪ www.perdeberg.co.za ▪ **T +27 (0)21-869-8244** ▪ F +27 (0)21-869-8245

Describing itself as 'the home of ethical winemaking', Saam ('Together') sources exclusive wines from selected growers stretching from Paarl across the Swartland to Durbanville for export.

Saam Single Vineyard Selection

★★★★☆ **Middelburg Chenin Blanc** ⊛ 🏠 🖉 From Perdeberg vineyard. Savoury **10** (★★★★) comes down a notch from impressive **09**, oaking still a dominant factor, needs time to meld with fruit.
Koopmanskraal Shiraz Await new, as for **Heldersig Shiraz-Viognier**. Discontinued: **Phisantekraal Sauvignon Blanc**.

Saam Quality range

Cabernet Sauvignon Not tasted, as for **Shiraz** & **Chenin Blanc**. **Pinotage** 🏠 🖉 ★★★ Juicy wild berries on lightish **11** offer real refreshment. Sleekly smooth with hint of oak spice. **Sauvignon Blanc** 🏠 🖉 ★★★ Shy, gentle **12** has faint dusty note, opening to surprisingly long finish. Understated but nicely balanced. — GdB

■ **Sabi Sabi** *see* Stellenrust

Sadie Family Wines

Location: Malmesbury ▪ Map: Swartland ▪ WO: Swartland/Stellenbosch/Olifants River/Piekenierskloof ▪ Est 1999 ▪ 1stB 2000 ▪ Tasting by appt ▪ Owner(s) The Sadie Family (Pty) Ltd ▪ Winemaker(s)/viticulturist(s) Eben Sadie (1999) ▪ 25ha (cinsaut, grenache n/b, mourv, syrah, tinta barocca, chenin, clairette, palomino, rouss, sem, verdelho, viog) ▪ 60t/8,000cs own label 50% red 50% white ▪ PO Box 1019 Malmesbury 7299 ▪ office@thesadiefamily.com ▪ www.thesadiefamily.com ▪ S 33° 31' 31.0" E 018° 48' 18.1" ▪ **T +27 (0)76-151-7131** ▪ F +27 (0)86-692-2852

One of three wine ventures of one of South Africa's most respected winemakers, Swartland-based Eben Sadie, the others being Sequillo (see separate listing) and Terroir al Limit in Priorat, Spain. The two Signature Series blends are complex and individual, having long reached icon status, while the Old Vine Series are more earthbound, respecting various old vineyard sites. The story of each is explained on the back labels, while the wine packaging remains almost austere in its classicism, as if proclaiming it's the wine inside that deserves your attention. Which it does in every case: naturally fermented, no fining or filtration, no mechanisation or new wood, and a true expression of place. For all of the vineyards date back to the last century, and some to the early part of it.

Signature Series

★★★★★ **Columella** As with complex **10**, shiraz-led with mourvèdre in **11** (★★★★★), offering trademark glossy dark fruit, scrub & violets, a lovely youthful freshness. Sleek & polished, the deep muscle tone promises a long life ahead.
★★★★★ **Palladius** Unfined/filtered, 24 months on lees, half in older barrel. Chenin-led 9-part blend, mainly Rhône whites, **11** is complex. A symphony of notes, major & minor, ending satisfyingly long. Take your time, it's worth it. Only 8 varieties in **10** (★★★★☆)!

Old Vine Series

★★★★☆ **Pofadder** ✓ Honouring cinsaut, the workhorse red grape of earlier times. From 43 year old vines, bunch ferment, unfined/filtered. Redcurrants & cherries on **12**, touch of scrub, & elegantly structured, the tannins mainly from the grapes, giving purity & length.

★★★★☆ **Soldaat** [NEW] ✓ Blueberries & violets, hint of Xmas cake, **12** is seductively perfumed, with the same fruit purity on the palate. Elegant, showcased with minimal trappings, an admirable lesson in thoughtful handling of old Piekenierskloof bushvine grenache.

★★★★☆ **Treinspoor** ✓ Tinta barocca from 39 year old vines. Plush wild red berries, forthcoming **12** (★★★★) is grippier than stellar **11**, needs a bit more time to harmonise. A good future ahead.

★★★★☆ **Mev. Kirsten** Ancient Stellenbosch chenin vineyard producing 1T off its 1 hectare. **12** more expressive than its sibling, melon & ginger preserve, quince, a deep waxy note, raw almond savouriness. Finishes fresh & ultra long, doesn't let go. Gorgeous.

★★★★★ **Skurfberg** ✓ Tiny yield off 80+ year old Olifants River dryland chenin vines. **12** is the mineral face of the variety, with subtle grapefruit, peach pip; quieter than **11**. Great purity achieved by minimal handling, natural ferment, bottle-age.

★★★★☆ **'T Voetpad** ✓ Semillon, chenin, palomino & muscat d'Alexandrie all from a tiny 106 year old vineyard, fermented together. Scents of poached apple, an intriguing fennel note, but **12**'s flavours are a zesty mix of passionfruit & melon, sleek & tightly focused.

★★★★☆ **Skerpioen** [NEW] ✓ Dried pear & mango, green olive tapenade, an unusual olive oil note, **12** presents its complexity quietly, layer upon layer, anchored by grapefruit freshness. A wonderful way to experience tiny 2T/hectare production of palomino & chenin. — CR

■ **Safari** *see* De Zoete Inval Estate

■ **Sainsbury** *see* Bosman Family Vineyards

Saltare

Location: Stellenbosch ▪ WO: Swartland/Paarl/Western Cape/Stellenbosch ▪ 1stB 2005 ▪ Tasting by appt ▪ Wines also available for tasting & sales every Saturday at the Stellenbosch Fresh Goods Market, Oude Libertas ▪ Owner(s) Christoff & Carla Pauw ▪ Cellarmaster(s)/winemaker(s) Carla Pauw (2005) ▪ 19t/2,200cs own label 15% red 15% white 70% MCC ▪ PO Box 2290 Dennesig Stellenbosch 7601 ▪ info@saltare.co.za ▪ www.saltare.co.za ▪ T +27 (0)21-883-9568 ▪ F +27 (0)88-021-883-9568

Dancing (it's what the Latin name means) is part of the spirit of Carla and Christoff Pauw's boutique winery - based in Stellenbosch but sourcing grapes from all over. The venture began in 2003 when Carla and friends crushed pinot noir and chardonnay for the first of her beloved bubblies - still one focus here.

★★★★ **Méthode Cap Classique Brut Rosé** Pretty, salmon pink **NV** sparkling from Stellenbosch pinot noir is bone-dry (no dosage), firm & stylish, with character from 2 years on lees. Label gives disgorgement date.

★★★★ **Méthode Cap Classique Brut Reserve** Chardonnay-led **NV** bubbly with pinot noir (mostly **09**) & 2 years on lees produce a fine improvement on last bottling. Complex yeasty aromas & dry, rich flavours given dimension from barrel-fermented component. Robertson, Stellenbosch grapes, like Brut Nature.

Syrah ★★★★ Bold **10** from organic Swartland vines, has splash carignan. Steps up from **09** (★★★★) with structured tannins & bright acidity to support spicy ripeness & lightly warm, rich finish. Only older oak. **Specialis** ⓘ ★★★★ Perfumed **08** blend merlot & cab plus a little cab franc. Juicy ripe fruit firmly underpinned by fresh, brisk acidity. WO Paarl. Previous was lavish **06** (★★★★). **Chenin Blanc** ★★★★★ Old Swartland vines deliver vibrant, pure-fruited, lightly oaked **11**. Huge advance on quirky, off-dry **10** (★★★★). Youthful, but will develop well, held by fine acidity, textured pithiness & lingering, focused mineral thread. **Old Vines Chenin Blanc** [NEW] ★★★★ More rustic than other bottling; **11** from barrel-fermented Paarl fruit, in less focused, broader, oxidative style with bruised apple character. **Méthode Cap Classique Brut Nature** ⌀ ★★★★ Pleasingly fresh **NV** sparkler mostly from **11** vintage, not quite as complex & persistent as last release, though breadth & character from 2 years lees & oaked portion. — IM

■ **Sandrivier** *see* Overgaauw Wine Estate

Santa Cecilia

Location: Riebeek-Kasteel ▪ Map: Swartland ▪ Est/1stB 2008 ▪ Tasting facility in The Wine Kollective: Mon-Sat 10-5 Sun 10-3 ▪ Closed Good Fri, Dec 25 & Jan 1 ▪ Gifts ▪ Farm produce ▪ Adjacent Bar Bar Black Sheep Restaurau-

rant ▪ Overnight facility 'The Santa Cecilia Boudoir' ▪ Owner(s) Anton Espost & Thys Greeff ▪ Winemaker(s) Anton Espost ▪ Viticulturist(s) Thys Greeff (Feb 2008), Outback Viticulture ▪ 2,000cs own label 30% red 70% white ▪ PO Box 61 Riebeek-Kasteel 7307 ▪ espost@telkomsa.net ▪ S 33° 23' 1.48" E 018° 53' 46.54" ▪ **T +27 (0)22-448-1008/+27 (0)82-776-9366**

It's hard to believe 'winemaker/bottle-washer' Anton Espost when he says his little cellar in Riebeek-Kasteel is 'struggling'. He has no plans to change anything, after all, and says his ultimate wine experience 'happens every evening'! He only wishes more people would try 'something natural and new' (like his Santa Cecilia wines) instead of the standard supermarket offering.

Sarah's Creek

Location: Robertson ▪ Closed to public ▪ Owner(s) Dirk C Malherbe ▪ Winemaker(s) Marga Malherbe ▪ 20ha (cab, merlot, sauv) ▪ PO Box 6531 Welgemoed 7538 ▪ info@sarahscreek.co.za ▪ www.sarahscreek.co.za ▪ **T +27 (0)76-838-6507**

In the Malherbe family since 1888, DCM Boerdery's wine brand is named Sarah's Creek after the freshwater stream on the Robertson home-farm where, generations ago, a young daughter was habitually waylaid by dragonflies and birds. 'Our handcrafted wines are the result of the same love of nature and simplicity.'

Saronsberg

Location/map: Tulbagh ▪ WO: Tulbagh/Coastal ▪ Est 2002 ▪ 1stB 2004 ▪ Tasting & sales Mon-Fri 8–5 Sat 10–2 ▪ Fee R25pp ▪ Closed Easter Fri/Sun, Ascension day, Dec 25 & Jan 1 ▪ Cellar tours by appt ▪ Olive oil ▪ BYO picnic ▪ Art works & sculptures on display ▪ Christmas in Winter Tulbagh festival (Jun) ▪ Self-catering guest cottages ▪ Owner(s) Saronsberg Cellar (Pty) Ltd ▪ Cellarmaster(s) Dewaldt Heyns (2003) ▪ Winemaker(s) Dewaldt Heyns (2002), with Jolandie van der Westhuizen (2011) ▪ Viticulturist(s) Chris Immelman (2012) ▪ 500ha/50ha (shiraz) ▪ 400t own label 70% red 30% white ▪ WIETA ▪ PO Box 361 Tulbagh 6820 ▪ info@saronsberg.com ▪ www.saronsberg.com ▪ S 33° 14' 48.2" E 019° 7' 2.0" ▪ **T +27 (0)23-230-0707** ▪ F +27 (0)23-230-0709

Next on cellarmaster and winemaker Dewaldt Heyns' bucket list, he jokes, is a bigger bucket – no doubt to cope with larger harvests as new vineyards come into production. Now in his 11th year at this quality-focused Tulbagh cellar embracing Rhône styles, he laughs when asked about his passions beyond wine: 'Excuse me?' His aim remains to provide consumers with a unique Saronsberg style, offering value for money at every price level (the shiraz is the top-seller, the viognier his personal favourite), and he modestly shrugs off any praise of his winegrowing prowess: 'Jan van Riebeeck was the first and only one that can really boast.' To boost the Saronsberg workers fund, staff are being trained to play a greater role in agri-tourism farm activities.

Saronsberg range

★★★★★ **Shiraz** 🄯 Worthy successor to **10**, perfumed & silky **11** shows house-style sombre red/black fruit & leashed power, accessible but commanding tannin structure for lengthy ageing.

★★★★☆ **Seismic** ⏱ Starry **08** cab (72%) with merlot, petit verdot & malbec. Ripe blueberry & fruitcake with earthy density, muscle from 20 months French oak, 100% new. Will reward 5+ years ageing. WO Coastal.

★★★★☆ **Full Circle** ⏱ Shiraz-led Rhône blend with grenache, mourvèdre, viognier. Bold & tannic **10** (★★★★) tad porty against **09**'s elegance, spice. As usual, drinks well now & can go for years.

★★★★ **Sauvignon Blanc** 🗐 🄯 Stylish **13** delivers typical Saronsberg richness & kaleidoscope of aromas & flavours (capsicum, greenpepper, khaki bush, passionfruit, lime). What a pick-me-up! WO Coastal.

★★★★ **Viognier** 🄯 Barrel fermented, portion with wild yeasts. Billows & shouts variety's peach & honeysuckle against spicy oak backdrop. As always, **12** fresh & finely crafted, lets pristine fruit shine.

★★★★ **Sauvignon Blanc Straw Wine** ⏱ Gorgeous dessert from air-dried grapes, **06** richly sweet with a shortbread seasoning, hidden strength from 22 months in oak.

Grenache NEW ★★★★ Wild scrub & gamey notes of the variety, **11** vibrant but not showy, elegant oaking & downy tannins. **Brut Méthode Cap Classique** ⏱ ★★★★ Classy **09** champagne-method sparkling from pinot noir & chardonnay improved on all-chardonnay **07** (★★★★). Elegant, truly dry & complex.

Provenance range

★★★★ **Shiraz** 🌿 Usually a modern, upbeat take on variety but **11** (★★★☆) more savoury, dense & tight, with dusty oak tannins. Misses something of the satisfying plumpness of **10**. WO Coastal, like next.

★★★★ **Rooi** 🌿 Bordeaux red blend consistently punches above its weight. Cedar-toned **11** rich & tarry, shows considerable substance, balance & form. Excellent now & will improve.

Shiraz Rosé 🍴 🌿 ★★★ Full of life, **13** is overtly fruity, spicy & dry. Versatile al fresco pink. — GdB,MW

■ **SA Rugby** *see* Ernie Els Wines

Sauvignon.com

Location: Durbanville ▪ WO: Western Cape ▪ Est/1stB 2010 ▪ Closed to public ▪ Owner(s) Thys & Tienie Louw ▪ Winemaker(s) Thys Louw & Mari Branders (both Jan 2010) ▪ Viticulturist(s) Div van Niekerk (Jan 2010) ▪ 40% red 60% white ▪ PO Box 27 Durbanville 7551 ▪ info@sauvignon.com ▪ www.sauvignon.com ▪ **T +27 (0)82-442-1317** ▪ F +27 (0)21-979-1802

With its pixellated vine leaf logo and active social media presence, Sauvignon. com is the brainchild of Diemersdal's internet-savvy cellarmaster, Thys Louw. Born in West Coast vineyards, this millennial brand is trotting the globe (Canada, Europe, Africa) and seeing considerable interest in its newer bag-in-box format.

Sauvignon Blanc ☺ 🍴 🌿 ★★★ Herby white peaches, packed with zesty fruit, **13** is summer fun in a bottle/box.

Cabernet Sauvignon 🍴 🌿 ★★★ Cassis & cream-toned **12** is fruity & uncomplicated, with supple tannins for easy quaffability. — CvZ

Savage Wines

Location: Cape Town ▪ WO: Western Cape ▪ Est 2006 ▪ 1stB 2011 ▪ Closed to public ▪ Owner(s) Duncan Savage ▪ Cellarmaster(s)/winemaker(s)/viticulturist(s) Duncan Savage (Jan 2006) ▪ 20t/2,000cs own label 40% red 60% white ▪ info@savagewines.com ▪ **T +27 (0)21-785-4019**

Duncan Savage, who has earned an enviable reputation as winemaker at Cape Point Vineyards, last year launched his own label. 'Savage by name but not by nature,' he says, accurately. Two blends, white and red, form the core, to be supplemented by some interesting varietal wines set to be released this year. Apart from saying that grapes are sourced from 'a number of altitude and maritime vineyards around the Western Cape', he's reluctant to go into more detail – lots of tiny parcels and these set to change from year to year.

Savage Wines range NEW

★★★★☆ **Red** Harmonious & complete Rhône blend, shiraz's (72%) pepper spice balancing grenache's black fruit & smidgen cinsaut's cherry gloss. Ripe & generous, but absence of new oak, & moderate alcohol, mean **11** is elegant rather than powerful, a pleasure to drink now & for many years.

★★★★☆ **White** Suave & assured barrel fermented (25% new oak) Bordeaux white blend sauvignon (70%) & semillon. **12** delicate oak spice & anise on grassy, waxy nose; fruit finely integrated with lees creaminess, taut acid thread ensures elegance within a full, generously weighted body. — GdB, GM

Savanha

This Spier-owned, mainly exported premium wine brand 'celebrates the vibrant energy of the South African sun, in a fun, relaxed and social way'.

Naledi range

★★★★ **Cabernet Sauvignon** Naledi is Sotho for 'star' & **11** certainly glitters: attractively compact & restrained berry fruit woven with firm tannins, dry & tangy, & in need of a few years to soften. WO W Cape.

★★★★ **Chardonnay** Sumptuous **12**, citrus fruit layered with leesy oatmeal & oak vanilla in rich & complex New World style. Barrel fermented/aged, 70% new oak. Tygerberg grapes.

Discontinued: **Merlot**, **Pinotage**.

Winemakers Selection

Cabernet Sauvignon-Merlot NEW ★★☆ Welcoming meaty/bacon fullness in previewed **12**. WO W Cape, as next. **Chardonnay-Chenin Blanc** NEW 🍷 ★★☆ Fleshy lemon & lime jostle with oak in tank sample **13**.

Savanha Sun range

> **Chardonnay** ☺🍷 ★★☆ Pre-bottling, unwooded **13** shows grippy citrus fruit & limy freshness.

Cabernet Sauvignon Not tasted, like **Merlot**. **Shiraz** 🍷 ★★ Baked plum character masks spice of business-like **12**. **Pinotage-Shiraz** 🍷 ★★ **12** packs tropical banana & clove flavour into light-bodied everyday red. **Shiraz-Cabernet Sauvignon-Pinotage** NEW 🍷 ★★ Light-hued **12** ex tank offers cinnamon spice & plummy fruit, dry finish. Unwooded. These all WO W Cape. **Pinotage Rosé** 🍷 ★★ Previewed **13** just-dry, savoury-tinged cherry styling that welcomes food; chill & bring on the tapas. **Chenin Blanc** 🍷 ★★ **13** is bottled sunshine, with fleshy apricot tang. **Sauvignon Blanc** 🍷 ★★ **13** juicy, fruity, easy-drinking. **Chenin Blanc-Sauvignon Blanc** NEW 🍷 ★★ Tank sample **13** has tropical melon tones held in check by tart acidity.

Frieda's Vine

Shiraz-Mourvèdre 🍷 ★★☆ Vanilla whiffs to berry-laden **12**, tad sweet but enough grip for food. Fairtrade certified & for export, like next. **Chenin Blanc-Viognier** 🍷 ★★☆ Aromatic, mediumweight **13** tank sample lively & dry. Both WO W Cape. — DS

Saxenburg Wine Farm

Location: Kuils River ▪ Map/WO: Stellenbosch ▪ Est 1693 ▪ 1stB 1990 ▪ Tasting & sales Mon-Fri 9–5 Sat/Sun 10–5 ▪ Fee R20 ▪ Closed Good Fri, Dec 25 & Jan 1 ▪ Cheese platters ▪ Gifts ▪ BYO picnic ▪ Conservation area ▪ Game park ▪ The Guinea Fowl Restaurant T +27 (0)21-906-5232 ▪ Saxenburg guest cottages (see Accommodation section) ▪ Owner(s) Adrian & Birgit Bührer ▪ Cellarmaster(s) Nico van der Merwe (Nov 1990) ▪ Winemaker(s) Nico van der Merwe (Nov 1990), with Edwin Grace (Jan 2005) ▪ Viticulturist(s) Donovan Diedericks (Apr 2008) ▪ 195ha/85ha (cabs s/f, malbec, merlot, ptage, shiraz, chard, chenin, sauv, viog) ▪ 650t/100,000cs own label 78% red 20% white 2% rosé ▪ Other export brands: Bosman's Hill, Gwendolyn ▪ PO Box 171 Kuils River 7580 ▪ info@saxenburg.co.za ▪ www.saxenburg.co.za ▪ S 33° 56' 47.9" E 018° 43' 9.4" ▪ **T +27 (0)21-903-6113**

The Swiss Bührer family's highly regarded estate in Stellenbosch's Polkadraai area has been producing standout wines under cellarmaster Nico van der Merwe since its modern reincarnation nearly a quarter of a century ago. In this time it has built an enviable reputation for classical styling, consistent quality and well-defined, focused product ranges. The elegant Cape Dutch buildings, some over 300 years old, have been carefully restored. Visitor facilities have recently been upgraded and, in addition to the popular Guinea Fowl Restaurant, now include a café-style tasting room and 'champagne lounge'.

Saxenburg Limited Release

★★★★★ **Shiraz Select** ⊕ Stunning depth & complexity of **09** (★★★★☆) excites. Beautifully judged weight & structure underscore rich, complex fruit in a dry, concentrated package. Seamless, complete & integrated now, but shows great ageing potential. A class act. Just a shade off magnificent **07**. No **08**.

Private Collection

★★★★☆ **Cabernet Sauvignon** **10** maintains superior standard of range. Supple, plush & elegant. Precision & remarkable balance, with fruits of the forest, herbal flecks & dark chocolate combining with plush oak & mouthwatering final grip. A classic.

★★★★☆ **Merlot** **10** (★★★★) just misses complexity of **09**, offering layers of plush black fruit, cardamom, dark chocolate with firm backbone & long spicy Christmas cake finish.

★★★★☆ **Shiraz** Vibrant **10** (★★★★) a step down from excellent vintage **09**. Bold & intense flavours of wild berry fruit, pepper, spicy oak & liquorice. Balanced, with good ageing potential.

★★★★ **Chardonnay** ✓ Opulent yet elegant barrel-fermented **12** maintains the pattern. Offers many intense layers of buttery citrus, crushed stone, vanilla & flowers; bold precise oaking (10 months French, only 10% new). A keeper.

★★★★ **Sauvignon Blanc** ✓🍷 **13** preview is dry, with concentrated grapefruit & lime flavours, & a good whiff of sea air. Refreshing minerality on the finish.

★★★★ **Méthode Cap Classique** ✓ Green-tinged **NV** (**09**) bubbly from chardonnay is dry, vibrant, with creamy texture & fine mousse. Intense pure flavours of lemon curd & apple pie leave you wanting more.

Pinotage ★★★☆ **11** back to form. Succulent black fruit, juicy & full, with loads of oak spice & punch. **Le Phantom Brut Cap Classique** Next awaited.

Guinea Fowl range

White ☺ 🍴 ★★★ Ripe fruit appeal on unoaked **13** chenin/viognier blend. Bouncy, with loads of flavour. Lees-ageing adds to creamy mouthfeel.

Red ✓ 🍴 ★★★★ 2nd-tier merlot, cab & shiraz blend, **12** is fresh & fruity with oaky vanilla to add to depth & body. Delicious everyday tipple. **Rosé** In abeyance.

Concept range

Grand Vin Rouge ☺ 🍴 ★★★ **NV** Bordeaux-style red is ripe & fruity, with hint of spice for picnic appeal.
Grand Vin Blanc ☺ 🍴 ★★★ Fun & fruity entry-level **NV** from sauvignon & chenin, bursts with ripe fruit & zesty acidity. — WB

Scali

Location: Paarl ▪ Map: Paarl & Wellington ▪ WO: Voor Paardeberg ▪ Est/1stB 1999 ▪ Tasting, sales & cellar tours Mon-Sat by appt ▪ Closed all pub hols ▪ B&B ▪ Owner(s) Willie & Tania de Waal ▪ Cellarmaster(s)/winemaker(s) Willie & Tania de Waal (Aug 1999) ▪ Viticulturist(s) Willie de Waal (Feb 1991) ▪ 270ha/70ha (cab, merlot, ptage, shiraz, chard, chenin, rouss, sauv, viog) ▪ 30t/4,000cs own label 67% red 33% white ▪ CERES Cert (vyds certified organic) ▪ PO Box 7143 Paarl 7620 ▪ info@scali.co.za ▪ www.scali.co.za ▪ S 33° 36' 70.6" E 018° 51' 49.5" ▪ **T +27 (0)21-869-8340** ▪ F +27 (0)21-869-8383

New to the de Waal's Scali boutique wine range is a 'méthode ancestrale' sparkling from chenin (a single fermentation completed in bottle rather than the two for méthode cap classique). Called Ancestor, it's a tribute to Hermanus Lambertus de Waal, who bought Schoone Oord with a 45 carat diamond in 1877, current owner Willie de Waal the fifth generation of his family to farm here.

★★★★ **Pinotage** ⏱ Engaging **08** shows red cherry, some earthiness; good fruit concentration, fresh acidity & densely packed tannins; year French oak, 20% new, an unobtrusive scaffolding.

★★★★ **Syrah** ⏱ Noble **08** (★★★★☆) has real sense of place; only 20% new oak (2 years French) attuned to De Waals' goal of fruit (not wood) expression, as was slightly higher 30% for **07**.

★★★★☆ **Blanc** ⏱ Super-dry **09** 50% chenin, 20% chardonnay with roussanne, sauvignon, viognier; year older oak. Intellectually demanding, hugely complex with great breadth, depth of flavour, intensity.

Ancestor NEW ★★★ Curious but not unappealing **12** sparkling is rich & broad, sweet, with a yeasty overtone. Moderate acidity, soft bubble. — CE

■ **Scarlett Organic** *see Seven Sisters*
■ **Schalk Burger & Sons** *see Welbedacht Wine Estate*

Schalkenbosch Wines

Location/map: Tulbagh ▪ WO: Tulbagh/Western Cape ▪ Est 1792 ▪ 1stB 2002 ▪ Tasting, sales & tours by appt ▪ Closed all pub hols ▪ Tour groups ▪ Walking/hiking & mountain biking trails ▪ Conservation area ▪ Self-catering cottages ▪ Owner(s) Platinum Mile Investments ▪ Cellarmaster(s)/winemaker(s) Gielie Beukes (Jun 2010) ▪ Viticulturist(s) Johan Wiese & Andrew Teubes ▪ 1,800ha/37ha (cab, shiraz) ▪ 140t/20,000cs own label 80% red 18% white 2% rosé ▪ BWI champion ▪ PO Box 95 Tulbagh 6820 ▪ info@schalkenbosch.co.za ▪ www.schalkenbosch.co.za ▪ S 33° 18' 49.7" E 019° 11' 59.9" ▪ **T +27 (0)23-230-0654/1488** ▪ F +27 (0)86-519-2605/+27 (0)86-654-8209

Last year, the Biodiversity & Wine Initiative again awarded Champion status to this Tulbagh farm with a conservation ethos: 'Our work in the cellar and vineyards has paid off,' says winemaker Gielie Beukes. He reports with satisfaction that China has been buying, and that Germany is now the winery's main European customer.

Schalkenbosch range

★★★★ **Cumulus** NEW ✓ 🌿 **10** impressive Bordeaux red with deep berry flavour, crisp acidity & cab's tightly wound, fine tannins. More approachable than sibling, will also improve.

★★★★ **Stratus** ✓ 🌿 Characterful shiraz-led flagship. **10** more muscular than last-tasted **07** yet still highlights house's affinity with Rhône varieties. Complex red fruits, lively acid & burly tannins; needs 2+ years.

Cuvée Brut Cap Classique Await next.

Edenhof range

Cabernet Sauvignon ☺ 🖿 ▨ ★★★ Cassis, cedar appeal on **11**, leaner than lithe previous bottlings. **Pinotage** ☺ 🖿 ▨ ★★★ Step-up **10** supple & succulent crowd pleaser; creamy texture ex portion American oak. **Nighthawk 409** ☺ 🖿 ▨ ★★★ Was 'Bin 409'. Expressive **11** mixes mainly spicy shiraz, 4 other Rhône varieties for easy enjoyment. WO W Cape.

Merlot NEW 🖿 ▨ ★★☆ **11** quite punchy, powerful; packed with meaty fruit & noticeable tannins. **Shiraz** 🖿 ▨ ★★☆ **11**'s firm tannins softened by ripe fruit & some sweet American oak. **Cabernet Sauvignon-Merlot** 🖿 ▨ ★★☆ 50/50 **11** combo has leafy, herbaceous notes on nose & palate. **Chardonnay** ⊕ 🖿 ▨ ★★☆ Attractive **12** unwooded, creamy aperitif. **Sauvignon Blanc** ⊕ 🖿 ▨ ★★☆ **12** achieves a good balance between ripe tropical fruit flavour & zesty acidity. **Viognier** ⊕ 🖿 ▨ ★★ Gently perfumed **12** was shade off the mark last edition; acerbic bite may have softened now. **Blanc de Blanc** 🖿 ★★ Blend of sauvignon, chenin & hanepoot; bone-dry & lightish (12% alcohol) **12**, satisfyingly vinous. WO W Cape.

Isis range

Dry Red Await next. **Rosé** ⊕ 🖿 ▨ ★★★☆ Savoury, leafy & dry **12** quite stylish, bright with tight structure, good length & juice. **Dry White** 🖿 ★★ Slimmer's friend **12** is low on sugar & alcohol, with pleasing texture from 4 months lees-ageing. WO W Cape. — CE,CvZ

■ **Scholtzenhof** see Ken Forrester Wines
■ **Schoone Gevel** see La Motte

Schultz Family Wines ▯

Location/WO: Stellenbosch ▪ Est 2002 ▪ Tasting by appt ▪ Closed all pub hols ▪ Owner(s) Rudi Schultz ▪ Cellar-master(s)/winemaker(s) Rudi Schultz (Jan 2002) ▪ Viticulturist(s) Dirkie Morkel ▪ 10t/1,340cs own label 100% red ▪ 8 Fraser Road Somerset West 7130 ▪ rudi@thelema.co.za ▪ **T +27 (0)82-928-1841** ▪ F +27 (0)21-885-1800

Rudi Schultz's 'day job' is the illustrious one of being winemaker for Thelema – but it allows him a little time for his own label. Here he is 'attempting to make hand-crafted ultra-premium wines at sensible prices'. The range is even expanding, with a cabernet and a cab-based blend, from the grower who has long supplied his fine syrahs, expected as the guide went to press.

★★★★ **Syrah** ▨ Ripe, dark-fruited **11** with smoky Asian spice notes. The round & supple palate shows intensity, intelligent oaking (15% new), & big but integrated 14.4% alcohol. More complexity with time.

★★★★☆ **Reserve Syrah** ▨ Expressive **10** has well-structured palate - fresh, with fine firm tannin (partly from 15% petit verdot addition) & rich spicy fruit. Pressed & aged in the same all-new barrels. Ripe, but lower alcohol than standard version. Both Bottelary grapes, naturally fermented. — JPf

Scrucap Wines

WO: Elgin/Western Cape/Coastal/Swartland/Durbanville/Stellenbosch ▪ Est 2011 ▪ Closed to public ▪ Cellar-master(s) Andries Burger (Paul Cluver Estate Wines), Chris & Andrea Mullineux (Mullineux Family Wines), JD Pretorius (Steenberg Vineyards), Charles Hopkins (De Grendel Wines) & Edouard Labeye (Winery of Good Hope) ▪ 20,000cs own label 40% red 40% white 10% rosé 10% MCC ▪ ksconsult@mweb.co.za ▪ www. luxislandresorts.com ▪ **T +27 (0)83-484-8781**

Guests of LUX* Resorts on Indian Ocean islands are invited to 'say farewell to corks and Old World wines and say hi to Scrucap, a collection of South African wines specially selected' for the hotel group. Consultant Kent Scheermeyer says the aim is to offer 'fresh, sexy' wines - a goal that should be met, considering the elite Cape sources: Paul Cluver, De Grendel, Steenberg, Winery of Good Hope and our 2014 Winery of the Year, Mullineux Family Wines.

★★★★ **Swartland Blend** 🖿 LUX* guests will be transported back to the Old World on tasting **12**, classy shiraz blend by Mullineux Family, with Rhône-like spicy flavour melange, supple structure.

★★★★ **Riesling** NEW 🖿 Featherlight (9.8% alcohol) **12** from Paul Cluver, showcases varietal aromatics & vitality. Semi-sweet styling, but appears fresher, courtesy finely tuned fruit/acid balance.

★★★★ **Popcap** ▨ Blanc de blancs sparkler from chardonnay in fresh, crisp, lighter style. Steenberg's **12** bracing green apple & citrus acidity tempered a year on lees; dry, refreshing, a super aperitif.

Pinot Noir 🍷 ★★★☆ Nicely proportioned **11** has dark cherry, bright acidity, fine tannins. Good fruit weight, oak carefully judged. By De Grendel. **Shiraz** 🍷 ★★★ Juicy & balanced, with appealing white pepper nuance to approachable **11** from Paul Cluver. **3 Valleys Blend** 🍷 🌿 ★★★ Muscular **11** offers grip at mealtime. Cab, cab franc & merlot blended by Steenberg. **Rosé** 🍷 ★★★ Lifted red fruit, some herbal character plus bright acidity on dry **13** from 50:50 combo cab & pinotage. By De Grendel. **Chardonnay** 🍷 ★★★★ Vivacious step up in **12** from Paul Cluver. Bright, fresh & balanced, with tangy marmalade flavours. **Chenin Blanc** 🍷 ★★★★ Chenin specialists The Winery of Good Hope made deeply satisfying **12**, with vivacious & delicious flavours of herb, melon & peach. **Sauvignon Blanc** 🍷 ★★★★ Paul Cluver's sprightly **12** has crisp herb & citrus tone. Fresh & balanced for summer enjoyment. **Sauvignon Blanc** 🍷 ★★★★ Rich & ripe **12** from De Grendel displays asparagus & bruised apple. Lacks some of the punch of **11** (★★★★★). — CE, TJ, DS, MW

Seal Breeze Wines

Location: Lutzville ▪ Map: Olifants River ▪ WO: Lutzville Valley ▪ Est 2004 ▪ 1stB 2005 ▪ Tasting, sales & cellar tours Mon-Fri 9-4 Sat 9-12 ▪ Closed Easter Fri-Mon, Ascension Day, Dec 25 & Jan 1 ▪ Meals/refreshments by prior arrangement ▪ Facilities for children ▪ Tour groups ▪ BYO picnic ▪ Owner(s) John & Joan Wiggins ▪ Cellarmaster(s) Joan Wiggins (Feb 2004) ▪ Winemaker(s) Joan Wiggins (Feb 2004), with Toy Brand (Feb 2006) ▪ Viticulturist(s) Joan Wiggins ▪ ±92ha/±70ha (cab, merlot, shiraz, chenin, cbard, hanepoot, sauv) ▪ 1,200t/1,560cs own label ▪ PO Box 33 Lutzville 8165 ▪ jwiggins@kingsley.co.za ▪ www.sealbreezewine.co.za ▪ S 31° 34' 50.1" E 018° 19' 9.8" ▪ **T +27 (0)84-505-1991** ▪ F +27 (0)27-217-1458

Since buying back the family farm on the diamond-rich West Coast, self-taught boutique vintner Joan Wiggins has vinified her Seal Breeze wines and shared her joy with others, hosting Journey of Hope breast cancer survivors during harvest and surprising buyers of her special magnums with a diamond in the bottle.

Cabernet Sauvignon ⊕ 🌿 Last edition, **10** too young & unknit to rate. **Merlot** ⊕ 🌿 ★★★ Charry oak seasoning to prune & date aromas, pre-bottling **10** lovely if unconcentrated milk chocolate flavours, warm afterglow. **Shiraz** ⊕ ★★★ Appealing meaty aroma & dusty overlay, **10** tannins still quite gruff when last tasted, may since have softened. **Sauvignon Blanc** ⊕ ★★★ **11** ripe lemon & passionfruit, engaging if unlingering fruity mouthful. — DB, MW

▪ **Season's Collection** *see* Orange River Wine Cellars
▪ **Secateurs** *see* AA Badenhorst Family Wines
▪ **Secret Cellar** *see* Ultra Liquors

Sedgwick's Old Brown

Venerable Distell brand, blend of jerepiko and dry sherry, in 200ml, 375ml, 750ml, 1L and 2L.

Sedgwick's Old Brown 🍷 ★★★ Fortified winter warmer since 1916. **NV**. Combo raisin, caramel & some sherry character; very ripe & sweet, delicious. — DB, HJ

▪ **Semara** *see* Wine-of-the-Month Club

Sequillo Cellars

Location: Malmesbury ▪ Map/WO: Swartland ▪ Est/1stB 2003 ▪ Tasting & sales Mon-Fri by appt ▪ Closed all pub hols ▪ Owner(s) Eben Sadie Trust & Cornel Spies Trust ▪ Cellarmaster(s)/winemaker(s) Eben Sadie (Jan 2003) ▪ 20ha (carignan, grenache, mourv, syrah, chenin, clairette, rouss, viog) ▪ 45t/6,000cs own label 50% red 50% white ▪ PO Box 1019 Malmesbury 7299 ▪ info@sequillo.com ▪ www.sequillo.com ▪ S 33° 31' 31.0" E 018° 48' 18.1" ▪ **T +27 (0)76-151-7131** ▪ F +27 (0)86-692-2852

Swartland's original winemaking star Eben Sadie (see also Sadie Family Wines) here partners with Australia-based Dr Cornel Spies. Sequillo, Latin for 'an arid dry place of great purity', aims to showcase Swartland terroir. Varieties used are Rhône/Mediterranean because they best suit conditions here and are blend-compatible, all handled with minimal intervention in the dryland vineyards and cellar. Labels have line-drawn designs which change each year and always contain a message about the natural way of farming versus its alternative. A work-in-progress - additional varieties joined the blends this year - but the main focus never wavers: integrity and balance.

★★★★☆ **Sequillo Red** Changing blend, mainly Rhône varieties, shiraz-led in **11** with cinsaut & 4 others. Reflecting the area & varieties, there is dusty cocoa, a core of dark wild fruit & then the clincher, juicy freshness & impressively supple tannins.

★★★★☆ **Sequillo White** Chenin & clairette blanche in a 5-part oaked blend selected to showcase the area. Made for enjoyment (says the winemaker) but **12**'s multi-layers impress as well. There's melon & quince, crushed almonds & tangy acidity promising a fine future. — CR

■ **Sereia** *see* Anatu Wines

Ses'Fikile

Location: Wellington ▪ Est/1stB 2006 ▪ Tasting at Wellington Wines by arrangement ▪ Owner(s) Ses'Fikile Wine Services ▪ Winemaker(s) Hugo Truter (Wellington Wines) ▪ 11,000cs own label 70% red 30% white ▪ PO Box 38055 Pinelands 7430 ▪ sesfikile@gmail.com

Brand owner and former teacher Nondumiso Pikashe partners with Wellington Wines to produce her good-value wines, whose brand name translates as 'We Have Arrived, In Style', for local and overseas winelovers.

■ **7even** *see* Zevenwacht

Seven Sisters

Location/map: Stellenbosch ▪ WO: Swartland ▪ Tasting & sales at Seven Sisters Farm, Welmoed Rd, off Annandale Rd, Lynedoch, Stellenbosch - phone ahead ▪ Owner(s) African Roots Wine ▪ Winemaker(s) Vivian Kleynhans ▪ PO Box 4560 Tygervalley 7536 ▪ vivian@africanrootswines.com ▪ www.sevensisters.co.za ▪ S 33° 59' 23.41" E 018° 46' 34.35" ▪ **T +27 (0)71-049-4109/+27 (0)83-624-0391** ▪ F +27 (0)86-514-5569

There really are seven sisters (soon to be joined by a brother), who descend from fisherman stock in the small West Coast town of Paternoster. They have taken on the wine world with their range of personality-focused, Swartland-sourced bottlings. Their new winery near Stellenbosch is up and running, and they will be planting their first vineyards soon.

Cabernet Sauvignon Carol ☺ 🍷 🍷 ★★★ Riper, softer **12** retains cherry fruit, adds body & poise.

Merlot June 🍷 🍷 ★★ **12** is light & uncomplicated. **Pinotage-Shiraz Dawn** 🍷 🍷 ★★★ **12** pleasant spicy berry flavours. Light bodied with rather brief finish. **Bukettraube Odelia** 🍷 🍷 ★★ Lightish, mildly sweet **13**. **Moscato Yolanda** NEW 🍷 🍷 ★★ Sweetly petillant & undemanding **12** from chenin. **Sauvignon Blanc Vivian** 🍷 🍷 ★★★ Nicely weighted **13** from Malmesbury vineyards offers area's dusty pebble notes with lemon & gooseberry fruit. **Sweet Rosé Twena** 🍷 🍷 ★★★ From hanepoot & pinotage, **12** has floral notes & hint of muscat. Discontinued: **Chenin Blanc Yolanda**. — GdB

Seven Springs Vineyards

Location: Hermanus ▪ WO: Overberg ▪ Est 2007 ▪ 1stB 2010 ▪ Closed to public ▪ Owner(s) Tim & Vaughan Pearson ▪ Winemaker(s) Riana van der Merwe (Nov 2009) ▪ Viticulturist(s) Peter Davison (Jul 2007, consultant) ▪ 12ha/±8ha (pinot, syrah, chard, sauv) ▪ ±56t/8,000cs own label 50% red 50% white ▪ Private Bag X15 Suite 162 Hermanus 7200 ▪ info@7springs.co.za ▪ www.7springs.co.za ▪ **T +27 (0)82-487-7572; UK +44 1789740502** ▪ F +27 (0)86-571-0623

Vinified offsite, the wines from Tim and Vaughan Pearson's 8ha vineyard on Shaws Mountain near Hermanus must be among the most blogged, tweeted and Facebooked in the world - in line with the UK-based but SA-passionate owners' belief that social media is key to marketing their young brand. No wonder that winemaker Riana van der Merwe shared online the step-by-step progress of her bottle of Pinot Noir, taken along while scaling Kilimanjaro last year!

Pinot Noir 🍷 🍷 ★★★★ Intense pure fruit expression on **12** follows debut **11** (★★★★). Pared down yet supple frame holds ripe, smoky raspberry fruit gently. Light & elegant. **Syrah** 🍷 🍷 ★★★★ Richly fruited **12** preview shows graphite minerality to pure plum & spice, integrated oak adds length. **Oaked Chardonnay** ⊕ 🍷 🍷 ★★★★ **11** maintains track record of previous with rich orange brûléed appeal framed by stylish oak. Smooth finish. **Unoaked Chardonnay** 🍷 🍷 ★★★ Vivacious citrus typical of the grape speaks

loudest on **12**. Light, fresh & zesty, for current enjoyment. **Sauvignon Blanc** ★★★★ Tangy green pineapple & peach freshness to **12**. Textured, rounded & full, with long aftertaste. — FM

Seven Steps Wines

Location: Cape Town ▪ WO: Western Cape/Elgin ▪ Est/1stB 2009 ▪ Tasting by appt only ▪ Owner(s) Travis Braithwaite & Pragasen Ramiah ▪ Cellarmaster(s)/winemaker(s) Travis Braithwaite ▪ (shiraz, sauv) ▪ 1,600cs own label 30% red 70% white ▪ PO Box 981 Sea Point Cape Town 8060 ▪ info@sevenstepswines.com ▪ www.sevenstepswines.com ▪ **T +27 (0)82-368-5270** ▪ F +27 (0)86-625-0109

A brand created by two entrepreneurs, Pragasen Ramiah and Travis Braithwaite, who is also the winemaker, sourced from across the winelands. The name comes from the last remaining concrete evidence of the old District Six in Cape Town.

Syrah ⊕ ★★★☆ Last **08** rose geranium scent, meaty hint, charry oak smoothed by few grams sugar. **Sauvignon Blanc** ⊕ ★★★★ Passionfruit with leafy nuance, **10** tangy appetite appeal. WO Elgin. — CR

■ **Sgt Pepper** *see* Teddy Hall Wines

Shannon Vineyards

Location/WO: Elgin ▪ Map: Elgin, Walker Bay & Bot River ▪ Est 2000 ▪ 1stB 2003 ▪ Tasting, sales & vineyard tour first weekend of the month (Oct-May), or by appt ▪ Owner(s) Stuart & James Downes ▪ Winemaker(s) Gordon Newton Johnson & Nadia Newton Johnson ▪ Viticulturist(s) Kevin Watt (consultant) ▪ 75ha/15.5ha (merlot, pinot, sauv, sem, viog) ▪ 100t/6,000cs own label 66% red 34% white ▪ BWI, Global GAP, IPW, Tesco's Natures Choice ▪ PO Box 20 Elgin 7180 ▪ james@shannonwines.com ▪ www.shannonwines.com ▪ S 34° 11' 3.9" E 018° 59' 3.6" ▪ **T +27 (0)21-859-2491** ▪ F +27 (0)21-859-5389

Located in Elgin Valley and owned by James and Stuart Downes, Shannon Vineyards first built an enviable reputation on the quality of the grapes supplied to several of South Africa's leading winemakers. (An invitation to the annual tasting and lunch at which Shannon-origin wines are compared and notes exchanged is highly prized.) Then, in 2009, the brothers' own label, vinified in Hemel-en-Aarde Valley by Gordon and Nadia Newton Johnson, debuted with a stellar trio of releases. Shannon wines have since enjoyed a 'second' reputation as among South Africa's finest, and most expressive of their cool, meticulously nurtured and very beautiful origin.

★★★★☆ **Mount Bullet Merlot** Among South Africa's top examples. **11** has the noble bearing & athletic build of **10**, & the suave fruit of earlier vintages. Beautifully dry & authoritative, already complex - violets, exotic spices, a sanguine note - will only show better with cellaring.

★★★★☆ **Rockview Ridge Pinot Noir** Effortless **12** follows on from **11**: ethereal yet convincing, with delicate black/red fruit perfume, icing sugar & wedding almonds complexity supported by enlivening minerality & elegant tannin.

★★★★☆ **Sanctuary Peak Sauvignon Blanc** **13** white peach fragrance, taut & gravelly; also-tasted **12** slightly riper & silkier; both well assembled, with 11% new-oaked semillon adding breadth without diminishing vibrancy. Crafted to improve with bottle-ageing, as mid-2013 tasting of earlier vintages showed.

★★★★ **Semillon** NEW! Toasty oak prelude to **12** opens & deepens to reveal lovely lemongrass aromas/flavours, tangy flourish on finish. Potential only hinted at mid-2013, deserves time to settle & unfurl; decant if uncorking now, don't over-chill.

★★★★ **Macushla Pinot Noir Noble Late Harvest** 'My Darling' deliciously idiosyncratic dessert picked at 38° Balling! (exclaims James Downes), naturally fermented in older oak. **12** (★★★★), first tasted since maiden **09**, tealeaf, spice savouriness juxtaposed with cherry sweetness. So easy to drink now, next year... or in 10. — CvZ

■ **Shepherd's Cottage** *see* Overgaauw Wine Estate

Ship

Another piece of Distell-owned South African wine patrimony, launched in 1929.

Ship ★★ Latest **NV** drops 'Sherry' from label but remains a raisiny jerepiko-style fireside comforter. — DB, HJ

Shoprite Checkers

Enquiries: Stephanus Eksteen ▪ 160,000cs own label 50% red 40% white 10% rosé ▪ PO Box 215 Brackenfell 7561 ▪ seksteen@shoprite.co.za ▪ www.shoprite.co.za ▪ **T +27 (0)21-980-4000** ▪ F +27 (0)21-980-4421

There's nothing odd about this southern African supermarket chain's in-house range: Odd Bins, selected by a panel tasting blind and produced to specifications, has become its second-biggest seller. The chain is also a major bidder at the annual Nederburg Auction, adding to its in-store 'Wine Route' stocks from over 80 leading Cape wine farms.

- ▪ **Short Story** *see Neethlingshof Estate*
- ▪ **Short Street** *see Valley Vineyards Wine Company*
- ▪ **Shortwood** *see Imbuko Wines*
- ▪ **Signal Cannon** *see Vondeling*

Signal Gun Wines

Location/WO: Durbanville ▪ Map: Durbanville, Philadelphia & Darling ▪ Est/1stB 2006 ▪ Tasting & sales Tue-Sat 9-5 Sun 9.30-4 ▪ Fee R20 ▪ Closed Good Fri, Dec 25 & Jan 1 ▪ Ke-Monate Wine Bar & Bistro (see Restaurants section) ▪ Conferences ▪ Conservation area ▪ Owner(s) WRM de Wit ▪ Cellarmaster(s)/winemaker(s) MJ de Wit (Jan 2006) ▪ Viticulturist(s) Walter Smith ▪ 210ha/95ha (cab, merlot, ptage, shiraz, chard, sauv) ▪ 19t/ 2,000cs own label 50% white 50% red ▪ PO Box 2359 Durbanville 7551 ▪ wine@signalgun.com ▪ www. signalgun.com ▪ S 33° 49' 13.26" E 018° 36' 40.32" ▪ **T +27 (0)21-976-7343** ▪ F +27 (0)86-611-8747

The range launched in 2006 by MJ de Wit as a mere 'hobby', with grapes off the old Hooggelegen family farm in Durbanville, soon developed into 'project Ke-Monate'. Its Sotho name appropriately meaning 'that's nice!', the venture includes tasting room, restaurant and, happily, more wines.

De Wit Family Reserve Wines NEW

WRM Shiraz ★★★☆ **10** comes across as selection of best barrels of standard version: more generous, more fruit intensity. Generally pleasing & rather elegant. **Sea Smoke Sauvignon blanc** ★★★★ Attractive & lively but lightweight & unlingering **12** has some charming ripe notes of blackcurrant & passionfruit.

Signal Gun Wines range

Merlot NEW ★★★★ Attractive warm, ripe aromas on **12**, leading to balanced palate with firmly gentle structure. Some herbal suggestions on finish. **Shiraz** ★★★★ 2 vintages tasted. **10**'s (★★★) spice & leather dominate a little sweet fruit; on lean side, with drying tannins. Riper **11** more warmly, fruitily generous & succulent. Both sensitively oaked, restrained. **Rosé** NEW 🍽 ★★★★ Successful, interesting **12** merlot, shiraz, sauvignon has a nice copper gleam. Balanced, dry & tasty, with light tannic grip. **Chardonnay** ⏱ 🍽 ★★★★ Flavourful **12** with tropical & citrus notes. Light oaking; bone-dry. **Sauvignon Blanc** ⏱ 🍽 ★★★★ Flavourful but not too fruity **12**, not intense, but crisply balanced & with a streak of stony elegance. — TJ

Signal Hill Wines

Location: Cape Town ▪ Map: Cape Peninsula ▪ WO: Stellenbosch/Coastal/Stellenbosch/Paarl/Piekenierskloof/ Constantia/Cape Point ▪ 1stB 1997 ▪ Tasting, sales & cellar tours Mon-Fri 11-6 Sat 12-4 in season ▪ Closed all pub hols ▪ Cheese platters, charcuterie & tapas during open hours ▪ Owner(s) Signal Hill Wines cc ▪ Cellarmaster(s)/winemaker(s)/viticulturist(s) Laurence Buthelezi ▪ 2ha (cab f, mourv, pinot, shiraz) ▪ 75% red 20% white 5% rosé ▪ Heritage Square, 100 Shortmarket Street, Cape Town 8001 ▪ info@winery.co.za ▪ www.winery.co.za ▪ S 33° 55' 15.06" E 018° 25' 5.54" ▪ **T +27 (0)21-424-5820** ▪ F +27 (0)21-422-5238

Long-time winemaker Laurence Buthelezi is now in charge of the wines and a part-owner of this city winery (with a remarkable and unique focus on tiny bottlings off city and Peninsula vineyards). Founder of the business and originator of the concept is the other co-owner, the irrepressible and innovative Frenchman, Jean-Vincent Ridon. The 'cellardoor' tasting room in the heart of Cape Town is now licensed as a wine bar offering other brands too.

Single Barrel range

★★★★ **Pinot Noir** ⏱ **10** lighter-footed style than **08** standard bottling, also from Stellenbosch fruit, with more appetising acidity & cranberry flavours imparting an elegant cool-climate feel.

★★★★ **1771 Heritage Vine** ⓕ One 240 year-old city centre chenin vine bore 20 bottles of this intriguing **11** curiosity: full of flavour, with a sweet impression despite low alcohol & sugar.

★★★★☆ **Pineau de Ludovic** ⓕ Contemplative **NV** aperitif; chenin-colombard blend spent a decade in barrel. 200g/l sugar & 16% alcohol on complex & delicious fortified wine. Stellenbosch/Paarl fruit.

Kalk Bay Blanc de Noir NEW ★★ Oxidative, light, bone-dry & tangy **12** from Cape Point cab franc.

Signal Hill range

★★★★☆ **Camps Bay Vineyard** Distinctive, intense wild berry fruit aromas in **10** (★★★★), from mourvèdre, leading to full, generous mouthful of sweet silky fruit, checked by supple tannins, persistent finish. Just 250 bottles off coastal suburban vines. Fine **09** was maiden harvest.

★★★★ **Petit Verdot** ⓕ Sharp **04** (★★★★) needed food to show best. **03** more seductive.

★★★★☆ **Clos d'Oranje** ⓕ Evocatively perfumed, individual **07** is bold but quite beautifully fresh, from tiny, apparently ungrafted shiraz vineyard in central Cape Town. **06** (★★★★★) more finely structured.

★★★★ **Grenache Blanc** ⓕ **08** subtle scents, silky, & savoury mineral core. From Piekenierskloof.

★★★★ **MCC Pinot Noir** ⓕ **06** disgorged on demand. Lovely mature aromas. Bone-dry, sulphured.

★★★★☆ **Empereur Rouge** ⓕ Delicious, ultra-sweet, warm & raisiny **06** from cab.

★★★★ **Crème de Tête Muscat d'Alexandrie NLH** ⓕ Last tasted was hedonistic **03**.

★★★★★ **Eszencia** ⓕ Magnificent **NV** (**02**), probably a one-off, sweet & rich, electrified by nervy acidity.

★★★★ **Mathilde Aszú 6 Puttonyos** Last **02** Tokaji lookalike from botrytised furmint & sauvignon.

★★★★ **Vin de l'Empereur** ⓕ Vivid **05** last-tasted botrytised dessert from muscat d'Alexandrie.

★★★★★ **Vin de l'Empereur Solera** ⓕ Unctuous, golden **NV** from 8 year-old solera of Constantia muscat d'Alexandrie. Layered complexity; sweetness (115g/l) balanced by integrated acidity. Dry, long & graceful finish.

Olympia Cabernet Franc ⓕ ★★★ **08** light-centred, with just a little fruit concentration & a rather uneasy structure. **Grenache Noir** In abeyance, as for **Malbec**, **Rosé de Saignée** & **The Threesome**. **Pinot Noir** ⓕ ★★★★ Fragrant, enticing **08** made in traditional earthy style with sure-footed presence & at same time a silky complex lightness from Stellenbosch fruit, a step-up from **07** (★★★★). **Syrah** ⓕ ★★★★ Fresh & fleshy **06**. **Straw Wine** ⓕ ★★★☆ **01** with super-viscous, almost syrupy texture. Mainly chardonnay, chenin & riesling, air-dried on straw mats ±8 weeks.

Buthelezi range

Tutuka Syrah Occasional release. — IM

■ **Signatures of Doolhof** *see* Doolhof Wine Estate

Sijnn ♀

Location/WO: Malgas ▪ Map: Southern Cape ▪ Est 2003 ▪ 1stB 2007 ▪ Tasting & sales at De Trafford Wines (see entry); and from April 2014 at Sijnn Sat 9-3 or by appt ▪ Closed all pub hols ▪ Owner(s) David & Rita Trafford, Simon Farr, Quentin Hurt ▪ Winemaker(s) David Trafford ▪ Viticulturist(s) Schalk du Toit (2002, consultant) ▪ 125ha/16ha (cab, mourv, shiraz, touriga nacional, trincadeira, chenin, rouss, viog) ▪ 50t/5,400cs own label 73% red 20% white 7% rosé ▪ PO Box 495 Stellenbosch 7599 ▪ info@sijnn.co.za ▪ www.sijnn.co.za ▪ **T +27 (0)21-880-1611** ▪ F +27 (0)21-880-1611

Nothing that co-owner and winemaker David Trafford does is without careful thought, as befits his architectural training. Sijnn (rhymes with 'sane') might look like an almost hobbyist project because of his holiday home there, but planting warm-country varieties in a cool climate like that of Malgas at the Breede River estuary (which he has) makes sense in the context of global warming. It's also part of the 'search for excellence outside the traditional areas' because David believes that 'that's where real interest lies'. For now, the wines are made at De Trafford in Stellenbosch, but an own cellar is on the cards.

★★★★★ **Syrah** NEW Captivating cool-climate shiraz. Intensity of dark spice & berry fragrance in **11** echoed in the layered flavours & fine-grained, mouthwatering tannins. Compelling in its delicacy & freshness. Natural ferment, unfined/filtered, like all these reds, & no new oak.

★★★★☆ **CWG Auction Reserve Syrah** NEW Fuller, more exuberant than **11** standard bottling. Hint of new oak (20% French) adds richer feel without curbing essential vigour, freshness & spicy fruit purity. Selection of best shiraz blocks.

★★★★ **Touriga Nacional** NEW **11** intrigues as a warm-climate grape in cooler area – it responds with elegance & freshness. Flowers, wild sage & liquorice; lithe & resilient, but mouthwatering ripe tannin.

★★★★ **Sijnn** ⚘ All-sorts blend with shiraz, touriga playing important roles, **10** is individualistic. Scrub & coffee, wild berries, it's hard to pin down but very easy to enjoy. The savoury oak grip makes it ideal for food.

★★★★☆ **White** Chenin proportion again increased (to 84%) in **12**, viognier adding a subtle spicy lift. Appealing purity, restraint & delicacy, yet also amplitude of mouthfeel, flavourful ripe fruit. Roundly dry. Natural ferment in small & 700-litre French oak; unfiltered.

Cabernet Sauvignon NEW ★★★ Tiny planting 'to see how cab performs', explains David Trafford, the grapes yet to find a permanent home. **10**'s straightforward dark berry fruit clipped short by austere tail. **Low Profile** NEW ★★★☆ Name alludes to profile holes dug to determine matching of variety to site. From touriga nacional; **11** less intense but seemingly bigger than varietally named version (though less alcohol), more plummy accessibility. **Saignée** ⚘ ★★★☆ Oaked rosé blend of mourvèdre with shiraz, trincadeira, **11** has scrub, cherry piquancy, savoury dryness. — AL

Silkbush Mountain Vineyards

Location: Wolseley ▪ WO: Breedekloof ▪ Est 2000 ▪ 1stB 2007 ▪ Closed to public ▪ Kingsbury Cottage (self-catering), www.silkbush.net/kingsbury ▪ Owner(s) Silkbush Holdings LP ▪ Winemaker(s) Bennie Wannenburg (2007, consultant) ▪ Viticulturist(s) Anton Roos (2000) ▪ 143ha/87ha (cabs s/f, malbec, merlot, mourv, p verdot, ptage, shiraz, sauv, sem, viog) ▪ 1,200t/10,000cs own label 100% red ▪ Other export brand: Lion's Drift ▪ PO Box 91 Breërivier 6858 ▪ anton@silkbush.net ▪ www.silkbush.net ▪ **T +27 (0)83-629-1735** ▪ F +27 (0)86-520-3261

Well-established and -reputed as a supplier of top-quality grapes to some of the Cape's majors, this Californian-owned spread below Breedekloof's Sybasberg (Silkbush Mountain) exports its own-brand wine to the US but is also now establishing a presence in Gauteng. Range expansions are in the planning.

Viognier NEW ☺ 🍽 🚫 ★★★ Unwooded **12** a textbook for the variety: apricot & peach perfumes, light-textured palate adorned with floral notes & fresh acidity. Perfect summer wine.

Pinotage ✓ 🍽 ★★★☆ Medium-bodied **09** has improved since sampled last year, shows tasty stewed fruit & long rooibos-spicy finish. Promising. **Shiraz** 🍽 🚫 ★★★ Revisited as bottled wine, aromatic **10** doing well, unusual cinnamon dusting to substantial red berry fruit. Should keep few more years. — GM

◾ **Silverhurst** see High Constantia Wine Cellar

Silvermist Vineyards ☕ ⚘ 📷

Location: Constantia ▪ WO: Constantia-Coastal/Constantia ▪ Est 1984 ▪ 1stB 2010 ▪ Closed to public for tasting ▪ Silvermist Mountain Lodge offering accommodation, conferences, weddings/functions, restaurant & wine sales ▪ Conservation area ▪ Owner(s) Constantia Ridge Estates (Pty) Ltd ▪ Cellarmaster(s)/winemaker(s)/viticulturist(s) Gregory Brink Louw (Jan 2005) ▪ 22ha/3ha (cab, shiraz, sauv) ▪ 5.2t/580cs own label 30% red 70% white ▪ Certified organic (BDOCA) ▪ PO Box 608 Constantia 7848 ▪ silmist@mweb.co.za ▪ www.silvermistvineyards.co.za ▪ **T +27 (0)21-794-7601** ▪ F +27 (0)21-794-7602

Silvermist, in the mountains above Constantia, is the only organically certified wine estate in the area and part of the Table Mountain National Park. Viticulturist/winemaker Gregory Louw and his team have spent over 12 years clearing alien vegetation, planting 3 ha of vines and recently bottling the fruits of their labour.

★★★★ **Rocket Dog Red** 🌶 Was 'Cab Sauv'. **11**'s cab gets 25% shiraz blended in at bottling. Overt sweet oak (100% new, 25% American) infused with wild scrub & pepper. New World, suavely approachable style.

Sauvignon Blanc 🌶 ★★★★ Focus more on structure & creamy-yet-crisp texture in **13**, with demure stonefruit & damp forest nuance. — MW

◾ **Silver Myn** see Zorgvliet Wines
◾ **Silversands** see Robertson Wide River Export Company

Silverthorn Wines

Location: Robertson ▪ WO: Robertson/Western Cape ▪ Est 1998 ▪ 1stB 2004 ▪ Closed to public ▪ Owner(s) Silverthorn Wines (Pty) Ltd ▪ Cellarmaster(s)/winemaker(s)/viticulturist(s) John Loubser (1998) ▪ 10.5ha/4ha (cab, shiraz, chard) ▪ 50t/3,000cs own label 66% white 34% rosé ▪ IPW ▪ PO Box 381 Robertson 6705 ▪

john@silverthornwines.co.za, karen@silverthornwines.co.za ▪ www.silverthornwines.co.za ▪ **T** +27 **(0)**21-712-7239 ▪ F +27 (0)21-712-7239

One of South Africa's relatively few bubbly-only producers, this small Robertson house was founded by Karen and John Loubser (he the champagne-loving GM and sometime winemaker of Steenberg, in far-off Constantia). Later investment by wine-loving bankers meant John was able to add a prestige cuvée and thus feel satisfied with a full complement of sparklings of his own. The Jewel Box takes the nickname of a cluster of stars in the Southern Cross - stars now fallen to earth.

★★★★ **Genie Rosé Brut** MCC sparkling most unusually from shiraz. Latest **NV** frivolous, joyful character. Bright red fruit mingle with interesting tones of cinnamon & some yeastiness. Crisp & dry, lipsmacking finish.

★★★★☆ **Jewel Box** Balance & class are obvious in chardonnay-driven **10** bubbly with 40% pinot. It is fine, rich & complex, with subtle notes of brioche, nuts & kaleidoscope of subtle fruit. Palate long & seamless, with a feeling of maturity (36 months on lees), yet vibrantly fresh & full of potential. WO W Cape.

★★★★☆ **The Green Man Blanc de Blancs** MCC sparkler from chardonnay. Elegant & intense **10** (★★★★★) aromas of green apple, pear & white flowers, plus gentle yeasty notes. Palate is fine & long, with typical blanc de blancs linearity. 32 months on lees. Fresh & steely. **09** also in focused style. — JPf

▪ **Simonay** see Simonsvlei International
▪ **Simonsbosch** see Koelenhof Winery

Simonsig Landgoed

Location/map: Stellenbosch ▪ WO: Stellenbosch/Western Cape ▪ Est 1953 ▪ 1stB 1968 ▪ Tasting & sales Mon-Fri 8.30-5 Sat 8.30-4 Sun 11-3 ▪ Fee R25pp (incl glass) ▪ Closed Easter Fri/Sun, Dec 25 & Jan 1 ▪ Cellar tours daily at 11 & 3 (booking advised) ▪ Cuvée restaurant (see Restaurants section) ▪ Facilities for children ▪ Tour groups ▪ Gifts ▪ Farm produce ▪ Conferences ▪ 4x4 Landrover experience ▪ Labyrinth vineyard ▪ Owner(s) Pieter, Francois & Johan Malan ▪ Cellarmaster(s) Johan Malan (1981) ▪ Winemaker(s) Debbie Thompson (Nov 1999) & Hannes Meyer (Jul 2009), with Charl Schoeman (Dec 2012) ▪ Viticulturist(s) Francois Malan (Jan 1981) & Tommie Corbett (Nov 2008), with Conrad Schutte (Vinpro) ▪ 300ha/210ha (cab, merlot, ptage, pinot, shiraz, chard, chenin, sauv) ▪ 2,500t/300,000cs own label 33% red 47% white 2% rosé 18% MCC & ±37,000cs for clients ▪ Brands for clients: Champany Inn, Malan Reeks, Rouana, The Warhorse, Wine of the Month Club, Woolworths ▪ BEE, BWI, HACCP 2009, IPW, SANAS ▪ PO Box 6 Koelenhof 7605 ▪ wine@simonsig.co.za ▪ www.simonsig.co.za ▪ S 33° 52' 12.1" E 018° 49' 31.7" ▪ **T** +27 **(0)**21-888-4900 ▪ F +27 (0)21-888-4909

Large in scale and status, the Malan family's estate near Koelenhof has been at the innovative forefront of the wine industry throughout the modern era. Frans Malan, visionary elder statesman of the Cape wine industry, who bought the farm in 1964, produced South Africa's first méthode champenoise bubbly over 40 years ago. A photo exhibit in their disgorging cellar commemorates the event. Around the same time, Frans was teaming up with like-minded trail blazers like Spatz Sperling (Delheim) and Niel Joubert (Spier) to create the Stellenbosch Wine Route. Frans' sons Francois, Johan and Pieter have ably run with the baton for some years now. And the next generation has just joined, Johan's son Michael making wine at Simonsig for the first time last year after qualifying in 2012.

★★★★☆ **Redhill Pinotage** Prestige counterpart to Merindol from single special vineyard, **10** reveals this variety's finer side. Plush, complex fruit is noble & focused, dominating all-new oak regime. Outperforms **09** (★★★★).

★★★★☆ **Merindol Syrah** 🎖 Sumptuous, decadent **11** reveals itself in stratified layers of peppery spice, black cherries, wild scrub & savoury meat, all borne on a hefty but supple frame. Premium selection from single-vineyard, built to impress, like **10** (★★★★★).

★★★★☆ **CWG Auction Reserve Heirloom Shiraz** 🎖 **11** ticks all the boxes. Spicy, with intense black fruit & rich savoury notes, finely knit tannins & noble bearing. Potent 15.7% alcohol is well modulated by powerful but elegant structure.

★★★★☆ **Tiara** Perennially classy flagship Bordeaux-style 5-way blend, **10** delivers on form. Uncompromisingly dark & serious, with spicy tobacco & Christmas-cake notes, bound by thick earthy, tannins. Should unfurl elegantly.

★★★★ **Frans Malan Cape Blend** 🎖 Definitive Cape Blend, **10** is 75% pinotage with cab & a splash of merlot. Smoky oak spices up sweetly generous fruit profile, with smooth, sleek tannin structure.

★★★★ **Aurum Chardonnay** ⏱ Prime vintage **09** (★★★★) swamped by potent oak, buttery/yeasty lees notes. Weighty, rich & ripe, may emerge in time, like last-tasted **07**.

★★★★ **Chenin Avec Chêne** 🌿 **12** (★★★★) more rigorously oaked than previous, but ripe tropical fruit still holds centre stage. Leaner than **10**.

★★★★★ **CWG Auction Reserve The Russety One Roussanne** NEW Intriguing interpretation of Rhône classic variety, oak-fermented **12** is gently but deftly handled in old barrels. Expressive, oily textured & spicy, with delightful nutty twist at end. Complex & finely detailed, demanding attention.

★★★★ **Kaapse Vonkel Brut Rosé** 🌿 Charmingly blush MCC sparkling, **12** from pinot noir & pinotage, dash pinot meunier, fruity appeal & fresh floral highlights. Creamy mousse, delicate biscuit underscore finesse.

★★★★☆ **Cuvée Royale** Change in form for MCC prestige bubbly from chardonnay: **08** is oaked (previous unwooded), showing appealing spices & yeasty notes on lengthy, complex palate. Statuesque bearing with seductive texture & long, elegant farewell.

★★★★ **Kaapse Vonkel Brut** 🌿 Pioneer MCC sparkler now in its 41st vintage, **11** still commands respect. Baked apple & biscuit, crisply dry, with elegant cream-of-tartar finish. Pinot & chardonnay, dash pinot meunier. WO W Cape.

★★★★ **Vin de Liza** ⏱ 🌿 Noble Late Harvest from sauvignon & semillon. After simpler **09** (★★★★), **10** satisfies with silky, gently unctuous charm.

★★★★ **Cape Vintage Reserve** ⏱ First recorded since **94** (LBV), all-shiraz port-style **09** is liquid Christmas pudding, complete with brandy! Dense, spicy & rich, made for cold winter nights.

Cabernet Sauvignon-Shiraz 😊 🍴 🌿 ★★★ Unpretentious & youthful, **12** has dense, ripe fruit tweaked with pinch of sugar on soft, user-friendly tannins. **Chenin Blanc** 😊 🍴 🌿 ★★★ Dependable, appealing & typically Stellenbosch, **13** follows form with yellow peaches, pineapple & melon fruit mix. **Adelberg Sauvignon Blanc** 😊 🍴 🌿 ★★☆ Competent, unassuming entry-level **13** is generously fruity.

Labyrinth Cabernet Sauvignon ✓ ★★★★ Earthy **09** is tinged with tealeaf, wrapped in thick tannins, but dominated by bold blackcurrant fruit which should soften & open with time in bottle. **Pinotage** 🌿 ★★★ **11** returns to form with ripe cranberries, sweet spices & aromatic edge. Unoaked, with expressive fruit, supple body. **Mr Borio's Shiraz** ✓ 🌿 ★★★★ Well-judged weight & ripeness produce an elegant, restrained yet expressive **11** after lesser **10** (★★★★). Bursts with spicy cherry & plum fruit, finishing lean & long. **Adelberg Cabernet Sauvignon-Merlot** ⏱ 🍴 🌿 ★★☆ Reliable, generously fruity **11** blend for everyday drinking. **The SMV** 🍴 ★★★ Shiraz & smidgens mourvèdre, viognier, mocha-styled **12** with hint of sweetness may not appeal to all tastes, but solid, plush fruit lends class. **Chardonnay** 🍴 🌿 ★★★★ Overtly oaky **12** has delicious lemon curd sublayers. Spicy, big boned & rich, promising better things to come. **Gewürztraminer** 🍴 🌿 ★★★★ Distinctively fragrant semi-sweet **13**, with dash of morio muscat, follows tried & trusted format. Spicy food soulmate. **Sunbird Sauvignon Blanc** ✓ 🍴 🌿 ★★★★ Pleasant spicy intensity on **13** is rounded off by 'oystershell' salty edge & creamy finish. Sleek & elegantly balanced. **Straw Wine** ⏱ 🌿 ★★★★ Boldly aromatic **11** sun-dried muscat ottonel is rich, sweet & ripe, with honeyed raisin fruit & clean, tight finish. — GdB

Simonsvlei International 🍷🍴🎿📷🎿♿

Location: Paarl ■ Map: Paarl & Wellington ■ WO: Western Cape ■ Est/1stB 1945 ■ Tasting & sales Mon-Fri 8–5 Sat 8.30–4.30 Sun (Sep-Jun) 11–3 ■ Fee R20pp ■ Cellar tours by prior arrangement ■ Closed Good Fri, Dec 25 & Jan 1 ■ Eat@Simonsvlei restaurant serving hot meals, snacks & refreshments ■ BYO picnic ■ Playground for children ■ Conference/function venue (80 pax) incl. equipment, break-away areas, lunches, etc. ■ Conservation area ■ Owner(s) 65 shareholders ■ Winemaker(s) Ryan Puttick (Nov 2010), with Mari de Jager (Jan 2012) ■ Viticulturist(s) Ryan Puttick (Nov 2010) & Francois van Zyl ■ 1,158ha (shiraz, chenin) ■ 7,400t ■ 48.5% red 48. 5% white 2% rosé 1% other ■ Brands for clients: Kelvin Grove, Ocean Basket, Woolworths ■ BWI, Fairtrade, HACCP, IPW, WIETA ■ PO Box 584 Suider-Paarl 7624 ■ info@simonsvlei.co.za ■ www.simonsvlei.com ■ S 33° 47' 24.9" E 018° 55' 49.1" ■ T +27 (0)21-863-3040 ■ F +27 (0)21-863-1240

Constituted in the aftermath of World War II to grow quality wines on a larger and sustainable scale, Simonsvlei took its name from the father of the South African wine industry, Simon van der Stel, and this Paarl area's vlei (wetlands) landscape. Co-founder Sonny le Roux in 1945 expressed a vision of 'quality wines at affordable prices' and that's still the mantra today. A 'rainbow' offering aims to please everyone, from grandpa and grandma with their sweet tooth to junior

jungle-gymming outside the cellardoor while dad and mom taste the charming easy-drinkers.

Hercules Paragon range

Cabernet Sauvignon ⑪ ★★★☆ Flagship of range, featuring occasional bottlings. **08**, first tasted since **05** (★★★★), elegant fruit profile & big oak vanilla which may since have settled & integrated. **Shiraz** ✓ ★★★★ Inviting mulberry, fynbos & spice on full-bodied juicy preview **12**, smooth crowd pleaser with a sweet spicy lift. **SMCV** ✓ ★★★★ Shiraz, mourvèdre, cinsaut & viognier **10** blend is soft & supple, packed with perfumed berry, savoury & earthy flavours. Charming & warm, invites spicy grilled meat dishes. Improves on last-tasted **08** (★★★★). **Sauvignon Blanc** ✓ 🍴 ★★★★ Pungent aromas, fresh **13** satisfies with generous flavour of lemon, lime & gooseberry, refreshing finish. Discontinued: **Méthode Cap Classique**.

New Generation range

Ja-Mocha Pinotage ✓ ★★★☆ Bright, ripe red berry fruit with strong whiffs of espresso on preview **12**. Smooth & rounded, with a firm grip. Will please fans of 'coffee' pinotage. **Toffee Chunk Syrah** ✓ 🖾 ★★★☆ **12** offers expected caramel & vanilla, plus ripe fruit flavours. Spicy & bold, with chunky tannins & smoky oak finish.

Premier range

Cabernet Sauvignon ☺ 🍴 ★★★ Succulent dark berries on **11**, soft ripe tannins & rounded balance, smooth ending. For everyday enjoyment. **Pinotage** ☺ 🍴 ★★★ Vibrant sweet ripe plum aromas on easy **12**, delights with berry & spicy coffee flavours. Try with biltong. **Cabernet Sauvignon-Merlot** ☺ 🍴 ★★★ **11** is deliciously smooth & soft with vibrant herb-dusted blackberry fruit slipping down easily. **Chardonnay** ☺ 🍴 🖾 ★★★ Fresh lemon curd flavours mingle with soft vanilla oak on harmonious & unassuming **12**. Excellent value. **Humbro Red Jerepiko** ☺ 🍴 ★★★ Bold, full-sweet **NV** fortified winter warmer with crystallised fruit & spice flavours, & delicious spirit grip to end.

Shiraz ✓ 🍴 ★★★★ Sweet-spicy mulberry on fresh & fruity **12**. Fynbos & white pepper add to savoury tail. Over-delivers - stock up! **Chenin Blanc** ✓ 🍴 ★★★★ Ripe tropical fruit & zingy pineapple flavours on unpretentious & delicious **13**, balanced by a mouthwatering fresh goodbye. Discontinued: **Bukettraube, Sauvignon Blanc, Humbro Hanepoot**.

Lifestyle range

Cabernet Sauvignon ☺ 🍴 🖾 ★★★ Soft, berry-fruited & easygoing **12** is for everyday sipping. Unoaked, as for rest of the range. **Merlot** ☺ 🍴 ★★★ **12** just-off-dry appeals with sweet sappy fruit flavours - an easy sip. **Pinotage** ☺ 🍴 🖾 ★★★ Fruity & lively **12**, dark chocolate on smooth picnic wine. **Shiraz** ☺ 🍴 ★★★ **12** rich brambleberry fruit, peppery spices with a tasty savoury goodbye. Over-achieves at the price. **Simonsrood** ☺ 🍴 ★★★ 4-way **NV** blend is fruity & smooth, with a hint of spice for easy sipping. **Simonsblanc** ☺ 🍴 ★★☆ Latest semi-dry **NV** from chenin tad off pace of previous but still light, easy & fresh, with a zingy tail.

Discontinued: **Charming Red, Blanc de Blanc, Sweet Chenin Blanc, Stein, Natural Sweet Rosé, Sweet Shiraz**.

Simonay range

Classic Red ★★ Soft berry flavour, smooth **NV** party wine. 5L bag-in-box, as all in this range. **Blanc de Blanc** ★★ Fragrant, fruity & fresh **NV** with zippy end. Moderate 12% alcohol. **Natural Sweet Rosé** ★☆ Feather-light pink **NV** sweetie. Discontinued: **Stein, Late Harvest**.

South Atlantic range

Discontinued: **Shiraz, Shiraz-Cabernet Sauvignon, Chardonnay, Sauvignon Blanc**.

Eco Glass Lifestyle range

Discontinued: **Cabernet Sauvignon, Chenin Blanc**. — WB

■ **Simplicity** *see* Weltevrede Estate
■ **Simply Red/White** *see* PicardiRebel
■ **Simply Wines** *see* Vins d'Orrance
■ **Sir George** *see* Napier Winery

Sir Lambert Wines

Location: Lamberts Bay ▪ Map: Olifants River ▪ WO: Western Cape/Lamberts Bay ▪ Est 2004 ▪ 1stB 2007 ▪ Tasting by appt in Lamberts Bay or Mon-Fri 9-5 Sat/Sun 9-3 at Diemersdal ▪ Closed Easter Fri/Sun, Dec 25 & Jan 1 ▪ Xamarin Guest House & Restaurant ▪ BYO picnic ▪ Conference & function venue (up to 250 people) ▪ Game drives ▪ Golf course ▪ Tour groups ▪ Conservation area ▪ 4x4 trail ▪ Facilities for children ▪ Owner(s) John Hayes, Johan Teubes & Thys Louw ▪ Winemaker(s) Thys Louw & Mari Branders ▪ Viticulturist(s) Johan Teubes (2004) ▪ 10ha (shiraz, sauv) ▪ 60t/6,000cs own label 10% red 90% white ▪ PO Box 27 Durbanville 7551 ▪ info@sirlambert.co.za ▪ www. sirlambert.co.za ▪ S 32° 5' 52.40" E 018° 18' 19.50" ▪ **T +27 (0)21-976-3361** ▪ F +27 (0)21-979-1802

Named after 19th century seafarer Sir Robert Lambert and the namesake Atlantic seaboard town where the vines are grown, this joint venture between Diemersdal cellar chief Thys Louw and partners John Hayes and Johan Teubes marks its 10th anniversary this year. The grapes are harvested by locals, not outside contractors, as part of the winery's ongoing support for the Lamberts Bay community.

★★★★ **Sauvignon Blanc** ✓ 🍽 📖 Bracing 'oystershell' & sea salt hints on maritime-grown **13**. Lovely fruit weight, depth & vinosity without sweetness, same moderate alcohol & minerality as **12**. WO Lamberts Bay.
The Admiral's Shiraz ✓ 🍽 📖 ★★★★ Tarry oak blows off reveal authentic black pepper & lively red fruit; **12** more than passes muster to sit at the Admiral's table! — CvZ

■ **Sir Robert Stanford Estate** *see Robert Stanford Estate*
■ **Six Hats** *see Citrusdal Wines*
■ **Sixpence** *see Opstal Estate*
■ **1685** *see Boschendal Wines*
■ **Sixty 40** *see Boland Kelder*

Sizanani Wines

Location: Stellenbosch ▪ WO: Aan-de-Doorns ▪ Est 2005 ▪ 1stB 2006 ▪ Tasting & sales at Bellevue Estate Stellenbosch ▪ Owner(s) Stellenbosch Wine and Logistics (Pty) Ltd ▪ CEO Annelize Tities ▪ Winemaker(s) Wilhelm Kritzinger & Anneke Potgieter (both 2005, Bellevue) ▪ Viticulturist(s) Dirkie Morkel (Feb 2005, Bellevue) ▪ 4,000cs own label 40% red 40% white 20% rosé ▪ PO Box 33 Koelenhof 7605 ▪ annelizepebbles@gmail.com ▪ www.sizanani-wines.co.za ▪ **T +27 (0)21-865-2055/+27 (0)72-511-8899** ▪ F +27 (0)21-865-2899

The employees of Stellenbosch estate Bellevue previously had a minority stake in the Sizanani brand but full ownership has been transferred to them. It used to be just another day in the vineyards, the new proprietors say, but now they have real control over their future and that of their children.

Pinotage ⚑ ★★ Red cherry & vague coffee note on nose & palate of light **08**. **Red Blend** Await next, as for **Cabernet Franc Rosé, Chenin Blanc** & **Sauvignon Blanc**. — RP

Skaap Wines

Location: Sir Lowry's Pass ▪ Map: Helderberg ▪ WO: Durbanville ▪ Est/1stB 2011 ▪ Private functions (lunch/dinner) by appt ▪ Swimming pool ▪ Tour groups ▪ Local art on display & for sale ▪ Conferences (up to 18 pax) ▪ Walks/hikes ▪ Mountain biking trail ▪ Conservation area ▪ 5-bedroom guesthouse, dining room with chef & 2 self-catering lodges ▪ Owner(s) Thierry Schaap ▪ Cellarmaster(s)/winemaker(s) Riaan Oosthuizen (Jan 2011) ▪ Vineyard manager(s) Jaco Mouton ▪ 17ha/4ha (shiraz, sauv) ▪ 1,100cs own label 30% red 70% white ▪ BWI, IPW ▪ PO Box 75 Sir Lowry's Pass 7130 ▪ info@skaapwines.com ▪ www.skaapwines.com ▪ S 34° 06' 11.35" E 018° 55' 05.87" ▪ **T +27 (0)21-858-1982/+27 (0)83-452-2083** ▪ F +27 (0)21-858-1983

Dutch banker Thierry Schaap has dryland vines on his prime Schapenberg site (Schaap and Schapen, meaning 'sheep', pure coincidence; 'Skaap' the Afrikaans version). Thierry and team are committed to sustainable farming, including local Sir Lowry's Pass village community involvement with a soup kitchen, children's foundation and amateur artists (whose beadwork is featured on the label).

★★★★ **Skaap 41 Sauvignon Blanc** 🍽 Gets 'Skaap 41' prefix in **12**. Concentrated grassy & fynbos with deepening layers of flint, herbaceousness & citrus. Shows Durbanville provenance with seabreezy undertone.
Shiraz ⚑ 🍽 ★★★★ Old & New World fans will come together (around a braai) over **11**, attractive spread of pepper-zested dark fruit, oak char & freshness. **Méthode Cap Classique Brut** ⚑ ★★★ Bottle-fermented sparkling from pinot noir & chardonnay; refreshing **11** is lightish, savoury & dry. — JP

Skilpadvlei Wines

Location/map/WO: Stellenbosch ▪ Est 2004 ▪ 1stB 2001 ▪ Tasting & sales Mon-Sat 8-5 Sun 8-4 ▪ Fee R15 ▪ Closed Dec 25/26 & Jan 1 ▪ Restaurant Mon-Sat 8-late Sun 8-4 ▪ Facilities for children ▪ Gift/décor shop ▪ Conferences ▪ Weddings & functions ▪ B&B guesthouse & self-catering cottages ▪ Owner(s) WD Joubert ▪ Cellarmaster(s) Koewie du Toit (consultant) ▪ Viticulturist(s) Johan Pienaar & Eben Archer (consultants) ▪ 78ha/55ha (cab, merlot, ptage, shiraz, chenin, sauv) ▪ 652t/12,000cs own label 80% red 20% white ▪ PO Box 17 Vlottenburg 7604 ▪ info@skilpadvlei.co.za ▪ www.skilpadvlei.co.za ▪ S 33° 57' 31.5" E 018° 45' 52.4" ▪ **T +27 (0)21-881-3237** ▪ F +27 (0)21-881-3538

From its ridge on the M12 into Stellenbosch, Skilpadvlei offers scenic vineyard vistas at almost every compass heading. Another reason 4th-generation owner Willie Joubert is upping the number of cottages to accommodate more visitors to this popular restaurant, functions, conference, wedding - and wine - venue.

Skilpaddop Dry Red Ⓟ ▤ ★ Previously, **09** was a herbal near-equal mix merlot & pinotage. **ML Joubert** ★★★☆ Spicy plum appeal of **09** ratchets quality up for shiraz, cab, merlot blend. Usual bold wood but will knit. **Cabernet Sauvignon-Shiraz** ▨ ★★☆ Cab cassis leads peppery shiraz in improved **11**. **Chenin Blanc** ▤ ▨ ★★☆ Appealing tangy, crisp & light peachy flavour on **12**. **Sauvignon Blanc** ▤ ▨ ★★☆ **12** grapefruit & zest appeal with dry flinty tail. — FM

■ **Skoon Vallei** *see* Eerste Hoop Wine Cellar

Slaley

Location/map: Stellenbosch ▪ WO: Simonsberg–Stellenbosch ▪ Est 1957 ▪ 1stB 1997 ▪ Tasting & sales Tue-Sun 10-4 ▪ Fee R20, waived on purchase ▪ Closed Good Fri, Dec 25/26 & Jan 1 ▪ Cellar tours by appt ▪ Bistro: light meals during tasting hours ▪ Farm produce ▪ Venue & conference facility with AV capacity ▪ Owner(s) Hunting family ▪ Winemaker(s) Ettienne Malan (Feb 2013) ▪ Viticulturist(s) Sean Burgoyne ▪ 240ha/51ha (cab, merlot, ptage, shiraz, chard, sauv) ▪ 320t/24-30,000cs own label 90% red 9% white 1% rosé ▪ IPW ▪ PO Box 119 Koelenhof 7605 ▪ info@slaley.co.za ▪ www.slaley.co.za ▪ S 33° 51' 53.7'' E 018° 50' 51.1'' ▪ **T +27 (0)21-865-2123** ▪ F +27 (0)86-529-2347

With three differently priced ranges and a selection of older vintage wines at peak drinking age, Slaley caters for its myriad visitors and fans. Added attraction is the newly opened bistro, with live music over weekends. New winemaker Etienne Malan, ex Rust en Vrede and Andreas, has settled in after a steep learning curve: his arrival coincided with the start of the 2013 harvest.

Hunting Family range

★★★★ **Merlot** Dark chocolate & meat extract add complexity to **07**'s rich dark fruit, while the serious oak regime (28 months, 40% new) provides spice & deep muscle tone for further cellaring.

★★★★ **Shiraz** ⓅLuscious berries & spice array, touch of wintergreen, doesn't quite cloak **06**'s (★★★☆) dry tannins, less seductive than **04**. No **05**.

★★★★ **Reserve Noble Late Harvest Chardonnay** Ⓟ Last was **07**, decadent & irresistible, concentrated honey/raisin character (from vine-dried grapes) perfect match for strong cheeses.

Pinotage Ⓟ ★★★★ Loads of dark fruit & opulent smoky tones, **07**'s freshening acidity keeps it juicy, lively. **Cabernet Sauvignon-Merlot** Ⓟ ★★★ When tasted, **07** equal blend had ripe fruit with tar, liquorice & nettle hints. Heady 15% alcohol needed time to integrate. **Chardonnay** Ⓟ ▨ ★★★★ Lacking the fruit of **09** (★★★★), barrel-fermented **10** has an attractive citrus & mineral profile, restrained slate-dry finish.

Broken Stone range

★★★★ **Pinotage** Ⓟ Vanilla from 70% American barrels enriches **06**'s mulberry fruit while leaving the supple juiciness intact. Admirable intensity yet elegant (13% alcohol), polished. No **05**.

Cabernet Sauvignon Ⓟ ★★★★ Lots going on in **06**, brambleberries, meaty notes, firm but ripe tannin, succulent drinkability. Enjoy now or keep a few years. **Shiraz** Ⓟ ★★★ Dark plum/prune ripeness with savoury spice, sturdily built **07** has a food-friendly firm grip. Could still age. **Cabernet Sauvignon-Shiraz-Pinotage** Ⓟ ★★★☆ Ripe & expressive, **07**'s cedar-dusted cassis nicely presented in a succulent, smoothly rounded body. Drinks well. **Sauvignon Blanc** Ⓟ ★★★ **11** gooseberries & litchi, sprinkle wild herbs, fresh & light.

Social range

Lindsay's Whimsy Cape Blend ⊕ 🍴 🍷 ★★★ Smoky hedgerow fruit, **10** charms with its gutsy rusticity. Equal pinotage & merlot, splash cab. **Lindsay's Whimsy Rosé** ⊕ 🍴 🍷 ★★★ Dry **10** from shiraz is light-hearted (12.9% alcohol) summer fare. — CR

Slanghoek Winery

Location: Rawsonville ▪ Map: Breedekloof ▪ WO: Slanghoek ▪ Est 1951 ▪ 1stB 1970 ▪ Tasting & sales Mon-Fri 9–5 Sat 10–1 ▪ Closed Easter Fri/Sun, Dec 25 & Jan 1 ▪ Cellar tours by appt ▪ Picnic baskets, booking required ▪ Slanghoek MTB Route, fee R20: 13km ride with optional extra, more challenging 4km ▪ Owner(s) 25 producers ▪ Cellarmaster(s) Pieter Carstens (Aug 2002) ▪ Winemaker(s) Nico Grundling & Paul Burger (Dec 2002/Dec 2008), with Jacques de Goede & Jaco Theron (Dec 2001/Oct 2007) ▪ Viticulturist(s) Callie Coetzee (Nov 2010) ▪ 1,830ha ▪ 30,000t/80,000cs own label 25% red 55% white 10% rosé 10% fortified ▪ Other export brand: Zonneweelde ▪ ISO 22000, BWI, IPW ▪ PO Box 75 Rawsonville 6845 ▪ info@slanghoek.co.za ▪ www.slanghoek.co.za ▪ S 33° 39' 1.1" E 019° 13' 49.0" ▪ **T +27 (0)23-344-3026** ▪ F +27 (0)23-344-3157

At the foot of the Slanghoek mountains lies this efficient and modern grower-owned winery. As one of the valley's biggest concerns, they often form part of the community's marketing and tourism activities like the popular Soetes & Soup festival, while their own events such as Blend & Bottle are in constant demand. Their Private Selection wines continue to prove popular both locally and overseas, providing excellent value-for-money.

Private Selection

★★★★ **Noble Late Harvest** ⊕ Honey & nougat nuanced **07** complex, well-knit, though lacks weight, vibrancy of previous. Mainly chenin, dash muscat d'Alexandrie; 9 months French oak.

> **Camerca** ☺ 🍴 ★★★ **11** Bordeaux red blend juicy, sweet fruited (& off-dry), lots of vibrant flavour for solo or table. **Chardonnay** ☺ 🍴 🍷 ★★★ **13** has curves in all the right places; rounded lemon preserve flavour, sweet buttery oak, dab sugar completes the Rubenesque profile. **Chenin Blanc** ☺ 🍴 🍷 ★★★ Hay & honey intro to **13**, tidy build with sugar & acid playing off each other, nice green apple/pear taste combo. **Sauvignon Blanc** ☺ 🍴 🍷 ★★★ Perhaps not a rockstar, but **13** is well made & flavourful, touch sugar makes for easy sipping.

Cabernet Sauvignon 🍷 ★★★ From dryland bushvines, **12** continues affable off-dry styling with portion new oak deftly folded into the soft red/blackcurrant fruit. Laudably moderate alcohol, as for most of the reds. **Merlot** 🍴 🍷 ★★★ New bottling of **10** touch firmer than previous, more food inclined, pleasant fresh-picked berry character. **Pinotage** 🍴 🍷 ★★★ Aromatic choc-cherry **11** is well padded with fruit, oak still settling mid-2013. **Shiraz** ✓ 🍷 ★★★★ Always the biggest (14.5% alcohol) of the unfortified wines, but **10** as well controlled as previous, alluring raspberry aroma, good savoury finish, finely judged wooding. **Crème de Chenin** ⊕ ★★★★ **10** Natural Sweet has dried apricots & bitter almond notes from small portion botrytis, gentle sweetness enlivened by lime tang. Worth seeking out. **Cuvée Brut** 🍷 ★★ Appley **NV** sparkling from chardonnay & chenin, bone-dry & very fresh. Tank fermented, like Vin Doux. **Vin Doux** 🍷 ★★ Frothy & grapey bubbles from hanepoot. Serve latest **NV** well chilled to counter syrupy sweetness. **Special Late Harvest** 🍴 🍷 ★★★ Muscat d'Alexandrie provides the lemons & flowers, sweet but clean flavours, uncloying finish in **13**. **Hanepoot Jerepigo** ✓ 🍷 ★★★★ They get it right every time: fresh, pleasing, aromatic, good weight & texture, usual slight nuttiness contrasting well with the tropical fruit flavours in **13**. **Red Muscadel** 🍷 ★★★ Appealing freshness in **13**'s crushed cranberry aroma, very sweet & warming, slightly unfocused leafy finish the only quibble. **Red Jerepiko** ✓ 🍷 ★★★★ Fortified dessert from pinotage. Crimson-hued **13** goes up a notch with its luscious & generous candied fruit flavour, balanced & supportive structure. **Cape Ruby** ★★ **12** port-style fortified from touriga with dark cherry aroma, fiery touch of brandy spirit, unlingering macerated fruit flavours.

Vinay range

Red 🍴 🍷 ★★ Latest **NV** blend (including pinotage) is elegantly fruited with contrasting blocky tannin. **Rosé** 🍴 🍷 ★★ New low-alcohol **NV** bottling from red muscadel is highly aromatic & not overly sweet. **Crispy White** 🍴 🍷 ★★ **NV** combo sauvignon, chenin, colombard is lightish, off-dry & floral. — DC

▪ **Slent** *see* Ayama Wines

Slowine

Location/map: Villiersdorp ▪ WO: Western Cape ▪ Est/1stB 2005 ▪ Tasting & sales at Villiersdorp Cellar (see entry) ▪ Owner(s) Villiersdorp Cellar ▪ Shareholders Beaumont Wines & Luddite Wines ▪ Technical team: Sebastian Beaumont & Niels Verburg ▪ Winemaker(s) Christo Versfeld, with André Bruyns (Dec 2009) ▪ Viticulturist(s) André Bruyns (Dec 2009) ▪ 300ha (merlot, chenin, sauv) ▪ 3,600t/40,000cs own label 40% red 40% white 20% rosé ▪ BWI, IPW ▪ PO Box 14 Villiersdorp 6848 ▪ marketing@slowine.co.za ▪ www.slowine.co.za ▪ S 33° 59' 11.2" E 019° 17' 48.5" ▪ **T +27 (0)28-840-1120** ▪ F +27 (0)28-840-1833

Slowine is a collaboration between owner Villiersdorp Cellar and shareholder wineries Luddite and Beaumont. Their motto urges us to slow down and relax… with slow food, slow wine and slow living. Appropriately, the emblem on the label is the endangered Geometric Tortoise, which the brand helps preserve.

Cabernet Sauvignon ☺ 🍽 🖫 ★★★ **11** steps up with cheery plum fruit, soft texture, hints of spice & juicy grip. **Merlot** ☺ 🍽 🖫 ★★★ Medium-bodied **11** offers bright juicy berries & good chewy tannins for everyday sipping. **Shiraz** ☺ 🍽 🖫 ★★★ Easy sipper **11** brims with dark berries & white pepper spicing. Ticks all drinkability boxes. **Chenin Blanc** ☺ 🍽 🖫 ★★★ **13** is vibrant, brims with white peach & tangy floral nuance in aftertaste. Alcohol a friendly 12%. **Sauvignon Blanc** ☺ 🍽 🖫 ★★☆ **13** zings with lemon, grapefruit & Granny Smith apple flavours. **Chenin Blanc-Sauvignon Blanc** ☺ 🍽 🖫 ★★★ Appeals with hints of blossom & grass, seamless zesty lemon conclusion. **13** lipsmacking & friendly.

Rosé 🍽 🖫 ★★★ Dry charmer from pinotage. **12** candyfloss & punnet of ripe red berries. — WB

▪ **Smokey Mountain** *see Wandsbeck Wyne Koöp Bpk*
▪ **Smook Wines** *see Anthony Smook Wines*

Snowfield Boutique Winery

Location: Sutherland ▪ WO: Western Cape ▪ Est 2012 ▪ 1stB 2011 ▪ Tasting, sales & cellar tours Mon-Sat by appt ▪ Fee R30pp, waived on purchase ▪ Closed Easter Fri/Sun & Dec 25 ▪ Meals/refreshments by appt ▪ Winter picnic baskets to be pre-booked ▪ Owner(s) Bi-Anne du Toit ▪ Winemaker(s) Bi-Anne du Toit (Aug 2008) ▪ (mourv) ▪ 1t/118cs own label 60% red 40% port ▪ PO Box 154 Sutherland 6920 ▪ harmoniekelder@gmail.com ▪ S 32° 28' 42.18" E 020° 38' 31.94" ▪ **T +27 (0)23-571-1137/+27 (0)78-165-8429** ▪ F +27 (0)23-571-1137

Raised in sunny Swartland, Bi-Anne du Toit completed her studies in winemaking in 2003 and, after marrying sheep farmer Louis, found herself in Sutherland, officially South Africa's second-coldest town. Undeterred, she planted a few rows of mourvèdre, and intends adding other varieties. Meanwhile she sources from Swartland and Goudini. Visitors can expect the warmest of welcomes.

Snowfield range NEW
Cabernet Sauvignon ★★★☆ Pleasant leafiness to **12**'s chocolatey dark fruit; medium body with good ripeness, healthy tannins are approachable & allow for few years cellaring. **Merlot** ★★★★ **12** impressive fruit concentration yet is still elegant, dry & savoury. Year older oak, as others in this range. **Icebreaker Cabernet Sauvignon-Merlot** ★★★★ Sombre bouquet of red & black fruit, oak notes & sweet spices on **12**, accessible & soft equal blend.

ZAHarmonie range NEW
The Maiden Cabernet Sauvignon ★★★ Briefly oaked, friendly **11** is a fresh & fruity uncomplicated sipper. **Anti-Freeze Cape Ruby** ★★★ Swartland touriga (90%) & shiraz in **NV** ripe & robust port-style, with candyfloss aroma & balanced sweetness. The result of realising 'something drastic had to be done' to overcome Sutherland's icy winters. — GdB, GM

▪ **Snow Mountain** *see Nabygelegen Private Cellar*
▪ **Social** *see Slaley*
▪ **Soek Die Geluk** *see Goedvertrouw Wine Estate*

SoetKaroo Wine Estate

Location: Prince Albert ▪ Map: Klein Karoo & Garden Route ▪ WO: Western Cape ▪ Est 2000 ▪ 1stB 2004 ▪ Tasting & sales Mon-Sat 9-1; afternoons by appt ▪ Closed Dec 25 ▪ Owner(s) Herman & Susan Perold ▪ Cellarmaster(s)/winemaker(s) Susan Perold (Jan 2007) ▪ Vineyard manager(s) Herman Perold ▪ 2t ▪ 56 Church Str

Prince Albert 6930 ▪ perold@netactive.co.za ▪ www.soetkaroo.co.za ▪ S 33° 13' 21.9" E 022° 1' 48.0" ▪ **T +27 (0)23-541-1768** ▪ F +27 (0)86-524-3801

Winemaker at this micro estate in Prince Albert, Susan Perold, calls her and husband Herman's business 'a hobby that got out of hand'. Their focus is on dessert wines, which they handcraft with 'meticulous/neurotic quality control'. Their Red Muscat d'Alexandrie is joined this edition by something equally rare: a Cape Vintage from petit verdot, both delicious and worth seeking out.

Red Muscat d'Alexandrie ★★★★ Pink-hued fortified dessert from unusual red hanepoot, smidgen (red) muscadel. Powerful perfumed grapiness but **12**'s flavours are more savoury, with a drier finish than expected.
Cape Vintage Touriga Nacional ★★★★ Xmas cake richness, cinnamon spice nose & flavours add to fortified **12**'s appeal. Opulent & full sweet, the oak subservient to the fruit; would benefit from a bit more grip.
Cape Vintage Petit Verdot ★★★ Unusual port-style **12** has the violets & blueberries of the variety, packaged in a succulent form, balancing tannins to anchor the richness & provide a rewarding future. — CR,CvZ

■ **Solms-Astor** *see* Solms-Delta

Solms-Delta

Location/map: Franschhoek ▪ WO: Western Cape ▪ Est 1690 ▪ 1stB 2004 ▪ Tasting & sales daily 9–5 ▪ Fee R20pp ▪ Closed Dec 25 & Jan 1 ▪ Cellar tours by appt ▪ Fyndraai Restaurant (see Restaurants section) ▪ Walking farm tours ▪ Dik Delta fynbos culinary garden ▪ Museum van de Caab & archaeological sites ▪ Harvest festival (Mar) ▪ Summer music concerts ▪ Delta draf/trap (Apr) ▪ Owner(s) Solms & Astor Family Trusts and Wijn de Caab Workers' Trust ▪ Winemaker(s) Hagen Viljoen (Nov 2012), with Joan Heatlie (Aug 2012) ▪ Viticulturist(s) Rosa Kruger (Jul 2011) ▪ 78ha/30ha (grenache n/b, mourv, shiraz, chenin, muscat d'A, muscat de F, rouss, sem, viog) ▪ 370t/80,000cs own label 63% red 33% white 4% rosé ▪ BWI, IPW ▪ PO Box 123 Groot Drakenstein 7680 ▪ info@solms-delta.co.za ▪ www.solms-delta.co.za ▪ S 33° 51' 51.0" E 018° 59' 23.8" ▪ **T +27 (0)21-874-3937** ▪ F +27 (0)21-874-1852

Recent arrivals at this progressive Franschhoek property, epitome of the 'rainbow wine nation', include winemakers Hagen Viljoen and Joan Heatlie, and general manager Mignon du Plessis. Future arrivals include more indigenous Sanga cattle, and a Cape genealogical research facility focusing on families of slave descent, reflecting Solms-Delta's commitment to the social history of its terroir. Helping excavate a 7,000 year-old site on the estate, Bennie Pietersen, long-time farm resident, showed an artefact to co-owner Mark Solms and said: 'Jy sien, Prof, my mense was hier voor joune!' (See, Prof, my people were here before yours!') The past is reflected, and honoured, all around this remarkable place – from the museum to the rural music programme, social history tourism, indigenous culinary garden, traditional cuisine, and, of course, wine.

Solms-Delta range

★★★★☆ **Africana** 🔄 From desiccated shiraz - a style specialised in here - shows tealeaf, raisin nuances & black plums. **11**, like **10**, great presence & lightness, dry finish despite few grams sugar. No **09**.
★★★★ **Hiervandaan** ✓ 🔄 Shiraz (portion vine-dried) blended with grenache & carignan, seasoned with 1% mourvèdre & 35% new oak (16 months). **11** as piquant & refreshing as **10**, with similar firm persistence.
★★★★ **Lekkerwijn** ✓ 🔄 Serious & consistently excellent rosé from free-run mourvèdre, viognier & grenache. **12** dry, full bodied & complex courtesy lees-maturation & barrel fermented portion.
★★★★☆ **Amalie** ✓ 🔄 Aromatic blend of viognier, grenache blanc, roussanne, barrel fermented. **12** white peach & dusty thatch aromas; rich & rounded, persistent. An individual wine, for contemplation. No **11**.
★★★★ **Koloni** ✓ 🔄 Muscat d'Alexandrie & vine-dried muscat de Frontignan fermented/aged in oak. Now bottled, **11** agreeably high-toned & nutty, with enlivening acidity & pithy grip, subtle sweetness. Good match for mature hard cheeses.
★★★★☆ **Gemoedsrus** ⊕ 🔄 'Peace of Mind' is a quirky take on port: vine-dried shiraz stiffened with husk spirit. **10** (★★★★) laced with cigarbox & cloves; lively but not as charming as **09**.

Solms-Astor range

Langarm ✓ 🔄 ★★★★ Characterful & complex interplay of pinotage, touriga, shiraz, mourvèdre. Improved **12** is just off-dry, packs in the flavour; keep case or 2 handy to impress your guests. **Vastrap** 🔲 🔄 ★★★ Older-oak-matured chenin with semillon, riesling. Dryness, briskness & pithy tail add to **12**'s thatchy appeal.

Cape Jazz Shiraz ★★★ Unusual in the Cape, a red sparkling. **NV**, semi-sweet, low in alcohol but high on flavour & texture; playful tannins & oak touch soak up sweetness. — CvZ

Solo Wines

Location: Stellenbosch ▪ WO: Western Cape ▪ Est/1stB 2009 ▪ Closed to public ▪ Wine sales by appt or tele-phonically ▪ Owner(s)/winemaker(s) Philip Costandius ▪ 50% red 50% white ▪ PO Box 241 Stellenbosch 7599 ▪ wine@solowines.com ▪ www.solowines.com ▪ **T +27 (0)82-802-5267**

A stalwart of the esteemed Cape Winemakers Guild ranks, Philip Costandius men-tions in passing that most of his time nowadays is taken up lending his considerable skills to others via contractual winemaking. Not flying quite as solo as the multi-talented Philip intended when he ventured out on his own some years ago.

Syrah ★★★★ Ripe plum elegance of **11** steps its game up on also-tasted **10** (★★★★) & previous. Supple, nuanced dry palate with well-judged oaking, just 10% new. Spicy & fresh. Long finish. **Viognier** ★★★★ **12** is silky smooth with rich peach & pineapple, ratcheting quality up from last-made **10** (★★★★). Creamy tex-ture from dab barrel fermentation & year in older oak. Fresh finish. — FM

Somerbosch Wines

Location: Stellenbosch ▪ Map: Helderberg ▪ WO: Stellenbosch/Western Cape ▪ Est 1950 ▪ 1stB 1995 ▪ Tasting & sales daily 9-5 ▪ Fee R20/6 wines, waived on purchase of any 3 btls; R40pp/ice cream & red wine tasting ▪ Closed Dec 25 & Jan 1 ▪ Cellar tours by appt ▪ Somerbosch Bistro: b'fast & lunch daily ▪ Facilities for children ▪ Farm produce ▪ Conferences ▪ Owner(s) Somerbosch Wines cc ▪ Cellarmaster(s)/winemaker(s)/viticulturist(s) Marius & Japie Roux (both 1995) ▪ 55ha/43ha (cab, merlot, shiraz, sauv) ▪ 350t 55% red 45% white ▪ PO Box 12181 Die Boord 7613 ▪ enquiries@somerbosch.co.za, sales@somerbosch.co.za ▪ www.somerbosch.co.za ▪ S 34° 0' 28.6" E 018° 49' 6.9" ▪ **T +27 (0)21-855-3615** ▪ F +27 (0)21-855-4457

The laid-back lifestyle of which the brothers Roux (Marius, Japie and Wrensch) are proponents is reflected in both wines and welcome on family farm Die Fonteine in the Helderberg foothills. Equally representative is the name of their flagship, Kylix, an ancient Greek earthenware drinking vessel, broad based and shallow for sipping supine.

Somerbosch range

★★★★ **Kylix** 🗎 First since **04**, **10** mainly cab with shiraz, merlot, accorded 100% new-oak treatment & it shows in spicy pencil shaving notes on backdrop of dark berries. Well made, should age rewardingly. **Cabernet Sauvignon** ⓘ 🗎 ★★★ Dry, well-structured **10** has lean, simple fruit. **Merlot** 🗎 ★★★ Good middle-of-the-road merlot, **10** sparingly oaked (like most of these reds) to show off ripe red fruit & firm full body. **Pinotage** ⓘ 🗎 ★★★ Uncomplicated meaty, vanilla **09** for everyday drinking. **Shiraz** 🗎 ★★★ Spicy, blueberry-laced, just-dry **10** with sprinkle of nutmeg & full yet restrained flavours. **Shiraz-Merlot** ⓘ 🗎 ★★★ Accessible, spicy **11** blend cheerfully youthful with plenty red fruit & spice. **Chardonnay** 🗎 ★★★ Fast-forwarding from **10** to **13**, there's citrus & green apple on offer with evident oak & a racy nutty conclusion. **Chenin Blanc** ⓘ 🗎 ★★★ Zippily fresh pineapple **12** perfect for summer picnics. WO W Cape. **Sauvignon Blanc** 🗎 ★★★ Slightly sweaty asparagus & lemon peel, tangy acidity but **13** is notch down from previous. **Méthode Cap Classique Brut** Next awaited. **Late Bottled Vintage Port** ⓘ ★★★ **06** from cab; warm-ing fireside sipper tasted a few years back.

Poker Hill range

Shiraz-Merlot 🗎 ★★ Equal blend in **11**, soft juicy berries for pleasant current drinking. **Semillon-Chenin Blanc** Await new vintage. — GM

Somerset Wines

Location: Somerset West ▪ Map: Helderberg ▪ WO: Western Cape ▪ Est 2010 ▪ 1stB 2011 ▪ Tasting & sales Mon-Fri 8.30-5 Sat 9-1 ▪ Closed all pub hols ▪ Tour groups ▪ Wine shop ▪ Owner(s) Boetie Rietoff, Greig Rietoff ▪ Cellarmaster(s) Francois van Zyl ▪ Winemaker(s) Ryan Elan-Puttick, with Jeff Wedgwood (consultant) ▪ 200,000cs 80% red 20% white ▪ PO Box 2240 Somerset West 7129 ▪ info@somersetbeverages.co.za ▪ www.somersetwine.com ▪ **T +27 (0)21-851-8188** ▪ F +27 (0)21-852-9563

Value-for-money wines sourced from established wineries in the Helderberg Basin, and all with easy names, designed to remove mystique and complication

from the drinking experience - this is due to the marketing savvy and experience of owner co-owner Boetie Rietoff. In the wine industry for over 40 years, he gives a portion of the sales to local charities and communities in need.

Lord Somerset range

Cabernet Sauvignon ▦ ▨ ★★★ Appealing ripe dark fruit in **12**, light body gives easy access. **Shiraz** NEW ▦ ★★★ Smoky, succulent dark fruit, unwooded **12** ends on a fresh note. **Merlot-Cabernet Sauvignon** ⓘ ▦ ▨ ★★★ Unwooded but backed by grape tannin, supports **11**'s red fruit. **Chenin Blanc Bushvine** ▦ ★★★ Apple-fresh **13** is crisply dry, with friendly 12.5% alcohol. **Sauvignon Blanc** ▦ ★★★ Gentle minerality in light-textured, food-friendly **13**. **Soft Smooth Red** ▦ ▨ ★★★ Light & juicy **NV**, lives up to its name. Touch of sweetness adds appeal.

Lady Somerset range

Stylish Elegant Red ☺ ▦ ▨ ★★★ Unoaked plummy **NV** from merlot/shiraz, nicely smooth & round. **Natural Sweet White** ☺ ▦ ★★★ Litchi flavoured **NV**, an appealing fresh lift to the tangy sweetness. Serve well chilled, good match for fruit desserts.

Crisp Dry White ▦ ★★★ Pear drops & a citrus tang, refreshing chardonnay/sauvignon **NV**. **Natural Sweet Red** ▦ ▨ ★★★ Ripe smoky plums, juicy & sweet **NV** anytime quaffer. **Natural Sweet Rosé** ▦ ★★★ Light & flirty **NV** lays on the charm with its red berry array. — CR

Somfula Wines

Location: Malmesbury ▪ Est/1stB 2009 ▪ Tasting by appt ▪ Closed Easter Fri/Sun/Mon, Dec 25/26 & Jan 1 ▪ Owner(s) Nokubonga Somfula ▪ 60% red 20% white 20% rosé ▪ c/o PO Box 1 Riebeek West 7306 ▪ bongis86@gmail.com ▪ www.somfulawines.co.za ▪ **T +27 (0)79-464-0204** ▪ F +27 (0)86-293-3443

Malmesbury-based Nokubonga 'Bongi' Somfula developed a love of wine while working as a wine label designer in Cape Town. With Pulpit Rock Winery near Riebeek-West, her intention is to market good quality, fruit-driven wines - currently a reserve cab, merlot and chardonnay - to fellow wine enthusiasts.

▪ **Sonata** see Waterstone Wines
▪ **Songloed** see Group CDV

Sonklip Wine

Location/map: Stellenbosch ▪ 1stB 2009 ▪ Tasting & cellar tours for groups only, by appt ▪ Owner(s)/winemaker(s) Frik Kirsten ▪ 200cs own label 100% red ▪ PO Box 6198 Uniedal 7612 ▪ sonklip@gmail.com ▪ S 33° 56' 3.55" E 018° 53' 44.95" ▪ **T +27 (0)21-887-5869** ▪ F +27 (0)21-887-5869

Engineer Frik Kirsten's later-in-life winemaking was inspired by a 2008 garagiste course and the 'thinking-out-the-box' approach of top Cape vintner Eben Sadie (whose vaunted Mev. Kirsten old-vine chenin comes from Frik's Stellenbosch family farm, Westridge). Frik elected to age his four '12 varietal wines longer and blend them, and the result is expected towards the middle of this year.

▪ **Sonop Organic** see African Terroir

Sophie & Mr P

Location: Elgin ▪ WO: Cape South Coast/Elgin/Stellenbosch ▪ Est/1stB 2009 ▪ Closed to public ▪ Owner(s) Andrew Gunn ▪ Cellarmaster(s) Werner Muller (May 2011) ▪ (cab, merlot, pinot, shiraz, sauv) ▪ 150t/20,000cs own label 10% red 85% white 5% rosé ▪ PO Box 527 Grabouw 7160 ▪ orders@sophie.co.za ▪ www.sophie.co.za ▪ **T +27 (0)28-284-9678** ▪ F +27 (0)28-284-9078

Production of these good-value wines with their catchy branding has more than doubled since the last edition, prompting Elgin-based owner Andrew Gunn and his Iona Vineyards team to source more widely around the Southern Cape Coast (while remaining 'as fastidious to quality as ever'). In addition to 'the most famous woman to never exist' (Sophie Te'blanche, a name stemming from a mis-pronunciation of 'sauvignon blanc'), the line-up now includes an Elgin-sourced pinot noir.

Mr P Pinot Noir NEW ✓ 🍴 ★★★★ Fun name & fun label playing on varietal name. Maiden **12** eminently quaffable in uncomplicated yet not facile style. Expressive cherry fragrance, fruitily fresh, properly dry. **Le Rouge** 🍴 ★★★ Near-equal blend shiraz, merlot & cab from Elgin, given popular spicy 'mocha' styling. Lovely freshness & abundant red fruit structured by well-integrated oak tannins in **11**. **Rosé** 🍴 🍷 ★★★ Dry **12**, nicely structured, uncomplicated & sufficiently light for chilled summer enjoyment. Stellenbosch WO. **Sophie Te'blanche** 🍴 ★★★ Popular sauvignon, with good reason. Vibrantly crisp, easygoing **13** dry & focused, though personality perhaps not quite as outgoing as previous. — AL,IM

■ **Sopiensklip** *see* Springfontein Wine Estate
■ **South Africa** *see* Wineways Marketing
■ **South African Soul** *see* Belbon Hills Private Cellar
■ **South Atlantic** *see* Simonsvlei International
■ **Southern Cape Vineyards** *see* Barrydale Winery & Distillery

Southern Right

Location: Hermanus ▪ Map: Elgin, Walker Bay & Bot River ▪ WO: Hemel-en-Aarde Valley/Walker Bay ▪ Est 1994 ▪ 1stB 1995 ▪ Tasting, sales & cellar tours Mon-Fri 9-5 Sat 9-1 ▪ Closed Easter Fri/Mon, Dec 25/26 & Jan 1 ▪ Fynbos reserve, renosterveld reserve & 3 wetlands ▪ Quad bike route ▪ Owner(s) Mark Willcox, Mikki Xayiya & Anthony Hamilton Russell ▪ Winemaker(s) Hannes Storm (2004) ▪ Viticulturist(s) Johan Montgomery (2005) ▪ 447ha/±36ha (ptage, sauv) ▪ 225-280t/30-40,000cs own label 20% red 80% white ▪ PO Box 158 Hermanus 7200 ▪ hrv@hermanus.co.za ▪ S 34° 24' 3.2" E 019° 13' 0.4" ▪ **T +27 (0)28-312-3595** ▪ F +27 (0)28-312-1797

In the 20 years since Hemel-en-Aarde Valley boutique vintners Southern Right embarked on their founding mission of redefining pinotage, co-owner Anthony Hamilton Russell believes, they've 'developed an international reputation for a more classic, restrained style of South Africa's national red grape'. Their other wine, Sauvignon Blanc, not only is a top seller but 'it certainly gets around! Most recently we learnt it is listed by a Michelin-starred restaurant in Greenland, and has been enjoyed in Antarctica by visiting scientists.'

★★★★☆ **Pinotage** 🍷 Reflects its maritime origin in cool violet & dark plum nuances, taut tannin frame. **12** (★★★★), despite soupçons 5 other varieties, shows characteristic strawberry tones, slight savoury complexity. Shade off poise & precision of last-tasted **10**.

★★★★☆ **Sauvignon Blanc 13** similar to less flamboyant but still accomplished **12**. Crisp 'wet pebble' minerality, persistent & dry, a lifted capsicum note in the conclusion. WO Walker Bay. — CvZ

Southern Sky Wines 🍷

Location: Paarl ▪ Map: Paarl & Wellington ▪ WO: Western Cape ▪ Est/1stB 2002 ▪ Tasting & sales by appt ▪ Owner(s) Andrew Milne ▪ Winemaker(s) Andrew Milne (Jan 2003) ▪ 20,000cs own label 95% red 5% white ▪ Other export brands: Golden Chalice, Hawk's Head, Les Fleurs, Rowlands ▪ PO Box 1312 Paarl 7624 ▪ andrew@ssw.co.za ▪ www.ssw.co.za ▪ S 33° 45' 8.78" E 018° 57' 42.55" ▪ **T +27 (0)21-863-4440** ▪ F +27 (0)21-863-0444

'Service is where we look to set ourselves apart,' says owner/winemaker Andrew Milne, bringing to his Paarl negociant business (achieving notable success in southeast Asia) the same passion he has for antique Cape furniture. 'I would drive to the ends of the earth to find an exceptional piece.'

Signature Selection
Tara Hill 🕐 ★★★★ Cab (88%) & petit verdot blend from Stellenbosch & Paarl. Serious effort, ably executed. **09** noble fruit on nose, pleasing earthy notes on palate. Quite fresh but well formed, smooth & concentrated.

Imagine range
Cabernet Sauvignon 🕐 🍴 ★★★ **08** shows some maturity but sweet berry fruit tastily intact for now & another year/2. **Shiraz** 🕐 🍴 ★★★ Ideal braai mate, ready-to-drink **08** has meaty charred oak notes already embedded. Just add T-bone steak.

Marimba range
Cabernet Sauvignon 🕐 ★★ A savoury version, **09** concentrated black cherry fruit, ends with a dried-fruit tang.

Almara range
Cabernet Sauvignon 🕐 ★★ Mediumweight **10** cab offering typical blackcurrant flavour & crisp acidity.

Capped with service

Superior service is about ability to adapt, refinement, perfection, innovation, and style. Most importantly, it is about meeting these high standards with no fuss.

As South Africa's largest metal and plastic closures manufacturer, Nampak Closures has a well established track record of delivering professional service. We have access to cross divisional packaging technology, expertise and market trends. We are supported by Nampak R&D, one of the most advanced packaging science and technology facilities in the southern hemisphere.

Our range of proudly South African screw caps, backed up by our superior personal service, are designed to give your wine a perfect sense of style that appeals to even the most sophisticated connoisseur.

Contact us on +27 21 507 8411

Nampak
Closures

www.nampak.com

Riedel recognises that the bouquet, taste, balance and finish of a wine is affected by the shape of the glass from which it is drunk. Over forty years ago Claus Riedel began his pioneering work to create stemware that would match and complement different wines and spirits.

"The Finest glasses for both technical and hedonistic purposes are those made by RIEDEL. The effect of these glasses on fine wine is profound.

I cannot emphasize enough what a difference they make."
Robert M.Parker Jr –
The Wine Advocate.

RIEDEL
THE WINE GLASS COMPANY

GRAPE ∴ VARIETAL SPECIFIC®

For more information & stockists in other areas please contact our Johannesburg Showroom:
Pilrig, 1 Rockridge Road, Parktown | Tel: +27 11 482 9178 | e-mail: riedel@reciprocal.co.za

www.reciprocal.co.za

A rainbow of backgrounds, nationalities and cultures, the Nick & Forti's wine brand was founded and is owned by **Fortunato 'Forti' Mazzone** (left), chef-patron of award-winning contemporary Italian eatery Ristorante Ritrovo in Waterkloof Heights, Pretoria, and **Nick van Huyssteen** (right), proprietor of Saronsberg winery outside Tulbagh, and vinified by Saronsberg cellarmaster Dewaldt Heyns (not pictured), a Swartland native and member of the Cape Winemakers Guild.

STUDY IN SWITZERLAND

DISCOVER THE ART OF HOSPITALITY AND BUSINESS MANAGEMENT IN SWITZERLAND

The wide variety of hospitality and business programmes combine quality academic standards with professional work experience and are tailored to the needs of this exciting industry.

The International Recruitment Forum will connect you with hospitality employers from around the world giving you access to the best career opportunities.

Choose the school and programme that suit you best and graduate with an Undergraduate or Postgraduate qualification.

- Hospitality
- Events
- Resort & Spa
- Tourism
- Hotel Design
- Culinary Arts
- Business
- Hotel Management

For further info about studying in Switzerland please contact:

Mrs. Diana Shires
T: 011 784 1533 or
072 257 0885
E: dshires@global.co.za
Facebook: LAURENT SEG

SWISS EDUCATION GROUP
Montreux | Switzerland | T +41 21 965 40 20
info@swisseducation.com | www.swisseducation.com

Hugo and Miwette Basson, co-owners of Swartland family winery Annex Kloof, see increasing numbers of beer drinkers enjoying wine and becoming immersed in wine culture. To abet the trend they're offering, among others, the opportunity for any member of the public to be mentored by winemaker **Hugo** (back left), with mentees **Altus van der Merwe** (right) and **Hennie Bosch** (front), vinifying a barrel of wine at the farm and overseeing it during it's 18-month maturation at Annex Kloof's cellar. The Bassons believe that such a hands-on experience will help make communities across the country more enthusiastic about the wine industry and prouder of South African wine.

Joris and **Natalie van Almenkerk** (centre), the Belgian owners of Elgin's showpiece winery, Almenkerk Wine Estate, since their advent in 2004 have transformed not only the property but also the lives of those who live on it, none more so than **Danver van Wyk** (left) and **Kholani Mkadeni** (right). Orchard workers under the old regime, today Danver is the assistant winemaker and Kholani the full-time cellar hand. Both live on the farm in their own houses, are members of the farm committee, and look after the daily running of the cellar.

The "Tavern of the Seas" no more...

*The Cape harbour was the "Tavern of the Seas" for many thirsty sailors
after long periods at sea.
The Marina Basin was a quarry and centuries later a luxurious site
for residential living.*

This is a place steeped in antiquity and its stories will forever be written in history.

HOME FROM HOME

Home from Home specialises in providing self-catering luxury accommodation
in the Marina, from one, two to three bedroom apartments.

Book Now
Tel: +27 21 418 2821 I Fax: +27 21 418 5100 IEmail: reservations@homefromhome.co.za
www.homefromhome.co.za

Spice Route
DESTINATION

A COLLECTION OF PRODUCERS

A carefully curated selection of artisans showcase their produce and share their knowledge with both the public and each other.

WINE TASTING

SUID AGTER PAARL ROAD, PAARL
GPS S 33°45'50.00 E 18°55'10.00
TEL. 021 863 5200
WEBSITE: *www.spiceroute.co.za*
TWITTER: *@SpiceRoutePaarl*
FACEBOOK: *SpiceRoutePaarl*

GRAPPA TASTING

RESTAURANTS

BILTONG TASTING

BEER TASTING

GLASS BLOWING STUDIO

CHOCOLATE TASTING

Co-founded with the primary objectives of education, employment, social cohesion and upliftment in mind by local entrepreneurs Mzoli Ngcawuzele of Mzoli's Place, a popular township restaurant, and Lungile Mbalo, the debut TOPS at SPAR Gugulethu Wine Festival, held on the rooftop of the Gugulethu Square Mall in May 2011, was hailed a major success by the 37 exhibitors, 120 media and 2,050 visitors who attended over the two evenings. Fast-forward to today and numbers have more than doubled to 4,555 visitors, who thoroughly enjoy this diverse, fun-filled and vibrant annual festival, which lives up to its slogan 'it's wine-devine in Gugs!'

HAUTE CABRIÈRE

Cellar Restaurant

F R A N S C H H O E K

Tel 021 876 3688 | Email restaurant@cabriere.co.za
Franschhoek Pass R45 Franschhoek 7690

WWW.CABRIERE.CO.ZA

As boutique wine farmers in Devon Valley, Devonair owners **Rina** and **Leon de Wit** (top right) say they are limited in what they can achieve in furthering an inclusive wine culture in South Africa. But they are actively involved in the community via their ownership of AmaZink Live theatre and restaurant in Khayamandi near Stellenbosch, described as 'not only a South African musical journey, but an experience that will uplift the spirit and get you "grooving" to the rhythm of the beat of local South African music.

www.jfhillebrand.com

100% GLOBAL 100% LOCAL

SINCE 1844
CELEBRATING
170 Years

No matter where you are in the world of wine, beer and spirits, you'll find JF Hillebrand is there – ready to respond to local issues and conditions, with an understanding of home-grown preferences and legislation. So while the reach of our 2000 professionals in 47 offices is 100% global, our touch remains 100% local.

100% BEVERAGE. 100% LOGISTICS.

JF Hillebrand Stellenbosch
T +27 21 809 2000
capetown@hillebrandgroup.com

JF Hillebrand
global beverage logistics

WOODED WHITE

South African brandy is made by distilling the finest quality wine followed by at least three years of maturation.

Chenin Blanc and Colombar are the most popular varietals, sourced mainly from warmer wine growing regions.

A **proud heritage** and comprehensive legislation ensure that South African brandy is widely regarded as the world's finest. The **IWSC Worldwide Best Brandy** trophy has been won by a South African brandy 11 times in the last 15 years!

SA
BRANDY
FOUNDATION

SHARE THE SPIRIT

Not for Sale to Persons Under the Age of 18

vineyard hotel & spa
the gourmet setting

Tastes of 2014

eat, sip, savour...

| diarise festivals | 02nd march | mcc festival |
| | 13th april | pinot noir festival |

diarise fridays	25th april	vineyard hotel's 5 wine partners
	09th may	cederberg
	23rd may	edgebaston
	06th june	simonsig estate
	20th june	beaumont wines
	04th july	graham beck wines
	18th july	ernie els wines
	08th august	creation wines
	22nd august	blackwater wine and david sadie
	05th september	thelema mountain vineyards
	19th september	boekenhoutskloof
	03rd october	saxenburg
	17th october	waterford estate
	31st october	constantia valley wines

Join us at the square and treat your tastebuds to a dining experience created by our chef to enhance the latest and greatest from top estates and fêted winemakers. Booking is essential for these popular events, call us on 021 657 4500 or e-mail us at eat@vineyard.co.za.

the SQUARE

WINE VILLAGE

HERMANUS

7 EXCUSES to stock up on wine at Cybercellar.com

Choose from 3,000+ wines
Cellar door prices
Free door-to-door delivery
Expert personal advice
Money-Back Guarantee
Access to exclusive and limited releases
Voted Number 1 online wine shop by Meininger's Wine Business International magazine

Cybercellar.com - where smart people buy wine.

CYBER CELLAR
WIDEST SELECTION, BEST PRICES – SINCE 1998

www.cybercellar.com

Not for Sale to Persons Under the Age of 18.

Ready Steady range
Red ⊕ 🖾 ★★ Lightish, juicy & pleasant **NV**, chiefly cinsaut & 3 others, mostly unwooded. — GdB,HJ

South Hill Vineyards

Location/WO: Elgin ▪ Map: Elgin, Walker Bay & Bot River ▪ Est 2001 ▪ 1stB 2006 ▪ Tasting Mon-Sun 10-4 ▪ The Gallery @ South Hill (original artworks) ▪ The Guest House and Pumphouse Cottage ▪ Function venue for conferences & weddings ▪ Conservation area ▪ Owner(s) South Hill Vineyards (Pty) Ltd ▪ Winemaker(s) Sean Skibbe (Jun 2005) ▪ Viticulturist(s) Andrew Teubes (Mar 2006, consultant) ▪ 57ha/28ha (cab, pinot, shiraz, chard, riesling, sauv, sem, viog) ▪ 130t/7,000cs own label 20% red 80% white ▪ PO Box 120 Elgin 7180 ▪ info@southhill.co.za ▪ www.southhill.co.za ▪ S 34° 13' 59.5" E 019° 6' 44.3" ▪ **T +27 (0)21-844-0888** ▪ F +27 (0)86-530-4065

This Elgin winefarm (with added attractions like art gallery, function venue and guesthouse) was, not long ago, home to neglected apple and pear trees. The fruit was replaced with vines on the varying slopes - some cooler, some warmer - according to suitability. Moving to rehabilitate the fynbos was another early act.

★★★★☆ **Cabernet Sauvignon** ⊕ 🍴 Elegant **10** (★★★★) shy aromas but intense flavours of black cherry, dark chocolate & touch of vanilla. Modest oaking. Lingering & fresh but not quite at level of **09**.
Cabernet Sauvignon Rosé ⊕ 🍴 ★★★★ Beautiful redcurrant & cherry on lightish & lively **12**. Intriguing mineral feel; bone-dry. **Sauvignon Blanc** Await next. **Blanc de Blancs Méthode Cap Classique** ⊕ ★★★★ Rich **08** sparkling from chardonnay. Aromas of ripe apple & melon lead to generous mouthful & a slight sweetness to conclude. — JPf

Spekulasie Landgoed  **NEW**

Location/map/WO: Swartland ▪ Est 2008 ▪ 1stB 2010 ▪ Tasting, sales & cellar tours Mon-Sat/pub hols by appt ▪ Fee R20 pp ▪ Light meals & refreshments ▪ Facilities for children ▪ Gift shop ▪ Farm produce ▪ Conferences ▪ Hiking trails ▪ Conservation area ▪ Accommodation ▪ Owner(s)/cellarmaster(s)/viticulturist(s) Johan & Linza Louw ▪ Winemaker(s) Linza Louw ▪ 220ha/27ha (cab, merlot, ptage, shiraz) ▪ ±120t/200cs own label 75% red 25% rosé ▪ PO Box 173 Malmesbury 7299 ▪ spekulasie@cornergate.com ▪ www.spekulasie-estate.co.za ▪ S 33° 23' 23.43" E 018° 35' 7.58" ▪ **T +27 (0)82-559-6066/+27 (0)72-375-7078**

Only a small amount of wine is handmade by Swartlanders Johan and Linza Louw in a 'petit little cellar' on their dryland bushvine estate, Spekulasie (most grapes go to Darling Cellars). The couple's wines, 'Old World styled and food friendly', are named after celebrated family members, notably progenitor Jan Pieterzoon, who arrived in the Cape in 1659 and founded an enduring vinegrowing tradition.

De Beatrix ✓ ★★★★ From shiraz, sparingly oaked in older wood. Lighter-styled **12** perfumed glassful of cherry, sweet spice, cinnamon & smoked meat, moderate alcohol & satisfying full conclusion. Worth seeking out. **De Pieterzoon** ★★★ Sunny, berry-rich pinotage & shiraz (79/21) blend, **12** with gentle texture & good finish, for early drinking. **The Elizabeth** 🍴 ★★★ Dry rosé from pinotage, **13** mild-mannered & floral, pleasant hints of sweet spice. — GdB, GM

■ **Spencer Bay** *see Namaqua Wines*

Spice Route Winery

Location: Malmesbury/Paarl ▪ Map: Paarl & Wellington ▪ WO: Swartland ▪ Est/1stB 1998 ▪ Tasting & sales Mon-Sun 9-5, last tasting 30min before closing ▪ Closed Good Fri, Dec 25 & Jan 1 ▪ Spice Route Restaurant (see Restaurants section) ▪ Tour groups by appt ▪ Red Hot Glass ▪ DV Artisan Chocolate Roastery & Espresso Bar ▪ Cape Brewing Company ▪ Barley & Biltong Emporium ▪ Wilderer's Distillery & La Grapperia Restaurant ▪ Owner(s) Charles Back ▪ Winemaker(s) Charl du Plessis (Dec 2001), with Licia Solomons (Jan 2006) ▪ 112ha (barbera, cab, carignan, grenache, merlot, mourv, petite sirah, ptage, sangio, shiraz, tannat, zin, chenin, rouss, sauv, sem, viog) ▪ 900t 60% red 40% white ▪ Fairtrade, IPW, WIETA ▪ PO Box 583 Suider-Paarl 7624 ▪ info@spiceroute.co.za ▪ www.spiceroutewines.co.za ▪ S 33° 45' 50.5" E 018° 55' 9.7" ▪ **T +27 (0)21-863-5200** ▪ F +27 (0)21-863-3797

The Spice Route label arose out of the conviction of Fairview's Charles Back that the Swartland was under-utilised. He acquired property in this region in the late 1990s keeping some old vines but also going on to pioneer some lesser known Mediterranean varieties. Ever the pragmatist however, Back says, 'Wine on its own is not a strong enough draw card to appeal to the average tourist' and the

wines now have a home in Paarl featuring a new tasting room, a restaurant, a 'bean-to-bar' chocolate maker, brewery, distillery and glass blowing studio. 'The success of inner-city markets point to a consumer hankering to connect with product. We're taking it one step further.'

★★★★ **Pinotage** ✓ ⌷ Consistent & appealing. **11** with usual seductive logan/blackberry note, bold but unobtrusive structure, subtle oaking, leaving succulent pure, fresh fruit. A keeper.

★★★★ **Shiraz** ✓ ⌷ Sweet fruited, ripe, full flavoured, full throttle... **10** is serious, not to be underestimated - it's a big, rich, oaky, assertive wine. Good New World expression.

★★★★ **Malabar** ⊕ **09** is opulent & ripe but more restrained than **07** (★★★★). Bold & rich, with a berry liqueur character, supported by smooth tannins. Neither up to lofty standard of **06** (★★★★☆). No **08**.

★★★★☆ **Chenin Blanc** ✓ ⊟ ⌷ Super expression of the variety, preview **13** is lush & silky, with kaleidoscopic crème brûlée, lemon, honey & vanilla. Already showing the same complexity as exceptional predecessor **11** (★★★★★). Fresh & vibrant, with restrained oak. No **12**.

★★★★ **Sauvignon Blanc** ✓ ⊟ ⌷ From night-harvested fruit, **12** attracts with tropical fruit aromas & herbaceous notes. Restrained, juicy acidity, refined & very enjoyable.

Mourvèdre ⊕ ⌷ ★★★★ Preview **10** fruity & balanced, with an earthy, dusty finish. Medium bodied, juicy & delicious. **Chakalaka** ✓ ★★★★ **11** has more gravitas than **10** (★★★★). Compact, delicious 6-way shiraz-led blend. Loads of restrained sweet fruit & fragrant spice, harmonious, groomed & well built. **Viognier** ✓ ⊟ ⌷ ★★★★ Spicy & fragrant oak-dusted peach melba builds in the mouth on **12**. Broad & rich, satisfying, with invigorating freshness. Livelier than last-tasted **10** (★★★). Discontinued: **Flagship Syrah**. — WB

Spier ♙ ♟ ☕ ⌂ 📷 ✕ ♿

Location/map: Stellenbosch ▪ WO: Western Cape/Coastal/Stellenbosch/Tygerberg ▪ Est 1692 ▪ 1stB 1770 ▪ Tasting 10-4.30 & sales 9-5 daily ▪ Tasting from R38 ▪ Facilities for children ▪ Tour groups ▪ Farm produce ▪ Conferences ▪ Manor House museum & The Heritage Walk ▪ Conservation area ▪ 4-star Spier Hotel & Spa ▪ Eight Restaurant, Eight to Go & Spier Hotel Restaurant (see Restaurants section) ▪ Owner(s) Enthoven family ▪ Cellarmaster(s) Frans Smit (Dec 1995) ▪ Winemaker(s) Johan Jordaan (reds, Jul 2007) & Jacques Erasmus (whites, Apr 2007), with Anthony Kock (2009) ▪ Wine procurement/winemaker(s) Johan de Villiers, Anton Swarts & Lizanne Jordaan ▪ Viticulturist(s) Johann Smit (Dec 1999) ▪ 650ha (barbera, cabs s/f, malbec, merlot, mourv, p verdot, ptage, shiraz, chard, chenin, sauv, sem, viog) ▪ 3,850t own label 65% red 31% white 3% rosé 1% MCC ▪ ISO 22000:2005, BWI, Fairtrade, IPW, Organic, WIETA ▪ PO Box 99 Lynedoch 7603 ▪ info@spier.co.za ▪ www.spier.co.za ▪ S 33° 58' 24.63" E 018° 47' 2.23" ▪ **T +27 (0)21-809-1100 (wine tasting)** ▪ F +27 (0)21-809-1930

'Consistent... and creative,' reflects cellarmaster Frans Smit on the heritage of Stellenbosch's Spier. Farmed since 1692, it's one of South Africa's oldest wine estates, with a wealth of history. The 21 gables on the property ('A history lesson in Cape Dutch architecture,' notes Frans) are celebrated in a top-end label. But, in the Enthoven family since 1996, the focus is on now, and the future. As 'custodians' rather than owners, they seek a 'closed loop' with and in the community, symbolised by '8', the name of an onsite restaurant. An example is the Creative Block project that sees local artists create small-format works which Spier markets on their behalf. Managing a patchwork of vineyards on the Stellenbosch home-farm and in the Helderberg, Paarl and Darling allows Frans and equally part-of-the-furniture viticulturist Johann Smit to create value at every level.

Frans K. Smit range

★★★★☆ **Frans K. Smit** Generous flagship Cape Blend (4 Bordeaux reds plus shiraz, pinotage) honours the cellarmaster on eve of his 20th year here. Inky **08**, suave forest floor fruit nestle in savoury tannins, 30 months 100% new oak still settling. A blockbuster from any angle. Coastal WO.

21 Gables range

★★★★☆ **Pinotage** ⌷ Outstanding expression of the variety; **11** juicy & velvet-smooth, easily absorbs grain sugar & 14.5% alcohol into fruit pastille profile. From home vineyards.

★★★★☆ **Chenin Blanc** ⊟ ⌷ Full bore **12** (★★★★) risks losing nuance of the grape; ripe fruit, 46% new oak, off-dry 6 g/l sugar & 14+% alcohol offer oodles of flavour though less silk than **11**. Tygerberg vines.

★★★★ **Sauvignon Blanc** NEW ⊟ Wake-me-up **13** like a dip in an icy lake, riveting grassy attack to tangy asparagus/canned pea fruit, super length of flavour. Refreshing, to say the least!

Creative Block range

★★★★ 5 ✓ 🗌 Cab & merlot lead **11** 5-way Bordeaux blend. Lots of power & a suggestion of sweetness but all well controlled by underlying minerality. WO Coastal, as is next.

★★★★ 3 ✓ 🗌 Shiraz & mourvèdre seasoned by splash viognier; some American oak, 60% new. **11** delectably spicy, sleek & smooth, with a savoury/green olive farewell.

★★★★ 2 🗌 Strident grassy muscularity of dominant sauvignon gets width & balance from 14% unoaked semillon in **13**; satisfying, but a yard off mineral **12** (★★★★★).

Private Collection

★★★★ **Shiraz** Energised spice of **11** captured in firm structure; maintains freshness with 50% new wood & 14.6% alcohol well contained.

Cabernet Sauvignon ★★★★ This range for export only. **11** gently leafy & herbaceous, blackcurrant fruit intact for now. Half new oak 18 months. Coastal WO, like Pinotage. **Merlot** ★★★★ Earthy, meaty profile of attractive **11** dominated mid-2013 by zealous wooding & enveloping tannins. **Pinotage** ★★★★ **11** a serious rendition of the variety, shows careful handling - half new barrels - with bold spicy, tropical features of the grape well framed by 14.7% alcohol. **Chardonnay** 🗌 ★★★★ Preview **12** laden with citrus fruit, swathed in oak vanilla (40% new); promises crispness, higher level pleasure when settled. **Sauvignon Blanc** 🗌 ★★★★ Broad summer melon features focused by piercing nettle notes, **13** palate softened by lees-ageing.

Methodé Cap Classique range

★★★★ **Méthode Cap Classique** Accomplished dry bubble from chardonnay, pinot noir & pinotage. **11** (★★★★) already quite evolved, misses tight mineral finish of **10**. WO Stellenbosch.

Vintage Selection

Cabernet Sauvignon Next awaited, as for **Sauvignon Blanc**. **Malbec-Cabernet Franc-Petit Verdot** NEW ★★★ This & next two blends for export. Bordeaux trio in tight, austere **12** preview; black berry fruit trussed in grippy tannins. **Shiraz-Mourvèdre-Viognier** NEW ★★★★ Lovely vibrancy to spicy mediumweight **12**. Pre-bottling, Rhône blend's piquant tone is most refreshing. **Chardonnay-Chenin Blanc-Viognier** NEW 🗌 ★★★ Ripe, sunny fruit promise in ex-tank **13**.

Signature range

Cabernet Sauvignon 😊 🗌 🗌 ★★★ Spearmint-brushed **12** is dark fruited, lightly oaked & refreshing for uncomplicated pleasure. **Merlot** 😊 🗌 🗌 ★★★ Floral **12** proffers unequivocal minty edge, sweet mulberry impression to technically dry tail. **Pinotage** 😊 🗌 🗌 ★★★ Quintessential banana & berry with acetone appeal, oak-licked **12** supple & commendably dry. **Shiraz** 😊 🗌 ★★★ Dark & brooding **12** a dinner companion; savoury, with black pepper freshness & dry tail. **Chardonnay** 😊 🗌 🗌 ★★★ Lipsmacking loquat character to crowd-pleasing **13** preview; tasty, very tasty! **Chenin Blanc** 😊 🗌 🗌 ★★★ **13** packed with white peach & melon, super fruit concentration in a moreish glassful. **Sauvignon Blanc** 😊 🗌 🗌 ★★★ Summery **13** wafts nettles & grass, zesty acidity livens tropical fruit in tail. —DS

Spioenkop Wines

Location: Elgin ▪ Map: Elgin, Walker Bay & Bot River ▪ WO: Western Cape/Elgin ▪ Est 2008 ▪ 1stB 2010 ▪ Tasting, sales & cellar tours by appt only ▪ Fee R20, waived on purchase (case of wine) ▪ Closed all pub hols ▪ Facilities for children ▪ BYO picnic ▪ Hiking trails ▪ Conservation area ▪ Weddings/functions ▪ Self-catering cottage ▪ Owner(s) Valuline 119 (Pty) Ltd, 5 shareholders ▪ Cellarmaster(s)/winemaker(s)/viticulturist(s) Koen Roose-Vandenbroucke (2008) ▪ ±47ha/10ha (ptage, pinot, chenin, riesling, sauv) ▪ 40t/5,000cs own label 20% red 80% white ▪ PO Box 340 Grabouw 7160 ▪ info@spioenkopwines.co.za ▪ www.spioenkopwines.co.za ▪ S 34° 14' 14" E 019° 3' 50" ▪ **T +27 (0)21-859-1458**

If you thought locals were passionate about South African terroir, clearly you've not met Spioenkop cellarmaster Koen Roose-Vandenbroucke, 'a rebel from Belgium who didn't move here for the sun, and isn't scared to do things differently'. Spioenkop, among Elgin's newer properties, according to Koen is 'adorable and simply gorgeous, a young world-class model who needed only a few years to master the catwalk.' Purity, elegance, sensuality and minerality are the winemaker/viticulturist's aims, and he's using artisanal tools and techniques - 'green' farming practices, long wild-yeast ferments, restrained oaking - to achieve them.

1900 range

★★★★☆ **Pinotage** Surpassing maiden **10** & quirky **11** (★★★★), **12** (★★★★★) is pinotage re-imagined: pure, subtle, elegant. Elgin & Stellenbosch fruit, red/black cherry, floral fragrance, attractive oak spice (well-judged 50% new wood). Medium bodied with fresh acidity & nicely grippy tannins. Natural ferment (as all).

★★★★ **Chenin Blanc** Sophisticated **12**, partly wooded, shows peach & apple, hint of spice, some burnt matchstick. Great concentration, driving acidity. Quite tight on tasting, should age a good few years.

★★★★ **Sauvignon Blanc 12** (★★★★) is more traditional SA in style with notes of asparagus & green pepper to go with cantaloupe. Rich & full with tangy acidity. Contains 14% semillon. Not as composed as **11**.

Sauvignon Blanc Barrel Selection In abeyance.

Spioenkop Wines range

★★★★ **Riesling** Slightly ponderous **12** (★★★★), lime, flint & hint of petrol. Rich & thick textured, with a dry savoury finish. Lacks finesse of **11**. WO Elgin, as next.

★★★★☆ **Sauvignon Blanc** Super-expressive, optimally ripe **12**, subtle lime, peach, green melon, granadilla & pineapple. Concentrated & rich but not at all blowsy. Should age extremely well. — CE

■ **Splattered Toad** *see* Cape Point Vineyards

Spookfontein Wines

Location: Hermanus ▪ Map: Elgin, Walker Bay & Bot River ▪ WO: Upper Hemel-en-Aarde Valley ▪ Est 2000 ▪ 1stB 2004 ▪ Tasting, sales & cellar tours by appt ▪ Two self-catering guest cottages ▪ Conservation area ▪ Owner(s) Spookfontein Wines cc (Mike Davis) ▪ Winemaker(s) Craig Sheard (Feb 2006) ▪ Viticulturist(s) Andries Gotze (Jan 2000) ▪ 313ha/±12ha (cabs s/f, merlot, pinot) ▪ 50t/2,000cs own label 100% red ▪ PO Box 12031 Mill Street Cape Town 8010 ▪ craig@spookfontein.co.za ▪ S 34° 21′ 19.5″ E 019° 17′ 20.8″ ▪ **T +27 (0)82-265-1071**

Much activity at this boutique winery in Upper Hemel-en-Aarde Valley, with a new tasting room planned for later on in the year. Winemaker Craig Sheard continues to farm organically and biodynamically, and reports a slight style change, the wines spending less time in oak to create a fresher, fruitier feel.

Cabernet Sauvignon ⊕ ★★★★ One of the Cape's leaner versions. Naturally fermented **08**'s mulberries & cream stretched over taut cab backbone. **Cabernet Franc** ⊕ ★★★★ **08**, while tending to the lean (unlike **07**), has plenty of sweet fruit flesh, easygoing tannins but sufficient tug for structure & interest. **Merlot** ⊕ ★★★★ Sugarplum note to step-up **08**'s mulberry & prune complexity. Only slightly herbal, very persistent & wonderfully dry (like most of these reds). **Pinot Noir** ⊕ ★★★ Fresh raspberry, earthy allure on **08** ex young single-vineyard. **Phantom** ⊕ ★★★★ Merlot-led (with cab & cab franc) **08** raises the bar on **07** (★★★★). Poised & lengthy, but greater grip & just the right amount of flavour without seeming worked. — CvZ

Spotswood Wines

Location/map/WO: Stellenbosch ▪ Est 2007 ▪ 1stB 2008 ▪ Tasting & sales by appt ▪ Owner(s) Spotswood family ▪ Cellarmaster(s)/winemaker(s) Guy Webber (Jan 2012, consultant) ▪ Viticulturist(s) Bill Spotswood (Sep 2007) ▪ 7.05ha/3ha (durif, shiraz, chard, viog) ▪ 28t/3,000cs own label 72% red 6% white 22% rosé ▪ Suite 200 Private Bag X4 Die Boord 7613 ▪ nick@limpro.co.za ▪ S 33° 59′ 2.0″ E 018° 51′ 35.0″ ▪ **T +27 (0)21-880-2893** ▪ F +27 (0)21-880-2893

Father and son Bill and Nick Spotswood bought a boutique property on the Blaauwklippen Road in 2007, already planted with (amongst others) durif – a variety rarely heard of in South Africa, but one which the Spotswoods believe has great potential, as enthusiastic attendees at wine shows in their hometown of Polokwane can attest.

Durif ⊕ 🌿 ★★★★ Variety, also known as petite sirah, shares its typical dark plum/prune fruit & juicy tannins in **11**. Still tight, brooding, deserves year/2 to unfurl & reveal all its charms. **Shiraz** 🌿 ★★★ Like previous, **12** a giant at 15+ alcohol but an affable one, will please many. Rounded, ripe & fruit-rich, well built if tad extracted. **Shiraz Reserve** Next awaited. **Dry Rosé** 🌿 ★★★ Summer picnic companion, **13** pomegranate & cranberry flavours, dry & fresh. **Viognier** NEW 🌿 ★★ **13** pick of the pair tasted. Delicate intro of peach & apricot, typical viognier warmth & body, nice spiciness. **12** (★★) textured & more savoury, a nutty overlay to the nectarine fruit. — DC

Springfield Estate

Location/map/WO: Robertson • Est/1stB 1995 • Tasting & sales Mon-Fri 8–5 Sat 9–4 • Closed Easter Fri/Sun, Dec 25 & Jan 1 • Cellar tours by appt • BYO picnic • Owner(s) Bruwer family • Cellarmaster(s)/viticulturist(s) Abrie Bruwer • Winemaker(s) Abrie Bruwer, with Johan van Zyl • 150ha (cabs s/f, merlot, p verdot, chard, sauv) • IPW • PO Box 770 Robertson 6705 • admin@springfieldestate.com • www.springfieldestate.com • S 33° 50' 12.1" E 019° 54' 54.0" • **T +27 (0)23-626-3661** • F +27 (0)23-626-3664

The Bruwers date their presence in the Cape back to the Huguenot Bruères who arrived in 1688. This eminent family estate in Robertson is more recent, but firmly established to the extent that nothing new seems to happen any more, says winemaker Abrie. 'Every year we plant vines, do something to the cellar, buy some new equipment...' And there are no secrets behind his success with grapes, like sauvignon blanc and cabernet, that seldom perform as well as this in these parts, let alone with such moderate alcohol levels. 'No tricks – just making the choices that lead to quality, the hundreds of little choices made each day.'

★★★★☆ **Méthode Ancienne Cabernet Sauvignon** Off 1979-planted vines, **06** enters its maturity with firm, serious majesty. Savoury bottle development adds complexity, but still some sweet, fresh fruit & cedary oak. Powerful & rich, strongly built, though just 13.2% alcohol. Good for another five years. No **05** made.

★★★★ **The Work of Time** ⏱ Time has softened the big tannins on **06** blend & added savoury complexity; herbaceous note part of the liveliness. Previous **04** (★★★★☆) led by cab franc, this by cab & merlot.

★★★★☆ **Méthode Ancienne Chardonnay** ⏱ Lively & exciting (& just a touch funky) naturally made **09** tasted a few years back. Full, ripe flavours absorb the new oak; rich, substantial, balanced.

★★★★ **Wild Yeast Chardonnay** Smooth-textured unwooded **10** (★★★☆) has ripe fruit with boiled-sweet overtones, but is sweeter & less concentrated than **09**. Less fresh too, despite a pleasant acidity.

★★★★ **Special Cuvée Sauvignon Blanc** 🏺 Confident (but never brash), balanced & aromatic **13** as usual the more subtle & interesting of the Springfield pair. Intense enough, but light-feeling.

Whole Berry Cabernet Sauvignon 🏺 ★★★★ Attractive fruity, vanilla notes on **11** tempered by cedary & herbal elements. Undemanding but not trivial - the plush, softly ripe tannins combining with acidity to give enough grip. **Life From Stone Sauvignon Blanc** 🏺 🏺 ★★★☆ **13** (tasted soon after bottling) less intense than **12** (★★★★), but enough crisply assertive passionfruit oomph to please its many admirers. — TJ

Springfontein Wine Estate

Location: Stanford • Map: Elgin, Walker Bay & Bot River • WO: Walker Bay • Est 1996 • 1stB 2004 • Tasting, sales & cellar tours Mon-Fri 8–5 Sat/Sun 9–4 • Closed Dec 25 & Jan 1 • Springfontein Eats Restaurant (see Restaurants section) • Tour groups • Farm produce • BYO picnic • Walking/hiking trail • Springfontein Guest House (see Accommodation section) • Owner(s) Johst & Jennifer Packard Weber, Jürgen & Susanne Schneider, with family & friends • Cellarmaster(s) Tariro Masayiti (Jan 2013) • Winemaker(s) Tariro Masayiti (Jan 2013), with Rohan Breytenbach (Dec 2012) • Viticulturist(s) Tariro Masayiti (Jan 2013), with Johannes Janse (Mar 2009) • 500ha/25ha (cab, p verdot, ptage, chenin) • 145t/20,000cs own label 80% red 18% white 2% rosé • PO Box 71 Stanford 7210 • info@springfontein.co.za • www.springfontein.co.za • S 34° 25' 38.5" E 019° 24' 32.7" • **T +27 (0)28-341-0651/+27 (0)72-371-7546** • F +27 (0)28-341-0112

This boutique winery is situated at a unique Stanford site with virgin limestone soils, set next to the sea and surrounded by fynbos. The conditions are particularly suited to pinotage and chenin, as their track record confirms, and under the leadership of new Tariro Masayiti, ex Nederburg white-wine maker, further quality advances can be expected. Horticulturist Hildegard Witbooi is part of the new team, to oversee removal of alien species in order to encourage growth of medicinal and culinary fynbos, as well as plant a vegetable and herb garden to supply the restaurant, where co-owner Jürgen Schneider is the chef.

Single Vineyard range

★★★★ **Jonathan's Ridge Pinotage** 🏺 Wild yeast fermented, unfiltered **10** (★★★★☆) improves on **09** with intense blueberry fruit, the oak adding savoury nuances, its firmness concealed, allowing the wine's smoothly polished lines to impress.

★★★★ **Jonathan's Ridge Mendocino Pinotage** Blueberries & salty liquorice, while the good tannin foundation offsets **10**'s ripeness. Adds restraint & focus without losing the polished varietal succulence.

★★★★ **Jil's Dune Chenin Blanc** ⓐ ⓦ Back on form after **10** (★★★☆), flaunting butterscotch & stonefruit, **11**'s sexy face hides a serious side - silky elegance, perfect fruit/acid balance & ageability.

Estate Wines
★★★★ **Ikhalezi Noble Late Harvest** ⓐ From chenin. Amber-hued **07** (★★★★☆) is one of a kind. Astonishingly rich at 372g/l sugar, it is so refreshed by racy acidity that it drinks beautifully; syrupy, tangy apricot with an added savoury roasted almond tone from new oak. 375ml. Even better than gorgeous **06** preview.
Special Red Occasional release. Discontinued: **Red**, **Ulumbaza**, **White**.

Terroir Selection
★★★★ **Cabernet Sauvignon** ⓦ Powerful blueberry/mulberry perfume demands attention, but the underpin is layers of complexity. Provençal herbs, liquorice, cappuccino, **10** (★★★★☆) is on another level to **09**, the final seduction a succulent, well-toned body, polished & long.

★★★★ **Petit Verdot** NEW ⓦ Fynbos & black pepper, hedgerow berries, there's a sense of wildness in **10** which will settle over time, its deep muscle tone promises a long future. Smooth & supple, already appeals.

★★★★ **Chardonnay Wild Yeast** Lovely combo orange rind & hazelnuts in **12** preview, creamy-savoury palate weight from 16 months lees-ageing in barrel. Care taken justified, this is individual, impressive. **Pinotage** ★★★☆ Ageing in 3 oak barrel types gives **09**'s black plums a vanilla & dried herb spicing, leaves an appealing juicy, curvaceous body. **Chardonnay** Await next. **Chenin Blanc** ✓ ★★★★ Oak fermented/matured **12** sample improves on **11** (★★★★) with quince & almond styling, a perfect integration of fruit & oak. Already delicious, will unfold further layers over time. **Sauvignon Blanc** ✓ ★★★★ Lime & fennel, **13** ex-tank is already scent-expressive, morphs into flinty minerality in its flavours, pure & long.

Sopiensklip range

Red ☺ ▦ ⓦ ★★★ Fruit-forward **10** showcases all 3 varieties, cab, shiraz & merlot in its plums & red berries, smoky spice & juicy appeal.

Pink ▦ ⓦ ★★★ From merlot in **12**, dry, full flavoured red berries, a herbal note. **White** ▦ ⓦ ★★★ Semillon/chardonnay in light unwooded **12**, melon & peach, soft & easy. — CR

Spring Grove Wines   ⓘ

Location/map/WO: Stellenbosch ▪ 1stB 2005 ▪ Tasting & sales by appt ▪ Owner(s) Parodi family ▪ Winemaker(s) Neil Moorhouse (2005) ▪ Viticulturist(s) Hannes Jansen van Vuuren (Mar 2008) ▪ 10ha/6.4ha (sangio, shiraz, pinot gris, sauv, viog) ▪ 41t/25,200L bulk ▪ PO Box 670 Vereeniging 1930 ▪ hannes@zorgvliet. com ▪ S 33° 54' 46.50" E 018° 56' 13.6" ▪ **T +27 (0)82-856-8717** ▪ F +27 (0)86-697-3938

Banhoek's Spring Grove, originally part of the Zorgvliet property, was purchased by David Parodi and family in 2005. After uprooting the vineyards, their Italian heritage encouraged them to include sangiovese and pinot grigio in the replant. The wines, bottled and bulk, are made at Zorgvliet by Neil Moorhouse.

★★★★ **Sauvignon Blanc** ⓐ ▦ Harmonious sample **11** (★★★★☆) fresh & enticing with lovely zesty mineral finish, though not as gutsy as **10**.

Sangiovese ⓐ ▦ ★★★★ Berries almost leap from the glass in delightfully fresh & youthful **10**, sweet fruit flavours tailored by ageing in older barrels. **Shiraz** ⓐ ▦ ★★★★ Barrel sample **09**'s succulent fruitiness underlined by savoury, spicy tannins; pleasing balance & some seriousness. **Pinot Grigio** ▦ Preview **13** too unsettled to rate. **Viognier** In abeyance. — IM

▪ **Spring Valley** see Old Vines Cellars
▪ **Spruitdrift** see Namaqua Wines
▪ **Stablemate** see Excelsior Estate

Stanford Hills Winery   🍾🍷☕⛺📷♿

Location: Stanford ▪ Map: Elgin, Walker Bay & Bot River ▪ WO: Walker Bay ▪ Est 1856 ▪ 1stB 2002 ▪ Tasting, sales & restaurant Thu-Mon & pub hols 11-5 Tue/Wed by appt only ▪ Grappa, olive oil, preserves ▪ Restaurant: chalkboard menu changes daily (exec chef Bridget Bartelman) ▪ Hiking/mountain biking trails ▪ Horse riding ▪ Fishing ▪ Whale watching flights from own airfield ▪ 5 self-catering cottages ▪ Owner(s) Stanford Hills Estate (Pty) Ltd ▪ Cellarmaster(s)/winemaker(s) Peter Kastner (Apr 2005) ▪ Viticulturist(s) Peter Kastner ▪ 131ha/12ha (ptage, shiraz, chard, sauv) ▪ 60t/4,000cs own label 66% red 34% white ▪ PO Box 1052 Stanford 7210 ▪

info@stanfordhills.co.za ▪ www.stanfordhills.co.za ▪ S 34° 25' 21.4" E 019° 28' 25.7" ▪ **T +27 (0)28-341-0841** ▪ F +27 (0)28-341-0286

It's a life less ordinary for Peter and Jami Kastner on their 131 ha property near Walker Bay, producing indigenous flowers for export, roses for the local market, olives and wine. The tasting room affords a view of the unspoilt surrounds and the comestibles on offer are delicious (the pork pie particularly memorable).

★★★★ **Jacksons Pinotage** ✓ Less substantial than **11**, unpretentious **12** (★★★☆) has pretty red cherry & fynbos perfume, sweet-fruited palate with gentle acidity & soft tannins.

Veldfire ⓐ 🖩 ★★★ **11** pinotage a little dusty from the oak staves used, a little fiery from the massive alcohol (15.7%), with lighter, sweeter fruit than the senior Pinotage - yet undeniably appealing. **Shiraz** NEW ★★★ Extravagant **12** with ultra-ripe black fruit & pepper. Sweet on entry, smooth textured, slightly hot on finish. Could do with more restraint. **Jacksons Chardonnay** ★★★☆ **12** overtly oxidative, yeasty & bready notes to go with ripe citrus. **11** (★★★★) was fresher. **Jacksons Sauvignon Blanc** Next awaited. — CE

Star Hill

Location: Montagu ▪ Map: Klein Karoo & Garden Route ▪ WO: Tradouw Highlands/Montagu ▪ Est 2005 ▪ 1stB 2009 ▪ Tasting & sales daily 9-3 ▪ Closed Dec 25 ▪ Cellar tours by appt ▪ Akkerboom farm stall & restaurant ▪ Facilities for children ▪ Gifts ▪ Farm produce ▪ Conference facilities on Killarney farm ▪ Walks/hikes ▪ Mountain biking ▪ Akkerboom self-catering cottages (www.akkerboomcountrycottages.com) ▪ Owner(s) Grant Hatch & Christopher Palmer Tomkinson ▪ Winemaker(s)/viticulturist(s) Lourens van der Westhuizen (consultant) ▪ 15ha (shiraz, chenin, sauv, viog) ▪ 1,000cs own label 40% red 60% white ▪ PO Box 342 Montagu 6720 ▪ starhill@tradouw.co.za ▪ www.starhillwines.com ▪ S 33° 54' 46.86" E 020° 29' 32.31" ▪ **T +27 (0)28-572-1610** ▪ F +27 (0)28-572-1644

'Tradouw Highlands' is not a Wine of Origin you see much on labels, so these wines should immediately pique the curiosity. They're from vineyards on a plain 723m up the Langeberg Mountains where the conditions, though harsh and dry, are perfect for vines, say owners Grant Hatch and Christopher Palmer Tomkinson. Vinification is by Robertson's Lourens van der Westhuizen.

★★★★ **Shiraz** ✓ Meaty **10** has **09**'s pepper & spice highlights, smooth & full. From single-vineyard fruit (as all these), a good Rhône-style expression of the variety.

★★★★ **Sauvignon Blanc** NEW ✓ **12**'s attraction lies in its lemon blossom, dried grass & dusty pebbles complexity. 14.3% alcohol is fairly bold but balanced, ends on a zesty note.

Chenin Blanc Wild Yeast ✓ ★★★★ Rounded **11** with vanilla & sherry-like notes, for early drinking with food. WO Montagu. **Viognier** Next awaited. — GdB,JP

Stark-Condé Wines

Location/map: Stellenbosch ▪ WO: Jonkershoek Valley/Stellenbosch/Elgin ▪ Est/1stB 1998 ▪ Tasting & sales Mon-Sun 10-4 ▪ Fee R30pp ▪ Closed Good Fri, Dec 25 & Jan 1 ▪ Postcard Café Tue-Sun 9.30-4 (see Restaurants section) ▪ Owner(s) Jonkershoek Cellars (Pty) Ltd ▪ Cellarmaster(s) José Conde (1998) ▪ Winemaker(s) José Conde (1998), with Elizma van Wyngaard (2012) ▪ Viticulturist(s) Andrew Klinck ▪ 250ha/40ha (cabs s/f, merlot, p verdot, shiraz) ▪ 150t/12,000cs own label 80% red 20% white ▪ PO Box 389 Stellenbosch 7599 ▪ info@stark-conde.co.za ▪ www.stark-conde.co.za ▪ www.postcardcafe.co.za ▪ S 33° 57' 13.83" E 018° 54' 37.59" ▪ **T +27 (0)21-861-7700/+27 (0)21-887-3665** ▪ F +27 (0)21-887-4340

The vineyard of the new Field Blend - with four varieties planted in eleven different soil types - is a mirror for the diverse influences shaping this South African front ranker. When patriarch Hans-Peter Schröder ended his seafaring days, he came home to Stellenbosch's Jonkershoek Valley via Tokyo with a Japanese wife and family. Enter son-in-law, Kansas City-born José Conde, a designer quick to learn the craft of fine wine. When José's maiden 1998 Cabernet scored five stars in this guide, we wondered: Would the star keep rising, or fizzle? Developments on the property - including the 'jewel box' tasting room and wife Marie Conde's Postcard Café - have been matched in vineyard and cellar, culminating in such accolades as Most Successful Producer at the 2013 Trophy Show. As we concluded previously: the star's here to stay - and impress.

Three Pines range

★★★★☆ **Cabernet Sauvignon** Extraordinary grace - a reflection of the fine single-vineyard site - defines the house style. Arresting **11** (★★★★★), tailored raspberry fruit folded into lithe texture, with echoing length of flavour. Like **10**, a rare combination of delicacy & power. Unfined/filtered; dabs merlot & petit verdot.

★★★★☆ **Syrah** From elevated home-vineyard noted for elegance. Alluring **11** (★★★★★), ethereal spices & layers of bramble fruit in a svelte body. Complex vinification: cold soak, portion whole-berry ferment, combo wild & commercial yeasts (local & Rhône), 40% new oak 2 years. Builds on success of fine **10**.

Stark-Condé range

★★★★ **Cabernet Sauvignon** Four mainly home-farm cab blocks, with dashes merlot, cab franc & petit verdot; **11** the epitome of Jonkershoek's signature red berry flavour profile, lipsmacking, succulent.

★★★★ **Syrah** Striking pepper spice & ripe, fleshy mulberry fruit grounded by tannin, **11** more accessible in youth than previous, & Three Pines version; no less enjoyable. Stellenbosch WO, as rest of range.

★★★★ **The Field Blend** NEW Roussanne, chenin, viognier & verdelho picked same day ex diverse 2 ha block. Individual **12** is perfumed, with weighty fruit & oak (40%, 5% new) freshened by acidity.

Oude Nektar In abeyance.

Pepin Condé range

★★★★ **Rowey Vineyards Pinot Noir** 🖾 In Pepin range as (Elgin) grapes not home grown, but with Stark-Condé finery & gravitas. **12** deep strawberry flavour layered with elegant tannin.

★★★★ **Chenin Blanc** 🍽🖾 **12** (★★★★) drier, less voluptuous than generously fruited **11**, but fresh & moreish. Stellenbosch dryland bushvines, 40% barrel fermented, 5% new.

Pinot Noir ✓ 🍽 🖾 ★★★★ Elegant cherry charm to earthy grip; delicacy of **12** belies depth of flavour. Enjoyable young, it will reward patience. WO Elgin. **Sauvignon Blanc** 🍽 🖾 ★★★★ Neither green nor tropical, but textured; **12**'s fine natural acidity balances oak richness (20%, old cask). WO Elgin. — DS

■ **Starlette** *see* Allée Bleue Wines

■ **Star Tree** *see* Orange River Wine Cellars

Steenberg Vineyards

Location: Constantia ▪ Map: Cape Peninsula ▪ WO: Constantia/Western Cape/Coastal ▪ Est 1990 ▪ 1stB 1996 ▪ Tasting & sales Mon-Sun 10–6 ▪ Tasting fees: R20pp, R50 for flagship range, waived on purchase ▪ Closed Good Fri & Dec 25 ▪ Cellar tours 11 & 3 daily ▪ Bistro Sixteen82 (see Restaurants section); Catharina's at Steenberg ▪ Steenberg Hotel & Spa; conferences; world-class golf course, walking trail ▪ Extensive merchandising area ▪ Annual festivals: Constantia Fresh (Feb), Spring it on Constantia (end Oct) ▪ Conservation area ▪ Owner(s) Graham Beck Enterprises ▪ Cellarmaster(s) JD Pretorius (Mar 2009) ▪ Vineyard manager(s) Johann de Swardt ▪ 60ha (merlot, nebbiolo, shiraz, sauv, sem) ▪ 312t/70,000cs own label 40% red 60% white ▪ WIETA ▪ PO Box 224 Steenberg 7947 ▪ info@steenbg.co.za ▪ www.steenberg-vineyards.co.za ▪ S 34° 4' 17.0" E 018° 25' 31.1" ▪ **T** +27 (0)21-713-2211 ▪ F +27 (0)21-713-2201

First farmed as 'Swaaneweide' in 1682 – three years before near neighbour, the iconic Groot Constantia – Steenberg's modern wine incarnation started when Johannesburg Consolidated Investments bought the prime Constantia land and began planting vineyards in 1990. A luxury golf course, premium housing estate and cellar followed, and Steenberg blazed onto the South African wine stage as a serious protagonist of sauvignon blanc in the mid-90s. After a spell in the Shamwari Holdings portfolio, operations came under the wing of Graham Beck, already an established premium wine brand, in 2005. Some corporate bedding down complete, the team is replanting the original sauvignon and semillon vines, and embracing the late Graham Beck's vision of a synergy between food and wine, reconceptualising the flagship Catharina's Restaurant – cleaner lines, lighter fare, more relaxed – amongst the diverse hospitality offering here.

Steenberg Vineyards range

★★★★ **Merlot** 🖾 Unequivocal **11** (★★★★) brims with trademark minty character that permeates its medium structure; more overt & less refined than **10**, will still be loved by many.

★★★★ **Nebbiolo** 🖾 Deceptively pale, outstanding **11** blossoms to show deliciously ripe & savoury sour cherry flavours given definition by firm tannin & acidity associated with the variety. Fabulous with food.

★★★★ **Shiraz** 🌿 Beguiling **11** elegant & expressive, with plenty of spice & earthiness in its smooth texture. Mediumweight, there's no threat of taste fatigue.

★★★★☆ **Catharina** 🌿 Selection of best of vintage; perfumed eucalyptus in powerful yet graceful blend. **11** (★★★★) compact merlot fruit lifted by 31% cab (plus splash shiraz), shade off **09**. No **10**.

★★★★ **Sauvignon Blanc** 🍴 🌿 Combination of fresh minerality & gravitas derived from lees-ageing & oak-fermented semillon component; **13** (★★★★) is stylish but lacks penetration of fabulously vibrant **12**.

★★★★ **The Black Swan Sauvignon Blanc** NEW 🌿 Replaces fabled Reserve bottling & contains 60% of original low-yielding Block 28, giving backbone to more vigorous grassy fruit ex younger vines; **12** cool-climate racy style filled out by subtle oak (10%) & lees-ageing.

★★★★☆ **Semillon** **12** (★★★★) shows the texture of barreled semillon, but not as rich, complex & weighty as **11**; usual minerality & savoury acidity keep the focus though.

★★★★☆ **Magna Carta** 🌿 Sauvignon's pristine layered herbaceous fruit & 40% semillon's richness perfectly combine with steely acidity & stony minerality in very fine **11**. Less aggressive than previous; eminently drinkable on release but will reward ageing. Oaked 9 months, 41% new.

★★★★☆ **John Loubser CWG Auction Reserve 'Thirteen'** NEW 🍴 🌿 GM John Loubser's CWG bottling of equal semillon ex Block 13A & Block 13B sauvignon, at auction in 2013! Co-fermented in older oak, aged 6 months at low 10°C; **11** complex, integrated, unfurling waxy patina, delicious zest on finish.

★★★★ **1682 Pinot Noir MCC** 🌿 Fragrant, beautifully textured dry rosé bubbly. Plush **10** (★★★★★) strikingly complex, glides ahead of less lavish **09**. Widely sourced grapes.

★★★★ **1682 Chardonnay MCC** ✓ 🌿 Blanc de blancs sparkler in fresh, crisp, lighter style. **12** with green apple & citrus zing tempered a year on lees; dry, refreshing, a super aperitif. WO W Cape.

Echo Red Blend 🍴 🌿 ★★★ Muscular **11** blend cab, cab franc & merlot offers grip at mealtime. WO Coastal. **Sphynx Chardonnay Barrel Fermented** 🍴 🌿 ★★★ **13** candied peel character, more charming than serious. Bought-in grapes (WO W Cape). **Rattlesnake Sauvignon Blanc Barrel Fermented** 🍴 🌿 ★★★ Wooded portion & dash semillon add dimension to lightly fruited **13** preview, acidity focuses brisk finish. **Sauvignon Blanc-Semillon** Occasional release. Discontinued: **Sauvignon Blanc Reserve**.

Klein Steenberg range

> **Cabernet Sauvignon** ☺ 🍴 🌿 ★★☆ Accessible **11**'s juicy fruit makes easy everyday quaffing.

Cabernet Sauvignon-Merlot-Cabernet Franc NEW 🍴 🌿 ★★★ Sturdy wood & firm cassis fruit leavened by merlot's succulence, **11** for export only. **Rosé** NEW 🍴 🌿 ★★ Raspberry-tinged **13**, from shiraz, modest & dry. This range WO W Cape. **Sauvignon Blanc** 🍴 🌿 ★★ Light **13** with splash of fruity colombard. — DS

■ **Steenbok** *see Riebeek Cellars*
■ **Steenhuis** *see Wine-of-the-Month Club*
■ **Steenrust** *see Stellenrust*
■ **STELL** *see Stellenrust*

Stellar Winery ▮🍷

Location: Vredendal ▪ Map: Olifants River ▪ WO: Western Cape ▪ Est 2000 ▪ 1stB 2001 ▪ Tasting & sales Mon-Fri 8–5 ▪ Closed all pub hols ▪ Cellar tours by appt ▪ Owner(s) Rossouw family, Stellar Empowerment Trust & others ▪ Cellarmaster(s) Berty Jones (Oct 2008) ▪ Winemaker(s) Klaas Coetzee (Aug 2010) & Mauritius Naude ▪ Viticulturist(s) Klaas Coetzee ▪ ±68ha/Stellar Farming & ±149ha/Independent organic producers (cab, merlot, ptage, ruby cab, shiraz, chenin, chard, muscat d'A, sauv) ▪ 11,900t ▪ Other export brands: African Star, Firefly, Ithemba, Moonlight Organics, Natural Star, Running Duck, Sunshine Organics, Green Drake ▪ Brands for clients: Ilula Gepa, La Place, Usapho ▪ Control Union (organic certification), Fair for Life (fairtrade) ▪ PO Box 4 Klawer 8145 ▪ info@stellarorganics.com ▪ www.stellarorganics.com ▪ S 31° 42′ 24.70″ E 018° 33′ 33.70″ ▪ **T +27 (0)82-317-6494** ▪ +27 (0)86-635-1968

Currently the world's largest producer of no-sulphur-added wines, this Fairtrade-accredited organic winery in new premises just outside Vredendal is 'part of the local community in all its diversity', says marketing co-ordinator Shelagh de Rosenwerth. Social development projects range from sunhats for fieldworkers to establishing organic vegetable gardens, while good neighbourliness extends to offering storage capacity to other local wineries during harvest. 'A company stands or falls by the people who are part of it,' says Shelagh,

revealing that Stellar workers own 26% of the business. Exciting new plans (following investment by the Industrial Development Corporation of South Africa) include tasting facilities.

Stellar Organic Reserve range

Pinot Noir ⏺ 🍴 🌿 📖 ★★ 'Forest floor' earthiness on austere **11** food wine. **Cabernet Sauvignon-Pinotage** ⏺ 🍴 🌿 📖 ★★★ Cab-led (70%) **11** packed with fruit but also strong tannins, tad foursquare. **Sauvignon Blanc-Semillon** 🍴 🌿 📖 ★★★ **13** reverses varieties on the label to reflect sauvignon dominance. Balanced & satisfying everyday unwooded white.

Stellar Organics range

Pinotage ☺ 🍴 🌿 📖 ★★★ Amiable **13** cherry & char appeal, tasty & easy to drink. **Chardonnay** ☺ 🍴 🌿 📖 ★★★ Improved **13**'s brisk citrus acidity enlivens apple crumble richness from very light oaking. Enjoy well chilled. **Sauvignon Blanc** ☺ 🍴 🌿 📖 ★★★ Bone-dry, moderate alcohol, **13** offers good persistent grassy flavour.

Cabernet Sauvignon 🍴 🌿 📖 ★★★ Country-food partner **13**, firm but ripe & sweet fruit flavours; lightly oak-staved, as most reds unless stated. **Merlot** 🍴 🌿 📖 ★★ Sweet-sour & savoury notes, **13** firm grip for grilled meats. **Shiraz** 🍴 🌿 📖 ★★★ No rough edges on step-up **13**; cherry flavours, light & breezy. **Rosé** 🍴 🌿 📖 ★★ Bracingly fresh & lightly flavoured, dry **13** is mostly colombard, dash pinotage for pinkness. **Chenin Blanc** 🌿 Await next. **Chenin Blanc-Sauvignon Blanc** 🍴 🌿 📖 ★★★ **13** drier than previous, floral & bouncy. **Sparkling Extra Dry** ⏺ 🌿 📖 ★★ Frothy, pleasant **12**, good partner (according to winemakers) for oysters or strawberries.

Stellar Organics No-Sulphur-Added

Pinotage ☺ 🍴 🌿 📖 ★★★ Sweet fruit & friendly grip on improved **13**, most generous of the reds but still decently dry.

Cabernet Sauvignon 🍴 🌿 📖 ★★★ Tobacco whiffs, black fruit & gentle tannic bite on easygoing **13**. **Merlot** 🍴 🌿 📖 ★★ Racy acidity on **13** choc-plum mealtime companion. **Shiraz** 🍴 🌿 📖 ★★ **13**'s tannin & acid slightly apart from the fruit, time/food could restore harmony. **Rosé** 🍴 🌿 📖 ★★ Meaty **13** lightly flavoured, zesty dry mouthful. **White** 🍴 🌿 📖 ★ **13** brief appley flavour to drink soonest.

Live-A-Little range

Slightly Sweet & Shameless ☺ 🍴 🌿 📖 ★★★ Grapey colombard stars in flirty **NV**, with the right amount of sweetness to get the party going.

Really Ravishing Red 🍴 🌿 📖 ★★★ Consistent charmer: **NV** gentle cherry fruit; brisk acid lift. **Rather Revealing Rosé** 🍴 🌿 📖 ★★ Latest **NV** zesty dry poolside refresher. **Wildly Wicked White** 🍴 🌿 📖 ★★★ Flowers & fresh-cut grass on appealing **NV**; zip of acidity good with deep-fried seafood.

Heaven on Earth range

★★★★ **Natural Sweet** 🌿 📖 Delicious honey-sweet dessert from air-dried muscat d'Alexandrie, usually older oak fermented but latest is unwooded. Indulgent sweetness brightened by dried apricot acidity in fresh & understated **NV**. — HJ, CvZ

Stellekaya Winery

Location/map: Stellenbosch ▪ WO: Stellenbosch/Western Cape/Elgin ▪ Est 1998 ▪ 1stB 1999 ▪ Tasting, sales & cellar tours Mon-Fri 10–4 ▪ Closed all pub hols; Dec 16 to Jan 2/3 ▪ Private luncheon & wine tasting with winemaker by arrangement (up to 6 pax) ▪ Owner(s) Dave & Jane Lello ▪ Winemaker(s) Ntsiki Biyela (Feb 2004) ▪ Viticulturist(s) Paul Wallace (Jan 2005, consultant) ▪ 23ha/15ha under vine ▪ 12,000cs own label 100% red ▪ Brands for clients: The Grand Beach Café ▪ IPW ▪ PO Box 12426 Die Boord Stellenbosch 7613 ▪ info@stellekaya.co.za ▪ www. stellekaya.co.za ▪ S 33° 56' 27.6" E 018° 50' 47.3" ▪ **T +27 (0)21-883-3873** ▪ F +27 (0)21-883-2536

Stellekaya ('House of Stars') is mainly a red-wine producer. Central to operations is winemaker Ntsiki Biyela, whose journey to get here was financially and culturally arduous. As a bursary student she understands the value of role models, which is why she is on the advisory board of the UK-funded Pinotage Youth Development Academy, focusing on the wine industry.

Premium Eclipse Collection

★★★★ **Merlot** ⊕ Such power in the berry, mint crisp flavours, one almost forgets how well made **08** is. Oak is in careful support, mainly older barrels, to retain the supple sleekness, fruit focus.

★★★★ **Pinot Noir** NEW ✓ Beguiling perfume on **11**, mulberries, chocolate, forest floor followed by the variety's trademark supple elegance. Very nicely made. WO Elgin.

★★★★ **Shiraz** ✓ Piquant red berries & cedar are **09**'s main focus, its youth apparent in the fruit's succulence. Tailored tannins give it a built-in future but it already drinks beautifully.

★★★★ **Orion** ⊕ Flagship cab-led Bordeaux blend. Heaps of concentration in **08**, intense blackcurrants & cigarbox, yet the palate remains juicy, streamlined, with supple tannins.

Cabernet Sauvignon ✓ ★★★★ With a dash of cab franc & half the oak barrels new, **09** improves on **08** (★★★★), showing depths of mellow dark berries & cigarbox, well-crafted oaking. Expect a long future. **Pinotage** ⊕ 🍷 📖 ★★★★ Only partial barrel ageing, which accounts for **10**'s ebullient fruitiness, youthfully vibrant palate appeal. WO Western Cape. **Aquarius** ⊕ ★★★★ Equal cab, merlot, cab franc in **11** shows succulent plums, peppery underbrush tones that add interest; firm but ripe tannins. **Cape Cross** ⊕ ★★★★ Cab domination shows in **08**'s lush blackcurrant, matches dry tannins but even better in a year. **Hercules** ⊕ ★★★★ Mainly sangiovese, dash cab gives **09** black cherry richness dusted with white pepper & the variety's renowned dry tannins. Bring on the food!

Boschetto range

Red ⊕ 🍷 ★★★ Mainly cab in appealing **09** with 3 partners; vibrant blackcurrants juicy counterpoint to oaking. **White** ⊕ 🍷 📖 ★★★★ White peach & fresh pear on exuberant **12**; brisk & breezy for summer enjoyment. — CR

Stellenbosch Hills Wines

Location/map: Stellenbosch ▪ WO: Stellenbosch/Polkadraai Hills ▪ Est 1945 ▪ 1stB 1972 ▪ Tasting & sales Mon-Fri 9–5 Sat/pub hols 10–3 ▪ Fee R10; R40 wine, biltong & droëwors tasting ▪ Closed Good Fri, Dec 25 & Jan 1 ▪ The Tank art gallery ▪ Owner(s) 16 members ▪ Cellarmaster(s) PG Slabbert (Jan 1997) ▪ Winemaker(s) Juan Slabbert (Jan 2009) ▪ Viticulturist(s) Johan Pienaar & Eben Archer (consultants) ▪ 715ha (cab, merlot, ptage, shiraz, chard, chenin, Muscat de Hambourg, sauv) ▪ 8,000t/200,000cs own label 68% red 30% white 2% other ▪ IPW ▪ PO Box 40 Vlottenburg 7604 ▪ info@stellenbosch-hills.co.za ▪ www.stellenbosch-hills.co.za ▪ S 33° 57' 38.2" E 018° 48' 1.8" ▪ **T +27 (0)21-881-3828** ▪ F +27 (0)21-881-3357

There's a wine to please every palate and pocket at this consumer-focused winery. 'Everyone in our rainbow nation is entitled to enjoy the style of wine they like best.' They're spreading this largesse by donating a percentage of sales generated by the popular Polkadraai range to the local Vlottenburg community.

1707 Reserve range

★★★★ **Red** Seriously vinified (100% new oak) & impressive blend shiraz & Bordeaux grapes in **10**. Generous & spicy, with complex layers of violets & juicy dark fruit in better balance with wood than last **08** (★★★★). **White** ★★★★ Chardonnay-dominated **12** showing some richness & complexity in palate laced with vanilla biscuit & dried pear. Elegant blend with crisp finish.

Stellenbosch Hills Cultivar Collection

Sauvignon Blanc ☺ 📖 ★★★ Food-friendly **13** over-delivers with greenpepper & crisp pineapple in fresh, balanced body.

Cabernet Sauvignon 📖 ★★★ More so than previous, **11** robust & dry for mealtime partnering. Dark chocolate, menthol & tobacco on a full body with firm tannins. **Merlot** 🍷 ★★★ Big & spicy braai wine, **10** layered with meaty, mocha & red berry flavours. **Pinotage** ⊕ 📖 ★★★ Tobacco & cedar perfumes, **10** rich dark berries & variety's firm tannins. **Shiraz** 📖 ★★★ Appealing everyday shiraz with trademark smoky leather & dark berry juiciness in **10**. **Chenin Blanc** 📖 ★★ Preview **13** shows leafy kiwifruit notes in spoolside sipper to be enjoyed young. **Muscat de Hambourg** ⊕ 📖 ★★★★ Now vintage-dated, **10** takes this unique-in-SA jerepiko-style fortified dessert to a new level. Eclipses previous **NV** (★★) bottling.

Polkadraai range

Pinotage-Merlot ☺ 📖 ★★★ Mellow mocha & prune tones make **12** a TV watching, undemanding quaffer. Polkadraai Hills WO, as all this range.

Polka Merlot-Shiraz ★★ With touches oak & spice, latest version of **12** 3L pack a step up from most bag-in-box reds. **Polka Sauvignon Blanc** ★★ **13** in 3L BIB an easy, uncomplicated sipper with floral wafts. **Chenin Blanc-Sauvignon Blanc** **13** tank sample to unformed to rate. **Pinot Noir Rosé Sparkling** ★★☆ Lively mousse, floral & raspberry sweetness make **13** a happy party wine. — DB

Stellenbosch Ridge

Location/map/WO: Stellenbosch ▪ Est 2004 ▪ 1stB 2005 ▪ Tasting & sales at Guardian Peak (see entry) ▪ Owner(s) Jean Engelbrecht ▪ Winemaker(s) Coenie Snyman (Jan 2005) ▪ Viticulturist(s) Dirkie Mouton (Jan 2010) ▪ 14t/ 3,000cs own label 100% red ▪ IPW ▪ PO Box 473 Stellenbosch 7599 ▪ info@rustenvrede.com ▪ www. stellenboschridge.com ▪ S 34° 0' 40.19" E 018° 50' 31.99" ▪ **T +27 (0)21-881-3881** ▪ F +27 (0)21-881-3000

This sophisticated blend is Rust en Vrede proprietor Jean Engelbrecht's homage to Stellenbosch, 'a unique town [and] birthplace and home to many of South Africa's greatest leaders, intelllectuals, artists, scientists, sportsmen and winemakers'.

★★★★☆ **Stellenbosch Ridge** Classic refinement & polish on **11** 4-way cab-led (63%) Bordeaux-style blend. Blue/black fruit suppleness & generosity backed by structure, concentration & inky cocoa depth. 18 months French oak, just 40% new, smoothly assimilated. — FM

Stellenbosch University Welgevallen Cellar

Location/map/WO: Stellenbosch ▪ Est 2001 ▪ 1stB 2009 ▪ Tasting Mon-Fri 9-4 ▪ Fee R10pp ▪ Closed all pub hols, Dec 25-Jan 10 ▪ Owner(s) Stellenbosch University ▪ Cellarmaster(s)/winemaker(s) Riaan Wassüng (Jan 2004) ▪ Viticulturist(s) Vaatjie Jacobs (Jan 1973) ▪ 11ha/10ha (cab, ptage, shiraz, chard, sauv) ▪ 4,600cs own label 68% red 32% white ▪ Department of Viticulture & Oenology Private Bag X1 Matieland 7602 ▪ winesales@sun.ac.za, rfw@sun.ac.za ▪ http://academic.sun.ac.za/viti_oenol/ ▪ S 33° 56' 22.38" E 018° 52' 1. 92" ▪ **T +27 (0)21-808-2925/+27 (0)83-622-6394**

In the premises where where Abraham Perold crossed pinot noir and hermitage (cinsaut) to create pinotage in the 1920s, Stellenbosch University oenology students today still learn their winecraft. Respect for tradition is an important part of this, the commercial label, as is value for money in the current climate.

Die Laan range

Rector's Reserve Occasional release. **Pinotage** ④ ★★★★ Pleasingly styled **10** has bright fruit & fine acid backbone. Oaking, almost half new, lends seriousness. **Cape Blend** ④ ★★★★ Well-constructed, ripe **10** from cab & pinotage with splash petit verdot is appetisingly fresh & savoury. **Rosé** NEW Not tasted, like **Chardonnay. Sauvignon Blanc** ④ ▦ ★★★ **12** tank sample was unsettled but showed typical crisp herbaceousness when last tasted. **Viognier** Await new.

Maties range

Rooiplein Await new. — IM

Stellenbosch Vineyards

Location/map: Stellenbosch ▪ Est 2004 ▪ Tasting & sales Mon–Fri 9-5.30 Sat 9–5 Sun 10–4 ▪ Fee R10pp ▪ Closed Good Fri, Dec 25 & Jan 1 ▪ The Duck Pond Restaurant (www.duckpond.co.za) ▪ Facilities for children ▪ Weddings/ functions ▪ Owner(s) 200+ shareholders ▪ Winemaker(s) Abraham de Villiers (Dec 2004) & Bernard Claassen (Feb 2005), with Justice Balula (May 2002), Felicity Seholoba (Jan 1993), Rudolph Steenkamp (2013) & Stefan Niemandt (2013) ▪ Viticulturist(s) Francois de Villiers (1998) ▪ 4,400t ▪ 55% red 35% white 10% rosé ▪ ISO 22000, Fairtrade, IPW, WIETA ▪ PO Box 465 Stellenbosch 7599 ▪ info@stellvine.co.za ▪ www.stellenboschvineyards.co.za ▪ S 33° 59' 26.06" E 018° 46' 2.21" ▪ **T +27 (0)21-881-3870** ▪ F +27 (0)21-881-3102

Formerly The Company of Wine People, Stellenbosch Vineyards' aim to build long-term relationships with global retailers is paying off: its distribution network now covers 66 countries! New MD Eduan Steynberg says a highlight has been partnering with Fairtrade-accredited grape grower Enaleni, UK distributor Enotria and global retailer Tesco to produce a Fairtrade wine for sale exclusively at Tesco. Back home, the company's Welmoed cellardoor has had a makeover, from revamped merchandising to new uniforms for the sales team. Brands Arniston Bay, Credo, Four Secrets, Versus and Welmoed are listed separately.

Stellendrift - SHZ Cilliers/Kuün Wyne ♀

Location/map: Stellenbosch ▪ WO: Stellenbosch/Western Cape ▪ Est 1995 ▪ 1stB 1996 ▪ Tasting, sales & cellar tours by appt ▪ Owner(s) Fanie Cilliers (SHZ Cilliers/Kuün Wines) ▪ Cellarmaster(s)/winemaker(s)/viticulturist(s) Fanie Cilliers (Nov 1995) ▪ 11,600cs own label 90% red 10% white ▪ PO Box 6340 Uniedal 7612 ▪ fcilliers@vodamail.co.za ▪ www.stellendrift.co.za ▪ S 33° 58' 54.92" E 018° 46' 15.91" ▪ **T +27 (0)21-887-6561/+27 (0)82-372-5180** ▪ F +27 (0)21-887-6561

Wine's in Stellenbosch-based Fanie Cilliers' blood – his forebears were French vignerons before they fled to the Cape in 1700; by 1709 they had 8,000 vines under cultivation. 'More mature, softer wines, competitively priced' is the goal of the man whose perfect wine moment is simply to be inside a maturation cellar.

Stellendrift range

Reserve Cabernet Sauvignon Await next, as for **Merlot-Cabernet Sauvignon Blitz**, **Cape Huguenot Merlot-Pinotage**, **Giant Sauvignon Blanc**. **Josué Merlot** 🗐 ★★★ Was just 'Merlot'. Improved **10**'s leafiness toned down by juicy pomegranate & berry fruit. **Kruispad Pinotage** ⊕ 🗐 ★★★ When last tasted, **05** was earthy & herbal, with integrated alcohol & firm tannins which should have softened by now. **VOC Syrah** ⊕ 🗐 ★★★★ White pepper & violets on improved **09**, 15% alcohol held in check by perfumed fruit, fresh acid & sweet oak aroma. **Rosa Rosaceae Red Select** NEW ★★★ For current drinking, **06** tastily marries cab's cranberry freshness & merlot's plummy fruit. **Cape White Savour** 🗐 ★★★ Chenin, sauvignon combo **12** nicely vinous, has pleasing 'oystershell' minerality. Drink soon.

Cilliers Cellars range

De Reijgersdaal Cabernet Sauvignon Await next, like **Elizabeth Couvret Merlot**. **Jacko's Pinotage-Cabernet Sauvignon** ⊕ ★★ **05** no spring chicken, yet when reviewed still juicy & accessible, toffee scent & sweet berry taste.

De Oude Opstal range

Cabernet Sauvignon Reserve ⊕ ★★★ Blackberry & dried fruit on earthy **05**, oak was still obvious when last we tasted. **Merlot-Cabernet Sauvignon** ⊕ ★★★ Previously we noted **04** as leaner, with herbal notes, best enjoyed soon. — HJ

Stellenrust 🍷🍽☕🏛📷

Location/map/WO: Stellenbosch ▪ Est/1stB 1928 ▪ Tasting & sales Mon-Fri 10–5 Sat 10–3 ▪ Bottelary property: tasting by appt only ▪ Closed Ash Wed, Easter Fri-Mon, Ascension Day, Dec 25/26 & Jan 1 ▪ Cellar tours by appt ▪ Farm-style platters & pre-arranged lunches/dinners ▪ BYO picnic ▪ Tour groups ▪ Grape 'stompings' ▪ Gifts ▪ Conferences ▪ Weddings/functions (300+ pax) ▪ Walking/hiking & mountain biking trails ▪ Art exhibition ▪ Owner(s) Stellenrust Family Trust ▪ Cellarmaster(s) Tertius Boshoff (Jan 2004) ▪ Winemaker(s) Tertius Boshoff (Jan 2004), with Christo van Rooyen (Feb 2012) ▪ Viticulturist(s) Kobie van der Westhuizen (Jan 2000) ▪ 500ha (cab, cinsaut, merlot, ptage, shiraz, chard, chenin, muscat d'A, sauv) ▪ 1,700t/300,000cs own label 69% red 30% white 1% rosé + 40,000cs for clients ▪ Other export brands: Steenrust, STELL, Steynsrust, Xaro ▪ Brands for clients: Cape Hill, Embrace, Lion's Pride, Ruyter's Bin, Sabi Sabi private game lodge ▪ HACCP 2005, Fairtrade ▪ PO Box 26 Koelenhof 7605 ▪ info@stellenrust.co.za ▪ www.stellenrust.co.za ▪ S 33° 59' 18.0" E 018° 50' 57.9" (Hberg) S 33° 51' 44.41" E 018° 46' 34.11" (Btlry) ▪ **T +27 (0)21-880-2283** ▪ F +27 (0)21-880-2284

Winemaker Tertius Boshoff and viticulturist Kobie van der Westhuizen are the dynamic duo driving Stellenrust. It's one of the Cape's larger family estates – with half of the 250-odd hectares of vines spread over Stellenbosch's 'Golden Triangle', the other vineyards high on the Bottelary Hills. The home-farm is old (with some pretty venerable vines), but the brand was built from scratch. Says Tertius: 'We started with no money and five barrels. We still don't have money, but eight years later at least we have more barrels.' There's a larger range of wines too: made in classic style – elegant and interesting. And remarkable value.

Super Premium range

★★★★☆ **Cabernet Franc** NEW ✓ 📖 The most elegant of grapes suits the house style. Delicate dry-leaf fragrance, with spice, tobacco & subtle red fruit on **10**. But not without force. Fresh acidity, firm but shapely tannins, give a supple, superior austere element. Should only grow with 5+ years in bottle.

★★★★ **Old Bushvine Cinsaut** NEW ✓ 🗐 📖 Bright, light-feeling **11**. Subtly intense red-fruit untrammelled by older oak. Supple, easy tannins & fresh acid unobtrusively shape it all. Delicious; should keep.

★★★★ **Cornerstone Pinotage** 📖 Almost pinot noir-like perfume on **10**, off old bushvines, leads to charming balance of sweet generosity & elegance, never jammy; the forceful tannins could do with bottle-age.

★★★★ **Peppergrinder's Shiraz** 📖 1952 vines give wild berry note & white pepper, spice aromas in **10**. Subtle flavours, refined - almost austere tannins needing time. Great vintage **09** (★★★★★) more aromatic.

★★★★ **Timeless** ✓ Cab-based blend with merlot & cab franc. **10** fresh, well balanced & lively, offering cool blackcurrant, cedar & tobacco. Good dry finish. Needs time to blossom. **09** (★★★★★) more intense.

★★★★ **Barrel Fermented Chardonnay** ✓ 📖 Tight, youthful **12** starts with note of butterscotch, but the lingering finish emphasises lemon-curd. Some pure-fruited, stony intensity on balanced, modestly rich palate.

★★★★☆ **48 Barrel Fermented Chenin Blanc** ✓ 📖 Name indicates vine age. Long, slow barrel ferment & botrytis addition enrich **12** (★★★★★), but oak & honeyed sweetness are subtle influences on the pure molten fruit. Persuasively structured & mouthwatering; endless finish. More complex & fascinating than **11**.

★★★★ **Chenin d'Muscat Noble Late Harvest** ④ Old chenin & muscat vineyards yield a light & vivacious elixir in **09**. Gentle apricot, almond & hint of perfume, subtly oaked. Delightful!

JJ Handmade Picalot 📖 ★★★★ As name hints, blends pinotage, cab, merlot. **10** has interest enough, but a little awkwardly balanced between sweet ripe fruit, drying tannins & big acid. **09** (★★★★) finer.

Premium range

Cabernet Sauvignon ✓ 📖 📖 ★★★★ Cedar & fynbos jostle with dark berries on **11**. Modest in the best sense; unshowy, approachable but quite serious-minded. **Merlot** 📖 📖 ★★★ Choc-mint on **11** has bright red fruit but a very strong tannin & acid structure making it rather lean & severe. **Pinotage** ✓ 📖 📖 ★★★☆ Clean fruity & savoury aromas on pleasing, ripe **12**, with an earthy edge. Easygoing & unshowy, but firmly built & serious enough. **Shiraz** ✓ 📖 📖 ★★★★ **11** a good example of the house's dry, elegant style without losing the attraction of fresh berry fruit. Sensitive, restrained oaking, as elsewhere in this range. **Simplicity** ✓ 📖 📖 ★★★☆ Shiraz takes on juicier fruit (complemented by cedar, tobacco notes) from minor partners cab & merlot in fresh **12**. **11** sold out untasted. **Chardonnay** ✓ 📖 📖 ★★★★ As usual, creamy pear & lime characters on lightly oaked, deft, balanced **13**. Quietly forceful & satisfying. **Chenin Blanc** ✓ 📖 📖 ★★★★ Chenin almost an estate speciality. **13**, radiant with fresh fruit; full, ripe, just-dry & intense but also mouthwatering. Very light oaking. Lengthy finish. Even ups **12** (★★★★). **Sauvignon Blanc** ✓ 📖 📖 ★★★★ From exuberant aromas to succulent finish, this racy **13** is packed with tangy flavour.

Kleine Rust range

Pinotage Rosé ☺ 📖 📖 ★★★ Nice partridge-eye colour on just-off-dry **13**, tangy & lightly fruity. **White** ☺ 📖 📖 ★★★ Forward **13** chenin/sauvignon full of flavour; softly off-dry but piquant. **Semi-Sweet** ☺ 📖 📖 ★★★☆ Scented, flavoursome **13** chenin/sauvignon blend; not heavy or cloying.

Red 📖 📖 ★★ Ripely fruity unoaked **12** blend, juicy but awkward. Fairtrade certified, as all except Semi-Sweet. — TJ

Stellenzicht Vineyards

Location/map/WO: Stellenbosch ▪ Est 1982 ▪ 1stB 1989 ▪ Tasting & sales Mon-Fri 9–5 Sat/Sun 10–4 ▪ Fee R25 ▪ Closed Good Fri, Dec 25 & Jan 1 ▪ Cellar tours by appt ▪ Owner(s) Lusan Premium Wines ▪ Winemaker(s) Guy Webber (Oct 1998), with Nataleé Botha (Aug 2010) ▪ Viticulturist(s) Quintus van Wyk ▪ 228ha/99ha (cabs s/f, malbec, merlot, p verdot, ptage, shiraz, chard, sauv, sem, viog) ▪ 795t/40,000cs own label 85% red 15% white ▪ BRC, HACCP, WIETA ▪ PO Box 104 Stellenbosch 7599 ▪ info@stellenzicht.co.za ▪ www.stellenzicht.co.za ▪ S 33° 59' 50.0" E 018° 51' 59.8" ▪ **T** +27 (0)21-880-1103 ▪ **F** +27 (0)21-880-1107

On the northern slopes of the Helderberg, Stellenzicht lives up to its name having a good view of the town of Stellenbosch. The area is unofficially known as the Golden Triangle, thanks to its ideal soils and climate for quality winegrowing. International banker and financier Hans-Joachim Schreiber purchased the property in 1981, and some 18 years later he and the forerunner of Distell formed Lusan Premium Wines, with Stellenzicht among its five properties. Long-time winemaker Guy Webber and his team have gained a name for pinotage, adding to their recognition as significant producers of both semillon and shiraz.

Stellenzicht Specialities range

★★★★ **Syrah** No waiting necessary for **07**, with savoury worn-in leather character & briskly dry finish. **Rhapsody** ★★★★ Boldly built pinotage-shiraz blend, **10** not shy in oaking either (all-new, 31 months). Dense, with sweetish spice & mint flavours. **Sémillon Reserve** Await next.

Cellarmaster's Release range

Petit Verdot (No Added Sulphites) ⓘ ★★★ Noble rusticity about 09. Concentrated dark fruit, slightly tart acidity, firm tannins. **Pinotage (No Added Sulphites)** ⓘ ★★★ Intense black cherry, malty note on 09. Rich & full, soft tannins, apparent sweetness due to 16%+ alcohol. **Chardonnay (No Added Sulphites)** ⓘ 🍽 ★★★ 10 has hint of citrus alongside yeasty, almost malty tones; fresh acidity lends verve.

Golden Triangle range

★★★★ **Pinotage** ⓥ Very soft, subdued mulberry fruit constrained by dominant sweet oak flavours & big 14.9% alcohol on 11 (★★★☆). Lacks acidity, structure of 10.

Cabernet Sauvignon ⓘ 🍽 ★★★ Herbal note along with dark fruit, malty note to awkward 10. **Shiraz** ★★★ Solid sweet red fruit, spice with hint vanilla on 10. Gentle tannins, assertive acid rather more bracing.

Sauvignon Blanc 🍽 ⓥ ★★★ Previewed 13 has modest tropical tones; may better integrate with racy acid once bottled. — AL

Sterhuis

Location/map: Stellenbosch ▪ WO: Bottelary ▪ Est 1980 ▪ 1stB 2002 ▪ Tasting, sales & cellar tours by appt ▪ Closed Christian hols ▪ Facilities for children ▪ Conservation area ▪ Owner(s) Kruger family ▪ Winemaker(s) Johan Kruger ▪ 100ha/40ha under vine ▪ 300t/12,000cs own label 25% red 75% white ▪ PO Box 131 Koelenhof 7605 ▪ johan@sterhuis.co.za ▪ www.sterhuis.co.za ▪ S 33° 54' 43.1" E 018° 46' 4.2" ▪ **T +27 (0)83-411-0757** ▪ F +27 (0)21-906-1195

Stellenbosch's Bottelary Hills are home to the Kruger family farm, whose name (literally 'Star House') was given by early colonists because it appears as if Venus rises above it. The boutique winery, into its second decade, continues to reflect winemaker Johan's and father André's focus on restrained and elegant top-end wines, including a standout chardonnay, supported by an appealing entry level.

★★★★ **Cabernet Sauvignon** ⓘ Good varietal character & freshness on 07 tasted a few years back.

★★★★☆ **Astra Red** ⓘ Some years back, 06 (★★★★) from cab & merlot was a bit lean, with modest fruit.

★★★★☆ **Chardonnay Barrel Selection** ⓥ Consistently a serious offering; 11 has riper yellow peach aromas, with inviting toasty oak spice, supported by a rounded mouthfeel & firm oak tannins. Earthy undertone adds interest, while acid backbone keeps fleshy parts in check.

★★★★ **Chenin Blanc** ✓ 🍽 ⓥ 11 from 40+ year old vines, their low yield giving a palate-driven wine with delicate aromas. Focused acidity & integrated oak, with clean dry end. Fine food wine.

★★★★ **Sauvignon Blanc** 🍽 ⓥ Two tasted: 12 more demure with seabreeze & quince, while 13 expresses delicate jasmine, ripe granadilla & lime. Both share a focused long & dry palate, with 15% barrelled component adding to complexity & length. 13 has fresher & brighter acidity.

★★★★☆ **Astra White** A third each of best barrels chenin, sauvignon & chardonnay. Oak spice & white chocolate lead to toasty, sweet-fruited & vanilla-rich 09. Bold in flavour & aroma with loads of oak tones needing to meld. Palate cleansed by tart orange peel & fresh lemon/lime zing.

★★★★ **Blanc de Blancs Méthode Cap Classique** ⓘ 09 sparkling from chardonnay. Ultra-dry, with fine mousse, rounded mouthfeel & integrated oak; continues to an almond/apple finish.

Merlot-Cabernet Sauvignon ☺ 🍽 ⓥ ★★★ Older oak adds serious tone to dry, approachable 10.

Merlot ★★★★ Sour plum intro on 09 followed by structured, firm palate requiring time to soften tannic austerity. In youth, best to decant. **Unwooded Chardonnay** ✓ 🍽 ⓥ ★★★★ White stonefruit & blossoms on inviting 13; ends fruity & dry, with good lingering acid freshness. **Chenin Blanc-Viognier** ✓ 🍽 ⓥ ★★★★ Inviting clean white peach & tropical intro on 12 followed by delicate spice complexity, fine fruit on good dry end. Not overblown - subtle oaking & modest alcohol. — JP

Stettyn Cellar

Location/map: Worcester ▪ WO: Western Cape ▪ Est 1964 ▪ 1stB 1984 ▪ Tasting & sales Mon-Thu 8–5 Fri 8-4.30 Sat (Oct-Mar) 10-1 ▪ Closed all pub hols ▪ Cellar tours from 1.30-4 by appt ▪ Lunch by arrangement (24 hrs in advance); or BYO picnic ▪ Facilities for children ▪ Vineyard tours R200pp ▪ Stettyn music evenings (±Oct) ▪ Owner(s) 4 major producers (3 family owned) ▪ Cellarmaster(s) Albie Treurnicht (Nov 2000) ▪ Winemaker(s) Albie Treurnicht (Nov 2000), with JM Crafford (Nov 2012) ▪ Viticulturist(s) Pierre Snyman (Vinpro) ▪ 400ha (cab, merlot, ptage, shiraz, chard, chenin, sauv) ▪ 7,500t/19,000cs own label 25% red 75% white + 6.1m L bulk ▪ Brands for clients: FirstCape; Felicité; The Griffin Range ▪ ARA, BEE, HACCP, IPW ▪ PO Box 1520 Worcester

6849 ▪ info@stettyncellar.co.za ▪ www.stettyncellar.co.za ▪ S 33° 52' 14.8" E 019° 22' 2.3" ▪ **T +27 (0)23-340-4220** ▪ F +27 (0)23-340-4220

Cellarmaster Albie Treurnicht says these are exciting times: they've completed a new R10 million red wine cellar, are exporting bulk wine to Germany, and have introduced a new bottled-wine range called Griffin specifically for Johannesburg. Chinese exports, buoyed by the exchange rate, are forging ahead.

Signature Reserve range

Shiraz-Cabernet Sauvignon 🖼 ★★★★ More serious styling than other ranges, **11** enticing bacon, smoke & pepper from shiraz (65%), cab's leafy notes; restrained oak detail from 22 months older barrels.

The Griffin range NEW

Pinot Grigio 🍴 🖼 ★★★ White stonefruit nuances on **13**, appealingly lean & lightish for sipping solo or with seafood. **Sauvignon Blanc** 🍴 🖼 ★★★ Greenpepper, fig & khaki bush nose & palate on patio staple **13**.

Millstone range

Stone Red ☺ 🍴 🖼 ★★★ Friendly & fruity for fireside fun. Cab with splashes cab franc, souzão, petit verdot & ruby cab in previewed **NV**. **Stone White** NEW ☺ 🍴 🖼 ★★★ Peach, apricot on zesty, nicely dry **NV**; easy-going but unusual blend chenin (75%), nouvelle, muscat d'Alexandrie.

Discontinued: **Chenin Blanc, Sauvignon Blanc**. — DB,CvZ

■ **Steynsrust** *see* Stellenrust
■ **Steytler** *see* Kaapzicht Wine Estate
■ **Stilfontein** *see* Eerste Hoop Wine Cellar

Stoep

Est/1stB 2001 ▪ Tasting, sales & tours by appt ▪ Owner(s) Zelpy 1023 (Pty) Ltd: 3 shareholders Gerrit Mars (SA), Sven Haefner (Swiss) & Daniel Hofer (Swiss) ▪ Cellarmaster(s)/winemaker(s) André Liebenberg (Romond) & Gerrit Mars ▪ 50% red 50% white ▪ gerritmars@mweb.co.za ▪ **T +27 (0)82-352-5583**

'It's the same old story,' says asset manager and brand co-owner Gerrit Mars between trips. Clearly the frequent flyer barely had a spare moment to sit on his own stoep and enjoy a glass of his red Bordeaux-style blend, vinified by André Liebenberg of Romond Vineyards, let alone bottle a chardonnay last year.

■ **Stonedale** *see* Rietvallei Wine Estate

Stonehill

Location/map/WO: Stellenbosch ▪ Est 1990 ▪ 1stB 2003 ▪ Tasting by appt ▪ Owner(s)/vineyard manager(s) Lorna Hughes ▪ Winemaker(s) Mark Carmichael-Green ▪ 4ha/3.2ha (cab, shiraz) ▪ 70% red 30% white ▪ PO Box 612 Stellenbosch 7599 ▪ llhughes@telkomsa.net ▪ S 33° 54' 4.8" E 018° 48' 56.4" ▪ **T +27 (0)73-420-3300** ▪ F +27 (0)21-865-2740

Tucked away in Stellenbosch's Devon Valley is Lorna Hughes' small vineyard, where, with husband Dave (an adviser to this guide), she indulges her passions for wine, rescue dogs and hiking. The winemaking is very hands-on, with interesting variations like her barrel-aged rosé, produced in boutique-scale volumes.

Bristle Red 🟡 ★★★ Modestly oaked, juicy **08** nicely structured & balanced cab-shiraz blend. **Dry Cabernet Sauvignon Rosé** ✓ 🍴 🖼 ★★★ Classy, lightly oaked **12** goes where few other rosés do: varietal character & body with real refreshment. Well priced, too. **Bristle White** 🟡 🍴 🖼 ★★★ Solid, ripe, wooded viognier, **11**'s peachy fruit prevails over lees creaminess & oak spices. Generous & appealing. —GdB

Stone Ridge Wines

Location/WO: Paarl ▪ Map: Paarl & Wellington ▪ Est 2002 ▪ 1stB 2003 ▪ Tasting by appt only ▪ Winemaker(s) Bertus Fourie (Jan 2010, consultant) ▪ Viticulturist(s) Jan Eksteen (2002) ▪ 300ha (cab, ptage, shiraz, chard, chenin, sauv) ▪ 20t/2,400cs own label 50% red 50% white ▪ PO Box 7046 Northern Paarl 7623 ▪ stoneridge@uitkijk.co.za ▪ S 33° 34' 19.72" E 018° 52' 45.48" ▪ **T +27 (0)82-324-8372** ▪ F +27 (0)21-869-8071

The Eksteen family have been growing wine grapes at their Voor Paardeberg property for six generations. With a passion for people, wine 'and everything in-between', viticulturist Jan Eksteen dreams of the day when his hard work pays off and Stone Ridge is a household name for quality and value.

Eksteen Family Vineyards Reserve range

★★★★☆ **Chenin Blanc Bush Vine 1977** ⓔ 🍴 Tropical notes & some pear on **10** from bushvines. Lees-ageing & sensitive oaking added complexity & depth to candied orange conclusion.

Shiraz ⓔ ★★★★ Barrel sample **10** from Paarl single-vineyard is ripe & smooth, with well-hidden 14.5% alcohol, integrated tannins. Black plum & pepper appeal.

Stone Ridge range

Cabernet Sauvignon Await next of this, **Merlot**, **Shiraz**, **Chardonnay** & **Sauvignon Blanc**. — CvZ

■ **Stone Road** see Louisvale Wines
■ **Stones in the Sun** see Dunstone Winery

Stonewall Wines

Location: Somerset West ▪ Map: Helderberg ▪ WO: Stellenbosch ▪ Est 1828 ▪ 1stB 1997 ▪ Tasting & sales by appt Mon-Fri 10–5 Sat 10–1 ▪ Closed Easter Fri-Sun, Dec 25/26 & Jan 1 ▪ Refreshments by appt ▪ Helderberg wine festival ▪ Owner(s) De Waal Koch ▪ Cellarmaster(s) Ronell Wiid (Jan 2000, consultant) ▪ Winemaker(s) De Waal Koch (Jan 2000) ▪ Viticulturist(s) De Waal Koch (Jun 1984) ▪ 90ha/70ha (cabs s/f, merlot, ptage, shiraz, chard, pinot gris, sauv) ▪ 300t/4,000cs own label 80% red 20% white ▪ PO Box 5145 Helderberg 7135 ▪ stonewall@mweb.co.za ▪ S 34° 1' 59.0" E 018° 49' 14.6" ▪ **T +27 (0)21-855-3675** ▪ F +27 (0)21-855-2206

The cellar behind the thick perimeter wall of this Helderberg property was built in 1828. Boutique owner-winemaker De Waal Koch, despite the tough economy, has taken care to renovate the white-gabled structure without sacrificing the 'olden times' atmosphere or the excellent original facilities, such as cement vats.

Cabernet Sauvignon ✓ 📷 ★★★★ Appealing ripe, concentrated dark berry fruit & milk chocolate in **11**. Firm tannin needs time to relax. **Rubér** ⓔ 📷 ★★★☆ Merlot, cabernet blend **10** displays juicy black fruit with firm dusty tannins in balance. A food wine. **Chardonnay** ✓ 📷 ★★★★ Pie crust & lemon curd flavours on **12** are generous & rounded, with a zingy citrus end. Over-delivers. **Valle Felice** ⓔ ★★★ Barrel-aged fortified dessert from merlot. **09** is light, fruity with a spirity grip. Serve chilled with soft cheese. — WB

StoneyCroft

Location/map/WO: Stellenbosch ▪ Est 2000 ▪ 1stB 2001 ▪ Tasting by appt ▪ Owner(s) John Stone ▪ Winemaker(s) Danie Steytler (2001), with Danie Steytler jnr (both Kaapzicht) ▪ Viticulturist(s) Gary Probert (Jan 2010, consultant) ▪ 4ha/3.5ha (cab, shiraz) ▪ 20t/3,000cs own label 100% red ▪ PO Box 239 Koelenhof 7605 ▪ john@stoneycroft.co.za ▪ www.stoneycroft.co.za ▪ S 33° 53' 24.41" E 018° 48' 19.78" ▪ **T +27 (0)21-865-2301/+27 (0)82-801-1804** ▪ F +27 (0)21-865-2360

The tiny shiraz vineyard on John Stone's Devon Valley farm, vinified by veteran vintners the Steytlers of nearby Kaapzicht, has been delivering the goods but is due for replacement next year. Meanwhile his cabernet, planted in 2011, is 'coming along well', promising its first crop for bottling this year.

★★★★ **Shiraz 09** (★★★★) sweet vanilla bouquet & plump berry palate well controlled by sappy grip & bitter-choc tail; ±15% alcohol perhaps just a little less balanced than **08** & previous. — CvZ

Stony Brook

Location/map: Franschhoek ▪ WO: Franschhoek/Western Cape/Elgin/Coastal ▪ Est 1995 ▪ 1stB 1996 ▪ Tasting by appt ▪ Fee R50 ▪ Sales Mon-Fri 10–5 Sat 10-1; enquire about pub hols ▪ Self-catering cottages ▪ Owner(s) Nigel & Joy McNaught ▪ Winemaker(s) Craig McNaught (2011), with Michael Blaauw (Jan 2008) ▪ Viticulturist(s) Paul Wallace (consultant) ▪ 23ha/14ha (cab, malbec, merlot, mourv, p verdot, pinot, shiraz, tempranillo, chard, sem, viog) ▪ 80t/10,000cs own label 56% red 40% white 4% rosé + 1,400cs for clients ▪ Brands for clients: Elgin Grove ▪ ISO 14001:2003 ▪ PO Box 22 Franschhoek 7690 ▪ info@stonybrook.co.za ▪ www.stonybrook.co.za ▪ S 33° 56' 28.7" E 019° 7' 4.1" ▪ **T +27 (0)21-876-2182** ▪ F +27 (0)86-664-2794

Nigel and Joy McNaught's small Franschhoek winery produces a large array of wines off their multi-varietal vineyards. It testifies to both enthusiasm and small-volume winemaking – fewer than 6,000 bottles of the Ghost Gum cabernet (named after a splendid 150-year-old tree), for example, and that's one of the larger bottlings. Craig McNaught has taken over from father Nigel as chief winemaker. Visitors must now make appointments to allow the family to continue giving the personal, informative tastings on which they pride themselves.

★★★★ **Syrah Reserve** Youthful **10** (★★★★☆) now a seriously styled & packaged Reserve bottling & step up on **09**. Intriguing, beguiling fragrance paves way for deeply spicy fruit gripped by resolute tannins from 28 months in cask; built for the long haul.

★★★★☆ **Ghost Gum** Single-vineyard cab **08** sees all-new oak treatment, altogether in balance with plush, pure red fruit. Surprisingly generous & inviting in youth, but has fruit & structure to develop.

★★★★ **The Max** ✓ Enticingly plush fruit in classy, well constructed cab-led **10** blend with merlot convincingly delicious & thoroughly harmonious. Accessible now, though structured for keeping.

★★★★ **SMV** Shiraz-based with mourvèdre & drop of viognier. Big, bold **09** with savoury tannins from judicious oaking adding shape to overtly spicy richness - the high alcohol a snug fit.

★★★★ **Snow Gum** ⊕ Individual 50/50 mourvèdre/malbec blend, the latter lifting former's earthy, gamey features on **09**. Broad & flavoursome, with a good rumble of chunky tannins. First since **07**.

★★★★☆ **Semillon Reserve** Seriously impressive **09** bottling of best 2 barrels - 3 year oaking evident in golden hue & slightly oxidative style. Broad pithy texture & exotic spiciness call for slow enjoyment with a meal.

★★★★ **Lyle** Elegance & complexity returns with **08**, after simplicity of **07** (★★★★). Persistent, creamy MCC spakling from own chardonnay & Stellenbosch pinot, raised in oak & with an astonishing 58 months on lees.

★★★★ **V on A** Tank sample dessert-style **11** in fine form. Beautifully balanced sweetness & acidity in lusciously rich barrel-fermented & matured viognier. Excellent partner for mature cheeses.

Shiraz ⊕ 🍷 ★★★★ The name, versus 'Syrah', & a hint of sweet oak vanilla reflects modern style of **08**. Big but balanced; straightforward spicy pizzazz. **Camissa** 🍷 ★★★☆ Succulent **10** cab-led blend with spicy shiraz & merlot. Portion new oak firms up flavours with lithe, savoury tannins. **Rosé** 🍷 ★★★★ Await next. **Sauvignon Blanc** 🍷 ★★★★ Engaging, just-dry **12** from Elgin in stylish mode: waves of flavour, bright acidity & minerality, with leesy texture & personality-laden finish. Great improvement on **11** (★★★). **Ghost Gum White** ★★★★ Ambitious **11** more about minerality, texture than fruit in food style. Sauvignon-semillon barrel-fermented blend, sweet & spicy, convincing step-up from **10** (★★★★). WO W Cape, like next. **The 'J'** 🍷 ★★★★ Lovely **11** combines pithy semillon, exotic viognier, both oaked, with sauvignon's freshness to offer sheer drinkability & interest. Discontinued: **Heart Of The Lees Sauvignon Blanc**. — IM

Storm Wines

🍷 **NEW**

Est 2011 ▪ 1stB 2012 ▪ Tasting by appt ▪ Closed Easter Fri/Sun, Ascension day, Dec 25/26 & Jan 1 ▪ Owner(s) Hannes Storm ▪ Winemaker(s)/viticulturist(s) Hannes Storm (Dec 2011) ▪ 3ha (pinot) ▪ 5t/550cs own label 100% red ▪ BWI, IPW, IPW ▪ PO Box 431 Hermanus 7200 ▪ hannes@stormwines.co.za ▪ **T +27 (0)28-312-1121/ +27 (0)82-325-4517**

Storm Wines is the story of two winemaking brothers, two continents and one grape: pinot noir. In Santa Barbara County, California, Ernst Storm since 2006 focuses on small lots from the Santa Rita Hills and Santa Maria Valley. Hannes, winemaker at Hamilton Russell, does likewise in Hemel-en-Aarde and Upper Hemel-en-Aarde (the '12 bottling missed our deadline). The siblings want their wines to express the unique fruit qualities born of their far-flung terroirs.

■ **Stormy Cape** see uniWines Vineyards

Stoumann's Wines

🍷 ☕ 📷

Location: Vredendal ▪ Map: Olifants River ▪ WO: Olifants River/Lamberts Bay ▪ Est 1998 ▪ 1stB 2008 ▪ Tasting, sales & cellar tours Mon-Fri 8-5 Sat by appt ▪ Closed all pub hols ▪ Cheese platters/meals/braai available on request ▪ Tour groups ▪ Farm produce ▪ Conferences ▪ Owner(s)/cellarmaster(s)/winemaker(s) Napoleon Stoumann ▪ Viticulturist(s) CG Stoumann (Jan 2010) ▪ 100ha (cab, merlot, muscadel r/w, ptage, ruby cab, shiraz, chard, chenin, cbard, hanepoot) ▪ 1,040t/4,000cs own label 50% red 40% white 10% rosé + 800,000L bulk ▪ IPW ▪ PO Box 307 Vredendal 8160 ▪ stoumanns@cybersmart.co.za ▪ www.stoumanns.co.za ▪ S 31° 41' 20.5" E 018° 30' 23.3" ▪ **T +27 (0)27-213-2323/+27 (0)83-236-2794** ▪ F +27 (0)27-213-1448

Conservation of the Cape Geometric Tortoise lies close to the heart of owner Napoleon 'Nappies' Stoumann and wife Annalise at their West Coast winery. The critically endangered critters, also known as 'suurpootjies', are to be seen in profusion, well cared for, doing their thing while you sample the Stoumann wines.

Cabernet Sauvignon ⓣ 🅥 ★★ Blackcurrant-infused **10**, nice & supple, slips down easily. **Shiraz** ⓣ 🅥 ★★★ Winter-warming **10**'s tannins are feisty, need time or a meaty accompaniment. **Vin de la Tortue** ⓣ 🅥 ★★★ **10** cab/shiraz combo has fruitcake appeal, is easy to drink. **Rosé Perlé Wine** Await next, also for **Chardonnay**. **Chenin Blanc** ⓣ 🅥 ★★★ Wallet-pleasing **12** preview satisfyingly dry & tangy, with yellow peach fragrance. **Sauvignon Blanc** ⓣ 🅥 ★★★ Cool-grown Lamberts Bay vines deliver bright acidity, fair flavour & complexity at moderate alcohol in pre-bottling **12**. **Hanepoot Jerepigo** ⓣ ★★★ **08** sunripe fortified sweetie offers honeyed ripe apricot, zippy lime acidity. **Red Jerepigo** ⓣ 🅥 ★ Fortified **NV** dessert from red muscadel, some tealeaf character but lacks the style's sweet succulence. — DB,CvZ

Strandveld Wines

Location/WO: Elim ▪ Map: Southern Cape ▪ Est 2002 ▪ 1stB 2003 ▪ Tasting, sales & cellar tours Mon-Thu 8–5 Fri 8-4 Sat 10-3 ▪ Closed Good Fri & Dec 25 ▪ Farm produce ▪ BYO picnic ▪ Walks/hikes ▪ Mountain biking ▪ Conservation area ▪ Two self-catering cottages ▪ Owner(s) Strandveld Vineyards & Rietfontein Trust ▪ Winemaker(s) Conrad Vlok (Dec 2004) ▪ Viticulturist(s) Tienie Wentzel (Oct 2009) ▪ 850ha/70ha (pinot, shiraz, sauv, sem) ▪ 246t/24,000cs own label 43% red 57% white ▪ BWI ▪ PO Box 1020 Bredasdorp 7280 ▪ info@strandveld.co.za ▪ www.strandveld.co.za ▪ S 34° 39' 59.2" E 019° 47' 26.8" ▪ **T +27 (0)28-482-1902/+27 (0)28-482-1906** ▪ F +27 (0)28-482-1902/+27 (0)28-482-1906

Another busy year – winemaker Conrad Vlok's 10th at Africa's most southerly vineyards, between Elim and Cape Agulhas – saw planting for phase two of a supply agreement with premier winery La Motte, plans for a Natural Sweet and MCC bubbly, and sustained local marketing. 'Home first' may be their mantra, but Germany is where Strandveld continues to boast its biggest European footprint, a small initial order recently went to Australia, and the US beckons.

Strandveld range

★★★★ **Pinot Noir** NEW 🅥 Violet-scented **10**'s plush berry fruit overlain with meaty notes, savoury spicing. Very satisfying glassful. Obvious but not intrusive grip courtesy deft 40% new oak touch.

★★★★☆ **Syrah** ✓ 🅥 Waves of Rhône-like savoury spice introduce **10**, with dashes grenache, mourvèdre, viognier. Powerful but contained & composed, ends elegantly with a smoked meat nuance & rock salt tang.

★★★★☆ **The Navigator** ✓ 🅥 Rhône-style blend salutes Henry the Navigator, patron of early Portuguese explorers. Shiraz & grenache (57/28) plus mourvèdre, viognier. Enticing **11**'s berry compote mingles with aromatic tobacco, spice & anise; finely tuned, has firm backbone for cellaring courtesy 40% new oak.

★★★★☆ **Sauvignon Blanc Pofadderbos** ✓ 🅥 Standout sauvignon from extreme-sounding 'Puff Adder Bush' single-vineyard. Subtlety & understatement define **12**, ethereal lime, asparagus & white nut nuances in fine & lithe body. Steely purity & persistent farewell.

★★★★☆ **Adamastor** ⓣ 🅥 Stately Bordeaux-style white flagship, slightly more sauvignon (51%) in lean & appealingly austere **11**. As in semillon-led **10** (57%), judicious partly new-oak seasoning. Should improve good few years.

Anders Sparrman Pinot Noir Occasional release.

First Sighting range

Shiraz ☺ 🍷 🅥 ★★★ Downscaled oaking, viognier-only seasoning differentiate this from sibling. **11**, now bottled, peppery scrub & flowers, honest cherry fruit. Juicy & fresh everyday glassful. **Shiraz Rosé** ☺ 🍷 🅥 ★★★ Unlikely combo strawberry shortcake & rosepetal works nicely on dry & spicy **13**.

Pinot Noir 🍷 🅥 ★★★ Toffee & lavender nuances on quince & cherry toned **11**. Though lighter than senior wine, satisfies at a friendly price. **Sauvignon Blanc** 🍷 🅥 ★★★ Generous **12** is nicely built, shows lees-imparted chalkiness, cut-grass & gooseberry interest. Enjoy well chilled. — WB, GdB

■ **String of Pearls** *see* Francois La Garde

Strydom Vintners

Location/WO: Stellenbosch ▪ Est 2012 ▪ 1stB 2009 ▪ Closed to public ▪ Owner(s) Louis & Rianie Strydom ▪ Cellarmaster(s) Rianie Strydom ▪ 8.5ha/6.5ha (cab, merlot, shiraz, sauv, sem) ▪ ±30t/1,000cs own label 50% red 50% white ▪ IPW ▪ PO Box 1290 Stellenbosch 7599 ▪ rianie.strydomvineyards@gmail.com ▪ T +27 (0)21-889-8553

This is an own label by leading husband-and-wife winemakers Louis and Rianie Strydom, both involved independently with prime Helderberg properties Ernie Els and Haskell/Dombeya respectively. Grapes grown on their small Simonsberg estate have gone into established brands to date, and they'll continue to sell off some fruit till they're ready to bottle their entire crop.

Retro ✓ ★★★★ Best wines of vintage determine blend; approachable **11** 50% merlot, equal parts cab, shiraz. Generous, fleshy mouthful of ripe, dark plummy fruit framed by seamless, fine tannins. No **10**. **09** (★★★☆). **The Freshman** 🛢 ★★★ Youthful apple blossom, greengage appeal on **13**. Full of zest & juiciness, with 10% semillon adding balanced weight. — AL

▪ **Stumble Vineyards** see Flagstone Winery
▪ **Suikerbosch** see Zidela Wines
▪ **Suikerbossie Ek Wil Jou Hê** see Boer & Brit

Sumaridge Wines   🍴🍷🥂🏠📷🍵⛷♿

Location: Hermanus ▪ Map: Elgin, Walker Bay & Bot River ▪ WO: Upper Hemel-en-Aarde Valley/Walker Bay ▪ Est 1997 ▪ 1stB 2000 ▪ Tasting & sales daily 10–3 ▪ Fee R25 for groups of 6+, waived on purchase ▪ Closed Easter Fri/Sun, Dec 25/26 & Jan 1 ▪ Seasonal tasting platter options plus kiddies platter, also available (Aug-May) as picnic ▪ Facilities for children ▪ Tour groups ▪ Conferences ▪ Weddings/functions ▪ Luxury self-catering guesthouse ▪ Conservation area ▪ Extensive nature trails ▪ Mountain biking ▪ Bass & fly fishing by arrangement ▪ Owner(s) Simon & Holly Turner-Bellingham ▪ Cellarmaster(s)/vineyard manager(s) Gavin Patterson (Jun 2005) ▪ Winemaker(s) Gavin Patterson (Jun 2005), with Reginald Maphumulo (Jun 2000) ▪ 210ha/42ha (cab f, malbec, merlot, ptage, pinot, shiraz, chard, sauv, sem, viog) ▪ 150t/20,000cs own label 45% red 50% white 5% rosé ▪ IPW ▪ PO Box 1413 Hermanus 7200 ▪ info@sumaridge.co.za ▪ www.sumaridge.co.za ▪ S 34° 22' 1.6" E 019° 15' 18.6" ▪ T +27 (0)28-312-1097 ▪ F +27 (0)86-623-4248

This increasingly impressive Hemel-en-Aarde producer is one of the longest established in the area, apart from the earliest pioneers. Zimbabwe-born Gavin Patterson has been the winemaker and vineyard manager since 2005, learning 'the peculiarities of this region – the land, the climate and its people'. A growing understanding of his vineyards means that, as well as persistently raising quality, he has been able to shift things, as he says, towards wines of individuality, expressive of the location (hence names like Epitome and Maritimus). Another significant move has been towards sustainable farming.

★★★★ Merlot 🛢 🌿 Delicate, youthful **11** - even more restrained than **09** (no **10**). Vanilla-infused plum & cassis aromas lead to firm but unevolved palate. Good potential for further development.

★★★★ Pinot Noir 🛢 Animated but restrained **11** (★★★★★), with a sense of maritime coolness & freshness - modest 13% alcohol helps here. Floral, earthy & red fruit aromas, but the wine still reach to reach full potential, unlike earlier-drinking **10**. Part wild-yeast ferment, part bunch-pressed.

★★★★ Epitome 🌡 Dark-fruited, savoury **09** from pinotage & shiraz (**08** also some merlot). Concentrated & flavourful, with soft tannins & good palate weight, but acidity needs a little time to integrate.

★★★★ Chardonnay 🌿 Rich **11**'s intense fruit, nut aromas lead to appealing, broad palate, with stonefruit & lemon curd added to the flavour equation. Noticeable 14.2% alcohol balanced by fresh acid. Should improve. **10** (★★★★★) tasted ex-tank showed even better few years back.

★★★★ Sauvignon Blanc 🛢 🌿 Vibrant **13** subtle yellow fruit with interwoven nettle & crushed stone. Zesty & thirst-quenching, though with some fullness from lees-ageing.

★★★★ Maritimus 🌿 **11** unusual mix sauvignon, chardonnay & dollops semillon & viognier. Apple, floral aromas lead to tight, mineral palate, uplifting finish. Wild yeast ferment, light oaking. **10** (★★★★) disjointed.

★★★★ The Wayfarer NEW Pinot-driven, salmon-pink **09** MCC bubbly (23% chardonnay) from Elgin. Yeast notes lifted by strawberry, apple, cherry. Bone-dry. 36 months lees lie-in shows in fine, persistent mousse.

Rosé 🛢 🌿 ★★★★ **13** another intensely coloured pink from merlot with cab franc & malbec. Happy wine, with aromas of plum, cherry & cassis; just off-dry but with a refreshing & cleansing acidity. — JPf

■ **Sumerton** *see* Zidela Wines

Summerhill Wines

Location/map/WO: Stellenbosch ▪ 1stB 2008 ▪ Tasting & sales Mon-Thu 9-4.30 Fri 9-2 ▪ Closed all pub hols ▪ Dorpstraat Restaurant Theatre open for dinner over weekends with live performances from 8.30-10 (bookings T +27 (0)21-889-9158 or info@dorpstraat.co.za) ▪ Tour groups (120 pax) ▪ Owner(s) Summerhill Wines cc, Charles R Hunting ▪ Winemaker(s) Hannes Meyer (whites, Simonsig) & Marius Malan (reds, Malanot Wines) ▪ Viticulturist(s) Paul Wallace (consultant) ▪ 15ha/3.5ha (merlot, shiraz, chenin) ▪ 24t/2,500cs own label 40% red 60% white ▪ PO Box 12448 Die Boord 7613 ▪ charles@summerhillwines.co.za, manager@ summerhillwines.co.za, reception@summerhillwines.co.za ▪ www.summerhillwines.co.za ▪ S 33° 52' 57.71" E 018° 50' 49.39" ▪ **T +27 (0)21-889-5015** ▪ F +27 (0)86-621-8047

Granted in 1837, Summerhill estate on Stellenbosch's Simonsberg foothills has been in the Hunting family for two generations. The property is home to the Dorpstraat Restaurant Theatre, adding novel dinnertime shows to the cellardoor offering. Watch for a maiden Shiraz Reserve, bottled as the guide went to press.

Sumsaré Wines

Location/map: Robertson ▪ Est 2008 ▪ 1stB 2007 ▪ Tasting, sales & tours by appt Mon-Fri 9-5 Sat 9-1 ▪ Closed Easter Fri-Mon, May 13, Pentecost, Dec 25/26 & Jan 1 ▪ Tour groups ▪ Facilities for children ▪ Farm produce ▪ BYO picnic ▪ Weddings ▪ Owner(s) Francèl Rabie, Johannes Erasmus, Danielle Jackson & Janine Joubert ▪ Winemaker(s) Lourens van der Westhuizen (Arendsig) ▪ Viticulturist(s) Briaan Stipp (Robertson Winery) ▪ 450ha/40ha (cab, ptage, ruby cab, shiraz, chard, chenin, cbard, muscadel w) ▪ 700t/±260cs own label 40% red 60% white ▪ PO Box 402 Robertson 6705 ▪ sumsare.wines@barvallei.co.za ▪ www.sumsarewines.co.za ▪ S 33° 54' 14.66" E 019° 40' 4.75" ▪ **T +27 (0)23-626-2152/+27 (0)82-221-6653** ▪ F +27 (0)86-505-8590

Spell 'Sumsaré' backwards, and you get 'Erasmus', the Robertson family behind the wine (and brandy) brand. Their home-farm, bought by Daniël Erasmus for his children, now has 2 ha under pinotage. 'The local cellar asked for it, and we have the right terroir.' New fire pits in the outside seating area add conviviality.

■ **Sunshine Organics** *see* Stellar Winery

Super Single Vineyards

Location/map: Stellenbosch ▪ WO: Stellenbosch/Sutherland-Karoo/Coastal ▪ Est/1stB 2004 ▪ Tasting Mon-Sat 10-5 ▪ Owner(s)/viticulturist(s) Daniël de Waal ▪ Winemaker(s) Daniël de Waal, with Kyle Zulch ▪ 60ha Canettevallei farm ▪ (cab, malbec, nebbiolo, p verdot, ptage, pinot, shiraz, tempranillo, riesling, sauv) ▪ 2,000cs own label 80% red 20% white ▪ PO Box 89 Vlottenburg 7604 ▪ marketing@ssvineyards.co.za ▪ www. supersinglevineyards.co.za ▪ S 33° 56' 29.73" E 018° 45' 15.20" ▪ **T +27 (0)72-200-5552 (Daniël)/+27 (0)82-556-0205 (Kyle)** ▪ F +27 (0)21-881-3026

Daniël de Waal - of the family from Uiterwyk farm and DeWaal Wines - has been building his own range for a decade, and with increased attention since the de Waal brothers agreed to concentrate more on their separate brands. Daniël's focus (from his Stellenboschkloof base) is on special and varied sites - hence the name. They're grouped as producing coastal wines and continental wines - the latter from pioneering, high-lying, far-inland vineyards near Sutherland in the Karoo.

Pella Coastal Wines

★★★★ **Cabernet Sauvignon** ⑤ After focused **08** (★★★★★), **09** has noble, dark & earthy Bordeaux overtones with rich ripeness & lovely dry finish. Slightly gawky oak spices should integrate with time.

★★★★ **Thomas Se Dolland Pinotage** Rich & round **10** from old vines plus a dash of malbec. Prominent fine-grained tannin & evident 60% new oak, which need time to integrate. **09** (★★★★) impressed a little less. **Merlot** NEW ★★★★ Simple blackberry, blackcurrant aromas on **11** lead to well-knit, succulent palate - but the oak (40% new) needs time to integrate. Has 15% cab. **The Vanilla** ★★★★ Mainly chenin with drop of viognier in oaked **12**. Aromas of quince, flowers, nuts &, yes, vanilla. Firmly built; friendly 12.8% alcohol. A year or so should increase harmony. **Sauvignon Blanc** NEW ★★★★ Fresh, slightly dusty **13** with green fig, capsicum aromas. Vibrant & dry, with reasonable intensity & length. WO Coastal.

Sutherland Continental Wines

★★★★ **Mount Sutherland Syrah** Spicy, meaty, promising **10** is rich & fresh, but with slightly angular tannin. Well-calculated oak. Needs time to integrate all parts. **11** also tasted: more fruit than spice here, with riper notes (& 14.4% alcohol versus 13.6%). — JPf

- **Sutherland** *see* Thelema Mountain Vineyards
- **Sutherland Continental** *see* Super Single Vineyards
- **Swallow** *see* Natte Valleij Wines

Swallow Hill Winery

Location: Greyton ▪ Map: Southern Cape ▪ Est 2009 ▪ 1stB 2013 ▪ Tasting, sales & cellar tours by prior arrangement ▪ Conservation area ▪ Owner(s) Di & Brian Dawes ▪ Cellarmaster(s) John Brian Dawes ▪ Winemaker(s) Di Dawes, with John Brian Dawes ▪ Viticulturist(s) Di Dawes & John Brian Dawes ▪ 45ha/2ha (tempranillo, viog) ▪ 2t own label 50% red 50% white ▪ IPW, SAWIS ▪ PO Box 299 Greyton 7233 ▪ swallowhill@thedawes.net ▪ www.thedawes.net ▪ S 34° 6' 10.10" E 019° 36' 35.46" ▪ **T +27 (0)82-423-9634**

One of a tiny handful of vineyards in Greyton, this 2 hectare organic parcel is farmed, and wines handcrafted by ex UK owners Di and Brian Dawes. The choice of viognier and tempranillo was to have something uncommon in South Africa, that would also adapt well to drought and the poor Greyton soils. Due for release within the currency of the guide, the wines will be aptly named First Swallow.

- **Swartland Stories** *see* Pulpit Rock Winery

Swartland Winery

Location: Malmesbury ▪ Map: Swartland ▪ WO: Western Cape/Swartland ▪ Est/1stB 1948 ▪ Tasting & sales Mon–Fri 9–5 Sat 9–2 ▪ Closed Mar 21, Easter Fri/Sun, Dec 25/26 & Jan 1 ▪ Facilities for children ▪ Tour groups ▪ Farm produce ▪ Owner(s) 60 producers ▪ Cellarmaster(s) Andries Blake (Dec 1995) ▪ Viticulturist(s) Claude Uren (Nov 2010) ▪ 2,689ha (cab, malbec, merlot, ptage, shiraz, chard, chenin, sauv) ▪ 20,000t 55% white 38% red 5% rosé 2% sparkling ▪ Brands for clients: Pick 'n Pay, Woolworths ▪ BRC, IFS, IPW, WIETA ▪ PO Box 95 Malmesbury 7299 ▪ suzanne@swwines.co.za ▪ www.swwines.co.za ▪ S 33° 27' 12.7" E 018° 45' 17.7" ▪ **T +27 (0)22-482-1134** ▪ F +27 (0)22-482-1750

Established in 1948 as a co-operative, this large-scale producer has adapted to the winds of change that blew so dramatically over the region. The business has unbundled, and now leases the winemaking facilities to Leeuwenkuil, who, in turn, produce the Swartland ranges on contract. This allows them to concentrate on the marketing aspects, and to offer bottling and laboratory services to outside customers. Although the range is extensive, care is taken in vinifying special batches separately to provide impressive regional character and well-defined tiers of quality.

Idelia range

★★★★ **Cape Blend** 🌱 Label suggests pinotage content, but undisclosed blend in barrel-matured **10** (★★★★) offers intense fruit beneath acetone whiff. Last-tasted **08** was better. Swartland WO.

Swartland Bushvine range

★★★★ **Shiraz** ⏱ 🌱 **10**, revisited as bottled wine, lives up to expectations. Substantial, ripe & full-bodied, but showing restraint.

Cabernet Sauvignon Next awaited, like **Chenin Blanc & Sauvignon Blanc. Pinotage** ⏱ 🌱 ★★★★ Sweetly spicy **10** shows improvement since last edition's preview. Vibrant, fruity enjoyment with satisfying weight & complexity. Follows last-tasted, lusciously fruity **08** (★★★★).

Swartland range

★★★★ **Cape Vintage** ✓ 🍷 Elegantly-shaped **08** port-style from tinta & shiraz, with touriga. Rich primary berry fruit, hints of caramel & spicy brandy-oak highlights. Shows deft handling. Swartland WO.

Chenin Blanc 😊 🍷 🌱 ★★★ Appealing ripe tropical fruit notes on freshly crisp, dry **13**. Good varietal definition. **Sparkling Rosè** **NEW** 😊 ★★★ Carbonated, almost-dry **NV** from pinotage is commendably full & fruit-driven, crisply satisfying.

Cabernet Sauvignon ⊕ 🍴 ▨ ★★★ Lively, medium-bodied **11** is fresh & youthful, showing leafy-tarry aromatic nose & well-defined berry fruit. **Merlot** 🍴 ▨ ★★ **12** is light, juicy & dilute. **Pinotage** 🍴 ▨ ★★★ Honest thrust of fresh, rosy cheeked wild berry fruit gives unwooded **12** charm & character. **Shiraz** 🍴 ▨ ★★★ Powerful mocha & mint notes on unwooded **12** mask fruit. **Tinta Barocca** 🍴 ▨ ★★★ Generous porty-peppery berry fruit on unwooded **12**, full of freshness & vigour. **Dry Red** 🍴 ▨ ★★ Uncomplicated, light & juicy **NV** anytime quaffer. **Blanc de Noir** 🍴 ▨ ★★★ Strawberry crush with rosepetals on off-dry **13** blush from pinotage. Swartland WO, like next. **Bukettraube** 🍴 ▨ ★★ Sweetly fruity **13** is balanced with crisp acidity. **Chardonnay** ⊕ 🍴 ▨ ★★★ Bright, fresh & fruity **12** faintly brushed with oak. **Sauvignon Blanc** ⊕ 🍴 ▨ ★★ Touch of sugar on **12** shows in sweet/sour granadilla fruit. **Cuvée Brut** ★★★ Hint of oxidation gives yeasty development impression & adds extra dimension to dry sauvignon **NV** bubbly. **Hanepoot** 🍴 ★★★★ Appealingly rich fortified **NV** fireside companion has enticing muscat fragrance & long, clean finish. Swartland WO, as next two. **Red Jerepigo** 🍴 ▨ ★★★★ Intensely sweet & spicy fortified **NV** from pinotage has molasses & black cherry syrup notes mingled with cocoa & raisins. **White Jerepigo** 🍴 ▨ ★★ Malty notes on fortified **NV** chenin winter warmer. **Cape Ruby** 🍴 ▨ ★★★ Port-style tinta & shiraz, pleasantly fruity **NV** has real ruby-style accessibility. Hints of cocoa on plum jam & spicy dates. Discontinued: **Merlot-Shiraz**, **Demi Sec**.

Contours Collection NEW

Merlot 🍴 ▨ ★★ Unwooded **11** is dilute & extracted. **Merlot-Cabernet Sauvignon** 🍴 ▨ ★★ Unoaked **11** is chewy with hint of sweetness. **Chenin Blanc** 🍴 ▨ Waxy-nutty oxidative notes on **12**. Dry, crisp; drink now. **Moscato** 🍴 ▨ ★★ Sweetly spicy, aromatic, petillant **NV** muscat d'Alexandrie, with low alcohol. **Sauvignon Blanc** ★★ Thin, tired **12** is quite ordinary.

D' Vine range

Cabernet Sauvignon-Merlot 🍴 ▨ ★ Forgettable, thin **NV**. **Rosé** 🍴 ▨ ★★ Sweet low-alcohol **NV** ex pinotage. **Chenin Blanc-Sauvignon Blanc** 🍴 ▨ ★★ Rather thin, tired off-dry **NV**. — GdB

■ **Sweet Darling** see Darling Cellars

SylvanVale Vineyards 🍷 ☕ 🏠 📷 🏃 ♿

Location/map: Stellenbosch ▪ WO: Devon Valley/Stellenbosch ▪ Est 1997 ▪ 1stB 1998 ▪ Tasting & sales daily 11–7 ▪ Fee R25 ▪ Open pub hols ▪ Flavours Restaurant: 120 seater (see Restaurants section); Vineyard Terrace; Cedarwood Bar & Lounge ▪ The Devon Valley Hotel: 50 rooms (see Accommodation section) ▪ Facilities for children ▪ Tour groups ▪ Conferences ▪ 6 banqueting venues (max capacity 98 pax) ▪ Walking/hiking trails ▪ Owner(s) Louis Group Hotels, Spas & Vineyards ▪ Winemaker(s) Mark Carmichael-Green (Sep 2003, consultant) ▪ Viticulturist(s) Lorna Hughes (1997, consultant) ▪ 8ha/4.3ha (cab, ptage, chenin) ▪ 6t/1,050cs own label 100% rosé ▪ PO Box 68 Stellenbosch 7599 ▪ info@sylvanvale.com ▪ www.sylvanvale.com ▪ S 33° 54' 12.5" E 018° 48' 57.7" ▪ **T +27 (0)21-865-2012** ▪ F +27 (0)21-865-2610

Upmarket Louis Group Hotels are in the happy situation of owning an own wine brand but also own vineyards: the Sylvanvale grapes are vinified to spec by seasoned consultant Mark Carmichael-Green, while the (recently replanted) vines share the scenic Stellenbosch premises of Devon Valley Hotel.

★★★★ **Pinotage Reserve** ⊕ Suitably mature, sweetish, violet-scented **05**, bold flavours ready to be enjoyed now. Oak maturation structures richly lush fruit flavours.
Cabernet Sauvignon ⊕ ★★★★ Accessible, refreshing **05** offers juicy fruit & sufficient structure (from mostly new oak) for seriousness in style & ageability. **Pinotage** ★★★ Returns to the guide with evolved, leather-toned **06**, delicate fruit beginning to fade in firm tannin & savoury acid structure. Enjoy drinking now.
Family Reserve Next awaited. **Dry Cabernet Sauvignon Rosé** ⊕ 🍴 ★★★ Characterful **11** is dry, crisp & appetising. Light oaking adds breadth. **Ghost Tree Sauvignon Blanc** ⊕ 🍴 ★★★ Delightfully fresh **11**, attractively light for summer lunchtime enjoyment. Koelenhof grapes. — IM

■ **Table Bay** see Ultra Liquors
■ **Table Mountain** see Distell
■ **Table View** see Rooiberg Winery

Tall Horse

Cheery labels and easy, fruit-forward style of this giraffe-themed DGB brand have clearly captured consumer tastes locally and overseas, where volumes are growing. Website www.tallhorsewines.com continues the quirky brand persona.

Tamboerskloof Wine – Kleinood Farm

Location/map/WO: Stellenbosch ▪ Est 2000 ▪ 1stB 2002 ▪ Tasting, sales & cellar tours by appt ▪ Fee R20, waived on purchase ▪ Closed all pub hols ▪ Owner(s) Gerard & Libby de Villiers ▪ Winemaker(s) Gunter Schultz (Sep 2007), with Julio Engelbrecht (Jan 2008) ▪ Viticulturist(s) Gunter Schultz (Sep 2007) ▪ 22ha/10ha (mourv, shiraz, rouss, viog) ▪ 70t/10,000cs own label 87% red 8% white 5% rosé ▪ BWI, IPW ▪ PO Box 12584 Die Boord 7613 ▪ admin@kleinood.com ▪ www.kleinood.com ▪ S 33° 59' 42.6" E 018° 52' 14.8" ▪ **T +27 (0)21-880-2527** ▪ F +27 (0)21-880-2884

The Afrikaans 'kleinood' means something small and precious - which is what boutique vintner/engineer Gerard de Villiers and wife Libby created in Stellenbosch's Blaauwklippen Valley. Libby harnessed tradition in the look and feel, while Gerard, with more than 150 winery process designs under his belt locally and abroad, handled the cellar. Inveterate surfer Gunter Schultz's focus on vineyard and wine is absolute, and environmentally sympathetic.

★★★★☆ **Syrah** ✓ Svelte **09** keeps the standard in refined, silky black fruit with twist of pepper, set against well-judged oak frame, just 26% new. Splashes mourvèdre & viognier add fresh spiciness to complex mouthful. Will age beautifully.

Katharien Syrah Rosé ⬛ ★★★★ Cherry blossom appeal on cranberry tangy palate of **13**. Vibrant yet full & creamy from older oak. Lingers long. **Viognier** ✓ ⬛ ★★★★ Nectarine & stonefruit richness to **12**, fresh & lively but creamy & full-bodied from supportive older oak & lees stirring. Accomplished, with confident dry end. — FM

Tanagra Private Cellar

Location/WO: McGregor ▪ Map: Robertson ▪ Est/1stB 2003 ▪ Tasting (wine/grappa), sales & cellar/distillery tours daily by appt ▪ Farm produce ▪ Boutique distillery (European style grappa & eau de vie) ▪ Luxury farm accommodation in 6 cottages (self-catering/B&B) ▪ Adjoining Vrolijkheid Nature Reserve ▪ Owner(s) Robert & Anette Rosenbach ▪ Cellarmaster(s)/winemaker(s) Robert Rosenbach & Lourens van der Westhuizen ▪ Viticulturist(s) Lourens van der Westhuizen ▪ 78ha/12.5ha (cabs s/f, merlot, ptage, shiraz, cbard) ▪ 120t/1,600cs own label 90% red 10% blanc de noir ▪ BWI, IPW ▪ PO Box 92 McGregor 6708 ▪ tanagra@tanagra-wines.co.za ▪ www.tanagra-wines.co.za ▪ S 33° 55' 29.6" E 019° 52' 15.9" ▪ **T +27 (0)23-625-1780** ▪ F +27 (0)23-625-1847

Handcrafting wines 'shaped by our unique fynbos-surrounded terroir', German owners Robert and Anette Rosenbach have joined the Biodiversity & Wine Initiative, recommending their new eco-friendly guest cottage, 'Faraway', as the best place to experience sustainable farming in the pristine McGregor landscape.

Cabernet Sauvignon ★★★ **12** full & flavoursome, with attractive dry tannin conclusion. Whole-berry natural ferment, only older oak, as for Shiraz & Carah. **Merlot** In abeyance, as for **Felicity**. **Shiraz** ★★★ Smoke & cherry-infused **12** has sweet fruit to counter firm tannin. **Heavenly Chaos** ⓓ ⬛ ★ Bordeaux red **11** on review had dried fruit notes, should be ready now. **Carah** ★★★ **12** cab & shiraz blend is bright & fresh, satisfying drinking now & for few years. **Cabernet Franc Blanc de Noir** NEW ★ **13** blush is bone-dry with food-styled racy freshness. Discontinued: **John's Medley**. — DC,JP

■ **Tangled Tree** see Van Loveren Family Vineyards

Tanzanite Wines

Location: Worcester ▪ WO: Western Cape ▪ Est 2006 ▪ Tasting Mon-Sat by appt ▪ Owner(s) Wentzel & Melanie van der Merwe ▪ Cellarmaster(s) Melanie van der Merwe (Apr 2006) ▪ 800cs own label ▪ PO Box 5102 Worcester 6850 ▪ melanie@tanzanitewines.co.za ▪ www.tanzanitewines.co.za ▪ **T +27 (0)23-347-0018** ▪ F +27 (0)86-694-0654

As the name suggests, Wentzel and Melanie van der Merwe's boutique venture is a rare gem, focusing exclusively on handcrafting small parcels of champagne-

method sparkling. Winemaker Melanie sources grapes and rents cellar space, and describes Tanzanite as 'minimalistic, passionate, reaching for the stars!'.

★★★★ **Méthode Cap Classique Brut Rosé NV (10)** bubbly with savoury, cranberry tone from 60% pinot noir & chardonnay. Retains delicacy & fresh refinement from 24 months on lees. Balanced, with good length.

★★★★☆ **Méthode Cap Classique ✓** Latest **NV (08)** sparkler richer than previous, with 48 months on lees & focused chardonnay (80%), pinot noir blend. Clean lemon & slatey freshness, refined balance with lingering farewell. Winemaker's food/occasion match: 'Made to celebrate life, so enjoy daily!' — MW

Tassenberg

Dry red affectionately known as 'Tassies'. Launched in 1936, the blend has varied over the years but not the affable persona. 750ml, 2L & 5L. By Distell.

Tassenberg ☺ 🍴 ★★★ Lightish **NV** cinsaut, cab, merlot is enduring favourite & all-rounder. —DB, HJ

Taverna Rouge

Big-selling budget-priced red blend by Distell; available in 750ml and 2L.

Taverna Rouge 🍴 ★★ Earthy **NV** tapas wine with red berry flavour & firm tannin finish. —DB, HJ

TCB Wines

Location: Rawsonville ▪ Map: Breedekloof ▪ WO: Western Cape ▪ Est 2002 ▪ 1stB 2008 ▪ Tasting, sales & cellar tours Mon-Fri 8-5 ▪ Fee R10pp ▪ Closed all pub hols ▪ Tour groups ▪ BYO picnic ▪ Conferences ▪ Self-catering units ▪ Owner(s) / manager TC Botha ▪ Cellarmaster(s)/winemaker(s) Christo Basson (Oct 2008) ▪ Viticulturist(s) Johan Slabber (Feb 1999) ▪ 190ha (cab, merlot, ptage, ruby cab, shiraz, chenin cbard, nouvelle, sauv, sem) ▪ 1,800t/600cs own label 70% red 30% white + 200cs for clients ▪ IPW ▪ PO Box 56 Rawsonville 6845 ▪ basson.christo8@gmail. com ▪ S 33° 42' 5.63" E 019° 18' 21.92" ▪ **T +27 (0)23-349-1748** ▪ F +27 (0)23-349-1325

Its home-farm in the hands of the sixth TC Botha farming here, there are no prizes for guessing the 'TCB' in the Breedekloof boutique's name. Christo Basson, now solo as cellarmaster, has impeccable qualifications, having gone from general cellar employee to cellar assistant, assistant winemaker to cellar chief.

Cape Sparrow Selection
Classic Red 🐦 🈂 ★★★ Cheerful **11** is lighter than previous, soft & fruity 5-way blend for early pleasure.

Wolfenberg range [NEW]
Shiraz ★★★ **11** ripe chocolate-laced dark cherries. Bold, juicy & toasty - perfect braai wine. **Sauvignon Blanc** Await new vintage. — WB

Teddy Hall Wines

Location/WO: Stellenbosch ▪ Closed to public ▪ Owner(s)/cellarmaster(s)/winemaker(s)/viticulturist(s) Teddy Hall ▪ PO Box 2868 Somerset West 7129 ▪ teddy@teddyhallwines.com ▪ www.teddyhallwines.com ▪ **T +27 (0)83-461-8111** ▪ F +27 (0)86-504-8178

Teddy Hall, Stellenbosch-based boutique producer specialising in chenin blanc, says of his approach: 'I make wines which I like and then hope the consumer enjoys them too.' He's certainly met with critical approval over the years, becoming Diners Club Winemaker of the Year in 2001 where the featured category was yes, you guessed it, chenin, and he won the annual Chenin Blanc Challenge run by the now defunct Wine magazine four times. When he's not making wine, you'll find him on his prized Harley-Davidson Softail.

Premium range
★★★★☆ **Hercùles van Loon Cabernet Sauvignon** Dense & brooding **09** includes 10% merlot. Cassis, violets & some earthy, slightly meaty notes. Rich & full but balanced. Pleasantly austere on the finish. 24 months in French oak, 50% new.

★★★★☆ **Dr Jan Cats Chenin Blanc Reserve** 🈂 Refined **11** with citrus, peach, subtle vanilla & some yeasty complexity. Just enough texture to ensure that the acidity is nicely coated while the finish is long & dry. Will only get better in bottle.

★★★★ **Brut Méthode Cap Classique** NEW 🍷 Pure & precise bottle-fermented sparkling from chardonnay. NV lemon & subtle brioche character, zippy acidity & lots of fine, long-lasting bubbles.

Sybrand Mankadan Chenin Blanc 🗄 🍷 ★★★★ Unshowy but satisfying **12** is unwooded but for 10% matured in older barrels. Peach & pear, bright acidity, bone-dry finish. **Jan Blanx Super White Cuvée** ⊕ 🗄 ★★★ NV is sauvignon-led but includes dashes semillon, chenin. Super-grassy but also hint of lime, bracing acidity. **Blanc de Blancs Méthode Cap Classique** ★★★★ An occasional release, **08** is champagne-method sparkling from chardonnay. Ripe citrus, liquorice & yeasty notes. Rich & full, soft mousse, tangy acidity.

Moments Collection

Winter Moments Shiraz-Cabernet Sauvignon 🗄 🍷 ★★★★ Shiraz-led 4-way blend **11** has bags of personality - black cherry, cassis, some herbal lift. Medium body, with nicely tart acidity & fine spicy tannins.
Summer Moments Chenin Blanc ⊕ 🗄 🍷 ★★★★ **11** punches above its weight, displaying great complexity. Notes of citrus, apple, peach & some waxiness, great acidity. Altogether more stylish than **10** (★★★).

Sgt Pepper range

Sgt Pepper 🗄 🍷 ★★★ Shiraz-led **10** is modest but likeable, with blackcurrant flavoured fruit-pastille quality about it. Juicy & fresh. — CE

◼ **Tembana Valley** *see* Rooiberg Winery

Tempel Wines

Location/WO: Paarl ▪ Map: Paarl & Wellington ▪ Est 2000 ▪ 1stB 2003 ▪ Tasting, sales & cellar tours by appt ▪ Fee R25 ▪ Guest lodge (B&B), with 5 cottages ▪ Owner(s)/winemaker(s) Alf Ljungqvist ▪ 6ha/4.2ha (ptage) ▪ 24t/ 1,700cs own label 85% red 15% white ▪ PO Box 7295 Noorder-Paarl 7623 ▪ sales@tempelwines.co.za ▪ www.tempelwines.co.za ▪ S 33° 40' 34.0" E 018° 58' 32.2" ▪ **T +27 (0)21-872-4065** ▪ F +27 (0)21-872-3883

Although Alf Ljungqvist sticks to the formula loved by his Scandinavian client base, he's not averse to trying something new. Last year he fermented petit verdot, shiraz, cab franc, malbec, sangiovese and zinfandel together as the makings of a cuvée now maturing in new oak for 24 months: 'Pretty unique!'

◼ **10 Chapters** *see* Thandi Wines
◼ **Terra Del Capo** *see* Anthonij Rupert Wyne
◼ **Terra Madre** *see* High Constantia Wine Cellar

Teubes Family Wines

Location: Vredendal ▪ Map: Olifants River ▪ WO: Western Cape/Olifants River ▪ Est 2010 ▪ 1stB 2011 ▪ Tasting & sales Mon-Fri 8-5 Sat 9.30-5 ▪ Fee R20 ▪ Closed Easter Sat/Sun, Dec 25 & Jan 1 ▪ Tour groups (up to 40 pax) ▪ Farm produce ▪ BYO picnic ▪ Conferences ▪ Walks/hikes ▪ Bergkraal 4x4 trail ▪ Mountain biking ▪ Conservation area ▪ Guest cottages ▪ Owner(s) Johan & Ella Teubes ▪ Cellarmaster(s) Sybrand Teubes ▪ Winemaker(s) Sybrand Teubes, with Isabel Teubes ▪ Viticulturist(s) Johan Teubes ▪ (cab, ptage, shiraz, chard, sauv) ▪ 300t ▪ PO Box 791 Vredendal 8160 ▪ sybrand@teubeswines.co.za ▪ www.teubeswines.co.za ▪ S 31° 43' 19.1" E 018° 30' 14.5" ▪ **T +27 (0)27-213-2377** ▪ F +27 (0)27-213-3773

Volumes continue to rise, reports Vredendal winemaker Sybrand Teubes, son of owners Johan and Ella, and slotting his wines into product tiers is an ongoing exercise. A new label, Teubes Family Collection, identifies a premium range sold at the cellardoor and in Gauteng, and includes Sybrand's maiden sauvignon.

Teubes Family Collection NEW

★★★★ **Sauvignon Blanc** From undisclosed but clearly special West Coast vineyard site, aromatic & poised **12** marries floral, passionfruit & blackcurrant notes with piquant acidity.
Pinotage Reserve ✓ ★★★★ Quintessential old-school pinotage aromas of banana, clean leather & strawberry on French-oak-matured **11** should please fans of the variety.

Limited Releases

Cabernet Sauvignon NEW ★★★★ Serious but approachable **10**, coconut-laced blackcurrant; evolved malty note & garnet hue suggest best enjoyed soon. WO Olifants River, as all these.

Malkopbaai range

Pinotage ⊕ 🍴 ★★★ Attractive **11** strawberry infused, supple tannins for easy sipping. **Sauvignon Blanc** ⊕ 🍴 ★★★ Early **12**, tasty if fleeting gooseberry & kiwi flavour, moderate alcohol. — HJ, CvZ

Thabani Wines

Location: Cape Town ▪ Closed to public ▪ Owner(s) Jabulani Ntshangase ▪ PO Box 1381 Stellenbosch 7599 ▪ jabspice@iafrica.com ▪ www.thabani.co.za ▪ **T** +27 (0)82-734-9409 ▪ F +27 (0)6-648-3676

Having started out as a wine shop assistant in New York almost four decades ago, Jabulani Ntshangase is an inspiration to the young black South Africans he mentors, each new university enrolment filling him with joy – hence the name Thabani ('Joyful') for his small range of mainly restaurant wines made to spec.

Thandi Wines

Location/map: Stellenbosch ▪ WO: Stellenbosch/Coastal/Western Cape ▪ Est 1995 ▪ Tasting & sales Mon-Thu 10-4 Fri 10-3 ▪ Fee R20pp ▪ Closed all pub hols ▪ Tour groups ▪ Owner(s) Thandi Wines (Pty) Ltd ▪ Fairtrade ▪ PO Box 597 Stellenbosch 7599 ▪ info@thandiwines.co.za ▪ www.thandiwines.com ▪ S 33° 57' 47.66" E 018° 47' 38.51" ▪ **T** +27 (0)21-881-3290 ▪ F +27 (0)86-577-2138

Positioned as an economic empowerment wine, with 250 farm employee families owning more than half the business, Thandi's vision is to become the world's leading social and ethical wine brand. There are a few firsts attached to the name: it was the country's first agricultural empowerment project (1999) and the world's first Fairtrade-accredited wine label (2003). The business has relocated to Stellenbosch's Eerstrivier Cellar, where there is a dedicated tasting room though there are still close ties with the restaurant on the Thandi farm in Elgin. The portfolio has also expanded to include Kumkani and 10 Chapters.

Kumkani range

★★★★ **Sauvignon Blanc** 🍴 📖 Appealing honeyed tone & stonefruit, with succulent texture on **11**. Now bottled, richer than previewed last time, with good length, ready for drinking. WO Coastal.

Pinotage 🍴 📖 ★★★ **11** smoky red fruit tempered into more savoury, leather tones by partial new-oak tannins. Supple structure with dry finish. **Shiraz** ⊕ 🍴 ★★★☆ **11** ex barrel, riper & bolder than previous. Ample fruit & spice with smoother profile & earlier accessibility. **10** held back for further maturation. **Chardonnay** ⊕ 🍴 📖 ★★★ Oak envelops succulent fruit in youthful **11**. Limy twist invites food. Time will harmonise & show true potential. **Infiniti Méthode Cap Classique Brut** ⊕ ★★★★ Sparkling from mostly chardonnay with pinots noir & meunier. **07** step up on last-tasted **04** (★★★☆). Rich & creamy, with ripe stonefruit, brioche & toasted nuts. WO W Cape.

Thandi Single Varietal range

Shiraz Rosé ☺ 🍴 📖 ★★★ Strawberry tone & flavour on just-dry **13** fresh quaffer.

Cabernet Sauvignon 🍴 📖 ★★★ Bold, rich & ripe-styled **11** has dark berry flavours, supple structure & dry food-friendly finish. **Shiraz** NEW ✓ 🍴 📖 ★★★☆ Mouthfilling rich & spicy flavours on **11**. Bright, lively drinkability with enough backbone for 3-5 years. **Sauvignon Blanc** 🍴 📖 ★★★☆ **13** crisp & refreshing tropical style, with creamy breadth & tangy finish. **Shiraz Rosé Sparkling** 📖 ★★☆ **13** crisply sweet & fragrant pink summer sparkler. Discontinued: **Pinot Noir, Chardonnay.**

Thandi Dual Varietal range

Shiraz-Cabernet Sauvignon Next awaited. **Chardonnay-Chenin Blanc** 🍴 📖 ★★★ Crunchy apple & ripe pear on succulent **13**. Finishes with pithy grapefruit grip. WO W Cape. Discontinued: **Cabernet Sauvignon-Merlot, Sauvignon Blanc-Semillon.** — MW

▪ **The Auction Crossing** *see* Auction Crossing Private Cellar
▪ **The Belief** *see* Thembi & Co
▪ **The Bernard Series** *see* Bellingham

The Berrio Wines

Location: Elim ▪ Map: Southern Cape ▪ WO: Elim/Western Cape ▪ Est 1997 ▪ 1stB 2002 ▪ Tasting & sales Mon-Fri 9-4.30 Sat 10-3 (booking essential) ▪ Closed Sun, Easter Fri/Sun, Dec 25/26 & Jan 1 ▪ Snack/lunch platters by prior booking ▪ Owner(s) Francis Pratt ▪ Cellarmaster(s)/winemaker(s) Francis Pratt (Feb 2009) ▪ Viticulturist(s) Andrew Teubes (Jan 2006, consultant) ▪ 2,276ha/±30ha (pinot, shiraz, sauv, sem) ▪ ±30t/20,080cs own label 20% red 80% white ▪ Fairtrade ▪ PO Box 622 Bredasdorp 7280 ▪ wine@theberrio.co.za ▪ www.theberrio.co.za ▪ S 34° 37′ 17.0″ E 019° 48′ 32.3″ ▪ **T +27 (0)28-482-1880** ▪ F +27 (0)86-603-2894

Owner and winemaker Francis Pratt has his eye on green matters as well as producing wines that will stand the test of time. He and fellow Elim vinegrowers have incorporated their farms into the Nuwejaars Wetland Special Management Area initiative to help preserve the unique fauna and flora of the Agulhas coastal area. Additional tasting locale staff from the local Elim community have been appointed and if all goes to plan they'll soon be pouring The Berrio's first shiraz.

★★★★ **Cabernet Sauvignon** ⓣ 🍴 First since 06, 09 (★★★★) surprisingly succulent for cool vintage. Tad herby, but plumped by fruit, sweet vanilla from some American oak. Portion Stellenbosch grapes.

★★★★ **Sauvignon Blanc** 🍴 🧺 Salty-mineral 12 in step with 11: bold yet refined, sweet-ripe passionfruit flavours overlain with textured citrus notes. Ageworthy, but we doubt you'll resist temptation.

★★★★☆ **The Weathergirl** 🍴 🧺 Flagship Bordeaux-style blend semillon & sauvignon, unwooded. Vibrant 12 intensely aromatic khaki bush & nettle, pinpoint balance & seamless elegance. Slightly more semillon (52%) than 11 but as shapely, & with fine tangy marmalade persistence. — WB, GdB

The Butcher Shop & Grill

Location: Sandton ▪ WO: Stellenbosch/Western Cape/Bot River/Durbanville/Elgin ▪ Owner(s) Alan Pick ▪ Shop 30 Nelson Mandela Square Sandton 2196 ▪ thebutchershop@mweb.co.za ▪ **T +27 (0)11-784-8676/7** ▪ F +27 (0)11-784-8674

Sandton's Butcher Shop & Grill proprietor Alan Pick has long been a prolific, high-profile Cape Winemakers Guild customer, and has built good relationships with its members. Some (as well as other estates) provide exclusive bottlings for his impressive top range, to complement his mostly carnivorous menu.

Limited Editions

★★★★ **Hartenberg The Snuffbox Merlot** ⓣ Austere 06 bold but classic, from prime single-vineyard. Oak (mostly new) seasons sour plum flavours & adds evolved but still firm tannins.

★★★★ **Morgenster** ⓣ Herb, cassis & eucalyptus toned 03 (★★★★★) dominated by cabs (sauvignon, franc 70%). When last tasted mid-2005, fruit, tannins & alcohol (14.3%) already well-aligned but needed time to integrate fully; should be ready now.

★★★★ **Vergelegen The Dani** ⓣ Labelled for the restaurant, 04 a fully mature, meaty & firm, ready to drink Bordeaux-styled red blend from this famous Stellenbosch estate.

★★★★ **Rust en Vrede The Sara** ⓣ Opulently ripe 07 shiraz-cab blend makes a big statement. Showily oaked, developed '1694 Classification' has reached peak, had muscular tannins which have softened. Drink up.

★★★★ **Vergelegen The Carine** ⓣ Ingratiatingly fruity 11 sauvignon is softer, less steely & bracing than the property's usual style.

★★★★☆ **Neils Verburg Shiraz-Cabernet Sauvignon** 🆕 Iron fist in velvet glove 09's firm oak backbone (100% new) cosseted by ripe, succulent, rounded black fruit. Smidgen mourvèdre, lovely spice accent for additional interest; deserves cellaring.

Discontinued: **Niels Verburg Shiraz**.

Pick's Pick range

★★★★ **Cabernet Sauvignon** From Durbanville's Diemersdal, brooding, inky notes on juicy & very ripe 12. Sweet fruit plumped by soft tannins (unusual for cab), gentle acidity. Very sippable, with or without a meal.

★★★★ **Sauvignon Blanc** 🍴 🧺 Lovely fruit purity on Jordan's 13, gooseberries & lime, with a core minerality showing on the flavours & finish, taut & focused. No 12.

Cabernet Sauvignon ★★★★ Ex Paul Cluver, 11 balanced & accessible with underlying seriousness. Bright & sappy red berried, with Elgin's cool fruited herbaceous signature herbaceous. Medium bodied, great with meaty fare. **Merlot** 🍴 🧺 ★★★★ Taking a step up from last-tasted 09 (★★★★), carefully made (80% new oak) 11 from Jordan offers ageing potential coupled with current enjoyment. Cassis & dark chocolate, its

sleekly curvaceous body ends dry & food friendly. **Protea Merlot** ★★★ By Anthonij Rupert Wyne, **12** has smoky red fruit & mint in firm, dry tannic embrace; needs one of Mr Pick's famous steaks! **Shiraz** 🗄 ★★★★ Succulent, plush & yielding **12**, spicy blue & plum fruit, light & fresh with medium body. **Shiraz** 🗄 ★★★★ Stepping up on **07** (★★★), **09** from Zevenwacht is full bodied, with ample savoury & spicy fruit clothed in dry amenable tannins. Splashes mourvèdre & grenache add interest. No **08**. **Classic French Blend** NEW ★★★★ Attractive cab-led Bordeaux-style blend by Morgenster. **12** shows pure concentrated fruit, elegant richness & a frisson of fine tannin. Satisfyingly drinkable. **Rosé** ⊕ 🗄 🖉 ★★★ Merlot blend ex Jordan, **11** preview was cranberry scented, light textured & zesty. Works both as an aperitif & with food. **Chardonnay** 🗄 ★★★ Lees-ageing adds richness & breadth to charming, easy-drinking **11** classy glassful courtesy The Winery of Good Hope. WO W Cape. **Protea Sauvignon Blanc** ★★★ Brisk & herbaceous **13** tank sample shade less fruity than previous, still refreshing. From Anthonij Rupert Wyne. **Cape White Blend** ⊕ 🗄 ★★★★ Last-tasted **09** chenin-viognier-chardonnay by Teddy Hall had intriguing perfume, flavours. Portion oaked. More delicious than **06** (★★★★). **Bubbly** 🖉 ★★★★ Delightfully dry verve & lemon zestiness from chardonnay, pinot & pinotage in NV MCC should put guests in a party mood. From Villiera. —IM, CE, TJ, AL, CM, CvZ, MW

◼ **The Cirrus Wine Company** *see* Cirrus Wines
◼ **The Collection** *see* Mooiplaas Estate & Private Nature Reserve
◼ **The Company of Wine People** *see* Stellenbosch Vineyards
◼ **The Cooperative** *see* Bosman Family Vineyards
◼ **The Den** *see* Painted Wolf Wines
◼ **The Diamond Collection** *see* Lutzville Cape Diamond Vineyards

The Drift Farm

Location: Napier ▪ WO: Western Cape/Overberg ▪ 1stB 2005 ▪ Wine sales Mon-Fri 8.30-4 ▪ Owner(s) Jack family ▪ Winemaker(s) Trizanne Barnard ▪ Viticulturist(s) Chris Keet (consultant) ▪ 204ha/12ha (barbera, malbec, pinot, shiraz, tannat, tinta barocca, touriga franca, touriga nacional, chard) ▪ WIETA ▪ PO Box 55 Napier 7270 ▪ info@thedrift.co.za ▪ www.thedrift.co.za ▪ **T +27 (0)86-150-2025** ▪ F +27 (0)86-563-9533

The focus on this Napier herb, olive and vegetable farm, run on organic principles, is moving closer to wine, and there can be no better team in place than winemaker Trizanne Barnard (Trizanne Signature Wines), viticulturist Chris Keet (Keet Wines) and co-owner Bruce Jack (Flagstone, Kumala). Plantings of a range of interesting varieties have not yet manifested in bottle but there is a '12 Pinot Noir whimsically named 'There Are Still Mysteries' on the horizon.

★★★★ **Bowwood Cabernet Sauvignon-Merlot** ⊕ Classic Bordeaux style, **05** sumptuous blackcurrant & leafy tobacco; well developed, drinking very well now. Agter Paarl grapes.

★★★★ **Riesling** ⊕ 🗄 Off cool Swartberg vines, **08** shows some development though still lively, fruity & a good expression of the variety. Lightish alcohol (±11%) perfect for lunchtime.

Year of the Rooster Rosé ✓ 🗄 🖉 ★★★★ From Douro/port grape touriga franca, dry, sleek (11% alcohol) **12** is gently perfumed but the brambleberries power up in the flavours & finish. WO Overberg. — CR

The Fledge & Co   🍴🍷

Location: Calitzdorp/Riebeek West ▪ WO: Calitzdorp ▪ Est 2007 ▪ 1stB 2010 ▪ Tasting & sales by appt at Boplaas ▪ Closed all pub hols ▪ Owner(s) Margaux Nel & Leon Coetzee ▪ Winemaker(s) Margaux Nel & Leon Coetzee (both Jan 2007) ▪ Viticulturist(s) Margaux Nel (Jan 2007) ▪ 12t/250cs own label 30% red 70% white ▪ IPW ▪ winemaker@boplaas.co.za, leon.mrfoo@gmail.com ▪ www.thefledge.co.za ▪ **T +27 (0)82-828-8416/ +27 (0)72-385-6503**

If you think of Klein Karoo as quiet and predictable, clearly you've not run into Leon Coetzee and Margaux Nel (she also winemaker at Calitzdorp's Boplaas). Ebullient and impassioned 'terroirists', they're intent on stirring things up by making 'individual, small batches of old-school wines [combining] New World freedom with Old World sensibility'. Latest hatchling is 'the Karoo's first ever straw wine', from 4 rows of muscat d'Frontignan intricately and slowly vinified in older barrels. The resulting Hatchi ('Bee' in Japanese) will certainly have the fans swarming.

★★★★ **Hatchi** NEW Delectable vine-dried Calitzdorp muscadel, naturally & carefully fermented. **12** honey, dried apricot & spice infusion. Only 350 (500 ml) bottles of vivacious sweetness (the winemakers insist) NOT to be consumed with pudding - instead pair with roast duck, Cape Malay, fine cheese & all things savoury.

HoekSteen Await next, as for **Vagabond**. — GdB,JP

The Foundry

Location/map: Stellenbosch ▪ WO: Stellenbosch/Coastal ▪ Est 2000 ▪ 1stB 2001 ▪ Tasting, sales & cellar tours by appt ▪ Closed all pub hols ▪ Owner(s) Chris Williams & James Reid ▪ Cellarmaster(s)/winemaker(s) Chris Williams (Nov 2000) ▪ Viticulturist(s) Chris Williams (Nov 2000), with growers ▪ 11ha (grenache, shiraz, rouss, viog) ▪ ±30t/4,000cs own label 40% red 60% white ▪ PO Box 12423 Die Board 7613 ▪ thefoundry@mweb.co.za ▪ www.thefoundry.co.za ▪ S 34° 1' 1.7" E 018° 45' 24.7" ▪ **T +27 (0)82-577-0491** ▪ F +27 (0)21-843-3274

Meerlust cellarmaster Chris Williams and Voor Paardeberg vinegrower (and local operations director of Accolade Wines) James Reid established this expanding joint venture well over a decade ago. Although Reid's farm is becoming 'home' to the label, the wines are as yet made at Meerlust - the original pair (Syrah and Viognier) and the Roussanne sourced in Stellenbosch, the fine Grenache Blanc from further inland. Williams talks of 'wines of purity, focus and distinction', which is the imprint they all in this portfolio bear.

★★★★☆ **Syrah** ⊕ Classy Cape interpretation of the northern Rhône, smooth & polished **08** bridges the spicy/fruity style divide, melds best of both in harmonious whole.

★★★★☆ **Grenache Blanc** 📖 **12** (★★★★★) beautifully layered, displaying aromas of lemon curd, white peaches & pear. The clean, gently oaked palate has generous, intense flavours of lemon, blackcurrant & crushed stone. Uplifting acidity gives great freshness & tension. From Voor Paardeberg fruit, as was **11**.

★★★★ **Roussanne** Delicate peach blossom & papaya on **12**, naturally fermented & matured in older oak (like Grenache). The fresh palate is not complex but has a sense of generosity & an attractive mineral element.

★★★★ **Viognier** Well proportioned, lightly oaked **12** offers apricot & intense floral aromas, leading to fantastic fresh nectarine & under-ripe apricot flavours, with a twist of lemon on the long finish. No **11**. — JPf

■ **The Game Reserve** see Graham Beck Wines

The Giant Periwinkle

Location: Bredasdorp ▪ Map: Southern Cape ▪ WO: Elim ▪ Est 2009 ▪ 1stB 2012 ▪ Tasting by appt only ▪ Owner(s) PJ Rabie snr & PJ Rabie jnr ▪ Cellarmaster(s) Johan de Kock (2011, consultant) ▪ Winemaker(s) Johan de Kock (2011, consultant) & Pierre Jacques Rabie jnr ▪ 0.06ha (sauv, pinot) ▪ ±292cs own label 66% red 34% white ▪ PO Box 415 Bredasdorp 7280 ▪ pjrabie@capebar.co.za ▪ **T +27 (0)21-426-2653** ▪ F +27 (0)21-422-2142

Co-owner Pierre Jacques Rabie junior's passion for boutique winemaking is matched by his love of angling, especially at Terrace Bay, Namibia, where a glass of his sauvignon and fresh-caught kabeljou constitute his perfect wine moment. A tasting venue and cellar will open on their Bredasdorp property this year.

The Giant Periwinkle range NEW

Sea Money Malbec 📖 ★★★ Polished **12**, opulent black berries held in check by spicy oak & slight medicinal edge. The Berrio fruit; Zoetendal for next two. **Kelp Forest Syrah** 📖 ★★★ Older-oak-touched **12** prune & date aromas, berry flavours; chunky tannins & dusting of spice perfect for winter stews. **21 Degrees Sauvignon Blanc** 📖 ★★★ Aromatic **12** lime & lemon scents, lean & taut - enjoy with... kabeljou. — WB, GdB

■ **The Goats do Roam Wine Company** see Goats do Roam Wine Company

The Goose Wines

Location: George ▪ Map: Klein Karoo & Garden Route ▪ WO: Upper Langkloof/Western Cape ▪ Est 2005 ▪ Tasting & sales by appt ▪ Meals/refreshments by appt ▪ Owner(s) Retief Goosen & Werner Roux ▪ Cellarmaster(s)/winemaker(s) Alwyn Liebenberg (Jan 2007) ▪ Viticulturist(s) Bennie Botha (Jan 2009) ▪ 500ha/21ha (cab, shiraz, sauv) ▪ 120t/18,666cs own label 66% red 34% white + 140cs for clients ▪ Brands for clients: Reuben's (Franschhoek & Robertson) ▪ HACCP ▪ PO Box 10 Oudtshoorn 6620 ▪ michele@thegoosewines.com ▪ www.thegoosewines.com ▪ S 33° 48' 53.5" E 022° 34' 23.4" ▪ **T +27 (0)82-610-2276** ▪ F +27 (0)86-543-1808

High in the Outeniqua Mountains near George is this cool-climate farm co-owned by renowned professional golfer Retief 'The Goose' Goosen. The Goose wines are all single-vineyards, while the Gander wines claim the Upper

Langkloof ward as their origin. All wines are still made off-site. Future plans include a local and export expansion programme, and a Goose Pinot Noir.

The Goose range

★★★★ **Expression** ⏱ Plush ripe-styled **09** from cab & shiraz. Dark plummy fruit has vibrant acid support, soft supple tannins. 30% new French oak. WO W Cape.

★★★★ **T-Box Sauvignon Blanc** ⏱ The weightiest of the 3 sauvignons, **11** spent 9 months in new oak. Citrus peel, spice & pure fruit in fine balance with wood, acid & alcohol. Dry & soft with apple-fresh finale.

Sauvignon Blanc ⏱ ★★★★ Shy bruised apple, lime & white pepper spice waft off delicate **11**. Lovely core of fruit follows to ultra-dry but soft end.

The Gander range

Cabernet Sauvignon NEW 🍴 🐷 ★★★★ Lead pencils, scrub, **10** is more savoury than fruity from the oaking, tannins firm but ripe. Will show more over time. **Shiraz** 🍴 🐷 ★★★ Creamy dark plums & whiffs of dried herbs, **11** has an appealing accessibility, the tannins supple, food friendly. **Sauvignon Blanc** ⏱ 🍴 🐷 ★★★★ Bone-dry, with lingering fresh & vibrant zing, **12** a step up from previous. — CR

■ **The Grand Beach Café** *see* Stellekaya Winery

The Grape Grinder

Location: Paarl ▪ WO: Western Cape/Coastal ▪ Est/1stB 2010 ▪ Closed to public ▪ Owner(s) Oliver Kirsten & Johan du Toit ▪ Cellarmaster(s)/winemaker(s) Pieter Carstens (Dec 2010, consultant) ▪ 51,000cs own label 80% red 20% white ▪ ISO 2009, BRC, WIETA ▪ PO Box 606 Paarl 7624 ▪ oliver@grapegrinder.com ▪ www.grapegrinder.com ▪ **T +27 (0)21-863-3943** ▪ F +27 (0)86-588-4338

Oliver Kirsten and Johan du Toit founded their Paarl-based wine business to showcase SA wines, with all their creativity and energy, to an international audience. Consumer focused, most of their wines have mass appeal though the newer ranges are increasingly concentrating on quality rather than quantity.

The Grape Grinder range

The Grinder Pinotage 🍴 🐷 ★★★☆ **12** far more subtle than name suggests & better for it. Fruit dominated (plums & damsons) given coffee tweaking & charry choc finish. **The Grinder Shiraz** NEW 🍴 🐷 ★★★ Perfumed **11** preview has pronounced meaty notes from 12% mourvèdre, black berries, good texture, smooth finish. WO Coastal.

The Milkwood range

Shiraz-Viognier 🍴 🐷 ★★★☆ Very expressive **12**, 2% viognier shows cumin, anise & blossom on nose. Suave & sophisticated, step up on previous.

The Wild Olive range

Old Vines Chenin Blanc 🍴 🐷 ★★★ Creamy quality to **13** from old Swartland vines, unwooded, improves previous. Baked lemon cheesecake, freshening acidity. — CM

■ **The Green House** *see* Bon Cap Organic Winery
■ **The Griffin** *see* Stettyn Cellar

The High Road

Location/map/WO: Stellenbosch ▪ Est/1stB 2003 ▪ Tasting & sales at Pane E Vino Food & Wine Bar Mon-Fri 10-6 Sat 10-5 ▪ Closed all pub hols ▪ Boardroom facilities ▪ Owner(s) Les Sweidan & Mike Church ▪ Winemaker(s) Mark Carmichael-Green (2004, consultant) ▪ Viticulturist(s) Paul Wallace (2004, consultant) ▪ 26t/4,000cs own label 100% red ▪ PO Box 4721 Cape Town 8000 ▪ wine@thehighroad.co.za ▪ www.thehighroad.co.za ▪ S 33° 56′ 27.1″ E 018° 50′ 49.1″ ▪ **T +27 (0)21-886-4288** ▪ F +27 (0)21-886-4288

Two one-time high-fliers from the world of insurance, Les Sweidan and Mike Church, turned to winegrowing and named their venture for 'the peaceful transition achieved when our country took the high road in 1994'. Specialists in small volumes of Bordeaux-style blends, they source grapes from Stellenbosch's 'Golden Triangle' and they're vinified close to the town centre.

★★★★ **Director's Reserve** Classic notes of pencil shavings & cassis emerge from **09** (★★★★☆) - half cab, with merlot & cab franc, while fine **08** had more cab. Well-balanced palate with fine tannin, ripe but fresh fruit, lingering finish. Subtle espresso & dark chocolate hint at the all-new oak, which is integrating well.

Classique ⓐ ★★★★ Dark-fruited, savoury **09** cab-led red blend with merlot & cab franc. Follows through well to interesting palate: firm, tannic & a touch rustic. Discontinued: **Reserve**. — JPf

The Hills

Location/map/WO: Stellenbosch ▪ Est/1stB 2006 ▪ Tasting & sales by appt ▪ Owner(s) The Victor Hills Family Trust ▪ Winemaker(s) Martin Meinert (Feb 2006, consultant) ▪ Viticulturist(s) Vic Hills (Jan 1998) ▪ 6ha/5ha (cab, pinot, shiraz, chenin) ▪ 40t/600cs own label 80% red 20% white ▪ PO Box 12012 Die Boord Stellenbosch 7613 ▪ vwhills@ iafrica.com ▪ S 33° 55' 04.1" E 018° 48' 47.1" ▪ **T +27 (0)21-865-2939** ▪ F +27 (0)21-865-2939

Chimanimani is a smallholding in Stellenbosch's prime Devon Valley where Vic Hills, whose family has owned the property since 1964, oversees 5ha of noble reds and a block of venerable chenin. The harvest is mostly sold but since 2006 a soupçon is made for the own-label by celebrated neighbour Martin Meinert.

Cabernet Sauvignon ✓ ★★★ Care & attention to detail evident in improved **09**, buffed by 2 years 33% new oak & showing fine dark fruit, balance & elegance. **Pinot Noir** ⓐ ★★★ Variety-true **10**, earthy cherries & hint of mint, light textured but generous, zesty & commendably dry. Ready now & good for few years. **Shiraz** ★★★ Medium-bodied **09** lush fruit aromas, ripe & soft on palate yet aftertaste is briefish. **Ensemble** ★★★ Repeating 60/40 cab/shiraz formula for 2nd-vintage **09** results in agreeably fruity cassis/plum combo but palate lacks stamina. **Chenin Blanc** ▤ ★★ Going up a notch, unchallenging **12** charms with waxy stonefruit flavours. — GM

The House of GM&Ahrens

Location/map: Franschhoek ▪ WO: Western Cape ▪ Est 2007 ▪ 1stB 2008 ▪ Tasting, sales & cellar tours by appt ▪ Closed all pub hols ▪ Meals/refreshments by appt ▪ Owner(s) Albert Ahrens & Gerrit Maritz ▪ Cellarmaster(s)/ viticulturist(s) Albert Ahrens (Jan 2007) ▪ 7t/700cs own label 100% MCC ▪ P O Box 5619 Helderberg 7135 ▪ info@gmahrens.co.za ▪ www.gmahrens.co.za ▪ S 33° 54' 14" E 019° 07' 08" ▪ **T +27 (0)79-196-6887**

This tiny méthode cap classique house in Franschhoek is a dedicated, single-minded partnership between Albert Ahrens (Goede Hoop winemaker) and lawyer Gerrit Maritz - with the input of bubbly expert Pieter Ferreira gratefully received. In its striking packaging, the sparkler is launched each year on Spring Day.

★★★★ **Vintage Cuvée** Fresh, bone-dry MCC bubbly takes a while to reveal full charms. **09** (★★★★★) shows greater complexity than **08**. Extended maturation (32 months) & multiple assemblage trials ensures this multi-regional, barrel-fermented pinot-led blend with chardonnay has the best chance of shining. — IM

The House of JC le Roux

Location/map: Stellenbosch ▪ WO: Western Cape ▪ 1stB 1983 ▪ Tasting & sales Mon-Fri 9-5 (May-Sep) & 9-6 (Oct-Apr) Sat 10-4 Sun 10-3 ▪ Fee R35-R75 ▪ Self tour available during opening hrs ▪ Closed Good Fri & Dec 25 ▪ Tour groups ▪ Gifts ▪ Le Venue restaurant (see Restaurants section) ▪ Owner(s) Distell ▪ Cellarmaster(s) Elunda Basson ▪ Winemaker(s) Elunda Basson (2007), with Hentie Germishuys (Oct 2002) ▪ Farm manager Willem Laubscher ▪ Viticulturist(s) Bennie Liebenberg (Jan 2000) ▪ 27ha own vyds ▪ 20% red 80% white ▪ ISO 9200 ▪ PO Box 184 Stellenbosch 7599 ▪ info@jcleroux.co.za ▪ www.jcleroux.co.za ▪ S 33° 54' 16.6" E 018° 48' 37.4" ▪ **T +27 (0)21-865-8200** ▪ F +27 (0)21-865-2585

Named after French Huguenot Jean le Roux, Distell's high-profile, dedicated sparkling-wine house operates from a 'lifestyle' cellar in Stellenbosch's Devon Valley. The range covers all levels, from standout méthode cap classique to sweet reds and non-alcoholic. Fruit is sourced from an extensive portfolio of suppliers and contracted growers as well as own vineyards. The venue has lots to offer visitors in search of something stylish and decadent in their tasting experience.

Méthode Cap Classique range

★★★★ **Scintilla** ⓐ Well-constructed, bone-dry, earthy **03** still youthfully fresh a decade after harvest. Seriously structured, complex citrus flavours in chardonnay-led blend, with pinot noir.

Pinot Noir Rosé ⓐ ★★★ Delicate pink **08** has developed, yeasty aromas. Fresh & subtly fruity, with decent structure, breadth & focus. **La Vallée Rosé** ★★★ Off-dry **NV** MCC, from mostly pinot noir with dash of chardonnay, has rosepetal fragrance with sweet red berry fruit. **Pinot Noir** ⓐ ★★★★ Steely **08** vinified pale & notably dry. Fresh, lean & steely style with enduring finish. **Brut** ★★★★ Latest bottling of pinot/chardonnay

NV has solid yeasty biscuit & apple pie character & pleasing roundness of body. **La Vallée ★★★** Semi-sweet pinot noir-based **NV** MCC has frothy mousse, baked apple fruit.

Sparkling range

La Chanson ★★ Sweet & nutty red **NV**, pinotage with dashes shiraz, cab franc. Low (7.5%) alcohol, as for all except Sauvignon. **La Fleurette ★★** Garish pink sweet & spicy **NV**. **Sauvignon Blanc** ⌂ **★★★** Perennially dependable bubbly. Near-dry **13** is cheerful & frothy, with generous but elegant fruit. **Le Domaine ★★** Sweetly aromatic, lightly frothy **NV** from sauvignon & muscat. — GdB

■ **The House of Krone** *see Twee Jonge Gezellen Estate-The House of Krone*
■ **The House of Mandela** *see House of Mandela*
■ **The Hughes Family** *see Hughes Family Wines*
■ **The Innings** *see Rietvallei Wine Estate*
■ **The Juno Wine Company** *see Juno Wine Company*

Thelema Mountain Vineyards　　　　　　　　

Location/map: Stellenbosch ▪ WO: Stellenbosch/Elgin/Western Cape ▪ Est 1983 ▪ 1stB 1988 ▪ Tasting & sales Mon-Fri 9–5 Sat 10–3 ▪ Fee R25/6 wines, waived on purchase ▪ BYO picnic ▪ Owner(s) McLean & Webb Family Trusts ▪ Cellarmaster(s) Gyles Webb (1983) ▪ Winemaker(s) Rudi Schultz (Dec 2000), with Duncan Clarke (Jan 2009) ▪ 250ha/95ha (cab, grenache, merlot, p verdot, pinot, shiraz, chard, muscat d'F, riesling, rouss, sauv, viog) ▪ 1,000t/ 100,000cs own label 40% red 60% white ▪ BWI ▪ PO Box 2234 Dennesig Stellenbosch 7601 ▪ info@thelema.co.za ▪ www.thelema.co.za ▪ S 33° 54' 30.0" E 018° 55' 23.4" ▪ **T +27 (0)21-885-1924** ▪ F +27 (0)21-885-1800

It's now over 30 years since the Webb and McLean families first converted an old fruit farm at the neck of the Banhoek Valley into a wine estate. Today, still in the same capable hands, Thelema is regarded as one of the pioneers of the region, blazing a trail that many have followed, often with stellar success. But standing still has never been part of Gyles Webb's philosophy and Thelema's Sutherland vineyards in up-and-coming Elgin are proving the canny foresight of this thoughtful and meticulous winemaker for a second time. Replanting is taking place in some of the original vineyards, with new clones and varieties coming onstream. A new reed bed filtration system has recently been introduced to continue the journey towards more sustainable ways of production.

Thelema range

★★★★☆ Cabernet Sauvignon ⊕ **09** tight (needs decanting) in youth, but the full fruit will expand in a few years & the hints of dusty tobacco oak be harmonised - it should keep a decade at least. Already fine, supple, with focused flavours, & the power expertly managed & balanced.

★★★★☆ The Mint Cabernet Sauvignon ⊕ ⌂ The herbal element behind the name shows pleasingly as ever on **10**. Big & forceful, all in balance - maybe a touch more severe & less graceful than the Cab Sauv (but that's a year older), though alcohol 0.5% lower, at 13.8%. Surely 10+ years ahead, satisfying all the way!

★★★★ Shiraz ⌂ Mulberries & blackcurrants on nose of elegant **10** coat a meatier palate (salami & cassoulet). Confident & assured, with well-integrated oak providing lots of drinking pleasure.

★★★★☆ Rabelais Intense, darkly-fruited **09** (★★★★★) with classic Bordeaux markers of cassis, cedarwood & hints of liquorice. Mainly cab with 15% petit verdot & dab of merlot, powerful structure given breadth by expressive fruit & freshening acidity. Good for another decade. Even finer than **08**.

★★★★ Chardonnay ▤ ⌂ Elegance & discreetness are the hallmarks of **12**, which combines a fresh fruit profile with very subtle oaking to great effect. Tangy & refreshing for current drinking pleasure.

★★★★ Ed's Reserve Chardonnay ⌂ Distinctive & unusual single-clone vineyard giving fragrant, muscat grape tones. **12** pairs limy citrus & elegant oaking with a sweet, creamy finish. Great partner for Asian food.

★★★★ Sauvignon Blanc ▤ ⌂ Fresh, green nettly nose on **13** still tight but opens up to tropical hints & citrus. Delicious texture & weight suggest worth waiting a year or two.

Merlot ⊕ ⌂ **★★★★** Bright, ripe & flavoursome but unfrivolous **10**; attractive aromas lead to a solid, chewy, slightly tannic mouthful. **Merlot Reserve** Next awaited. **Mountain Red** ▤ ⌂ **★★★** Shiraz-dominated **11** in pleasing dark-fruit melange topped by liquorice & spice. WO W Cape. **Muscat de Frontignan** ▤ ⌂ **★★★** Tank sample (unfortified) **13** is off-dry, light, frilly lunchtime quaffer with litchi & rosepetals. **Riesling** ▤ ⌂ **★★★★** Well-balanced & back-on-form **11** is packed with fresh limes & some waxy intensity. Touch of sweetness, showing some development already. **Rhine Riesling Late Harvest** ⊕ **★★★★ 09** in customary light style; easily gratifying but neither very sweet nor very acidic. Satisfying & even

dryish feel as it lingers. 375 ml. **Vin de Hel Muscat Late Harvest** ⊠ ★★★★ Rich & grapey **10** steps up on **09** (★★★☆) to show spiced currant buns & candied peel on the nose. Marmalade freshness & zip balance out sugar, sweep through to clean finish.

Sutherland range

★★★★ **Chardonnay** ▤ ⊠ **11** fragrant, flowery nose with honeyed oatmeal notes & caramelized yellow fruits. Showy rather than particularly subtle, but with more than enough character to back it all up.

★★★★ **Sauvignon Blanc** ▤ ⊠ Lean & green nose of **13** trickles on to rounded mid-palate where touch of sugar adds richness. Elegant wine, again showing signs of further improvement to come.

★★★★ **Viognier-Roussanne** ⓘ ▤ Herbal, peachy complexity on lovely aromas & lingering flavours of **10** (★★★★★) - even finer than **09**. Despite ripeness, viognier subtle rather than overblown presence in effective, restrainedly rich, modestly oaked blend. Should only gain with few years in bottle.

Pinot Noir ⊠ ★★★ Charry notes & spiced plums/cherries on fresh **12**. Oak a little bothersome, but ripe, appealing fruit should pull it through. **Syrah** ⓘ ★★★★ **09** especially attractive to sniff. Notably ripe flavours with sweet fruit; firm build, well-balanced oak. **Cabernet Sauvignon-Petit Verdot** ⓘ ★★★★ Big, ripe, rather solid & chunky **09** packed with fruit & savoury flavours. More forceful than previous vintage. **Shiraz-Grenache Rosé** **NEW** ▤ ⊠ ★★☆ Slight & delicate **13** preview, refreshing cherries & floral highlights. **Riesling** ⓘ ▤ ▤ ★★★★ Elegantly steely, even austere **11** - but technically only just dry, with a few grams sugar for richness. Dried peach & citrus notes. Great with food. — CM

The Liberator   **NEW**

WO: Stellenbosch/Swartland ▪ Est 2010 ▪ 1stB 2008 ▪ Closed to public ▪ Owner(s) Richard Kelley & Eduard Haumann ▪ 50% red 50% white ▪ rk@abswineagencies.co.uk ▪ www.theliberatorwine.com ▪ T +44 (0)1476-870717

Rick the Cape Crusader, aka UK-based Richard Kelley MW, who lived and worked in the winelands for several years, returns regularly to 'liberate' hidden wine gems. But rather than a superhero in a cloak, it's a 'rather tatty Harris Tweed jacket' he sports, his superpower is his 'blessed palate' and his mission 'to procure these precious vinous orphans and consign them to a better home'. Each wine is an 'Episode' with its own story told on the website.

★★★★ **The Francophile Chenin Blanc** ▤ ⊠ Layered **12** taut & dry, with just a hint of rock salt, whiff of vanilla oak from partial wooding in large older vats. Cellar 3+ years or decant. By DeMorgenzon.

★★★★ **The Bird Has Flown** **09** rich, complex & full-bodied chenin with extra detail from viognier, chardonnay & clairette, all ex Swartland. Savoury & firm, for fine dining. Producer? Top secret.

★★★★ **The Pie Chart** ▤ ⊠ Deftly oaked Bordeaux-style white from leading Cape exponent Tokara. **11** beautifully poised, sauvignon's (65%) minerality emphasising semillon's waxiness & lemongrass tone.

The Francophile Syrah ▤ ⊠ ★★★★ Billed as 'pure & naked example of syrah', unwooded **12** is polished, silky & slippery. By DeMorgenzon. **The Connoisseur** ⊠ ★★★ Shiraz (60%) & grenache in old-oak-matured **11**, with red berry jam, tar & smoke highlights; finishes warm & sappy. From Zevenwacht. **The Bandolier** ★★★ Savoury equal partnership mourvèdre & shiraz/syrah, **09** purposefully big & bold to mimic the style of Bandol, where the former is king. By Tokara. — DC,JP

■ **The Light** see Arniston Bay
■ **The Marais Family** see Wonderfontein

The Mason's Winery

Location/WO: Paarl ▪ Map: Paarl & Wellington ▪ Est/1stB 2001 ▪ Tasting & sales by appt at Proviant Restaurant, adjacent to cellar ▪ Owner(s) JA Clift (Pty) Ltd - Clift family ▪ Cellarmaster(s)/winemaker(s)/viticulturist(s) Derek Clift (2001) ▪ 47ha/4ha (shiraz) ▪ 30t/2,000cs own label 100% red ▪ Main Street Suider-Paarl 7646 ▪ masons@cliftgranite.co.za ▪ www.cliftgranite.co.za ▪ S 33° 45' 20.5" E 018° 57' 42.6" ▪ T +27 (0)83-228-7855 ▪ F +27 (0)21-863-1601

Derek Clift, who tends the vines on the Paarl family farm and produces wine in a cellar on the town's main road, is sulphur-intolerant, so understandably uses it minimally. Now he's responding to others' wishes in making a shiraz with (only just) less than 15 percent alcohol: 'It's a matter of tailoring my wine-making ideals for the demands of the new consumer.'

Mason's Shiraz ★★★ Smoky, savoury, headily alcoholic & seriously oaked **11** - first tasted since **07**.
Voëltjiegat Shiraz Occasional release. **Klipkapper Chenin Blanc** Await next. — IM

Thembi & Co

Location: Paarl ▪ Est/1stB 2009 ▪ Tasting by appt ▪ Owner(s) Thembi Tobie ▪ Winemaker(s) Jaco Brand (Citrusdal Cellars) ▪ Fairtrade ▪ thembi@thembiwines.co.za ▪ www.thembiwines.co.za ▪ **T** +27 (0)22-921-2235/+27 (0)83-277-5117

Though this is a black empowerment venture, medical nursing assistant turned entrepreneur Thembi Tobie says its long-term success is based on offering excellent products backed up by world-class service. 'I find people choose your wine because they like your label and what's in your bottle. That's all that matters.'

The Belief range

Pinotage ⊕ ★★★ Uncomplicated & friendly **11** offers up blueberry & raspberry succulence & light spice. **Shiraz** ⊕ 🍽 ★★★ Fruit pastille appeal on soft & gentle **11** charmer. Christmassy spice & plum notes. Medium body & length. **Chardonnay** ⊕ ★★★ Approachable tangy mouthful of citrus with touch of honey on **11**. **Chenin Blanc** Await new vintage.

Thembi range

Pinotage Next awaited, as for **Shiraz**, **Chardonnay** & **Chenin Blanc**. — FM

▪ **Thembu** see House of Mandela
▪ **The Mentors** see KWV Wines
▪ **The Naked Vine** see Hornbill Garagiste Winery
▪ **The Old Man's Blend** see Groote Post Vineyards
▪ **The Pavillion** see Boschendal Wines

The Rhino of Linton Park

Location: Wellington ▪ WO: Western Cape ▪ Tasting & sales by appt at Linton Park (see entry) ▪ Owner(s) Camellia PLC UK ▪ Cellarmaster(s) Hennie Huskisson (2007) ▪ Winemaker(s) JG Auret (2007) ▪ Viticulturist(s) Rudolf Jansen van Vuuren (2012) ▪ PO Box 1234 Wellington 7654 ▪ sales@lintonparkwines.co.za ▪ www.rhinowines.com ▪ **T** +27 (0)21-873-1625 ▪ **F** +27 (0)21-873-0851

Once a plentiful fynbos type in the Cape, renosterveld today is highly endangered - much like the rhinos which share the name. Wellington producer Linton Park merges a variety of interests in The Rhino label, in that it is Fairtrade accredited, forms part of the home-farm's employee empowerment scheme, and benefits Save The Rhino through the donation of a portion of profits.

Red Rhino range

Cabernet Sauvignon ⊕ 🍽 🖉 ★★★★ **11** offers fruitcake appeal, serious savoury dryness & depth. Firm yet lithe structure allows for few years ageing. **Merlot** 🍽 ★★★ Spice & Xmas cake with light herb brush on uncomplicated **12**. **Pinotage** 🍽 🖉 ★★★ Juicy raspberry simplicity on light-bodied **12** easy drinker. **Shiraz** ⊕ 🍽 🖉 ★★★★ Cushioning effect of layered blue & black berries on **11**'s dryness is instant, fleshing out the squeeze of tannins in firm frame. **Cape Red** 🍽 ★★★ Fynbos edge to red & black berries of **12** 50/50 merlot & shiraz. Soft tannin hug on finish. Unoaked, as most of these.

Pink Rhino range

Rosé ⊕ 🍽 🖉 ★★★ Lightish & fresh **12**, tangy fynbos on off-dry pink from chardonnay & cab.

White Rhino range

Chardonnay ☺ 🍽 ★★★ Tangy lime & lemon succulence to **12** uncomplicated quaffer.

Chenin Blanc 🍽 ★★★ Green pineapple vibrancy to uncomplicated & juicy **13**. **Sauvignon Blanc** ⊕ 🍽 🖉 ★★★ Green citrus zing & gooseberry on **12**, zesty & fresh. **Cape White** 🍽 ★★ Equal sauvignon & chardonnay on citrusy, light **13**. — FM

▪ **The Royal** see Valley Vineyards Wine Company
▪ **The Ruins** see Bon Cap Organic Winery
▪ **The Sadie Family** see Sadie Family Wines
▪ **The Shore** see Arniston Bay

■ **The Spice Route Winery** *see* Spice Route Winery

The Three Foxes

Location: Riebeek-Kasteel ▪ WO: Swartland ▪ Est/1stB 2004 ▪ Tasting by appt at Mullineux Wines ▪ Owner(s) Pascal Schildt, Olivier Schildt & Chris Mullineux ▪ Winemaker(s)/viticulturist(s) Chris Mullineux (Jan 2004) ▪ 1. 2ha (carignan, mourv, syrah, chenin, clairette) ▪ 6t/800cs own label 80% red 20% white ▪ PO Box 369 Riebeek-Kasteel 7307 ▪ info@the-three-foxes.com ▪ www.the-three-foxes.com ▪ **T +27 (0)82-333-6888** ▪ F +27 (0)82-121-1333-6888

Outside his day job of making precisely focused wine for Mullineux Family Wines, Chris Mullineux collaborates with brothers Pascal and Olivier Schildt on these unfettered projects, to produce wines entirely free of constraints like marketability, replication, volumes or even general stylistic direction. Rather like improvised jazz music, the end results are mostly very satisfying.

★★★★ **Castillo Syrah** ✓ ⅓ **10** (★★★★★) well crafted from low-yielding Swartland vines, delivers a cornucopia of alluring spices, with lovely freshness. Both intense & restrained, achieves elegant balance that belies 14.6% alcohol. Step up on **09**.
Mourvèdre NEW ⅓ **11** not ready for tasting. Discontinued: **Sangiovese**, **Roussanne**. — MW

■ **The Tin Mine** *see* Zevenwacht

The Township Winery

Location: Philippi ▪ Map: Cape Peninsula ▪ WO: Western Cape/Paarl ▪ Est 2009 ▪ 1stB 2010 ▪ Tasting Mon-Fri 10-4 ▪ Owner(s) The Township Winery cc ▪ Cellarmaster(s) Wilhelm van Rooyen (Oct 2009, consultant) ▪ 800cs own label 100% white ▪ PO Box 63 Philippi 7781 ▪ kate@jambela.co.za ▪ S 34° 0' 1.02" E 018° 35' 37. 71" ▪ **T +27 (0)21-371-6083** ▪ F +27 (0)21-371-6083

Entrepreneurial property developer Kate Jambela is combining viticultural land-use opportunities in the depressed neighbourhoods of the Cape Flats with an innovative community winemaking project. Happily, vintage 2014 of Philippi Sauvignon will be the first to contain juice from homesteader vines in Philippi, Nyanga and Crossroads. 'And, for the first time, you'll be able to taste the wine on site and take our 60-second cellar tour, maybe even twice, just in case you missed something. It's for free and all in one room.'

The Township Winery range

Philippi Merlot NEW ⅓ ★★★★ **12** preview has ripeness & focus, with mulberry notes & creamy tannins. Impressive poise, weight & balance. Shows potential once settled. **The Flats Pinotage** NEW 🗒 ⅓ ★★★ Soundly crafted, with wild berry fruit, **12** delivers pure varietal character in a light, spicy package. **Philippi Shiraz** NEW ⅓ ★★★☆ High-toned leafy aromas on debut **12** barrel sample evolve to appealing, dense plum pudding fruit. From Paarl vineyards. **Philippi Sauvignon Blanc** ⑤ 🗒 ⅓ ★★★★ Asparagus, grassy character beginning to dominate **10** on retaste. Roasted nuts & nettles spice up full, nicely balanced palate. Drink now. **The Flats Viognier** NEW 🗒 ★★★☆ Unoaked debut **12** shows typical oily texture & body but loses focus on fruit.

Dido range

★★★★ **Cabernet Sauvignon** ⑤ Drink-now **04** impressed previously with brooding black fruit & tealeaf herbaceousness. Wellington grapes, as all unless noted.
Pinotage ⑤ 🗒 ★★★ When last tasted, **09** was fresh, youthful, with vibrant berry fruit, restrained tannins. Some Darling vines. **The Storm Mourvèdre-Shiraz** ⑤ 🗒 ★★★ Light-bodied **09** last time showed feisty cherry fruit, hints of pepper & spices. **Pinot Grigio** ⑤ 🗒 ⅓ ★★★★ Charming, smoothly rounded body, **10** couches beeswax & stonefruit notes. Forthright & elegant. **Sauvignon Blanc** ⑤ 🗒 ★★★ **09**, from Durbanville, was lean & steely on review, with restrained gooseberry flavour. Discontinued: **Hamilcar Merlot**, **Shiraz**. — GdB

■ **The Tree Series** *see* Bellingham

Theuniskraal

Location/map/WO: Tulbagh ▪ Est 1705 ▪ 1stB 1947 ▪ Tasting & sales Mon–Fri 9–12 & 1–4, Sat 10–1 ▪ Closed Easter Sat/Sun, Dec 25 & Jan 1 ▪ Owner(s)/viticulturist(s) Jordaan family ▪ Cellarmaster(s) Andries Jordaan (1991) ▪ Winemaker(s) Andries Jordaan (1991) & Wagner Jordaan ▪ 140ha total ▪ BWI ▪ PO Box 34 Tulbagh 6820 ▪ tkraal@lando.co.za ▪ www.theuniskraal.co.za ▪ S 33° 13' 41.3" E 019° 8' 7.1" ▪ **T +27 (0)23-230-0687/89** ▪ F +27 (0)23-230-2284

A venerable Tulbagh label and South Africa's first white-wine estate, Theuniskraal has been farmed by the Jordaan family since 1927. Tradition and modernity happily intertwine here: probes monitor soil moisture and weather stations watch the sky while snail-munching ducks earn eco credits as 'integrated pest managers'.

> **Moscato Rosé** ☺ 🏚 📖 ★★★ Was 'Rosé'. Muscat ottonel the star of party-starting **13** preview; light, peachy & pleasantly sweet with blush from shiraz. **Bouquet Blanc** ☺ 🏚 📖 ★★★ Aromatic Natural Sweet from gewürztraminer & muscat de Frontignan. **13** Turkish Delight & sweet melon, lightly chill for picnic/patio pleasure.

Prestige 🏚 📖 ★★ **12** ruby cab-based easy-drinker shade less generous than previous. **Cape Riesling** 🏚 📖 ★★★ Cape institution since 1948, from grape aka crouchen blanc. Pink musk sweet **13** not as distinctively Granny Smith apple as previous. **Semillon-Chardonnay** 🏚 📖 ★★ **13** near-equal unwooded combo slips down easily but lacks distinctive character. — CvZ,CE

■ **The Village Walk** *see* Franschhoek Cellar
■ **The Warhorse** *see* Simonsig Landgoed

The Wine Fusion

Location: Wellington ▪ WO: Western Cape/Wellington ▪ Est 2007 ▪ Closed to public ▪ Cellarmaster(s) Graham Knox (Dec 2007) ▪ Winemaker(s) Various ▪ 1.5m L bulk 60% red 40% white ▪ c/o Wine Masterpieces (Pty) Ltd PO Box 1209 Wellington 7654; TWF 90 London Rd London SE16LN UK T +44 2077171569 ▪ graham@ thewinefusion.com ▪ **T +27 (0)21-447-4476/+27 (0)83-625-2865** ▪ F +27 (0)21-447-4476

In an innovative take on entrepreneurial wine-selling, Wellington-based Graham Knox gathers a team of winemakers to produce singular and evocatively named wines, bottled offshore.

★★★★ **Linley's Pure Chardonnay-Viognier** ⊕ 🏚 Peach, tangerine, zesty citrus lead to soft creamy palate. **11**'s off-dry appeal balanced by crisp acid, giving a rounded richness. Only a splash viognier. **The Director's Cut Merlot** ⊕ 🏚 ★★★ Fruity & tangy **11**, with wood spice & zingy freshness. **Highwire Summit Pinot Noir** ⊕ 🏚 ★★★ Austere **10** from Elgin, lifted tealeaf aroma, dry & light with acidic bite. **Vermeulen & Knox High Hills Pinot Noir** NEW 🏚 ★★★ **11** combines both cool-climate freshness & darker berry elements from warmer Paarl. Vibrant & bone-dry for food. WO W Cape. **The Grid Single Vineyard Optenhorst Pinotage** NEW 🏚 ★★★ Toffee allure combines with banana aromas on firm & dry **10**. Structured palate is well-suited dinner partner. WO Wellington. **Desert & Dunes Shiraz** ⊕ 🏚 ★★★ Spice route allusions in wine's name echoed in white/black pepper aromas of **11**, tight-coiled Swartland & Durbanville fruit cushioned by gram sugar. **The Alabama Pinotage-Zinfandel** NEW 🏚 ★★★★ Lively & fresh **12** mostly from pinotage (75%), but has juicy & spicy support from zinfandel component. WO Wellington. **Red Ocean Chardonnay** ⊕ 🏚 ★★★ Soft & easy unwooded style has lovely balance but **11** lacks verve. **The Quest Semillon** NEW 🏚 ★★★ Unwooded **12** shy & a little unlingering, allow time to uncoil. **The Puddingstone** ⊕ 🏚 ★★★★ Rhône-inspired white. **11** from marsanne, grenache blanc & roussanne, with typical broad stonefruit softness. Ready to enjoy. — JP

The Winery of Good Hope

Location: Stellenbosch ▪ Map: Helderberg ▪ WO: Stellenbosch/Swartland/Western Cape/Elgin/Stellenbosch ▪ Est/1stB 1998 ▪ Tasting & sales Mon–Fri 9-5 by appt ▪ Closed all pub hols ▪ Owner(s) Alex Dale, Andrew Openshaw, Yalumba, Edouard Labeye, Cliff Roberson, Ben Radford, Heather Whitman ▪ Cellarmaster(s) Edouard Labeye (1998) ▪ Winemaker(s) Jacques de Klerk (Oct 2009), with Tubby May (2002) ▪ Viticulturist(s) Edouard Labeye, Jacques de Klerk & Gus Dale ▪ ±100ha (cab, carignan, cinsaut, grenache, merlot, pinot, shiraz, chard, chenin, viog) ▪ 500t/80,000cs own label 50% red 50% white ▪ Brands for clients: Pick's Pick ▪ Level

1 BEE, IPW, WIETA ▪ Postnet Suite 124 Private Bag X15 Somerset West 7129 ▪ thewineryofgoodhope@
thewineryofgoodhope.co.za ▪ www.thewineryofgoodhope.com ▪ S 34° 0' 57.5" E 018° 49' 2.6" ▪ T +27
(0)21-855-5528 ▪ F +27 (0)21-855-5529

This Stellenbosch-based winery has possibly the most owner nationalities of any in
the Cape (Brits, Frogs, Ozzies, not to mention locals). As for the diverse range of
wines from diverse areas, one main varietal strand, pinot noir, probably owes
much to founder and MD Alex Dale's story - he's English born but Burgundy bred.
The other focus, chenin blanc, resulted from Alex's early awareness of its quality
here. For all the wines, a more 'natural' approach is increasingly evident, as is the
environmentally responsible vineyard work. Minimal intervention in the cellar,
lower alcohol levels, less power, less oak. So, a real sense of values here. Social concerns are also central, with the Land of Hope range going entirely to support a trust
benefitting previously disadvantaged employees and their families.

Radford Dale range

★★★★☆ **Merlot** ⚕ 🍴 🌿 Good, ripe aromas & flavours on **10** (★★★★), with herbal twist to sweet fruit;
forceful, dense-textured & big, but perhaps less intense than **09** so slightly drying oak tannins less harmonised.

★★★★☆ **Freedom Pinot Noir** 🍴 🌿 Dark, pure-fruited fragrance on **12** with earthy note, & ripe, sweet
fruit. But this version, more than most in the Cape, not about immediate, easy sensuous charm. All is balanced,
but a few years needed for the fruity intensity & serious structure to offer their harmonised best. From Elgin.

★★★★☆ **Pinot Noir AD** ⚕ 🍴 🌿 Selection released after 3 years. **10** from Elgin starting last year to
flaunt cherry perfume, with savoury forest-floor undertones. Complex & deep, tannic but richly delicate. Needs
time.

★★★★ **Frankenstein Pinotage** 🍴 🌿 Another un-monstrous, perfumed & pure-fruited version in **12**,
but less showy than **11**. Soft-textured, sweetly juicy (but bone-dry); drily assertive tannins need a few years.

★★★★ **Nudity** NEW 🍴 Shiraz from organic Voor Paardeberg vines, **12** in spirit of 'natural wine', even
avoiding sulphur. Spice & pure red fruit, more elegant & fresh than rich. Firm tannins. Will benefit from time.

★★★★ **Syrah** 🍴 🌿 Was 'Shiraz', & **11** does have a French accent. On elegant, restrained side, with lovely
flavours & already a complexity which should increase. Fairly moderate alcohol; slightly drying tannin.

★★★★ **Black Rock** 🍴 **11** a typical Swartland blend of shiraz, cinsaut, carignan. Sweet fruit, spice & dry
herbs. Perhaps the most easily delicious of the serious shiraz-based wines, balanced, fairly delicate. No **10**.

★★★★☆ **Gravity** 🍴 🌿 Forceful, forward **10** from shiraz, cab, merlot offering spice and bright red & black
berries on a firmly structured base. Successfully balances the claims of fresh fruitiness & savoury depths to give
some early complexity supported by good oaking. Will benefit from some years in a cool dark place.

★★★★☆ **Chardonnay** ✓ 🍴 Perhaps less knife-edged & delicate than previous, richer **12** does offer a fine
element of stony minerality, with enough acidity to balance a seductive softness, before a long finish of subtle
lime. Oaking is subtle & supportive, contributing to a characterful version of chardonnay.

★★★★☆ **Renaissance Chenin Blanc** 🍴 🌿 As usual, elegant, stony intensity on **12** deriving from old,
unirrigated bushvines, untrammelled by the mostly older oak. More delicate this year? A touch more austere
than Vinum, but with an apricot-tinged charm to its silk-textured finesse. 12.5% alcohol; dry; long finish.

★★★★ **Viognier** 🍴 Less oak showing on **12** than previously, so an even finer version of the less showily
perfumed, drier & less alcoholic style of viognier. Altogether subtle & serious & very pleasing.

★★★★☆ **Vine Dried Viognier** ⚕ 🍴 🌿 Intense but not overdone **11** dessert wine; subtle oaking, fresh
acidity & modest 12% alcohol in good balance with rich texture & fine mineral tension.

Shiraz-Merlot 🍴 ★★★★ Spicy, firm shiraz with berried merlot. Somewhat light fruit, but **11**'s alcohol in
better balance than previous; dry, lean finish.

Land of Hope range

★★★★☆ **Cabernet Sauvignon** ⚕ 🍴 Adds 'Reserve' with **11** (★★★★), previewed very young last year.
Solid ripe fruit & long finish hint at future complexity, but dominated by oak & drying tannin. Time might harmonise. Followed plush **09**.

★★★★ **Reserve Pinot Noir** ⚕ 🍴 🌿 Enticing red-fruit & savoury scents on **11** from Elgin &
Stellenbosch. Less intensity than Radford Dales, but lovely cherry fruit, savoury elegance & light, firm grip.

★★★★ **Reserve Chenin Blanc** 🍴 🌿 From Helderberg bushvines, **12** back on charming form after oaky
11 (★★★☆). Velvet texture, pure sweet fruit (melon, straw, cool earth), fresh & subtly oaked; clean, dry finish.

Vinum range

★★★★ **Cabernet Sauvignon** ⓐ 🍶 🖩 Delicious, bright, savoury flavours lurk behind the youthful tannic austerity of **11**, with greater harmony to come after a few years in bottle.

★★★★ **Chenin Blanc** 🍶 🖩 Supple, subtle & fresh, **12** (★★★★★) off old bushvines finer & less flamboyant than **11**, yet with a lovely core of sweet peach & citrus (clementine, perhaps). Oaking unobtrusive, mostly adding texture & breadth – it's the concentrated fruit that gives the lingering pleasure of the finish.

The Winery of Good Hope range

★★★★ **Granite Ridge Reserve** ⓐ 🍶 **09** from shiraz the most serious in this range, but still combines fairly easy drinkability with character & interest. Less powerful than lithe; ripe but not pushy; clean & fresh.

Oceanside Cabernet Sauvignon-Merlot ☺ 🍶 🖩 ★★★ Don't forget to sniff! The aroma's the most delightful part of pleasantly fruity, modestly oaked **12**. Lightweight, soft but grippy palate. **Unoaked Chardonnay** ☺ 🍶 🖩 ★★★ As always, **12** is easy-drinking but dry, firm, lightly rich & rather classy, with zingy citrus fruit. Stellenbosch & Robertson vines.

Pinot Noir Reserve 🍶 🖩 ★★★★ From Elgin & Stellenbosch grapes, **12** is emphatically forward & suggests power more than grace. Dark fruit balances big tannin & acid. A year or two might well justify a higher rating. **Bush Vine Pinotage** 🍶 🖩 ★★★★ Bright, attractively fruity & fragrant **12**, unoaked to preserve its easygoing, fresh pleasure-giving sweetness (but bone-dry & not jammy). Good grip, though. **Mountainside Shiraz** 🍶 ★★★☆ Tank sample of soft, very lightly oaked **12** offers ripely sweetish fruit. Might still pull itself together more. **Bush Vine Chenin Blanc** ⓐ 🍶 🖩 ★★★★ Herbs, melon & peach among the mouthfilling flavours of vivacious & delicious **12**; balanced & fresh for easy but deeply satisfying pleasure. — TJ

■ **The Wingnut** *see* Chateau Naudé Wine Creation

The Wolftrap

This increasingly successful brand, previously listed under Boekenhoutskloof, is still made (in large volumes) by that eminent winery - and still at the forefront of offering exceptional value for money. Grapes are sourced from Swartland for the red, and Swartland, Stellenbosch and Piekenierskloof for the white.

The Wolftrap ☺ 🍶 🖩 ★★★ Continues elegant combo shiraz, mourvèdre, viognier, **12** fresh, with bright fruit expression offering complexity & value.

The Wolftrap White ✓ 🍶 🖩 ★★★★ Clever dry blend of viognier plus dollops chenin & grenache blanc. **12** over-delivers with ripe stonefruit intricacy. — JP

■ **Thierry & Guy** *see* Fat Bastard

Thokozani Wines   🍾 ☕ ⛺ 📷

Location/WO: Wellington ▪ Map: Paarl & Wellington ▪ Est/1stB 2005 ▪ Tasting & sales daily 10-5 ▪ Closed Dec 25 ▪ Cellar tours by appt ▪ Seasons Restaurant ▪ Tour groups ▪ Conferences ▪ Walks/hikes ▪ Mountain biking trail ▪ 4-star Thokozani Cottages ▪ Owner(s) Diemersfontein employees, external investors & Diemersfontein Wines ▪ Cellarmaster(s) Francois Roode (Sep 2003) ▪ Winemaker(s) Francois Roode (Sep 2003), with Lauren Hulsman (2011) ▪ Viticulturist(s) Waldo Kellerman (Aug 2007) ▪ 180ha/60ha (cabs s/f, grenache, malbec, mourv, p verdot, ptage, roobernet, shiraz, chenin, viog) ▪ 60t/8,000cs own label 40% red 40% white 20% rosé ▪ WIETA ▪ PO Box 41 Wellington 7654 ▪ info@thokozani.co.za ▪ www.thokozani.co.za ▪ S 33° 39' 41.1" E 019° 0' 31.1" ▪ **T +27 (0)21-864-5050** ▪ F +27 (0)21-864-2095

This Wellington empowerment partnership between Diemersfontein employees, external investors and Diemersfontein Wines is more than just a range of wine. It owns land, offers event and hospitality facilities, and provides professional training and development to its employees. Thokozani ('Celebration') has an enthusiastic following in Europe and, increasingly, at home.

★★★★ **CCV** ✓ 🍶 🖩 Unwooded blend of chenin with dollops chardonnay & viognier; **12** (★★★★) citrus fruit given creamy texture by lees-ageing; tasty, but shade off last-tasted **10**.

Rosé ☺ 🍶 🖩 ★★★ Previewed **13** dances with bright summer fruit; acid tang lifts the semi-dry tail.

SMV 🖩 ★★★ Shiraz, mourvèdre & viognier. **12** tarry gloss to choc-mocha profile; robust oak; for food. —DS

Thorne & Daughters Wines   ♣ NEW

Est 2012 ▪ 1stB 2013 ▪ Closed to public ▪ Owner(s) John & Tasha Seccombe ▪ Cellarmaster(s)/winemaker(s)/viti-culturist(s) John Seccombe (Dec 2012) ▪ 7t/800cs own label 14% red 86% white ▪ PO Box 96 Elgin 7180 ▪ john@thorneanddaughters.com ▪ www.thorneanddaughters.com ▪ **T +27 (0)76-036-7116** ▪ F +27 (0)86-246-2923

Thorne & Daughters was started by John Seccombe and wife Tasha at the end of 2012. Prior to that, they spent a stint in the UK, Seccombe acquiring a Viticulture & Oenology degree in Sussex while also doing harvests all over the world. Going forward, the approach is to take on small parcels of grapes wherever they may be found. The 'Thorne' in T&D comes from John's middle name, linked to the family for some four centuries.

■ **Thorntree Wines** *see Doran Vineyards*
■ **1000 Miles** *see Mulderbosch Vineyards*
■ **Three Graces** *see Women in Wine*
■ **Three Peaks** *see Mount Vernon Estate*
■ **Three Pines** *see Stark-Condé Wines*
■ **Three Rivers** *see Bon Courage Estate*

Thunderchild

Location/WO: Robertson ▪ Est 2003 ▪ 1stB 2008 ▪ Wines available from Rooiberg Winery, Ashton Cellar, Robertson Winery, Ashton Wine Boutique, Affie Plaas Farmstall, Platform 62, Tanagra Winery, De Wetshof Winery & La Verne Wine Boutique - see individual cellars for opening times ▪ Owner(s) Thunderchild Wingerd Trust ▪ Cellarmaster(s) Various Robertson winegrowers ▪ 5ha (cabs s/f, merlot) ▪ PO Box 770 Robertson 6705 ▪ info@thunderchild.co.za ▪ www.thunderchild.co.za ▪ **T +27 (0)23-626-3661** ▪ F +27 (0)23-626-3664

Bearing the motto 'In aid of humanity', Thunderchild is made pro bono by sympathetic Robertson wineries and sold from their cellardoors. After audited costs, all proceeds are ploughed into the education of the children of Die Herberg Home.

Thunderchild ★★★★ Savoury Bordeaux red blend, naturally fermented, **09** is led by merlot (50%) with both cabs; dark berry & cocoa fusion, pliable tannins for easy imbibing. — JP,DB

Tierhoek   ♥ 🏛 🏠 📷

Location: Citrusdal ▪ Map: Olifants River ▪ WO: Piekenierskloof ▪ Est 2001 ▪ 1stB 2003 ▪ Tasting, sales & cellar tours on the farm Mon-Fri 8.30-4.30 by appt; alternatively tasting & sales in Sandveld Huisie restaurant cnr Church & Muller Str Citrusdal Mon-Fri 8.30-4.30 Sat 8.30-1.30 ▪ Fee R20, waived on purchase ▪ Closed all pub hols ▪ BYO picnic ▪ Walks/hikes ▪ Conservation area ▪ Guest house (sleeps 9) ▪ Owner(s) Shelley Sandell ▪ Cellarmaster(s) Roger Burton (Oct 2006) ▪ Winemaker(s) Riandri Visser (Jan 2013), with Basie Snyers (Oct 2006) ▪ Viticulturist(s) Ryno Kellerman (Aug 2006), advised by Johan Viljoen ▪ 700ha/16ha (grenache, mourv, shiraz, chard, chenin, sauv) ▪ 70t/6,000cs own label 40% red 60% white ▪ BWI, IPW ▪ PO Box 53372 Kenilworth 7745 ▪ info@tierhoek.com ▪ www.tierhoek.com ▪ S 32° 23' 27.49" E 018° 51' 24.14" ▪ **T +27 (0)21-674-3041/+27 (0)82-536-7132** ▪ F +27 (0)86-731-6351

This remote winery, set in Piekenierskloof's breathtaking landscape, was established by Shelley and the late Tony Sandell in 2001. Huge boulders made way for new vineyards, but the 60-year-old ungrafted grenache and 40-year-old chenin, says new winemaker Riandri Visser, 'still deliver amazing grapes with plenty of character'. The watchword is 'natural' – no pesticides or herbicides in those vineyards, and spontaneous fermentation and minimal use of sulphur.

Tierhoek range

★★★★ **Grenache** 🎨 Intense **11** (★★★★★) is tighter & more focused than **10**. Beautiful aromas of raspberries, spice & tree sap. The palate is well layered, with a very fine but firm tannin structure, & a broad finish. As with all, natural ferment & only older oak barrels used.

★★★★ **Syrah-Grenache-Mourvèdre** 🎨 Big, powerful **12** shows some alcoholic warmth (15%) & is less precise & fresh than Grenache - but interesting & different. Pleasant aromas, intense flavours.

★★★★ **Chardonnay** ⊕ 🎨 Vigorous, fresh & clean **11** with restrained aromas of lime blossom & crushed stone, unobscured by the older oak used. Fairly intense, though light-feeling.

★★★★ **Chenin Blanc** 🔖 Dry, lightly oaked **12** (previous off-dry) offers quince, mandarin & melon aromas. Full-flavoured & well-shaped palate. Wild ferment; 30% matured in old oak for added breadth.

★★★★ **Sauvignon Blanc 13** tank sample has aromas & flavours tending to the tropical & yellow fruits side, plus subtle flinty undertones. Attractive & interesting; should develop a few years. Tiny oak influence.

★★★★☆ **Straw Wine** 🔖 Incredibly imposing **NV** (made in solera system) with nearly 300 grams of residual sugar & just 9.5% alcohol. Intense aromas of marmalade, quince, Asian spices. Forceful, rich & creamy, the long-lingering finish with lovely dried apricot notes.

Piekeniers range

Red In abeyance. **Sauvignon Blanc** Await next. **White** 🔖 🔖 ★★★★ Sample **13** from sauvignon, chardonnay & viognier has aromas from ripe melon to grass & flowers. Disjointed still - should be integrated after bottling. — JPf

- ■ **Timbili** *see* Ernst Gouws & Co Wines
- ■ **Timothy White** *see* La Petite Vigne
- ■ **Tin Cups** *see* Wineways Marketing
- ■ **Tin Mine** *see* Zevenwacht
- ■ **Title Deed** *see* Croydon Vineyard Residential Estate
- ■ **Tobias** *see* Bryan MacRobert Wines

Tokara

Location/map: Stellenbosch • WO: Stellenbosch/Western Cape/Walker Bay/Elgin • 1stB 2001 • Tasting & sales Mon-Fri 9–5 Sat/Sun 10–3 • Closed Easter Fri/Mon & Dec 25 • Tokara Restaurant Tue-Sun lunch 12.30-2.30 & dinner 7-9.30 • Delicatessen Tue-Sun 10-4 • Facilities for children • Gift shop • Art exhibitions • Owner(s) GT & Anne-Marie Ferreira • Winemaker(s) Miles Mossop (Jan 2000), with Dumisani Mathonsi (Jan 2004) • Viticulturist(s) Aidan Morton (Nov 2000) • 104ha (cabs s/f, grenache, malbec, merlot, mourv, p verdot, ptage, shiraz, chard, chenin, sauv, sem) • 705t/100,000cs own label 40% red 59% white 1% rosé • PO Box 662 Stellenbosch 7599 • wine@tokara.com • www.tokara.com • S 33° 55' 2.9" E 018° 55' 13.7" • **T +27 (0)21-808-5900** • F +27 (0)21-808-5911

Great wine is made in the vineyard rather than the cellar – a principle more often quoted than put into practice. At banker GT Ferreira's Tokara it's more than words. Viticulturist Aidan Morton is working with Stellenbosch University boffins to implement new techniques in vineyard management in order to achieve the flavour profile wanted from Tokara's cool-climate sauvignon blanc vineyards in Elgin and Walker Bay. And at the Stellenbosch home-farm they're working on some red-wine vineyards, wanting 'to achieve wines of balance and ripeness with lower alcohols'. Great grapes are not quite enough, of course - it helps to have Miles Mossop's excellence in the cellar. Altogether, Tokara's combination of classicism and modernity seems to give finer results each year.

Reserve Collection

★★★★☆ **Pinotage 11**'s great fruit handles all-new French oak better than showy **10** (★★★★), giving more delicately perfumed charm. Ripe, juicy & rich, but despite big alcohol there's more lightness & restraint than in many examples & a fine balance. Should keep well.

★★★★ **Syrah** NEW Notably ripe fruit on **10** gives full flavour & very gentle, soft tannin structure, but not a great intensity. Less powerful affect than scary 15.4% alcohol suggests; balance is good.

★★★★☆ **Director's Reserve Red** Cab with dollops petit verdot, merlot & malbec in **10**, with oak more prominent & vintage giving slightly less harmony & generosity than in superbly balanced **09**, though lots of power. Firm, almost severe tannins should soften with few years in bottle.

★★★★ **Stellenbosch Chardonnay** ✓ 🔖 **12** (★★★★★) more outgoing than **11**, with some tropical notes (ripe pineapple, even) added to citrus. Rich, supple & lively, with acid balancing the ripeness. Already harmonious, with flavours that last & last. Like next, about a third new oak.

★★★★ **Walker Bay Chardonnay** 🔖 Hints of smoky complexity on **12**, more steely than Stellenbosch version - this year lighter & a touch less expressive. Elegant, though - both charming & racy, posed & balanced.

★★★★★ **Walker Bay Sauvignon Blanc** 🔖 Unusual delicacy on **13**, with subtle pear, floral & blackcurrant notes. Refined & unshowy, with a restrained intensity & a thrilling, mineral acidity focusing the fresh fruit flavours. Lighter-feeling than equally superb **12**.

★★★★☆ **Elgin Sauvignon Blanc** ▤ **13** more emphatic & gutsy than the Walker Bay version, with a winning balance between green pungency & tropical flamboyance that results in both intensity & poised elegance. Both these will benefit from at least a few years in bottle.

★★★★★ **Director's Reserve White** ▤ Like **11**, 70/30 sauvignon/semillon blend in **12**. Ripe blackcurrant-tinged fruit from former dominant mid-2013; lemony semillon adds breadth to complex palate. Oak integrated & supportive. Altogether complete: expressive & refined. Should gain yet more harmony & grace.

★★★★☆ **Noble Late Harvest** Rich gorgeousness as usual on **12** from oaked sauvignon. Silky, lively & fresh, the sweetness disciplined in a tightly structured balance. Alcohol lower than many (12%). WO W Cape.

Tokara range

★★★★ **Sauvignon Blanc** ✓ ▤ ⌾ Zesty aromas (green-tinged & tropical) leap out, & liveliness continues to lingering passionfruit finish on **13**. Not complex, but as deft & satisfying as they come. WO W Cape.

Cabernet Sauvignon ★★★★ Easy to enjoy this generously expressive **11**, more impressive than **10** (★★★★), with its casual charm & elegance draped over a softly firm structure. Ripe & full, well oaked. **Shiraz** ▤ ★★★★ Dollop mourvèdre on neatly wooded **11**. Juicy tannins just enough to control the ripe, sweet fruit without detracting from easy but burly friendliness. **Grenache Rosé** ▤ ★★★ Bone-dry, refreshing **13** ex tank. Restrainedly elegant rather than thrustingly fruity, with earthy element & good grip. Like next, WO W Cape. **Chardonnay** ✓ ▤ ★★★★ Rich, forthcoming aromas on **12**, the tangy, limy fruit untrammelled by the older oak used. Forthright, bone-dry & pleasing. **Noble Late Harvest** Occasional release.

Brandy range NEW

5 Year Potstill ★★★☆ Attractive youthful mix dried fruit & floral notes, with nutty, clean oak support & a hint of sweetness. Smoothly bright, not too fiery. — WB, TJ

■ **Tooverberg** *see* Klein Parys Vineyards

Topaz Wine   🍷

Location/map: Stellenbosch ▪ WO: Elgin/Wellington/Paarl ▪ Est 2000 ▪ 1stB 2001 ▪ Tasting & sales Sat 10-2 (Sep-Apr), or by prior arrangement ▪ Owner(s) Topaz Wine Company (Pty) Ltd, shareholders Tanja Beutler, Anthony Hill & Christopher Cosgrove ▪ Winemaker(s) Topaz winemaking team ▪ 1,200cs own label 80% red 20% white ▪ IPW ▪ PO Box 804 Somerset Mall 7137 ▪ tanja@topazwines.co.za ▪ www.topazwineco.com ▪ S 33° 50' 55.67" E 018° 51' 26.19" ▪ **T +27 (0)21-855-4275** ▪ F +27 (0)86-612-6118

Local pioneers of garagiste winecrafting, the Topaz team have launched an online course for 'every South African to learn more about wine in a fun edutaining way'. They also help smaller industry players with their admin, and run team building events. Oh yes - and they make wines, including a new Rhône-style red.

★★★★ **Pinot Noir** ⌾ Toasty, charry oak currently masks **12**'s bright, elegant sour cherry Elgin fruit; lively acidity gives structure & carries savoury mineral finish.

★★★★ **Shiraz** Previously 'Syrah' - last tasted by that name was elegant **07**. Smoothly textured spicy **12** (★★★★) exhibits Elgin's cool-climate pepperiness & finishes with appetising savoury acidity.

★★★★ **Custom Crush** ▤ ⌾ Stern **11** (★★★★) from Wellington cab, latest offering under recession-beating label, not as plush & complex as **08** blend with cab franc.

★★★★ **Shiraz-Mourvèdre** NEW ⌾ Floral, dry, complex **12** blend offers charm & interest in rich, rounded flavours, effectively checked by good acidity. Older oak imparts supple structure to lush Paarl fruit.

★★★★ **Viognier** ▤ ⌾ Rich, lightly oxidative **12** (★★★★) flaunts variety's ripe fleshiness & warmth, while happily retaining Elgin's trademark mineral edge. Like previous **09**, subtly oaked. — IM

Topiary Wines

Location/map/WO: Franschhoek ▪ Est 2005 ▪ 1stB 2006 ▪ Tasting & sales Mon-Sat by appt ▪ Closed Easter Sun, Dec 25/26 & Jan 1 ▪ Meals/refreshments & cellar tours on special request ▪ BYO picnic ▪ Small tour groups ▪ 1. 7km fynbos hiking trail ▪ Conservation area ▪ Owner(s) Roy & Hilary Andrews ▪ Cellarmaster(s)/winemaker(s) Mark Carmichael-Green (Nov 2010, consultant) ▪ Viticulturist(s) Wouter van der Merwe (Jan 2013), with Paul Wallace (consultant) ▪ 63ha/20ha (cab, shiraz, chard, chenin) ▪ 65t/8,000cs own label 72% red 15% rosé 13% MCC + 25,000L bulk ▪ IPW ▪ PO Box 108 La Motte 7691 ▪ Phone ahead for wheelchair access point ▪ topiarysales@telkomsa.net ▪ www.topiarywines.com ▪ S 33° 51' 52.2" E 019° 2' 39.0" ▪ **T +27 (0)21-867-0258** ▪ F +27 (0)86-750-1742

The address might be Franschhoek but the surroundings set it apart, for family-owned boutique winery Topiary lies in the foothills of the Wemmershoek Mountains, against a nature reserve. The name comes from 30 different topiary designs in the garden, some featured on the charming labels.

★★★★ **Cabernet Sauvignon** ⓐ Seductive perfume array - black plum, scrub, sweet spice - but the palate is the main attraction: fruit rich, lush, smooth textured. **08** ready now, can keep a few years.

★★★★ **Shiraz** ⓐ Tar & wild berries in **08**, follows in **07**'s footsteps with its succulence & silky smooth body. Drinking so well, hard to resist or cellar.

Cabernet Sauvignon-Shiraz ⓐ ★★★★ Despite 54% cab, **07** has the dark fruit, gamey profile of shiraz. Underpinned by firm tannins, will keep 3-5 years. **Rosé** ⓐ 🖼 🖼 ★★★★ Fresh berry & rosewater perfume, flavour brightens up **11**'s just-dry cerise-hued shiraz/cab mix. **Blanc de Blancs Brut** Await next. — CR

■ **Tormentoso** see MAN Family Wines
■ **Torres Claude** see Crows Nest
■ **Totus** see Trajan Wines
■ **Touch of Oak** see Rijk's
■ **Towerkop** see Ladismith Winery & Distillery
■ **Township Winery** see The Township Winery

Trajan Wines

Location: Stellenbosch ▪ WO: Coastal/Western Cape ▪ Est 2005 ▪ 1stB 2008 ▪ Closed to public ▪ Owner(s) Trajan Wines (Pty) Ltd ▪ Winemaker(s) Mark van Schalkwyk (Sep 2005) ▪ Viticulturist(s) Mark van Schalkwyk ▪ 10,000cs own label 70% red 30% white ▪ Fairtrade ▪ PO Box 1498 Stellenbosch 7599 ▪ info@trajanwines.co.za ▪ www.trajanwines.co.za ▪ **T +27 (0)83-505-2681** ▪ F +27 (0)86-299-4281

Established in 2005 by wine enthusiasts with dreams of an own brand and community service, Stellenbosch's Trajan since 2008 has focused increasingly on its premium range Totus ('Complete'). Fairtrade accredited for 7 years, the brand funds a crèche/daycare school and pledges to continue helping those in need.

Totus range

Cabernet Sauvignon ⓐ 🖼 ★★★★ Ripe, fruity **09**'s sweet berries dominated by oak spices when tasted. Good structure & balance should prevail, given time. **Pinotage** ⓐ 🖼 ★★★ High-toned & piercing, with opulent fruit & easygoing body, **09** displays balanced ripeness. Riebeek & Stellenbosch grapes. **Shiraz** ⓐ 🖼 ★★★★ Riebeek & Paarl grapes for **09**, made in super-ripe, big-bodied style, expressing red fruit jam & confectionery. **Shiraz-Mourvèdre** ⓐ 🖼 ★★★★ Appealing **08** partnership mid-2010 was full of spicy warmth, gamey red fruit extras. Well structured without heaviness. **Chenin Blanc** ⓐ 🖼 🖼 ★★★ Appealing **10** shows sunny ripeness, deftly handled oak lends body & form without dominating. **Sauvignon Blanc** ⓐ 🖼 🖼 ★★★★ Classy, nicely balanced **11**, typical Durbanville fruit character, ripe & supple, with leesy weight & crisp acidity. — GdB

■ **Transkaroo-Bring My Huis Toe/Take Me Home** see Boer & Brit
■ **Travino** see Klawer Wine Cellars

Tread Lightly by Backsberg ♀

Location: Paarl ▪ WO: Paarl/Western Cape ▪ Est/1stB 2010 ▪ Tasting, sales & cellar tours at Backsberg Estate (see entry) ▪ Owner(s) Michael Back ▪ Winemaker(s) Alicia Rechner (Jun 2012) ▪ Viticulturist(s) Clive Trent (Jul 1992) ▪ PO Box 537 Suider-Paarl 7624 ▪ info@treadlightly.co.za ▪ www.treadlightly.co.za ▪ S 33° 49' 42.9" E 018° 54' 56.9" ▪ **T +27 (0)21-875-5141** ▪ F +27 (0)21-875-5144

The team at forward-thinking Paarl estate Backsberg are focused on reducing carbon emissions and treading lightly on this planet, and leading almost all comers in their innovative PET (plastic) bottles. Lightweight and shatterproof, the packaging is flying high... with British Airways on domestic flights in South Africa.

PET range

Rosé NEW ☺ 🖼 🖼 ★★★ Tangy cranberry debut for **12** grenache, chardonnay, viognier mix. Uncomplex sweetly pink fun quaffer. **Sauvignon Blanc** ☺ 🖼 🖼 ★★★ Seamless **12** has developed in bottle. Rounded lemon curd vitality & appeal. Friendly with bright acid & dry finish.

Cabernet Sauvignon NEW ⬚ ⓥ ★★★★ Heaps of spicy blackberry, fruitcake appeal on **10**. Density & depth on well-framed body. Long friendly finish. **Merlot** ⬚ ⓥ ★★★★ Steady as she goes for eco-friendly **11** with hedgerow fruit & tobacco. Textured length & presence, toned body. **Chenin Blanc** ⬚ ⓥ ★★★ Previewed last year, now-bottled **12** has improved a notch. Ripe pear, crisp apple & zesty freshness. — FM

⬛ **Tribal** see African Terroir

Trizanne Signature Wines

Location: Cape Town ▪ WO: Elim/Coastal/Western Cape ▪ Est 2008 ▪ 1stB 2009 ▪ Closed to public ▪ Wine sales via website ▪ Owner(s)/winemaker(s) Trizanne Barnard ▪ 1,600cs own label 40% red 60% white + 1.5m L bulk wine export ▪ 14 van der Horst Avenue Kommetjie 7975 ▪ info@trizanne.co.za ▪ www.trizanne.co.za ▪ **T +27 (0)21-783-0617/+27 (0)82-383-6664** ▪ F +27 (0)86-669-0913

Internationally experienced winemaker Trizanne Barnard makes careful choices about where she sources grapes, all having to conform to her standard of environmentally sustainable production. That Elim features high on her list is no accident, and she now also supplies a sauvignon from there to an American exporter. The continually evolving range includes a more widely sourced new label Clearsprings for the UK market.

Trizanne Signature Wines range

★★★★ **Coastal Syrah** ✓ ⓥ Gets 'Coastal' prefix. In contrast to sibling, **10** has black plums, meaty scrub tones, a ripeness reflected in the plush palate, smooth & round. Deft oaking keeps the balance, adds definition.

★★★★ **Elim Syrah** NEW ✓ ⬚ With cooler-climate tones than its sibling, **09** is taut, tightly focused, its piquant wild red berries enhanced by forest floor earthiness, tobacco spicing. Streamlined, fresh, lovely.

★★★★ **Elim Sauvignon Blanc** ✓ ⬚ ⓥ New 'Elim' prefix. House-style salty minerality in **12**, & intriguing fynbos, English meadow green note that boosts freshness, individuality. Drinks well, perfect seafood match.

Sauvignon Blanc-Semillon Next awaited.

Clearsprings Wines NEW

Sauvignon Blanc ⬚ ★★★★ Export only. With gooseberries & mango, **13** declares its ripeness. Fulfils sauvignon's expectation by finishing fresh & clean. — CR

Truter Family Wines

Location: Wellington ▪ WO: Western Cape ▪ Est 2008 ▪ 1stB 2010 ▪ Closed to public ▪ Owner(s) Hugo & Celeste Truter ▪ Winemaker(s) Hugo Truter ▪ 1,000cs own label 50% red 50% white ▪ hugo@truterfamilywines.co.za ▪ www.truterfamilywines.co.za ▪ **T +27 (0)83-639-6288**

Small quantities of wine are made under the Agaat ('agate' in English) label of Hugo and Celeste Truter, both trained winemakers, who always wanted to produce handcrafted wines focusing on blends rather than 'boring' single cultivars. The first vintage well past, they are relieved that the 'novice' tag can be dropped.

Agaat range

★★★★ **Christina** ⓣ ⬚ ⓥ Sauvignon plus nouvelle, chenin & viognier in finely crafted **12**; crisp & clean, with good palate weight. Tasted ex tank.

John David ✓ ⬚ ★★★★ Brightly fruited but also with cocoa powder perfume. **12** Cape Blend of cab, pinotage & shiraz is filled with youthful, fresh verve. — JP

⬛⬛⬛ Cellar Calitzdorp 🍷🍸🎍♿

Location/WO: Calitzdorp ▪ Map: Klein Karoo & Garden Route ▪ 1stB 2003 ▪ Tasting, sales & tours Mon-Fri 8-4 Sat 8-2 Sun by appt ▪ Closed Easter Fri-Mon, Apr 27, May 1, Dec 25 & Jan 1 ▪ Honey & olive oil ▪ BYO picnic ▪ Owner(s) Ashley & Pat Mason ▪ Cellarmaster(s)/viticulturist(s) Ashley Mason ▪ Winemaker(s) Ashley Mason, with Johan Julies ▪ 0.5ha (souzão, tinta, touriga, hanepoot) ▪ 4t/600cs own label 100% red ▪ PO Box 7067 Newton Park 6055 ▪ tttcellars@iafrica.com ▪ S 33° 31' 50.94" E 021° 41' 44.88" ▪ **T +27 (0)44-213-3114** ▪ F +27 (0)44-213-3114

The Mason family were thrilled with the Port & Wine Challenge gold for dad Ashley's 2010 Cape Vintage, plus Klein Karoo regional show silvers for both it and their best-selling Red Muscadel. The peripatetic Port Elizabeth electrical

contractor, who commutes to his Calitzdorp farm, dreams of winelands travel further afield: California, Portugal, France, Italy.

Cabernet Sauvignon ⓟ 11 a tad wild & funky, will have its fans. **LTD** Await next, as for **Shiraz, Hilltop Red, Chenin Blanc, Muscat d'Brigne** & **Red Muscadel. Dry Red** ⓟ ★★ Shiraz & splash cab, cloves & some berries on high-toned, brief **NV. Calitzdorp Collage** NEW ★★★★ Characterful Calitzdorp Blend marries equal parts touriga & tinta with 20% souzâo. 12 preview is spicy, with leather notes & robust tannins firmly embracing dense fruit. **Hanepoot** Previewed **NV** too unformed to rate. **Cape Ruby** Unrated **NV** work-in-progress. **Cape Vintage** 📷 ★★★ Convincing port-style 13 barrel sample repeats successful recipe of half touriga with tinta & souzâo. Rich & dense, needs brief abstinence for spirit to fully integrate. **Cape White** ★ Port-style from chenin, **NV** preview high-toned barley sugar whiffs. — HJ,CvZ

■ **Tukulu** *see* Earthbound

Tulbagh Winery

Location: Tulbagh/Porterville • Map: Tulbagh • WO: Tulbagh/Western Cape/Coastal • Est 1906/2006 • 1stB 1910 • Tulbagh Cellar: Tasting & sales Mon-Fri 8-5 Sat & pub hols 9-1 Sun at Paddagang Wine Shop 11-3 • Porterville Cellar: Tasting & sales Mon-Fri 8-5 • Closed Easter Fri-Sun & Dec 25/26 • Cellar tours by appt • Gifts • Farm produce • BYO picnic • Conferences • Walks/hikes • Mountain biking in the area • Owner(s) 86 members • Cellarmaster(s) /Production manager Naude Bruwer (Jan 2010) • Winemaker(s) Porterville: Rudi Wium (Aug 2011); Tulbagh: Helena Neethling (Jun 2010) • Viticulturist(s) Elizabeth Cloete (Dec 2011) • 1,230ha (cab, merlot, ptage, shiraz, chenin, chard, sauv) • 14,500t/100,000cs own label 65% red 30% white 5% rosé & 8m L bulk + 40,000cs for clients • Brands for clients: Grimont (Germany), Millberg (UK/France) • IPW • PO Box 85 Tulbagh 6820; PO Box 52 Porterville 6810 • info@tulbaghwine.co.za • www.tulbaghwine.co.za • S 33° 15' 8.8" E 019° 8' 36.5" • **T** +27 (0)23-230-1001 (Tulbagh); +27 (0)22-931-2170 (Porterville) • **F** +27 (0)23-230-1358; +27 (0)22-931-2171

This grower-owned venture runs two cellars: one in historic Tulbagh, the other near Porterville in big-sky Swartland. The dynamic management team (including new winemaker Rudi Vium, viticulturist Elizabeth Cloete and just-married marketing/sales manager Lourens Relihan) intend repeating 2013's 10% production increase every year. They'll get help from niche varieties (barbera, malbec, petit verdot) supplied by the Moravia Empowerment Project in nearby Piketberg, as well as from the new irreverently named Flippenice blends and, of course, the winery's top seller, Tulbagh Shiraz-Pinotage.

Klein Tulbagh Reserve range

Cabernet Sauvignon Await next, as for **Merlot. Pinotage** ⓟ 📷 ★★★ Fynbos-nuanced 11's fruit in grip of firm oak tannin mid-2012; would benefit from year/2 in bottle. WO Coastal. **Shiraz** 📷 ★★★ Now bottled, 10 is overtly oaky, with sweet spices, rich candied berry fruit & bold 15% alcohol.

Tulbagh range

Cabernet Sauvignon 🍴 📷 ★★★ Mulberry & pencil shavings appeal on step-up 11; nicely shaped if a tad brief. Lightly oak-staved, as most reds in range. **Merlot** 🍴 📷 ★★ Previewed last time, 12 now shows a brisk cherry centre, dusty tannic finish. **Pinotage** 🍴 📷 ★★★ 12 raises the bar with ample raspberry taste, friendly tannin; lightly chill for summer fun. **Shiraz** 🍴 📷 ★★★ 12 old-fashioned but pleasing BBQ sipper with charry oak, meaty nuances & strong tannin grip. **Shiraz-Pinotage** 🍴 📷 ★★ 12 spicy berry & oak scents, gentle sweetness for uncomplicated quaffing. WO Coastal. **Rosé** Await next, as for **Chardonnay, Sauvignon Blanc, Sauvignon** & **Port. Chenin Blanc** 🍴 📷 ★★ Ripe melons & tropical fruit, crisp acidity & tinned pineapple end on 13. **Colombard-Chenin Blanc** 🍴 📷 ★★★ 13 easy-drinker is floral, bright & curvaceous courtesy few grams sugar. **Pinotage Doux** 📷 ★★ Drops 'Sparkling' from name but 12 remains a sparkler, frothy & sweet. WO Coastal. **Sauvignon Blanc Brut** 📷 ★★★ Attractive varietal Granny Smith apple & grass notes on improved 13 dry sparkling. **Muscat Ottonel Doux** NEW 📷 ★★ Friendly 12 muscatty bubbly for the sweet-toothed.

Paddagang range

Paddapoot Hanepoot 📷 ★★ Fortified sweetie 12 delivers lemon & honey fireside enjoyment. **Sopkoppie Rooi Muskadel** NEW 🍴 📷 ★★ Jasmine highlights on delightfully grapey if unlingering 12 fortified dessert. WO W Cape, as next. **Brulpadda Port** ⓟ ★★★ **NV** sweet fortified from pinotage & ruby cab.

Flippenice range NEW

Cabernet Sauvignon-Merlot ▦ ▨ ★★ 60/40 **NV** combo, amicable liquorice-toned quaffer. These WO Coastal. **Chenin Blanc-Sauvignon Blanc** ▦ ▨ ★★ Soft baked apple & almond notes on light & quaffable 60/40 **NV**.

Secluded Valley range NEW

Shiraz-Pinotage ▨ ★★ Supple & easygoing picnic mate in **NV** bag-in-box (3L), as next. **Chenin Blanc** ▨ ★★ **NV** offers very light red apple flavour. Like sibling, WO W Cape.

Porter Mill Station range

Reserve Cabernet Sauvignon ① ▦ ▨ ★★★ Back-on-track **11** (with 'Reserve' now in name) mixes dark berries & vanilla oak, medium body & slight tannic touch from wood staves. WO W Cape, export only as for all in this range. **Pinotage** ① ▦ ▨ ★★★ Mulberry & coffee enticement on decently dry **11**. **Shiraz** Not tasted. **Chenin Blanc** ① ▦ ▨ ★★ Engaging spring meadow aromas on lightish **11**, flavours fading, drink up. **Sauvignon Blanc** ① ▦ ▨ ★★★ Improved **11** for those who don't like their sauvignon too fruity; mineral, dry & pithy. — GdB,MW

■ **Tullie Family Vineyards** *see* Lanner Hill

Twee Jonge Gezellen Estate-The House of Krone

Location/map: Tulbagh ▪ WO: Western Cape ▪ Est 1710 ▪ 1stB 1937 ▪ Tasting & sales Mon-Fri 10-4 Sat & selected pub hols 10-2 ▪ Annual festivals: Christmas in Winter (Jun) & Summer Elegance (Dec) ▪ Owner(s) TJG Estate (Pty) Ltd ▪ Cellarmaster(s) Nicky Krone ▪ Winemaker(s) Matthew Krone (2000), with Stephan de Beer (2008) ▪ Viticulturist(s) Rosa Kruger ▪ PO Box 16 Tulbagh 6820 ▪ info@tjg.co.za ▪ www.houseofkrone.co.za ▪ S 33° 14' 18.1" E 019° 6' 51.8" ▪ **T +27 (0)23-230-0680** ▪ F +27 (0)23-230-0686

The 'Two Young Companions' farm in Tulbagh was a beacon of innovation in the local wine industry for decades: pioneers of cold fermentation, tradition-method sparkling wines, late disgorgement, night harvesting... Once best known for aromatic white wines and innovative blends, the emphasis has shifted to the now near-exclusive focus on méthode cap classique. Krones and their forebears have resided on the picturesque property since its establishment in 1710. Youngest-generation Matthew and Luke have recently taken over the reins of winemaking and marketing respectively, with dad Nicky presiding over the cellar and matriarch Mary helping drive the brand.

Krone range

★★★★ **Rosé Cuvée Brut** Strawberry shortbread, fine dry conclusion on **09** (★★★★) salmon-hued MCC bubbly from pinot (60%), chardonnay. Like more harmonious **08**, elegant partner for charcuterie or dessert.

★★★★ **Borealis Cuvée Brut** ① Always a stately sparkler from pinot noir & chardonnay; 55/45 in appealing & uplifting **09**. Bruised apple, clean yeasty notes & truly 'brut' dry conclusion.

★★★★☆ **Nicolas Charles Krone Marque 1** ① Standout **NV** multi-vintage (**01**, **02**, **03**) sparkling from 50/50 pinot noir/chardonnay; last-tasted disgorgement matured 7 years on lees. Restrained, with pinot richness, chardonnay freshness on palate, persistent bone-dry farewell.

Chardonnay-Pinot Noir NEW ☺ ▦ ★★★ House's signature grapes in a non-sparkling blend, for 'special everyday moments'. Unwooded **12** is tasty, dry, with generous berry fruit, pear & lime complexity. — GdB,MW

Twelve Apostles Winery   NEW

Est/1stB 2009 ▪ Tasting by appt only ▪ Owner(s)/winemaker(s) Chris & Charles Lourens ▪ 3-5t/±650cs own label 50% red 50% white ▪ Brands for clients: Kanah Winery ▪ SAWIS ▪ PO Box 16007 Panorama 7506 ▪ info@ twelveapostleswinery.co.za ▪ www.twelveapostleswinery.co.za ▪ **T +27 (0)82-375-2884** ▪ F +27 (0)86-510-2431

Cape Town father-and-son team Chris and Charles Lourens describe themselves as 'garagiste winemakers in the true sense of the word; winelovers with a passion for the art and history of small-scale winemaking'. From basket-pressing hand-sorted grapes (sourced widely) to organising one-on-one tastings with

winelovers, the civil engineer and online wine marketer swear by 'keeping it real by keeping it small, because when it becomes "work", the passion goes'.

■ **24 Rivers** see Valley Vineyards Wine Company
■ **Twin's Peak** see Lateganskop Winery
■ **Two Centuries** see Nederburg Wines
■ **Two Cubs** see Knorhoek Wines

Two Oceans   🍷 🍸

Location: Stellenbosch ▪ WO: Western Cape ▪ Tasting & sales at Bergkelder ▪ Owner(s) Distell ▪ Cellarmaster(s) Deon Boshoff & Andrea Freeborough ▪ Winemaker(s) Justin Corrans, Pieter Badenhorst, Bonny van Niekerk, Elize Coetzee & Natasha Williams ▪ Viticulturist(s) Bennie Liebenberg, Annelie Viljoen & Drikus Heyns ▪ Distell PO Box 184 Stellenbosch 7599 ▪ info@distell.co.za ▪ www.twooceanswines.co.za ▪ **T** +27 (0)21-809-7000

Sold in 80 countries, popular Distell-owned Two Oceans is widely applauded for its good value and embrace of modern attributes like eco-minded lighterweight bottles and lower alcohol levels (the untasted Quay 5 range is a kilojoule-busting 5.5% by volume). Winemaker Natasha Williams recently joined the team, which has access to fruit from across the Western Cape and is advised by viti expert Drikus Heyns, trained locally and in France.

Shiraz Rosé ☺ 🗄 ★★☆ Like previous, **13** boiled sweets & flowers, dryish & creamy, hard to resist. **Sauvignon Blanc** ☺ 🗄 🖉 ★★☆ Pleasant semi-dry poolside quaffer, despite being slightly more straightforward in **13**. Sweet-sour tropical fruit has an interesting savoury element.

Pinot Noir ✓ 🗄 ★★★☆ After standout, variety-true **12** (★★★★), **13** pre-bottling seems just a shade less cultivar specific but perfectly pleasant, well made & excellent value. **Pinotage** ★★★☆ Goes up a level in ex-tank **13** on the strength of pure, concentrated fruit, bright acidity, beautifully soft tannins, aided by touch sugar. **Shiraz** ★★★☆ Another improved label under this brand, aiming for - & achieving - easier-drinking style. **13** preview generous sweet ripe berry fruit, dusting of spice, attractively light & fresh feel. **Cabernet Sauvignon-Merlot** 🗄 ★★★ **13** showing bit more cab brawn than previous, merlot's slightly thatchy note amid the black fruit, chewy tannins. **Soft & Fruity Red** 🗄 ★★★ **13** delivers honest drinkability with red & black berry smells & tastes. **Shiraz-Cabernet Sauvignon** 🖉 ★★★ Dark-fruited **12** slightly weightier & chewier incarnation, but still appealing everyday semi-dry red. **Chardonnay** 🗄 ★★★ **13**, pre-bottling, is nicely poised between apple crumble richness, toasty oak & zesty citrus fruit. **Pinot Grigio** Await next. **Semillon-Chardonnay** 🗄 ★★★ From tank, improved **13** is attractively fresh, fragrant & fruit filled, its oak a subtle backdrop. **Chenin Blanc-Sauvignon Blanc** 🗄 ★★★ Tasty & balanced combo of quince & lime, previewed **13** big step up, deft 80/20 blend surprisingly serious for entry-level wine. **Sauvignon Blanc-Chenin Blanc** [NEW] ★★★ Harmonious **13**, fresh grassy gooseberry flavours, soft & easy to drink. **Fresh & Fruity White** 🗄 🖉 ★★★ 3-way blend is fresh & fruity as advertised, **13** lightish guava-laced sweetness. — DB, HJ

■ **Two Tunns** see Valley Vineyards Wine Company
■ **Tygerberg** see Altydgedacht Estate
■ **Uiterwyk Estate** see DeWaal Wines

Uitkyk Estate   🍴 🍷 ☕ 📷 🎎 ♿

Location/map: Stellenbosch ▪ WO: Simonsberg–Stellenbosch/Stellenbosch ▪ Est 1712 ▪ 1stB 1957 ▪ Tasting & sales Mon-Fri 9–5 Sat/Sun 10–4 ▪ Tasting fees: R15/5 wines; R20/brandy & chocolate truffle; R40/brandy, chocolate truffle & fruitcake ▪ Closed Good Fri & Dec 25 ▪ Facilities for children ▪ Tour groups ▪ Gift shop ▪ Cheese platters during tasting hours ▪ Gourmet picnic baskets, to be booked 24hrs in advance ▪ Conferences ▪ 4x4, hiking & mountain biking trails ▪ Conservation area ▪ Manor House museum ▪ Owner(s) Lusan Premium Wines ▪ Cellarmaster(s) Estelle Lourens (Oct 2000) ▪ Winemaker(s) Estelle Lourens (Oct 2000) ▪ Brandy master Estelle Lourens (Jan 2000) ▪ Viticulturist(s) Rudi Buys (2001) ▪ 591ha/140ha (cab, shiraz, chard, pinot grigio, sauv) ▪ 772t/18,400cs 55% red 45% white (Uitkyk) & 71,000cs 53% red 45% white 2% rosé (Flat Roof Manor) ▪ BWI champion, WIETA ▪ PO Box 104 Stellenbosch 7599 ▪ info@uitkyk.co.za ▪ www.uitkyk.co.za ▪ S 33° 51' 24.8" E 018° 51' 50.7" ▪ **T** +27 (0)21-884-4416 ▪ F +27 (0)21-884-4717

Established in 1929 by Prussian nobleman Hans von Carlowitz, this Lusan-owned wine estate on prime Simonsberg slopes combines the 18th-century manor house's history with modern winemaking, eco-mindedness and a family-friendly

atmosphere. Recent diversification into Aberdeen Angus stud farming has seen viticulturist/farm manager Rudi Buys become a recognised cattle judge!

Uitkyk Estate range

Carlonet ⚖ ★★★★ Venerable Old-Cape cab label given thoroughly modern styling in **10**, with soupçon shiraz. Takes **09**'s (★★★★) ripeness & power to next level, with 14.7% alcohol, tannin that tightly grips blackberry fruit mid-2013, needing time. **Shiraz** ⏱ ⚖ ★★★★ **10**, with 13% cab, in ripe dark-berried idiom. Obvious oaking adds to full-bodied palate, but lacks freshness & balance for higher rating, ends sweetish. Stellenbosch WO. **Shiraz-Cabernet Sauvignon** ★★★ Showing plenty of extracted plum fruit, **09**'s dark-toned palate is sweet/sour, tending more to sweet in the conclusion. **Chardonnay** ⚖ ★★★★ More power than most years, but **12**'s lemon butter richness well contained within bright & vibrant structure. Very young still - deserves time to settle. **Chenin Blanc** NEW ⚖ ★★★ Barrel-fermented (20% with native yeasts) **12** is zesty & lively if not majorly concentrated, a savoury undertone gives food affinity. **Sauvignon Blanc** ⚖ ★★★★ Hardly out the starting blocks, **13** ex tank already shows lithe athleticism, needing only bit of time for green-spectrum fruit to fully reveal itself.

Brandy range NEW

★★★★ **10 Year Grand Reserve Brandy** Smart 10-year-matured pure postill estate brandy, unusually from clairette, cinsaut & chenin grapes. Plenty of oak vanillin & spice to accompany the fruit, though not great complexity. Smooth, rich, round & balanced. — WB, DC, TJ

■ **Uitvlucht** see Montagu Wine & Spirits Co
■ **Ukuzala** see Mountain River Wines

Ultra Liquors

Location: Cape Town ▪ WO: Stellenbosch/Robertson/Coastal/Paarl/Western Cape/Darling ▪ Owner(s) Colin Robinson ▪ Winemaker(s) Various ▪ 426 Main Rd Wynberg Cape Town 7824 ▪ marknorrish@ultraliquors.co.za, dale@bordelais.co.za ▪ **T +27 (0)21-797-4341** ▪ F +27 (0)21-797-4351

'Big on palate, small on pocket' is the motto in the Ultra Wine Division, liquor retail chain turned specialist wine merchant. 'It dictates our selection process,' says general manager Mark Norrish, delighted at recent competition results and listings highlighting the wines' value. Mark is equally pleased that while sales of own-labels Table Bay and Secret Cellar grow rapidly, consumers are also increasingly trying different wines: 'They just love our policy of refunding any bottle they are not entirely happy with.'

Table Bay range

Sauvignon Blanc ☺ ⚖ ★★★ A fairly serious sauvignon with super-appealing guava & white pear aromas, **13** good flavour intensity & zippy finish.

Cabernet Sauvignon ⏱ ★★★★ Brooding & dark, with seaweed/iodine notes, **09** offers real character. Shows elegance way above its station. WO Coastal, as for all in this range unless noted. **Merlot** ⚖ ★★★ Firmer & more savoury this time, **11** dusty, leafy & olive-like notes, dry tannins. Drink with char-grilled meat. **Chenin Blanc** ⏱ 🍽 ⚖ ★★★ **12** has layers of dried apricots & honey melon, borne on light, breezy body. Charmingly honest. **Méthode Cap Classique Brut** NEW ✓ ★★★★ For the bargain hunter, **NV** bubbly from chardonnay & splash pinot noir over-delivers completely with loads brioche & marmalade flavour. Ex Robertson, as the other sparklings here. **Méthode Cap Classique** ⏱ ★★★★ Traditional-method bubbly, mostly chardonnay, **NV** repeats previous fresh crispness, apple fruitiness. Perfect breakfast tipple. **Méthode Cap Classique Blanc de Blancs** NEW ✓ ★★★★ **NV** chardonnay fizz similar to Brut in showing richness & secondary character from lees-ageing. Buttery apple crumble, ripe lime & sweet biscuits. Good intensity, tangy finish. Discontinued: **Shiraz, Starboard Red, Spinnaker White.**

Secret Cellar range

Cabernet Sauvignon-Shiraz No.112 NEW ☺ ★★★ Concentrated, extracted winter fireside wine, **11** jammy, ripe dark fruit good partner for cheese. Will benefit from decanting.

Cabernet Sauvignon Selection 633 Next awaited, as for **Cabernet Sauvignon Reserve, Shiraz Selection 480, Shiraz Selection 275, Shiraz Reserve, Shiraz & Méthode Cap Classique Blanc de Blancs. Cabernet Sauvignon No. 466** NEW ★★★ For drinking soon, **08** offers greenpepper, fynbos & eucalyptus in a drying body held together - for now - by good tannin frame. **Share The Secret Merlot** ⏱ ★★★ Baked fruit

with chocolate notes on **11**, backed up with ripe tannins. Juicy & quaffable. WO Robertson. **Merlot Reserve** ⊕ ★★★★ Leafy & (attractively) lean, with hint of mint, **09** presents healthy ripe fruit on elegant structure. WO W Cape. **Merlot No. 459** NEW ★★★ Big, serious **08** with dusty notes, coffee oak & stewed fruit. Showing signs of age - best enjoyed soonest. **Share the Secret Merlot No. 060** NEW 🗒 ★★★ Fresh & appetising **11**, juicy ripe fruit with berry spice & bright core, dry finish. Robertson WO. **Pinotage No.435** NEW ★★★ As for most in range, surprises with seriousness & weight. Variety's banana & smoke in **08** plus strong mocha notes from oak. Drinkable, but has structure to evolve. **Shiraz No. 343** NEW ✓ ★★★★ White pepper, violets & black berries - all well-defined & balanced. **11** appetising, fresh. **Share The Secret Red Blend No. 695** 🗒 📖 ★★ Gets 'No. 695' suffix this ed. Leafy NV Bordeaux-style blend with savoury meaty body & dry body. Drink soon with hearty food. WO Coastal. **Cabernet Sauvignon-Merlot** ⊕ ★★ Rather tired **06** ex Paarl vines doesn't ring any bells. **Petit Verdot-Cabernet Sauvignon-Malbec** NEW ✓ 📖 ★★★★ Enticing **12** blend with opulent fruit - plum, cassis, mulberry - along with spicy perfume. Chewy tannins make for mouthwatering grip, perfume follows to long finish. Bright & moreish. **Chardonnay No. 473** NEW ✓ ★★★★ For fans of buttery, rich chardonnays, **08** shows development in nutty complexity, savoury tone & toasty oak. In balance now, but drink soon. Punches above the price point. **Sauvignon Blanc** ✓ 🗒 📖 ★★★★ **12** shows its Darling origins, along with bottle-age characters of sweet grass, asparagus & baked lime. Age complexity continues on palate with tinned pea & khaki bush. Serious food wine, not a tutti-frutti quaffer. **Méthode Cap Classique Rosé No. 350** NEW ★★★ Pink bubbles from classic varieties & dollop pinotage. **10** savoury flavours along with some red fruit in light frame. Good persistent dry mousse. WO Paarl. **Méthode Cap Classique Brut No. 558** ✓ ★★★★ Gets 'No. 558' moniker this ed. From Paarl, **09** bottle-fermented sparkling from pinot noir/chardonnay. Creamy, balanced & well made. Straightforwardly pleasing. **MCC Blanc de Blancs No. 428** NEW ✓ ★★★★ Budget-friendly champagne-method sparkling. **07**, from chardonnay, with toasty yeasty notes. Paarl vines. Discontinued: **Cabernet Franc-Petit Verdot Selection 299**. — HJ

■ **Umfiki** *see Goudini Wines*

Umkhulu Wines

Location: Paarl ▪ Est/1stB 2000 ▪ Closed to public ▪ Owner(s) Fiona Phillips ▪ 5,000cs own label 100% red ▪ PO Box 304 Pearl Valley Paarl 7646 ▪ fiona@umkhulu.com ▪ www.umkhulu.com ▪ **T +27 (0)83-257-6353** ▪ F +27 (0)86-646-1852

'Umkhulu', in both Xhosa and Zulu, means 'the big one' and therefore an apt moniker for the bold red wines under this label. Owned by Fiona Phillips, it remains solely an export brand.

★★★★☆ **Pinotage** ⊕ Firmish tannins add texture to modern **04**'s slightly sweet fruit.
★★★★ **Tian** ⊕ Cab-led Bordeaux blend. Last **03** (★★★★) shy, light textured; **02** was dense & extracted.
Malbec ⊕ ★★★★ **05**'s exuberant mulberry fruit curtailed by tannins when last tasted. **Shiraz** ⊕ ★★★★ Last **04** was straightforward & rich. **Ubuntu** ⊕ ★★★★ Cape Blend pinotage, merlot, petit verdot in pliable **05**. **Akira** ⊕ ★★★★ **03** mixed cab, petit verdot & pinotage for generous sipping a while back. **Njalo** ⊕ ★★★ Few years ago **05**'s tannins needed time or food. Combo merlot, shiraz, pinotage. — CvZ

United Nations of Wine

Location: Sandton ▪ WO: Western Cape ▪ Est/1stB 2005 ▪ Closed to public ▪ Owner(s) Dogwood Trust ▪ Cellar-master(s)/winemaker(s) David John Bate (Jun 2005) ▪ 60,000cs own label 30% red 70% white ▪ Fairtrade; CarbonNeutral ▪ 8 Royal Ascot Lane Sandown Sandton 2196 ▪ info@unitednationsofwine.com ▪ www. unitednationsofwine.com ▪ **T +27 (0)11-884-3304** ▪ F +27 (0)11-883-0426

Producer-distributor of 'fun, friendly, affordable' wines largely for export (recently including Hong Kong, Singapore, Canada), UNOW 'secretary general' David John Bate received Fairtrade accreditation to partner his carbon-neutral production rating.

Frisky Zebras range

Captivating Cabernet Sauvignon ⊕ 🗒 ★★★ Cassis-laden NV, flavoursome & approachable. **Mystic Merlot** ⊕ 🗒 ★★ Shy & firm NV, needs hearty fare. **Seductive Shiraz** 🗒 📖 ★★★ Supple & spicy NV, has savoury red berried appeal. **Sublime Chardonnay** ⊕ 🗒 ★★★ Engaging & friendly NV, succulent butter-scotch & melon fullness tweaked by lime. **Sultry Chenin Blanc** ⊕ 🗒 ★★★ Fruit-filled NV quaffer exudes joie de vivre. **Sensuous Sauvignon Blanc** 🗒 📖 ★★ NV is plump & tropical, with warm afterglow despite only 12% alcohol. Note: Dusty Rhino, G Spot, Harmony Tree & Luscious Hippos ranges not tasted. — MW

uniWines Vineyards

Location: Rawsonville ▪ Map: Breedekloof ▪ WO: Breedekloof/Western Cape ▪ Est/1stB 2007 ▪ Tasting & sales Mon-Thu 8–5 Fri 8-4 Sat & pub hols 10–2 ▪ Closed Easter Fri-Mon, Dec 25/26 & Jan 1 ▪ Cellar tours Mon-Fri & by appt Sat/during harvest ▪ Tour groups ▪ BYO picnic ▪ Conferences ▪ Soetes & Soup festival (Jul) ▪ Breedekloof outdoor festival (Oct) ▪ Owner(s) 50 shareholders ▪ Cellarmaster(s) Nicolaas Rust (Oct 2008) ▪ Winemaker(s) WS Visagie (Nov 2010), Hattingh de Villiers (Sep 2010), Schalk van der Merwe (Dec 2007), Christo Smit (Jan 2001) & Madre Fullard (Apr 2013) ▪ Viticulturist(s) Gert Engelbrecht (Aug 2009) ▪ 6,000+ha/ha (cab, cinsaut, merlot, ptage, shiraz, chard, chenin, cbard, sauv) ▪ 45,000t/200,000cs own label 50% red 50% white + 100,000cs for clients ▪ Brands for clients: Cape Nelson, Cape Promise, Fairtrade Original, Stormy Cape ▪ ISO 22000:2008, BWI, Fairtrade, IPW, WIETA ▪ PO Box 174 Rawsonville 6845 ▪ info@uniwines.co.za ▪ www.uniwines.co.za ▪ S 33° 43' 16.7" E 019° 21' 0.0" ▪ **T +27 (0)23-349-1110** ▪ F +27 (0)86-529-1392

Fifty producer-shareholders contribute to this extensive, widely accredited winery, operating from three large Breedekloof cellars: Groot Eiland, Nuwehoop and Daschbosch, and vinifying 45,000 tons of grapes. Mostly bulk, the production also features the Daschbosch reserves (soon to include a Rhône-style red and a white blend), and Palesa Fairtrade range, including 1.5L pouches and a husk brandy.

Daschbosch range
Procavia Cabernet Sauvignon-Merlot ⓥ ★★★★ Stylish flagship blend, **11** is elegant without intensity, fruity without complexity & nicely spiced with oak. WO W Cape.

Ankerman range
Cabernet Sauvignon-Merlot ⓘ 🍴 ⓥ ★★★ **11** juicy-fruity, unassuming light-bodied 50-50 blend. **Chenin Blanc-Chardonnay** 🍴 ⓥ ★★ **12** shows oxidative notes on neutral, oak-touched palate. **Nectar de Provision Red** ⓥ ★★★ Powerful sweetness (200+ g/l sugar) & nutty brandy aromas in **NV** jerepigo, merlot-based version of Cognac's Pineau des Charentes. **Nectar de Provision White** ⓥ ★★★★ Fortified colombard with hefty 180g/l sugar is quirky but appealing. Malty sugarcane & spicy brandy. Solera matured, thus **NV**, as for red sibling.

Groot Eiland range
Cabernet Sauvignon ⓘ ★★★ **09** shows promising black fruit, but lean body fades quickly. **Merlot** ⓘ ★★★ Sweet, minty fruit with softly textured tannins, **09** fades to lean, brief finish. **Pinotage** ⓘ ★★★ Juicy & ripe **09** had supple tannins when last tasted, ideal for pasta partnering. **Shiraz** Next awaited. **Shiraz-Pinotage** ⓘ ⓥ ★★★★ Spicy & aromatic cooked fruit on **11** shows dominance of pinotage in this Cape Blend. Substantial & satisfying. **Sauvignon Blanc** 🍴 ⓥ ★★★ Appealing grassy notes on **13**, with crisp acidity, tart gooseberry fruit. Freshness, lower alcohol from early harvest. Discontinued: **Shiraz Rosé**, **Chardonnay**, **Chenin Blanc**.

Meander range
Merlot-Shiraz 🍴 ⓥ ★★ Stalky, nutty **12** has tangy blackcurrant fruit, light body. **Moscato** ⓥ ★★★ Frothy sweet **13** muscat d'Alexandrie in traditional Asti style. **Chenin Blanc-Sauvignon Blanc** NEW 🍴 ⓥ ★★★ Lots of fresh pineapple fruitiness on **13** poolsider. Discontinued: **Chenin Blanc-Colombar**.

Palesa Fairtrade range

Sauvignon Blanc ☺ 🍴 ⓥ ★★★ **13** shows bright kiwi fruit with gentle acid nudge.

Merlot 🍴 ⓥ ★★★ Earthy notes & juicy fruit on slender body, **11** is for lighter moments. **Pinotage** 🍴 ⓥ ★★ Honest, light & fruity **11** for summer quaffing. **Chenin Blanc** ⓘ 🍴 ★★★ Fresh & enticingly tropical **11** brims with fruit. Rounded body, gentle acid. Summer delight. **Moscato** ⓘ 🍴 ⓥ ★★ Screwcap version of Meander, above. **12** light, sweet & slightly sparkling. — GdB

■ **Upington** see Orange River Wine Cellars

Upland Organic Estate

Location/WO: Wellington ▪ Map: Paarl & Wellington ▪ Est 1990 ▪ 1stB 1996 ▪ Tasting, sales & tours by appt ▪ Closed Easter Fri-Mon & Dec 25 ▪ Self-catering cottages ▪ Distillery: brandy & grappa ▪ Organic olives, olive oil, dried fruit & nuts ▪ Craft workshop ▪ Owner(s) Edmund & Elsie Oettlé ▪ Cellarmaster(s) / brandy master(s) Edmund Oettlé ▪ Winemaker(s)/viticulturist(s) Edmund Oettlé ▪ 46ha/10ha (cab, chenin, cbard, crouchen) ▪ 20t/1,200cs own label 100% red & 2,000L brandy ▪ QCS organic certification ▪ PO Box 152 Wellington 7654 ▪

info@organicwine.co.za ▪ www.organicwine.co.za ▪ S 33° 40′ 19.9″ E 019° 2′ 40.0″ ▪ **T +27 (0)82-731-4774** ▪ F +27 (0)21-873-5724

Wellington owner/winemaker Edmund Oettlé proposes a new sort of wine competition: 'One that's based on how you feel the next morning!' Organic and sulphur-free do the trick, he insists, adding that careful production has resulted in an innovation for Upland: sulphur-free organic cabernets that last in the bottle.

Upland Organic Estate range
Cabernet Sauvignon ⓘ 🌿 ★★★ Core of dark savoury fruit on **09** bridled by firm structure. Needs time & good hearty fare. Organic, & claimed sulphite free, as is the port. **Tandem Cape Ruby** ⓘ 🌿 ★★★ **07** port-style from cab. Pleasant liquorice tone but quite stern for a Ruby.

Brandy range NEW
★★★★ **Undiluted Cask Strength Potstill Brandy** 🌿 100% potstill, 13 years in oak. The only local brandy in this undiluted style (62% alcohol). Says the distiller: 'No colour, flavourants, sugar, not even water added.' Intense perfumed, fruit-rich nose; lovely, long flavours. Smooth despite the power. For small sips!
Pure Potstill Brandy 🌿 ★★★★ 12 years in oak. Attractive fruity aromas, flavours; harmonious, elegant & fresh, but not too complex. These uniquely organic brandies from chenin & crouchen.

Grappa-Styles NEW
Grapé 🌿 ★★★★ Another rare organic spirit offering. Inviting aromas of nut, fynbos & herbs. Quite rustic & powerful in style, but a nice fat texture & long finish. From cab. — WB, MW, TJ

Usana 🍷

Location/map: Stellenbosch ▪ WO: Stellenbosch/Elgin ▪ Est/1stB 2003 ▪ Tasting & sales by appt ▪ Owner(s) JP & Pierre Winshaw ▪ Winemaker(s) Jasper Raats (2012, consultant), with Hendrien de Munck (2010, consultant) ▪ Viticulturist(s) Deon Joubert, Nikki Joubert & Pierre Winshaw ▪ 300ha/60ha (cabs s/f, malbec, merlot, chard, pinot gris, sauv) ▪ 29t/4,000cs own label 15% red 85% white ▪ PO Box 68 Lynedoch 7603 ▪ jp@usanawines.co.za, pierre@usanawines.co.za ▪ www.usanawines.co.za ▪ S 33°56′29.7″ E 018°46′16.3″ ▪ **T +27 (0)83-650-9528**

The brand name is a Xhosa word meaning 'New Beginning', and its current custodians, brothers JP and Pierre Winshaw, from a renowned Stellenbosch wine-growing family, contract with Longridge to vinify the wines. Reflecting on 'a busy year finding our feet', JP says 'the main goal is to open a tasting room and hopefully a deli where we can sell our pasture-reared beef and chicken eggs'.

★★★★ **The Fox Cabernet Sauvignon** ✓ Sweet cassis, vanilla highlights on brisk & tightly wound **10**. Juicy enough for now, fruit depth & tannin structure for 3+ years development. Enjoy solo or take to the table.
★★★★ **Sauvignon Blanc** 🏛 Unknit **13** tank sample unfair to rate conclusively. Shows satisfying lees nutty creaminess, brisk acidity & full body. **12** was a gravelly mealtime companion.
Barrel Fermented Chenin Blanc NEW ★★★ Toasty oak dominates **12**'s nose & palate, masks the fruit, adds to a sweet, slippery impression on the finish. Fermented/aged 8 months, 34% new. **Pinot Gris** 🏛 ★★★★ **13** provisionally rated preview shows ginger nuances, pleasing vinosity, texture & length. — CvZ

◼ **Usapho** see Stellar Winery

Uva Mira Vineyards 🍷🥂☕📷♿

Location/map/WO: Stellenbosch ▪ Est 1997 ▪ 1stB 1998 ▪ Tasting & sales Mon-Fri 9-5 Sat/Sun 10-4 ▪ Fee R30 ▪ Closed Good Fri, Dec 25 & Jan 1 ▪ Cheese platters & savoury meat platters ▪ Olive oil ▪ Tour groups ▪ Conservation area ▪ Owner(s) Denise Weedon ▪ Winemaker(s)/viticulturist(s) Christiaan Coetzee (2012) ▪ 140ha/30ha (cabs s/f, merlot, shiraz, chard, sauv) ▪ 100t/14,000cs ▪ IPW ▪ PO Box 1511 Stellenbosch 7599 ▪ info@uvamira.co.za ▪ www.uvamira.co.za ▪ S 34°1′31.3″ E 018°51′26.1″ ▪ **T +27 (0)21-880-1683** ▪ F +27 (0)21-880-1682

Christiaan Coetzee, who came across from KWV to Denise Weedon's Helderberg eyrie towards the end of 2012, says attention to detail, both in vineyard and cellar, is what matters to him. 'I want to assure people that they're getting a true expression of our terroir wherever in the world they may be.' And what terroir it is! Incorporating the highest vineyards in the area, over 50% of the property is left wild and is home to a wide array of animals and birds.

Vineyard Selection

★★★★ **Syrah** Clearly an ambitious offering but oak (vanilla, sawdust) is the over-riding impression mid-2013. Does **10** (★★★☆) have the fruit concentration of more balanced **08** for happy maturation? No **09**.

★★★★☆ **Red Blend** ⓘ Layered brilliance, complex aromas & classy oak attractions on **07**. Fresh, deep flavours beautifully balanced with cab-focused structure. Merlot, cab franc, shiraz add savoury conclusion.

★★★★☆ **Single Vineyard Chardonnay** **12** in the house's usual flamboyant style. Very flavourful, with notes of lemon, orange & vanilla. Sweet, rich & thick texture offset by bright acidity. Oak (90% new) currently prominent but good fruit concentration suggests all should harmonise with time.

Cellar Selection

★★★★ **Sauvignon Blanc** ⓘ 🖳 These usually tasted ex-tank, so ratings provisional. **12** sample in usual bracing, tangily dry style; still taut, yet to exhibit full flavour, lees-enriched dimension. **11** sold out untasted.

Merlot-Cabernet Sauvignon ⓘ ★★★★ Maturing savoury edge to previewed **08**'s dark plum, berry fruit adds to complexity. Opulent yet fresh, for delicious current drinking. Step up on **07** (★★★★). — CE

Vaalvlei Wines

Location: Stanford ▪ Map: Elgin, Walker Bay & Bot River ▪ WO: Walker Bay ▪ Est 2005 ▪ 1stB 2008 ▪ Tasting & sales Mon-Sat 11-5 by appt ▪ Closed Good Fri & Dec 25 ▪ Self-catering cottages ▪ Fly-fishing ▪ Owner(s) Terblanche family ▪ Cellarmaster(s)/viticulturist(s) Naas Terblanche (Mar 2005) ▪ Winemaker(s) Naas Terblanche (Mar 2005) & Josef Dreyer (Aug 2005, Raka), advised by Charl van Teijlingen CWM (Mar 2008) ▪ 50ha/3ha (shiraz, sauv) ▪ 19t/650cs own label 40% red 60% white ▪ PO Box 92 Stanford 7210 ▪ info@vaalvlei.co.za ▪ www.vaalvlei.co.za ▪ S 34° 26' 56.11" E 019° 33' 07.05" ▪ **T +27 (0)28-341-0170/+27 (0)72-782-3431**

The Terblanche family farm near Stanford on the Walker Bay coastline lures fly-fishermen and shelters the endangered Western Leopard Toad, thanks in part to passionate conservationist (and winemaker/viticulturist) Naas Terblanche. More new French oak is being used for the shiraz, and a maiden port-style is due soon.

Shiraz Reserve ★★★ Displaying similar DNA of sweet fruit, vanilla, exotic spice & bold alcohol, vintage-boosted **11** is a notch up on previous. **Shiraz** Next awaited. **Sauvignon Blanc** 🖳 ★★★ Previewed **13**, pungent lime, passionfruit & kiwi, cool-climate structure supports the fruit, minerality uplifts the finish. — HJ

Val de Vie Wines

Location: Paarl ▪ Map: Paarl & Wellington ▪ WO: Western Cape/Coastal ▪ Est 2003 ▪ 1stB 2004 ▪ Tasting & sales Tue-Fri 8-5 Sat/Sun & pub hols 10-4 ▪ Cellar tours by appt ▪ Closed Good Fri, Dec 25 & Jan 1 ▪ Platters by prior arrangement ▪ Polo Club Restaurant (see Restaurants section) ▪ Conservation area ▪ Owner(s) Val de Vie Wines (Pty) Ltd ▪ Winemaker(s) Harold Versfeld ▪ Vineyard manager(s) Naas Engelbrecht ▪ 14ha (carignan, cinsaut, grenache n/b, mourv, petite sirah, shiraz, clairette, marsanne, rouss, viog) ▪ 75t/8,500cs own label 60% red 40% white ▪ PO Box 6223 Paarl 7620 ▪ wine@valdevie.co.za ▪ www.valdevie.co.za ▪ S 33° 48' 15.0" E 018° 58' 4.0" ▪ **T +27 (0)21-863-6100** ▪ F +27 (0)21-863-2741

One of several wine-themed residential estates in the winelands, Paarl's wine-and-polo Val de Vie has a special focus on the Rhône, the vineyards being a virtual tour of that French valley with almost a dozen varieties planted and more to come. The goal is to be a benchmark Rhône producer, and make winelovers aware of 'the quality that can be produced by previously lesser-known varieties'.

Val de Vie range

★★★★ **Shiraz** ⓘ **08**'s smoky mulberry & plum appeal follows similar **07**. Rounded yet muscled & firm. Dark char depth & density. Oak shows restraint, 70% new for 11 months. Long finish. WO Coastal.

★★★★ **Ryk Neethling** ⓘ Pepper & spice abound on taut & toned **10** from shiraz, mourvèdre, carignan, grenache & cinsaut. Rich & savoury, with restrained black fruit wrapped around a firm body of tannin.

★★★★☆ **Val de Vie** ⓘ Premium-priced flagship, mainly mourvèdre (50%), shiraz & dabs grenache, carignan & cinsaut. **07** last time was ripe & concentrated yet elegant, 80% new wood already assimilated.

★★★★ **GVC** ⓘ 🖳 Graceful **08** blend of grenache blanc (50%), viognier & clairette blanche. Vanilla (from 100% new oak, 7 months on lees) layered with citrus & stonefruit freshness.

Polo Club range

> **Filly Rosé** ☺ ▦ ★★★ Was just 'Filly'. Rosepetals & soft red fruit flavours on friendly (10.5% alcohol) off-dry **12** from 5 red/white varieties. WO Coastal. **Chenin Blanc** NEW ☺ ▦ ★★★ Floral wafts & bright, crisp apple flavours on uncomplicated **12**. Hint of oak & lees-ageing adds some complexity. **Sauvignon Blanc** ☺ ▦ 🈂 ★★★ Upfront grass & greenpepper aromas, **13** bristles with fresh citrus flavours, ends with bracing lemon lift. Darling grapes.

Cabernet Franc ✓ ★★★★ Beautifully dry **11** a step up from **10** (★★★☆). Elegant red berry, savoury fynbos & dried herb flavours with precise oaking for balance & structure. **Craftsman** ⓟ ▦ ★★★★ 08 five-way Rhône-style blend is earthy & spicy, with succulent black fruit. Semi-dry, with a refreshing acid counterweight. Discontinued: **Polo White**. — WB

Val du Charron

Location/WO: Wellington ▪ Map: Paarl & Wellington ▪ Est 2007 ▪ 1stB 2009 ▪ Tasting daily 10-4 ▪ Sales Mon-Fri 8-5 Sat/Sun 10-4 ▪ Cellar tours during tasting hours ▪ Breakfast & lunch daily; dinner by appt ▪ Tour groups ▪ Conferences/functions (100 pax) ▪ Walks/hikes ▪ Mountain biking trail ▪ 4-star guesthouse (stay@vdcwines.com) ▪ Owner(s) Val du Charron Wines (Pty) Ltd ▪ Winemaker(s) Bertus Fourie (Apr 2010, consultant) ▪ Viticulturist(s) Heinie Nel (Apr 2010, consultant) ▪ 43ha/21ha (cab, ptage, shiraz, chard, chenin) ▪ 200t ▪ Other export brands: Girlfriends Wine ▪ IPW ▪ PO Box 890 Wellington 7654 ▪ ce@vdcwines.com ▪ www.vdcwines.com ▪ S 33° 37' 28.14" E 019° 2' 55.32" ▪ **T +27 (0)21-873-1256** ▪ F +27 (0)86-509-4865

Formerly a Wellington fruit farm, the track record since conversion to wine doubtless has bemused (as well as delighted) the owners, who have actuarial and construction backgrounds. A recent finalist in the Exporter of the Year Awards, other accolades include good ratings at numerous local and overseas competitions. To encourage visitors, the lawns and gardens have been expanded for picnics and winetasting, and a wellness centre established.

Estate Reserve range NEW

Cabernet Sauvignon 🈂 ★★★☆ Opulent blackcurrant in **12** sample vies with firm but ripe tannins from 80% new oak. Gives a well defined finish. **Shiraz** 🈂 ★★★★ Scrub & hedgerow fruit in deftly oaked (80% new) **12** preview. Already drinks well, has a good future. Nudges next level. **Chardonnay** ▦ 🈂 ★★★★ White peach with citrus nuances, **12**'s oaked pinot gris portion adds interest. Good length & freshness. **Pinot Gris** ▦ 🈂 ★★★★ Dashes of chenin & viognier in oak-fermented **12** sample. Sleekly distinctive with aromatic & savoury appeal.

Theater of Wine range

★★★★ **Four White Legs** ✓ ▦ 🈂 Well-crafted blend, mainly chenin, nouvelle, sauvignon, pinot gris in **12** with different oaking including acacia. Elegant, poised, its savoury earthiness brightened by greengage. **Erasmus** ✓ ▦ ★★★★ Merlot/pinotage blend with 3 others gives **12** sample supple berry richness, the oak backbone ensures good ageing future. **Black Countess** 🈂 ★★★ Shiraz with mainly Rhône varieties, pre-bottled **12** is a juicy, smooth, dark-toned charmer. — CR

- **Valley Green** see Hannay Wines
- **Valley Road Vintners** see Ross Gower Wines

Valley Vineyards Wine Company

Location: Riebeek-Kasteel ▪ Est/1stB 2009 ▪ Closed to public ▪ Owner(s) Richard Addison & Richard James ▪ ±100,000cs own label 40% red 40% white 15% rosé 5% other ▪ Other export brands: Two Tunns; Lion Ridge; Short Street ▪ PO Box 2175 Riebeek-Kasteel 7307 ▪ raddison@valleyvineyardswine.com ▪ www.valleyvineyardswine.com ▪ **T +27 (0)71-238-6765**

Wine partners Richard James and Richard Addison, specialists in Argentina and South Africa respectively, combine their knowledge and long experience to select wines from mainly those countries for their United Kingdom merchant house. Their South African brands, including 24 Rivers, Mischief Maker, The Royal and Post Tree, are all sourced from Swartland.

Van Biljon Wines

 NEW

Location/map/WO: Stellenbosch ▪ Est 2004 ▪ 1stB 2013 ▪ Tasting, sales & cellar tours Mon-Sat by appt ▪ Closed all pub hols ▪ Self-catering Tarentaal Cottage (see Accommodation section) ▪ Owner(s) Anton & Julia van Biljon ▪ Winemaker(s) Christopher Keet (Oct 2008, consultant), with Anton van Biljon (Jan 2011) ▪ Viticulturist(s) Christopher Keet (Oct 2008, consultant) ▪ 7ha/3ha (cabs s/f, malbec, merlot, p verdot) ▪ 15t/500cs own label 100% red ▪ IPW ▪ PO Box 1292 Hermanus 7200 ▪ info@vanbiljonwines.co.za ▪ www.vanbiljonwines.co. za ▪ S 33° 58' 4.98" E 018° 45' 8.39" ▪ **T +27 (0)21-882-8445** ▪ F +27 (0)28-313-0435

All bodes well for Anton and Julia van Biljon, owners of a small property on Stellenbosch's Polkadraai Hills. With illustrious neighbours like De Toren and Reyneke, they hope their wines will reach similar heights, and as part of this vision, they've secured the services of much-awarded winemaker/viticulturist Chris Keet (Keet Wines). The vineyards were planted in 2004 with the Bordeaux 'big five' red varieties, well-suited to the granite soils, and this edition sees the first release under the own label, vinified in the newly equipped cellar.

★★★★☆ **Cinq** 🍷 Elegant & aristocratic Bordeaux red, **11** cabs sauvignon (50%) & franc, merlot & malbec, showing rich oaky spices (though only 10% new wood) on sweet-ripe black fruit. Finely shaped but substantial, the enduring finish & healthy tannins auguring well. Impressive, deserves time. — GdB, GM

■ **Van Hunks** see Oudtshoorn Cellar - SCV

Van Loveren Family Vineyards

🍷🥂🏠📷♿

Location/map: Robertson ▪ WO: Robertson/Western Cape ▪ Est 1937 ▪ 1stB 1980 ▪ Tasting & sales Mon-Fri 8. 30-5 Sat 9.30-3 Sun 11-2 ▪ Closed Easter Fri/Sun, Dec 25 & Jan 1 ▪ Cellar tours ▪ Garden tours ▪ Food & wine tasting platters ▪ Fish Eagle hiking trail ▪ MTB trails (bike rental available) ▪ Self-catering farm cottage ▪ Christina's @ Van Loveren bistro (closed Tue) ▪ Owner(s) Nico, Wynand, Phillip, Hennie, Bussell & Neil Retief ▪ Cellarmaster(s) Bussell Retief ▪ Winemaker(s) Danelle Conradie (Jan 2007), with Malcolm Human (Jan 2012) ▪ Viticulturist(s) Neil & Hennie Retief ▪ 500ha (cab, merlot, mourv, muscadel r/w, ptage, pinot noir/gris, ruby cab, shiraz, touriga nacional, chard, chenin, cbard, gewürz, morio muscat, nouvelle, sauv, sem, viog) ▪ 7,700t/ 2,400,000cs own label 33% red 33% white 34% rosé ▪ Brands for clients: Woolworths ▪ BWI, Fairtrade, IPW ▪ PO Box 19 Klaasvoogds 6707 ▪ info@vanloveren.co.za ▪ www.vanloveren.co.za ▪ S 33° 52' 31.3" E 020° 0' 9. 1" ▪ **T +27 (0)23-615-1505** ▪ F +27 (0)23-615-1336

Hennie and Jean Retief bought this Robertson farm in 1937 but it took until 1980 for sons Nico and Wynand to launch the first wine, a Premier Grand Cru, under the Van Loveren label. In an area then better known for jerepigo and brandy, the dry white was an innovation, an attribute maintained by their children. Today's extensive range contains many novelties, from the Four Cousins magnums, introduced in 2000, to the recently launched Tangled Tree range in recyclable plastic bottles. Don't expect the Retiefs' thinking out of the box to end there.

Christina Van Loveren Limited Releases

★★★★ **Sauvignon Blanc** 🍷 Interesting lemon sage & grassy aromas, lemon & almond flavours on sweet-sour **12** (★★★☆). Tense, poised, with flinty finish but, unlike **11**, a bit brief. WO W Cape.

★★★★ **Noble Late Harvest Rhine Riesling** ⏲ 09 (★★☆) barley sugar & apricots; softer acidity, creamier than zingy 08. Lacks wonderful presence of previous examples at less than 11% alcohol.

Cabernet Sauvignon ★★★★ Firmly structured **11** has sufficient fruit, chalky tannin & cab acidity to improve with few years ageing. WO W Cape as next. **Shiraz** ★★★ Pretty blackberry fruit, meaty seasoning on **11** overwhelmed by oak char & tar mid-2013, 14.5% alcohol sweetens its finish. **Chardonnay** ★★★ Barrel-fermented **12**'s vanilla butteriness enlivened by lemony acidity. Similar elegant drinkability to standout **10** but shade less gravitas. **Méthode Cap Classique Brut** ★★★ Traditional-method sparkling from chardonnay (86%) & pinot. Latest NV intense citrus & brioche, good weight, lacking some complexity and length of previous.

Van Loveren range

★★★★ **Red Muscadel** ⏲ 🍷 12 (★★★☆) signature red fruit pastille character, delightfully clean & uncloying but misses the complexity & enduring length of **11**.

Blue Velvet Pinot Noir NEW ☺ 🍴 🖩 ★★★ Lightly oaked **12**'s tannins youthfully gawky but lovely pure pinot fruit, very sippable & reasonably priced. **Cramond Cabernet Sauvignon-Merlot** ☺ 🍴 🖩 ★★★ **12** likeable & characterful; lively red fruit, creamy oak nuance & mint. **Blackberry Cabernet Sauvignon-Shiraz** ☺ 🖩 ★★★ **12** as advertised: dark fruited & friendly, sparingly oak-staved for early drinkability. **Special Late Harvest Gewürztraminer** ☺ 🍴 🖩 ★★★ **13** textbook gewurz: rosepetals, Turkish Delight, litchi; genteel sweetness for solo enjoyment or spicy foods.

Merlot 🖩 ★★★ **12** not too leafy, not too fruity; medium bodied, bright & just right. **African Java Pinotage** 🖩 ★★ **13** full-bore 'coffee' styling, juicy red fruit & mouthfilling sweetness. **River Red** 🍴 🖩 ★★★ Unoaked ruby cab (80%) & merlot, versatile bistro companion. **13** sweet-savoury, just enough grip to match pizza & pasta, too. **Blanc de Noir Shiraz** 🍴 🖩 ★★ Unwooded & dry **13**, berries & spice, brief but cheerful. **Blanc de Noir Red Muscadel Blush** 🍴 🖩 ★★ **13** slightly sweeter, less fruity than usual. **Cape Riesling** ⊕ 🍴 🖩 ★★ Fresh & tangy **12**, slender body lightly brushed with oak. **Chardonnay** 🍴 🖩 ★★ Underplayed fruit, obvious vanilla on lightly oak-staved **13**. **Chenin No. 5** 🍴 🖩 ★★ **13** repeats successful formula: zesty acidity + moderate alcohol = easy sippability. **Neil's Pick Colombar** 🍴 🖩 ★★ Honours viti man Neil Retief. Off-dry **13** with kiwi/guava charm & bracing freshness needing butter-based braaied snoek. **Pinot Grigio** ⊕ 🍴 🖩 ★★ Shade less excitement in **12**, with fleeting pear nuance. **Sauvignon Blanc** 🍴 🖩 ★★ Brisk **13**'s capsicum & grass flavours very brief. **Cramond Sauvignon Blanc-Chardonnay** 🍴 🖩 ★★ Unoaked **13** picnic white, fruity, savoury & herby flavours make versatile food partner. **Blanc de Blanc** 🍴 🖩 ★★ Improved **13** summer quaffer from colombard & sauvignon, with lemon & herb freshness. **Cape Ruby** ⊕ 🔆 🖩 ★★★ NV fortified port-style from touriga shows commendable dryness, seamless spirit integration for winter warmth.

Four Cousins range

Dry Red ★★ From ruby cab & merlot, charmingly rustic unoaked **NV** braai companion. **Dry White** 🍴 ★★ Colombard & sauvignon duo, **NV**, Thai curry match. **Extra Light White** 🍴 ★ Lemony & light **NV** gets the nod from Weigh-Less. **Natural Sweet Red** ★★ **NV** bit rough around the edges despite sweet & round centre. **Sweet Rosé** ★★ Strawberry sherbet & quaffing fun delivered by latest **NV**. **Light Natural Sweet Rosé** 🍴 ★★ Cherry & cranberry on sweet, low-alcohol **NV** endorsed by Weigh-Less. **Natural Sweet White** 🍴 ★★ Low-alcohol (8.5%) & softly fragrant **NV** for the sweet toothed. Note: above variously available in 500ml, 750ml & 1.5L.

Five's Reserve range

Cabernet Sauvignon ⊕ 🖩 ★★ **12** unfettered by oak, packed with juicy blackcurrant. **Pinotage** ⊕ 🖩 ★★ Rustically charming **12**, pure black cherry flavour uncluttered by wood. **Merlot Rosé** 🍴 🖩 ★★ Bone-dry & aromatic **12** for chilled sunset sipping. **Chenin Blanc** ⊕ 🍴 🖩 ★★ Guava & peach appeal, amenable **12** not as markedly dry as previous.

Tangled Tree range

Chocolate Cabernet Sauvignon ☺ 🍴 🖩 ★★★ Get-together-with-mates **12** much improved, bright & cheerful, grippy. Reds lightly staved; all these in light-weight PET bottles.

Spicy Shiraz 🍴 🖩 ★★ Sweetish & fruit-filled **12** has sufficient grip for the BBQ. Takes step up, as does next. **Moscato Rosé** 🍴 🖩 ★★ Turkish Delight on **13** sweet but balanced crowd pleaser from red muscadel. **Butterscotch Chardonnay** 🍴 🖩 ★★ Aptly named **13**, vanilla & creamy-sweet flavours. **Tropical Sauvignon Blanc** 🍴 🖩 ★★ As per back label text, **13** delivers banana, pineapple & guava in easy-drinking package.

Papillon Sparkling range

Vin Doux ⊕ ★★ NV sparkling from red muscadel offers lots of bubbly sweetness. **Brut** ⊕ ★★★ Latest NV uncomplex but easy & charming celebratory sparkler. **Demi-Sec** ★★ Fizzy semi-sweet **NV** (latest from white muscadel, hence no pink hue) uncomplicated grapey fun.

Four Cousins Sparkling range

Sauvignon Blanc Brut ☺ 🖩 ★★★ Latest NV sparkler ups the ante with grass & lemon complexity, zesty dry tail.

Red ⊕ ★★ Carbonated NV from ruby cab touch plain but cheery. **Blush** ⊕ ★★ Cranberries lifted by lively acidity in NV, semi-sweet & frothy. **White** ⊕ ★★ Sweet end on fragrant NV bubbly.

Brandy range NEW

Brandy 🍾 ★★★ 5 year old blended brandy (50% potstill) from chenin & colombard. Peaches, caramel & fresh fruit flavours - cheerful & charming, some dry elegance. Good on the rocks. — WB, DC, TJ, MW

Van Ryn   NEW

These are Distell's flagship brandies, at home in the century-old visitor-friendly Van Ryn distillery near Stellenbosch. Custodian Marlene Bester is one of a team of six distillery managers reporting to production director, Johan Venter, a globally acknowledged spirits expert. Winner of many World's Best Brandy awards, Van Ryn's skilful marketing introduces palates to premium brandy's versatility: neat, in cocktails and with gourmet food (from chocolate to charcuterie).

★★★★☆ **Vintage 10 Year** Testimony to the quality possible for a Vintage Brandy - that is, with a component of matured (not potstill) spirit. Youthful, with a showy array of fruit aromas, plus some sandalwood & vanilla from oak. The mature & fruity parts marry appealingly. Assertive, rich, lively.

★★★★★ **12 Year Distillers Reserve** 100% potstill brandy, like all below. Deep colour, with mahogany gleam. Fragrant, delicate aromas of fruit, herbs, flowers lead to full, richly powerful but gentle palate, then a long, sustained finish. Complete, balanced, triumphant.

★★★★☆ **15 Year Fine Cask Reserve** Delicate & penetrating aromas - rather less fruit, but more floral notes than 12YO (rose, violet, lavender), & rather more restrained in effect though still in the richer style of this house. Refined, complex finish. These all from chenin & colombard, widely sourced.

★★★★★ **20 Year Collectors Reserve** Concentrated nose of dark berries, dried fruit & spice. Spice, especially, repeated on the palate along with apricot & prune amidst the complexity. Reminiscences of oak but never intrusive. Mellow, silky & very rich, with forthright finish.

★★★★★ **Au.Ra** South Africa's longest-matured - & by a long way rarest & priciest - brandy: 30 year minimum maturation. Even smoother, more sumptuously mouthfilling than others in range, but retaining elegance. Full spicy, dried fruit complexity splendidly supported by oak. Sets a local standard for excellence. — WB, TJ

■ **Vansha** see Ridgeback
■ **Van Zijls Family Vintners** see Imbuko Wines

Van Zylshof Estate   🍷🍴&

Location: Bonnievale ▪ Map/WO: Robertson ▪ Est 1940 ▪ 1stB 1994 ▪ Tasting & sales Mon-Fri 9-5 Sat 9-1 ▪ Closed Good Fri, Ascension day, Dec 25 & Jan 1 ▪ Cellar tours by appt ▪ Owner(s) Van Zylshof Trust ▪ Cellarmaster(s)/winemaker(s)/viticulturist(s) Andri van Zyl (Mar 1993) ▪ 37ha/32ha under vine ▪ 450t/±8,000cs own label 15% red 80% white 5% rosé ▪ PO Box 64 Bonnievale 6730 ▪ vanzylshof@lando.co.za ▪ www.vanzylshof.co.za ▪ S 33° 56' 18.5" E 020° 6' 23.4" ▪ **T +27 (0)23-616-2401** ▪ F +27 (0)23-616-3503

Three generations work together on this Bonnievale family arm, focusing on easy-drinking wines, epitomised by the delightful chenin. Second-generation Andri van Zyl maintains South Africa's USP is the fusion of Old and New World wine styles, though his ultimate taste experience remains a 1968 Burgundy enjoyed in 1979.

★★★★ **Riverain Unwooded Chardonnay** 🍾 13 (★★★) has the grapefruit & pineapple complexity of concentrated yet light-hearted 12 preview but lacks its verve.

Chenin Blanc ☺ 🍾 ★★★ Delicious 13 offers white peach, nectarine & dried pineapple complexity & persistent lemony aftertaste. Stock up for summer!

Cabernet Sauvignon-Merlot 🍾 ★★★ Herbaceous nuance on plummy, chocolate-infused 12 everyday red. **Chardonnay** 🍾 ★★★ 13 preview faint yellow stonefruit aroma, lovely texture & lingering zesty finish. **Sauvignon Blanc** ✓ 🍾 ★★★★ Generous & engaging 13 ex tank takes big step up. Herby/spicy lift to tropical fruit salad aromas & flavours, bouncy acidity for all-day enjoyment. Discontinued: **Rosé**. — DB, JP

Vaughan Johnson's Wine & Cigar Shop

Location: Cape Town ▪ Map: Cape Peninsula ▪ WO: Paarl ▪ Est/1stB 1985 ▪ Sales Mon-Fri 9-6 Sat 9-5 Sun 10-5 ▪ Open pub hols ▪ Gifts, souvenirs, spirits & beer available ▪ Owner(s) Vaughan Johnson ▪ PO Box 50012 Waterfront 8002 ▪ vjohnson@mweb.co.za ▪ www.vaughanjohnson.co.za ▪ S 33° 54' 19.15" E 018° 25' 10.68" ▪ **T +27 (0)21-419-2121** ▪ F +27 (0)86-509-6401

Vaughan Johnson's Wine & Cigar Shop has long been a landmark at Cape Town's V&A Waterfront. Proprietor Vaughan Johnson is a champion of customer service, and his belief that 'three times the price is not always three times the quality' is evident in his own range, trimmer now and still offering smile-faced value.

Good Everyday Cape Red ☺ 🍱 ★★★ Dark-fruited & eminently drinkable **NV** Bordeaux blend from cab franc, merlot, cab & petit verdot.

Good Everyday Cape White 🍱 ★★★ 11 combo sauvignon & chenin offers unfruity easy quaffing. — JP

Veenwouden Private Cellar   🍷

Location: Paarl ▪ Map: Paarl & Wellington ▪ WO: Paarl/Coastal ▪ Est 1989 ▪ 1stB 1993 ▪ Tasting, sales & cellar tours by appt ▪ Fee R100, waived on purchase ▪ Owner(s) The Van Der Walt Trust ▪ Cellarmaster(s) Marcel van der Walt ▪ Winemaker(s) Marcel van der Walt, with Faried Williams ▪ Viticulturist(s) Marcel van der Walt, with Sias Louw ▪ 14ha/12.5ha (cabs s/f, malbec, merlot, p verdot, pinot) ▪ ±100t/11,000cs own label 90% red 10% white ▪ PO Box 7086 Northern Paarl 7623 ▪ admin@veenwouden.com ▪ www.veenwouden.com ▪ S 33° 41' 7.0" E 018° 57' 52.4" ▪ **T +27 (0)21-872-6806** ▪ F +27 (0)21-872-1384

This small-scale family wine venture between Paarl and Wellington celebrated two special events last year: two decades of making wine, and more especially for Marcel van der Walt, ex golfing professional who took over as winemaker after their maiden vintage, the release of their first pinot noir. Like all their wines, it bears their hallmark classic restraint, with potential to develop. A project that resonates with a proudly South African theme is Marcel's wine collaboration with renowned jazz musician Hugh Masekela. The sales of this wine help fund a music bursary for a previously disadvantaged child.

Reserve Collection

★★★★ **Merlot** 🏵 **12** with a splash of cab franc shows refinement despite 14.5% alcohol. Cool red fruit & mint, deftly oaked. Balanced, silky tannins already tempting, with charm for 4-6 years.

★★★★ **Syrah** Similar fresh spicy tone to **11**, but preview of **12** (★★★★) shows less fruit intensity. Bright & sappy, with supple tannins.

★★★★ **Classic** Cab-led quintet of Bordeaux varieties, **10** more restrained than **09**. Tart savoury fruit sheathed in chalky tannins. Refined, all elements in place, just needs time's smoothing hand.

Chardonnay ⓦ ★★★★ Fruit-driven **11**, just 5% oaked for extra flesh. Accessible, with attractive citrus vitality, gently rounded, dry.

Hugh Masekela Collection

★★★★ **Hugh Masekela** ⓦ Harmonious merlot-based **10** blend with cab, shiraz. Invitingly rich, savoury with caressing velvet feel, gentle grip. Easy as 'listening to Hugh's soul soothing sounds of Jazz', as per back label.

Premium Collection

Pinot Noir NEW ★★★★ **12** earthy red fruit with savoury, smoky infusion, focused by brisk acidity. Elegant, but taut & introverted in youth. Time & decanting will reveal greater charm. **Chardonnay** Await next.

Vivat Bacchus Collection

Red ⓦ ★★★★ Velvety, approachable merlot-based **11** with a little shiraz; fresh red plums, spicy flavours polished with French oak, 20% new. WO Coastal, like next. **Sauvignon Blanc-Chenin Blanc** NEW 🍱 🏵 ★★★ Demure sauvignon-led **12** is waxy & crisp with a clean almondy finish. Discontinued: **Chenin Blanc**. — MW

■ **Veldt** see Robertson Wide River Export Company

Vendôme   🍷📷♿

Location/WO: Paarl ▪ Map: Paarl & Wellington ▪ Est 1692 ▪ 1stB 1999 ▪ Tasting & sales by appt ▪ Closed all pub hols ▪ Conferences/functions (up to 150 pax) ▪ Owner(s)/winemaker(s)/viticulturist(s) Jannie le Roux ▪ 40ha (cabs s/f, merlot, shiraz, chard, chenin, cbard, sauv, sem) ▪ 5t/600cs own label 50% red 50% white ▪ PO Box 36 Paarl 7645 ▪ lerouxjg@icon.co.za ▪ www.vendome.co.za ▪ S 33° 45' 27.8" E 018° 58' 42.4" ▪ **T +27 (0)21-863-3905** ▪ F +27 (0)21-863-0094

Farmed by the Le Roux family for 10 generations, this Berg riverside property in Paarl was named to honour their Huguenot heritage and ancestral home in central France. Vigneron Jannie le Roux focuses on blends, none ready for tasting.

■ **Vera Cruz Estate** *see* Delheim Wines

Vergelegen Wines

Location: Somerset West ■ Map: Helderberg ■ WO: Stellenbosch/Western Cape ■ Est 1987 ■ 1stB 1991 ■ Tasting & sales daily 9.30–4.30 (gate closes at 4) ■ Cellar tours daily at 10.30, 11.30 & 3 (Nov–Apr); 11.30 & 3 (May–Oct) ■ Tasting R30/6 wines (excl Vergelegen Red & White), R10 each for flagship wines; Cellar tour R20pp incl tasting of 4 premium range wines ■ Closed Good Fri, May 1 & Dec 25 ■ Camphors Restaurant, Stables Bistro & Camphor Forest Picnic (see Restaurants section) ■ Facilities for children ■ Gift shop ■ Historic Cape Dutch homestead; library; exhibition corridor ■ 313 year old camphor trees (National Monuments since 1942) ■ Conservation area ■ 18 gardens including Camellia Garden of Excellence & children's adventure garden & maze ■ Owner(s) Anglo American plc ■ Winemaker(s) André van Rensburg (Jan 1998) ■ Viticulturist(s) Niel Rossouw (Apr 1995) & Dwayne Lottering (Nov 2003) ■ 3,000ha/158ha (cab, merlot, sauv) ■ 900t/120,000cs own label 58% red 42% white ■ ISO 9001, ISO 14001, OSHAS 18000, BWI champion, WIETA ■ PO Box 17 Somerset West 7129 ■ info@vergelegen.co.za ■ www.vergelegen.co.za ■ S 34° 4' 38.33" E 018° 53' 30.03" ■ **T +27 (0)21-847-1334** ■ F +27 (0)21-847-1608

'We're a wine business that represents the layered history on which Cape culture was founded. We've introduced innovation and change, but in a manner that showcases our heritage,' says Vergelegen MD Don Tooth. Others would argue that Vergelegen is a trailblazer, winemaker André van Rensburg consistently raising the bar in the world arena with his complex white and red blends, and precise single varieties. Most agree Vergelegen the property is an icon, its stark, white octagonal winery a lone sentry on a hill flanked by dramatic mountains. In its sights are the famous wind-buffeted Schaapenberg vineyard and False Bay beyond. Behind are the estate's sweeping farmlands, with not only vines but also the fruit trees which now belong to an empowerment enterprise. Below, close to the historic manor house, are 300+ year old camphor trees, National Monuments since 1942, 18 gardens (including new East Garden and its children's play area), modernised winetasting centre and two fine restaurants. As we said: iconic.

Flagship range

★★★★☆ **Vergelegen V** Now 100% cab, 100% new-oaked. Regal **09** taut & savoury with cassis centre, mineral lift; should take years to unfold. **08** also reviewed, as complete & well defined; slightly bigger (14.5% alcohol) no less fresh & thrilling; also for the long haul. **07** was mostly cab with merlot, cab franc.

★★★★☆ **Vergelegen GVB Red** Was 'Red'. Masterly Bordeaux blend always fine & dry with measured tannic grip. 98% cab with splash merlot in **08** quite the package, demonstrates André van Rensburg's command of a challenging vintage. More merlot (10%) plus 88% cab, 2% cab franc in also-tasted **07**; leafier but with similar restraint. Like plush **06**, handsome **05** (★★★★★), both should improve many years. All-new oak.

★★★★☆ **Vergelegen GVB White** 🍷 Previously 'White'; pioneering barrel fermented/aged semillon-sauvignon blend. Whiff blackcurrant & brimstone on **12**; tighter & pithier, as pedigreed & classy as **11**. Here, toasty oak layered with semillon's lemon, sauvignon's fig. Both reviewed, both 55+% semillon, ageworthy & showing delicate 'wet stone' minerality of **10**.

Reserve range

★★★★☆ **Cabernet Sauvignon** Exquisite spice, cedar & lead pencil **08** with dashes merlot, cab franc. Heady 14.6% alcohol in sync with seductive fruit, stately tannins. Poised **07** (★★★★) was not as concentrated as this or **06**.

★★★★☆ **Merlot** 🍷 Consistently one of the Cape's finest. Creamy **10** inviting plum, milk choc; soft yet with satisfying grip. Accomplished **08** a study in finessed fruit & complexity. **09** sold out untasted.

★★★★☆ **Shiraz** 🍷 Scaling the heights of **06**, latest **10** has an impressive structure & length, no pushover. Lily, red berry & dusty oak complexity; sleeker than ripe **07** (★★★★). No **09**, **08**.

★★★★☆ **DNA** Cab franc leads in serious nod to Bordeaux. Youthful **09** plusher, better integrated, more accessible than stern but vibrant **07** (★★★★) also reviewed. Dense core soaks up 100% new oak. **06** was quietly persuasive. No **08**

★★★★☆ **Chardonnay** Powerful oak-derived biscuit, vanilla & nougat nuances on **11** (★★★★) countered by signature citrus grip, savoury end. Less complex & riveting than **10**, still worth ageing 5+ years.

★★★★☆ **Sauvignon Blanc Schaapenberg** 🈲 Named for 24 year old hillside vineyard overlooking False Bay. **12** cool & classy: blackcurrant & knife-edge acidity; hallmark 'oystershell' minerality found in reserved **11**.

★★★★ **Semillon** 🈲 Not as grassy as some, **11** (★★★★☆) is richer (from 25 year old vineyards, barrel ferment & ageing) yet with focused acidity to refresh, extend the finish. Will improve 3+ years. **08** fruitier; heralded departure from previous more savoury & oxidative styling.

★★★★ **MMV** ⏱ Individual MCC sparkler from chardonnay & pinot noir. **08** biscuity, savoury & austere; not as creamy as many others. WO W Cape.

★★★★☆ **Semillon Straw Wine** NEW 🈲 Shimmering gold dessert from vine- & pallet-dried grapes, fermented on skins/stems, aged 14 months older barrels. Nuts, glacé pineapple & varietal lanolin on hedonistic **11**. Bolt of tangy lime accentuates barley sugar, cuts sweetness for a clean, lingering finish. 375 ml.

Premium range

★★★★ **Shiraz** 🈲 **10** carbon copy of **09**: peppery hints, lily/red fruit scents; supple yet with sufficient body; only 30% new oak.

★★★★ **Cabernet Sauvignon-Merlot** 🈲 Drops cab franc from name (but not from blend; also dab petit verdot; **10** highly perfumed with lavender, plum. Fruitier than **09**, soft & rounded for easy drinking with friends.

★★★★ **Chardonnay** 🍴 🈲 Part-oaked **12**'s (★★★★) fruit-sweetness countered by toast & biscuit aromas, flavours; stock up for summer. Standout **11** had masterly lemon-vanilla touches.

★★★★ **Sauvignon Blanc** 🍴 🈲 Attractive **13** aperitif, fig/nettle nose & palate, ebullient acidity. As elegant & stylish as **12**. Both with weight from few months lees-ageing & dab semillon. — CvZ

Vergenoegd Wine Estate   🍴☕📷🎿♿

Location/map: Stellenbosch ▪ WO: Stellenbosch/Western Cape ▪ Est 1696 ▪ 1stB 1972 ▪ Tasting & sales Mon-Fri 9–5 Sat/Sun 9.30–4 ▪ Fee R15 ▪ Closed Good Fri, Dec 25 & Jan 1 ▪ Cellar tours by appt ▪ Facilities for children ▪ Tour groups ▪ Wine-related gifts ▪ Fresh duck eggs in spring ▪ 6 boule courts ▪ Guided historical walks & duck tours by appt ▪ Bird hides ▪ Conservation area ▪ Pomegranate Restaurant open for lunch Tue-Sun, dinner by appt ▪ Owner(s) Vergenoegd Trust ▪ Cellarmaster(s) John Faure (Nov 1983) ▪ Winemaker(s) Marlize Jacobs (Dec 2007) ▪ Viticulturist(s) Marlize Jacobs (Dec 2007), advised by Drikus van der Westhuizen (2004) ▪ 300ha (cabs s/f, malbec, merlot, p verdot, shiraz, tinta, touriga) ▪ 500t ▪ 94% red 3% white 3% rosé ▪ BWI, IPW ▪ PO Box 1 Faure 7131 ▪ info@vergenoegd.co.za ▪ www.vergenoegd.co.za ▪ S 34° 2' 2.8" E 018° 44' 20.1" ▪ **T +27 (0)21-843-3248** ▪ F +27 (0)21-843-3118

This is one of the oldest farms in Stellenbosch - just five kilometres from False Bay - and owned by the Faure family since 1820. Sixth-generation John Faure is the current cellarmaster, honouring tradition while meeting the demands of the modern market. He speaks of the Vergenoegd philosophy: 'If a wine is not ready to be consumed, then it is not ready to be released.' In fact, few locals have a proven track record of long-term ageability like Vergenoegd Cabernet. Buy a bottle of '99 vintage available ex cellardoor (see below) and taste for yourself.

Vintage Collection

★★★★ **Cabernet Sauvignon** ⏱ For development rather than easy gratification. **99**, with 10% cab franc, showing vintage's earlier approachability but also sombre flavours over firm tannins & acid.

★★★★☆ **Shiraz** ⏱ Exceptional **99** explodes in mouth with dark cherries, ripe plums & the whole herbarium – truly amazing bouquet: complex, aromatic, exciting. New-oak portion sensitively notched down to 70%, preserving fruit. All in range tasted some years back.

★★★★☆ **Reserve** ⏱ **99** shade more forward, concentrated than some previous; wild herb redolence with red berry, cassis & eucalyptus complexity; blend cab (75%), merlot & cab franc, all-new oak, 18-20 months. **Merlot** Await next. **Terrace Bay** In abeyance.

Classic range

★★★★ **Cabernet Sauvignon** Ripe & ready **07** shows cassis, blackberry liqueur & earthy undertones. Bold & intense but balanced, with well-judged oak. Despite a drop of touriga, a classic SA cab.

★★★★ **Merlot** ⏱ In usual house style, **07** has classic shaping. Ripe earthy plums & sushi wrapper notes. Fresh palate with fine tannin structure & intelligent oaking. Drops of malbec, cab franc aid complexity.

★★★★ **Shiraz** ⏱ Ripe **06** with 8% touriga. Beautiful game, truffle & leather undertones; attractively rustic palate shows intensity & weight, with a nice warming finish. Harmonious, ready to drink.

★★★★ **Vergenoegd Estate Blend** ⏱ Previously 'Vergenoegd'. **06** Bordeaux-style blend rewards the patient. Usual firm structure & earthy tones uplifted by fresh redcurrant, tar & spicy plum. Integrated oak.

★★★★☆ **Old Cape Colony Cape Vintage** Drops 'Port' from name. Powerful yet elegant **06** from tinta & touriga offers complex aromas of berries, spice & chocolate. The palate seems quite savoury for port, is subtle, with well-measured tannins & an appealing sense of restraint. Long warming finish.

Terrace Bay ⊛ ★★★☆ **06** a slightly earthy, easygoing 5-way red blend with some intensity, length, interest.

Runner Duck range

Red ✓ 🍴 📖 ★★★☆ Intriguing **11** from touriga, malbec, cab franc & tinta. Rich & delicious, no new oak interferes with the Asian-spiced dark fruit. Real interest & character. **Rosé** 🍴 📖 ★★ Now bottled, malbec-based dry **12** shows plush, soft red berry fruit, blood orange undertones. **White** 🍴 📖 ★★★ Sauvignon's zesty acidity, grassy freshness balanced by ripe tropical fruit on uncomplicated **13** for summery pleasure. WO W Cape.

Limited Edition range

Cabernet Franc Await next. **Malbec** Await next. **Tawny Port** ⊛ ★★★ Sweetly rich & rustic once-off **99** from tinta barocca tasted a few years back. — JPf

---

Verlieft Wines

Location: Stellenbosch ▪ Est 2010 ▪ Tasting & sales by appt ▪ Closed Easter Fri-Mon, Dec 25/26 & Jan 1 ▪ Owner(s) Roos Family Wines ▪ Cellarmaster(s) Dirk Roos ▪ PO Box 104 Stellenbosch 7605 ▪ dirk@verlieftwines. com ▪ www.verlieftwines.com ▪ **T +27 (0)82-904-6886**

The Roos family, boutique brand owners in Stellenbosch, enjoy 'collaborations with artists and other interesting people'. Hence the venture with New York artist Jason Oliva on the label artwork for Verlieft's upcoming The Astronaut Bordeaux blend. Next are a muscat de Frontignan dessert, barrel-aged 13 years, and supper club events featuring rare wines and vintages from around the world.

Versailles

Location: Wellington ▪ Map: Paarl & Wellington ▪ WO: Western Cape ▪ Est/1stB 2004 ▪ Tasting, sales & tours by appt ▪ Conservation area ▪ Owner(s) Annareen de Reuck (Malan) ▪ Vineyard manager(s) M Joseph ▪ 100ha (cab, cinsaut, merlot, shiraz, chenin, cbard, riesling) ▪ ±1,200t ▪ PO Box 597 Wellington 7654 ▪ adereuck@ ezinet.co.za, orders@versailleswines.co.za ▪ www.versailles.co.za ▪ S 33° 37' 34.98" E 018° 59' 37.11" ▪ **T +27 (0)21-873-2618/+27 (0)82-898-9314** ▪ F +27 (0)86-502-1482

Owner Annareen de Reuck is the scion of the Malan family which helped establish the Wellington grower-owned cellars now merged into Wellington Wines. Small parcels of her Versailles grapes are vinified in the old estate cellar.

Merlot Await next, as for **Shiraz**, **Cabernet Sauvignon-Merlot** & **Chenin Blanc**. **Sauvignon Blanc** 🍴 📖 ★★★ Khaki bush, dusty fig nuances on budget-priced **13**; brisk, lightish for al fresco enjoyment. —DB

Versus

Easy-drinking brand (www.versuswines.com) of Stellenbosch Vineyards, billed (in the spirit of this edition's theme) as 'true rainbow nation wines - for everyone'.

Original range

Red ☺ 🍴 ★★☆ Soft & fruity **12** preview from shiraz, ruby cab & merlot, unoaked for immediate enjoyment. WO W Cape, as all below.

Rosé 🍴 📖 ★★ Tropical, juicy semi-dry **13** mainly from shiraz. **White** 🍴 📖 ★★ Mainly chenin & colombard **13** is earthy, dryish. This range also in 2-litre pouches.

Naturally Sweet range

Red 🍴 📖 ★ Latest **NV** strawberry nuanced, unlingering. **Rosé** 🍴 📖 ★★ Understated aromas & flavours on latest **NV**. **White** 🍴 📖 ★★ Muted lemon tones on gentle **NV**. These all light 9.5% alc. —CvZ

▪ **Vertex Reserve** *see* Bonnievale Wines

Viceroy

One of South Africa's most enduring blended brandies, with the added fillip of five years' barrel maturation (unusual in its category), Viceroy has historic ties to what was once the Van Ryn Wine & Spirit Company, dating back to the mid-1800s. It subsequently became part of Distell's extensive stable of brandies.

5 ★★★★ A more serious blended brandy (30% potstill), & smoother & more complex than 5 years ageing would usually imply. Fruity enough, clean & bright. Pleasing whether sipped or diluted. — WB, TJ

■ **Victoria Bay** *see* Darling Cellars

Vierlanden Boutique Family Cellar [NEW]

Location: Durbanville ▪ Map: Durbanville, Philadelphia & Darling ▪ WO: Swartland ▪ Est 2009 ▪ 1stB 2010 ▪ Tasting, sales & cellar tours Mon-Sat by appt ▪ Fee R55 ▪ Closed all pub hols ▪ Conferences ▪ Owner(s) Vierlanden Boutique Wines cc ▪ Cellarmaster(s) Esther van Tonder (Jan 2009) ▪ Winemaker(s) Esther van Tonder (Jan 2009), Marius van Tonder & PJ Geyer ▪ 1ha/0.25ha (cab) ▪ 4t/±650cs own label 60% red 40% white ▪ Le Petit Jem, 17 on Murray, Vierlanden Heights, Durbanville 7550 ▪ vierlandencellar@gmail.com ▪ www.vierlandencellar.com ▪ S 33° 48' 21. 44" E 018° 39' 35.36" ▪ **T +27 (0)21-975-7286** ▪ F +27 (0)21-975-7286

The four garagistes vinifying small parcels from selected terroirs in a thatched cellar in Durbanville's Vierlanden area - Danel van Tonder, wife Esther, younger brother Marius and winemaker friend PJ Geyer - liken their personalities to the four elements, saying: 'Our combined efforts and energy produce balanced wines of great expression and character that pair beautifully with food.'

ThatchRoof 📷 ★★★ Merlot & cab combo (56/44) from Swartland vines, **11** very ripe & full, also shows cab's leafy notes, burly tannins. Needs year/2 to meld. — GdB, GM

Vilafonté

Location/map: Stellenbosch ▪ WO: Paarl ▪ Est 1996 ▪ 1stB 2003 ▪ Tasting, sales & tours by appt ▪ Owner(s) Mike Ratcliffe, Zelma Long & Phil Freese ▪ Winemaker(s) Zelma Long & Martin Smith (May 2010) ▪ Viticulturist(s) Phil Freese (1996) & Edward Pietersen (2006) ▪ 17ha (cabs s/f, malbec, merlot) ▪ 60t/4,000cs own label 100% red ▪ Unit 7C Lower Dorp Street Bosman's Crossing Stellenbosch 7600 ▪ info@vilafonte.com ▪ www.vilafonte.com ▪ S 33° 56' 26.8" E 018° 50' 49.8" ▪ **T +27 (0)21-886-4083** ▪ F +27 (0)21-883-8231

The establishment of Vilafonté in the mid 1990s, with two eminent American wine people investing, represented a signal mark of confidence in Cape terroir. Phil Freese, who consults to some of California's grand wineries (and some South African ones too), designed and continues to direct their Paarl vineyards while Zelma Long, with an illustrious reputation as a winemaker, is in charge of the cellar on the outskirts of Stellenbosch town. Both are frequent visitors and fully involved (as the plush elegance, rather Napa-like, of the two red wines perhaps attests), with the help of Martin Smith as resident winemaker and the redoubtable Mike Ratcliffe (also of Warwick), the managing partner in the venture.

★★★★☆ **Series C** 🕒 Intense black fruit aromas, cassis & almond notes on plush & concentrated **10** - cab-dominated as always, with 25% cab franc, merlot, malbec. Opulent, brocaded textures & real mid-palate weight are defining features of this iconically styled wine, a near clone to super-rich, finely balanced **09**.

★★★★☆ **Series M** 🕒 M is still for merlot (49%) in **10**, with malbec & cab. Profound & vinous, rendered approachable by sweet redcurrant aromas, juicy accessibility. Light caramel notes, dryish tannins confirm substantial oaking. Elegance, spice remain hallmarks in **10** - finer, less intense than **09**. — MF

Viljoensdrift Wines & Cruises

Location/map/WO: Robertson ▪ Est/1stB 1998 ▪ Tasting, sales & river cruises at Riverside venue Mon-Fri 9-5 Sat 10-4 & 1st Sun/month 10-3; open 7 days/week during peak season ▪ Closed Good Fri, Dec 25 & Jan 1 ▪ Deli - create your own picnic ▪ Facilities for children ▪ Tour groups ▪ Conferences ▪ Owner(s) Fred & Manie Viljoen ▪ Winemaker(s) Fred Viljoen, with Zonia Lategan ▪ Viticulturist(s) Manie Viljoen ▪ 240ha/120ha (cab, ptage, shiraz, chard, chenin, sauv) ▪ 200t/±160,000cs own label 55% red 40% white 4% rosé 1% port + 15,000L for clients ▪ Other export brands: Elandsberg, Riverscape, Vuurgloed ▪ BWI, IPW, WIETA ▪ PO Box 653 Robertson

6705 ▪ wines@viljoensdrift.co.za ▪ www.viljoensdrift.co.za ▪ S 33° 52' 8.4" E 019° 59' 13.6" ▪ **T +27 (0)23-615-1901 (cellar)/+27 (0)23-615-1017 (tasting/cruises)** ▪ F +27 (0)23-615-3417

Fred Viljoen, co-owner of bucolic Robertson family estate Viljoensdrift, loves to go to their tasting area on the Breede River on Saturdays, 'crack a bottle of wine and talk to visitors' as they take trips on the riverboat Uncle Ben. Dams are full, Fred smiles, and harvest 2013 was 'excellent', boding well for the future.

River Grandeur range

Cabernet Sauvignon Await next. **Merlot** 🎫 **12** preview too unformed to rate. **Pinotage** 🍷 🎫 ★★★ Banana & toasty oak seasoning, extended spicy tail on plummy **12** perfect for easy sipping. **Shiraz** ⏰ 🎫 ★★★ Rusticity part of the charm of supple & savoury **11**. **Cape Blend** ⏰ 🍷 🎫 ★★★ Well-crafted & affable merlot-led **11**, succulent & smooth, thread of lively acidity keeps the pastille-like flavours light & buoyant. **Chardonnay** 🍷 🎫 ★★★ Wood-driven styling (100% new American oak staves) for **13**, modest yet flavoursome aperitif with citrus & coconut highlights. **Sauvignon Blanc** 🍷 🎫 ★★ Capsicum & sherbet on crisp, lightish (12% alcohol) **13** picnic libation.

Viljoensdrift range

Villion ⏰ ★★★ NV méthode cap classique sparkling showing deepish yellow hue, nutty/honeyed bottle-age. **Muskapino Sweet Sparkling Rosé** ⏰ 🎫 ★★ Splash pinotage adds colour to muscat de Frontignan in sweet & frothy party-starting **12**. **Cape Vintage Reserve** ⏰ ★★ Port-style fortified from tinta with souzão, **09** Christmas mince pie character & still-integrating spirit mid-2012. Discontinued: **Rosé**. — MW,DC

▪ **Villa San Giovanni** *see* Zandvliet Wine Estate & Thoroughbred Stud
▪ **Villa Verde** *see* Seven Oaks

Villiera Wines

Location/map: Stellenbosch ▪ WO: Stellenbosch/Western Cape ▪ Est/1stB 1983 ▪ Tasting, sales & cellar tours Mon-Fri 9–5 Sat 9–3 ▪ Closed Good Fri, Dec 25 & Jan 1 ▪ MCC & Nougat pairings; Dalewood cheese platters & soft drinks; or BYO picnic ▪ Conferences (up to 40 pax) ▪ Wildlife sanctuary ▪ Game drives & birding R150pp (R75 for children under 15) incl. tasting & self-guided tour of cellar, book ahead ▪ Owner(s) Grier family ▪ Cellarmaster(s) Jeff Grier (1983) ▪ Winemaker(s) Christiaan Visser (Dec 2008) ▪ Viticulturist(s) Simon Grier ▪ 400ha/210ha (cab, merlot, ptage, pinot, shiraz, chard, chenin, sauv) ▪ 1,800t/120,000cs own label 28% red 37% white 35% MCC; 28,000cs for Marks & Spencer; 42,000cs for Woolworths ▪ Other export brand: Groot Geluk (Belgium) ▪ HACCP, WIETA ▪ PO Box 66 Koelenhof 7605 ▪ wine@villiera.com ▪ www.villiera.com ▪ S 33° 50' 14.4" E 018° 47' 34.4" ▪ **T +27 (0)21-865-2002/3** ▪ F +27 (0)21-865-2314

There's always been more to the wine business than just wine at this quintessential family estate at the edge of the Stellenbosch district, since it was founded by cousins Jeff and Simon Grier just over 30 years ago. Good value to go with the quality, for a start. But Villiera has long been known for its ethical practices in relation to both society (through a range of upliftment projects) and the environment (viticulturist Simon Grier's responsible vineyard management, as well as a large wildlife sanctuary). As to the wines, the range is large and varied, the style always unpretentious and dedicated to drinkability as well as quality. There's something of a focus on sparkling wines, for which cellarmaster Jeff Grier has established an enviable reputation.

Villiera Wines range

★★★★ **Monro** Nicely matured, plush-textured & accessible **09** merlot-led Bordeaux blend with both cabs; sweet expressive ripe dark fruit both structured & softened by 2 years in all-new barrels. No **08** made.

★★★★ **Bush Vine Sauvignon Blanc** ✓ 🎫 'Traditional' not now in name. **13** achieves fresh herbaceousness through careful viticulture. Tasty, crisply succulent fruit well-harmonised with savoury acidity.

★★★★☆ **Inspiration** ⏰ 🎫 Botrytised chenin, riesling dessert. Last-tasted **10**'s fresh acid controls richness.

Merlot ☺ 🎫 ★★★ Dash of touriga adds spicy intrigue & interest to nicely ripe, plummy **11**; vibrant finish has savoury herbal edge. **Pinotage** ☺ 🎫 ★★★ Freshly youthful **11**, hint of mocha mixed with red fruit's inviting juiciness; underpinned by firm but pliable tannins. **Chenin Blanc** ☺ 🎫 ★★★ Lightly honeyed **13** offers satisfyingly spicy ripe peach & apple, focused by lovely acidity. **Gewürztraminer** ☺ 🎫 ★★★ Pure Turkish Delight on off-dry **13**, appealingly spicy & flavourful. Perfectly light for lunchtime.

Cabernet Sauvignon ✓ 📓 ★★★★ Smart, lively **11** offers abundant succulent sweet fruit, seasoned in oak; intriguing spicy, herbal edge adds interest. **Traditional Barrel Fermented Chenin Blanc** Await next. **Rhine Riesling** ⓣ ★★★★ Last tasted was ethereal, spicy, off-dry **09**. **Sauvignon Blanc** ✓ 🏠 📓 ★★★★ Flavoursome **13** appealingly fresh & juicy, with crisp acidity, less serious than standout **11** (★★★★) but nonetheless harmonious, vibrant & delightful. WO W Cape. Discontinued: **Fired Earth**.

Villiera Méthode Cap Classique range

★★★★ **Brut Natural** ⓣ Quietly-spoken charm in clean, delicate **09** sparkler. Bone-dry, no dosage yet manages soft, refined edge. Persistent mousse carries bright pure-fruited citrus flavours. No sulphur used.

★★★★☆ **Monro Brut** Classy, deliciously creamy & persistent **08** barrel-fermented chardonnay-pinot sparkling softer than much-lauded cool-vintage **07** (★★★★★) & not quite as thrilling - though shows great dimension & complexity from 4 years on lees.

Tradition Brut Rosé 📓 ★★★ Salmon-coloured, earthy & harmonious **NV** sparkling toned by pinotage, with chardonnay & both pinots. Satisfying weight & flavour. **Starlight Brut** NEW 📓 ★★★★ **NV** sparkler is dry & light (9.5% alcohol) without losing flavour. Lovely balance, focus, creaminess from chardonnay, with pinot meunier & pinotage. **Tradition Brut** ✓ 📓 ★★★★ Ever-popular stalwart **NV** bubbles from chardonnay, pinot & pinotage; delightfully dry verve & zippy lemon freshness for any celebration. Discontinued: **Reserve Brut Rosé, Brut Special Dosage**.

Down to Earth range

Red ☺ 📓 ★★★ Temptingly perfumed & flavoured **12** touriga, shiraz blend is vibrant & tasty with gorgeous grip. Over-delivers on price. **White** ☺ 🏠 📓 ★★★ Invitingly fresh, dry & crisp **13** sauvignon-semillon blend for everyday quaffing. —IM

Villiersdorp Cellar

Location/map: Villiersdorp • WO: Western Cape • Est 1922 • 1stB 1974 • Tasting & sales Mon-Fri 8–5 Sat 9-1 • Fee R10 for groups of 7+ • Closed Easter Fri-Mon & Dec 25/26 • Kelkiewyn Restaurant (see Restaurants section) • Farm produce • Walks/hikes • Mountain biking & 4x4 trails • Tractor museum open on request • Owner(s) 40 growers • Winemaker(s) Christo Versfeld, with André Bruyns (Dec 2009) • Viticulturist(s) André Bruyns (Dec 2009) • 300ha (merlot, chenin, sauv) • 3,600t/19,000cs own label 30% red 30% white 30% rosé 10% fortified • BWI, IPW • PO Box 14 Villiersdorp 6848 • marketing@slowine.co.za • www.villiersdorpcellar.co.za • S 33° 59' 11.2" E 019° 17' 48.5" • **T +27 (0)28-840-1120** • F +27 (0)28-840-1833

Villiersdorp Cellar and its 40 vinegrower owners are blessed with immense scenic beauty including the huge Theewaterskloof Dam, which lends its name to the well-priced unfortified Dam Good wines, now co-vinified (along with the separately listed Slowine range) by ex-Springfontein winemaker Christo Versfeld.

Dam Good range

White ☺ 🏠 📓 ★★★ Friendly **13** (12.6% alcohol) has fragrant fruit (mainly chenin), ends with dry lemon flick. **Rosé** ☺ 🏠 📓 ★★★ **13** pretty pink Natural Sweet with pinotage's strawberry tones.

Red ⓣ 🏠 📓 ★★★ **10** mainly merlot/shiraz, dark fruit, soft spice, pleasant grip of tannin.

Villiersdorp Cellar range

Treintjiewyn Hanepoot Jerepiko ☺ 📓 ★★★ 'Little Tractor' **NV** fortified dessert oozes orange rind, watermelon & sunshine. Slippery, luscious, but a cloying farewell.

Cape Ruby 📓 ★★ NV more 'high-alcohol red' than dinkum port-style. Light hearted & sweet. — WB

■ **Vinay** see Slanghoek Winery
■ **Vin du Cap** see Vrede Wines

Vinimark

Stellenbosch • Closed to public • Directors Tim Rands, Cindy Jordaan, Geoff Harvey, Gys Naudé, Rudiger Gretschel & Guy Pause • Exports: Geoff Harvey • geoff@vinimark.co.za • PO Box 441 Stellenbosch 7599 • www.vinimark.co.za • **T +27 (0)21-883-8043/4** • F +27 (0)21-886-4708

Wine merchants marketing, selling and distributing various ranges with local partners, including Robertson Winery, Kleindal, Long Beach and Silversands, some listed separately.

■ **Vin Maison** *see* Maison

Vins d'Orrance ▮▮

Location: Constantia ▪ WO: Western Cape ▪ Est/1stB 2000 ▪ Tastings by appt ▪ Owner(s) Christophe & Sabrina Durand ▪ Cellarmaster(s)/winemaker(s) Christophe Durand ▪ 11ha ▪ 30t/4,666cs own label ▪ PO Box 23923 Claremont 7735 ▪ christophe@vinsdorrance.co.za ▪ www.vinsdorrance.co.za ▪ **T +27 (0)21-683-7479** ▪ F +27 (0)86-588-2989

Christophe Durand arrived from France in 1995 to import barrels, but soon started buying in grapes – they now come from diverse terroirs across the Cape - and vinifying them in rented space in Constantia. Classically oriented, with a stylish je ne sais quoi, his wines salute his daughters Ameena and Anais, with Kama ('sensual pleasure' in Sanskrit) for his wife Sabrina, of South African Indian origin.

Vins d'Orrance range

★★★★☆ **Syrah Cuvée Ameena** Polished blend of Elgin's elegant florality & pepper with Perdeberg's deep, dark, spicy fruit, these two shiraz components perfectly integrated with judicious portion new oak. Complex **11** flaunts mineral vibrancy & a fine thread of acidity throughout.

★★★★☆ **Chardonnay Cuvée Anaïs** Ultra-stylish, classy **12** in usual elegant guise from half Elgin & Franschhoek fruit. Resolutely steely grip contains intense citrus fruit core which promises to unfurl with time. Seamless oak detail completes.

★★★★☆ **Chenin Blanc Kama** Name now has variety first. Subtly oaked (no new barrels) **12** from old Swartland single-vineyard exceedingly reticent, but shaped for interesting evolution. Change in style from sensual richness in **11** to a more cerebral one here, with a bone-dry, lean, fino-like tanginess & structure.

Simply Wines range NEW

Simply Red 🏠 ⓥ ★★★ Nicely ripe & simple **10** an aromatic shiraz-based blend. **Simply White** 🏠 ⓥ ★★★ Pleasingly straightforward chenin-viognier **12** for easy, chilled summery enjoyment. — IM

■ **Vinum** *see* The Winery of Good Hope
■ **Vior** *see* Malanot Wines

Virgin Earth

Location: Riversdale ▪ WO: Langeberg-Garcia/Philadelphia/Coastal/Overberg ▪ Est 2002 ▪ 1stB 2003 ▪ Closed to public ▪ Owner(s) Kobus du Plessis ▪ Winemaker(s) Piet Kleinhans (Sep 2008) & Joseph Gertse (Jan 2000) ▪ Viticulturist(s) Rudi Benn (Jan 2001) & Hendrik Otto (2004) ▪ 13,000ha/21ha (cabs s/f, merlot, p verdot, shiraz, sauv, sem, verdelho, viog) ▪ 70,000cs own label 40% red 45% white 15% rosé ▪ Fairtrade, organic in conversion, WIETA ▪ PO Box 451 Melkbosstrand 7437 ▪ sales@havanahills.co.za ▪ www.havanahills.co.za ▪ **T +27 (0)21-972-1110** ▪ F +27 (0)21-972-1105

About 320 km distant from its West Coast sibling property, Havana Hills, the Virgin Earth home-farm is situated on the foothills of the Langeberg. This part of Klein Karoo has its own appellation, Langeberg-Garcia, and it's ons of the smallest wine wards in South Africa. Most of the 13,000 ha estate has been kept natural, and a game park established where numerous species of wild antelope roam.

★★★★ **Pinot Noir** Philadelphia grapes as usual for **11** (★★★★), true to type & perfect for the uninitiated. Red fruit, hint of vanilla, some farmyard pong. Fruit driven, bright acidity, no real tannic grip. Lacks class of **09**. No **10**.

★★★★ **High 5ive** ✓ Cab-led Bordeaux blend but for 2% shiraz. **10** (★★★★) red & black fruit, some attractive herbal character. Trades off a little sugar, tannins are soft & fine. Lacks gravitas of **08**. No **09**.

★★★★ **Noble Late Harvest** ⓦ From semillon, last **08** ticked all the boxes: deeply rich & full flavoured; apricot, pineapple, good length. Deliciously easy to drink. 30% in seasoned barrels. 500 ml.

Pinotage ★★★★ Slightly rustic **10** shows red fruit but also an earthy note. Medium bodied with firm tannins & a savoury finish. Not as lipsmacking as **09** (★★★★). **Lost Barrel Shiraz** ⓦ ★★★ Last was **07**, with smoky dark fruit, plump, & nice tannin grip. Designed to please now & next few years. Overberg WO. **Shiraz-Viognier** NEW ★★★ **11** is a pizza & pasta sort of wine with prominent oak tending to dominate black cherry fruit. **Chenin Blanc**

🏠 ★★★ Undemanding but likeable **13** is sauvignon-esque being lightly fruity with racy acidity despite few grams sugar. Coastal WO. **Pepper Tree Sauvignon Blanc** ✓ 🏠 ★★★★ Cleverly assembled **13** has good concentration & zip, high sugar playing off against high acidity. Notes of lime & peach before some white pepper on the finish. Better resolved than **12** (★★★★). **Succulent** ⊕ ★★★★ Wooded off-dry semillon, viognier blend. When last tasted **10** had waxy melon styling, full-bodied yet retained freshness. Delicious on release, could age few years. Improved on aptly named **08** (★★★★). **Sauvignon Blanc-Semillon** NEW ✓ 🏠 ★★★★ **12** impresses with the purity of its fruit rather than any great complexity. Intense lime, a good line of acidity before a savoury finish. 50/50 blend, just off-dry. **Viognier MCC** ⊕ ★★★ Bubbles enhancing peachiness, **08** previously was not your usual méthode cap classique style sparkling. Flavourful enough for creative food pairing. — CE

Virginia

For over 40 years, a consistent semi-sweet white, widely sourced, by Distell. 2 & 5L.

Virginia 🏠 ★ Like its front label, **NV** quaffer is straightforward & unvarying from year to year. — DB, HJ

■ **Vivat Bacchus** *see* Veenwouden Private Cellar

Vleiland Wines

Location: Vredendal ▪ Map: Olifants River ▪ Est 2004 ▪ 1stB 2005 ▪ Tasting & sales by appt Mon-Fri 8-5 Sat 8-12 ▪ Closed Easter Fri-Mon, Dec 25 & Jan 1 ▪ BYO picnic ▪ Farm produce ▪ Walks/hikes ▪ 4x4 & mountain bike trails ▪ Owner(s) Nico Laubscher snr, Alette Laubscher, Nico Laubscher jnr ▪ Winemaker(s)/viticulturist(s) Nico Laubscher ▪ 60ha (cab, ptage, shiraz, chenin, cbard, sauv) ▪ 790t/560cs own label 100% red ▪ PO Box 627 Vredendal 8160 ▪ alzanne@mylan.co.za ▪ S 31° 44' 42.24" E 018° 32' 8.16" ▪ **T +27 (0)27-213-2525/+27 (0)82-905-1640** ▪ F +27 (0)27-213-2825

Grape growers at Vredendal, the Laubscher family last year acquired West Coast farm Lochheim, with 32 ha of vines, and some of the grapes from these might find their way into the smidgen made for the Vleiland own-label by Nico Laubscher jnr. 'Maybe pinotage,' he muses, to join his cab-shiraz (the latest 2012 untasted).

Vondeling

Location: Paarl ▪ Map: Paarl & Wellington ▪ WO: Voor Paardeberg ▪ Est 2001 ▪ 1stB 2005 ▪ Tasting & sales Mon-Fri 10-5 ▪ Wedding/function/conference venue & chapel ▪ Owner(s) Richard Gower, Julian Johnsen & Anthony Ward ▪ Cellarmaster(s) Matthew Copeland (Jul 2007) ▪ Winemaker(s) Emile van der Merwe (Dec 2011), with William Mofokeng (Jan 2005) ▪ Viticulturist(s) Magnus Joubert (Jul 2012) ▪ 115ha (cabs s/f, carignan, grenache r/w, malbec, merlot, mourv, p verdot, shiraz, chard, chenin, muscat de F, sauv, viog) ▪ 950t/90,000cs own label 40% red 50% white 10% rosé ▪ Other export brand: Signal Cannon ▪ PO Box 57 Wellington 7654 ▪ admin@vondelingwines.co.za ▪ www.vondelingwines.co.za ▪ S 33° 35' 22.50" E 018° 52' 45.00" ▪ **T +27 (0)21-869-8595** ▪ F +27 (0)21-869-8219

Continual development at this British-owned progressive property. It's now open to the public, with a dedicated tasting centre, and a small chapel for weddings has been completed. Behind the scenes is serious commitment to conservation and sustainability, a full-time botanist employed to geo-tag, catalogue and DNA fingerprint endangered fynbos. Vondeling is also home to the Voor Paardeberg Sustainability Initiative and Fire Protection Association. On the wine side, due early this year is a single-ferment méthode ancestrale sparkling.

★★★★ **Erica Shiraz** 🏠 🌿 With soupçons 4 other Rhône varieties, **10** has all the right touches, scrub, white pepper, hint of chocolate, folded into plush dark fruit. Supple tannins give a platform for ageing.

★★★★ **Chardonnay** ✓ 🏠 🌿 Bunch pressing, wild yeast ferment, 10 months in barrel, **11** is seriously made. Citrus peel, dried peach & almonds, lees-ageing creamy & softly curvaceous, this is delicious.

★★★★ **Sauvignon Blanc** ✓ 🏠 🌿 Nice combo lemon leaf & flintiness in elegant **13**, all pointing to vibrant freshness, excellent seafood compatibility. Back on track after less intense **12** (★★★☆).

★★★★ **Babiana** ✓ 🏠 🌿 Half chenin with 3 others, wild ferment & oak, **11** (★★★★☆) has lovely melon & dried pear, oatmeal & silky curvaceous lines, improves on also-tasted **10**, which shows how well these wines age. Deeper flavours here, melon preserve & crushed nuts, but enough intrinsic freshness for a continued future.

Petit Rouge ☺ 🍽 🈂 **★★★** Merlot/cab mix for earlier drinking, as **12**'s name implies. Plump mulberries, juicy, a dash of cedar & nice grip.

Cabernet Sauvignon Next awaited, as for **Petit Blanc** & **Sweet Carolyn**. **Baldrick Shiraz** 🍽 🈂 **★★★☆** Smoky & dark **12**'s floral, dried herb notes are from mourvèdre & viognier but the fleshy smoothness is shiraz's own. Discontinued: **Cabernet Sauvignon-Merlot**. — CR

Vrede en Lust Wine Farm

Location: Paarl ▪ Map: Paarl & Wellington ▪ Est 1688 ▪ 1stB 2002 ▪ Tasting & sales daily 10–5 ▪ Closed Good Fri & Dec 25 ▪ Tours 10–4 by appt ▪ Lust Bistro & Bakery ▪ Guest accommodation in three deluxe suites & manor house ▪ Tour groups by appt ▪ Conferences, functions & weddings ▪ Play area for children ▪ Pétanque courts ▪ Owner(s) Buys family ▪ Winemaker(s) Susan Erasmus (2006), with Ansoné Stoffberg (2009) ▪ Viticulturist(s) Etienne Buys (Jun 1998) ▪ 275ha total ▪ Vrede en Lust: 66ha (cab, grenache, malbec, merlot, p verdot, shiraz, chard, viog); Casey's Ridge, Elgin: 88.9ha (cabs s/f, merlot, shiraz, chard, chenin, pinots g/n, riesling, sauv, sem, viog); Ricton: 127ha (cab, cinsaut, ptage, shiraz, chard) ▪ 811t/48,000cs own label ▪ WIETA ▪ PO Box 171 Groot Drakenstein 7680 ▪ info@vnl.co.za ▪ www.vnl.co.za ▪ S 33° 50' 15.9" E 018° 57' 13.4" ▪ **T +27 (0)21-874-1611** ▪ F +27 (0)21-874-1859

Family-owned Vrede en Lust, noted for its rich and stylish cellardoor experience, has opened a new bistro and bakery named Lust, which Nicola Momberg, marketing manager, commends as 'a culinary delight and a feast for the eye'.

■ **Vredehoek** see Koopmanskloof Wingerde
■ **Vredelust** see Koopmanskloof Wingerde

Vredenheim Wines

Location/map/WO: Stellenbosch ▪ Tasting & sales Mon-Sat 9-4.45 ▪ Closed Good Fri, Dec 25 & Jan 1 ▪ Restaurant Barrique T +27 (0)21-881-3001 ▪ Hudson's Coffee Shop T +27 (0)21-881-3590 ▪ Conferences/functions ▪ Vredenheim Angus Stud ▪ Big Cats Park ▪ Jaguar cars for hire ▪ Curio shop ▪ Guesthouse ▪ Owner(s) Bezuidenhout family ▪ Winemaker(s) Kowie du Toit ▪ Viticulturist(s) Kalie Kirsten ▪ 80ha under vine ▪ 20,000cs own label 60% red 40% white ▪ PO Box 369 Stellenbosch 7599 ▪ wine@vredenheim.co.za ▪ www.vredenheim.co.za ▪ S 33° 57' 38.2" E 018° 48' 29.4" ▪ **T +27 (0)21-881-3637** ▪ F +27 (0)21-881-3296

Love for wild animals prompted the Bezuidenhout family owners to open a Big Cats Park at their Stellenbosch estate so visitors can observe lion, leopard, cheetah and lynx while enjoying Vredenheim wines. Gardens, food, curios, a nursery and in-cellar conferencing broaden an unusually diverse visitor offering.

Merlot ☺ 🍽 **★★★** Fruitcake, sweet plums & dark chocolate on smooth **11** sipper. **Pinotage** ☺ 🍽 🈂 **★★★** Rich & fruity **11** is rounded, succulent & spicy. Over-delivers on value. **Shiraz** ☺ 🍽 🈂 **★★★** Leather, smoke & mocha abound on vibrant **11**, dark fruit & punchy spice up the enjoyment. **Vredenvonkel** ☺ **★★★** Light-bodied, fruity, off-dry **NV** pink sparkler for party fun.

Cabernet Sauvignon ⓕ 🍽 **★★★** Ripe berry & chocolate flavours, **10** good structure & grip, easy to like. **Reserve** ⓕ 🍽 **★★★★** Polished **08**, from shiraz & cab, sweet fruit & soft tannins, lovely balance. **Rosé** ⓕ **★★** Step-up **NV** from sauvignon & splash shiraz, semi-sweet, soft & piquant. Serve well chilled. **Sauvignon Blanc** ⓕ 🍽 **★★★** Fresh, zesty **12**, tropical fruit flavours for pleasant everyday drinking. — WB

Vredevol Private Wine Cellar

Location: Klawer ▪ WO: Coastal ▪ Est 2010 ▪ 1stB 2008 ▪ Closed to public ▪ Owner(s) Johan & Anne-Mari le Hanie ▪ Cellarmaster(s)/winemaker(s) Johan van Wyk (Jul 2010) ▪ 30ha ▪ 1,000cs own label 50% red 50% white ▪ PO Box 12695 Die Board 7613 ▪ vredevol.wines@vodamail.co.za ▪ **T +27 (0)21-887-1277** ▪ F +27 (0)21-887-1288

While a new barrel maturation cellar at their Klawer winery and an Out of Region range are still on the agenda, boutique vignerons Johan and Anne-Mari le Hanie's melot-cab is still from Coastal fruit vinified at Stellenbosch's Blue Creek.

Merlot-Cabernet Sauvignon ★★★★ Was 'Bordeaux Blend'. Well-constructed **11**'s mixed berries delicious now but bolstered by sufficient structure, chalky tannic grip, to improve few years. — GdB, GM

Vrede Wines

Location/map/WO: Stellenbosch ▪ 1stB 1998 ▪ Tasting & sales by appt only ▪ Owner(s) Duplenia Plase/ Kleintjie Bellingan Family Trust ▪ Production & marketing by Vin du Cap International (Pty) Ltd ▪ Viticulturist(s) Russel Gerber ▪ 74ha (cab, merlot, shiraz, chenin, sauv, viog) ▪ 500t/14,000cs own label 60% red 40% white ▪ PO Box 7271 Stellenbosch 7599 ▪ info@vredewines.co.za ▪ www.vredewines.co.za ▪ S 33° 50' 37.8" E 018° 48' 31.4" ▪ **T +27 (0)21-865-2257** ▪ F +27 (0)21-865-2257

Vin du Cap manages the production and marketing of the portfolio from the 75 ha of vineyards on Stellenbosch's Vrede property. Attractively and classically attired, each wine is intended to be 'a voyage of discovery'.

Vineyard Select range NEW

> **Syrah** ☺ ▨ ★★★ White pepper-dusted **10**'s meaty stewed tomato & robust tannins are made for country food. **Lourentius van Andringa** ☺ ▨ ★★★ Cab-led Bordeaux blend with merlot (25%), cab franc (5%). **10** fullish, with dense ripe fruit core, good finish.

Cabernet Sauvignon ★★★ Mint & menthol accents to blackcurrant pastilles, **09** ideal partner for roast lamb. **Andrea** ▨ ★★★ Aromatic Cape Blend mainly cab & pinotage, splash petit verdot. Mint, plums & American oak vanilla in friendly **10**.

Charmé range

Cabernet Sauvignon ▤ ▨ ★★ Rhubarb & savoury notes on drink-soon **11**. **Shiraz** ▨ ★★ Leathery/ savoury **11** will appeal to fans of the unfruity old-Cape style. — GdB, GM

Vriesenhof Vineyards

Location/map: Stellenbosch ▪ WO: Stellenbosch/Piekenierskloof ▪ Est 1980 ▪ 1stB 1981 ▪ Tasting & sales Mon-Thu 10–4 Fri 10–3.30 Sat by appt ▪ Fee R25 ▪ Closed all pub hols ▪ Cellar tours by appt ▪ Owner(s) Landgoed Vriesenhof (Pty) Ltd ▪ Cellarmaster(s) Jan Coetzee ▪ Winemaker(s) Nicky Claasens (2008), with Richard Phillips (2001) ▪ Viticulturist(s) Coetzee Ehlers ▪ 60ha/45ha (cabs s/f, grenache, merlot, pinot, ptage, chard) ▪ 300t/34,000cs own label 90% red 10% white ▪ PO Box 155 Stellenbosch 7599 ▪ info@vriesenhof.co.za ▪ www.vriesenhof.co.za ▪ S 33° 58' 16.7" E 018° 52' 2.8" ▪ **T +27 (0)21-880-0284** ▪ F +27 (0)21-880-1503

Rugby legend Jan 'Boland' Coetzee bought his farm on the slopes of Stellenbosch Mountain, just outside the town, in 1980, but purchases, long leases, land swaps and new plantings have changed its shape over the years. Working with Nicky Claasens in the cellar, Jan's winemaking approach remains resolutely traditional, avoiding upfront fruitiness and maintaining a proper dryness in their adherence to a model of classic austerity. Just the Grenache is allowed a little fruity flamboyance - but that's not from Stellenbosch fruit, after all!

Vriesenhof range

★★★★ **Cabernet Sauvignon 09** (★★★☆) firmly old-school, as was previous **06**. There's good but muted fruit presence, with a leathery, savoury overlay. Smooth, with solid tannins. In magnums only. Should keep.

★★★★☆ **Grenache** As usual, **11** from Piekenierskloof combines deliciousness with the firm structure one expects at Vriesenhof, with the half-new oak in balance with the fruit flavours. Sophisticated & serious as well as easily delightful, with a long, properly dry finish.

★★★★ **Pinot Noir 09** released after **10** (tasted last year). Most attractive cherry & berry fruit, though not showy or intense; well balanced, with mild tannins & fresh acidity. **11** (★★★★) also well structured, but more earthy, with the fruit a little dulled.

★★★★ **Chardonnay** Always made in a restrained, steely style. **12** no exception - balanced & fresh, the fruit well supported by unobtrusive new oak; clean, limy conclusion.

Pinotage ★★★ Light perfume on seriously oaked **09**, but sweet fruit flavours on heavy textured palate rather reined-in. Dry, grippy finish. **08** (★★★) also tasted, similar but less charm, less fruit. **Kallista** ★★★☆ **09** Bordeaux blend another old-style offering, stressing savoury/leathery notes over the pleasant berry fruit. Firm, classic structure. No **08**. **07** (★★★) also tasted: more awkward; reduced fruit leaves that structure too exposed.

Paradyskloof range

Cabernet Sauvignon ⊕ ★★ Modest-fruited **10**; dry, rather austerely dull & fleeting. All these wines tasted last year. **Pinot Noir** ⊕ ★★★ **11** a pleasant, easy 'dry red'. Quietly fruity, a touch jammy, with good acidity & a little tannic grip. **Pinotage** ⊕ ★★★ **11** light-hearted & friendly, though the sweet fruit controlled by

strong tannins & bone-dry finish. **Grenache-Malbec-Shiraz** Await next. **Chardonnay** ⓦ ★★★ As usual, in same classic mould as Vriesenhof version, but **11** a little lighter fruited & easier. Balanced & fresh, attractive weight & texture. **Muscat d'Alexandrie** ⓦ ★★★ Light, bright & not too sweet **08** from rather rare red hanepoot - 50 year old vines. Tawny coloured; just 15% alcohol. — TJ

Vruchtbaar Boutique Winery

Location/map/WO: Robertson ▪ Est/1stB 2001 ▪ Tasting, sales & cellar tours Mon-Sat by appt ▪ Closed all pub hols ▪ Owner(s) Alwyn & Francois Bruwer ▪ Cellarmaker(s)/winemaker(s) Francois Bruwer ▪ Viticulturist(s) Briaan Stipp (consultant) ▪ 35ha (cab, merlot, ptage, ruby cab, chard, chenin, sauv) ▪ 400t/±874cs own label 62% red 38% white ▪ PO Box 872 Robertson 6705 ▪ vruchtbaar@mweb.co.za ▪ S 33° 48' 17.7" E 019° 51' 43. 6" ▪ **T +27 (0)82-739-5553/+27 (0)82-335-1152** ▪ F +27 (0)23-626-2334

Last year topped even the previous year's record, with 'huge yields from every block', says cellarmaster Francois Bruwer. 'We expected fruit quality to decline, but that was not so - it was exceptional.' Most of the family boutique's fruit goes to Robertson Winery 'and they were very happy, agreeing it was outstanding'.

★★★★ **Cabernet Sauvignon** ⓦ Concentrated **08** preview fruit-filled sipper with modern styling. Dense & lingering, with tannins giving form. Rating provisional. Last **06** was integrated, polished & harmonious.

★★★★ **Chenin Blanc Limited Edition** ⓦ In contrast to sinuous **08**, bold **09** (★★★★) not for the faint-hearted: ripe tropical tones lashed with buttery oak, warming 15% alcohol.

Pinotage ⓦ ★★★ Quintessential banana & strawberry on **09**. Dense, delivers power but with noticeable sweetness. **Island Red** ⓦ ★★☆ Happy **NV**, bright & refreshing, light tannin for everyday sipping. Cab & pinotage. **Chardonnay** ⓦ Await next, as for **Chenin Blanc Unwooded** & **Noble Late Harvest**. — CvZ

Vukani Wines

Location: Plettenberg Bay ▪ WO: Durbanville/Robertson/Stellenbosch ▪ Est 2005 ▪ Tasting & sales daily 9-5.30 ▪ Fee varies per wine ▪ Owner(s) Peter & Caroline Thorpe ▪ Cellarmaster(s)/winemaker(s) Anton Smal ▪ Viticulturist(s) Peter Thorpe ▪ ±2,800cs own label 56% red 44% white ▪ PO Box 1606 Plettenberg Bay 6600 ▪ peter@vukaniwines.com, danny@bramonwines.co.za ▪ www.bramonwines.co.za ▪ S 33° 57' 25.0" E 023° 28' 50.8" ▪ **T +27 (0)44-534-8007** ▪ F +27 (0)44-534-8007

Vukani ('Wake Up') is a 2005 empowerment project established by the owners of Bramon farm in Plettenberg Bay, specialising in training previously disadvantaged farmers in the area in viticulture and winemaking. Wines are listed in restaurants, guest houses and hotels locally, with some exported.

Cabernet Sauvignon ⓦ ★★★ **10** showed cab's firm grip when reviewed, needed food to cushion the tannins. **Pinotage** ⓦ ★★★ Ripe & sweet-fruited **11**, from Robertson grapes embellished with oak staves. **Chenin Blanc** ⓦ ★★★ Easygoing tropical quaffer **11** perfect for summer lunches. WO Stellenbosch. — IM

▪ **Vusani** see House of Mandela

Vuurberg

Location/map: Stellenbosch ▪ WO: Stellenbosch/Western Cape ▪ Tasting, sales & cellar tours by appt ▪ Closed all pub hols ▪ Owner(s)/cellarmaster(s) Sebastiaan Klaassen ▪ Winemaker(s) Donovan Rall (Oct 2010) ▪ 8ha (cabs s/f, malbec, merlot, p verdot, chenin, viog) ▪ 4,000cs own label 50% red 50% white ▪ PO Box 449 Stellenbosch 7599 ▪ info@vuurberg.com ▪ www.vuurberg.com ▪ S 33° 54' 28.9" E 018° 56' 52.7" ▪ **T +27 (0)82-387-6235**

Donovan Rall, known for non-conformist yet highly acclaimed wines under his own label, has been at this Banhoek boutique winery since 2010. 'Our wines are very different to our neighbours'. Unusual blends made as naturally as possible.' It's all about arriving at an end-product with a 'distinctly South African vibe'.

Vuurberg Reserve ⓦ ★★★☆ **09** from half petit verdot plus cab, merlot, malbec - a really tasty ensemble. Bit less woody than **08**, but also big, bold. **White** ⓦ 🍷 ★★★★ **11** 7-way blend with chenin to the fore. Yellow fruit, spice (from a third new oak), firm line of acidity. Needed time when last reviewed. WO W Cape. — CE

▪ **Vuurgloed** see Viljoensdrift Wines & Cruises

▪ **W** see Whalehaven Wines

Waboomsrivier Wine Cellar

Location: Worcester ▪ Map: Breedekloof ▪ Est 1949 ▪ Tasting & sales Mon-Fri 8-5 ▪ Closed all pub hols ▪ Cellar tours by appt during harvest ▪ Cellarmaster(s) Bennie Wannenburg (Sep 2005) ▪ Winemaker(s) Wim Viljoen (Sep 1991), with André Landman (Jan 2013) ▪ Viticulturist(s) Pierre Snyman (Vinpro) ▪ ±1,106ha ▪ 19,872t ▪ ISO 22000:2011 ▪ PO Box 24 Breërivier 6858 ▪ sales@waboms.co.za ▪ www.waboomsrivier.com ▪ S 33° 31' 43.08" E 019° 12' 35.24" ▪ **T +27 (0)23-355-1730** ▪ F +27 (0)23-355-1731

Situated in the mountain and river wonderland of the upper Breede River Valley, grower-owned Waboomsrivier describes itself 'a bulk-wine cellar which uses traditional and modern technology to perfection'. A tiny portion of its production appears under the Wagenboom own-label, not ready for tasting this edition.

■ **Wagenboom** *see* Waboomsrivier Wine Cellar

Waka Waka Wines

Location/WO: Paarl ▪ Est 2011 ▪ 1stB 2010 ▪ Tasting & sales at Perdeberg Winery ▪ Owner(s) REH Kendermann & Perdeberg Winery ▪ Cellarmaster(s) Albertus Louw (Oct 2008) ▪ Winemaker(s) Riaan Möller (Dec 2006) & Carla Herbst (Jun 2008) ▪ Viticulturist(s) Jaco Engelbrecht (Nov 2011) ▪ PO Box 214 Paarl 7620 ▪ info@perdeberg.co.za ▪ www.perdeberg.co.za ▪ **T +27 (0)21-869-8244** ▪ F +27 (0)21-869-8245

Invoking Shakira's catchy theme song for FIFA World Cup 2010, this joint venture between Perdeberg Winery and REH Kendermann is for export only, mainly to the US and Germany. Listen for the blare of a vuvuzela as you take your first sip!

Shiraz-Cabernet Sauvignon 🍴 📖 ★★ Rough & ready quaffer, **10** shows rhubarb through tough tannins. **Sauvignon Blanc** ⊕ 🍴 📖 ★★★ Vibrantly youthful **12**. Light bodied, with commendably moderate alcohol. **Sauvignon Blanc-Chenin Blanc** 📖 ★★ Unpretentious, lean & light **12**, showing time in bottle. — GdB

Walker Bay Vineyards

Location: Stanford ▪ Map: Elgin, Walker Bay & Bot River ▪ WO: Walker Bay ▪ Est 1997 ▪ 1stB 2007 ▪ Tasting & sales Mon-Sat 10-5 Sun 11-4 ▪ Fee R20 wine/beer ▪ Closed Good Fri & Dec 25/26 ▪ Cellar tours by appt ▪ Micro brewery ▪ Restaurant ▪ BYO picnic ▪ Facilities for children ▪ Tour groups ▪ Owner(s) Birkenhead Holdings Ltd (Isle of Man) ▪ GM Reinhard Odendaal ▪ Winemaker(s)/viticulturist(s) Reinhard Odendaal ▪ 300ha/24ha (cab, merlot, p verdot, pinot, shiraz, chard, sauv, sem) ▪ 90t/12,000cs own label 40% red 60% white ▪ PO Box 530 Stanford 7210 ▪ info@birkenhead.co.za ▪ www.birkenhead.co.za ▪ S 34° 26' 30.5" E 019° 27' 40.5" ▪ **T +27 (0)28-341-0183** ▪ F +27 (0)28-341-0196

Lovers of beer as well as wine are catered for at this estate near Stanford, where they call themselves 'the first wine and brewing estate in the Southern Hemisphere'. Water lovers can also smile, as there's a water-bottling plant alongside the winery and Birkenhead micro-brewery. Liquid assets galore, in fact.

Cabernet Sauvignon ★★★ Charry oak & austere acidity dominate **11**'s savoury fruit. **Amesteca** ⊕ ★★★ Petit verdot-led (unusually) Bordeaux red. Smoothly integrated **10** offers simple fresh ripe fruit & agreeably firm tannins. **Rosé** ⊕ Tank sample **12** was too unsettled to rate last edition. **Chardonnay** ⊕ 🍴 ★★ **11** a fruity, lightly oaked quaffer. **Chardonnay** Await the next unwooded version. **Sauvignon Blanc** 🍴 ★★☆ Lean, light & dry, this cool-climate **12** perfect for seafood. — IM

Wandsbeck Wyne Koöp Bpk

Location/map/WO: Robertson ▪ Est 1965 ▪ 1stB 1986 ▪ Tasting & sales Mon-Fri 8–5 Sat/Sun by appt ▪ Closed all pub hols ▪ Cellar tours by appt ▪ Facilities for children ▪ Owner(s) 21 members ▪ Cellarmaster(s) Jacques du Toit (Jun 2008) ▪ Winemaker(s) Adriaan Foot (Jan 2009) ▪ Viticulturist(s) Hennie Visser ▪ 516ha (cab, cinsaut, merlot, ruby cab, shiraz, chenin, chard, cbard, sauv) ▪ 8,000t/4,000cs own label 43% red 29% white 14% rosé 14% other + 6m L bulk ▪ IPW ▪ PO Box 267 Robertson 6705 ▪ info@wandsbeckwyne.co.za ▪ www. wandsbeckwyne.co.za ▪ S 33°55' 60.0" E 019°36' 34.4" ▪ **T +27 (0)23-626-1103** ▪ F +27 (0)23-626-3329

At this small but expanding cooperative in Agterkliphoogte Valley, the focus is shifting slightly from bulk wine to introducing consumers to 'top-quality bottled wines at affordable prices'. Hence the more attractive, visitor-friendly cellardoor (jungle gym, al fresco seating) and major upgrade to the production facilities.

Cabernet Sauvignon ⊕ ★★★ Nutty/vanilla overlay on sweet plums of amicable **09**. **Revelation Red** ⊕
🍴 📷 ★★★ Soft & plump easy-drinker from merlot, **12** bright raspberry core. **Symphony** 🍴 📷 ★★☆
Natural Sweet-style wine perlé rosé from shiraz, showing delicate bubbles & candyfloss sweetness in **13**. **Sauvignon Blanc** 🍴 📷 ★★ Faint sherbet character on lean, lively **13**. **Revelation White** 📷 ★★★ Pleasant
grassy **13** chenin/chardonnay mix with waxy overtone, unwooded. **Muscadel** ⊕ 📷 ★★★ Fortified dessert
loses 'Red' from the label. **10** all sunshine & raisins, well-knit fortification. — DC,MW, CvZ

Warwick Estate

Location/map: Stellenbosch • WO: Simonsberg–Stellenbosch/Western Cape/Coastal • Est 1964 • 1stB 1983 •
Tasting & sales daily 10–5 • Cellar tours by appt • 'Big 5' vineyard safari on horseback • Gourmet picnics in summer; tapas inspired winter menu • Facilities for children • Gifts • Conferences • Conservation area • Owner(s)
Ratcliffe family • Winemaker(s) Nic van Aarde (May 2011) • Viticulturist(s) Ronald Spies (Nov 2001) • 110ha/
70ha (cabs s/f, merlot, ptage, shiraz, chard, sauv) • 300t/80,000cs own label 60% red 40% white • BWI,
WIETA • PO Box 2 Elsenburg 7607 • info@warwickwine.com • www.warwickwine.com • S 33° 50' 27" E 018°
51' 54.0" • **T** +27 (0)21-884-4410 • F +27 (0)21-884-4025

As second generation head of the Ratcliffe family estate, marketing-savvy Mike
Ratcliffe understands the value of forging closer ties with consumers. The
Warwick Wine Club now offers membership in the USA, UK and EU, supported by
the revamped website with its social media focus, and the world's biggest travel
website Tripadviser.com, for the past 3 years in a row, has voted Warwick the #1
Stellenbosch winery to visit, a deserved accolade taking into account the many
activities on offer. The 'Lady' theme of the labels was inspired by matriarch
Norma Ratcliffe, one of the first women winemakers in the country and the first
woman invited to join the prestigious Cape Winemakers Guild. To come is a Napa
Valley-inspired charity auction early in 2014.

★★★★ **The First Lady Cabernet Sauvignon** ✓ 📷 Softened & spiced by 15% shiraz, earlier drinking
than the other reds but **11** is no less delicious. Bright red fruit, juicy palate & enough grip to add definition, match
food. WO W Cape.

★★★★☆ **Blue Lady** NEW 📷 100% cab, only in the best years, a vineyard & barrel selection, handsome **10**
demands to be taken seriously. Graphite & salty liquorice, cedar, a berry mix, its tannins still youthfully firm.
Designed for ageing, will unfold further over time.

★★★★★ **Cabernet Franc** 📷 **10** succulent berries are seamed with dark chocolate, herb/scrub nuances
adding seductive complexity. Supple tannins give immediate access but - like **09** - there's a long future ahead,
expensive oaking saw to that.

★★★★ **Old Bush Vines Pinotage** 🍴 📷 Dark-toned **11** offers blueberry & chocolate appeal, the variety's expected succulence. Tannins are in support as a foundation, finishing dry, food ready & ageworthy.

★★★★☆ **Trilogy** 📷 Cab-led Bordeaux-style red blend & flagship, **10** combines cassis, cocoa-rich dark
chocolate & exotic spice, anchored by fine-grained tannins. Given serious attention, 26 months French barrels,
60% new, promises a good future.

★★★★ **Three Cape Ladies** 📷 Cape Blend with pinotage, cab & shiraz working well together in **11**.
Creamy dark fruit, touch of liquorice & well structured palate, with enough grip to provide a serious note.

★★★★ **White Lady Chardonnay** 📷 New name & label, **12** (★★★★★) improves on the house style
hazelnuts & citrus peel of **11**. Lots of care taken, wild yeast ferment/maturation in third new French wood, has
layers of interest, perfect balance & extensive length.

★★★★ **The First Lady Unoaked Chardonnay** ✓ 🍴 📷 White peach & citrus, nicely rounded body, **12**
oozes character & appeal. Good example of chardonnay not needing oak adornment. Dab viognier. WO W Cape.

★★★★☆ **Professor Black Sauvignon Blanc** 🍴 📷 Reductively made to showcase varietal intensity,
structurally elegant **12** has passionfruit, greengage, even sage & a thrilling mineral freshness on the finish that
cries out for oysters, shellfish. Soupçon semillon from Durbanville.

The Black Lady Syrah Next awaited. — CR

Waterford Estate

Location/map: Stellenbosch • WO: Stellenbosch/Western Cape/Elgin • Est/1stB 1998 • Tasting, sales & cellar tours
Mon-Fri 9–5 Sat 10–5 • Tasting fees: R40/standard; R45/chocolate; R50/The Jem (current vintage only); R200/
reserve; R250/wine walk & R550/wine drive, pre-booking essential • Closed Good Fri, Dec 25 & Jan 1 • Tea/coffee/

soft drinks & chocolates ▪ 14ha BWI conserved land ▪ Owner(s) Jeremy & Leigh Ord; Kevin Arnold (partner) ▪ Cellarmaster(s) Kevin Arnold (1998) ▪ Winemaker(s) Mark le Roux (Jul 2009) ▪ Viticulturist(s) Tollie van der Spuy (Jun 2012) ▪ 120ha/60ha (barbera, cab, sangio, shiraz, tempranillo, chard, sauv) ▪ 503t/80,000cs own label 51% red 45% white 3% rosé 1% other ▪ PO Box 635 Stellenbosch 7599 ▪ info@waterfordestate.co.za ▪ www.waterfordestate.co.za ▪ S 33° 59' 54.6" E 018° 52' 12.7" ▪ **T +27 (0)21-880-5300** ▪ F +27 (0)21-880-1007

This stylish property in Stellenbosch's Blaauwklippen Valley was founded when IT magnate Jeremy Ord and wife Leigh bought a sizeable section of the old Stellenrust farm. Eminent Kevin Arnold was a partner from the beginning, establishing vineyards (resurrecting old ones too) and planning the grand new winery – a European-looking design executed in rock and wood off the farm. Kevin, as cellarmaster, ensures continuity as Mark le Roux takes over as winemaker from Francois Haasbroek. Work continues on developing the flagship The Jem as an expression of the estate - with seven of the farm's 11 grape varieties it is an unusually comprehensive reflection of soils, aspects and climates there. The Library Collection of small parcels of mature wines, mostly one-offs, reflects continuing experimentation in the cellar.

Waterford Estate range

★★★★☆ **Cabernet Sauvignon** ⊛ Sleekly muscular **09** youthful & tight last year, needing 5+ years to express the fruit shown by flavour persistence. Impressive, but forceful tannins a touch forbidding in youth.

★★★★☆ **Reserve Chardonnay** ⊛ Single-vineyard, natural ferment **11** less forthcoming in mid-2012 than standard version, but subtly exudes quality. Restrained but forceful, with oaky note over the citrus & fruit intensity veined by insistent acidity - really well balanced. Will benefit from ageing.

★★★★☆ **The Jem** ⊛ Cab & shiraz plus 5 other varieties in rich & grand **09**. Supple & silky, refined but generous & modern in its fruit insistence - all superbly balanced on quite a big scale. Will develop further complexity & harmony with good few years but readier to drink in youth than the cab and cab-heavy blends.

★★★★ **Chardonnay** As usual, **12** is unshowy, mild, smooth & elegant, with modest oaking (& everything else) just as it should be for early drinking - though it'll keep.

★★★★ **Sauvignon Blanc** ⊛ Ripe granadilla & citrus (tangerine rather than grapefruit) in restrained mode on balanced, fresh & not too intense **11**. Tasty, but a little less impressive than **10** (★★★★☆).

Rose Mary Await next.

Library Collection

★★★★☆ **Edition: 3BB** NEW Cab-based **09** with cab franc & merlot is serious, even stern, like some classic Bordeaux. Forthright tannins should soften & harmonise in 5+ years. Decant now & drink with food.

★★★★ **Edition: BW** NEW More severity than easy charm on unwooded **09** 'Bordeaux White'; lemony, waxy semillon firmly in charge, hints of aromatic sauvignon. Fruit intensity should allow for few years in bottle.

Edition MB ⊛ ★★★★ Shiraz-based blend. **04** showed marked ripeness a few years back - tasty, but slightly unharmonious with dry tannic presence.

Waterford range

★★★★☆ **Kevin Arnold Shiraz** ⊛ Lovely dark notes on **09** (berries, olive) along with cedary element (but no new oak used) that should integrate with the few years needed for this powerful, assertive wine to relax. Strong tannins drying in youth, beneath sweet fruit & rich but fine-grained texture. Has 10% mourvèdre.

★★★★ **Heatherleigh Family Reserve** ⊛ Lightly oaked muscat-based **NV** dessert (up to 5 vintages), with chenin, chardonnay, viognier. Fragrant, charmingly delicate & not too sweet. Some Swartland grapes.

Elgin Pinot Noir ⊛ ★★★★ Good varietal character on **11**; insubstantial, but some charm; nicely dry. Less toasty than previous. **Elgin Sauvignon Blanc** ⊛ 🏛 ★★★★ **13** more complex than **12** (★★★☆), also with showy, ripe tropical fruit plus winning blackcurrant. Lean & refined rather than rich.

Pecan Stream range

Chenin Blanc ☺ 🏛 ★★★ Mildly fruity **13** with usual pleasing peach-tinged perfume from dollop of oak-aged viognier. Fresh, charming & easy. **Pebble Hill** ☺ 🏛 ★★★ Shiraz-based 3-way blend is ripe, easygoing & full-flavoured **10** - but not gushing or simply fruity, partly thanks to nicely firm structure. **Sauvignon Blanc** ☺ 🏛 ★★★ **13** in usual ripe, tasty style. Balanced & deft, but straightforward & unlingering. These all WO W Cape. — TJ

◾ **Waterhof** *see* Waterstone Wines

Waterkloof

Location: Somerset West ▪ Map: Helderberg ▪ WO: Stellenbosch ▪ Est 2004 ▪ 1stB 2005 ▪ Tasting & sales daily 10-5 ▪ Fee R30/6 wines ▪ Closed Good Fri, Dec 25 & Jan 1 ▪ Cellar tours by appt ▪ The Restaurant at Waterkloof (see Restaurants section) ▪ Walking/hiking trails ▪ Conservation area ▪ Art collection on display ▪ Tutored horse riding tours with ploughman's platter & wine tasting ▪ Owner(s) Paul Boutinot ▪ Cellarmaster(s) Nadia Barnard (Jan 2013) ▪ Winemaker(s) Nadia Barnard (Jan 2013), with Jacques van der Vyver (Jan 2012) ▪ Viticulturist(s) Christiaan Loots (Jan 2010) ▪ 149ha/56ha (cabs s/f, grenache, merlot, mourv, p verdot, shiraz, chard, chenin, sauv, sem, viog) ▪ 450t/20,000cs own label 50% red 45% white 5% rosé ▪ BWI champion ▪ PO Box 2093 Somerset West 7129 ▪ info@waterkloofwines.co.za ▪ www.waterkloofwines.co.za ▪ S 34° 5' 55.4" E 018° 53' 22.8" ▪ **T +27 (0)21-858-1292** ▪ F +27 (0)21-858-1293

During the course of last year, Nadia Barnard took over as winemaker at this handsome property owned by British wine merchant Paul Boutinot. She was the obvious replacement for Werner Engelbrecht (who left due to changed family circumstances) as she had been his assistant since December 2008. 'I've been at the farm since before the buildings went up. I've got lots of pride in what Waterkloof stands for.' And what does it stand for? After a long worldwide search, Paul decided on the property as being capable of 'truly fine wine with a defining sense of origin'. Significantly, the 56 ha under vine are all farmed biodynamically and official certification is underway.

Waterkloof range

★★★★☆ **Sauvignon Blanc** ⊕ 🕮 **10** open & expressive, with flavours expanding & proliferating as they linger. Some invisible sugar softens acidity, adds breadth. Takes Circumstance version to higher level.

Circle of Life range

★★★★ **Red** ⊕ 🍴 **09** 80% merlot & shiraz, plus 4 others. Touch more elegant than **08**, but also sophisticatedly easy-going. Deep & subtle & delicious too, for early unfrivolous pleasure.

★★★★ **White** 🍴 🕮 **12** 56% sauvignon, rest chenin, chardonnay & semillon, is intellectual & mid-2013 not ready with its favours. Notes of lime, peach & spice before savoury finish.

Circumstance range

★★★★☆ **Cinsaut Noir** NEW Gorgeous **12** with red berries, fynbos & spice. Great fruit purity, soft but sufficient acidity & fine tannins. 30% new oak effortlessly absorbed. Medium bodied & extremely enticing.

★★★★☆ **Syrah** ⊕ 🍴 🕮 **10** as usual a star of the range, flaunting its floral-spicy charm, yet serious - & modest in the best sense of the word. Quietly assertive, succulent & satisfying, with a sweet edge to its juicy fruit & dry finish. Approachable, but should respond well to ±5 years in bottle.

★★★★ **Sauvignon Blanc** ⊕ 🍴 🕮 Always a characterful, slightly different version. Intense fruit character & some weight on **12**, but not flamboyant, with a savoury element & a big structuring acidity.

Cabernet Sauvignon 🍴 🕮 ★★★★ **10** the most successful yet, nudging higher rating. Carries its big alcohol lightly & lithely. Good sweet fruit but dry finish. **Merlot** ⊕ 🍴 🕮 ★★★★ **10** far from plump varietal stereotype - a bit lean & tannic rather, but herbal element restrained. Respectable rather than exciting. **Cape Coral Mourvèdre** 🍴 🕮 ★★★ Understated **12** dry rosé has earthy, spicy notes to go with subtle strawberry. Bunch pressed, spontaneous ferment in tank. **Chardonnay** Await next. **Chenin Blanc** 🕮 ★★★ Barrel-fermented **12** explicitly not about primary fruit but rather texture, secondary flavour. Some peach but also yeasty, earthy notes. **Viognier** 🕮 ★★★ Unconventional **12** was bunch pressed, underwent spontaneous ferment in old, large barrels. Vague peach & spice notes, gentle acidity. — CE

■ **Waterlilly** see Bloemendal Estate

Waterstone Wines

Location: Somerset West ▪ Map: Helderberg ▪ WO: Western Cape/Stellenbosch/Coastal ▪ Est/1stB 2007 ▪ Tasting, sales & cellar tours by appt ▪ Closed all pub hols & Dec 15-Jan 3 ▪ Tour groups ▪ Self-catering accommodation ▪ Owner(s) Pim de Lijster & Reino Kruger ▪ Winemaker(s) Annamarie Fourie & Burger Badenhorst ▪ 41ha (cab, merlot, ptage, shiraz, chard, chenin, sauv) ▪ 80,000cs own label 65% red 35% white ▪ Other export brand: Compadre ▪ PO Box 1560 Somerset West 7129 ▪ info@waterstonewines.co.za ▪ www.waterstonewines.co.za ▪ S 34° 2' 0.3" E 018° 48' 34.8" ▪ **T +27 (0)21-842-2942** ▪ F +27 (0)86-505-8691

From a Helderberg base, Waterstone negociant house is 'slowly taking over the world one country at a time,' laughs administrator Inga Rix, explaining that co-

owner Reino Kruger is tirelessly visiting 'selected clients from Africa to Asia' in line with the winemaker-turned-businessman's drive 'to understand specific market needs and to supply them with premium products at every price point'.

KFK range NEW

Cabernet Sauvignon ★★★☆ Satisfying **10**, precise tannin & bright acidity provide counterpoint to vanilla-infused dark fruit. Warm but quite juicy. Stellenbosch WO, as for all these. **Shiraz** ★★★ Pastille-like ripe fruit & vanilla greet you, firm savoury tannins frame roasted red fruits, slightly drying palate suggests **07** best opened soon. **Chardonnay** ★★★ Green-tinged unwooded **11** is lightish, balanced & fresh, green melon, lime & sushi-friendly hint of savoury. **Sauvignon Blanc** ★★★☆ Blending green & tropical tones, **10** is still quite fresh & zippy, slight creaminess to palate cleansed by zesty acid.

Africa Five Collection NEW

Pinotage ✓ ★★★☆ Very youthful looking **08**, warming, sweet fruited & powerful: slick, crowd-pleasing styling, with fresh tannin cleaning up the liqueur-like fruit. Stellenbosch WO, as all these. **Shiraz Reserve** ★★★ **09** covers the bases with sweet, savoury, earthy & herbaceous characters all featuring; concludes on sweet, drying, alcoholic note. **Cabernet Sauvignon-Shiraz** ★★★ Leafy cab fruit meets spicy shiraz in ripe, warming **11**, unexpectedly firm tannin needs time or a plate of hearty food.

Waterhof range

Cabernet Sauvignon Reserve ★★★☆ Seriously styled **10** shows vintage power & warmth (14.6% alcohol), with contrasting herbaceous edge to dense plum fruit. **Shiraz Reserve** ⓢ ★★★ **07** harks back to Old Cape with sweet-sour flavours, but good length & balance. **Chardonnay Reserve** ⓢ ★★★ Creamy, faint lemon & lime flavours on **11**; unconcentrated finish. **Sauvignon Blanc Reserve** ⓢ ★★★☆ Showing good varietal character & balance at commendably moderate alcohol, **10** still standout in range. WO Stellenbosch, like all this range.

Cape Royale range NEW

Cabernet Sauvignon ★★ Sweet & simple but not charmless **NV**, red/blue berry fruit slathered with vanilla. **Merlot** ★ Sweet-fruited & spicy **NV** with herbaceous overtone & warming conclusion. **Shiraz** ★★ **NV** leans towards savoury in olive/saline character, lots of wood evident throughout. **Sauvignon Blanc** ★ Some grass & lime in fresh, uncomplicated off-dry **NV**.

Cape Discovery range

Cabernet Sauvignon ★★ Sweet overripe fruit, oaky spice & nutty tannin in **NV**. **Merlot** NEW ★★ Sweet/sour **NV** with very ripe fruit yet strong puckering tannins. **Pinotage** ★★ Vibrantly fruity **NV**, warm berries, chocolate & mocha hint, surprising burst of tannin on finish. **Shiraz** NEW ★ Sweet stewed fruit contrasts with hard acid & tannin in latest **NV**. **Chardonnay** ★ Dusty peach & honey in unconcentrated **NV**, unwooded. **Sauvignon Blanc** ★★ Off-dry styling as before, **NV**'s sugar cushions high acid & pithy texture, accents tinned pea & kiwi fruit flavour.

Sonata range

Cabernet Sauvignon ⓢ 🍴 ★★★ Improved **10** raspberry & clean leather wafts, rounded tannins; neat dinner companion. Stellenbosch vines, as all these. **Shiraz** NEW ★★★ Very ripe & powerful **11**, with warming finish & slightly smoky character to berry fruit. **The Ludwig** ⓢ 🍴 ★★ Gruff **04** blend; raisiny, dominated by merlot. **Chenin Blanc** ⓢ 🍴 ★★★ Reticent floral & thatch nose on fresh **11**; chill for maximum enjoyment. **Sauvignon Blanc** ⓢ 🍴 ★★★ Bottled, **11** offers nettles, fresh hay; palate-cleansing sweet-sour acidity.

Africa range

Bomvu ⓢ 🍴 ★★★ Easy-drinking, refreshing **11** cab/shiraz, bright red fruit & friendly grip. **Ifula** 🍴 ★★ With beaded bottle-neck, pleasant **12** off-dry chenin & sauvignon mixes lemons & flowers with firm acidity.

Africa Five range

Sauvignon Blanc ☺ ★★★ Fresh bowl of apple & kiwi fruit, some grassiness, in zesty & balanced **12**.

Cabernet Sauvignon ★★ Steakhouse red **12** with firm tannins & slightly herbaceous red fruit flavours. **Merlot** ★★★ Well-shaped, ripe-fruited **12**, leafy redcurrant, zippy acid & chewy tannin, touch warming conclusion. **Pinotage** ⓢ ★★★ Lovely strawberry, faint acetone varietal character on **11**. Sleek & light footed. **Shiraz** ⓢ 🍴 ★★ **11** woody, with juicy sweet tail. **Cape Premier Red** ★★ Perfect campfire sipper, latest **NV**'s dark & brooding cherry liqueur flavours will warm cockles, stimulate conviviality. **Chardonnay** ⓢ

★★★ Lemon tones, some creaminess on evanescent **11**. **Chenin Blanc ★★** Hay & lemon-toned **12**, straightforward off-dry quaffer.

Zulu 8 range NEW

Cabernet Sauvignon ★★ Vibrant red-fruited **11**, quite ripe, soft candy-toned finish. **Merlot ★★ 11** light red-fruit aromas & fairly firm flavours, pleasant weekday supper red. **Pinotage ★★** Not overdone coffee/mocha tones to dark cherry fruit, **11** appealing & sleek. **Shiraz ★★** Versatile food red: **11** mouthfilling spicy fruit, hint of milk chocolate, prominent but amenable tannin. **Cabernet Sauvignon-Shiraz ★★** Dark fruit & pliable tannin, **11** unpretentious anytime red. **Sauvignon Blanc ★★** Hints of apple & jasmine on **11**, undemanding & noticeably sweet.

Opener's range

> **Merlot** ☺ 🍴 **★★★** Fun, fruity **12**, with obvious sweetness, appealing red/purple fruits & touch of herbs. **Shiraz** NEW ☺ 🍴 **★★★** Range's ubiquitous sweetness relatively well hidden in **12**, loaded with red fruit & spice, enough tannin to balance. **Chenin Blanc** ☺ 🍴 **★★★** Grain sugar plumps the palate of tropical & orchard fruit in **12**, bright & fresh, nice pithy grip.

Dry Red Occasional release. **Rosé** 🍴 **★★** Salmon-hued **13** from sauvignon & pinotage, giving plum/mulberry & asparagus taste spectrum, quite sugary - serve very cold. **Sauvignon Blanc** 🍴 **★★** Clean apple & grass flavours, **12** noticeable crispness on palate. **Cabernet Sauvignon** 🍴 **★★** Semi-sweet styling gives friendly persona, abetted by corner coffee shop aromas, but **12** misses freshness of range mates.

Golden Vine

Discontinued: **Shiraz**, **Cape Premier Red**. — DC

Waverley Hills Organic Wines & Olives 🍴🍷☕🎋📷🎋⛟

Location/map/WO: Tulbagh ▪ Est 2006 ▪ 1stB 2004 ▪ Tasting, sales & cellar tours Mon-Fri 8-5 Sat 10-4 Sun 11-3 ▪ Closed Easter Fri/Mon & Dec 25 ▪ Restaurant Tue-Fri 9-4 Sat 10-4 Sun 11-3 & Wed/Fri evenings ▪ Picnic baskets by appt; or BYO picnic ▪ Facilities for children ▪ Tour groups ▪ Farm produce ▪ Conferences ▪ Wedding venue & chapel ▪ Walks/hikes ▪ Mountain biking ▪ Conservation area ▪ Fynbos nursery & eco-centre ▪ Owner(s) Brenn-O-Kem (Pty) Ltd ▪ Cellarmaster(s) Johan Delport (Oct 2008) ▪ Winemaker(s) Richard Sewell (Jan 2013), with Andre Ewerts (Jul 2008) ▪ Viticulturist(s) Johan Greeff (May 2012) ▪ 80ha/30ha (cab, grenache, merlot, mourv, shiraz, chard, pinot gris, sauv, sem, viog) ▪ 230t/20,000cs own label 75% red 15% white 5% rosé 5% MCC ▪ Other export brand: Dixon's Peak ▪ BWI Champion, WIETA 2-star ▪ PO Box 71 Wolseley 6830 ▪ info@waverleyhills.co.za ▪ www.waverleyhills. co.za ▪ S 33° 24' 21.2" E 019° 14' 19.6" ▪ **T +27 (0)23-231-0002** ▪ F +27 (0)23-231-0004

This beautiful eco-friendly Tulbagh estate added a grenache and fortified cab to their slate last year. Music concerts in their restaurant are proving popular and they now also offer picnic baskets to order. They believe that sustainability includes not only the land but the environment, people, community and ethics.

> **Sauvignon Blanc-Semillon** ☺ 🍴 🌿 🈚 **★★★** Appealing candied pineapple & citrus rind on gently waxy **13** tank sample. Moderate 12% alcohol does lunchtime.

Cabernet Sauvignon 🌿 🈚 **★★★** Tight cherry/berry fruit, tarry core on **11** mealtime companion. **Cabernet Sauvignon No Added Sulphites** 🍴 🌿 🈚 **★★** Now bottled, meat & coffee infused **12** needs a hearty food partner. **Grenache** NEW 🍴 🌿 🈚 **★★★ 13** barrel sample shows promise of **12** Grenaches du Monde award winner. Soft, pliant & easy, peppery & herbaceous notes from smidgens & viognier. **Shiraz** 🌿 🈚 **★★★** Juicy **11** preview exceptionally ripe & oak-sweet crowd pleaser. **CW Reserve Shiraz** 🌿 🈚 **★★★★** From a tiny parcel yielding smaller-than-usual grapes & bunches. Blackberry compote, spicy tobacco on intense now-bottled **10**; lengthy & balanced vanilla-oak finish for solo enjoyment. **Cabernet Sauvignon-Merlot** 🌿 🈚 **★★★** Succulent fruit, supple tannins in **11** 56/44 combo. 'Perfect with choc desserts' say the Waverley team. **Shiraz-Mourvèdre-Viognier** 🌱 🌿 🈚 **★★★ 10** full bodied (15.4% alcohol) & flavoursome, needs country food to cushion the very dry tannins. **Cabernet Sauvignon-Shiraz** 🍴 🌿 🈚 **★★★ 11** with hint of clove, burly tannins would handle anything off the BBQ. **Rosé** 🌱 🍴 🌿 🈚 **★★** Strawberries-&-cream, tangy acidity on improved **11** make for easy summer dry sipping. **Pinot Grigio** 🌱 🍴 🌿 🈚 **★★** Crisp acidity softened by touch sugar on earthy **12** tank sample. **Viognier-Semillon-Chardonnay** 🌿 🈚 **★★★★** Previewed **12** raises the bar: sandalwood, pine needles & flowers, generous palate enlivened by dash sauvignon, smooth & balanced conclusion. Older oak aged, portion cask fermented. **Méthode Cap Classique Brut** 🌿 🈚 **★★★★** Celebratory bubbly **11** from chardonnay continues upward

of chardonnay/semillon **10**. Intense brioche notes from 19 months lees-ageing, creamy bubbles, lengthy lemon aftertaste. **Rooi Jerepiko** NEW 🍷 ☕ 🌀 Dessert from cab fortified with house-distilled spirit, achieving organic status. **12** preview too unformed to rate. — CvZ,CE

■ **Waverley TBS** ▪ *see* Cape Promise
■ **Weathered Hands** *see* Dewaldt Heyns Family Wines

Webersburg Wines

Location/map: Stellenbosch ▪ WO: Stellenbosch/Western Cape ▪ Est 1995 ▪ 1stB 1996 ▪ Tasting, sales & cellar tours Mon-Fri 10-5 Sat/Sun 10-4 ▪ Fee R40 ▪ Closed Ash Wed, Easter Fri-Mon, Dec 25/26 & Jan 1 ▪ French country bistro ▪ Tour groups ▪ Historic buildings: Manor House 1786; cellar & Jonkershuis 1796 ▪ 5-star Cape Dutch guesthouse ▪ Conferences ▪ Weddings/functions ▪ Owner(s) Fred Weber ▪ Winemaker(s)/viticulturist(s) Matthew van Heerden ▪ 20ha/5ha (cab) ▪ 30t/4,000cs own label 80% red 20% white ▪ PO Box 3428 Somerset West 7129 ▪ info@webersburg.co.za ▪ www.webersburg.co.za ▪ S 34° 0' 22.1" E 018° 50' 34.5" ▪ **T +27 (0)21-881-3636** ▪ F +27 (0)21-881-3217

With the beautifully restored Cape Dutch cellardoor in the Helderberg foothills now offering (in addition to weddings, functions and luxury accommodation) French country food and, by appointment, private tastings and dinners in the family owners' own cellar, one can understand the steady stream of visitors here - and the viability of the new pair of sparklings, part of a classic-leaning wine portfolio overseen by seasoned winery chief Matthew van Heerden.

★★★★☆ **Cabernet Sauvignon** ✓ Released after sufficient oak & bottle age to ensure market readiness, complex **08** reflects the vintage in its deep plummy fruit but the supple elegance & finesse is the cellar's own.

★★★★ **Sauvignon Blanc** ✓ 🏠 Grassy fresh greeting but **12** offers more, lime & passionfruit flavours, intense & pure. Lots going on here, a wine to savour.

★★★★ **Webersburg Brut** NEW ✓ 3-variety sparkler, **NV** intense citrus & honey biscuit styling, seam of acidity giving freshness you'd expect from a celebration drink. Elegance & length. WO W Cape, like Rosé.
Webersburg Await next. **Webersburg Brut Rosé** NEW 🌀 ★★★☆ **NV** classic dry bottle-fermented bubbly, pinot noir-led. Gentle red berries, ending fresh-fruity, fine bubbles brightening the experience. — CR

Wedderwill Wine Estate 🍷🍴🌲🏠📷♿

Location: Sir Lowry's Pass ▪ Map: Helderberg ▪ WO: Stellenbosch ▪ Est 1992 ▪ 1stB 1997 ▪ Tasting, sales & tours Mon-Thu 9-4 Fri 9-2 Sat/pub hols by appt only ▪ Farm produce ▪ BYO picnic ▪ Guided walks/mountain bike tours T +27 (0)82-462-3624 Di Marais ▪ Game reserve ▪ Conservation area ▪ Conference/function facilities ▪ Lalapanzi Lodge T +27 (0)21-858-1982 & Cape Country Living T +27 (0)21-858-1607 ▪ Owner(s) Neil Ian Jowell & Cecil Jowell ▪ Cellarmaster(s) Nico Vermeulen ▪ Winemaker(s) Nico Vermeulen (Jun 2004) ▪ Viticulturist(s) Wolfgang von Loeper (Apr 2004) ▪ 400ha/41ha (cab, merlot, shiraz, sauv) ▪ 80-100t/30,000cs own label 60% red 40% white ▪ BWI champion, Carbon Neutral, Control Union Organic, Demeter Biodynamic, IPW ▪ PO Box 75 Sir Lowry's Pass 7133 ▪ sales@wedderwill.co.za ▪ www.wedderwill.co.za ▪ S 34° 5' 55.0" E 018° 56' 42.0" ▪ **T +27 (0)21-858-1558** ▪ F +27 (0)21-858-1461

Wine is just one of the attractions at this idyllic family estate draped over the lower reaches of the Hottentots-Holland mountains near Sir Lowry's Pass. It's about bringing nature into all aspects of living, using technology to bring sustainability to winemaking, and experiencing life in balance. Ongoing initiatives to restore, reinstate and protect their natural heritage include alien vegetation control, river course rehabilitation and protection of endemic fauna.

★★★★ **Syrah** Was 'Shiraz'. **08** continues Rhône style & form of **07**, albeit with high-toned whiff. Floral scents mingle with white pepper to spice up surprisingly youthful plummy fruit.

★★★★ **Sauvignon Blanc** ⊚ **12** (★★★☆) misses previous mark with curious marzipan notes laced with khaki bush & gooseberry, flabbier acid profile after better **11** & previewed **10** (★★★★★).

17degreeC 🏠 ⊚ ★★★ Some wild notes on brisk, characterful **12**, shiraz & 5 Bordeaux reds. Cheerful & fruity braai companion. **12degreeC** 🏠 ⊚ ★★★ Muscat/raisin scent on dry, light **12**, sauvignon-led 5-way blend. Discontinued: **Wedderwill**. — GdB

Wederom Boutique Winery

Location/map/WO: Robertson • Est 2002 • 1stB 2003 • Tasting, sales & cellar tours by appt • Fee R20pp tasting/tour • Closed Good Fri & Dec 25 • Meals by appt • Tour groups • Gifts • Farm produce • Conferences • Weddings/functions • Hikes • Conservation area • Italian prisoner of war museum • Hanepoot Huisies guesthouse • Owner(s) Philip & Almien du Toit • Cellarmaster(s)/winemaker(s)/viticulturist(s) Philip du Toit • 111ha/±17ha (cinsaut, merlot, shiraz) • ±130t/838Ls own label 100% red + 42t grapes for clients • IPW • PO Box 60 Robertson 6705 • wederom@myisp.co.za • www.wederom.co.za • S 33° 49' 5.5" E 019° 47' 15.8" • **T +27 (0)23-626-4139** • F +27 (0)23-626-3306

Philip du Toit makes wine chiefly for wholesale, but bottles some of his favourite shiraz 'mainly for family and visitors', says daughter Joyce. As of the '11 vintage, there will be only one bottling, namely the Salvadori, Philip's tribute to the Italian POWs who tended the vines here in the 1940s.

Shiraz ⊕ ★★★ Smoked meat & red fruit, **10**'s savouriness & firm flavours perfect for Du Toits' suggested oxtail, game birds & strong cheeses. **Salvadori Vino Rosso Shiraz** ⊕ ★★★ Exuberant, charry **10** as advertised: 'whole day, everyday drinking wine'. — CvZ,MW

■ **Wedgewood Wines** see Nordic Wines

Welbedacht Wine Estate

Location: Wellington • Map: Paarl & Wellington • WO: Wellington/Western Cape • Est/1stB 2005 • Tasting, sales & cellar tours Mon-Fri 9-5 Sat 9-1 • Fee R15 • Closed Dec 25 & Jan 1 • No. 6 Restaurant @ Welbedacht (see Restaurants section) • Picnics • Facilities for children • Tour groups • Gifts • Conferences • Welbedacht Cricket Oval • Bradgate Manor House (see Accommodation section) • Owner(s) Schalk Burger Family Trust • Winemaker(s) Flip Smith (Jan 2013) • Viticulturist(s) Tony Julies (Jan 2007, consultant) • 140ha/130ha (19 varieties r/w) • 1,300t • 75% red 20% white 5% rosé • IPW • PO Box 51 Wellington 7654 • tiaan@welbedacht.co.za • www.meerkatwines.co.za, www.schalkburgerandsons.co.za • S 33° 34' 39.8" E 019° 1' 12.8" • **T +27 (0)21-873-1877** • F +27 (0)86-669-5641

Welbedacht and neighbouring farm Af-en-Toe were purchased by the Burger family in the 1990s, though both properties date back to the 1800s; added attractions on both farms are decades-old chenin and cinsaut vines. After careful restoration of the manor house and old cellar, the decision was taken in 2005 to start making their own wines. The Burgers were encouraged in this move by the success of other producers who made award-winning wines from their fruit. Schalk Burger snr and his family have enjoyed similar success under their own label, many of the wines' names reflecting the family's sporting prowess.

Schalk Burger & Sons Proprietors Reserve range

★★★★ **No. 6** ⊕ Striking shiraz-led 6-way mix. **06** (★★★★★) plush fruitcake & plum spice, big & bold but harmonious, lithe as a flank brushing off a tackler. 2 years older French oak. Step up on **05**.

★★★★ **Myra** ⊕ Last tasted was **07** viognier, chenin, chardonnay blend. Oxidative styling, rich & satiny.

Mon René 🍷 ★★★★ Elegant MCC bubbly from chardonnay has fine bead, extra-dry finish. In latest **NV** 5% barrel-fermentation adds nutty, creamy breadth. Named for Burger daughter.

Welbedacht Estate range

★★★★ **Cabernet Sauvignon Barrique Select 09** (★★★★) shows some development in its ripe, slightly jammy berry fruit. Firmly built, but lacks concentration, refinement of **08** to warrant long ageing.

★★★★ **Merlot Barrique Select** ⊕ **08** tasted a few years back. Ripe mulberry & cocoa depth, soft texture yet firm structure. Stylish, refined & lengthy.

★★★★ **Bohemian Syrah** ⊕ 📖 Just 'Syrah' last time. Plush fruit vies with fresh acid in **08**, made for long haul. Nuanced, deep, smoky & spicy with dry tannin & solid centre. Has concentration, length.

★★★★ **Cricket Pitch** ⊕ Gentle but structured blend of cab, merlot & cab franc. Striking cassis & cigar spice on **08**'s rich, soft palate a few years ago. Harmony of fruit, acid & wood. **07** (★★★★) preview needed time.

★★★★ **Hat Trick** 🍷 Structured, concentrated **10**, first since **07**, absorbs 75% new oak. Harmonious mix pinotage & grenache with merlot, their rich, dark fruit still embraced by firm yet balanced tannins.

Pinotage ⊕ ★★★★ Refined, just-dry **10** charms with dark cherry features, supple mouthfeel. Carefully managed & integrated tannins add form, freshness. Follows drying **09** (★★★★). **Patriot** ⊕ ★★★ Merlot-led Bordeaux quartet in showy style. Early-drinker **08** fronted by spicy oak, with ripe fruit spread smoothly to

sweetish conclusion. **Chardonnay Barrel Fermented** 🍷 📷 ★★★★ **10** offers plenty of savoury satisfaction in its soft, creamy texture. 40% unoaked to lift fruit, freshen. **Chenin Blanc Barrel Fermented** 🍷 📷 ★★★★ **10** shows promising bruised apple, oxidative notes but yet to reveal the full textural dimension usually afforded by 40 year old vines. Worth a few years' wait. **Sauvignon Blanc** ⊕ 🍷 ★★★ For those who like some perkiness but unshowy fruit in sauvignon, **12** fits the bill.

Meerkat range

> **Chenin Blanc** ☺ 🍷 📷 ★★★ Lovely fruit purity, length on **13**. Gentle freshness, dry finish add to drinkability.

Pinotage ⊕ 🍷 📷 ★★★ Forthcoming raspberry juiciness on **11**; straightforward but with good substance. Fruitily sweet close balances bold alcohol. **Burrow Blend** 🍷 📷 ★★★ Straightforward, fruit-driven, pinotage-led **11**. Few grams sugar soften any rough edges. **Pinotage Rosé** ⊕ 🍷 ★★ Gently fresh, sweetish **12**. **Sun Angel Semi-Sweet** 🍷 📷 ★★ Honey notes on chardonnay **NV**. Soft, uncloying sweetness. **Sauvignon Blanc** 🍷 📷 ★★★ Quaffable, lightish **12** (new bottling since last year) has quiet flinty tones, unaggressive freshness. WO W Cape. — AL

Welgegund Wines

Location: Wellington ▪ Map: Paarl & Wellington ▪ WO: Wellington/Western Cape/Paarl ▪ Est 1800 ▪ 1stB 1997 ▪ Tasting & sales by appt at Welgegund farm ▪ B&B cottage with pool & tennis court ▪ Walks ▪ Wine sales & cellar tours at Boutique Baratok (see entry) ▪ Owner(s) Alex & Sheila Camerer ▪ Cellarmaster(s)/winemaker(s)/viticulturist(s) Daniël Langenhoven (Jun 2008) ▪ 35ha/15ha (carignan, cinsaut, ptage, chenin) ▪ 84t/640cs own label 62% red 38% white ▪ PO Box 683 Wellington 7654 ▪ sales@welgegund.co.za ▪ www.welgegund.co.za ▪ S 33° 39' 38.3" E 019° 2' 13.6" ▪ **T +27 (0)21-873-2123** ▪ F +27 (0)21-873-2683

Alex and Sheila Camerer bought this Wellington farm, whose name means 'Well Bestowed', some 30 years ago. It was established in 1800, however, and much later was part of Rhodes Fruit Farms, when apricots were the main crop. Today vines dominate, though not all of the grapes are vinified under the Camerers' own label.

★★★★ **Pinotage** ⊕ Bright hue, buchu & cherry aromas mark **10**. Silkiness clipped by fine, freshening tannins; long savoury tail. Like next, tasted a few years back.

★★★★☆ **Chiara** ⊕ 🍷 Grenache blanc joins chenin, chardonnay, sauvignon & viognier in **10** oaked blend. Haunting complexity on aromas & suave, smooth-textured palate. WO Paarl.

Ricco ⊕ ★★★★ Shiraz-led **09** blend with splash barbera. Soft core, smooth, with 15.2% alcohol glow, sweetness. WO W Cape. Discontinued: **Divina Carignan-Pinotage Rosé**. — AL

Welgeleë Boutique Wedding & Wine Farm

Location: Paarl ▪ Map: Paarl & Wellington ▪ Est 1999 ▪ 1stB 2003 ▪ Tasting & sales daily 9–5 ▪ Picnics by appt ▪ Function venues (±45 & 160 pax) ▪ Owner(s) Liris Trust (Chris & Lidea Meyer) ▪ Winemaker(s) Chris Meyer ▪ Viticulturist(s) Chris & Lidea Meyer ▪ 26ha/3ha (shiraz) ▪ 600cs own label 100% red ▪ PO Box 439 Klapmuts 7625 ▪ chris@welgelee.com ▪ www.welgelee.com ▪ S 33° 47' 45.3" E 018° 53' 35.4" ▪ **T +27 (0)21-875-5726** ▪ F +27 (0)86-592-2806

Chris and Lidea Meyer ceased circumnavigating the world's oceans to settle on this small Paarl wine estate, tapping into the market for winelands weddings and country conferences. Contributing to the farm's charm – it's home to the couple's two children, pack of dogs and field full of horses – is a handmade shiraz.

Welgemeend Estate

Location: Paarl ▪ Map: Paarl & Wellington ▪ WO: Paarl/Coastal ▪ Est 1974 ▪ 1stB 1979 ▪ Tasting, sales & cellar tours Mon-Fri 10–4 Sat 10–2/by appt in winter ▪ Closed all pub hols ▪ Owner(s) Welgemeend Estate (Pty) Ltd ▪ Winemaker(s) Lizette Steyn-James (Mar 2007), advised by Louis Nel ▪ Viticulturist(s) Lizette Steyn-James (Mar 2007) ▪ 16ha/11ha (cabs s/f, grenache, malbec, merlot, ptage, shiraz) ▪ 24t own label 100% red ▪ PO Box 1408 Suider-Paarl 7624 ▪ info@welgemeend.co.za ▪ www.welgemeend.co.za ▪ S 33° 47' 50.8" E 018° 53' 8.5" ▪ **T +27 (0)21-875-5210** ▪ F +27 (0)86-654-3806

Once home to Billy Hofmeyr, who produced the first Cape Bordeaux blend in the late 1970s, this Paarl red-wine property has stayed true to the terroir compatibility

by three of its four wines being variations of the original blend. Another benefit of that early vision is the older vineyards, showcased in the wines on offer. The young, enthusiastic team's new vision? An earlier-drinking range.

Estate Reserve ⊕ ★★★★ First commercial Cape Bordeaux red blend in 1979. Merlot-led **06** appeals with cassis, violets, backed by firm dry tannin, 2 years oaking. **Douelle** ⊕ ★★★★ Mainly malbec & cab, giving **06**'s fruit a tarry, liquorice character. Well structured, enough flesh to handle the dry tannins. **Soopjeshoogte** ✓ ★★★★ Classic 4 Bordeaux varieties in **07** give red berries, lead pencils, slight minty note. Succulent, perfect drinking age. WO Coastal, like next. **Amadé** ✓ ★★★★ Individual **06**, shiraz with pinotage, grenache, cab. Glossy dark fruit, savoury accessibility & enough tannin for food. — CR

■ **Welgevallen Cellar-Stellenbosch University** *see* Stellenbosch University Welgevallen Cellar

Welgevallen Wines

Location/map/WO: Stellenbosch ▪ Est/1stB 2000 ▪ Visits Mon-Fri 10–2 ▪ Closed pub & school hols ▪ Owner(s) Paul Roos Gymnasium Old Boys Union ▪ Winemaker(s)/viticulturist(s) Wouter Pienaar & Tinnie Momberg (consultants) ▪ 800cs own label 75% red 25% white ▪ c/o Paul Roos Gymnasium Old Boys Union Suidwal Stellenbosch 7600 ▪ oldboys@prg.wcape.school.za ▪ www.paulroos.co.za ▪ S 33° 56' 31.2" E 018° 51' 41.1" ▪ **T +27 (0)21-883-8627** ▪ F +27 (0)21-883-8627

Named after the farm on which Stellenbosch's prestigious Paul Roos Gymnasium was built in 1866, this is a selection of wines donated by old boys who have gone on to become winemakers and estate owners. Sales generate funds enabling talented boys from economically disadvantaged families to attend the school.

Pinotage ⊕ ★★★★ **09** succulent & smooth, worth seeking out as much for palate appeal as for noble (fund-raising) intentions. **Cabernet Sauvignon-Merlot** Await next. **Sauvignon Blanc** ⊕ 🍴 ★★★ Reticent **11** delivers gravelly texture & weight absent in previous. — CvZ

Wellington Wines 🍷 ♿

Location/WO: Wellington ▪ Map: Paarl & Wellington ▪ Est 1941 ▪ Tasting & sales Mon-Fri 8–5 Sat 8.30–12.30 ▪ Closed all pub hols ▪ Cellar tours by appt ▪ Owner(s) 70 shareholders ▪ Production manager Gert Boerssen (Oct 1980) ▪ Winemaker(s) Pieter-Niel Rossouw (Jun 2009), Chris Smit (Nov 2005), Hugo Truter (Oct 2005) & Fritz Smit (Jan 2009) ▪ Viticulturist(s) Marko Roux (Nov 2008) ▪ 2,400ha ▪ 27,000t ▪ 60% red 40% white ▪ BWI, BRC, Fairtrade, IPW, WIETA ▪ PO Box 509 Wellington 7654 ▪ sales@wellingtonwines.com ▪ www.wellingtonwines. com ▪ S 33° 38' 17.7" E 018° 59' 20.6" ▪ **T +27 (0)21-873-1582** ▪ F +27 (0)21-873-3194

Wellington has stepped out from under the shadow of Paarl as a Wine of Origin district, and the formation of Wellington Wines by merging neighbours Wamakersvallei and Wellington Cooperative and, now, Bovlei Cellar (see entry), has added critical mass to the enterprise. With access to thousands of hectares courtesy of their combined 100+ growers, the mega-winery crushes thousands of tons a year, making a broad range of styles at various quality levels.

La Cave range

★★★★ **Pinotage** 🗍 **11** matches standard of **10** and **09**. Red cherry spice & vibrancy but on a gently rounded, textured palate. Despite all-new oak, wood is harmonious to end.

★★★★ **Cape Blend** ⊕ 🗍 Maiden **10** a 3-way pinotage, shiraz, cab mix. Layered black fruit melange that, while succulent & fresh, glides silkily to an intense, long finish.

Cabernet Sauvignon ⊕ 🗍 ★★★★ Boldly fruited **10** a step up on lighter **09** (★★★★). Chalky tannic squeeze adds structure while whole remains lithe & elegant. Savoury, supple & long. **Shiraz** ⊕ ★★★★ Lovely tug between ripe black fruit & earthy char on **10**'s rounded palate. Medium body, fine tannin & length. **Méthode Cap Classique** [NEW] ★★★★ **11** all-chardonnay sparkler is dry, crisp & clean, with limestone & brioche nuances. Focused & long, with a finish that keeps on giving. Ideal food fizz.

Wellington Wines range

> **Chardonnay** ☺ 🍴 🗍 ★★★ Juicy orange & peach ease to lightly tangy unwooded **13**. A quaffer. **Chenin Blanc** ☺ 🍴 🗍 ★★★ **13** improves on previous with ripe pineapple & nectarine. Well balanced, with long, dry, fruited finish.

Cabernet Sauvignon ✓ ▤ ⊘ ★★★★ Gentle & genteel **11** has ripe brambly flavour with a tobacco leaf depth. Wood frames fruit well & adds a chalky grip. **Pinotage** ▤ ⊘ ★★★ Yielding, plush **11** has cherry & plum generosity with a mocha sheen. Rounded & easy, soft texture on lingering tail. **Shiraz** ▤ ⊘ ★★★ **11**'s blueberry compote appeal is framed with good structure & definition. Lithe & limber, it ticks all the boxes. **Moscato Frizzante** NEW ▤ ⊘ ★★★ Sweet grapey spritz to low-alcohol **NV** from hanepoot. Light & fun.

Bain's Way range

Merlot ▤ ⊘ ★★★ **12** is strident in its mulberry & cocoa intensity. Succulent but with firm, balancing structure. Long smoky aftertaste. **Rosé** NEW ▤ ★★★ Cranberry & cherry simplicity to **NV** semi-dry pink from pinotage. Light & easy. **Chenin Blanc** NEW ▤ ⊘ ★★★ Grapefruit tang on maiden **13**. Light, but with a dry finish. **Sauvignon Blanc** ▤ ⊘ ★★★ **13** up a notch; lively grass & pepper typicity. **Viognier** ▤ ⊘ ★★★ Peach & nectarine on tangy, textured unwooded **13**. Succulent & fresh, it's a good, uncomplicated example of the grape. **Brut Sparkling Wine** NEW ⊘ ★★★ **NV** sparkler shows chenin to best effect in lively, zesty flavours. Light bodied, with bread, biscuit notes on dry finish. **Fishermans Jerepigo** ▤ ★★★ Sweet jasmine & muscat ripeness on **NV** fortified fishing companion from hanepoot. Sweet but not cloying. Long sultana-rich tail. **Jagters Port** ⊘ ★★★ Choc-covered raisins & spicy plums on **NV** fortified from pinotage. Gentle grip of spirit makes it light, dry & rich. — FM

Welmoed

This well-priced, easy-drinking range takes its name from the venerable Stellenbosch property Welmoed, once owned by courageous rebel Jacobus van der Heyden and now home of brand owner Stellenbosch Vineyards.

Heyden's Courage range

Bushvine Pinotage NEW ▤ ⊘ ★★★★ Inviting **12** preview greater depth & complexity than standard bottling; firm tannic structure padded by concentrated fruit augurs well for 3+ years ageing. **Red** ▤ ⊘ ★★★★ Previewed **11** Bordeaux blend with creamy texture & firm, precise tannins. Should impress further with year/2 cellaring. Some Darling grapes. **Bushvine Chenin Blanc** NEW ▤ ⊘ ★★★★ Barrel-fermented (40%) **13** extank shows impressive fruit richness, satisfying weight, long conclusion. Provisionally rated. WO Stellenbosch, like most above. **White** ✓ ▤ ⊘ ★★★★ Now bottled, **11** ups ante with asparagus, grapefruit & tropical complexity, pebbly conclusion. Mainly sauvignon & 4 others, 40% barrel fermented for extra mouthfeel. WO Coastal.

Welmoed range

Merlot ☺ ▤ ⊘ ★★★ Step-up **12** plummy, with meat & chocolate notes, light tannins for early drinkability. **Pinotage** ☺ ▤ ⊘ ★★★ Candyfloss & strawberry appeal on **12** anytime pick-me-up; light - if tad furry - tannins. **Chardonnay** ☺ ▤ ⊘ ★★★ **13** citrus-toned sipper gains breadth & depth from older-oaked portion, vivacity from bouncy acidity.

Cabernet Sauvignon ▤ ⊘ ★★ **12** has herbaceous, lean styling; needs food. Like all these reds, from Stellenbosch fruit & oak-staved. **Shiraz** ▤ ⊘ Floral **12** tank sample still gripped by firm tannin at tasting time; too unformed to rate. **Rosé** ▤ ⊘ ★★ Dry **13** fresh strawberry & rose aromas, flavours. WO W Cape, as all whites & sparkling. **Chenin Blanc** ▤ ⊘ ★★★ Good vinosity & palate weight from lees-ageing on faintly floral **13**. **Sauvignon Blanc** ▤ ⊘ ★★★★ **13** perfect al fresco partner: cool, green fruited, characterful & not overly acidic. **Viognier** ▤ ⊘ ★★ Light & fresh **13** preview dusted with spice, dried apricots; amiable anytime companion. **Sparkling Brut** ⊘ ★★★ Granny Smith apple appeal on frothy **NV** dry fizz ex chenin with dollops chardonnay, sauvignon. — CvZ

Welmoed Estate 🍷 🏛 📷 ♿

Location: Bonnievale ▪ Map: Robertson ▪ WO: Robertson/Western Cape ▪ Est 1912 ▪ 1stB 1945 ▪ Tasting & sales Mon–Fri 8–5 Sat 9–3.30 ▪ Closed Easter Fri/Sun, Dec 25/26 & Jan 1 ▪ Cellar tours & underground tasting by appt ▪ Walks/hikes ▪ Conservation area ▪ Weddings/functions ▪ 4 self-catering guest cottages ▪ Owner(s) Lourens Jonker ▪ Cellarmaster(s) Philip Jonker (Jan 1997) ▪ Viticulturist(s) Francois Viljoen (consultant) ▪ 360ha/106ha (cab, merlot, pinot, shiraz, chard, cbard, gewürz, sauv) ▪ 1,300t/50,000cs own label 15% red 75% white 10% other ▪ Brands for clients: Woolworths ▪ BWI ▪ PO Box 6 Bonnievale 6730 ▪ info@weltevrede.com ▪ www. weltevrede.com ▪ S 33° 56' 30.9" E 020° 3' 4.4" ▪ **T** +27 (0)23-616-2141 ▪ F +27 (0)23-616-2460

Chardonnay has long been the focus – in still and sparkling form – of the Bonnievale estate farmed by the Jonker family for more than a century. Ever-thoughtful and contemplative cellarmaster Philip Jonker revels in the diversity

of soils in Robertson, and the proximity to the Breede River. The Jonkers share their bounty with guests, offering wedding, function and conference facilities, and accommodation. The family also share with employees via the Weltevrede Aansporingstrust, an empowerment initiative.

Estate range

Bedrock Black Syrah ✓ 🗌 ★★★☆ Noticeable oak on perfumed **12** seamlessly integrated with the peppery fruit, elegant & fine conclusion. **Poet's Prayer Chardonnay** Await next. **Place of Rocks Chardonnay** ⊕ 🗌 🗌 ★★★ Fresher, fruitier styling takes **11** up a rung, engaging yellow peach & sweet pear notes, 100% new oak no impediment to current enjoyment. **Gewürztraminer** In abeyance. Discontinued: **The Travelling Stone Sauvignon Blanc**.

Philip Jonker Brut Cap Classique Collection

★★★★ **Entheos** 🗌 Aptly named bottle-fermented sparkler ('Energy of Spontaneous Laughter'). Dry **NV** from chardonnay (60%) & pinot noir is fruitier, less rich, than vintage-dated sibling. Lively & fresh.

Lindelize ⊕ ★★★☆ Rosé champagne-method bubbly named for Philip Jonker's wife; current **NV** is 100% pinot noir, hence the meaty/savoury element, fine firm structure. **The Ring** ★★★★ Buttered toast, apple crumble nuances on improved **09** celebratory bubbles from chardonnay. Like **07** (★★★★), impressive leesy richness despite being bone-dry, fine mousse completes the package. No **08**. Discontinued: **Aletheia**.

Simplicity range

Cherrychoc Merlot ☺ 🗌 ★★★ **12** ticks all the party-starting boxes: sweet fruit, silky texture, friendly tannins & affordable price. **Cigarbox Shiraz** 🆕 ☺ 🗌 🗌 ★★★ **12**'s plush red fruit spiced with cedar oak; 'perfect match for steak' says Philip Jonker. **Vanilla Chardonnay** ☺ 🗌 🗌 ★★☆ Vanilla by name, vanilla in style... **12** slips down easily with food or solo.

Trop!co Sauvignon Blanc ⊕ 🗌 🗌 ★★☆ Whiff of pepper lifts tropical appeal of breezy **12**. WO W Cape.

Heritage range

Oupa se Wyn ⊕ 🗌 ★★★☆ **11** fortified dessert from muscats Hamburg & de Frontignan. 'Grandad's Wine' a delightful fireside treat. **Ouma se Wyn** 🗌 ★★★ 'Granny's Wine', from old white muscat de Frontignan vines, for the sweet-toothed: **12** raisined, syrupy; enjoy chilled with twist of lemon for freshness. — HJ,MW

Welvanpas   🍴🍵🎋📷🎿

Location/WO: Wellington ▪ Map: Paarl & Wellington ▪ Est 1704 ▪ 1stB 1994 ▪ Tasting & sales Tue-Fri 8–5 Sat/Sun 8–3 ▪ Fee R10pp ▪ Closed Easter Fri-Mon, Dec 16-Jan 2 ▪ Die Ou Meul coffee shop open daily ▪ Facilities for children ▪ Tour groups ▪ History package incl lunch & talk on Piet Retief family ▪ Farm produce ▪ BYO picnic (day permit R20pp) ▪ Walks/hikes ▪ Bains mountain bike trails ▪ Owner(s)/viticulturist(s) Dan Retief ▪ Cellarmaster(s) Dan Retief (Jan 1993) ▪ Winemaker(s) Dan Retief (Jan 1990), with Neels Kruger (Jan 1999) ▪ 260ha/50ha (11 varieties r/w) ▪ 25t own label 80% red 15% white 5% rosé ▪ PO Box 75 Wellington 7654 ▪ welvanpas@gmail.com ▪ S 33° 37' 59.9" E 019° 4' 12.5" ▪ **T +27 (0)21-864-1239** ▪ F +27 (0)21-864-1239

Welvanpas owner and cellarmaster Dan Retief is a descendant of Great Trek leader Piet Retief, so it's fitting that this Wellington wine estate offers 'history packages' featuring interesting chats about local lore over lunch at onsite Die Ou Meul coffee shop, recently enlarged to cater to children and bike riders.

Cabernet Sauvignon ⊕ 🗌 ★★★ **10** cranberry & dark cherry notes, savoury end. **Shiraz** ⊕ 🗌 ★★★ Robust **09** toasty tobacco & liquorice aromas; on review, needed year/2 to knit. **Revival Red** Next awaited, as for **De Krakeelhoek Rood**, **Suzanne Rosé**, **Chardonnay**, **Sauvignon Blanc** & **Amity**. — MW

◼ **Weskus** *see Winkelshoek Wine Cellar*

Westbridge Vineyards   🍾🍵⌂📷

Location/map: Stellenbosch ▪ Est 1998 ▪ 1stB 1999 ▪ Tasting & sales by appt only (T 083-631-2229) ▪ Muldersvlei Stables B&B ▪ Chapel/wedding/conference venue ▪ Sunday lunch (booking required) ▪ Owner(s) JC Starke & Muldersvlei Estates ▪ Winemaker(s) Ian Starke ▪ Viticulturist(s) Julian Starke ▪ 3ha cab (chenin & sauv bought in) ▪ 40t/6,000cs own label 50% red 50% white ▪ PO Box 66 Muldersvlei 7607 ▪ wine@muldersvlei.co.za ▪ www.muldersvlei.com ▪ S 33° 49' 30.2" E 018° 50' 17.6" ▪ **T +27 (0)21-884-4433** ▪ F +27 (0)86-624-7446

No wines were made last harvest as building took up much of winemaker Ian Starke's time. The pub and grill at Stellenbosch family farm Muldersvlei, with its guesthouse accommodation and venue for conferences and weddings, took longer than expected to complete and the opening had to be rescheduled.

■ **Westerdale** *see Kronendal Boutique Winery*

Whalehaven Wines

Location: Hermanus ■ Map: Elgin, Walker Bay & Bot River ■ WO: Coastal/Elgin ■ Est/1stB 1995 ■ Tasting & sales Mon-Fri 9.30–5 Sat/Sun 10.30–2.30 ■ Fee R30pp for wine tastings, R60pp for paired tastings ■ Tours by appt ■ Tour groups (up to 50 pax) ■ Private tasting room can be booked for small functions/corporate events (up to 14 pax) ■ Owner(s) Bottega family ■ Winemaker(s) Reino Thiart ■ Vineyard manager(s) Tim Clark ■ 120t capacity ■ Private Bag X14 Hermanus 7200 ■ wine@whalehaven.co.za, info@bottegafamilywine.co.za ■ www. whalehaven.co.za, www.bottegafamilywine.co.za ■ S 34° 24' 36.9" E 019° 11' 60.0" ■ **T +27 (0)28-316-1633** ■ F +27 (0)28-316-1640

Undergoing extensive renovations at press time, the facilities at the Bottega family's artisan winery on Hermanus' 'whale coast' were being transformed into a Wine Experience Centre, with handcrafted decor and myriad attractions like private tastings in the Winemaker's Lab and various 'tasting boards' showcasing aromatic aspects of the wines. Renewed focus on local terroir/varieties will see new premium cool-climate pinot noir, chardonnay and sauvignon releases.

Whalehaven range
Cabernet Franc ★★★ Dusty dark fruit, dried herbs & toasty oak on rich & full-bodied **09**. **Merlot** ★★★ **10** a step-up: good fruit concentration, soft tannin structure & savoury goodbye. **Pinot Noir** ★★★ **10**, from Elgin grapes, medium bodied with fresh acidity, bold tannins & vanilla oak overpowers pristine fruit. **Pinotage** ★★★☆ **10** dark & dusty black fruit, prominent oak balances fruit sweetness, nicely tart farewell. **Chardonnay** ★★☆ Soft **11** is barely there, dilute apple flavours for quick sipping. WO Elgin. **Sauvignon Blanc** 🏞 ★★☆ Hay & floral wafts, bracing acidity on light-bodied **13**. **Sauvignon Blanc-Semillon** ⏱ ★★★ Light & tangy **10**, crisp green-fruit flavours; creamy vanilla from oaked semillon portion. Harmonious, but does not linger. **Viognier-Chardonnay** ⏱ 🏞 ★★★ 2 vintages reviewed. Floral-toned **10** mouthfilling richness balanced by crisp acidity. **12** same flavour profile with more zingy appeal, less breadth. Both perfect for summer enjoyment.

W range
Old Harbour Red ⏱ 🏞 ★★ Gluggable merlot-driven **10** more appealing than previous. **Pinotage Rosé** 🏞 🖌 ★★★ Sweet & spicy strawberry, dry finish on perky **13**. — WB

■ **Whispering Jack** *see Flagstone Winery*
■ **White River** *see Bergsig Estate*

Wildehurst Wines

Location: Koringberg ■ Map/WO: Swartland ■ Est 2006 ■ 1stB 2009 ■ Tasting & sales daily at The Wine Kollective, Riebeek-Kasteel ■ Closed Dec 25 & Jan 1 ■ Cellar tours & tasting by appt at 1 Main Road, Koringberg ■ Owner(s) Chris & Joanne Hurst ■ Winemaker(s) Marais de Villiers (Nov 2008, consultant), with Gerard Havercroft (May 2013) ■ Viticulturist(s) John Loxton (2006, consultant) ■ 0.5ha/±0.3ha (shiraz, viog) ■ 1.8t/422cs own label 35% red 53% white 12% rosé ■ PO Box 103 Koringberg 7312 ■ wildehurst@gmail.com ■ www.wildehurst.co.za ■ S 33° 01' 10.10" E 018° 40' 26.42" ■ **T +27 (0)22-423-8396 (winery)** ■ F +27 (0)22-423-8396

It wouldn't be unreasonable to expect something interesting and characterful from a tiny, isolated shiraz-viognier vineyard (other varieties are brought in) and winery at the foot of the Koringberg, in the heart of the vast Swartland. Especially when the wine is made with all the naturalness and passion proper to a member of the radical Swartland Independent organisation. Expectations met.

★★★★ **Red** ⏱ **10** previewed last year as Shiraz-Mourvèdre, which are its components, with drop viognier for fragrance. Characterful & different, with light-footed charm; sweet-fruited but ends dry. Fine structure.
★★★★ **Chenin Blanc** Lightly oaked **12** from Perdeberg grapes now happily in bottle. A winning combo of silky richness & subtle fruit - with peachy notes from a drop of viognier. Long-lingering finish.
Velo Red ★★★ Previewed as Grenache-Shiraz last year. **11** also with viognier. Shows a little better bottled, but big dry tannins still win over the charming, sweetish, light fruit. **Rosé** ★★★★ Sophisticated, savoury,

bone-dry **12** with a nice tannic tug, sampled last year, now bottled. Packed with flavour & personality. Same grapes as the red wines, plus chenin. Natural ferment, only older oak barrels - as for all these wines. — TJ

Wildekrans Wine Estate

Location/WO: Bot River ▪ Map: Elgin, Walker Bay & Bot River ▪ Est/1stB 1993 ▪ Tasting, sales & cellar tours Mon-Fri 8.30–5 Sat/Sun 11-3 ▪ Closed Dec 25 ▪ Tour groups ▪ Picnics to order ▪ Conferences/functions ▪ Walks/hikes ▪ Mountain biking ▪ Birding ▪ Conservation area ▪ Self-catering cottages ▪ Owner(s) Wildekrans Trust ▪ Winemaker(s) William Wilkinson (2006) ▪ Viticulturist(s) Braam Gericke (2008) ▪ 1,015ha/70ha (ptage, pinot, chard, chenin) ▪ 350t own label 55% red 40% white 5% rosé; ±13,200cs for clients ▪ WIETA ▪ PO Box 31 Botriver 7185 ▪ wines@wildekrans.com ▪ www.wildekrans.com ▪ S 34° 9' 42.6" E 019° 0' 36.0" ▪ **T +27 (0)28-284-9902** ▪ F +27 (0)21-413-0967

This extensive property in Bot River Valley was originally established as a mixed farming operation. Many of the old buildings survive and have been restored, including the original cellar. The farm's suitability for wine grapes was realised in the early 1990s, since when vineyards have been in the mix with the abundant fauna and indigenous flora. The staff, who have their own block of pinotage, which they planted and look after, vinified the maiden 2013 harvest into a rosé.

Barrel Selection Reserve range

★★★★ **Pinotage** 🌱 **11** full bodied yet smoothly structured. In youth, toasty oak (50% new) & sweetish finish detract from pretty raspberry undertones; may settle with year or 2.

★★★★ **Cape Blend** 🌱 Whole more than the sum of **11**'s equal parts shiraz & pinotage with 20% cab. Restrained mint, spice & chocolate aromatic weave; good fresh lift, nip of tannin & finishing sweetness.

Shiraz 🌱 ★★★★ Comfortably rich feel to mint-laced **11**. Big 15% alcohol, dense tannin carpet smoothed by few grams sugar. **Chenin Blanc** 🌱 ★★★★ Gentle-fruited **12** has balanced freshness, complementary oak & medium body. Off-dry: sweetness a little too obvious in youth - may mellow, merge with year or 2. **Sauvignon Blanc** 🌱 ★★★★ A bit of bottle age & oak spice add aromatic character to fresh, food-friendly **11**.

Méthode Cap Classique range

Méthode Cap Classique 🌱 ★★ Creamy, but **10** champagne-style sparkling ex chenin rather lacks fruit. — AL

Wilderer Private Distillery

Location: Paarl ▪ Map: Paarl & Wellington ▪ Est/1stB 1995 ▪ Tasting, sales & distillery tours daily 10-5 ▪ Fee R25 ▪ Closed Dec 25 & Jan 1 ▪ Restaurant open for lunch & dinner Tue-Sun ▪ Facilities for children ▪ Gift shop ▪ Owner(s) Helmut Wilderer & Christian Wilderer ▪ Brandy master Helmut Wilderer (1995) ▪ 2ha ▪ ±2,000cs (6x500ml) ▪ PO Box 150 Paarl-Simondium 7670 ▪ info@wilderer.co.za ▪ www.wilderer.co.za ▪ S 33° 48' 1.12" E 018° 57' 5.81" ▪ **T +27 (0)21-863-3555** ▪ F +27 (0)86-546-3053

German restaurateur Helmut Wilderer's early forays into distilling a 'house schnapps' morphed into a fully-fledged eaux de vie distillery and restaurant in the Cape winelands in the early 1990s. Now in partnership with son Christian, with a second distillery (and requisite eatery) at The Spice Route Destination in Paarl, Helmut crafts grappa-styles as well as fruit, herbal fynbos and other 'new, unusual' post-prandial pleasures in Ulrich Kothe custom-built copper column stills.

★★★★ **Grappa Pinotage Barrique** From 2011, a year in oak giving gold-straw colour & refining, softening the delicate fire. Clean, bright, subtle nutty & red-fruit perfume; gently unctuous, smooth & balanced.

★★★★ **Grappa Muscato Barrique** Obvious rosepetal, grapey fragrance & flavours might limit appeal of focused & fresh 2012 bottling to muscat lovers. Full flavours, integrated spirit. Gold colour from oak-ageing.

★★★★☆ **Shiraz Barrique Reserve** Light pink-tinged gold. Refined, delicate, with complex aroma & flavour - including delicious hints of berry & choc-mint alongside typical husk notes. Lightly viscous & smooth, the spirit integrated & tamed by time in oak barrels. From 2012 vintage. Premium Husk Spirit, like both above.

Grappa Tempranillo ★★★★ Fresh, pure & enticing aromas on 2013 edition (all in range indicate vintage on bottle). Lightly slippery, focused & pleasing, but perhaps a little fiery & lacking intensity of flavour. — WB,TJ

William Everson Wines

Location: Grabouw ▪ Map: Elgin, Walker Bay & Bot River ▪ WO: Elgin/Stellenbosch/Paarl ▪ Est/1stB 2001 ▪ Tasting, sales & tours by appt ▪ Self-catering accommodation (www.mentmor.co.za) ▪ Owner(s)/winemaker(s)

William Everson ▪ 4t/800cs own label 60% red 40% white ▪ 2281 Essenhout Avenue Klipkop Grabouw 7160 ▪ william@eversonwine.co.za, william@eversonscider.com ▪ www.eversonwine.co.za, www.eversonscider. com ▪ S 34° 8' 44.01" E 019° 1' 1.21" ▪ **T +27 (0)82-554-6357** ▪ F +27 (0)86-662-4045

William Everson, 'proud to be a garagiste', has launched a shiraz/mourvèdre blend at his Grabouw home where he makes wine, literally, in the garage. He says the wine forms a nice balance with his apple and pear cider business. The products are available at the Woodstock Old Biscuit Mill Saturday Market, Cape Town.

Stellenbosch Cabernet Sauvignon ⓘ ★★★ **09** earthy tones mixed with sour cherry flavours, when last tasted needed more time to fill out. **Paarl Shiraz** ⓘ ★★★ Fruity & rounded **08** abounds with dark ripe berries & warm plums. **Elgin Shiraz** ⓘ ★★★ Smoky/leathery **09** more elegant, subtle & crisp than previous. **Poplar Overberg Shiraz** NEW Available but not reviewed, as for **Poplar Cabernet Sauvignon. Shiraz-Mourvèdre** NEW ★★★ From two Elgin farms, **10** is coming together nicely, showing leathery dark chocolate & a pleasant firmness. Allow more time to show full potential. **One Barrel Chardonnay** Await new vintage. Discontinued: **Stone's End Pinot Noir, Sauvignon Blanc, Sauvignon Blanc-Chardonnay.** —GM

■ **Willowbrook** *see* Wine-of-the-Month Club

Windfall Wine Farm   ▮❢🍴🎋

Location/map/WO: Robertson ▪ Est 1998 ▪ 1stB 2006 ▪ Tasting, sales & tours by appt ▪ Closed all pub hols ▪ BYO picnic ▪ Owner(s) Bianca Weingartz, Sarah Alexander & Jaco de Wet ▪ Cellarmaster(s) Kobus van der Merwe (Jan 2006, consultant) & Jaco de Wet ▪ Winemaker(s) Kobus van der Merwe (Jan 2006, consultant), with Van Zyl de Wet (Jan 2009, consultant) ▪ Viticulturist(s) Jaco de Wet (Jan 2003) ▪ ±288ha/30ha (cab, merlot, pinot, ruby cab, chard, chenin, sauv) ▪ 534t/550cs own label 75% red 25% white ▪ PO Box 22 Robertson 6705 ▪ info@ windfallwine.co.za ▪ www.windfallwine.co.za ▪ S 33° 56' 33.37" E 019° 38' 42.98" ▪ **T +27 (0)83-320-8473** ▪ F +27 (0)86-743-4162

Named and once owned by cricket legend Eddie Barlow, this boutique winery in Agterkliphoogte Valley is extending and diversifying its portfolio with a new chenin blanc (which missed our deadline), extra virgin olive oil and postill brandy undergoing maturation. 'A wine for every person and palate' is the brand promise.

Sauvignon Blanc ☺ 🍴 🚫 ★★★ Commendably light & dry, **13** delivers attractive spread of grass, melon & pineapple, crisp acidity for invigorating sipping.

Cabernet Sauvignon ★★★ Leafy **09** has appealing berry notes, is light enough (12% alcohol) for all-day enjoyment. **Shiraz** 🚫 ★★★ Easygoing **10** ripe & generously layered with plum pudding notes, mocha & chocolate. **Barrel 41** ★★★ Cab/shiraz blend **10** raises the bar with fragrant, juicy red berries & touch of savoury. **Mendola** ⓘ ★★★ Long-gestated méthode cap classique sparkling from chardonnay, **07** genteel caramelised apple aroma & creamy bubbles; drink soon. — DB,CvZ

Windmeul Cooperative Cellar   ▮❢☕📷♿

Location: Paarl ▪ Map: Paarl & Wellington ▪ WO: Paarl/Coastal/Aan-de-Doorns ▪ Est 1944 ▪ 1stB 1945 ▪ Tasting & sales Mon-Fri 9-5 Sat 9-3 ▪ Closed all pub hols ▪ Cellar tours by appt ▪ Farmers' market every 1st Sat of each month, with fresh produce & meals ▪ Owner(s) 42 members ▪ Cellarmaster(s) Danie Marais (Oct 1999) ▪ Winemaker(s) Francois van Niekerk (Dec 2004), with Liani Theunissen (Dec 2010) ▪ Viticulturist(s) Anton Laas (Oct 2007) ▪ 1,700ha ▪ 13,500t/12,000cs own label 54% red 44% white 1% fortified + 800cs for clients ▪ PO Box 2013 Windmeul 7630 ▪ windmeul@iafrica.com ▪ www.windmeulwinery.co.za ▪ S 33° 40' 18.1" E 018° 54' 30.6" ▪ **T +27 (0)21-869-8100/8043** ▪ F +27 (0)21-869-8614

Monthly farmers' markets are a feature at this Paarl winery, and the team are using the popular events to showcase their Reserve wines during winemaker-conducted tastings. These limited-release bottlings, available only ex cellardoor, are key to Windmeul's aspiration of rising above the perception that grower-owned wineries can make only 'good-value' wines - an ambition the solid block of red text below (and the winery's first five star rating) should help achieve.

Reserve range

★★★★☆ **Pinotage** ✓ Fragrant **12** oozes succulent cocoa-dusted blueberries, fynbos & cinnamon spice from new French barrels (as for other reds in range). Generous & elegant, with a polished tannin structure built for 8+ years.

★★★★ **Shiraz** ⓦ A serious wine, **10** needs time. Ripe (15% alcohol) but masked by fruit & oak. Organic notes in awarded **09** add to the complexity, supple tannins supply definition. Both improve on **08** (★★★★).

★★★★☆ **The Legend** ✓ Cab-led (with petit verdot & merlot) Bordeaux-style blend **11** boasts lovely notes of tobacco, crushed herbs & cedar, overlying a rich rounded palate of blackcurrant fruit. Wonderful expression of the vintage. Ageworthy.

★★★★ **Cape Blend** ✓ Exceptional, voluptuous **12** (★★★★★) trumps **10** with ripe black plum fruit & fleshy body. Mainly & unashamedly pinotage (60%) & it shows, with cab's stylish & serious structure. Smooth, with fragrant notes of vanilla oak. Enjoy now & for many years.

★★★★ **Chardonnay** ⓦ Concentrated citrus & buttered toast, **11** though mouthfilling & rich, has enough acid to balance the overall structure. Will reward ageing for few years.

★★★★ **Chenin Blanc** ✓ Knockout citrus & tropical aromas mingle with sweet vanilla oak (50% new French). **12**'s intense, concentrated & focused, with a delicious freshness. Super value, stock up!

Cabernet Sauvignon ⓦ ★★★★ Heaps of potential in **10**, ups the ante, molten berries counter the tannins, give a smoothly textured effect. Drink now till ±2018. Meatier **09** (★★★★) has similar palate appeal.

Windmeul range

★★★★ **White Muscadel** ⓦ Fragrant, vibrant orange peel on fresh **10** fortified dessert. Slippery, dense & concentrated, with a delicious alcohol grip balancing sweetness. Great debut! WO Coastal.

Merlot ☺ ★★★ 2 vintages reviewed: step-up **11** offers juicy, sweet plum flavours, dusting of oak & spicy grip. **12** in the same vein with a delicious vibrancy. Both perfect for fireside enjoyment. **Pinotage** ☺ ★★★ Bright spicy plum & blueberry fruit on well-made **11**, firm body is good for a few years. **Shiraz** ☺ ★★★ Charming & warming **11** oozes juicy black fruit with a delicious spicy edge. Ticks all quaffing boxes. **Chardonnay** ☺ ★★★ Ripe baked apple & tropical notes delight on **13**, brush of oak adds harmony & generosity. Try with feta & spinach tart. **Chenin Blanc** ☺ ★★★ Crunchy apple flavours on crisp, dry unoaked **13** summer sipper. **Sauvignon Blanc** ☺ ★★★ Zesty fruit salad & greener leafy notes on **13**.

Cabernet Sauvignon Next awaited. **Cabernet Sauvignon-Merlot** ⓦ ★★★ Crowd-pleasing **10** up a notch with spicy plum fruit & smooth end. **Port** ⓦ ★★★ Lightish & juicy-sweet berry fruit, touch of spice on **09**. WO Coastal. — WB

■ **Winds of Change** see African Terroir

Wine Concepts 🍷

Location: Cape Town/Johannesburg ▪ Tasting & sales Mon-Fri 9–7 Sat 9.30–4.30 ▪ Owner(s) Michael Bampfield-Duggan, Derick Henstra, Peter Fehrsen, Neil & Sue Proudfoot, Corlien Morris ▪ Winemaker(s) Derick Henstra & Peter Fehrsen ▪ Cardiff Castle cnr Kildare & Main St Newlands 7700 ▪ newlandshop@wineconcepts.co.za ▪ www.wineconcepts.co.za ▪ **T +27 (0)21-671-9030 (Newlands)/+27 (0)21-426-4401 (Gardens)/+27 (0)11-440-5498 (Blue Bird, Jhb)** ▪ F +27 (0)21-671-9031/+27 (0)88-021-426-4401/+27 (0)11-440-5398

Derick Henstra and Peter Fehrsen, co-owners of Wine Concepts specialist wine shops in Cape Town and Johannesburg, themselves make wine with the help of Nabygelegen's James McKenzie from grapes sourced from high-lying vineyards. Their Black Block Pinot Noir 2013 is due this year, only from Wine Concepts stores.

■ **Wine Lover's Collection** see Anura Vineyards

Wine-of-the-Month Club

Location: Cape Town ▪ Est 1986 ▪ MD Tai Collard ▪ Private Bag X2 Glosderry 7702 ▪ wineclub@wineofthemonth.co.za ▪ www.wineofthemonth.co.za ▪ **T +27 (0)21-709-6300** ▪ F +27 (0)86-674-4690

Wine-of-the-Month Club, South Africa's original and still leading wine mail-order business, distributes third-party wines selected by its expert panel as well as own-label brands such as Berg en Dal, Giant's Peak, Montebello, Semara, Steenhuis and Willowbrook.

■ **Winery of Good Hope** see The Winery of Good Hope

Wines of Cape Town

Location: Bellville ▪ Map: Durbanville, Philadelphia & Darling ▪ Est 2007 ▪ Tasting by appt ▪ Owner(s) DS Sarnia (Pty) Ltd ▪ 80% red 20% white ▪ Other export brand: Dolphin Sands ▪ Brands for clients: Diamond Creek, Bushman's Creek, Dolphin Bay ▪ 71 Sonneblom Street Stellenridge Bellville 7530 ▪ sales@winesofcapetown.com ▪ www.winesofcapetown.com ▪ **T +27 (0)21-876-2129** ▪ F +27 (0)21-876-3486

A negociant business based in Bellville, Wines of Cape Town specialises in mainly red private-label wines for clients in Asia and Africa. It also exports its own brand of 'good-value, well-made wines', Dolphin Sands, now available in 6L packaging with branded dispenser that chills the contents optimally.

Wine Village-Hermanus

Location: Hermanus ▪ Map: Elgin, Walker Bay & Bot River ▪ Est 1998 ▪ 1stB 2004 ▪ Open Mon–Fri 9–6 Sat 9–5 Sun 10–3 ▪ Closed Good Fri & Dec 25 ▪ Owner(s) Paul & Cathy du Toit ▪ ±2,000cs 50% red 50% white ▪ PO Box 465 Hermanus 7200 ▪ wine@hermanus.co.za ▪ www.wine-village.co.za ▪ S 34° 24' 40.7" E 019° 12' 1.9" ▪ **T +27 (0)28-316-3988** ▪ F +27 (0)86-509-4931

Paul and Cathy du Toit opened their specialist wine shop, Wine Village, at the entrance to Hermanus' Hemel-en-Aarde Valley in 1998. They are constantly on the lookout for good-quality, easy-drinking wines to bottle under their own Are We Having Fun Yet? label, of which no new bottlings were in sight at press time.

Wineways Marketing

Location: Kuils River ▪ WO: Swartland/Stellenbosch/Western Cape ▪ Est 2000 ▪ Closed to public ▪ Owner(s) Carl Schmidt, Stephen Vermeulen & Fanie Marais ▪ Winemaker(s) Andries Blake (Swarland) & Bernard Claassen (Stellenbosch Vineyards) ▪ 400,000cs own label 60% red 40% white ▪ Plot 689, Zinfandel Street, Saxenburg Park 2, Blackheath 7580 ▪ info@wine-ways.co.za ▪ www.wine-ways.co.za ▪ **T +27 (0)21-905-7713/6/9** ▪ F +27 (0)86-509-9587

While the Leipoldt 1880 Merlot-Cabernet, which pays tribute to well-known Afrikaans writer Louis Leipoldt, has done well since its release a year ago, the Black Tie and Coral Reef ranges, now retailing in all nine provinces, remain the best sellers of Stellenbosch negociant house Wineways. 'We're very happy both with the product and the feedback from customers,' says co-owner Carl Schmidt.

Mountain Shadows range

Merlot ☺ ★★★ NV 3L pack is harmonious & friendly, with red berry appeal. **Pinotage** ☺ 🗒 ★★★ Ripe & plump **11**, juicy & just off-dry. **Chenin Blanc** ☺ 🗒 ★★★ **12** fresh, crisp fruit salad medley. Friendly summer style. WO W Cape, like next; rest of range WO Stellenbosch. **Sauvignon Blanc** ☺ 🗒 ★★★ Early picked freshness & bright fruit on **12**'s well-rounded quaffer.

Cabernet Sauvignon 🗒 ★★ Bright & dark-berried **12**, balanced for easy enjoyment. **Merlot** 🗒 🗒 ★★ Food-styled **12** is tart & minty. **Shiraz** ⊕ 🗒 🗒 ★★ Good mix of fruit & savoury notes in **11** meal mate. **Merlot-Cabernet Sauvignon** ★★★ NV juicy & poised, with supple structure. Amiable entertainer. Also in 3L box.

Coral Reef range

Pinotage ☺ ★★★ Dark & spicy **12**, well proportioned & supple for satisfying drinking.

Cabernet Sauvignon 🗒 ★★ Leaner **12** has sweet-sour tone. **Merlot** ★★ **12** bright, juicy fruit pastille flavours with clean sappy finish. **Merlot-Cabernet Sauvignon** 🗒 ★★ **12** is taut & herbaceous. **Sauvignon Blanc** 🗒 🗒 ★★ **13** light & smooth tropical-toned summer tipple. **Shiraz Natural Sweet** ★★ **12** cinnamon-spiced sipper.

Tin Cups range

Sweet Rosé 🗒 🗒 ★ **12** serve lightly chilled for an easy sundowner. **Sauvignon Blanc** 🗒 🗒 ★★ **13** has light melon tones. **Smooth Red** 🗒 🗒 ★★ **12** easy sweet/savoury quaffer. Discontinued: **Merlot-Cabernet Sauvignon**.

Leipoldt 1880 NEW

Merlot-Cabernet Sauvignon ★★ Lighter-styled, approachable **NV** shows juicy mint & cassis.

Black Box range

Shiraz ☺ 📵 ★★★ Fresh & flavoursome **NV** is appealingly drinkable. This range all 5L bag-in-box.

Merlot ★★ Lean **NV** has a tart cherry tone. **Pinotage** ★★ **NV** plump & juicy. Amiable just-off-dry crowd pleaser. **Merlot-Cabernet Sauvignon** 📵 ★★ Chunky, firm **NV** with tangy berry flavours, for robust fare.

Black Tie range

Pinotage ☺ 📵 ★★★ Ripe brambleberries on bright & juicy **12**.

Cabernet Sauvignon 📵 ★★ Brusque **12** has a sweet/sour tone. **Merlot** 📵 ★★ **12** tart & savoury pizza mate. **Merlot-Cabernet Sauvignon** 📵 ★★★ Richly fruited **12**, well constructed, fresh & satisfying. **Sauvignon Blanc** 🏠 📵 ★★ Refreshing **13** tropical summer sipper. **Shiraz Natural Sweet** ★★ **12** spicy & sweet.

South Africa range

Discontinued: **Cabernet Sauvignon**, **Merlot**, **Merlot-Cabernet Sauvignon**, **Shiraz Natural Sweet**. — MW

Winkelshoek Wine Cellar

Location: Piketberg ▪ Map: Swartland ▪ Tasting & sales Mon-Fri 9-4 Sat 9–12 ▪ Gifts ▪ Owner(s) Hennie Hanekom & Jurgens Brand ▪ Cellarmaster(s) Hennie Hanekom ▪ Winemaker(s) Hennie Hanekom (1984) ▪ PO Box 395 Piketberg 7320 ▪ info@winkelshoek.co.za ▪ S 32° 54' 22.4" E 018° 46' 2.0" ▪ **T +27 (0)22-913-1092** ▪ F +27 (0)22-913-1095

This cellar's easy-drinkers are available for tasting and sale from the visitor centre near the intersection of the N7 and R44 roads outside Piketberg. The wines, untasted this edition, include Weskus Dry Red, Sweet Rosé, Grand Cru, Blanc de Blanc and Late Harvest; and the Cap Vino Red (unwooded) and White (chenin).

Winters Drift

Location/WO: Elgin ▪ Map: Elgin, Walker Bay & Bot River ▪ Est 2004 ▪ 1stB 2010 ▪ Tasting Tue-Fri 9-4 Sat 10-4 & every first Sun of the month ▪ Platform 1 eatery ▪ Conservation area ▪ Owner(s) Molteno Brothers (Pty) Ltd ▪ Cellarmaster(s) Kobie Viljoen (shiraz, Gabriëlskloof) & Koen Roose (pinot/chard/rosé/sauv, Spioenkop) ▪ Viticulturist(s) Christiaan Cloete (Jan 2011) & Francois Viljoen (Vinpro) ▪ 1,600ha/±54ha (grenache, merlot, mourv, pinot, shiraz, chard, sauv, sem, viog) ▪ 460t/7,000cs own label 40% red 50% white 10% rosé ▪ PO Box 128 Elgin 7180 ▪ gerhard@wintersdrift.com ▪ www.wintersdrift.com ▪ S 34° 08' 59.42" E 019° 02' 22.61" ▪ **T +27 (0)21-859-3354** ▪ F +27 (0)21-859-4893

This relatively new venture is right on track, from the tasting facility in the old Elgin station, filled with memorabilia from bygone days, and the new eatery, Platform 1, to building brand awareness. The adjacent railway buildings are being renovated to host conferences, cooking courses and seminars. The brand owner, Molteno Brothers, is a non-profit, so net income goes back to the community.

★★★★ **Pinot Noir** NEW ✓ 📵 **12** debuts in convincing style with pretty much everything you need in young pinot: ample bright cherry fruit, touches of varietal spice & farmyard funk, hint of oak, fine dry tannins.

Rosé ☺ 🏠 📵 ★★★ Step-up **12** from merlot. Maraschino cherry & toffee hint at sweetness, but reined in nicely by chalky fresh acidity.

Shiraz NEW ✓ 📵 ★★★★ Elegant shiraz with medium body & attractively austere flavours of leafy cassis & pomegranate pointing to cool provenance. **11** has benefited from bottle-maturation at cellar, will reward further ageing. **Chardonnay** ✓ 🏠 📵 ★★★★ Oak noticeable in buttered toast & marmalade, merging on **12** palate with combo sweet/sour & ripe fruit for tangy-clean effect, ready to drink. **Sauvignon Blanc** 🏠 📵 ★★★ Retains fuller styling in **12**, though fruit tone is greener (grapefruit, melon, some capsicum) & acidity more food- than solo-cordial. — HJ

Withington

Location: Darling ▪ Map: Durbanville, Philadelphia & Darling ▪ WO: Darling/Coastal/Paarl ▪ Est 2001 ▪ 1stB 2003 ▪ Tasting & sales at Darling Wine Shop Mon-Sat 10-6 (10-7 in summer) Sun 11-2 ▪ Closed Mar 21, Easter

Fri/Sun & Dec 25/26 ▪ Fresh West Coast oysters served when available ▪ Owner(s) Withington family ▪ 6,000cs own label 70% red 30% white + 8,000cs for clients ▪ Brands for clients: Cape Diversity, Greendale ▪ PO Box 236 Darling 7345 ▪ mail@withington.co.za ▪ www.withington.co.za ▪ S 33° 22' 28" E 018° 22' 38" ▪ **T +27 (0)22-492-3971/+27 (0)74-194-1711** ▪ F +27 (0)86-516-4010

Having spent many years marketing wines for well-known producers, Charles Withington set up shop for his wine brand in Darling, the country town renowned for its annual Spring flowers. He's blossomed too, greeting visitors to his wine shop and tasting room with natural bonhomie - which usually translates into a sale!

Withington range

Carignan ⊕ 🍷 ★★★ Overtly plummy, ripe **10** similar to previous. Cheerful, sunny & appealing take on variety. WO Coastal. **Shiraz-Cabernet Sauvignon** ⊕ 🍷 ★★★ Likeable, easy-drinking **09** shows vintage's ripeness, with sweet cherry & plum fruit, soft tannins. Paarl fruit. **Chardonnay** ✓ 🍷 ★★★☆ Rich pineapple & honeyed citrus notes on **12**. Medium body with integrated acid & ripe fruit, long finish. **Semillon** ⊕ ★★★ Unwooded **10** follows form, striking nettle & greenpepper notes backed by fullish, lanolin-oily body.

Darlington range

Malbec ☺ 🍷 🍷 ★★★ Juicy raspberry & blueberry vibrancy to **12**. Light, gentle & uncomplicated, with clean dry finish. **Chardonnay** NEW ☺ 🍷 🍷 ★★★ **12** has tropical-styled citrus lightness & easy-drinking appeal. Seamless & rounded to dry end.

Pinotage Next awaited. Note: Greendale & Living Rock ranges untasted. — FM

Withoek

Location/WO: Calitzdorp ▪ Map: Klein Karoo & Garden Route ▪ Est/1stB 1996 ▪ Tasting, sales & cellar tours by appt ▪ Self-catering cottages ▪ Walks ▪ Conservation area ▪ Owner(s) Geyser family ▪ Winemaker(s) Fanie Geyser ▪ Viticulturist(s) Johannes Mellet ▪ 454ha/30ha (cab, p verdot, ruby cab, shiraz, tinta, touriga, chenin, cbard, hanepoot, muscadel) ▪ ±300t/800cs own label 50% red 50% fortified ▪ PO Box 181 Calitzdorp 6660 ▪ withoek@telkomsa.net ▪ www.withoek.blogspot.com ▪ S 33° 32' 24.1" E 021° 40' 59.8" ▪ **T +27 (0)44-213-3639** ▪ F +27 (0)86-628-7853

A significantly smaller crush at this 'small, intimate' Calitzdorp family winery after Mother Nature delivered a hail storm in February. Still, co-owner Fanie Geyser says they had a very successful Port Festival with sales increasing nicely. Their stock is low as they weren't able to produce their usual quantities.

Cabernet Sauvignon ⊕ Artisanal **10** slightly spritzy. **Shiraz** ⊕ ★★ Tasted mid-2010, **09** had beefy alcohol & dry tannin from 11 months oak. **Sauvignon Blanc** ⊕ ★★ Amiable **11** grassy & fresh, with satisfying vinosity. **Kairos Muscadel** ⊕ ★★★ Fortified dessert from mainly white muscadel, dash red for pinkish hue. **10**'s watermelon & honeyed notes appeal but fade fast. **Fick's Ruby Port** ⊕ ★★ Raisin & dusty spices on uncomplex **NV**. **Geyser Cape Ruby** ⊕ ★★ Rustic **NV** port-style fireside sipper. **Geyser Cape Vintage** ⊕ ★★★ House's 3rd port-style offering; cranberry & tealeaf-toned **10** makes up for lack of tannin grip with a fiery tail. — CE,JP

▪ **Witklip** see Eerste Hoop Wine Cellar
▪ **Wolfenberg** see TCB Wines

Wolfkloof

Location/map: Robertson ▪ Est 1883 ▪ 1stB 2004 ▪ Tasting, sales & cellar tours by appt ▪ Meals by appt; or BYO picnic ▪ Tour groups ▪ Conferences (40 pax) ▪ Weddings/functions (100 pax) ▪ Hiking trail ▪ Art & craftwork ▪ Owner(s) JC Kannemeyer ▪ Cellarmaster(s)/winemaker(s) Jan Kannemeyer ▪ Viticulturist(s) Hennie Visser (consultant) ▪ 360ha/4ha (merlot, chard) ▪ 10t/1,000cs own label 40% red 40% white 20% rosé + 180cs for clients ▪ PO Box 40 Robertson 6705 ▪ info@wolfkloof.co.za ▪ www.wolfkloof.co.za ▪ S 33° 47' 28.1" E 019° 52' 1.4" ▪ **T +27 (0)74-339-5008** ▪ F +27 (0)86-554-4894

Jan Kannemeyer's boutique vintning story began in 2004 when he concluded he couldn't call himself a vinegrower and not make wine. Merlot - all of one barrel - was his first attempt and the variety is still favourite. Production has reached 10 tons, all made as naturally as possible and bottled under his JC Kannemeyer label.

Wolvendrift Private Cellar

Location/map: Robertson ▪ Est 1903 ▪ Tasting & sales Mon-Fri 8.30–4.30 Sat 10–1 ▪ Closed Easter Fri-Mon, May 1, Dec 25/26 & Jan 1 ▪ Cellar tours by appt ▪ Refreshments/meals by pre-booking ▪ Facilities for children ▪ Tour groups ▪ Walking/hiking trails ▪ Conservation area ▪ Weddings & functions ▪ Owner(s) Michael Klue ▪ Winemaker(s) Jan Klue (Jan 2003) ▪ Viticulturist(s) Jan Swart (Jan 2000) ▪ 120ha (cab, merlot, chard, chenin, cbard, sauv) ▪ 45% red 45% white 10% fortified ▪ PO Box 24 Robertson 6705 ▪ info@wolvendriftwines.co.za ▪ www.wolvendriftwines.co.za ▪ S 33° 55' 0.1" E 020° 0' 9.0" ▪ **T +27 (0)23-616-2890** ▪ F +27 (0)23-616-2396

Robertson's Kleu family are creating an increasingly attractive cellardoor offering on their Breede River shores, with overseas tour groups being hosted for pre-booked cheese-and-wine tastings or meals-and-tastings. Casual visitors are also made welcome and treated to 'hospitality, tranquility and breathtaking views'.

Women in Wine

Location: Stellenbosch ▪ WO: Western Cape ▪ Closed to public ▪ PO Box 12869 Die Boord Stellenbosch 7613 ▪ info@womeninwine.co.za ▪ www.womeninwine.co.za ▪ **T +27 (0)21-872-8967** ▪ F +27 (0)21-872-8967

Established by a group of black female professionals inspired by quality wines and the empowerment of women in the winelands, this collective's current focus is on growing relationships with strategic business partners and managing the brand within South Africa.

Three Graces Reserves

Euphrosyne Cabernet Sauvignon ⊕ ★★★ Striking & graceful labels a feature throughout. **08** commands attention with its substance & grip, ideally kept year/2 or matched with full-flavoured food. **Thalia Merlot** ⊕ ★★★ **09** takes SA merlot's sometimes herbaceous quality to the max: leafy, minty, very dry & lean. A love/hate wine, but we urge: try! **Aglaia Chardonnay** ⊕ ★★★ Opulent & mouthfilling, **09**'s sweet-seeming honeyed lemon cream character is surprisingly assertive, needs rich food or chilling for solo. — JP,CvZ

Wonderfontein

Location/map/WO: Robertson ▪ Est ca 1884 ▪ Tasting by appt only ▪ Sales Mon-Fri 9–6 Sat 9–1 ▪ Tour groups ▪ Conferences/events (40-80 guests), picnic facilities, 4×4 trail & other attractions ▪ Owner(s) Paul René Marais ▪ Winemaker(s) Stefan Bruwer ▪ Viticulturist(s) Gert Visser, Gerald Stemmet & Bennie Stemmet, advised by Brian Stipp ▪ 270ha (cab, merlot, ptage, pinot, ruby cab, shiraz, chard, chenin, sauv) ▪ 5,500t/6,000cs own label 10% red 80% white 1% rosé 9% fortified ▪ PO Box 4 Robertson 6705 ▪ henk@wonderfonteinestate.co.za ▪ www.wonderfonteinestate.co.za ▪ S 33°49' 3.5" E 019° 52' 2.1" ▪ **T +27 (0)23-626-2212** ▪ F +27 (0)23-626-2669

The fifth-generation Marais winegrowers' relatively recent boutique label is focusing on champagne-method bubbly. Pinot noir has been picked for a possible Brut Rosé to partner the chardonnay Brut introduced last year. An underground storeroom, sometimes used for honey processing, is being readied for riddling.

★★★★ **Paul René MCC Brut** ⊠ **NV** bottle-fermented sparkling from chardonnay packed with personality. Lively mousse, lemon & lime vibrancy, elegant dry conclusion.

La Bonne Vigne Shiraz ☺ ▦ ⊠ ★★★ Herbs & plums in **11**, soft & undemanding pizza/pasta red. **La Bonne Vigne Sauvignon Blanc** ☺ ▦ ⊠ ★★★ **13** lightish, pineapple-toned book club staple.

The Marais Family Merlot ⊕ ▦ ★★★ Spice-dusted **10** ideal for early enjoyment, juicy plum gently wrapped with tannin. **La Bonne Vigne Merlot** ▦ ⊠ ★★ Chocolate & coffee scented **11** for casual sipping. **La Bonne Vigne Rosé** ⊕ ▦ ★★★ Friendly **NV** (**12**) ups the quaffability level with ripe strawberry flavours & hint of sweetness. **Wonderfontein Red Muscadel** ⊠ ★★★★ **11** lovely example of this fortified dessert style, endless raisin & fig flavours, tangy spirit lift on finish. **White Muscadel** NEW ⊠ ★★★ Pretty bouquet of flowers & honey, touch melon on generous & syrupy **12** after-dinner treat. — CvZ,DB

Woolworths

WO: Various ▪ Selector Allan Mullins T +27 (0)21-407-2777 AllanMullins@woolworths.co.za ▪ Buying manager Ivan Oertle T +27 (0)21-407-2762 IvanOertle@woolworths.co.za ▪ Owner(s) Woolworths Holdings ▪ Woolworths House 93 Longmarket Street Cape Town 8000 ▪ www.woolworths.co.za ▪ **T +27 (0)21-407-9111** ▪ F +27 (0)21-407-3958

Upmarket retail network Woolworths introduced their respected wine selections in 1985, and the list, like Topsy, has grown and grown. Even with a combined 40-plus years in the wine department, Allan Mullins and Ivan Oertle's enthusiasm for offering customers something new and exciting thankfully doesn't wane. Their latest project is the Single Vineyard range, where the whole wine team is involved, from selecting sites and varieties to harvesting, vinifying, maturing and blending. A label upgrade, new imports and a new Fairtrade initiative under the My Village banner, which will see selected suppliers make contributions to winelands charities for every bottle sold, are just a few more projects in hand. No wonder the team has had to be expanded: Rebecca Constable has recently joined as Wine & Beverage Product Developer.

Cabernet Sauvignon range

★★★★ **DD Cabernet Sauvignon** NEW Dark & brooding **11** 1.5L magnum by Diemersdal is restrainedly confident. Nicely ripe, with lifted acidity, well-managed tannins. Cellar with confidence for 5+ years.

★★★★☆ **Exclusive Cabernet** ① Unshowy **08** (★★★★) from Grangehurst, carefully judged to allow for lighter fruit. Smooth tannins, shortish finish suggest best enjoyed early. **07** richer, longer lived.

★★★★ **Cabernet Sauvignon Reserve** ② Full, rich **11** has measured blackcurrant fruit woven with ripe, pliable tannin. Understated tobacco & herbal notes, with the firm grip of its Diemersfontein origin.

★★★★ **Cabernet Sauvignon Reserve** ✓ Waves of complex flavours lift mocha-toned **11**; plump berry fruit in elegant structure, accessible now but will reward patience. Crafted at Spier.

> **Longmarket Cabernet Sauvignon** ☺ ② ★★★ Improving on previous, **12** offers dark berry, mint chocolate & coffee highlights on plummy palate. From Bergsig, as is next. **Tell It Like It Is Cabernet Sauvignon** ☺ ▤ ② ★★☆ Unoaked sweet juicy red berries, slight grip on smooth, light & easy **12**.

The Hutton Cabernet Sauvignon ★★★☆ Named for dominant soil type from which grapes are sourced. Cassis mingles with chocolate & vanilla courtesy Spier's oaking of **11**. **10** sold out untasted. **NSA Organic Running Duck Cabernet Sauvignon** ▤ ❀ ② ★★☆ Easy-sipping **13** with tobacco spicing. Fairtrade certified, as all the Stellar Winery bottlings for Woolworths. **Cabernet Sauvignon** ✓ ② ★★★☆ Lively **11** from Villiera delivers abundant succulent sweet fruit seasoned in oak; appealingly spicy herbal edge adds interest.

Merlot range

★★★★ **Merlot Reserve** ① Firmly structured **09** from Morgenhof shows dark cherries, blackberries, & slight herbaceous note. Powerful, with integrated acidity but warmish finish ex 14.8% alcohol.

★★★★ **Exclusive Selection Merlot** ▤ ② Carefully made, including 80% new French oak, Jordan's **11** has the cassis & dark chocolate notes you'd expect, plus a sleekly curvaceous body, ending dry & food friendly.

★★★★ **Shannon Merlot** NEW ② Plummy, honeyed **12**'s plush palate has a hint of oak char, sufficient tannic grip to extend the finish. Concentrated but vivacious, like also-tasted **11** by Shannon Vineyards.

> **Merlot** ☺ ② ★★★ Savoury **11** from Villiera; dash touriga adds spicy intrigue & interest to ripe plum flavours & vibrant finish.

Koffie Klip Merlot ★★★☆ Named for dominant soil type in the vineyard, ripe **11**'s plum fruit cosseted by 60% new French oak, slightly spirituous farewell (14.7% alcohol). By Spier. **NSA Organic Swooping Falcon Merlot** ▤ ❀ ② ★★ **13** by Stellar Winery needs hearty food to offset racy freshness. **Merlot** ② ★★★ Still youthful grip on La Motte's **12** only a slight distraction from underlying supple flesh, dark plum, cedary tones. **Longmarket Merlot** ① ★★★ Easy, fresh & round **11** shows succulent red berries. From Simonsvlei. **Tell It Like It Is Merlot** ① ▤ ★★ Wellington Wines-sourced, barrel-matured **11** is light & basic. **Organic Merlot** ✓ ❀ ② ★★★★ Rich choc-mulberry on **12** ramps up quality on **11** (★★★★). Graphite earthiness underpins velvety texture & deep, broad, structured palate. By Laibach. **Light Merlot** ▤ ② ★★ Succulent **12** has decent grip; low alcohol & off-dry, from Spier. **Breath Merlot** ▤ ② ★★★ Plum & cherry chocolate vibrancy on **12** from Wellington Wines. Gentle & soft but with structure & density. Good length. **Jordan No Added Sulphur Merlot** NEW ▤ ② ★★★ Minty red berries with a herbal top note in unoaked **12** gives a food wine with its grape tannin grip.

Pinot Noir range

★★★★ **Pinot Noir Reserve** ① Challenging **11** (★★★★) vintage, shows a smoky, savoury nuance with some earthiness. Less oak, leaner fruit & body than **10**. From Paul Cluver.

★★★★ **Limited Release CM Pinot Noir** ② Catherine Marshall's **12** combination of clones & soils creates a lithe, silk-textured pinot with lovely fruit purity & complexity. Persuasive, elegant styling.

Limited Release Pinot Noir Next awaited. **Cabrière Pinot Noir ★★★** Soft berry notes & integrated oak complement the mellow russet hue of **09**, tasty, but misses purity, detail of cherry-toned **08**. From Haute Cabrière. **DMZ Pinot Noir** 🍷 📖 **★★★** From DeMorgenzon, **12** bigger, more sturdy than previously tasted **10** (**★★★★**). Straightforward ripe cherry features. **11** sold out untasted. **Longmarket Pinot Noir** Await next.

Pinotage range

★★★★ Simonsig Pinotage 📖 **12** (**★★★★**) is dense & brimming with berry compote fruitiness. High-toned aromatics spice up well-structured & focused body. Follows appealingly juicy **10**. **11** sold out untasted.
★★★★ Reyneke Pinotage NEW ☺ 📖 Gorgeous aromas on this **11** biodynamic wine; bright fruit on supple, round palate. Seriously built - the tannins need a year or two. A bracing bitter hint on the end.

> **NSA Organic Glowing Firefly Pinotage** ☺ 🍷 ⚙ 📖 **★★☆ 13** fruity, amiable & plump but ends dry. From Stellar Winery.

Light Pinotage NEW 🍷 **★** Spier's sweet plum fruit on **13**, unfettered by tannin or low (9%) alcohol. **Coffee Pinotage** 🍷 📖 **★★☆** Close your eyes & **12** tastes of, well, coffee, with a sweet feel for an easy glide. From Diemersfontein. **Pinotage** 📖 **★★★** Roasted coffee & bright red fruit in balanced, supple tannined **11**. From M'Hudi. **Tell It Like It Is Pinotage** 🍷 📖 **★★★** Exotically perfumed **12** has sweet fruit, fine tannins. Made for uncomplicated drinking by Ken Forrester. **Longmarket Pinotage** 📖 **★★☆** From Rooiberg Winery, **12** taut & dry, savoury mealtime companion. **Exclusive Selection Pinotage** 📖 **★★★** By Bellevue, a softer-styled pinotage, with profusion of red fruit, **12** smooth & ready to drink ('with red or white meat - it's versatile' say winemakers). **Pinotage Reserve** 📖 **★★★★** Plummy **12** carries 70% new French oak (1 year) wearily mid-2013; chunky fruit awaits softening of tannin with time. From Diemersfontein.

Shiraz range

★★★★ Shiraz Reserve 📖 **10** (**★★★★**) light fruited & a little shorter than **09**. Playful red fruit combine with spice, ending dry. From Darling Cellars.

> **Chocolate Shiraz** ☺ 📖 **★★★** Bearing Diemersfontein's plummy stamp, generous **12** brims with bonhomie. It could even partner chocolate cake.

Organic Hunting Owl Shiraz ⊕ ⚙ **★★★** Succulent red berry fruit pads out tad stalky grape tannins on unoaked **11**. For early quaffing, ex African Terroir. **Hercules Paragon Shiraz** ⊕ ✓ **★★★★** Inviting mulberry, fynbos & spice on full-bodied juicy preview **12** from Simonsvlei; smooth food wine with a sweet spicy lift. **Pumphouse Shiraz ★★★★** By Backsberg. Spicy plum succulence & depth covers nicely firm frame of earthy & richly fruited **09**; follows French-styled **08** (**★★★★**). **Longmarket Redstone Shiraz** ⊕ 📖 **★★☆** Consistent, juicy everyday tipple has faint savoury, hay notes in **12**. Ex Rooiberg Winery. Discontinued: **Light Shiraz**.

Niche Red Cultivars

★★★★ Nederburg Grenache ✓ 📖 Deep, rich but bright red berries, fynbos & nutmeg, **12** from Nederburg ticks all the drinkability boxes. Harmonious & silky, dollop carignan adds complexity.
★★★★ Limited Release Malbec 📖 By Bellevue, **10** returns to form after **09** (**★★★**) with excellent concentration of red fruit, layered flavours of berry, molasses & mocha, sound platform of tannin for cellaring.
★★★★ Malbec Reserve 📖 Perfumed **12** proffers nutmeg & blackcurrant profile contrasted & balanced by sleek tannin. Year 60% new oak; needs few years to unfurl. By Diemersfontein.
★★★★ Granite Blocks Cabernet Franc ⊕ 📖 **10** powerful & concentrated mouthful of black fruit & some truffle notes. Ripe berries lent a savoury edge with fragrant herbs of lavender & rosemary. By Raats Family.
Cabernet Franc Reserve ✓ 📖 **★★★★** Juicy **11** shows perfumed red fruit & tangy, firm structure. Alcohol unobtrusive. Food styled & rewards decanting. By Paul Cluver.

Red Blends

★★★★ Cabernet Sauvignon-Merlot Reserve 📖 **11** shows more fruit opulence & accessibility than **10** while retaining elegant balance & structure. Engaging & well crafted, from Neil Ellis.
★★★★☆ Cobblers Hill Bordeaux blend barrel selection from Jordan. **09** is a silky, succulent triumph, the spice & plush fruit interwoven. So easy to drink one could overlook the sleek musculature.
★★★★ The Ladybird Red ⊕ ⚙ **10** from Laibach follows in **09**'s footsteps. 5-way Bordeaux combo. Ripe but still refreshing, tobacco leaf & earth nuances to firm body & slight chunky texture.
★★★★ Warwick Cape Lady ✓ 📖 Shiraz-led with pinotage, 3 others, **11**'s hedonistic spiced dark fruit & smooth fleshy palate is designed to please. Not for long ageing, but why resist something so delicious?
★★★★ Grenache-Shiraz-Mourvèdre **09** (**★★★★**) includes 12% mourvèdre for the first time. Unfussy but pleasing with red & black fruit plus some gentle spice. Not as winning as **08**. By Ken Forrester.

Juicy Red ☺ ★★★ Raspberry caramel appeal on **NV** unoaked mourvèdre, cinsaut mix by Wellington Wines.

Exclusive Selection Cabernet Sauvignon-Merlot 📖 ★★★☆ Mouthfilling **11** offers milk chocolate, cedarwood complexity, lingering red plum conclusion. By De Wetshof. **Grand Rouge** 📖 ★★★ La Motte's lively, sweet-fruited **11** provides easy-drinking satisfaction. Cab-led Bordeaux blend, rounded by older oak. **Cabernet Sauvignon-Merlot** 📖 ★★★★ As usual, in **11** Delheim gives a balanced, structured & satisfying blend; fruity & friendly - but not over-eager. **Allan Mullins Red 'My Song'** Next awaited. **Parlotones Giant Mistake** 🍴 📖 ★★★ Succulent smoky black fruit on **11** 5-way cab/shiraz-led mix from Wellington Wines. Soft tannic grip but ripe plum tail. **Longmarket Shiraz-Pinotage** 📖 ★★ Earthy, dusty **12** uncomplicated sipping, by Spier. **Capstone Shiraz-Cabernet Sauvignon** ⓘ ◎ ★★★ Ripe-fruited, savoury & serious **09** from biodynamic producer Reyneke more interesting than **08** (★★★★). Spicy, floral aromas, then a supple but grippy palate needing year or two to flesh out. **Shiraz-Cabernet Sauvignon** ✓ 📖 ★★★★ Mocha-toned **11** has spicy interest & medium build; less assertive than previous. Ex Diemersfontein. **Cape Red** 🍴 ★★★ Fresh, light-bodied **NV** red from Wellington Wines. Juicy plum & berries with chocolate nuance makes it punch above its weight. **Cabernet Sauvignon-Shiraz Reserve** 📖 ★★★★ Wholesome **11** from La Motte. Smooth, rich fruit & tastily savoury finish. Will give pleasure for good few years. **Goshawk's Chant** ✓ 🍴 📖 ★★★★ Bordeaux base with unusual red grape roobernet; diffident **11** ex Diemersfontein offers attractive black fruit purity with lingering oak grip. **The Portuguese Connection** ⓘ ★★★☆ Marries Portuguese grapes touriga & tinta with cab in spicy, juicy **11**. Quite robust, enjoy with hearty food now or age few years to soften. From Boplaas. **Natural Sweet Red** ⓘ 🍴 📖 ★★ Faintly berry-toned, cab-led low-alcohol **12** quaffer from Spier. **Juicy Sweet** 📖 ★★ Dusty plums & spice on soft sweet red, best served chilled. **NV** 3-way blend by Bergsig.

Rosé Wines

Pierre Jourdan Tranquille Blush ☺ 🍴 ★★★ Fragrant pale pink rosé from pinot & chardonnay. Current **NV** cherry spice, faintly smoky. Light, just-dry & zesty. By Haute Cabrière. **Cape Rosé** NEW ☺ 🍴 ★★★ Friendly freshness & raspberry, pomegranate appeal to **NV** pinotage quaffer ex Wellington Wines.

Longmarket Blanc de Noir 🍴 📖 ★★★ From Robertson Winery, fruitful **13** very dry, for serious dinner tables or chilled al fresco sipping. **Light Pinot Noir Rosé** ⓘ 🍴 📖 ★★★ Just-dry, zingy, strawberry **12** from Villiera for summer drinking. Only 9.5% alcohol. **Longmarket Rosé** ⓘ 🍴 📖 ★★★ Undemanding blush quaffer in light, off-dry style. **12** ex Villiera. **Pinotage-Shiraz Rosé** 🍴 📖 ★★★ Mildly fruity, just off-dry **13** from Delheim with a nice earthy tug for interest. **Zesty Rosé** 📖 ★★ Perfumed fruity berries, zippy acid on very light off-dry **NV** from Bergsig. **Parlotones We Call this Dancing** ⓘ 🍴 ★★★ Characterful dry 27-way (!) pink, **12** generous strawberry fruit. Fresh semi-dry fun-times quaffing from Wellington Wines. **Natural Sweet Rosé** 🍴 ★ By Spier, **13** low-alcohol sweet sipper from shiraz needs chilling. Discontinued: **NSA Organic Diving Hawk Rosé.**

Chardonnay range

★★★★ **Chardonnay Reserve** 📖 On track after **10** (★★★), **11** blooms in the glass to reveal an integrated & perfectly poised wine with delicate oak spice seasoning. Shows De Wetshof's mastery of the variety.

★★★★ **Abacus Chardonnay** ✓ 📖 Composed, lemon-toned **12** from Spier; taut & dry, wet clay & 'oystershell' mineral notes give much enjoyment now & for next year or two. **11** sold out before tasting.

★★★★ **Chardonnay Lightly Wooded** 📖 Proving that character & flavour is possible with partial oaking, Jordan's **12** offers citrus & crushed almonds, a lovely smooth-textured freshness.

★★★★☆ **Elgin Chardonnay** 🍴 📖 Elgin's provenance shines through on **12** from Neil Ellis. Vivacious, with lovely fruit intensity & length. Oak is seamlessly integrated into pear & lime flavours. Zesty, fresh & satisfying.

★★★★ **Exclusive Selection Chardonnay** 📖 Tropical fruit & limy freshness give **13** ex Jordan taste appeal, offers a good alternative to wooded chardonnay.

★★★★ **Wild Yeast Chardonnay** 📖 Ripe fruit with boiled-sweet overtones, smooth-textured unwooded **10** (★★★★) is sweeter, less intense than **09**. Less fresh too, despite a pleasant acidity. From Springfield.

Organic Feeding Duck Chardonnay 🍴 🐝 📖 ★★★ Deft light oaking gives tasty apple pie note to citrus fruit of **13**. By Stellar Winery. **Longmarket Chardonnay** 📖 ★★★ From Robertson Winery, **13** lusciously ripe yellow stonefruit with vanilla overlay from oak, slight sweetness which makes it very easy to drink. **The Ladybird Chardonnay** ⓘ 🍴 🐝 📖 ★★★★ Rich citrus flavour burst but restraint evident in oak sheen on zesty organic **11** ex Laibach. Vibrant & integrated. **Vanilla Chardonnay** NEW 🍴 📖 ★★★ Easy-sipping semi-dry **12** exudes cream & vanilla fudge appeal; from Weltevrede. **Limestone Hill Chardonnay** 📖 ★★★★ Made-for-oysters **12** by De Wetshof goes up a notch with clean lime aromas, crisp citrus notes &

elegant minerality. **Tell It Like It Is Chardonnay** 🍱 📖 ★★★ Unwooded **13** by Weltevrede raises the bar with zesty citrus/peach attraction & a touch of savoury. **Light Chardonnay** 🍱 ★ Lemony unwooded **12** ends sweet; low alcohol from Spier.

Chenin Blanc range

★★★★ **Chenin Blanc Sur Lie** ✓ Stylish & complex **12** from Simonsig off-dry & unwooded, expressing delightfully ripe fruit salad bolstered by lees richness & delicate perfume. Way better than price suggests.

★★★★ **Chenin Blanc** 📖 Buttered toast richness (14 months oak, 45% new) to fruit-filled **12** from Spier. Tasty, but obvious sweetness (7.4 g/l RS) makes you wish for a bite of acidity.

Chenin Blanc Reserve 📖 Unshowy **12** has subtle notes of peach & spice. Good palate weight, finishes pleasantly dry. By Ken Forrester. **Tell It Like It Is Chenin Blanc** 🍱 ★★★ **12** will have broad appeal given its ripe peach character, moderate acidity. By Ken Forrester. **Longmarket Chenin Blanc** 🍱 📖 ★★★ Thatch & floral notes on crisp **13**, by Rooiberg Winery. **M'hudi Chenin Blanc** ⊕ 🍱 📖 ★★★ Full-flavoured **11** blends tropical & light herbaceousness in engagingly rich fruitiness, balanced by zesty acidity. From M'Hudi. **Light Chenin Blanc** 🍱 ★★ Low-alcohol **12** by Spier is gently tropical, off-dry but doesn't cloy. **Noble Late Harvest Chenin Blanc** Not tasted. Discontinued: **The W (Chenin Blanc)**.

Sauvignon Blanc range

★★★★ **Sauvignon Blanc Reserve** 📖 From Groote Post, very different to its own sauvignons, **12** is gooseberry toned with minerality to the fore on the palate & finish. Good match for seafood, fine dining.

★★★★ **Exclusive Selection Sauvignon Blanc** Stylish, restrained **12** ex Durbanville vines by Cape Point Vineyards shows creamy smoothness from long lees-ageing. Very mineral with hints of passionfruit.

★★★★ **Exclusive Selection Nitida Sauvignon Blanc** ⊕ 🍱 Consistently delicious example from Nitida Cellars. Some Darling fruit in **12**, gooseberries, with a fynbos edge adding focus, individuality.

★★★★ **Lonely Blue Gum Sauvignon Blanc** 🍱 📖 Restrained grass & herb notes, crisp mouthful smoothed by creamy lees of **13** (★★★★) by Spier. Not quite as persistent & steely as oyster-ready **12**.

★★★★ **Elgin Sauvignon Blanc** 🍱 📖 **12** from Neil Ellis, returns to form after plumper **11**, showcasing Elgin's cooler fruit intensity. Tangy stonefruit & minerality, balanced for satisfying drinkability.

Wet Rocks Sauvignon Blanc ☺ 📖 ★★★ **12** is crisp & lemon-toned, light 11.8% alcohol - perfect lunchtime companion. Ex Bergsig. **Tell It Like It Is Sauvignon Blanc** ☺ 📖 ★★★ Bergsig's **13** upfront tropical fruit salad flavours, zippy fresh farewell. Also-tasted **12** (★★★) gooseberry & hay aromas/flavours, lifting lemon grip.

Organic Swooping Swallow Sauvignon Blanc 🍱 🌿 📖 ★★★ Full, lively grassy flavours on bone-dry **13** ex Stellar Winery. **Sauvignon Blanc Bush Vine** ★★★☆ Tropical **13** takes step up with floral complexity, clean & zippy conclusion. From Darling Cellars. **Longmarket Sauvignon Blanc** 📖 ★★★ Refreshing grapefruit & yellow citrus, bone-dry, with lowish alcohol: **13** a summer fridge staple. By Robertson Winery. **Light Sauvignon Blanc** 🍱 ★ **13** is light in all respects, including 7% alcohol. By Spier. **La Motte Sauvignon Blanc Organically Grown** 🌿 Await next. **Breath Sauvignon Blanc** 🍱 📖 ★★★ Fig & lime, with zesty freshness on **12** from Wellington Wines. Lively, with a clean, dry tail. **DD Sauvignon Blanc** NEW ★★★★ Fig & quince aromas, perky acidity, lemon boiled sweet tastes on **13** everyday sipper from Diemersdal, in 1.5L magnums.

Niche White Cultivars

★★★★ **Ferricrete Riesling** ✓ 🍱 📖 **12** (★★★★☆) featherlight kiss of lime & ginger, German-style finessed intensity from Paul Cluver's low-yielding vines, grown on namesake ferricrete soils. Up on **11**.

Limited Release Gewürztraminer 🍱 📖 ★★★★ Rosepetal & Turkish Delight on uncloying semi-dry **12**, with clean waxy grip. Great fusion food partner ex Paul Cluver. **Pinot Grigio** ⊕ 🍱 📖 ★★ Pear-toned **12** barely there, brief. Ex Van Loveren. **Exclusive Selection Viognier** NEW 🍱 ★★★★ **11** is admirably tidy for the variety, peach & a hint of oak spice, tangy acidity. By Ken Forrester. **Moscato Light** ⊕ 🍱 📖 ★★ **12** a spicy, spritzy, sweet & low-alcohol charmer from Villiera. Discontinued: **NSA Rhine Riesling**.

White Blends

★★★★☆ **Allan Mullins White My Song** Clever, serious & lovely **12** blend of Reyneke (Stellenbosch) sauvignon & Cape Point Vineyards semillon. The former offers aromatic tropical zest, the latter adds citrus-toned breadth. Fresh, lively & elegant, with a tight, steely core beneath the suave, silky texture. Will develop.

★★★★☆ **DMZ White** 🍱 📖 **12** echoes viognier, roussanne, chenin blend (no chardonnay) of **11** in bigger, firmer style. Slightly riper dried fruit, spice features, too, but well offset by freshness, tangy dry conclusion Natural ferment in older oak. By DeMorgenzon.

★★★★ **Nitida Cellars Sauvignon Blanc-Semillon Reserve** ⊛ 🍴 🄯 Gooseberry & leafy-toned white Bordeaux blend, **12** has nervy elegance; fresh & focused. Portion oak fermented.

Cape White ☺ 🍴 ★★☆ Granadilla & peach tang on **NV** chenin, chardonnay mix from Wellington Wines.

NSA Organic Fluttering Butterfly White 🍴 ✿ 🄯 ★ By Stellar Winery, **13** unlingering Granny Smith apple flavour to drink soonest. **Longmarket Chardonnay-Viognier** 🄯 ★★ Uncomplicated everyday enjoyment from Spier. Lightly oaked **12** has lemon lift. **Longmarket Sauvignon Blanc-Semillon** 🄯 ★★ Waxy, developed **12** from Spier. Unwooded. **Longmarket Sauvignon Blanc-Chenin Blanc** 🍴 🄯 ★★☆ Tank sample zesty, spicy & dry Villiera **13** blend for everyday drinking. **Zesty White** ★★ Granadilla & guava life on citrusy dry, quaffing **NV** from Wellington Wines. **Natural White** NEW Not tasted. **Bianca Light** 🍴 ★★ **13** grapey off-dry, low-alcohol blend from Spier. **Zesty Sweet** 🄯 ★★ Tropical fruit on light white **NV** quick-sip by Bergsig. **Parlotones Push Me To The Floor** ⊛ 🍴 ★★★★ Aromatic, oxidative chenin-based 4-way blend by Wellington Wines, **10** shows body & complexity. Marzipan notes on spicy fragrance. Enjoy soon. **Chardonnay-Pinot Noir** ⊛ ✓ 🍴 ★★★★ Fresh & elegant **13** ex Haut Cabrière blushes discreetly, offers savoury flavours with sweet-sour edge, perfect for versatile food partnering. **Natural Sweet White** 🍴 ★★ Ex Spier **13** sweet colombar delight, low 9% alc. **Natural White** NEW 🍴 🄯 Not tasted. **Chenin Blanc-Pinotage** NEW 🍴 🄯 ★★★ Quirky chenin-led white blend, unwooded **13** from Simonsig is boldly fruity, oddly appealing. WO Stellenbosch.

Méthode Cap Classique Sparkling range

★★★★☆ **Exclusive Selection Pinot Noir Rosé NSA** ✓ 🄯 Simonsig's blush **12** is persistently dry, with dense, creamy texture. Refined but generously opulent, with delightful layers of baked berries & shortbread.

★★★★ **Blanc de Blancs Brut** ⊛ Voluptuous **NV** from Villiera, for those who enjoy generously styled MCC; dry but plenty flavour & richness delivered on wave of fresh creamy mousse.

★★★★ **Brut Natural** ⊛ Great charm in whistle-clean, delicate chardonnay **09** from Villiera. Bone-dry, yet a soft, refined edge. Persistent mousse carries pure-fruited citrus flavours. No added sulphur.

★★★★ **Krone Borealis Cuvée Brut** ⊛ From MCC specialist The House of Krone. **09** in style: bruised apple, creamy mousse, emphatic dryness. 55/45 chardonnay, pinot blend. As engaging as elegant **08**. **Ladybird Brut Méthode Cap Classique** NEW 🄯 ★★★ Cranberry & raspberry tang on **11** traditional-method sparkling from Laibach. Broad, leesy palate with red fruit typical of pinotage. Clean, dry end. **Brut Rosé** 🄯 ★★★ Delicately coloured harmonious **NV** Villiera blend toned by pinotage, with chardonnay & both pinots. Satisfying weight. **Krone Rosé Cuvée Brut** ★★★★ Perennial favourite from The House of Krone. **09** salmon-hued MCC bubbly's biscuit tones heighten the sippability of 60/40 pinot noir/chardonnay marriage. **Brut** ✓ 🄯 ★★★☆ Ever-popular, consistent **NV** MCC from chardonnay, pinot & pinotage ex Villiera offers delightfully dry verve & zippy lemon freshness. Discontinued: **Vintage Reserve Brut**.

Sparkling Wines

Spumante Rosé ★★★ Peach & strawberry sweetness in pretty, much-improved **NV** pink fizz. By Rooiberg Winery, as all these. **Spumante Brut** ★★ Uncomplicated dry **NV** celebratory bubbly with tropical overlay. **Organic Sauvignon Blanc Brut** ✿ 🄯 ★ **13** foamy dry party wine with quiet lemongrass tone. **Spumante Doux** ★★ Grapey & frothy **NV** pick-me-up.

1L Box range

Dry Red ★★ All-sorts **NV** for easy sipping. By Simonsvlei, as all these. **Off-Dry Rosé** ★★ Bright, juicy berry-fruited **NV** chenin with spice from pinotage. Serve chilled. **Crisp White** ★★ **NV** from chenin, dry, with ripe apple flavours. **Light White** ★ **NV** from chenin, dry, light in all departments. **Semi-Sweet** ★☆ Soft easy **NV** sipper from chenin.

2L Box range

Longmarket Merlot 🄯 ★★ Light plummy fruit on **12** quaffer. By Simonsvlei, like Cab-Merlot. **Longmarket Cabernet Sauvignon-Merlot** ★★ Ripe berry tones on easy **12** picnic companion. **Longmarket Chardonnay** 🄯 ★★★ **13** deliciously ripe yellow stonefruit, some vanilla from oak, slight sweetness for easy drinkability. By Robertson Winery, as for Pinot Grigio & Sauvignon. **Longmarket Pinot Grigio** 🄯 ★★★ **13**'s zesty lemon-lime flavour is perfect for seafood. **Longmarket Sauvignon Blanc** 🄯 ★★ Zippy **13** straightforward but pleasant grapefruit aromas & flavours.

3L Box range

Light Red ★★ Off-dry **NV** party starter, mainly shiraz, low ±9% alcohol. By Simonsvlei, as for all. **Dry Red** ★★ Soft, easy **NV** berry-flavoured sipper. **Light Rosé** ⓦ ★★ Low-alcohol light-berried **NV** from shiraz. **Light White** ★ Dry, low-alcohol **NV** al fresco tipple. **Crisp White** ★★ Softly dry **NV** from chenin, bright & zippy.

5L Box range

Dry Red ★★ Undemanding smooth & spicy **NV** quaffer. By Simonsvlei, as all these. **Blanc de Blanc** ★★ Lightish, friendly & dry **NV** from chenin. **Stein** ★★ Off-dry **NV** from chenin, light, with zingy apple taste. — Various tasters

■ **Workhorse (Marks & Spencer)** see Ken Forrester Wines
■ **Wyma Vineyards** see Cape Hutton
■ **Xaro** see Stellenrust
■ **Xenna** see Annex Kloof Wines
■ **Y** see Yonder Hill

Yardstick Wines   🍷

Location/map: Stellenbosch ▪ WO: Western Cape ▪ Est/1stB 2009 ▪ Tasting by appt ▪ Owner(s) Peter Tempelhoff, Charles Banks & Adam Mason ▪ Winemaker(s) Adam Mason ▪ Yardstick 800cs & Marvelous 6,000cs ▪ 50% red 50% white ▪ adam@marvelouswines.com, peter@marvelouswines.com ▪ www.yardstickwines.com ▪ marvelouswines.com ▪ S 33° 53' 22.8" E 018° 49' 8.3" ▪ **T +27 (0)82-924-3286 (Adam)/+27 (0)82-578-5320 (Peter)** ▪ F +27 (0)21-881-3372

Comic book names continue but the wines are anything but jokey, packing a punch worthy of a 'Ka-pow!' speech bubble! Mulderbosch winemaker Adam Mason and McGrath Collection chef Peter Tempelhoff continue to bolster their range of food-friendly wines from unique pockets of fruit found in cool climes like Agter Witzenberg at 900m above sea level.

Yardstick range

★★★★ **Pinot Noir**  Delicate yet sinewy **12** (★★★★★) a notch up on maiden **11**. Still powerful forest floor flavours & steadily tautening tannic grip. Lovely integration & fresh succulence. Mix of Elgin, Ceres fruit with carbonic maceration twist.

★★★★ **Chardonnay**  Fleshy ripe citrus sashays confidently on polished oak platform in **12**. Ticks all boxes: length, depth, breadth, rounded, approachable & crisply fresh. A delight.

Marvelous range

Kaboom!  ★★★★ Confident return for **12** preview of 4-way cab franc-led blend. Step up on last-tasted **10** (★★★★). Fynbos edge to Christmas cake ripeness. Genteel, with dry graphite mineral tail. **Shazam!**  ★★★★ Tangy plum, blackberry spice **12** preview of shiraz-led cinsaut, mourvèdre, viognier mix. Juicy, focused & firm. **Le Mullét** NEW ★★★ From chenin, its nectarine sweetness brushed away by fresh acidic lift on **13**. Rounded & rich, long balanced finish. **Ka-Pow!** ★★★★ Harmonious 6-way white blend, mainly chenin in **13** tank sample. Lively freshness but full & broad too. Crisp, dry & characterful. Textured & poised. Step up on 3-way **12** (★★★). — FM

Yonder Hill

Location: Somerset West ▪ Map: Helderberg ▪ WO: Western Cape/Stellenbosch ▪ Est 1989 ▪ 1stB 1993 ▪ Tasting & sales Mon-Fri 9–4 Sat (Oct-Mar) 10-2 ▪ Closed all pub hols ▪ Tour groups ▪ Gift shop ▪ Olives & olive oil tasting ▪ Owner(s) Naudé family ▪ Cellarmaster(s)/winemaker(s) Pieter Kruger (2013) ▪ Viticulturist(s) Francois Hanekom ▪ 14ha/10ha (cabs s/f, merlot, p verdot) ▪ 80t/20,000cs own label 95% red 5% white ▪ PO Box 914 Stellenbosch 7599 ▪ wines@yonderhill.co.za ▪ www.yonderhill.co.za ▪ S 34° 2' 22.5" E 018° 49' 40.2" ▪ **T +27 (0)21-855-1008** ▪ F +27 (0)21-855-1006

This small family farm lies on the lower slopes of the Helderberg, with views across False Bay. The speciality is the red-grape Bordeaux varieties, but they bring in sauvignon and shiraz for the good-value Y range. A replanting programme has already seen new vineyards coming into production – for new viticulturist Francois Hanekom to nurture, and for new winemaker Pieter Kruger to turn into wines resting in the underground barrel cellar.

Yonder Hill range

★★★★☆ **Merlot** Oak dominates infant **11** (★★★★) - but more elegant, less opulent than last-tasted **09**. It's nonetheless dense & deep fruited, with a tannic firmness & drying finish that time could well harmonise.

★★★★ **Inanda** 📖 **12** (★★★★) cab-based Bordeaux-style blend less powerful & sombre than last-tasted **09**. Pleasing aromas, but on the lean side, with fruit somewhat dwarfed by the grippy structure.

★★★★☆ **Nicola** Like **08**, **09** (★★★★) a cab-based blend. Fuller, more powerful & intensely fruit-rich than others in range, coping well with the slightly overdone, spicy all-new oak. Good length. Needs 5+ years.

Y range

> **Merlot** ☺ 📖 ★★★ Ripe, cheerful, juicy **13** is easy & warmly engaging, with a vivifying jolt of acidity & a nice grip. These all WO W Cape. **Shiraz** ☺ 📖 ★★★ Spicy-fruity, bright charm on **13** tasted ex tank (as all the range). Lightweight fruit nicely uncluttered by any oak influence. **Sauvignon Blanc** ☺ 📖 ★★★ Forwardly fruity **13** happily combines grassiness & ripe tropical notes in easygoing bundle. — TJ

■ **ZAHarmonie Wine Cellar** *see* Snowfield Boutique Winery

■ **Zalze** *see* Kleine Zalze Wines

Zanddrift Vineyards

Location/WO: Paarl ▪ Map: Paarl & Wellington ▪ Est 1995 ▪ 1stB 2006 ▪ Tasting & sales Mon-Fri 9-1 & 2-5 ▪ Function venue ▪ Owner(s) Windsharp Trading 23, Koh Seow Chuan (Singapore) ▪ Winemaker(s)/vineyard manager(s) Christo Jacobs ▪ 8.5ha (cab, shiraz) ▪ PO Box 1302 Suider-Paarl 7624 ▪ zanddrift@telkomsa.net ▪ http://zanddrift.webs.com/ ▪ S 33° 45' 39.20" E 018° 59' 11.41" ▪ **T +27 (0)21-863-2076/+27 (0)82-256-5006** ▪ F +27 (0)86-530-1892

Zanddrift Vineyards is a Singapore-owned boutique winery near Paarl. Its limited area under vine – less than 9 ha – affords vineyard manager and winemaker Christo Jacobs the opportunity to continually try new techniques to boost quality. The wines are bottled as Chapel Cellar, a nod to the chapel-like visitor locale.

Chapel Cellar range

Cabernet Sauvignon Await next. **Shiraz** ⓧ 📖 ★★★ **07** high-toned red fruit, zesty acidity. — CvZ

Zandvliet Wine Estate & Thoroughbred Stud

Location: Ashton ▪ Map/WO: Robertson ▪ Est 1867 ▪ 1stB 1975 ▪ Tasting & sales Mon-Fri 9–5 Sat 10-2 ▪ Closed Easter Fri/Sun, Dec 25/26 & Jan 1 ▪ Tour groups ▪ Private tastings presented by cellarmaster/winemaker in Zandvliet House R55pp by appt only ▪ BYO picnic ▪ Owner(s) Paul & Dan de Wet ▪ Cellarmaster(s) Paul de Wet (1971) ▪ Winemaker(s) Jacques Cilliers (Dec 2011) ▪ Viticulturist(s) Dan de Wet (1993) ▪ 830ha/148ha (cab, shiraz, chard, cbard, sauv) ▪ 1,134t/90,000cs own label 47% red 49% white 5% rosé + 4,000cs for clients ▪ Export brands: Enon, Cogmanskloof ▪ Ranges for clients: Cogmanskloof Cape Muscat, Rijckholt (Netherlands); Villa San Giovanni ▪ PO Box 36 Ashton 6715 ▪ info@zandvliet.co.za ▪ www.zandvliet.co.za ▪ S 33° 50' 50.7" E 020° 2' 13.7" ▪ **T +27 (0)23-615-1146** ▪ F +27 (0)23-615-1327

Wine and horses – who could ask for more? Not the de Wets, who are passionately involved with both on their family farm in Robertson. Dan looks after the vineyards and the horses while brother Paul has been joined in the cellar by Jacques Cilliers, now hitting his stride after his second vintage at the estate. New labels have been designed for popular 'My Best Friend' range and the premium range of Hill of Enon is looking 'very promising'.

Zandvliet Estate range

★★★★ **Kalkveld Chardonnay** ⓧ 100% new French oak sets this apart from standard bottling. **10** restrained & savoury, some earthy notes.

Kalkveld 'Hill of Enon' Shiraz Await new. **Kalkveld Shiraz** ★★★★ Cherry & plum, leathery complexity on French-oaked **08**, from vineyard on chalky soils. **Shiraz** ⓧ ★★ **09** for fans of full-bore, super-ripe reds, warmth from high alcohol better with food than solo. **Chardonnay** ⓧ 📖 🎨 ★★★ Appealing **12** has sweet vanilla charm from brief sojourn in oak, undemanding flavours. **VLW Cape Vintage Shiraz** 🎨 ★★★★ Port-style winter warmer takes step up **11** with rum-&-raisin/cherry cola melange, peppery tannins, integrated spirit.

Le Bistro range

Cabernet Sauvignon ⏺ 🍴 📖 ★★★ Plum & prune aromas on ripe, accessible **10**, light bodied for any-time enjoyment. **Chardonnay Unwooded** ⏺ 🍴 ★★★ Creamy **12** ripe & easy sipper with peach & pear flavours. **Sauvignon Blanc** ⏺ 🍴 📖 ★★ Picked early, **12** very dry & bracing. **Crème** 🍴 📖 ★★ Bone-dry **13**, softly floral blend colombard (80%) & sauvignon.

My Best Friend range

Red 🍴 📖 ★★★ Improved **10** mainly cab, dollop shiraz: leafy overlay on plum & blackcurrant, good savoury tannins, smidgen sugar well integrated. **Shiraz Rosé** 🍴 📖 ★★ As in **12**, **13** ultra-dry & lightish; previous were slightly sweet. **Semi-Sweet** ⏺ 🍴 📖 ★★ From chenin, **12** soft curry companion. **White** 🍴 ★★ Delicate lemon & floral appeal in chill-and-enjoy **13**. Mostly chardonnay, chenin & two others. — DC,MW

- ▪ **Zandwijk** *see* Kleine Draken
- ▪ **Zaràfa** *see* Mountain River Wines
- ▪ **Z-Collection** *see* Zevenwacht
- ▪ **Zebra Collection** *see* Rooiberg Winery
- ▪ **Zee** *see* Anura Vineyards
- ▪ **Zellerhof** *see* Huguenot Wine Farmers
- ▪ **Zenith** *see* Kumala

Zevenwacht

Location: Kuils River ▪ Map/WO: Stellenbosch ▪ Est 1980 ▪ 1stB 1983 ▪ Tasting & sales Mon-Fri 8.30–5 Sat/Sun 9.30–5 ▪ Fee R35 incl glass ▪ Closed Dec 25 ▪ Cellar tours by appt ▪ Restaurant (see Restaurants section) ▪ Picnics in summer ▪ Facilities for children ▪ Gift shop ▪ Conferences ▪ Weddings/banqueting ▪ Walking & mountain biking trails ▪ 4x4 trail by appt ▪ Conservation area ▪ Mangwanani spa ▪ 4-star country inn (see Accommodation section) ▪ Owner(s) Harold Johnson ▪ Winemaker(s) Jacques Viljoen (May 2005) ▪ Viticulturist(s) Eduard van den Berg (Jan 2001) ▪ 473ha/100ha (cabs s/f, grenache, merlot, mourv, ptage, primitivo, shiraz, chard, chenin, gewürz, muscat de F, rouss, sauv, sem, viog) ▪ 657t/100,000cs own label 48% red 48% white 4% rosé ▪ BWI, IPW ▪ PO Box 387 Kuils River 7579 ▪ info@zevenwacht.co.za ▪ www.zevenwacht.co.za ▪ S 33° 55' 46.0" E 018° 43' 38.2" ▪ **T +27 (0)21-900-5700** ▪ F +27 (0)21-903-3373

Family-owned Zevenwacht outside Kuils River has developed into a multifaceted entertainment and conference venue with panoramic views of Table Mountain and the ocean. Wine, is however their core business, with growing export markets, especially China. Winemaker Jacques Viljoen is more upbeat than ever, with the mentorship of experienced Chris Keet, and the potential of their range of terroirs and quality wines. Some new wooded whites have been released, and there would have been more grenache for their classy Rhône red had the baboons not had a quarter of the crop for breakfast!

Flagship range

★★★★ **Merlot** ✓ 📖 **10** exudes varietal appeal, with rich chocolate, berry & mint flavours. Balanced & well groomed, with underlying seriousness. Good potential over 3-5 years.

Cabernet Sauvignon ✓ 📖 ★★★★ **11** has a supple structure with complementary cassis & cedar. Balanced & approachable, enjoy over the next 4-6 years. **Syrah** ✓ ★★★★ A step up on **08** (★★★★), **09** is full bodied with ample savoury & spicy fruit, clothed in dry, amenable tannins. Splashes of mourvèdre & grenache add interest. Ageworthy. **Chardonnay** NEW ✓ 🍴 📖 ★★★★ **12** rich pear & lime in tangy fusion. Medium bodied, with integrated oak & fresh farewell. Vivacious food partner. **Chenin Blanc** 🍴 📖 ★★★★ **12** focused apple & almond flavours, threaded with acidity, from 31 year old vines. Oak a tad dominant, time should harmonise. **Sauvignon Blanc** 🍴 📖 ★★★ Fresh-cut grass & crunchy apple on easy-drinking **13**. **Semillon Straw Wine** Next awaited. Discontinued: **Primitivo**.

Z-Collection

★★★★ **CMC** 📖 **10** elegant, cab-led Bordeaux blend with merlot & cab franc, has a good core of cassis & spice, interwoven with fine-grained tannins. Shows inherent balance & ageing potential.

★★★★ **Gewürztraminer** 📖 Unusual wood-fermented/aged **12**, a shade off **11** (★★★★★). Dry, still exudes varietal perfume & spice, with creamy lees breadth absorbing some of the flavour & charm.

★★★★ **360° Sauvignon Blanc** ✓ 🍴 📖 **12** (★★★★★) surpasses leaner **11**. Quivers with pungent fruit intensity & freshness, from lofty sea-facing vines. 10% barrel aged portion & 6 months lees-ageing add richness. Lovely balance & verve, with long flinty farewell.

SGM ⓦ ★★★★ Mainly shiraz, with grenache & mourvèdre. **10** raises the bar on **09** (★★★★). Lithe & balanced, with good structure, from focused vineyard & cellar treatment. Tempting now, but will age.

The Tin Mine Collection

★★★★ **Red** ✓ 🍴 ⓦ **11** mainly shiraz with grenache & mourvèdre. Riper, full bodied & without 2010's primitivo. Flavoursome & balanced now, but enough backbone for 3-5 years enjoyment.

★★★★ **White** ✓ 🍴 ⓦ **12** harmonious, aromatic quartet, mostly chardonnay & chenin, with viognier & roussanne. A mix of oak adds subtle richness. Mouthfilling & creamy, lifted by fresh acidity.

7even range

Pinotage ⊕ 🍴 ⓦ ★★ Confected **11** shows dark cherry fruit, oak-derived coffee. **Rood** 🍴 ⓦ ★★☆ Amiable **11** shiraz-dominated 4-way blend is ripe & spicy with a smoky nuance. **Rosé** 🍴 ⓦ ★★☆ **13** is a fresh, off-dry pink, mostly merlot & zinfandel. **Sauvignon Blanc** NEW 🍴 ⓦ ★★ Light & quaffable **13** has a gentle tropical & grassy tone. **Bouquet** 🍴 ⓦ ★★☆ Viognier-led **13** has floral charm in crisp, off-dry style. Discontinued: **Blanc**. — MW

Zidela Wines

Location: Stellenbosch ▪ WO: Western Cape ▪ Est 2001 ▪ 1stB 2002 ▪ Closed to public ▪ Owner(s) Danie Kritzinger, Herman Nell, Jaco Kritzinger & Erik Kritzinger ▪ 60% red 30% white 10% rosé ▪ 8,000,000 litres for clients ▪ PO Box 3021 Matieland 7602 ▪ info@zidelawines.co.za ▪ www.zidelawines.co.za ▪ **T +27 (0)21-880-2936** ▪ F +27 (0)21-880-2937

Jaco Kritzinger, co-owner of Stellenbosch wine trade and export company Zidela, reports further growth in sales of bottled wine to the Low Countries, a small initial export to China, discussions with contacts in Australia, and intentions to target the US.

Sumerton range NEW

Cabernet Sauvignon-Pinotage 🍴 ⓦ ★★☆ BBQ mate **12** drinks easily thanks to pinotage's ripe strawberry flavours, none of cab's sometimes sticky tannins. **Sauvignon Blanc** 🍴 ⓦ ★★☆ Peardrop aromas & tastes on **13** chilled-out summer sipper.

Mooiberg range NEW

Cabernet Sauvignon ⓦ ★★☆ Walnut & olive whiffs on fruity **12**, firm tannins give grip & food compatibility. **Sauvignon Blanc** ⓦ ★★☆ Attractive musk sweet overtone to **13**'s khaki bush & cut grass, zesty acidity & satisfying vinosity for laid-back enjoyment.

Suikerbosch range

Reserve Shiraz Await next, like **Reserve Chardonnay**. **Shiraz-Merlot** 🍴 ⓦ ★★ Strong tannins, tart cranberry finish on **12** near-equal blend. **Rosé** 🍴 ⓦ ★★☆ Attractive rosepetal nuance on off-dry & flavoursome **13**, for chilled relaxation. **Chenin Blanc** 🍴 ⓦ ★★☆ Back-in-production **13** spicy lemongrass aromas & lowish alcohol for Asian-style lunches. **Golden Muscat** 🍴 ★★ **12** perfumed, gently sweet muscat d'Alexandrie, to be enjoyed soon.

Zidela range

Cabernet Sauvignon ★★ Unoaked **13**'s fruity mouthful caged by cab's firm tannins. **Merlot** Await next, as for **Pinotage, Shiraz, Bouquet Blanc** & **Sauvignon Blanc. Chenin Blanc** 🍴 ⓦ ★★★ Forthright white peach aromas & flavours, **13** a brisk but balanced safari companion. — CvZ

Zoetendal Wines   🍷 🏛 📷

Location/WO: Elim ▪ Map: Southern Cape ▪ Est 2002 ▪ 1stB 2004 ▪ Tasting, sales & cellar tours by appt only ▪ Closed Easter Fri/Sun, Dec 25 & Jan 1 ▪ Conservation area ▪ Draaihoek self-catering guesthouse ▪ Owner(s) Johan & Elizan de Kock ▪ Cellarmaster(s)/winemaker(s)/viticulturist(s) Johan de Kock ▪ 790ha/8.5ha (shiraz, sauv) ▪ 39t/4,000cs own label 15% red 85% white ▪ BWI, IPW ▪ PO Box 22 Elim 7284 ▪ info@zoetendalwines.co.za ▪ www.zoetendalwines.co.za ▪ S 34° 36' 1.0" E 019° 47' 20.9" ▪ **T +27 (0)28-482-1717** ▪ F +27 (0)28-482-1720

It's been a decade since sheep and grain farmer turned winegrower Johan de Kock, the pioneer of the Elim ward, bottled the first wines under the Zoetendal label. Now Johan (co-owner with wife Elizan) intends downscaling production for the boutique brand, and winetastings and cellar tours will be by appointment. He will, however, sell his grapes to other producers.

Shiraz ⓘ ★★★☆ Sweet fruit, hint char on firm **09**, commendably dry & savoury. **Sauvignon Blanc** ✓ 🖩 🍷 ★★★★ Reminding how well Elim sauvignons age in bottle, gooseberry & pear toned **12** shows restrained minerality, fine fruit/acid balance; interesting salty tang. — WB,GdB

Zonnebloem

Location: Stellenbosch ▪ WO: Stellenbosch/Coastal/Western Cape ▪ Est 1893 ▪ Wine sales at Die Bergkelder Wine Centre ▪ Owner(s) Distell ▪ Cellarmaster(s) Deon Boshoff (Feb 2010) ▪ Winemaker(s) Bonny van Niekerk (reds, Oct 2007) & Elize Coetzee (whites, Jun 2010), with Bradley van Niekerk (whites) & Natasha Williams (whites, Aug 2008) ▪ Viticulturist(s) Annelie Viljoen (Jun 2008) ▪ (cab, merlot, shiraz, chard, sauv, sem) ▪ 9,000t/±440,000cs own label 59% red 41% white ▪ ISO 9002, Fairtrade ▪ PO Box 184 Stellenbosch 7599 ▪ info@zonnebloem.co.za ▪ www.zonnebloem.co.za ▪ **T +27 (0)21-809-7000** ▪ F +27 (0)21-886-4879

One of South Africa's most enduring and best-loved wine brands continues its upwards curve of quality under the leadership of Deon Boshoff. The young cellarmaster believes a key reason for Zonnebloem's success is time - how long it has taken the Distell-owned label to build relationships with its growers (many now into the fourth generation of supplying grapes) added to the measured, no-rush approach in the cellar. 'Our attention to detail pays off in the long run.'

Limited Editions

★★★★ **Pinotage** 🍷 Very lovely **10** is a welcome return after absence. Perfumed nose, moist plumcake flavours, chewy pliable tannins. Plenty of elegance & polish. From Stellenbosch fruit, all-new oak.

★★★★ **Sauvignon Blanc** 🍷 **12** now showing nice development, good for another year. Coastal WO.

★★★★ **Semillon** 🍷 Pungent pine needles, peppers & limes on the nose of elegant, unwooded **13**. From a single vineyard in Malmesbury, racy citrus acidity is balanced by creamy intensity. Plenty more to come here.

★★★★ **Sauvignon Blanc-Semillon** 🍷 Delicious drinking on **12** with pungent gooseberries & hay plus some waxy notes. Showing some development but should be more to come as layered, complex finish hints. Coastal WO.

Cabernet Sauvignon ⓘ ★★★★ 100% new oak for this top-line version. Dark chocolate & spiced blackcurrant nose on **09** with whiffs of eucalyptus & herbs. Well-managed tannins, good length. **Shiraz** ⓘ ★★★★ **09** sweet concentrated fruit with some meaty/hammy notes, more intense than **08** (★★★★). Dark chocolate, plums, damsons, currants all lifted by well-integrated acidity & all-new oak. Lots of drinking pleasure. **Chenin Blanc** Occasional release.

Zonnebloem range

> **Chardonnay** ☺ 🖩 🍷 ★★★ Nicely balanced mouthful of lemons & limes on **12**. Fragrant & fruity, with a soft kiss of wood & an almond blossom finish. Coastal WO. **Sauvignon Blanc** ☺ 🖩 🍷 ★★★ Pungent cat's pee aromas on **13** yielding to fresh & fruity flavours of citrus & tropical fruit. Thoroughly enjoyable. WO W Cape, like next. **Blanc de Blanc** ☺ 🖩 🍷 ★★★ Summer in a glass! Almost-dry **13** offers crisp, fresh gooseberries & grapefruit & pleasing lowish alcohol for all-day quaffing.

Cabernet Sauvignon 🍷 ★★★ **11** lacks some of the character of previous. Black fruit, dry finish. **Merlot** 🍷 ★★★ **11** missing exuberance of last release; some black fruit, soft tannins. **Pinotage** 🍷 ★★★ Spicy cherries & dark chocolate on **11** make for pleasant everyday quaffing. Fairly short & dry. **Shiraz** 🍷 ★★★★ Well-made, everyday crowd pleaser **11** has savoury nose, perfume & dried meat. Cheery chocolate twist in tail. **Shiraz-Mourvèdre-Viognier** ⓘ 🍷 ★★★★ Casserole aromas of dried & spiced meats, **10** broadens to blackcurrant sweetness with lively acidity & pleasing length. **Lauréat** ⓘ 🍷 ★★★★ Enduring label switches to Bordeaux blend plus 10% shiraz in **10**. Sweet plum clafoutis aromas with some spiced cherries. Soft tannins surround black berries with pleasing grip on finish. — CM

■ **Zonneweelde** *see Slanghoek Winery*

Zonquasdrift Estates

Location: Riebeek-Kasteel ▪ Map: Tulbagh ▪ WO: Swartland ▪ Est 2001 ▪ 1stB 2009 ▪ Tasting Mon-Fri by appt ▪ Closed all pub hols ▪ Sales at Riebeek Cellars ▪ Owner(s) Alexander & Antoinette Mettenheimer ▪ Cellarmaster(s) Zakkie Bester (Riebeek Cellars) ▪ Winemaker(s) Eric Saayman (Riebeek Cellars) ▪ Viticulturist(s) Gustav Andrag (Sep 2005) ▪ 360ha/53ha (mourv, shiraz, chard, chenin, cbard, grenache blanc, muscadel) ▪ 600t/100cs own label

100% white ▪ HACCP, IPW ▪ PO Box 7 Riebeek-Kasteel 7307 ▪ info@zonquasdrift.co.za ▪ S 33° 20' 35.00" E 018° 58' 32.00" ▪ **T +27 (0)22-448-1078/+27 (0)82-896-4430** ▪ F +27 (0)86-606-2049

When Alexander and Antoinette Mettenheimer bought Zonquasdrift farm in the Swartland in 2001, they realised the value of the chenin blanc vines dating back to 1962. A precious 100 cases are now made at nearby Riebeek Cellars, with tastings and tours by appointment and sales at Riebeek.

Chenin Blanc ✪ 🔲 ★★★☆ Single-vineyard handled with care & allowed full (unoaked) expression: preview **11** blossom perfume, stonefruit & lime, lovely intensity, weight & texture. A label to watch. — CE, CvZ

Zorgvliet Wines

Location/map: Stellenbosch ▪ WO: Banghoek ▪ Est/1stB 2000 ▪ Tasting & sales Mon-Fri 9–5 Sat/Sun 10–5 pub hols 10–4 ▪ Closed Good Fri & Dec 25 ▪ Fee R20pp, waived on purchase ▪ Cellar tours by appt ▪ Zorgvliet Picnic Sep-Apr ▪ Facilities for children ▪ Tour groups ▪ Gifts ▪ Conferences ▪ Walks/hikes ▪ Zorgvliet Country Hotel (17 rooms) ▪ Owner(s) Van der Merwe family ▪ Winemaker(s) Neil Moorhouse (Jan 2003), with Ruben Adams ▪ Viticulturist(s) Hannes Jansen van Vuuren ▪ 131ha/46ha (cabs s/f, merlot, p verdot, pinot, shiraz, tannat, chard, chenin, sauv, sem, viog) ▪ 250t/25,000cs own label 50% red 40% white 7% rosé 3% MCC + 200t for clients ▪ PO Box 1595 Stellenbosch 7599 ▪ winecellar@zorgvliet.com ▪ www.zorgvlietwines.com ▪ S 33° 54' 41.7" E 018° 56' 32.0" ▪ **T +27 (0)21-885-1399** ▪ F +27 (0)21-885-1318

Now into his second decade at the winemaking helm of this family-owned winery in Stellenbosch's stunningly scenic Banhoek Valley, Neil Moorhouse is bullish about the differences that larger-format oak barrels installed prior to harvest have made on the flagship white and red blends - and indeed all the wines. 'The flagships are the ultimate representation of Banhoek terroir,' he says, and is something he and co-owner Mac van der Merwe are committed to. Ensuring that things stay fresh, new UK importers Boutinot have assisted in launching the new Enigma range, modelled on a kiwi concept of pink Sauvignon.

Zorgvliet range

★★★★ **Cabernet Sauvignon** 🔲 Soft, velvety berry compote & spice on **09**. Fine piquant tannin from 20 months in French oak, just 38% new. Leaner than last-tasted **08**, but lithe & supple.

★★★★ **Cabernet Franc** 🔲 **12** preview has intense graphite & turned earth character with cocoa & fynbos scents. Maintains tone set by last-made **09**. Concentrated & focused, with long fruited tail.

★★★★☆ **Richelle** 🔲 Red flagship from cab (50%), cab franc, merlot, petit verdot. Complex hedgerow & bramble fruit to **09**. Smooth & refined with genteel, harmonious use of oak (22 month French). Tannins are fine & dry. Structured, textured mouthful with a long, rich aftertaste.

★★★★ **Single Vineyard Sauvignon Blanc** 🔲 Gets 'Single Vineyard' prefix for **13** preview, generously tropical with kiwi & fig but flint & lime zest add tension. Structured & taut yet rich & rounded too.

★★★★ **Simoné** 🔲 White flagship, semillon leads sauvignon in flinty **11** oaked blend. White pepper vies with peach & lemon curd vibrance. Lively yet rounded & full to end. Not as expressive as bold **10** (★★★★★). **Petit Verdot** 🔲 ★★★★ Spicy red cherry appeal on **10**. Deeply concentrated & long, French oak (none new) well integrated. No **09**. **Blanc de Blancs** ★★★★ Méthode cap classique sparkling from chardonnay. **10** leapfrogs not-yet-ready **09**. Crisp 'oystershell' & limestone/yeast tang. **Natural Sweet Sauvignon Blanc** ✪ ★★★ Muted richness on **10**. Brûlée & oatmeal over grapefruit marmalade. Variety's acidity noticeable on clean, dry finish.

Silver Myn range

Sauvignon Blanc ☺ 🔲 🚫 ★★★ Tangy granadilla & lime cordial vibrance to **13**. Dab semillon (4%) adds interest & texture. Dry flinty finish.

Argentum 🔲 ★★★ Intense black fruit & clove spice on **11** preview of five-way blend of merlot, cab, cab franc, petit verdot & malbec. **Cabernet Franc Rosé** Next awaited. Discontinued: **Cabernet Sauvignon, Merlot**.

Enigma by Zorgvliet NEW

Sauvignon Blanc Rosé ☺ 🔲 🚫 ★★★ Cheerful raspberry & grapefruit tang to **13** quaffer. Refreshing, crisp & pleasantly pink (from dash cab franc) yet dry on the finish. — FM

David Biggs

David has been writing about wine for more than 30 years, since attending two Gilbeys courses in 1979, before the establishment of the Cape Wine Academy. He qualified officially as a wine judge in 2000. He has been a judge in every Veritas competition since its inception, is a founder member of the Wine-of-the-Month tasting panel, and regularly judges the Muscadel Championship and the Terroir Wine Awards. David was invited to be a judge at the Vinitaly international wine competition in Verona in 2012. In 2011 he was declared a 'Living Legend' in the Cape wine industry by the South African National Wine Show Association. He is a regular contributor to Good Taste magazine and runs the wine website www.davidbiggsonline.com.

Winifred Bowman

A qualified physiotherapist and biomedical scientist, and holder of a PhD in Education, Winnie developed an interest in wine during her student days at Stellenbosch University and later through frequent travels to international winegrowing areas. She is a Cape Wine Master, and judges wine regularly at local and international competitions. She also presents corporate and private wine tastings, teaches and writes about wine and food. Wine is Winnie's passion and she enjoys every moment talking about or tasting it.

David Clarke

Starting out in fine wine retail in his native Melbourne, David moved to the UK and spent most of a two-year visa working at the Harrod's wine department in Knightsbridge. Returning to Australia (with South African wife in tow), he made the move into restaurants where he worked and qualified as a sommelier. During the next five years, David worked mostly in degustation-only fine dining restaurants. Since 2011 he has been an adviser to the retail and hospitality industries. Before arriving in South Africa in 2013, he was the executive officer for Sommeliers Australia (the sommeliers' association of Australia). David was part of the selection panel for the Nederburg Auction 2013 and is currently sommelier at Burrata, Cape Town.

Greg de Bruyn

Greg is an architect by profession, practicing in and around the Cape wine industry. He allowed wine to beguile him into leaving Johannesburg in 1999 to seek his future amongst the vines, first to establish and run a wine estate, and later as a specialist consultant in winery construction. He qualified as a wine judge in 1996 and a Cape Wine Master in 2000. Greg has sat on many of the major South African competitions and assessment panels, and

has contributed to several publications and websites.

Christian Eedes

Christian Eedes is a freelance winewriter and founder of Whatidranklastnight.co.za. A Stellenbosch University graduate with an Honours degree in Philosophy, he has also completed a wine evaluation course and a small-scale winemaking programme run by that institution's Department of Viticulture & Oenology. He has judged at the Trophy Wine Show since 2007 and sits on numerous other competition panels.

Michael Fridjhon

The Louis Roederer Awards International Wine Columnist for 2012, Michael is South Africa's leading wine industry authority and the country's most widely published winewriter. A former advisor to the Minister of Agriculture and past chairman of the South African Wine Industry Trust, he is currently visiting professor of Wine Business at the University of Cape Town's Graduate School of Business. An internationally recognised wine judge, he is chair of, among others, the Trophy Wine Show and the Five Nations Challenge (2012) in Sydney. He has authored or contributed to over 35 books, and has been a taster for this guide since the early 1980s.

Higgo Jacobs

Before, during and after studying and qualifying in Law at Stellenbosch University, Higgo spent nine years on either side of the cellar door: first making wine, then marketing and exporting it. Today, certified with the Court of Master Sommeliers, he is general secretary and founding member of the South African Sommelier Association (SASA), co-ordinator of the Nederburg Auction selection tastings and tasting director for Top 100 SA Wines. He consults within the hospitality industry, is a senior judge at the International Wine Challenge (IWC), and tastes for local publications and competitions.

Tim James

Tim has been writing about wine long enough for him to realise that it's no longer just a hobby. With a home-base on www.grape.co.za, he contributes to various local and international publications, including a column for the Mail & Guardian and frequent articles in the London-based World of Fine Wine. Tim is a Cape Wine Master and has twice won the SA Wine Writers Annual Award. He declines to participate in large competitive tastings but has been a taster (and associate editor) for this guide for many years. His book on SA wine appeared in 2013.

Angela Lloyd

Writing, lecturing, broadcasting and making wine are some of Angela's undertakings during her 30

years' professional involvement with wine. Even so, it is still just one interest in her life though closely allied to another, cooking. When not tied to her laptop, Angela loves the outdoors: she grows vegetables, fruit and indigenous flowers in her and her husband's garden, while her daily walks with Syrah, their black Labrador, keep them both fit. Reading, cinema, theatre, music, rugby and cricket are other interests crammed into a busy life.

Cathy Marston

Cathy hails from Yorkshire, UK, and after completing her degree in English at Cambridge University, she joined Adnams Wine Merchants, passing all the Wine & Spirit Education Trust exams, culminating in Diploma. She came to South Africa in 2001, and opened and ran The Nose Restaurant & Wine Bar, selling it after seven successful years. Cathy now concentrates on tasting, writing for local and international publications, and wine education. She is an associate of the Institute of Wines & Spirits and is the Approved Programme Provider in Africa for the Wine & Spirit Education Trust.

Fiona McDonald

Chronicling the dramatic changes that have taken place in the South African wine landscape for the past two decades has been not only a privilege but a pleasure for trained journalist Fiona. Editor of Wine magazine for eight years and a freelance wine writer for the past five, she got into wine 'by accident'. It started in the 1990s by helping a colleague organise The Mercury Wine Week for a number of years while working as a reporter and night news editor on the KwaZulu-Natal newspaper. Today Fiona serves as a judge and jury president at various international wine competitions, among them the International Wine Challenge, International Wine & Spirit Competition, Decanter World Wine Awards and Concours Mondial, and edits Cheers and Whisky magazines.

Gregory Mutambe

Gregory's voyage into wine and food began at one of the handful of wineries in his home country, Zimbabwe, where he worked as a cellarhand. He then trained and worked in Johannesburg and Cape Town, and currently is the sommelier at 12 Apostles Hotel & Spa, overseeing an award-winning wine list. Gregory has judged for the South African Airways and Nederburg Auction selections, and is an associate judge for this year's Best Value Wine Guide. He has emerged as regional winner in the Jeunes Sommeliers Competition Bailliage du Cap and finalist in the Bollinger Exceptional Wine Service Award, and is enrolled in the Cape Wine Master programme.

Ingrid Motteux

Love of wine and a growing aversion to hospital basements led Ingrid to give up a successful career in nuclear medicine to work first as a vineyard labourer, then as a lecturer and wine writer. Her wine interest took formal shape during more than a decade abroad, where she attained the UK WSET Diploma and, soon after, the Cape WSET Wine Judge certification. An associate of the Institute of Wines & Spirits, Ingrid judges for the International Wine Challenge and runs an independent wine consultancy, Winewise, advising some of Africa's top game lodges.

Jörg Pfützner

German-born Jörg is an internationally trained and certified sommelier living in South Africa. Having worked at top restaurants in Hamburg and Cape Town, he started his own businesses: The Riesling Club, whose members have access to top European bottlings; and Fine Wine Events, which celebrates wine with specifically themed fine-wine and food tastings and festivals. Since completing his postgraduate diploma in Wine Business Management, Jörg continues to present and lecture locally and abroad, as well as manage a group of private cellars.

James Pietersen

As a Stellenbosch University student, James helped organise his law professor's cellar. 'In exchange, he opened a few great bottles and I fell in love with wine.' James has since pursued his passion, first as Vineyard Connection's wine buyer, consultant to Singita Game Lodge and lately as the head sommelier for Belthazar in Cape Town, also responsible for the wine program at Balducci's restaurant. He judges for the Trophy Wine Show and several other competitions.

Christine Rudman

Christine's love affair with wine might have started late, in her 30s, when she joined Stellenbosch Farmers' Winery after a Johannesburg FMCG marketing career, but she rapidly made up for lost time. Enrolling in the Cape Wine Academy, she achieved her Cape Wine Masters qualification in 1986; left SFW to run the CWA for seven years; and has since been occupied with consultancy work, wine judging, lecturing and writing. She has written A Guide to the Winelands of the Cape, travels widely, tastes on international panels and looks forward to working with wine for years to come.

Dave Swingler

Co-author of One Hundred Wines - An Insiders' Guide to South African Wine and drinks contributor to Posh Nosh, Dave has been blending his love of wine and words for this guide since the 1990s. A long-standing member of the International Wine & Food Society, Dave was director of wine for the IWFS

Cape Town Festival, is the South African consultant for its Annual Vintage Chart and current chair of the Cape Town branch. Dave has over the years consulted to restaurants, game lodges and convention centres, taught wine courses and contributed to various radio, print and other media.

Cathy van Zyl

Cathy started her wine journey on a bicycle: she asked her husband to ride South Africa's famed Argus Cycle Tour with her; he accepted if she attended a wine course with him. She has since notched up 15 more Cycle Tours and gone on to pass the Master of Wine examination. Cathy judges locally and internationally, has recently taken on the position of chair of the Institute of Masters of Wine's education committee, occasionally contributes to wine journals and web sites around the world, but spends most of her wine-time as associate editor of this guide.

Meryl Weaver

The Cape winelands lured Meryl away from her legal career and, more than 20 years later, she remains firmly under their spell. She has conducted wine presentations abroad on SA wine on behalf of Wines of South Africa, lectures for the Cape Wine Academy, tastes and writes about wine, and judges for various wine competitions and magazines. Meryl qualified as a Cape Wine Master and has graduated with distinction from the Wine Judging Academy. She ensures, however, that the vinous learning curve continues by visiting wine-producing countries, combining some of her other passions, food and travel.

Here we summarise the wines featured in the A–Z section, with their ratings, sorted first by wine style, in alphabetical order, and then by producer or brand. New wines in **bolder type**. **NS** = no star; **NT** = not tasted; **NR** = tasted but not rated; **D** = discontinued. Where wineries produce more than one version of a particular style, the number of versions is indicated in brackets after the name. A number of wines were tasted as pre-bottling barrel or tank samples, and therefore ratings are provisional. Refer to the A–Z for details.

Barbera

★★★★ Fairview, Idiom, Merwida

★★★☆ Altydgedacht, Hofstraat ★★★ Bovlei **NT** Hidden Valley

Biodynamic

★★★★★ Reyneke (Chenin blanc wooded, dry)

★★★★☆ Reyneke (4) (Shiraz/syrah, Red blends, Cape Bordeaux, Red blends, shiraz/syrah-based, Sauvignon blanc wooded)

★★★★ Woolworths (2) (Pinotage, Red blends, shiraz/syrah-based), Weltevrede (2) (Sparkling, Méthode cap classique, white, dry, Sparkling, Méthode cap classique, white, dry), Reyneke (Pinotage)

★★★☆ African Terroir (Shiraz/syrah, Fairtrade), Wedderwill (Sauvignon blanc unwooded) ★★★ Weltevrede (2) (Merlot, Muscadel, white, fortified), African Terroir (2) (Cabernet sauvignon, Merlot, Fairtrade), Wedderwill (Red blends, shiraz/syrah-based) ★★☆ Wedderwill (White blends, unwooded, dry) **D** Woolworths (Chenin blanc wooded, dry)

Blanc de noir

★★★★ **Aaldering**, Lynx, Mellasat ★★★ Aan de Doorns, Altydgedacht, Arra, Blaauwklippen, Boschendal, Buitenverwachting, **Deux Frères**, **Flagstone**, Groot Constantia, Lovane, Peter Falke, Woolworths ★★☆ Klawer, Landskroon, Nieuwedrift, Swartland ★★ Asara, Boucheron, De Redley, Landskroon, **Lithos**, **Signal Hill** ★☆ Van Loveren (2) ★ **Tanagra NT** Lovane, Maison, Mount Abora, Tempel **NR** Lemberg

Brandy

★★★★★ Boplaas, KWV Brandies (2), Oude Meester, Van Ryn (3)

★★★★☆ Boplaas (2), Klipdrift, KWV Brandies, Oude Meester (2), Oude Molen, Van Ryn (2)

★★★★ Avontuur, Backsberg (2), Barrydale, De Compagnie (2), **Flight of the Fish Eagle**, Imoya, Kaapzicht, KWV Brandies, Laborie, Ladismith, Mons Ruber, Nederburg, Oude Molen, Richelieu, Uitkyk, Upland

★★★☆ Backsberg, Barrydale (2), Boplaas, Collison's, De Compagnie, Klipdrift (2), KWV Brandies, Oude Meester, Oude Molen (2), Tokara, Upland (Organic), Viceroy ★★★ Chateau VO Extra Fine, Grundheim, Kingna Distillery, Limosin, Louiesenhof (2), Olof Bergh Solera, Van Loveren, Blaauwklippen (2), **D'Aria**, Mons Ruber, Richelieu

Bukettraube

★★★☆ Cederberg ★★ Nuweland, Swartland ★☆ Seven Sisters **D** Simonsvlei

Cabernet franc

★★★★★ Raats, Warwick

★★★★☆ BLANKbottle, Buitenverwachting, Nelson, Rainbow's End, Raka, **Stellenrust**

★★★★ Alluvia, Anthonij Rupert, Avontuur, CK Wines, Doolhof, Druk My Niet, Hillcrest, Knorhoek, Lovane, Mont du Toit, Ormonde, Raats, Rainbow's End, Val de Vie, Zorgvliet

★★★☆ Benguela Cove, Hermanuspietersfontein, Lynx, Môreson, Oldenburg, Philip Jordaan, Spookfontein, Woolworths ★★★ Bushmanspad, Hannay, Idiom, Signal Hill, Whalehaven **NT** Audacia, High Constantia, KWV, La Petite Ferme, Leopard Frog, Longridge, Maison de Teijger (2), My Wyn, Ridgeback, Vergenoegd **NR** Claime d'Or **D** Mooiplaas, Plaisir

Cabernet sauvignon

★★★★★ Boekenhoutskloof, Cederberg, Delaire, **Ernie Els**, Neil Ellis, Stark-Condé

★★★★☆ Anthonij Rupert, Bilton, Dalla Cia, Darling Cellars, De Trafford, Delaire, Dombeya, Edgebaston, Eikendal, Flagstone, Fleur du Cap, Glen Carlou, Glenelly, Graham Beck, Grangehurst, Guardian Peak, **Hartenberg**, House of Mandela, Kleine Zalze, Knorhoek (2), Le Riche (2), Louis, Meerlust, Nederburg, Restless River, Rickety Bridge, Rudera (2), **Rust en Vrede**, Rustenberg, Saxenburg, Springfield,

Springfontein, Teddy Hall, Thelema (2), Vergelegen (2), **Warwick**, Waterford, Webersburg

★★★★ Akkerdraai, Alluvia, Annandale, Arra (2), Bartinney, **Bayede!**, Belfield, Bergsig, Bilton, Bon Courage, Bon Terroir, Botanica, Brenaissance, Buitenverwachting, Cape Chamonix, Cape Hutton, Cederberg, Chateau Naudé, Conviction, De Meye, De Wetshof, Delheim, Devonvale, Dornier, Druk My Niet, Edgebaston, Eerste Hoop, Ernie Els, Fairview, Glen Carlou, Goedverwacht, Graceland, Graham Beck, Groenland, Groot Constantia, Guardian Peak, Hartenberg, Hoopenburg, Jordan, Journey's End, Kaapzicht, Kanonkop, Katbakkies, Klawer, Kleine Zalze, Kloovenburg, KWV, L'Avenir, La Motte, La Petite Ferme, Landskroon, Lanzerac, Le Bonheur, Le Riche, Linton Park, **M'hudi**, Marianne, MC Square, Meinert, Miravel, MolenVliet, Mont du Toit, Mooiplaas, Morgenhof, Namaqua, **Napier**, Nederburg, Neil Ellis, Niel Joubert, Nitida, Noble Hill, Nuy, **Oldenburg** (2), Org de Rac (Organic), Overgaauw, **Perdeberg**, Rainbow's End, Raka, Remhoogte, Rickety Bridge, Ridgeback, Rust en Vrede, Savanha, South Hill, Stark-Condé, Stellekaya, Sterhuis, Super Single Vineyards, The Butcher Shop, The Township Winery, The Winery of Good Hope (2), Tokara, Topiary, Usana, Vergenoegd (2), Vruchtbaar, Warwick, Wellington Winery, Windmeul, **Woolworths** (4), Zorgvliet

★★★☆ Agterplaas, Alto, Altydgedacht, **Amani**, Amares, AntHill, Anthonij Rupert, Arra, Asara, Avontuur, Backsberg, Beau Joubert, Bernheim, Blaauwklippen, Boschheim (2), Boschkloof, Bosman, Bovlei, Brampton, Carisbrooke, Catch Of The Day, Chennells, **Claime d'Or**, Conradie, Constantia de Tulbagh, **De Bos** (Fairtrade), **De Breede** (Organic), Devon Hill, Devonair (2), DeWaal, Dormershire (2), Durbanville Hills, Eaglevlei, **Esau**, Excelsior, Feiteiras, Fort Simon, Glenelly, Goede Hoop, Groenland, Hathersage, Haut Espoir, Hildenbrand, Holden Manz, Hout Bay, Jacques Smit, Journey's End, Juno, Kyburg, La Kavayan, Laborie, Lyngrove, Lynx, MAN Family, McGregor, Middelvlei, Mitre's Edge, Mont Rochelle, **Morgenster**, Mount Rozier, Mountain Ridge, Nederburg, Neil Ellis Meyer-Näkel, Nuweland, Onderkloof, Opstal, **Ormonde**, Osbloed, Plaisir, Porcupine Ridge, Post House, Rietvallei, Robertson, Rooiberg, Ross Gower, Simonsig, Simonsvlei, Slaley, **Snowfield**, Spier, Spookfontein, Springfield, Stellenrust, Stonewall, SylvanVale, **Teubes** (2), The Berrio, The Butcher Shop, **The Goose**, The Rhino,

Trajan, **Tread Lightly**, Uitkyk, Ultra Liquors, **Val du Charron**, Van Loveren, Villiera, Vriesenhof, Waterkloof, **Waterstone** (2), Welbedacht, Wellington Winery, Woolworths (2), Zevenwacht, Zonnebloem ★★★ Abbottshill, African Terroir (2) (Biodynamic, Fairtrade), Allesverloren, Annex Kloof, Anura, Ayama, Beau Joubert, Bellingham, Bergsig, Boland (2), Bon Courage, Bonview, Boplaas, Botha, Bovlei, Bushmanspad, **Cape Dreams**, De Meye, Desert Rose, Die Mas, Diemersfontein, Doolhof, Douglas Green, Du Toitskloof, **Earthbound** (Organic, Fairtrade), Elgin Vintners, Fairview, **False Bay**, Fernskloof, Fleur du Cap, Galleon, Grande Provence, Helderberg, Het Vlock Casteel, Hoopenburg, Hunneyball, Jacobsdal, Jason's Hill, Joubert-Tradauw, Kaapzicht, Kanu, Klein Parys, Kleine Draken (Kosher), Kleine Zalze, Koopmanskloof, Kranskop, **La Chaumiere**, Landskroon, Le Manoir de Brendel, Leopard's Leap, Lindhorst, Linton Park (3), Lovane, Maastricht, MAN Family, Meerendal, Merwida, Mon Rêve, Montagu Wine Cellar, Mooi Bly, Mostertsdrift, Napier, **Nederburg** (2), Obikwa, Olifantsberg, Orange River, **Ormonde** (2), Painted Wolf, Perdeberg, Retief, Riebeek, Rietvallei, Schalkenbosch, Seven Sisters, **Sijnn**, Simonsvlei, Slowine, Southern Sky, Stellenbosch Hills, Stellendrift, Swartland, Thandi (Fairtrade), The Hills, Upland (Organic), Vredenheim, Waterstone, Windfall, Women in Wine, Woolworths, Zandvliet ★★★☆ African Pride, African Terroir (2) (Organic), Alvi's Drift, Arniston Bay, Audacia, Bayede!, Bonnievale, Boplaas, Brandvlei, Cape Dreams, Clairvaux, Cloof, Darling Cellars, De Doorns, De Krans, De Wet, Desert Rose, Drostdy-Hof, Du Preez, Durbanville Hills, **Eagle's Cliff**, Eikehof, Excelsior, Fat Bastard, Franschhoek Cellar, Goedvertrouw, **Group CDV**, **House of Mandela** (2), Klein Roosboom, KWV, La Petite Provence, Ladismith, Long Mountain, Lutzville, Malanot, Manley, Montpellier, Moordenaarskop, Neethlingshof, New Beginnings, Niel Joubert, Org de Rac (Organic), **Overhex** Phizante Kraal, Place in the Sun (Fairtrade), Pulpit Rock, Riebeek, Roodezandt, Rooiberg, Ruitersvlei, Sauvignon.com, Simonsvlei, Slanghoek, **Snowfield**, Somersbosch, Somerset Wines, Spier, Steenberg, Stellar (2) (Organic, Fairtrade), Stellenzicht, Tanagra, Tulbagh Winery (2), **Ultra Liquors**, United Nations, uniWines, Van Loveren, **Vrede**, Vukani, Walker Bay Vineyards, Wandsbeck, Waverley Hills (Organic), Welvanpas, William Everson, Woolworths (2) (Organic, Fairtrade), **Zidela**, Zonnebloem ★★ Barrydale, Bergwater, Blomendahl, Blue Crane, Calitzdorp, Cranefields, Goudini, Imbuko,

Kleinfontein, Landzicht, Louisvale, Lovane, Mount Vernon, Mountain River, Namaqua, Org de Rac (Organic), Oude Compagnies Post, Pulpit Rock, Quest, **Robertson** (4), Southern Sky, Stoumann's, Van Loveren (Fairtrade), Vriesenhof , Waterstone, Waverley Hills (Organic), Welmoed, Wineways, Zidela ★★ Ashton, Langverwacht, Long Mountain, Nuy, Southern Sky, Vrede, **Waterstone** (3), Wineways (2) ★ Jonkheer **NS** TTT Cellar, Withoek **NT** African Pride, African Terroir, AlexKia, Benguela Cove, Bernheim, Blomendahl, Bonfoi, Breëland, Callender, Camberley, Cape Rock, Citrusdal, Clovelly, Crows Nest, De Villiers, Domaine Brahms, Du Preez, DuVon, Escapades, Govert, Havana Hills, Herold, High Constantia, Hildenbrand, Hofstraat, KWV, L'Olivier, La Bri, La Petite Vigne, Laibach, Landzicht, Le Pommier, Libby's Pride, Lovane, Maison de Teijger (3), Marklew, Maske, Melkboomsdrift, Mimosa, Miravel, Mont Rochelle, Moordenaarskop, Mountain River, Nederburg, Nietvoorbij, Rico Suter, Rosendal, Saam, Savanha, Spier, Stark-Condé, Stellendrift (2), Stone Ridge, Swartland, Tulbagh Winery, Ultra Liquors (2), Valley Vineyards, Viljoensdrift, Vondeling, **William Everson**, Windmeul, Zanddrift **NR** Fairvalley (Fairtrade), Seal Breeze **D** African Terroir (Organic), Bloemendal, Botha, Calais, David Frost, Galleon, Group CDV, Hornbill , Klein Constantia, Laibach, Ormonde, Perdeberg, Roodezandt, Simonsvlei, Wineways, Zorgvliet

Cape Riesling

★★★ Theuniskraal ★★ Van Loveren **NT** Calais **D** Goudini

Carignan

★★★☆ **Blackwater**, Fairview ★★★ Bovlei, Koopmanskloof, Withington **NT** BLANKbottle **D** BLANKbottle

Chardonnay unwooded

★★★★ **Bayede!**, De Wetshof, Glen Carlou, GlenWood, Groote Post, Warwick, Woolworths

★★★★ Bouchard Finlayson, **Cape Chamonix**, Constantia Uitsig, De Wetshof, Diemersdal, Doolhof, Eikendal, Fairview, False Bay, Glenelly, Kloovenburg, Louisvale, Meerendal, **Môreson**, Springfield, Sterhuis, Withington, Woolworths (2)
★★★ AlexKia, Arniston Bay, Bellpost, Brampton, Brandvlei, **Clouds**, Dalla Cia, De Wetshof, Delheim, Eagle's Cliff, Eaglevlei, Hildenbrand, **Jean Daneel**, Jordan, Kleine Zalze, La Petite Ferme, Landskroon,

Langverwacht, Lutzville, Middelvlei, Mont Rochelle, Mostertsdrift, Neethlingshof, **Org de Rac** (Organic), **Plettenvale**, Rietvallei, Seven Springs , Stellar (Organic, Fairtrade), Stellenzicht, The Butcher Shop, The Winery of Good Hope, Van Zylshof, Vriesenhof , **Waterstone**, Women in Wine, Zonnebloem ★★★ African Terroir (Organic), Ayama, Backsberg (Kosher), Blomendahl, Bon Courage, Boplaas, Bovlei, Burgershof, Cape Dreams, Cloof, Cloverfield, **De Bos** (Fairtrade), De Krans, De Meye, Die Mas, Koopmanskloof (Fairtrade), Leeuwenberg, Leopard's Leap, McGregor, New Beginnings, Ormonde, Riebeek, Rooiberg, Savanha, Schalkenbosch, Somersbosch, Spier, The Rhino, The Wine Fusion, Wellington Winery, Woolworths, Zandvliet ★★ Ashton, Calais, Graham Beck, **House of Mandela** (Fairtrade), La Couronne, **Nuweland**, Welbedacht ★★ Group CDV (3), Jonkheer, Ladismith ★ Org de Rac (Organic), Waterstone, Woolworths **NT** African Pride, African Terroir, Eerste Hoop, Goudini, Highgate, Kanu, Karusa, Libby's Pride, Malanot, **Place in the Sun** (Fairtrade), Re'Mogo, Stone Ridge, Tulbagh Winery, United Nations, Valley Vineyards (2), Walker Bay Vineyards **NR** Franschhoek Cellar, Long Mountain **D** Asara, Elgin Ridge (Organic), Groot Parys (Organic), Rustenberg, uniWines

Chardonnay wooded

★★★★★ Cape Chamonix, Hamilton Russell, Newton Johnson, **Richard Kershaw**

★★★★☆ Ataraxia, Bartinney, Boschendal, Bouchard Finlayson (2), Buitenverwachting, Cape Chamonix, Cape Point, Constantia Uitsig, Creation, Crystallum, De Wetshof (2), Edgebaston, Eikendal, Elgin Vintners, Fleur du Cap, Glen Carlou, **GlenWood** (2), Groot Constantia, Hartenberg, Haskell, Iona, Jordan (2), Julien Schaal, Koelfontein, La Motte, Lanzerac, Lourensford, **Môreson**, Mulderbosch, Nederburg, Neil Ellis, Oak Valley, Paul Cluver, Quoin Rock, Restless River, Rupert & Rothschild, Rustenberg, Saxenburg, Springfield, Sterhuis, The Winery of Good Hope, Tokara, Uva Mira, Vins d'Orrance, Warwick, Waterford, Woolworths

★★★★ Almenkerk, Anura, Babylonstoren, Badsberg, **Boschendal**, Bouchard Finlayson, **Corder**, Crystallum, De Wetshof, Delaire, Diemersdal, **Domaine Coutelier**, Dombeya, Ernst Gouws, Glen Carlou, Glenelly, Grande Provence, Groote Post, Hartenberg, Haut Espoir, Havana Hills, **Hermit on the Hill**, Hoopenburg, House of Mandela, JH Meyer, Jordan, Joubert-Tradauw, Journey's End (2), Kleine Zalze, Kloovenburg, KWV (2), La Petite Ferme,

Lanzerac, Le Riche, Longridge, Meerlust, Meinert, Migliarina, Mont Rochelle (2), Muratie, Napier, Newton Johnson, Ormonde, Paul Cluver, Plaisir, Rustenberg, Savanha, Springfontein, Stellenrust, Sumaridge, Thelema (3), Tierhoek, Tokara, Vergelegen, Vondeling, Vriesenhof , Waterford, Windmeul, Woolworths (3), Yardstick, Zandvliet

★★★☆ Aaldering, Amani, Anthonij Rupert, Bergsig, Boland, Bon Courage, Brenaissance, Brothers, Callender, Chateau Naudé, Delheim, Domaine des Dieux, Doolhof, Durbanville Hills, Eerste Hoop, Fairview, Fernskloof (Organic), Flagstone, Freedom Hill, Goedverwacht, **Goudini**, Hildenbrand, **Holden Manz**, Journey's End, Kanu, Kloovenburg, Kranskop, KWV, La Bri, La Chaumiere, La Vierge, Laborie (2), Le Bonheur, Linton Park, **Lothian**, **Louiesenhof**, Louisvale (2), Lourensford, Lyngrove, Maison, Mellasat, Merwida, Mimosa, **Môreson**, **Mountain River**, Mulderbosch, Nabygelegen, Nederburg, Niel Joubert, Nitida, Noble Hill, Oldenburg, Onderkloof , Ormonde, Osbloed, Overgaauw, Passages, Pulpit Rock, Rhebokskloof, Rickety Bridge, Rietvallei, Rooiberg, Scrucap, Seven Springs , Signal Gun, Simonsig (2), Slaley, Spier, Stanford Hills, Stellenrust, Stonewall, Tokara, Uitkyk, **Ultra Liquors**, **Val du Charron**, Veenwouden, Vergelegen, Welbedacht, Winters Drift, Woolworths (Organic), **Zevenwacht** ★★★ African Terroir, Alkmaar, Alvi's Drift, Anthonij Rupert, Anura, Ashton, Avontuur, Backsberg, **Baleia Bay**, Boland, Boschendal, Boschkloof , Cape Classics, Claime d'Or, Clos Malverne, **Credo**, Darling Cellars, De Wet, Douglas Green, Drostdy-Hof, Elgin Heights, Excelsior, Fairvalley (Fairtrade), Fat Bastard, Goedvertrouw, Graham Beck, Hillock, Jonkheer, Klawer, KWV, Ladera, Linton Park, Lord's, Louiesenhof, Lourensford, MAN Family, Meerendal, Morgenhof, Mount Rozier, Mount Vernon, Nederburg, Newstead, Niel Joubert, Nuy, Olsen, Orange River, Overhex, Rhebokskloof, Riebeek, Robertson (3), Simonsvlei, Steenberg, Thandi, Two Oceans, Van Loveren, Viljoensdrift, Welmoed, Weltevrede, Windmeul, **Withington**, Woolworths (3) (Organic), Zandvliet ★★★ **Asara**, Calitzdorp, Cloverfield, Du Preez, Du Toitskloof , Durbanville Hills, Eikehof, Fleur du Cap, Goedverwacht, Hathersage, Hoopenburg, Klein Parys, Kumala, Montpellier, Obikwa, Org de Rac (Organic), Pulpit Rock, Slanghoek, Swartland, Thembi & Co, United Nations, Van Zylshof, Waterstone (2), Weltevrede, Whalehaven, **Woolworths** ★★ African Terroir (Organic), Barrydale, Bonnievale, De Zoete Inval, Kingsriver, Kleine Draken (Kosher), Walker Bay

Vineyards ★★ African Terroir, Long Mountain, Montagu Wine & Spirits, Van Loveren (2) ★ Four Fields **NT** Bonfoi, Buffalo Creek, Citrusdal, Clovelly, Crows Nest, DeMorgenzon, Felicité, Fort Simon, Four Paws, Galleon, Goede Hoop, Groot Parys (Organic), Hill & Dale, Imbuko, Jason's Hill, Lazanou (Organic), Lorraine, Lutzville, Marklew, MC Square, Mooi Bly, Mountain Oaks (Organic), Nelson, Nietvoorbij, Olifantsberg, **Robertson** (2), Rosendal, Springfontein, **Stellenbosch University**, Stoumann's, Sumsaré, Thembi & Co, Veenwouden, Vruchtbaar, Waterkloof, Weltevrede, Welvanpas, William Everson, Wolfkloof, Zidela **NR** Bellingham **D** Asara, Bloemendal, Conradie, De Wetshof, Kaapzicht, L'Avenir, Lord's, Rijk's (2), Simonsvlei, Thandi

Chenin blanc off-dry/semi-sweet (w & u/w)

★★★★☆ DewaldtHeyns, Ken Forrester, Knorhoek, Rijk's, Rudera

★★★★ Diemersfontein, Kanu, Ken Forrester, Lutzville, Saam, Spier, Woolworths (2)

★★★☆ Franschhoek Cellar, **Groot Parys** (Organic), Katbakkies, Knorhoek, **Perdeberg**, Simonsig, Trajan, Wildekrans ★★★ Botha, Du Toitskloof , Flagstone, Landskroon (2), Nederburg (2), Robertson, Virgin Earth, **Yardstick** ★★★ Boschendal, Breëland, Drostdy-Hof, Goudini, Kanu, Ken Forrester, **Laborie** (Light & low-alcohol), Lutzville, Nelson, Nuweland, Robertson, Simonsvlei, Waterstone ★★ Bon Courage, Bottelary, Cloverfield, Obikwa ★★ Bonnievale (2) (Perlé, Light & low-alcohol), Brandvlei, Hillock, Landzicht, Leopard's Leap, **Seven Sisters** (Light & low-alcohol), **Tulbagh Winery**, Waterstone, Woolworths (3) (Light & low-alcohol), Zandvliet **NT** Robertson, Summerhill, Valley Vineyards **D** Bottelary, Goudini, Leopard's Leap, MAN Family, Simonsvlei (3), Zidela

Chenin blanc unwooded dry

★★★★☆ **Bayede!**, Old Vines

★★★★ Annex Kloof, Babylon's Peak, Babylonstoren, Beaumont, Cederberg, **De Bos** (Fairtrade), Maison, Mooiplaas, Raats, Teddy Hall

★★★☆ Alvi's Drift, Arra, Barton, Chateau Naudé, De Meye, Fairview, Groote Post, Hazendal, Ken Forrester, Kleine Zalze, La Chataigne, Laibach, Le Pommier, Mooi Bly, Napier, Neethlingshof, Nieuwedrift, Scrucap, Simonsvlei, Stellekaya, The Winery of Good Hope, Zonquasdrift ★★★ Ayama, Backsberg, Bellingham, Blaauwklippen, Boland, Bovlei, Cloof,

Darling Cellars, David Frost Signature, DeWaal, **Eagle's Cliff**, **Earthbound** (Organic, Fairtrade), Ernie Els, Fairview, False Bay, Fish Hoek, Groenland, Halala, Hawksmoor, Kaapzicht, Klein Parys, Kleine Zalze, Koopmanskloof (Fairtrade), KWV, La Petite Ferme, Landskroon, Leeuwenkuil, Leopard's Leap, Lula, Lyngrove, Mellasat, Nordic, Olsen, Ormonde (2), Perdeberg, Phizante Kraal, Pulpit Rock, Rickety Bridge, Simonsig, Slowine, Somerbosch, Spier, Stoumann's, Swartland, The Grape Grinder, Tread Lightly, Ultra Liquors, United Nations, uniWines, Van Zylshof, Villiera, Welbedacht, Wellington Winery, Woolworths (2), Zidela ★★★ African Pride, Badsberg, Bergsig (2), Blomendahl, Bottelary, Brandvlei, Croydon, De Krans, **Diemersfontein**, Dornier, Douglas Green (2), Eagle's Cliff, Fairvalley (Fairtrade), False Bay, Glenview, Group CDV, **Hoopenburg**, Klein Parys, Kleine Zalze, **Knorhoek**, Long Mountain, MAN Family, McGregor, Montagu Wine & Spirits, Monterosso, Mountain River, New Beginnings, Niel Joubert, **Nuy**, **Onderkloof** , Orange River, **Overhex** (2), Rhebokskloof, Riebeek, Roodezandt, Rooiberg, Skilpadvlei, Slanghoek, Somerset Wines, The Rhino, Vaughan Johnson, Waterstone, **Wellington Winery**, Welmoed, Windmeul, Wineways, Woolworths, Zidela ★★ Aan de Doorns, Ashton, Botha, Calais, De Wet, Klawer, Koopmanskloof (Fairtrade), Langverwacht, Montagu Wine Cellar, Montpellier, Nuy, Robert Stanford, Savanha, Stellenbosch Hills, The Hills, Tulbagh Winery (2), Van Loveren (2) ★★ African Terroir, Bayede!, **House of Mandela** (Fairtrade), Ladismith, Long Mountain, Woolworths (3) ★ Woolworths (2) (Light & low-alcohol) ★ Drostdy-Hof **NT** Cape Dreams, Catch Of The Day, Citrusdal, Delheim, Diners Club Bartho Eksteen , Domaine Brahms, Dornier, Dragonridge, DuVon, Freedom Hill, Groot Parys (2) (Organic), Jacques Smit, Jason's Hill, L'Avenir, **Luddite**, Maske, Oude Denneboom, Ruitersvlei, Saam, Sizanani, Stellar (Organic), **Swartland**, The Fledge, The Mason's, Thembi & Co (2), TTT Cellar, United Nations, Valley Vineyards (3), Versailles, Vruchtbaar, Waboomsrivier, Westbridge, Zonnebloem **D** Ernst Gouws, Group CDV (2), Môreson, Napier, Nederburg, Seven Sisters, Simonsvlei, Stettyn, Ultra Liquors, uniWines, Vaughan Johnson, Veenwouden

Chenin blanc wooded, dry

★★★★★ **Alheit**, Beaumont, Botanica, DeMorgenzon, Jean Daneel, **Kleine Zalze**, **Mullineux**, **Opstal**, Reyneke (Biodynamic), Sadie, Stellenrust

★★★★☆ Alheit, Cederberg, David, Delaire, Donkiesbaai, KWV (2), L'Avenir, Lammershoek, Raats, Remhoogte, Rijk's, Sadie, Saltaré, Spice Route, Stone Ridge, Teddy Hall, The Winery of Good Hope (2)

★★★★ AA Badenhorst, Allée Bleue, Andy Mitchell, Anthonij Rupert, Bellingham, Bosman (Fairtrade), **Catherine Marshall**, **Credo**, De Trafford, Doran, Eenzaamheid, Fort Simon, Graham Beck, Groot Parys (2) (Organic), **Hawksmoor**, Jordan, Ken Forrester, Kleine Zalze, Lazanou (Organic), **Maison**, Morgenhof, Mount Abora, **Mulderbosch** (4), Nederburg, Old Vines, Oldenburg, Perdeberg, Post House, Remhoogte, **Reverie**, Rickety Bridge, Ridgeback, Rijk's, Rudera, Signal Hill, Spioenkop, Springfontein (2), Stellenrust, Sterhuis, **The Liberator** (2), The Winery of Good Hope, Tierhoek, Wildehurst, Windmeul

★★★☆ **Andy Mitchell**, Anura, Arniston Bay, Avondale (Organic), Beau Joubert, **Beaumont**, Bellevue, Black Pearl, **BLANKbottle**, Boland, **Bryan MacRobert**, Crios Bríde, **DeMorgenzon**, Fleur du Cap, Graham Beck, L'Avenir, Longridge, Meerhof, Mooiplaas, Mullineux, Nabygelegen, Paardebosch, Painted Wolf (2), Raka, Riebeek, Rudera, **Saltaré**, Star Hill, Stark-Condé, Super Single Vineyards, Teddy Hall, Vruchtbaar, Welbedacht, **Welmoed**, Zevenwacht ★★★ Agterplaas, Anthonij Rupert, Cape Classics, **Darling Cellars**, Druk My Niet, Jacaranda, M'hudi, MAN Family, Rietvallei, **Uitkyk**, **Val de Vie**, Waterford, Waterkloof, Woolworths ★★☆ Koelenhof, Kumala, **Usana**, Vukani ★★ Hawksmoor **NT** Aeternitas, Barry Gould, Domaine Brahms, Hildenbrand, Jean Daneel, Lateganskop, Leopard Frog, Linton Park, Malanot, Môreson, Orange River, Robert Stanford, **Sumsaré**, Swartland, Villiera **NR** Chateau Naudé, Dagbreek **D** BLANKbottle, De Trafford, Hazendal, Lord's, Woolworths

Cinsaut

★★★★☆ Sadie, **Waterkloof**

★★★★ Stellenrust

★★★☆ BLANKbottle, Osbloed ★★ Landskroon **NT** Howard Booysen **D** BLANKbottle

Colombard

★★★★ Micu Narunsky

★★★ Aan de Doorns ★★★☆ Langverwacht, McGregor, Montagu Wine Cellar, Nuy, Orange River, Rooiberg ★★ Bon Courage, Goedwacht, Van Loveren ★★ Hartswater (2) ★ Stellar (Organic, Fairtrade), Woolworths **D** Nuy

Fairtrade

★★★★ Nederburg (Red blends, shiraz/syrah-based), **The Winery of Good Hope** (Shiraz/syrah), Bosman (2) (Red blends, shiraz/syrah-based, White blends, wooded, dry), Stellar (Vin de paille, Organic), De Bos (Chenin blanc unwooded dry), Bosman (Chenin blanc wooded, dry), **The Township Winery** (Merlot)

★★★★ Nederburg (Sauvignon blanc unwooded), Fairview (Pinotage), Thandi (2) (Shiraz/syrah, Sauvignon blanc unwooded), De Bos (2) (Cabernet sauvignon, Sauvignon blanc unwooded), Place in the Sun (Sauvignon blanc unwooded), African Terroir (Shiraz/syrah, Biodynamic), **The Township Winery** (Shiraz/syrah) ★★★ Stellar (2) (White blends, unwooded, dry, Chardonnay unwooded, Organic), Nederburg (Pinotage), Thandi (Cabernet sauvignon), Stellenrust (White blends, off-dry/semi-sweet (w & u/w)), Thandi (White blends, unwooded, dry), De Bos (Pinot noir), **Earthbound** (2) (Cabernet sauvignon, Chenin blanc unwooded dry, Organic), Fairvalley (3) (Pinotage, Chardonnay wooded, Sauvignon blanc unwooded), Koopmanskloof (2) (Shiraz/syrah, Chenin blanc unwooded dry), African Terroir (2) (Cabernet sauvignon, Merlot, Biodynamic), **The Township Winery** (Pinotage) ★★★ Woolworths (2) (Cabernet sauvignon, Sauvignon blanc unwooded, Organic), Stellar (10) (Cabernet sauvignon, Pinotage, Shiraz/syrah, Sauvignon blanc unwooded, White blends, off-dry/semi-sweet (w & u/w), Cabernet sauvignon, Pinotage, Pinotage, White blends, off-dry/semi-sweet (w & u/w), White blends, off-dry/semi-sweet (w & u/w), Organic), Thandi (2) (Rosé dry, Sparkling, Non-MCC, rosé, dry), Stellenrust (Rosé off-dry/semi-sweet), De Bos (Chardonnay unwooded), **Earthbound** (3) (Pinot noir, Pinotage, Sauvignon blanc unwooded, Organic), Fairvalley (Chenin blanc unwooded dry), Savanha (2) (Red blends, shiraz/syrah-based, White blends, unwooded, dry), United Nations (Shiraz/syrah), Koopmanskloof (Chardonnay unwooded), uniWines (2) (Merlot, Sauvignon blanc unwooded), Place in the Sun (3) (Cabernet sauvignon, Merlot, Shiraz/syrah), **The Township Winery** (Viognier) ★★ Van Loveren (Cabernet sauvignon), Stellar (6) (Merlot, Rosé dry, Merlot, Shiraz/syrah, Rosé dry, Rosé off-dry/semi-sweet, Organic), Stellenrust (Red blends, with pinotage), **House of Mandela** (2) (Pinotage, Chardonnay unwooded), De Bos (Merlot), United Nations (Sauvignon blanc unwooded), Koopmanskloof (Chenin blanc unwooded dry),

uniWines (Pinotage) ★★ **House of Mandela** (Chenin blanc unwooded dry) ★ Woolworths (Colombard, Organic), Stellar (Colombard) **NT** Overhex (3) (Shiraz/syrah, Rosé dry, Pinot gris/grigio), **Place in the Sun** (Chardonnay unwooded) **NR** Fairvalley (Cabernet sauvignon)

Gamay noir

★★★ Asara (Nouveau), Kleine Zalze **D** Altydgedacht

Gewürztraminer

★★★★ Nederburg, Neethlingshof, Paul Cluver, Zevenwacht

★★★★ Simonsig, Woolworths ★★★ Altydgedacht, Bergsig, Bovlei, Delheim, Villiera ★★★ Bon Courage ★★ Montpellier **NT** Weltevrede **D** Buitenverwachting, Group CDV

Grappa-Styles

★★★★☆ Dalla Cia, Wilderer Private Distillery

★★★★ Dalla Cia (2), Wilderer Private Distillery (2)

★★★★ Dalla Cia, Upland (Organic), **Wilderer Private Distillery** ★★★ Klein Constantia

Grenache blanc

★★★★★ AA Badenhorst, The Foundry

★★★★ Signal Hill

NT KWV

Grenache noir

★★★★☆ David, Neil Ellis, **Sadie**, Tierhoek, Vriesenhof

★★★★ Hermit on the Hill, **Momento**, Woolworths

★★★★ Diemersdal, Lynx, **Saronsberg** ★★★ Nuweland, **Waverley Hills** ★★★ Franki's, Hermit on the Hill **NT** Esau, Nederburg, Signal Hill **D** BLANKbottle

Hanepoot fortified

★★★★☆ Goudini, Muratie, Signal Hill

★★★★ Aan de Doorns, Boplaas, Calitzdorp, Constantia Uitsig, Ladismith, Nuweland, Opstal

★★★★ Badsberg, Calitzdorp, De Wet, Du Preez, Eaglevlei, Goudini, Mon Rêve, Orange River, Slanghoek, SoetKaroo, Swartland ★★★ Boplaas, Clairvaux, Die Mas, Du Toitskloof , Kaapzicht, Koelenhof , Stoumann's, Villiersdorp, Vriesenhof

★★☆ Grande Provence ★★ Bergwater, Landzicht, Tulbagh Winery **NT** Bovlei, Klawer, Waboomsrivier **NR** TTT Cellar **D** Simonsvlei

Hanepoot unfortified

★★☆ Overhex, uniWines (Perlé), **Wellington Winery** ★★ Cape Classics (Light & low-alcohol), Riebeek (Perlé, Light & low-alcohol), **Swartland** (Light & low-alcohol), uniWines ★☆ Zidela

Hárslevelü

★★★★ Lemberg

Icewine

★★☆ Kaapzicht

Jerepigo red

★★★★☆ Blaauwklippen

★★★★ Badsberg, Laborie

★★★☆ De Krans, Feiteiras, **Nuweland**, Slanghoek, Solms-Delta, Swartland ★★★ Grundheim, Orange River, Simonsvlei, Stonewall, uniWines ★★☆ Botha, **Grundheim**, Hartswater, Montagu Wine & Spirits (2) ★★ Die Mas ★ Stoumann's **NT** Camberley, Landzicht **NR** Waverley Hills

Jerepigo white

★★★★☆ Signal Hill

★★★★ Botha, Calitzdorp

★★★☆ Backsberg, Feiteiras, Namaqua, Niel Joubert, Opstal, Orange River, Riebeek, uniWines ★★★ Die Mas, Montagu Wine & Spirits, Sedgwick's Old Brown, Wellington Winery ★★☆ Brandvlei, Chateau Naudé ★★ Hartswater, Ship, Swartland **NT** Lateganskop **NR** Nuweland

Kosher

★★★ Backsberg (Sparkling, Méthode cap classique, white, dry), Kleine Draken (Cabernet sauvignon) ★★☆ Backsberg (3) (Merlot, Pinotage, Chardonnay unwooded), Kleine Draken (2) (Merlot, Natural Sweet, red, Light & low-alcohol) ★★ Backsberg (Sweet red, Sacramental), Kleine Draken (5) (Red blends, Cape Bordeaux, Chardonnay wooded, Sauvignon blanc unwooded, Natural Sweet, white, Sacramental wine, Sacramental, Light & low-alcohol) ★☆ Kleine Draken (Rosé off-dry/semi-sweet) **NT** Kleine Draken (Sparkling, Non-MCC, white, off-dry/semi-sweet)

Late Harvest

★★★★ Thelema

★★★☆ Thelema ★★★ Montagu Wine Cellar ★★ Jonkheer ★★ Kellerprinz, Overmeer Cellars, Pick n Pay, Robertson **NT** Landau du Val, Nederburg **D** Delheim, Simonsvlei

Light & low-alcohol

★★★★★ Nederburg (2) (Natural Sweet, white, Noble Late Harvest), Fleur du Cap (Noble Late Harvest)

★★★★☆ Neethlingshof (Noble Late Harvest), Durbanville Hills (Noble Late Harvest), Hermanuspietersfontein (Noble Late Harvest), Jordan (Natural Sweet, white), Paul Cluver (Noble Late Harvest), Tierhoek (Vin de paille)

★★★★ Delaire (Noble Late Harvest), Paul Cluver (Riesling), **Scrucap** (Riesling)

★★★☆ Villiera (Sparkling, Méthode cap classique, white, dry), Altydgedacht (Noble Late Harvest) ★★★ Leopard's Leap (Muscadel, white, unfortified), Clos Malverne (Sparkling, Non-MCC, white, dry), Somerset Wines (Natural Sweet, white) ★★☆ Overhex (White blends, off-dry/semi-sweet (w & u/w)), **Laborie** (Chenin blanc off-dry/semi-sweet (w & u/w)), Orange River (Vin de paille), **Wellington Winery** (Hanepoot unfortified, Perlé), Drostdy-Hof (Natural Sweet, white), **Orange River** (Sparkling, Non-MCC, white, off-dry/semi-sweet), Solms-Delta (Sparkling, Non-MCC, red, off-dry/semi-sweet), **Badsberg** (Light & low-alcohol, Perlé), Grünberger (Natural Sweet, white), Klawer (Sparkling, Non-MCC, rosé, off-dry/semi-sweet), Kleine Draken (Natural Sweet, red, Kosher), Somerset Wines (Natural Sweet, rosé), **Alvi's Drift** (2) (Sparkling, Non-MCC, rosé, off-dry/semi-sweet, Sparkling, Non-MCC, white, off-dry/semi-sweet), **Imbuko** (Muscadel, white, unfortified) ★★ Woolworths (2) (Merlot, Natural Sweet, red), Robertson (3) (Natural Sweet, rosé, Natural Sweet, rosé, Natural Sweet, white), Overhex (Rosé off-dry/semi-sweet), Van Loveren (Rosé off-dry/semi-sweet), Woolworths (Red blends, Cape Bordeaux), Boplaas (Perlé wines), Robertson (Sauvignon blanc unwooded), Lutzville (Natural Sweet, rosé), **Swartland** (Hanepoot unfortified), **Laborie** (Rosé off-dry/semi-sweet), Arniston Bay (White blends, off-dry/semi-sweet (w & u/w)), Fleur du Cap (White blends, off-dry/semi-sweet (w & u/w)), Drostdy-Hof (Natural Sweet, rosé), Perdeberg (Sparkling, Non-MCC, rosé, off-dry/semi-sweet), **De Krans** (Perlé wines, Perlé), De Wet

(Muscadel, white, unfortified, Perlé), Flat Roof Manor (Rosé off-dry/semi-sweet), Cape Classics (Hanepoot unfortified), Kleine Draken (2) (Natural Sweet, white, Sacramental wine, Sacramental, Kosher), Robertson (Sauvignon blanc unwooded), Riebeek (Hanepoot unfortified, Perlé), Pearly Bay (5) (Rosé off-dry/semi-sweet, Rosé off-dry/semi-sweet, White blends, off-dry/semi-sweet (w & u/w), Sparkling, Non-MCC, rosé, off-dry/semi-sweet, Sparkling, Non-MCC, white, off-dry/semi-sweet), JC le Roux (2) (Sparkling, Non-MCC, red, dry, Sparkling, Non-MCC, white, off-dry/semi-sweet), **Robertson** (2) (Sparkling, Non-MCC, rosé, off-dry/semi-sweet, Sparkling, Non-MCC, white, off-dry/semi-sweet), Slanghoek (Rosé off-dry/semi-sweet)
★★ Woolworths (Chenin blanc off-dry/semi-sweet (w & u/w), Group CDV (Natural Sweet, white), Woolworths (2) (White blends, off-dry/semi-sweet (w & u/w), Natural Sweet, white), Van Loveren (4) (Natural Sweet, red, Natural Sweet, rosé, Natural Sweet, rosé, Natural Sweet, white), Robertson (Natural Sweet, red), Douglas Green (Natural Sweet, rosé), Woolworths (2) (Red blends, shiraz/syrah-based, Rosé off-dry/semi-sweet), Botha (White blends, off-dry/semi-sweet (w & u/w)), Lutzville (Natural Sweet, red), Arniston Bay (2) (Rosé off-dry/semi-sweet, Sweet red), Swartland (Rosé off-dry/semi-sweet), Drostdy-Hof (Natural Sweet, red), Bonnievale (Chenin blanc off-dry/semi-sweet (w & u/w), Perlé), Jonkheer (2) (Perlé wines, Perlé wines, Perlé), Grünberger (Natural Sweet, rosé), Versus (2) (Natural Sweet, rosé, Natural Sweet, white), Obikwa (2) (Natural Sweet, red, Natural Sweet, white), **Rooiberg** (Sauvignon blanc unwooded), **Seven Sisters** (Chenin blanc off-dry/semi-sweet (w & u/w)), JC le Roux (Sparkling, Non-MCC, red, off-dry/semi-sweet) ★
Woolworths (4) (Pinotage, Natural Sweet, rosé, Chardonnay unwooded, Sauvignon blanc unwooded), Van Loveren (White blends, unwooded, dry), Woolworths (2) (Chenin blanc unwooded dry, Chenin blanc unwooded dry), Bonnievale (Rosé off-dry/semi-sweet, Perlé), Landzicht (Natural Sweet, white), **Riebeek** (Sweet red, Perlé), Versus (Natural Sweet, red) ☆ Drostdy-Hof (Chenin blanc unwooded dry), Robertson (Merlot), Riebeek (Rosé off-dry/semi-sweet) **NT** Lutzville (Natural Sweet, white)

Malbec

★★★★ Anura, Bellevue, Diemersfontein, **Dornier**, Druk My Niet, Hillcrest, Mooi Bly, Paul Wallace, Raka, Woolworths (3)

★★★☆ Annex Kloof, Doolhof, Flagstone, Mount Vernon, Neethlingshof, Umkhulu ★★★ Blaauwklippen, Bushmanspad, Fairview, **La Couronne**, Ormonde, **The Giant Periwinkle**, Withington ★★★ Bovlei, **Maison de Teijger**, **Malanot** ★★ **Paardebosch NT** High Constantia, Hildenbrand, Le Pommier, Maison de Teijger (3), Signal Hill, Vergenoegd **D** Audacia, Plaisir

Merlot

★★★★☆ Bein, **Catherine Marshall**, Eagles' Nest, Groot Constantia, Laibach, **Lourensford**, Meerlust, Red Tape, Shannon, Vergelegen

★★★★ Amani, Anthonij Rupert (2), Anura, Bein (2), Boland, Buitenverwachting, Catherine Marshall, Creation, De Trafford, De Wetshof, Delaire, DeWaal, Dombeya, Durbanville Hills (2), Eikendal, Fleur du Cap, Glen Carlou, GlenWood, Graceland, Hartenberg, Hazendal, Hillcrest, Jordan, Journey's End, Laibach, Lanzerac, Linton Park, Marianne, Morgenhof, **Morgenster**, Nabygelegen, Noble Hill, Oldenburg, Rainbow's End, **Remhoogte**, Rickety Bridge, Rust en Vrede, Rustenberg, Saxenburg, Slaley, Stellekaya, Sumaridge, The Butcher Shop (2), **The Township Winery** (Fairtrade), The Winery of Good Hope, Veenwouden, Vergenoegd, Welbedacht, **Woolworths** (4) (Organic), Yonder Hill, Zevenwacht

★★★☆ Akkerdal, Annandale, Ayama, Backsberg, **Bayede!**, Blaauwklippen, **Bloemendal**, Boschkloof , Botanica, Bovlei, **Cloof**, Clos Malverne, Doolhof, Dornier, Du Preez, Elgin Vintners, Ernst Gouws, Excelsior, Fairview (2), False Bay, Fort Simon (2), Fraai Uitzicht 1798, Glenelly, Groenland, Guardian Peak, Hathersage, Hout Bay, Kaapzicht, Kloovenburg, **Knorhoek**, Kyburg, La Bri, La Petite Ferme, Laborie, **Lanner Hill**, Linton Park, Longridge, Lourensford, Meerendal, Meinert, Miravel, Muratie, Nederburg, Nico van der Merwe, Niel Joubert, Org de Rac (Organic), **Ormonde**, Passages, Post House, Raka, **Red Tape**, Ridgeback, **Rosendal**, **Signal Gun**, **Snowfield**, Spier, Spookfontein , Steenberg, Sterhuis, **Super Single Vineyards**, Thelema, Tread Lightly, Ultra Liquors, Waterkloof, Woolworths
★★★ African Terroir (Biodynamic, Fairtrade), Altydgedacht, Anura, Asara, Bellingham, Bellpost, Bilton, Blaauwklippen, Blue Crane, Boland, Boschendal, Botha, Bovlei, Brenaissance, Cape Classics, D'Aria, Darling Cellars, De Meye, DeWaal, Diemersdal, Du Preez, Dunstone, Ernie Els, Fish Hoek, Flagstone (2), Flat Roof Manor, Fleur du Cap, Fraai Uitzicht 1798, Franschhoek Cellar, Goede Hoop, Graham Beck, Groote Post, Group CDV, Havana Hills,

Herold, Het Vlock Casteel, Hoopenburg, **House of Mandela**, Jason's Hill, Jordan, Klawer, Klein Parys, Kleine Zalze, Kleinfontein, Koelenhof , **Koopmanskloof**, KWV, L'Auberge, L'Avenir, **Lievland**, Lindhorst, Lomond, Lyngrove, Lynx, M'hudi, Manley, Middelvlei, Mon Rêve, Mont du Toit, Mont Rochelle, Mzoli's, Nederburg, Neethlingshof, **Nuweland**, Old Vines, Org de Rac (Organic), Ormonde (2), Oude Compagnies Post, Overgaauw, Overhex, Perdeberg, Plaisir, Porcupine Ridge, Pulpit Rock, Quest, Retief, Riebeek, Rooiberg, **Ruitersvlei**, Seal Breeze, Slowine, Somersbosch, Stellenbosch Hills, Stellenrust, **Ultra Liquors** (2), Van Loveren, Villiera, Waterstone, Wellington Winery, Weltevrede (Biodynamic), Whalehaven, Windmeul, **Woolworths** (4), Yonder Hill ★★★ Anthonij Rupert, Arra, Audacia, Backsberg (Kosher), Badsberg, Bayede!, Bellingham, Blomendahl, Boland, Bottelary, De Grendel, Delheim, Desert Rose, Die Mas, Douglas Green, Drostdy-Hof, Du Toitskloof , Durbanville Hills, Eikehof, Excelsior, Goudini, **Group CDV**, Kanu, Klein Roosboom , Kleine Draken (Kosher), Kranskop, La Couronne, La Petite Provence, Ladismith, Landskroon, **Landzicht**, Le Manoir de Brendel, Leopard's Leap, Louisvale, MAN Family, Mount Rozier, Namaqua, Obikwa, Place in the Sun (Fairtrade), Riebeek, **Schalkenbosch**, Simonsvlei, Slanghoek, Spier, Stellendrift, The Butcher Shop, The Rhino, The Wine Fusion, **Ultra Liquors** (2), uniWines (2) (Fairtrade), Vredenheim, Wandsbeck, Waterstone, Welmoed, Wineways, Women in Wine, Wonderfontein, Woolworths, Zonnebloem ★★ African Pride, African Terroir (2) (Organic), Arniston Bay, Barrydale, Bernheim, **Bonnievale**, Bonview, Boplaas, Burgershof, Calitzdorp, Cape Dreams, **De Bos** (Fairtrade), Glenview, Goedvernacht, Group CDV, **Halala**, Hoopenburg, **Long Mountain**, **Lula**, Niel Joubert, Robertson (3), Rooiberg, Seven Sisters, Stellar (2) (Organic, Fairtrade), **Waterstone**, Wineways, Woolworths (3) (Organic, Light & low-alcohol) ★★ Asara, Bergwater, Cranefields, Hill & Dale, Jonkheer, Lutzville, Pulpit Rock, **Swartland** (2), Tulbagh Winery, United Nations, **Waterstone**, Wineways (3), Wonderfontein, Woolworths ★ **Waterstone** ★ Robertson **NT** AlexKia, Barton, Bonfoi, Buffalo Creek, Calais, Callender, Camberley, De Breede (Organic), De Villiers, Devon Hill, Domaine Brahms, Escapades, High Constantia (2), Hofstraat, Holden Manz, Ken Forrester, Klein Parys, KWV, Libby's Pride, Linton Park, Maison de Teijger (3), Marklew, Maske, Meerendal, Mitre's Edge, My Wyn, Nederburg, Nietvoorbij, Painted Wolf, Quoin

Rock, **Re'Mogo**, Ross Gower, Savanha, Stellendrift, Stone Ridge, Tanagra, Thelema, Tulbagh Winery, Valley Vineyards (2), Vergenoegd, Versailles, Westbridge, Wolfkloof, Zidela **NR** Bergwater, Viljoensdrift **D** Bloemendal, David Frost, Hornbill , KWV, Mooiplaas, Namaqua, Org de Rac (Organic), Remhoogte (2), Savanha, The Township Winery, Wineways, Zorgvliet

Mourvèdre

★★★★ Beaumont, Raka, Signal Hill

★★★☆ Arra, Fairview, Hawksmoor, **Hermit on the Hill**, Spice Route ★★★ **Boschheim**, Bovlei, MAN Family ★★☆ Arra, Oude Compagnies Post ★★ Idiom **NT** Stony Brook **D** BLANKbottle

Muscadel, red, fortified

★★★★☆ Boplaas, Nuweland, **Nuy**, Rietvallei, Robertson

★★★★ Badsberg, Boplaas, Namaqua, Nuy, Orange River, Rooiberg

★★★☆ Aan de Doorns, Bon Courage, Calitzdorp, Clairvaux, De Wet, Du Toitskloof , Karusa, Klawer, Rietvallei, Van Loveren, Weltevrede, Wonderfontein ★★★ Boland, Boplaas, KWV, Landzicht, McGregor, Montagu Wine Cellar, Reiersvlei, Roodezandt, Slanghoek ★★★ BurCon, **Die Mas**, Jonkheer, Montagu Wine & Spirits, Wandsbeck ★★ Ashton, Grundheim, **Tulbagh Winery NT** Excelsior Vlakteplaas, Klein Parys, TTT Cellar, Wolvendrift

Muscadel, white, fortified

★★★★★ Alvi's Drift

★★★★☆ **Boplaas** (2), De Krans, Monis, Nuy

★★★★ Calitzdorp, De Krans, De Wet, Ladismith, Lutzville, Windmeul

★★★☆ Graham Beck, Jonkheer, Klawer, Merwida, Orange River ★★★ Bon Courage, Boplaas, Clairvaux, De Wetshof, **Die Mas**, Excelsior Vlakteplaas, Jonkheer, McGregor, Montagu Wine Cellar, Namaqua, Weltevrede (Biodynamic), Withoek ★★★ Grundheim, **Wonderfontein** ★★ Montagu Wine & Spirits **NT** La Couronne, Landzicht, Mostertsdrift **D** Montagu Wine & Spirits, Robertson

Muscadel, white, unfortified

★★★★ The Fledge

★★★ Karusa (2), **Leopard's Leap** ★★★ Imbuko (Perlé, Light & low-alcohol), Thelema ★★ De Wet

Muscat de Hambourg fortified
★★★★ Stellenbosch Hills

Muscat Ottonel unfortified
NT Zidela

Natural Sweet, red
★★★★ Adoro ★★★ Blomendahl (2) ★★☆ Arra, Kleine Draken (Light & low-alcohol, Kosher), Somerset Wines ★★ Darling Cellars, Woolworths ★★ 4th Street, Drostdy-Hof (Light & low-alcohol), Kanu, Lutzville (Light & low-alcohol), Obikwa (Light & low-alcohol), Robertson (2) (Light & low-alcohol), Rooiberg, Van Loveren (Light & low-alcohol), Wineways (2) ★ Versus NT Bosman, Cape Hutton D Wineways

Natural Sweet, rosé
★★★★☆ Groot Constantia

★★★ Seven Sisters, Somerset Wines (Light & low-alcohol), Villiersdorp ★★ Drostdy-Hof (Light & low-alcohol), Lutzville (Light & low-alcohol), Nelson, Pick n Pay, Robertson (4) (Light & low-alcohol), Rooiberg ★★ 4th Street, Darling Cellars, Douglas Green (Light & low-alcohol), Grünberger (Light & low-alcohol), Landzicht, Simonsvlei, Van Loveren (2) (Light & low-alcohol), Versus ★ Woolworths D Simonsvlei

Natural Sweet, white
★★★★★ Nederburg

★★★★☆ Badsberg, Jordan (Light & low-alcohol), Klein Constantia, Perdeberg, Quoin Rock

★★★★ Boschendal, Glen Carlou, Stony Brook

★★★★ Cloof, Meerendal, Rickety Bridge ★★★ Quando, Rooiberg, Somerset Wines (Light & low-alcohol), Zorgvliet ★★★ 4th Street, Arra, Drostdy-Hof (Light & low-alcohol), Grünberger (Light & low-alcohol), Theuniskraal ★★ Darling Cellars, Douglas Green, Goudini, Kleine Draken (Light & low-alcohol, Kosher), Lord's, Orange River, Robertson (3) (Light & low-alcohol) ★★ Group CDV (Light & low-alcohol), Obikwa (Light & low-alcohol), Van Loveren (Light & low-alcohol), Woolworths ★ Landzicht NT Buitenverwachting, Dornier, Highlands Road, Le Pommier, Lutzville (Light & low-alcohol), Ridgeback D Kaapzicht

Nebbiolo
★★★★☆ Steenberg

★★★★ Idiom, Morgenster

★★★★ Du Toitskloof ★★★ Dagbreek

Noble Late Harvest
★★★★★ Delheim, Fleur du Cap (Light & low-alcohol), KWV, Nederburg (2) (Light & low-alcohol), Signal Hill

★★★★☆ Asara, Boekenhoutskloof, De Wetshof, Durbanville Hills (Light & low-alcohol), Hermanuspietersfontein (Light & low-alcohol), Joostenberg, Lourensford, Lutzville, Miles Mossop, Neethlingshof (Light & low-alcohol), Paul Cluver (Light & low-alcohol), Post House, Rudera, Springfontein, Tokara, Villiera

★★★★ Badsberg, Beaumont, Blaauwklippen (2), Bon Courage, Cape Point, Delaire (Light & low-alcohol), Fort Simon, Hartenberg, Kanu, Ken Forrester, L'illa, Longridge, Mulderbosch, Namaqua, Shannon, Signal Hill (3), Simonsig, Slaley, Slanghoek, Stellenrust, Virgin Earth, Waterford

★★★★ Altydgedacht (Light & low-alcohol), Blaauwklippen, Kranskop ★★★ Du Toitskloof , Hildenbrand ★★★ De Grendel, Van Loveren NT Avontuur, Badsberg, Darling Cellars, Groote Post, Morgenhof, Nitida, Tokara, Vruchtbaar, Woolworths

Non-muscat, white, fortified
★★★★ Haute Cabrière

Nouveau
★★☆ Asara (Gamay noir)

Nouvelle
NT Darling Cellars

Organic
★★★★☆ Avondale (White blends, wooded, dry), Lazanou (Shiraz/syrah)

★★★★ Woolworths (2) (Merlot, Red blends, Cape Bordeaux), Avondale (2) (Red blends, shiraz/syrah-based, Sparkling, Méthode cap classique, white, dry), Org de Rac (3) (Cabernet sauvignon, Shiraz/syrah, Sparkling, Méthode cap classique, white, dry), Stellar (Vin de paille, Fairtrade), Reyneke (Sauvignon blanc unwooded), Upland (Brandy), De Breede (Shiraz/syrah), Groot Parys (3) (Chenin blanc wooded, dry, Chenin blanc wooded, dry, Vin de paille), Laibach (Red blends, Cape Bordeaux), Lazanou (Chenin blanc wooded, dry), Silvermist (Red blends, other), Bon Cap (Red blends, shiraz/syrah-based)

★★★★ Woolworths (Chardonnay wooded), Avondale (3) (Shiraz/syrah, Red blends, other, Chenin blanc wooded, dry), Org de Rac (Merlot), Bon Cap (2) (Red blends, with pinotage, Sparkling, Méthode cap classique, white, dry), **Upland** (Brandy), **De Breede** (2) (Cabernet sauvignon, Red blends, Cape Bordeaux), **Groot Parys** (2) (Rosé dry, Chenin blanc off-dry/semi-sweet (w & u/w)), Elgin Ridge (Sauvignon blanc unwooded), Fernskloof (Chardonnay wooded), **Upland** (Grappa-Styles), Joostenberg (Red blends, shiraz/syrah-based), Laibach (White blends, wooded, dry), Lazanou (Red blends, shiraz/syrah-based), Mountain Oaks (Pinotage), Reyneke (White blends, wooded, dry), Silvermist (Sauvignon blanc unwooded), Waverley Hills (3) (Shiraz/syrah, White blends, wooded, dry, Sparkling, Méthode cap classique, white, dry) ★★★ Woolworths (Chardonnay wooded), Avondale (Rosé dry), Van Loveren (Port, red), Stellar (2) (White blends, unwooded, dry, Chardonnay unwooded, Fairtrade), **Org de Rac** (3) (Merlot, Shiraz/syrah, Chardonnay unwooded), **Groot Parys** (2) (Pinotage, Sparkling, Méthode cap classique, white, dry), **Earthbound** (2) (Cabernet sauvignon, Chenin blanc unwooded dry, Fairtrade), Lazanou (2) (Viognier, White blends, unwooded, dry), Mountain Oaks (Red blends, Cape Bordeaux), African Terroir (Viognier), Bon Cap (2) (Sauvignon blanc unwooded, White blends, off-dry/semi-sweet (w & u/w)), Upland (Cabernet sauvignon), **Waverley Hills** (4) (Grenache noir, Shiraz/syrah, Red blends, shiraz/syrah-based, White blends, wooded, dry) ★★★ Woolworths (4) (Cabernet sauvignon, Pinotage, Shiraz/syrah, Sauvignon blanc unwooded, Fairtrade), Stellar (11) (Red blends, with pinotage, Cabernet sauvignon, Pinotage, Shiraz/syrah, Sauvignon blanc unwooded, White blends, off-dry/semi-sweet (w & u/w), Cabernet sauvignon, Pinotage, Pinotage, White blends, off-dry/semi-sweet (w & u/w), White blends, off-dry/semi-sweet (w & u/w), Fairtrade), Org de Rac (3) (Cabernet sauvignon, Chardonnay wooded, Red blends, Cape Bordeaux), De Breede (Red blends, Cape Bordeaux), **Earthbound** (3) (Pinot noir, Pinotage, Sauvignon blanc unwooded, Fairtrade), **Joostenberg** (Rosé dry), African Terroir (Chardonnay unwooded), Bon Cap (3) (Pinotage, Rosé dry, Sparkling, Non-MCC, white, dry), Upland (Port, red), Waverley Hills (3) (Cabernet sauvignon, Red blends, Cape Bordeaux, Red blends, other), African Terroir (3) (Cabernet sauvignon, Shiraz/syrah, Red blends, with pinotage) ★★ Woolworths (Merlot), Stellar (8) (Pinot noir, Merlot, Rosé dry, Sparkling, Non-MCC, white, dry, Merlot, Shiraz/syrah, Rosé dry, Rosé off-dry/semi-sweet, Fairtrade), Org de Rac (2) (Rosé dry, Cabernet sauvignon), Bon Cap (Port, red), Mountain Oaks (Red blends, with pinotage), African Terroir (Chardonnay unwooded), Waverley Hills (2) (Cabernet sauvignon, Rosé dry), African Terroir (5) (Merlot, Pinotage, Chardonnay wooded, Sauvignon blanc unwooded, Sparkling, Non-MCC, rosé, dry) ★★ Waverley Hills (Pinot gris/grigio) ★ Woolworths (2) (Colombard, Sparkling, Non-MCC, white, dry, Fairtrade), Stellar (Colombard, Fairtrade), Org de Rac (2) (Rosé dry, Chardonnay unwooded), African Terroir (2) (Rosé dry, White blends, unwooded, dry) **NT** Woolworths (Sauvignon blanc unwooded), Stellar (Chenin blanc unwooded dry), La Motte (Sauvignon blanc unwooded), Bon Cap (Viognier), De Breede (Merlot), Groot Parys (4) (Chardonnay wooded, Chenin blanc unwooded dry, Rosé dry, Chenin blanc unwooded dry), Lazanou (Chardonnay wooded), Mountain Oaks (3) (Rosé dry, Chardonnay wooded, White blends, unwooded, dry), Reyneke (Red blends, shiraz/syrah-based), Porseleinberg (Shiraz/syrah) **NR** Joostenberg (White blends, wooded, dry), **Waverley Hills** (Jerepigo red) **D** Woolworths (Rosé dry), Org de Rac (Merlot), Groot Parys (Chardonnay unwooded), Elgin Ridge (Chardonnay unwooded), African Terroir (Cabernet sauvignon)

Perlé Wines

★★★ Group CDV (White blends, off-dry/semi-sweet (w & u/w), Perlé), **Wellington Winery** (Hanepoot unfortified, Perlé, Light & low-alcohol), **Badsberg** (Light & low-alcohol, Perlé, Light & low-alcohol), De Wet (Rosé off-dry/semi-sweet, Perlé), uniWines (Hanepoot unfortified, Perlé), **Imbuko** (Muscadel, white, unfortified, Perlé, Light & low-alcohol), Wandsbeck (Rosé off-dry/semi-sweet) ★★ Louiesenhof (Rosé off-dry/semi-sweet, Perlé), **De Krans** (Perlé wines, Perlé, Light & low-alcohol), De Wet (Muscadel, white, unfortified, Perlé, Light & low-alcohol), Grünberger (Perlé wines, Perlé), Riebeek (Hanepoot unfortified, Perlé, Light & low-alcohol), uniWines (Hanepoot unfortified, Perlé), Du Toitskloof (2) (Rosé off-dry/semi-sweet, White blends, off-dry/semi-sweet (w & u/w), Perlé) ★★ Bonnievale (Chenin blanc off-dry/semi-sweet (w & u/w), Perlé, Light & low-alcohol), Jonkheer (2) (Perlé wines, Perlé wines, Perlé, Light & low-alcohol) ★ Bonnievale (Rosé off-dry/semi-sweet, Perlé, Light & low-alcohol), **Riebeek** (Sweet red) ★ Riebeek (Rosé off-dry/semi-sweet) **NT** Bergsig (Perlé wines) **D** Darling Cellars (Perlé wines)

Petit verdot

★★★★ Anura, Asara, Du Preez, KWV, Raka, **Springfontein**

★★★☆ Doolhof, Hillcrest, Lovane, Signal Hill, Zorgvliet ★★★ Bellevue, Maison de Teijger, Stellenzicht ★★☆ Definitum **NT** BLANKbottle, Calais, Darling Cellars, Haut Espoir, Havana Hills, Maison de Teijger, My Wyn, Nederburg, Rico Suter, TTT Cellar **D** Nabygelegen

Petite sirah/durif

★★★★ Fairview

★★★☆ Spotswood ★★★ Karusa

Pinot gris/grigio

★★★★ Eagle's Cliff

★★★☆ Anthonij Rupert, De Grendel, Nederburg, The Township Winery, Usana, **Val du Charron** ★★★ Fairview, Idiom, **Stettyn** ★★☆ Flat Roof Manor, Hill & Dale, Robertson, Woolworths ★☆ Obikwa, Van Loveren, Waverley Hills (Organic), Woolworths **NT** Overhex (Fairtrade), Two Oceans **NR** Spring Grove

Pinot noir

★★★★★ Newton Johnson (2)

★★★★☆ **Blackwater**, Botanica, Bouchard Finlayson (2), Cape Chamonix, Creation, **Crystallum** (3), Hamilton Russell, Iona, **Litigo**, Meerlust, **Newton Johnson** (2), Shannon, Sumaridge, The Winery of Good Hope (2), Yardstick

★★★★ **AntHill**, Catherine Marshall (2), **Cederberg**, Creation, Dalla Cia, De Wetshof, Edgebaston, Flagstone, Glen Carlou, Groote Post, La Chaumiere, La Vierge, **Lothian**, Muratie, **Newton Johnson** (2), Oak Valley, Paul Cluver (2), Seven Springs , Signal Hill (2), Stark-Condé, **Stellekaya**, **Strandveld**, The Winery of Good Hope, Topaz, **Winters Drift**, Woolworths

★★★☆ Backsberg, **Blackwater**, **Boschendal**, **Boschheim**, **Claime d'Or**, **Clouds**, De Grendel, Domaine des Dieux, **Driefontein**, **Driehoek**, **Eagle's Cliff**, Elgin Vintners, Felicité, Grande Provence, Herold, **Karusa**, Kleine Zalze, **Maison de Teijger** (3), Meerendal, **Ormonde**, Paul Cluver, Peter Falke, Scrucap, **Sophie & Mr P**, Stark-Condé, The Winery of Good Hope, Two Oceans, **Veenwouden**, Virgin Earth, Vriesenhof, Waterford, Woolworths ★★★ Avontuur, Barrydale, Bon Courage, **De Bos** (Fairtrade), Ernst Gouws, Glen Carlou, Haute Cabrière (2), Hoopenburg, JH Meyer, **La**

Vierge, Lemberg, **Lomond**, Lord's, **Maastricht**, Maison de Teijger (2), Nabygelegen, **Ormonde**, Quando, Robertson, Strandveld, The Hills, **The Wine Fusion**, Thelema, Vriesenhof, Whalehaven, Woolworths (2) ★★☆ **Baleia Bay, Dâbar, Earthbound** (Organic, Fairtrade), Maison de Teijger, Mofam, Rietvallei, Spookfontein , The Wine Fusion, **Van Loveren** ★★ Goedvertrouw, Highlands Road, **Kranskop**, Stellar **NT** Andy Mitchell (2), Beau Joubert, Callender, Fryer's Cove, Herold, Longbarn, Maison de Teijger, Malanot, Strandveld, Woolworths (2) **D** Thandi, William Everson

Pinotage

★★★★★ Chateau Naudé, Rijk's, Spioenkop

★★★★☆ Beyerskloof, Cape Chamonix, **Cecilia**, DeWaal, Diemersfontein, Fairview, **Flagstone** (2), Grangehurst, Kaapzicht (2), Kanonkop, L'Avenir, Lanzerac, Meerendal, Nederburg, Pulpit Rock, Simonsig, Spier, Springfontein, Tokara, Umkhulu, Windmeul

★★★★ **Aaldering** (2), Allée Bleue, Altydgedacht, Arra, Bayede!, Bellingham, Beyerskloof, Boland, Bosman, Conradie, Croydon, De Zoete Inval, DeWaal, Diemersdal (2), Dornier, Durbanville Hills, Eikendal, Escapades, Groot Constantia, Hawksmoor, Hidden Valley, **Hornbill** , Karusa, Kleine Zalze, KWV, L'Avenir, Laibach, Lammershoek, Lanzerac, Longridge, **M'hudi**, Meerendal, Middelvlei, Môreson, Namaqua, Neethlingshof, Neil Ellis, Painted Wolf (2), **Perdeberg** (2), Reyneke (Biodynamic), Rijk's (2), Rooiberg, Scali, Slaley, Southern Right, Spice Route, Springfontein, Stellenrust, Super Single Vineyards, Swartland, SylvanVale, The Winery of Good Hope, Warwick, Welbedacht, Welgegund, Wellington Winery, Wildekrans, **Woolworths** (Biodynamic), Zonnebloem

★★★☆ **Alkmaar**, Annex Kloof, Anura (2), Barista, Beaumont, Bellevue, Bergsig, Beyerskloof, Bovlei, Camberley, **Cape Dreams**, Clos Malverne (2), Darling Cellars, Delheim, Devon Hill, Diemersfontein, Doolhof, Eagle's Cliff, **Ernst Gouws**, Fairview (Fairtrade), False Bay, **Fat Bastard**, Flagstone, Fort Simon, Goede Hoop, Graham Beck, Hofstraat, Jonkheer, Ken Forrester, KWV, **Leeuwenberg**, Lemberg, Lindhorst, **Lutzville**, Lyngrove, Maastricht, Malanot, Manley, Meinert, **Miravel**, Mooiplaas, Mountain Oaks (Organic), Nederburg, Neil Ellis, Nuweland, Olifantsberg, Onderkloof, Passages, Raka, Remhoogte, Rhebokskloof, Robertson, Romond, Saxenburg, Silkbush, Simonsvlei, Slaley, Spier, Springfontein, Stanford Hills, Stellekaya,

Stellenbosch University, Stellenrust, Stellenzicht, **Teubes**, The Grape Grinder, **The Wine Fusion**, The Winery of Good Hope, Two Oceans, Virgin Earth, **Waterstone**, Welgevallen, **Welmoed**, Whalehaven, Woolworths (2) ★★★ Allée Bleue, **Amani**, Anthonij Rupert, Avontuur, Ayama, Backsberg, Bellingham, Bergheim, Blomendahl, Boland, Breëland, Calitzdorp, **Chateau Naudé**, Cloof (2), Darling Cellars, DeWaal, **Doran**, Douglas Green, Drostdy-Hof, Du Toitskloof, Durbanville Hills, Fairvalley (Fairtrade), Fairview, Fish Hoek, Franschhoek Cellar, Freedom Hill, **Groot Parys** (Organic), Hawksmoor, Hoopenburg, **House of Mandela**, Jacobsdal, Jason's Hill, Klein Parys, Kleine Zalze, **Knorhoek** (2), Lemberg, Louiesenhof, M'hudi, MAN Family, Merwida, **Nederburg** (2) (Fairtrade), Neethlingshof, Nitida, **Nuy**, Obikwa, **Old Vines**, Olsen, Orange River, Oude Compagnies Post, Overhex, **Paardebosch**, Painted Wolf, Perdeberg, Pulpit Rock, Rickety Bridge, Riebeek, Saam, Schalkenbosch, Simonsig, Simonsvlei, Slanghoek, Stanford Hills, Stellenbosch Hills, Stellendrift, Stellenzicht, Swartland, SylvanVale, Teubes, Thandi, **The Township Winery** (2) (Fairtrade), Thembi & Co, Trajan, Tulbagh Winery (2), **Ultra Liquors**, uniWines, Villiera, Vredenheim, Vriesenhof (2), Vruchtbaar, Welbedacht, Wellington Winery, Windmeul, Wineways, Woolworths (3), Zonnebloem ★★★ Aan de Doorns, Alvi's Drift, Anura, Arniston Bay, Arra, Backsberg (Kosher), **Barnardt Boyes**, Bernheim, **Black Elephant**, Boland, Bon Cap (Organic), Bon Courage, Boplaas, Botha, Bovlei, Burgershof, Cape Dreams, **Darling Cellars**, De Wet, Die Mas, Eagle's Cliff, **Earthbound** (Organic, Fairtrade), Fleur du Cap, Freedom Hill, Goudini, Graham Beck, Group CDV, Hawksmoor, Imbuko, Klawer, Klein Parys, Kleine Zalze, Koelenhof, Koopmanskloof, KWV, **La Couronne**, Ladismith, Landskroon, Lateganskop, Le Manoir de Brendel, Lutzville, Lyngrove, MAN Family, McGregor, Montagu Wine & Spirits, Morgenhof, Mountain River (2), Niel Joubert, **Nuy**, Rhebokskloof, Robertson, **Rooiberg** (2), Simonsvlei, Somersbosch, Spier, Stellar (3) (Organic, Fairtrade), The Rhino, Tulbagh Winery, Viljoensdrift, Vukani, Waterstone, Welmoed, Wineways (2), Woolworths (3) (Organic) ★★ African Pride, African Terroir (3) (Organic), Café Culture, **Doran**, Group CDV (2), Hill & Dale, **House of Mandela** (Fairtrade), Koopmanskloof, Long Mountain, Mount Vernon, Namaqua, New Beginnings, Oude Compagnies Post, Riebeek, Sizanani, uniWines (Fairtrade), Van Loveren, **Waterstone** (2), Wineways, Zevenwacht

★★ Ashton, Bayede!, Blomendahl, Bovlei, Imbuko, Long Mountain, Van Loveren ★ Jonkheer, Long Mountain, **Woolworths NT** African Terroir, Badsberg, Bellevue, Bergsig, Boer & Brit, Buffalo Creek, Calais, Citrusdal, De Villiers, De Zoete Inval, Devon Rocks, Domaine Brahms, Eenzaamheid, Fernskloof, Four Paws, Govert, Hazendal (2), Klein Parys, L'Auberge, L'Avenir, Malanot (2), Marianne, Marklew, Mountain River, Nietvoorbij, Re'Mogo, Reiersvlei, Rico Suter, Ruitersvlei, Stellenbosch University, Tempel, Thembi & Co, United Nations, Valley Vineyards, Waboomsrivier, Westbridge (2), Withington, Zidela **D** Bloemendal, De Krans, Hornbill, Savanha

Port, pink

★★★ Boplaas ★★★ De Krans

Port, red

★★★★★ Axe Hill, Boplaas, De Krans, JP Bredell, KWV

★★★★☆ Boplaas (3), De Krans (2), Vergenoegd

★★★★ Allesverloren, **Anura**, Bergsig, Boplaas (3), De Krans, De Wet, Delaire, Jonkheer, JP Bredell, Knorhoek, Landskroon, Monis, Morgenhof, Muratie (2), Overgaauw, Peter Bayly, Quinta, Simonsig, Swartland

★★★☆ Aan de Doorns, Annandale, Axe Hill, Backsberg, Bergsig (2), Beyerskloof, Boplaas (2), Calitzdorp, Clairvaux, De Wet, Douglas Green, Du'SwaRoo, Flagstone, Groot Constantia, Grundheim (2), Jacques Smit, Kaapzicht, Louiesenhof, Maison, Monis, Montagu Wine & Spirits, SoetKaroo, Zandvliet ★★★ Anura, Badsberg, Beau Joubert, Beaumont, **BLANKbottle**, Boland, Botha, Calitzdorp, Catherine Marshall, De Zoete Inval, Die Mas, **Druk My Niet**, Du Toitskloof, Holden Manz, Koelenhof, KWV, Louiesenhof, My Wyn, **Orange River**, Riebeek, Rooiberg, **Snowfield**, SoetKaroo, Swartland, TTT Cellar, Van Loveren (Organic), Vergenoegd, Wellington Winery, Windmeul ★★ Allée Bleue, Bernheim, Bon Courage, Bovlei, Elemental Bob, Fairview, Grundheim, Peter Bayly, Somersbosch, Tulbagh Winery, Upland (Organic), Withoek ★★ Bon Cap (Organic), **Highlands Road**, Karusa, Klawer, Montpellier, Reiersvlei, Slanghoek, Viljoensdrift, Villiersdorp, Withoek (2) ★★ **Bergwater**, Bonnievale, Landzicht ★ McGregor **NT** Alto, Annex Kloof, De Zoete Inval, Du'SwaRoo, Goede Hoop, JP Bredell (2), Lovane, Nietvoorbij, Robertson, Tulbagh Winery **NR** TTT Cellar **D** Hout Bay, Montagu Wine & Spirits, Muratie, Ridgeback, Ultra Liquors, Villiera

Port, white

★★★☆ Axe Hill ★★★ Boplaas, De Krans, Grundheim, Karusa ★★ Peter Bayly ★ TTT Cellar **NT** My Wyn

Red blends, Cape Bordeaux

★★★★★ Cape Chamonix, Dalla Cia, Eikendal, Fleur du Cap, Keet, Thelema

★★★★☆ Allée Bleue, **Anthonij Rupert** (2), Bartinney, Beaumont, Buitenverwachting, Constantia Glen, Darling Cellars, De Toren, Delheim, Diemersdal, **Dornier** (2), Druk My Niet, Gabriëlskloof, Grangehurst, Groot Constantia, Hartenberg, Haskell, Hermanuspietersfontein, Hidden Valley, Hillcrest, Jordan (2), Kaapzicht, Kanonkop, KWV, Laibach, Lynx, Meerlust, Miles Mossop, Morgenster (2), Mulderbosch, Muratie, Mvemve Raats, Nabygelegen, Neethlingshof, Nico van der Merwe, Nitida, Peter Falke, Raats, **Remhoogte**, Reyneke (Biodynamic), Romond, Rupert & Rothschild, Saronsberg, Simonsig, Stellenbosch Ridge, Stony Brook, The Butcher Shop, The High Road, Tokara, **Van Biljon**, Vergelegen (2), Vergenoegd, Vilafonté (2), Warwick, **Waterford**, Windmeul, Woolworths, Zorgvliet

★★★★ Aaldering, Allée Bleue, **Arra**, Asara, Backsberg, **Beau Constantia**, Belfield, Bellevue, Beyerskloof, Boschkloof , Buitenverwachting, Camberley (2), Capelands, CK Wines, Cloof, Clos Malverne, Constantia Glen, Constantia Uitsig, Creation, Damarakloof, De Toren, **DeMorgenzon**, DeWaal, Diemersdal, Dombeya, Durbanville Hills, Epicurean, Equitania, Ernie Els, Glen Carlou, Grande Provence, **Grangehurst** (2), JP Bredell, Knorhoek, La Bri, La Motte, La Petite Ferme, Laibach (Organic), Le Bonheur, Le Riche, **Leopard's Leap**, Lovane, Malanot, Meerhof, Meerlust, MolenVliet, Mooiplaas, Môreson, Morgenhof, Namaqua, Napier, Nederburg (2), Neil Ellis, Nelson, Noble Hill, Noble Savage, Oak Valley, Ormonde, Overgaauw, **Painted Wolf**, Raka, Ridgeback, Robert Stanford, Russo, Saltaré, Saronsberg, **Schalkenbosch**, Spier, Spookfontein , Springfield, Stellekaya, Stellenrust, Stony Brook, The Butcher Shop, The Drift, Uva Mira, Veenwouden, Vergelegen, Vergenoegd, Villiera, Welbedacht, Woolworths (2) (Organic), Yardstick, Yonder Hill, Zevenwacht

★★★☆ Amani, Anura, Avontuur, **Barton**, **Beau Constantia** (2), Black Oystercatcher, Cape Chamonix, Cloof, De Breede (Organic), De Grendel, **De Toren**, **Deux Frères**, Doolhof (2), Dornier, Eagles' Nest, Elgin Vintners, Emineo, Four Fields,

Gabriëlskloof, **Goudini**, Havana Hills, Hermanuspietersfontein, **Hillcrest**, **Hillock**, Holden Manz, Jakob's Vineyards, Kanu, Klein Constantia, **Klein Roosboom** , Kleinfontein, L'Avenir, La Vierge, Laborie, Le Joubert, Linton Park, Louis, Louisvale, Lynx, Malanot, Marianne, Mimosa, **Miravel**, Mzoli's, Neethlingshof, Nelson, Nick & Forti's, Nomada, **Oldenburg**, Orange River, Rosendal, Rustenberg, **Snowfield**, Southern Sky, Stellekaya, Sterhuis, Stonewall, **The Butcher Shop**, The High Road, Thelema, Thunderchild, Topaz, **Ultra Liquors**, Umkhulu (2), uniWines, Vredevol, Vriesenhof , Vuurberg, Welbedacht, Welgemeend (3), Welmoed, Woolworths (2), Yonder Hill ★★★ Agterplaas, Alkmaar, Ashton, Audacia, Avontuur, Badgerberg, Bayede!, Beau Joubert, Beyerskloof, Blomendahl, Boschkloof , Brenaissance, D'Aria, Doolhof, **Doran**, Douglas Green, Eagle's Cliff, Goedverwacht, Idiom, Jacaranda, Jordan (2), Journey's End, Ken Forrester, Klein Parys, Kleine Zalze, Knorhoek, **Leeuwenberg**, Leopard Frog, Leopard's Leap, Louiesenhof, Lourensford, MolenVliet, Monterosso, Morgenhof, Mostertsdrift, Mountain Oaks (Organic), Nordic, Passages, Rainbow's End, Rietvallei, Rosendal, Saxenburg, Scrucap, Simonsvlei, Slaley, Slanghoek, **Spier**, Steenberg, Stellendrift, The Winery of Good Hope, Two Oceans, Vondeling, **Vrede**, Walker Bay Vineyards, Woolworths, Zorgvliet ★★★ Akkerdal, Anura, Arniston Bay, Asara, Bon Courage, **Cape Classics**, Darling Cellars, De Breede (Organic), Diemersdal, Diemersfontein (2), **Doran**, Douglas Green, **Fernskloof**, Glen Carlou, **Hathersage**, Havana Hills, Jason's Hill, La Petite Provence, McGregor, Montpellier, Mooiplaas, Org de Rac (Organic), Overgaauw, Perdeberg, Rhebokskloof, Riebeek, Rooiberg, Schalkenbosch, Simonsig, Somerset Wines, **Steenberg**, **Stellendrift**, Sterhuis, uniWines, Van Loveren, Van Zylshof, Vaughan Johnson, **Vierlanden**, Waverley Hills (Organic), Windmeul, Wineways (2) ★★ Bonnievale, Craighall, Hoopenburg, Kleine Draken (Kosher), La Couronne, Morgenhof, **Tulbagh Winery**, Ultra Liquors (2), **Wineways** (2), Woolworths ★★ Overhex, Robertson, **Swartland**, Wineways ★ Lathithá, Swartland, Tanagra **NT** Akkerdal, Alluvia, Alto, Amani, Barry Gould, Bernheim (2), BLANKbottle (2), Boer & Brit, Bonfoi, Camberley, Crows Nest, Equitania, Govert, Hathersage, High Constantia, Jean Daneel, Maison de Teijger (2), Môreson (2), Natte Valleij, Nederburg, Nico Vermeulen, Nietvoorbij (2), Noble Hill, Old Vines, Rico Suter, Rosendal, Ruitersvlei, Springfontein, Stellendrift, Tanagra, Vendôme (2), Versailles, Webersburg, Welgevallen, Wolfkloof,

Wolvendrift, Woolworths **NR** Claime d'Or **D** David Frost, Druk My Niet (2), Eagles' Nest, Hornbill , Iona, Kronendal, KWV, Main Street, MC Square, Meerendal, Tanagra, Thandi, The High Road, Ultra Liquors, Vondeling, Wedderwill, Wineways (2)

Red blends, other

★★★★★ Bouchard Finlayson, Delaire, Ken Forrester

★★★★☆ Anwilka, Ataraxia, Bilton, De Trafford, Druk My Niet, Ernie Els (2), Fairview, Graham Beck, Jean Daneel, Ken Forrester, **Klein Constantia**, Lourensford, Nederburg (2), Nico van der Merwe, Rust en Rede, The Winery of Good Hope, Uva Mira, Val de Vie, Waterford

★★★★ Akkerdal, Alto, Amani (2), Anatu, Annandale (2), Anwilka, Backsberg (2), Beau Joubert, Bergsig, BLANKbottle, Boplaas, Boschendal, **Bryan MacRobert**, Capaia, De Krans, De Meye, Eikendal, **Glen Carlou**, Graceland (2), Hout Bay, Keermont, Ken Forrester, Klein Gustrouw, KWV, Le Bonheur, Lingen, Marianne, Micu Narunsky, Mont du Toit (3), Morgenster, Nabygelegen, Neil Ellis Meyer-Näkel, Nietgegund, **Osbloed** (2), **Perdeberg**, Plaisir, Rustenberg, Silvermist (Organic), Somersbosch, Steenberg, Stony Brook, Strydom, The Goose, Veenwouden, Waterkloof

★★★★ Adoro, Akkerdal, Anthonij Rupert (2), Ashton, Avondale (Organic), Axe Hill, Babylonstoren, Badsberg, Blaauwklippen (2), Black Oystercatcher, BLANKbottle, Boplaas, Boschheim, Brothers, Capaia, Casa Mori, Cederberg, Chateau Libertas, Clos Malverne, Desert Rose, Dormershire, Durbanville Hills, Edgebaston, **Escapades**, Fairview, Faraway House, Flagstone, Franki's, GlenWood, Goats do Roam (2), Groote Post, Guardian Peak, Hartenberg, Haut Espoir, Havana Hills, Idiom, Jacques Smit, Joostenberg, Kaapzicht, Kanu, Kyburg, La Kavayan, La Vierge, Leopard Frog, Lutzville, Mary Le Bow, Mont du Toit, Nederburg, Noble Hill, **Osbloed**, **Peter Falke**, Plaisir, Rhebokskloof, Roodeberg, Saxenburg, Skilpadvlei, Stellekaya, Stellenrust, Stony Brook, Swartland, Topiary, **TTT Cellar**, Val de Vie, Veenwouden, Vergenoegd (2), Virgin Earth, Woolworths (4), Zonnebloem ★★★ Arra, Audacia, Avontuur, Backsberg, Bayede! (2), Blomendahl, Blue Crane, Bon Courage, Boschendal, **Bushmanspad**, Cloof, Dornier, Du Toitskloof , Goede Hoop, **Graceland**, Hermanuspietersfontein, Hermit on the Hill, Hill & Dale, **Holden Manz**, Idiom, Koopmanskloof, Kumala (3), La Petite Ferme, Landskroon, Leeuwenjacht, Lievland, Micu

Narunsky, Mon Rêve, Mont Rochelle, Napier, Raka, Ridgeback, **Rosendal**, Simonsig, Sophie & Mr P, Springfontein, Stonehill, Tanagra, The Rhino, The Township Winery, Thelema, **Ultra Liquors**, Van Loveren, Villiera, Waterstone, Woolworths ★★★ Aan de Doorns, Allée Bleue, Almenkerk, **BLANKbottle**, Blouvlei, Bonnievale, Botha, Burgershof, Camberley, Crows Nest, **Darling Cellars**, David Frost Signature, De Zoete Inval, Goudini, Highlands Road, Idiom, Klein Parys, Kumala, Landskroon, **Leeuwenberg**, Lynx, **Mitre's Edge**, Mzoli's, Robertson, Rustenberg, Simonsvlei, Skilpadvlei, Somerset Wines, Stettyn, Stoumann's, Tassenberg, TCB Wines, The Hills, Van Loveren, Versus, Villiersdorp, Waterstone, Waverley Hills (Organic), Wildehurst, Windfall, Woolworths, Zandvliet ★★ African Terroir, Angels Tears, Ashton, **Barnardt Boyes**, Beaumont, Bergwater (2), Boland, Calais, Cranefields, Du'SwaRoo, KWV, Landskroon (2), Leopard's Leap, Main Street, Oude Compagnies Post, Southern Sky, Stellenbosch Hills, Swartland, Taverna Rouge, Theuniskraal, uniWines, **Waterstone** (2), Whalehaven ★★ Barrydale, Bonne Esperance, Brandvlei, Calais, **Du'SwaRoo**, Kumala, Mountain River, Peter Bayly, Pick n Pay, Robertson (2), Roodezandt, Simonsvlei, Van Loveren, Woolworths (3) ★ Overmeer Cellars **NT** Abbottshill, African Terroir, Akkerdal, Bonnievale, Buffalo Creek, Cape Rock, Clovelly, **Gilga**, Govert, Herold, Jean Daneel, Klein Constantia, Libby's Pride, Melkboomsdrift, Montagu Wine Cellar, Natte Valleij, Nederburg (2), Nuy, Quoin Rock, Retief (2), Rico Suter (2), Roodeberg, Ruitersvlei, Schalkenbosch, Signal Hill, Tierhoek, TTT Cellar, Vergenoegd, Vleiland, Vriesenhof , Waterstone, Welvanpas (2), Westbridge, Withington **NR** Ariston Bay, **Catch Of The Day**, Delheim **D** Babylon's Peak, Bottelary, De Krans, Group CDV, Hazendal, Hornbill , Newton Johnson, Overgaauw, Remhoogte, Swartland, Vaughan Johnson, Waterstone

Red blends, shiraz/syrah-based

★★★★☆ AA Badenhorst, Anatu, **Arra**, Asara, Boekenhoutskloof, Cape Rock, Creation, **David**, Glenelly, Iona, La Motte, Lammershoek, **Luddite** (2), **Neil Ellis**, Reyneke (Biodynamic), Rust en Rede, Sadie, **Savage**, Sequillo, Strandveld, Welbedacht

★★★★ AA Badenhorst, Akkerdal, Avondale (Organic), Ayama, BABISA, Babylon's Peak, Barton, Beaumont, Bellingham, Black Pearl, BLANKbottle, Bon Cap (Organic), Bosman (Fairtrade), Bovlei, Bushmanspad, Cecilia, Crios Bríde, Darling Cellars,

Deux Frères, Domaine des Dieux, Eagle's Cliff, Eaglevlei, Edgebaston, Emineo, Ernie Els, Fable, Goats do Roam, Grangehurst, Groenland, Guardian Peak, Havana Hills, Hermanuspietersfontein, Hermit on the Hill, Hidden Valley, Hoopenburg, Hughes Family, Kronendal, KWV, La Motte, Landskroon, **Leopard's Leap**, Meerhof, MolenVliet (2), Mont Destin, Mullineux, Nederburg (Fairtrade), Neil Ellis, Newton Johnson, Nico Vermeulen, Oude Denneboom, Painted Wolf, **Paradisum**, Post House, Rall, Ridgeback, Saronsberg, Schalkenbosch, Scrucap, Sijnn, Simonsvlei, Solms-Delta, Spice Route (2), Spier, Stellenbosch Hills, Stony Brook, The Butcher Shop, The Winery of Good Hope, Tierhoek, **Topaz**, Val de Vie, Wildehurst, Woolworths (Biodynamic), Zevenwacht (2)

★★★★ Alkmaar, Annex Kloof, Auction Crossing, Axe Hill, Babylon's Peak, Beaumont, Bilton, **Blackwater**, Boschendal, Brenaissance, **Credo**, Diemersfontein, **Eenzaamheid** (2), Feiteiras, Flat Roof Manor, Four Paws, Groenland, Heron Ridge, Idiom, Joostenberg (Organic), Kaapzicht, Karusa, Kleine Zalze, Kloovenburg, Lazanou (Organic), Le Joubert, Leeuwenkuil, Leopard's Leap, Louis, Lourensford, Lynx, Mont Destin, Mount Babylon, Naughton's, Nico van der Merwe, Noble Hill, Nuweland, Ormonde, Painted Wolf, Rickety Bridge, Ridgeback, Rietvallei, Rosendal, **Spier**, Stettyn, Teddy Hall, The Grape Grinder, The Winery of Good Hope, Trajan, uniWines, Vredenheim, Waterford, Welgegund, Woolworths, Yardstick, Zonnebloem ★★★ Arniston Bay, Arra, Ayama, Beau Joubert, Bernheim, Boschendal, Cape Point, D'Aria, **Darling Cellars** (2), DeMorgenzon, Doolhof, Drostdy-Hof, Eagle's Cliff, Eenzaamheid, Eikendal, Freedom Hill, Graham Beck (2), Hermanuspietersfontein, Jacaranda, Juno, Kanu, Karusa, Kleine Zalze, Koelenhof, Kumala, **Lanzerac**, Lindhorst, Lourensford, MAN Family (2), Manley, Muratie, Nederburg (2), Porcupine Ridge, Post House, Robert Stanford, Schalkenbosch, Simonsig, Somersbosch, Teddy Hall, **The Liberator**, The Wolftrap, Thokozani, Two Oceans, Uitkyk, Val du Charron, Waterford, Waverley Hills (Organic), Wedderwill (Biodynamic), **William Everson**, Withington ★★★ **Andy Mitchell**, Arniston Bay, Bellingham, D'Aria, De Wet, Drostdy-Hof, Excelsior, **Groenland**, Hazendal, **Jean Daneel**, Kanu, Klawer, Kleine Zalze, Leopard Frog, Longridge, **Maske**, Old Vines, **Oude Compagnies Post**, **Pulpit Rock**, Savanha (Fairtrade), **The Liberator**, **Vins d'Orrance**, **Virgin Earth**, Zevenwacht ★★ Allesverloren, **Barnardt Boyes**, Hoopenburg, Kleine Zalze, Lynx, Malan Family, Overhex,

Savanha, Somersbosch, Tulbagh Winery, Waka Waka ★★ TTT Cellar, Woolworths (Light & low-alcohol), Zidela **NT** Abbottshill, Akkerdal, AntHill, Boer & Brit, Boscheim, Cape Rock, Du'SwaRoo, Govert, Haskell, Hawksmoor (2), Hazendal, Joostenberg, La Ferme Derik, Le Joubert, Lindhorst, Malanot (2), Neil Ellis, Orangerie, Oude Compagnies Post, Reiersvlei, Retief, Reyneke (Organic), Riebeek, Saam, Summerhill, Thandi, Valley Vineyards (2) **D** Bottelary, Catherine Marshall, Croydon, Graham Beck, KWV, La Vierge, Orange River, Rijk's (2), Simonsvlei, Springfontein, Ultra Liquors, Zidela

Red blends, with pinotage

★★★★★ Windmeul

★★★★☆ Ashbourne, Beyerskloof, Bosman, Kaapzicht (2), Lanzerac, Meinert, Spier

★★★★ Altydgedacht, Alvi's Drift, **Anura**, Beaumont, Beyerskloof, Brampton, Clos Malverne (2), Devon Hill, Doolhof, Eaglevlei, Emineo, Flagstone, Goede Hoop, Grangehurst, **Hornbill**, Idiom, Klein Parys, **Meerendal**, Middelvlei, Post House, Raka, Rijk's, Rupert & Rothschild, Simonsig, Sumaridge, Warwick, Welbedacht, Wellington Winery, Wildekrans, Woolworths

★★★★ Bon Cap (Organic), Croydon (2), Domaine Brahms, Durbanville Hills, Eaglevlei, **Eenzaamheid**, **Hawksmoor** (2), La Chataigne, Lindhorst, Lyngrove (2), Maske, Remhoogte (2), Rooiberg, Slaley, Solms-Delta, Stellekaya, Stellenbosch University, Stellenrust, Stellenzicht, **The Wine Fusion**, Truter Family, Umkhulu, Val du Charron, Viljoensdrift, Welgemeend ★★★ Anura, Arniston Bay, Arra, Asara, Bergsig, Bernheim, Cloof (2), **Clos Malverne**, **Die Mas**, Doolhof, Douglas Green, Du Toitskloof (2), **Esau**, Flagstone, Freedom Hill (2), Groot Constantia, Hillock, Kanonkop, Kumala, L'Avenir, Lateganskop, Leeuwenberg, Leopard Frog, **Lithos**, **Marianne** (2), **Meinert**, Mellasat, Middelvlei, Mostertsdrift, Mount Vernon, Opstal, Oude Compagnies Post, Stellekaya, Two Oceans, Umkhulu, **Vrede**, Woolworths ★★☆ African Terroir (Organic), Cloof, Conradie, De Krans, Drostdy-Hof, Du Preez, Faraway House, **Fernskloof**, Kumala, Lemberg, Louiesenhof, **Overhex** (2), Rooiberg, **Savanha**, Seven Sisters, Slaley, **Spekulasie**, Stellar (Organic), Stellenbosch Hills, Vruchtbaar, Welbedacht, Zidela ★★ BurCon, De Doorns, Dragonridge, Jonkheer, Koelenhof , Mountain Oaks (Organic), Pearly Bay, Savanha, Slanghoek, Stellendrift, Stellenrust (Fairtrade), **Tulbagh Winery**, Waterstone, Woolworths ★★ Douglas Green, Montagu Wine & Spirits ★ Skilpadvlei **NT** African

Pride, Bellevue, Bernheim, BLANKbottle, Bon Cap, Domaine Brahms, Lorraine, Marklew, Mountain River, Nordic, Obikwa, Re'Mogo, Sizanani, Stellendrift, SylvanVale, Waboomsrivier **D** Credo, Fairview, Hornbill , Leeuwenberg, Mellasat, Simonsvlei, Springfontein

Riesling

★★★★☆ Woolworths

★★★★ Groote Post, Hartenberg, Klein Constantia, Nitida, Paul Cluver (2) (Light & low-alcohol), **Scrucap** (Light & low-alcohol), The Drift

★★★☆ Altydgedacht, De Wetshof, Fairview, **Hartenberg**, Howard Booysen, Jordan, **Meinert**, Nederburg, Osbloed, Spioenkop, Thelema (2), Villiera ★★★ BLANKbottle, La Vierge ★★☆ **Lothian NT** Howard Booysen, Rosendal, Ross Gower **D** Woolworths

Rosé dry

★★★★ **Cape Rock**, Croydon, Grangehurst, Solms-Delta

★★★☆ Anatu, Arumdale, Cederberg, De Meye, Delaire, DeMorgenzon, Desert Rose, Goats do Roam, **Groot Parys** (Organic), Hermanuspietersfontein, Holden Manz, Lammershoek, Morgenster, **Rivendell**, Romond, Schalkenbosch, **Signal Gun**, Sijnn, South Hill, Stonehill, Tamboerskloof, The Drift, Topiary, Wildehurst ★★★ Almenkerk, Anatu, Avondale (Organic), Avontuur, Barton, Beaumont, Bein, Beyerskloof, **Bloemendal**, Blomendahl, Brampton, Bushmanspad, Clouds, Dunstone, Eikendal, Elgin Vintners, Feiteiras (2), Fort Simon, Hawksmoor (2), Herold, Hill & Dale, Hillcrest, Hout Bay, Jacaranda, Jordan, Kanonkop, Kleine Zalze, L'Avenir, La Petite Ferme, La Petite Vigne, Leeuwenjacht, **Leopard's Leap**, Nederburg, Noble Hill, Painted Wolf, Rainbow's End, Raka, Robert Stanford, Sophie & Mr P, Strandveld, SylvanVale, The Butcher Shop, Tokara, Waterkloof, Whalehaven ★★★ Babylonstoren, Beau Belle, Beau Joubert, Black Oystercatcher, Bon Cap (Organic), Bosman, Claime d'Or, De Grendel, **De Krans**, Diemersdal, Doolhof, Dornier, Douglas Green, Durbanville Hills, Escapades, Fairview, **Foothills**, **Joostenberg** (2) (Organic), Kloovenburg, Knorhoek, Koopmanskloof, La Chataigne, La Couronne, Le Bonheur, Leopard Frog, Mount Vernon, Muratie, New Beginnings, Niel Joubert, **Nuweland**, Plettenvale, Quando, Rickety Bridge, Ridgeback, Riebeek, Saronsberg, Scrucap, Slaley, Slowine, **Spekulasie**, Spotswood, Springfontein,

Thandi (Fairtrade), **Thelema**, Vergenoegd, Woolworths, **Zorgvliet** ★★ African Pride, Ayama, Bellingham, Bernheim, Cloof, **Doran**, Du'SwaRoo, Eerste Hoop, Group CDV, Hoopenburg, Kleine Zalze, Koopmanskloof, **Leeuwenberg**, Leopard's Leap, Marianne, Mellasat, Mont Rochelle, Mooiplaas, **Mountain River**, Org de Rac (Organic), Pulpit Rock, **Rhebokskloof**, Savanha, Stellar (2) (Organic, Fairtrade), Waverley Hills (Organic), Welmoed ★★ False Bay, Overhex, **Steenberg**, Zandvliet ★ African Terroir (Organic), **Group CDV**, Koelenhof , Org de Rac **NT** Abbottshill, African Terroir, **Allesverloren**, Andy Mitchell, Blomendahl, Blouvlei, Cape Dreams, Citrusdal, Dormershire, Dragonridge, Felicité, Fernskloof, Groot Parys (Organic), Group CDV, Haut Espoir, High Constantia (2), Highlands Road, Hildenbrand, Klein Constantia, La Ferme Derik, Land's End, Le Pommier, Mitre's Edge, Mountain Oaks (Organic), **Nuweland**, Oude Compagnies Post, Overhex (Fairtrade), Perdeberg, Signal Hill, Sizanani, **Stellenbosch University**, Stony Brook, Waterford, Wolfkloof, Zorgvliet **NR** Lord's, Walker Bay Vineyards **D** De Krans, De Wetshof, Devonair, Group CDV (2), Nabygelegen, Welgegund, Woolworths

Rosé off-dry/semi-sweet

★★★☆ AA Badenhorst, Eaglevlei, Sumaridge ★★★ Allée Bleue, Anura, Backsberg, Fish Hoek, Haute Cabrière, Karusa, Ladismith, **Lanzerac**, Lourensford, Meinert, **Merwida**, Mulderbosch, Noble Savage, Opstal, Ross Gower, **Tread Lightly**, Val de Vie, Winters Drift, Wonderfontein, Woolworths (2) ★★★ Badsberg, **Beau Belle**, Blaauwklippen, Blomendahl, Bovlei, Darling Cellars, De Wet (Perlé), Eagle's Cliff, Franschhoek Cellar, Gabriëlskloof, Goedverwacht, Graham Beck, Hazendal, **Hillock**, Kumala (2), KWV, Meerendal, Morgenhof, Nederburg, Nelson, **Nuweland**, Obikwa, Orange River, Rooiberg, Stellenrust (Fairtrade), The Rhino, Theuniskraal, Thokozani, Two Oceans, Wandsbeck (Perlé), **Wellington Winery**, **Woolworths** (3), Zevenwacht, Zidela ★★ Amani, Arniston Bay, Asara, Autumn Harvest Crackling, Bergsig, **Bergwater**, Boland, Bon Courage, Botha, Bottelary, Brandvlei, Calitzdorp, D'Aria, Delheim, Douglas Green, Du Toitskloof (Perlé), Flat Roof Manor (Light & low-alcohol), Goudini, Imbuko, **Kanu** (2), Ken Forrester, Kleinfontein, Koelenhof , **Laborie** (Light & low-alcohol), Lathithá, **Leeuwenkuil**, Louiesenhof (Perlé), MAN Family, Overhex (Light & low-alcohol), Pearly Bay (2) (Light & low-alcohol), Rhebokskloof, Slanghoek (Light & low-alcohol), Stellar (Organic,

Fairtrade), Van Loveren (2) (Light & low-alcohol), Versus, Vredenheim, Waterstone, Welbedacht, Woolworths (2) ★★ Angels Tears, Arniston Bay (2) (Light & low-alcohol), Drostdy-Hof, Graça, Hartswater, Jonkheer, Kleine Draken (Kosher), **Long Mountain**, McGregor, **Montagu Wine & Spirits**, **Ruitersvlei**, Swartland (Light & low-alcohol), Woolworths ★ Ashton, Bonnievale (Perlé, Light & low-alcohol), Cellar Cask, Overmeer Cellars, Wineways ✦ Riebeek **NT** Benguela Cove, Bovlei, Buffalo Creek, Devon Rocks, Havana Hills, Lorraine, Lutzville, Mountain Ridge, Mzoli's, Nietvoorbij, Pick n Pay, Robertson, Saxenburg, Stoumann's, Tulbagh Winery, Welvanpas **NR** Mostertsdrift **D** Beau Belle, Drostdy-Hof, Goedverwacht, Havana Hills, Lanzerac, Merwida, uniWines, Van Zylshof, Viljoensdrift, Zidela

Roussanne

★★★★★ Simonsig

★★★★ Bellingham, Painted Wolf, The Foundry

★★★☆ Rustenberg **D** The Three Foxes

Ruby cabernet

★★★☆ Nuweland ★★★ Bellpost, Orange River, Robertson (2) ★★★ Langverwacht, Lutzville ★★ Ladismith ★★ Barrydale, Hartswater, McGregor ★ Long Mountain **NT** Kingsriver

Sacramental Wines

★★ Backsberg (Sweet red, Sacramental, Kosher), Kleine Draken (Sacramental wine) ★★ **Landzicht** (Sacramental wine)

Sangiovese

★★★★ Anura

★★★☆ Anthonij Rupert, Fairview, Idiom, Monterosso, Spring Grove ★★★ Dragonridge, Raka ★★★ Bovlei ★★ Koelenhof **D** The Three Foxes

Sauvignon blanc unwooded

★★★★★ Klein Constantia, Kleine Zalze, Tokara

★★★★☆ Ataraxia, Bartinney, **Boschendal**, Buitenverwachting (2), Constantia Glen, Corder, De Grendel, Delaire, Diemersdal (2), Flagstone, Fleur du Cap, Fryer's Cove, Graham Beck, Groote Post, **Hillcrest** (2), Phizante Kraal, Rivendell, Southern Right, Spioenkop, Strandveld, Tokara, Vergelegen, Warwick

★★★★ Aaldering, Allée Bleue, Almenkerk, Anthonij Rupert, Anura, Benguela Cove, Black

Oystercatcher, **Boplaas**, Boschendal, Bouchard Finlayson (2), Bramon, Brampton, Brunia, Capaia, Cape Hutton, Catherine Marshall, Cederberg (2), Constantia Mist, Constantia Uitsig, Dalla Cia, Darling Cellars, De Grendel, Delaire, Domaine des Dieux, Driehoek, Durbanville Hills, Eagle's Cliff, Elgin Heights, Fairview, Garden Route, GlenWood, Groot Constantia, Groote Post, Havana Hills, Hermanuspietersfontein (2), Hidden Valley, Hillock, Izak van der Vyver, Jordan, Klein Constantia, **KWV** (4), Lanner Hill, Lanzerac, **Le Bonheur**, Lomond (3), Longridge, Louis, Meinert, Merwida, Nederburg, Neethlingshof, Neil Ellis, Nitida (2), **Ormonde**, Packwood, Plaisir, Reyneke (Organic), Robert Stanford, Robertson, Saronsberg, Saxenburg, Sir Lambert, Skaap, Spice Route, **Spier**, Springfield, **Star Hill**, Stony Brook, Sumaridge, **Teubes**, Thandi, The Berrio, The Butcher Shop, Thelema (2), Tokara, Trizanne, Uva Mira, Vergelegen, Villiera, Virgin Earth, Vondeling, Waterford (2), Waterkloof, Webersburg, Woolworths (4), Zonnebloem, Zorgvliet

★★★☆ Adoro, African Pride, Alluvia, Altydgedacht, Alvi's Drift, Annandale, Anura, Arumdale, Asara, Avontuur, Bayede!, **Bloemendal**, Blomendahl, Boplaas, Bushmanspad, Callender, Claime d'Or, Clos Malverne, Clouds, Creation, Crios Bríde, Darling Cellars, **David Frost**, **De Bos** (Fairtrade), De Wetshof, Doolhof, Dunstone, Durbanville Hills, Eagles' Nest, Elgin Grove, Elgin Ridge (Organic), Elgin Vintners, **Excelsior**, Fort Simon, Fryer's Cove, Grande Provence, Groenland, **Guardian Peak**, Hannay, Hartenberg, Hill & Dale, Hillock, Hout Bay, Kaapzicht, Karusa, Ken Forrester, Klein Constantia, Klein Gustrouw, L'Avenir, La Chataigne, La Motte, La Petite Ferme, Laborie, Land's End, Le Bonheur, Lindhorst, Longbarn, Lourensford, Lutzville, Maastricht, Meerendal, Mofam, Morgenhof, Mulderbosch, **Nederburg** (2) (Fairtrade), Neethlingshof, Neil Ellis, Newstead, Nico Vermeulen, Noble Hill, Nuweland, Oak Valley, Old Vines, **Ormonde** (3), Overgaauw, Peter Falke, Place in the Sun (Fairtrade), Quando, **Rare Earth**, Ridgeback, Rietvallei, Ross Gower, Rustenberg, Scrucap (2), Seven Springs, Seven Steps, **Signal Gun** (2), Silvermist (Organic), Simonsig, Simonsvlei, Spier, Spioenkop, Spring Grove, Springfield, Springfontein, Stellenrust, **Super Single Vineyards**, Thandi (Fairtrade), The Goose (2), The Township Winery, Trajan, **Trizanne**, Uitkyk, Ultra Liquors, Van Loveren, Van Zylshof, Villiera, **Waterstone** (2), Wedderwil (Biodynamic), Welmoed, **Woolworths** (3), Zoetendal ★★★ African Terroir, Almenkerk, Anthonij Rupert, Avontuur, Ayama, Backsberg, Barton, Bellingham, Bergsig,

Blouvlei, Bon Cap (Organic), Boschendal, Boschkloof , Botha, **Breëland**, Brenaissance, Brothers, Cape Classics, Cape Point, Catch Of The Day, Cloof, Conradie, D'Aria, De Wetshof, DeWaal, Diemersdal, Dornier, Douglas Green, Du Preez, Du Toitskloof , Durbanville Hills, Eagle's Cliff, Ernie Els, Fairvalley (Fairtrade), False Bay (2), Flagstone, Fleur du Cap, Fort Simon, Four Paws, Franschhoek Cellar, **Fryer's Cove**, Galleon, Glen Carlou, Graham Beck, Hathersage, Havana Hills, Helderberg, Herold, Imbuko, Journey's End, Kanu, Ken Forrester, Klawer, Kleine Zalze, Kloovenburg, Knorhoek, Kranskop, KWV, Le Pommier, Lorraine, Louis, Louisvale, LuKa, Lutzville, Lyngrove, MAN Family, Miravel, Monterosso, Mooiplaas, Mount Rozier, Nabygelegen, Nederburg, Nelson, Noble Savage, Nomada, Onderkloof , Overhex, PaardenKloof, Perdeberg, Porcupine Ridge, Raka, Rickety Bridge, Rietvallei (2), Rosendal (3), Saam, Sauvignon.com, Seal Breeze, Seven Sisters, Sophie & Mr P, Spier, Stellenzicht, Stoumann's, Strandveld, SylvanVale, Teubes, The Butcher Shop, **The Giant Periwinkle**, Tread Lightly, Tulbagh Winery, Ultra Liquors, uniWines, Vaalvlei, Val de Vie, Versailles, Waka Waka, Waterford, Welbedacht, Welgevallen, Windfall, Winters Drift, Wonderfontein, Woolworths (3), Yonder Hill, Zevenwacht, **Zidela**, Zonnebloem, Zorgvliet ★★★ African Pride, Andersons, Angels Tears, Arniston Bay, **Asara**, **Baleia Bay**, Beau Joubert, Bergwater, Bilton, Blaauwklippen, Blue Crane, Boland, Bon Courage, Bonnievale, **Boplaas** (2), Bovlei, Cloverfield, Dâbar, De Wet, Delheim, Die Mas, Diemersdal, Du Preez, **Earthbound** (Organic, Fairtrade), Fairview, Fish Hoek, **Foothills**, Glenview, Goede Hoop, Goedvertrouw, Goedverwacht, Goudini, Hoopenburg, House of Mandela, Juno, Klein Parys, **Knorhoek**, Koopmanskloof, La Petite Vigne, Landskroon, Leopard's Leap, Lievland, Linton Park, Lord's, Louiesenhof, Lourensford, Mount Vernon, Mountain River (2), Muratie, Namaqua, Niel Joubert, Orange River, Reiersvlei, Robertson, Schalkenbosch, Simonsig, Skilpadvlei, Slaley, Slanghoek, Slowine, Somerbosch, Somerset Wines, Stellar (Organic, Fairtrade), Stellenbosch Hills, Stellenbosch University, **Stettyn**, The Rhino, The Township Winery, Two Oceans, uniWines (Fairtrade), Vredenheim, Walker Bay Vineyards, Waterstone (2), Welbedacht, Wellington Winery, Weltevrede, Whalehaven, Windmeul, Wineways, Woolworths (2) (Organic, Fairtrade), **Zidela** ★★ Aan de Doorns, African Terroir (2) (Organic), Badsberg, **Black Elephant**, Boland, Boplaas, Burgershof, Calais, Cape Dreams, Clairvaux, Corder,

Craighall, D'Aria, Drostdy-Hof, **Eagle's Cliff**, Excelsior, Flat Roof Manor, Highlands Road, Hoopenburg, Imbuko, Jonkheer, Klein Roosboom , Kleine Draken (Kosher), Koelenhof (2), La Couronne, Ladismith, Langverwacht, Lateganskop, Libby's Pride, McGregor, Nuy, Obikwa, Rhebokskloof, Riebeek, **Robertson** (4) (Light & low-alcohol), Roodezandt, Rooiberg, Ruitersvlei, Savanha, Steenberg, Stellenbosch Hills, Swartland, United Nations (Fairtrade), Van Loveren (2), Wandsbeck, Waterstone, Wineways (2), Withoek, Woolworths, **Zevenwacht** ★★ Ashton, Barrydale, Bayede!, Brandvlei, Jonkheer, Long Mountain, Montagu Wine & Spirits, **Rooiberg** (Light & low-alcohol), Viljoensdrift, **Waterstone** (2), Wineways, Zandvliet ★ **Montagu Wine Cellar**, **Waterstone**, Woolworths **NT** African Terroir (2), Akkerdal, Alluvia, Badgerberg, Barry Gould, **Bayede!**, Bellevue, Boer & Brit, Bonfoi, Buffalo Creek, Calitzdorp, Camberley, Citrusdal, Devon Hill, Dormershire, Durbanville Hills (2), DuVon, Ernst Gouws, Freedom Hill, Hazendal, Het Vlock Casteel, High Constantia (2), Jason's Hill, Kingsriver, Klein Roosboom , L'Olivier, La Motte (Organic), Linton Park, Mimosa, Montpellier, Môreson (2), Mountain Ridge, Nederburg (2), Noble Hill, Nuweland, Post House, Rico Suter, Sizanani, South Hill, Spier, Stanford Hills, Stellendrift, Sumsaré, Swartland, TCB Wines, Tierhoek, Tulbagh Winery, United Nations, Valley Vineyards (2), Waboomsrivier, Welvanpas, Wolvendrift, Woolworths (Organic), Zidela **NR Flagstone**, Usana **D** Bloemendal (2), Boschendal, De Villiers, Delheim, Goedverwacht, Goudini, KWV, La Vierge, M'hudi, Perdeberg, Saam, Simonsvlei (2), Steenberg, Stettyn, Weltevrede, William Everson

Sauvignon blanc wooded

★★★★★ Cederberg, Mulderbosch

★★★★☆ Cape Point, Diemersdal, **Hermanuspietersfontein**, Hermit on the Hill, Iona, Nederburg, Quoin Rock (2), Reyneke (Biodynamic), Shannon, Waterkloof, Zevenwacht

★★★★ Black Oystercatcher, Bloemendal, Buitenverwachting, Cape Chamonix, Cape Point, Diners Club Bartho Eksteen , Eikendal, Hermanuspietersfontein, Hermit on the Hill, Jordan, Le Pommier, Lourensford, Meerendal, **Neil Ellis**, Newton Johnson, Paul Cluver, Rickety Bridge, **Steenberg**, Sterhuis, The Butcher Shop, The Goose, Tierhoek

★★★★ Backsberg, D'Aria, Dombeya, **Driefontein**, Edgebaston, Escapades, Gabriëlskloof, Glen Erskine,

Painted Wolf, Stark-Condé, Steenberg, Wildekrans
★★★ Amani, Marianne, Steenberg ★★☆ Fat Bastard, Opstal ★★ Robertson ★★ Swartland NT African Terroir, DeMorgenzon, Leeuwenberg, Mont Rochelle, Spioenkop, Stone Ridge NR Lemberg D Cape Chamonix, Neil Ellis, Stony Brook

Semillon unwooded

★★★★ Lutzville, Zonnebloem

★★★☆ Ormonde ★★★ Withington ★★☆ The Wine Fusion NT Nederburg D Bloemendal

Semillon wooded

★★★★★ Constantia Uitsig

★★★★☆ Boekenhoutskloof, Cederberg, Lanner Hill, Stony Brook, Vergelegen

★★★★ Anthonij Rupert, Dornier, Fairview, Fleur du Cap, GlenWood, KWV, Shannon, Steenberg

★★★☆ Escapades, Hathersage, Rickety Bridge
★★★ Franschhoek Cellar, Haut Espoir, La Chataigne NT Eaglevlei, Hildenbrand, Landau du Val, My Wyn, Nitida, Stellenzicht

Sherry-Styles

★★★★ KWV Sherry-Styles (2), Monis

★★★☆ Douglas Green (3), Monis (2) ★★ Landzicht

Shiraz/syrah

★★★★★ Cederberg, Delheim, Eagles' Nest, Fable, Hilton, Mont Destin, Mullineux (2), Raka, Rust en Vrede, Saronsberg, Sijnn, Stark-Condé

★★★★☆ AA Badenhorst, Arra, Avontuur, Boekenhoutskloof, Boschdal, Cirrus, De Grendel, De Trafford, Fairview (4), Flagstone, GlenWood, Groote Post, Hartenberg (3), Haskell, Hermit on the Hill, Julien Schaal, La Motte, Lazanou (Organic), Lomond (2), Lourensford, Luddite, Metzer, Mullineux, Muratie (2), Nico van der Merwe, Quoin Rock, Rainbow's End, Reyneke (Biodynamic), Rijk's, Robertson, Rudera, Rustenberg, Saxenburg, Scali, Schultz Family, Signal Hill, Sijnn, Simonsig (2), Solms-Delta, Stony Brook, Strandveld, Tamboerskloof, The Foundry, The Three Foxes, Vergelegen, Vergenoegd, Vins d'Orrance, Waterford, Waterkloof

★★★★ Aaldering, Akkerdal, Almenkerk, Andreas, Annandale, Anthonij Rupert, Anura (2), Arra, Babylonstoren, Belfield, Bellingham, Bilton, Blaauwklippen (2), Bloemendal, Boland, Bon

Courage, Boschendal, Boschkloof, Boschrivier, Cederberg, Cloof, Creation, D'Aria, De Breede (Organic), De Trafford, DeanDavid, Delaire, Delheim, DeMorgenzon, DewaldtHeyns, Diemersdal, Dombeya, Driehoek, Dunstone, Eagle's Cliff, Elgin Vintners, Ernie Els, Gabriëlskloof, Graham Beck, Groot Constantia, Hartenberg, Haskell, Haut Espoir, Hermit on the Hill, Heron Ridge, Hildenbrand, Hilton, Hoopenburg, House of Mandela, Joostenberg, Katbakkies, Keermont, Kleine Zalze (2), Koelfontein, KWV, La Petite Ferme, Laborie, Ladera, Lammershoek (2), Land's End, Lomond, Longridge, M'hudi, Maastricht, Maison, Malanot, Meerhof, Metzer, Middelvlei, Migliarina, MolenVliet, Mooiplaas, Mountain Ridge, Nabygelegen, Namaqua, Nederburg, Nico van der Merwe, Niel Joubert, Nuy, Oak Valley, Org de Rac (Organic), Ormonde, Oude Denneboom, Perdeberg, Quoin Rock, Remhoogte, Rhebokskloof, Rickety Bridge, Ridgeback, Rijk's (2), Rivendell, Robert Stanford, Robertson, Rooiberg, Rust en Rede, Saltaré, Saxenburg, Schultz Family, Simonsig, Solo, Spice Route, Spier, Star Hill, Stark-Condé, Steenberg, Stellekaya, Stellenrust, Stellenzicht, Super Single Vineyards, Swartland, The Butcher Shop, The Winery of Good Hope (3) (Fairtrade), Thelema, Tokara, Topiary, Trizanne (2), Val de Vie, Vergelegen, Vergenoegd, Vondeling, Wedderwill, Welbedacht, Windmeul, Zevenwacht, Zonnebloem

★★★☆ African Terroir (Biodynamic, Fairtrade), Allée Bleue, Allegria, Allesverloren, Alto, Altydgedacht, Amares, Annex Kloof, Anthonij Rupert, Asara, Audacia, Avondale (Organic), Ayama (2), Babylon's Peak, Backsberg, Bayede!, Beau Belle (2), Bellpost, Benguela Cove, Bergheim (2), Bernheim, Bizoe, Blaauwklippen, Black Elephant, Black Pearl, Blackwater, Blue Crane, Bon Courage, Bonnievale, Boplaas (2), Boschendal, Bovlei, Brampton, Brenaissance, Brothers, Cape Dreams, Cape Rock, Cloof, Credo, Darling Cellars (2), De Meye, Devonvale, Diners Club Bartho Eksteen , Domaine Brahms, Doolhof, Du Preez, Durbanville Hills, Eerste Hoop, Elgin Heights, Ernst Gouws, Fairview, Faraway House, Fish Hoek, Fort Simon, Franschhoek Cellar, Freedom Hill, Gabriëlskloof, Garden Route, Glen Carlou, Glenelly, Goede Hoop, Graceland, Grande Provence, Groenland (2), Guardian Peak, Hartenberg, Hawksmoor, Hermit on the Hill, Heron Ridge, Hillock, Jacques Smit, Jordan, Joubert-Tradauw, Journey's End, Kaapzicht, Karusa, Katbakkies, Kloovenburg, Knorhoek, KWV, Kyburg, La Bri, La Chaumiere, La Couronne, La Vierge, Laborie (2), Landskroon, Leeuwenberg, Lindhorst, Linton

Park (2), Lorraine, Louiesenhof, Lourensford, Lyngrove, Lynx, Marianne, Meerendal (2), Metzer, Mont du Toit, Mont Rochelle, **Mount Pleasant**, Naughton's, Nederburg, Neil Ellis, Nelson (2), Nick & Forti's, Nieuwedrift, Nitida, Noble Hill, Olifantsberg, **Ormonde**, Perdeberg, Peter Falke, Plaisir, Porcupine Ridge, Pulpit Rock, Rhebokskloof, Riebeek (2), Rietvallei, **Rustenberg**, Saronsberg, Seven Springs , Seven Steps, **Signal Gun** (2), Signal Hill, Simonsvlei (3), Sir Lambert, Skaap, Slaley, Slanghoek, **Spekulasie**, Spring Grove, Stellendrift, Stellenrust, Stone Ridge, StoneyCroft, Stony Brook, **Thandi** (2) (Fairtrade), The Butcher Shop, **The Liberator**, The Rhino, **The Township Winery** (Fairtrade), Thelema, Tokara, Topaz, Trajan, Two Oceans, Uitkyk, **Ultra Liquors**, Umkhulu, Uva Mira, **Val du Charron**, Veenwouden, Vondeling, Waverley Hills (Organic), Wellington Winery, Weltevrede, Wildekrans, William Everson, **Winters Drift**, Woolworths (3), Zandvliet, Zoetendal, Zonnebloem ★★★ Abbottshill, Amani, Arumdale, Beau Joubert, Boland, Botha, Bovlei, Brunia, Bushmanspad, Cape Dreams, Cape to Cairo, Catch Of The Day, Chateau Naudé, Chennells, Claime d'Or, Corder, David Frost Signature, David Frost, De Meye, Desert Rose, Devonvale, Diemersfontein, Doran, Dormershire (2), Drostdy-Hof, Du Toitskloof , Durbanville Hills, Excelsior, Fairview, Fleur du Cap, **Foothills**, Fort Simon, **Fraai Uitzicht 1798**, Freedom Hill, Graham Beck, Group CDV, Havana Hills (2), Hill & Dale, Hofstraat, Hoopenburg, Hout Bay, Jordan, Juno, Kanu, **Klein Roosboom** , Koopmanskloof (Fairtrade), Kranskop, Kumala, La Terre La Mer, Ladismith, Landskroon, Le Fût, Leeuwenkuil, Lemberg, Lievland, **Londinium**, Lord's, Lyngrove, Malanot, MAN Family, Manley, Mount Rozier, Namaqua, Nederburg, Neethlingshof, New Beginnings, Niel Joubert, Oldenburg, Orange River, Org de Rac (Organic), Ormonde, Oude Compagnies Post, **PaardenKloof**, Perdeberg, Phizante Kraal, Pulpit Rock, Rijk's, Robertson (3), Rooiberg, **Rosendal**, Scrucap, Silkbush, Simonsvlei, Slaley, Slowine, Somersbosch, Southern Sky, Spier, **Stanford Hills**, Stellenbosch Hills, Stellenzicht, Strandveld, **TCB Wines**, **The Giant Periwinkle**, The Goose, **The Grape Grinder**, The Hills, The Wine Fusion, Thembi & Co, Tulbagh Winery (2), Vaalvlei, Van Loveren, Virgin Earth, **Vrede**, Vredenheim, **Waterstone** (4), Waverley Hills (Organic), Wellington Winery, **Weltevrede**, Welvanpas, William Everson, Windmeul, Woolworths, Yonder Hill, Zanddrift ★★★ African Pride (2), African Terroir (2) (Organic), Alvi's Drift, Arniston Bay, Arra, **Asara**, Ashton, **Beau Belle**, Bergwater, Blomendahl,

Bonview, De Wet, DeWaal, Die Mas, **Doran**, **Dunstone**, Eerste Hoop, **Esau**, False Bay (2), Fat Bastard, **Four Secrets**, Franschhoek Cellar, Goedverwacht, Halala, Het Vlock Casteel, **House of Mandela** (2), Jason's Hill, Kingsriver, Klein Parys, Koelenhof, KWV, **Langverwacht**, Le Manoir de Brendel, Leopard's Leap, Lula, Lutzville (2), Mellasat, Mitre's Edge, Obikwa, **Overhex**, Place in the Sun (Fairtrade), Rhebokskloof, Riebeek, Roodezandt, Schalkenbosch, Seal Breeze, **Somerset Wines**, Spotswood, Stellar (Organic, Fairtrade), Stoumann's, Swartland, Tanagra, The Mason's, The Winery of Good Hope, United Nations (Fairtrade), Viljoensdrift, **Waterstone**, Wederom (2), Windfall, Wineways, Wonderfontein, Woolworths (2) (Organic) ★★ African Terroir, Barrydale, Bellingham, Blomendahl, **Brandvlei**, Calitzdorp, Cape Classics, Clairvaux, Douglas Green, Du'SwaRoo, Eikehof, Excelsior, Goudini, Imbuko, Jonkheer, Klawer, Kumala, Langverwacht, Mountain River, Overhex, Reiersvlei, Savanha, Stellar (Organic, Fairtrade), Van Loveren, Vrede, **Waterstone** (2), Wineways, Zandvliet ★★ **Axe Hill**, Bonnievale, Cranefields, **Waterstone**, Withoek ★ Jonkheer, Long Mountain, McGregor, **Waterstone NT** Aeternitas, African Pride, African Terroir (2), Andy Mitchell (2), AntHill, Axe Hill, **Bayede!**, Bellevue, Bonfoi, Calais, Camberley, Cameradi, Citrusdal, Clovelly, Corder, Crows Nest, De Villiers, Devon Hill, Dispore Kamma (2), Du Preez, Du'SwaRoo, DuVon, Escapades, Fernskloof, Galleon, Gilga, GlenWood (2), Hawksmoor, Hazendal, Holden Manz, KWV, Le Manoir de Brendel, Leopard Frog, Libby's Pride, Linton Park, MC Square, Melkboomsdrift, Mimosa, Montpellier, Mooi Bly, Mountain River, My Wyn, Nederburg, Neil Ellis, Nietvoorbij, Onderkloof , Overhex (Fairtrade), Painted Wolf, Porseleinberg (Organic), Post House, Rico Suter, Ross Gower, Ruitersvlei, Saam (2), Signal Hill, Spotswood, Stellenbosch University, Stone Ridge, Sumsaré, The Mason's, Thembi & Co, TTT Cellar, Tulbagh Winery, Ultra Liquors (4), United Nations (3), uniWines, Vaalvlei, Versailles, Warwick, Westbridge, **William Everson**, Zandvliet, Zidela (2) **NR** Cloverfield, Welmoed **D** Anatu, Ashton, Avontuur, Beau Belle, Cape Classics, Iona, Le Pommier, Leeuwenberg, Mooiplaas, Ormonde, Rainbow's End, Simonsvlei, Spice Route, The Butcher Shop, The Township Winery, Ultra Liquors, Waterstone, Woolworths

Sparkling, Méthode cap classique, red, dry

★★★ Nitida, **Woolworths NT** Camberley

Sparkling, Méthode cap classique, rosé, dry

★★★★☆ Am베loui, Bon Courage, CharlesFox, Steenberg, Woolworths

★★★★ Ayama, Boschendal, Chabivin, Chateau Naudé, Colmant, De Wetshof, Domaine des Dieux, Du Preez, Fairview, Graham Beck, Klein Optenhorst, L'Avenir, Lourensford, Mount Babylon, Saltaré, Silverthorn, Simonsig, Sumaridge, Tanzanite

★★★☆ Allée Bleue, Anthonij Rupert, Barrydale, Graham Beck, Groote Post, Laborie, Pongrácz, Rickety Bridge, Twee Jonge/Krone, Webersburg, Weltevrede, Woolworths ★★★ Francois La Garde, Karusa, Leopard Frog, Plettenvale, JC le Roux (2), Villiera, Woolworths ★★★ Haute Cabrière, Namaqua, Packwood, Ultra Liquors NT Môreson, Ross Gower D Villiera

Sparkling, Méthode cap classique, rosé, off-dry/semi-sweet

★★ Tulbagh Winery

Sparkling, Méthode cap classique, white, dry

★★★★★ Bon Courage, Klein Constantia

★★★★☆ Am베loui, Boschendal, Bramon, Cederberg, Colmant (2), Graham Beck (2), Groot Constantia, Lourensford, MC Square, Pongrácz, Silverthorn, Simonsig, Tanzanite, The House of GM, Twee Jonge/Krone, Villiera

★★★★ Anura, Avondale (Organic), Avontuur, Bon Courage, Boschendal (2), Buitenverwachting, Chabivin (2), CharlesFox, Constantia Uitsig, Darling Cellars, De Grendel, De Wet, De Wetshof, Domaine des Dieux, Du Preez, Francois La Garde, Genevieve, Glen Carlou, Haute Cabrière, Hout Bay, KWV, La Motte, Laborie, Meerendal, Morgenhof, Muratie, Niel Joubert, Org de Rac (Organic), Quoin Rock, Saltaré, Saronsberg, Saxenburg, Scrucap, Signal Hill, Simonsig, Steenberg, Sterhuis, Stony Brook, Teddy Hall, Thandi, JC le Roux, Twee Jonge/Krone, Vergelegen, Villiera, Webersburg, Weltevrede (2) (Biodynamic), Wonderfontein, Woolworths (3)

★★★☆ Allée Bleue, Ayama (2), Backsberg, Badgerberg, Bon Cap (Organic), Boplaas, Chabivin (2), Crios Bríde, Graham Beck, Haute Cabrière, Hazendal, Hoopenburg, Huis van Chevallerie, Klein Parys, Laborie, Leopard's Leap, Longridge, Lovane, Mooiplaas, Môreson, Nitida, Pongrácz, Rhebokskloof, Rickety Bridge, Ross Gower, Saltaré, Spier, Teddy Hall, The Butcher Shop, JC le Roux (2), Ultra Liquors (5), Villiera (2) (Light & low-alcohol), Waverley Hills (Organic),

Welbedacht, Wellington Winery, Woolworths, Zorgvliet ★★★ Backsberg (Kosher), Graham Beck, Groot Parys (Organic), Haute Cabrière, Karusa, Ken Forrester, Leopard Frog, Lord's, Montpellier, Nieuwedrift, Riebeek, Robertson, Van Loveren, Viljoensdrift, Virgin Earth, Windfall ★★★ Haute Cabrière, Koelenhof , La Chaumiere, Skaap ★★ Diners Club Bartho Eksteen , Plaisir, Wildekrans NT Altydgedacht, Boer & Brit, Cape Chamonix, De Zoete Inval, Elgin Heights, Francois La Garde, High Constantia, Highlands Road, Kanu, Klein Parys, Klein Roosboom , Môreson (3), My Wyn, Nico van der Merwe, Old Vines, Perdeberg, Re'Mogo, Saxenburg, Schalkenbosch, Somersbosch, Topiary, Ultra Liquors D Simonsvlei, Villiera, Weltevrede, Woolworths

Sparkling, Méthode cap classique, white, off-dry/semi-sweet

★★★★★ Silverthorn

★★★★ Colmant, Roodezandt

★★★☆ South Hill ★★★ Graham Beck ★★★ JC le Roux

Sparkling, Non-MCC, red, dry

★★ JC le Roux (Light & low-alcohol), Van Loveren
★☆ Alvi's Drift

Sparkling, Non-MCC, red, off-dry/semi-sweet

★★★ Four Secrets ★★★ Robertson, Solms-Delta
★★ Café Culture, JC le Roux

Sparkling, Non-MCC, rosé, dry

★★★ Knorhoek, Thandi ★★ African Terroir (Organic), Boplaas NT African Terroir D Beyerskloof

Sparkling, Non-MCC, rosé, off-dry/semi-sweet

★★★ Bayede!, Orange River, Swartland ★★☆ Aan de Doorns, Alvi's Drift (Light & low-alcohol), Bergwater, Bon Courage, Cold Duck (5th Avenue), Goedverwacht, Klawer (Light & low-alcohol), Kloovenburg, Rhebokskloof, Rooiberg, Stellenbosch Hills, Vredenheim, Woolworths ★★ Arniston Bay, Bovlei, KWV, Pearly Bay (Light & low-alcohol), Perdeberg (Light & low-alcohol), Robertson (Light & low-alcohol), Van Loveren (2) ★☆ Koelenhof , Viljoensdrift ★ Ashton NT Jason's Hill, Overhex

Sparkling, Non-MCC, white, dry

★★★☆ AA Badenhorst ★★★ Clos Malverne (Light & low-alcohol), Du Toitskloof , Nederburg,

Wellington Winery ★★★ Arniston Bay, **Bergwater**, Bon Cap (Organic), Bovlei, Goudini, Obikwa, Orange River, Perdeberg, Riebeek, **Robertson**, Tulbagh Winery, Van Loveren, Welmoed ★★ Bonnievale, KWV, Slanghoek, Stellar (Organic), Woolworths ★ Woolworths **NT** African Terroir, Bergsig, Goedverwacht, Merwida, Overhex **D** Altydgedacht, Klein Parys

Sparkling, Non-MCC, white, off-dry/semi-sweet

★★★ **Scali**, Swartland, JC le Roux ★★★ **Alvi's Drift** (Light & low-alcohol), Badsberg, Botha, Koelenhof , Nuy, Opstal, **Orange River** (Light & low-alcohol), Van Loveren ★★ KWV, Pearly Bay (Light & low-alcohol), **Robertson** (Light & low-alcohol), Rooiberg (2), Slanghoek, JC le Roux (Light & low-alcohol), Van Loveren, Woolworths ★★ Grand Mousseux, **Tulbagh Winery**, Van Loveren **NT** African Terroir, Kleine Draken (Kosher), Overhex **D** Rhebokskloof, Swartland

Special Late Harvest

★★★★ Nederburg

★★★★ Backsberg, Drostdy-Hof, Robertson ★★★ Fairview, Roodezandt ★★★ Badsberg, Bon Courage, Slanghoek, Van Loveren **NT** Bergsig, Bovlei

Sweet red

★★★★☆ Signal Hill

★★★★ Dormershire ★★★ Beau Belle, David Frost Signature, **Laborie**, Overhex, Perdeberg, Somerset Wines ★★ Backsberg (Sacramental, Kosher), Bottelary, Kumala, Louiesenhof, **RED ESCape**, Waterstone, Woolworths ★★ Arniston Bay (Light & low-alcohol), Cloverfield, Hartswater, Imbuko, Robertson, Wineways ★ Cellar Cask, Pick n Pay, **Riebeek** (Perlé, Light & low-alcohol), Robertson **NT** Lynx, Tulbagh Winery **D** Simonsvlei

Sylvaner

★★★ Overgaauw

Tannat

★★★★ Glen Carlou, Mooi Bly ★★★ Fairview

Tempranillo

★★★★ Dornier ★★★ De Krans

Tinta barocca

★★★★ Sadie

★★★ **BLANKbottle**, Boplaas, De Krans, Jeu, Nuweland, Swartland ★★★ Allesverloren, Boplaas **NT** Reiersvlei

Touriga nacional

★★★★ De Krans, **Sijnn**

★★★★ Boplaas, Dagbreek, **Overgaauw**, **Sijnn** ★★★ Allesverloren, Bergsig, Reiersvlei ★★★ Calitzdorp ★★ Ladismith

Verdelho

★★★★ Feiteiras ★★★ **Flagstone D** Anura

Vin de paille

★★★★★ Mullineux

★★★★★ Alluvia, **Donkiesbaai**, Fairview, **Meinert**, Nuweland, Rustenberg, The Winery of Good Hope, Tierhoek (Light & low-alcohol), Vergelegen

★★★★ De Trafford, Goede Hoop, Groot Parys (Organic), Lemberg, Maison, Saronsberg, Stellar

★★★★ Signal Hill, Simonsig ★★★ **La Motte**, Naughton's ★★★ Orange River **NT** Fairview, Hazendal, Keermont, Mellasat, Vondeling, Zevenwacht **D** Fairview

Viognier

★★★★★☆ **Buitenverwachting**, Eagles' Nest, Elgin Vintners

★★★★★ Alvi's Drift, Backsberg, Beau Constantia, Bilton, Creation, Diemersfontein, Fairview, Flagstone, Fleur du Cap, Four Paws, Gabriëlskloof, Idiom, Kanu, Katbakkies, Kranskop, Lourensford, Lynx, **Mellasat**, Nick & Forti's, Painted Wolf, Ridgeback, Saronsberg, Solo, Spice Route, Tamboerskloof, The Foundry, The Winery of Good Hope

★★★★ Anura, Arra (2), Babylonstoren, Bellingham, De Grendel, **Glen Erskine**, **Hermit on the Hill**, Hilton, Klawer, La Petite Ferme, Maison, Montpellier, Niel Joubert, Stonehill, Topaz, **Woolworths** ★★★ African Terroir (Organic), Auction Crossing, Ayama, Blaauwklippen, **Calais**, Cloof, Corder, DeWaal, Excelsior, Fairview, Fort Simon, Graham Beck, Karusa, Katbakkies, Lazanou (Organic), **Lutzville**, Noble Hill, **Nuweland**, Rhebokskloof, Robertson, **Silkbush**, Waterkloof, Wellington Winery ★★★ Boplaas, Chennells, Eerste Hoop, **La Petite Vigne**, Le Joubert, **The Township Winery** (Fairtrade), Welmoed ★★ Arra, La Bri, Schalkenbosch **NT** Bon Cap (Organic), Citrusdal, High Constantia (2), Iona, Jason's Hill, KWV, La Ferme Derik, Leopard Frog, Lorraine, Lynx,

My Wyn, Naughton's, Nederburg, Riebeek, Spring Grove, Star Hill, Stellenbosch University, The Fledge **D** African Terroir, Brampton, Lemberg, Riebeek

White blends, off-dry/semi-sweet (w & u/w)

★★★★ BLANKbottle, Hughes Family, Solms-Delta, The Butcher Shop, The Wine Fusion, Virgin Earth

★★★☆ Amani, Boschendal, Buitenverwachting, Edgebaston, Painted Wolf, Slanghoek, Stony Brook, **Virgin Earth**, Woolworths (2) ★★★ Altydgedacht, Boland, Bon Cap (Organic), Douglas Green, **Havana Hills**, Kanu, KWV, Montpellier, Nederburg, Onderkloof , Overhex, Robertson, Stellenrust (Fairtrade), Zonnebloem ★★★ Arniston Bay, Bayede!, Boschendal (2), De Wetshof, Drostdy-Hof, Du Toitskloof , Graça, Group CDV (Perlé), Leeuwenjacht, Malan Family, Obikwa, Overhex (Light & low-alcohol), **Pulpit Rock**, Robertson, Stellar (Organic, Fairtrade), Stellenrust, Tulbagh Winery, Two Oceans, Zevenwacht ★★ Angels Tears, Arniston Bay (Light & low-alcohol), Barrydale, Bergwater, Bonne Esperance, Bovlei, Du Toitskloof (Perlé), Fleur du Cap (Light & low-alcohol), Jonkheer, Koelenhof , Kumala (2), Opstal, Overmeer Cellars, Pearly Bay (2) (Light & low-alcohol), Rooiberg, Slanghoek, **Tulbagh Winery**, Waka Waka, Waterstone, Woolworths (2) ★★ Botha (Light & low-alcohol), Drostdy-Hof, Ladismith, Morgenhof, Pick n Pay (2), Robertson (2), Ruitersvlei, Swartland, Versus, Woolworths (2) (Light & low-alcohol) ★ Cellar Cask, Kupferberger Auslese, Landzicht, Virginia **NT** African Terroir (2), Bonnievale, TTT Cellar **D** De Krans, KWV (2), Simonsvlei, Zevenwacht

White blends, other, unwooded, dry

★★★☆ Neil Ellis ★★★ Beaumont, **Stettyn** ★★☆ Overhex

White blends, other, unwooded, off-dry/semi-sweet

★★ Imbuko ★☆ Ruitersvlei

White blends, unwooded, dry

★★★★☆ Ashbourne, The Berrio

★★★★ Bouchard Finlayson, Elgin Vintners, Groote Post, Lammershoek, Spier, Truter Family, **Waterford**, Woolworths, Zonnebloem

★★★☆ Allée Bleue, **Ashbourne**, Ayama, Barton, Bovlei, Buitenverwachting, Creation, **Doran**,

Douglas Green, Flagstone, Grande Provence, Groot Constantia, Karusa, **Namaqua**, Quando, The Wine Fusion, Thokozani ★★★ Ayama, Barrydale, Bon Courage, Boschendal, De Zoete Inval, **Foothills**, Four Paws, Glen Carlou, Goats do roam, **Group CDV**, Hathersage, Jordan (2), Kaapzicht, Knorhoek, Koopmanskloof, Kumala, Ladismith, **Lanzerac**, Lazanou (Organic), Leeuwenjacht, Longridge, **Louisvale**, Mooiplaas, **Nabygelegen** (2), Napier, Noble Hill, Old Vines, Opstal, Post House, Saxenburg (2), Slowine, Solms-Delta, Stellar (Organic, Fairtrade), Strydom, Teddy Hall, Thandi (Fairtrade), **Twee Jonge/Krone**, Two Oceans, Vergenoegd, Villiersdorp, Whalehaven (2) ★★☆ African Pride, Asara, Beau Joubert, Beyerskloof, Cloof, Darling Cellars, **Diemersfontein** (2), Doolhof (2), Eikendal, Goede Hoop, Hazendal, **Imbuko**, Kanu, Kumala (3), Landskroon, MAN Family, Rustenberg, Savanha (Fairtrade), Somerset Wines, **Spier**, Springfontein, Stellendrift, **Two Oceans**, uniWines, **Veenwouden**, Villiera, **Vins d'Orrance**, Wedderwill (Biodynamic), Woolworths (2) ★★ African Terroir, Arniston Bay, Ashton, Avontuur, **Barton**, Kumala, Mountain River, Obikwa, Pick n Pay (2), **Robertson** (5), **Savanha**, Schalkenbosch (2), Simonsvlei, The Rhino, Theuniskraal, uniWines, Van Loveren (3), Woolworths (2), Zandvliet ★★ Arniston Bay, Bovlei, Drostdy-Hof, Leopard's Leap, Nuy, Oom Tas, Wandsbeck, Zandvliet ★ African Terroir (Organic), Van Loveren ★ Overmeer Cellars **NT** African Terroir (2), Buffalo Creek, Hildenbrand, Jean Daneel, Joostenberg, Klein Parys, KWV, Lateganskop, Mountain Oaks (Organic), Nederburg, Nico Vermeulen, Oude Denneboom, **Re'Mogo**, Rico Suter, Robertson, Somersboch, Vendôme, Vondeling, Welvanpas, Withington, **Woolworths NR** Stellenbosch Hills **D** Altydgedacht, Babylon's Peak, Bloemendal, Breëland, Cape Chamonix, Overgaauw, Overhex, Thandi, uniWines

White blends, wooded, dry

★★★★★ Cape Point, **Cederberg**, David, DeMorgenzon, Fable, Fairview, Flagstone, Miles Mossop, Nederburg, Nitida, Rall, Sadie, Tokara

★★★★☆ AA Badenhorst, Adoro, Anatu, Avondale (Organic), Black Oystercatcher, Cape Chamonix, Cape Point, Cape Rock, Constantia Glen, Constantia Uitsig, Darling Cellars, Delaire, Ernst Gouws, Groot Constantia, Hermanuspietersfontein, Lammershoek, Lomond, Lourensford, Mullineux, Newton Johnson, Oak Valley, **Sadie** (2), **Savage**, Scali, Sequillo, Sijnn, Solms-Delta, **Steenberg** (2), Sterhuis, Strandveld,

Thelema, Vergelegen, Vins d'Orrance, Vondeling, Welgegund, Woolworths (2)

★★★★ Allée Bleue, Altydgedacht, Alvi's Drift, Backsberg, Bergheim, BLANKbottle (2), **Bloemendal**, Bosman (Fairtrade), Celestina, Dornier, Du Toitskloof , Escapades, **Fleur du Cap**, Gabriëlskloof, Keermont, La Ferme Derik (2), La Vierge, Lanner Hill, Leeuwenkuil, **Lemberg**, Lomond, **Môreson**, Muratie, Neethlingshof, Nico van der Merwe, Paardebosch, Quoin Rock, Rietvallei, **Stark-Condé**, Stony Brook, Sumaridge, **The Liberator**, Val de Vie, Val du Charron, Waterkloof, Welbedacht, Yardstick, Zevenwacht, Zorgvliet

★★★☆ Alvi's Drift, Anatu, Anura, Bellingham, D'Aria, De Grendel, Drostdy-Hof, Eerste Hoop, Glen Erskine, Haute Cabrière, Hermit on the Hill, **Idiom**, Joostenberg, La Ferme Derik, Laibach (Organic), **Leopard's Leap**, Malanot, Manley, Metzer, Morgenster, **Nuweland**, **Osbloed**, Perdeberg, Porcupine Ridge, Raka, Reyneke (Organic),

Stellenbosch Hills, Sterhuis, The Wolftrap, Tierhoek, Vuurberg, Waverley Hills (Organic), Welmoed ★★★ **AntHill**, Bellpost, **Darling Cellars**, Doolhof, Highlands Road, Hildenbrand, Hillock, Karusa, **Namaqua**, Nederburg (2), Ridgeback, Two Oceans, Waverley Hills ★★☆ Bellingham, Bergheim, Craighall, **Jean Daneel**, Kumala (2), Olifantsberg, **Savanha** ★★ Elemental Bob, Kumala, Nomada, Woolworths ★☆ Klein Parys **NT** AA Badenhorst, Babylon's Peak, Beau Constantia, Bizoe, Dragonridge, **Gilga**, Hildenbrand, Klein Constantia, Mountain Oaks, My Wyn, Nederburg, Orangerie, Steenberg, Trizanne, Withington **NR** Joostenberg **D** Credo, Druk My Niet (2), Ormonde, Rijk's, Springfontein, Val de Vie, William Everson

Zinfandel/Primitivo

★★★★ Idiom

★★★☆ Blaauwklippen (2), Glen Carlou **D** Zevenwacht

Overview

According to the latest available data (2012), South Africa is the 8th largest wine-producing nation by volume. France, with 16.8% of global production, is the biggest, followed by Italy (16%) and Spain (11.8%). South Africa, with ±1,004m litres (excluding grape juice and grape juice concentrate), in 2012 contributed 4% of global volume, slightly up from 3.6% in 2011, though the number of wine-grape growers in South Africa continued to decline (3,440 compared with 3,527 the previous year). The overall number of wine cellars crushing grapes is steady at 582, while the number of private cellars crushing grapes continues to rise, from 505 in 2011 to 509. (Producing wholesalers crushing grapes again are slightly down, to 23, while co-operatives — 'producer cellars' in officialese — dropped further, to 50). Though their number continued to decline marginally in 2012, to 251, micro-cellars vinifying fewer than 100 tonnes still constituted ±43% of all producers and thus remained a potent force in the industry.

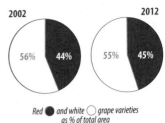

Red ● and white ○ grape varieties as % of total area

followed by chardonnay (70) and, interestingly, muscats d'Alexandrie and de Frontignan (62/52), knocking consumer favourite sauvignon back to 6th place (50). Pinotage, with 427 ha, again outpaced shiraz (204 ha) as most-planted red-wine variety, followed by ruby cab (126), supplanting cab (114), and newly fashionable 'legacy' grape cinsaut (68). As ever, much more chenin is uprooted than planted, but the variety still leads the overall hectareage table, with ±18% of the total 100,093 ha under vine. Cab, with ±12%, remains the leading red. The percentage of very young vines (under 4 years) again increased fractionally in 2012 to 8.2%, while 18.3% are older than 20, slightly more than previously.

Vineyards

Adjusted official figures reveal a significant decline in new vineyard establishment over the past decade, from 5,714 to 2,285 ha in 2012, while the rate of uprooting remained fairly steady at an average of ±4,000 ha per annum. In 2012, planting for red wine overtook that for white (1,179 ha vs 1,105), though white-wine grape chenin retained its entrenched position as most-planted variety (486 ha added). Colombard remained the second most-planted white-wine variety, with 283 ha,

Exports

After three consecutive years of decline, exports in 2012 jumped to a ten-year high of 417,2 m litres, or ±48% of South Africa's total wine production.

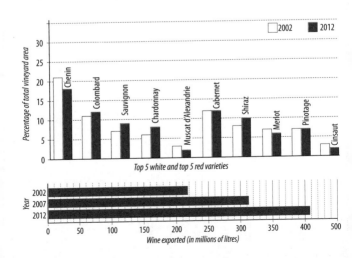

Top 5 white and top 5 red varieties

South African Wine Industry – Ten-Year Overview

	2003	2004	2005	2006	2007	2008	2009	2010	2011	2012
Number of wineries	505	561	581	576	560	585	604	573	582	582
Total vine area (excl sultana) (hectares)	98 605	100 207	101 607	102 146	101 957	101 325	101 259	101 016	100 568	100 093
Producing area 4 yrs & older (excl sultana) (hectares)	82 719	85 331	87 284	89 426	91 326	92 503	93 285	93 198	92 621	91 867
Avg yield (tons/hectare)	14.91	15.38	13.42	14.55	14.80	15.41	14.45	13.53	14.06	15.4
Avg grape price – producer cellars/co-ops (R/ton) (2011/2012 est)	1624	1458	1387	1362	1434	1522	1918	1814	1933	1981
Avg grape price – excl producer cellars/co-ops (R/ton)	4041	4133	3593	3128	2971	3173	3917	3949	3801	3930
Grapes crushed (millions of tons)	1.23	1.31	1.17	1.30	1.35	1.43	1.35	1.26	1.30	1.41
Total production (millions of litres)	956.0	1 015.7	905.2	1 013.0	1 043.5	1 089.0	1 033.4	984.8	1 012.8	1 095.1
Domestic sales (millions of litres)	333.7	338.4	334.2	337.4	355.5	355.8	338.3	346.4	352.7	361.2
Consumption per capita (litres SA wine)	7.2	7.3	7.1	7.1	7.4	7.3	6.9	6.9	7.0	7.0
Export volume (millions of litres)	238.5	267.7	281.1	271.7	312.5	411.7	395.6	378.5	357.4	417.2
Stock (millions of litres)	336.8	363.7	339.4	403.1	425.2	357.2	361.7	351.0	413.9	433.0
Stock : sales ratio	0.57:1	0.59:1	0.54:1	0.65:1	0.64:1	0.47:1	0.49:1	0.48:1	0.59:1	0.56:1

Chenin and (overtaking sauvignon) chardonnay topped the list of most-exported varietal wines (bottled and bulk), with in-vogue pinks, cab, shiraz, pinotage and merlot also in demand. Russia and the US in 2012 edged the Netherlands and Denmark out of the top five markets for SA wine (packaged and bulk), with stalwarts the UK, Germany, Sweden retaining their top three slots . When it comes to packaged wine only, the UK, Sweden, Germany and the Netherlands still top the list, followed by the holy grail of many exporters, the US and Canada.

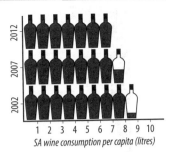

SA wine consumption per capita (litres)

Local wine consumption

South African domestic per-capita wine consumption in 2012 increased fractionally for the third year in a row, from 6.97L to 6.98L. But wine's combined market share (natural, fortified and sparkling) of ±16% remains substantially lower than beer (±57%). Brandy's ±6% share is slowly declining, while whisky's ±6% represents steady incremental growth. Of natural wine sold in South Africa during 2012 (including locally bottled imports), a steady 49% is in glass, of which about half is in the standard 750ml bottle. Wine in bag-in-box accounts for a rising ±27% of total sales, plastic containers ±22% and Tetra packs ±2%. Foil bags — the notorious *papsakke*, now carefully regulated — represent only 0.3% .

Note

Statistical data was provided by SA Wine Industry Information & Systems.

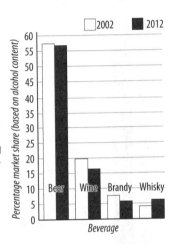

Wine Industry Organisations

African Vintners Alliance Marketing: Vivian Kleynhans ▪ T +27 (0)71-049-4109 ▪ ava@africanrootswines.com
Established to create an enabling environment for emerging black-owned wineries.

Agricultural Ethical Trade Initiative of SA (WIETA) CEO: Linda Lipparoni ▪ T +27 (0)21-880-0580 ▪ F +27 (0)21-880-0580 ▪ linda@wieta.org.za; info@wieta.org.za ▪ www.wieta.org.za
Multi-stakeholder, non-profit, voluntary organisation established in 2002 to promote ethical trade in wine, fruit, cut flowers and general agriculture. WIETA has adopted a code of labour standards for the industry, and its main task is to support, enhance and promote members' ethical performance and best practice through training, technical assessments and ethical inspections to assess compliance. WIETA recently adopted an ethical seal which has been endorsed by the wine industry in recognition of wine supply chains' ethical commitment to good working conditions on farms and in cellars.

ARC Infruitec-Nietvoorbij Manager: Johan van Zyl ▪ Public relations officer: Derusha Rangasamy ▪ T +27 (0)21-809-3100 ▪ F +27 (0)21-809-3400 ▪ infocape@arc.agric.za ▪ www.arc.agric.za
Internationally-regarded one-stop research institute, committed to provide sustainable technologies to the developing and commercial agricultural sectors in South Africa, through leading and dynamic research, technology development and technology transfer.

Biodiversity & Wine Initiative (BWI) See WWF-SA Biodiversity & Wine Initiative.

Cape Estate Wine Producers' Association (CEWPA) Secretary: Elsabe Ferreira ▪ T +27 (0)21-

863-1599 ▪ F +27 (0)21-8631552 ▪ elsabe@ efpromosies.co.za

Cape Port Producers' Association Chair: Carel Nel ▪ **T +27 (0)44-213-3326** ▪ F +27 (0)44-213-3750 ▪ boplaas@mweb.co.za

Cape Winemakers Guild (CWG) Chair: Jeff Grier ▪ General Manager: Kate Jonker ▪ **T +27 (0)21-852-0408** ▪ F +27 (0)21-852-0409 ▪ info@ capewinemakersguild.com ▪ www.capewinemakersguild.com

Independent, invitation-only association, founded in 1982 to promote winemaking excellence among its members. Since 1985, the CWG has held a highly regarded annual public auction. Established in 1999, the Nedbank CWG Development Trust supports social development in the winelands through its Protégé Programme, aimed at transforming the industry by cultivating and mentoring promising young winemakers and by offering Billy Hofmeyr AGRI Seta bursaries to final year Viticulture & Oenology students.

Chardonnay Forum of South Africa Chair: Matthew van Heerden ▪ matthew@webersburg.co.za ▪ **T +27 (0)21-881-3636 / +27 (0)82-520-9338** ▪ F +27 (0)21-881 3217

Chenin Blanc Association (CBA) Chair: Ken Forrester ▪ **T +27 (0)21-855-2374 / +27 (0)82-783-7203** ▪ F +27 (0)21-855-2373 ▪ ken@ kenforresterwines.com ▪ www.chenin.co.za ▪ Manager: Ina Smith ▪ T +27 (0)82-467-4331 ▪ F +27 (0)86-672-8549 ▪ ina.smith@iafrica.com ▪ @CheninBlancAsso

Fairtrade Africa - Southern Africa Network (FTA-SAN) Regional manager: Benjamin Cousin ▪ T +27 (0)21-448-8911 ▪ b.cousin@fairtrade.net ▪ www.fairtradeafrica.net.

FTA-SAN represents Southern African Fairtrade producers in the global Fairtrade system on issues related to governance, new price setting, standards consultation and making standards more relevant to local farming practices. FTA-SAN supports producers with their development program, market access and promotes south-south trade and intra-Africa trade.

Fairtrade Label South Africa (FLSA) Executive director: Boudewijn Goossens ▪ T +27 (0)21-448-8911 ▪ info@fairtradesa.org.za ▪ www.fairtradesa.org.za

The local marketing and promotion organisation for Fairtrade. FLSA was established in 2009 and promotes ethical farming practices and trade in South Africa through the international Fairtrade label. Wine is one of the key Fairtrade products, and an increasing number of local farms and wineries choose Fairtrade as the endorsement for their sound ethical and environmental practises. See also Fairtrade Africa Southern Africa Network.

Garagiste Movement Coordinator: Tanja Beutler ▪ **T +27 (0)21-855-4275** ▪ F +27 (0)86-612-6118 ▪ tanja@topazwines.co.za

Institute of Cape Wine Masters Chair: Andy Roediger ▪ **T +27 (0)83-250-9821** ▪ Secretary: Margaret Fry ▪ T +27 (0)83-628-6511 ▪ F +27 (0)86-611-7150 ▪ capewinemasters@gmail.com ▪ www.capewinemasters.co.za

Successful completion of examinations set since 1983 by the Cape Wine & Spirit Education Trust and, latterly, the Cape Wine Academy, have qualified 82 Cape Wine Masters. Their Institute holds seminars, runs tasting workshops, charts trends and names a Wine Personality of the Year

Integrated Production of Wine (IPW) Manager: Daniël Schietekat ▪ **T +27 (0)21-889-6555** ▪ F +27 (0)866-903-224 ▪ daniel@ipw.co.za ▪ www.ipw.co.za

Innovative, widely supported initiative aimed at producing wine in an environmentally sustainable, profitable way by means of guidelines for both farm and cellar, embracing all aspects of grape production, winemaking and biodiversity conservation. See also WWF-SA Biodiversity & Wine Initiative and Sustainable Wine South Africa.

Méthode Cap Classique Producers' Association Chair: Peter Ferreira ▪ bubblesferreira@gmail.com ▪ Admin: Elsabe Ferreira ▪ **T +27(0)21-863-1599** ▪ F +27 (0)21-863-1552 ▪ info@capclassique.co.za

Muscadel SA Chair: Henri Swiegers ▪ **T +27 (0)23-344-3021** ▪ F +27 (0)86-617-9443 ▪ winemaker@badsberg.co.za ▪ Vice-chair: André Scriven ▪ **T +27 (0)23-626-1664** ▪ andre@ rooiberg.co.za

Pinotage Association Chair: Beyers Truter ▪ T +27 (0)21-865-1235 ▪ F +27 (0)21-865-2683 ▪ reception@beyerskloof.co.za ▪ Manager: Elsabe Ferreira T +27 (0)21-863-1599 ▪ F +27 (0)21-863-1552 ▪ admin@pinotage.co.za ▪ www.pinotage.co.za

Sauvignon Blanc Interest Group of South Africa (SBIG) Secretary: Pieter de Waal ▪ **T +27 (0)83-357-3864** ▪ F +27 (0)21-948-3441 ▪ sbig@dw.co.za

Shiraz South Africa Chair: Edmund Terblanche ▪ **T +27 (0)82-770-2929** ▪ F +27 (0)21-876-3446 ▪ et.cellar@la-motte.co.za ▪ Secretary: Sandra Lotz ▪ **T +27 (0)82-924-7254** ▪ F +27 (0)86-267-4333 ▪ info@shirazsa.co.za

South African Black Vintners Alliance See African Vintners Alliance

South African Port Producers' Association (SAPPA) See Cape Port Producers' Association

South African Sommelier Association (SASA) Chair: Neil Grant ▪ General secretary: Higgo Jacobs ▪ info@sommeliers.org.za, membership@ sommeliers.org.za ▪ www.sommeliers.org.za

Membership driven, non-profit, voluntary private

organisation established in 2012 to promote a culture of fine wine, food and service excellence in South Africa; formalise the profession of sommelier; and provide a forum for dialogue, exchange of ideas, knowledge and skills.

South African Wine Industry Information & Systems (SAWIS) Executive Manager: Yvette van der Merwe ▪ **T +27 (0)21-807-5703** ▪ F +27 (0)86-559-0274 ▪ info@sawis.co.za
Responsible for the collection, processing and dissemination of industry information. Administers the Wine of Origin (WO) system and manages the Information Centre, a comprehensive information resource base for the South African wine and brandy industry.

South African Wine Industry Trust (SAWIT) Chair: Sharron Marco-Thyse ▪ CEO: Charles Erasmus ▪ **T +27(0)21-889-8101** ▪ F +27 (0)86-503-6222 ▪ sawit@live.co.za ▪ www.sawit.co.za
The vision of SAWIT is the creation of a transformed wine industry that is sustainable and vibrant, populated by an empowered worker community that shares equitably in growth and prosperity.

Southern Africa Fairtrade Network (SAFN) See Fairtrade Africa Southern Africa Network

Sustainable Wine South Africa www.swsa.co.za ▪ Contact details as for individual organisations. Alliance between the Wine & Spirit Board (WSB), Integrated Production of Wine (IPW), Biodiversity & Wine Initiative (BWI) and Wines of South Africa (WOSA), driving the industry's commitment to sustainable, eco-friendly production.

Wine & Spirit Board Chair: Sibongile Nkomo ▪ Secretary: Hugo van der Merwe ▪ **T +27 (0)21-889-6555** ▪ F +27 (0)21-889-5823 ▪ hugo@ wsb.org.za
Mainly administers the Wine of Origin, Estate Brandy and Integrated Production of Wine (IPW) schemes.

Wine & Agricultural Ethical Trade Association (WIETA) See Agricultural Ethical Trade Initiative.

Wines of South Africa (WOSA) Chair: Johann Krige ▪ T/F +27 (0)21-884-4656 ▪ wine@ kanonkop.co.za ▪ CEO: Siobhan Thompson ▪ **T +27 (0)21-883-3860** ▪ F +27 (0)21-883-3861 ▪ info@wosa.co.za ▪ www.wosa.co.za, www.varietyisinournature.com
Generic marketing organisation, responsible for

raising the profile of SA wine in key export markets. See also WWF-SA Biodiversity & Wine Initiative and Sustainable Wine South Africa.

Wine Industry Development Association (WIDA) Executive Manager: Denver Williams ▪ **T +27 (0)21-872-9181** ▪ F +27 (0)2-872-4560 ▪ denver@wida.co.za ▪ www.wida.co.za
Promotes transformation through social development, human resource development and training, economic empowerment, and industrial relations, and protects the interests of vulnerable communities in the industry.

Wine Industry Network of Expertise & Technology (WINETECH) Executive manager: Gerard Martin ▪ **T +27 (0)21-807-3099** ▪ F +27 (0)21-807-3385 ▪ marting@winetech.co.za
Coordinates the research, training and technology transfer programmes of participating institutions and individuals, to improve the competitiveness of the wine industry.

WWF-SA Biodiversity & Wine Initiative (BWI) bwi@wwf.org.za ▪ www.wwf.org.za/bwi ▪ Programme manager: Martin Albertus ▪ **T +27 (0)21-882-9085** ▪ F +27 (0)865-359-433 ▪ malbertus@wwf.org.za ▪ Senior extension officer: Joan Isham ▪ **T +27 (0)21-886-4080** ▪ F +27 (0)865-359-433 ▪ jisham@wwf.org.za
Pioneering conservation partnership between the wine industry and conservation sector, aiming to protect places of outstanding conservation value and iconic species, and to maintain living and productive landscapes. This is achieved by steering expansion away from threatened natural vegetation and fostering a culture of sustainable production through ecologically-sound land use practices. Demonstrating laudable commitment and buy-in, producers have set aside highly threatened natural areas well in excess of the industry's 100,093 ha vineyard footprint. Today, thanks to the WWF Biodiversity & Wine Initiative (BWI), South African wines lead the world in production integrity, environmental sustainability and conservation. Consumers can support accredited BWI members by buying wines displaying the colourful 'conservation in action' logo, depicting a sugarbird and a protea. See also Integrated Production of Wine and Sustainable Wine South Africa.

Winegrowing Areas

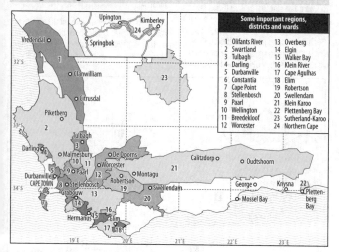

	Some important regions, districts and wards	
1 Olifants River	13 Overberg
2 Swartland	14 Elgin
3 Tulbagh	15 Walker Bay
4 Darling	16 Klein River
5 Durbanville	17 Cape Agulhas
6 Constantia	18 Elim
7 Cape Point	19 Robertson
8 Stellenbosch	20 Swellendam
9 Paarl	21 Klein Karoo
10 Wellington	22 Plettenberg Bay
11 Breedekloof	23 Sutherland-Karoo
12 Worcester	24 Northern Cape

From modest beginnings in the Dutch East India Company's 17th-century gardens below Table Mountain, South Africa's vineyards now cover 100,093 ha and more than 100 official appellations. Changes to the Wine of Origin (WO) scheme of 1972/3 saw 'geographical units' incorporated into the WO classification alongside 'regions', 'districts' and 'wards' (the latter have the smallest footprint of the WO areas, following earlier amendments to the 'estate' legislation). Below are brief notes on the most important grape cultivation zones. Information supplied by Wines of South Africa (WOSA) and SA Wine Industry Information & Systems (SAWIS), and reflects 2012 data for the WO areas. **Note:** Area maps are not to the same scale.

Breedekloof Large (12,759 ha) Breede River Valley district producing mainly for brandy industry and merchant trade, but also featuring some quality-focused boutiques and family estates with reputations for pinotage, chardonnay and semillon. Major varieties (ha): chenin (2,805), colombard (1,861), chardonnay (994), sauvignon (942), pinotage (872). See under Robertson for climate, geology etc.

Cape Point Small (±31 ha), cool district on mainly western slopes of the Cape Peninsula. Recognised for sauvignon and semillon. Sauvignon (19), cab (5), shiraz (4), semillon (2), chardonnay (1). See also Constantia below.

Cape South Coast 'Umbrella' region (2,779 ha) for Cape Agulhas, Elgin, Overberg, Plettenberg Bay,

Swellendam and Walker Bay districts, and Herbertsdale, Napier and Stilbaai East wards.

Cederberg 70 ha ward in the Cederberg Mountain range, with some of South Africa's remotest and highest vineyards (950-1,100 m). Best known for shiraz (14 ha) and sauvignon (11). Chenin (9) chardonnay (8), cab (7).

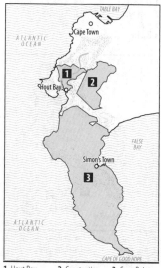

| 1 Hout Bay | 2 Constantia | 3 Cape Point |

Central Orange River
This ward along the Orange River (Gariep) is a production zone within the Northern Cape Geographical Unit. Altitude: 500-1,000 m; temp 25.3°C; rain: 250/208 mm; geology: granite, dolorite, shale, alluvial. Overwhelmingly a white-grape area but red plantings are increasing. Sultana (7,122),

colombard (2,384), chenin (980), villard blanc (209), muscat d'Alexandrie (155).

Constantia Premier viticultural ward on the eastern flank of the Cape Peninsula, cooled by south-easterly sea breezes. Recognised for whites generally, notably sauvignon, semillon and muscat. Altitude: 100-300 m;

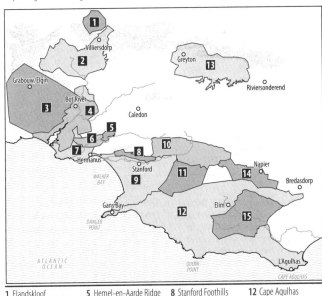

1 Elandskloof	5 Hemel-en-Aarde Ridge	8 Stanford Foothills	12 Cape Agulhas
2 Theewater	6 Upper Hemel-en-Aarde	9 Walker Bay	13 Greyton
3 Elgin	7 Hemel-en-Aarde Valley	10 Klein River	14 Napier
4 Bot River		11 Sunday's Glen	15 Elim

1 Voor Paardeberg	4 Simonsberg-Paarl
2 Wellington	5 Franschhoek
3 Paarl	

1 Polkadraai Hills	5 Stellenbosch
2 Bottelary	6 Simonsberg-Stellenbosch
3 Devon Valley	7 Jonkershoek Valley
4 Papegaaiberg	8 Banghoek

temp (Mean February Temperature, MFT) 20.6°C; rain: total/summer 1,056/335 mm; geology: granite (sandstone). Major varieties: sauvignon (180), merlot (44), cab (40), chardonnay (25), shiraz (23).

Darling District (2,811 ha) encircling the eponymous West Coast town, best known for the wines from its higher-lying ward, Groenekloof, long the source of top sauvignon; growing reputation for reds, especially shiraz. Groenekloof: cab (472), shiraz (346), sauvignon (307), chenin (207), pinotage (188).

Durbanville Ward within the Tygerberg district, with solid reputation for striking merlot and sauvignon. The latter (413) is the dominant variety, followed by cab (240), merlot (235), shiraz (213) and chardonnay (93). Altitude: 150-350 m; temp 22.4°C; rain: 481/140 mm; geology: shale.

Elgin Cool upland district within the Cape South Coast region, yielding aromatic whites and elegant reds. Altitude: 200-250 m; temp 19.7°C; rain: 1,011/366 mm; geology: shale (sandstone). Sauvignon (334), pinot noir (108), chardonnay (99), shiraz (82), cab (62).

Elim Maritime ward within the Cape Agulhas district, its 146 ha of vineyards are arrayed around the old mission village of Elim near Africa's most southerly point. Sauvignon (83), shiraz (31), pinot noir (11), semillon (9), cab (4).

Franschhoek Valley A district with 1,254 ha under vine, recognised for cab and semillon. Sauvignon (190), cab (188), chardonnay (182), shiraz (171), merlot (117).

Hemel-en-Aarde See Walker Bay

Klein Karoo Scrubby semi-arid region (2,480 ha), reliant on irrigation. Recognised for excellent 'ports', and fortifieds generally. Calitzdorp district: muscat d'Alexandrie (82), colombard (66), chenin (30), cab (23), shiraz (17). Tradouw ward: chardonnay (15), merlot (11), colombard (10), sauvignon (10), shiraz (10). Interesting stirrings in tiny Langeberg-Garcia

district (41), and Upper Langkloof (50) and Tradouw Highlands (10) wards.

Northern Cape See Central Orange River.

Olifants River Quality moves are afoot in this north-westerly Cape grape-growing region (9,910 ha), particularly in the Bamboes Bay 'micro-ward' (just 6 ha) and Lutzville Valley district (3,067) nearer the coast, as well as the cool upland ward of Piekenierskloof (470). Inland, a climate conducive to organic cultivation is being exploited to that end. Altitude: 20-100 m; temp 23°C; rain: 139/47 mm; geology: mainly schist and alluvial deposits. Koekenaap ward (Lutzville Valley): chenin (295), colombard (213), sauvignon (167), cab (69), muscat d'Alexandrie (37). Piekenierskloof: pinotage (68), chenin (51), palomino (49), grenache noir (47), sauvignon (38).

Orange River See Central Orange River

Paarl This district has many mesoclimates, soils and aspects, and thus succeeds with a variety of styles and grapes. Altitude: 100-300 m; temp 23.2°C; rain: 945/273 mm; geology: granite and shale. Paarl proper is recognised for shiraz and, more recently, viognier and mourvèdre grown on warmer slopes. Chenin (1,476), cab (983), shiraz (917), pinotage (564), cinsaut (402). The following are wards: Simonsberg-Paarl, on the warmer slopes of the Simonsberg, recognised for red blends, shiraz and chardonnay. Cab (320), chardonnay (216), sauvignon (183), shiraz (178), merlot (120). Voor Paardeberg, long an uncredited source of top-quality grapes, now becoming a star in own right. Cab (374), shiraz (323), chenin (225), merlot (204), pinotage (179).

Philadelphia A ward of Tygerberg, cooled by the Atlantic air and noted for cab, merlot and Bordeaux-style reds. Cab (225), sauvignon (139), shiraz (65), merlot (65), chardonnay (37). See under Durbanville for climate, geology etc.

Robertson Traditionally a white-wine district, increasingly recognised for shiraz and cab. Chardonnay,

1 Montagu	**5** Malgas	**9** Langeberg-Garcia	**12** Calitzdorp	**15** Outeniqua
2 Stormsvlei	**6** Buffeljags	**10** Still Bay East	**13** Prince Albert Valley	**16** Upper Langkloof
3 Swellendam	**7** Tradouw	**11** Herbertsdale	**14** Swartberg	**17** Plettenberg Bay
4 Tradouw Highlands	**8** Klein Karoo			

sauvignon and sparkling remain stand-outs. Altitude: 150-250 m; temp 23°C; rain: 280/116 mm; geology: shale and alluvial. Colombard (2,180), chardonnay (2,117), chenin (1,680), sauvignon (1,532), cab (1,469).

Stellenbosch To many, this intensively farmed district is the wine capital of South Africa. Key contributors to quality are the cooler mountain slopes, varied soil types and breezes off False Bay which moderate summer temperatures. Altitude: 200-400 m; temp

21.5°C; rain: 713/229 mm; geology: granite (sandstone). Jonkershoek Valley, a ward east of Stellenbosch town, is recognised for cab and cab blends. Cab (62), merlot (24), chardonnay (24), shiraz (19), sauvignon (15). Simonsberg-Stellenbosch, in the south-western foothills of the Simonsberg Mountain, is especially recognised for cab, cab blends and pinotage, and reds generally. Cab (332), sauvignon (190), merlot (169), shiraz (153), chardonnay (121). North-west of Stellenbosch town are four adjoining

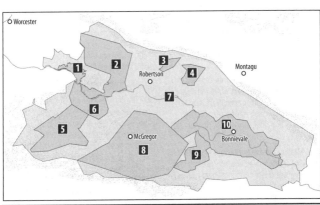

1 Eilandia	3 Hoopsrivier	5 Agterkliphoogte	7 Robertson	9 Boesmansrivier
2 Vinkrivier	4 Klaasvoogds	6 Le Chasseur	8 McGregor	10 Bonnievale

1 Swartland	4 Durbanville	7 Tulbagh
2 Darling	5 Malmesbury	
3 Philadelphia	6 Riebeekberg	

1 Lutzville Valley	6 Olifants River
2 Bamboes Bay	7 Citrusdal Mountain
3 Lamberts Bay	8 Citrusdal Valley
4 Vredendal	9 Piekenierskloof
5 Spruitdrift	10 Cederberg

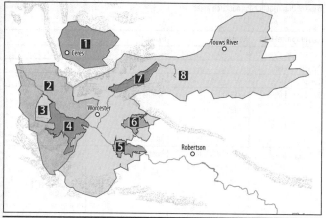

1 Ceres Plateau
2 Breedekloof
3 Slanghoek
4 Goudini
5 Scherpenheuvel
6 Nuy
7 Hex River Valley
8 Worcester

wards: Papegaaiberg - chardonnay (28), sauvignon (22), chenin (21), pinot gris (12), cabernet (12); Devon Valley, recognised mainly for red blends - merlot (143), cab (135), sauvignon (119), shiraz (79), pinotage (68); Bottelary, noted for pinotage, shiraz and warm-blooded blends - chenin (459), cab (363), sauvignon (316), shiraz (274), pinotage (253); the most westerly ward, Polkadraai Hills - sauvignon (162), cab (155), shiraz (130), merlot (92), chenin (75); and Banghoek, the mountain amphitheatre above the village of Pniel - cab (75), shiraz (44), merlot (30), sauvignon (30), chardonnay (22). The remainder of the Stellenbosch district, as yet officially undemarcated, includes Stellenboschberg, Helderberg and Faure, recognised for red blends, chenin and sauvignon. Cab (1,676), shiraz (1,229), sauvignon (1,107), merlot (965), chenin (678).

Swartland Traditionally associated with full-bodied reds, but latterly also with chenin and Mediterranean-style red and white blends, this sunny district north of Cape Town has two wards, Malmesbury and Riebeekberg, plus a large unappellated area. Riebeekberg: chenin (213), shiraz (180), pinotage (179), chardonnay (132), cab (103). Malmesbury: cab (715), shiraz (565), pinotage (488), chenin (472), sauvignon (318). 'Swartland': chenin (1,878), shiraz (848), cab (778), pinotage (734), chardonnay (386). Altitude: 100-300 m; temp 23.3°C; rain: 523/154 mm; geology: granite and shale.

Tulbagh Inland district, traditionally known for sparkling and lightish whites, acquiring reputation for quality reds and serious white blends. Altitude: 160-400 m; temp 24°C; rain: 551/175 mm; geology: sandstone boulderbeds and shale. Chenin (234), colombard (182), shiraz (133), cab (119), chardonnay (81).

Walker Bay Highly regarded maritime district southeast of Cape Town, recognised for pinot noir, pinotage, sauvignon and chardonnay. Altitude: 100-250 m; temp 20.3°C; rain: 722/322 mm; geology: shale, granite and sandstone. Sauvignon (269), shiraz (129), pinot noir (125), chardonnay (105), cab (79). Bot River, Hemel-en-Aarde Ridge, Hemel-en-Aarde Valley, Sunday's Glen, Upper Hemel-en-Aarde Valley and new Stanford Foothills are wards.

Wellington District in the Coastal region increasingly reputed for shiraz and gutsy red blends. Chenin (952), cab (759), shiraz (609), pinotage (408), chardonnay (312).

Worcester District producing chiefly for the brandy industry and merchant trade, but small quantities bottled under own labels often represent good quality/value. Recognised for everyday reds/whites and fortifieds. Chenin (1,875), colombard (1,087), chardonnay (556), shiraz (410), sauvignon (370). See under Robertson for climate, geology etc.

Wine of Origin-defined production areas
(New appellation/s in bold.)

Geographical Unit	Region	District	Ward
Eastern Cape	—	—	St Francis Bay
KwaZulu-Natal	—	—	—
Limpopo	—	—	—
Northern Cape	—	Douglas	—
	—	—	Central Orange River
	—	—	Hartswater
	—	—	Rietrivier (Free State)
	—	Sutherland-Karoo	—
Western Cape	Breede River Valley	Breedekloof	Goudini
			Slanghoek
		Robertson	Agterkliphoogte
			Boesmansrivier
			Bonnievale
			Eilandia
			Hoopsrivier
			Klaasvoogds
			Le Chasseur
			McGregor
			Vinkrivier
		Worcester	Hex River Valley
			Nuy
			Scherpenheuvel
	Cape South Coast	Cape Agulhas	Elim
		Elgin	—
		Overberg	Elandskloof
			Greyton
			Klein River
			Theewater
		Plettenberg Bay	—
		Swellendam	Buffeljags
			Malgas
			Stormsvlei
		Walker Bay	Bot River
			Hemel-en-Aarde Ridge
			Hemel-en-Aarde Valley
			Stanford Foothills
			Sunday's Glen
			Upper Hemel-en-Aarde Valley
		—	Herbertsdale
		—	Napier
		—	Stilbaai East
	Coastal	Cape Point	—
		Darling	Groenekloof
		Franschhoek Valley	—
		Paarl	Simonsberg-Paarl
			Voor Paardeberg
		Stellenbosch	Banghoek
			Bottelary
			Devon Valley
			Jonkershoek Valley

Geographical Unit	Region	District	Ward
Western Cape *(continued)*	Coastal *(continued)*	Stellenbosch *(continued)*	Papegaaiberg Polkadraai Hills Simonsberg–Stellenbosch
		Swartland	Malmesbury Riebeekberg
		Tulbagh	—
		Tygerberg	Durbanville Philadelphia
		Wellington	—
		—	Constantia Hout Bay
	Klein Karoo	Calitzdorp	—
		Langeberg-Garcia	—
		—	Montagu
		—	Outeniqua
		—	Tradouw
		—	Tradouw Highlands
		—	Upper Langkloof
	Olifants River	Citrusdal Mountain	Piekenierskloof
		Citrusdal Valley	—
		Lutzville Valley	Koekenaap
		—	Bamboes Bay
		—	Spruitdrift
		—	Vredendal
—	—	—	Cederberg
—	—	**Ceres Plateau**	Ceres
—	—	—	Lamberts Bay
—	—	—	Prince Albert Valley
—	—	—	Swartberg

Boberg (fortified wines from Franschhoek, Paarl and Tulbagh). Source: SAWIS

Grape Varieties

Below are brief notes on some of the grape varieties mentioned in the guide, and their contribution to the national vineyard (statistics from SA Wine Industry Information & Systems — SAWIS). See under Wine-growing Areas for details of the most widely planted and best-performing varieties in the major vine cultivation zones.

Red-wine varieties

Cabernet sauvignon Adaptable and internationally planted black grape making some of the world's finest and longest-lasting wines. And retaining some of its inherent qualities even when overcropped in less suitable soils and climates. Can stand alone triumphantly, but frequently blended with a wide range of other varieties: traditionally, as in Bordeaux, with cab franc, merlot and a few minor others, but also in SA sometimes partnering varieties such as shiraz and pinotage. Number of different clones, with differing characteristics. ±11% of total vineyard area.

Cabernet franc Like its descendant cabernet sauvignon, with which it is often partnered, a classic part of the Bordeaux blend, but in SA and elsewhere — particularly in the Loire — also used for varietal wines. Tiny, stable vineyard area (±1%).

Carignan Hugely planted in the south of France, where it is not much respected. But there, as in SA, older, low-yielding vines can produce pleasant surprises. Insignificant vineyard area.

Cinsaut (noir) 'Cinsault' in France. Another of the mass, undistinguished plantings of southern France, which only occasionally comes up trumps. Used to be known locally as hermitage, the name reflected in its offspring (with pinot noir), pinotage. About 2% of vineyard area.

Gamay noir Although it produces some serious long-lived wines in Beaujolais, its use for (mainly) early- and easy-drinking 'nouveau' wines there, often using

carbonic maceration, is the model mostly copied in SA. Insignificant vineyard area.

Grenache (noir) The international (ie French) name for the Spanish grape garnacha. Widespread in Spain and southern France, generally used in blends (as in Rioja and Châteauneuf), but occasionally solo. A favourite for rosés. When vigour restrained, capable of greatness, but this is rare. Tiny plantings here. (White/pink versions also occur.)

Malbec Once a significant part of Bordeaux's blend, now most important in Cahors in western France (where it is known as cot), and as Argentina's signature variety. In SA a few varietal and blended examples; very small plantings.

Merlot Classic blending partner (as in Bordeaux) for cabernet, fashionable around the world, where it tends to be seen as an 'easier' version of cab — although this is perhaps because it is often made in a less ambitious manner. Merlot varietal wines increasingly common in SA too. ±6% of vineyard area.

Mourvèdre Internationally known by its French name, though originally Spanish (monastrell). In Australia and California also called mataro. Particularly successful in some serious southern French blends, and increasingly modish internationally. Minuscule plantings here.

Nebbiolo Perhaps the greatest red grape to have scarcely ventured from its home — Piedmont in this case, where it makes massive, tannic, long-lived wines. Minute plantings here.

Petit verdot Use of this excellent variety in the Médoc limited by its late ripening. Now appearing in some local blends, and a few varietals. 0.7% of vineyard area.

Pinotage A 1920s cross between pinot noir and cinsaut ('hermitage'). Made in a range of styles, from simply fruity to ambitious, well-oaked examples. 6.4% of vineyard area.

Pinot noir Notoriously difficult grape to succeed with outside its native Burgundy, but South Africa, along with the rest of the New World, now produces some excellent examples. Slightly increasing 1% of the vineyard.

Ruby cabernet US cross between cabernet sauvignon and carignan, designed for heat tolerance. Rather rustic, used mostly in cheaper blends. ±2% of vineyard area.

Shiraz Better known as syrah outside South Africa and Australia (and on some local labels too). Internationally increasing in popularity, with northern Rhône and now also Australia as its major domiciles. Made in a variety of styles — generally wooded. ±10% of vineyard area.

Tinta barocca Elsewhere spelt 'barroca'. One of the important Portuguese port-making grapes, which is now its primary role in SA, usually blended. Also used for some varietal unfortified wines, and namelessly in some 'dry reds'. 0.2% of vineyard area.

Touriga nacional Important Portuguese port-making grape, now usefully grown here for similar ends, along with tinta franca, tinta roriz (tempranillo) and souzão. Tiny plantings.

Zinfandel The quintessential Californian grape (of European origin, and the same as Italy's primitivo), used here in a small way for some big wines. Tiny plantings.

White-wine varieties

Chardonnay In SA, as elsewhere, many new vineyards of this grape have come on-stream, with wines showing a wide range of styles, quality and price. Generally used varietally, but also in blends, and for sparkling. (Heavily) wooded in more ambitious wines. ±7% of vineyard area.

Chenin blanc SA has more chenin (locally also called steen) than even France's Loire Valley, the variety's home. Used here for everything from generic 'dry white' to ambitious sweet wines, to brandy. Increasing numbers of table-wine successes in recent years, as well as inexpensive flavoursome easy-drinkers. ±17% of vineyard area.

Colombar(d) One of the mainstays of brandy production in South Africa, colombard (usually without the 'd' in SA) is also used for numerous varietal and blended wines, ranging from dry to sweet — seldom wooded. Steady ±11% of vineyard area.

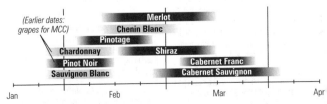

Approximate ripening dates in the Stellenbosch area for some important grape varieties

Gewürztraminer Readily identifiable from its rose-petal fragrance, best known in its Alsatian guise. In South Africa usually made off-dry. Insignificant vineyard area.

Hanepoot Traditional Afrikaans name for muscat d'Alexandrie, South Africa's most planted muscat variety (see also muscadel below). ±2% of vineyard area (some for raisins and table grapes), slowly declining.

Muscadel Name used here for both muscat de Frontignan and muscat blanc à petits grains (both red and white versions). The grape associated with the famous Constantia dessert wines of the 18th century today is used chiefly for dessert and fortified wines and for touching up blends. Red and white versions total about 1% of vineyard area.

Muscat See Hanepoot and Muscadel.

Riesling The name by itself now refers to the great German grape (as it does in this guide). Previously, the grape had to carry the prefix 'Rhine' or 'weisser', and the 'riesling' was an official SA synonym for the inferior crouchen blanc, also known as Cape riesling and mostly used anonymously in blends, occasionally varietally. Rhine riesling often off-dry here, in blends or varietally, some excellent botrytised dessert examples. Crouchen: 0.5% of vineyard area, steady; Rhine: small but steady 0.2%.

Sauvignon blanc Prestigious vine most associated with eastern Loire regions, Bordeaux and New Zealand — whose wines have helped restore fashionability to the grape. The SA version no longer a poor relation of these. Usually dry, but some sweet wines; sometimes wooded, more often not (former sometimes called fumé blanc/blanc fumé). ±9% of vineyard area.

Semillon Spelt sémillon in French. Sometimes heavily wooded, sometimes sweet, more often in blends. ±1% of vineyard area, including rare red version.

Viognier Increasingly fashionable variety internationally, spreading out from its home in the northern Rhône, now showing promise here. Usually wooded. Still tiny plantings.

Competitions, Challenges & Awards

An increasing number of wine competitions, awards and challenges are run by liquor industry bodies, independent companies, publishing houses and individuals. Below are the main national events:

Absa Top Ten Pinotage Competition Run annually by the Pinotage Association and a major financial institution to help set international quality targets for growers of pinotage. Local/overseas judges. See under Industry Organisations for contact details.

Amorim Tsogo Sun Cap Classique Challenge Annual competition to appoint SA's top bottle-fermented sparkling wines. Mostly local judges. ▪ elsabe@efpromosies.co.za ▪ www.capclassique.co.za ▪ T +27 (0)21-863-1599 ▪ F +27 (0)21-863-1552

Best Value Wine Guide SA judges gather annually to select the best-value wines under R80 based on quality. Sponsored by Ultra Liquors, results are published in the Best Value Wine Guide, distributed with Getaway magazine. ▪ bestvalue@ramsaymedia.co.za ▪ www.bestvaluewineguide.co.za ▪ T +27 (0)21-530-3151

CAPPA Port & Wine Challenge Organised by the Cape Port Producers' Association to award best in class and gold medals in each of the port categories, and select the Top 10 Portuguese-style wines. Local judges. ▪ info@boplaas.co.za ▪ www.capeportproducers.co.za ▪ T +27 (0)44-213-3326 ▪ F +27 (0)44-213-3750

Christian Eedes Cabernet Sauvignon Report Founded 2012 and presented by Sanlam Private Investments, the Cabernet Sauvignon Report scrutinises the category's 60 front-runners, included by invitation only. Local tasters. ▪ christian.eedes@ gmail.com ▪ www.whatidranklastnight.co.za ▪ T +27 (0)83-454-3644

Christian Eedes Chardonnay Report Launched 2011 in association with Sanlam Private Investments, the Chardonnay Report follows the format of the Christian Eedes Cabernet Sauvignon Report. See that entry for details and contact numbers.

Classic Wine Trophy See Taj Classic Wine Trophy

Diners Club Winemaker of the Year Inaugurated in 1981, this prestigious competition features a different category each year. The Young Winemaker of the Year recognises the winning entrant aged 30 years or younger. Local panel with some overseas representation. ▪ winemaker@dinersclub.co.za ▪ www.dinersclub.co.za ▪ T +27 (0)21- 795-5400 ▪ F +27 (0)21-794-8185

Getaway Ultra Liquors Best Value Wine Awards See Best Value Wine Guide

Michelangelo International Wine Awards sponsored by Rotolabel Well-established competition (1997) with strong international emphasis: 16 accredited judges from around the globe, and foreign as well as South African wines competing under OIV rules for 15 trophies as well as the newly established Platinum awards and Gran d'Or, gold and silver medals. ▪ lorraine@michelangeloawards.com ▪ www.michelangeloawards.com ▪ T +27 (0)82-556-8679 ▪ F +27 (0)86-555-8061

Muscadel Award for Excellence Annual competition aimed at raising consumer awareness and recognising quality in the creation, packaging and promotion of SA's muscadel wines. Local judges. ▪ winemaker@badsberg.co.za, andre@rooiberg.co.za ▪ **T +27 (0)23-344-3021 / +27 (0)23-626-1664** ▪ F +27 (0)23-344-3023

Nedbank Green Wine Awards A three-part competition, recognising the best wine made from certified organically grown grapes, wines made from BWI certified farms and the producer with the best environmental practices. Results are published in the Nedbank Green Wine Awards booklet. Local judges. ▪ kathryn.frew@ramsaymedia.co.za ▪ www.greenwineawards.com ▪ **T +27 (0)21-530-3308**

Old Mutual Trophy Wine Show Convened by Michael Fridjhon and sponsored by Old Mutual. Seeks to identify the best wines in SA and award trophies to the top gold medal winner in the major classes, as well as the top producer overall. Local and international judges. ▪ alex@outsorceress.co.za ▪ www.trophywineshow.co.za ▪ **T +27 (0)11-482-5936** ▪ F +27 (0)11-507-6027

Perold Absa Cape Blend Competition Launched in 2011 and aimed at creating a signature style for Cape Blends (see SA Wine Styles section). Local judges. Contacts as for Absa Top Ten Pinotage.

SAPPA Port Challenge See Cape Port Challenge

South African Airways (SAA) Wine Awards Annual selection of wines to fly with the national carrier (drinkability in flight conditions an important consideration). The top red, white, bubbly and port each receive a trophy. Local and overseas palates. ▪ BongiSodladla@flysaa.com, YolandeSchutte@flysaa.com ▪ **T +27 (0)11-978-9304 / +27 (0)11-978-3982** ▪ F +27 (0)11-978-3115

SA National Bottled Wine Show See Veritas

South African Terroir Wine Awards Only wines that truly portray a specific terroir can enter, making this a highly exclusive competition. The best wines certified as from single vineyards, units registered for the production of estate wine, wards in SA's officially recognised winegrowing areas, as well as small districts that are not divided into wards, are awarded. SA's top 5 estate wines are also honoured. Seven local judges. ▪ mlab@iafrica.com ▪ www.terroirwineawards.co.za ▪ **T +27 (0)21-975-8166**

South African Young Wine Show Inaugurated 1975 to gauge the quality of embryo wines, prior to finishing and bottling, thereby also recognising wineries which sell their products in bulk. The grand champion receives the General Smuts Trophy. Local judges. ▪ information@veritas.co.za ▪ www.youngwineshow.co.za ▪ **T +27 (0)21-863 1599** ▪ F +27 (0)21-863-1552

TAJ Classic Wine Trophy Established in 1998 to recognise ageworthy, elegant and well-made SA wines. Staged in partnership with the TAJ Hotel Cape Town and La Revue du Vin de France. Overseas judges. ▪ info@classicwinetrophy.co.za ▪ www.classicwinetrophy.co.za ▪ **T +27 (0)21-683-7479** ▪ F +27 (0)86-588-2989

Top 100 South African Wines National fine-wine challenge that aims to identify the best 100 wines of South Africa using mainly Master of Wine judges. Separately the Top 100 wine list challenge identifies winning restaurants lists. The winners are showcased in a hardcopy book and on the website, and made available for public and trade tasting both in SA and internationally. ▪ info@top100sawines.com ▪ www.top100sawines.com ▪ **T +27 (0)21-787-9880** ▪ F +27 (0)86-627-5588

Trophy Wine Show See Trophy Wine Show

Veritas SA's biggest competition for market-ready wines, awarding double-gold, gold, silver and bronze medals across a wide range of categories. Local palates with some overseas input. ▪ information@veritas.co.za ▪ www.veritas.co.za ▪ **T +27 (0)21-863 1599** ▪ F +27 (0)21-863-1552

Winemakers' Choice Awards Gives winemakers from all wine regions the opportunity to judge the products of their peers. A Diamond Award is given to all winning wines; trophies and a cash prize are also awarded to the best white and red on show. ▪ robyn@winemakerschoice.co.za ▪ www.winemakerschoice.co.za ▪ **T +27 (0)21-887-2377 / +27(0)82-301-4509**

Wine Education

Cape Wine Academy Long-established general wine education body. Based in Stellenbosch and Johannesburg with satellites in Durban, Pretoria, Bloemfontein, Kenya and Zimbabwe. Runs wine theory and tasting courses with examinations at several levels, as well as training for front-of-house sales staff and sommeliers . Also presents corporate tastings. ▪ www.capewineacademy.co.za ▪ Stellenbosch: **T +27** (0)21-889-8844 ▪ F +27 (0)21-889-7391 ▪ michelle@capewineacademy.co.za ▪ Johannesburg: **T +27 (0)11- 024-3616** ▪ F +27 (0)11- 440 2157 ▪ busi@capewineacademy.co.za

University of Stellenbosch Garagiste Winemaking Course The premium short course for people interested in producing quality small-scale

wines at home or simply expanding their wine knowledge. Attendees receive a set of notes; observe the use of garagiste winemaking equipment; taste different vinifications; bottle their own wine; and receive a certificate from Stellenbosch University. ▪ wdutoit@sun.ac.za ▪ **T +27 (0)21-808-2022** ▪ F +27 (0)21-808-4781

Wine Tasting Academy Run by Michael Fridjhon and the University of Cape Town's Graduate School of Business, this intensive 3-day tasting and wine judging course aims to increase the number of competent wine judges at work in the local industry. ▪ crossley@reciprocal.co.za

WSET in South Africa The industry standard for wine education in 60 countries, the UK-based Wine & Spirit Education Trust's courses cater for beginners up to wine industry professionals. In-situ training for front-of-house staff is also offered and, for those wanting to take their wine education to the highest level, WSET is the direct path to the Master of Wine (MW) qualification. Stand-alone spirits courses also available. WSET are the only internationally recognised wine courses available and offered throughout Africa. ▪ info@thewinecentre.co.za ▪ www.thewinecentre.co.za ▪ **T +27 (0)72-390-9166**

Service Excellence Training Runs wine courses for staff in the licensed restaurant trade to improve their knowledge of viticulture and wine service. ▪ mfine@icon.co.za ▪ www.bevtrainsa.co.za ▪ **T +27 (0)82-932-9430 / +27 (0)21-782-5472**

A-Code Numbers & Codes

Many wines appear on the market under brand names, with, at first glance, no reference to their producers or purveyors. However, consumers need not buy 'blind', and may trace a wine's provenance by checking the official 'A-number' which appears on the bottle or pack. This identity code tells you either who produced the wine, or who sourced it for resale. In the latter case, an enquiry to the merchant should elicit the source. The list keeps growing and being revised, and is too lengthy to reproduce in this guide. Via the online SAWIS portal (**www.sawis.co.za**), it is possible however to search the list of A-codes, as well as the certification codes issued for each wine by the Wine & Spirit Board, for details about the production area, variety and vintage.

Recent Cape Vintages

South African wines do not exhibit the major vintage variations seen in some winegrowing areas. There are, nevertheless, perceptible differences from year to year. Dry, hot summers are the norm but a variety of factors make generalisations difficult and possibly misleading.

2013 Biggest crop to date; moderate conditions yielded good to very good reds and whites, lighter alcohol levels.

2012 Unusually dry, hot January strained unirrigated vineyards; otherwise good to very good vintage for both reds and whites; moderate alcohol levels.

2011 Yet more variable than the last, impossible to generalise. As in 2010, producer's track record should guide the buying/cellaring decision.

2010 A real test of the winegrower's savvy, and one of the toughest recent harvests to call. Be guided by producer's track record.

2009 Perhaps one of the greatest vintages. Late, gruelling, but whites and reds both stellar.

2008 Long, wet, late and challenging but also unusually cool, favouring elegance in reds and whites.

2007 Elegant, structured whites; smaller red-grape berries gave intense colour and fruit concentration.

2006 Perhaps the best white-wine vintage in a decade — particularly expressive sauvignon and chenin. Fleshy, mild-tannined reds, with lower alcohols.

2005 Particularly challenging. Concentrated if alcoholic reds; mostly average whites, some exceptions.

2004 Cooler dry conditions yielded elegant, often ageworthy wines with lower alcohols, softer tannins.

2003 Outstanding, especially for reds — concentrated and structured, and often slow to show their best.

Older Vintages

2002 Challenging and patchy, but top producers show fine concentration and moderate alcohols.
2001 Some excellent reds — fruity and concentrated, best are long lived. Flavourful if alcoholic whites.
2000 Powerful, concentrated reds, befitting a hot year; the best have kept very well. Whites generally less impressive, not for long ageing.
1999 Fat, alcoholic reds with ripe fruit for earlier drinking. Generally not too much excitement among the whites.
1998 Excellent red vintage with enough fruit for extended cellaring; whites generally not for keeping.
1997 Among coolest and latest vintages on record. Supple, elegant reds; some excellent and stylish whites.
1996 Generally awkward reds, not for keeping; whites, except for top NLHs, best drunk up.
1995 For many, the vintage of the 90s. Concentrated reds, some still maturing spectacularly.
1994 Hottest, driest vintage in decades; variable quality; new-clone cabs and early ripening reds fared well.
1993 Without serious mishaps; some excellent sauvignons; above-average reds.
1992 Coolish season, favouring whites, especially sauvignon; the reds (notably pinotage) very good;
1991 Dry, warm to hot, favouring early to mid-season ripeners; some long-lasting reds.
1990 Uneven year, alternately cool and warm; average whites and reds; not for further ageing.
1980s: even years (82, 84, 86) usually more favourable for reds; uneven years, marginally cooler, favoured whites, but 'white' years 87 and, especially, 89 produced remarkable reds.
1970s: again, even years generally favoured whites. Best was 74; but top wines from some other vintages are still delicious.
1960s and earlier yielded some astonishingly long-lived wines.

South African Wine Styles

Blanc de blancs White wine made from white grapes only; also used for champagne and méthode cap classique.

Blanc fumé or **fumé blanc** Dry white from sauvignon, usually but not necessarily wooded (nor smoked, smoky).

Blanc de noir A pink wine (shades range from off-white through peach to pink) made from red grapes. See also Rosé.

Blend See Varietal wine and Cape Blend.

Brut See Sugar or sweetness, and Sparkling wine.

Cap classique See Sparkling wine.

Cape Blend Evolving term, increasingly used to denote a (red) blend with pinotage, the 'local' grape making up a significant part of the assemblage; sometimes simply a blend showing a distinct 'Cape' character; occasionally used for chenin-based blends.

Carbonated See Sparkling wine.

Cultivar Grape variety (a contraction of 'cultivated variety').

Cuvée French term for the blend of a wine.

Demi-sec See Sugar or sweetness.

Dessert wine A sweet wine, often to accompany the dessert but sometimes pleasurably prior, as in the famous Sauternes/foie gras combo.

Dry to sweet See Sugar or sweetness.

Estate wine Term now reserved for wine originating from an officially registered 'unit for the production of estate wine' (see www.sawis.co.za for current list).

Fortified wines Increased in alcoholic strength by the addition of spirit, by SA law to minimum 15% alcohol by volume.

Grand cru See Premier Grand Cru.

Jerepiko or **jerepigo** Red or white wine, produced without fermentation; grape juice is fortified with grape spirit, preventing fermentation; very sweet, with considerable unfermented grape flavours.

Kosher See Winemaking terms section.

Late Harvest Sweet wine from late-harvested and therefore sweeter grapes. See Sugar or sweetness.

Méthode cap classique (MCC) See Sparkling wine.

Noble Late Harvest (NLH) Sweet dessert wine (still, perlé or sparkling) exhibiting a noble rot (botrytis) character, from grapes infected by the *botrytis cinerea* fungus. This mould, in warm, misty autumn weather, attacks the skins of ripe grapes, causing much of the juice to evaporate. As the berries wither, their sweetness and flavour become powerfully concentrated. SA law dictates that grapes for NLH must be harvested at a minimum of 28° Balling and residual sugar must exceed 50g/L.

Nouveau Term originated in Beaujolais for fruity young and light red, usually from gamay and made by the carbonic maceration method. Bottled soon after vintage to capture the youthful, fresh flavour of fruit and yeasty fermentation.

Perlant, perlé, pétillant Lightly sparkling, usually carbonated wine.

Port Fortified dessert with excellent quality record in South Africa since late 1980s, partly through efforts of Cape Port Producers' Association which has adopted 'Cape' to identify the local product. Following are CAPPA-defined styles: **Cape White**: non-muscat grapes, wood-aged min 6 months, any size vessel; **Cape Pink**: non-muscat varieties, pink hue, barrel/tank-aged min 6 months; **Cape Ruby**: full bodied, fruity; min 50% barrel/tank-aged 6-36 months; **Cape Vintage**: fruit of one harvest; dark, full-bodied; tank/cask-aged min 1 year; must be certified, sold in glass, vintage dated; **Cape Vintage Reserve**: as for Vintage, but 'superior quality'; **Cape Late Bottled Vintage** (LBV): fruit of single year, full-bodied, slightly tawny colour, barrel/bottle aged min 3 years (of

which min 2 years in oak); **Cape Tawny**: min 80% wood matured, amber-orange (tawny) colour, smooth, slightly nutty taste; **Cape Dated Tawny**: single-vintage tawny.

Premier Grand Cru Unlike in France, not a quality rating in SA — usually an austerely dry white.

Residual sugar See Sugar or sweetness.

Rosé Pink wine, made from red or a blend of red and white grapes. The red grape skins are removed before the wine takes up too much colour.

Single-vineyard wine Classification for wines from officially registered vineyards, no larger than 6ha in size and planted with a single variety.

Sparkling wine Bubbly, or 'champagne', usually white but sometimes rosé and even red, given its effervescence by carbon dioxide — allowed to escape in the normal winemaking process. **Champagne** undergoes its second fermentation in the bottle. Under an agreement with France, SA does not use the term, which describes the sparkling wines from the Champagne area. Instead, **méthode cap classique** (MCC) is the SA term to describe sparkling wines made by the classic method. **Charmat** undergoes its second, bubble-forming fermentation in a tank and is bottled under pressure. **Carbonated** sparklers are made by the injection of carbon dioxide bubbles (as in fizzy soft drinks). See also Sugar or sweetness.

Special Late Harvest (SLH) SA designation for a lighter dessert-style wine. There is no legal stipulation for residual sugar content, but if the RS is below 20g/L, the label must state 'extra dry', 'dry', 'semi-dry' or 'sweet', as the case may be. The minimum alcohol content is 11% by volume.

Stein Semi-sweet white wine, usually a blend and often confused with steen, a grape variety (chenin blanc), though most steins are at least made partly from steen grapes.

Sugar or sweetness In still wines: extra-dry or bone-dry wines have less than 2.5g/L residual sugar, undetectable to the taster. A wine legally is dry up to 5g/L. Taste buds will begin picking up a slight sweetness, or softness, in a wine — depending on its acidity — at about 6g/L, when it is still off-dry. By about 8–9g/L a definite sweetness can usually be noticed. However, an acidity of 8–9g/L can render a sweet wine fairly crisp even with a sugar content of 20g/L plus. Official sweetness levels in SA wine are listed in the table opposite.

Varietal wine From a single variety of grape. Legislation requires the presence in the wine of 85% of the stated variety or vintage. Blends may name component parts only if those components were

vinified separately, prior to blending; then they are listed with the larger contributor(s) named first. If any one of the blend partners is less than 20%, percentages for all the varieties must be given. Blends may be vinified separately in any recognised WO area; component areas may be named, as above except the threshold is 30%.

Vintage In SA primarily used to denote year of harvest. Not a quality classification (a 'vintage' port in Europe means one from an officially declared great port-grape year).

Wine	Sugar (g/l)
Still wines	
Extra-dry	≤ 2.5
Dry	≤ 5
Semi-dry	5 ≤ 12
Semi-sweet	> 5 <30
Late Harvest	≥ 20
Special Late Harvest (SLH)	—
Natural Sweet (or Sweet Natural)	> 20
Noble Late Harvest (NLH)	> 50
Naturally dried grape wine (straw wine)	> 30
Sparkling wines	
Brut nature	<3
Extra brut	<6
Brut	<12
Extra-dry	12–17
Dry	17–32
Semi-sweet	32–50
Sweet	> 50

Brandy, Husk Spirit & Sherry-styles

Brandy and Husk Spirit

Brandy was last covered by Platter's in the 1998 edition, though it was not rated then. In this edition it is, along with sherry-style wine and husk spirit (the latter better known as grappa, though the European Union restricts that name to the Italian original, as it does 'sherry' to the Spanish original).

These categories were tasted by small panels (Winnie Bowman and Tim James for brandy and grappa; Winnie Bowman and Christine Rudman for sherry), with constant reference to Dave Hughes, perhaps the country's most experienced judge of spirits. The panel also nominated the winners of five stars — these did not go through the same five-star board that the wines did. This applies also to those brandies which are listed above the names of other individual tasters in winery entries.

Unlike what might happen in some spirits competitions, these were rated on one scale, not on different scales for each category. Assessments were conducted sighted, as for the wines.

South African brandy is divided into three main stylistic categories. Put simply and reductively these are as follows:

- Blended Brandy must by law contain at least 30% brandy distilled in a potstill and aged for at least three years in oak barrels. The remaining component will be of unmatured wine spirit (made in a continuous still). More often than not, these brandies are intended to partner mixers or to play a role in cocktails. The alcohol by volume (ABV) content must be at least 43% (in practice it usually is 43%).

- Vintage Brandy (a small category) must have at least 90% blended brandy, where the brandy and wine spirit are aged for at least eight years. Up to 10% neutral wine spirit is permitted.

- Potstill Brandy has a potstill component of at least 90%. Up to 10% neutral wine spirit may be added, but this rarely happens. As for Vintage Brandy, the ABV level must be at least 38% (and tends in practice to vary between 38% and 41%).

Estate Brandy is brandy in any of the above categories in which all stages of production, from vineyard to maturation, have taken place on one property (as for 'estate' wine).

Husk Spirit will have an ABV level of at least 43% and not be matured; Premium Husk Spirit must be at least 40% ABV, and be matured in oak for between three and six months.

Sherry-Style Fortified Wines

There are eight classes of sherry-style wines described in South Africa's Liquor Products Act.

The colour of these wines must range – depending on the class – from pale straw to amber. Their aromas and flavours must be 'nutty' and 'woody'.

Five of the eight classes must have a discernible flor yeast and/or wood character. In addition, these classes should:

- In the case of Fino, the residual sugar shall not exceed 20 g/l, and the alcohol content must not exceed 16%. It should have an almond flavour.

- The alcohol content of an Amontillado must be at least 16%, and it should have a flavour of hazelnuts.
- Oloroso must have rich, nutty flavours; a minimum of 50 g/l residual sugar, and at least 16% alcohol by volume.
- The residual sugar content of a Pale Dry wine cannot exceed 30 g/l, and its alcohol content should exceed 16%.
- Similarly, the alcohol content of a Pale Cream must exceed 16%, but its residual sugar can only range between 30 g/l and 80 g/l.
- The remaining three classes need only exhibit a discernable wood character.

- In addition, the residual sugar and alcohol content of a Medium Cream must be between 80 g/l and 115 g/l, and above 16% respectively.
- A Full Cream wine must have at least 115 g/l residual sugar, and an alcohol content above 16%.
- A muscat character and an aldehyde content of at least 80 mg/l, a residual sugar content of at least 100 g/l, and at least 16% alcohol by volume is necessary for an Old Brown. This may also only be sweetened with concentrated must, or with fortified wine with a residual sugar content of at least 180 g/l.

Winetasting Terms

Short of a ready description? Here are a few frequently-used words, phrases and explanations that may be helpful. See also Winemaking terms; SA wine styles.

Accessible, approachable Flavours and feel of the wine are harmonious, easily recognised; it is ready to drink.

Aftertaste The lingering flavours and impressions of a wine; its persistence — the longer, the better.

Alcoholic 'Hot' or, in excess, burning character caused by imbalanced or excessive alcohol. Also simply spiritous.

Astringent Mouth-puckering sensation in the mouth, associated with high tannin (and sometimes acid); also bitter, sharp.

Aroma Smells in the bouquet, or nose, especially the odours associated with the grape rather than the winemaking process.

Attack First sensations on palate/nose — pungent, aggressive, quiet etc.

Austere Usually meaning unyielding, sometimes harsh. Sometimes, more favourably, to imply a notable restraint/refinement.

Backbone The wine is well formed, firm, not flabby or insipid.

Baked 'Hot', earthy quality. Usually from scorched/ shrivelled grapes which have been exposed too long to the sun, or from too warm a barrel fermentation, especially in some whites.

Balance Desirable attribute. The wine's chief constituents — alcohol, acid, tannin, fruit and wood (where used) — are in harmony.

Bead Bubbles in sparkling wine; a fine, long-lasting bead is the most desirable. See also Mousse.

Big Expansive in the mouth, weighty, full-bodied, as a result of high alcohol or fruit concentration.

Bite or **grip** Imparted by tannin, acid and/or alcohol, important in young wines designed for ageing. If overdone can impart undesirable bitterness, harshness or spirity 'glow'.

Bitter Sensation perceived mainly on the back of the tongue, and in the finish of the wine. Usually unpleasant, though an accepted if not immediately admired character of certain Italian wines. Sometimes more positively associated with the taste of a specific fruit or nut, such as cherry-kernel or almond.

Body Fullness on the palate.

Botrytis/ed Exhibits a noble rot/botrytis character, from grapes infected by the *botrytis cinerea* fungus.

Bottle-age Negative or positive, depending on context. Positively describes development of aromas/ flavours (ie complexity) as wine moves from youth to maturity. Much-prized attribute in fine whites and reds. Negatively, bottle age results in a wine with stale, empty or even off odours.

Buttery Flavour and texture associated with barrel-fermented white wines, especially chardonnays; rich, creamy smoothness.

Claret Another name for a dry red Bordeaux or Bordeaux-like red.

Classic Showing characteristics of the classics of Bordeaux, Burgundy etc; usually implying balance, elegance, subtlety.

Coarse Rough, unbalanced tannins, acid, alcohol or oak.

Complexity Strong recommendation. A complex wine has several layers of flavour, usually developing with age/maturation. See Bottle age.

Concentration See Intensity.

Confected Over-elaborately constructed, artificial, forced; sometimes overly sweet.

Corked, corky Wine is faulty; its flavours have been tainted by yeast, fungal or bacterial infections, often but not necessarily from the cork. It smells damp and mouldy in its worst stages — but sometimes it's barely detectable. In a restaurant, a corked wine should be rejected and returned immediately; producers are honour-bound to replace corked wine.

Creamy Not literally creamy, of course; more a silky, buttery feel and texture.

Crisp Refers to acidity. Positively, means fresh, clean; negatively, too tart, sharp.

Deep and **depth** Having many layers; intense; also descriptive of a serious wine.

Dense Well-padded texture, flavour packed.

Deposits (also sediment or crust) Tasteless and harmless tartrates, acid crystals or tannin in older red wines. Evidence that wine has not been harshly fined, filtered or cold-stabilised.

Dried out Bereft of fruit, harder constituents remaining; tired.

Earthy Usually positive, wine showing its origins from soil, minerals, damp leaves, mushrooms etc.

Easy Undemanding (and hopefully inexpensive).

Elegant Stylish, refined, 'classic'.

Esters Scents and smells usually generated by alcohols and acids in wine. A wine may be 'estery' when these characteristics are prominent.

Extract An indication of the 'substance' of a wine, expressed as sugar-free or total extract (which would include some sugars). 18g/L would be low, light; anything much above 23g/L in whites is significant; the corresponding threshold for reds is around 30g/L.

Fat Big, full, ample in the mouth.

Finesse Graceful, polished. Nothing excessive.

Finish The residual sensations — tastes and textures — after swallowing. Should be pleasant (crisp, lively) and enduring, not short, dull or flat. See also Length.

Firm Compact, has good backbone.

Flabby Usually, lacking backbone, especially acid.

Flat Characterless, unexciting, lacks acid. Or bubbly which has lost its fizz.

Fleshy Very positive, meaning a wine is well fleshed out with texture and grape flavours.

Flowery, **floral** Flower-like (ie the smell of rose, honeysuckle, jasmine etc). Distinct from 'fruity' (ie smell/taste of papaya, cantaloupe, grape! etc).

Forward rather than shy; advancing in age too; mature.

Fresh Lively, youthful, invigorating. Closely related to the amount of acid in the wine and absence of oxidative character: a big, intensely sweet dessert without a backbone of acidity will taste flat and sickly; enough acid and the taste is fresh and uncloying.

Fruity See Flowery.

Full High in alcohol and extract.

Gamey Overripe, decadent, not universally unattractive; also meaty, 'wild'.

Gravel/ly With suggestions of mineral, earthy quality; also firm texture.

Green Usually unripe, sour; also herbaceous; sometimes simply youthful.

Grip Structure, firm on palate, in finish. Acid, tannin, alcohol are contributors.

Heady Usually refers to the smell of a wine. High in alcohol; intense, high-toned.

Herbaceous Grassy, hay-like, heathery; can also indicate under-ripeness.

Hollow Lacking substance, flavours.

Honey or **honeyed** Sometimes literally a honey/beeswax taste or flavour; a sign of developing maturity in some varieties or more generally a sign of bottle-age.

Hot Burning sensation of alcohol in finish.

Intensity No flab, plenty of driving flavour; also deep colour.

Lean Thin, mean, lacking charm of ample fruit; also, more positively, compact, sinewy.

Lees/leesy Taste-imparting dead yeast cells (with grape skins and other solid matter) remaining with wine in tank/barrel (or bottle in the case of *méthode champenoise* sparkling wines) after fermentation. The longer the wine is 'on its lees' (*sur lie*) the more richness and flavour it should absorb.

Light/lite Officially wines under 10% alcohol by volume; also light in body (and often short on taste); a health-conscious trend in both reds and whites.

Lively Bouncy, fresh flavours.

Long or **length** Enduring; wine's flavours reverberate on the palate long after swallowing.

Maderised Oxidised and flat; colour is often brownish. Over-mature.

Meaty Sometimes suggesting a general savouriness; but also literally the aroma of meat — raw, smoked etc.

Mousse Fizz in sparkling wines; usually refers also to quality, size and effervescence of the bubbles. See also Bead.

Mouthfeel, **mouthfilling** Texture, feel; racy, crispness (fine with appropriate dishes) or generous, supple, smooth.

Neutral What it says, neither here nor there.

New World Generally implies accessible, bold, often extrovert (in terms of fruit and use of oak). **Old World** embraces terms like subtle, complex, less oaky, more varied and generally more vinous (than fruity). See also Classic.

Oaky Having exaggerated oak aromas/flavours (vanilla, spice, char, woodsmoke etc). Oak balanced by fruit in young wines may lessen with age, but over-oaked young wines (where fruit is not in balance) will become over-oaked old wines.

Palate Combination of flavour, taste and texture of a wine.

Pebbly See Gravelly.

Perfumed or **scented** Strong fragrances (fruity, flowery, animal etc)

Plump Well fleshed in a charming, cherubic way.

Porty Heavy, over-ripe, stewed; a negative in unfortified wine.

Rich Flavourful, intense, generous. Not necessarily sweet.

Robust Strapping, full-bodied (but not aggressive).

Rough Bull-in-a-china-shop wine, or throat sandpapering quality.

Round Well balanced, without gawkiness or jagged edges.

Sharp or **tart** All about acid, usually unbalanced. But occasionally sharpish, fresh wine is right for the occasion.

Short or **quick** Insubstantial wine, leaving little impression.

Simple One-dimensional or no flavour excitement.

Stalky Unripe, bitter, stemmy.

Stewed Over-ripe, cooked, soft, soggy fruit.

Structure Vague word, usually refers to the wine's make up (acid, tannin, alcohol) in relation to its ageing ability; if a wine is deemed to have 'the structure to age' it suggests these principal preservatives are in place.

Stylish Classy, distinguished; also voguish.

Supple Very desirable (not necessarily subtle); yielding, refined texture and flavours. See also Mouthfeel.

Tannic Tannins are prominent in the wine, imparting, positively, a mouth-puckering, grippy, tangy quality; negatively, a harsh, unyielding character.

Tension Racy, nervous fruity-acid play on the palate.

Terpene(s)/terpenoid Strong, floral compounds influencing the aromas of especially riesling, gewürztraminer and the muscats; with bottle-age, terpenes often develop a pungent resinous oiliness.

Texture Tactile 'feel' in the mouth: hard, acidic, coarse and alcoholic; or, smooth, velvety, 'warm'.

Toasty Often used for barrel-fermented or -aged wines showing a pleasant biscuity, charry character.

Vegetal Grassy, leafy, herby — in contrast to fruity, flowery, oaky. Overdone, a no-no.

Yeasty Warm bakery smells, often evident in barrel-fermented whites and *méthode champenoise* sparkling wines, where yeasts stay in contact with the wine after fermentation.

Winemaking Terms

A few brief reference explanations. See also sections Winetasting Terms, SA Wine Styles.

Acid and **acidity** The fresh — or, in excess, sharp or tart — taste of wine. Too little acid and the wine tastes dull and flat. In SA, winemakers are permitted to adjust acidity either by adding acid — at any stage before bottling — or by lowering the acid level with a de-acidifier. See also Volatile acid and Malolactic.

Alcohol Essential component of wine, providing fullness, richness and, at higher levels, sometimes an impression of sweetness. Also a preservative, helping keep wines in good condition. Produced by yeasts fermenting the sugars in the grape. Measured by volume of the total liquid. Most unfortified table wines in SA have between 11% and 14.5% alc by vol; fortifieds range from ±16% to 21%. A variation of up to 1% between the strength stated on the label and the laboratory analysis is permitted by local law. Various techniques (such as reverse osmosis and 'spinning cone', also the addition of water) exist to address the increasingly important issue of high alcohol levels in wine, and some are legal in SA (though not for export to, eg, Europe).

Barrels (**barrel-aged**; **barrel-fermented**) Wines are transferred into barrels to age, pick up oaky flavours etc. When must or fermenting must is put into barrels, the resulting wine is called barrel-fermented. A barrel or cask is generally a 225–500L oak container; *barrique* is a French word for a 225L barrel; a pipe, adapted from the Portuguese *pipa*, usually indicates a vessel of 530–630L; vat is a term generally used for larger (2,000–5,000L) wooden vessels.

Batonnage See Lees.

Biodynamic See Organic.

Blend A wine made from two or more different grape varieties, vintages, vineyards or containers. Some of the world's finest wines are blends.

Bottles While the 750ml (75cl) bottle is now the most widely used size of container for wine, it is by no means the only one. Smaller bottles (375 & 500ml) are popular with restaurants and airlines, and larger sizes are prized by collectors because of their novelty value and/or their tendency to promote slower wine ageing. The following are the larger bottle sizes (note: some no longer in production):

Capacity		Bordeaux	Champagne/Burgundy
litres	*bottles*		
1.5	2	Magnum	Magnum
3	4	Double magnum	Jéroboam
4.5	6	Jéroboam	Rehoboam
6	8	Impériale	Methuselah
9	12	—	Salmanazar
12	16	—	Balthazar
15	20	—	Nebuchadnezzar

Brettanomyces or '**brett**' Naturally occurring yeast, usually associated with red wine and regarded as a spoilage factor, because its growth triggers the formation of volatile acids, phenols and other compounds which, in sufficient concentration, impart a range of unpleasant characters, from barnyard to sweat to cheese. At low concentrations, can enhance complexity and character.

Carbonic maceration or **maceration carbonique** Method of fermenting wine without first crushing the grapes. Whole clusters with stalks etc are put into closed vat; intracellular fermentation occurs within the grape berries, which then burst.

Chaptalisation Originally French term for the addition of sugar to grape must to raise the alcohol of a wine. Selectively legal in northern Europe, where acid adjustments are not allowed as they are in SA. Winemakers in both hemispheres bend the rules.

Charmat Method of making sparkling wine in a sealed tank (*cuvée close*) under pressure. Easier, cheaper than *méthode champenoise*.

Chips See Oak chips.

Cold ferment 'Cold' is a relative term; applied to fermentation of mainly white wines in temperature-controlled tanks, it refers to a temperature around usually 13–16°C. The benefits, especially important in a warm country, include conserving the primary fruit aromas and ensuring fermentation is carried out steadily and thoroughly.

Cold soak or **cold maceration**. Red winemaking method carried out prior to fermentation. Skins and juice are held, usually for a few days, at a sufficiently cool temperature to prevent fermentation. The theory is that this extracts more favourable colour and aromas than after fermentation.

Cold stabilisation Keeping a wine at about –4°C for a week or more to precipitate tartaric acid and 'clean up' the wine, preventing later formation of (harmless) tartrate crystals in bottle. Some winemakers believe this process damages flavour and prefer to avoid it.

Disgorgement (*dégorgement* in French) Important stage in the production of traditionally fermented sparkling where accumulated sediment (or lees), which could cloud the finished wine, is removed from the neck of the bottle.

Dosage The sugar added to sparkling wine after the second fermentation.

Fermentation The conversion of sugar in grapes into alcohol and carbon dioxide, a function of enzymes secreted by yeasts. Wild yeasts occur in vineyards and wineries, but in modern Cape winemaking cultured yeasts are normally added to secure the process. Beyond about 15% of alcohol, yeasts are overwhelmed and fermentation ceases, although it usually is stopped (for instance by cooling, filtration or the addition of alcohol) before this stage. See also Malolactic.

Filtration Removes last impurities including **yeast** cells. Done excessively, can thin a wine. Some traditionalists bottle without cold- or protein-stabilisation or filtration.

Fining and **protein stabilisation** Fining is ridding wine of suspended particles by adding substances that attract and draw the particles from the wine.

Flash-pasteurisation See Kosher.

Free run After grapes have been de-stalked and crushed, juice runs freely.

Garage wine Generic term for wine made in minuscule quantities, sometimes literally in a garage; a grower of such wine is sometimes called a *garagiste*.

Glycerol Minor product of alcoholic fermentation; from the Greek for sweet. Has an apparent sweetening effect on even dry wines and also gives a viscous, mouthfilling character.

Icewine Sweet, concentrated wine from grapes picked and pressed while frozen. Not a recognised category for SA wine production.

Kosher Wine made 'correctly', i.e. under rabbinical supervision, to be suitable for use by religious Jews. Vinification and any initial movement of the wine must be done by an observant Jew. Flash-pasteurisation, increasingly by means of new flavour-preserving processes such as Thermoflash, renders the resulting *meshuval* wine (literally 'boiled' or 'cooked') fit for handling by non-Jews.

Leafroll virus Virus (or complex of viruses), widespread throughout the winegrowing world, which causes the vine to perform below its potential and thereby produce wine which is lower in colour, body and flavour than that derived from virus-free or 'cleaned-up' plants.

Lees Spent yeast cells and other matter which collect at the bottom of any container in winemaking. Yeast autolysis, or decomposition, can impart richness and flavour to a wine, sometimes referred to as leesy. Lees stirring or *batonnage* involves mixing the bed of lees in a barrel or tank through the wine, which is said to be *sur lie*; it is employed primarily on barrel-fermented white wines. The main effects of mixing lees and wine are to prevent off-odours developing from lack of oxygen, to limit the amount of wood tannin and oak character extracted, and to increase flavour.

Malolactic fermentation (malo) Occurs when bacteria convert malic into lactic acids. This reduces the acidity of a wine, a normal and healthy process, especially in reds — provided, of course, it occurs before bottling.

Maturation Ageing properties are closely related to tannin and/or fixed acid content of a wine. A relatively full red wine with tannin has lasting power. With age, it may develop complexity, subtlety and smooth mellowness. Lighter wines with lower tannins are drinkable sooner but probably will not reach the same level of complexity. A number of Cape whites mature well over several years, but most are best drunk in their fruity youth, up to 18 months.

Méthode champenoise Classic method of making champagne by inducing secondary fermentation in the bottle and producing fine bubbles. Due to French restrictions on terminology, Cape sparkling wines made in this way are called méthode cap classique (MCC).

Micro-oxygenation Technique enabling introduction of precise, controlled doses of oxygen to must/wine. Advocates claim softer tannins, more stable colours and other advantages.

Oak chips, either in older barrels or stainless steel tanks, are used increasingly in SA, as are oak **staves**. Still frowned on by some purists, the 'additives' approximate the flavour effects of a new barrel, far more cheaply, more easily handled.

Oak-matured See Barrels.

Organic viticulture/winemaking Increasingly popular alternative to 'conventional' or 'industrialised' winegrowing, emphasising natural and sustainable farming methods and cellar techniques. A variant is biodynamic viticulture, influenced by anthroposophy, focused on improving wine quality through harmony with nature and its rhythms.

Oxidation Change (usually for the worse) due to exposure to air, in whites often producing dark yellow or yellowish colour (called maderisation), altering, 'ageing' the taste. Controlled aeration is used to introduce acceptable and desirable development in wine.

Pasteurisation See Kosher.

pH A chemical notation, used in winemaking and evaluation. The pH of a wine is its effective, active acidity — not in volume but by strength or degree. The reading provides a guide to a wine's keepability. The optimum pH in a wine is somewhere between 3.1 and 3.4 — which significantly improves a wine's protection from bacterial spoilage, so permitting it to mature and develop if properly stored.

Racking Drawing or pumping wine off from one cask or tank to another, to leave behind the deposit or lees.

Reductive Wine in an unevolved, unoxidised state is said to be 'reductive'; usually with a tight, sometimes unyielding character. The absence of air (in a bottled wine) or the presence of substantial sulphur dioxide (anti-oxidant) levels, will inhibit both oxidation and reduction processes, which are linked and complementary.

Reverse osmosis A specialised filtration technique, now permitted in SA for various purposes, including the removal of water from wine. See also Alcohol.

Skin contact After crushing and de-stemming, white grapes may be left for a period with the juice, remaining in contact with skins (before being moved into the press, from which the grape juice is squeezed). Some winemakers believe the colours and flavours in and under the grape skins should be maximised in this way; others believe extended (or any) contact can lead to coarseness, even bitterness.

Spinning cone See Alcohol.

Sulphur dioxide (SO₂) Sterilising agent and preservative, near-ubiquitous in winemaking since antiquity, now strictly controlled. In SA, max total SO₂ level for dry wines is 150–160mg/L; for wines with 5+ g/L sugar it is 200mg/L; and botrytis-style wines 300 mg/L. Any wine with more than 10mg/L total SO₂ must carry the warning 'Contains sulphites' (or 'sulfites') on the label.

Sur lie See Lees.

Tannin Vital preservative in wine, derives primarily from the grape skins. Necessary for a red wine's longevity. A young wine's raw tannin can give it a harshness, but no red wine matures into a great one without tannin, which itself undergoes change, combines with other substances and mellows. Tannin leaves a mouth-puckering dryness about the gums, gives 'grip' to a wine. A wooded wine will usually also contain some wood tannin.

Tartrates Harmless crystals formed by tartaric acid precipitating in non-cold-stabilised wine. Because of lack of public acceptance, usually avoided through cold stabilisation.

Terroir Important, controversial (and in SA overused) French term embracing soil, climate, topography and other elements which constitute the natural environment of a vineyard site and give it a unique character.

Thermovinification/Thermoflash See Kosher.

Unfiltered See Filtration.

Virus or **virused** See Leafroll.

Volatile acid (VA) The part of the acidity which can become volatile. A high reading indicates a wine is prone to spoilage. Recognised at high levels by a sharp, 'hot', vinegary smell. In SA, most wines must by law be below 1.2g/L of VA; in practice, the majority are well below 1g/L.

Whole-bunch pressing or **cluster pressing** Some SA cellars use this age-old process of placing whole bunches directly in the press and gently squeezing. The more usual method is to de-stem and crush the berries before pressing. Whole-bunch pressing is said to yield fresher, cleaner must, and wine lower in polyphenols which, in excess, tend to age wines faster and render them coarser.

Wood-fermented/matured See Barrels.

Yeasts Micro-organisms that secrete enzymes which convert or ferment sugar into alcohol. See fermentation.

Wine Routes, Trusts & Associations

For localised information about regional official wine routes and wineries, contact these organisations:

Breedekloof Wine & Tourism ▪ T +27 (0)23-349-1791 ▪ F +27 (0)23-349-1720 ▪ info@breedekloof.com ▪ www.breedekloof.com

Constantia Valley Wine Route ▪ T +27 (0)83-679-4495 (Carryn Wiltshire) ▪ info@constantiafoodandwine.co.za ▪ www.constantiavalley.com

The Darling Wine & Art Experience ▪ www.darlingtourism.co.za

Durbanville Boutique Wine Association ▪ T +27 (0)83-357-3864 ▪ F +27 (0)21-948-3441 info@durbanvilleboutiquewine.co.za ▪ www.durbanvilleboutiquewine.co.za

Durbanville Wine Valley Association ▪ T +27 (0)83-310-1228 ▪ info@durbanvillewine.co.za ▪ www.durbanvillewine.co.za

Elim Winegrowers ▪ T +27 (0)28-482-1902/+27 (0)82-328-3824 (Conrad Vlok) ▪ conrad@strandveld.co.za

Franschhoek See Vignerons de Franschhoek

Green Mountain Eco Route (Elgin/Bot River) ▪ T +27 (0)21-844-0975 ▪ F +27 (0)21-844-0970 ▪ info@greenmountain.co.za ▪ www.greenmountain. co.za

Helderberg See Stellenbosch

Hermanus Wine Route & Hemel-en-Aarde Winegrowers Association ▪ T +27 (0)83-305-7319 (Frieda Lloyd) ▪ frieda@hermanuswineroute.com ▪ T +27 (0)28-312-3862 (Bevan Newton Johnson) ▪ bevan@newtonjohnson.com ▪ www.hermanuswineroute.com

Klein Karoo Wine Route ▪ T +27(0)44-272-7492 / +27 (0)82-214-5910 ▪ F +27 (0)86-528-4055 (Ellen Marais) ▪ info@kleinkaroowines.co.za ▪ www.kleinkaroowines.co.za

Northern Cape Wine Association See Orange River Wine Route

Olifants River Vodacom Wine Route ▪ See West Coast Wine Route

Orange River Wine Route ▪ T +27 (0)54-337-8800 (Jorine van Niekerk/Elene Swanepoel) ▪ F +27 (0)54-332-4408 ▪ admin@orangeriverwines.com, info@owk.co.za

Paarl Wine Route ▪ T +27 (0)21-863-4886 / +27 (0)82-787-4118 ▪ F +27 (0)21-863-4883 ▪ info@paarlwine.co.za ▪ www.paarlwine.co.za

Robertson Wine Valley ▪ T +27 (0)23-626-3167 / +27 (0)83-701-5404 ▪ F +27 (0)23-626-1054 ▪ manager@robertsonwinevalley.com ▪ www.robertsonwinevalley.com

Stellenbosch American Express Wine Routes ▪ T +27 (0)21-886-4310 ▪ F +27 (0)21-886-4330 ▪ info@wineroute.co.za ▪ www.wineroute.co.za

Santam Swartland Wine & Olive Route ▪ T +27 (0)22-487-1133 ▪ F +27 (0)22-487-2063 swartlandinfo@westc.co.za ▪ www.swartlandwineandolives.co.za

Tulbagh Wine Route ▪ T/F +27 (0)23-230-1348/75 ▪ tulbaghinfo@lando.co.za ▪ www.tulbaghwineroute.com ▪ www.tulbaghtourism.co.za

Vignerons de Franschhoek ▪ T +27 (0)21-876-2861 ▪ F +27 (0)21-876-2768 ▪ marketing@franschhoek.org.za, office@franschhoek.org.za ▪ www.franschhoek.org.za

Walker Bay Wine Wander ▪ T +27 (0)28-316-3988 ▪ F +27 (0)86-509-4931 ▪ wine@hermanus.co.za

Wellington Wine Route ▪ T +27 (0)21-864-2479 ▪ F +27 (0)21-873-4607 ▪ wine@wellington.co.za ▪ www.wellington.co.za

West Coast Wine Route ▪ T +27 (0)82-611-3999 / +27 (0)27-201-3376 / F +27 (0)27 213 4819 ▪ monika@namaquawestcoast.com ▪ www.namaquawestcoast.com

Worcester Wine Route ▪ T +27 (0)23-342-8710 ▪ F +27 (0)86-771-4468 ▪ info@worcesterwineroute.co.za ▪ www.worcesterwineroute.co.za

Winelands Tourism Offices

For additional accommodation options, brochures and local advice, contact the information offices and/or publicity associations of the wine areas you plan to visit.

Breedekloof Wine & Tourism ▪ T +27 (0)23-349-1791 ▪ F +27 (0)23-349-1720 ▪ info@breedekloof.com ▪ www.breedekloof.com

Calitzdorp Tourism ▪ T +27 (0)44-213-3775 ▪ F +27 (0)86-569-1447 ▪ tourism@calitzdorp.org.za ▪ www.calitzdorp.org.za

Cape Town Tourism ▪ Contact Centre: T +27 (0)86-132-2223

Cape Town Tourism (Head-Office) ▪ T +27 (0)21-487-6800 ▪ F +27 (0)21-487-6859 ▪ capetown@capetown.travel

Somerset West ▪ T +27 (0)21-840-1400 ▪ F +27 (0)21-840-1410 ▪ somersetwest@cape-town.travel

Elgin Valley Tourism T +27 (0)21-848-9838 ▪ F +27 (0)86-660-0398 ▪ info@elginvalley.co.za ▪ www.elginvalley.co.za

Franschhoek Wine Valley ▪ T +27 (0)21-876-2861 ▪ F +27 (0)21-876-2768 ▪ info@franschhoek.org.za, office@franschhoek.org.za ▪ www.franschhoek.org.za

Hermanus Tourism Bureau ▪ T +27 (0)28-312-2629 ▪ F +27 (0)28-313-0305 ▪ hermanustourism@hermanus.co.za ▪ www.hermanustourism.info

McGregor Tourism ▪ T +27 (0)23-625-1954 ▪ info@tourismmcgregor.co.za ▪ www.tourismmcgregor.co.za

Northern Cape Tourism ▪ T +27 (0)53-832-2657 ▪ F +27 (0)53-831-2937 ▪ northerncapetourism@telkomsa.net ▪ www.northerncape.org.za

Paarl Tourism Association ▪ T +27 (0)73-708-2835 ▪ F +27 (0)86-590-871 ▪ info@paarlonline.com ▪ www.paarlonline.com

Paarl Tourist Information Centre ▪ T +27 (0)21-872 4842 ▪ F +27 (0)21-872-9376 ▪ paarlinfo@drakenstein.gov.za ▪ www.drakenstein.gov.za

Robertson Tourism Association ▪ T +27 (0)23-626-4437 ▪ F +27 (0)23-626-4290 ▪ info@robert-son.org.za ▪ www.robertsontourism.co.za

Route 62 ▪ T +27 (0)23-616-3563 ▪ F +27 (0)23-616-3422 ▪ info@route62.co.za ▪ www.route62.co.za

Saldanha Bay Tourism Organisation ▪ info@sbto.co.za, marketing@sbto.co.za, dave@sbto.co.za ▪ www.capewestcoastpeninsula.co.za

Saldanha: T +27 (0)22-714-2088 ▪ F +27 (0)22-714-4240 ▪ saldanha@sbto.co.za

Hopefield: T/F +27 (0)22-723-1720 / +27 (0)73-187-6764 ▪ hopefield@sbto.co.za

Langebaan: T +27 (0)22-772-1515 ▪ F +27 (0)22-772-1531 ▪ langebaan@sbto.co.za ▪ www.capewestcoastpeninsula.co.za

Vredenburg: T +27 (0)22-715-1142 ▪ F +27 (0)22-715-1141 ▪ vredenburg@sbto.co.za

Paternoster: T/F +27 (0)22-752-2323 ▪ paternos-ter@sbto.co.za ▪ www.capewestcoastpeninsula.co.za

St Helena Bay: T +27 (0)76-661-2046 ▪ sthelenabay@sbto.co.za

Jacobs Bay: T +27 (0)22-714-2088 ▪ F +27 (0)22-714-4240 ▪ jacobsbaai@sbto.co.za

Stellenbosch 360 ▪ T +27 (0)21-883-3584 ▪ F +27 (0)21-882-9550 ▪ info@stellenbosch360.co.za ▪ www.stellenbosch.travel

Wellington Tourism ▪ T +27 (0)21-873-4604 ▪ F +27 (0)21-873-4607 ▪ info@wellington.co.za ▪ www.wellington.co.za

West Coast Peninsula Tourism Bureau See Saldanha Bay Tourism Organisation

Worcester Tourism Association ▪ +27 (0)23-342-6244 /+27 (0)76-200-8742 ▪ info@worcestertourism.com ▪ www.worcestertourism.com

Specialist Wine Tours

Adamastor & Bacchus Cape Gourmet Wine & Culinary Tours ▪ English, Afrikaans, Dutch, Norwegian, German ▪ www.adamastorbacchus.com ▪ johnford@iafrica.com, jarche@iafrica.com ▪ T +27 (0)21-439-3169 / +27 (0)83-229-1172

African Story Wine Tours ▪ English ▪ info@africanstorytours.com ▪ www.africanstorytours.com ▪ T +27 (0)73-755-0444 / +27 (0)79-694-7915

African Trax Tours ▪ English ▪ africantrax@telkomsa.net ▪ www.africantrax.co.za ▪ T +27 (0)83-692-8873

African Wonder Tours ▪ Afrikaans, English, French, Italian, German ▪ info@africanwonder.co.za ▪ www.africanwonder.co.za ▪ T +27 (0)82-325-1485

Amber Tours ▪ English ▪ lesleyc@wol.co.za ▪ www.ambertours.co.za, www.lesleycox.co.za ▪ T +27 (0)83-448-7016

Bizoe Wine Tours ▪ Afrikaans, English ▪ info@bizoe.co.za ▪ www.bizoe.co.za ▪ T +27 (0)21-843-3307 / +27 (0)83-709-3957 ▪ F +27 (0)86-653-8186

Capefuntours ▪ English ▪ capefuntours@icon.co.za ▪ www.capefuntours.co.za ▪ T +27 (0)21-782-5472 / +27 (0)82-932-9430 ▪ F +27 (0)21-782-5472

Cape Fusion Tours ▪ English ▪ cazcape@mweb.co.za, info@capefusion.co.za ▪ www.capefusiontours.com ▪ T +27 (0)21-461-2437 / +27 (0)83-235-9777 ▪ F +27 (0)86-672-5877

'C' the Cape Tours ▪ English, Afrikaans ▪ cherylscott@ballmail.co.za, cherylscott66@yahoo.com ▪ www.tourguide.co.za/-cheryl ▪ T +27 (0)21-433-2545 / +27 (0)83-698-5483 ▪ F +27 (0)21-433-2545

Double Gold Wineland Tours ▪ English ▪ kimdg@cybersmart.co.za, kimdg@absamail.co.za ▪ T +27 (0)21-785-5094 / +27 (0)82-293-3176

D'Vine Wine & Dine ▪ pauline.nel@dvinewinedine.co.za ▪ www.dvinewineanddine.co.za ▪

+27 (0)73-972-7830 / +27 €(0)21-975-4851 ▪ +27 (0)86-601-1238

Exclusively African Tours ▪ English, Dutch (German, Swedish, French on request) ▪ ian@travelxa.com ▪ www.holidaystosouthafrica.co.uk ▪ T +27 (0)21-5314887 ▪ F +27 (0)86-609-0896

Go! Shuttles & Tours ▪ English, German, Afrikaans, French and Italian ▪ info@goshuttle.co.za, nic@gotours.co.za ▪ www.gotours.co.za ▪ T +27 (0)72-368-3455 ▪ F +27 (0)86-548-2375

Gourmet Travels ▪ English, German ▪ rainer@gourmettravels.co.za ▪ www.gourmettravels.co.za ▪ T +27 (0)82-449-7666 ▪ F +27 (0)86-542-0542

Gourmet Wine Tours ▪ English ▪ sflesch@iafrica.com ▪ www.gourmetwinetours.co.za ▪ T +27 (0)21-705-4317 / +27 (0)83-229-3581 ▪ F +27 (0)21-706-0766

Greatest Africa (Cape wine tours) ▪ richard@greatestafrica.co.za ▪ www.greatestafrica.co.za ▪ T +27 (0)21-855-5244 / +27 (0)83-650-5661

Happy Holiday Wine Tours ▪ English, Afrikaans & German on request ▪ john@happyholiday.co.za ▪ www.happyholiday.co.za ▪ T +27 (0)84-705-1383

Janet Malherbe ▪ English, German, French & Flemish ▪ janetm@mweb.co.za ▪ www.janetmalherbe.webs.com ▪ T +27 (0)82-553-8928 ▪ T/F +27 (0)21-862-1484

Judy Krohn Personal Itineraries & International Wine Experience ▪ English, German ▪ judithk@lantic.net ▪ www.judykrohn.co.za ▪ T +27 (0)84-500-1941 / +27 (0)21-851-7009

Klaus Schindler See Schindler's Africa

Luhambo Tours ▪ English, Afrikaans, German ▪ info@luhambotours.com ▪ www.luhambotours.com ▪ T +27 (0)21-551-0467 / +27 (0)82-306-4141

Ocean & Vine Adventures & Tours ▪ English, translator on request ▪ wayne@wine.co.za, oceanv@netactive.co.za ▪ www.prowinetours.co.za ▪ T +27 (0)21-559-6906 / +27 (0)82-900-6999 ▪ F +27 (0)21-559-6906

Percy Tours ▪ English, Afrikaans & some French & German ▪ travel@percytours.com ▪ www.percytours.com ▪ T +27 (0)72-062-8500 / +27 (0)28-316-4871

Redwood Tours ▪ English, Afrikaans ▪ info@redwoodtours.co.za ▪ www.redwoodtours.co.za ▪ T +27 (0)21-886-8138 / +27 (0)82-443-6480

Schindler's Africa ▪ German, English ▪ schindler@kapstadt.de ▪ www.kapstadt.de/schindlers-africa ▪ T +27 (0)83-270-3449

Southern Destinations ▪ English ▪ info@southerndestinations.com, vanessa@southerndestinations.com ▪ www.southerndestinations.com ▪ T +27 (0)21-671-3090 ▪ F +27 (0)21-674-7481

Taste the Cape Travel & Tours ▪ English, other languages upon request ▪ info@tastethecape.co.za ▪ www.tastethecape.co.za ▪ T +27 (0)21-715-3559 / +27 (0)79-812-0220

Tri Active Events Management (Green Mountain Eco Route) ▪ English, Afrikaans ▪ info@triactive.co.za ▪ www.triactive.co.za ▪ T +27 (0)21-844-0975 / +27 (0)83-456-2181 ▪ F +27 (0)21-844-0970

Tsiba Tsiba Wine Tours & Travel ▪ Dutch, English, French, German, Spanish ▪ info@tsibatsiba.co.za ▪ www.tsibatsiba.co.za ▪ T +27 (0)82-956-8104

Vineyard Ventures English, Afrikaans, German; other languages on request ▪ vinven@iafrica.com ▪ www.vineyardventures.co.za ▪ T +27 (0)21-434-8888 / +27 (0)82-920-2825 ▪ F +27 (0)86-579-9430

Vintage Cape Tours ▪ English, Afrikaans, Dutch, French, German, Italian, Spanish ▪ info@vintagecape.co.za, jade@vintagecape.co.za ▪ www.vintagecape.co.za ▪ T +27 (0) 84-513-3066 ▪ +27(0)21-913-2358 ▪ F +27 (0)86-690-8572

Walker Bay Wine Wander ▪ English, Afrikaans, French, German ▪ wine@hermanus.co.za, travel@percytours.com ▪ T +27 (0)28-316-3988 / +27 (0)72-062-8500 ▪ F +27 (0)86-509-4931

Wanderer Wines ▪ English, German, French, Italian ▪ wines@wanderer.co.za ▪ www.wanderer.co.za ▪ T +27 (0)82-878-1176 ▪ F +27 (0)86-648-0352

Wellington Wine Walk ▪ English, Afrikaans ▪ info@winewalk.co.za ▪ www.winewalk.co.za ▪ T +27 (0)83-313-8383

Wine Desk ▪ Scheduled (small group) and private day tours led by specialist wine guides. Available in most languages for private tours ▪ info@winedesk.co.za, ligia@winedesk.co.za ▪ www.winedesk.co.za ▪ T +27 (0)21-424-6364 / +27 (0)82-822-6127 ▪ F +27 (0)86-607 2980

Wine Escapes ▪ info@wineescapes.co.za ▪ www.wineescapes.co.za ▪ T +27 (0)83-453-2670

WineFairy ▪ English ▪ info@winefairy.co.za, katie@winefairy.co.za ▪ www.winefairy.co.za ▪ T +27 (0)79-892-2859

Winemaker-led Tasting Tours ▪ English; translators on request with sufficient notice ▪ vitis@mweb.co.za ▪ www.winetastingtours.co.za ▪ T +27 (0)82-322-3733

Restaurants in the Winelands and Cape Town

Below are some dining out options in Cape Town and the winelands. These are paid entries. The venues supplied information on their cuisine, menus and attractions, which was then edited for consistency of style. For more restaurants among the vines, consult the A–Z section of the guide for wineries which offer light lunches, picnics etc. Look for the 🍷 symbol beside the individual entries. Unless stated to the contrary, all allow you to bring your own (BYO) wine — the corkage fee is indicated at the start of each entry. Should you wish to know about wheelchair access, please discuss with the relevant restaurant.

Index of restaurants
Listed alphabetically, with region.

Bot River

Gabriëlskloof Restaurant & Deli Gabriëlskloof, N2, Swart River Road, Bot River ▪ Overberg-inspired country fare ▪ Deli stocked with homemade treats ▪ Open Wed–Mon 9–5 ▪ Closed Tue, annual holiday from mid-May to first week of June & Dec 24/25 ▪ Booking advised ▪ Children welcome ▪ Major credit cards accepted ▪ No BYO ▪ Owners Frans & Mariaan Groenewald ▪ Executive chef Frans Groenewald ▪ Ideal venue for special occasions/weddings ▪ restaurant@gabrielskloof.co.za ▪ www.gabrielskloof.co.za ▪ S 34° 14' 19.88" E 019° 15' 9.69" ▪ **T +27 (0)28-284-9865** ▪ F +27 (0)86-504-0310

The only way to enjoy the no-fuss comfort food and appetising wine and food-pairing platters prepared by the hands-on owners of this friendly farm restaurant is to take in the scenery and slow down. Passionate about freshness, they source most of their produce locally, with menus changing according to season and availability. A perfect place for a lazy lunch on the stoep, or round a cosy fireplace in winter. (See also A–Z section.)

Bredasdorp

The Fig Tree Restaurant De Hoop Nature Reserve, Bredasdorp ▪ World Heritage site ▪ Open daily 8am–10pm: breakfast, lunch, dinner, snacks, teas, coffees and cakes ▪ Licenced, no BYO ▪ Owners Stephens, Trieloff & Zeeman families ▪ Executive chef Marcia Tyobeka ▪ manager@dehoopcollection.co.za ▪ www.dehoopcollection.co.za ▪ S 34° 27' 17.96" E 020° 23' 57.74" ▪ **T +27 (0)28-542-1253** ▪ F +27 (0)28-542-1679

Visit this unique eco-tourism destination and enjoy culinary creations inspired by the natural surroundings, and lovingly crafted into a seasonal menu by Marcia Tyobeka. Relax on a shaded terrace while bontebok and eland graze nearby, or take a picnic down to the pristine beach with its rugged coastline and white dunes — a prime whale-watching site. Day visitors welcome. (See also Accommodation section for De Hoop Collection.)

Camps Bay

Azure Restaurant The Twelve Apostles Hotel and Spa, Victoria Road, Camps Bay, Cape Town ▪ Member of Leading Hotels of the World ▪ SA influenced, modern French cuisine ▪ Open daily for breakfast 7–10.30, lunch 12.30–3.30 & dinner 6–10.30 ▪ Booking advised ▪ Children welcome ▪ Major credit cards accepted ▪ No BYO ▪ Owners Red Carnation Hotel Collection ▪ Executive chef Christo Pretorius ▪ restaurants@12apostles.co.za ▪ www.12apostleshotel.com ▪ S 33° 8' 59.37" E 018° 21' 31.43" ▪ **T +27 (0)21-437-9029** ▪ F +27 (0)21-437-9055

Nautical-themed cliffside restaurant that has it all: mesmerising ocean views; cuisine that focuses

attention on the plate. Sustainable fish, organic herbs from the garden. Enticing creations from exec chef Christo Pretorius; inviting options from internationally honoured owner Bea Tollman's cookbook. Leisurely English breakfasts; à la carte lunches or dinners; with weekend buffet lunches on the Atlantic-facing terrace — the perfect spot for spectacular sunsets and cocktails. (See also Accommodation section.)

Cape Town

Aubergine Restaurant 39 Barnet Street, Gardens, Cape Town ▪ Classical cuisine with innovative twists & Asian influence ▪ Outdoor terrace ▪ Lunch Wed–Fri 12–2 (Sep–Apr), dinner Mon–Sat 6–10 ▪ Closed Sun ▪ Booking advised ▪ Children 5+ welcome ▪ Major credit cards accepted ▪ No BYO ▪ Owner/chef Harald Bresselschmidt ▪ info@aubergine.co.za ▪ www.aubergine.co.za ▪ S 33° 55' 55.20" E 018° 24' 57.60" ▪ **T +27 (0)21-465-0000** ▪ F +27 (0)86-671-0835

Warmly sophisticated restaurant revolving round wine-pairing. A 10 000-bottle cellar (selected for food compatibility) allows chef/patron Harald Bresselschmidt's keen palate and culinary skills full scope. Whether fish, seafood, prime aged local meat or tasty vegetarian options, dishes accent flavour, aroma and texture, with degustation menus offering flavour-teasers like seared scallops topped with lardo, and souffléd berry and vanilla pancake enhanced by almond sabayon and champagne.

Auslese 115 Hope Street, Gardens, Cape Town ▪ Wines paired with tapas-sized dishes in classic yet innovative style ▪ Booking essential, open for pre-booked functions only ▪ Children welcome ▪ Major credit cards accepted ▪ BYO by arrangement ▪ Owner/chef Harald Bresselschmidt ▪ info@auslese.co.za ▪ www.auslese.co.za ▪ S 33° 55' 55.20" E 018° 25' 4.80" ▪ **T +27 (0)21-461-9727** ▪ F +27 (0)86-671-0835

Wanting to match gems from your wine collection, but can't cook? Organising anything from corporate events to a private birthday party or wine launch? Aubergine's elegant venue in a refurbished historic house close to the restaurant, is custom-designed for functions. Owner Harald Bresselschmidt will tailor the occasion for you, creating delectable tapas-style dishes to complement wines, either your own or from his 10 000-bottle cellar.

Azure Restaurant see under Camps Bay

Balducci's Ristorante and Royal Sushi Bar Shop 6162, Lower level, V&A Waterfront, Cape Town ▪ Italian, Sushi, Trendy ▪ Open daily 12 noon to late ▪ Booking advised ▪ Children welcome ▪ Major credit cards accepted ▪ No BYO ▪ Owners Ian Halfon & Doron Duveen ▪ info@slickrestaurants.com ▪ www.balduccis.co.za ▪ S 33° 54' 14" E 018° 25' 16" ▪

T +27 (0)21-421-6002/3 ▪ F +27 (0)21-421-6010

Popular ristorante offering generous helpings of 'great value home-cooked food', attentive service and view of the Waterfront buzz. Specialities include wood-fired gourmet pizzas, butter chicken pasta, veal Milanese, kingklip pescato and grainfed beef from sister restaurant Belthazar; end with signature Lindt white chocolate cheesecake. The adjacent Royal Sushi Bar menu has an Asian section featuring favourites like Tom Yum soup and salmon with citrus yuzo sauce. *Wine Spectator* Award of Excellence 2013; TripAdvisor Award of Excellence 2013.

Bascule Whisky, Wine and Cocktail Bar Cape Grace, West Quay Road, V&A Waterfront, Cape Town ▪ Bistro/Tapas ▪ Open daily 10am–close ▪ Major credit cards accepted ▪ Corkage R80 wine/R250 Champagne ▪ Owner Cape Grace ▪ Executive chef Malika van Reenen ▪ bascule@capegrace.com ▪ www.capegrace.com ▪ S 33° 54' 29" E 018° 25' 12" ▪ **T +27 (0)21-410-7082** ▪ F +27 (0)21-419-7622

Newly refurbished, this popular meeting place for whisky connoisseurs and Cape Town's see-and-be-seen set stocks a global collection of over 500 whiskies and impressive selection of fine Cape wines. The new look combines contemporary chic with comfort; a tapas menu, served in the bar area or on the sun-drenched deck tempts appetites, and the stylish setting alongside the V&A yacht basin encourages lingering over sundowners. (See also Accommodation section.)

Belthazar Restaurant and Wine Bar Shop 153, Lower level, V&A Waterfront, Cape Town ▪ Steak house, seafood restaurant, wine bar ▪ Open daily 12 noon to late ▪ Booking advised ▪ Children welcome — no prams ▪ Major credit cards accepted ▪ No BYO ▪ Owners Ian Halfon & Doron Duveen ▪ info@slickrestaurants.com ▪ www.belthazar.co.za ▪ S 33° 54' 14" E 018° 25' 16" ▪ **T +27 (0)21-421-3753/6**

Indulge your palate at this multiple award-winning restaurant and world's biggest wine-by-the-glass bar, where sommeliers serve over 200 of the Cape's finest wines by the glass and offer knowledgeable advice on a spoilt-for-choice 600-label winelist. Pair sought-after vintages with specialities ranging from prime cuts of aged and butter-tender export quality grain-fed 28 day matured beef to game and the freshest South African and Mozambican shellfish. *Wine Spectator* Award 2013; TripAdvisor Award of Excellence 2013.

Bistro Sixteen82 see under Constantia

Buitenverwachting Restaurant, Courtyard & Coffee Bloc see under Constantia

Burrata Restaurant The Old Biscuit Mill, 373–375 Albert Road, Woodstock, Cape Town ▪ Contemporary Italian ▪ Mon (1 Oct–30 Apr only) 6pm–10pm, Tue–Fri 12pm–10pm, Sat 10am–3pm & 6pm–10pm ▪ Closed Sun, Easter & Dec 25 ▪ Booking advised ▪ Children welcome ▪ Major credit cards accepted ▪ Corkage R65 (1 bottle per table) ▪ Owners Neil Grant & Barry Engelbrecht ▪ Head chef Annemarie Steenkamp ▪ info@burrata.co.za ▪ www.burrata.co.za ▪ S 33° 55' 38.83" E 018° 27' 25.78" ▪ **T +27 (0)21-447-6505** ▪ F +27 (0)86-528-6209

Head Chef Annemarie Steenkamp (ex-Le Quartier Français) interprets seasonal ingredients, using Italian techniques to create dishes that speak of freshness and integrity. Sample the difference an imported wood-fire oven makes in producing Neapolitan pizzas that rely on the quality (not quantity) of toppings, and let joint-owner Neil Grant (Chairman of the South African Sommeliers Association) encourage you to join him in exploring the magic of food and wine via the ever-changing winelist. Best emerging Italian restaurant Africa and the Middle East 2012 — voted by World's 50 Best restaurant academy.

Den Anker Restaurant Pierhead, V&A Waterfront, Cape Town ▪ French/Belgian cuisine ▪ Open daily 11am–10.30pm (kitchen); 11am–12pm (bar) ▪ Booking advised ▪ Children welcome ▪ Visa & MasterCard accepted ▪ No BYO ▪ Owner E de Visscher ▪ denanker@mweb.co.za ▪ www.denanker.co.za ▪ **T +27 (0)21-419-0249** ▪ F +27 (0)21-419-0251

Buzzing quayside venue that opened with the waterfront and grew with it. Latest update highlights Belgian beers, including exclusive Belgian-brewed Den Anker, with tastings and menu pairing as new drawcards (there's also a well-chosen winelist). Watch basking seals from indoors or terrace tables, where a tapas menu is a must. Evergreen best-seller is moule & frites but don't ignore seafood platters, steaks and SA specialities.

Karibu Restaurant Shop 156, The Wharf Centre, V&A Waterfront, Cape Town ▪ South African fine dining ▪ Open daily 11am–11pm ▪ Booking advised ▪ Children welcome ▪ Major credit cards accepted ▪ No BYO ▪ Owners Olivier family ▪ Executive chef Jamie Rowntree ▪ kariburestaurant@mweb.co.za ▪ www.kariburestaurant.co.za ▪ **T +27 (0)21-421-7005/6** ▪ F +27 (0)21-421-7012

Welcome to the gateway of Africa, set between the picturesque view of Table Mountain and the tranquil blue waters of the Atlantic Ocean. A traditional South African menu with Cape Malay influences, including a variety of local seafoods, steaks, venison (try the giant venison skewer), ostrich fillet, bobotie, potjiekos, and delicious vegetarian dishes, accompanied by an award-winning wine list,

featuring the best South African wines. Diners Club Wine List Diamond Award 2009-'13, *Wine Spectator* Award 2012 -'13, Top 100 Wine List Good Value Award 2012 -'13, Top 100 Wine List Outstanding Award 2012.

Savoy Cabbage Restaurant & Champagne Bar
101 Hout Street, Cape Town ▪ Contemporary cuisine ▪ Lunch Mon–Fri 12–2.30, dinner Mon–Sat 7–10.30 ▪ Closed Sun ▪ Booking essential ▪ Major credit cards accepted ▪ Air-conditioned ▪ Corkage R45 ▪ Owner Caroline Bagley ▪ savoycab@iafrica.com ▪ www.savoycabbage.co.za ▪ S 33° 55' 12.31" E 18° 25' 05.45" ▪ **T +27 (0)21-424-2626** ▪ F +27 (0)21-424-3366

Now 15 years young and as popular as ever, this city-centre venue boasts a string of accolades and plaudits from international critics. Expect exposed brick and high ceilings; evergreen favourites as menu fixtures; and daily-changing taste treats like 'Three little pigs' with pan-fried loin, smoked fillet and sticky glazed belly; or house-smoked Norwegian salmon on buckwheat crêpe, with grapefruit jelly and Keta caviar. Intelligent boutique winelist.

Signal Restaurant Cape Grace, West Quay Road, V&A Waterfront, Cape Town ▪ Cape cosmopolitan cuisine ▪ Open daily for breakfast 6–11, lunch 12–3 & dinner 6.30–10 ▪ Booking advised for breakfast & dinner ▪ Children welcome ▪ Major credit cards accepted ▪ Corkage R80 wine & sparkling/R250 Champagne ▪ Owner Cape Grace ▪ Executive chef Malika van Reenen ▪ signal@capegrace.com ▪ www.capegrace.com ▪ S 33° 54' 29" E 018° 25' 12" ▪ **T +27 (0)21-410-7080** ▪ F +27 (0)21-419-7622

Explore Cape Town's tastes and flavours in masterly mixes of herbs, spices and sustainable local ingredients under a mirrored, chandelier-hung ceiling. The à la carte carries combos like butter-tender Chalmar beef fillet with slow-roasted short-rib and goats cheese arancine; and seared scallops with confit duck and toasted fennel velouté. Or opt for tasting menus (meat-orientated and vegetarian) offering wine-pairing from an excellent, terroir-orientated wine list. Voted within 101 Best Hotel Restaurants Around the World, The Daily Meal 2012; Outstanding Award In The Top 100 SA Wine List Awards 2012; Winner of the Master of the Trade Routes Culinary Challenge 2012. (See also Accommodation section.)

Societi Bistro 50 Orange Street, Gardens, Cape Town ▪ French & Italian inspired, bistro ▪ Mon–Sat & pub hols 12–11 ▪ Closed Sun ▪ Booking advised ▪ Children welcome ▪ Major credit cards accepted ▪ Corkage R30 ▪ Owners Peter Weetman & Tammy Botbyl ▪ Executive chef Stéfan Marais ▪ info@societi.co.za ▪ www.societi.co.za ▪ S 33° 55' 44.70" E 018° 24'

47.21" ▪ **T +27 (0)21-424-2100** ▪ F +27 (0)21-424-1140

Societi Bistro is a neighbourhood 'local'. More than cuisine, it's a way of life: savouring an unhurried meal in the company of family and friends. To hospitable owners Tammy and Peter, the bistro is an extension of their home — 'and a sanctuary for Capetonians and visitors looking for a home from home'. Flavour-packed specialities change frequently, but perennial best-sellers are fillet au poivre and dreamy cheesecake. Alto Top 10 Places to Eat in Cape Town; SASSI Seafood Circle Trailblazer.

Sotano by Caveau 121 Beach Road, Mouille Point, Cape Town ▪ Mediterranean, classic tapas ▪ Open daily 7am–10.30pm ▪ Booking advised ▪ Children welcome ▪ Major credit cards accepted ▪ No BYO ▪ Owners Brendon Crew, Marc Langlois & Jean Muller ▪ Executive chef Russell Jalil ▪ info@sotano.co.za ▪ www.sotano.co.za ▪ S 33° 54' 7.49" E 018° 23' 58.37" ▪ **T +27 (0)21-433-1757**

Mediterranean-inspired food stars at this vibey seaside eatery. Sip bubbly watching the sunset from the outside deck and nibble an array of tapas like lamb koftas, halloumi and patatas bravas. Hearty mains feature signature paella; tempting lighter options include salads and flat breads with creative toppings. Try spicy Lebanese shakshouka for something different, and don't miss yummy eggs Benedict at brunch. The winelist's well-curated.

The Square Restaurant Vineyard Hotel & Spa, Colinton Road, Newlands, Cape Town ▪ Eclectic contemporary cuisine ▪ Sushi prepared by skilled Sushi chefs ▪ Breakfast Mon–Sat 6.30-10.30, Sun/pub hols 7.30–11; lunch 12–2.30 & dinner 6.30–10 daily ▪ Booking advised ▪ Children welcome ▪ Major credit cards accepted ▪ Corkage R60 still wine, R75 sparkling wine ▪ eat@vineyard.co.za ▪ www.vineyard.co.za ▪ S 33° 58' 44.68" E 18° 27' 30.71" ▪ **T +27 (0)21-657-4500** ▪ F +27 (0)21-657-4501

Their varied, eclectic cuisine is framed by the tranquil ambience of this glass-roofed restaurant and sushi bar, softened by trees and soothing water fountain in the heart of the Vineyard Hotel. Sushi is offered at lunch and dinner, while both classic and creative dishes feature on à la carte menus, matched by a multi award-winning winelist presenting major estates as well as 'off-the-beaten-track' choices. Diners Club Winelist Diamond Award 2009 -'13. (See also Accommodation section.)

Constantia

Bistro Sixteen82 Steenberg Vineyards, Steenberg Road, Tokai ▪ Contemporary bistro ▪ Open daily for breakfast 9–11.30, lunch 12–4 & tapas 4.30–8.30 ▪ Closed July ▪ Booking advised ▪ Children welcome ▪

Major credit cards accepted ▪ Corkage R50 ▪ Owner Graham Beck Enterprises ▪ Executive chef Brad Ball ▪ reservations@bistro1682.co.za ▪ www.steenberg-vineyards.co.za ▪ S 34° 4' 17.0" E 018° 25' 31.1" ▪ **T +27 (0)21-713-2211** ▪ F +27 (0)21-713-2201

Executive chef Brad Ball serves flavour-packed contemporary bistro fare from an ever-changing blackboard menu for lunch, while tempting tapas allows you to enjoy small plates from around the world. Pair dishes with award-winning wines in a sophisticated setting with tasting bar and lounge, or on patios beside reflecting pools and landscaped fynbos gardens. Do try the beef tataki with green ginger, coriander, chilli and lime. American Express Platinum Fine dining Awards: 2011 & '12; *Eat Out* Best Bistro's SA: 2011 & '12; *Wine Access* magazine: 20 of the World's Best Winery Restaurants. (See also A–Z section.)

Buitenverwachting Restaurant, Courtyard & Coffee Bloc Klein Constantia Road, Constantia, Cape Town ▪ Global cuisine ▪ Breakfast daily (mid Aug–end Jun); lunch Tue–Sat (mid Aug–end Jun)/Mon–Sat (Nov–mid Apr); dinner Thu–Sat (mid Aug–mid Sep)/Tue–Sat (mid Sep–end Oct)/Mon–Sat (Nov–mid Apr)/Thu–Sat (mid Apr–end Jun); open most public holidays, phone ahead ▪ Closed Sun, annual closure July-mid Aug ▪ Booking advised ▪ Children welcome ▪ Major credit cards accepted ▪ Corkage R55 ▪ Owners Mueller family ▪ MD Lars Maack ▪ Executive chef Edgar Osojnik ▪ restaurant@buitenverwachting.com ▪ www.buitenverwachting.com ▪ S 34° 2' 30.4" E 018° 25' 1.5" ▪ **T +27 (0)21-794-3522** ▪ F +27 (0)21-794-1351

Restaurant, courtyard and coffee bloc are seamless blends of relaxing bistro, casual and a more austere fine-dining experience. Sliding glass windows to the newly refurbished Glass Terrace open to a jaw-dropping view of vineyards mountain-climbing, while tantalising menus match this spectacular backdrop. Ideal for a light or full lunch or dinner — don't miss innovative mielie, spinach and wild African garlic soup with organic lamb tapas. American Express Platinum Fine Dining Restaurant 2013; TripAdvisor Certificate of Excellence 2010 -'13; South African Tourism Best Wine Farm Fine dining Restaurant 2012; 15 Year Achievement Award, American Express 2012. (See also A–Z section.)

Constantia Uitsig Restaurant Constantia Uitsig, Spaanschemat River Road, Constantia, Cape Town ▪ Italian & Mediterranean with a hint of the East ▪ Open daily for lunch 12–2.15, dinner 7–9.15 ▪ Closed month of July, Dec 25 eve & Jan 1 lunch ▪ Booking advised ▪ Children welcome ▪ Major credit cards accepted ▪ BYO restricted to one bottle/table ▪ Corkage R60/wine, R100/Champagne ▪ Owner Constantia Uitsig Holdings (Pty) Ltd ▪ Executive chef Clayton Bell

▪ restaurant@uitsig.co.za ▪ www.constantia-uitsig.com ▪ S 34° 2' 51.9" E 018° 25' 27.5" ▪ **T +27 (0)21-794-4480** ▪ F +27 (0)21-794-3105

Consistency coupled with a relaxed ambience has ensured this eatery's popularity for 20 years. Well-seasoned, flavourful food, enjoyed against a mountain backdrop in the heart of the Constantia Valley, makes regulars of locals and visitors alike. Best-selling dishes, influenced by Italy and the Med with hints of the East, include sweetbreads, beef sirloin with mushroom and truffle cream sauce, and Constantia Uitsig fruit Pavlova. TripAdvisor top 10 restaurants 2012; 2 stars *Rossouw's Restaurants* 2012. (See also Accommodation & A–Z sections.)

Jonkershuis Constantia Restaurant Groot Constantia Wine Estate, Groot Constantia Road, Constantia ▪ Bistro/Cape Malay ▪ Mon–Sat & pub hols 9am–9pm, Sun 9am–4pm ▪ Booking advised — please call to check winter trade hours (May–Aug) ▪ Children welcome ▪ Function room with historic charm ▪ Major credit cards accepted ▪ Corkage R50 ▪ Owners Chris Coetzee, Peter Weetman, Tammy Botbyl & Laurence Burgess ▪ Executive chef Laurence Burgess ▪ info@jonkershuisconstantia.co.za ▪ www.jonkershuisconstantia.co.za ▪ S 34° 01' 37.03" E 018° 25' 28.84" ▪ **T +27 (0)21-794-6255** ▪ F +27 (0)86-532-6961

Capture the flavours of the Cape in the historic core of Groot Constantia wine estate. Dine alfresco under ancient oaks overlooking the Constantia valley and False Bay; in the courtyard under vines; or choose the welcoming interior, where a double-sided fireplace adds warmth to an ambience of history and charm. The delicately spiced Cape Malay dishes will entice you — and don't miss the baked cheesecake. Alto Top 10 Places to Eat in Cape Town; SASSI Seafood Circle Trailblazer. (See also A–Z section.)

La Colombe Restaurant Constantia Uitsig, Spaanschemat River Road, Constantia, Cape Town ▪ French cuisine influenced with Asian fusion ▪ Open daily for lunch 12.30–2.30, dinner 7–9.30 ▪ Closed Sun eve (winter); Dec 31 dinner & Jan 1 ▪ Booking advised ▪ Children welcome at lunch ▪ Major credit cards accepted ▪ BYO restricted to one bottle per table of four guests ▪ Corkage R45/wine, R70/Champagne ▪ Owner Constantia Uitsig Holdings (Pty) Ltd ▪ Head chef Scot Kirton ▪ lacolombe@uitsig.co.za ▪ www.constantia-uitsig.com ▪ S 34° 2' 51.9" E 018° 25' 27.5" ▪ **T +27 (0)21-794-2390**

Subtle palate-pleasing flavours are the enticing hallmarks of head chef Scot Kirton and his talented kitchen team. Perfectly-presented dishes retain their classic base, with creative play enhancing seasonal ingredients. New is a taste-tantalising culinary journey through the Western Cape (with map) to reduce the restaurant's carbon footprint by supplier

partnerships closer to home. Do choose the inspired wine-pairing from vibrant front-of-house manager, French Jennifer Whittle. 3 stars in *Rossouw's Restaurants* 2013; 10th in *Eat Out*/DStv Food Network Restaurant Awards 2012; 7th in *Eat Out* Awards 2013. (See also Accommodation & A–Z sections.)

River Café Constantia Uitsig, Spaanschemat River Road, Constantia, Cape Town ▪ Rustic café-style dining ▪ Open daily for breakfast 8.30–11.30, lunch 12.30–4.30 ▪ Booking advised ▪ Children welcome ▪ Major credit cards accepted ▪ Corkage R45/wine, R70/sparkling ▪ Restaurant manager Ruby Wagner ▪ Executive chef Craig Andersson ▪ rivercafe@ uitsig.co.za ▪ www.constantia-uitsig.com ▪ S 34° 2' 51.9" E 018° 25' 27.5" ▪ **T +27 (0)21-794-3010** ▪ F +27 (0)86-504-0108

Country comfort in the heart of Constantia. Relax in the child-friendly bright and cosy rooms, or outside under the pergola in the courtyard on a summer's afternoon. A popular spot for brunch, scrumptious breakfasts (eggs Benedict a must) and delicious classic-style lunches from simple, fresh, and light seasonal ingredients. The rustic café-style venue is also ideal for birthday parties, special functions or business conferences. (See also Accommodation & A–Z sections.)

Volare Peddlars on the Bend, Spaanschemat River Road, Constantia ▪ Italian cuisine ▪ Open daily 12 noon to 11pm ▪ Closed Dec 24 eve & Dec 25 ▪ Booking advised ▪ Children welcome ▪ Major credit cards accepted ▪ Corkage R30 ▪ Owners Mike van der Spuy & Peter Fleck ▪ Executive chef Carl Penn ▪ info@ peddlars.co.za ▪ www.peddlars.co.za ▪ **T +27 (0)21-794-7747** ▪ F +27 (0)21-794-2730

Peddlars' thriving bambino, Volare, (to soar or fly), now occupies the renovated restaurant with walk-in wine cellar. Experienced exec chef Carl Penn, ex 95 Keerom and Il Leone Mastrantonio, produces mouth-watering Italian cuisine: try T-bone steak sliced off the bone, with garlic and rosemary, or pan-seared veal, white wine and mixed mushroom cream. You'll find Peddlars' favourites in the garden area or 'Bicycle Shop' bar. Diners Club Platinum Wine List Award 2012.

Durbanville

Cassia Restaurant, Bar & Function Venue Nitida Wine Estate, Tygerberg Valley Road (M13), Durbanville ▪ Trendy/Continental ▪ Mon–Sat 9–9.30, Sun 9–3 ▪ Closed Sun eve ▪ Booking advised ▪ Children welcome ▪ Major credit cards accepted ▪ Corkage R40 ▪ Owners Warren Swaffield & Bernhard Veller ▪ info@cassiarestaurant.co.za ▪ www.cassiarestaurant.co.za ▪ **T +27 (0)21-976-0640/+27 (0)21-975-3825** ▪ F +27 (0)21-976-0645

Ideal for visitors wanting a true taste of the winelands, this welcoming wine estate eatery, only 20 minutes from central Cape Town, is a firm favourite with locals. Portions are generous, views panoramic, décor stylish, and a sunny deck beckons. Best-selling speciality is Durbanville Wine Valley's regional dish — lamb sosaties with cumin pumpkin stampkoring and pumpkin pickle — which pairs happily with highly-rated Nitida wine. (See also A–Z section.)

De Grendel Restaurant De Grendel Wines, 112 Plattekloof Road, Panorama ▪ Modern South African cuisine ▪ Lunch Tue–Sun 12–2.30, dinner Tue–Sat 7–9.30, Sun & pub hols lunch only ▪ Closed Mon ▪ Booking advised ▪ Children welcome at lunch ▪ Major credit cards accepted ▪ No BYO — De Grendel wines available at cellar door prices ▪ Owner Sir David Graaff ▪ Executive chef Ian Bergh ▪ restaurant@degrendel.co.za ▪ www.degrendel.co.za ▪ S 33° 51' 2.5" E 018° 34' 18.4" ▪ **T +27 (0)21-558-7035** ▪ F +27 (0)21-558-7083

From farm to fork and vineyard to glass against the spectacular backdrop of Table Mountain and Table Bay. Rather than flash-in-the-pan trends on this historic farm, today's 'hunter gatherer' chef Ian Bergh brings a deliciously inventive edge to dishes. Constantly changing menus revolve round fresh farm produce: pasture-fed organic meats, free-range chicken, guinea fowl, just-picked greens, yoghurt and honey. All enhanced by award-winning De Grendel wines. (See also A–Z section.)

Diemersdal farm eatery Diemersdal Wine Estate, M58 (Koeberg Road), Durbanville ▪ Farm style tapas, plat du jour ▪ Lunch daily 12–3, dinner Thu–Sat 6–10 (Oct–Apr)/Fri 5–9 (May–Sep) ▪ Booking advised for Sundays & large groups ▪ Children welcome ▪ Visa & MasterCard accepted ▪ Corkage R30 ▪ Executive chef Nic van Wyk ▪ restaurant@diemersdal.co.za ▪ www.diemersdal.co.za ▪ S 33° 48' 04.35" E 018° 38' 24.69" ▪ **T +27 (0)21-976-1810** ▪ F +27 (0)86-514-5577

True farm hospitality in a converted stable on a 315 year-old wine estate. Chef Nic van Wyk's food speaks of the seasons, with ingredients straight from the kitchen garden and orchard. Relish his gutsy flavours in plats du jour and tapas platters, classic bistro combinations and traditional Sunday roasts with all the trimmings, fresh from the veggie patch. Diemersdal's award-winning wines are available at cellar-door prices. (See also A–Z section.)

Joostenberg Bistro see under Stellenbosch

Ke-Monate Wine Bar & Bistro Hooggelegen Farm, Vissershok Road, Durbanville ▪ Bistro/Tapas ▪ Open for breakfast, lunch and dinner Tue–Sat 9–late, Sun & pub hols 9–4 ▪ Closed Mon ▪ Booking advised ▪ Children welcome ▪ Conference & function venues ▪ Major

credit cards accepted ▪ Corkage R50 ▪ Owners MJ & Estani de Wit ▪ Executive chef Tamara Kuun ▪ info@ke-monate.com ▪ www.signalgun.com ▪ S 33° 49' 13.26" E 018° 36' 40.32" ▪ **T +27 (0)21-976-7343** ▪ F +27 (0)86-611-8747

The view from Hooggelegen Farm, one of the oldest family owned wine farms in Durbanville, is panoramic; the tasty bistro fare pairs happily with the farm's popular Signal Gun wines, or boutique labels from the Durbanville Wine Valley. Consult the blackboard menu for best-sellers from tapas to pizzas, or go with live music and theme evenings: pasta on Wednesdays and Mexican on Thursdays and Fridays. (See also A–Z section for Signal Gun Wines.)

Elgin

Flavours Restaurant at Mofam River Lodge Off Appletiser Road, Elgin/Grabouw ▪ French & Italian inspired dishes with local twist ▪ Open Tue–Sun 8am–9pm; Mondays only for stay-over guests ▪ Booking advised ▪ Children welcome ▪ Major credit cards accepted ▪ Corkage R20 ▪ Owners Sharon & Derek Moore ▪ Executive chef Gordon Manuel ▪ info@mofam.co.za ▪ www.mofam.co.za ▪ S 34° 13' 42.06" E 018° 59' 18.30" ▪ **T +27 (0)21-846-8345** ▪ F +27 (0)86-295-0084

Enjoy French- and Italian-inspired dishes in a light, airy and wide-windowed restaurant on the grassy banks of the Palmiet River. Seasonal, fresh and locally sourced ingredients, offset by the stylish white interior, complement the natural beauty of the setting, and exec chef Gordon Manuel's signature twist shows in specialities like rump steak in rosemary butter, Elgin free-range chicken breast and a best-selling gourmet beef burger.

The Pool Room at Oak Valley Oak Valley Estate, R321, Oak Avenue, Elgin ▪ Mediterranean-country ▪ Lunch Tue–Sun & pub hols 12–3.30, dinner Fri–Sat 6.30–10 ▪ Closed Jun–Aug ▪ Booking advised ▪ Children welcome ▪ Major credit cards accepted (excl. AMEX) ▪ No BYO ▪ Owners The AG Rawbone-Viljoen Trust ▪ Executive chef Jacques Barnard ▪ poolroom@oak-valley.co.za ▪ www.oakvalley.co.za ▪ S 34° 9' 24.4" E 19° 2' 55.5" ▪ **T +27 (0)21-859-4111** ▪ F +27 (0)21-859-3405

Freshness rules and a custom-built grill takes centre stage. Relax on the terrace, relishing country inspired cuisine, with ingredients sourced from the farm where possible, and crafted into mouthwatering dishes by chef Jacques Barnard. Feast on grass-fed beef steaks and burgers, charcuterie from acorn-fed pork, just-picked vegetables and artisanal breads from the wood-burning oven. Favourite lunchtime platter combines these delights with highly-acclaimed Oak Valley wines. (See also A–Z section.)

Franschhoek

Allée Bleue Bistro & Restaurant Intersection R45 & R310, Groot Drakenstein ▪ Bistro fare & winetasting light lunches ▪ Bistro open daily 8–6 (happy hour from 4–6); restaurant daily 10–4 ▪ Booking advised ▪ Children welcome ▪ Visa & MasterCard accepted ▪ No BYO ▪ Wine Tasting Courtyard for light al fresco meals in summer ▪ Both venues available for small private functions ▪ Picnic area ▪ Herb tours ▪ Owners Wilfred & Elke Dauphin ▪ Bistro now under new chef Attila Allmann & his wife Maryna ▪ functions@alleebleue.com ▪ www.alleebleue.co.za ▪ S 33° 51' 55.22" E 18° 58' 56.22" ▪ **T +27 (0)21-874-1021** ▪ F +27 (0)21-874-1850

Eating options are growing at Allée Bleue. There's a new family feel to the bright bistro, but focus remains on fresh, seasonal fare, now with a continental slant. For herb-rich light lunches, visit the restaurant next to the relocated winetasting centre, overlooking the herb gardens. The gatehouse will convert into a deli selling farm produce, while the courtyard will still offer light alfresco meals in summer. (See also Accommodation & A–Z sections.)

Backsberg Restaurant see under Paarl

cosecha Restaurant Noble Hill Wine Estate, Klapmuts-Simondium Road, Simondium, Paarl ▪ Latin-inspired, Californian influences ▪ Open Wed–Mon 10–5 & most pub hols ▪ Closed Tue; 2 weeks in Aug ▪ Picnics ▪ Booking advised ▪ Children & friendly, well-behaved pets welcome ▪ Major credit cards accepted (excl. Diners Club) ▪ Corkage R50 ▪ Pepper and vegetable garden ▪ Owner Noble Hill Trust ▪ info@cosecharestaurant.com, wines@noblehill.com ▪ www.cosecharestaurant.com ▪ S 33° 49' 38.31" E 018° 56' 12.57" ▪ **T +27 (0)21-874-3844** ▪ F +27 (0)21-874-2948

Bringing the farm-fresh flavours of the family's southwestern roots to Cape Town, cosecha (harvest) reflects the al fresco eatery's location adjoining the winery crushing and sorting area. Feast on traditional or contemporary Latin-inspired treats like tableside guacamole with house-made tortilla chips; breakfast on huevos rancheros; lunch on beef enchiladas, kingklip tacos, or bocaditos (small plates) to share. Daily specials feature just-picked peppers, herbs and vegetables. (See also A–Z section.)

Franschhoek Kitchen at Holden Manz Wine Estate 3 Green Valley Road, Franschhoek ▪ Contemporary country ▪ Lunch Tue–Sun & pub hols 11–3, dinner Tue–Sat 6–close ▪ Closed Mon ▪ Booking advised ▪ Children welcome ▪ Visa & MasterCard accepted ▪ Corkage R50 ▪ Owners Gerard Holden & Migo Manz ▪ Executive chef Maryna Frederiksen ▪ restaurant@holdenmanz.com ▪ www.holdenmanz.com ▪ S 33° 56' 7" E 19° 6' 54" ▪ **T +27 (0)21-876-2729** ▪ F +27 (0)21-876-4624

Executive chef Maryna Frederiksen delights in fresh local produce, using estate-grown vegetables and fruit to create dishes inspired by her passion for local sustainable food (try the oak barrel-planked trout) to complement award-winning Holden Manz wines. Her cuisine is regionally inspired to offer a true 'slow food' experience to guests: enjoy lunch on the deck overlooking vineyards, or a gourmet picnic beside the Franschhoek river. (See also Accommodation & A–Z sections.)

Fyndraai Restaurant @ Solms-Delta Delta Road, off R45, Groot Drakenstein, Franschhoek Valley ▪ Traditional Cape cuisine ▪ Open daily 9–5 ▪ Closed Dec 25 & Jan 1 ▪ Booking advised ▪ Children welcome ▪ Major credit cards accepted ▪ No BYO ▪ Owners Solms Family Trust, Astor Family Trust & The Wijn de Caab Workers Trust ▪ Executive chef Shaun Schoeman ▪ restaurant@solms-delta.co.za ▪ www.solms-delta.co.za ▪ www.facebook.com/solmsdelta ▪ Twitter @solms_delta ▪ S 33° 52' 23.8" E 018° 59' 21.3" ▪ **T +27 (0)21-874-3937 ext 115** ▪ F +27 (0)21-874-1852

Culinary heritage meets modern innovation. The herb-rich menu pays tribute to the diverse cultures that contributed to SA cuisine, from ingredients used aeons ago by the valley's indigenous Khoe inhabitants to the influence of the 'Cape Malay' slaves and contemporary Afrikaner boerekos. Enjoy a brandewyn and wildeknoffel béarnaise with wildekruie-coated steak, or for an overview, order the tasty tapas platter. Winner: Great Wine Capitals Best of Wine Tourism — Innovative Wine Tourism Experience 2012. (See also A–Z section.)

Haute Cabrière Restaurant Haute Cabrière, Franschhoek Pass (Lambrechts Road/R45), Franschhoek ▪ Contemporary South African ▪ Lunch Tue–Sun; dinner Tue–Sat (summer) & Fri–Sat (winter) ▪ Closed Mon ▪ Booking advised ▪ Children welcome ▪ Major credit cards accepted ▪ No BYO ▪ Owner Haute Cabrière ▪ Executive chef Ryan Shell ▪ restaurant@cabriere.co.za ▪ www.cabriere.co.za ▪ S 33° 54' 51.63" E 019° 8' 7.90" ▪ **T +27 (0)21-876-3688**

Soaring arches and a view over the cathedral-like barrel maturation cellar enhance an experience centred round 'the true marriage of food and wine'. The menu offers guests an ever-changing selection of wholesome meals and tasting menus, prepared from the freshest seasonal and — where possible — locally sourced ingredients, paired with the Estate's wines or Méthode Classiques. Outdoor tables overlook the valley; winter brings a warming fire. KLINK Wine Tourism Award 2012 — Winner: Beyond Expectations. (See also A–Z section.)

Mange Tout & Country Kitchen Mont Rochelle Hotel & Mountain Vineyards, Dassenberg Road, Franschhoek ▪ **Mange Tout** — international cuisine: breakfast daily 7–10.30, lunch Sat–Sun 12.30–2.30 & dinner Wed–Sun 7–9.30 ▪ **Country Kitchen** — rustic bistro: Mon–Tue 10–9 & Wed–Sun 10–7 ▪ Booking advised ▪ Children welcome ▪ Major credit cards accepted ▪ No BYO ▪ Owners Erwin Schnitzler & Rwayitare family ▪ Executive chef Maki Mahki ▪ info@montrochelle.co.za ▪ www.montrochelle.co.za ▪ S 33° 92' 05.20" E 019° 10' 50.53" ▪ **T +27 (0)21-876-2770** ▪ F +27 (0)21-876-3788

Both elegant and rustic restaurants to suit your mood. Mange Tout offers spectacular valley views, varied menus with a delightfully French slant that reflects support of organic and free range farming, showcasing local produce in imaginative vegetarian options. Informal Country Kitchen specialises in tasty bistro fare, around the fireplace in winter, celebrating summer on the terrace, or with a winelands picnic in the garden. Diners Club Diamond winelist award 2011. (See also Accommodation & A–Z sections.)

Monneaux Restaurant Main Road, Franschhoek ▪ Contemporary cuisine ▪ Open daily for breakfast, lunch & dinner ▪ Underground cellar available for functions ▪ Booking advised ▪ Children welcome ▪ Major credit cards accepted ▪ Corkage R45 ▪ Owner Jean-Pierre Snyman ▪ Executive chef Louis Jansen ▪ info@fch.co.za ▪ www.fch.co.za ▪ S 33° 54' 0.64" E 019° 6' 16.55" ▪ **T +27 (0)21-876-3386** ▪ F +27 (0)21-876-2744

A restaurant ranked among Franschhoek's top, offering a contemporary take on the classics. Enjoy lunch on the fountain terrace under a spreading pepper tree; dinner in the elegantly relaxed dining room in the manor house. Set on the site of Franschhoek's first perfumery, today it's the scent of chef Louis Jansen's cooking that inspires: feast on seared Franschhoek salmon trout sashimi, wasabi mayonnaise, caviar and chives. Diners Club Diamond Winelist Award Winner 2012. (See also Accommodation section for Franschhoek Country House & Villas.)

Paulina's at Rickety Bridge Rickety Bridge Wine Estate, R45 Main Road, Franschhoek ▪ formerly The Restaurant in the Vines ▪ Bistro global ▪ Open daily 12–4 ▪ Closed Jan 1 ▪ Booking advised ▪ Children welcome ▪ Major credit cards accepted ▪ No BYO ▪ Owner Rickety Bridge ▪ Executive chef Melissa Bruyns ▪ functions@ricketybridge.com ▪ www.ricketybridge.com ▪ S 33° 53' 58.5" E 019° 5' 27.6" ▪ **T +27 (0)21-876-2129** ▪ F +27 (0)21-876-3486

The new-look restaurant, honouring the original owner of the estate, provides simple, tasty bistro-style fare, offering full and half portions that double as starters, allowing diners to sample and share. Using fresh produce from the herb and vegetable garden, executive chef Melissa Bruyns (ex Haute Cabrière and Westin Grand) allows ingredients to

speak for themselves: try crispy pork belly, Franschhoek trout burgers and vegetable tempura. (See also Accommodation & A–Z sections.)

Pierneef à La Motte La Motte Wine Estate, R45, Main Road, Franschhoek ▪ Traditional Cape Winelands cuisine ▪ Lunch & Winelands teas Tue–Sun 9–5; dinner Thu–Sat from 7 with fine dining Chef's Menu option ▪ Closed Mon; 3-week winter break (Jun/July) & Christian religious holidays ▪ Booking advised ▪ Children welcome ▪ Major credit cards accepted ▪ Corkage R50 ▪ Owner Hanneli Rupert-Koegelenberg ▪ Executive chef Chris Erasmus ▪ pierneef@la-motte.co.za ▪ www.la-motte.co.za ▪ S 33° 53' 0.91" E 019° 4' 21.57" ▪ **T +27 (0)21-876-8800** ▪ F +27 (0)21-876-3446

Pair food with fine wine in a tranquil garden setting, where seasonal menus, inspired by the past, echo the creativity of SA artist, JH Pierneef. Fresh ingredients, including greens from the estate's biologically-farmed vegetable garden, are transformed into new favourites: try best-selling Cape bokkom salad. Inviting Winelands tea tempts with a wide choice of teas, confectionery and traditional 'soet sopie' or glass of sparkling wine. American Express Top Fine Dining Winelands Restaurant 2013; SA wine list of the year 2012 (three flutes winner); Diner's Club Platinum wine list of the year 2012. (See also A–Z section.)

Restaurant @ Glen Carlou see under Paarl

The French Connection Bistro 48 Huguenot Street, Franschhoek ▪ French bistro ▪ Open daily for lunch 12–3.30 & dinner 6.30–9.30 ▪ Closed for dinner on Dec 25 ▪ Booking advised ▪ Children welcome ▪ Major credit cards accepted ▪ Corkage R40 (1 bottle per 4 guests) ▪ Chef/patron Matthew Gordon ▪ GM Jason Ratner ▪ info@frenchconnection.co.za ▪ www.frenchconnection.co.za ▪ S 33° 54' 36.49" E 019° 7' 8.31" ▪ **T +27 (0)21-876-4056** ▪ F +27 (0)86-591-4988

Matthew Gordon's popular bistro in the heart of the Franschhoek village offers a relaxed culinary experience with top-quality French classics like slow-roasted crispy duck with raspberry vinegar jus; superb steaks (try the fillet mignon with three-mushroom sauce), plus the freshest fish and local produce. Friendly, informative staff ensure that French Connection remains one of the most popular stops in the 'Gourmet Capital of the Cape'. American Express Platinum Fine Dining Award 2006 -'12; Diners Club International Wine List Award 2011 -'13; Tripadvisor Certificate of Excellence for 2012 & 2013.

The Restaurant at Grande Provence Grande Provence Heritage Wine Estate, Main Road, Franschhoek ▪ Fine dining French cuisine with Asian influence ▪ Lunch 12–3 daily; dinner 7–9 daily in summer, Mon–Sat/pub hols in winter ▪ Closed 15 Jul–5 Aug ▪ Booking advised ▪ Children welcome ▪ Major credit cards accepted ▪ No BYO ▪ Owner Alex van Heeren ▪ Executive chef Darren Badenhorst ▪ reservations@grandeprovence.co.za ▪ www.grandeprovence.co.za ▪ S 33° 53' 57.6" E 19° 06' 10.5" ▪ **T +27 (0)21-876-8600** ▪ F +27 (0)21-876-8601

Past elegance fuses with contemporary chic in this sophisticated, girder-exposed restaurant where innovative cuisine hits all the high notes. Menus, flavoured with global influences, change weekly to highlight fresh local produce. Treat your taste buds to specialities like butter-poached lobster tail in cream of coral bisque, with barrel smoke dome, or buchu and balsamic braised lamb neck, tomato ragoût, pistachio butter and sage pommes croquette. American Express Platinum Fine Dining Award 2011-'13. (See also Accommodation & A–Z sections.)

Hout Bay

Pure Restaurant Hout Bay Manor, Baviaanskloof Road, Hout Bay ▪ Bistro-inspired South African cuisine, with a modern twist ▪ Lunch daily 12–3, dinner Tue–Sat & pub hols 6.30–10.30 ▪ Closed Sun eve & Mon ▪ Booking advised ▪ Children welcome ▪ Major credit cards accepted ▪ No BYO, extensive wine list ▪ Occasional Wine & Dine evenings with live band ▪ Owner Susan Struengmann ▪ Head chef Philip Arno Botes ▪ pure@houtbaymanor.co.za ▪ www.pure-restaurant.co.za ▪ S 34° 2' 35.52" E 018° 21' 38.46" ▪ **T +27 (0)21-791-9393** ▪ F +27 (0)21-790-0118

Comfortably seating 70 guests in style, Pure is tranquil in a sea-washed palette of creams, whites, marble and fine art, living up to its name and gracious manor house setting. Bistro-inspired SA cuisine promises delectable dishes from light summer menus to winter warming specials. Book for the occasional Wine & Dine evening accompanied by toe-tapping tunes as a live band entertains you as you dine. Diners Club Diamond Winelist award 2012. (See also Accommodation section.)

Kuils River

Zevenwacht Restaurant see under Stellenbosch

Paarl

Backsberg Restaurant Backsberg Estate Cellars, Klapmuts-Simondium Road, Klapmuts ▪ Country cuisine ▪ Open daily 9.30–3.30 ▪ Booking advised ▪ Children welcome ▪ Major credit cards accepted ▪ No BYO ▪ Owner Michael Back ▪ Executive chef Linda Abrahams ▪ restaurant@backsberg.co.za, info@backsberg.co.za ▪ www.backsberg.co.za ▪ S 33° 49' 42.9" E 018° 54' 56.9" ▪ **T +27 (0)21-875-5952/-5141** ▪ F +27 (0)21-875-5144

Pair country-style, home-grown and homemade food with award-winning wines at this rustic,

family-friendly venue set in lush gardens with a mountain view. The fresh, simply prepared seasonal menu offers tasty specialities like lamb stew and chicken pie. Book ahead for the Sunday buffet lunch starring spit-roasted Karoo lamb. It's legendary — and so are the roast potatoes. Enjoy live music and a log fire in winter. (See also A–Z section.)

Bosman's Restaurant Plantasie Street, Paarl ▪ Global cuisine ▪ **Bosman's Restaurant:** dinner daily 7–9 (mid Dec–end Mar) & Thu–Sun (1 Apr–mid Dec); no children under the age of 4 ▪ **Bistro Allegro:** open daily for lunch & dinner; children welcome ▪ Breakfast served daily in the Manor House ▪ Booking advised ▪ Major credit cards accepted ▪ No BYO ▪ GM Anja Bosken ▪ Executive chef Roland Gorgosilich ▪ reserve@granderoche.co.za ▪ www.granderoche.co.za ▪ S 33° 45' 02" E 18° 57' 35" ▪ **T +27 (0)21-863-5100** ▪ F +27 (0)21-863-2220

Bosman's Restaurant, in the Boland's gabled Grande Roche Hotel, is the perfect place for fine dining. Enjoy culinary delights from a choice of inviting menus, compiled by creative, Michelin-star trained executive chef Roland Gorgosilich. Specialities like red-wine marinated springbok loin with vodka-parsnip purée, sautéed brussels sprouts, cep sauté, pumpernickel flan and juniper berry-port wine jus are complemented by splendid wines from the superbly stocked cellar. Diners Club winelist Diamond Award 2013; Wine Spectator's Best of Award of Excellence 2013; American Express Platinum Fine Dining Restaurant Award 2012. (See also Accommodation section for Grande Roche Hotel.)

cosecha Restaurant see under Franschhoek

Harvest restaurant at Laborie Laborie Wine Farm, Taillefer Street, Paarl ▪ Contemporary South African cuisine ▪ Lunch daily 12–3, dinner Wed–Sat 6.30–9 ▪ Booking advised, especially in summer ▪ Children welcome, jungle gym & kiddie menu ▪ Caters for weddings, corporate functions, and conferences ▪ Major credit cards accepted ▪ Corkage R50 ▪ Owner KWV (Pty) Ltd ▪ Consulting chef Matthew Gordon ▪ info@laboriewines.co.za ▪ www.laboriewines.co.za ▪ S 33° 45' 57.64" E 018° 57' 31.84" ▪ **T +27 (0)21-807-3095**

Friendly, relaxed restaurant, seating 80 inside and a further 100 on the terrace, overlooking Laborie's immaculate vineyards. The appetising menu is drawn from South Africa's cultural mosaic, presented in a modern idiom: perennial best-sellers are chef Matthew Gordon's famous duck, steaks and mussels (when in season). This is a favourite wedding venue with the added benefits of scenic backdrops, attentive service and secure parking. KLINK

award for Best Bistro or Café on a Wine Farm. (See also Accommodation & A–Z sections.)

Joostenberg Bistro see under Stellenbosch

Marc's Restaurant 129 Main Street, Paarl ▪ French bistro ▪ Open Mon–Sat 10–10, pub hols — please call to check ▪ Closed Sun, Easter Mon, 2 weeks during winter school hols, Dec 25 & Jan 1 ▪ Booking advised ▪ Children welcome ▪ Major credit cards accepted ▪ Corkage R40 ▪ Chef/patron Marc Friederich ▪ info@marcsrestaurant.co.za ▪ www.marcsrestaurant.co.za ▪ **T +27 (0)21-863-3980** ▪ F +27 (0)21-863-3990

Just turned 11, this popular Paarl 'fixture' hasn't changed much, save for a touch of traditional dishes from Alsace (owner Marc's home) and a shorter, more flexible Paarl-orientated winelist and menu. But while the French bistro favourites, grills, best-selling paella and crisp-based, fun-topped pizzas are still available, the restaurant's carbon footprint has been reduced, replaced by local free-range meat, sustainable fish, organic veg and herbs. TripAdvisor certificate of excellence 2012.

Polo Club Restaurant at Val de Vie Estate Val de Vie Estate, R301, Jan van Riebeeck Drive, Paarl ▪ Contemporary country cuisine ▪ Open Tue, Thu & Sun 9–4, Wed, Fri & Sat 9–9 ▪ Closed Mon ▪ Booking advised ▪ Children welcome ▪ Major credit cards accepted (excl. AMEX) ▪ Corkage R40 ▪ Owners Jan Morne Bosch & Nicolas Hendrik Hendrikse ▪ Executive chef Edmore Ruzoza ▪ restaurant@valdevie.co.za ▪ www.valdevie.co.za ▪ S 33° 48' 15.0" E 18° 58' 4.0" ▪ **T +27 (0)21-863-6174** ▪ F +27 (0)21-863-2741

This relaxed, bistro-style restaurant overlooking pristine polo fields offers a variety of eating experiences. Entertain guests or enjoy family lunch on the terraces; make sundowners a light tapas meal with innovative cocktails. The chic Italian-style bar is a popular rendezvous for both polo players and residents; evenings offer fine dining, and Sunday lunch is sumptuous. Specialities range from chicken liver pasta to slow-cooked lamb shank. (See also A–Z section.)

Restaurant @ Glen Carlou Glen Carlou, Simondium Road, Klapmuts ▪ Contemporary cuisine with French & African influences, paired with Glen Carlou wines ▪ Open daily 11–3 ▪ Closed Good Fri & Dec 25 ▪ Booking advised ▪ Children welcome ▪ Major credit cards accepted ▪ BYO by arrangement, corkage R50 ▪ Weddings & events welcomed ▪ Contemporary art on display ▪ Wine tasting daily ▪ Six-course canapé and wine tasting by appointment ▪ Owner Hess Family Wine Estates ▪ Executive chef Johan Stander ▪ restaurant@glencarlou.co.za ▪ www.glencarlou.co.za ▪ S 33° 48' 44.85" E 018° 54' 12.88" ▪ **T +27 (0)21-875-5528** ▪ F +27 (0)21-875-5314

Family-friendly venue geared for lazy Sunday lunches and business meetings, with spectacular

view from sunlit veranda or from behind glass in winter, the stylish interior cosily lit and fire-warmed. Seasonal menus — with palate-tempters from spicy lamb croquettes, apricot salsa and pineapple yoghurt to vegetarian options — support SASSI. All wines are offered by the glass: best-selling crème brûlée sings with Natural Sweet Chenin Blanc. Klink Wine Tourism Awards Top 5 Best Bistro on a Wine Farm. (See also A–Z section.)

Spice Route Restaurant Spice Route, Suid-Agter Paarl Road, Suider-Paarl ▪ Contemporary, eclectic ▪ Open Mon–Fri, Sun & pub hols 11–6 (kitchen closes at 5.30) ▪ Sat 11–8.30 (kitchen closes at 8) ▪ Closed Dec 25 & Jan 1 ▪ Booking advised ▪ Children welcome ▪ Major credit cards accepted ▪ Corkage R50 ▪ Owners Andy Küng & Charles Back ▪ Executive chef Andy Küng & executive head chef Marion Kumpf ▪ restaurant@spiceroute.co.za ▪ www.spicerouterestaurant.co.za ▪ S 33° 45′ 50″ E 018° 55′ 10″ ▪ **T +27 (0)21-863-5222** ▪ F +2 (0)21-863-2591

Take a tantalising culinary journey, exploring the fusion between spice, food and wine in a relaxed mountainside restaurant with panoramic view. Discover the delights of traditional South African cooking infused with the subtle seasoning of the Spice Route and trading empire of the Dutch East India Company; each dish carefully crafted to complement award-winning Spice Route wines. Do try korma curry served in a tagine. (See also A–Z section.)

The Goatshed Restaurant Fairview Wine & Cheese Farm, Suid-Agter Paarl Road, Suider-Paarl ▪ Farmstyle Mediterranean ▪ Open daily 9–5 (kitchen closes at 4.30) ▪ Closed Dec 25 & Jan 1 ▪ Booking advised ▪ Children welcome ▪ Major credit cards accepted ▪ Corkage R50 ▪ Owners Andy Küng & Charles Back ▪ Executive chef Andy Küng ▪ goatshed@fairview.co.za ▪ www.goatshed.co.za ▪ S 33° 46′ 22.00″ E 018° 55′ 24.50″ ▪ **T +27 (0)21-863-3609** ▪ F +2 (0)21-863-2591

Named for Fairview's 1000-strong goat herd, this rustic, hospitable restaurant in one of the farm's old wine cellars pulls the crowds with light and tasty lunches from locally-sourced seasonal produce, spilling on to a terrace in summer. Enjoy highly-rated Fairview wines with Chalmar beef, chicken pie and springbok salad; or pick a platter from some 25 farm cheeses with just-baked breads, including more-ish Goatshed ciabatta. (See also A–Z section.)

Robertson

Bodega de Vinho Rooiberg Winery, on Route 60 between Worcester & Robertson, Robertson ▪ Continental/country cuisine ▪ Open Mon–Fri 8–5.30, Sat 9–4 ▪ Closed Sun, Good Fri, Dec 25 & Jan 1 ▪ Booking

advised ▪ Children welcome ▪ Pet friendly garden ▪ Bakery ▪ Major credit cards accepted ▪ No BYO ▪ Owner Rooiberg Winery ▪ Executive chef Deon le Roux ▪ bodega@rooiberg.co.za ▪ www.rooiberg.co.za ▪ S 33° 46′ 35.3″ E 019° 45′ 42.9″ ▪ **T +27 (0)23-626-1243** ▪ F +27 (0)23-626-3295

You can't miss it: look out for a 9m high red chair on Route 60. Let the dogs and kids out (there's grass and a jungle gym) and settle in — the name translates as 'a convivial meeting place serving food and wine'. Apart from light lunches and wine pairing, just-baked breads and alluring pastries, from pain-au-chocolat to copenhagens and ciabattas, are reason enough to stop. (See also A–Z section.)

Fraai Uitzicht 1798 Klaas Voogds East, on R60 between Robertson & Montagu ▪ Contemporary, fusion, Mediterranean influences ▪ Open Wed–Sun lunch from 12 & dinner from 6 (Mon–Tue dinner for resident guests only) ▪ Closed mid Jun–end Aug, Dec 24/31 & Jan 1 ▪ Booking advised ▪ Children 12+ welcome ▪ Major credit cards accepted ▪ No BYO ▪ Owners Karl Uwe & Sandra Papesch ▪ Executive chef Sandra Papesch ▪ info@fraaiuitzicht.com ▪ www.fraaiuitzicht.com ▪ S 33° 47′ 43.13″ E 20° 0′ 17.99″ ▪ **T +27 (0)23-626-6156** ▪ F +27 (0)86-662-5265

Experience fine dining in an award-wining restaurant, where attentive hosts, spectacular views across vineyards and informal décor add to the charm. Share the conviviality of a cosy fire, or in summer, enjoy the tranquillity of the umbrella-shaded veranda. The creative six-course menu offers seasonal treats showcasing fresh vegetables and herbs from the garden, complemented by Robertson Valley's best wines, including handcrafted Fraai Uitzicht 1798 Merlot. American Express Platinum Fine Dinning award — 11 consecutive years. (See also Accommodation & A–Z sections.)

Somerset West

96 Winery Road Restaurant see under Stellenbosch

Avontuur Estate Restaurant Avontuur Estate, R44, Somerset West ▪ Contemporary country, rustic ▪ Open Mon–Fri 9–5, Sat/Sun 9–4; dinner Wed/Fri/Sat (summer) & Wed/Fri (winter) ▪ Closed Good Fri, Dec 25 & Jan 1 ▪ Booking advised ▪ Children welcome ▪ Major credit cards accepted ▪ No BYO ▪ Chefs/patrons Zunia Boucher-Myers & Melanie Paltoglou ▪ openhand@polka.co.za ▪ www.avontuurestate.co.za ▪ S 34° 1′ 33.2″ E 018° 49′ 23.8″ ▪ **T +27 (0)21-855-4296** ▪ F +27 (0)21-855-4600

Tourism 4-star rated, this hands-on welcoming restaurant offers vine-shaded tables with a view. The good-value new menu, tempting tastebuds with dishes like tomato fondue, or pan-fried duck liver with caramelised beetroot, now includes vegan and

vegetarian options, plus a no-guilt, gluten free daily bake. Regulars can relax: their favourites — including signature crispy duckling in Van der Hum sauce, and deep-fried ice-cream — are still listed. Voted no 1 Restaurant on Tripadvisor for the Helderberg area. (See also A–Z section.)

The Restaurant at Waterkloof Waterkloof Estate, Sir Lowry's Pass Village Road, Somerset West ▪ Contemporary, with a French fusion ▪ Lunch daily in summer & Tue–Sun in winter, orders in by 2pm; Dinner Mon–Sat in summer & Tue–Sat in winter, orders in by 9pm ▪ Closed Dec 25 & Jan 1 ▪ Booking advised ▪ Major credit cards accepted ▪ No BYO ▪ Owner Paul Boutinot ▪ Executive chef Grégory Czarnecki ▪ restaurant@waterkloofwines.co.za ▪ www.waterkloofwines.co.za ▪ S 34° 5' 55.4" E 018° 53' 22.8" ▪ **T +27 (0)21-858-1491** ▪ F +27 (0)21-858-1293

A 'glass box' restaurant seemingly suspended in space, with panoramic views over vineyards and False Bay; elegant cuisine that matches the setting. Grégory Czarnecki, a chef with a 3-star Michelin background, creates contemporary French-inspired dishes that engage all six senses, using fresh farm ingredients and prime local produce. His perfectly-judged flavour combinations pair seamlessly with wines from the estate. Allow time to savour your meal. Tripadvisor Certificate of Excellence 2012–'13. (See also A–Z section.)

Vergelegen Vergelegen Wine Estate, Lourensford Road, Somerset West ▪ **Camphors at Vergelegen** (à la carte/contemporary/global) lunch Wed–Sun 12–3, dinner Fri & Sat 6.30–9; **Stables at Vergelegen** (bistro) open Mon–Sun for breakfast 9.30–11.30, lunch 11.30–3.30, tea/coffee & cakes 9.30–4; Fri-Sat (Nov–Apr) kitchen closes at 7pm; **Forest Picnic** (luxury/elegant picnic) baskets available Nov–Apr between 12.15–1.30 ▪ Estate closed Good Fri, May 1 & Dec 25 ▪ Booking advised ▪ Forest Picnic & Stables specifically child-friendly ▪ Major credit cards accepted ▪ No BYO ▪ Owners Anglo American plc ▪ Executive chefs PJ Vadas at Camphors & Gary Richardson at Stables ▪ info@vergelegen.co.za ▪ www.vergelegen.co.za ▪ S 34° 4' 37.0" E 018° 53' 30.6" ▪ **T +27 (0)21-847-1346 Camphors Restaurant / Forest Picnic; T +27 (0)21-847-2156 Stables Bistro**

Experience the world of Vergelegen first-hand: from spectacular formal gardens to arts and culture, wine tasting and cellar tours, and restaurants to suit all tastes. A recent major revamp of the estate's culinary hospitality saw a 'new kid on the farm': family friendly Stables, offering bistro-style treats from pastries to pizzas (junior sizes available), generous burgers, juicy steaks and delectable desserts. The original Lady Phillips morphed into

Camphors at Vergelegen (named after the magnificent camphor trees standing guard in front of the old homestead) where chic blends seamlessly with tradition, and award-winning classic wines are perfectly paired with enticing, classically-grounded global cuisine. The perennially popular forest picnic in the shadows of a centuries old camphor forest provides relaxation for adults while children amuse themselves with an exciting treasure hunt. (See also A–Z section.)

Stanford

Springfontein Eats Restaurant Springfontein Wine Estate, Springfontein Road, Stanford ▪ Michelin-quality for locavores ▪ Lunch Wed–Sun, dinner Tue–Sat ▪ Closed Mon, July & August ▪ Booking advised ▪ Children welcome ▪ Major credit cards accepted ▪ No BYO ▪ French & German spoken ▪ Owners Weber & Schneider families ▪ Executive chef Jürgen Schneider ▪ hospitality@springfontein.co.za ▪ www.springfontein.co.za ▪ S 34° 25' 38.5" E 019° 24' 32.7" ▪ **T +27 (0)28-341-0651** ▪ F +27 (0)28-341-0112

Unfamiliar with the term 'locavore'? Then visit Springfontein estate, where Jürgen and Susanne Schneider (WSET Diploma), after managing restaurants in the world's top locations, have joined owners Johst and Jennifer Weber. Their just-opened restaurant offers 'locavore fare': fresh herbs, vegetables and fruits grown or foraged from the farm. Savour flavour-treats like sweet potato mousse with wood-sorrel foam; box of oxtail stuffed with mushroom and mash, and triptychon of carrots. Michelin-starred in Germany since 1998. (See also Accommodation & A–Z sections.)

The Tasting Room Stanford Hills Estate, Stanford ▪ Global cuisine ▪ Open Thu–Mon & pub hols 11–5 ▪ Closed Tue/Wed ▪ Booking advised ▪ Children welcome ▪ No credit card facilities ▪ No BYO ▪ Fishing ▪ Self-catering cottages ▪ Hiking trails ▪ Owners Peter & Jami Kastner ▪ Executive chef Bridget Bartleman ▪ jami@stanfordhills.co.za ▪ www.stanfordhills.co.za ▪ S 34° 25' 21.4" E 019° 28' 25.7" ▪ **T +27 (0)28-341-0841** ▪ F +27 (0)28-341-0286

Taste Stanford Hills wines and virgin olive oil before relishing farm-fresh fare in a quaint, rustic restaurant with gorgeous valley views, overlooking a dam. Small, inviting blackboard menus change daily: expect home-made pastas, soups, gourmet burgers, mezze platters and tempting desserts. Catch-and-release Bass fishing (take your own gear); boats for paddling and lawns for lazing; pull-down blinds and fireplace to ensure cosy lunches on chilly days. (See also A–Z section.)

Steenberg

The Brasserie see under Tokai

Stellenbosch

96 Winery Road Restaurant Zandberg Farm, Winery Road, off the R44 between Stellenbosch & Somerset West ▪ Country cuisine with influences from around the world ▪ Lunch daily 12–3.30, dinner Mon–Sat 6.30–9 ▪ Closed Good Fri, Dec 26 & Jan 1 ▪ Booking advised ▪ Children welcome ▪ Major credit cards accepted ▪ Corkage R45 ▪ Owners Ken Forrester, Allan Forrester, Martin Meinert & Natasha Wray ▪ Executive chef Natasha Wray ▪ wineryrd@mweb.co.za ▪ www.96wineryroad.co.za ▪ S 34° 1′ 36.2″ E 018° 48′ 32.3″ ▪ **T +27 (0)21-842-2020** ▪ F +27 (0)21-842-2050

Relaxed family friendly venue, where you can share good times, great food and some world-class wines. Opening in May 1996, the rustic restaurant rapidly established a reputation for consistency, fresh, seasonal organic produce and prime matured beef: specialities include Hollandse pepper fillet flambéed at the table. Signature dish is evergreen duck and cherry pie, and chocolate, chocolate, chocolate with vanilla bean ice-cream as a dreamy finale. Wine Spectator Grand Award 2012; Tripadvisor Award of Excellence 2011 -'13; Diners Club Platinum Winelist Award 2012.

Avontuur Estate Restaurant see under Somerset West

Barouche Restaurant Blaauwklippen Vineyards, on the R44 between Stellenbosch & Somerset West, opposite Techno Park ▪ Modern country cuisine (breakfast/lunch) & fine dining (dinner) ▪ Summer: Mon/Tue/Sat/Sun/pub hols 9–3, Wed–Fri 9–9 & Tapas Lounge 4–7; Winter: Wed–Fri 12–3, Sat/Sun/pub hols 9–3 ▪ Closed Mon–Tue in winter & Jan 1 ▪ Booking advised ▪ Children welcome ▪ Major credit cards accepted ▪ Corkage R45 ▪ Family Market every Sun 10–3 ▪ Horse-drawn carriage rides ▪ Picnics available with 24hrs notice ▪ Cellar tours & wine tasting at the Wine Centre ▪ Weddings, functions & conferences ▪ Owners Blue Lion GmbH, Munich ▪ hospitality@blaauwklippen.com, mail@blaauwklippen.com ▪ www.blaauwklippen.com ▪ S 33° 58′ 23.3″ E 018° 50′ 51.0″ ▪ **T +27 (0)21-880-8222/0133** ▪ F +27 (0)21-880-1246/0136

Match the true taste of South Africa to Blaauwklippen wines in beautiful surroundings. At Barouche, a relaxed, family friendly space with large outdoor terrace overlooking a jungle gym and paddocks, fresh, locally sourced seasonal ingredients are creatively combined in inviting, light and wholesome menus. Dishes, based on the South African kitchen with a modern focus, update traditional recipes. Family Day Out Award for Best Child-Friendly Venue on a Wine Farm at the inaugural KLINK Tourism Awards 2013, plus Supernova

Award for the nominee with the most votes overall. (See also A–Z section.)

Café Blanc de Noir Brenaissance Wine & Stud Estate, Devon Valley Road, Stellenbosch ▪ Fresh/Café style/European ▪ Open Wed–Sat 11am–10pm, Sun 11am–5pm; Wed & Thu 11am–9pm in winter ▪ Booking advised ▪ Children welcome ▪ Major credit cards accepted ▪ Corkage R50 ▪ Owners Tom & Hayley Breytenbach ▪ Manager Adam Sivoglou ▪ café@brenaissance.co.za ▪ www.brenaissance.co.za ▪ S 33° 55′ 4.31″ E 018° 49′ 7.82″ ▪ **T +27 (0)21-200-2644**

Experience interactive pizza and wine-pairing in a chic café set in plum orchards, overlooking vineyards and the Stellenbosch Mountains. Focus is on providing a relaxing, happy space, from the open-plan interior, filled with home touches, to well-trained, friendly staff. Menus centre round farm-fresh ingredients, specialising in gourmet wood-oven pizzas, salads, wraps and 'family secret' cakes, to enjoy with award-winning Brenaissance wines and local craft beer. (See also Accommodation & A–Z sections.)

Chez Shiraz Devonvale Golf & Wine Estate, Bottelary Road, Stellenbosch/Koelenhof ▪ French/continental cuisine ▪ Open daily 7am–10pm ▪ Booking advised ▪ Children welcome ▪ Major credit cards accepted ▪ No BYO ▪ Owner JJ Provoyeur ▪ Executive chefs Benito & William ▪ info@devonvale.co.za, events@devonvale.co.za ▪ www.devonvale.co.za/restaurant ▪ S 33° 52′ 59.6″ E 018° 48′ 15.0″ ▪ **T +27 (0)21-865-2080** ▪ F +27 (0)21-865-2113

As Devonvale Golf & Wine Estate's restaurant and the hotel's à la carte restaurant, Chez Shiraz welcomes guests to buffet-style breakfasts, light lunches on the outdoor Terrace overlooking the golf course, and elegant dining in a typical French-style restaurant. Part of the charm is the enchanting atmosphere and French menu: an ideal setting for sitting back, relaxing, and enjoying delectable meals with sumptuous wines. (See also Accommodation & A–Z sections.)

Cuvée Simonsig Wine Estate, Kromme Rhee Road, Stellenbosch ▪ Contemporary cuisine ▪ Lunch Tue–Sat 12–3 Sun 12–2; dinner Wed, Fri & Sat 7–10 ▪ Closed Mon ▪ Booking advised ▪ Children welcome ▪ Major credit cards accepted ▪ No BYO ▪ Owners Francois, Johan & Pieter Malan ▪ Head chef Lucas Carstens ▪ cuvee@simonsig.co.za ▪ www.simonsig.co.za ▪ S 33° 52′ 14.19″ E 018° 49′ 34.92″ ▪ **T +27 (0)21-888-4932** ▪ F +27 (0)21-888-4909

This hospitable signature restaurant captivates with a mix of nostalgia and Cape Dutch modernism, embracing French Provençal flavours, home-grown South African tastes and Asian touches. Match Simonsig wines to back-to-basics, garden-fresh food from head chef Lucas Carstens, grounded in sustainability and just-picked ingredients. Fresh

linefish pairs with oriental mushroom linguine and prawn bisque, and new-taste Malva pudding goes gourmet with milk-tart ice-cream and brandy Anglaise. (See also A–Z section.)

Delaire Graff Restaurant Delaire Graff Estate, R310 Helshoogte Pass, Banhoek Valley, Stellenbosch ▪ Bistro-chic, modern Mediterranean ▪ Lunch daily 12–2.30, dinner Wed–Sat 6–9 ▪ Booking advised ▪ Children 12+ welcome ▪ Major credit cards accepted ▪ Corkage R80 ▪ Owner Laurence Graff ▪ Executive chef Christiaan Campbell ▪ reservations@delaire.co.za ▪ www.delaire.co.za ▪ S 33° 55' 20.4" E 018° 55' 26.0" ▪ **T +27 (0)21-885-8160** ▪ F +27 (0)21-885-1270

The dining experience is holistic, from the moment you enter the estate to the service ethic permeating the restaurant. Executive chef Christiaan Campbell's seasonal and organic 'bistro-chic' cuisine turns food into an art form (desserts are a creative triumph) and experienced sommeliers will guide you through the winelist. Relax, soak up the magnificent setting, and admire the superb collection of contemporary SA art and sculpture. (See also Accommodation & A–Z sections.)

Flavours Restaurant at The Devon Valley Hotel Devon Valley Road, Devon Valley, Stellenbosch ▪ Contemporary Cape cuisine ▪ Open daily 6.30am–11pm ▪ Booking advised ▪ Children welcome ▪ Major credit cards accepted ▪ Corkage R35 — BYO not encouraged ▪ Owner Louis Group Hotels, Spa's & Vineyards ▪ Executive chef Markus Schwemberger ▪ flavours@devonvalleyhotel.com ▪ www.devonvalleyhotel.com ▪ S 33° 54' 12.64" E 18° 48' 53.03" ▪ **T +27 (0)21-865-2012** ▪ F +27 (0)21-865-2610

Flavour comes first — followed by a picturesque setting. Contemporary Cape cuisine, served in a gentle understated ambience, focuses on bold flavours and fresh, clean tastes. Lunch offers light items as well as daily specials (try home-made ice-cream), while dinner best-seller is herb-crusted rack of Karoo lamb with potato rösti and pinotage jus. Pair dishes with the award-winning winelist to make any meal a special occasion. Diners Club Wine List of the Year Diamond Award 2012 (their fourth consecutive annual Diamond Award). (See also Accommodation section & A–Z for SylvanVale.)

Guardian Peak Winery & Grill Guardian Peak Wines, Annandale Road, Stellenbosch ▪ Bistro with a focus on prime quality steak ▪ Lunch Mon–Sun 12–3.30, dinner Wed–Sat 6.30–10, wine tasting Mon–Sat 9–5 & Sun 11–5 ▪ Closed Dec 25 ▪ Booking advised ▪ Children welcome ▪ Major credit cards accepted ▪ No BYO ▪ Owner Jean Engelbrecht ▪ info@guardianpeak.com ▪ www.guardianpeak.com ▪ S 34° 0' 40.19" E 018° 50' 31.99" ▪ **T +27 (0)21-881-3899** ▪ F +27 (0)21-881-3388

For a hospitable Stellenbosch Winelands experience, relax at tables on a wide veranda with vineyard vistas. Wine-inspired lunches and dinners match hearty, wholesome dishes (including tasty vegetarian options), but focus is on prime-quality steak and venison: choices from the grill include fillet, rump, and rib-eye, with tempting sauces. Treat yourself to a 'Portfolio Tasting' with wines from Guardian Peak's greater portfolio, sold under separate brands. (See also A–Z section for Guardian Peak, Stellenbosch Ridge, Cirrus & Donkiesbaai.)

Indochine Restaurant Delaire Graff Lodges & Spa, Delaire Graff Estate, R310 Helshoogte Pass, Banhoek Valley, Stellenbosch ▪ Asian-inspired cuisine ▪ Open daily for lunch 12.30–2.30 & dinner 6.30–9.30 ▪ Booking advised ▪ Children welcome ▪ Major credit cards accepted ▪ Corkage R80 ▪ Owner Laurence Graff ▪ Executive chef Christiaan Campbell ▪ guest.relations@delaire.co.za ▪ www.delaire.co.za ▪ S 33° 55' 20.4" E 018° 55' 26.0" ▪ **T +27 (0)21-885-8160** ▪ F +27 (0)86-626-4403

Savour Asian-inspired cuisine with a contemporary yet delicate twist, in a soothing space and deck with wraparound views over the valley below towards Table Mountain. Only the finest ingredients are used, with menus featuring fresh organic produce from the estate greenhouse: don't ignore the tantalising side-dishes. Flavours are lively, aromatic and robust while maintaining a style of eating synonymous with vitality, wellness and healthy living. (See also Accommodation & A–Z sections.)

Joostenberg Bistro Klein Joostenberg, R304, Muldersvlei ▪ French bistro ▪ Open daily from 8–5 ▪ Closed Dec 25 & Jan 1 ▪ Booking advised ▪ Children welcome ▪ Major credit cards accepted ▪ Corkage R35 ▪ Owners Susan & Christophe Dehosse, Philip Myburgh ▪ Executive chef Christophe Dehosse ▪ bistro@joostenberg.co.za ▪ www.joostenberg.co.za ▪ **T +27 (0)21-884-4208** ▪ F +27 (0)21-884-4141

Craving freshly prepared traditional bistro dishes? Look no further. The specialities & best-selling dishes will set you salivating: coq au vin; bouillabaisse; pork sausages from own farm-reared pork, apple sauce and mash; terrine and jambon persillée — with highly rated Joostenberg wines. The venue is relaxed, spacious and family friendly, with tables set on a vine-shaded stoep in summer and beside a huge fireplace in winter. (See also A–Z section.)

Lanzerac Wine Estate 1 Lanzerac Road, Stellenbosch ▪ European-influenced classics with an African twist ▪ Dinner parties, corporate functions, tastings or special events ▪ 2 restaurants ▪ Open daily 7am–11pm (last order taken at 10pm) ▪ Booking advised ▪ Children welcome ▪ Major credit cards accepted ▪ Corkage R45 ▪ GM Hans Steyn ▪ Executive chef Stephen Fraser ▪ info@lanzerac.co.za ▪ www.lanzerac.co.za ▪ S 33° 56'

14.7" E 018° 53' 35.5" ▪ **T +27 (0)21-887-1132** ▪ F +27 (0)21-887-2310

Dine in elegance, in a stately ambience hung with portraits of past governors. The Governors Hall, the hotel's main à la carte restaurant, opens its impressive wood-panelled doors daily to welcome guests to a gastronomic explosion of international and local cuisine, served with carefully selected, award-winning wines. Generous buffet-style breakfast and appetising lunches are also served daily, with alfresco meals offered at the Terrace Restaurant. (See also Accommodation & A–Z sections.)

Le Venue at the House of JC le Roux The House of JC le Roux, Devon Valley Road, Devon Valley, Stellenbosch ▪ Chic country fare with MCC and sparkling wines ▪ Open daily 9–3 ▪ Booking advised ▪ Children welcome ▪ Gourmet braai ideal for private functions ▪ Major credit cards accepted ▪ No BYO ▪ Owner Distell ▪ Executive chef Renshaw Adams ▪ levenue@hsvhospitality.com ▪ www.levenue.co.za ▪ S 33° 54' 16.6" E 018° 48' 37.4" ▪ **T +27 (0)21-865-8200** ▪ F +27 (0)21-865-2610

Escape to scenic Devon Valley, to the al fresco deck of a stylish new venue: the result of a makeover that literally raised the roof of the House of JC le Roux. Pair award-winning Méthode Cap Classique and sparkling wines with bubbles-enhancing treats such as truffle-centred scrambled egg with all the indulgent extras; oysters and sushi, and wine-rich desserts like La Fleurette crème brûlée. (See also A–Z section.)

Makaron Restaurant Majeka House, 26-32 Houtkapper Street, Paradyskloof, Stellenbosch ▪ French/contemporary cuisine ▪ Open daily for lunch 12–2.30, dinner 7–9.30 ▪ Closed month of Jun; Wed from 1 Apr–30 Sep ▪ Booking advised ▪ Children welcomè ▪ Major credit cards accepted ▪ Corkage R50 ▪ Owners Karine Dequeker-van der Merwe & Lloyd van der Merwe ▪ Executive chef Tanja Kruger ▪ reception@majekahouse.co.za ▪ www.majekahouse.co.za ▪ S 33° 58' 04.07" E 018° 51' 39.64" ▪ **T +27 (0)21-880-1549** ▪ F +27 (0)21-880-1550

Sophisticated cuisine in a stylish setting. The restaurant leads onto a sheltered garden terrace, ideal for alfresco dining. But the food's the star. Resident chef Tanja Kruger shows her creative skill in contemporary dishes grounded in the French classics, delightfully plated and impeccably served. Flavour fuses with eye-appeal in constantly changing menus accenting seasonality and prime local produce. Allow time to linger over your meal. (See also Accommodation section.)

Morgenhof Restaurant Morgenhof Wine Estate, Klapmuts Road (R44), Stellenbosch ▪ Country cuisine ▪ Open Mon–Fri 9–4, Sat/Sun 9–3 ▪ Closed Mon (May–end Aug), Good Friday, Dec 25 & Jan 1 ▪

Booking advised ▪ Children welcome ▪ Major credit cards accepted ▪ No BYO ▪ Owner La Tour International Investments t/a Morgenhof Wines ▪ Executive chef Thys Esterhuysen ▪ meryka@morgenhof.com ▪ www.morgenhof.com ▪ S 33° 53' 38.5" E 018° 51' 39.2" ▪ **T +27 (0)21-889-2024** ▪ F +27 (0)21-889-5266

Popular year-round venue where flavour sets seasonal menus from exec chef Thys Esterhuysen. Relax at garden tables in summer; under a vine canopy in winter sunshine; or banishing the chill beside log fires indoors, enjoying signature dishes like chicken salad; best-selling venison, or hearty oxtail ragoût, Irish crushed potatoes and tasty jus. (See also Accommodation & A–Z sections.)

Postcard Café @ Stark-Condé Wines Stark-Condé Wines, Jonkershoek Valley, Stellenbosch ▪ Simple & fresh, country-style lunch & cakes ▪ Open Tue–Sun 9.30–4 ▪ Closed Mon, Good Fri, Dec 24/25 & Jan 1 ▪ Booking advised ▪ Visa & MasterCard accepted ▪ No BYO ▪ Owner Marie Condé ▪ postcardcafe@stark-conde.co.za ▪ www.postcardcafe.co.za ▪ S 33° 57' 14.00" E 018° 54' 38.00" ▪ **T +27 (0)21-861-7703** ▪ F +27 (0)21-887-4340

Small, relaxed café, set against a picture-postcard mountain backdrop, offers simple, country-style treats. Light Asian chicken salad, crispy fried prawns with lemon cream dressing, and springbok braised in red wine are best-sellers; homemade desserts are legendary. Best reserve your baked cheesecake, pear and blueberry crumble or apple pie before lunch in case it sells out. Award-winning Stark-Condé wines available by the glass at cellar door prices. (See also A–Z section.)

Rust en Vrede Restaurant Rust en Vrede Wine Estate, Annandale Road (off R44), Stellenbosch ▪ Fine dining, contemporary take on the classics ▪ Dinner Tue–Sat from 7pm to close ▪ Closed Sun/Mon, Good Fri & Dec 25 ▪ Booking advised ▪ Major credit cards accepted ▪ No BYO ▪ Owner Jean Engelbrecht ▪ Executive chef John Shuttleworth ▪ dining@rustenvrede.com, info@rustenvrede.com ▪ www.rustenvrede.com ▪ S 33° 59' 54.0" E 018° 51' 22.5" ▪ **T +27 (0)21-881-3757** ▪ F +27 (0)21-881-3000

Dine in sought-after style in the wine estate's historic cellar, where décor and a see-it-all open-plan kitchen, plus the finest glasses and custom-designed tableware, enhance creative four- and six-course gourmet menus. Executive chef John Shuttleworth brings original touches to a range of perfectly-plated dishes, while internationally-acclaimed sommelier Joakim Hansi Blackadder adds his expertise to the innovative wine-matching experience; not all of the wines South African. *San Pellegrino* Top 100 in the world 2009 -'11, 2013; *Eat Out* Best Service Awards

2009 -'11, 2013; 3 stars in *Rossouw's Restaurants* 2009 -'13. (See also A–Z section.)

Spier Restaurants Spier, R310 Baden Powel Road, Stellenbosch ▪ **Eight Restaurant** Tue–Sun 10am–4.30pm & **Eight to Go** 10am–5pm; **Hotel Restaurant** 6.30am–10.30pm daily ▪ Children welcome ▪ Major credit cards accepted ▪ No BYO ▪ Executive chef Lorrianne Heyns ▪ info@spier.co.za ▪ www.spier.co.za ▪ S 33° 58' 24.63" E 018° 47' 2.23" ▪ **T +27 (0)21-809-1100**

Three choices, each offering a different eating experience, but all making the most of zingingly fresh organic produce from Spier farm and local suppliers. At the **Hotel Restaurant,** where chicken and meat dishes are sought-after specialities, linger over breakfast, lunch or dinner, or relax with a glass of wine with bar snacks on the terrace. For the ultimate harvest table or farm-style braai, visit airy and eco-conscious **Eight,** where farm-to-table food is combined in healthy and delicious dishes that turn heartier and warming in winter. If you're into picnics and ready-to-eat food, lovingly prepared to the same principles, book a picnic and sandwiches from **Eight to Go,** which offers an appetising, wholesome feast to enjoy with a bottle of award-winning Spier wine on the shady farm lawns. (See also A–Z section.)

Terroir Restaurant Kleine Zalze Wines, R44, Technopark, Stellenbosch ▪ Provençal ▪ Lunch daily 12–2.30, dinner Mon–Sat 7–9 ▪ Closed Sun eve ▪ Booking advised ▪ Children welcome ▪ Major credit cards accepted ▪ Corkage R50 ▪ Owner Kleine Zalze Wines ▪ Chef Michael Broughton ▪ terroir@kleinezalze.co.za ▪ www.kleinezalze.co.za ▪ S 33° 56' 16.51" E 018° 51' 06.70" ▪ **T +27 (0)21-880-8167** ▪ F +27 (0)21-880-0862

The terroir is decidedly Cape in flavour and setting; so are the food-friendly, highly-rated Kleine Zalze wines. Though deceptively simple dishes are French-inspired, fresh seasonal ingredients are local, showcasing chef Michael Broughton's award-winning culinary skill and impeccably judged sauces. The relaxed ambience encourages lingering over chalkboard offerings like miso glazed salmon with leek and champagne sauce, or pork belly with rhubarb and 'truffle mac' (macaroni). *Eat Out* Awards' Top 10 2006 -'07, 2009 -'12. (See also A–Z section.)

The Big Easy Restaurant & Wine Bar 95 Dorp Street, Stellenbosch ▪ Up-market and contemporary ▪ Open for breakfast, lunch & dinner Mon–Fri 7.30am–10pm, Sat/Sun/pub hols 8.30am–10pm ▪ Retail store open daily from 9–5 (for proprietor's wines at cellar door prices) ▪ Closed Dec 25 ▪ Booking advised ▪ Children welcome ▪ Major credit cards accepted ▪ No BYO ▪ Owners Jean Engelbrecht, Ernie Els, Johann Rupert,

Paul Harris & Giuseppe Cuicci ▪ info@thebigeasy.co.za ▪ www.thebigeasyrestaurant.co.za ▪ S 33° 56' 21.67" E 018° 51' 28.52" ▪ **T +27 (0)21-887-3462** ▪ F +27 (0)21-887-3470

Relax and enjoy hearty meals in a laid-back ambience rich in history. Setting is a gracious Cape Dutch manor house with interleading rooms; service is friendly and efficient, and constantly changing menus celebrate seasonal flavours. Prime chargrilled rump, sirloin and fillet are best-sellers, sharing top spot with a speciality burger. But do try the mushroom risotto with truffle cream, and the sinful 70% chocoholic platter. (See also A–Z section.)

Vergelegen see under Somerset West

Wild Peacock Food Emporium 32 Piet Retief Street, Stellenbosch ▪ Brasserie — Del Foods and Mediterranean ▪ Open Mon–Tue 7.30–6, Wed–Fri 7.30–10pm, Sat/Sun 8–4 ▪ Booking advised evenings ▪ Children welcome ▪ Major credit cards accepted ▪ No BYO ▪ Owner Baker Family Trust ▪ foodemporium@wildpeacock.co.za ▪ www.wildpeacock.co.za ▪ S 33° 56' 24" E 018° 51' 34" ▪ **T +27 (0)21-887-7585** ▪ F +27 (0)86-577-3663

This enticing French-style brasserie-cum-deli oozes temptation, whether shopping for specialities like oysters, snails, fresh duck, quail, fish, free-range poultry, artisanal cheeses and fine wine, or sitting down to eat. Breakfasts are scrumptious; lunches deliciously light or a filling, flavoursome *plat de jour* (pots of Ma Baker's mussels are a must). Excellent, well-priced wine-by-the-glass selection, plus a specialised retail wine boutique focused on the Stellenbosch area. Winner of 'Best Food Outlet in the South' at the Eat Out produce awards 2013.

Zevenwacht Restaurant Zevenwacht Wine Estate, Langverwacht Road, Kuils River ▪ Contemporary global cuisine with modernist influences ▪ Breakfast Mon–Fri 7–10, Sat/Sun & pub hols 8–11; lunch 12–3 & dinner 6–10 daily ▪ Garden picnics ▪ Booking advised ▪ Children welcome ▪ Major credit cards accepted ▪ No BYO ▪ Owner Manie Wolmarans ▪ Executive chef Wesley Peters ▪ restaurant@zevenwacht.co.za ▪ www.zevenwacht.co.za ▪ S 33° 55' 47" E 018° 43' 43" ▪ **T +27 (0)21-900-5800** ▪ F +27 (0)21-903-5257

Tantalise tastebuds in a friendly, relaxed manor house set beside a tranquil lake. Locally sourced ingredients add seasonal appeal to specialities from folded ravioli of mushroom and ricotta, wild rocket and white truffle cream, to entrecote of pork, slow-braised belly and basil-infused crackling with sage and walnut pomme purée, wilted baby pak choi and tomato foam. End indulgently with Belgian white chocolate and lavender brûlée. (See also Accommodation & A–Z sections.)

Tokai

The Brasserie Shop 1, Forest Glade House, Main Road, Tokai ▪ European with French influences ▪ Mon–Fri & pub hols 11.30am–10pm, Sat 9am–10pm, Sun 9am–3pm ▪ Booking advised ▪ Children welcome ▪ Major credit cards accepted ▪ Corkage R30 from 2nd bottle ▪ Owners Chris Coetzee, Peter Weetman, Tammy Botbyl, Stéfan Marais & Julie Galvin ▪ Executive chef Stéfan Marais ▪ info@brasseriect.co.za ▪ www.brasseriect.co.za ▪ **T +27 (0)21-712-1363** ▪ F +27 (0)86-532-6961

The name may have changed, but this unpretentious, accessible neighbourhood 'local' has retained its welcoming home-away-from-home ambience, large marbled diner's bar and popular chef's table in the open-plan kitchen. Flavour-packed favourites change regularly, but the core menu remains focused on the evergreen specialities: home-made pastas, risotto, steak au poivre, mussels and artisanal pizzas. Regulars are greeted by name; there's no rush, and the winelist's well-chosen.

Tulbagh

Readers Restaurant 12 Church Street, Tulbagh ▪ Global contemporary, fusion of flavours ▪ Lunch & dinner Wed–Mon ▪ Closed Tue ▪ Booking advised ▪ Children welcome ▪ Major credit cards accepted (excl. AMEX) ▪ Corkage R25 ▪ Owner Carol Collins ▪ readers@iafrica.com ▪ www.readersrestaurant.co.za ▪ S 33° 17' 14.20" E 019° 08' 19.18" ▪ **T +27 (0)23-230-0087**

Combine history with fresh cordon bleu delights. The oldest house in Church Street, Reader's, was revitalised in 1997 as a restaurant under Silwood-trained chef Carol Collins. 'The best bobotie in town' remains a menu fixture, but try a speciality such as lamb strudel or lightly-smoked salmon trout with pickled ginger and wasabi butter. Unique flavoured ice creams are a definite must. SA Top 100 award-winning restaurant 2012 & '13. TripAdvisor Certificate of Excellence award 2013.

Villiersdorp

Kelkiewyn Restaurant Main Road (R43), Villiersdorp ▪ South African/European cuisine ▪ Breakfast & lunch Mon–Fri 9–4, Sat/Sun 8–4; smart-casual dinners with live piano Wed–Sat 6–10 ▪ Closed some pub hols — call first ▪ Booking advised Sat/Sun ▪ Children welcome ▪ Major credit cards accepted ▪ Corkage R35 ▪ Chef/patron Harry van Kamp ▪ hjvankamp@gmail.com ▪ S 33° 59' 10.37" E 019° 17' 49.07" ▪ **T +27 (0)28-840-0900**

Popular small-town restaurant with associates in Finland and a chef/patron with international experience in executive functions and food-wine pairing. Fresh ingredients are sourced from the valley and tasty dishes combining South African and European influences can be paired with wines from the Villiersdorp Cellar. All Slowine is available by the glass: relish it with the house speciality — a Slowine burger with Slowine caramelised onions. (See also A–Z section.)

Wellington

No. 6 Restaurant @ Welbedacht Wine Estate Oakdene Road, Wellington ▪ Mediterranean & traditional South African ▪ Open Tue–Sat 10–late, Sun 10–3 ▪ Closed Mon, Good Fri & Dec 25 ▪ Children welcome ▪ Major credit cards accepted (excl. AMEX) ▪ No BYO ▪ Owner Schalk Burger ▪ no.6@welbedacht.co.za ▪ www.schalkburgerandsons.co.za ▪ S 33° 34' 39.8" E 019° 1' 12.8" ▪ **T +27 (0)21-873-1877** ▪ F +27 (0)86-669-5641

This gregarious venue for winelovers, sports-lovers and Springbok supporters is a favourite haunt of sporting greats. Integrated into the Welbedacht wine cellar, the down-to-earth restaurant is closely linked to the surrounding vineyards and the wine that complements flavourful food. Best-sellers are tapas, bobotie and other exotic dishes. (See also Accommodation section for Bradgate Manor House & A–Z section.)

The Stone Kitchen Dunstone Winery, Bovlei Road, Wellington ▪ Country cuisine ▪ Open Wed–Sun 9–4 & dinner by reservation ▪ Closed Mon/Tue ▪ Booking advised on Sun ▪ Children welcome ▪ Major credit cards accepted ▪ Corkage R50 ▪ Owner Abigail Wallis ▪ food@dunstone.co.za ▪ www.stonekitchen.biz ▪ S 33° 38' 5.3" E 019° 3' 36.8" ▪ **T/F +27 (0)21-873-6770**

The mood's relaxed; the setting is the most beautiful valley in Wellington — and fresh valley produce rules the country-style, family food on the café-style blackboard menu. Tables in the cool of the cellar offer a glimpse of winemaking during harvest, and alfresco settings are geared for those wanting to take advantage of the spectacular mountain views, expanse of lawn and fun kid's play area. (See also Accommodation section for Bovlei Valley Retreat & A–Z section.)

Accommodation in the Winelands and Cape Town

Featured below are some guest lodges, hotels, country inns, B&Bs and self-catering cottages in the winelands, many of them on wine farms (look for the 🛏 symbol beside the individual entries in the A–Z section of this guide). These are paid entries. The venues supplied information on their facilities and attractions, which was then edited for consistency of style. Unless stated to the contrary, all speak English and Afrikaans, have parking and gardens/terraces. Rates are for standard double rooms unless otherwise specified — for example per person (pp) or breakfast included (B&B). Tourism Grading Council of South Africa (TGCSA) ratings where provided. Should you wish to know about wheelchair access, please discuss with the relevant venue.

Index of accommodation

Listed alphabetically, with region.

Ashton

Pat Busch Mountain Reserve   see under Robertson

Bot River

Barton Villas   Barton Vineyards, R43 Hermanus Road, Bot River ▪ TGCSA 4-star self-catering ▪ 3 villas: 3 or 4 bedrooms per villa ▪ Seasonal rates from R1,900–R4,500 per villa ▪ Major credit cards accepted ▪ Fully equipped kitchen, dishwasher, washing machine & tumble dryer ▪ Pool ▪ Jacuzzi ▪ Tennis ▪ Walks/hikes ▪ Birding ▪ Cellar tours ▪ Wine tasting ▪ Secure parking ▪ Fireplace ▪ DSTV ▪ WiFi ▪ Owner Peter J Neill ▪ info@bartonvineyards.co.za ▪ www.bartonvineyards.co.za ▪ S 34° 15' 43.8" E 019°

10' 29.2" ▪ **T +27 (0)28-284-9283** ▪ F +27 (0)28-284-9776

Unwind in the heart of the Kogelberg Biosphere Reserve near Bot River, where views from three Tuscan-style self-catering villas encompass surrounding mountains, vineyards, olive groves and lavender fields. Each has a spacious open-plan kitchen, dining room, Jacuzzi and view-rich outdoor pool. Just one hour's drive from Cape Town International Airport and 20 minutes from Hermanus, this is a perfect base for exploring the Western Cape. (See also A–Z section.)

Bredasdorp

De Hoop Collection De Hoop Nature Reserve, Bredasdorp ▪ 35 units ▪ From R690pp DB&B ▪ Major credit cards accepted ▪ Restaurant ▪ Conferences ▪ Weddings/functions ▪ Pool ▪ Tennis court ▪ Whale watching ▪ Mountain biking ▪ Walks/hikes ▪ Birding ▪ Boule court ▪ TV (lounge) ▪ WiFi ▪ Owners Stephens, Trieloff & Zeeman families ▪ reservations@ dehoopcollection.co.za ▪ www.dehoopcollection.co.za ▪ S 34° 27' 17.96" E 020° 23' 57.74" ▪ **T +27 (0)21-422-4522** ▪ F +27 (0)28-542-1679

Opt out. Enjoy an outdoor experience that embraces sea, sand dunes, vlei, rare fynbos and mountains. Bird life extends from wading birds to endangered vultures; close-up encounters could include bontebok, Cape mountain zebra, eland, baboons and ostrich. Take scenic game drives; watch whales in season; mountain bike; discover fynbos plains or walk along the deserted coastline; snorkel in turquoise rock pools — or simply enjoy the beach. (See also Restaurants section for The Fig Tree Restaurant.)

Caledon

Boschrivier Farm Accommodation see under Stanford

Calitzdorp

The Retreat at Groenfontein Groenfontein Road, District Calitzdorp (20km from Calitzdorp, off Route 62) ▪ TGCSA 3 & 4-star guest house; AA Quality Assured highly recommended ▪ 8 rooms — garden & standard ▪ Low season: R540–R720pps DB&B; high season: R740–R990pps DB&B ▪ Visa & MasterCard accepted ▪ Restaurant (problem diets catered for, advise when booking) ▪ Pool ▪ Children & pets welcome ▪ Mountain biking ▪ Walking trails ▪ Birding ▪ River with rock pools ▪ Star gazing ▪ Secure parking ▪ Fireplace ▪ Safe ▪ WiFi & TV in lounge ▪ French, German, Italian & Swedish spoken ▪ Owner Marie Holstensson & Grant Burton ▪ info@groenfontein.com ▪ www.groenfontein.com ▪ S 33° 26' 15.6" E 021° 47' 20.9" ▪ **T +27 (0)44-213-3880** ▪ F +27 (0)86-271-5373

A consistent award-winner, this welcoming, personally run 3 and 4-star graded Victorian farmhouse offers both standard and garden rooms. You'll enjoy personal pampering, hearty breakfasts and tasty dinners. The inviting lounge and dining room overlook sweeping lawns and the majestic Swartberg. Take leisurely walks, challenging trails, explore the rock pools in the bird-rich river, or simply chill out at the pool, absorbing up the peace and silence.

Camps Bay

The Twelve Apostles Hotel and Spa Victoria Road, Camps Bay, Cape Town ▪ TGCSA 5-star hotel, part of the family-run Red Carnation Hotel Collection ▪ Member of Leading Hotels of the World ▪ 55 guest rooms, 15 suites & presidential suite ▪ Seasonal rates: R2,182.50–R2,932.50pps B&B, single R4,165–R5,665 B&B ▪ Major credit cards accepted ▪ Azure Restaurant; The Café Grill; The Leopard Bar ▪ Banqueting & conferences ▪ Weddings ▪ Spa ▪ Sauna ▪ Gym ▪ Jacuzzi ▪ 2 pools (1 heated) ▪ 16-seater cinema ▪ Hiking trails ▪ Helipad ▪ Wine tasting ▪ Secure parking ▪ Shuttle service ▪ Children and dogs welcome ▪ Air-conditioning ▪ TV ▪ DVD player ▪ WiFi ▪ Safe ▪ French & German spoken ▪ Owners Red Carnation Hotels ▪ bookta@ 12apostles.co.za ▪ www.12apostleshotel.com ▪ S 33° 58' 59.37" E 018° 21' 31.43" ▪ **T +27 (0)21-437-9000** ▪ F +27 (0)21-437-9055

This 5-star luxury boutique hotel, set on the mountainside between Table Mountain National Park and the Atlantic breakers, has a world-beating location: don't miss the sunset as you sip cocktails on the deck. Individually decorated rooms combine sophistication with serenity; food at Azure restaurant brings the ocean to your plate; a cinema, two pools and world-class spa beckon. Eight minutes by helicopter to the V&A Waterfront. Hotel group founder/president Mrs Beatrice Tollman was recognised as European Hotelier of the Year at the European Hospitality Awards 2012; top international and local awards for 2013 include *Travel + Leisure* (USA) 'World's Best Service': No. 1 City Hotel in Africa and the Middle East; *TripAdvisor* Travelers' Choice: Top 25 Hotels in Africa; Top 25 Hotels in South Africa (2); Top 25 Luxury Hotels in South Africa; Top 25 Hotels for Service in South Africa; *Travel + Leisure* (USA) 500 'The World's Best Hotels'; Top 50 hotels worldwide (41); *Condé Nast Traveler* (USA) Gold List: South Africa — Best Hotels & Resorts; Azure Restaurant American Express Platinum Fine Dining Award. (See also Restaurants section.)

Cape Town

Brooklands House 3 Surbiton Road, Rondebosch, Cape Town ▪ TGCSA 4-star guest house ▪ 4 en-suite rooms ▪ Low season from R495pps B&B, high season from R595pps B&B ▪ Major credit cards accepted ▪ Small conferences & weddings ▪ Pool ▪ Boule court ▪ Secure parking ▪ Shuttle service ▪ Walks/hikes ▪ Birding ▪ Cellar tours ▪ Wine tasting ▪ Ceiling fans ▪ Fireplace ▪ Digital safes ▪ Satellite TV ▪ DVD player ▪ WiFi ▪ Owners Philip & Sandra Engelen ▪ brooklands@ mweb.co.za ▪ www.brooklands-guesthouse.co.za ▪ **T/ F +27 (0)21-689-3594**

Charming Victorian villa, within walking distance of some 7 restaurants, near Newlands rugby and cricket grounds, and less than 15 mins drive from CT

international airport. Breakfast in the sunroom overlooking the garden; dine by prior arrangement; in winter relax beside the drawing room fire. If you're planning Winelands excursions, consult your hosts, wine enthusiasts who planted a petit shiraz vineyard beside the boule court.

Cape Grace Hotel West Quay Road, V&A Waterfront, Cape Town ▪ TGCSA 5-star hotel ▪ 120 rooms ▪ From R5,683–R7,288 per room B&B ▪ Major credit cards accepted ▪ Signal Restaurant; Bascule Whisky, Wine and Cocktail Bar ▪ Luxury yacht charters ▪ Conferences ▪ Weddings/functions ▪ Spa ▪ Sauna ▪ Gym ▪ Outdoor heated pool ▪ Secure parking ▪ Shuttle service ▪ Air-conditioning ▪ Under-floor heating ▪ Satellite TV ▪ DVD player ▪ X-Box Playstation ▪ iPod docking station ▪ WiFi ▪ Lavazza coffee machines in mid-priced rooms & suites ▪ Safe ▪ French, German, Korean, Portuguese, Xhosa & Zulu spoken ▪ Owner Cape Grace ▪ info@capegrace.com ▪ www.capegrace.com ▪ S 33° 54' 29" E 018° 25' 12" ▪ **T +27 (0)21-410-7100** ▪ F +27 (0)21- 419-7622

Setting is a private quay of an international yacht marina, against the backdrop of Table Mountain, between Cape Town's working harbour and bustling Victoria & Alfred Waterfront. Ambience is gracious, capturing the essence of the Cape in furnishings and fabrics that combine local creativity with seductive luxury, reinforcing the warm atmosphere and personalised service that have for years defined the hotel. Cape contemporary restaurant and whisky bar. Showered with annual awards. Latest are: Conde Nast Traveler 2013 Gold List and on the Platinum List (hotels that have made the list for five consecutive years). Rated second of the 25 Best Hotels in the World by Trip Advisor's Travelers Choice 2013; in top 50 of Travel + Leisure's Top 500 list 2013; in the top 3 honeymoon accommodations in Southern & Eastern Africa Live the Magic of Africa 2013. (See also Restaurants section.)

Taj Cape Town Cnr Wale Str & St Georges Mall, Cape Town ▪ TGCSA 5-star hotel ▪ 176 luxury rooms & suites which include a two-bedroom, split-level Presidential suite ▪ Rates on request ▪ Major credit cards accepted ▪ Bombay Brasserie, Mint The Local Grill, Twankey Bar ▪ Weddings, functions and conferences: 7 banqueting & meeting rooms ▪ Jiva Grande Spa ▪ Fully equipped fitness centre ▪ Sauna ▪ Gym ▪ Indoor heated lap pool ▪ Jacuzzi ▪ Walks/hikes ▪ Wine tasting ▪ Secure parking ▪ Shuttle service ▪ Air-conditioning ▪ TV ▪ DVD player ▪ iPod docking station ▪ WiFi ▪ Safe ▪ Indian, Thai, Xhosa & Zulu spoken ▪ Owner Taj Hotels, Resorts & Palaces ▪ sales.capetown@tajhotels.com ▪ www.tajhotels.com ▪ **T +27 (0)21-819-2000** ▪ F +27 (0)21-819-2001

A luxury hotel in the vibrant heart of Cape Town, retaining the architecture and meticulously restored features of two of the Mother City's significant historic buildings. Seventeen new storeys house suites and guestrooms with magnificent mountain and city views, while banqueting and meeting rooms blend past elegance with state-of-the-art technology. Culinary temptations include the Indian specialty Bombay Brasserie, relaxed all-day dining restaurant MINT, and the Champagne, Guinness and Seafood Twankey Bar. Diners Club Platinum Winelist Award 2013 Mint The Local Grill; Diners Club Diamond Winelist Award 2013 Bombay Brasserie; TripAdvisor Travellers' Choice winner 2012 & 2013.

The Twelve Apostles Hotel and Spa see under Camps Bay

Vineyard Hotel & Spa Colinton Road, Newlands, Cape Town ▪ TGCSA 4-star deluxe ▪ 207 rooms ▪ Double from R2,450pps B&B; single from R1,990 B&B ▪ Major credit cards accepted ▪ 3 restaurants: The Square, Myoga & Splash Café ▪ Conferences ▪ Angsana Spa ▪ Health & fitness centre ▪ 2 pools: outdoor & heated indoor ▪ TV ▪ Air-conditioning ▪ Free in-room WiFi ▪ Dutch, French, German & Xhosa spoken ▪ Owners Alexander & George Petousis ▪ hotel@vineyard.co.za ▪ www.vineyard.co.za ▪ S 33° 58' 44.68" E 018° 27' 30.71" ▪ **T +27 (0)21-657-4500** ▪ F +27 (0)21-657-4501

Start your Cape Town adventure from one of its most historic and beautiful settings — the 120 year-old Vineyard Hotel, on the eastern slopes of Table Mountain, near Kirstenbosch Botanical Gardens, the sporting mecca of Newlands, and a short drive from the city. Stroll the idyllic riverside estate, unwind at the internationally-known spa or indulge in top Cape wines and gourmet food at two award-winning restaurants. (See also Restaurants section for The Square.)

Constantia

Constantia Uitsig Hotel and Spa Constantia Uitsig Wine Estate, Spaanschemat River Road, Constantia, Cape Town ▪ TGCSA 4-star hotel ▪ 16 rooms ▪ Low season from R875pps B&B, high season from R1,925pps B&B ▪ Major credit cards accepted ▪ Three restaurants: Constantia Uitsig Restaurant, La Colombe & River Café ▪ The Wine Shop ▪ Wine tasting ▪ Conferences ▪ Weddings/functions ▪ Spa ▪ Sauna ▪ Pool ▪ Walks/hikes ▪ Birding ▪ Secure parking ▪ Air-conditioning ▪ Ceiling fans ▪ Fireplace ▪ Under-floor heating ▪ TV ▪ DVD player ▪ WiFi ▪ Safe ▪ Owner Constantia Uitsig Holdings (Pty) Ltd ▪ reservations@uitsig.co.za ▪ www.constantia-uitsig.com ▪ S 34° 2' 51.9" E 018° 25' 27.5" ▪ **T +27 (0)21-794-6500** ▪ F +27 (0)21-794-7605

A perfect resting place for the discerning traveller. This serene hotel, set among the vineyards of a private wine estate in the shadow of Table Mountain, is

just 20 minutes from Cape Town city centre and the V&A Waterfront. Charmingly furnished rooms overlook tranquil gardens; heartfelt hospitality is backed by friendly service, and three restaurants on the estate offer a tempting choice of eating options. (See also Restaurants & A–Z sections.)

Darling

Darling Lodge Guest House 22 Pastorie Street, Darling ▪ TGCSA 3-star B&B; Greenwood Guide; Portfolio Collection ▪ 6 rooms ▪ Seasonal rates R400–R490pps B&B, single R550–R750 B&B ▪ Visa & MasterCard accepted ▪ Lunch & dinner available on request ▪ Conferences ▪ Weddings/functions ▪ Pool ▪ Tennis ▪ Golf ▪ Horse riding ▪ Mountain biking ▪ Walks/hikes ▪ Birding ▪ Cellar tours ▪ Wine tasting ▪ Secure parking ▪ Shuttle service ▪ Ceiling fans ▪ Safe ▪ WiFi ▪ Guest lounge with DSTV, DVD player, iPod docking station, honesty bar & fireplace ▪ German, Swiss German & French spoken ▪ Owners Stephan Moser & Oliver Studer ▪ info@darlinglodge.co.za ▪ www.darlinglodge.co.za ▪ S 33° 22' 44.16" E 018° 22' 42.73" ▪ **T +27 (0)22-492-3062** ▪ F +27 (0)22-492-3665

Charmingly restored Victorian House in the gentle Darling Valley offers a welcoming blend of old and new in an environment of vineyards, pastures, wheat fields and spectacular wildflower displays. Enjoy the areas' award-winning wines and olives in a gorgeous garden with inviting pool. An hour from Cape Town and minutes from the Atlantic Ocean. Winelands, beaches, whale watching, golf, art galleries, Evita se Perron nearby.

Franschhoek

Allée Bleue Hospitality Intersection R45 & R310, Groot Drakenstein ▪ TGCSA 5-star MESE ▪ 6 rooms ▪ **Kendall Cottage** (5-star) accommodates 4 guests (R1,800); 15 guests for cocktail-style function ▪ **Manor House** (luxury) accommodates 4 guests (two double suites at R2,800 per suite); 40 guests for functions ▪ **Mill House** (4-star) ▪ Rates R400–R900pps B&B ▪ Visa & MasterCard accepted ▪ Allée Bleue Bistro & Restaurant ▪ Picnics ▪ Conferences ▪ Weddings/functions ▪ Herb garden tours ▪ Walks/hikes ▪ Cellar tours ▪ Wine tasting ▪ Secure parking ▪ Air-conditioning ▪ Fireplace (Kendall & Manor House) ▪ TV ▪ DVD player ▪ WiFi ▪ Safe ▪ German spoken ▪ Owners Wilfred & Elke Dauphin ▪ functions@ alleebleue.com ▪ S 33° 51' 55.22" E 18° 58' 56.22" ▪ **T +27 (0)21-874-1021** ▪ F +27 (0)21-874-1850

A choice of accommodation to suit your taste and pocket, from the luxury of the gabled Manor House (two double suites and ideal for weddings) and charming Sir Herbert Baker-designed Kendall cottage, to the comfort of B&B in an old Mill House. All this on a serene wine and fruit estate, complete with wine tasting centre; two restaurants; and herb tours followed by herb-centred lunch. (See also Restaurants & A–Z sections.)

Cabrière Cottage 47 Cabrière Street, Franschhoek ▪ 1 self-catering cottage, with 2 en-suite bedrooms ▪ Seasonal rates: R1,100–R1,300 per room ▪ No credit card facilities — cash or pre-payment via EFT ▪ Plunge pool ▪ Mountain biking ▪ Ceiling fans ▪ Fireplace ▪ DSTV ▪ DVD player ▪ iPod docking station ▪ WiFi ▪ Safe ▪ Owners Matthew & Nicky Gordon ▪ info@ cabrierecottage.com ▪ www.cabrierecottage.com ▪ **T +27 (0)82-455-6411/+27 (0)21-876-4444** ▪ F +27 (0)86-503-2294

Restful self-catering Cabrière Cottage, at the heart of the mountain-ringed Franschhoek village, offers visitors the ideal base for exploring all that the beautiful valley has to offer. The upmarket cottage, with private garden and plunge pool, has two comfortable en-suite bedrooms, spacious open-plan lounge with fireplace, and fully-equipped kitchen — plus the amenities expected by today's travellers: DSTV satellite television, iPod docking station and DVD player.

Franschhoek Country House & Villas Main Road, Franschhoek ▪ TGCSA 5-star country house ▪ 26 rooms ▪ Seasonal rates from R900–R1,300pps B&B ▪ Major credit cards accepted ▪ Monneaux Restaurant ▪ Conferences ▪ Weddings/functions ▪ Spa ▪ Two pools (one heated) ▪ Horse riding ▪ Walks/hikes ▪ Cellar tours ▪ Wine tasting ▪ Secure parking ▪ Shuttle service ▪ Air-conditioning ▪ Ceiling fans ▪ Fireplace ▪ Under-floor heating ▪ TV ▪ DVD player ▪ Free WiFi ▪ Safe ▪ Owner Jean-Pierre Snyman ▪ info@fch.co.za ▪ www.fch.co.za ▪ S 33° 54' 0.64" E 019° 6' 16.55" ▪ **T +27 (0)21-876-3386** ▪ F +27 (0)21-876-2744

Five-star boutique hotel with top-rated Monneaux restaurant in a restored manor house and former perfumery dating back to 1890, on the outskirts of the village, surrounded by vineyards and majestic mountains. Laze at one of the two pools (one heated), enjoy a massage, visit the boutique winefarms in Franschhoek, or take a shuttle service to the charming town. Just an hour's drive from Cape Town. (See also Restaurants section.)

Holden Manz Country House Holden Manz Wine Estate, 3 Green Valley Road, Franschhoek ▪ TGCSA 5-star country house ▪ 5 rooms ▪ Seasonal rates from R1,452–R2,396pps B&B ▪ Visa & MasterCard accepted ▪ Franschhoek Kitchen ▪ Weddings/functions ▪ Spa with revitalising Africology products ▪ Pool ▪ Air-conditioning ▪ Fireplace ▪ Under-floor heating ▪ TV ▪ iPod docking station ▪ WiFi ▪ Safe ▪ French & German spoken ▪ Owners Gerard Holden & Migo Manz ▪ info@ holdenmanz.com ▪ www.holdenmanz.com ▪ S 33°

56' 7" E 19° 6' 54" ▪ **T +27 (0)21-876-2738** ▪ F +27 (0)21-876-4624

5-star tranquility overlooking vineyards. Restrained architecture and soothing, art-filled spaces; ultra-modern en-suite bathrooms offering a near spa-indulgence; muted wall shades and extra-large, sleep-inducing pillows. On warmer days, enjoy a private garden tea in the five guest suites, three of which have their own terraces. On cooler evenings, sip a glass of Holden-Manz award-winning red wine in your suite in front of a crackling log fire. (See also Restaurants & A–Z sections.)

Mont Rochelle Hotel & Mountain Vineyards

Dassenberg Road, Franschhoek ▪ 16 rooms & 6 suites ▪ Seasonal rates: R2,300–R3,500 per room B&B ▪ Major credit cards accepted ▪ Two restaurants: Mange Tout & Country Kitchen ▪ Conferences ▪ Weddings/functions ▪ Spa ▪ Sauna ▪ Gym ▪ Pool ▪ Jacuzzi ▪ Horse riding ▪ Mountain biking ▪ Hiking ▪ Boule court ▪ Cellar tours ▪ Wine tasting ▪ Secure parking ▪ Air-conditioning ▪ Under-floor heating ▪ TV ▪ DVD player ▪ WiFi ▪ Safe ▪ German spoken ▪ Owners Erwin Schnitzler & Rwayitare Family ▪ info@montrochelle.co.za ▪ www.montrochelle.co.za ▪ S 33° 92' 05.20" E 019° 10' 50.53" ▪ **T +27 (0)21-876-2770** ▪ F +27 (0)21-876-3788

Elegant boutique hotel with wrap-round views of vineyards and mountains, plus fine dining and rustic restaurants. Attention to detail is paramount: sink into comfort in individually decorated rooms and luxury suites, each with every convenience. Expect fresh flowers, homemade chocolates and a welcome drink upon arrival, daily local newspaper and scrumptious breakfast every morning. South African Winelist of the year 2012 – 3 Flutes (Western Cape); Tripadvisor Award of Excellence 2012 - '13. (See also Restaurants & A–Z sections.)

Rickety Bridge Manor House

Rickety Bridge Wine Estate, R45 Main Road, Franschhoek ▪ TGCSA 4-star B&B/guest house ▪ 3 rooms on request ▪ Visa & MasterCard accepted ▪ Paulina's restaurant ▪ Conferences ▪ Weddings/functions ▪ Pool ▪ Walks/hikes ▪ Boule court ▪ Cellar tours ▪ Wine tasting ▪ Secure parking ▪ Air-conditioning ▪ Under-floor heating ▪ DSTV ▪ WiFi ▪ Safe ▪ Owner Rickety Bridge ▪ shani@ricketybridge.com ▪ www.ricketybridge.com ▪ S 33° 53' 58.5" E 019° 5' 27.6" ▪ **T +27 (0)21-876-2994** ▪ F +27 (0)21-876-3673

Relax in the stylishly renovated 19th century rooms of this luxury guest house, warmed by personal attention. The patina of the past encourages it: yellow-wood beamed ceilings and pine floors polished with layers of history; Cape Dutch furniture, fire-warmed lounge and country kitchen. Sleep late (it's easy to do) and take breakfast in the quaint

breakfast room or beside the pool in a purple-mountain setting. (See also Restaurants & A–Z sections.)

The Owner's Cottage & La Provençale at Grande Provence

Grande Provence Heritage Wine Estate, Main Road, Franschhoek ▪ TGCSA 5-star guest house ▪ 7 rooms in total ▪ Seasonal rates: Owner's Cottage R2,500–R3,500 per room B&B & La Provençale R2,075–R2,500 per room B&B ▪ Major credit cards accepted ▪ Restaurant ▪ Pool ▪ Jacuzzi ▪ Walks/hikes ▪ Cellar tours ▪ Wine tasting ▪ Secure parking ▪ Air-conditioning ▪ Fireplace ▪ Under-floor heating ▪ TV ▪ DVD player ▪ iPod docking station ▪ WiFi ▪ Safe ▪ Owner Alex van Heeren ▪ reservations@grandeprovence.co.za ▪ www.grandeprovence.co.za ▪ S 33° 53' 57.6" E 19° 06' 10.5" ▪ **T +27 (0)21-876-8600** ▪ F +27 (0)21-876-8601

Two inviting choices: luxurious **Owner's Cottage** and simpler, stylish **La Provençale**. The beautifully appointed cottage has four rooms, a deluxe suite, conservatory, lounge, swimming and spa pool area. Soothing in a grey and white palette, rooms offer an indulgent experience; lush lawns edge the swimming pool. Relaxing La Provençale offers contemporary comfort in two double en-suite bedrooms separated by a lounge, private gardens and pool. (See also Restaurants & A–Z sections.)

Whale Cottage Franschhoek

11 Akademie Street, Franschhoek ▪ 7 rooms ▪ Low season R350–R450pps B&B; high season R550pps B&B ▪ Visa & MasterCard accepted ▪ Small conferences, weddings & functions ▪ Pool ▪ Tennis ▪ Golf ▪ Horse riding ▪ Mountain biking ▪ Hiking ▪ Birding ▪ Cellar tours ▪ Wine tasting ▪ Secure parking ▪ Shuttle service ▪ Air-conditioning ▪ TV ▪ WiFi ▪ German spoken ▪ Owner Chris von Ulmenstein ▪ winelands@whalecottage.com ▪ www.whalecottage.com ▪ S 33° 54' 41" E 019° 07' 22" ▪ **T +27 (0)21-433-2100** ▪ F +27 (0)21-433-2101

Welcome to a whale of a stay at Whale Cottage Franschhoek, a country house with delightful garden, beautiful mountain views and babbling brook, in the heart of South Africa's mountain-ringed gourmet village. Close to restaurants Reuben's and Le Quartier Français, 5 minute drive to excellent winefarm restaurants, the Franschhoek Artisanal Food Route, MCC Route, and Wine Route.

Hermanus

Barton Villas see under Bot River

Hout Bay

Hout Bay Manor

Baviaanskloof Road, Hout Bay ▪ TGCSA 5-star boutique hotel ▪ 19 rooms ▪ Seasonal rates from R1,920–R3,200 per room B&B ▪ Major credit cards accepted ▪ Pure Restaurant ▪ Conferences ▪ Weddings/functions ▪ Inzolo Wellness Suite ▪ Heated

pool ▪ Secure parking ▪ Shuttle service ▪ Air-conditioning ▪ Under-floor heating ▪ TV ▪ DVD player & iPod docking station on request ▪ WiFi ▪ Safe ▪ Xhosa & Zulu spoken ▪ Owner Susan Struengmann ▪ reservations@houtbaymanor.co.za ▪ www.houtbaymanor.co.za ▪ S 34° 2' 35.52" E 018° 21' 38.46" ▪ **T +27 (0)21-790-0116** ▪ F +27 (0)21-790-0118

Relax, be spoilt, unwind and immerse yourself in tranquil luxury in the Republic of Hout Bay. Gracious Hout Bay Manor, built in 1871 and beautifully restored, offers 19 individually decorated en-suite rooms and a casually elegant restaurant and function venue, 'Pure'. An intimate boardroom is ideal for executive meetings or private dinners, while the Inzolo Wellness Suite encourages self-indulgence with massages, facials and other pampering therapies. (See also Restaurants section.)

Kuils River
Saxenburg Estate see under Stellenbosch
Zevenwacht Country Inn see under Stellenbosch

Montagu
Les Hauts de Montagu Guest Lodge 3km from Montagu on Route 62 to Barrydale ▪ TGCSA 4-star country lodge ▪ 10 en-suite rooms ▪ Seasonal rates: R625–R850pps B&B ▪ Visa & MasterCard accepted ▪ Weddings/functions ▪ Small chapel ▪ Pool ▪ Mountain biking ▪ 8 hiking trails ▪ Birding ▪ Boule court ▪ Secure parking ▪ Shuttle service ▪ Ceiling fans ▪ Fireplace ▪ Under-floor heating ▪ Safe ▪ TV ▪ WiFi ▪ French spoken ▪ Owners Myriam & Eric Brillant ▪ info@leshautsdemontagu.co.za ▪ www.leshautsdemontagu.co.za ▪ S 33° 80' 58.96" E 020° 15' 77.23" ▪ **T +27 (0)23-614-2514** ▪ F +27 (0)23-614-3517

Take time out in a peaceful 4-star lodge on a 600 ha olive farm on the slopes of the Langeberg, offering spectacular views of surrounding mountains and olive groves, and bird-rich hiking trails through fynbos. Romantic thatched cottages with spacious en-suite rooms have quaint Victorian bathtubs, plus outdoor showers that make the most of the view. Two hours from Cape Town on the scenic Route 62.

Paarl
Druk My Niet Wine Estate Guest Cottages Bodal Road, Daljosafat, Paarl ▪ 3 self-catering cottages ▪ Rates per cottage per night: Protea R1,000 (sleeps 2), Guava R1,600 (sleeps 4), Fynbos R2,600 (sleeps 6) ▪ Major credit cards accepted ▪ Pool ▪ Walks/hikes ▪ Cellar tours ▪ Wine tasting ▪ Air-conditioning (Fynbos) ▪ Fireplace ▪ TV ▪ WiFi ▪ Safe ▪ German spoken ▪ Owners Georg & Dorothee Kirchner ▪ carlien@dmnwines.co.za ▪ www.dmnwines.co.za ▪ S 33° 41' 23.26" E 019° 1' 40.23" ▪ **T +27 (0)21-868-2393** ▪ F +27 (0)21-868-2392

Break away — and wake to the sound of birds on a boutique wine farm, where original buildings (still extant) date back to 1692. Three charming thatched cottages, fully equipped for self-catering, offer all mod cons from air-conditioning to washing machine and WiFi. Enjoy unspoiled vistas over vineyards and Paarl valley; taste wines, walk or hike; or simply laze at the pool, soaking up the peace. (See also A–Z section.)

Grande Roche Hotel Plantasie Street, Paarl ▪ TGCSA 5-star hotel; Satour 5-star silver ▪ 28 rooms ▪ Low season R2,430–R3,800 per room B&B; High season R3,430–R5,300 per room B&B ▪ Major credit cards accepted ▪ Bosman's Restaurant & Bistro Allegro ▪ Conferences ▪ Weddings ▪ Functions ▪ Fitness room ▪ 2 heated pools ▪ Tennis court ▪ Walks/hikes ▪ Wine tasting ▪ Secure parking ▪ Air-conditioning ▪ Under-floor heating ▪ TV ▪ DVD player ▪ WiFi ▪ Safe ▪ German, Shona & Xhosa spoken ▪ GM Anja Bosken ▪ reserve@granderoche.co.za ▪ www.granderoche.co.za ▪ S 33° 45' 02" E 18° 57' 35" ▪ **T +27 (0)21-863-5100** ▪ F +27 (0)21-863-2220

The only SA member of Small Luxury Hotels of the World, this award-winning luxury estate hotel is a legend for hospitality, attention to detail, beautiful gardens, and culinary delights. Set against a mountain backdrop, it's a relaxing base from which to explore the Cape. Laze at the pools, visit the fitness centre, enjoy excellent golf nearby or tour the numerous wine farms in close proximity. Diner's Club winelist Diamond Award 2013. (See also Restaurants section.)

Laborie Guest House Laborie Wine Farm, Taillefer Street, Paarl ▪ 11 rooms ▪ From R585–R960pps B&B ▪ Full English breakfast included in room rates ▪ Major credit cards accepted ▪ Harvest restaurant ▪ Conferences ▪ Weddings/functions ▪ Pool ▪ Walks/hikes ▪ Boule court ▪ Cellar tours ▪ Wine tasting ▪ Secure parking ▪ Shuttle service ▪ Air-conditioning ▪ TV ▪ DVD player ▪ WiFi ▪ Safe ▪ German spoken (request prior to arrival) ▪ Owner KWV (Pty) Ltd ▪ info@laboriewines.co.za ▪ www.laboriewines.co.za ▪ S 33° 45' 57.64" E 018° 57' 31.84" ▪ **T +27 (0)21-807-3093**

Relax in Cape French-style elegance, surrounded by history. Spacious individually furnished guest rooms (one in the gracious, architecturally important Manor House, built in 1750 and proclaimed a national monument in 1977), overlook sweeping lawns, vineyards and the majestic Drakenstein. Exclusive dinners at the Manor House may be arranged for a maximum of 40 guests, and the farm's popular Harvest restaurant specialises in contemporary Cape cuisine. (See also Restaurants & A–Z sections.)

Mooi Bly Horse Shoe at Bo Dal Road, Dal Josafat, Paarl ▪ 5 self-catering cottages (each sleeping up to 6) ▪ Breakfast can be booked upfront ▪ From R220–R450pppn, depending on length of stay, season & number of guests ▪ Visa & MasterCard accepted ▪ Pool ▪ Walks/hikes ▪ Cellar tours ▪ Wine tasting ▪ Fan ▪ Fireplace ▪ TV ▪ Dutch spoken ▪ Owners Wouters family ▪ info@mooibly.com ▪ www.mooibly.com ▪ S 33° 41' 14" E 019° 01' 17" ▪ **T/F +27 (0)21-868-2808, C +27 (0)82-371-2299**

'Mooi Bly' translates as 'keep well'. You'll not only keep well but stay well at these delightful thatched cottages on a family wine farm on the Du Toitskloof mountain slopes. Surrounded by vineyards, secluded in a large garden with swimming-pool, all are spacious, fully-equipped, charmingly furnished and serviced on a regular basis. Just 10 minutes to Paarl and Wellington and 30 to Stellenbosch and Franschhoek. (See also A–Z section.)

Riebeek Kasteel

The Royal Hotel 33 Main Street, Riebeek Kasteel ▪ AA Superior Hotel ▪ 10 rooms ▪ Low season R695pps B&B, high season R750pps B&B ▪ Major credit cards accepted ▪ Restaurant ▪ Conferences ▪ Weddings/functions ▪ Golf ▪ Walks/hikes ▪ Cellar tours ▪ Wine tasting ▪ Secure parking ▪ Air-conditioning ▪ Under-floor heating ▪ Safe ▪ TV ▪ DVD player ▪ WiFi ▪ Owners Robert & Carminda Brendel ▪ info@royalinriebeek.com ▪ www.royalinriebeek.com ▪ S 33° 22' 59.51" E 018° 53' 47.80" ▪ **T +27 (0)22-448-1378** ▪ F +27 (0)22-448-1073

The extensively refurbished Royal has catered for both national and international guests for over seven generations (today's visitors welcome mod-cons like air-conditioning and under-floor heating). The restaurant offers menus highlighting fresh local ingredients, the winelist is extensive, and the 'longest stoep south of the Limpopo', once the spot for G&T's, now accommodates guests sipping house wine from the region, with the hotel on the label.

Robertson

Ballinderry, The Robertson Guest House 8 Le Roux Street, Robertson ▪ TGCSA 4-star guest house ▪ 7 rooms ▪ Low season R450–R680pps B&B; High season R490–R700pps B&B; single on request ▪ Major credit cards accepted ▪ Restaurant only for stay-over guests, bookings 24-hrs in advance ▪ Pool ▪ Secure parking ▪ Air-conditioning ▪ DSTV ▪ WiFi ▪ Safe ▪ Dutch/Flemish, French & German spoken ▪ Owners Luc & Hilde Uyttenhove ▪ info@ballinderryguesthouse.com ▪ www.ballinderryguesthouse.com ▪ S 33° 48' 02.40" E 019° 53' 13.58" ▪ **T +27 (0)23-626-5365** ▪ F +27 (0)86-742-8692

Relish fine wines and delectable food at this contemporary guest house in the heart of Robertson, where hands-on Belgian owners, Luc and Hilde, pamper guests with personal service. The thatched villa in a large and tranquil tropical garden offers five double rooms and two pool suites. Near the region's best-known wineries and an 18-hole golf course. Champagne breakfast included in room rates; dinner reservations essential.

Fraai Uitzicht 1798 Klaas Voogds East, on R60 between Robertson & Montagu ▪ TGCSA 4-star guest house ▪ 9 units consisting of luxury cottages & garden suites ▪ From R550pps B&B ▪ Major credit cards accepted ▪ Restaurant ▪ Pool ▪ Walks/hikes ▪ Birding ▪ Cellar tours ▪ Wine tasting ▪ Secure parking ▪ Air-conditioning ▪ Fireplace, under-floor heating, TV & DVD player (cottages only) ▪ WiFi for resident guests in restaurant area ▪ German, Xhosa & Zulu spoken ▪ Owners Karl Uwe & Sandra Papesch ▪ info@fraaiuitzicht.com ▪ www.fraaiuitzicht.com ▪ S 33° 47' 43.13" E 20° 0' 17.99" ▪ **T +27 (0)23-626-6156** ▪ F +27 (0)86-662-5265

Fraai Uitzicht lives up to its name 'Beautiful View'. Stylishly appointed guest cottages and suites overlook the Robertson Wine Valley, Sonderend Mountains, fruit orchards and vineyards — some at the door. Comfort characterises Cape Dutch-style cottages with reed ceilings; cottages beside the historic wine cellar retain the period charm of the 1800s, and individually appointed suites with private entrances, offer spacious bedrooms and all en-suite facilities. (See also Restaurants & A–Z sections.)

Pat Busch Mountain Reserve Klaasvoogds West, Robertson ▪ 7 self-catering cottages & 1 large farmhouse ▪ Rates from R240–R395pppn ▪ Visa & MasterCard accepted ▪ Conferences ▪ Weddings/functions ▪ Jacuzzi ▪ Mountain biking ▪ Hiking ▪ 4x4 route ▪ Birding ▪ Swimming & fishing in mountain dams ▪ Boule court ▪ Cellar tours ▪ Wine tasting ▪ Air-conditioning ▪ Ceiling fans ▪ Fireplace ▪ WiFi ▪ German spoken ▪ Owners Stephan & Lindi Busch ▪ cottages@patbusch.co.za ▪ www.patbusch.co.za ▪ S 33° 46' 34" E 019° 59' 47" ▪ **T +27 (0)23-626-2033** ▪ F +27 (0)86-573-2156

Escape to an unspoiled reserve, ringed by mountains, at the end of a country road. Owned and managed by husband and wife Stephan and Lindi Busch, this peaceful getaway offers self-catering accommodation in cosy cottages, large farmhouse and two exclusive units sleeping a total of 48 guests. The rustic banquet hall and meadows are an ideal venue for events from conferences to retreats or weddings.

The Robertson Small Hotel 58 Van Reenen Street, Robertson ▪ TGCSA 5-star hotel ▪ 10 suites ▪ Low season from R850pps B&B, high season from R950pps B&B; single supplement R200 ▪ Major credit cards

accepted ▪ Reuben's at The Robertson ▪ The Wellness Room ▪ 2 pools ▪ Secure parking ▪ Air-conditioning ▪ Under-floor heating ▪ TV ▪ DVD player ▪ iPod docking station ▪ WiFi ▪ Electronic safe ▪ Complimentary mini-bar contents ▪ Wheelchair-friendly with suite specifically for the disabled ▪ Owners Tim Rands, Gys Naude & Marc Kent ▪ GM Riaan Kruger ▪ reservations@therobertsonsmallhotel.com ▪ www.therobertsonsmallhotel.com ▪ S 33° 48' 00.8" E 019° 52 47.6" ▪ **T +27 (0)23-626-7200** ▪ F +27 (0)23-626-1680

Sophisticated outer-city hospitality at its best. Natural hues and rich textures cocoon air-conditioned luxury suites in tranquillity, while eclectic furnishings fuse modern design with space and comfort. The Victorian manor house is home to a cosy bar-lounge and state-of-the-art wine cellar, backdrop to signature restaurant, Reuben's at the Robertson. Manicured lawns and inviting pools encourage relaxation; the pampering wellness room will revitalise body and spirit. Best Luxury Country Hotel in South Africa — World Luxury Hotel Awards 2012.

Route 62
Les Hauts de Montagu see under Montagu

Somerset West
Eikendal Lodge see under Stellenbosch

Somerton Manor Guesthouse 13 Somerset Street, Bridgewater, Somerset West ▪ TGCSA 4-star guesthouse ▪ 12 rooms ▪ Low season R475pps B&B, high season R650pps B&B ▪ Major credit cards accepted ▪ Conferences ▪ Weddings/functions ▪ Spa ▪ Sauna ▪ Gym ▪ Pool ▪ Jacuzzi ▪ Birding ▪ Cellar tours ▪ Wine tasting ▪ Secure parking ▪ Shuttle service ▪ Air-conditioning ▪ Ceiling fans ▪ Fireplace ▪ Under-floor heating ▪ Safe ▪ TV ▪ DVD player ▪ WiFi ▪ Dutch & German spoken ▪ Owner Antonie van den Hurk ▪ info@somerton.co.za ▪ www.somerton.co.za ▪ S 34° 5' 27" E 18° 51' 23" ▪ **T +27 (0)21-851-4682** ▪ F +27 (0)21-851-4672

Styled with Cape Dutch elegance, blending old world charm with modern facilities. Luxurious en-suite bedrooms; Jacuzzi, sauna, and heated-swimming pool; gym to keep toned. Wine from the cellar to enjoy in the tranquil garden, lapa, or on the veranda. A golfer's paradise: 20 courses nearby and reduced green fees at Erinvale golf club. 30 minutes from Cape Town international airport, with easy access to major tourist attractions.

Stanford
Boschrivier Farm Accommodation Remhoogte, Caledon (on the R326 between Caledon & Stanford) ▪ Self-catering ▪ 4 rooms ▪ Rate R800 per night up to 6 people, then R150pp extra up to 9 people & R200 cleaning fee ▪ Major credit cards accepted ▪ Restaurant ▪ Mountain biking ▪ Hiking trails ▪ 4x4 route ▪

Birding ▪ Fishing ▪ Canoeing ▪ Wine tasting ▪ Fireplace ▪ Safe ▪ TV ▪ DVD player ▪ Owner NJT de Villiers ▪ drnjtdevilliers@mweb.co.za ▪ S 34° 23' 19.4" E 019° 37' 51.0" ▪ **T +27 (0)28-341-0630/+27 (0)23-347-3313** ▪ F +27 (0)23-342-2215

Take time out on a working winefarm at the foot of the Klein River mountain range. The typical veranda-shaded farmhouse, dating back to 1689, offers four comfortable bedrooms with spectacular views; relaxing lounge with fireplace; modern kitchen and braai facilities. Self-cater or breakfast in the farm restaurant, taste wine, mountain-bike through vineyards, hike through wild flowers and fynbos, or canoe on the dam or river. (See also A–Z section.)

Springfontein Guest House Springfontein Wine Estate, Springfontein Road, Stanford ▪ 7 rooms ▪ R1,200pps B&B ▪ Major credit cards accepted ▪ Restaurant ▪ Conferences ▪ Weddings/functions ▪ Pool ▪ Tennis court ▪ Golf course ▪ Horse riding ▪ Walks/hikes ▪ Birding ▪ Fishing ▪ Cellar tours ▪ Wine tasting ▪ Secure parking ▪ Shuttle service ▪ Fireplace ▪ WiFi ▪ French & German spoken ▪ Owners Weber & Schneider families ▪ hospitality@springfontein.co.za ▪ www.springfontein.co.za ▪ S 34° 25' 38.5" E 019° 24' 32.7" ▪ **T +27 (0)28-341-0651** ▪ F +27 (0)28-341-0112

Johst and Jennifer Weber of Springfontein, have joined forces with Jürgen and Susanne Schneider, owners and executive directors of Michelin Star restaurants and a Relais and Château Hotel in Germany. Well-known for owning 'the last Michelin star before Moscow', the Schneiders are now shooting for SA's first 'Michelin Star' for Springfontein. Expect terroir-driven wines; a nature-driven kitchen; and sustainable rooms from guesthouse to delightful cottages. Jürgen Schneider, executive chef of Gutshaus Stolpe, Relais & Château Restaurant and Hotel: Michelin Star 1998–2000; 1999–today Michelin Star as executive chef of Strahlenberger Hof, Schriesheim, Germany. (See also Restaurants & A–Z sections.)

Stellenbosch
Brenaissance Wine & Stud Estate Devon Valley Road, Stellenbosch ▪ 9 suites ▪ Seasonal rates: Vineyard suites R750–R950 per room; Luxury/bridal suite R1,200–R1,950 per room ▪ Picnic breakfast box R100pp extra ▪ Major credit cards accepted ▪ Café Blanc de Noir ▪ Conferences ▪ Weddings/functions ▪ Walks/hikes ▪ Birding ▪ Wine tasting ▪ Air-conditioning ▪ TV (Vineyard suites) ▪ WiFi ▪ Owners Tom & Hayley Breytenbach ▪ stay@brenaissance.co.za ▪ www.brenaissance.co.za ▪ S 33° 55' 4.31 E 018° 49' 7.82" ▪ **T +27 (0)21-200-2537**

Escape to serenity. This secluded Devon Valley estate offers visitors & guests a unique destination encompassing premier wines, opulent venues, luxury

accommodation, chic Café Blanc de Noir (think wine, gourmet pizzas and craft beer) and a sighting of their Boran Cattle Stud. An ideal base for exploring the region, or simply enjoying the tranquil gardens and views of vineyards, plum orchards, surrounding mountains and bird-life. (See also Restaurants & A–Z sections.)

Caledon Villa 7 Neethling Street, Stellenbosch ▪ TGCSA 3-star guest house ▪ Portfolio 'great comfort'▪ National monument ▪ 15 rooms ▪ Low season R440-R500pps B&B, high season R525–R600pps B&B ▪ Visa & MasterCard accepted ▪ Conferences ▪ Pool ▪ Secure parking ▪ Shuttle service ▪ Air-conditioning & fireplaces in some rooms ▪ Ceiling fans ▪ TV ▪ WiFi ▪ Safe ▪ German spoken ▪ Owners Johan & Ode Krige ▪ info@caledonvilla.co.za ▪ www.caledonvilla.co.za ▪ S 33° 56' 15" E 018° 51' 55" ▪ **T/ F +27 (0)21-883-8912**

Explore the historic heart of Stellenbosch with its restaurants, shops and art galleries on foot from this splendid Edwardian house. The owner's in-depth research into history, culture, genealogy, wine and art is reflected in the character and ambience of the villa. Enjoy the colour-play of sunset on the mountains from the roof terrace and expect expert assistance in the planning of any outings and tours!

Delaire Graff Lodges & Spa Delaire Graff Estate, R310 Helshoogte Pass, Banhoek Valley, Stellenbosch ▪ TGCSA 5-star lodges; Relais & Chateaux ▪ 10 lodges (8 x 1-bedroom/2 x 2-bedroom) ▪ Seasonal rates: Luxury Lodge (vineyard view) R8,600–R10,920 B&B; Deluxe Lodge (garden view) R7,750–R9,820 B&B ▪ Rates include daily newspaper, Delaire wine tasting in wine lounge, daily transfers to and from Stellenbosch, guided vineyard walks & art tours, evening sparkling wine & canapés served in each lodge, cinema room (max 10 guests) ▪ Major credit cards accepted ▪ Delaire Graff & Indochine Restaurants ▪ Art collection ▪ Weddings/functions ▪ Spa ▪ Sauna ▪ Gym ▪ Pool ▪ Jacuzzi ▪ Mountain biking ▪ Hiking ▪ Cellar tours ▪ Secure parking ▪ Each lodge has private heated pool, butler's kitchen, en-suite bedrooms & separate sitting area ▪ Air-conditioning ▪ Fireplace in Owner's Lodge ▪ Under-floor heating in bathroom ▪ LED flat screen TV ▪ DVD player ▪ iPod docking station ▪ WiFi ▪ Safe ▪ German & Spanish spoken ▪ Owner Laurence Graff ▪ lodge.reservations@delaire.co.za ▪ www.delaire.co.za ▪ S 33° 55' 20.4" E 018° 55' 26.0" ▪ **T +27 (0)21-885-8160** ▪ F +27 (0)86-626-4403

Indulge yourself in an idyllic setting. Secluded luxury lodges on the Helshoogte mountain slopes, each with a private plunge pool and sweeping views across vineyards and mountains, invite complete relaxation. Enjoy art and design, gourmet cuisine, award-winning wines and revitalise at a world-class spa. For the more active, excursions include vineyard walks, wine tasting and visits to the nearby historic towns of Stellenbosch and Franschhoek. Best of Wine Tourism award for accommodation 2012 & '11. (See also Restaurants & A–Z sections.)

Devonvale Golf Lodge Devonvale Golf & Wine Estate, Bottelary Road, Stellenbosch/Koelenhof ▪ TGCSA 4-star lodge & hotel ▪ 60 rooms ▪ Seasonal rates from R980–R1,300 per room ▪ Buffet breakfast R100pp ▪ Major credit cards accepted ▪ Chez Shiraz restaurant ▪ Conferences ▪ Weddings/functions ▪ Spa ▪ Gym ▪ Pool ▪ Golf course ▪ Mountain biking ▪ Walks/ hikes ▪ 4x4 route ▪ Birding ▪ Fishing ▪ Boule court ▪ Wine tasting ▪ Secure parking ▪ Shuttle service ▪ Air-conditioning ▪ TV ▪ DVD player ▪ WiFi ▪ Safe ▪ German spoken ▪ Owner JJ Provoyeur ▪ hotel@devonvale.co.za ▪ www.devonvale.co.za/accommodation ▪ S 33° 52' 59.6" E 018° 48' 15.0" ▪ **T +27 (0)21-865-2080** ▪ F +27 (0)21-865-2113

Relax to a warm welcome in a spectacular vineyard setting, against the backdrop of the Simonsberg. Stylish, comfortable accommodation ranges from hotel rooms ideal for the business traveller, to self-catering apartments and luxurious holiday houses. Unwind: enjoy the championship golf course or boule court; laze at the pool; revitalise at the spa; go birding or fishing, or sample Provoyeur wines in the comfortable restaurant bar. (See also Restaurants & A–Z sections.)

Eendracht Hotel 161 Dorp Street, Stellenbosch ▪ TGCSA 3-star hotel ▪ AA Travel superior hotel ▪ 15 rooms ▪ Seasonal rates R499–R649pps B&B ▪ Major credit cards accepted ▪ Pool ▪ Air-conditioning ▪ TV ▪ Free uncapped high-speed internet ▪ Safe ▪ Owner Daniël Lutz ▪ info@eendracht-hotel.com ▪ www.eendracht-hotel.com ▪ S 33° 56' 19.13" E 018° 51' 46.15" ▪ **T +27 (0)21-883-8843** ▪ F +27 (0)21-883-8842

Experience the historic ambience of Dorp Street in the comfort of a delightfully restored, owner-run village hotel with award-winning service and friendly coffee bar offering breakfast, light lunch and traditional SA treats. Within easy walking distance of over 30 restaurants, antique shops, museums, and art galleries. Easy access to numerous golf courses; centrally placed for the Stellenbosch Wine Route; 30 minutes to CT International Airport. AA Accommodation Award — winner in small hotel/inn category 2009 -'11 and Hall of Fame 2012.

Eikendal Lodge Eikendal Vineyards, R44, between Somerset West & Stellenbosch ▪ TGCSA 4-star country house; AA Superior ▪ SATOUR approved ▪ 9 rooms ▪ Low season R580pps B&B, high season R998pps B&B; single supplement +10% ▪ Major credit cards accepted ▪ Restaurant ▪ Conferences ▪ Weddings/

functions ▪ Pool ▪ Mountain biking ▪ Walks/hikes ▪ Birding ▪ Fly fishing ▪ Cellar tours ▪ Wine tasting ▪ Willie Haas cheetah outreach facility ▪ Secure parking ▪ Shuttle service ▪ Air-conditioning ▪ TV ▪ WiFi ▪ Safe ▪ Owner Rudolf Saager ▪ info@eikendallodge.co.za ▪ www.eikendallodge.co.za ▪ S 34° 00' 51.16" E 018° 49' 42.42" ▪ **T +27 (0)21-855-3617** ▪ F +27 (0)21-855-3862

Relax and enjoy a custom-tailored, authentic Winelands experience, with fine wines and true hospitality. Surrounded by vineyards, the welcoming lodge has nine spacious en-suite rooms, each with private terrace. Breakfast al fresco against the backdrop of the Helderberg; in season, savour complimentary evening snacks and wine. Take a cellar tour and taste wines; meet cheetah cubs (seasonal); learn to fly-fish or hike through unspoiled fynbos. Regional Winner in annual AA Accommodation Awards, in the Country-Style Retreats category; InnKeeper.com silver plaque, awarded to establishments upholding exceptional service standards. (See also A–Z section.)

Laibach Vineyards Lodge　Laibach Vineyards, R44, Klapmuts Road, Stellenbosch ▪ TGCSA 4-star self-catering ▪ 5 apartments ▪ R495pps; single R850 ▪ Major credit cards accepted ▪ Pool ▪ Walks/hikes ▪ Wine tasting ▪ Secure parking ▪ Ceiling fans ▪ Fully-equipped small kitchen with bar fridge, microwave and induction plate ▪ LCD satellite TV ▪ WiFi ▪ Safe ▪ Owners Laibach Family ▪ info@laibachwines.com ▪ www.laibachwines.com ▪ S 33° 50' 41.67" E 018° 51' 43.88" ▪ **T +27 (0)21-884-4511** ▪ F +27 (0)21-884-4848

Self-cater surrounded by organic vines on a 50 ha working wine farm, where five comfortably spacious, fully-equipped apartments, each with an en-suite bathroom with shower, open on to a view-rich deck. Taste wines, hike or walk, or laze at the pool. Only 40 minutes from Cape Town, 15 from Paarl and Stellenbosch and 20 from Franschhoek. Beaches, golf courses, restaurants and wine farms within easy reach. (See also A–Z section.)

Lanzerac Hotel & Spa　1 Lanzerac Road, Stellenbosch ▪ TGCSA 5-star hotel ▪ 48 rooms & suites ▪ Seasonal rates from R1,225–R1,790pps B&B ▪ Major credit cards accepted ▪ Governors Hall & The Terrace Restaurants ▪ Esquire Cigar & Whiskey Lounge ▪ Die Taphuis ▪ Conferences ▪ Weddings/functions ▪ Spa & Wellness Centre ▪ Sauna ▪ Pool ▪ Jacuzzi ▪ Horse riding ▪ Mountain biking ▪ Walks/hikes ▪ Birding ▪ Cellar tours ▪ Wine tasting & cellar tours ▪ Secure parking ▪ Shuttle service ▪ Air-conditioning ▪ Under-floor heating ▪ Satellite TV ▪ WiFi ▪ Minibar ▪ Safe ▪ GM Hans Steyn ▪ info@lanzerac.co.za ▪ www.lanzerac.co.za ▪ S 33° 56' 14.7" E 018° 53'

35.5" ▪ **T +27 (0)21-887-1132** ▪ F +27 (0)21-887-2310

Established over 300 years ago, this serene five-star hotel on a 155 ha working wine estate is perfectly placed for exploring the winelands. Spacious, antique-filled bedrooms and suites lead onto private patios with magnificent views. Dine elegantly or casually to suit your mood; taste wine and pair with delicacies at the Lanzerac Cellar; rejuvenate at the spa: appropriately, all therapy oils are based on grapes. (See also Restaurants & A–Z sections.)

Lovane Boutique Wine Estate & Guesthouse　Polkadraai Road (M12), Vlottenburg, Stellenbosch ▪ TGCSA 4-star guesthouse ▪ 9 rooms ▪ Low season R262.50–R553pps B&B, high season R400–R750pps B&B ▪ Major credit cards accepted (excl. Diners) ▪ Conferences ▪ Pool ▪ Cellar tours ▪ Wine tasting ▪ Secure parking ▪ Air-conditioning ▪ Satellite TV ▪ WiFi ▪ Safe ▪ Owners Philip & Gail Gous ▪ info@lovane.co.za ▪ www.lovane.co.za ▪ S 33° 57' 09.74" E 018° 48' 02.38" ▪ **T +27 (0)21-881-3827** ▪ F +27 (0)21-881-3546

Just 5 km outside Stellenbosch, this 4-star rated, comfortable guesthouse offers air-conditioned rooms with stylish décor. Wake to views of mountains and vineyards; enjoy a homemade breakfast in the dining area or outside on the wooden deck. Relax at the pool, taste wine in the boutique cellar, or explore the area: the guesthouse is ideally placed for visiting historic Stellenbosch or top wine farms nearby. (See also A–Z section.)

Majeka House　26–32 Houtkapper Street, Paradyskloof, Stellenbosch ▪ TGCSA 5-star country house ▪ 22 rooms ▪ Low season from R900pps B&B; high season from R1,150pps B&B ▪ Major credit cards accepted ▪ Makaron Restaurant ▪ Conferences ▪ Sanctuary Spa with full range of treatments, sauna, steamroom & fitness centre ▪ 2 pools + 1 heated indoor pool ▪ Jacuzzi ▪ Secure parking ▪ Air-conditioning ▪ DSTV ▪ DVD player ▪ WiFi ▪ Lavazza coffee machine ▪ Mini bar ▪ Safe ▪ French spoken ▪ Owners Karine Dequeker-van der Merwe & Lloyd van der Merwe ▪ reservations@majekahouse.co.za ▪ www.majekahouse.co.za ▪ S 33° 58' 04.07" E 018° 51' 39.64" ▪ **T +27 (0)21-880-1549** ▪ F +27 (0)21-880-1550

One of the most stylish boltholes in the Cape Winelands, this owner-managed and blissfully private 5-star country house combines a prime location with luxurious accommodation, thoughtful service, a sophisticated bar and restaurant, professionally run spa and spacious grounds. An ideal base for exploring historical Stellenbosch with its museums, galleries and café culture, with numerous well-known vineyards and restaurants along the Stellenbosch wine route in easy distance. International A'Design

Award and bronze medal in the interior design category 2012. (See also Restaurants section.)

Morgenhof Manor House Morgenhof Wine Estate, Klapmuts Road (R44), Stellenbosch ▪ 5 en-suite rooms ▪ Seasonal rates: R395–R495pps B&B ▪ Major credit cards accepted ▪ Restaurant ▪ Conferences ▪ Weddings/functions ▪ Pool ▪ Horse riding ▪ Mountain biking ▪ Walks/hikes ▪ Cellar tours ▪ Wine tasting ▪ Secure parking ▪ Fireplace ▪ Under-floor heating ▪ Tea & coffee making facilities ▪ Self-catering kitchen ▪ Owner La Tour International Investments t/a Morgenhof Wines ▪ wendy@morgenhof.com ▪ www.morgenhof.com ▪ S 33° 53' 38.5" E 018° 51' 39.2" ▪ **T +27 (0)21-889-2034** ▪ F +27 (0)21-889-5266

Experience the relaxed food and wine lifestyle of a wine estate dating back to 1692. The gracious gabled manor house, refurbished with en-suite rooms and well-equipped self-catering kitchen, allows you to absorb the past in comfort. Breakfast in the cosy coffee shop or under the vines; lunch is available at the estate restaurant. Centrally located on the R44 just 4 km outside Stellenbosch. (See also Restaurants & A–Z sections.)

Natte Valleij Farm Natte Valleij, Klapmuts Road (R44), between Stellenbosch and Paarl ▪ TGCSA 3-star B&B & self-catering ▪ 2 cottages — both private with patio and BBQ — Vineyard cottage (sleeps 6) & Cellar cottage (sleeps 2 adults + 2 children) ▪ B&B R390pp; self-catering varies depending on cottage, season & length of stay ▪ Owners Charles & Charlene Milner ▪ milner@intekom.co.za ▪ www.nattevalleij.co.za ▪ S 33° 50' 3.6" E 018° 52' 43.2" ▪ **T +27 (0)21-875-5171**

Step into the past. Ideal for families or a group of friends, this historic wine farm in the prime wine-making 'Muldersvlei bowl' area, with a magnificent Cape Dutch homestead, was the original land grant of the area. Relaxing rural ambience; secluded pool set in the large garden. Wonderful walking through vineyards or the neighbouring game reserve where wildebeest, zebra, springbok, bontebok, gemsbok and eland graze. (See also A–Z section.)

Saxenburg Estate Polkadraai Road, Kuils River ▪ 3 self-catering apartments: bachelor, 1-bedroom & 3-bedroom ▪ R680 per room ▪ Major credit cards accepted ▪ The Guinea Fowl Restaurant ▪ Conferences ▪ Weddings/functions ▪ Pool ▪ Walks/hikes ▪ Wine tasting ▪ Secure parking ▪ Fireplace ▪ TV ▪ DVD player ▪ WiFi ▪ Safe ▪ German spoken ▪ Owners Bührer family ▪ info@saxenburg.co.za ▪ www.saxenburg.co.za ▪ S 33° 56' 47.9" E 018° 43' 9.4" ▪ **T +27 (0)21-903-6113** ▪ F +27 (0)21-903-3129

Shed stress in the idyllic surroundings of a view-rich working farm only 20 minutes from Cape Town International Airport, 30 minutes from Cape Town and 10 from Stellenbosch. Three inviting, colour-bright and fully secure Cape Dutch-style apartments share a swimming pool and are fully equipped for self-catering (including barbeque facilities). Should you choose to relax rather than cook, book at the estate's popular restaurant. (See also A–Z section.)

Sugarbird Manor Devon Valley Road, Stellenbosch ▪ TGCSA 4-star guesthouse ▪ 9 rooms ▪ Seasonal rates: double R1,000–R1,450 per room B&B; single R700–R1,160 B&B ▪ Major credit cards accepted ▪ Conferences ▪ Weddings ▪ Pool ▪ Hiking ▪ DSTV ▪ Air-conditioning & ceiling fan ▪ Owner Ginny Povall ▪ reservations@sugarbirdmanor.co.za ▪ www.sugarbirdmanor.co.za ▪ S 33° 54' 18.5" E 018° 49' 25" ▪ **T +27 (0)21-865-2313/+27 (0)76-340-8296**

Comfortable meets chic; welcoming detail meets delightful destination. Eclectic in design, this 4-star guesthouse on a protea and wine farm adds a respectful twist of city sophistication to the Cape Wineland's country roots. Whether for a long holiday or short break, the 21 ha of gorgeous flowers and vineyards provides a perfect base for exploring the Winelands — or just chilling out in quiet luxury. (See also A–Z section for Botanica Wines.)

Tarentaal Cottage Tarentaal Farm, Polkadraai Road, Stellenbosch ▪ Self-catering cottage (sleeps 4) ▪ Seasonal rates from R1,250–R1,650 per unit ▪ No credit card facilities ▪ Mountain biking ▪ Hikes ▪ Birding ▪ Secure parking ▪ Air-conditioning ▪ Fireplace ▪ TV ▪ DVD player ▪ Manager Luzanne Gerstner ▪ info@tarentaalcottage.co.za ▪ www.tarentaalcottage.co.za ▪ S 33° 58' 4.98" E 018° 45' 8.39" ▪ **T +27 (0)71-484-0248** ▪ F +27 (0)28-313-0435

Relax and enjoy the vineyard tapestry surrounding you in a self-catering cottage on a boutique wine farm. Stellenbosch central is 10 minutes away: stroll down Dorp Street with its coffee shops, restaurants and galleries; or taste wine on the many wine farms nearby. The fully furnished cottage is open-plan, with undercover porch and braai facility, and serviced after 10 days, to allow for holiday privacy. (See also A–Z section for Van Biljon Wines.)

The Devon Valley Hotel Devon Valley Road, Devon Valley, Stellenbosch ▪ TGCSA 4-star hotel ▪ 50 suites ▪ Seasonal rates from R525–800pps B&B ▪ Major credit cards accepted ▪ Flavours Restaurant ▪ Conferences ▪ Weddings/functions ▪ 2 Pools ▪ Jacuzzi ▪ Mountain biking ▪ Walks/hikes ▪ Birding ▪ Boule court ▪ Wine tasting ▪ Secure parking ▪ Shuttle service ▪ Air-conditioning ▪ Ceiling fans ▪ Fireplaces (some) ▪ TV ▪ WiFi ▪ Safe ▪ German spoken ▪ Owner Louis Group Hotels, Spa's & Vineyards ▪ info@devonvalleyhotel.com ▪ www.devonvalleyhotel.com ▪ S 33° 54' 12.64" E 18° 48' 53.03" ▪ **T +27 (0)21-865-2012** ▪ F +27 (0)21-865-2610

For 'handmade hospitality' discover this award-winning haven, hidden in a shady, green and peaceful corner of the Stellenbosch winelands. The 50 stylish suites reflect the contemporary-cum-colonial feel of the hotel, enjoying unobstructed views of mountains, vineyards and olive groves, while the spacious luxury rooms and executive suites in the Manor House are the hotel's premier offering, ideal for a romantic escape or a rejuvenating retreat. Tripadvisor Travellers Choice award 2013. (See also Restaurants section & A–Z for SylvanVale.)

The Residence and Cottage at Haskell Vineyards
Annandale Road, Lynedoch, Stellenbosch ▪ Seasonal rates: Residence R2,065–R2,650 & Cottage R950-R1,350; rates discounted for stays of 3 weeks or longer ▪ Major credit cards accepted ▪ Long Table Restaurant ▪ Conferences ▪ Weddings/functions ▪ Mountain biking ▪ Walks/hikes ▪ Birding ▪ Cellar tours ▪ Wine tasting ▪ Secure parking ▪ Air-conditioning ▪ Ceiling fans ▪ Fireplace ▪ DSTV ▪ DVD player ▪ iPod docking station ▪ WiFi ▪ Owner Preston Haskell ▪ theresidence@haskellvineyards.com ▪ www.haskellvineyards.com ▪ S 34° 0' 13.9" E 018° 51' 38.4" ▪ **T +27 (0)21-881-3895** ▪ F +27 (0)21-881-3986
Two view-rich, tempting accommodation options: the spacious, two-bedroom, two-bathroom The Residence, surrounded by vines, where the stylish interior, created by a leading local interior designer, exudes contemporary comfort; or the loft-style cottage, ideal for two guests. Both within walking distance of the farm's unpretentious Long Table restaurant, where flavoursome food and a creative winelist with Haskell and Dombeya wines, is available in a convivial ambience. (See also A–Z section.)

Zevenwacht Country Inn Zevenwacht Wine Farm, Langverwacht Road, Kuils River ▪ TGCSA 4-star country house ▪ Total 38 rooms: 1 honeymoon suite (deluxe), 12 Country Inn luxury suites, 7 x 3-bedroom cottages, 1 x 4-bedroom self-catering chalet ▪ Low season from R380pps B&B; high season from R455pps B&B ▪ Major credit cards accepted ▪ Restaurant ▪ Gift shop ▪ Picnics ▪ Conferences ▪ Weddings/functions ▪ Mangwanani Spa ▪ Sauna ▪ Pool ▪ Tennis court ▪ Mountain biking ▪ Walks/hikes ▪ 4x4 route ▪ Birding ▪ Cellar tours ▪ Wine tasting ▪ Secure parking ▪ Shuttle service ▪ Air-conditioning ▪ TV ▪ WiFi ▪ Tea/coffee making facilities ▪ Hairdryer ▪ Trouser press ▪ Safe ▪ Xhosa spoken ▪ Owner Harold Johnson ▪ info@zevenwacht.co.za ▪ www.zevenwacht.co.za ▪ S 33° 55' 47" E 018° 43' 43" ▪ **T +27 (0)21-900-5700** ▪ F +27 (0)21-906-1570
A choice of accommodation on a multi-faceted wine farm, from luxury suites in the Country Inn to vineyard cottages and self-catering chalet with spectacular views of Table Bay and False Bay. Restaurant in the historic manor house open daily for breakfast, lunch and dinner; garden picnics also available. Facilities for weddings, launches and conferences; cheesery, wine tasting centre, gift shop and Mangwanani African Day Spa. Superior Accommodation: Fine Country Estates. (See also Restaurants & A–Z sections.)

Wellington

Bovlei Valley Retreat Bovlei Road, Wellington ▪ TGCSA 4-star guest house ▪ 5 guest suites in converted stables/farm cottage and 1 self-catering cottage ▪ Seasonal rates R550–R850pps B&B ▪ Major credit cards accepted ▪ The Stone Kitchen restaurant ▪ Weddings/functions ▪ Pool ▪ Mountain biking ▪ Walks/hikes ▪ Birding ▪ Fishing ▪ Boule court ▪ Cellar tours ▪ Wine tasting ▪ Secure parking ▪ Air-conditioning ▪ Fireplace ▪ Under-floor heating ▪ DSTV ▪ DVD player ▪ iPod docking station ▪ WiFi ▪ Safe ▪ Owners Abbi & Lee Wallis ▪ info@bvr.co.za ▪ www.bvr.co.za ▪ S 33° 38' 5.3" E 019° 3' 36.8" ▪ **T/F +27 (0)21-864-1504**
Idyllic retreat on a working wine & fruit estate at the foot of the Limietberg mountains. Self-cater in a farm cottage, or relax in delightfully converted guest suites. Breakfast overlooking mountains; lunch lazily at the winery restaurant; take afternoon tea in the rose and lavender-scented garden; taste wine with nibbles at sunset and enjoy gourmet dining from the in-house chef. (See also Restaurants section & A–Z section for Dunstone Winery.)

Bradgate Manor House 2 Commissioner Street, Wellington ▪ TGCSA 3-star B&B ▪ 6 en-suite rooms ▪ R400–R450pps B&B ▪ Major credit cards accepted (excl. AMEX) ▪ Tennis court ▪ Cellar tours & wine tasting at Welbedacht Wine Estate ▪ Secure parking ▪ Air-conditioning ▪ TV ▪ DVD player ▪ WiFi ▪ Safe ▪ Owners Schalk & Myra Burger ▪ myra@welbedacht.co.za ▪ www.bradgatemanor.co.za ▪ **T +27 (0)21-873-1877**
Sojourn in Victorian splendour. Built in 1903 in imposing British colonial style, Bradgate was named after the home of England's nine-day queen, Lady Jane Grey. It remained a private home until the Burger family moved to Welbedacht wine estate in 2001, renovating and adding modern conveniences, but leaving most of the family antiques and paintings. (See also Restaurants for No. 6 & A–Z sections.)

Druk My Niet Wine Estate Guest Cottages see under Paarl

Mooi Bly
see under Paarl

Disabled Access in SA Wineries

The guide's accessibility audit initiative first featured in the 2002 edition and then, as now, intended to verify that venues which are open to the public at set times, and aim to be disabled friendly, in fact are accessible.

'Accessibility for All' is the intent of the initiative, not only wheelchairs which the international icon seems to suggest, but a much wider section of the special-needs community including people who are visually impaired, the hearing impaired, the elderly, children in prams and others.

The accessibility audit project is carried out in conjunction with the Disability Solutions team of Guy Davies, who initiated the project in 2000, and Jeremy Hazell, the leg-man for this guide. The evaluations cover both new and recently upgraded venues, and the results are incorporated into the relevant producer entries in the A-Z section of this book, in the form of the universally recognisable wheelchair icon, as well in the look-up tables which accompany the maps.

Wineries open only by appointment are excluded, as it is felt that in these cases visitors can ascertain their individual requirements when making an appointment.

It is worth noting that the audits cover fours aspects, namely parking, the tasting area, toilet facilities and cellar tours, if offered. The focus is on the tasting area, however, and in the A-Z directory we display the wheelchair icon for wineries whose tasting areas is considered accessible.

While Guy and Jeremy base their assessments on the principles of universal design (making things safer, easier and more convenient for everyone), they try to be sensitive to the practical implications for each winery. In agricultural, rural and historical settings it is often a real challenge to ensure that access conforms to international standards.

The 2002 guide featured 104 wineries that had been assessed and shown in the guide as accessible. The 2014 guide has 253 wineries featured as

being accessible. This does illustrate the willingness of the wine industry to make the effort to be inclusive of a wider audience. The guide believes that the right attitude to accommodating visitors at venues is very important, with 'friendly' being the key word.

Wine Tourism is an integral part of South Africa's tourism offering, in which service is king. Accessibility should be seen as a core service.

An amusing anecdote from Guy's earlier farm visits occurred at the establishment that had a precipitous stairway from the car park down to the tasting room, with no ramp in sight. On phoning the farm, Guy was asked to wait a few minutes. The owner arrived with four employees to carry him down to the tasting room, with the explanation that We are wheelchair friendly because we all smile when we carry disabled peoples down the stairs! While we don't accept this as a legitimate access method, disabled people do respond very positively to a helpful and positive attitude.

Bear in mind that wineries which are not flagged as accessible in the A-Z or the map tables do not necessarily have deficient or non-existent disabled facilities; it might simply be that we are not in a position to comment on them.

With Jeremy crisscrossing the winelands every year with his wheelchair and hand-controlled car, assessment of accessibility at wine tasting venues is a continual work in progress. So we invite readers who have any comments and suggestions about the project to please contact Jeremy Hazell through our offices or directly on his mobile +27 (0)82-377-3498, or email jeremy@disability.solutions.co.za.

We'd like to take the opportunity to wish our readers pleasant and safe travels around the winelands. Do connect with us on Twitter (@ wineonaplatter) or Facebook (www.facebook.com/platterswineguide) and share your experiences with us. We're looking forward to hear from you.

WINELANDS MAPS

The maps in this section show locales where wine is available for tasting/sale either at set times or by appointment. The larger-scale map below shows the areas covered by the maps, and the table starting on the next page lists some details for prospective visitors.

Areas covered by the maps

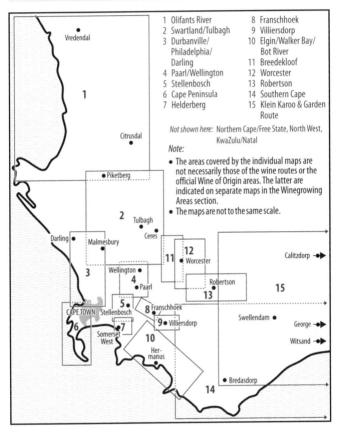

1 Olifants River	8 Franschhoek
2 Swartland/Tulbagh	9 Villiersdorp
3 Durbanville/ Philadelphia/ Darling	10 Elgin/Walker Bay/ Bot River
4 Paarl/Wellington	11 Breedekloof
5 Stellenbosch	12 Worcester
6 Cape Peninsula	13 Robertson
7 Helderberg	14 Southern Cape
	15 Klein Karoo & Garden Route

Not shown here: Northern Cape/Free State, North West, KwaZulu/Natal

Note:
- The areas covered by the individual maps are not necessarily those of the wine routes or the official Wine of Origin areas. The latter are indicated on separate maps in the Winegrowing Areas section.
- The maps are not to the same scale.

Some distances from Cape Town (kilometres)

Calitzdorp	370	Paarl	60	Tulbagh	120
Franschhoek	75	Robertson	160	Vredendal	300
Hermanus	120	Stellenbosch	45	Worcester	110

Key for maps

- ═══ Main access roads
- ── Roads
- ······ Gravel roads

R62 R60 Road numbers

● Towns

Details of Locales Shown on Maps

The tables below are intended to facilitate winery visits by providing summary information about all the winetasting venues which are open to the public, either at set times or by appointment, and appear on our winelands maps. Venues are listed by region, and details provided include a **map grid-reference**, if applicable; whether the particular venue is **open only by appointment** (T); **open on Saturdays and/or Sundays** (√ = at set times; T = by appointment); **open on public holidays** (X = closed all public holidays; otherwise assume open all or some holidays); and whether **meals/refreshments are available** (BYO = bring your own picnic). Other details include availability of **accommodation, cellar tours** and **facilities for children**. Venues which have tasting facilities **friendly to individuals with reduced mobility**, as audited by our disability consultants, are highlighted. **Other languages spoken** (besides English and Afrikaans) are also noted (Danish = da, Dutch/Flemish = nl, French = fr, German = de, Hebrew = he, Hungarian = hu, Italian = it, Japanese = ja, Mandarin = mdr, Norwegian = nn, Portuguese = pt, Romanian = ro, Russian = ru, Setswana = tn, Spanish = sp, Swedish = sv, Swiss = gsw, isiXhosa = xh, isiZulu = zu). For more information, **particularly items marked with an asterisk**, see the A-Z and Restaurants/Accommodation sections. For **GPS coordinates**, where known, for wineries open to the public, see the relevant A-Z entries.

Breedekloof Map Map	Grid reference	Open by appt. only	Open Saturdays	Open Sundays	Open public holidays	Meals/refreshments	Accomodation	Cellar tours	Disabled friendly	Child friendly	Languages spoken
Aufwaerts Co-operative		T									
Avondrood Vineyards			T			T/BYO*	√	√		√	
Badsberg Wine Cellar			√		X	T/BYO*		√*	√	√	
Bergsig Estate			√			√		T	√	√	
Botha Wine Cellar			√			BYO		T	√		
Breëland Winery		T*				T/BYO*	√	T			
Dagbreek		T			X	BYO		T			
De Breede Organic Vineyards		T									
Du Preez Estate			√		X	BYO		T*	√		
Du Toitskloof Winery			√			√/BYO*		T	√		de
Goudini Wines			√			√*		T			
Jason's Hill Private Cellar			√			√		T	√	√	
Kirabo Private Cellar			T		X	T/BYO		√		√	
Ladera Artisan Wines		T*				T*		T			sp
Lateganskop Winery								T			
Lorraine Private Cellar					X	T/BYO*		√			
Merwida Winery			√				√		√		
Mountain Oaks Organic Winery		T						T			
Mountain Ridge Wines					X	BYO			√		
Olifantsberg Family Vineyards		T*									
Opstal Estate			√	T		√*		√	√	√	
Rico Suter Private Cellar		T				T/BYO*	√	T			de/fr/it
Slanghoek Winery			√			T*		T	√		de
TCB Wines					X	BYO	√	√			

	Grid reference	Open by appt. only	Open Saturdays	Open Sundays	Open public holidays	Meals/refreshments	Accomodation	Cellar tours	Disabled friendly	Child friendly	Languages spoken
uniWines Vineyards			✓			BYO		✓*	✓		
Waboomsrivier Wine Cellar					✗			T*			
Cape Peninsula Map											
Ambeloui Wine Cellar		T									
Beau Constantia			✓	✓							
Buitenverwachting			✓		✗	✓		T	✓		
Cape Point Vineyards			✓	✓		✓*		✓	✓	✓	
Cape to Cairo Wines		T									
Constantia Glen			✓	✓		✓*					
Constantia Mist	T*					BYO	✓				
Constantia Uitsig			✓	✓		✓	✓		✓		
Eagles' Nest			✓	✓		✓			✓		
Emineo Wines		T									
Groot Constantia Estate			✓	✓		✓		✓	✓	✓	de/fr/nl
High Constantia Wine Cellar			✓			T/BYO		✓			
Hout Bay Vineyards		T						T		✓	de
Klein Constantia Estate			✓	✓*					✓		fr/sv
Mzoli's Wines			✓	✓		✓					xh
Signal Hill Wines			✓*		✗	✓		✓			fr
Steenberg Vineyards			✓	✓		✓	✓	✓	✓		
The Township Winery											
Vaughan Johnson's Wine & Cigar Shop											
Durbanville, Philadelphia & Darling Map											
Altydgedacht Estate			✓			✓		T		✓	
Bloemendal Estate			✓	✓		✓			✓		
Capaia Wine Estate			T	T	✗	✓		✓			de
Cloof Wine Estate			✓			✓*		T	✓		
D'Aria Winery			✓	✓		✓	✓				nl
Darling Cellars			✓					T	✓	✓	xh
De Grendel Wines			✓	✓		✓		T	✓		
Diemersdal Estate			✓	✓		✓/BYO		T			
Durbanville Hills			✓	✓		✓		✓*	✓	✓	
Groote Post Vineyards			✓	✓		✓/BYO*		✓	✓	✓	
Hillcrest Estate			✓	✓		✓		T			
Klein Roosboom			✓	✓		✓/BYO*		✓	✓		
Kronendal Boutique Winery		T	✓			✓*		T	✓		
Lanner Hill		T*									
Meerendal Wine Estate			✓	✓		✓	✓	T	✓	✓	xh/zu
Nitida Cellars			✓	✓		✓			✓	✓	
Nomada Wines			✓	✓							

	Grid reference	Open by appt. only	Open Saturdays	Open Sundays	Open public holidays	Meals/refreshments	Accomodation	Cellar tours	Disabled friendly	Child friendly	Languages spoken
Ormonde Private Cellar			✓			T/BYO*		T*	✓	✓	
Phizante Kraal			✓								
Russo Family Vintners			T		×			✓			
Signal Gun Wines			✓	✓		✓					
Vierlanden Boutique Family Cellar		T*			×			T*			
Wines of Cape Town		T									
Withington			✓	✓							

Elgin, Walker Bay & Bot River Map

	Grid reference	Open by appt. only	Open Saturdays	Open Sundays	Open public holidays	Meals/refreshments	Accomodation	Cellar tours	Disabled friendly	Child friendly	Languages spoken
Alheit Vineyards		T									
Almenkerk Wine Estate			✓	✓		✓/BYO*		✓*			nl/fr
Arumdale Cool Climate Wines			✓	✓							
Ashbourne		T						T			
Ataraxia Wines			✓	✓*							
Barry Gould Family Wines		T				T*	✓	T		✓	
Barton Vineyards			✓				✓	✓	✓		
Beaumont Wines			✓				✓	✓	✓		
Belfield Wines		T						T			
Benguela Cove			✓*			BYO		✓			
Blomendahl Vineyards		T									de
Boschrivier De Villiers Family Vineyards			✓			✓/BYO	✓	✓			
Bouchard Finlayson			✓		×	✓/BYO*		✓	✓		de/fr
Catherine Marshall Wines		T				T		T			
Charles Fox Cap Classique Wines		T*	✓	✓				✓*		✓	
Corder Family Wines			T	T	×						
Creation Wines			✓	✓		✓		✓	✓	✓	de/fr
Dispore Kamma Boutique Winery		T						T			
Domaine des Dieux			✓*	✓*							
Eerste Hoop Wine Cellar		T*						T			
Elgin Ridge		T*				✓/BYO*		T*			fr
Elgin Vintners		T									
Feiteiras Vineyards		T									pt
Gabriëlskloof			✓			✓		T	✓	✓	
Glen Erskine Estate		T				BYO		T			de
Goedvertrouw Estate		T				T	T			✓	
Hamilton Russell Vineyards			✓					T			tn/xh
Hannay Wines			T	T		T/BYO*		T			
Hermanuspietersfontein Wynkelder			✓	✓*		✓*	✓	T	✓		
Highlands Road Estate			✓	✓		✓		✓	✓	✓	
Hornbill Garagiste Winery			✓			✓	✓	✓			
Iona Vineyards			T		×			✓			

	Grid reference	Open by appt. only	Open Saturdays	Open Sundays	Open public holidays	Meals/refreshments	Accomodation	Cellar tours	Disabled friendly	Child friendly	Languages spoken
Jakob's Vineyards		T									
La Vierge Private Cellar			✓	✓		✓		T	✓		fr
Lothian Vineyards		T*					✓				sp
Luddite Wines			T	T				T	✓		nl
Mofam Wines			✓	✓		✓	✓			✓	
Mount Babylon Vineyards		T						T			
Newton Johnson Vineyards			✓		X	✓			✓		
Oak Valley Wines			✓	✓		✓	✓		✓		it/fr
Oneiric Wines		T				BYO					
Oude Molen Distillery			T	T	T						
PaardenKloof		T*						T			xh
Paul Cluver Estate Wines			✓						✓		
Paul Wallace Wines		T*									
Raka			✓			BYO		T	✓		
Restless River		T			X	T/BYO*		T			
Rivendell			✓	✓		✓				✓	
Robert Stanford Estate			✓	✓		✓*				✓	
Ross Gower Wines		T					✓				fr/de
Shannon Vineyards		T*									
South Hill Vineyards			✓	✓			✓		✓		
Southern Right			✓					✓	✓		
Spioenkop Wines		T			X	BYO	✓	T		✓	fr/nl
Spookfontein Wines		T					✓	T			
Springfontein Wine Estate			✓	✓		✓/BYO	✓	✓			
Stanford Hills Winery			✓	✓		✓*	✓		✓		
Sumaridge Wines			✓	✓		✓	✓		✓	✓	
Vaalvlei Wines		T*					✓				
Walker Bay Vineyards			✓	✓		✓/BYO		T	✓	✓	
Whalehaven Wines			✓	✓				T			
Wildekrans Wine Estate			✓	✓		T*	✓	✓	✓		
William Everson Wines		T					✓	T			
Wine Village-Hermanus			✓	✓					✓		
Winters Drift			✓	✓*		✓					

Franschhoek Map

	Grid reference	Open by appt. only	Open Saturdays	Open Sundays	Open public holidays	Meals/refreshments	Accomodation	Cellar tours	Disabled friendly	Child friendly	Languages spoken
Akkerdal Wine Estate					X		✓				
Allée Bleue Wines			✓	✓		✓	✓	T	✓	✓	de
Anthonij Rupert Wyne			✓	✓*		✓			✓		
Bellingham			✓	✓		✓*					
Black Elephant Vintners		T						T			
Boekenhoutskloof Winery					X				✓		xh

	Grid reference	Open by appt. only	Open Saturdays	Open Sundays	Open public holidays	Meals/refreshments	Accomodation	Cellar tours	Disabled friendly	Child friendly	Languages spoken
Boschendal Wines			✓	✓		✓		✓	✓	✓	
Cape Chamonix Wine Farm			✓	✓		✓	✓	T	✓		
Colmant Cap Classique & Champagne		T*						T	✓		fr
Dieu Donné Vineyards			✓	✓		✓		T*			
Eikehof Wines			✓*					✓*			
Four Paws Wines		T									
Franschhoek Cellar			✓	✓		✓/BYO*		✓			
GlenWood			✓*	✓*		✓		✓	✓		
Grande Provence Heritage Wine Estate			✓	✓		✓	✓	✓*	✓		
Haut Espoir		T			×			T	✓		
Haute Cabrière			✓	✓		✓		✓*	✓		fr/de
Holden Manz Wine Estate			✓	✓		✓	✓	✓	✓		de
La Bri Estate			✓			✓*		✓			
La Chataigne			✓	✓	×		✓				sv
La Chaumiere Estate		T						T			
La Couronne Wines			✓			✓*				✓	
La Motte			✓			✓			✓	✓	xh
La Petite Ferme Winery			✓*	✓*		✓	✓	✓			
La Petite Vigne		T						T			
Landau du Val		T									
Le Manoir de Brendel			✓	✓		T*	✓			✓	
Leopard's Leap Family Vineyards			✓	✓		✓				✓	
Lynx Wines			T	T	T	BYO		✓*			de/sp
Maison			✓	✓		✓					
Mont Rochelle			✓	✓		✓	✓	✓			
Môreson			✓	✓		✓		✓			
My Wyn			T	T	T	T*		✓			
Plaisir de Merle			✓	T*		✓*	✓*	✓	✓	✓	de
Rickety Bridge Winery			✓	✓		✓	✓	✓	✓	✓	
Solms-Delta			✓	✓		✓		T			
Stony Brook			✓*		T		✓		✓		
The House of GM&Ahrens		T			×	T		T			
Topiary Wines		T				T/BYO		T	✓		
Helderberg Map											
Aeternitas Wines		T			×						
Anatu Wines		T			×			T			fr/he
Avontuur Estate			✓	✓		✓		T	✓		de/pt
BLANKbottle		T*									
Cape Classics		T									
Chennells Wines		T*			×			T			de/sp

	Grid reference	Open by appt. only	Open Saturdays	Open Sundays	Open public holidays	Meals/refreshments	Accommodation	Cellar tours	Disabled friendly	Child friendly	Languages spoken
Conspirare		T									
Croydon Vineyard Residential Estate			✓					T	✓	✓	
Driefontein		T			×						
Eikendal Vineyards			✓	✓		✓*	✓	✓	✓	✓	de
Equitania		T			×	BYO					
Fish Hoek Wines											
Flagstone Winery			✓					T	✓		
Foothills Vineyards		T				T	✓				
Grangehurst			✓*	✓*			✓				
Hathersage		T*			×						
Helderberg Wijnmakerij					×						
Heron Ridge		T			×	T*		T			
Idiom Wines		T*									it
Journey's End Vineyards		T*				T/BYO*		T			
JP Bredell Wines		T									
Ken Forrester Wines			✓	✓*		✓*			✓		
Kumala											
Le Riche Wines			T		×			✓			de
Lithos Wines		T			×			T			
Longridge Wine Estate			✓			✓		T			
Lourensford Wine Estate			✓	✓		✓		✓	✓		
Lyngrove		T	✓	✓		✓*	✓				
Micu Narunsky Wines		T									
Miravel		T			T	T	✓				nl/fr
Moordenaarskop		T						T			
Morgenster Estate			✓	✓							
Mount Rozier Estate		T*					✓	T			
Onderkloof		T					✓	T			
Osbloed Wines		T*						T*			
Pfeifer's Boutique Wines		T									gsw/de
Post House Vineyards			T		×	BYO	✓	✓	✓		
Romond Vineyards		T*					✓	T*			
Skaap Wines						T*	✓			✓	nl
Somerbosch Wines			✓	✓		✓		T	✓	✓	
Somerset Wines			✓	×							
Stonewall Wines		T*				T					
The Winery of Good Hope		T			×						fr/sv
Vergelegen Wines			✓	✓		✓		✓*	✓	✓	
Waterkloof			✓	✓		✓		T	✓		
Waterstone Wines		T			×		✓	T			
Wedderwill Wine Estate			T		T	BYO	✓	✓*	✓		de

	Grid reference	Open by appt. only	Open Saturdays	Open Sundays	Open public holidays	Meals/refreshments	Accomodation	Cellar tours	Disabled friendly	Child friendly	Languages spoken
Yonder Hill			✓*		✗				✓		
Klein Karoo & Garden Route Map											
Andersons Wines		T			✗						
Axe Hill		T						T			
Barrydale Winery & Distillery			✓			BYO		T			
Bergwater Winery			✓	✓		T/BYO	✓	T	✓		
Boplaas Family Vineyards			✓					T		✓	
Bramon Wines			✓	✓		✓		T	✓	✓	
Calitzdorp Cellar			✓			T/BYO		T	✓		
De Krans			✓			✓/BYO*			✓	✓	
Domein Doornkraal			✓			✓*	✓				
Du'SwaRoo		T*			✗						
Excelsior Vlakteplaas		T									
Fernskloof Wines			✓	T*		BYO	✓			✓	sp
Garden Route Wines			✓*						✓		
Grundheim Wines			✓						✓		
Herold Wines			✓			✓*	✓	✓	✓	✓	
Hillock Wines			✓	✓		✓/BYO	✓	✓			
Jakkalsvlei Private Cellar			✓			✓/BYO					
Joubert-Tradauw Wingerde & Kelder			✓			✓	✓	✓	✓	✓	
Karusa Vineyards			✓			✓		✓			
Ladismith Winery & Distillery			✓			✓		T	✓		
LuKa Wine Estate											
Mimosa Boutique Wines			✓	✓		✓	✓		✓	✓	de/gsw
Mons Ruber Wine Estate			✓		✗	BYO					
Montagu Wine & Spirits Co			✓						✓		
Montagu Wine Cellar					✗				✓		
Newstead Lund Family Vineyards		T				T*					zu
Packwood Wines					✗	T*	✓				
Peter Bayly Wines		T						T			
Plettenvale Wines		T					✓				
Quinta do Sul		T									
Reiersvlei			✓			T*		✓			
SoetKaroo Wine Estate			✓						✓		de
Star Hill			✓	✓		✓	✓	T		✓	
The Goose Wines		T				T					
TTT Cellar Calitzdorp			✓	T		BYO		✓	✓		
Withoek		T					✓	T			
KwaZulu-Natal Map											
Abingdon Wine Estate		T*	✓	✓		✓*	✓	T			

	Grid reference	Open by appt. only	Open Saturdays	Open Sundays	Open public holidays	Meals/refreshments	Accomodation	Cellar tours	Disabled friendly	Child friendly	Languages spoken
Highgate Wine Estate			✓	✓		✓				✓	de
Northern Cape, Free State & North West Map											
Bezalel-Dyasonsklip Wine Cellar			✓			✓*		✓		✓	nl
Die Mas van Kakamas			T	T		T/BYO*	✓	✓*	✓		
Douglas Wine Cellar					×			T			
Hartswater Wine Cellar								T			
Landzicht GWK Wines					×	T		T*			
Orange River Wine Cellars			✓		×			✓*	✓		
Olifants River Map											
Bellpost		T						T			
Cape Rock Wines		T				BYO		T			
Cecilia Wines		T									
Cederberg Private Cellar			✓	✓*		BYO	✓				
Desert Rose Wines		T									
Driehoek Wines			✓			BYO	✓			✓	
Fryer's Cove Vineyards			✓			✓/BYO*		✓	✓		
Klawer Wine Cellars			✓		×	BYO			✓	✓	
Lutzville Cape Diamond Vineyards			✓			✓		✓	✓		de
Matzikama Organic Cellar		T									
Melkboomsdrift Wines						✓*	✓				
Namaqua Wines			✓			✓*		✓*	✓	✓	
Seal Breeze Wines			✓			T/BYO		✓	✓	✓	
Sir Lambert Wines		T*				✓/BYO*	✓			✓	
Stellar Winery					×			T			
Stoumann's Wines			T		×	T		✓			
Teubes Family Wines			✓			BYO	✓	T			
Tierhoek		T*			×	BYO*	✓	T*			
Vleiland Wines		T*				BYO					
Paarl & Wellington Map											
African Terroir	C1	T			×			T			fr
Alkmaar Boutique Vineyard	G2		✓					T			
Andreas Wines	G1	T*			×		✓	T			sv
Anura Vineyards	C7		✓	✓		✓		✓	✓		de
Arra Vineyards	C8		✓								
Avondale	F6	T*						T	✓		
Ayama Wines	B2	T			×	T/BYO					it
Babylonstoren	D8		✓	✓		✓*	✓	T	✓		
Backsberg Estate Cellars	D8		✓	✓		✓/BYO		T	✓	✓	
Bayede!	E6		T	T	×						
Bergheim	E6	T									

	Grid reference	Open by appt. only	Open Saturdays	Open Sundays	Open public holidays	Meals/refreshments	Accomodation	Cellar tours	Disabled friendly	Child friendly	Languages spoken
Bernheim Wines	D1, E3	T			×			T	✓		
Black Pearl Vineyards	D5	T*					✓	T*	✓		
Blouvlei Wyne	G2		T		×			✓*			de
Boer & Brit	G2										de/fr/nl/sp/xh
Boland Kelder	E4		✓					T	✓		
Bosman Family Vineyards	G1	T						T			
Boutique Baratok	E5		✓	✓	×	✓		✓			
Bovlei Cellar	G2		✓						✓		
Calais Wine Estate	F4	T*					✓				
Crows Nest	D3		T	T	T	T/BYO		✓		✓	
Damarakloof	A7	T*									
De Compagnie Wine Estate	H1	T*			×	BYO	✓	T*			
De Villiers Wines	E6	T									
De Zoete Inval Estate	E6	T									
Diemersfontein Wines	F2		✓	✓		✓	✓	T			
Diners Club Bartho Eksteen Academy	C3	T				T/BYO		T		✓	
Domaine Brahms Wineries	C3	T			T			T			
Doolhof Wine Estate	H1		✓	✓		✓*	✓	T	✓		
Doran Vineyards	D1	T*	✓	✓					✓		
Druk My Niet Wine Estate	F4	T			×	T/BYO	✓	T			de
Dunstone Winery	H1		✓	✓		✓	✓	✓		✓	
Eenzaamheid	B5	T									
Fairview	D6		✓	✓		✓		✓			
Freedom Hill Wines	F7		✓	✓*				✓			
Glen Carlou	D7		✓	✓		✓		T	✓	✓	de
Groot Parys Estate	E5	T									nl
Hawksmoor at Matjieskuil	A7	T*				T*	✓				fr/de/ja
Hildenbrand Wine, Olive & Art Estate	G2		✓	T*		✓	✓	✓			de
Imbuko Wines	F4		T		×	T*					
Jacaranda Wine & Guest Farm	F1		✓			T*	✓				fr/de/mdr
Jacques Smit Wines	F2	T						T		✓	
Joostenberg Wines	A8		✓*	✓*		✓		T	✓	✓	
Juno Wine Company	E5		✓			✓					
Klein Optenhorst	H1	T									
Klein Parys Vineyards	E5		✓					✓		✓	
Kleine Draken	D6				×	T*		T	✓		
KWV	E6		✓	✓		✓*		✓	✓		de
La Ferme Derik	D3	T					✓	T			
Laborie Wine Farm	E6		✓	✓		✓		✓			de
Landskroon Wines	D6		✓*			BYO	✓	T*		✓	
Lazanou Organic Vineyards	F1	T*				T*					

	Grid reference	Open by appt. only	Open Saturdays	Open Sundays	Open public holidays	Meals/refreshments	Accomodation	Cellar tours	Disabled friendly	Child friendly	Languages spoken
Le Fût	F5	T									
Le Joubert	E4	T									
Lindhorst Wines	D7	T*				T*	✓	T	✓		
Linton Park Wines	G1	T*			X	BYO		T*			
Longbarn Winery	F2							T			
Maske Wines	G2	T				BYO					de
Mellasat Vineyards	G5		✓	✓		T*		T	✓		
Mon Rêve Estate	D7	T				BYO		T		✓	fr/de
Mont du Toit Kelder	G2			T	X	BYO*	✓	✓/*			de
Mooi Bly Winery	F4					BYO	✓	T			nl
Mount Vernon Estate	C7		✓					✓	✓		
Nabygelegen Private Cellar	H1		✓		X		✓	✓			
Napier Winery	G2		✓			✓*		✓	✓		
Nederburg Wines	F5		✓	✓*		✓*		✓	✓		de
Nelson Family Vineyards	D3	T			X		✓	T	✓	✓	
Niel Joubert Estate	C8	T*			X						
Noble Hill Wine Estate	D8		✓	✓		✓		T	✓	✓	fr
Olsen Wines	G5	T				T*					
Oude Denneboom	C2	T					✓				
Painted Wolf Wines	E6	T*				T*					fr
Perdeberg Winery	B3		✓			T/BYO*		T*			xh
Retief Wines	E4	T			X						
Rhebokskloof Wine Estate	D3		✓	✓		✓		T	✓	✓	
Ridgeback	D3		✓	✓		✓	✓	T		✓	
Ruitersvlei Wines	D6		✓			✓	✓		✓	✓	
Rupert & Rothschild Vignerons	D8		✓					✓	✓		
Scali	C1	T			X		✓	T			
Simonsvlei International	D7		✓	✓*		✓/BYO		T	✓	✓	
Southern Sky Wines	E5	T									
Spice Route Winery	D6		✓	✓		✓					
Stone Ridge Wines	D1	T									
Tempel Wines	E3	T					✓	T			de/fr/sv
The Mason's Winery	E6	T				✓*					
Thokozani Wines	F2		✓	✓		✓	✓	T			
Upland Organic Estate	G3	T			T		✓	T			de
Val de Vie Wines	F7		✓	✓		✓*		T			
Val du Charron	H1		✓	✓		✓	✓	✓	✓		
Veenwouden Private Cellar	E3	T						T			
Vendôme	E6	T			X					✓	
Versailles	E1	T						T			
Vondeling	C1										

	Grid reference	Open by appt. only	Open Saturdays	Open Sundays	Open public holidays	Meals/refreshments	Accomodation	Cellar tours	Disabled friendly	Child friendly	Languages spoken
Vrede en Lust Wine Farm	D8		√	√		√	√	T*	√	√	
Welbedacht Wine Estate	F1		√			√	√	√	√	√	de
Welgegund Wines	G2	T					√				
Welgeleë	D7		√	√		T					
Welgemeend Estate	C7		√*	×				√	√		
Wellington Wines	E2		√	×				T	√		
Welvanpas	H1		√	√		√/BYO				√	nl
Wilderer Private Distillery	D7		√	√		√*		√		√	de
Windmeul Cooperative Cellar	D3		√		×	√*		T			
Zanddrift Vineyards	E6										
Robertson Map											
Arendsig Handcrafted Wines		T				BYO	√	T			
Ashton Kelder			√					T	√	√	
Bon Cap Organic Winery				√		√	√	√	√	√	
Bon Courage Estate			√			√		√	√	√	
Bonnievale Wines			√			√*		√	√	√	
Buffalo Creek Wines			√	T				√*			
BurCon Wines		T*				√	√			√	
Bushmanspad Estate						BYO	√				nl
Cape Dreams		T						T			
Clairvaux Private Cellar					×	BYO		T	√		
Cloverfield Private Cellar								√			
De Wetshof Estate			√					T*	√		
DuVon Private Cellar		T					√	T			
Esona Boutique Wine			√								
Excelsior Estate			√			T/BYO	√			√	
Fraai Uitzicht 1798			√	√		√*	√				de
Goedverwacht Wine Estate			√			T/BYO*		√			
Graham Beck Wines			√	√				√			
Jonkheer		T*			×		√	T			
Kingsriver Estate			√	√		√/BYO	√	√			nl
Kleinhoekkloof		T*									
Kranskop Wines			√			BYO		√			de
Langverwacht Wynkelder				×				√	√		
Le Grand Chasseur Wine Estate		T		×				√			
Lord's Wines			T*	T*				√			
McGregor Wines			√			BYO		T	√		
Mooiuitsig Wine Cellars							√	T			
Quando Vineyards & Winery		T		×							de
Rietvallei Wine Estate			√			√*		T	√		

	Grid reference	Open by appt. only	Open Saturdays	Open Sundays	Open public holidays	Meals/refreshments	Accomodation	Cellar tours	Disabled friendly	Child friendly	Languages spoken
Robertson Winery			✓	✓				T			
Roodezandt Wines					✗			T	✓	✓	
Rooiberg Winery			✓			✓			✓	✓	
Rosendal Winery			✓	✓		✓	✓	✓	✓		nn
Springfield Estate			✓			BYO		T			
Sumsaré Wines		T*				BYO		T*		✓	
Tanagra Private Cellar		T*					✓	T			de
Van Loveren Family Vineyards			✓	✓		✓	✓	✓	✓		
Van Zylshof Estate			✓					T	✓		
Viljoensdrift Wines & Cruises			✓	✓*		✓*				✓	fr
Vruchtbaar Boutique Winery		T			✗			T			
Wandsbeck Wyne Koöp Bpk			T	T	✗			T	✓	✓	de
Wederom Boutique Winery		T			T	T	✓	T			de
Weltevrede Estate			✓				✓	T	✓		
Windfall Wine Farm		T			✗	BYO		T			
Wolfkloof		T				T/BYO		T			
Wolvendrift Private Cellar			✓			T		T	✓	✓	
Wonderfontein		T*									
Zandvliet			✓			BYO			✓		

Southern Cape Map

	Grid reference	Open by appt. only	Open Saturdays	Open Sundays	Open public holidays	Meals/refreshments	Accomodation	Cellar tours	Disabled friendly	Child friendly	Languages spoken
Andy Mitchell Wines		T						T			
Black Oystercatcher Wines			✓	✓		✓*	✓	✓	✓	✓	
Brunia Wines		T*				✓*					
Jean Daneel Wines		T				✓		T			de
Lismore Estate Vineyards		T								✓	
Lomond		T*			✗	✓	✓				
Strandveld Wines			✓			BYO	✓	✓			
Swallow Hill Winery		T						T			de/fr/sp
The Berrio Wines		T*				T*					
The Giant Periwinkle		T									
Zoetendal Wines		T					✓	T			

Stellenbosch Map

	Grid reference	Open by appt. only	Open Saturdays	Open Sundays	Open public holidays	Meals/refreshments	Accomodation	Cellar tours	Disabled friendly	Child friendly	Languages spoken
Aaldering Vineyards & Wines	D4			✓*	✗			T			
Akkerdraai	E8			✓							de
Allegria Vineyards	B6	T					✓				nl/de/gsw
Alluvia Winery & Private Residence Club	H5		✓	✓		T*	✓	T		✓	
Alto Wine Estate	E8		✓	✓		T*					
Amani Vineyards	B6		✓			✓/BYO*		✓	✓	✓	
Amares Wines	G4	T*			✗	T*		T*			nl
Annandale Wines	E8		✓			BYO		✓	✓		

	Grid reference	Open by appt. only	Open Saturdays	Open Sundays	Open public holidays	Meals/refreshments	Accomodation	Cellar tours	Disabled friendly	Child friendly	Languages spoken
Asara Wine Estate & Hotel	D6		✓	✓		✓	✓	T	✓	✓	de
Audacia Wines	E7		✓	✓		✓*			✓	✓	
Bartinney Private Cellar	H5				×			T	✓		
Beau Belle	C7	T*				T/BYO*	✓	T*			
Beau Joubert Vineyards & Winery	B6		T		×	BYO	✓	T			
Bein Wine Cellar	B6	T						T			de/fr
Bellevue Estate Stellenbosch	C3		✓								
Beyerskloof	E3		✓			✓		T	✓		
Bilton Wines	E8		✓	✓				T*	✓	✓	
Blaauwklippen Vineyards	E6		✓	✓		✓		T	✓	✓	de
Bonfoi Estate	C5	T			×	BYO			✓		
Boschheim	E5	T									de
Boschkloof Wines	C6		✓			BYO		✓			
Botanica Wines	D4	T*				✓*	✓				
Brampton	F5		✓			✓*					
Brenaissance	D4		✓	✓		✓	✓			✓	
Camberley Wines	H5		✓	✓		T/BYO	✓	T			
Cape Hutton	E7	T						T			
Carisbrooke Wines	C6				×						
Casa Mori	D3	T				T		T			it/fr
Chabivin Champagne & MCC House	E7		✓	✓		✓					fr
Cirrus Wines	E8		✓	✓							
Clos Malverne	D4		✓	✓		✓		✓*	✓		
Clouds Wine Estate	G5		✓			✓*	✓				
Clovelly Wines	D4	T						T			
Dalla Cia Wine & Spirit Company	E5		✓			✓					it
De Meye Wines	E1	T*	✓	✓		✓*		T*	✓		
De Toren Private Cellar	B6	T						T			
De Trafford Wines	G8		✓		×			✓*			
Delaire Graff Estate	G5		✓	✓		✓	✓	T*	✓		
Delheim Wines	F2		✓	✓		✓	✓	✓	✓	✓	de
DeMorgenzon	C5		✓	✓				T			
Deux Frères Wines	E3		✓			BYO					
Devon Rocks	D3	T					✓	T			de/sv
Devonair	D3	T			×		✓				
Devonvale Golf & Wine Estate	D3	T*				✓	✓		✓		de/fr
DeWaal Wines	C5		✓*								
Die Bergkelder Wine Centre	E5		✓					✓	✓		
Domaine Coutelier	D4	T			×			T			fr
Dombeya Wines	E8		✓	✓		✓*	✓	T	✓	✓	
Donkiesbaai	E8		✓	✓							

	Grid reference	Open by appt. only	Open Saturdays	Open Sundays	Open public holidays	Meals/refreshments	Accomodation	Cellar tours	Disabled friendly	Child friendly	Languages spoken
Dormershire Estate	A5		✓		✗			✓			
Dornier Wines	F7		✓	✓		✓*	✓	T	✓	✓	
Eaglevlei Wine Estate	E1		✓	✓		✓*			✓	✓	
Edgebaston	F3	T									
Elgin Heights	C6	T									
Ernie Els Wines	F8		✓			✓*		✓	✓		
Ernst Gouws & Co Wines	D1		✓						✓	✓	de
Escapades Winery	B4	T									
Fort Simon Wine Estate	C4		✓		✗	✓*		T	✓		
Francois La Garde	E5	T									
Gilga Wines	D5	T									
Glenelly Cellars	F4		✓					T	✓		de/fr
Goede Hoop Estate	C3		✓			T/BYO*			✓		
Graceland Vineyards	E7	T*			✗						
Groenland	B3		✓			BYO		T	✓		
Guardian Peak Wines	E8		✓	✓		✓					
Hartenberg Estate	C4		✓	✓*		✓*		T	✓	✓	de
Haskell Vineyards	E8		✓	✓		✓*	✓	T	✓	✓	
Hazendal	B3		✓	✓		✓		✓*	✓	✓	de/ru
Hidden Valley Wines	F8		✓	✓		✓		✓	✓		
Hoopenburg Wines	E1				✗	BYO	✓	✓			
Jacobsdal	B6	T*									
Jordan Wine Estate	C5		✓	✓		✓*		T*	✓		
Kaapzicht Wine Estate	B4		✓				✓	T			de
Kanonkop Estate	F2		✓			T/BYO*			✓		
Kanu Private Cellar & Vineyards	E3				✗						
Katbakkies Wine	D5	T*			✗						
Keermont Vineyards	F8	T						T			
Klein DasBosch	F7	T*				✓					
Kleine Zalze Wines	E6		✓	✓		✓	✓		✓		
Knorhoek Wines	F3		✓	✓		✓*	✓	✓	✓	✓	
Koelenhof Winery	D1		✓			BYO		T	✓	✓	de
Kyburg Wine Estate	D4	T					✓	T			fr/de
Laibach Vineyards	F1		✓*				✓	T			
Lanzerac	G5		✓	✓		✓	✓	✓	✓		
L'Avenir Vineyards	E3		✓			BYO	✓	T	✓	✓	fr
Le Bonheur Wine Estate	F1			✓	✓						
Le Pommier Wines	H4	T*				✓	✓			✓	
Lievland Estate	F1	T				T*	✓	T	✓		
L'Olivier Wine & Olive Estate	D5	T					✓				
Louiesenhof Wines	E4		✓	✓		✓*	✓		✓	✓	de

	Grid reference	Open by appt. only	Open Saturdays	Open Sundays	Open public holidays	Meals/refreshments	Accomodation	Cellar tours	Disabled friendly	Child friendly	Languages spoken
Louisvale Wines	D4				x	BYO		✓	✓		
Lovane Boutique Wine Estate	D6		✓	✓	x		✓	✓			
Malanot Wines	E8	T						T*	✓		
Marianne Wine Estate	G1		✓	✓		✓	✓	✓	✓		de/fr
Marklew Family Wines	F1	T						T			
Meerlust Estate	B8		✓		x			T			
Meinert Wines	D4	T*			x						de
M'hudi Wines	B1	T*									tn/xh/zu
Middelvlei Estate	E4		✓	✓		✓*	✓	T	✓	✓	
Mitre's Edge	F1	T*					✓	T			
MolenVliet Wine & Guest Estate	H4	T					✓				
Mont Destin	G1	T			x			T			de/fr
Monterosso Estate	E4	T			T			T			it/zu
Mooiplaas	B4		✓			T*	✓				
Morgenhof Wine Estate	F3		✓	✓		✓	✓	T	✓	✓	de/fr
Mostertsdrift Noble Wines	E4	T				T*		T		✓	
Mulderbosch Vineyards	C6		✓	✓		✓*					fr
Muratie Wine Estate	F2		✓	✓		✓	✓	T			
Mvemve Raats	B6	T			x						
Natte Valleij Wines	F1		✓		x		✓	✓		✓	
Neethlingshof Estate	D5		✓	✓		✓*		✓	✓	✓	de
Neil Ellis Wines	G5		✓			✓*		✓			
Nico van der Merwe Wines	B6	T									fr/de
Nietvoorbij Wine Cellar	F4				x						
Oldenburg Vineyards	H5		✓*			✓*		✓			
Origin Wine	D3	T									fr/de
Overgaauw Wine Estate	D5		✓					✓			
Peter Falke Wines	E8		✓	✓		✓*		T			
Quoin Rock Winery	F3		✓	✓		✓*					
Raats Family Wines	B6	T			x						
Rainbow's End Wine Estate	H5	T				BYO		T			
Remhoogte Wine Estate	E3		✓			✓*	✓	T			
Re'Mogo Wines	E4		T*						✓		
Reyneke Wines	B6		T		T			✓*	✓		
Rudera Wines	G6	T									
Rust en Vrede Estate	E8		✓			✓		✓			
Rustenberg Wines	G4		✓	✓					✓		
Saxenburg Wine Farm	A5		✓	✓		✓/BYO	✓				
Seven Sisters	D7	T									
Simonsig Landgoed	E2		✓	✓		✓		✓*	✓	✓	
Skilpadvlei Wines	C6		✓	✓		✓	✓		✓	✓	

	Grid reference	Open by appt. only	Open Saturdays	Open Sundays	Open public holidays	Meals/refreshments	Accomodation	Cellar tours	Disabled friendly	Child friendly	Languages spoken
Slaley	E2		✓	✓		✓		T			
Sonklip Wine	G5	T*						T			
Spier	C7		✓	✓		✓	✓		✓	✓	de/xh
Spotswood Wines	F7	T									
Spring Grove Wines	H4	T									
Stark-Condé Wines	G6		✓	✓		✓			✓		ja
Stellekaya Winery	E5				×	T*		✓	✓		zu
Stellenbosch Hills Wines	D6		✓						✓		
Stellenbosch Ridge	E8		✓	✓							
Stellenbosch University	F6				×						
Stellenbosch Vineyards	C7		✓	✓		✓			✓	✓	xh
Stellendrift - SHZ Cilliers/Kuün Wyne	C7	T						T			
Stellenrust	E7		✓			✓/BYO*		T			xh
Stellenzicht Vineyards	E7		✓	✓				T			
Sterhuis	C4	T						T	✓	✓	
Stonehill	D4	T									
StoneyCroft	D3	T									
Summerhill Wines	E3				×	✓*			✓		
Super Single Vineyards	C5		✓								
SylvanVale Vineyards	D4		✓	✓		✓	✓		✓	✓	de/xh
Tamboerskloof Wine — Kleinood Farm	F7	T			×			T			
Thandi Wines	D6				×						
The Foundry	B8	T			×			T			
The High Road	E5		✓		×						
The Hills	D4	T									
The House of JC le Roux	D4		✓	✓		✓		✓*	✓		
Thelema Mountain Vineyards	G4		✓			BYO			✓		
Tokara	G4		✓	✓		✓			✓	✓	
Topaz Wine	F2		✓*								de/fr
Uitkyk Estate	F2		✓	✓		✓*			✓	✓	
Usana	C5	T									
Uva Mira Vineyards	F8		✓	✓		✓			✓		
Van Biljon Wines	B6	T			×		✓	T			
Vergenoegd Wine Estate	B8		✓	✓		✓*		T	✓	✓	xh
Vilafonté	E5	T						T			
Villiera Wines	D1		✓			✓/BYO*		✓	✓		fr
Vrede Wines	D1	T									
Vredenheim Wines	D6		✓			✓	✓		✓		
Vriesenhof Vineyards	F7		T		×			T			
Vuurberg	H4	T			×			T			
Warwick Estate	F1		✓	✓		✓*		T	✓	✓	

	Grid reference	Open by appt. only	Open Saturdays	Open Sundays	Open public holidays	Meals/refreshments	Accomodation	Cellar tours	Disabled friendly	Child friendly	Languages spoken
Waterford Estate	F7			✓				✓	✓		
Webersburg Wines	E8		✓	✓		✓	✓	✓	✓		
Welgevallen Wines	F5				✗			✓			
Westbridge Vineyards	E1	T				T*	✓				
Yardstick Wines	C6	T									
Zevenwacht	B5		✓	✓		✓	✓	T	✓	✓	xh
Zorgvliet Wines	H4		✓	✓		T*	✓	T	✓	✓	
Swartland Map											
AA Badenhorst Family Wines		T			✗		T	T			
Abbottshill		T				BYO		T			
Allesverloren				✓		✓*		T	✓	✓	
Annex Kloof Wines			✓	✓		BYO		T			
Babylon's Peak Private Cellar		T				T/BYO*	✓	T	✓		
Bryan MacRobert Wines		T			✗						
David		T									
Dragonridge		T				T/BYO	✓	T		✓	
Franki's Vineyards		T			✗	T/BYO	✓	T			
Het Vlock Casteel			✓			T*			✓		
Hofstraat Kelder		T						T			
Hughes Family Wines		T									sp
Huis van Chevallerie		T									de/fr/it
Kloovenburg Wine & Olives			✓	✓*		BYO	✓	✓*	✓		
Lammershoek Winery		T				T/BYO		T			de
Meerhof Family Vineyards		T									
Mount Abora Vineyards		T									
Mullineux Family Wines		T	✓*					T			
Nieuwedrift Vineyards			✓			T/BYO		✓		✓	
Orangerie Wines		T						T			
Org de Rac			✓			T/BYO		✓			de
Paardebosch Wines		T			✗	BYO		T			
Pulpit Rock Winery			✓			BYO	✓	T	✓		
Riebeek Cellars			✓	✓		BYO		T			
Sadie Family Wines		T									
Santa Cecilia			✓	✓		✓*	✓				
Sequillo Cellars		T*			✗						
Spekulasie Landgoed		T			T	✓	✓	T		✓	
Swartland Winery			✓						✓	✓	
Wildehurst Wines			✓	✓				T*			
Winkelshoek Wine Cellar			✓						✓		

	Grid reference	Open by appt. only	Open Saturdays	Open Sundays	Open public holidays	Meals/refreshments	Accomodation	Cellar tours	Disabled friendly	Child friendly	Languages spoken
Tulbagh Map											
Blue Crane Vineyards			T					T			
Constantia de Tulbagh		T			X			T			
Drostdy-Hof Wines			√						√		
Fable Mountain Vineyards		T						T			
Koelfontein			√		X	BYO	√				
Lemberg Wine Estate			√	√		T/BYO*	√	√	√		
Manley Private Cellar			√			√	√	T			
Montpellier			√		X	√/*	√	√		√	
Oude Compagnies Post Private Cellar		T						T			
Rijk's			√				√	T	√		
Saronsberg			√			BYO	√	T			
Schalkenbosch Wines		T			X		√	T			de
Theuniskraal			√						√		
Tulbagh Winery			√*	√*		BYO		T	√		
Twee Jongegezellen/Krone			√								de
Waverley Hills Organic Wines & Olives			√	√		√/BYO*		√	√	√	
Zonquasdrift Estates		T*			X						
Villiersdorp Map											
Badgerberg Estate		T*				√*					
Cranefields Wine		T									
Faraway House Wine Estate		T									
Slowine			√			√			√		
Villiersdorp Cellar			√			√			√		
Worcester Map											
Aan de Doorns Cellar			√		X			T*	√		
Alvi's Drift Private Cellar		T			X			T			
Auction Crossing Private Cellar			√		X	√		T		√	
Brandvlei Cellar			√		X				√		
Conradie Family Vineyards			√	√		√/BYO	√	√		√	
De Doorns Wynkelder (Koöp) Bpk			√						√		
De Wet Winery			√		X	BYO		T	√		
Eagle's Cliff Wines-New Cape Wines					X	√*			√	√	
Leipzig Winery			√	√		√*	√	√*		√	ru
Nuy Wine Cellar			√			BYO			√		
Overhex Wines International			√	√		√*		T	√	√	
Stettyn Cellar			√*		X	T/BYO*		T*	√	√	

Northern Cape, Free State & North West

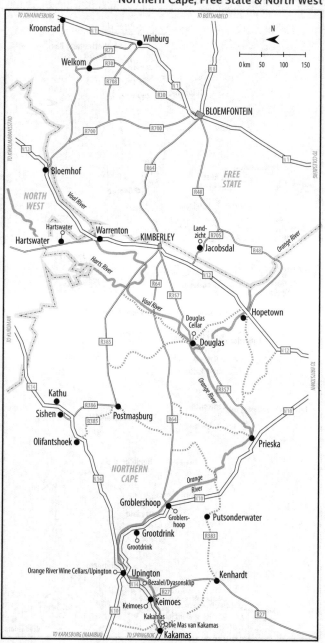

Klein Karoo & Garden Route

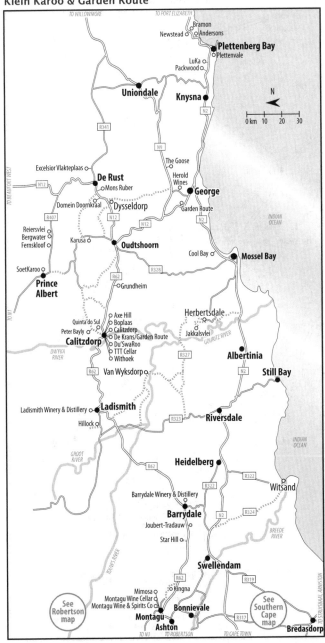

TO WILLOWMORE

TO PORT ELIZABETH

Bramon
Newstead ○ ● Andersons
Plettenberg Bay
● Plettenvale
LuKa ○
Packwood ○

N

0 km 10   20   30

Uniondale   **Knysna** ●

N2

R341

N9

Excelsior Vlakteplaas ○
The Goose ○
De Rust ●
○ Mons Ruber
Herold
Wines ○
George ●

TO BEAUFORT WEST

N12

Domein Doornkraal
Dysseldorp
N12
Garden Route ○
N12

R407
Reiersvlei ○
Bergwater ○
Fernskloof ○
Karusa ○
Oudtshoorn ●
Cool Bay ○
Mossel Bay ●

INDIAN OCEAN

SoetKaroo ○
R62
R328

Prince Albert ●
○ Grundheim

○ Axe Hill
○ Boplaas
Quinta do Sul ○ ○ Calitzdorp
Peter Bayly ○ ○ De Krans/Garden Route
Calitzdorp ● ○ Du'SwaRoo
○ TTT Cellar
○ Withoek

Herbertsdale ○

TO N1

DWYKA RIVER

Jakkalsvlei ○
GOURITZ RIVER

Albertinia ●

R62 Van Wyksdorp ○
R327
Still Bay ●

Ladismith Winery & Distillery ○
Ladismith ●
R323
Riversdale ●
Hillock ○

INDIAN OCEAN

GROOT RIVER

R62
Heidelberg ●
R322

Witsand ●
R322
R324

Barrydale Winery & Distillery ○
Barrydale ●
N2
Joubert-Tradauw ○
BREEDE RIVER

Star Hill ○

TO'INUS RIVER

Swellendam ●
R319

R62
Mimosa ○ ○ Kingna
Montagu Wine Cellar ○
Montagu Wine & Spirits Co ○
Bonnievale ●

See Robertson map

Montagu ●
Ashton ●
R317
Bredasdorp ●

See Southern Cape map

TO N1
TO ROBERTSON
TO CAPE TOWN

TO STRUISBAAI, ARNISTON

KwaZulu-Natal

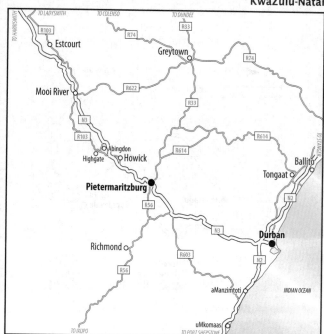

Southern Cape

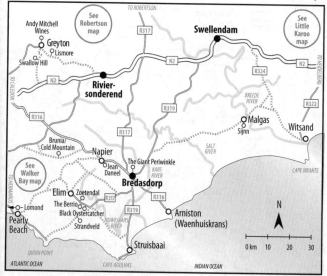

Robertson

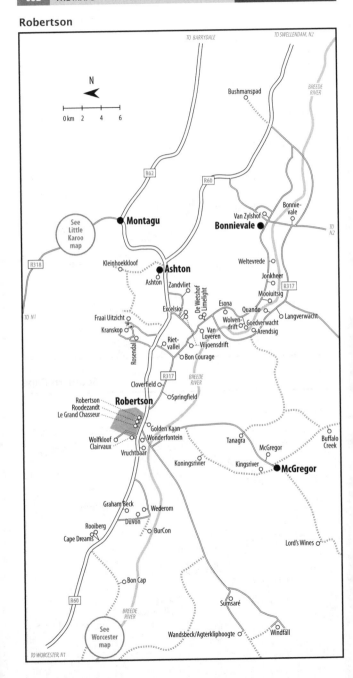

Olifants River & West Coast

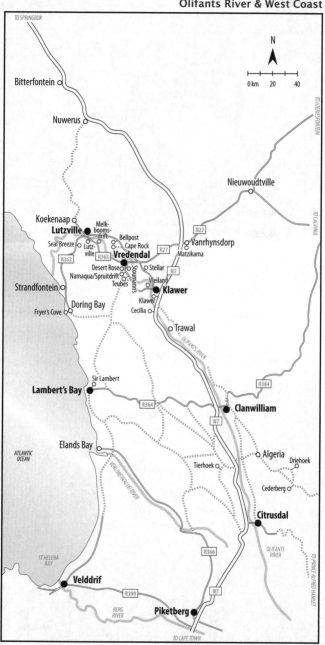

N

0 km   20   40

TO SPRINGBOK

TO LOERIESFONTEIN

TO CALVINIA

Bitterfontein

Nuwerus

Nieuwoudtville

Koekenaap
Lutzville
Melk-
booms-
drift
Seal Breeze
Lutz-
ville
Bellpost
Cape Rock
Vredendal
Desert Rose
Namaqua/Spruitdrift
Teubes
Stoumann's
Stellar
Vleiland
Klawer
Klawer
Cecilia
R362
R363
R27
R27
N7
Vanrhynsdorp
Matzikama

Strandfontein
Doring Bay
Fryer's Cove

Trawal

OLIFANTS RIVER

R364

Sir Lambert
Lambert's Bay
R364
Clanwilliam
N7

ATLANTIC
OCEAN

Elands Bay
Tierhoek
Algeria
Driehoek

Cederberg

KRULDENVALLELRIVER

Citrusdal

OLIFANTS
RIVER

R366

TO PRINCE ALFRED HAMLET

ST HELENA
BAY

Velddrif
R399

BERG
RIVER

Piketberg
N7

TO CAPE TOWN

Cape Peninsula

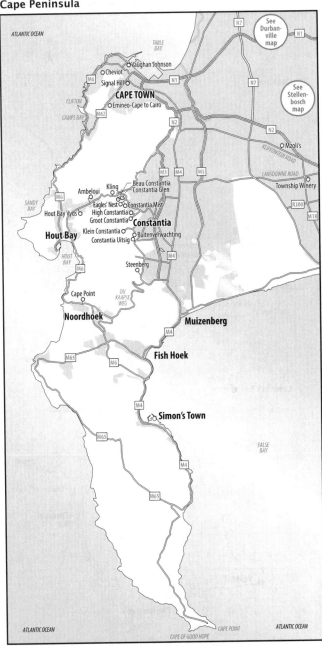

Durbanville, Philadelphia & Darling

Breedekloof

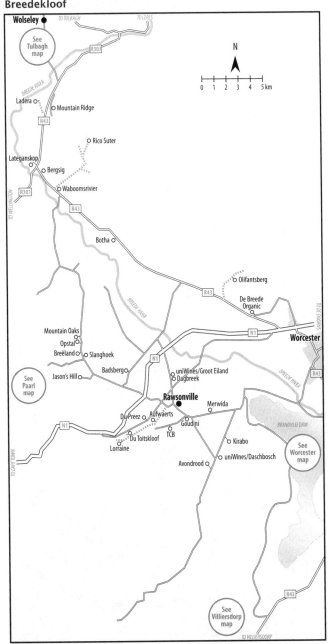

Worcester

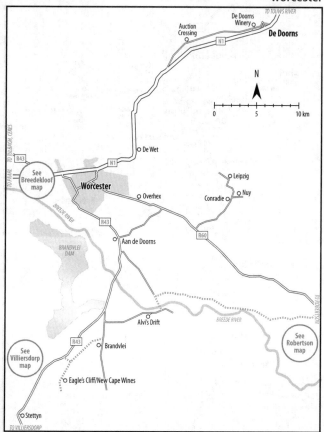

Villiersdorp

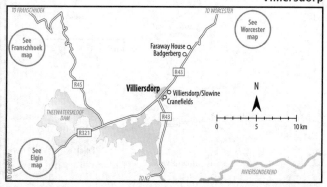

Franschhoek

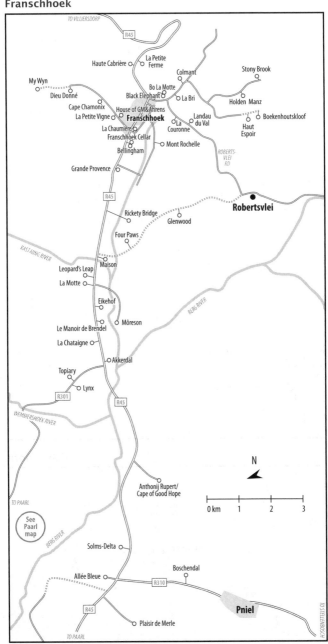

Elgin, Walker Bay & Bot River

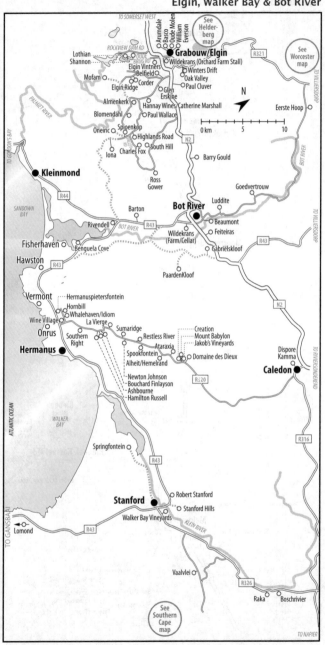

Swartland

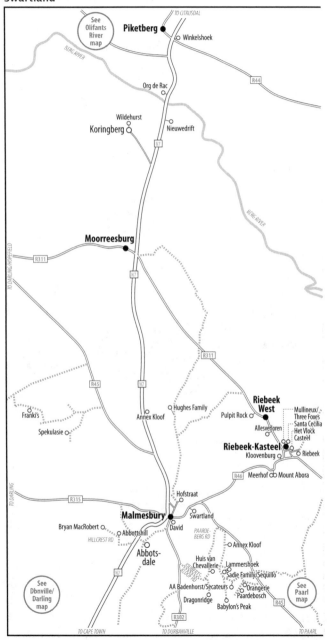

Tulbagh

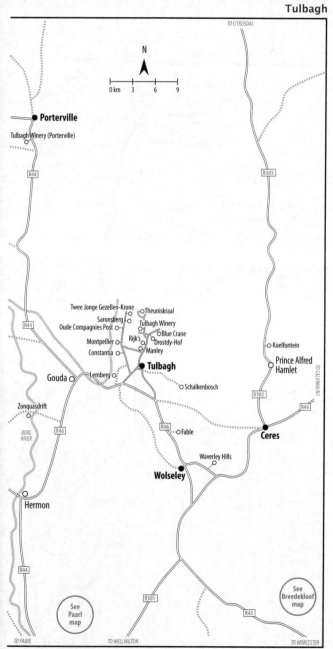

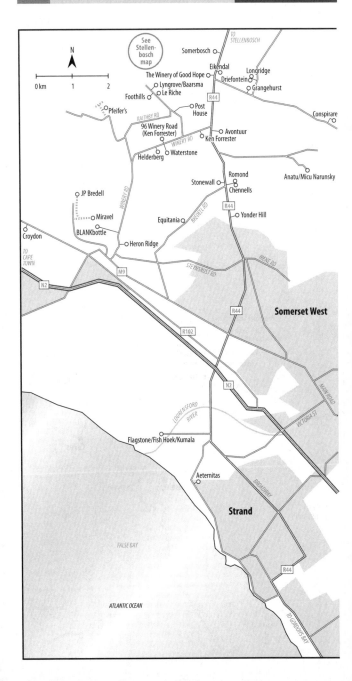

Helderberg

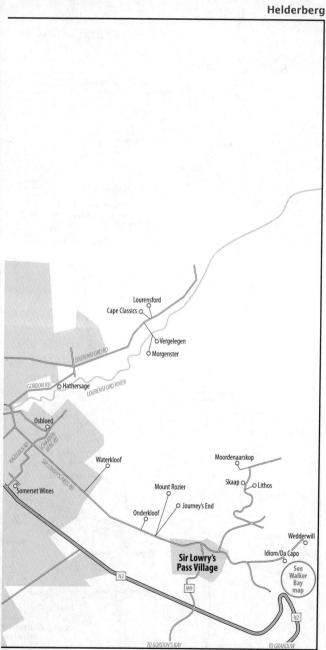

Lourensford

Cape Classics

Vergelegen

Morgenster

LOURENSFORD RD

GORDON RD   Hathersage

LOURENSFORD RIVER

Osbloed

SCHAPEN-BERG RD

Waterkloof

Moordenaarskop

Skaap   Lithos

HAZELDAL RD

SIR LOWRY'S PASS RD

Somerset Wines

Mount Rozier

Onderkloof   Journey's End

Wedderwill

Idiom/Da Capo

Sir Lowry's Pass Village

See Walker Bay map

N2

M9

N2

TO GORDON'S BAY   TO GRABOUW

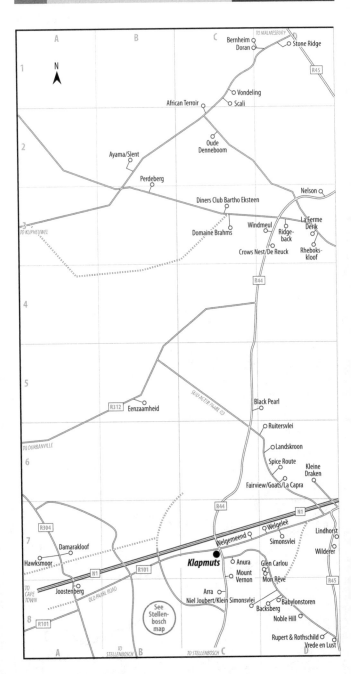

N

TO MALMESBURY

Bernheim
Doran
Stone Ridge

R45

Vondeling
Scali

African Terroir

Oude Denneboom

Ayama/Slent

Perdeberg

Diners Club Bartho Eksteen

Nelson

TO KLIPHEUWEL

Domaine Brahms
Windmeul
Ridge-back
La Ferme Derik

Crows Nest/De Reuck
Rheboks-kloof

R44

R312 Eenzaamheid

SUID AGT.R (N44) CR

Black Pearl

Ruitersvlei

TO DURBANVILLE

Landskroon

Spice Route
Kleine Draken

Fairview/Goats/La Capra

R44
N1

R304

Welgeleë

Welgemeend
Simonsvlei
Lindhorst

Damarakloof

Wilderer

Hawksmoor
N1
R101
Klapmuts
Anura
Glen Carlou
R45

TO CAPE TOWN
Joostenberg
OLD PAARL ROAD
Mount Vernon
Mon Rêve

Arra
Niel Joubert/Klein Simonsvlei
Babylonstoren

R101
Backsberg

See Stellenbosch map

Noble Hill

Rupert & Rothschild
Vrede en Lust

TO STELLENBOSCH
TO STELLENBOSCH

Paarl & Wellington

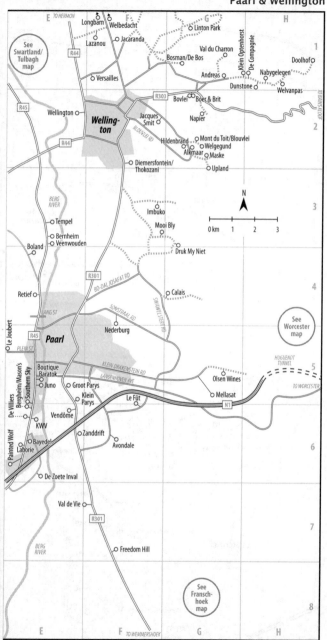

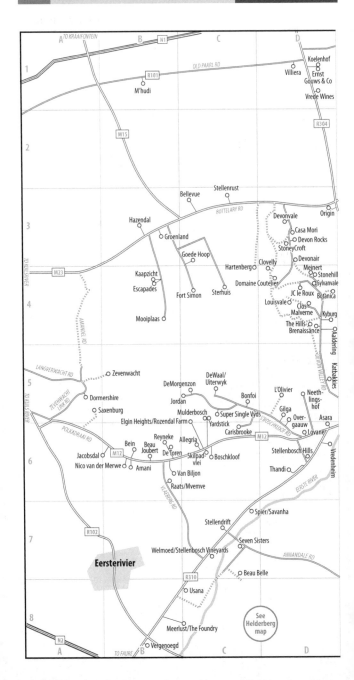

Stellenbosch

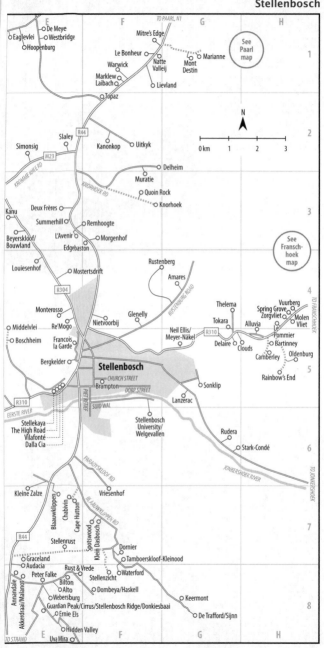

TO PAARL, N1

De Meye
Westbridge
Eaglevlei
Hoopenburg

Mitre's Edge
Le Bonheur
Marianne
Warwick
Natte Valleij
Mont Destin
Marklew
Laibach
Lievland
Topaz

See Paarl map

N

0 km   1   2   3

Slaley
Simonsig
R44
Kanonkop
Uitkyk
Delheim
Muratie
Quoin Rock
Knorhoek
Kanu
Deux Frères
Summerhill
Remhoogte
Beyerskloef/Bouwland
L'Avenir
Morgenhof
Edgebaston
Louiesenhof
Mostertsdrift

KNORHOEK RD
KROMME RHÉE RD
M23

See Franschhoek map

Rustenberg
Amares
RUSTENBURG ROAD
Monterosso
Re'Mogo
Nietvoorbij
Glenelly
Thelema
Vuurberg
Spring Grove
Zorgvliet
Molen Vliet
Middelvlei
Tokara
Alluvia
Boschheim
Francois la Garde
Neil Ellis/Meyer-Näkel
R310
Pommier
Bartinney
Delaire
Clouds
Oldenburg
Bergkelder
Camberley
TO FRANSCHHOEK
R304

Stellenbosch
CHURCH STREET
Brampton
DORP STREET
Rainbow's End
PIET RETIEF
SUID WAL
Sonklip
Lanzerac
EERSTE RIVER
R310
Stellekaya
The High Road
Vilafonté
Dalla Cia
Stellenbosch University/Welgevallen
Rudera
Stark-Condé
JONKERSHOEK RIVER
TO JONKERSHOEK

PARADYSKLOOF RD
Kleine Zalze
Vriesenhof
Blaauwklippen
Chabivin
Cape Hutton
BLAAUWKLIPPEN RD
R44
Stellenrust
Spotswood
Kleij Dasbosch
Dornier
Graceland
Rust & Vrede
Tamboerskloof-Kleinood
Audacia
Peter Falke
Stellenzicht
Waterford
Bilton
Alto
Dombeya/Haskell
Webersburg
Keermont
Annandale
Akkerdraai/Malang?
Guardian Peak/Cirrus/Stellenbosch Ridge/Donkiesbaai
Ernie Els
De Trafford/Sijnn
TO STRAND
Hidden Valley
Uva Mira